W9-DIV-764

FIRSTHAND AMERICA

FIRSTHAND AMERICA

Brandywine Press • St. James, New York

A History of the United States

FIFTH EDITION ☆ COMBINED EDITION

DAVID BURNER

VIRGINIA BERNHARD

STANLEY I. KUTLER

Dedication

For Thomas R. West

Text copyright © 1980, 1985, 1991, 1992, 1994, 1996, 1998

Library of Congress Cataloguing in Publication Data

Main entry under title:

Firsthand America

Includes bibliographical references and index.
1. United States—History. I. Burner, David,
1937–   . II. Burner, David, 1937–   . American
people.
vol. 1, ISBN 1-881089-77-0, 600 pp.
vol. 2, ISBN 1-881089-78-9, 640 pp.
Combined edition, ISBN 1-881089-76-2, 1120 pp.

Telephone Orders: 1-800-345-1776

PRINTED IN THE UNITED STATES OF AMERICA

First Printing 1998

About the Fifth Edition . . .

All comprehensive United States survey textbooks, including this one, give full coverage to standard political, economic, diplomatic, and legal events. But these elements of history are largely the story of elites. This textbook also provides social history captured in the recognizable lives of ordinary people. Presidents, congressmen, and corporate executives are quoted throughout the book. So are soldiers, slaves, indentured servants, cowboys, working girls and women, and civil rights activists. *Firsthand America,* using more than 2,000 quotations, therefore gives due place both to the traditional leaders and to the myriad Americans never named in formal histories.

In this fifth edition of *Firsthand America,* many of the firsthand quotations are placed in the margins in a contrasting color. This strategy is undertaken in cases where the materials might interrupt the main text narrative. The two-color format also improves the maps and graphs, and there are more of both. New dramatic incidents, including "A New World," "Liberty and Slavery," "The Trail of Tears," a Klan lynching in South Carolina, and the Oklahoma City bombing, improve the text along with innumerable smaller changes.

This fifth edition of *Firsthand America* contains a dialogue between two historians at the conclusion of each chapter. Contributors include Joyce Appleby, Bernard Bailyn, Michael Barnhart, Michael Les Benedict, Ira Berlin, Paul Boyer, Gene M. Brack, David Burner, Hosoya Chihiro, Catherine Clinton, Peter Collier, Paul Conkin, John S. D. Eisenhower, Peter G. Filene, David Hackett Fischer, Elizabeth Fox-Genovese, Paul Fussell, Eugene Genovese, Lawrence Goodwyn, Patricia Guerrin, Oscar Handlin, Louis R. Harlan, Joan Hoff, David Horowitz, Carol P. Karlsen, Maury Klein, Thomas J. Knock, Alan M. Kraut, Walter LaFeber, Suzanne Lebsock, William Leuchtenburg, Manning Marable, Drew McCoy, Forrest McDonald, James M. McPherson, James Mooney, Gary B. Nash, Stephen Nissenbaum, Shari Osborn, Nell Irvin Painter, Edward Pessen, Thomas Reeves, Robert V. Remini, Martin Ridge, Daniel T. Rodgers, Michael Paul Rogin, Kirkpatrick Sale, Richard H. Sewell, Martin J. Sherwin, Kenneth M. Stampp, Richard B. Stott, Stephan Thernstrom, Hans L. Trefousse, Irwin Unger, Thomas R. West, Sean Wilentz, Gordon S. Wood, and Donald Worster.

Acknowledgments

We are eager to receive comments on the fifth edition of this textbook from both teachers and students. We welcome corrections, suggestions, news of omissions, and general criticisms, which may be addressed to any of the authors. Or call the toll-free number of Brandywine Press at 1-800-345-1776.

For various kinds of help and encouragement thanks are gratefully extended to the following critics now teaching the United States history survey course: Francine Medeiros, Gus Seligmann, Jr., Thomas Schoonover, Lee Annis, Gary Bell, Ihor Bemko, Rick Donohoe, Gretchen Eick, Pat Gerster, Marilyn Halter, Barbara Posadas, John Belohlavek, Susan Hellert, Lottie Wilson, James E. diestler, Raymond Hauser, Michael Mills, Chuck Wallenberg, James Mooney, Harlan Hoffman, Michael Krenn, Virginia Leonard, Elizabeth Kessel, Frank Alduino, Eric Jacobsen, Jane Johnson, Howard Jones, Cary Wintz, Lena Boyd-Brown, Louis Williams, Merline Pitre, Kathleen Munley, Patricia Mulligan, Mario Perez, Stan Phipps, Michael Kopanic, Robert Sayre, Constance Schulz, Marcia Synnott, Michael Strickland, James Willis, Kelly Woestman, Charles Zelden, Carl Meier, Anthony B. Miller, Ben Johnson, Raymond Wilson, Drew Holloway, Ron Hays, John H. Hutson, Stuart Knee, S. Carol Berg, Charles O'Brien, Douglas Firth Anderson, and Kathleen Byrne.

Special thanks for the preparation of the manuscript are due to the tireless perfectionists Renzo Melaragno, Susan Masayda Senter, Lisa Kochis, Robert Fisher, and Roberta Poynton of Brandywine Corporation of Waterbury, Connecticut, and to the firm's helmsmen Charles and Ron Peach.

The Authors

American Letter for Gerald Murphy

It is a strange thing—to be an American
Neither an old house it is with the air
Tasting of hung herbs and the sun returning
Year after year to the same door and the churn
Making the same sound in the cool of the kitchen
Mother to son's wife, and the place to sit
Marked in the dusk by the worn stone at the wellhead—
That—nor the eyes like each other's eyes and the skull
Shaped to the same fault and the hands' sameness.
Neither a place it is nor a blood name.
America is West and the wind blowing.
America is a great word and the snow,
A way, a white bird, the rain falling,
A shining thing in the mind and the gulls' call.
America is neither a land nor a people,
A word's shape it is, a wind's sweep—
America is alone: many together,
Many of one mouth, of one breath,
Dressed as one—and none brothers among them:
Only the taught speech and the aped tongue.
America is alone and the gulls calling.

It is a strange thing to be an American.
It is strange to live on the high world in the stare
Of the naked sun and the stars as our bones live.
Men in the old lands housed by their rivers.
They built their towns in the vales in the earth's shelter.
We first inhabit the world. We dwell
On the half earth, on the open curve of a continent.
Sea is divided from sea by the day-fall. The dawn
Rides the low east with us many hours;
First are the capes, then are the shorelands, now
The blue Appalachians faint at the day rise;
The willows shudder with light on the long Ohio:
The lakes scatter the low sun: the prairies
Slide out of dark: in the eddy of clean air
The smoke goes up from the high plains of Wyoming:
The steep Sierras arise: the struck foam
Flames at the wind's heel on the far Pacific.
Already the noon leans to the eastern cliff:
The elms darken the door and the dust-heavy lilacs. . . .

This, this is our land, this is our people,
This that is neither a land nor a race. We must reap
The wind here in the grass for our soul's harvest:
Here we must eat our salt or our bones starve.
Here we must live or live only as shadows.
This is our race, we that have none, that have had
Neither the old walls nor the voices around us,
This is our land, this is our ancient ground—
The raw earth, the mixed bloods and the strangers,
The different eyes, the wind, and the heart's change,
These we will not leave though the old call us.
This is our country-earth, our blood, our kind.
Here we will live our years till the earth blind us—

—ARCHIBALD MACLEISH

About the Points of View . . .

This country, as the poem by Archibald MacLeish reprinted opposite this page of your textbook has it, was born on a naked continent, and it has neither a single race nor a single family nor a single ancient tradition to make it a unity. The ancestors of some of us were here before Columbus, and their descendants have been driven from home after home by European immigrants or their offspring. Other Americans came in the wretched holds of slave ships. Countless others, from Europe, had a somewhat better and yet a miserable journey, packed in the poorer recesses of ships that also provided luxurious quarters for wealthy travelers. Asians among us have Chinese ancestors who worked on the railroads that bound the country in the nineteenth century, or Japanese who labored on California farms amidst vicious discrimination against them. More recently we have added to our numbers Southeast Asians, refugees from a war that we did not begin but enormously escalated, and along with them Koreans whose shops are becoming a visible feature of our cities. And we are also the migrants from south of our borders and from the Caribbean, children of various racial and national strains that have mixed over the centuries since Columbus. What we have to make us a nation besides the physical fact of dwelling here is an idea of what it means to be an American. And that in itself is a ceaseless question for debate.

This country was born of ideas, and innumerable Americans beginning with the Pilgrim and Puritan migrants to New England have thought that the very point of being here was to live one or another of them. A good way of summarizing them is to see in American history a continuing quarrel or partnership between the claims of individualism and the claims of community.

The American economy, for example, has championed the virtues of the self-contained individual: industry, foresight, ambition. It has at the same time been an immensely cooperative venture, stretching across the continent a tight web of roads, factories, electronic communication, and more recently computer networks. It is in contributing skills and effort to this web that personal industry and ambition have found much of their expression. Americans have craved private property. Yet twentieth-century American political conflicts have been over how to extend, limit, tax, or reconstruct institutions of private property for the general good. As popular phenomena, too, these polarities in American culture have varied in specific content. A labor organization is a community of sorts, but so is a lynch mob. A union-breaking financial buccaneer is an individualist of one kind; another sort is a southern small-town newspaper editor, denouncing the bigotry of his subscribers.

As opponents or as partners, individualism and community have in differing ways furnished much of our national political questioning. As an illustration of the breadth of the argument, this text provides a running debate among several dozen prominent American historians. The ability to read controversial argument and gain from the reading is at the heart of a college education. Hence the points of view in *Firsthand America*.

No number of interpretations, of course, could cover all the issues over which American historians have quarreled. This is particularly true today, as the tools of history become increasingly multilayered, while popular argument over the future of the nation grows both angrier and more confused than it has been for some time. It is the hope of the contributors to *Firsthand America* that readers will enjoy following the arguments of scholars as they struggle to give some clarifying order to the endlessly diverse and restless facts of history.

About the Authors . . .

DAVID BURNER has published several books on twentieth-century America including *Making Peace with the 60s* (1996), *John F. Kennedy and a New Generation* (1988), *Herbert Hoover: A Public Life* (1979), and *The Politics of Provincialism: The Democratic Party, 1918–1932* (1968). He is currently writing a history of the American environmental movement for Princeton University Press.

VIRGINIA BERNHARD has published a historical novel, *A Durable Fire*, set in seventeenth-century Virginia and Bermuda, as well as a biography of a Texas governor's daughter. Her scholarly articles have appeared in *New England Quarterly, Virginia Magazine of History and Biography,* and *Journal of Southern History.* She has coedited the 1992 University of Missouri Press *Southern Women: Histories and Identities* and teaches at the University of St. Thomas in Houston. Professor Bernhard has served on the Advanced Placement test development committee for United States history.

STANLEY I. KUTLER is E. Gordon Fox professor of American Institutions at the University of Wisconsin and editor since its inception of the influential *Reviews in American History.* Kutler brings to the book his familiarity with the most recent interpretations of American history from colonial times to the present. A constitutional historian, his published books include *Privilege and Creative Destruction: The Charles River Bridge Case, Judicial Power and Reconstruction Politics,* and *The Wars of Watergate.* Kutler's most recent book is *Abuse of Power: The New Nixon Tapes* (1997).

Contents

9 Sectionalism and Party 1816–1828 / 279

10 The Jacksonian Era 1828–1840 / 307

11 An Age of Reform / 337

12 Westward Expansion: The 1840s / 371

13 Impending Crisis: The 1850s / 409

24   The New Deal / 805

Preface: The Bonus Army of 1932, 805

Points of View: A New Deal But Not a New Deck? 834

25   Diplomacy and War 1933–1945 / 837

Preface: Kristallnacht, 837

Points of View: Did the United States Provoke the Japanese into World War II? 874

26   Postwar Politics and the Cold War / 877

Preface: Hiroshima and Nagasaki, 877

Points of View: Why Did We Drop the Atomic Bomb? 904

27   Consensus and Division: 1953–1965 / 907

Preface: The Greensboro Sit-Ins, 907

Points of View: JFK—A Question of Character? 942

28   American Society and the Vietnam War / 945

Preface: The Kent State Massacre, 945

Points of View: Was the Generation of the Sixties Destructive? 976

29 New Boundaries / 979

Appendixes / I

Glossary / XXV

Succeeding in History Courses / XXXIII

Index / XLIII

Cristoforo Colombo. Painter unknown. *(Courtesy, Uffizi Galleria, Firenze)*

1
Europe, Africa, and the Americas

Christopher Columbus did not "discover" America. He was not even the first European to reach the New World. The Vikings, sailing in their small boats from Scandinavia around A.D. 1000, had reached Iceland and Greenland, but their brief presence there had no discernible effect on the rest of the world. The voyages of Columbus, on the other hand, set in motion an economic, cultural, intellectual, and political transformation that eventually revolutionized Europe, colonized the Americas, and ushered in the modern age.

Son of a Genoese weaver, Columbus was an extraordinary weaver of dreams. He envisioned himself sailing beyond the sunset, far beyond the horizons of his native Italy. Columbus was a fine mariner but an inaccurate geographer. Both qualities helped him to sell his dream to the monarchs of Spain. He badly underestimated the circumference of the globe, placing Asia about 2,400 miles from the Canary Islands of the eastern Atlantic: the actual distance is more than 10,000 miles, most of it vast oceans. Besieging King Ferdinand of Aragon and Queen Isabella of Castile, Columbus finally got his ships, his crews, and his quest for riches. On August 2, 1492, he sailed from Spain, setting his course west across the uncharted Atlantic Ocean, hoping to reach the fabled lands of the East Indies of Asia by sailing westward around the globe.

Instead, Columbus reached a "new world." It was not on any

HISTORICAL EVENTS

1100
Islamic forces conquer Morocco, western Algeria, Ghana, and parts of Spain and Portugal

Early 1200s
Mongols' Genghis Khan begins raids on China, Europe, and Islamic worlds

1260
Islamic forces stop Mongol invasion outside of Egypt

1348
Bubonic plague strikes Europe

1415
Prince Henry of Portugal begins explorations

1453
Constantinople falls to the Turks

1469
Queen Isabella and King Ferdinand marry, uniting Spain

1485
Henry VII becomes King of England

1487
Dias rounds the southern tip of Africa

continued

1

map, and it was inhabited by millions of people whose languages and cultures were completely unknown to Europeans. Arriving on the island of San Salvador in the Caribbean on October 12, 1492, Columbus, believing that he had reached the East Indies, met some natives he called "Indians." He had no way of knowing that there was a vast mainland to the west. He would have been astonished to learn that there were approximately twelve to sixteen million native Americans living in what we now call Central and South America. Another five million or more inhabited North America.

Much to Columbus's disappointment, he could not find a sea route to the Far East from Europe. After further voyages in 1493, 1498, and 1502, he died in 1504 believing that he had failed in his

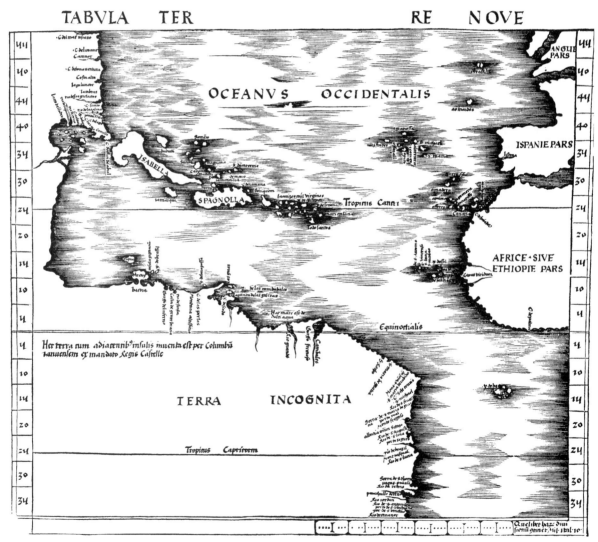

Tabula Terre Nove, **Map of the New World, ca. 1507–1513.** *(N. Phelps Stokes Collection. Prints Division. The New York Public Library, Astor, Lenox and Tilden Foundations)*

mission. He never knew that deep in the interior of the mainland beyond the Caribbean islands lay not the riches of China and Japan, but the fabulous treasures of the Aztec and the Inca empires. Their cities—the Aztecs' Tenochtitlán, where modern Mexico City now stands, and the Inca capital at Cuzco, high in the Andes Mountains of Peru—were flourishing centers of trade and culture at the time of Columbus's voyages. Before the Aztecs, the Mayan civilization, with sophisticated mathematics, astronomy, and architecture, had bloomed from about A.D. 300 to 900 in what is now Guatemala and the Yucatán peninsula. Royal palaces and ornate temples lavishly decorated with gold and silver, spacious public squares, gardens, terraces, paved roads, canals, and efficient systems of government existed in both Central and South America long before the first Europeans arrived in the Western Hemisphere. In North America, in the lands watered by the Rio Grande River, the Pueblo towns with their multilevel adobe structures, and in the valley of the Mississippi River, the huge earthen pyramids of the Mound Builders, abandoned before the coming of the Europeans, testified to the vitality of native cultures.

With the arrival of three small ships in 1492, the course of these native peoples' history, as well as that of Europe, would be forever changed. Christopher Columbus, whose given name means "Christ-bearer," saw himself as carrying Christianity to pagan peoples across the ocean. Christianity, in fact, would in its various institutions transform the Americas. In exchange, Europe was to be transformed by the Western Hemisphere. Much of the New World's first effect on the Old World was by way of its extraordinary wealth in resources. Gold and silver set in motion an economic revolution. Maize, or Indian corn, sometimes called the bread of the Americas, squash, beans, pumpkins, tomatoes, chili peppers, and chocolate enhanced European diets; and potatoes became a major sustenance to a growing European population. Tobacco altered Europe's social customs and helped colonial economies. Furs such as beaver pelts created fashions in dress. From the Old World to the New came hogs, horses, cattle, iron and steel weapons and tools, and wool for clothing and blankets, as well as beads, mirrors, alcohol, and other manufactured goods. But along with the knives, guns, axes, and copper kettles that changed the Stone Age societies of the Americas came another less welcome and accidental import: European diseases.

Smallpox, the scourge of Europe, was unknown in the Western Hemisphere until Europeans came. Native peoples had no immunity to this often fatal and always disfiguring disease. Indians were equally susceptible to plagues, measles, diphtheria, cholera, and typhus. They died by the millions. European bacteria and viruses reduced the native population of the Americas by as much

HISTORICAL EVENTS

1501
Vespucci explores east coast of South America

1513
De León explores Florida
• Balboa sights the Pacific

1517
Martin Luther posts his "Ninety-Five Theses," beginning Protestant Reformation

1519
Piñeda explores Texas Gulf Coast
• Cortés conquers Aztecs in Mexico

1522
Magellan's crew completes circumnavigation of globe begun in 1519

1524
Verrazano explores northeast coast of North America

1529–36
Henry VIII of England (1509–1547) uses Parliament to separate England from Rome

1532
Pizarro conquers Incas in Peru

1535
Cartier names the St. Lawrence River

Early 1540s
Coronado and de Soto search for gold in southern and western North America

1542
Cabrillo explores the North American west coast

1556
Philip II becomes King of Spain

1558
Elizabeth I becomes Queen of England

1565
St. Augustine founded by the Spanish

About 1570
Five Nations of Iroquois form confederation

1588
English defeat the Spanish Armada

as seventy-five to ninety percent. No wonder many early explorers described the new land as a "wilderness," and later historians would write of a "virgin land."

Europe's contacts with the lands across the sea initiated another kind of virus: the transatlantic slave trade. On his first voyage Columbus brought back seven Indians to display before his fascinated countrymen, "to learn our language and return . . . or to be kept as captives." A few years later a Spanish decree of 1503 allowed the enslavement of Indians in the Caribbean. In the 1520s Spaniards visiting the coast of what is now the Carolinas captured Indians there and sold them as slaves in Santo Domingo. By the 1500s European traders who had "discovered" Africa a few years before Columbus's first voyage were bringing African captives to work as slaves on the New World's lands. That trade in Africans, much of it provided by African slave dealers, grew from hundreds, to thousands, to millions. Over the next 350 years an estimated ten to fifteen million African men, women, and children were transported to the Americas against their will. Another four to six million died on the way.

The First North Americans

For perhaps forty thousand years, people had been living in the world the Europeans called "new." Stone tools, spear points, and other artifacts unearthed at sites in modern-day Pennsylvania, Wisconsin, New Mex-

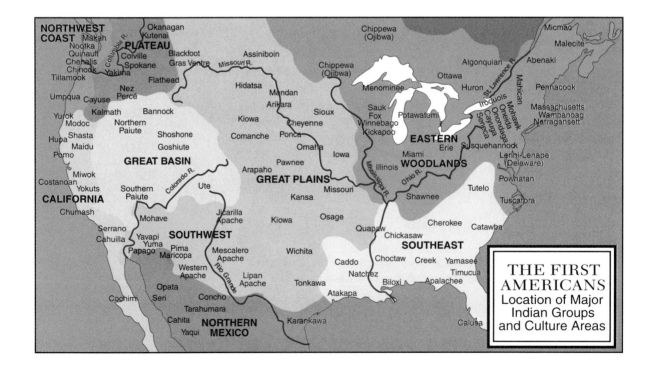

"They have likewise a notable way to catche fishe in their Rivers, for whear as they lack both yron, and steele, they faste unto their Reedes or longe Rodds, the hollowe tayle of a certain fishe like to a sea crabbe in steede of a poynte, wehr with by nighte or day they stricke fishes, and take them opp into their boates."—Thomas Hariot (1590). John White, *The Manner of Their Fishing*, drawing 1585. *(Courtesy, British Museum, London)*

ico, and Virginia show that human habitations were scattered across North America as early as ten or twenty thousand years ago. The first inhabitants had arrived from Asia thousands of years before that, gradually migrating into the interiors of North and South America.

The story of the millions of pre-Columbian Indians who inhabited the Americas is a puzzle for anthropologists, archaeologists, and historians. For the thousands of years before the Europeans arrived, there are no written records. The Mayans, whose culture flourished in Central America for six centuries prior to A.D. 900, made sophisticated mathematical calculations, accurate solar calendars, and pictorial representations, but they did not leave any written narratives. Neither did the Aztecs, who ruled Mexico from A.D. 1200 to 1500. The Incas governed an empire that extended from modern Ecuador to Chile by 1500 and built stone structures without mortar that survived earthquakes, but they had no alphabet. The history of these people, like that of the countless others who preceded them, is hidden in artifacts: carved images, strings of beads, pictographs. Painted pebbles dating from 6500 B.C. to A.D. 1400 have been found in the Pecos River valley in Texas, but the meaning of their linear designs remains a mystery.

In North America alone scholars have identified over 150 different language groups. These primitive North Americans were seed gatherers and game hunters. Some ten thousand years ago they learned to remove flakes from stone, making spears with what are called "Folsom points." Such weapons made them more efficient hunters. Yet they continued where possible to drive big game such as mammoths, bison, deer, and antelope off cliffs or into swamps preparatory for the kill. Gradually diets diversified to include raccoon, opossum, shellfish, and sea animals. As the Ice Age retreated about twelve thousand years ago and the continent dried, great forests grew in the north and east of North America; the bow and arrow aided in the kill of small, swift woodland animals. Hooks, nets, and weirs caught fish and snared ducks. Desert Indians relied increasingly on plants, ground seeds, berries, bulbs, and nuts. About seven thousand years ago North American natives, like peoples elsewhere around the world, developed agriculture. In comparison with modern technologies, basic agriculture seems simple. But in contrast with hunting and the gathering of wild plants, it is a major, sophisticated control of the environment. Efficiency in food growing increased populations and quickened village life. Plant domestication emerged first in the Mexican highlands, and then spread north and south. It probably reached the peoples north of Mexico about three thousand years ago.

Peoples of the Northwest   In the coldest regions of North America dwelt the Inuits, or Eskimos. They were and are uncommon among human beings in their ability to accommodate themselves, by remarkable adaptations of clothing, housing, and

While Europeans were developing an interest in science and commerce, peoples half a world away were expressing cultures of their own. Mask. Nootka people. West Vancouver, Canada.
(Courtesy, The Menil Collection, Houston)

A North Pacific Coast Indian village as depicted in a nineteenth-century painting by Arthur A. Jansson. Indians in this region probably never developed agriculture, relying instead on fishing and hunting for food.
(Courtesy, American Museum of Natural History)

hunting, to regions of snow, ice, and long winters. Most quickly associated with Alaska, they spread across the extreme north of the continent and into Greenland. The Indians of the Far North, across Canada and Alaska, were few. Divided into two major language groups, Algonquian and Athabascan, they included such tribes as Algonquian, Beaver, Chippewa, Cree, Chowo, and Yellowknife by present designations. Since the growing season was short for agriculture, they gathered berries, plants, and nuts, and hunted caribou, moose, deer, elk, musk-ox, and buffalo. Nomadic Indians used portable tepees; others built sturdy log homes. The Far North Indians appear to have fought rarely.

A unique hunter-gatherer culture existed in the northwest corner of the present-day United States. The Northwest Coast Indians, their population stretching from northern California to southern Alaska, probably never developed agriculture. The Bella Coola, Chinook, Kwakiutl, Nootka, Quinault, and Tlingit Indians harvested the oceans and rivers, taking salmon, inland trout, shellfish, sea lions, sea otter, and whales. In the lush forests, they hunted bear, caribou, deer, elk, and moose. Unlike most Indians north of Mexico, these people were not egalitarian. A few families accumulated wealth in canoes, blankets, or hammered copper sheets. Lavishing wealth brought power over others, and these extraordinarily competitive Indians therefore held ceremonial feasts called "potlatches"; the hosts fed their guests and displayed, gave away, or even destroyed valued possessions. Like the hunter-gatherer Far North Indians, the Northwest Coast tribes had no pottery; they used wood for masks, grave markers, and utensils. The abundant redwoods, cedars, firs, and pines served as posts, beams, siding, and gables for their homes, and as raw material for the huge sixty-foot seagoing canoes that could carry up to sixty men. Religious dramas kept alive the myths surrounding the Northwest gods.

Indians of the West More technologically primitive tribes occupied the Great Basin of America—the region between the Rockies and the Sierra Nevada Mountains which comprises present-day Utah, Nevada, and southern and eastern Oregon. The climate was arid and the soil, without the use of complex irrigation systems, was unsuited for agriculture. Also, the desert did not support the big game populations to sustain a hunting economy. The people of the Great Basin—the Utes, Paiutes, Goshiutes, Modocs, Bannocks, and Shoshones—were foragers, living off the roots, insects, berries, rabbits, and small rodents they were able to collect or catch. They were nomadic, moving in small groups of twenty to thirty and sleeping under portable lean-tos. They lived a marginal economic existence in which starvation was always a threat.

A kaleidoscope of hundreds of small tribes lived along the California coast from what is today San Francisco south to San Diego. Although these Indians were neither hunters nor farmers, they enjoyed an adequate food supply. Most of them either foraged for clams and shellfish along the bays, inlets, and beaches of the Pacific Ocean or collected acorns from the oak tree forests. The weather was temperate and the food supply reliable for the California Indians. They lived in villages and handcrafted some of the finest basketry in the world.

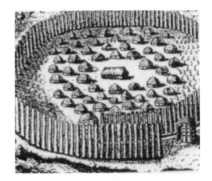

The longhouse (bottom), made from bark stretched over a wood frame, was the standard home of the Iroquois. Most Algonquians of the eastern woodlands lived in wigwams (top), which were made by bending tree boughs and covering them with animal skin. Most Plains Indians lived in small, durable tepees (middle), usually made from buffalo hides.
(Courtesy, New York Public Library)

Columbus's voyages heralded an era of European expansionism that led to the development of new frontiers across the world. The first depiction of native Americans suggests Europe's fascination with the New World inhabitants. Note the elaborate ship, asserting the superiority of European culture. Unidentified artist. *Insula hyspana.* Woodcut, 1493. From *Carolus Verardus, In laudem serenissimi Ferdinandi* (Basel, 1494). *(Courtesy, Beinecke Rare Book and Manuscript Library, Yale University, New Haven, Connecticut)*

The land between the Mississippi River and the Rocky Mountains belonged to the Plains Indians. Until the mid-1500s the Plains Indians preferred a more settled agricultural life in villages near rivers. By the end of the sixteenth century the Plains Indians had domesticated the wild ponies, descendants of horses brought by the Spanish. They quickly became superb horsemen. As mounted warriors and hunters they would roam the plains for nearly three hundred years. When they stayed in their permanent villages, they built homes of log framing covered with brush and dirt. While traveling, they lived in portable tepees.

A combination of hunter-gatherer and settled agrarian culture occupied much of the Southwest. These Indians showed remarkable ability to adapt to the arid buttes, mesas, and steep canyons in the northern part of this area and the flatter desert country to the south. The Anasazi, whom the Navaho call "the Ancient Ones," and their general descendants, the Pueblos, Hopi, and Zuni, built cliff dwellings, some with as many as 800 units, centering around the point where Colorado, Utah, New Mexico, and Arizona meet. This more advanced agrarian culture developed specialization in work, yet sophistication did not lead to hierarchy: religious and military leaders worked much like anyone else. Pueblos were peaceable, preferring to pull up the ladders to their adobe homes when attacked. When an Anasazi killed someone, even in self-defense, elaborate purification preceded his reentry into the village. This peaceful, advanced culture faded, possibly because of a prolonged thirteenth-century drought and growing population pressures from the north.

Indians of the Midwest and the East

From about 400 B.C. to A.D. 1500, in the Mississippi and Ohio river valleys, in parts of what are now Wisconsin, Michigan, Missouri, Illinois, Indiana, Ohio, Louisiana, and on the Gulf Coast, a culture known as the Mound Builders flourished. It left behind hundreds of huge earthen mounds, some in the shapes of birds and snakes. Many were used as burial mounds. Ornaments and tools of bone, shell, and copper suggest that the Mound Builders traded with areas as far away as Mexico. From about A.D. 900 to 1500 the peoples along the Mississippi Valley built enormous flat-topped earthen pyramids, some containing exquisitely-made jewelry, pottery, and agricultural implements.

On the eve of European discovery several Indian cultures dominated the third of the continent bordering the Atlantic. The eastern Algonquians occupied the Atlantic Coast from Labrador to North Carolina. Deep in the interior, on the Western Great Lakes, a northern and western Algonquian culture shared many of the traits of its eastern relatives. The Iroquois peopled the area between the two Algonquian cultures, from the Great Lakes to the central Appalachians. They included the Hurons, located north of the lakes; the Five Nations (Cayuga, Onondaga, Oneida, Mohawk, and Seneca) of the Mohawk Valley; and a conglomerate of related tribes including the Cherokee, Tuscarora, Moneton, and Monacan in the central and southern Appalachian Mountains. The Muskogean culture occupied the lowlands of southeastern North America.

The Iroquois   The Five Nations Iroquois confederation, founded around 1570, numbered perhaps 10,000 people by the year 1600. Its purpose was to eliminate blood feuds and cope with conflicts with nearby Algonquians, which may have resulted from population growth generated by improved agriculture. According to Iroquois legend, the leader credited with solving these problems was a chief named Hiawatha. He apparently lost relatives around 1450 and, rather than taking blood revenge, recommended that a ritual bereavement replace the vendetta, that retaliations be forbidden, and that a council of forty-nine chiefs make decisions for all the villages. Thereafter villages of the Five Nations were bound together for internal peace and external defense. Communal sharing extended to land use, the hunt, and the home. Although plowed by a family, the land was not owned, and while one hunter might outdo another, the kill was distributed. Families might live together in one house, but no single family owned it.

Women dominated familial lineages and were influential in Iroquois politics, although the Senecas did not give women the right to vote or serve on tribal councils until the 1960s. The families included the oldest female and her daughters, immature male children, and sons-in-law. Married men joined the family of their wives. Women initiated divorce by throwing their husbands' belongings outside. In politics women influenced village decisions behind the scenes. The women farmed, controlling the villages while the men warred, fished, and hunted; women could sometimes veto military expeditions by refusing to supply footwear or food.

Although the Iroquois did compete among themselves in hunting, fishing, and fighting, child raising encouraged egalitarianism. Youngsters were rarely punished physically, and were expected to err as they imitated adults. This freedom continued as the children matured. Without specialized legal personnel, laws, or jails, acceptable behavior was maintained by the ostracism and consensus that are typical of many small agricultural communities.

Among themselves, then, the Iroquois were civilized people, in some ways more civilized than the Europeans. Yet they do not deserve to be romanticized as a lost, virtuous civilization destroyed by white invaders. Like Europeans and white Americans, they could be as ruthless toward people outside their polity and culture as they were civil to their own kind. Algonquians and others knew the Iroquois as cruel warriors.

Indians of the South and Southeast   South of the Iroquois, from Chesapeake Bay to the Gulf Coast were other tribes, some belonging to the Algonquian-speaking groups and the rest to the Muskogean language peoples in what is now the southeastern United States. The Susquehannocks, powerful in the Chesapeake Bay region, had links to the Iroquois, as did the Tuscaroras, who in 1720 became the sixth nation in the Iroquois confederation. Among the eastern Algonquians were the Delawares and the Powhatans, the latter being the Indians who met the English settlers at Jamestown in 1607. All of these tribes grew corn and vegetables, made pottery, hunted game with bows and arrows, fished, and lived in large communal houses made from reeds and saplings. The Muskogean groups to the south included the Cherokee, Caddo, Creek, Natchez, Chickasaw, Choctaw, and Seminole tribes. They, like the Algonquians, grew corn, dressed in deerskins, and were skilled at weaving and ceramics. Though these tribes had their own leaders, many with organized systems of tribute and considerable skills in making war, each tribe maintained a separate identity and had no interest in uniting with others.

The World Stage

At the time of Columbus's discovery of America, Europe was in a state of unending warfare. Europeans fought Europeans as well as Africans and Asians. Wars in defense of rival claims never ceased. Whatever unity held within European Christendom rested upon the hostility and contempt with which Europeans viewed all other racial, religious, and cultural groups. The contempt was unjustified. Europe, being one of the least unified, was also one of the most primitive and least potent of the world's major cultures. For some centuries its home territory had been shrinking.

In the twelfth century, the great civilizations had arrived at a temporary stalemate. Islam, the religion arising in Arabia early in the seventh century A.D., proclaimed Muhammad its prophet and the Koran (*qur'an,* or "book") its central religious text. Like Jews and Christians, Muslims believed in one God. They obeyed strict laws defining personal conduct and social justice, and yet were respectful of other religions, notably Judaism and Christianity, which they defined as true but incompletely understood faiths. Convinced that this world and this life are open to ordering by right reason and right conscience, Islam fostered philosophy, science, and such arts as did not violate the injunction against graven images. Islamic scholars in Spain, much of which had fallen under Muslim control, had a large part in providing the Christian West with philosophical texts of ancient Greece. For centuries Islam nurtured the most dynamic and aggressive culture on the planet. But after subduing the Iberian peninsula in Europe, all of North Africa, and southern Asia as far as northern India, Islam had temporarily spent its force. The Muslims retained a commanding superiority over the Europeans in science, technology, warfare, and general learning. It was the Muslims, in fact, who preserved the works of the ancient astronomer Ptolemy, whose estimates of the earth's size guided Columbus. In China, where printing, paper money, and gunpowder had already been invented, the Sung dynasty had presided over a culture differing from both the Islamic and the Christian world in the West but impressive on its own. Chinese philosophy flourished along with highly refined arts. But in the 1120s the Sungs lost half their territory through war and rebellion, and before the end of the twelfth century central Asia had spawned a new Mongol Empire that would rule for a hundred years.

The thirteenth century belonged to a fierce warrior army out of Asia. In the space of forty years, under the leadership of their ruler, Genghis Khan, the Mongols swept over two continents, totally subjugating China and pressing into both Europe and the Islamic world. In 1260 Islamic forces stopped them just short of Egypt. Thenceforth, the Mongols expanded no more; they held on for a century and then abruptly declined.

The European Economy

The Mongol occupation stimulated Europe's economy and in ways that would have vast consequences. When the Mongols seized land to the east, the wealthiest and most advanced centers in Europe were the great city-states of northern Italy. Venice and Genoa in particular had gained large profits by supplying and transporting the armies of the Crusades, a series of Christian wars against Islamic territory along the eastern Mediterranean and particularly in the ancient Holy Land. Venice and Genoa then established themselves as the principal trading centers for the importation of spices, silks, and other commodities from the Far East. During the Mongol years, the trade route for these many necessities and luxuries from the East had to shift southward, out of reach of the Mongol Empire, and a segment of that route went from the Byzantine Empire, the easternmost portion of the Christian world, by sea to Venice and Genoa. To exploit this trade, the Italians borrowed extensively from the technological and scientific storehouse of the Muslims. They learned to construct and use sails in a way that enabled vessels to sail toward the wind, and acquired a knowledge of mathematics, astronomy, and navigation that was far superior to any then current in Europe.

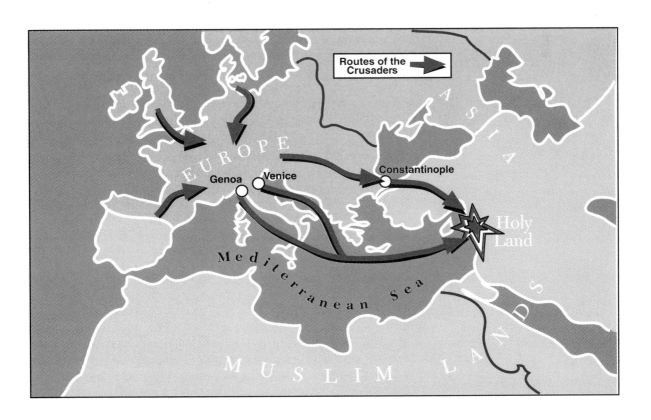

Late in the thirteenth century a Venetian, Marco Polo, spent nearly twenty years in the Far East, mostly in service at the court of Genghis Khan's grandson, the emperor Kublai Khan. Marco Polo's journal gave Europeans their first direct information about the geography and civilization of the Orient, quickened their curiosity, and introduced them to a host of Chinese technological and scientific advances, including gunpowder. Through such borrowings, and by their own ingenious improvements on them, the Italians started Europe along the way to the technological superiority that would, in time, make Europeans masters of the world.

The Ottoman Turks
But Europe's time of world power was yet to come. At the beginning of the fourteenth century, just as the menace of the Mongols was abating, the Muslims rose again, this time under the Ottoman Turks. Before this wave of Islamic zeal had spent itself, the Ottoman Empire would dominate a land mass extending ten thousand miles, from the Danube River to the Red Sea, and including North Africa, Egypt, Syria, Persia, and the Arab peninsula. Through their advanced seamanship, the Muslims dominated the entire Indian Ocean as well.

This expansion had drastic effects on economic conditions in Europe. Eastern commodities could no longer be carried overland to Constantinople, the city that today, as Istanbul in Turkey, is on both sides of the water between eastern Greece and Asia Minor. They now went by water to the Red Sea or the Persian Gulf, and thence overland, through a series of what were in effect toll stations, to Mediterranean ports in Africa and Asia Minor. The price of spices rose greatly, with severe consequences to Europe. Spices—cinnamon, cloves, pepper—were a necessity, not a luxury. Europe suffered from a chronic shortage of winter feed for cattle, and the spices were needed as preservatives for the huge amount of livestock slaughtered every autumn. The population of Europe, moreover, began to increase rapidly at this time, which meant that Oriental spices were becoming scarcer and dearer as the demand was becoming greater. By 1453, when Constantinople fell to the Turks, old trade patterns with the East had been thoroughly disrupted, and Europe's strength was at its lowest in centuries.

The European Social Setting
In the centuries preceding the entrance of the New World of America into the life of the Old, Europe was almost completely rural. Peasant life followed the seasons, along with recurrent celebrations determined by tradition and the Christian calendar. Society was strictly hierarchical, with rigid social classes and a Christian church equally structured from bishops down to clergy. Basic literacy was unavailable to the masses. Disease and other calamities threatened life at earlier ages than the more industrialized peoples of the world expect today. Craftsmen clustered in towns and sorted themselves into guilds—a carpenters' guild, a guild of goldsmiths, and so forth—that controlled standards for entrance and regulated quality and quantity of production.

Of misery, there was more than enough. Agricultural work wrestled from the earth often just enough food to fill stomachs, and sometimes less. Any shift in rain pattern or temperature could bring famine. The thinness of the margin that nature left for human survival got its most dramatic demonstration in the bubonic plague of 1348, which wiped out more than one-third of the people of Europe, townsfolk and villagers alike. This and reappearances of the disease kept the population down for more than a century—incidentally easing pressure on the land and thereby bettering the lives of the survivors. That it took such a disaster to improve the ratio of people to land indicates the delicacy of the balances of soil, effort, and biology amidst which Europeans eked out as many years of life as they could.

Yet there is another side to this grim European existence. Festivity and celebration informed the lives of Europeans. Both peasants and craftsmen worked by a less rigorous schedule than people of recent times. European immigrants to the United States in the late nineteenth century, inheritors of countless generations of labor on the land, would have difficulty adjusting to the clock-timed schedules of American factories. Training for work must have been difficult enough: peasants had to grasp the varied knowledge of planting, reaping, and the management of animals, and learning a craft meant being sent to live in the household of a craftsman. But the skills learned in either case were customary, handed down; they did not elicit the kind of formal literate and mathematical schooling that the work of present-day urban society requires.

The Renaissance
Another way of life and thought was forming in the larger European towns, especially in Italy. Beginning in the fifteenth century, the phenomenon known as the Renaissance, the rebirth, radically altered the thinking of the classes having the luxury of literate and educated thought, and in time was to transform the existence of peasants and day laborers as well.

For centuries Christians in western Europe had labored under the belief that humankind is miserably weak and sinful, subject to the overwhelming forces of temptation and physical nature. The Renaissance was a time in which a small portion of the European populace discovered, or rediscovered from the texts of the ancient Greeks, the powers of human creativity and the openness of nature to investigation and control. Yet the Renaissance itself was devoutly Christian, and harmonious with this Christianity that affirms the goodness of creation and the high place in it that is assigned to humanity.

The economic source of the Renaissance was the flourishing of Italian towns in the sea trade with Arabia, India, and the Far East. Their part in that commerce was to provide sea transport from the eastern Mediterranean, where goods arrived after overland travel. Perhaps the richness of the silks, the spices, and the other goods that passed through their hands on the way to the rest of Europe stimulated the imaginations of Venetian and Genoan merchants and townspeople. It must have revealed to them the splendid things of which nature and human skill are capable. Wealthy families paid painters and other artists for productions that today remain as tributes to the Renaissance.

In the midst of European peoples almost completely rural, Italian merchant cities offered the daily rush of activity, the interchange of

Printing and Exploration

The development of printing coincided with the age of discovery. Instead of shutting up explorers' accounts of their discoveries in dusty letter files, the fifteenth-century printing presses of Europe—Johannes Gutenberg's 1444 press in Mainz, Germany, was the first—broadcast them to the world. The technology of printing spread quickly through Europe, and eight million copies of books were printed by the end of the sixteenth century.

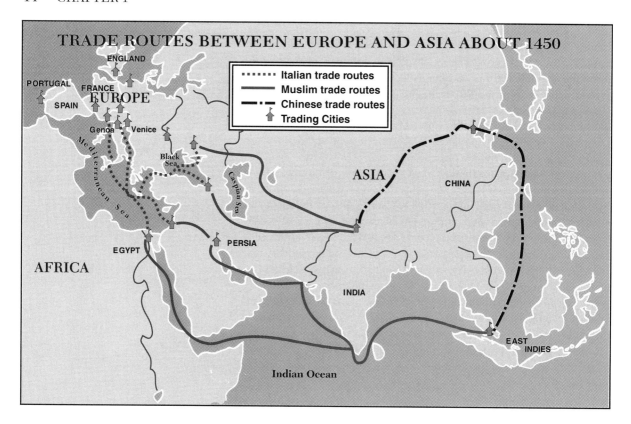

ideas, the vigor that make urban centers places of artistic and intellectual work. Towns too were centers of craftsmanship, from the simplest utilitarian kinds to the most refined metalworking. Renaissance artists belonged to this community of craftsmen, taking joy in the act of making, whether a great painting or the ornate salt dish that the sixteenth-century artist Benvenuto Cellini wrought of gold.

As thin as the line between craft and art was that between art and science. The Renaissance achievement of perspective in painting capturing the sense of depth on a two-dimensional canvas, was an aesthetic accomplishment. But it also reflected an essentially scientific curiosity about how the eye perceives space. The poet, painter, sculptor, and architect Michelangelo did not think it outside his province to examine the motion of horses, and so he did careful sketches of the leg positions of the animals as they ran.

This salt dish made from gold is attributed to Benvenuto Cellini.
(Courtesy, Melville Library)

The Reformation   In the sixteenth century began a religious movement, the Reformation, that like the Renaissance changed European thought and behavior. In 1517 a German priest, Martin Luther, nailed to the door of the cathedral at Wittenberg—a common way of opening a debate—his Ninety-Five Theses, defining what he saw as abuses of the Catholic Church. In the years that followed, Luther developed a theology denying that the earthly Church and its sacraments are the means to salvation. That, Luther insisted, comes of God's freely given grace and the believer's response in faith. The theologian John Calvin emphasized the individual's utter dependence on God's will. The Reformation captured much of northern Europe, setting Protestant countries against Catholic and generating conflicts within nations, including hostilities among the creeds and sects into which Protestantism itself splintered.

On the surface, the Reformation would seem opposite to the Renaissance in its definition of the human condition. The Renaissance celebrated the powers of intellect and talent; Protestantism brooded over the fallenness and helplessness of humanity. But the Reformation too increased productive activity. Protestant morality demanded work: not only strenuous but constant, methodical, carefully planned effort, a subjugation of the wayward impulses of the individual. The Renaissance awakened among artists and craftsmen an exuberant expression of human energies. Protestantism encouraged work for restraining and giving form to energies that might otherwise turn malicious. But together the two movements turned Christians to the world and the ways human skill and effort can master it. Without the scientific investigation and technological experimenting of the Renaissance and the Reformation, the European settlement of the Americas would have taken a far different course.

Africa

As Europe went through its long stretch of largely self-isolated history, much of the land known, even in the twentieth century, as the "Dark Continent" was growing wealthy, learned, and powerful. Yet Africa to Europeans was a land of "savages" that held riches, and the route to riches, that they coveted and as Christians felt entitled to.

Geography and Climate   Man is believed to have originated from 4 to 1.5 million years ago in the high grasslands of eastern and central Africa. Gradually these early human beings spread out across Africa and to other continents.

The size of Africa is remarkable. It stretches 5,000 miles from its northernmost to its southernmost point and it is 4,600 miles at its greatest breadth. Several distinct geographical regions divide the continent. Starting with the northern coast, a narrow, fertile strip runs along the Mediterranean from the Atlantic to the Gulf of Tunis, east of present-day Algeria. A band of savanna or grassland runs beneath it and a bit farther east. Below this expands the Sahara, covering more than four million square miles, too dry to farm but larger than all of the United States by about 400,000 square miles. The central area beneath the Sahara, called the Sudan, is covered with grasslands down to the Equator, where they meet rain forests and mountains. The Kalahari Desert covers a large region near the southern tip. Grasslands, mountains, desert, and semi-desert complete the landscape in the southern region. The population of Africa in 1500 was approximately 78 million, nearly the same as that of Europe.

In many respects Africa is the most inhospitable of the populated continents. The ability of Africans to build complex cultures and survive

Figure of kneeling African woman with child. Western Sudan: Djenne culture. *(Courtesy, The Menil Collection, Houston)*

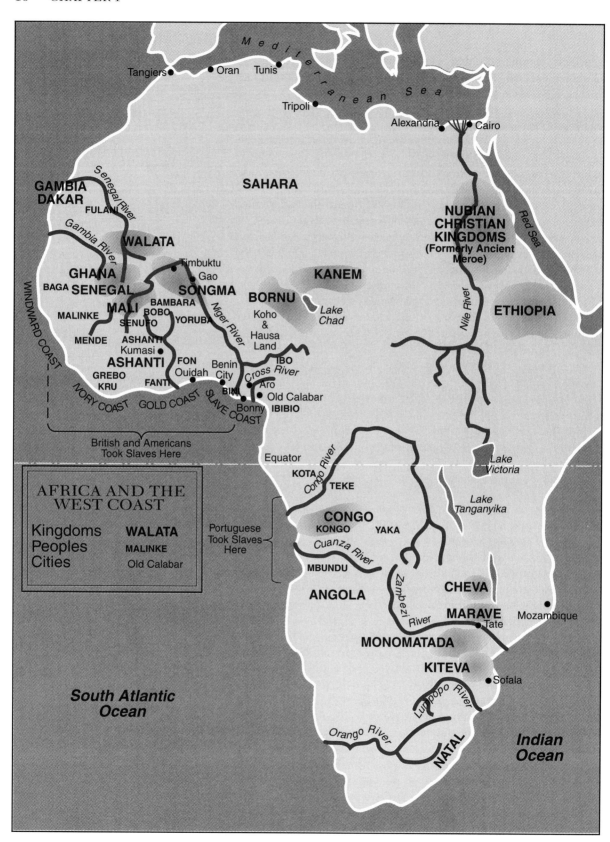

AFRICA AND THE WEST COAST

Kingdoms   **WALATA**
Peoples   **MALINKE**
Cities   Old Calabar

many hardships realizes the scope of human enterprise and purpose. The natural geography kept intruders away from its interior until the nineteenth century. Its deserts are hostile to habitation and travel. Throughout the whole of the continent, a plateau that rises swiftly from the coastline leaves few natural harbors. Even where entry is possible, the traveler is blocked by the desert, semi-desert, or nearly impenetrable forest that stands beyond the coast.

Africa has some of the world's longest and widest rivers, but the high elevation south of the equator makes river navigation difficult. Africans learned to adapt to a climate that ranged from the hot, dusty, dry summer weather and cold winter nights and bone-chilling winds of the desert to the hot and humid rain forest. In northern and southern Africa were areas with mild, rainy winters and warm summers, but diseases thrived for which the Europeans had no tolerance. The half-inch tsetse fly carried the deadly sleeping sickness that prevented animal transport as a means of travel south of the Sahara, and so interior travel was primarily on foot with porters. The interior was divided by the Great Rift Valley, a series of cliffs and troughs that separated the tribes on either side of it. The ability to eke a living out of this formidable landscape and not only to maneuver, but also to profit from its tangled interiors required skills that Africans developed over many thousands of years. It was a triumph of human ingenuity and persistence.

Empires Rise and Fall Ancient Egypt is the African civilization most commonly known, but the continent nurtured numerous empires and states growing, shifting, and overlapping, then falling and rebuilding. What they held in common was an interest in trade among communities far and near, the development and refinement of artistic endeavors, and slavery.

The Nile Valley, whence sprang the civilization of ancient Egypt, had soil so fertile that it required but a minimum of labor to farm more productively than anywhere else in the continent or perhaps the world. The surrounding desert sands made ideal storage for cereal crops, in underground bins, and domesticated animals had ample riverside pastures to graze upon. These conditions created the opportunity for society to grow to a high population density. Records place some early dynasties as far back as 5000 B.C., and archaeologists have found hieroglyphics and skillfully wrought gold from that period.

The Egyptians learned to work copper as well as gold and created advanced tools, carefully constructed furniture, and the huge crosscut saws that enabled them to cut large stones and to build the immense tombs, the pyramids, that housed their Pharaohs after death. For builders the Pharaohs used slaves. Typically these were war captives from neighboring populations, although from 3000 B.C. onward, slaves were also regularly bought and sold—as they were in many parts of the world.

Ancient Egypt was the largest and most advanced among the enduring civilizations in northern Africa. Others arose somewhat concurrently. Egyptian traders carried information and skills to Greece, Rome, Arabia, and India as well as to the regions west and south of them

Gou, god of war, a metal sculpture from the Fon culture in Dahomey. *(Courtesy, New York Public Library)*

in Africa. Meroë was the seat of a power, the kingdom of Kush, that rose to greatness. Iron making began in Kush, for the area, located south of the Nile Valley, was rich in iron ore. With iron weapons and iron tools, the kingdom became the richest and most influential in Africa during the first and second centuries A.D. Ancient Egypt had begun its decline long before that, finally falling in 332 B.C. to Alexander the Great. Later it became a province of the Roman Empire.

Generally, in Africa north of the equator, centralized states with hereditary rulers developed, while in regions isolated from exchange with other cultures, more egalitarian, decentralized communities came about essentially for ecological reasons. These were ruled, or rather regulated, by kinship groups such as clans and family lineages, and overall developed more slowly than the Sudan and northern Africa.

In those areas, civilization rolled forward swiftly. By the first century A.D., Greek merchants were trading with Axum, a rival of Meroë in the hills in the northern part of modern Libya. Art flourished throughout these rising civilizations. The rulers of Axum built stone obelisks as high as ninety feet, in addition to fine temples and palaces. In the fourth century A.D., the King of Axum imported iron weapons with which his armies were able to attack and destroy Meroë. Along the west coast, the kingdom of Ghana was formed about A.D. 200, reaching its height many centuries later. Since around the birth of Christ, both Jews and Christians settled along the coast of North Africa, and until early in the seventh century Christianity won some converts in North Africa and within Egypt and Meroë. The pattern of emerging rival states that traded, competed, and warred with one another was interrupted by the arrival of Arabs, aflame with the spirit of Islam and the will and means to conquer and convert.

African Art (1200–1700). This figure is decorated with Indian Ocean cowrie shells, which were used as currency in many parts of Africa. *(National Museum of Denmark, Department of Ethnography)*

Muslim Invaders

In A.D. 639, Muslim invaders swept through Egypt, easily subduing the country within two years. Thence they marched westward, were temporarily turned back by the Berbers, and eventually made their way into Berber territory and converted many. From there they conquered Spain and Portugal. In the eleventh century they seized all of North Africa and parts of both western and eastern coasts. It became the "Maghreb," or western part of the Arab world, and even the Berbers, who struggled to maintain their own language and racial identity, gave themselves over to the Arab religion, dress, speech, and customs. The vast Arab empire thus created had an enormous impact on Africa, bringing to it a unifying religion and many cultural elements critical to Africa's development up to the fifteenth century.

The conquest was followed by a period of political stability and economic growth. The Muslims brought learning to Africa at a time when much of Europe was illiterate and impoverished. Through them information about astronomy, advanced mathematics, medicine, clear and strict rules for governing and behaving, and a keenly managed and sophisticated system of trade passed to Africans. They also ran an active slave trade. Captives were sold throughout North Africa, into areas of Arabia, Spain, and Portugal, and to countries involved in the Arabs'

Indian Ocean trade route. Tens of thousands of slaves were dispersed this way.

The stability and trade engendered by the Muslim invasions and Islamic rule stimulated the rise of yet more African empires. The states that rose up during the period from about the eighth century to the fourteenth—the Hausa and Kanem-Baru, the Mali and Songhai, the Congo (also written *Kongo*) and Guinea—each had its goods to contribute to the trading system, each collected fees from those traveling through it, and each had fierce rivalries and frequent wars with the others. These states grew powerful and rich, their coffers built on international trade that went on, largely uninterrupted, until new waves of invasions began in the twelfth century.

The African   The decentralized regions of Africa, whose popula-
Slave Trade   tion met the harsh ecological challenge of their en-
                       vironments by engaging in subsistence agriculture,
were especially vulnerable to slave traders. These societies lacked central government structures and standing armies to protect themselves from the more powerful and predatory neighbors on their borders. As these neighbors took captives to sell as slaves, slavery became an essential part of African trade.

African slavery existed long before the Europeans initiated the transatlantic slave trade. From the seventh to the nineteenth century, more than a thousand years, Africans were bought and sold as slaves. In Islamic Africa as well as a few other areas, slaves of children could gradually free themselves, as could slave soldiers through the process of manumission preached in the Koran. In previous centuries many slaves had intermarried with their captors and so became integrated into a tribe. But this potential for liberation slowly changed. A general rule evolved that proclaimed that slaves born in captivity could not be sold, and this increased the need for slaves bought or stolen elsewhere. It also expanded the slave population to such an extent that, in some areas, slaves began to outnumber free people two or even three to one. Wars among the large states, or by large communities upon smaller ones (there were, according to one estimate, some one thousand smaller states), put more slaves into the rapidly expanding market, many of them needed as soldiers. The trade brought even more wealth to those states able to participate in it, and with that wealth came intensified rivalries and insatiable greed. The slave trade was profitable because of the trading networks and because slaves often cost little or nothing at the beginning of the market chain. The system could not work without African knowledge of the wild to traverse the unwelcoming land, African warriors to capture slaves, African merchants to facilitate the sales, and carefully managed agreements among populations and states.

Arab Africa controlled the spice trade and a large portion of the slave trade. Western and central Africans controlled the gold and the supply of slaves, as well as the flow of trade. So poised, Africa seemed to have everything that Europe wanted and needed, and it was available legitimately through trade, or illegitimately through plunder.

The diversity of the trade and the distance spanned to support that

One slave trader explained his operation:

"In the daytime we called at the villages we passed, and purchased our slaves fairly; but in the night we . . . broke into the villages and, rushing into the huts of the inhabitants, seized men, woman, and children promiscuously."

trade were stupendous given the time, difficulties, and dangers of travel. Yet European and African trade goods were distributed all over the northern half of the continent. While such trade had existed before the Arab invasions, Arab occupation and influence briskly increased commerce and made it more sophisticated. A merchant in the 1400s might start his trans-Saharan trek with beads and Egyptian cottons and exchange those at the first stop for camels. There he could pick up minerals, selling them for kolo nuts from the Yoruba kingdom on the southern edges of the savanna. Those he might sell to merchants in the centrally located Hausa states, picking up cotton and leather goods in that vicinity. Going eastwards again, he would perhaps exchange his merchandise for ostrich feathers and slaves, selling those in his home city, from which he might have been absent for as long as ten years.

Salt from the north and gold from the south were the most valuable commodities. Copper, cloth, beads, jewelry, horses, cattle, and dried fruit also came from the north, while commodities such as knives and swords, spices, and rugs came to East Africa and then west via the Arabian Indian Ocean trade, in exchange for gold, ivory, slaves, and skins. Through East Africa also came new foods from Indonesia, many of which—banana and coconut, for example—enabled the populations there to spread farther south and west. Iron, weaving, pottery, leather goods, slaves, grains, dried fish and mollusks, medicines, and baskets were but a few of the many goods that moved from south and west to north and east. Besides gold, cowrie shells from the Indian Ocean, iron bars, brass weights, and bolts of cotton cloth were used for currency, as was direct barter. An obligation to care for the elderly, widows, and orphans was pervasive throughout African society.

Olaudah Equiano. *(Courtesy, Collection of Hugh Cleland)*

OLAUDAH EQUIANO

Olaudah Equiano was kidnapped as a boy from what is now the Benin province of Nigeria. He was sold to British slavers in 1756, brought to Barbados, and then to Virginia. After service in the French and Indian War, he was able to buy his freedom and lived to publish his uniquely detailed memoirs in 1789. This part of his story, describing his capture in the 1700s, is a classic account of an experience shared by millions of Africans from the 1500s to the early 1800s.

[W]hen the grown people in the neighborhood [of Benin] were gone far in the fields to labor, the children assembled together in some of the neighboring premises to play; and commonly some of us used to get up a tree to look out for any assailant, or kidnapper, that might come upon us—for they sometimes took those opportunities of our parents' absence, to attack and carry off as many as they could seize. One day as I was watching at the top of a tree in our yard, I saw one of those people come into the yard of our next neighbor but one to

kidnap, there being many stout young people in it. Immediately on this I gave the alarm of the rogue, and he was surrounded by the stoutest of them, who entangled him with cords, so that he could not escape till some of the grown people came and secured him. But, alas! ere long it was my fate to be thus attacked, and to be carried off, when none of the grown people were nigh. . . .

The first object which saluted my eyes when I arrived on the coast, was the sea, and a slave ship, which was then riding at anchor, and waiting for its cargo. These filled me with astonishment, which was soon converted into terror, when I was carried on board. I was immediately handled, and tossed up to see if I were sound, by some of the crew; and I was now persuaded that I had gotten into a world of bad spirits, and that they were going to kill me. . . . When I looked round the ship too, and saw a large furnace of copper boiling, and a multitude of black people of every description chained together, every one of their countenances expressing dejection and sorrow, I no longer doubted on my fate; and, quite overpow-

Portugal's Crusade by Sea

Europe desperately needed a way of coping with the Muslims and trading with the East. Portugal found it. The people of that tiny kingdom, free for two centuries from Muslim domination but struggling for survival in a rocky and barren land, had turned to the sea, first as fishermen, then as traders. As seagoing traders whose home base was on the Atlantic, not the Mediterranean, they understandably thought of an indirect route to the spices that Europe needed. With Africa's gold and ivory Europe could buy spices. If Europeans could find a sea route around Africa to the East, they could bypass the Muslims who controlled North Africa's trade and establish trade directly with the black rulers of West Africa and the Sudan.

Geography was a reason Portugal and Spain were the leaders in the late fifteenth-century expansion of Europe. The Iberian peninsula, which Portugal and Spain occupied, jutted well out into the Atlantic and constituted the southwesternmost region of the continent of Europe. Seventy years before Columbus sailed, Portuguese and Spanish sailors had pushed far out into the Atlantic. The Canary Islands, which are located approximately seventy miles off the coast of West Africa, became Spanish territory in the 1420s. At the same time the Azores, a group of islands almost eight hundred miles out into the Atlantic, became Portuguese colonies. Portugal and Spain were both maritime powers long before the rest of Europe was even beginning to look westward beyond its shores.

It is also important that the two European powers were among the first to consolidate into nation-states. In the twelfth century, Portugal

---

ered with horror and anguish, I fell motionless on the deck and fainted. When I recovered a little, I found some black people about me, who I believed were some of those who had brought me on board, and had been receiving their pay; they talked to me in order to cheer me, but all in vain. I asked them if we were not to be eaten by those white men with horrible looks, red faces, and long hair. They told me I was not. . . .

I was soon put down under the decks, and there I received such a salutation in my nostrils as I had never experienced in my life: so that, with the loathsomeness of the stench, and crying together, I became so sick and low that I was not able to eat, nor had I the least desire to taste any thing. I now wished for the last friend, death, to relieve me; but soon, to my grief, two of the white men offered me eatables; and, on my refusing to eat, one of them held me fast by the hands, and laid me across, I think the windlass, and tied my feet, while the other flogged me severely. I had never experienced any thing of this kind before, and although not being used to the water, I naturally feared that element the first time I saw

it, yet, nevertheless, could I have got over the nettings, I would have jumped over the side, but I could not; and besides, the crew used to watch us very closely who were not chained down to the decks, lest we should leap into the water; and I have seen some of these poor African prisoners most severely cut, for attempting to do so, and hourly whipped for not eating. This indeed was often the case with myself. In a little time after, amongst the poor chained men, I found some of my own nation, which in a small degree gave ease to my mind. I inquired of these what was to be done with us? they gave me to understand, we were to be carried to these white people's country to work for them. I then was a little revived, and thought, if it were no worse than working, my situation was not so desperate; but still I feared I should be put to death, the white people looked and acted, as I thought, in so savage a manner; for I had never seen among any people such instances of brutal cruelty; and this not only shown towards us blacks, but also to some of the whites themselves.

had become an independent kingdom, and when Queen Isabella of Castile married King Ferdinand of Aragon in 1469, the two most powerful political entities in Spain came together. Both Spain and Portugal enjoyed the political unity and the economic resources necessary for exploration and colonization.

Both, moreover, were possessed of a crusading zeal unknown in the rest of Europe. In the eighth century, the Moors from North Africa had invaded Iberia, and they carried their Arabic, Muslim culture deep into Spain and Portugal. Over the next seven hundred years, Christian monarchs fought a bloody war to drive the Moors back into North Africa. In the process Spain acquired a religious identity bordering on fanaticism, imbued with a passion for expelling the infidels and upholding the Christian faith: a passion that after the Protestant Reformation would be committed to the defense of Roman Catholicism. Portugal expelled the last of the Moorish armies in 1245. Ferdinand and Isabella did not get rid of the Moors until 1492.

In the year Columbus headed for "the Indies," then, Spain and Portugal possessed the unity, maritime skills, and resources needed for exploration and empire.

Marine Monsters: from Olaus Magnus, Historia de Gentibus Septentrionalibus, 1555. (*Courtesy, New York Public Library*)

Prince Henry the Navigator   The man who directed Portugal's efforts to take advantage of the possibilities for pioneering by sea was Prince Henry the Navigator. Henry began his explorations in 1415. At the age of twenty-one this extraordinary young man retired from the court and from politics, became governor of the southernmost province of Portugal, and began building a strange settlement there, on Cape St. Vincent—"where endeth land and where beginneth sea." For the next forty years he gathered sailors, astronomers, mapmakers, instrument makers, and shipbuilders from all over Europe, and subsidized expeditions to explore the west coast of Africa, seeking to reach India by ocean. Overcoming the fears of superstitious sailors that ships would run into boiling hot waters at the equator, the grand and audacious Portuguese undertaking was only temporarily set back by Henry's death in 1460. In 1487 Bartholomeu Dias, his ship blown off course by a gale, rounded the southern tip of Africa. Then from 1497 to 1499, Vasco da Gama made his celebrated voyage around the Cape of Good Hope to India with a four-vessel fleet, returning two years later with a cargo of pepper and cinnamon. Within twenty more years Henry's dream was fulfilled, for Portugal had established a maritime empire that extended the full breadth of the Indian Ocean.

Other Europeans, inspired by the Portuguese, sought to share trade in the East. None reckoned that they could overtake Portugal in the race around Africa, but several thought they might find an alternate course. It was reasonably well known that the earth was round, and not knowing of the existence of America, they thought that a daring sailor might easily reach the Orient by sailing west from Europe. The most persistent of seamen who so reasoned was Christopher Columbus. His voyages profited from Prince Henry's development of a small sailing ship, the caravel. Its hull design and sail plan enabled the caravel to sail faster than earlier ships. Now mariners could go as far as they wished with assurance that they could return. And so Columbus made his spectacular voyages, thinking that he was finding the Orient but in fact opening a new continent to Europeans.

The Spanish Empire

The consequence of Columbus's voyages was a flurry of efforts by other Europeans to capitalize on his findings. The Portuguese did little, for they were convinced that Columbus had not reached Asia. Other European monarchs, including the Kings of England and France, backed voyages upon Columbus's mistaken belief that he had found the Indies, or a passage to them. Henry VII of England sponsored trips by the Italian John Cabot (Giovanni Caboto) in 1497 and 1498. Cabot explored the American coast from Labrador to Chesapeake Bay and discovered vast areas teeming with fish, but found neither spices nor a passage to India. Henry's England profited little from these and later explorations by John Cabot's son Sebastian. French and Venetian efforts were likewise unprofitable, and both states had pressing preoccupations, and so they, like England, soon abandoned the search for the Indies. Hence, for nearly a hundred years Spain had a virtual monopoly on exploration and discovery in the New World.

Explorers for Spain   The greatest of explorers sailing under the Spanish flag was, of course, Columbus himself. Columbus made four voyages in all: 1492–93, 1493–96, 1498–1500, and 1502–04. He visited most of the major islands of the Caribbean, the northern coast of South America, and the Central American mainland from Honduras to Panama, and planted colonies in several of these places. In Cuba one of Columbus's sailors reported "many people, with a firebrand in the hand, and herbs to drink the smoke thereof." By the 1600s tobacco smoking would become the rage all over Europe. In activities other than navigation, Columbus proved inept. He so neglected and mismanaged the colonies that he had to be removed as governor; and when he died in 1506 he was still convinced that what he had explored was part of Asia. Columbus's reports of the new land's abundance and its natives' childlike innocence planted in the European mind the image of an earthly paradise, a lost Eden inhabited by noble savages, that would shape ideas about the New World for centuries to come.

One of Columbus's contemporaries, an Italian navigator named Amerigo Vespucci, first convinced Europeans that Columbus had discovered a new continent. In 1507 a German cartographer, impressed by Vespucci's writings, named the new land "America" in his honor. Vespucci's detailed descriptions of terrain, plants, and people added greatly to European knowledge and understanding of the shape and size of the New World. Henceforth all Europe knew America for what it was, a new continent and a barrier between Europe and Asia.

Nothing of any recognized value had yet been found in America, and so the problem now was to find a strait through a land mass of unknown size. In 1513 a Spanish explorer, Juan Ponce de León, visited what is now the southeastern United States. He named the area Florida,

Sailing through the rich Grand Bank fisheries off Labrador, the explorer John Cabot wrote in his diary of "cod so thick they sometimes stayed my ship."

After sailing along the coast of what is now South America in 1501, Vespucci described the land and its people:

"The inhabitants of the New World do not have goods of their own, but all things are held in common. They live together without King, without government, and each is his own master. . . . If the terrestrial paradise be in any part of this earth, I esteem that it is not far distant from these parts."

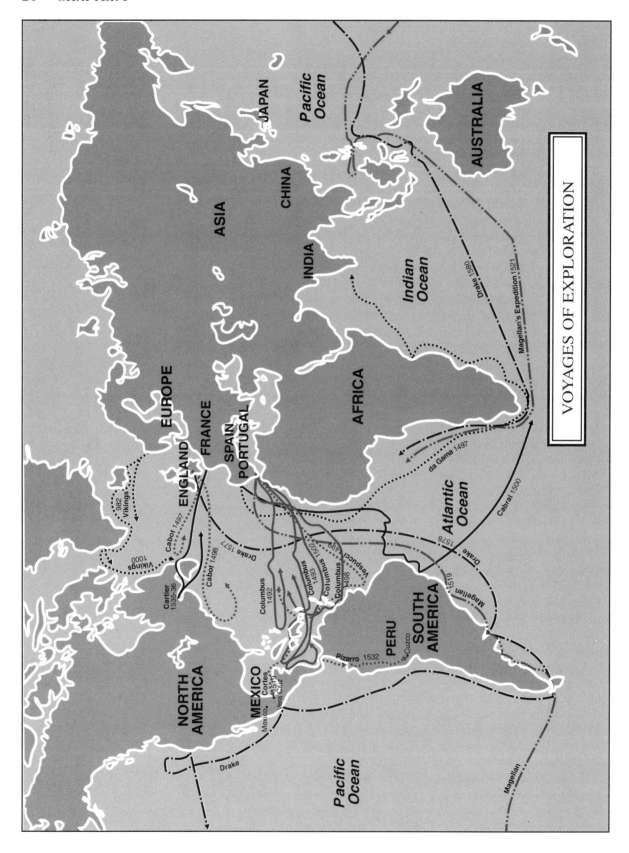

VOYAGES OF EXPLORATION

roughly translatable as "land of flowers." A chance discovery in 1513 stimulated the search for a passage to the Orient. Vasco Núñez de Balboa, a Spanish adventurer, led a band of followers in search of gold in Central America, crossed the Isthmus of Darien, and sighted the Pacific. Spain promptly planted a colony in the vicinity, and explorers, encouraged to learn that the two oceans were separated only by an extremely narrow strip of land, renewed their hopes. After the coast of Central America and Mexico had been fairly thoroughly cruised, it appeared that the most promise of finding a route lay to the south. And in 1519 Ferdinand Magellan, a Portuguese sailing under Spanish auspices, set out on a monumental voyage. On September 20 he embarked with five small ships and 275 men; three years later, on September 8, 1522, one worm-eaten ship and eighteen survivors sailed upriver into the harbor at Seville. Magellan had been killed by natives in the Philippines, but his place in history was assured. His expedition had discovered a passage to the Pacific lying between the southern tip of South America and the islands now named Tierra del Fuego: the narrow waterway has been named the Strait of Magellan. Thence the voyagers had sailed across the Pacific, through the Indian Ocean, around Africa, and back to Spain.

The first journey to circle the globe, it added enormously to Europe's knowledge of the world and demonstrated for all time that it was not feasible for Spain to try to compete with Portugal in the East by sailing west. The route was simply too difficult; and besides, by the time Magellan's vessels reached the Indian Ocean the Portuguese had already established the bases that made them dominant in the entire area. In 1519, while Magellan's ships were nearing Tierra del Fuego, another voyage of discovery brought the first Europeans to what is now the Texas Gulf Coast. Searching like Magellan for a route to the Orient, Alonso Alvarez de Piñeda and his 270 men visited the mouth of the Rio Grande River before returning to Spain.

Beginnings of World History   The exploratory voyages of the Spanish and Portuguese were seminal events in the history of the world. Until 1492 there was no "world," at least of a global stretch. Europeans, Asians, and Africans had only the vaguest notions of one another's existence, and the people of North America, South America, Australia, and the Pacific Islands were cut off almost completely. There were some tenuous commercial connections. European traders exchanged goods with West Africans. Arab businessmen in East Africa regularly crossed the Indian Ocean to trade with India. Italian merchants worked through traders in the Middle East to acquire Chinese products. And the Islamic religion by the fourteenth century was moving west into North Africa and east into Indonesia and the Philippines. What the Spanish and Portuguese voyages of exploration managed to do was bring together all of the previously separate regions of the world.

The process of creating a global community, of course, would take centuries to complete, but after 1500 no one part of the world was isolated from its distant neighbors. Religions, technologies, products, services, animals, plants, and people began spreading from one conti-

The Great Temple of Tenochtitlán reconstructed by Ignacio Marquina from descriptions by Spanish conquerors and existing Aztec monuments. *(Courtesy, American Museum of Natural History)*

Bartolomé de Las Casas (1474–1566) spent most of his long life attempting to protect native Americans against the massacres, tortures, slavery, tribute, and forced labor imposed on them by their Spanish conquerors. Modern scholars generally accept the accuracy of Las Casas's shocking portraits of devastation, some of which he personally witnessed. Today, however, many view these horrors not as the outcome of some peculiar Spanish cruelty but as characteristic of the "Columbian encounter" between Europeans and other cultures in the age of exploration and conquest.

"The natives are likewise the most delicate people, weak and of feeble constitution, and less than any other can they bear fatigue, and they very easily die of whatsoever infirmity; so much so, that not even the sons of our Princes and of nobles, brought up in royal and gentle life, are so delicate as they; although there are among them such as are of the peasant class. They are also a very poor people, who of worldly goods possess little, nor wish to possess: and they are therefore neither proud, nor ambitious, nor avaricious. . . .

Among these gentle sheep, gifted by their Maker with the above qualities, the Spaniards entered as soon as they knew them, like wolves, tigers, and lions which have been starving for many days, and since forty years they have done nothing else; nor do they otherwise at the present day, than outrage, slay, afflict, torment, and destroy them with strange and new, and divers kinds of cruelty, never before seen nor heard of, nor read of. . . . The reason why the Christians have killed and destroyed such infinite numbers of souls, is solely because they have made gold their ultimate aim."

nent to another, and so did disease, exploitation, and war. World history, in the sense of an interaction of all regions of the globe, had begun.

The Aztecs, Maya, and Incas

The early Spanish settlements in the West Indies proved reasonably prosperous, establishing some economies based on cattle raising with Spanish labor and others founded on sugar planting with Indian slave labor. But raising cattle and growing sugar were not the kinds of activities that quickened the imagination or filled the treasuries of the Spanish monarchs. Far more exciting were rumors of highly civilized kingdoms in the interiors of Mexico, Central America, and northwestern South America, and of their stores of gold and silver. An expedition set out in 1519 to find, conquer, plunder, and Christianize these kingdoms. In command was Hernán Cortés, a thirty-two-year-old soldier and adventurer.

The Aztec Indians had dominated the valley land of Mexico since the early 1300s. From their capital city of Tenochtitlán, now Mexico City, they sent out war parties to exact tribute from other tribes. In the capital the Aztecs had surgeons and hospitals as advanced as the best in Europe, but they also practiced human sacrifice. They worshiped many gods but particularly Quetzalcoatl, the feathered serpent, and the blood-thirsty Hummingbird. In the space of only four days the Aztecs once sacrificed from 20,000 to 60,000 human beings at the altar in Tenochtitlán. In 1519 as news of the Spanish encroachments reached them, the court astrologers forecast a war of the gods and the emperor Montezuma II stepped up the ritual killings. When the emperor finally realized that the Spanish were not gods, he fought ably and might have held them off. But during the siege of his city, smallpox imported from Europe decimated the Indian population. In a matter of months Cortés had penetrated the heart of the Aztec Empire, though it took two years to complete the systematic looting and destruction of Tenochtitlán and the total conquest of the Aztec people. The Aztecs, like the later Indian tribes Europeans encountered in America, had developed no immunity against the perennial European epidemics. Between 1500 and 1600 the native population of the New World declined, by various estimates, from as much as 70 to 90 percent.

After subduing the Aztecs, Cortés's men moved on to seize the Mayan lands of the southeastern Mexican peninsula of Yucatán and the present Central American republic of Guatemala. From about A.D. 300 to 900 the Maya had a culture advanced in architecture and representative arts and notable in astronomy: their calendar remains a marvel. Though the Maya, like the Aztecs, were warriors, the Aztecs had militarily overshadowed them. The relation between the empire-building Aztecs and the artistic Maya has been roughly compared to that between ancient Rome, skilled in organization and administration, and the culturally sophisticated Greek city-states. But the Maya had their own form of organization in the form of an aristocratic priesthood that lived off the labor of the populace. By the time of the Spanish conquest, Maya civilization had long since passed its greatness. Descendants of a people subjected to a priestly caste were now to be subject to adventurers and then to a Spanish colonial aristocracy. Even in the twentieth century, the Maya of Central America would live under regimes distinguished for the ruthlessness of their dominant classes and the military and police in the service of the wealthy.

South of the Maya and the Aztecs, the Incas ruled an area stretching from what is now modern-day Colombia through Peru to Chile, a distance equal to that from New York City to the Panama Canal. Inspired by rumors of Incan gold, in 1532 Francisco Pizarro, an illiterate adventurer in the service of the Spanish crown, entered Peru with a force of fewer than two hundred men. He seized and executed the Incan ruler, Atahualpa, placing himself at the head of an empire of six or eight million souls and fabulous riches of gold and silver. Pizarro was mur-

This description of a Peruvian garden, written by the illegitimate son of an Inca princess and a Spanish laborer, appeared in a work published in England in 1625:

"This Garden was in the Incas time a Garden of Silver and Gold, as they had in the Kings' houses, where they had many sorts of Hearbes, Flowers, Plants, Trees, Beasts great and small, wilde, tame: Snakes, Lizards, Snailes, Butterflies, small and great Birds, each set in their place. They had . . . Fruit-trees with the fruite on them all of Gold and Silver, resembling the naturall. They had also in the house heapes of wood, all counterfeit of Gold and Silver, as they had in the house royal: likewise they had great statues of men and women, and children . . . All the Vessel[s] . . . for the Temple's service, Pots, Pans, Tubs, Hogsheads, was of Gold and Silver, even to the Spades and Pickaxes for the Garden."

Machu Picchu, the fabled "Lost City of the Incas," clings to a ridge high in the Andes Mountains above the Urubamba Valley, eighty-five hundred feet above sea level. Built by the Incan ruler, Pachacuti, about 1450 and mysteriously abandoned around the time of the Spanish conquest, it was never found by the *conquistadores*. Once a vital part of the vast Inca Empire in the 1400s, Machu Picchu remained unknown to the outside world until a Yale history professor named Hiram Bingham discovered it in 1911. *(Braniff International)*

dered by one of his own men in 1541, but Peru, like most of South and Central America, would remain under Spanish rule for nearly three hundred years. Only Brazil, awarded to Portugal by the Treaty of Tordesillas in 1494, was outside Spain's vast New World domain.

In the years after Columbus, Spanish *conquistadores,* far outnumbered by the Aztecs, Incas, and other native peoples, subdued them with relative ease. Indian warriors on foot with weapons made of stone and bone were no match for Spaniards on horseback with steel swords and guns. With superior technology, and with bravado, cunning, and occasional treachery, the Spanish made themselves masters of all they invaded. They also deliberately destroyed most of the Indian cultures and imposed their own. Human sacrifice gave way to Holy Communion as intrepid friars and priests converted the natives to Christianity. Ornate Spanish buildings built by Indian laborers rose on the stone foundations of native structures. Roman Catholic churches, their altars carved by native artisans and encrusted with Indian gold and silver, replaced temples to the sun and moon. With remarkable efficiency and considerable cruelty, the Spanish established an empire that filled their coffers with gold and silver, while rumors of yet undiscovered New World treasures swept through Europe.

Coronado wrote to his monarch of the peoples in the kingdoms he visited:

"The people of the towns seem to me to be of ordinary size and intelligent, although I do not think that they have the judgment and intelligence which they ought to have to build their houses in the way in which they have, for most of them are entirely naked except the covering of their privy parts. . . ."

Exploration of the West   In the 1540s Hernando de Soto and Francisco Vásquez de Coronado separately explored parts of the present-day United States for gold. De Soto, after landing on the west coast of Florida, led his men into North Carolina, turning westward and ending somewhere at or just west of the Mississippi River, in what is now Tennessee, where he died in 1542. Ultimately, over three hundred of his followers made their way back to Mexico via the Mississippi River. Coronado moved northward out of Mexico and probably traveled as far as Kansas. When he returned he made clear that the fabled "seven Cities of Cíbola," cities said to be made of gold, did not exist and that there was little else in the area to attract settlement.

Spanish exploration of the California coast also occurred in the 1540s. In 1542 Juan Rodriguez Cabrillo, a Portuguese explorer in the employ of Spain, hoped to discover the Northwest Passage between the Pacific and the Atlantic. He first sailed into San Diego Bay and later went northward, perhaps as far as Oregon. Following Sir Francis Drake's claiming of California for the English, the Spaniards, fearing they might lose the region, sent Sebastián Vizcaíno in 1602 to report about California to the Spanish monarch. Vizcaíno recommended to the King that Spain establish colonies there, but further Spanish activity along the West Coast would await the passing of nearly a century.

Early French Explorations   In 1524 King Francis I of France sent an Italian navigator, Giovanni da Verrazano, to explore the coast of North America. Hoping to find a passage to the East Indies, Verrazano tried the Hudson River (where a bridge bears his name today), and other places from New York to Newfoundland, to no avail. But he did establish France's claim to the region, which he named "New France."

By 1535 a French explorer, Jacques Cartier, had discovered and named the St. Lawrence River. He also made friends with the Huron Indians there, who told him of a fabulously rich kingdom far upriver. Cartier then invited the King of the Hurons to return home with him and meet the King of France. After hearing the Indian King's story Francis I sent Cartier in 1541 with ten ships to explore the St. Lawrence. The expedition sailed as far as the site of present-day Montreal, but failed to find the storied kingdom. Far to the south, another group of Frenchmen in 1564 established a colony, Fort Caroline, near present-day Jacksonville, Florida. French Protestants, called Huguenots, remained in this colony until the Spanish massacred them. In 1565 the Spanish founded St. Augustine, the first permanent settlement in what would one day become part of the United States.

England: The Sceptered Isle

Henry VII   When Henry VII, the first King belonging to the House of Tudor, ascended the throne in 1485, the royal treasury had been depleted by a long civil war, the War of the Roses.

Henry might have been expected to secure his position in the traditional way, allying himself with groups of nobles. Instead, he built up the independent power of the Crown by taking a number of commoners into the government. As the principal instrument for his attack on the nobility he created the Court of the Star Chamber, through which people could be seized, tried without a jury, and punished by fines that amounted to confiscation of their property. In these early days the Star Chamber functioned and was looked upon as a protector of the common people against the tyranny of the nobles. By its means Henry weakened and divided the nobility. To replenish the royal treasury, Henry managed his fiscal affairs efficiently and frugally: for the 1497 voyage to America he paid John Cabot £10. He chose his wars carefully, acting only when he was likely not only to win, but also to reap profit from plunder. By the time he died in 1509 his dynasty was firmly secured, and the royal treasury was the richest in all Europe.

Henry VIII   Henry VII's son and successor, Henry VIII, began his reign by dissipating the royal treasury in little more than a decade. Then a number of circumstances induced Henry to a radical measure. Of the six children borne by Henry's wife Catherine of Aragon, only one daughter survived and Catherine was unable to have more. And so the Tudor dynasty was in danger of having no male successor to the throne. In addition, Henry fell passionately in love with Anne Boleyn, who was willing to marry the King but refused to become his mistress. Henry turned to the Pope with a request for an annulment of his marriage. That might have been granted except that the Pope was virtually a prisoner of Catherine of Aragon's nephew, who was both King Charles I of Spain and Emperor Charles V of the Germanic political entity known as the Holy Roman Empire. The King had the unfaithful

English Exploration

The English clergyman Richard Hakluyt in 1584 presented her majesty, Elizabeth I, reasons for the state to take a hand in the western voyages:

"The soil yieldeth . . . all the several commodities of Europe, . . . that by trade of merchandise cometh into this realm.

The passage thither and home is neither too long nor too short, but easy and to be made twice in the year.

The passage . . . is safe passage, and not easy to be annoyed by prince or potentate whatsoever.

This enterprise may stay the Spanish King from flowing over all the face of America, if we seat and plant there in time. . . . How easy a matter may it be to this realm, swarming at this day with valiant youths, . . . to be lords of all those seas, . . . and consequently to abate the pride of Spain.

This voyage, albeit it may be accomplished by bark or smallest pinnace, . . . yet . . . the merchant will not for profit's sake use it but by ships of great burden; so as this realm shall have by that means ships of great strength for the defense of this realm. . . .

By making of ships and by preparing of things for the same, . . . by planting of vines and olive trees, and by making of wine and oil, by husbandry, and by thousands of things there to be done, infinite numbers of the English nation may be set on work, to the unburdening of the realm with many that now live chargeable to the state at home. . . .

We shall by planting there enlarge the glory of the gospel, and from England plant sincere religion, and provide a safe place to receive people from all parts of the world that are forced to flee for the truth of God's word. . . ."

Catherine beheaded and secretly married Anne Boleyn. In 1529 Henry called Parliament into a historic session that lasted seven years. Before it was dissolved, the King had created the Church of England, or Anglican Church, and broke all ties with Rome and the Roman Catholic faith.

That opened the way for a solution to Henry's financial problems. He confiscated the property of the church monasteries, which brought him nearly a sixth of all the land in England. The releasing of land from the control of the Church, the consequent growth in the number of landholders, and the commercial activity that the sale of the lands awakened together energized the English economy.

The break gained for England the zealous enmity of its traditional ally, Spain. That enmity intensified with the accession of Philip II to the Spanish throne in 1556. Philip was fanatically dedicated to using all the wealth and power of the Spanish Empire to suppress Protestantism.

Elizabeth I   Queen Elizabeth, Henry VIII's daughter by Anne Boleyn, ascended the throne in 1558 after a turbulent and bloody eleven-year interval in which her half-brother Edward and her Roman Catholic half-sister Mary each occupied the throne for just over five years. By then England's internal order and external relations had been fundamentally rearranged.

Elizabeth faced spiraling prices and had no more monasteries to confiscate. One solution was for England to obtain a share of Spain's gold and silver through direct trade with Spanish colonies, and for Elizabeth to augment her treasury either by taxing or licensing this trade or by going into secret partnership with the English traders.

For a while such undertakings were entrusted to private enterprise. The first outsider to exploit this market was the Englishman John Hawkins. The two Old World commodities most in demand in Spanish America were cloth and slaves, the first a product of England and the other easily obtainable in Portuguese West Africa. In 1562 Hawkins acquired three hundred black slaves and sailed with them to the Caribbean, receiving payment in sugar and hides, which he sold profitably in Europe. On his second venture the Queen and several members of her Privy Council were Hawkins's secret partners, and he again made an enormous profit. Subsequent ventures were handicapped by a Spanish crackdown and by 1569 trade was thoroughly closed to outsiders. Within another four years, more or less open conflict between the Catholic and the Protestant countries had begun, the Dutch having allied themselves with England. For the next thirty years, British and Dutch ships engaged in smuggling to Spanish America and in systematic plunder of Spanish shipping.

The greatest of the English captains in these enterprises was Sir Francis Drake, kinsman of Hawkins. Drake conducted a brilliant and profitable privateering raid in 1573, viewed the Pacific Ocean from the Isthmus of Panama, and resolved "to sail an English ship in these seas." He launched his most spectacular venture five years later. With secret authorization and an investment from the Queen he crossed the Atlantic, passed through the Strait of Magellan, plundered Spanish shipping

Sir Walter Raleigh, encouraged by Queen Elizabeth to colonize North America, explored a new region which was named Virginia in honor of the monarch known to history as the Virgin Queen.
(Courtesy, New York Public Library, Picture Collection)

off South America, captured a shipload of Peruvian silver, explored the Pacific coast of North America, crossed to the East Indies, concluded a treaty with a sultan who was at war with the Portuguese, bought several tons of cloves, and sailed home by the Portuguese route around Africa, returning with a magnificent treasure of £2,500,000. Meanwhile, Elizabeth encouraged Martin Frobisher and John Davis in their exploration of North America for a northwest water passage to Asia, and granted Humphrey Gilbert and his half-brother Walter Raleigh a charter to colonize "remote heathen and barbarous lands not actually possessed by any Christian prince or people," and providing for settlers to "enjoy all the privileges of free denizens and persons native of England." When Drake came home from his spectacular circumnavigation of the world in 1581, the Queen knighted him on the quarterdeck of his ship, the *Golden Hind,* and rejected all attempts by Spain to recover the stolen booty.

Open war with Spain soon followed. Spain under Philip II had had more than enough of Elizabethan sea dogs, and the somber Catholic zealot Philip was committed to rewinning Protestant England and Scotland for the Roman Catholic Church.

Naval warfare began in 1584. Elizabeth sent troops to Protestant Dutch states to aid in their struggle to retain independence from the Spanish crown. Drake set forth with more than twenty men-of-war to attack the Spanish position in America. In the ensuing year Drake wreaked considerable devastation in the West Indies and sacked Santo Domingo. In 1587 he conducted an audacious raid that sank much of the Spanish fleet in its home harbor at Cádiz.

Philip of Spain then ordered the construction of an "Invincible Armada" of 132 vessels carrying 3,165 cannon. The British hurriedly prepared for defense by constructing a fleet less heavily armed but more numerous and far better suited to fighting in rough seas. In a great naval battle in July 1588 the British outmaneuvered the Spanish in the English Channel and defeated the great Armada. Most of the Spanish vessels that escaped fled north hoping to return home by circling the British Isles, only to be destroyed by a storm off the Scottish Hebrides Islands.

At the time of Elizabeth's death in 1603, the English people, a scant three million but proud, aggressive, and prosperous, had gathered the energy that would propel them into virtual domination of the Western world.

While the Spanish were planting their colonies in the New World, Englishmen had given comparatively little attention to colonization. In the late sixteenth and the early seventeenth centuries, however, the idea of colonization found its promoters and publicists. The English after 1600 began crossing in large numbers to North America and the West Indies. In the first century of colonization, some 400,000 Britons embarked for the New World. Some searched for wealth, and some for a modest prosperity in the new lands. Many came for reasons connected with the religious controversies of the seventeenth century. Both the economic and the religious motives would leave their marks on American history, but first the English, like the Spanish, had to come to terms with the native Americans.

Population and Colonization

The emergence of England as a modern nation-state reflected more than changes in the role of the monarchy or the growth of a centralized bureaucracy. It also involved profound economic and social changes. In the first half of the sixteenth century British exports of woolen goods grew enormously. This new source of prosperity caused English landlords to shift from farming to sheepherding on a wide scale, a change that altered the society as well as the economy of the English countryside. Small farmers, most of them tenants, were driven from the land. These people wandered from place to place looking for work.

Colonies seemed the perfect solution to this and other new problems. Not only would they lead to increased trade, but they would also provide a place for the surplus population to go in the chartered trading colonies.

The Columbian Exchange

Death and Devastation

European exploration of the Americas brought about the worst demographic disaster in world history. Smallpox and other diseases for which the New World's natives had no immunity devastated regions from Canada to Chile, reducing Indian populations by as much as ninety percent by the eighteenth century. Within fifty years after Columbus, epidemics had killed off nearly all the native inhabitants of Santo Domingo, Haiti, and much of Mexico. After Francis Drake's ships visited the Caribbean and Florida in 1585, Indians in those regions died in great numbers, believing that "it was the Inglisshe God that made them die so fast." There were 150,000 Timucuan Indians in Florida when Europeans first came, but by the end of the seventeenth century their population had been reduced to around three thousand. In New Mexico the Pueblo Indians numbered around 130,000 in 1539 when Europeans first visited them; by 1706 there were 6,440 left.

As the years passed the native populations of the Americas were replaced by Europeans in three major patterns. In Central and South America the Spanish and Portuguese intermarried with highland Indians and lowland black slaves to form the mixed-race groups called mestizo, mulatto, and zambo. The English, French, and Dutch in the West Indies and the English on the southeast coast of the present-day United States, failing to enslave the Indians, established hierarchical societies based on the labor of blacks imported from Africa. And in the Northeast, English along with Dutch, German, French, and other European colonists and a few black slaves lived on farms or in villages separate from Indian communities.

Animal and food plant exchanges accompanied encounters between Indians and Europeans. Domesticated animals—pigs, goats, horses, cattle, and sheep—accompanied Europeans to America, along with wheat, rye, barley, oats, rice, melons, coffee, dandelions, sugar cane, and olives. Much of this was to the eventual benefit of the Indians. Another import was alcohol, bringing destructive consequences. The plants that American Indians made available to the rest of the world now constitute one-third of the world's food supply: Indian corn, beans, squash, pumpkins, tomatoes, peppers, and potatoes, the last an extraordinarily important food. The rich importation of American food was a factor in the growth and economic advance of the European population in modern times. Tobacco, drugs such as cocaine, novocaine, and quinine, and the strains of cotton in modern use also entered the world market from the Americas.

Some of the biological exchange also involved microscopic life in the form of diseases. Indians had developed no immunity to measles, chicken pox, smallpox, and whooping cough, from which they had been isolated by three thousand miles of ocean. These diseases devastated American Indians, killing far more than did conquest. And Europeans may have contracted syphilis from Americans or possibly Africans. The first recorded case appeared in Cádiz, Spain, soon after Columbus returned from America. In any event, as many as ten million Old World people died of syphilis within the next fifteen years.

Technical and Cultural Exchange

Central and South American gold and silver enriched European monarchies and stimulated trade and industry. European merchants prospered from the trade in American agricultural raw materials. America provided a storehouse of information in the natural sciences and contributed to the intensification of scientific inquiry. Europeans who prided themselves on such things as written languages, advanced weapons, and Christianity looked down on Indians. But others were captivated by the notion of the "noble savage" and took that mythic creation into political and moral philosophies that furthered modern concepts of liberty and democracy. The very idea of a new and open land enlarged the vision of human possibility.

In America, Europeans adopted Indian ways. Besides eating Indian foods, they wore moccasins, snowshoes, ponchos, and parkas, plied rivers and lakes with canoes, and rested in hammocks. They played lacrosse, built homes of adobe, and rode on dogsleds and toboggans. The early European settlers followed Indian trails, smoked native tobacco, and used native medicines. Indian names entered English usage. They would serve for about half of the eventual state names from Connecticut and Alabama to Iowa, Texas, and Wyoming and were used for many rivers and cities.

In addition to declining in numbers, the original Americans underwent enormous cultural changes. Indian lands shrank as the plow, lumbering, cattle, and sheep permanently transformed the eastern woodlands. Other changes in Indian life were largely a matter of choice. European knives and guns improved hunting. The horse gave the Plains Indians mobility to hunt buffalo and raid settlements. Iron pots replaced pottery and baskets. Sheep made possible the beautiful wool blankets of the Navahos. The iron hoe and plow increased agricultural productivity, and the metal fish hook enhanced catches. Many natives also responded to the lure of profit from the fur trade. European demand for pelts soon outstripped the animal population near the sea coast, and some tribes had to abandon older settlements in favor of new ones farther inland, eventually depleting animals there, too. In North America, Indians were not conquered and enslaved to the extent that occurred in Latin America, and so were able to maintain a largely separate racial and cultural existence. They interacted with the Europeans primarily in trade and war, with disastrous results for both sides.

Suggested Readings

The 500th anniversary of Columbus's 1492 voyage inspired a vigorous scholarly debate over the meanings of the initial encounters between Europeans and the indigenous peoples of the Americas. See William D. Phillips, Jr. and Carla Rahn Phillips, *The Worlds of Christopher Columbus* (1992), Donald T. Gerace, ed., *Columbus and His World* (1987), Paolo Emilio Taviani, *Christopher Columbus: The Grand Design* (1985), and Cecil Jane, ed., *The Four Voyages of Columbus* (1988). *The Columbian Exchange* (1972) by Alfred W. Crosby, Jr., shows how ways of life were altered in both hemispheres; see also Crosby's *Ecological Imperialism: The Biological Expansion of Europe, 900–1900* (1986). Kirkpatrick Sale gives the anti-Columbus view in *The Conquest of Paradise: Christopher Columbus and the Columbian Legacy* (1990). See also Tzvetan Todorov, *The Conquest of America: The Question of the Other* (1984).

Any study of the voyages of discovery can begin with Samuel Eliot Morison's works, *The European Discovery of America: The Northern Voyages, A.D. 500–1600* (1971) and *The European Discovery of America: The Southern Voyages, A.D. 1492–1616* (1974). A beautifully illustrated book on this period is Richard Humble, *The Explorers* (1979).

Colin G. Calloway's *New Worlds for All: Indians, Europeans, and the Remaking of Early America* (1997) explores the ways in which the cultures of indigenous peoples and immigrants affected each other. See also Karen O. Kupperman, *Settling with the Indians: The Making of English and Indian Cultures in America* (1980). Francis Jennings's *The Founders of America: How Indians Discovered the Land, Pioneered in It, and Created Great Classical Civilizations* (1993) is a provocative antidote to European-centered accounts. See also A. M. Joseph, Jr., ed., *America in 1492* (1992), David Carrasco, *Quetzalcoatl and the Irony of Empire* (1982), Brian M. Fagan, *The Great Journey: The People of Ancient America* (1987), and Robert Silverberg, *Mound Builders of Ancient America: The Archaeology of a Myth* (1968). Other recommended works are D. B. Quinn, *North America from Earliest Discovery to First Settlements* (1977), Samuel Eliot Morison's *Admiral of the Ocean Sea* (1942), a biography of Columbus, and James Axtell, *The European and the Indian* (1981) and *After Columbus* (1988).

On the Spanish in North America see David Weber, *The Spanish Frontier in North America* (1992), Joseph P. Sanchez, *Forging the Old Spanish Trail, 1678–1850* (1997), and Donald E. Chipman, *Spanish Texas, 1519–1821* (1992). See also John Miller Morris, *El Llano Estacado: Exploration and Imagination on the High Plains of Texas and New Mexico, 1536–1860* (1997).

John Thornton's *Africa and Africans in the Making of the Atlantic World, 1400–1680* (1992) is a pathbreaking study. See also Roland Oliver, *The African Experience* (1991), Phyllis Martin and Patrick O'Meare, eds., *Africa* (1986), and Anthony Sillery, *Africa: A Social Geography* (1972).

Christopher Columbus— The Conqueror of Paradise?

Kirkpatrick Sale

On his first voyage Columbus found himself in the middle of an old-growth tropical forest the likes of which he could not have imagined before, its trees reaching sixty or seventy feet into the sky, more varieties than he knew how to count much less name, exhibiting a lushness that stood in sharp contrast to the sparse and denuded lands he had known in the Mediterranean, hearing a melodious multiplicity of bird songs and parrot calls—why was it not an occasion of wonder, excitement, and the sheer joy at nature in its full, arrogant abundance? . . .

One measure that Colón [Columbus] could make, and did so frequently, was the utilitarian: if he was not up to describing natural beauty or distinguishing trees, he was a master at determining the potential use and value of all that he saw, even when (as so often) he was deluding himself. Nature for him was all one form of treasure or another, whether aloes, mastic, spices, cinnamon, nutmeg, dyes, or medicines, or gold and silver and pearls—it hardly mattered as long as it could be sold in Europe.

Colón was nothing more than "a businessman" describing resources for potential markets. Large European mammals were brought over on the Second Voyage. Nothing of the kind (nothing larger than a small dog) lived in the Caribbean, no competing species of any sort, so there were no established diseases to threaten them and, with the exception of sheep and goats, they bloomed spectacularly. Cattle reproduced so successfully on Española that, it was said, thirty or forty stray animals would multiply to three or four hundred in a couple of years. . . . Pigs were so numerous by 1500, just seven years after the first four pairs were introduced, that according to Las Casas they were called *infinitos*.

All these voracious animals naturally dominated and then destroyed native habitats, rapidly and thoroughly, with human help and without. The record is inadequate, since none among the colonists, even those who would take on the job of describing native species for audiences at home, ever noted the extensive alteration of the environment that was taking place literally beneath their feet. Las Casas, however, does mention that a certain grass common in Española at the turn of the century had vanished just forty years later, a victim of the hungry herds, and we may presume there were many similar floral die-outs. Crosby, without specifics, considers that the spread of these large species "doubtlessly had much to do with the extinction of certain plants, animals . . . and even the Indians themselves" who lost out "in the biological competition with the newly imported livestock." . . .

Many of those who know well the cultures that once existed in the New World have reason to be less than enthusiastic about celebrating the event that led to the destruction of much of that heritage and the greater part of the people who produced it; some have insisted on labeling the events of 1492 an "encounter" rather than a "discovery" and having it so billed for 1992; some others have chosen to make it an occasion to direct attention to native American arts and achievements, and others still are planning to protest the entire goings-on as a wrongful commemoration of an act steeped in bloodshed, slavery, and genocide.

And some of those who have sought to draw attention to the environmental destruction wrought in the aftermath of the Discovery, particularly members of various Green movements in the industrialized world, have decided to use the occasion to draw into question the nature of a civilization that could take the earth so close to ecocide.

Kirkpatrick Sale, *The Conquest of Paradise* (New York: Alfred A. Knopf, 1990). Reprinted by permission.

A century ago, the United States celebrated the exploits of Columbus proudly. Some 24 million people—which amounted to about 40 percent of the U.S. population at the time—attended a great international exposition in Chicago marking the event. There, at a meeting of the American Historical Association, the young historian Frederick Jackson Turner delivered his famous paper on "The Significance of the Frontier in American History," sounding an appropriate theme for the commemoration of the explorer who opened up the most significant frontier in world history: the entire Western Hemisphere.

The 500th anniversary of 1492, by contrast, has touched off enormous controversy and endless political wrangling. The National Council of Churches has announced that 1992 should not be a time for celebration at all but rather for "repentance" for a great historical crime. Columbus, in the council's view, was a monster akin to Hitler, having been responsible for an "invasion and colonization with legalized occupation, genocide, economic exploitation, and a deep level of institutional racism and moral decadence."

The story of the European discovery, invasion, and conquest of the Western Hemisphere—a process that began with Columbus in 1492—certainly is not all sweetness and light. Crimes and follies are in the history of every people, including those who did not leave behind written records allowing historians to demonstrate their sins in detail. The Columbus story, like every other momentous historical event, calls not for easy moralizing and finger pointing but for an appreciation of a complex clash of cultures that was crucial to the emergence of the modern world we inhabit. . . .

Painful though it might be to accept, much of history is the story of what the strong have done to the weak—and of shifts in the bases of power that undermine the position of the once-strong and lead to their decline and fall. It would be nice if that were not so, but it has been so thus far in human history.

Contrary to romantics like Sale, who contrast the warlike Europeans of 1492 with the supposedly pacific natives, the history of the societies of the Western Hemisphere before Columbus fits this mold, too. Conquest and domination were not corruptions that Europeans introduced into a New World Eden. The great empires of the Aztecs in Mexico, the Incas in Peru, and those of the Mayas much earlier were not formed by a process of peaceful persuasion but by superior force. And their rule was as cruel and exploitative as anything Europeans were guilty of in the New World; in some ways more cruel. . . .

The newest addition to the indictment against Columbus is that he committed "ecocide." The native peoples of the Western Hemisphere, some current environmentalists claim, revered nature and lived in harmony with it. The European invaders instead raped and pillaged the land with reckless abandon.

Since environmentalists have been a healthy voice in contemporary public policy debates, it is regrettable to find some of them taking such a simplistic position on complex historical problems. It is generally true that the native peoples who lived at the most primitive technological level did less to alter the physical environment, for better or worse, than those who developed a more complex economy. But even small, semi-nomadic tribes practiced slash-and-burn agriculture, felling trees by stripping their bark along the base, letting them die and fall, and then setting them on fire. They violated the precept "Save the trees" and created some ugly scenes on the landscape, including forest fires burning out of control.

Reprinted with permission from the Spring 1992 issue of the *American Educator*, the quarterly journal of the American Federation of Teachers.

JAMESTOWN IN 1622
VIRGINIA

Jamestown, founded in 1607, fared better than the Roanoke settlement. Though ravaged by disease and Indian attacks, the settlement survived and Virginia became the preeminent southern colony. (*Courtesy, American Historical Society*)

John Smith, one of the original settlers of Jamestown, wrote a history of the colony. Smith's presidency of the local council was critical for the survival of the settlement. (*Scribner's Archives*)

A portrait of Pocahontas, painted in 1616, when she was 21. (*Courtesy, Smithsonian Institution*)

North America

THE STARVING TIME

In the fall of 1609 a group of English colonists huddled fearfully inside the log palisade of a small fort on the banks of a river. They had named this river the James, in honor of their King, James I. The local Indians called it the Powhatan, which was also the name of their ruler. The site of the fort was Jamestown, in the new colony of Virginia. It was the first permanent English settlement in the New World, a project undertaken by British businessmen who had formed the Virginia Company. A marshy, mosquito-infested place, it was nonetheless safe from Indian attacks, so the English thought, and it was close to a river that flowed to the ocean—the way back home.

Drought, disease, and death had plagued Jamestown from the beginning. Of the 104 men and boys carried by the ships *Susan Constant, Discovery,* and *Godspeed,* and left there in April 1607, only 38 were alive the following January. Governed by an unwieldy and bickering council, they quarreled over their meager food supply, refused to work, grew sick from drinking the brackish water of the James, and antagonized the Indians. The next year, a brash twenty-seven-year-old named John Smith became president of the council and declared that "he that will not work shall not eat." Through his friendship with Pocahontas, the twelve-year-old daughter of Wahunsonacock, the ruler of the surrounding tribes, Smith made a fragile peace with the Indians. Settlers exchanged glass beads with them for baskets of corn. The Virginia Company sent more colonists (including the first "Gentlewoman and woman servant" to arrive at Jamestown), but more died, and

continued

HISTORICAL EVENTS

1626
Dutch establish settlement called New Amsterdam

1630
Members of the Massachusetts Bay Company arrive in Massachusetts

1634
Maryland founded

1636
Roger Williams establishes Providence (Rhode Island)

1637–38
Pequot War

1638
Anne Hutchinson banished from Massachusetts

1642–47
Civil war in England (Puritans vs. Royalists)

1649
Maryland passes Toleration Act
• Charles I executed

1651
First Navigation Act

1660
Charles II becomes King of England: the Restoration • Navigation Act

1662
Half-Way Covenant enacted in Massachusetts

1664
Charles II seizes New York from Dutch

1669
Locke and Ashley write "The Fundamental Constitutions of Carolina"

1675–76
King Philip's War

1676
Bacon's Rebellion

1680
Pueblo Revolt in New Mexico
• Virginia and Maryland export seventeen million pounds of tobacco

1682
Penn publishes *Frame of Government*

continued

Smith himself was severely wounded by an exploding bag of gunpowder. In October 1609 he left for England, never to return.

Now, two years after the founding of the settlement, the colonists at Jamestown still had not managed to raise enough corn to see them through a winter, or to placate the Indians whose lands they occupied. John Smith was gone, and Pocahontas no longer came to visit the English. Now the inhabitants of the fort cowered inside, fearing the Indians outside its walls.

As cold weather approached, so did starvation. According to one of the colonists reporting on what has been remembered as the Starving Time, "Having fed upon horses and other beasts as long as they lasted we were glad to make shift with vermine, as dogs, cats, rats, and mice . . . boots, shoes, or any other leather . . . and those being spent and devoured, some were forced to search the woods and to feed upon serpents and snakes and to dig the earth for wild and unknown roots where many of our men were cut off and slain by savages. . . . And one of our colony murdered his wife, ripped the child out of her womb and threw it in the river and after chopped the mother in pieces and salted her for his foode. . . ." Once, when some of the men went in search of food, the Indians killed them and left them for the English to find: the mouths of the corpses had been stuffed with bread. Yet while the Jamestown colonists were shivering inside their log enclosure, thirty or forty of their countrymen, who had been sent to build a fort thirty miles downriver at Point Comfort, spent the winter in relative plenty. When spring came, there were "not past sixty men, women, and children" left in the fort at Jamestown.

In May 1610 two small ships arrived, carrying 150 more colonists, the survivors of a shipwreck in Bermuda. Among them was Virginia's new deputy governor, Sir Thomas Gates. Horrified at the condition of the people at Jamestown, Gates ordered the abandonment of the fort. But as his two ships made for the open sea, they were met by a longboat announcing the arrival of Lord De La Warr, the new governor, with more colonists—and enough food to feed the starving survivors. All returned, rejoicing, to the fort at Jamestown. England at last had a foothold on the coast of North America. But the English had made lasting enemies of the Indians.

Early Southern Settlements

The Roanoke Colony

Jamestown was not the first English effort to plant a colony in the New World. Late in the sixteenth century a group of adventurers, among them the courtier Sir Walter Raleigh, had developed plans for establishing settlements in the New World. Lusty and aggressive, the mercantile and maritime adventurers of the time were eager to exploit the American continent that Europeans only a few decades earlier had considered no more than an annoying obstacle on the route to the Orient.

In 1584 under Raleigh's sponsorship a voyage explored the coast of what is now North Carolina. One of the leaders of this expedition wanted to name the new land "Wingandacoa," a word he had heard the Indians use, but Raleigh chose "Virginia," in honor of Elizabeth, the Virgin Queen.

In 1585 Raleigh sent over a hundred men to establish a settlement at Roanoke, a small wooded island off the coast of present-day North Carolina. They quarreled with the Indians and returned home after a year. In 1587 Raleigh, still determined to set up a colony, sent 117 settlers, this time including seventeen women, under the leadership of John White, whose watercolors of the Indians and wildlife would furnish Europeans with some of their first views of the New World. At Roanoke, White's daughter Elenora, wife of Ananias Dare, gave birth to a girl, "the first Christian born in Virginia." The infant was named Virginia.

Sometime between 1587, when John White and the supply ships left Roanoke, and 1590, when he was finally able to return, Virginia Dare and all the rest of the colonists vanished. Research released in 1998 on the rings of centuries-old bald cypress trees suggest they—and a tribe of neighboring Indians—had the misfortune to be there during the worst three-year drought in some eight hundred years. Certainly this would have upset Raleigh's plans for a flourishing plantation agriculture. England's war with Spain and the battle of the Spanish Armada in 1588 had prevented a resupply mission to Roanoke until 1590. The letters CROATOAN the settlers left carved in a tree suggest some kind of involvement with a more southerly Indian tribe, perhaps a flight by stormy seas. Years later an English settler reported that coastal Indians told him that "several of their ancestors were white People."

Other reports from America nevertheless whetted English appetites for more colonizing ventures. One account described the shellfish as "exceeding good and very great," and characterized the Indians as "courteous" and "gentle of disposition." Another found the Atlantic coast's crabs "rather better in taste than ours, one able to suffice four men." In 1603 a sea captain exploring what would become New Hampshire reported seeing "goodly groves and woods and sundry beasts, but no people."

New Settlers   After the troubles of Jamestown's initial years, the Virginia Company and its investors were determined to see the colony prosper. Hardships and disease—salt poisoning from the saline James River, dysentery, typhoid—took a fearful toll. One colonist thought that "more doe die here of the disease of their mind, then of their body." In order to attract more investors and more settlers, the Company granted a "headright" of fifty acres of land per person to all individuals who came on their own or brought others to Virginia. With aggressive recruiting the Company poured some 3,500 newcomers into the colony between 1618 and 1621, more than twice the number who had emigrated since 1607.

At its own expense the Company undertook to send to Virginia a

---

HISTORICAL EVENTS

1684
Massachusetts becomes a royal colony

1685
James II becomes King of England and creates the Dominion of New England

1688
Glorious Revolution • James II dethroned

1689
William and Mary become monarchs of England • Bill of Rights passed

1690
Locke's *An Essay Concerning Human Understanding* and *Two Treatises of Government*

1696
Navigation Act

John White's journal records his fruitless search for the lost settlers of Roanoke:

"We espied towards the north end of the island the light of a great fire through the woods, to which we presently rowed. When we came right over against it, we let fall our grapnel [anchor] near the shore, & sounded with a trumpet call, & afterwards many familiar English tunes of songs, and called to them friendly, but we had no answer. . . .

In all this way we saw on the sand the print of the savages' feet of 2 or 3 sorts trodden that night, and as we entered up the sandy bank upon a tree, in the very brow there were curiously carved these fair Roman letters, C R O: which letters presently we knew to signify the place, where I should find the planters seated, according to a secret token agreed upon between them & me. . . ."

Barbarism and cruelty occurred on both sides of the encounters between the English and the Indians in Virginia. George Percy recorded an incident of English treatment of a captured Indian queen and her children in 1610.

"And after we marched with the queen and her children to our boats again . . . my soldiers did begin to murmur because the queen and her children were spared. So upon the same a council being called it was agreed upon to put the children to death the which was effected by throwing them overboard and shooting out their brains in the water. Yet for all this cruelty the soldiers were not well pleased and I had much to do to save the queen's life for that time."

John Smith's General History of Virginia recorded the Indian uprising that took place in the spring of 1622.

"On the Friday morning that fatal day, being the two and twentieth of March . . . as at other times they came into our houses, with deer, turkeys, fish, fruits, and other provisions to sell us, yea in some places sat down at breakfast with our people, whom immediately with their own tools they slew most barbarously, not sparing either age or sex, man, woman or child, so sudden in their execution, that few or none discerned the weapon or blow that brought them to destruction . . . and by this means fell that fatal morning . . . three hundred forty seven men, women, and children, most by their own weapons, and not being content with their lives, they fell again upon the dead bodies, making as well as they could a fresh murder, defacing, dragging, and mangling their dead carcasses into many pieces, and carrying some parts away in derision, with base and brutish triumph."

variety of craftsmen and a number of female settlers, "young maids" who would make the colony's economy more self-sufficient and its life more tolerable. The Company relaxed its rules, provided that settlers continue to be governed by English law and have the rights of Englishmen, and gave settlers a voice in the management by allowing them to elect representatives to an assembly. The House of Burgesses, the first colonial legislature in North America, began meeting in 1619.

Also in that year, according to a letter written by colonist John Rolfe, a Dutch ship brought "20 and odd Negroes, which the governor and cape merchant bought . . . at the best and easiest rate they could." These were not the first blacks in Virginia; a census a few months earlier recorded 32 blacks—15 men and 17 women—before the arrival of the Dutch ship. The status of these people is not clear from the existing records, and it is possible that Virginia's blacks were treated much the same as the colony's white servants. The origins of slavery in North America are obscure, and the institution itself evolved slowly as the number of blacks in Virginia and other colonies grew in the seventeenth century.

Despite the determined efforts of the Virginia Company, the colony had not flourished. As the English tobacco fields spread, the Indians feared the loss of their lands, and in 1622 a surprise attack on English settlements killed 347 men, women, and children. A muster of English colonists in 1625 recorded a population of only about 1,210, including 23 blacks. The shocking mortality rate and the Virginia Company's virtually empty treasury led to a dissolution of the Company in 1624, and Virginia became a royal colony governed directly by the crown. Relations with the Indians worsened. One colonial official exulted that "now we have just cause to destroy them by all means possible." On one occasion, the colonists lured a band of peaceful Indians into drinking a toast with poisoned wine, killing "some two hundred." Indian-English relations were unstable for much of the seventeenth century.

Beginnings of New England

On the eve of European settlement, the Indian population of New England was possibly as large as 25,000, a density of about one person per four acres. The various tribes, none larger than 4,000 people, lived in relatively settled territories, moving between winter, summer, and autumn quarters to sustain their mixed farming and hunting economy and to escape into more sheltered valleys for the winters. During the winter of 1616–17 an epidemic of smallpox suddenly decimated many of the tribes, including the Massachusetts Indians, after whom the European colony would derive its name. No Indian would have connected this mysterious visitation with the occasional and usually friendly encounters with European fishermen drying their catches on the beaches in summer or trading a few items for furs and skins or food. But these were the source of the disease that wiped out as much as one-third of the area's population. Early settlers in New England found the land largely cleared of natives.

Religious persecution brought in 1620 the first permanent English colonists to present-day Massachusetts. By the 1630s thousands of religious dissenters known as Puritans were making their way across the Atlantic.

In England in the early 1600s the Separatists, so called for their desire to separate from the Church of England, incurred the wrath of King James I, who succeeded Elizabeth I in 1603. He declared that a Separatist was like "a rat to be trapped and tossed away." James was as good as his word. In Lincolnshire in 1607, the same year Jamestown, Virginia, was being settled, a Separatist leader named William Brewster and his young friend, seventeen-year-old William Bradford, were among those imprisoned for several months.

The Pilgrims and the Mayflower Compact

In 1611 Brewster, Bradford, and a small group of Separatists fled to the Netherlands, and in 1620 cemented an agreement with the London Company of Virginia to finance their emigration to America. In September 1620 the 180-ton *Mayflower* left Plymouth Sound with 102 men, women, and children. On November 9, they reached Cape Cod. The grateful Pilgrims celebrated their first Thanksgiving in October 1621. To secure their government in this unknown land, the leaders of these Separatists had drafted on shipboard an agreement that has come to be known as the Mayflower Compact. Every adult male who intended to be a part of the Separatist community signed it, and it has held a special place in the American imagination ever since as a model for the formation of government by free consent. And since contrary winds put the Pilgrims at Cape Cod, well outside the bounds of their London Company charter, that Company document could not serve as the basis of their government. The Pilgrims named their colony Plymouth, after the English seaport they had left behind. In 1691 Plymouth colony would become part of the larger Puritan colony of Massachusetts.

Despite the many obvious cultural differences and the language barrier between English settlers and Indians, the Pilgrims and after them the larger Puritan settlement in Massachusetts Bay received a generally friendly welcome. Puritans also made an effort to convert the Indians to Christianity. Trade, Indians perceived, made tribes rich and powerful and usually ended with their acquiring firearms. At first the needs of the two cultures seemed compatible. The English settlers carefully drew up land titles granting the Indians the right to continue to hunt or fish.

The Massachusetts Bay Colony

The Massachusetts Bay Company, organized in 1629 by a group of well-to-do English Puritans, received from the King a charter granting it land in present-day New England and elsewhere to the south. Hostile like his father to the Puritans, James's son and in 1625 his successor, Charles I, was doubtless happy to send some of them to the opposite shores of the Atlantic, also using them to populate and enrich parts of his American domain. Members of the Company signed a document, known as the Cambridge Agreement, to settle with their families in the

William Bradford, governor of Plymouth Colony, recorded in his journal the arrival in 1620 of the Pilgrims:

"Being thus arrived in a good harbor, and brought safe to land, they fell upon their knees and blessed the God of Heaven who had brought them over the vast and furious ocean, and delivered them from all the perils and miseries thereof, again to set their feet on the firm and stable earth, their proper element. . . . They now had no friends to welcome them nor inns to entertain or refresh their weatherbeaten bodies; no houses or much less town to repair to, to seek for succour. . . . And as for the season it was winter, and they that know the winters of that country know them to be sharp and violent, and subject to cruel and fierce storms, dangerous to travel to known places, much more to search an unknown coast. Besides, what could they see but a hideous and desolate wilderness, full of wild beasts and wild men—and what multitudes there might be of them they knew not."

Housing in Massachusetts Bay was primitive at first. Some colonists borrowed from the Indians and built wigwams. According to a settler's recollection:

"We built us our wigwam, or house, in one hour's space. It had no frame, but was without form or fashion, only a few poles set together, and covered with our boat's sails, which kept forth but a little wind, and less rain and snow."

Others dug cellars. The Puritan historian Edward Johnson wrote that they

"burrow themselves in the Earth for their first shelter under some Hillside, . . . make a smoaky fire against the Earth at the highest side, and thus . . . provide for themselves, their Wives, and little ones, keeping off the short showers from their Lodgings, but the long ones penetrate through to their great disturbance."

Some years later, Johnson described the finished houses, observing that

"the Lord hath been pleased to turn all the wigwams, huts, and hovels the English dwelt in at their first coming into orderly fair, and well-built houses, well furnished many of them, together with Orchards filled with goodly fruit trees, and gardens with variety of flowers."

new land, provided that they be allowed to take the charter and government of the Company with them. Nothing in the charter required the Company to maintain headquarters in England, and the transfer was arranged. This meant, in effect, that the structure of the Massachusetts Bay Company was to become the local government of the colony itself. The Company elected as its governor John Winthrop, a solid country squire. In 1630 Winthrop and ten other members of the Company had set sail for America with a fleet of eleven ships carrying 800 adults and children with them. They arrived in Massachusetts in July 1630. In the next decade, as persecutions of Puritans increased, more than 20,000 would come to New England. From the start, the immigration of families distinguished the settlement of New England. The presence of nearly as many women as men among the Puritans guaranteed that the settlement would grow in population. Women assured the accomplishment of basic domestic tasks necessary for survival. Perhaps because of that, these New England colonists, with the exception of those at Plymouth the first winter, did not suffer the dreadful mortality of Virginia's early years. By the end of 1630 the Puritans had established six towns in addition to Boston.

The Massachusetts Bay Company, like other English business corporations of the time, was governed by its voting members, or "freemen." At first the only members were the stockholders, but the government of the Company and therefore of the colony soon admitted as freemen all male members of Puritan congregations. Like the original government, this extended body was constituted on the assumption that men only were fitted for governance and would naturally speak for the women of their families. The charter provided that Company members gather as a General Court four times a year, and that between times management be in the hands of a governor, deputy governor, and council of eighteen "assistants," all elected annually by the freemen. As the colony expanded, legislation by the entire body of freemen became unwieldy, and after 1634 they annually elected representatives from each settlement. Government of the church was the domain of the male members of the church congregation; and the government of the town

Pilgrims Going to Church, a nineteenth-century painting by George Boughton. The original Massachusetts settlements were governed by and for the orthodox, but by the 1660s other settlers and congregations were laying the basis for religious pluralism. *(Courtesy, The New-York Historical Society. From the Robert L. Stuart Collection)*

was also their domain. Gaining admission to a congregation, however, was not automatic: the candidate had to give convincing indications of having experienced divine grace.

New England Democracy

It is easy, and in part correct, to trace American democracy to early New England institutions. But the Mayflower Compact, the government of Massachusetts Bay, and the church polity of the New England congregations did not spring from anything close to a conscious modern democratic theory. Each of the three came out of its own special circumstances and needs.

The *Mayflower* colonists were going to be far beyond the reach of established authority, and therefore the Pilgrim leaders feared that some of the settlers might "use their owne libertie, for none had the power to command them." A need for law and order, not a desire for democratic government, inspired the Mayflower Compact. To agree among themselves to have a government was a simple, necessary act. And the Compact did not project an independent government: it specifically declared allegiance to the King of England.

The suffrage in Massachusetts Bay represented the fusion of the organization of a business company with that of the New England Puritan congregations. That English joint-stock companies gave a vote to each shareholder for the conduct of business was a practical arrangement among people who had chosen to pool their resources for some enterprise. The purpose of such companies was not to establish a democracy, nor was democracy the purpose of the settlers who turned the shareholder voting system into a political system for the colony. Seventeenth-century Massachusetts Bay had few if any advocates of democracy. "If the people be governors," asked Puritan divine John Cotton, "who shall be governed?"

Within the Puritan and the Separatist congregations, members were spiritual equals, of a sort. While women could be full members of congregations, they could not be ministers or members of the governing body of the church, and they could not voice their opinions too loudly. The Puritan concept of equality derived from the doctrine, which no modern democrat would accept, that the members of the church congregations must be confined to the elect, selected for salvation from the beginning of time. Members were spiritual equals, but only because there can be no inequality among saints.

Yet even if the early institutions of New England did not derive from any philosophical notions of equality or democracy, they deserve a place in the history of American democracy. The manner of their formation represents the way in which many of the nation's political and social institutions came into being—neither by theory nor by ancient custom but by matter-of-fact response to conditions and needs.

Puritan Theology

Economic ambition had combined with religion in the founding of the New England colonies and many settlers had land or opportunity as their motive. The prevailing creed, however, was Puritan. This creed was heavily influenced by the French theologian John Calvin, best known for his belief in predestination: that those who were to be saved had been so chosen from the beginning of time. Calvin's premise might be taken to mean that there was no need to make any effort to be moral and good since salvation had already been granted. Not so: orthodox ministers in Massachusetts observed that religious conversion, an intense personal experience of salvation, would be attended by diligent pursuit of a "calling" or earthly occupation and a life of fervent prayer and good works. Industriousness, charity, and the other virtues were considered a consequence of salvation, a continuing act of gratitude, a joyful expression of the faith of the saved or, as Calvinists called them, the elect. The New England Puritans believed that God had made a covenant, or agreement, with the faithful to provide them with a clear and orderly redemption. Not only individuals but whole congregations and entire communities considered themselves as having entered into a convenant with God, promising to live together in love and harmony.

Not all Puritans reasoned the same way, and not all agreed even on the principle of cooperation among congregations. One who shared few of the values of the Pilgrims was Thomas Morton, an adventurer whose followers fraternized with the Indians and enjoyed drinking freely and dancing around a maypole at Mt. Wollaston, near Plymouth. The colonists disapproved of his conduct and shipped him back to England in 1628. Settlers who shared Puritan values but disputed specific points of the colony's religious practices were a good deal more troublesome.

New England Society   The Separatist Pilgrims at Plymouth and then the much larger body of Puritans around Massachusetts Bay continued to live as they had in England in tightly knit communities. The rural life of England had itself been close, peasants living in villages and working the surrounding fields under arrangements that made individual land tenancy subordinate to the will and need of the whole village. Those arrangements remained, reinforced by the Puritan determination to establish a model society on Christian principles, or, as John Winthrop called it, a "city upon a hill."

That model included enacting into Massachusetts law the injunctions against drunkenness (but not drinking in itself), adultery, murder, theft, and violations of the Sabbath. Neither these laws nor the powerful moral consensus of the community itself was sufficient to prevent New Englanders from committing the normal range of sins or worldly behavior; but they gave a certain righteous definition to the Puritan experiment.

Puritans would not have understood the modern tendency to distinguish between private and public morality. To be selfish toward your neighbor was a sin, exactly as was a private act of what Puritans considered sexual misconduct. Puritans were driven by a morality of work. But work, besides being a way of restraining otherwise rebellious impulses, was supposed to be for the common good. It was therefore not merely obedience to tradition that dictated the landed arrangements of Massachusetts Bay villages. Upon the signing of a contract, pledging the seriousness of their endeavor, a number of Puritans would receive from the Massachusetts General Court the authorization to form a town.

John Winthrop. *(Courtesy, New York Public Library)*

As early as 1630 John Winthrop was reminding the first Puritans of their mission:

"Wee must consider that wee shall be as a citty upon a Hille. The eyes of all people are uppon us. Soe that if wee shall deale falsely with our God in this worke wee have undertaken, and soe cause him to withdraw his present help from us, wee shall be made a story and a by-word through the world."

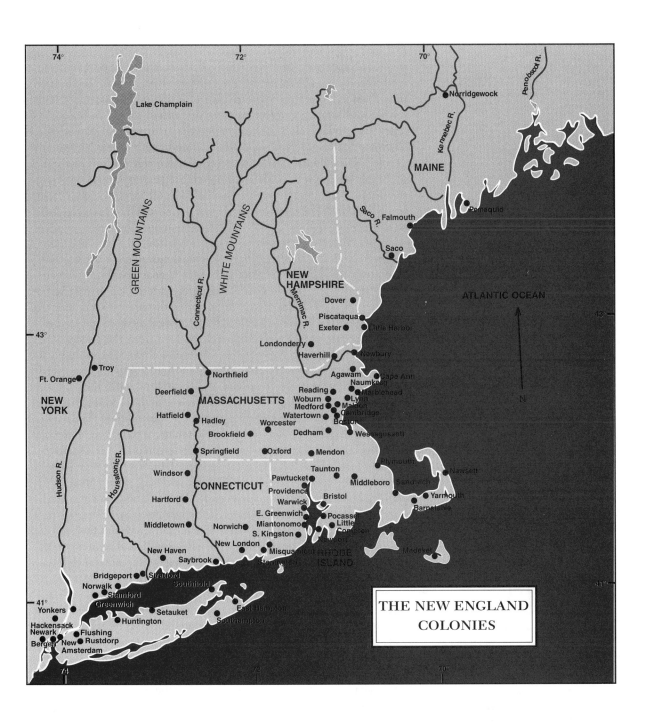

THE NEW ENGLAND
COLONIES

The responsible villagers would then apportion land to individuals on the basis of the size of the recipient's family and the usefulness of the land grant to the village as a whole. It was a remarkable fusion of private property and social obligation.

The word "Puritan" has come to be used, with some justification, to imply a rigid morality and a gloomy existence. But Puritans believed that conscience and effort could bring into good order both the individual self and the external world. Revering the Bible, which the printing press had made available to the masses, and other religious writings, they encouraged literacy, and communities supported common schools. Literacy brought not only Scripture reading but a degree of secular culture. The more educated Puritans read and wrote poetry. New Englanders developed a bright if decorous social life. They engaged in lively and profitable commerce—which in time, for better or for worse, broke up the original communal organization of the land. And it appears that, surely for the worse, they were early practitioners of the American habit of lawsuits.

A PURITAN MEDICAL REMEDY, 1656

"For all sorts of agues, I have of late tried the following magnetical experiment with infallible success. Pare the patient's nails when the fit is coming on; and put the parings in a litle bag of fine linen and tie that above a live eel's neck, in a tub of water. The eel will die and the patient will recover."

William Bradford, the Puritan historian, referred in his *History of Plimmouth Plantation* to Roger Williams as "a man godly and zealous, having many precious parts but very unsettled in judgment."

Roger Williams and Rhode Island

In 1631 Roger Williams, a clergyman of great personal charm, arrived in Massachusetts and became minister of the congregation at Salem. He began immediately to point out the numerous defects he saw in the Massachusetts scheme of things, declared the colony's charter invalid because it had not purchased the land from the Indians, and delivered such seditious doctrines as that no government should have authority over religious matters. When large numbers began to share those views the government found it necessary to banish him, lest the foundation for all authority in Massachusetts be undermined. In 1636 he went down the coast to Narragansett Bay, established a settlement he named Providence, which he said would be a "shelter for persons distressed of conscience," and for almost half a century presided as the spiritual head of what became the colony of Rhode Island and Providence Plantations—a haven for religious nonconformists. Roger Williams is sometimes mistaken for an early secular liberal. He was not. His opposition to government coercion of conscience was founded in a Separatist theology that had little specifically in common with the language of present-day defenders of civil liberties. But his sense of the integrity of private judgment does suggest something of later defenses of freedom of conscience.

Roger Williams, banished from Salem for arguing that government has no authority over religious matters, founded Providence, Rhode Island.
(Courtesy, Ewing Galloway, New York)

Anne Hutchinson

In 1638 the colony's authorities tried and banished another religious dissident. Anne Hutchinson, the daughter of a minister, wife of a prosperous cloth merchant, and mother of eleven children, had arrived with her family in 1634. She soon emerged as a charismatic amateur theologian. Holding informal meetings in her home to discuss the Sunday sermons, she argued that faith was more important than works in assuring salvation. She espoused a variety of what is commonly called Antinomianism, which by a rough translation means "against the law." It amounts to the belief that when love of Christ burns in the human spirit, the cold law of reason, custom, and government no longer prevails. Anne Hutchinson's interpretation of Puritan theology challenged the very foundations of the community.

The words of this formidable and eloquent woman found a receptive audience. Even the most learned ministers had difficulty in countering the hair-splitting logic of her reasoning. As increasing numbers of Bostonians embraced Anne Hutchinson's doctrines, she became even more dangerous to the established authorities than Roger Williams had been. Moreover, in a society where women were supposed to be submissive and subservient to men, Anne Hutchinson spoke confidently. John Winthrop described her as "a woman of a haughty and free carriage, of a nimble wit and active spirit . . . more bold than a man." Spurred on by Winthrop, the authorities reacted sharply, accusing her and her followers of heresy. She was condemned by both civil and religious leaders and banished. She and her family, along with a number of loyal followers, moved to Rhode Island.

In the 1630s other Massachusetts colonists settled elsewhere, many simply out of an urge to have more room to move around in, physically and politically. In 1635 a group settled along the Connecticut River. The Reverend Thomas Hooker led his flock west also, to establish Hartford. In 1639 these new settlements, choosing to place themselves outside the jurisdiction of Massachusetts, drew up an agreement called the *Fundamental Orders of Connecticut*. Under this charter they established their own government, which differed from that in Massachusetts in a single important feature: suffrage was not confined to church members.

Puritans and Indians   In the early 1600s the Narragansett Indians of Connecticut and their neighbors were threatened by a powerful and warlike tribe from the upper Hudson River that had pushed its way into the Connecticut Valley. These people earned by their behavior the name Pequot: "destroyer" in the Algon-

***The Red Fox*, James Hope.**
(Courtesy, Museum of Fine Arts, Boston)

quian dialects of New England. By the 1630s they dominated the valley, terrorizing and exacting tribute from the neighboring tribes. But potential allies—white settlers equipped with modern firearms—were now arriving from Europe.

An eighteenth-century poet chronicler of the Pequot War made his sympathies clear:

First, helpless Stone! they bade thy
    bosom bleed,
A guiltless offering at th' infernal shrine.
Then, gallant Norton! the hard fate was
    thine,
By ruffians butcher'd, and denied a
    grave
Thee, generous Oldham! next the doom
    malign
Arrested; nor could all thy courage save
Forsaken, plunder'd, cleft, and burried
    in the wave.

The Pequot War

Misunderstandings nonetheless turned into resentments and finally conflict. Neither Puritan governors nor tribal sachems could control all that occurred in each trading venture or settlement. Massachusetts court records are full of attempts to punish and make restitution for the deception, sharp dealings, kidnappings, and little battles that marked many encounters between newcomers and natives. By the early 1630s the number of English colonists was far larger than that of any single Indian tribe; by mid-decade there were probably as many English as Indians in New England. And as the Massachusetts Bay colony grew in size, the disposition to impose order on Indians grew likewise. When settlement expanded into the Connecticut Valley, where the Pequots had already shredded the tissue of intertribal diplomacy, war broke out.

The war has been attributed to the killing of three Englishmen. That John Stone had already been banished from New England under penalty of death for larceny, adultery, and attempted murder of the governor of Plymouth lends some force to the Pequot claim that his killing was under dire provocation. Walter Norton was in cahoots with Stone; and John Oldham, apparently, met his fate at the hands of the Narragansetts—who remained allied to the colonists—rather than the Pequots. But the Puritans, goaded by their Indian allies, dispatched ninety men under John Endicott on a mission of destruction.

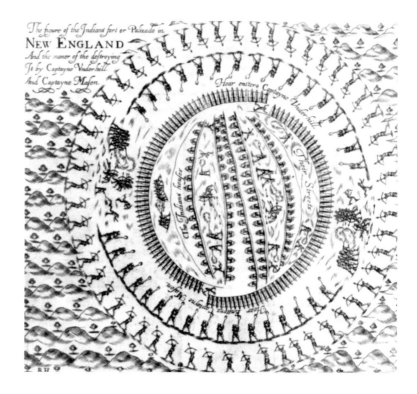

Diagram of the attack on the Pequot fort on Mystic River. Led by Captains John Mason and John Underhill the colonial forces set fire to the fort, burning alive all of the men, women, and children inside it. From an illustration, artist unknown, accompanying John Underhill's *Newes from America,* **London, 1638.** *(Courtesy, Rare Book Room, New York Public Library)*

Endicott's orders included putting to death all Indian men on Block Island. When the band of Englishmen with guns was frustrated by the Indians' retreat into swamps, they fired all their wigwams, destroyed all their possessions, then wantonly "destroyed some of their dogs." The Pequots replied in kind. Ambushing five men near Saybrook, they dispatched three immediately and roasted one alive; "the other came down drowned to us . . . with an arrow shot into his eye through his head." Similar fates befell about thirty white settlers in the next year before skirmishes and ambushes turned into a full-scale war of extermination, whose genocidal intent was expressed in the Reverend Thomas Hooker's admonition "not to do this work of the Lord's revenge slackly."

The Pequot War was not an early version of cowboys and Indians. There was not a white and an Indian side. The climactic battle pitted Mohegans, Narragansetts, and Englishmen against the Pequot fort on Mystic River within which somewhere between 400 and 700 men, women, and children perished by fire, musket ball, or arrow in less than an hour's time on May 26, 1637. God, so the Puritan commander reported, had "laughed his Enemies and the Enemies of his People to Scorn, making them as a fiery Oven. . . . Thus did the Lord judge among the Heathen, filling the Place with dead Bodies."

New England and the Chesapeake   From the beginning the settlers in New England differed fundamentally from those in Virginia and in Maryland, the Chesapeake Bay colonies. The New Englanders lived in small, close-knit towns and villages with a common Puritan theology and devotional life. The Chesapeake colonists lived on small farms and plantations, located, as one of them put it, "scatteringly, as a choice veine of rich ground invited them, and the further from neighbours the better." They were united in little more than a devotion to tobacco as a money-making crop. Maryland, founded in 1634 as a haven for England's persecuted Roman Catholics, also attracted Protestants, but economics proved a better magnet than religion for drawing new colonists to the Chesapeake.

Maryland was the first proprietary colony, a colony founded not by a joint-stock company as were Virginia and Massachusetts Bay but by a close-knit group, a family, or an individual. Later the Carolinas, New York, New Jersey, Pennsylvania, and Georgia also would begin as proprietary colonies. In Maryland's case it was the family of George Calvert, Lord Baltimore. Calvert, a devout Roman Catholic, was also a good friend of King Charles I, who gave him a large grant of land in America. After his death in 1632, his son, Cecil, the second Lord Baltimore, carried out the plan for a colony in America. Lord Baltimore had the authority to set and collect rents, issue legal writs, appoint administrative officials, confirm laws, and supervise the defense of the colony. The only important limitation required the proprietor to make laws "with the advice, assent, and approbation of the freemen of the province," a provision that led Baltimore to establish an elective assembly similar to Virginia's House of Burgesses. The colony remained small. Founded with 2,000 colonists in 1634, it had fewer than 6,000 in 1660. Most heads of families were small planters, cultivating tobacco for export.

The Maryland Toleration Act of 1649, despite its advanced provisions, was nevertheless a document of the seventeenth century. It stated in part:

"Therefore . . . enacted that noe person or persons whatsoever within this Province, or the Islands, Ports, Harbors, Creeks, or havens thereunto belonging professing to believe in Jesus Christ, shall from henceforth bee any waies troubled, Molested or discountenanced for or in respect of his or her religion nor in the free exercise thereof within this Province or the Islands thereunto belonging nor any way compelled to the beleife or exercise of any other Religion against his or her consent, soe as they be not unfaithful to the Lord Proprietary, or molest or conspire against the civill Government established or to bee established in this Province under him or his heires. . . . [S]uch person or persons soe offending, shalbe compelled to pay trebble damages to the party soe wronged or molested, and for every such offence shall also forfeit 20^{s} sterling in money or the value thereof. . . , Or if the parties soe offending as aforesaid shall refuse or bee unable to recompense the party soe wronged, or to satisfy such ffyne or forfeiture, then such offender shalbe severely punished by publick whipping & imprisonment."

Roman Catholics never settled in Maryland in large numbers, and Protestants soon sought greater influence. During the 1640s England was in civil war. On the one side were the forces of Parliament, dominated by the Puritans and seeking to set up a republic and a state church purified of remnants of Catholic theology and practice. On the other was the army of King Charles I, defending the existence of monarchy along with the established church. That church was Protestant and technically considered Rome to be an enemy. But it was close enough to Catholicism in sacraments, liturgy, and hierarchy to have a degree of affinity with England's remaining Roman Catholics, at least so long as Puritans were a common foe. In 1649 the Maryland assembly adopted an act, framed by Lord Baltimore in response to pressures in England and America and in response to his own conscience, that guaranteed religious toleration to all Christians. Maryland, like the New England colonies and Virginia, felt the shock waves from civil war and revolution in England.

A Moment of American Independence: 1642–1660

In 1642 the Puritan Parliament in England began open warfare with the monarchy, holding it to be the defender of an unpurified church. Parliament triumphed in 1647, and in 1649 executed Charles I. Then for eleven years a nation without a monarch was given over to experimentation in politics and in the shaping of a virtuous Protestant society. Parliament made the country into a Commonwealth that soon gave way to a Protectorate under Oliver Cromwell, who had been the essential leader of the Puritan forces. In 1660, not long after the death of Cromwell and the succession of his son to the Protectorate, Parliament invited a Stuart to resume the monarchy, and Charles II became King after years of exile in Europe.

From the Civil War until the restoration of the Stuarts, England was occupied with argument, war, and experiment, and the colonies were orphaned, virtually independent of the mother country. During these times they matured institutionally and socially.

The Chesapeake colonies of Virginia and Maryland, and the settlements in New England, evolved largely on their own, and then during the twenty years of the English Civil War the government largely ignored them. With little outside interference, the early British colonies developed a powerful sense of independence and self-sufficiency.

When the war broke out, the Puritan magistrates in New England formally dissolved their connections with the Crown. Various of the colonies, partly to establish more regular and consistent relations with the Indians in the wake of the Pequot War of 1637–38, formed the New England Confederation for mutual defense and general cooperation. Rhode Island was excluded, on the ground that it was a sinkhole of depravity and heresy. The sense of a common identity among the members of the Confederation hardened through their isolation from England. During the turmoil in England the New Englanders took to the sea, ventured into occasional trading activities with the West Indies, and therein laid the foundations for New England's robust maritime future.

During the 1650s both New England and the Chesapeake continued to grow. The outbreak of the Civil War had cut off the flow of

The Massachusetts General Court declared in 1650:

"Wee humbly conceive that the laws of England are bounded within the four seas, and doe not reach America. The subjects of his majesty here being not represented in Parliament, so we have not looked at ourselves to be impeded in our trade by them."

Puritans to New England, but by the time the war ended in 1647 the population of Massachusetts and the other New England colonies was increasing as fast as ever. In New England, where so many hundreds of Puritans had brought their families, that increase was largely due to a high birthrate. In Virginia and Maryland, women were scarcer, and family life took longer to develop. But a steady stream of immigrants swelled the population of the Chesapeake colonies. Some of the immigrants were fugitives from the Puritanical repression that was unfolding in England during the 1650s. Maryland's Toleration Act of 1649, guaranteeing freedom to all Christians, pulled immigrants of all denominations to Maryland.

The Half-Way Covenant After about 1650, New England's economy began to boom. Industriousness, furthered perhaps by a Puritan commitment to the virtue of diligence, had brought material prosperity to John Winthrop's "citty upon a Hille." This quickening of economic activity turned heads away from the Puritan founders' original purpose and attracted profit seekers who remained outside the religious community. And by the 1650s Puritans uneasily noticed that many of their children were not undergoing the conversion experience required for church membership. If the trend continued, Puritans feared, a dangerously large portion of the population would soon be outside the church.

In 1662 a meeting of Puritan ministers arrived at a solution to the problem of declining church membership. The ministers agreed to admit the grown children of church members into partial fellowship even though they could not give evidence of grace. To preserve the church's purity, the ministers excluded these "halfway" members from participation in the sacrament of Holy Communion. This Half-Way Covenant did revive lagging church membership, but it also showed that the Puritans' early dreams were yielding to practicality. Churches must be kept filled, even though, as one Concord man complained, "in the extreme seasons of heat and cold we were ready to say of the Sabbath, 'Behold what a weariness.'" The colony of Massachusetts was no longer a community of saints.

Boston by the late 1660s was, in the observation of a merchant, a town

"furnished with many fair shops; their materials are brick, stone, lime, handsomely contrived, with three meeting houses or churches, and a town-house built upon pillars where the merchants may confer; in the chambers above they keep their monthly courts. Their streets are many and large, paved with pebble stone, and the south-side adorned with gardens and orchards. The town is very rich and populous, much frequented by strangers; here is the dwelling of their governor. On the northwest and northeast two constant fairs are kept for daily traffic [trade] thereunto. On the south there is a small but pleasant Common where the gallants a little before sunset walk with their *Marmalet*-madams . . . till the nine o'clock bell rings them home to their respective habitations, when presently the constables walk their rounds to see good orders kept, and to take up loose people."

New Colonies

While New England and the Chesapeake colonies were establishing settlements, other colonies were taking shape—some founded for religious reasons and some for a variety of other motives. Until the middle of the seventeenth century the division of British North America into colonies had been on a patchwork basis. In 1660, when a Parliament tired of the disruptiveness of the Puritan period brought back the Stuart monarchy, some settlements had no official sanction. The new King, Charles II, had to give these some legal status, and he also wished to reward his loyal supporters. His government and that of his successor James II also proceeded to provide for further colonization.

Earlier in the century lands lying within the present states of New Hampshire and Maine had gone to individual proprietors receiving

The Thirteen Original Colonies

Name	Founded by	Year	Made Royal	Status at Revolutionary War
1. Virginia	London Company	1607	1624	Royal
2. New Hampshire	John Mason and others	1623	1679	Royal
3. Massachusetts	Separatists and Puritans	1620–30	1691	Royal
4. Maryland	Lord Baltimore	1634	———	Proprietary (controlled by proprietor)
5. Connecticut	Emigrants from Massachusetts	1635	———	Charter
6. Rhode Island	Roger Williams	1636	———	Charter
7. North Carolina	Virginians	1653	1729	Royal (separated informally from S.C., 1691)
8. New York	Dutch	1613–24		
	Duke of York	1664	1685	Royal
9. New Jersey	Berkeley and Carteret	1664	1702	Royal
10. South Carolina	Eight nobles	1670	1719	Royal
11. Pennsylvania	William Penn	1681	———	Proprietary
12. Delaware	Swedes	1638	———	Proprietary
13. Georgia	James Oglethorpe	1733	1752	Royal

authority from the Crown, but that authority was shadowy and from time to time Massachusetts Bay had extended its government to settlers there. By 1679 New Hampshire became a royal colony, while Maine stayed with Massachusetts until 1820.

Connecticut and Rhode Island were quickly provided for. In 1662 the towns in the Connecticut Valley received a charter from Charles. The charter, to the displeasure of New Havenites, placed the strict Puritan town of New Haven within the same colony as the more liberal settlements of the Connecticut Valley. The Puritan government of England at Roger Williams's urging had given a patent to Rhode Island. In 1663 Charles granted a charter to that democratic collection of towns. The grant confirmed the policy of religious freedom that had made Rhode Island a haven for religious dissenters. Their charters gave to Connecticut and Rhode Island the privilege of governing themselves. Therein appeared a colonial form, the charter colony, taking its place alongside the proprietary colony such as Maryland, owned by a single individual or small group, and the colony owned by a joint-stock company, like Massachusetts. Before long the British American mainland would contain more royal colonies, with governors appointed by the Crown.

New York   Since the early 1600s the Dutch West India Company had owned New Netherland, the territory that is now the state of New York. A collection of Dutch, English, other Europeans, Africans, and Indians dwelt in the little village of New Amsterdam on the island of Manhattan, in a later century to become

This 1651 engraving, the earliest known view of Manhattan Island, shows the fort of New Amsterdam in the 1620s. Indians are bringing beaver pelts in their canoes to sell to the Dutch.

one of the world's greatest cities: The future New York City lived off the fur and land trade and whatever other commerce the colony could offer. Farther up the Hudson River were the beginnings of a system that would leave its mark on New York society for two centuries and more, in which patroons—the word suggests the English "patron"—presided over huge farming estates and their workers. The Dutch West India Company had extended over New Netherland a loose control and provided local self-government and freedom of religion. The company was not able to turn a profit from the fees, taxes, and duties it imposed on the colony, and in 1654 it went bankrupt.

Charles II, continuing the commercial conflict with the Netherlands that the Puritan Commonwealth had entered, in 1664 seized New Netherland bloodlessly, the allegedly hot temper of its governor, Peter Stuyvesant, proving to have some mixture of prudence. (The Dutch would briefly retake the colony in the 1670s.) Charles II gave the province to his brother James, the Duke of York, and it became New York; the town of New Amsterdam also took that name. James's lieutenant in the colony proceeded to work out a set of laws. The scheme gave the freeholders—in essence, the landholders—of the colony the vote for town officials, but ensured that the Duke would hold ultimate power. There was to be freedom of religion, though each town was required to sustain a church. To two supporters, Lord Berkeley and Sir George Carteret, the Duke transferred the nearby conquered territory that received the name New Jersey. It was so named in honor of Carteret's earlier defense of the English Channel island of Jersey against the Puritans. Berkeley and Carteret then provided freedom of religion and granted to the freeholders the right to elect representatives who, along with a governor and council appointed by the proprietors, would legislate for the colony. The proprietors retained the authority to annul the laws.

Peter Stuyvesant. *(New-York Historical Society, New York City)*

The Carolinas   In 1663 a group that included Berkeley and Carteret became the proprietors of Carolina. In a charter of 1665, the King affirmed the right of the inhabitants to liberty of religion. The proprietors provided for a legislature elected by the freeholders, but retained the right to revoke laws. In 1669 Lord Ashley, one of the proprietors, and his secretary, the political philosopher John Locke, designed "The Fundamental Constitutions of Carolina," conceiving an elaborate and fanciful scheme for the colony, with a hereditary nobility and a feudal serfdom that were never realized. Toward the end of the century Carolina was centered in two unconnected locations: in the north, benefiting from migration from Virginia, a society of small farmers; and in the south, around the seaport of Charles Town (Charleston), a cluster of Virginians, migrants from the northern colonies, English immigrants, Scots, French Protestants called Huguenots, and planters from Bermuda and the British West Indies. The economy of the southern part of Carolina subsisted in part on the fur trade with the Indians, and the settlers around Charles Town were beginning to grow rice with slave labor. North and South Carolina both possessed self-government under ultimate proprietary control, but each would eventually become a royal colony with a Crown-appointed governor.

Pennsylvania   In 1681 an upper-class Quaker, William Penn, received from Charles II a proprietary grant to "Pennsylvania." Penn had already joined other Quakers in purchasing from Carteret the proprietary rights to part of New Jersey.

The Quakers, so called for the trembling religious fervor among their earlier members, believed that within each individual is a seed of truth and enlightenment. In pious living, contemplation, and a state of receptivity, a person can allow this seed to grow and spread its spiritual light. Quakers lived, then, in a condition of expectancy and inner questioning. Many Quakers were conspicuous for rejecting outward forms, customs, and social hierarchy. It was a common practice among Quakers, for example, to address even people of high social station with the familiar "thou" and "thee." They were persecuted in England and in Massachusetts Bay.

Penn's grant derived in part from the earlier friendship between Charles and Penn's father; Charles owed Penn for services rendered by

GABRIEL THOMAS'S ACCOUNT OF PENNSYLVANIA

Gabriel Thomas was a Quaker living in Pennsylvania during the late seventeenth century. Like many Quakers, he acted as a salesman for the new colony:

"The *Air* here is very delicate, pleasant, and wholesome; the *Heavens* serene, rarely overcast, bearing mighty resemblance to the better part of *France;* after Rain they have commonly a very clear Sky, the Climate is something Colder in the depth of Winter, and Hotter in the height of Summer; (the cause of which is its being a Main Land or Continent; the Days also are two Hours longer in the shortest Day of Winter, and shorter by two Hours in the longest Day of Summer) than here in *England,* which makes the Fruit so good, and the Earth so fertil.

The Corn-Harvest is ended before the middle of *July,* and most Years they have commonly between Twenty and Thirty Bushels of Wheat for every one they Sow. Their Ground is harrowed with Wooden Tyned Harrows, twice over in a place is sufficient; twice mending of their Plow-Irons in a Years time will serve. Their Horses commonly go with out being shod; two Men may clear between Twenty and Thirty Acres of Land in one Year, fit for the Plough, in which Oxen are chiefly us'd, though Horses are not wanting, and of them Good and well shap'd. A Cart or a Wain may go through the middle of the Woods, between the Trees without getting any damage, and of such Land in a convenient place, the Purchase will cost between *Ten* and

Penn's Treaty with the Indians, **by Benjamin West. The Quaker William Penn's historic treaty with the Delaware Indians in 1682 created a peaceful settlement in Pennsylvania.** *(Courtesy, Pennsylvania Academy of Fine Arts)*

the father, an admiral, and the grant was made in payment of that debt. The charter to Pennsylvania required that William Penn enforce British trading acts, permit appeals from Pennsylvania courts to the King, submit all Pennsylvania laws to the King for approval, and upon request from twenty colonists, provide a minister of the established Church of England. The King reserved the power to impose taxes "by act of Parliament." In all other respects Penn was free to govern his colony as he pleased.

In an elaborate *Frame of Government* (1682), Penn provided that the governorship of the colony would go to the proprietor or his deputy, and that legislative power would be vested in a council and an assembly, both elected by the freeholders of the colony. He proposed to earn an income from his colony by collecting rents from the settlers, and to attract the settlers by advertising widely the good land, free government, and religious liberty available in the colony. The campaign was an immediate success. Quakers flocked to Pennsylvania from England, Holland, Germany, Wales, and Ireland. Many people of other beliefs

Fifteen Pounds for a Hundred Acres. Here is much Meadow Ground. Poor People both Men and Women, will get near three times more Wages for their Labour in this Country, than they can earn either in *England* or *Wales.* . . .

[There are also] Land Fowl, of most sorts, *viz. Swans, Ducks, Teal,* (which two are the most Graceful and most Delicious in the World) *Geese, Divers, Brands, Snipe, Curlew;* as also *Eagles, Turkies* (of Forty or Fifty Pound Weight) *Pheasants, Patridges, Pidgeons Heath-Birds, Black Birds;* and that Strange and Remarkable Fowl, call'd (in these Parts) the Mocking-Bird, that Imitates all sorts of Birds in their various Notes. And for Fish, there are prodigious quantities of most sorts, *viz. Shadds Cats Heads, Sheeps-Heads, Herrings, Smelts, Roach, Eels, Perch.* As also the large sort of Fish, as *Whales* (of which a great deal of Oyl is made) *Salmon, Trout, Sturgeon, Rock, Oysters,* (some six Inches long) *Crabs, Cockles,* (some as big as Stewing *Oysters* of which are made a Choice Soupe or Broth) *Canok* and *Mussels,* with many other sorts of Fish, which would be too tedious to insert.

There are several sorts of wild *Beasts* of great Profit, and good Food; *viz. Panthers, Woolves, Fither, Deer, Beaver, Otter, Hares, Musk-Rats, Minks, Wild Cats, Foxes, Rackoons, Rabits,* and that strange Creature, the *Possam,* she having a false Belly to swallow her Young ones, by which means she preserveth them from danger, when any thing comes to disturb them. There are also *Bears* some *Wolves,* are pretty well destroy'd by the *Indians,* for the sake of the Reward given them by the *Christians* for that Service."

went as well, and a group of German Mennonites, driven from their homes by the continental religious wars, also immigrated to Pennsylvania. The capital, Philadelphia, the City of Brotherly Love, had by 1720 a population of 10,000, and by the 1770s would be the largest city in North America.

Penn also possessed deeds to what is now Delaware, though the grounds of his legal claim to govern "the Territories," as the lower region was called for a while, were unclear. In the first decade of the eighteenth century, Delaware, settled in part by Swedes, in effect would separate from Pennsylvania, though both colonies continued to have the same governor. In 1776 Delaware was to become a separate state.

Spanish explorations inspired by the French expedition to the Gulf Coast in the late seventeenth century gave the state of Texas its name. In 1686 Spaniards traveling in what is now east Texas met some hospitable Hasinai Indians, members of the Caddo nation. The Hasinai used a word for "friend" that sounded to Spanish ears like "tejas." The Spaniards, thinking themselves in the "great kingdom of the Tejas," called the entire region by that name.

Spanish and French Settlements

While England was colonizing much of the North Atlantic coast, other seventeenth-century European powers were settling portions of North America. Besides the Dutch in New Netherland (later New York) and the French in Canada, there were Spanish settlements in the Southwest. In 1598 Juan de Oñate had led a large expedition to the Rio Grande River into what is now New Mexico to claim that region for Spain. On August 20, 1598, Oñate and his entire company gathered with the priests to give thanks for their safe journey and successful settlement. Some say that this, and not the Pilgrims' more famous celebration in 1620, was the first Thanksgiving celebrated by Europeans in North America. The Spaniards also brought livestock with them: six hundred longhorn cattle and four hundred horses. Descendants of these longhorns were to become a legendary breed in Texas, and the descendants of the horses, the wild mustangs, would transform the Plains Indians into skilled horsemen and fearsome mounted warriors. Oñate's expedition led to the founding of Santa Fe, New Mexico, in 1609. Don Pedro de Peralta and a group of Franciscan missionaries established the settlement, but they were not the first to live there: the town was built on the site of an ancient Indian village.

Santa Fe was the northern outpost of Spain's vast empire. A branch of this main Spanish road led eastward across Texas to the French settlement on the Red River at Natchitoches, Louisiana, founded in 1713. Still another branch road went west to the Gila River and the Gulf of California. Along these roads, traders, Indians, and Spanish missionaries extended the influence of New Spain in North America.

By the early 1700s there was a scattering of small Spanish missions and presidios or forts in the river valleys of what are now the states of Texas, New Mexico, and Arizona. Jesuit and Franciscan priests worked at converting the Indians to Christianity, and Indians worked at growing beans and corn and meat cattle to supply the settlements' needs. Both enterprises had mixed results. In general, the Indians were not enthusiastic about leaving their native gods for a Christian deity, and the missions, far from the headquarters of New Spain in Mexico and even farther from the center of power in Spain, languished for want of converts and supplies.

In 1680 the Pueblo Indians of the upper Rio Grande valley staged a successful revolt against the Spanish settlers. Under the charismatic leader Popé, Indians killed priests, burned missions, and invaded the

Spanish capital at Santa Fe. Over four hundred Spanish colonists were killed, and the survivors fled. The refugees found safety at a place they called El Paso del Norte (the Northern Pass), now modern Juárez, Mexico, across the Rio Grande from the present city of El Paso, Texas.

Besides the Pueblo revolt, a French incursion into the Gulf of Mexico in 1685 potentially threatened New Spain. In 1682 a French explorer named Robert Cavelier, Sieur de La Salle, had traveled south from French outposts in Canada and claimed the Mississippi River Valley for France, calling the entire region Louisiana, after King Louis XIV. Two years later, supported by a grateful King Louis, La Salle sailed into the Gulf of Mexico, planning to establish a colony at the mouth of the Mississippi. Instead, his three ships missed their destination by about four hundred miles, arriving in early 1685 at Matagorda Bay near what is now the town of Port O'Connor in south Texas. The expedition's supply ship ran aground trying to enter the shallow bay, and another returned to France, leaving La Salle with 180 colonists and one small ship to search in vain for the Mississippi River. Their search ultimately proved unsuccessful, and disease and hostile Indians took their toll. In 1686 the French colonists' one remaining ship was wrecked in a storm. By 1687 only twenty settlers remained at Fort St. Louis as La Salle and seventeen others set off in search of help from a French outpost in Illinois. Discord as well as disease plagued these Frenchmen, and La Salle in 1687 was murdered by his disgruntled followers. In 1688 Indians attacked the few survivors at Fort St. Louis and destroyed the fort.

A year later the Spanish explorer Alonso de Leon, sent to search for Fort St. Louis, found the deserted site. All that remained were the main building, six huts of mud and buffalo hide, torn books, broken trunks, and parts of muskets. The Spaniards buried the remains of three dead bodies, two men and a woman. De Leon and his men also found eight cast-iron cannons, which they buried to keep them safe for future use.

Three major archaeological discoveries in the 1990s, three centuries after La Salle's ill-fated visit to Texas, verified the French presence on the Gulf Coast. In 1995 the wreckage of one of La Salle's ships, the sixty-five-ton *La Belle*, wrecked in 1686, was discovered in twelve feet of murky water in Matagorda Bay in south Texas. This shipwreck is one of the most significant ever found in North America. An eight-hundred-pound bronze cannon bearing the crest of King Louis XIV, and other recovered artifacts verified the ship's identity: *La Belle* had been a gift to La Salle from the French monarch. In 1996 a ranch hand with a metal detector unearthed three of the cannons that the Spanish had buried at Fort St. Louis in 1689. Archaeologists working in the same spot recovered all eight of the cannons, and the site of the long-lost French fort was conclusively identified. In 1998 the wreck of La Salle's supply ship *Aimable*, of three hundred tons, was discovered under water near the narrow channel of Cavallo Pass, the entrance to Matagorda Bay where the vessel had run aground in 1685.

The Colonies and the Crown

The Navigation Acts and Mercantilism

In 1651 the government of the Puritan Commonwealth passed a Navigation Act aimed at building up the shipping of England and the empire. The government was particularly interested in excluding from English and colonial ports the ships of the Netherlands, a fellow Protestant nation with which the Commonwealth was in close economic competition. The Act provided that no ships except those belonging to the people of England or her colonies could carry Asian, African, or American goods into England or the colonies.

After Charles II restored the English monarchy in 1660, his ministers and Parliament, building on principles established by the Navigation Act, enacted a broad program designed to stimulate England's economic growth and to transform into a world empire the scattered American settlements and East Indian trading posts. The primary aim of this mercantilist program was to make England and its overseas colonies a vast, closed trading area, as self-sufficient as possible, pro-

By the 1620s Virginia was exporting in considerable quantity a valuable crop, tobacco, which appealed to Europeans. King James I published a pamphlet that denounced smoking as "a custom loathsome to the eye, hateful to the nose, harmful to the brain, dangerous to the lungs, and in the black stinking fumes thereof, the nearest resembling the horrible smoke of the pit that is bottomless." But the King's perception failed to dissuade seventeenth-century smokers, some of whom may have read a 1614 pamphlet by an Edinburgh physician. He claimed that tobacco would cure asthma, shortness of breath, coughs, ulcers, colic, "yea almost all diseases," and that smoking "prepareth the stomach for meat, it maketh a clear voice, it maketh a sweet breath, it cleareth the sight, it openeth the ears, it comforteth the nerves. . . ." Whatever the eventual impact on European lungs, tobacco ensured a long and prosperous history for the preeminent southern colony.

tected by an enlarged navy, and serviced by an expanded merchant fleet. Each part of the empire was supposed to specialize in supplying the products and services for which it was best suited, and thereby contribute to the well-being of all the other parts and to the strength of the whole. The colonies would provide the mother country with materials that England could not produce economically, such as lumber, naval stores, fish, tobacco, indigo, and West Indian sugar. The colonial products were supposed to be sent only to Britain, but would have a monopoly on the English market. Insofar as was feasible, the colonies were not to engage in manufacture. Instead they would buy their finished goods from England. All products would be subject to customs duties and be carried only in English or colonial ships.

Two major acts laid the legal foundations of the system: the Navigation Act of 1660 and the Staple Act of 1663. The Navigation Act restricted all colonial trade to vessels owned and manned primarily by Englishmen or British colonists, and required that certain named articles produced in the colonies—tobacco, sugar, indigo, and ginger—be shipped only to Britain or to another English colony. The Staple Act required that most goods imported into the colonies, whether they originated in Britain or in foreign parts, must be shipped from a British port. The Staple Act aimed to benefit the Crown by increasing the customs revenues on exports from England. It was supposed also to help English exporters by giving them a monopoly of the colonial market (even as the Navigation Act gave colonial producers a monopoly of the English market). And it was intended to protect the colonists by confining their trade to shipping lanes that could be patrolled and protected by the English navy.

A Trade Boom   For all the laxity of its enforcement, the new commercial system was an immediate success. English commerce boomed and the merchant fleet became the largest and most profitable the nation had yet known. Besides the mainland colonies, England's island possessions prospered under this new system. These included Bermuda, founded in 1612, and the West Indies colonies of St. Christopher (1624), Barbados (1627), Nevis (1628), Montserrat and Antigua (1632), and Jamaica (1655). The West Indies, booming with the rapid expansion of slavery and sugar production, welcomed the naval protection afforded by the new system, for the Caribbean had been teeming with pirates. The Chesapeake colonies, Virginia and Maryland, paid perhaps a bit more for freight than they had before, and tobacco prices continued to decline until the 1690s. But the establishment of a great central marketing system in England facilitated an enormous increase in production that in the long run more than compensated. By 1680, for example, the Chesapeake colonies were exporting over seventeen million pounds of tobacco a year. The New England colonies, being free to elect their own governors, were also free to ignore the Acts of Trade when it was to their advantage. Thus they profited from trade with the enclosed imperial market as well as from the protection of the English navy, and otherwise did as they pleased. Consequently, the merchant fleet of New England, built by a burgeoning new local industry, grew even faster than that of Old England.

After what is known as the Restoration, the return of the Catholic Charles II to the British throne in 1660, the colonies cultivated the independence that they had already enjoyed when England, first under the Puritan Commonwealth and then under the Protectorate, left them for the most part alone. The Massachusetts Bay Puritan Colony led the way.

Charles II's resumption of discrimination against those who dissented from the Church of England also promoted New England's prosperity. A new wave of dissenters went to America in flight from this policy, and in the 1660s the population of New England increased from about 33,000 to some 52,000.

Resistance to the Crown From the outset of the Restoration, Massachusetts was troublesome. It secretly harbored three of the men condemned to death for the execution of Charles I (though there was a £100 bounty on their heads and anyone caught assisting them would be executed). Massachusetts ignored the Navigation Acts; and it violated its charter by retaining on its statute books a number of laws, particularly those concerning religion, contrary to the laws of England. Very early, Charles II sent orders commanding Massachusetts to make its laws conform to those of England. The colony did temporarily stop persecuting the Quakers—it had executed three— and did modify its laws concerning suffrage, but neither action was taken in response to the King's orders, which the colonial assembly flatly ignored. And so, when the British mission to seize New Netherland from the Dutch was dispatched in 1664, Charles sent four commissioners along to investigate the New England governments.

The commissioners encountered no difficulty in Plymouth, Connecticut, or Rhode Island, but when they arrived in Boston they met a reception at once icy and bold. The magistrates referred the commissioners to the Massachusetts Bay Charter of 1629, refused to submit to investigation, and publicly forbade the citizens to offer any testimony. The commissioners returned to England, and three of them recommended to the King that the charter be revoked. The open defiance might have provoked not only a revocation of the charter but armed suppression of the colony as well. But the confrontation came just at the time England was suffering from the London plague, a great fire in that city, and military reverses abroad. For the next six years Massachusetts, together with the other colonies, was largely ignored, and could take advantage of the situation.

In 1667, when the price of tobacco fell to a low of less than half a penny a pound, New England's merchants began a practice they would continue off and on until the American Revolution. When it was to their advantage, they ignored the mother country's Acts of Trade. Tobacco by the late 1660s was a staple of the colonies' transatlantic trade, but its transport and sale were strictly regulated. Tobacco was subject to a customs duty of two pennies per pound, and could be shipped only to England, there to be taxed and put into English vessels bound for the European market. Under normal circumstances about half the tobacco shipped from the colonies to London was re-exported to the European continent through Holland. Though the English market had dwindled, European demand for tobacco continued. So the merchants of New

England, disregarding the Navigation Acts, loaded the Chesapeake's tobacco aboard their own vessels and sailed directly to Holland, where they and the colonial tobacco planters made handsome if illegal profits.

Virginia, of all the colonies most committed to the monarchy, and New England, the least, were equally dissatisfied with the government in London. By late in the seventeenth century, colonists in the two regions were to be in close to open rebellion against the English government. Both, too, had found something else to worry about: renewed hostilities with the Indians.

Indian Affairs

Indian Migration

The ultimate wellspring of the trouble was the ambition of France. Since the massacre of 1622 in Virginia and the Pequot War of 1637–38 in Massachusetts, the Indians had gradually and peacefully retreated to the interior rather than face the fire of English muskets. But in the late 1660s the French adopted a broad strategy of encircling the English colonies with settlements along the St. Lawrence, the Great Lakes, and the Mississippi, and forged alliances with the Indians between their own settlements and those of the English. The five Iroquois nations of New York had long been enemies of the French and their Indian allies. Hence the new French policy forced the Iroquois back. They, in turn, pushed back the Algonquian tribes of New England and the Susquehannocks of Pennsylvania, with the result that in the 1670s New England Indians clashed with the English to the east, and the Susquehannocks engaged in hostilities with the colonists to the south.

New England and King Philip's War

In New England the fighting was known as King Philip's War (1675–76). Philip (Metacomet), a Wampanoag chieftain whose own people were already hemmed in between rival governments and land speculators in Rhode Island and Massachusetts, was pressed to the point of desperation by the Iroquois drive; and just at that time the Massachusetts government ordered the Indians to disarm. They responded in the only way they could, by attacking the English settlements.

The Indians did not fight according to the rules of formal territorial warfare, European-style: a contest in which the only combatants and subjects of attack were uniformed armies and both sides campaigned until one or the other surrendered. They crept up on unsuspecting villages, setting fire to houses and barns, driving away or killing livestock as well as unsuspecting colonists, and then retreating into the forests. Town after town was laid waste in the winter of 1675–76. The Indians fought only intermittently, and they regarded everyone, women and children included, as fair prey. There was considerable barbarism on both sides. But the colonists had the advantage of superior arms and superior organization. Not everyone was eager to fight. Two Boston men said they "would be hanged drawne and quartered rather than goe." The New England Confederation mobilized about a thousand men and conducted a relentless campaign. By 1676 the Indians had been thor-

King Philip. *(Courtesy, Smithsonian Institution)*

oughly defeated, though at great cost: King Philip's War destroyed over 20 towns and cost the English settlers a sixth of their adult males. During the entire campaign, the English government sent no help.

Instead of help, a special agent of Charles II, Edward Randolph, arrived in Boston to convey new royal instructions and to investigate the enforcement of the Navigation Acts. The obstinate Massachusetts General Court refused to recognize Randolph as customs officer, set up its own customs office, and imprisoned the deputies Randolph had appointed. When the colony did not satisfactorily reform its behavior, court proceedings began. In 1684 the Massachusetts Bay Company lost its charter and Massachusetts became a royal colony.

A map of Virginia in 1612, showing Powhatan. *(Courtesy, Smithsonian Institution)*

Virginia and the Powhatan Confederacy   After the bloody Powhatan uprising of 1622 in Virginia, throughout the 1620s and 1630s the Virginia militia methodically attacked native villages, destroying people, homes, and food supplies. Not until the mid-1630s did peace return. The aged Opechancanough, chief of the Powhatan Confederacy, then struck in 1644, his warriors killing more than 500 of Virginia's 8,000 settlers. With superior numbers and technology, the English quickly crushed the rebellion, capturing and killing Opechancanough and destroying the Powhatan Confederacy.

In a treaty that was to become typical of future such transactions between Indians and non-Indians in the United States, the English colonists and Virginia natives agreed in 1646 to end hostilities. For a variety of reasons, the colonists wanted to move the Indians to distant lands so that the two communities would be permanently separated. Some colonists supported such a plan because it would liberate native lands for development, while others saw it as a way to protect both Indians and Europeans from future violence. The treaty moved the tidewater tribes north of the York River and promised them permanent tenure on their new land. They were to be protected by Virginia courts and were expected to serve in the colonial militia. The reservation system in America had begun.

The reservation system would dominate for nearly three hundred years the relations between Indians and whites. The typical pattern was for white Americans to choose for an Indian tribal reservation land that they did not find desirable. Then over time new settlers, new technologies, or new discoveries of natural resources would make that piece of land suddenly valuable to whites. Violence or legal maneuvering would begin again as whites tried to settle on the reservations and Indians tried to prevent them. The Indians would then be moved to a new reservation farther west, until white land hunger brought still another cycle of invasion and removal.

Virginia and Bacon's Rebellion   In the summer of 1675, bands of Susquehannock Indians, fleeing the Iroquois, crossed the Potomac River into Virginia. Relations between the backcountry Indians and the Virginia planters deteriorated until a planter's herdsman was killed, several Indians (including five Susquehannock chiefs under a flag of truce) were killed in retaliation, and the whole Potomac frontier erupted in raids and counterraids.

Thomas Mathew of Virginia described the colonists' fears of Indians after a scare in 1675:

"In these frightfull times the most Exposed small families withdrew into our houses of better Numbers. . . . Neighbours in Bodies Joined their Labours from each plantation to others alternatively, taking their Arms into the Fields, and Setting sentinels; no Man Stirrd out of Door unarm'd."

As part of the restored royal authority, according to Governor William Berkeley of Virginia, Indians became subjects of the King, on an equal footing with the English colonists, and were therefore entitled to the protection of royal justice. No warfare upon the Indians was to be tolerated, despite the Indian attacks—which Berkeley regarded as minor frontier incidents and impediments to the lucrative fur trade. Berkeley met the crisis by raising funds to rebuild the frontier forts and to pay and equip a band of mounted rangers, and by prohibiting fur trade by any but a handful of traders whom he himself licensed. The new tax was ill calculated to please the frontiersmen, and the new trade regulations threatened the ambitions of a number of frontier fur traders, land seekers, and border barons.

The malcontents soon raised a leader who was willing to defy the governor: Nathaniel Bacon, recent settler in the interior of Virginia, artful demagogue, unscrupulous lawyer who had been trained at the Inns of Court in London. Bacon held that the Indians were not subjects of the Crown but were outside the law and could be attacked by any Englishman so disposed. In May 1676, without a commission from the governor, Bacon marched at the head of an expedition that descended upon the Roanoke River to destroy a Susquehannock village. He was promptly accused of treason, but the governor pardoned him when he acknowledged his offense.

"Bacon's Laws" Meanwhile Bacon, along with a goodly number of other radicals, was elected to the House of Burgesses. They proceeded to push through a series of enactments, collectively known as "Bacon's laws," which reversed most of Berkeley's policies by liberalizing voting, tax, and religious regulations. Bacon himself had little or nothing to do with all this. Instead, he took up his military career again. He raised an army of 500 men, marched on the colonial capital at Jamestown, forced Berkeley to commission him as a militia captain, and set about looking for more Indians to kill.

The planters professed no allegiance at all to Parliament, and their loyalty to the Crown had become only formal, devoid of any personal commitment. When Governor Berkeley again declared Bacon a rebel, many planters swore their allegiance to that frontiersman. In 1676, they held to their oath, enabling Bacon to drive Berkeley's forces out of Jamestown and burn the village to the ground. Loyalist forces threatened rebel families, and Bacon used loyalists' wives as hostages during his attack on Jamestown. The rebellion revealed class tensions as well as political differences. One female partisan of Berkeley wrote to a friend that the "differences within our selves [are] far greater [than with the Indians]."

Order was restored in the ensuing months, largely as a result of Bacon's death from the "bloody flux" (dysentery) in October. Berkeley regained control and proceeded to hang twenty-three of the rebels, causing Charles II to remark, "The old fool has hanged more men in that naked country than I have done for the murder of my father." The King sent a royal commission to Virginia to investigate the rebellion, and the seventy-year-old Berkeley was recalled to England, but he died before he could give his side of the story.

The Dominion of New England

With the death of Charles II in 1685, his brother James became King. James carried forward the project for the establishment of royal rule, and for bringing some coherence to the government of the colonies. He created the Dominion of New England. New Hampshire, Massachusetts, Plymouth (not yet absorbed into Massachusetts), Connecticut, Rhode Island, New York, and the Jerseys were all to be governed by one governor and his council, without the interference of representative assemblies. James appointed as governor of the Dominion Sir Edmund Andros, a former governor of New York and a staunch Church of England man, who arrived in Boston during 1686. "The fox," said the Puritan clergyman Cotton Mather, "has been made master of the hen house."

Sir Edmund Andros   The new system made a great deal of administrative sense. It had a defensive purpose as well. James II feared that the French in North America would threaten England's colonies, and wanted the Dominion of New England to unite those independent-minded colonists under one firm hand. For the first and only time in the history of the English empire in America, England had a colonial system that was, at least on paper, as efficient as those of France and Spain.

Andros's administration was in many respects both shrewd and enlightened. He left most of the existing laws in force. He respected the established churches and schools—though in his attempts to provide for the Church of England he antagonized Puritans. His observance of Christmas, which Puritanism rejected for savoring of ritual and Catholicism, drew the indignant notice of Samuel Sewall. A prominent and devout Puritan, Sewall made a dour comment in his diary on December 25, 1686 (a Sunday): "The Christmas keepers had a very pleasant day." For the most part Andros left the towns in control of their own local affairs: and the town and congregation constituted the primary unit of government in New England. Andros could also govern with a strong hand. He offered the merchants of his Dominion, for example, the protection of the Royal Navy if they cooperated with him. He also levied taxes without legislative approval, but they were no larger than they had been when duly elected representatives levied them. Andros further encroached upon the principle of local self-government by ordering that town meetings be held no more than once a year and that control of the militia be vested in the governor. But the towns customarily met officially only once a year anyway (they met once a week as church congregations, and that Andros did not change), and as it happened Andros never had occasion to call out the militia.

In short, Andros's innovations directly challenged the professed principles of the New Englanders, but altered little their daily lives. It is uncertain whether this experiment in enlightened despotism would have won over New Englanders inclined to hostility toward outside rule, and more especially rule by a communicant of the Church of England. The Dominion of New England was never put to the full test, for the Crown power that it needed for support collapsed.

Edmund Andros, governor of the Dominion of New England from 1686–1688, being taken prisoner in Boston. Though this was triggered by rumors of a popish plot, opposition to Andros stemmed from the colonists' belief that he was limiting local self-government. *(Courtesy, Scribner's Archives)*

James II's undoing came in 1688 after he alienated his strongest supporters by attempting to go too far too fast in his efforts to restore Roman Catholicism. Even the Tories, the party more sympathetic to the privileges of the Crown, were antagonists. Rich country gentry, who made up much of the strength of the Tories, were wedded to the Church of England. Some of them feared that full restoration of the Roman Church might include restoration of its lands, which happened now to belong to them. Even then, James might have prevailed but for a sudden change in the prospects for the royal succession.

The Glorious Revolution   James was in his fifties and his only children were two daughters, Mary and Anne, both by his first wife and both devoutly Protestant; his second wife, an Italian princess and a Catholic, had borne him no children. Most Englishmen, however much they despised the King, therefore thought it better to wait out the papist storm as they had the Puritan, on the theory that little permanent harm could be done before James died and the Crown passed to a Protestant. But in June 1688 the Queen had a son, and that opened the possibility of a permanent Catholic succession. English Protestantism seemed endangered: and so a group of prominent Englishmen conspired to invite William of Orange of Holland, husband of James's daughter Mary, to rescue England from Roman Catholicism. William accepted and on November 5 landed with a force of about 14,000. Great numbers of royal troops deserted, and much of the remainder of James's army refused to obey their Catholic commanders. James was left defenseless, and in December he fled to the continent. Eight weeks later William and Mary became joint sovereigns of England. The whole tame affair acquired a flamboyant title: the Glorious Revolution.

Governor Andros was in Maine when he got news of William's landing, and he returned to Boston to prevent an anti-royalist response. But he had neither army nor police, and rioting broke out in response not to James's removal but to rumors of a popish plot. Andros fled to the local fort, but before the end of the day he and the other royal officials surrendered and were jailed. A Puritan oligarchy governed the colony for two months, until a new General Court could be elected. In July Andros was ordered to return to England.

As soon as the news of Boston's uprising reached New York that colony too was swept with a great fear of a popish plot, and three of its counties, those populated mainly by Puritans, threw out the royal officials and elected their own. In New York, Jacob Leisler, a successful German trader, led a group that ousted Andros's deputy governor and established a provisional government. At first Leisler had little backing outside the city, but soon Indian raids in the upper part of the colony inspired by the French lent gruesome reinforcement to the rumors of a papist and Indian campaign to massacre Protestants. Leisler offered discipline, order, and military strength, and became in fact governor of the entire colony for two years, until a new royal governor arrived. Then Leisler and his son-in-law were hanged and drawn and quartered for treason.

The Jerseys and Pennsylvania adjusted to the new regime in England with little drama. In Maryland a group of colonists calling themselves the Protestant Association forced the resignation of the governor appointed by the Catholic Lord Baltimore, brought back the assembly, which had been dissolved, and petitioned the Crown to take over the colony. In Virginia the dominant planters announced their support of William and Mary and their confidence that James's governor would be removed, which soon happened. Settlers in northern Carolina turned on the proprietary governor, who fled to Charles Town and temporarily set up a government there. Soon afterward the proprietors suspended him.

The Ideology of Revolution   The philosopher of the English revolution was John Locke. At the behest of various champions of the revolution, Locke published in 1689 and 1690 several essays, notably the *Second Treatise of Civil Government* and *An Essay Concerning Human Understanding*. Locke reasoned that man had once lived in a state of nature, in accordance with the laws of nature, which endow man with rights to life, personal freedom, and the property that he accumulates through honest labor. But in the natural state the strong prey upon the weak, and so men had formed societies and created governments. Governments exist by virtue of voluntary agreements, or contracts, between governed and governors, and their function is to protect the individual's natural rights to life, liberty, and property. The conclusion to which this argument points is that the government of James II broke the contract by depriving people of their natural rights, in effect declaring war upon his subjects. The people therefore had no recourse but to overthrow James's government and to establish a new contract with a new sovereign, William of Orange, who seemed more likely to abide by his agreements.

To make legitimate the Glorious Revolution, a Convention Parliament proclaimed early in 1689 a Declaration of Rights that a formal Parliament enacted, under the title of Bill of Rights; William and Mary approved it later the same year. The Bill of Rights established, for all time, limits upon the English monarchy and judiciary. The Crown could no longer make or suspend laws, levy taxes, or maintain standing armies without the consent of Parliament, which was guaranteed frequent meetings, free elections, and free debate. Some ecclesiastical courts were eliminated and others had their powers reduced, and in all courts every person was guaranteed trial by jury and protected from excessive bails and forfeiture of estates before conviction.

Equally important were measures to regularize, modernize, and render more flexible the system of public finance, which had previously occasioned such destructive conflict between the Crown and Parliament. Henceforth Parliament did not merely grant monies, but controlled their expenditure as well. To that end, it began to make specific appropriations for specific purposes, and to require estimates and accounts of expenditures.

Crown and Parliament, restructuring the government at home, attempted also to bring order to affairs in the colonies.

The Suffrage in the Colonies

While seventeenth-century European nations—with the partial exception of England—were becoming more autocratic, Americans were opening their political system to wide participation. That did not come of some radical democratic ideology. The colonies went on the fairly conservative conviction that participation in political decisions should be left to property owners. Since in the colonies ownership of property was widespread, so was the proportion of voters to the whole population. In the early settlement of Massachusetts Bay, the vote was vested in male members of Puritan congregations, and this too made for a fairly broad electorate. The eventual ideological commitment among Americans to popular rule resulted in good measure from their practical experience of it.

England Tries Again: The Navigation Act of 1696
In 1696 King William III of England commissioned the Board of Trade to supervise commerce, recommend appointments of colonial officials, and review colonial laws to see that none interfered with trade or conflicted with the laws of England. Since the 1660s the colonists had taken advantage of England's political preoccupations to profit from illegal trade. Enforcement of the earlier Navigation Acts had depended more upon private morality, supplemented by generous rewards to informers, than upon efficient administrative machinery. The new Navigation Act of 1696 sought to change that. Colonial governors were now held responsible, on penalty of forfeiture of office, for violations of the law. Regular customs officers were appointed for each colony, whereas previously there had been only a few officers who moved about from one colony to another. Trials for violations of the law were to be in admiralty courts, where proceedings were not encumbered by juries.

But the new system could not overcome the physical circumstances in English America, which were not conducive to efficient supervision of trade. Effective customs operations require concentration of shipping, and in much of America such concentration was not feasible. Tobacco, for example, by far the most valuable product of the mainland colonies, was normally loaded on ships directly at the plantations along the rivers of Virginia and Maryland and on Chesapeake Bay. Short of placing customs officers on every plantation or stationing armed ships at every river and inlet, it was virtually impossible to prevent masters of vessels from carrying tobacco anywhere they pleased.

For the enforcement of anything like the Navigation Acts England had as yet no tradition of civil service, royal or parliamentary, in the colonies or at home. Posts were filled through influence, bribery, or other corrupt means as quickly as through regard for honest and efficient administration. Colonial service attracted the least savory of a generally unsavory lot, not only because life in the colonies was far from desirable to most courtiers, but also because the rewards for legitimate service there were small. In all the mainland colonies except Virginia the governor was dependent upon the local assembly for his salary, and the customs officers were paid out of fees and fines, not the royal treasury. Accordingly, many of those who filled imperial positions were quite amenable to bribes, offered in exchange for looking the other way.

By and large, the imperial commercial system worked when it was to the mutual advantage of the colonies and the mother country to abide by it; which is to say, it worked for about three-quarters of the trade affected by the Navigation Acts. Otherwise it was generally ignored, except when the Royal Navy was not engaged in war and had nothing better to do than police the seas against pirates and smugglers.

In the years following the Glorious Revolution colonial governments underwent reorganization. Connecticut and Rhode Island retained their self-government, and the Penn family, after losing the original charter to Pennsylvania, regained the proprietorship of that colony. In 1691 the Crown took over Maryland, though the Calvert family retained property rights there. But then the Calverts converted from Roman Catholicism to the Church of England, and in 1715 they were given back proprietary rights to the government of Maryland. In the colony founded as a refuge for Roman Catholics, people of that faith lost the right to vote. Virginia, Massachusetts, and New Hampshire were now royal colonies. In 1702 New Jersey too became a Crown colony, and by 1729 North Carolina and South Carolina were separate Crown colonies.

Within a few years after the Glorious Revolution, then, British North America had the kind of government and the relationships to Great Britain that would determine its course until the American Revolution. In the eighteenth century governors and councils appointed by the monarch would often clash with elected assemblies that alone had the authority to tax the colonists, and therefore had the authority to withhold money from a governor in the pursuit of his policies. The Navigation Acts, with further legislation in the eighteenth century, would in time lead to major conflict with the government in Great Britain. The foundations had been laid for a grand but restless empire.

Suggested Readings

The study of the massive migration of Europeans to America must begin with Bernard Bailyn's *The Peopling of America: An Introduction* (1985). Patricia Seed's insightful *Ceremonies of Possession in Europe's Conquest of the New World, 1492–1640* (1995) explores the different ways in which the Spanish, English, Dutch, and French staked their cultural claims on the lands they colonized. See also David Hackett Fischer's provocative study, *Albion's Seed: Four British Folkways in America* (1989) and James Horn, *Adapting to a New World: English Society in the Seventeenth Century Chesapeake* (1994). Karen O. Kupperman's 1984 study, *Roanoke: The Abandoned Colony*, is a well-reasoned account of the lost settlers. Alden Vaughan, *American Genesis: Captain John Smith and the Founding of Virginia* (1975) and Edmund S. Morgan, *American Slavery, American Freedom: The Ordeal of Colonial Virginia* (1975), are classic works on early Virginia. Newer studies include Everett Emerson, *Captain John Smith* (1993) and A. J. Leo LeMay, *Did Pocahontas Save John Smith?* (1992).

On the founding of New England, Edmund Morgan's *The Puritan Dilemma: The Story of John Winthrop* (1958) has become a classic, as has John Demos, *A Little Commonwealth: Family Life in Plymouth Colony* (1970). Demos explores new territory in *The Unredeemed Captive: A Family Story from Early America* (1994). Useful town studies include Darrett Rutman, *Winthrop's Boston* (1965), Kenneth Lockridge, *A New England Town: The First Hundred Years* (1970), and Philip Greven, *Four Generations: Population, Land, and Family in Colonial Andover, Massachusetts* (1970).

Early New England's rich intellectual history may be sampled in Kenneth Silverman's *Cotton Mather: Puritan Priest* (1988), Sacvan Bercovitch, *The American Jeremiad* (1978), and the classic *Errand into the Wilderness* (1956) by Perry Miller. The standard study of the Anne Hutchinson controversy is still Emery Battis, *Saints and Sectaries: Anne Hutchinson and the Antinomian Controversy in the Massachusetts Bay Colony* (1962). See also Kenneth Lockridge, *Literacy in Colonial New England* (1974).

An important environmental study is William Cronon's *Changes in the Land: Indians, Colonists, and the Ecology of New England* (1984). Alden Vaughan's *New England Frontier: Puritans and Indians, 1620–1675* (1965) examines the confrontation of cultures, as does Gary B. Nash in *Red, White, and Black: The People of Early North America* (1992). Alfred A. Cave's *The Pequot War* (1996) is a recent account of that New England conflict.

On Virginia's Indians see Helen Rountree, *The Powhatan Indians of Virginia: Their Traditional Culture* (1989), and an important collection of essays edited by Peter Wood and others entitled *Powhatan's Mantle: Indians in the Colonial Southeast* (1989). See also Douglas Deal, *Race and Class in Colonial Virginia: Indians, Englishmen, and Africans on the Eastern Shore during the Seventeenth Century* (1993). Daniel Richter's *The Ordeal of the Longhouse: The Peoples of the Iroquois League in the Era of European Colonization* (1992) is a sympathetic study of northern tribes.

See the provocative new study by Jill Lepore, *King Philip's War* (1997). On Bacon's Rebellion see Stephen Webb's *The End of American Independence* (1983) and Wilcomb Washburn, *The Governor and the Rebel: A History of Bacon's Rebellion in Virginia* (1957).

Cultural Influences on the Early Colonies

David Hackett Fischer

Our society is dynamic, changing profoundly in every period of American history; but it is also remarkably stable. The search for the origins of this system is the central problem in American history. . . .

The organizing question here is about what might be called the determinants of a voluntary society. The problem is to explain the origins and stability of a social system which for two centuries has remained stubbornly democratic in its politics, capitalist in its economy, libertarian in its laws, individualist in its society and pluralistic in its culture. . . .

During the very long period from 1629 to 1775, the present area of the United States was settled by at least four large waves of English-speaking immigrants. The first was an exodus of Puritans from the east of England to Massachusetts during a period of eleven years from 1629 to 1640. The second was the migration of a small Royalist elite and large numbers of indentured servants from the south of England to Virginia (ca. 1642–75). The third was a movement from the North Midlands of England and Wales to the Delaware Valley (ca. 1675–1725). The fourth was a flow of English-speaking people from the borders of North Britain and northern Ireland to the Appalachian backcountry mostly during the half-century from 1718 to 1775.

These four groups shared many qualities in common. All of them spoke the English language. Nearly all were British Protestants. Most lived under British laws and took pride in possessing British liberties. At the same time, they also differed from one another in many other ways: in their religious denominations, social ranks, historical generations, and also in the British regions from whence they came. They carried across the Atlantic four different sets of British folkways which became the basis of regional cultures in the New World.

By the year 1775 these four cultures were fully established in British America. They spoke distinctive dialects of English, built their houses in diverse ways, and had different methods of doing much of the ordinary business of life. Most important for the political history of the United States, they also had four different conceptions of order, power and freedom which became the cornerstones of a voluntary society in British America.

Today less than 20 percent of the American population have any British ancestors at all. But in a cultural sense most Americans are Albion's seed, no matter who their own forebears may have been. Strong echoes of . . . British folkways may still be heard in the major dialects of American speech, in the regional patterns of American life, in the complex dynamics of American politics, and in the continuing conflict between four different ideas of freedom in the United States. The interplay of four "freedom ways" has created an expansive pluralism which is more libertarian than any unitary culture alone could be. . . . The legacy of four British folkways in early America remains the most powerful determinant of a voluntary society in the United States today.

Reprinted from David Hackett Fischer, *Albion's Seed: Four British Folkways in America* (New York: Oxford University Press, 1989). Reprinted with permission.

"God is English." Thus John Aylmer, a pious English clergyman, exhorted his parishioners in 1558, attempting to fill them with piety and patriotism. That thought, though never stated so directly, has echoed ever since through our history books. As schoolchildren, as college students, and as presumably informed citizens, most of us have been brought up on what has passed for the greatest success story of human history, the epic tale of how a proud, brave offshoot of the English-speaking people tried to reverse the laws of history by demonstrating what the human spirit, liberated from the shackles of tradition, myth, and oppressive authority, could do in a newly discovered corner of the earth. . . .

This is ethnocentric history, as has been charged frequently and vociferously in the last few decades, both by revisionist white historians and by those whose citizenship is American but whose ancestral roots are in Africa, Asia, Mexico, or the native cultures of North America. Just as Eurocentrism made it difficult for the early colonizers and explorers to believe that a continental land mass as large as North America could exist in the oceans between Europe and Asia, historians in this country have found it difficult to understand that the colonial period of our history is the story of a minority of English colonizers interacting with a majority of Iroquois, Delawares, Narragansetts, Pequots, Mahicans, Catawbas, Tuscaroras, Creeks, Cherokees, Choctaws, Ibos, Mandigos, Fulas, Yorubas, Ashantis, Germans, French, Spaniards, Swedes, Welsh, and Scots-Irish, to mention only some of the cultural strains present on the continent. . . .

[A] fuller and deeper understanding of the colonial underpinnings of American history must examine the interaction of many peoples, at all levels of society, from a wide range of cultural backgrounds over a period of several centuries. For the "colonial period" this means exploring not only how the English and other Europeans "discovered" North America and transplanted their cultures there, but also how societies that had been in North America and Africa for thousands of years were actively and intimately involved in the process of forging a new, multistranded culture in what would become the United States. Africans were not merely enslaved. Native Americans were not merely driven from the land. As Ralph Ellison, the African American writer, has reasoned: "Can a people . . . live and develop for over three hundred years by simply *reacting*? Are American Negroes simply the creation of white men, or have they at least helped to create themselves out of what they found around them?" To include Africans and Indians in our history in this way, simply as victims of the more powerful Europeans, is hardly better than excluding them altogether. It is to render voiceless, nameless, and faceless people who powerfully affected the course of our historical development as a society and as a nation.

To break through the notion of Indians and Africans being kneaded like dough according to the whims of the invading European societies, we must abandon the notion of "primitive" and "civilized" people. There is still some utility in pointing out differences in technological achievement—the Europeans' ability to navigate across the Atlantic and their ability to process iron and thereby to manufacture guns, for example. But if we take these achievements as constituting the marks of a "superior" culture coming into contact with an "inferior" one, we unconsciously step in a mental trap in which Europeans are the active agents of history and the African and Indian people are the passive victims.

. . . "Savages we call them," wrote Benjamin Franklin more than two centuries ago, "because their Manners differ from ours, which we think the Perfection of Civility; they think the same of theirs." To think of Indians simply as victims of European aggression is to bury from sight the rich and instructive story of how Narragansetts, Iroquois, Delawares, Pamunkeys, Cherokees, Creeks, and many other nations, which had been changing for centuries before Europeans touched foot on the continent, responded creatively and powerfully to the newcomers from across the ocean and in this way reshaped themselves while reshaping the course of European settlement.

Gary B. Nash, *Red, White, and Black: The People of Early North America*, 3rd ed. (Englewood Cliffs, N.J.: Prentice Hall, 1992). Reprinted with permission.

Gallows Hill, Salem, Massachusetts, where the "witches" were hanged.

70

The Developing Colonies

THE SALEM WITCHES

In 1692 the Devil assaulted the seaport town of Salem, Massachusetts, north of Boston. This village of a few hundred people was invaded by scores of warlocks and witches, men and women who had covenanted with the Devil to make mischief, to drive little children mad, to sicken and kill livestock and people. One witch, it seemed, had caused the deaths of fourteen members of a single family. The jails bulged with over a hundred prisoners awaiting trial, including a four-year-old child bound for nine months in heavy iron chains. Twenty-seven people eventually came to trial; the court hanged nineteen—fourteen women and five men—as witches. One man refused to enter a plea, and suffered *peine forte et dure:* heavy weights were laid on Giles Cory's body until, still refusing the plea, he was pressed to death.

The trouble had begun innocently enough: "Conjuration with sieves and keys, and peas, and nails, and horseshoes" at first seemed harmless activities with which to pass the New England winter. But these games turned serious when grim-visaged parents tried to discover what was causing their children's "fits" and "distempers."

Everyone knew about witchcraft. Witches and their male counterparts the warlocks had made a pact with the Devil. They "wrote in his book," joining his legions for the thrill of conjurations, midnight frolics, obscure or perhaps obscene rituals, and the power to harm their neighbors. Do not "suffer a witch to live," the Bible commanded, and in Europe, tens of thousands, most of them women but many men as well, had been executed as the Evil One's followers.

HISTORICAL EVENTS

1636
America's first college founded (Harvard)

1692
Salem witch hunts

1699
Wool Act

1704
America's first newspaper published (*Boston News-Letter*)

1712
Slave uprising in New York City

1715
Yamasees of South Carolina rebel

1718
Spanish founded San Antonio • French founded New Orleans

1732
Hat Act

1733
Sugar Act • last British colony in America founded (Georgia)

1734
The Great Awakening begins in Massachusetts

1735
The Zenger Case

continued

Before 1692, the Devil had paid small attention to New England. Forty-four cases, three hangings—such was the entire history of New England witchcraft before the malady spread to nine adolescent girls in Salem. Under intense questioning, and responding to this attention with yet further manifestations of demoniac possession, the girls named three women as the source of their sufferings. These were likely candidates.

Sarah Good, daughter of a well-to-do innkeeper, had steadily tumbled down the social ladder; she was in 1692 a surly, pipe-smoking beggar whose "muttering and scolding" seemed to cause cows to die. Sarah Osborne's name swirled in contention and scandal: her battle with her own sons for control of her first husband's estate, her liaison with the Irish indentured servant who became her second husband.

And there was Tituba, the Indian slave woman, who represented a culture both fascinating and frightening to the Puritans. She had been brought to Massachusetts from Barbados in 1680 by the Reverend Samuel Parris, and when the girls accused her of witchcraft, her testimony sent waves of fear throughout Salem. For five days, she regaled her questioners with stories of comportings with the Devil, with witches Sarah Good, Sarah Osborne, and with two Boston women she did not name. Tituba told of nightly spectral meetings and rides through the air. In vivid, fearsome detail, Tituba described one of Satan's minions as "a thing all over hairy, all the face hairy and a long nose," a creature "about two or three foot high." She had seen the Devil's "book," she said, and although she could not read, she had counted nine names in it. Drawing on the Indian and African lore she had learned in the West Indies, Tituba told her fearful, fascinated audiences what she thought they wanted to hear.

Tituba's dark complexion and dark hair reminded her Puritan hearers that she was an Indian—one of a people they associated with Satanic practices. They were more than willing to accept her imaginative fantasies as truth. As Tituba tried to protect herself, she unfolded a tale of Satanic conspiracy that confirmed the deepest suspicions of the anxious Puritan community. A recent biography of Tituba points out that it was this Indian slave woman's confession, not her alleged teaching of witchcraft practices to the young girls, that so inflamed the Puritan community.

Soon the girls, shrieking, contorting, sobbing hysterically, dredged up still more names. Not all were outcasts like Sarah Good, Sarah Osborne, and Tituba; not all were from Salem. The jails groaned; the gallows rope snapped. The madness, for the better part of a year, infected a whole society. When the accusers began to name prominent citizens—some Boston clergymen, for instance, and the governor's wife—the Reverend Cotton Mather, his father, the Reverend Increase Mather, and some other ministers recommended the cessation of the trials. (Cotton Mather, as was common in the seventeenth century, believed in witches, but he also believed in science. He would have his day in 1721, when to combat popular fears of the new medical practice of inoculation for smallpox, he allowed his son to be inoculated.) Reason returned to Salem; probing questions were asked; the jailed were sent home and pardoned.

The girls' part in it is easiest to explain. The life of young girls in Massachusetts Bay was dull in the best of times. "I am not fond," wrote Cotton Mather, "of proposing *Play* to children, as a Reward of any diligent Application to learn what is good; lest they should think *Diversion* to be a better and nobler Thing than *Diligence*." While young men, sent to school and taught to pray and work, could at least look forward to the adventure of choosing careers, girls could do little more than wonder "what trade their sweethearts should be of." It is understandable that when the little girls dabbled in magic with Tituba, their slightly older friends and relatives joined the only excitement midwinter had to offer. (Many teen-aged girls—including most of the "afflicted" ones— did not live at home where parents might spoil them, but were sent to relatives' or neighbors' houses to learn their adult roles and to be evenly disciplined.) Once the adults began to fuss over their fits, how could the young resist pursuing their adventure and showing their power over the adult community, particularly over the married women who laid on endless chores and discipline? Even these antics would have been relatively harmless had not the adults panicked.

One explanation that has been offered of the witchcraft turmoil in Salem is that it fed upon local conflicts. People from differing political and clerical factions hurled accusations back and forth. For Salem was an angry place. Town and countryside were sharply diverging. Conservative backcountry farmers smarted under the growth of commercial capitalism and its accompanying secular style. Sons coming of age found difficulty establishing themselves as land became increasingly scarce. The values of Puritanism itself seemed more and more in question as ministers bemoaned the "declension" from the piety of the colony's founders three generations before. And from 1684 to 1691 the colony of Massachusetts had been without a charter. Would the old land claims be valid under a new one? Would voting still be restricted to church members? Nearly every adult must have been startled at a changing world crowding in on what had been for two generations a largely fixed culture. Men and women who were supposed to practice Christian unity engaged year after year in lawsuits over boundaries and legacies. Like the witches, they were at war with their neighbors, disrupting the church and government, bursting the old molds. Were they too possessed? How much easier it must have been to blame everything on the literal bewitchment of enemies rather than on their own bewitchment with the new and perhaps dubious values and goals that were transforming John Winthrop's "citty upon a Hille" into a secular society.

One recent writer correlates the witchcraft scare with an Indian war that began in 1689. Here was a main cause of dislocation. People who survived the frontier massacres abandoned their exposed positions and retreated to older settlements. Fear of Indian attack spurred by French Catholics to the north was quite thoroughly mixed up with fear of the Devil in the minds of seventeenth-century Protestants.

Massachusetts a few years after the Salem trials passed an act reversing the convictions of those executed. Though this did not help the victims, it lifted a stigma from the townspeople. No community before had ever issued a repentance for destroying witches.

New England Colonies

Everyday Life The early New England settlers gathered into communities that duplicated something of the physical arrangement of the English villages they had known. An English family did not live in isolation on the land it worked. Homes were close together in the village, and each family worked plots of the surrounding lands. The system was well suited to the needs of the first generation in New England. On a stubborn soil in a harsh winter climate and under threat of Indian attack, that generation sought to establish a stable and comfortable life. For several decades in Massachusetts, attendance at church was required of everyone, including nonmembers; and the centrality of the churches in the life of the colony was further reason for the colonists to cluster into villages. By the eighteenth century, however, young men seeking farm land had to go farther afield, or be content with smaller plots as fathers parceled out family holdings to sons. Neighbors sometimes coveted one another's land, and social tensions rose. But the village pattern that had developed in the early years left its permanent stamp on New England. The system of town meetings, in which local citizens directly make decisions that elsewhere in the country are left to elected or appointed officials, persists to this day.

Even in the seventeenth century New England, at least in its most settled portions, contained one of the most remarkably well-educated populaces in the English world. Harvard College, America's first institution of higher learning, was founded in 1636, primarily to educate young men for the clergy. The government of Massachusetts Bay had the towns provide free elementary schools—although girls were not expected to benefit from them and women's literacy lagged far behind that of men. Sermons could employ an imagery beautiful in its home-

Boys and girls alike read the New England Primer, published in 1691:

In *Adam's* fall
We sinned all.

Thy life to mend
This *Book* attend.

The *Cat* doth play
And after slay.

A *Dog* will bite
The thief at night.

An *Eagle's* flight
Is out of sight.

The idle *Fool*
Is whipped at school.

As runs the *Glass*,
Man's life doth pass.

spun plain style, and educated New Englanders read not only religious but secular literature written in the language of everyday life. Sermons and history dominated colonial reading, but there was also an audience for poetry that ran from the religious doggerel of Reverend Michael Wigglesworth's "Day of Doom" to the delicate lyrics of Anne Bradstreet's "To My Dear and Loving Husband." Colonists also read newspapers, beginning in 1704 with the *Boston News-Letter* and the *New England Courant* (run by Benjamin Franklin's brother) in 1721.

Scholars have rejected the notion that New Englanders were black-clad haters of life, the world, and pleasure. The diarist Samuel Sewall might grumble at Edmund Andros for celebrating Christmas, but Sewall and other Puritans enjoyed good food and drink. In 1725 the *Boston News-Letter* complained that people "could hardly hear the minister's first prayer for the rustling of silk gowns and petticoats." That same year a horse race on Boston Common offered a prize of "a velvet Saddle with Silver Lace." Most New Englanders did not even wear black, although they would have been happy to do it. Black was the color not of grimness but of wealth and prominence. As New England's economy matured, colonial merchants found it necessary to buy large quantities of manufactured goods from England. The region was almost entirely dependent upon the mother country for clothing, for almost all tools beyond the most primitive, for muskets and other firearms, and for clocks, compasses, and a host of other instruments. The New Englanders drank oceans of tea and used considerable quantities of spices, which could be legally obtained only through the East India Company in London; and despite recurring waves of puritanical hostility toward the consumption of luxuries, they sought and bought the finer things of life when they were able.

New England settlers imported English class distinctions, yet here as in other matters the land and conditions of the New World modified the institutions of the old. Class distinction in New England meant not the presence of a powerful aristocracy but a somewhat milder component of the English system of class, a deference on the part of the majority toward people of greater wealth, schooling, and political position. But class distinctions were difficult to maintain. As one New England minister observed, "The Misery and Iniquity of it is, the inferior sort of People will be clad in as Costly Attire as the Rich and Honourable."

Prosperity   The years from about 1715 to 1755 were a time of great prosperity. New England's commercial success was not based upon hauling freight or directly upon the slave trade. The colonial merchants were never more than marginally engaged in either of these maritime activities. The key to the New Englanders' system was the great sugar plantations of the West Indies. These were not self-sufficient, for it was uneconomical to waste the labor of slaves on growing staple food when it could be bought so cheaply and land was so valuable. The sugar islands were also deficient in timber suitable for providing the bare necessity of wood products, even including staves for making containers in which to ship their sugar. By supplying the West

If ever two were one, then surely we,
If ever man were lov'd by wife, then thee;
If ever wife was happy in a man,
Compare with me ye women if you can.
—Anne Bradstreet
d. 1672

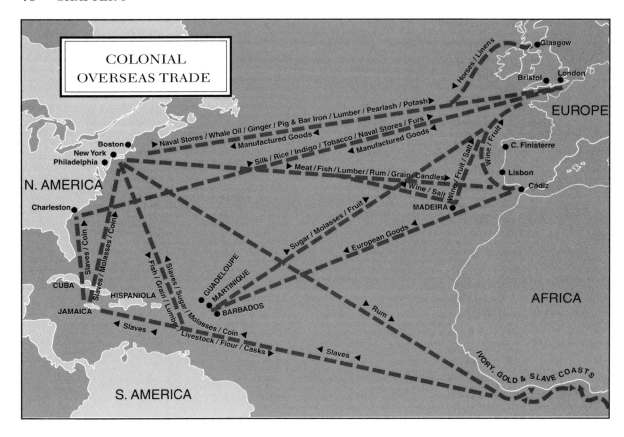

COLONIAL
OVERSEAS TRADE

Indies, New England's entrepreneurs made enough profit not only to pay what they owed for imports, but to provide employment for their whole population.

New England farmers produced fruit, beef, pork, butter, and cheese for the West Indian market, and many also raised cattle, horses, and chickens for live export. Fishing expanded enormously and became highly commercialized after 1715. By the 1730s as many as 150 new fishing vessels were being built annually, and the number of people employed in the fisheries was more than 5,000. Whaling developed as an additional specialty in some places, notably Nantucket, where it was even more valuable than fishing.

In the early days, when settlements were concentrated along the seacoast and immediately to the interior from Boston and the other ports, farmers produced marketable timber from the trees they felled to clear their lands for the plow. But timber is a bulky commodity and the only practical way to transport it is by river; and south of Salem the Massachusetts coast was almost entirely devoid of streams that extended as much as five miles into the interior. New settlers in towns beyond that distance developed the practice of burning the trees they felled and making the ashes into potash; this could easily be carried to port towns for merchants who found a ready market for it in England. But the change also meant that the supply of lumber from Massachusetts and Connecticut dwindled just at the time the demand for lumber products in the West Indies was expanding rapidly. For this growing market, a commercial lumber industry was developed after about 1720 in New Hampshire and the province of Maine, where there were magnificent stands of white pine and the river systems afforded convenient transportation.

The merchants of New England secured their provisions for the West Indies from the local farmers by selling them goods imported from England, but the owners of fishing fleets and lumber camps and their employees consumed little of such commodities. The fishermen and lumber workers did, however, consume one thing abundantly, and that was rum. Accordingly, New England merchants made a practice of importing West Indian molasses for part of the goods they sold in the islands; the molasses was then manufactured into rum to trade for more lumber or fish.

Payment of the duty on molasses that the British government imposed under the Sugar Act of 1733 would have been detrimental to New York and Pennsylvania and ruinous to New England. So merchants did what American businessmen would do ever after when British law ran counter to their interests: they simply ignored the law. It was easy enough to do, for Britain's machinery for collecting customs and preventing smuggling in America was as yet primitive, and many customs officials were amenable to bribery. The passage of the Sugar Act of 1733, therefore, in no way altered the course of New England's economic growth, except to place the entire economy upon illegal foundations.

Middle Colonies

New York, Pennsylvania, New Jersey, and Delaware contained by the mid-eighteenth century a varying mix of population. People of Dutch ancestry in New York were retaining their ethnic identity, Scotch-Irish and Germans had settled in Pennsylvania west of the Quakers, and there were Swedes to their south. Philadelphia was a principal landing place for immigrants who in the eighteenth century moved to British America by the hundreds of thousands. Each successive wave of immigrants sought land for settlement in the immediate vicinity, until all the cheaply available land in the middle colonies was taken up and it became necessary to push toward the interior and toward the backcountry of the South.

German Immigrants   Many if not most German immigrants came as indentured servants—also called redemptioners— paying for their passage by binding themselves to serve as laborers for a number of years before becoming freemen and ordinary settlers. Then, migrating to the backcountry, former German redemptioners settled in a broad area extending twenty to a hundred miles west of the Delaware River. They picked the choicest lands, especially those in the limestone valleys, cleared their farms slowly but thoroughly, and built solid buildings upon them. Because of the care with which they proceeded, by the time they were able to produce for market they could bring in regular and bountiful harvests. Their princi-

Gottlieb Mittelberger, a German immigrant, described the arrival of indentured servants in Philadelphia around 1750:

"When the ships finally arrive in Philadelphia after the long voyage only those are let off who can pay their sea freight or can give good security. The others, who lack the money to pay, have to remain on board until they are purchased and until their purchasers can thus pry them loose from the ship. In this whole process the sick are the worst off, for the healthy are preferred and are more readily paid for. The miserable people who are ill must often still remain at sea and in sight of the city for another two or three weeks."

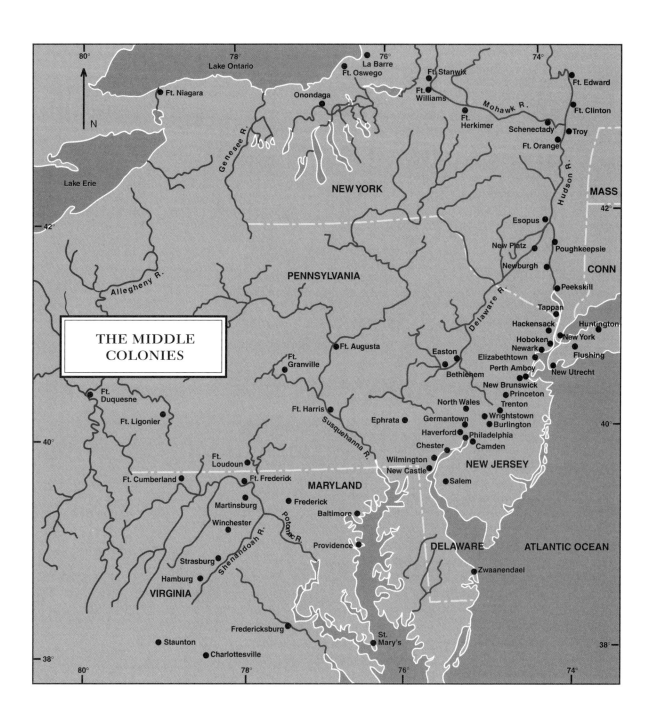

THE MIDDLE
COLONIES

pal crop was wheat, which became the second great staple (or third, if New England fish is counted) to be produced in British North America. Virginia tobacco of course was the first.

The Germans continued to arrive at a steady rate, around 2,000 a year, from 1717 until about 1750. By the 1730s they were beginning to overflow the middle colonies. Thenceforth, they proceeded to the Pennsylvania backcountry and headed south, settling the Cumberland Valley in Pennsylvania and Maryland and much of the Shenandoah Valley of Virginia.

By and large, wherever they went the Germans kept to themselves, retaining their own ways and making no effort to become involved in the political or social life of the colonies they inhabited. They tended to cluster in groups that had little to do even with one another. They represented a wide variety of religious sects, Reformed, Mennonite, Dunker, Moravian Brethren, and even Roman Catholic.

The Scotch-Irish   Considerably more numerous and far more disruptive were the descendants of the Scottish Protestants from Ulster in the North of Ireland. The total number of Scotch-Irish immigrants was around 250,000.

The first wave headed for New England. The Ulstermen, like the Puritans, were Calvinist, though the congregation-based church polity of New England was incompatible with the Scotch-Irish polity, with its more centralized Presbyterian church structure. Boston and its vicinity, at any rate, had no excess land and no shortage of labor; the inhabitants feared that immigrants would become just so many paupers to feed from the resources of their meager land; and New Englanders generally regarded the Ulstermen as less civilized. A few thousand immigrants of the first wave landed in Boston and, with difficulty, founded settlements around Worcester and along the Merrimac Valley of New Hampshire, but irate mobs greeted at the docks subsequent Scotch-Irish intended settlers and refused to let them land. Here was an early instance of a phenomenon that continues to this day: hostility on the part of an established American ethnic group to the immigration of another.

The remainder of the first wave of Ulstermen and the overwhelming majority of future shiploads headed for Philadelphia, along with the Germans. The Scotch-Irish also followed the same routes to the interior, but there the resemblance between them and the Germans ends. For reasons of preference as well as circumstance, the two groups of immigrants did not mix. The pattern of settlement, all the way down through the Virginia valley, was that the German firstcomers farmed staples on the rich bottom lands and the Ulstermen who came later raised cattle and corn on the hillsides and poorer lands.

By the late 1730s Ulstermen were filling the Shenandoah Valley of Virginia. Late in the next decade they were spilling out over the Piedmont Plateau of southern Virginia and central North Carolina. A decade later they were invading the uplands of South Carolina.

In constant friction with the Indians, Scotch-Irish often did not hesitate to slaughter them or involve colonial authorities in wars with them. They became avid politicians, skillful and disputatious, and regu-

As late as the mid-eighteenth century the practice of indentured servitude was still common as this newspaper account indicates:

Philadelphia, April 14, 1748.

Run away from Samuel Lippincott of Northampton in the county of Burlington, an Irish servant Maid, named Mary Muckleroy, of a middle Stature: Had on when she went away, a blue and white striped gown, of large and small stripes, cuffed with blue, a white muslin handkerchief, an old blue quilt, a new Persian black bonnet, a new pair of calf-skin shoes, a fine Holland cap, with a cambrick border, an old black short cloak lined with Bengal, blue worsted stockings, with white clocks, a very good fine shirt, and a very good white apron. She took with her a sorrel horse, about 14 hands high, shod before, and paces very well. It is supposed there is an Irishman gone with her. Whoever takes up and secures the said woman and horse, so that they may be had again, shall have Three Pounds reward, and reasonable charges paid by

Samuel Lippincott
—The Pennsylvania Gazette

larly demanded a voice in the lawmaking process when the law affected their way of life, but they disregarded the law when it did not suit them. While many Scotch-Irish showed what frontiersmen could be at their worst, others had a zeal for education deriving from their Presbyterianism, and founded schools and colleges on a scale that no other group of Americans ever approached.

Economic Life in the Middle Colonies   Amidst enormous growth in population—from more than 75,000 in 1715 to 400,000 by the 1750s—the economic and political life of the middle colonies developed rapidly. The economy grew even faster than the population and, as had been the way in New England and the tobacco colonies, proceeded along two lines: development of small-scale production of tools and other equipment for the expanding population, and development of production for trade in international markets.

In the colonies to the north and the south, by far the biggest portion of the business was selling land, but in the middle colonies the population at large could not participate in this lucrative enterprise. In New York the governors and assemblies continued the policy, originated by the Dutch, of granting land only in huge tracts—and only to themselves and their friends and relations. The great patroons, as the Dutch called them, who received the grants were interested more often in leasing the lands than in selling them. In Pennsylvania and Delaware the land belonged originally to the Penn family as proprietors, and all proceeds from sales and rentals went to them. In New Jersey, too, the land belonged to small groups of proprietors, and though the system of land disposition was always complex the profits from land sales went to these small groups.

Indians in the Middle Colonies   King Philip's War in 1675–76 had all but destroyed the Indian communities in New England, but in the middle colonies relations between Indians and whites evolved differently, for a while at least. By the time the English took over in 1664, the Dutch in southern New York and the Swedes in New Jersey had nearly eliminated the Indians as a force. In Pennsylvania the situation was different. A persecuted people dedicated to nonviolence and the belief that all men and women were children of God, the Quakers along with their leader William Penn wanted a colony in which everyone could live in harmony. They respected the right of the Delaware Indians to the land and purchased it from them only after careful negotiations. Word spread, and in the 1690s and early 1700s the Tuscaroras, Shawnees, and Miamis all migrated to Pennsylvania. Eventually, as Scotch-Irish Presbyterians, German Lutherans, and more English Protestants pushed west in Pennsylvania and squatted on tribal land, tensions increased. And when the colonial rivalry for control of the Ohio Valley erupted during the 1750s between the English and the French, open warfare commenced between the Indians and the European settlers, who were far distant in space and mind from the Quaker establishment of eastern Pennsylvania. Eventually, the Indians of Pennsylvania, like those of New England, New York, and New

ESTIMATED POPULATION OF AMERICAN COLONIES:
1630 TO 1750

	1630	1650	1670	1690	1730	1750
White						
New England	1,796	22,452	51,521	86,011	211,233	349,029
Middle Colonies	340	3,786	6,664	32,369	135,298	275,723
Southern Colonies	2,450	22,530	49,215	75,263	191,893	309,588
Black						
New England	0	380	375	950	6,118	10,982
Middle Colonies	10	515	790	2,472	11,683	20,736
Southern Colonies	50	705	3,370	13,307	73,220	204,702
Total White	4,586	48,768	107,400	193,643	538,424	934,340
Total Black	60	1,600	4,535	16,729	91,021	236,420

Jersey, were either killed or driven to points west, where their children awaited the arrival of the next generation of white settlers.

Philadelphia   The supply of craftsmen, the abundance of raw materials, and the insatiable market combined in the middle colonies to breed a thriving industry in farm implements, locks, guns, nails, and other hardware, as well as clocks, flints, glass, stoneware, paper, and woodwork. The port of Philadelphia burgeoned: by the mid-1730s several hundred vessels were entering and clearing the port every year. At first most of these vessels belonged to others, but then Philadelphians began to acquire their own ships. With this development came another, the establishment of a shipbuilding industry and such linked activities as importing and processing naval stores and manufacturing ropes, anchors, and sails.

By the 1730s, Philadelphia, like New York City to a lesser extent, had begun to emerge as a major export and import center. Among the exports were beef and pork, which, along with the livestock, were produced mainly by the Scotch-Irish. These products found ready markets on the sugar plantations of the West Indies. More important were wheat and flour, produced by the industrious Germans and the scores of mills that sprang up along the Delaware and Schuylkill rivers. The Navigation Acts did not confine colonial wheat and flour to the English market. Some went to the West Indies and much to the European continent, where Philadelphia merchants could acquire bills of exchange and goods for trade in England. This made Philadelphia a principal importing center for English manufactures in North America.

Quaker   William Penn's plans late in the seventeenth century
Influences for Pennsylvania had been ambitious. The colony
                would be a place of love and harmony. Penn had
established friendly relations with the Indians. The very act of establishing a government that could back up its laws with force meant, of

course, that whether or not Penn, like other Quakers, would oppose all wars among nations, he was not prepared to practice a Quakerism of total nonresistance at home. Yet one of his schemes provided that imprisonment would be humane and seek the reformation of criminals. For a short period Pennsylvania actually attempted a system of imprisonment for reform of criminals—an experiment that prefigured the modern penitentiary. The earliest Quakers had been given to fits of emotionalism accompanied by disruptive behavior, but Penn prized more sober virtues and conduct. An account that he wrote of Pennsylvania, translated into German, Dutch, and French and published on the European continent as well as in Britain, invited solid, industrious farmers and craftsmen to settle in the colony. His Quakerism, then, cherished the compound of spirituality and virtuous worldliness that has been characteristic of the Society of Friends ever since.

After Penn's death the colony became quite different from the harmonious commonwealth he had envisioned. The presence of the Scotch-Irish on the frontier guaranteed that the Indians would receive something other than the treatment Penn would have wanted for them. The tide of immigration made the Quakers a minority in the colony, though a wealthy and powerful one, and Quakers lost favor with the proprietors when the sons of William Penn left the Society of Friends for the Church of England. To promote and protect their interests in the face of these reversals, the Quakers gathered allies and formed a political faction called variously the Quaker party and the Anti-Proprietary party. Their wealth and influence normally gave them control of the legislature. Arrayed against them in the Proprietary party were the Scotch-Irish, many frontiersmen, and a considerable number of non-pacifist Germans.

New York   By the late eighteenth century Philadelphia would be the second largest city and second busiest port in the entire English-speaking world. New York's port also thrived, though it developed much more slowly. The colony's restrictive immigration and land policies kept New York City from developing anything like Philadelphia's business of transporting and supplying newcomers, and it also had a smaller productive base for its international trade. But the Iroquois Indians in New York's interior did trap some furs themselves and also served as middlemen between the Albany traders and many of the western Indians, who trapped in enormous quantities and were eager to sell.

In contrast to the popularly based politics of Pennsylvania, politics in New York was aristocratic. The colony did have numerous and vociferous lower elements, fighting one another as well as the upper classes and clamoring for a voice in government. But the lower classes largely canceled one another out in antipathies among Scotch-Irish and New Englanders and New Yorkers, among Presbyterians and Congregationalists and Dutch Calvinists, among tenant farmers and squatters and the plain folk of the city. Such of these inhabitants as could vote were normally easy for the landed aristocrats to manage, for they voted orally, in public, and were therefore amenable to bribery and pressure when mere deference failed to secure their vote.

Southern Colonies

The upper South, unlike New England, had land suitable for the growth of a great commercial staple crop. And since Virginia planters had never been interested in setting up villages with churches as the focus of their life, society in Virginia spread out into tobacco plantations of various sizes—the average was about 200 acres. The majority of Virginia's colonists were small farmers, the independent yeomen whom Thomas Jefferson, years later, would call "the chosen people of God."

Economic Boom in Virginia   In the early 1730s there began a remarkable economic boom in Virginia. Before it had ended the entire area from Pennsylvania to Georgia had been transformed.

Part of the boom was in tobacco prices. The plantation system spread rapidly, and slavery spread with it. An enormous volume of importations as well as natural increase doubled the number of slaves in Virginia to 60,000 in 1740, pushed it substantially past 100,000 in 1750, and took it to 140,000 in 1760.

Meanwhile, land sales surged in Virginia. When the Penn family in the 1730s raised the prices and rents on Pennsylvania lands, Scotch-Irish and German immigrants flooded to the west and south. As they poured southward down the great valley of Virginia, North Carolina and Virginia both promised freedom of worship for Presbyterians, and Virginia and Maryland liberalized their land policies. These measures stimulated a thriving sale of land, and Virginia in particular moved to capitalize on it. Planters and other influential inhabitants of the old tidewater settlements began to realize that there was as much money to be made from selling land as from selling tobacco, and perhaps a great deal more. The members of the House of Burgesses, in collaboration with the governor and his council, began to grant large blocks of interior lands to themselves: sometimes for nominal sums, sometimes for nothing, sometimes in exchange for their services in attracting new settlers to the colony.

The social system that evolved in Virginia was designed to ensure the primacy of a class that can best be termed gentry. The gentry were not of the same class as the royal officials, and did not possess the wealth of the largest planters and land speculators. But by education and the size of their lands they stood apart from their neighbors and from the Scotch-Irish and Germans of the backwoods. Their position of leadership came in large part from the willingness of their humbler neighbors to grant it to them, a habit of deference on the part of the lowly toward people of education and political training. That deference was easily given, for the gentry were generous to those below them. A Fairfax County candidate for the House of Burgesses named George Washington once provided 160 gallons of liquor for the county's 400 voters and, after an election, invited his supporters to a victory ball and supper.

The Carolinas and Georgia   Early in the eighteenth century the institution of slavery was rapidly spreading in another quarter, on the rice plantations of South Carolina (and, a little later, of Georgia). Slavery was a part of life in South Carolina almost as

In 1716 Virginia's Governor Spotswood and a party of Virginians explored the Blue Ridge Mountains. One of them, John Fontaine, noted in his journal:

"We had a good dinner, and after it we got the men together, and loaded all their arms, and we drank the King's health in champagne, and fired a volley; the Princess's health in burgundy, and fired a volley; and all the rest of the Royal Family in claret, and a volley. We had several sorts of liquors, viz., Virginia red wine and white wine, Irish whiskey, brandy, shrub, two sorts of rum, champagne, canary, cherry, punch, water, cider, etc. I sent two of the rangers to look for my gun, which I dropped in the mountains. . . ."

A visitor to Virginia in the 1680s described life there:

"They usually plant tobacco, Indian corn, wheat, peas or beans, barley, sweet potatoes, turnips, which grow to a monstrous size and are very good to eat. They make gardens as we do in Europe. . . . So much timber have they that they build fences all around the land they cultivate. A man with fifty acres of ground, and others in proportion, will leave at least twenty-five wooded, and of the remaining twenty-five will cultivate half and keep the other as a pasture and paddock for his cattle. . . . Some people in this country are comfortably housed; the farmers' houses are built entirely of wood."

Of the houses of the wealthier planters, this observer commented:

"Those who have some means, cover them inside with a coating of mortar in which they use oyster shells for lime; it is as white as snow, so that although they look ugly from the outside, where only the wood can be seen, they are very pleasant inside, with convenient windows and openings. They have started making bricks in quantities, and I have seen several houses where the walls were entirely made of them. . . . They build also a separate kitchen, a separate house for the Christian slaves, one for the Negro slaves, and several to dry the tobacco. . . ."

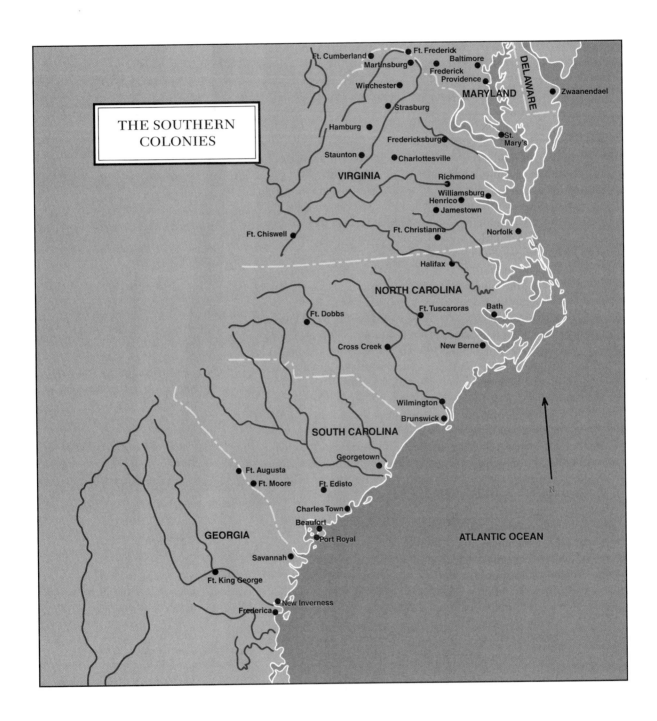

THE SOUTHERN
COLONIES

soon as the colony passed beyond its primitive frontier stage. Many of the early settlers were immigrants from Barbados, where slavery had long been firmly established, and they brought their slaves with them. Of the roughly 3,900 inhabitants of the colony in 1690, about 1,500 were slaves. Then, in the early decades of the eighteenth century the South Carolinians began large-scale rice cultivation in the coastal swamps, and with a phenomenal increase in rice production, slavery increased apace. South Carolina exported 394,000 pounds of rice in 1700 and 43,000,000 in 1740; in the same years the number of slaves in the colony increased from 2,400 to 30,000. From 1720 until the Civil War, slaves outnumbered whites about two to one in South Carolina.

Rice was grown in the coastal swamps, where the climate was hot and humid and malaria and other diseases were common. The work was possible only for strong young adult males, and even many of these died from overwork and disease. For the few slaves, most of them women and children, who lived in or near the master's house and worked as menial servants, life was tolerable, but for the field hands it was monstrous. Despite a law permitting any white to shoot on sight a slave who left his plantation without a written pass from his owner, many a Carolina slave escaped from his master and found refuge among the Creek and Seminole Indians to the south. There were isolated uprisings, and in 1739 slaves on several plantations rose in a rebellion that was not put down until twenty-one whites and forty-four blacks had been killed and scores more of both races had been wounded. Thirty more slaves were killed in the Stono Rebellion that same year.

In the early 1700s North Carolina rapidly became even more separate socially and economically from its sister colony. Plantation slavery was slow to take root, for the colony was covered with thick pine forests, was too dry to permit rice cultivation, and lacked the access to the sea that was then necessary to the growth of tobacco plantations. Until well into the eighteenth century North Carolina's principal products were the naval stores that could be extracted from the pines: tar, pitch, rosin, turpentine, and masts and spars. After 1705, the British government subsidized the production of all these commodities.

Georgia, founded in 1733, the last British colony to be established in America, developed slowly until the 1760s. In 1732 James Oglethorpe, a Tory member of Parliament, had received a charter to plant the colony. He conceived of it as a refuge for paupers and debtors, and as a laboratory for experiments in social and religious reform. But for the first twenty years of its existence the colony served mainly as a buffer between South Carolina and the hostile Indians to the immediate south along with the Spanish colony in Florida. Thereafter, Georgia began to develop on a more permanent basis, largely through the establishment of slavery and a rice plantation system much like that of South Carolina.

William Byrd. *(Courtesy, Library of Congress)*

The Virginia planter William Byrd looked down upon the backcountry denizens of North Carolina and Virginia, condemning them for their idleness:

"Indian corn is of so great increase, that a little pains will subsist a very large family with bread, and then they may have meat without any pains at all, by the help of the low grounds and the great variety of mast that grows upon the high-land. The men for their parts, just like the Indians, impose all the work upon the poor women. They make their wives rise out of their beds early in the morning, at the same time that they lie and snore, till the sun has run one third of his course, and dispersed all the unwholesome damps. Then, after stretching and yawning for half an hour, they light their pipes, and, under the protection of a cloud of smoke, venture out into the open air; though if it happens to be ever so little cold, they quickly return shivering into the chimney corner. When the weather is mild, they stand leaning with both their arms upon the cornfield fence, and gravely consider whether they had best go and take a small heat at the hoe: but generally find reasons to put it off till another time."

Indians in the Southern Colonies   In the southern colonies occurred tribal resentment at the proliferation of English settlements similar to the fury of the New England Indians. Bacon's Rebellion in Virginia in 1676 aimed at nothing less than the destruction or expulsion of the Virginia tribes. Although Governor

William Berkeley eventually crushed this rebellion, the assault on the Indians continued in the 1670s and 1680s. By 1690, only 1,000 of an original 30,000 Indians were still in Virginia. The others either were dead or had moved, voluntarily and involuntarily, into the western forests.

There were no powerful Indian confederacies in Maryland, and the tribes living along the southern seaboard had been defeated and driven away in the seventeenth century. But it was not that easy in the Carolinas. In 1711 the Tuscaroras in North Carolina finally rebelled after years of exploitation at the hands of fraudulent traders and slave-raiding parties, as well as the inexorable expansion of English settlement. After two years of hard fighting, a colonial militia finally crushed Tuscarora resistance, killing hundreds of Indians and enslaving hundreds more. The survivors moved north and eventually settled Pennsylvania or joined the tribes of the Iroquois Confederacy in New York.

The Yamasee of South Carolina rebelled in 1715. Once friendly allies with the English, the Yamasee were outraged when English traders cheated them and seized and sexually exploited their wives and daughters, while English settlers presumptuously took control of tribal land. In their uprising, the Yamasee gained the support of several other tribes, including the Creeks and Catawbas, and inflicted heavy casualties on the colonists, at one point threatening the very future of South Carolina. With the assistance of the Cherokees, the colonial militia finally ended the rebellion by a nearly genocidal assault on the Yamasee. Relations with the Creeks later improved after the founding of Georgia in 1733. The relationship of James Oglethorpe, the proprietor, with a mixed-blood woman named Mary, a close relative of a Creek chief, helped alleviate tensions between the Creeks and the English.

An Indian is taken into slavery by South Carolinians in the late seventeenth century. *(Courtesy, The Illustrated London News)*

Slavery

Through most of the seventeenth century slavery was not of major importance on the American mainland. There was a perpetual shortage of labor in most of the colonies, but as long as the farm unit remained small and was worked by the owner alongside his family and such indentured servants as he could afford, servants who spoke English were preferred to others. At first even large planters shunned slaves as expensive and subject to a high mortality in a new land.

For a time, then, the black population in the English colonies grew only slowly. The first blacks in the English colonies had arrived in Virginia in the early 1600s. But in that colony at midcentury, out of a population of 15,000 there were only about 300 blacks in Virginia and not all of these were slaves. In Virginia's early years some of them lived as free men and women, and some acquired land of their own. As late as 1671 there were still no more than 2,000 in Virginia within a population of 40,000 and fewer than 7,000 slaves in all the mainland colonies combined.

But then in the 1680s and the following decades a series of developments combined to establish slavery firmly, though still on a modest scale, in the tobacco-growing colonies of Virginia and Maryland, and at the same time to establish a prosperous gentry as the governing class. A change in the laws of both colonies finally made it legal and even easy to buy land in large tracts. Despite rapid increase in production, tobacco prices remained fairly high from 1684 to 1703. In these circumstances small farm units began to give way to sizable plantations, where workers could be employed efficiently in gangs. At just this time, the Royal Africa Company and other groups of English merchants were beginning to dominate the African slave trade and were looking for markets. Competition among slave traders of several nations, moreover, temporarily reduced the profits of supplying blacks for West Indian sugar plantations, so the English were willing to sell slaves in Virginia and Maryland at bargain prices. After moving up and down the coast of West Africa acquiring slaves, the English slave ships turned west and headed for America. The trip across the Atlantic was the dreaded "Middle Passage." Hundreds of slaves were crowded into the dark, damp holds of a slave ship for months at a time, with subsistence diets, little or no exercise, and no sanitary facilities. The mortality rate from flu, dysentery, pleurisy, pneumonia, and smallpox was devastating. Thousands of Africans died from what the shipowners called "fixed melancholy," a severe mental depression. As many as ten to fifteen million slaves were transported from Africa to all the colonies in the Western Hemisphere between 1600 and 1800, and another four to six million died on the way. The vast majority of the survivors ended up working the sugar plantations of Brazil, Cuba, Hispaniola, and Puerto Rico, but during the colonial period approximately 400,000 came to British North America.

The Character of Colonial Slavery

In the beginnings of colonial settlement, Africans and whites had needed to work closely together to survive. West Africa, the homeland of most of the slaves, was a settled area in which agriculture, mining, and handicrafts were well established, and slaves from there adapted reasonably well to work on American farms and plantations. Since West Africa resembled the South in climate and flora, Africans made conspicuous contributions to the economy. They helped introduce rice cultivation to South Carolina, and Guinea corn was mixed with native Indian varieties. Experienced in animal husbandry, Africans were put in charge of the livestock. The use of gourds for drinking, grass and reeds for baskets and mats, and palmetto leaves for fans, brooms, and chairs all came from Africa. Familiar with swamps and marshes, Africans dominated fishing and passed on to Europeans their knowledge

Percentage of African Americans in the Total Population of the British Colonies, 1660–1780

Year	New England	Middle Colonies	Upper South	Lower South	West Indies
1660	1.7	11.5	3.6	2.6	42.0
1700	1.8	6.8	13.1	17.6	77.7
1740	2.9	7.5	28.3	46.5	88.0
1780	2.0	5.9	38.6	41.2	91.1

LIST OF THE SLAVES who died on board the ship *St. John* from 30th June to 29th October in the year 1659.

1659	Men	Women	Children
June 30	3	2	
July 1	2	1	
3		1	
5		2	1
6		1	
7	1		
8	2	1	
9	2		
10		2	
12		1	
13	2		1
14	1		
16	3	2	
17	2		
18	3	1	
19	1	3	
20	1		
21	1	1	
23		2	
24	1	1	
25	2	1	
26	1		
28	3		
29		2	
Aug. 2	2		
3	1		
6	1		
8	2		1
9		1	
11		1	
16	1 man leaped overboard		
18	1		
20		1	
22		1	
23		1	
24	1		
29	1		
31	1	1	
Sept. 3		1	
6	2		
7	1		
8	1	1	
13	1	1	
14	2	2	1
16	1		
19	1		
23		2	
24	1	3	
26		1	
Oct. 1	2		
3	1	1	
4		1	
10	1	2	
12	1		
13		1	
19		1	
23	1		
29	1		
	59	47	4

As this eighteenth-century advertisement suggests, tobacco-smoking was popular in Europe. Tobacco profits, based on the labor of slaves, were popular in Virginia.

Among slaves, resistance mixed with acquiescence. An English visitor in 1746 observed that

"a *new Negro*, if he must be broke, either from obstinacy, or, which I am more apt to suppose, from greatness of soul, will require more hard discipline than a young spaniel. You would really be surprised at their perseverance; let an hundred men show him how to hoe, or drive a wheelbarrow; he'll still take the one by the bottom, and the other by the wheel, and they often die before they can be conquered."

of temporarily poisoning rivers and streams with quicklime to catch fish. Europeans feared alligators, but Africans knew that, like the crocodiles back home, they could be used to protect livestock. Africans also introduced to the colonies the use of certain herbs and natural medicines, dominated the fur trade as Indians disappeared, and served in the colonial militias well into the 1700s.

Slavery acquired in time a sharper legal definition. A Virginia law of 1662 declaring that "all children born in this country shall be held bond or free only according to the condition of the mother" ensured that children of slave women would be slaves as well. Other legislation restricted slaves from "walking abroad on nights meeting together" without their master's permission. By the early eighteenth century slavery was fully defined as a legal institution in the colonies. Virginia and Maryland were importing thousands of African slaves and laying the foundation for the plantation system of southern agriculture. In 1710 there were well over 30,000 slaves in Maryland and Virginia in a total population of about 120,000. By 1740 the numbers had grown to 84,000 blacks in a population of 296,000. New England, by contrast, had only 8,500 blacks in a population of nearly 290,000. Slavery spread throughout the colonies, but never in the concentration it achieved in the plantation economies of the South.

On a tobacco plantation the atmosphere was generally healthy and the labor to be done, though fussy and tedious, was not backbreaking. It became possible and profitable for a plantation owner to encourage both breeding and some semblance of family life among his slaves. Around the 1720s the slave population in the Chesapeake colonies began to reproduce itself, kinship networks formed, and a slave community developed. Slaves on small plantations might visit friends or relatives on larger ones; husbands and wives (slave marriages were not recognized by law) if owned by different masters might spend Sundays together.

Opinions of Slavery   The English who settled in North America did not go there with the intention of enslaving other human beings for life. After all, chattel slavery did not exist in England. But in English America by the end of the seventeenth century it was a well established institution. From Puritan clergymen in New England to rice planters in Georgia, slave holders could be found in every colony. New Englanders, who did not need a large labor force, nonetheless held slaves and perceived slavery as one of the conditions appropriate to the human race. South of New England, farmers and planters who desperately needed labor turned to slavery when supplies of white servants dwindled.

Few colonists protested the use of slaves. Quakers in Pennsylvania denounced slavery, but many Quakers themselves acquired slaves. A Puritan pamphlet attacking slavery, Samuel Sewall's *The Selling of Joseph,* was published in Boston in 1701, but the Reverend Cotton Mather informed a group of Boston slaves that slavery was "what God will have to be the thing appointed for you."

In the Northeast, where by the middle of the eighteenth century a small but substantial portion of the populations of Boston, Philadelphia, New York City, and Newport, Rhode Island were slaves, most worked as craftsmen, laborers, or personal servants rather than as field workers. In New York City in 1712 a slave uprising involving two dozen blacks resulted in the deaths of nine whites. Punishment was swift and cruel: thirteen slaves were hanged, one left to die in chains, three burned at the stake, one burned over a slow fire for ten hours, and one broken on the wheel.

In the colonies as a whole, white indentured servants could look forward to freedom and perhaps to entry into the propertied classes. A large part of the population could vote or otherwise engage in local government. And yet, while so much of British civilization was becoming freer in North America, the new land had begun to cultivate the institution of slavery, unknown in Britain for centuries. Freedom and slavery were growing up together.

John Woolman, a prominent Quaker, wrote in his diary:

"A neighbor received a bad bruise in his body and sent for me to bleed him, which having done, he desired me to write his will. Amongst other things he told me to which of his children he gave his young Negro. I considered the pain and distress he was in, and knew not how it would end, so I wrote his will, save only that part concerning his slave and carrying it to his bedside read it to him. I then told him in a friendly way that I could not write any instrument by which my fellow creatures were made slaves without bringing trouble on my own mind. I let him know that I charged nothing for what I had done, and desired to be excused from doing the other part in the way he proposed. We then had a serious conference on the subject; at length, he agreeing to set her free, I finished his will."

The Great Awakening and the Enlightenment

In the 1730s, a new enthusiasm for religion and moral reform appeared almost simultaneously in continental Europe, Great Britain, and the colonies. The message was essentially the same, whatever its form: that the way to salvation lay not in faithful performance of sacraments and rituals as the Catholics and Anglicans had always maintained, or a life of good works, but simply in opening the heart to God through prayer. A simple and total act of faith in God's goodness and mercy would bring to the faithful an unspeakably profound experience of personal conversion and salvation. And while good works were not the means to

The Rev. Jonathan Edwards awakened many congregants to their plight in sermons such as "Sinners in the Hands of an Angry God" *(Courtesy, Library of Congress)*

The eloquent British revivalist preacher George Whitefield fueled the Great Awakening on his evangelical tours. *(Courtesy, National Portrait Gallery)*

redemption, they would follow, issuing from the cleansed and grateful heart of the convert. As John Winthrop and those who banished Anne Hutchinson had argued in the 1630s, any such doctrine is potentially dangerous to an established social order, for it implicitly vests in individuals the capacity to judge the moral rectitude of their own behavior.

In the colonies the Great Awakening had its beginnings in 1734, when the Reverend Jonathan Edwards, pastor of the church in the small frontier town of Northampton, Massachusetts, a community of about 200 families, noted a "religious concern on people's minds." As the winter of 1734 progressed, Edwards noticed that "There was scarcely a single person in the town, either old or young, that was left unconcerned about the great things of the eternal world. Those that were wont to be the vainest, and loosest, and those that had been most disposed to think and speak slightly of vital and experimental religion, were now generally subject to great awakenings." Edward's account of the Northampton revival, *A Faithful Narrative of the Surprising Work of God,* published in 1737, may have prepared the way for the preaching of George Whitefield, the eloquent young English clergyman who arrived in America in 1739.

George Whitefield

Various French, German, and Dutch ministers were associated with revivalism, and John and Charles Wesley were the most important figures involved in England. The most influential of all in British America was George Whitefield.

After receiving some training at Oxford, Whitefield had persuaded his bishop of the Church of England to ordain him before he was of the customary age. In his maiden sermon, this restless, charismatic preacher raved and exhorted, sang and shouted, wept and thundered. Whitefield made his first evangelical tour to America in 1739 at age twenty-five, preaching under the open air and converting hundreds in Georgia. He returned two years later to conduct a great revival in New England. The New England and mid-Atlantic tour was the greatest triumph of Whitefield's career, though he made several successful trips to America during the next thirty years. In 1740 the populace was ready for him, if only out of restlessness, boredom, or economic troubles.

Enthusiastic Religion

The impact of the Great Awakening was not quite what the ministry that welcomed Whitefield had expected. The number of active participants in church affairs doubled, trebled, and quadrupled, and for the first time in years religion attracted the enthusiasm of the young. But much of New England became divided into fiercely hostile camps of "Old Lights," or defenders of the existing order, and "New Lights," who embraced the new piety.

The Great Awakening had its philosophical connections with more sober forms of Protestantism that had preceded it. Puritans, like other Protestants, had taken the conversion experience very seriously. Even after the Half-Way Covenant of 1662, which accepted as restricted church members the unconverted children of full members, a conversion experience was a requirement for full admission. But the Puritan congregations had not demanded the violent outpourings of emotion that revivalism usually identifies with religious experience. The New Lights sought to convert through their sermons, thereby taking what had been an intensely private experience and making it public. People cried out—presumably under the conviction of sin. They wept, they groaned, they fell to their knees. Some lost consciousness. And, most critically, the excitement was contagious. Whole gatherings experienced the drama of conversion together. The Great Awakening was the earliest instance of a recurrent phenomenon in American Protestantism. Like the Great Awakening, moreover, American religion since has emphasized the experiential component of religion. In breaking open churches that had been stable and undivided, the Awakening is suggestive of the tendency within Protestantism to multiply churches and sects. And the Awakening introduced America to a movement that John and Charles Wesley were spreading within the Church of England: a faith that stressed both religious feeling and a consequent morality of self-discipline and hard work. Soon, adherents to that form of piety left the Anglican church and formed their own, the Methodist. In the nineteenth century the Methodist and Baptist churches, well adapted in structure, practice, and belief to spread to the frontier and the backcountry, would become two of the largest denominations both in cities and in the countryside. Throughout Great Britain and the United States, Methodism had a powerful influence on popular morality, spreading habits of sobriety, thrift, and diligence, turning its members to acts of social reformation. Numbers of Methodists in the northern states, for example, were active in the antislavery movement, and later generations worked for prohibition of alcohol. In Britain, Methodists had an important part in the labor movement.

The Enlightenment   The energies of revivalism were directed against reason, or at least the cool, detached reason that opposed bursts of emotion. But there began in Europe around the middle of the eighteenth century a movement, called the Enlightenment, that celebrated reason and viewed the times as an age of social and scientific rationality. The Enlightenment soon reached American shores.

It began to glimmer there in the glass jars of Benjamin Franklin's electrical experiments in Philadelphia. In 1749 Franklin was "chagrined a little that we have hitherto been able to discover nothing in the way of use to mankind," but by 1752, with his now-famous kite experiment, he had proved that lightning and electricity were one and the same. His practical invention of the lightning rod soon followed. On one occasion he nearly electrocuted himself attempting to roast a turkey. By the late 1750s Franklin had acquired an international reputation for his contributions to science.

In its European form the Enlightenment practiced an abstract kind of thinking known as deductive logic, a reasoning that begins with general principles and then applies these to particular cases or details. Philosophers of the Enlightenment, for example, abstractly defined large, general "laws of nature," which could be laws governing the material world or natural laws fixed in human beings. Having deter-

In Philadelphia Whitefield managed to affect even that lover of reason, Benjamin Franklin, who recorded in his Autobiography:

"I happened . . . to attend one of his sermons, in the course of which I perceived he intended to finish with a collection, and I silently resolved he should get nothing from me. I had in my pocket a handful of copper money, three or four silver dollars, and five pistoles in gold. As he proceeded I began to soften, and concluded to give the coppers. Another stroke of his oratory made me ashamed of that, and determined me to give the silver; and he finished so admirably, that I empty'd my pocket wholly into the collector's dish, gold and all."

George Whitefield and John Wesley promised salvation to those who opened their hearts to God through prayer. To them was offered eternal life in the New Jerusalem depicted in this drawing; to others the door to Hell stood open. *(Courtesy, Scribner's Archives)*

GEORGE WHITEFIELD'S PREACHING

Nathan Cole, a farmer and carpenter of Connecticut, sought out the evangelist George Whitefield.

"There came a messenger and said Mr. Whitfield preached at Hartford and Weathersfield yesterday and is to preach at Middeltown this morning at 10 o clock. I was in my field at work [and] I dropt my tool that I had in my hand and run home and run thru my house and bade my wife get ready quick to goo and hear Mr. Whitfield preach at Middeltown. And [I] run to my pasture for my hors with all my might, fearing I should be too late to hear him. I brought my hors home and soon mounted and took my wife up and went forward as fast as I thought my hors could bear, and when my hors began to be out of breath I would get down and put my wife on

the Saddel, and bid her ride as fast as she could, and not Stop or Slak for except I bade her. And so I would run until I was almost out of breth, and then mount my hors again, and so I did severel times to favour my hors. . . .

When we came within about half a mile of the road that comes down from Hartford, Weathersfield and Stepney to Middeltown, on high land, I saw before me a Cloud or fog, rising—I first thought—off from the great river. But as I came nearer the road I heard a noise, something like a low rumbling thunder, and I presently found it was the rumbling of horses feet coming down the road and this Cloud was a Cloud of dust made by the running of horses feet. It arose some rods into the air over the tops of the hills and trees. And when I came

---

mined the laws of nature that applied to human beings, Enlightenment thinkers considered what particular kind of government would best serve or express these laws. The European Enlightenment would make for great advances in science. Its political thought, much of which presumed that the laws of nature make all human beings equal in rights, contributed to the modern political revolutions seeking freedom and legal equality.

Empiricism   Numbers of American writers were much under the influence of the political as well as the scientific Enlightenment in Europe, talked of the general "laws of nature," and argued in the language of the Enlightenment for liberty and equality. But some historians have identified a difference in emphasis between the European Enlightenment and its American counterpart. Americans tended more than European philosophers of the time to follow not deductive reasoning but a kind of thought that is now called empiricism, a reasoning that begins with the observation of particular details rather than with speculation about general principles. American thinkers confined much of their work to looking at plants and animals, to experimenting with gadgets, and to solving practical problems of government.

Empiricism produced early and important scientific studies in America. In 1715 eleven-year-old Jonathan Edwards studied a spider's habits and recorded his observations in an essay, "Of Insects." But he forsook science for theology. Late in the seventeenth and early in the eighteenth century the New Englanders Thomas Brattle and Thomas Robie made a number of astronomical observations that proved useful to Newton and other Europeans, and the Royal Society in London published papers by John Banister, Cotton Mather, and Paul Dudley on American flora and fauna. Eliza Lucas Pinckney's observations pioneered the cultivation of indigo, which became widespread as a cash crop. Mathematical observations of note came from John Winthrop IV, Ezra Stiles, and David Rittenhouse. Possibly as important as these scientific

within about twenty rods of the road, I could see men and horses Slipping along in the Cloud like shadows. And when I came nearer it was like a stedy streem of horses and their riders, scarcely a horse more than his length behind another, all of a lather and fome with swet, ther breth rooling out of their noistrels. . . . Every hors semed to go with all his might to carry his rider to hear the news from heaven for the saving of their Souls. It made me trembel to see the Sight.

We went down in the Streeme. I herd no man speak a word all the way, three mile, but evry one presing forward in great haste. And when we gat down to the old meating house, thare was a great multitude. It was said to be 3 or 4000 of people assembled together.

We gat off from our horses and shook off the dust, and the ministers was then coming to the meating house. I turned and looked toward the great river and saw the fery boats running swift forward and backward, bringing over loads of people. The ores rowed nimble and quick. Everything—men, horses and boats—all seamed to be struglin for life. The land and the banks over the river looked black with people and horses all along the 12 miles. I see no man at work in his field, but all seamed to be gone.

When I see Mr. Whitfield come upon the Scaffold, he looked almost angellical—a young, slim, slender youth before some thousands of people, and with a bold, un-daunted countenance. And my hearing how God was with him everywhere as he came along, it solomnized my mind, and put me in a trembling fear before he began to preach, for he looked as if he was Cloathed with authority from the great God."

discoveries were the media through which scientific knowledge was introduced and spread.

Higher Education The most advanced were the colleges, along with philosophical and scientific societies, notably the American Philosophical Society, established in Philadelphia in 1743. Most colleges started during the colonial period were founded by religious groups. Harvard (1636) and Yale (1701) were what is now termed Congregationalist, the word that has come to designate New England churches of Puritan ancestry that placed church government in the hands of the congregation. William and Mary (1691) and King's College (1754, later renamed Columbia) were founded by Anglicans. Rhode Island College (1764, later Brown) was Baptist, Queen's College (1766, later Rutgers) was Dutch Reformed, and the College of New Jersey (1746, later Princeton) was Presbyterian. The only nonsectarian college founded in the colonial period was Franklin's Academy, established in 1754, which became the University of Pennsylvania in

Captains from Surinam, by John Greenwood. *(Courtesy, Art Museum of St. Louis)*

AN EARLY HARVARD RIOT

College students have long complained about the quality of food in university dining rooms. If this very first American instance in 1639 of an incipient food riot is typical, they have good reason for their complaint. Mistress Eaton, the cook and author of this letter, was wife of Harvard's first headmaster, Nathaniel Eaton. Both lost their jobs when students protested the severe discipline that Mr. Eaton dispensed and the atrocious food that his wife served.

"For their breakfast, that it was not so well ordered, the flour not so fine as it might, nor so well boiled or stirred, at all times that it was so, it was my sin of neglect, and want of that care that ought to have been in one that the Lord had intrusted with such a work. Concerning their beef, that was allowed them, as they affirm, which, I confess, had been my duty to have seen they had it, and continued to have had it, because it was my husband's command; but truly I must confess, to my shame. I cannot remember that ever they had it, nor that ever it was taken from them. And that they had not so good or so much provision in my husband's absence as presence, I conceive it was because he would call sometimes for butter or cheese, when I conceived there was no need of it; yet, forasmuch as the scholars did otherways apprehend, I desire to see the evil that was in the carriage of that as well as in the other, and to take shame to myself for it. And that they sent down for more, when they had not enough, and the maid should answer, if they had not, they should not, I must confess, that I have denied them cheese, when they sent for it, and it have been in the house; for which I shall humbly beg pardon of them, and own the shame, and confess my sin. And for such provoking words, which my servants have given, I cannot own them, but am sorry any such should be given in my house. And for bad fish, that they had it brought to table,

1791. Dartmouth became a college in 1769 after having been established much earlier as an Indian missionary school. King's College and Franklin's Academy introduced practical courses in agriculture, navigation, and astronomy.

Higher education was available to a much wider spectrum of classes in the colonies than in England, though the prestigious institutions of higher learning were reserved for males. During the eighteenth century, a few private academies for women were founded, but systematic attempts to provide even for the education of upper-class girls would not emerge until after the Revolution. The colonies did produce some well-educated and even learned women, but it was typical among them to have benefited from private instruction from tutors who had been hired for their brothers or cousins. Female literacy lagged far behind the rate among men.

The Press and the Zenger Case

On the popular level, scientific and other information was spread mainly through newspapers. Laws in Massachusetts and Connecticut required every town to provide a school at which children could learn reading and writing. Elementary schools, established most zealously by Congregationalists and Presbyterians, gave America a much higher literacy rate than Europe possessed: ninety percent or more could sign their names in New England, fifty to sixty percent in Virginia.

In 1725 the British mainland colonies had only five newspapers. Then along with the rapid expansion of commerce and land settlement came a proliferation of papers: by 1765 there were twenty-five. Four-page weeklies were filled with advertisements, notices of arrivals and departures of ships, and reprints of news that had appeared months earlier in European journals. But as time went by the colonial news-

I am sorry there was that cause of offence given them. I acknowledge my sin in it. And for their mackerel, brought to them with their guts in them, and goat's dung in their hasty pudding, it's utterly unknown to me; but I am much ashamed it should be in the family, and not prevented by myself or servants, and I humbly acknowledge my negligence in it. And that they made their beds at any time, were my straits never so great, I am sorry they were ever put to it. For the Moor his lying in Sam. Hough's sheet and pillowbier, it hath a truth in it: he did so one time, and it gave Sam. Hough just cause of offence; and that it was not prevented by my care and watchfulness, I desire [to] take the shame and sorrow for it. And that they eat the Moor's crusts, and the swine and they had share and share alike, and the Moor to have beer, and they denied it, and if they had not enough, for my maid to answer, they should not, I am an utter stranger to these things, and know not the least footsteps for them so to charge me; and if my servants were guilty of such miscarriages, had the boarders complained of it unto myself, I should have thought it my sin, if I had not sharply reproved my servants, and endeavored reform. And for bread made of heated, sour meal, although I know of but once that if was so, since I kept house, yet John Wilson affirms it was twice: and I am truly sorry, that any of it was spent amongst them. For beer and bread, that it was denied them by me betwixt meals, truly I do not remember, that ever I did deny it unto them; John Wilson will affirm, that, generally, the bread and beer was free for the boarders to go unto. And that money was demanded of them for washing the linen, it's true it was propounded to them, but never imposed upon them. And for their pudding being given the last day of the week without butter or suet, and that I said, it was miln of Manchester in Old England, it's true that I did say so, and am sorry, they had any cause of offence given them by having it so. And for their wanting beer, betwixt brewings, a week or half a week together, I am sorry that it was so at any time, and should tremble to have it so, were it in my hands to do again."

papers printed more and more articles, written by their readers, in which the nature of man, society, and government was endlessly explored. So it was largely through the newspapers that Americans formed their opinions of themselves and their world. Following the English lead, the colonies also began to produce a few journals such as the *Lady's Magazine* and the *Gentleman's and Lady's Town and Country Magazine* that catered to the female members of polite society.

Colonial America provided an important incident in the development of freedom of the press. In 1735 John Peter Zenger faced a charge of libel for publishing in his newspaper an attack by the former chief justice of New York on actions of the governor of the colony. The counsel for Zenger argued that since the statements printed in the paper were true were not libelous. The jury agreed, and returned a verdict of not guilty. The effect of the verdict was to establish the principle that only false statements are libelous, and thereby to free newspapers to widen the range of their commentary and criticism.

The lawyer Andrew Hamilton argued the case for John Peter Zenger:

"Power may justly be compared to a great river which, while kept within its due bounds is both beautiful and useful; but when it overflows its banks, it is then too impetuous to be stemmed, it bears down all before it and brings destruction and desolation wherever it comes. If this then is the nature of power, let us at least do our duty, and like wise men use our utmost care to support liberty. . . . The question before the court and you gentlemen of the jury is . . . the cause of liberty . . . by . . . writing Truth."

The American Character

An English visitor in Connecticut in 1750 remarked of Americans that "their government, religion, and manners all tend to support an equality. Whoever brings in your victuals sits down and chats with you." Europeans were inclined to view Americans as bumpkins lacking the social graces. The commercial and urban sectors and the more well-to-do planters were in fact quite sophisticated in their awareness of events on both sides of the Atlantic. They had to be. Their prosperity depended on knowledge of European markets; their political well-being on the doings of factions within the British Parliament. And having a higher literacy rate than perhaps any nation of Europe, Americans read newspapers and exchanged letters avidly.

British America was diverse not only in ethnic and religious background but in regions and societies changing over time, from the plantations of the Virginia tidewater section a century and a half old to the newly-plowed red fields of Georgia, from the urban bustle of Boston and Philadelphia to the remote villages and farms on the frontier. Multiple forms of social stratification existed. Each community—the town in New England, the manor in New York, the county or parish elsewhere—had its own hierarchy, which sometimes did and sometimes did not correspond to the gradations of power and status in the colony as a whole.

A Woman's Place   According to the Puritan leader John Winthrop, a woman's husband "is her lord, and she is subjected to him, yet in a way of liberty, not of bondage: and a true wife accounts her subjection her honor and freedom." A Puritan clergyman likened the family to "a little commonwealth" with the father as its undisputed head. Women when they married normally lost whatever property rights they might have had. As the eighteenth-century British jurist William Blackstone put it: "Husband and wife are one and that one is the husband." Husbands were expected to govern their wives with gentleness and love whenever possible, but an unruly wife required stronger measures.

The laws of Massachusetts differed from those of England in restricting the husband's right to correction. Wife-beating with a stick that was larger than one inch in diameter was prohibited. But even the gentler laws of the new world did not interfere with "corrections" or "chastisements" administered with switches of the proper size. And the Puritan emphasis on the responsibility of the individual to God did not encourage women's equality in religious institutions. Puritan fathers were especially fond of St. Paul's dictum: "Women, keep silent in the churches." By the end of the seventeenth century, women usually outnumbered men in church congregations, and in the nineteenth century the predominance of women in church attendance would be noticeable in many congregations, but it did not open to women the role of minister or church leader. And women were almost entirely excluded from all forms of politics.

The inferiority of women to men, like women's necessary subordination to men, was the dominant view of gender relations and one of

Puritan women in their Sunday best. Some wore masks to protect themselves from wind and sun.
(Courtesy, Scribner'sArchives)

the most widely shared assumptions throughout the colonies. It has nonetheless been argued that women enjoyed a better position in the New World than women in the old, then or earlier. This view rests in part on the assumption that since women remained in short supply throughout the seventeenth century they were especially valued. But there is little evidence to suggest that simply because the authorities tried very hard to encourage women to go to the colonies the reigning idea of women's nature and worth actually changed very much. The incentives offered to women had to do more with improving their social and economic position among other women than with improving the status of women relative to men.

The distinction between male and female remained a fundamental determinant of an individual's social opportunities, but in any given instance wealth, inherited social status, and family membership could outweigh gender. Women of high social stature were desirable as wives for ambitious men seeking to ally themselves to influential families. Family connections could also permit women, either married or single, to take significant political roles in exceptional circumstances. Most women, however, spent their lives firmly under the governance of their fathers, husbands, and male kin to whom they were considered constitutionally and intellectually inferior.

Indentured Servants and Slave Women

Female indentured servants were doubly subordinate. Indentured women were seldom allowed to marry, and in some places the "secret marriage of servants" was forbidden by law. Masters reserved the right to lengthen the period of service if the woman became pregnant. The possibility of marrying better than they might have married in England was the major attraction for single female immigrants. But delaying marriage for the normal minimum of the seven years of indenture often meant that the female servant might marry only after several of her childbearing years had passed and after brutal work in a harsh climate had perhaps undermined her health.

The hardships that weighed on female indentured servants weighed even more heavily on slave women who lacked the minimal rights and promise of eventual freedom that masters accorded to indentured servants. Initially, slave women were as scarce relative to slave men as indentured females were to indentured men. African societies placed a high value on women, or at least on their productive and reproductive abilities, and so African slave-traders often withheld women from the slave trade. Many women who were transported to the New World had been separated from their families. In the early years of slavery in the colonies, the ratio of men to women was too high for the newly enslaved population to reproduce itself. Only in the eighteenth century did a considerable community of slaves begin to take shape in the Chesapeake colonies and South Carolina. By then, some slave women were forming stable unions with slave men and bearing their children. But the legality of slave marriages was never recognized in law. And slave women, even more than indentured women, lacked any resources to oppose sexual exploitation by the master or other white males. Most slave colonies forbade interracial sex, but enough black women bore mulatto chil-

A Virginia colonist advised single women to

"sojourn in a house of good honest repute, for by their good carriage, they may advance themselves in marriage . . . loose persons seldome live long unmarried, if free, yet they match with as desolate as themselves, and never live handsomly or are ever respected."

In 1756 a young serving-girl in Maryland wrote to her father that she was "toiling almost day and night," had "scarce any thing but Indian corn and salt to eat," and had "no shoes nor stockings to wear . . . what rest we can get is to rap ourselves up in a blanket and ly upon the ground."

A poem speaks in the voice of an indentured servant who, after recalling her happier days in England, laments her condition in the New World:

In weeding Corn or feeding Swine,
I spend my melancholy Time,
Kidnap'd and Fool'd, I thither fled,
And to my cost already find,
Worse Plagues than those I left behind.

Jersey Nanny, **by John Greenwood.** *(Courtesy, Museum of Fine Arts, Boston)*

dren—either because they had been raped, or because they had established a relationship with a man who was not black—to make the status of mulatto children a pressing legal question. In most Latin American slaveholding countries many masters acknowledged their mulatto offspring and freed them, so a distinct class of free mulattoes emerged. In English America, such acknowledgments and manumissions were less common: there were many mulatto slaves, and free mulattoes simply joined the class of free blacks.

Women's Legal Rights   The law severely circumscribed the status of most women whether their status be slave, indentured, or free. Only adult single or widowed free women could act in their own name or hold or dispose of property for themselves. These legal barriers to all forms of female independence derived primarily from the English common law, which assigned all minor children to the authority of their fathers and viewed all married women as "femmes coverts"—or, literally, covered women. New World practice apparently modified the severity of this legal doctrine; some widows who remarried signed contracts with their husbands-to-be prior to marriage and thus preserved control of their own property. In Braintree, Massachusetts, John French upon his marriage to Eleanor Veazie in 1683 had to agree "not to meddle with or take into his hand any part of her estate wherein she is invested by her former husband. . . ." Women were also known to act in a legal capacity on their own or their family's behalf. Wills reveal that at least some women did bequeath property to heirs of their own choosing. Law in some colonies such as Massachusetts and Connecticut also permitted women somewhat easier access to divorce than they had in England, and the records reveal that at least some women took advantage of the opportunity. But formal divorce was never common; some colonies prohibited it absolutely except by act of the legislature.

In a predominantly rural society, most women had few opportunities to live comfortably on their own. Men had difficulty managing an agricultural household without a woman; women alone faced even greater obstacles. But by the eighteenth century, some single and widowed women were running small businesses, managing shops, or otherwise supporting themselves and perhaps their children. And whatever the limitations imposed by the law, in practice married free women probably enjoyed considerable feelings of importance to the survival of their households. Their work was as essential to the survival and solvency of those households as was that of their men. White women who survived their childbearing years had on the average about eight children. Some bore more, and many lost one or more in childbirth or infancy. In addition to this vital contribution, most women shouldered a significant portion of the labor necessary to the household. They were responsible for cooking, for the making of many household necessities such as candles and soap, for washing, for sewing, and frequently for making clothes. This labor could include heavy tasks, among them carrying the water for cooking and washing from stream or well to the house. Women also usually assumed responsibility for certain kinds of agricultural labor, such as milking cows, tending gardens, and keeping chickens. When circumstances required, especially at harvest time, they worked in the fields beside men.

The woman of the day who enjoyed the greatest freedom did not work alongside her husband, but could enjoy the more leisured life of the colonial aristocracy. She might acquire something of the more serious education provided for her brothers. By the eighteenth century, she was likely to have silver instead of pewter, an ample supply of linen for beds and tables, silks and laces to wear, looking glasses, cupboards and chests from Europe, books, periodicals, and more. But the comfort of her life depended upon the labor of other women—slaves or servants—who performed the tasks from which wealth had liberated her.

The Young   In a land where labor was scarce, offspring also contributed to the livelihood of the family. Colonial Americans had little if any concept of a time of suspension between childhood and maturity that today goes by the name of adolescence. But if family responsibilities came early, the opportunities of a new land also frequently pulled the young away from home.

Every colony had laws demanding obedience from young offspring; the potential punishment for disobedience in Massachusetts and Connecticut was nothing less than death. In New Haven in 1656, for example, the law stated that "If any child or children above sixteen year[s] old, and of competent understanding, shall curse, or smite, his, her, or their natural father or mother, each such child shall be put to death. . . ." "Stubborn rebellious" sons sixteen or older who refused to obey the "voice and chastisement" of their parents were also subject to the death penalty. Existing records do not reveal that any court ever resorted to such extreme punishment. In fact, by allowing such cases to be tried, these laws guarded against parental abuse at the same time that they sought to curb recalcitrant youth. Colonial law reflected the belief that the community, acting through the courts, had an interest in maintaining order within individual families.

New England also assumed the burden of providing formal education. A Massachusetts statute of 1641 anticipated the nineteenth-century community provision of schooling for all members of society. And as society became more secular, so did education; the inculcation of civic virtue and good citizenship took priority over religious instruction.

Yet most young people learned pedagogical and vocational skills within their families. If a son did not want to learn his father's trade, he might be apprenticed into another family for study under the direction of the master. Whatever young colonials failed to absorb from elders they had to learn on their own. Colonial newspapers and almanacs, such as Ben Franklin's *Poor Richard's Almanac*, served as early home study guides.

Courtship   Though marriages were often arranged by parents or at least had to have parental approval, courtship had its prescribed rituals. The custom of "bundling," a betrothed couple's spending the night in bed together—but fully clothed—was much practiced, especially during the cold New England winters. Particularly in the cities, courting customs changed rapidly, disturbing the older

Alice Mason, 1670. Massachusetts. Artist unknown. Puritans focused on the moral development of their children. (*National Park Service, Adams National Historic Site, Quincy, Massachusetts*)

Courtship and marriage across racial boundaries were discouraged, and in some colonies illegal. A 1691 Virginia law aimed to prevent

"that abominable mixture and spurious issue which hereafter may increase in this dominion, as well by negroes, mulattoes, and Indians intermarrying with English, or other white women, as by their unlawful accompanying with one another. . . ."

Such couples were to be "banished and removed from their dominion forever."

Compare the lyricism of the English "Greensleeves" ("Alas, my love / You do me wrong / To cast me off / Discourteously. . . .") with the blunter expression of "Springfield Mountain," the first popular folk song known to be native to the colonies in both words and music:

On Springfield Mountain there did
  dwell
A lovelie youth I knowed him well. . . .
He had scarce mowed half round the
  field
When a poison serpent bit at his
  heel. . . .
They took him home to Mollie dear,
Which made him feel so verie queer. . . .
She also had a rotten tooth
And so the poison killed them both.

generation, shocking rural visitors, and even surprising foreign observers. A young man described a party he went to in Quaker Philadelphia: "Seven sleighs with two ladies and two men in each, preceded by fiddlers on horseback" rode to a public house where "we danced, sung, and romped and ate and drank, and kicked away care from morning till night, and finished our frolic in two or three sideboxes at the play." A British traveler in Virginia in 1755 reported that "dancing is the chief diversion here," and another was shocked at the widespread dancing of "jigs." Claiming that the dance was borrowed from the slaves, the proper Englishman found it "without method or regularity: a gentleman and lady stand up, and dance about the room, one of them retiring, the other pursuing, then perhaps meeting, in an irregular fantastical manner." Serenading under the window of a favored lady also came into vogue during the late colonial period. Sometimes the gentlemen first lubricated their throats at a local tavern, yet women reportedly considered the midnight visitation, however predictably inharmonious, a high compliment.

Like folk songs everywhere, those of colonial America revolved around courtship, unrequited love affairs, or doomed lovers. Many American ballads came from Britain. "Greensleeves" was one of the most popular and graceful tunes, and it provided the melody for about eighty different sets of lyrics.

English Colonies at Midcentury

Indians, Africans, and Europeans

The wars of the 1600s and early 1700s had either killed or driven most of the Indians out of the thirteen colonies and into the western frontier. There were still large groups: Cherokee, Creeks, Choctaws, and Chickasaws on the North Carolina and Georgia frontiers, and surviving members of the Iroquois Confederacy in upstate New York and western Pennsylvania. But the rest of the Indians were gone. They were living near the foothills of the Appalachian Mountains or had already crossed the mountains.

In 1750 blacks, both slave and free, made up a fifth of the population of Britain's mainland colonies. In the southern colonies, however, the population consisted of just under two blacks for every five whites. In the northern colonies in 1750, less than one person in twenty was black. Of the entire black population in all of the colonies, only one in twenty was free.

By 1750 America had become an ethnic kaleidoscope of competing racial, religious, and linguistic groups. Although representatives of most groups were scattered throughout the colonies, there were visible ethnic concentrations in particular regions.

English settlers lived everywhere, but they were especially dense along the Atlantic seaboard of all thirteen colonies and throughout New England. Although they shared a heritage of language and national origins, the English settlers were deeply divided along religious lines. Most of the English residents of New England were Congregationalists—of Puritan descent—but in the middle colonies dwelt sizable numbers of Anglicans and Quakers. Anglicans dominated the English settlements of the South, although Maryland still had a contingent of Roman Catholics.

The Scotch-Irish were Presbyterians. Their greatest numbers were in the western reaches of the colonies, from Pennsylvania south to Georgia. Although they spoke English, the Scotch-Irish did not have much else in common with their neighbors on the eastern seaboard. Political life in the colonies with large Scotch-Irish populations was characterized by extreme factional struggles between the English settlers on the East Coast and the Scotch-Irish settlers on the western frontier.

The German settlers in colonial America were largely confined to Pennsylvania and Maryland, where they prized the rich limestone soil. Most Germans were Lutheran or "Dutch" Reformed, but significant numbers of Quakers, Moravians, and other groups stressing personal, inward devotion lived among them. The Germans retained their language and separate identity throughout the colonial period: among some of their descendants in Pennsylvania, a form of the German language survives today. By 1750 approximately 200,000 people of German descent lived in America. The Germans of south central Pennsylvania became known as "Pennsylvania Dutch," "Dutch" referring, as with the Dutch Reformed Church, not to natives of the Netherlands but to the *Deutsch*, as Germans speak of themselves in their own language.

The Dutch of the Netherlands were still located in the New York colony, where their ancestors had settled back in the 1620s or later. Approximately 60,000 people of Dutch descent resided in New York City and on farms bordering the Hudson River between New York City and Albany. Several thousand other Dutch lived on the west side of the Hudson River in New Jersey. Most were Dutch Reformed in religion and earned reputations for hard work, prosperity, and clannishness.

The Colonies and the Empire By the middle of the eighteenth century the thirteen contiguous British colonies clustered on the North American mainland contained well over a million inhabitants. The Board of Trade, a fifteen-member agency of the Crown, exercised general supervisory power over the entire overseas empire. It selected most royal officials for the colonies and reviewed all legislation passed by the colonial assemblies. Of about 8,500 colonial laws passed in the entire period prior to 1776, all were at least nominally reviewed and 469 were rejected. The Board had established vice-admiralty courts in five mainland colonies, with jurisdiction over the acts of Parliament and the various orders concerning trade, other maritime activity, and the conservation of timber for the Royal Navy. For a time appeals from these courts went to the High Court of Admiralty in London. After 1748, the Admiralty court shared jurisdiction with the Board of Trade. Appeals from colonial courts on all other matters went to the King's Privy Council. All told, something like 1,500 court decisions were appealed prior to 1776. This jerry-built structure, cumbersome enough in theory, was doubly so in practice, for officials were generally slipshod, inefficient, and negligent in executing their duties. That left the royal governors as the principal instruments of the royal will in the colonies, but since the governors normally received their salaries from the local legislatures they were prone to identify themselves less with the Crown than with the richer and more powerful colonials.

The Imperial System and Mercantilism The system of imperial regulation that the colonies followed or evaded as expediency demanded was not merely an effort to build up the prosperity of the mother country at the expense of the colonies. It aimed at protecting the empire as a whole and encouraging each part to do what it could do best.

The Navigation Acts gave a monopoly of the carrying trade within the empire to ships of England and the colonies, with crews made up mostly of colonists or Englishmen. The acts not only protected the American carrying trade but stimulated the shipbuilding industry in British America. Another measure of the imperial system gave the tobacco colonies a monopoly for their product. The Wool Act of 1699, the Hat Act of 1732, and the Iron Act of 1750 did shield producers in the home country against potential competition from American makers of these goods. But at the moment there was not enough colonial production of wool, hats, or iron to make them competitive with British products. The Molasses Act injured the colonial manufacture of rum, or would have done so if colonists had obeyed it, but its object was to protect other colonists, those of the British West Indies, against foreign competition.

The imperial system, then, was designed to nourish the whole empire and each of its parts. But to colonists aware that the imperial system was the work of a government in which they had no direct voice, every item of the system that seemed to clash with their interests could turn them suspicious of the motives of the mother country. In the meantime, Britain and the colonies alike profited from a vast, enclosed common market.

The informal adhesives of the empire were somewhat stronger than the formal. The colonies and the mother country had common enemies, France and Spain, and that alone was enough to cement the empire. Beyond such tangible considerations were common language, customs, constitutional and legal institutions, and above all pride in a heritage of freedom, of sharing the celebrated "rights of Englishmen."

Political Theory All British subjects, whether they resided in England or the colonies, shared a pride in the British constitution. This unwritten foundation of Britain's political system was an aggregation of custom, law, and precedent developed over centuries. By the 1700s it had achieved a fine balance among the classic forms of government: monarchy, rule by the one; aristocracy, rule by the few; and democracy, rule by the many. Englishmen believed that each needed to be checked by the other two, or it would degenerate into an evil: monarchy would fall into tyranny, aristocracy into selfish domination by the wealthy and powerful, democracy into mob rule. The British government, according to this concept, contained an element of each of the three forms. The Crown represented rule by the one; the House of Lords represented the titled aristocracy, the privileged few; the House of Commons represented the democracy. In the British system, the theory went, each of the three was properly restrained by the other two.

Theory was one thing, practice another. The House of Commons did represent, directly or indirectly, a considerable range of British public opinion. But it was not democratic. For the most part only the propertied classes, and not all individuals within these, had the privilege of voting for members of the Commons. And the Commons did not balance neatly against the Lords. Interests represented in the House of Commons could be as hostile to one another as to the aristocracy. The monarchy in the later years of the century did wield much power, but it was no longer able to rule by sheer sovereign will and command. Its strength now lay in its ability to influence Parliament through the appointments and other royal favors at its disposal.

Much of what remained of the presence of the Crown in British political thought was a fiction that theorists thought it convenient to abide by. It was believed that for every country, there must be a sovereignty, a single individual source of all legal authority. The British throne, so tradition claimed, constituted this sovereignty within the empire. Whatever legitimate power the Lords, the Commons, or the courts possessed was by grant of authority from the monarch. Those who held to this idea were perfectly aware that in fact Parliament could pretty much do as it pleased, constrained only by the monarch's power to make appointments and to influence parliamentary votes. But champions of the King believed that the idea of a monarchy from which all legitimate authority flows made for loyalty, unity, and obedience to law.

Eighteenth-century observers perceived the politics of their time as a corruption of a system that had once been pure. Beginning in the 1720s, when party politics was developing in the mother country, political essays attacking the King's ministers and claiming evil designs against English liberties were common in London periodicals. Literate and concerned colonists read these, too, and kept a watchful eye on ministerial policies. By the 1760s it would take little to convince Americans that they, too, were endangered by a vast, evil conspiracy of corrupt officials to take away the sacred rights of Englishmen everywhere. The belief that an ideal government should combine three elements—monarchy, aristocracy, and democracy—and that the British system had once possessed the right combination persisted into the early days of the independent United States. It would be a model for the Constitution, the President providing government by the one, the Senate—for which the Constitution did not require popular elections—embodying rule by the few, and the House of Representatives supplying rule by the many.

By 1750 the governments of the royal colonies—all the colonies except Rhode Island and Connecticut—also appeared to reflect the structure of the British government. The governor, appointed by the Crown, had the authority to veto legislation passed by the colonial assembly and to call or dissolve the assembly. The governors' powers in the colonies were not identical to those of the monarch in Britain, but the governors, like the Crown, could be described as providing government by the one. While some governors were upper-class Americans, the Crown commonly appointed someone from Britain. A council, drawn for the most part from among the wealthier or more distinguished colonists and in most royal colonies appointed by the governor, could amend or reject measures passed by the other branch of the colonial legislature, called in most colonies the assembly, and served as the highest court in the colony. The assembly provided government by the many. Throughout British America between fifty and seventy-five percent of adult white males possessed enough property to vote for members of that branch of government.

How Much Democracy? Why were the colonies so much more nearly democratic politically than Great Britain? No passionate commitment to the idea of universal equality had moved proprietors, companies, and colonial leaders to provide for broad distribution of the right to vote, or led Kings and the rest of the British government to accept the arrangement. Voting in much of England was restricted to people owning at least a "forty-shilling freehold" (land that produced a yearly income of forty shillings). But land was scarce in England, and comparatively few people could vote. In America land was abundant, and a modest property requirement comparable to that in England was easily met. Thus the franchise in the colonies was wider by accident, not by design. Not only was voting more widespread in America, but the number of voters was constantly growing as new immigrants became settlers, as new communities formed and elected their own representatives to colonial legislatures. And so much of colonial British America enjoyed a democracy that had little ideology to it, representing instead something of British tradition and much of the reality of colonial life.

Still, the colonies were not democratic by modern standards. People voted, but governors not chosen by the people could veto legislation. Wealthy elites ruled, but ordinary folk were untroubled by that rule, since, being democratic by circumstance rather than by ideology, they had no philosophical reason to be troubled; they were prepared to offer to people of wealth and standing a certain deference.

By no means all white American males could vote. There were laborers and seamen with almost no property, and paupers with none. Women were similarly disfranchised, but there is no record of their having protested their condition. Since in principle married women could own no property without very special legal arrangements, and since officially no women performed military service, they could not claim the two main justifications for a vote. Colonists of both genders widely shared the assumption that public affairs were the business of men. And finally, throughout British America the institution of slavery mocked whatever democracy white Americans practiced.

And so democracy in British America was incomplete and, in considerable part, unintentional.

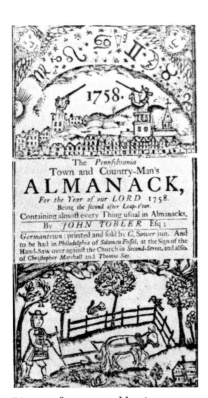

Literate farmers and businessmen craved practical information and made almanacs best-sellers. Nathaniel Low wrote in 1786: "No book we read (except the Bible) is so much valued, and so serviceable to the community. Almanacs serve as clocks and watches for nine-tenths of mankind." (Courtesy, New York Public Library)

Suggested Readings

On the development of New England and the Chesapeake colonies, see Michael Zuckerman, *Peaceable Kingdoms: New England Towns in the Eighteenth Century* (1970) and Allan Kulikoff, *Tobacco and Slaves: The Development of Southern Culture in the Chesapeake, 1680–1800* (1986). See also Lois Green Carr, Philip D. Morgan, and Jean B. Russo, *Colonial Chesapeake Society* (1989), Francis Bremer, *The Puritan Experiment* (1976), Stephen Foster, *Their Solitary Way: The Puritan Social Ethic in the First Century of Settlement in New England* (1971), Charles Hambrick-Stowe, *The Practice of Piety: Puritan Devotional Literature in Seventeenth-Century New England* (1982).

As for witchcraft, Bernard Rosenthal's *Salem Story: Reading the Witch Trials of 1692* (1993), sees adolescents and elders collaborating in a scheme of lies and fraud. Paul Boyer and Stephen Nissenbaum find the cause in social and economic tensions in *Salem Possessed: The Social Origins of Witchcraft* (1974), while Carol Karlsen offers a feminist view in *The Devil in the Shape of a Woman: Witchcraft in Colonial New England* (1987). Elaine Breslaw offers a fresh perspective in *Tituba, Reluctant Witch of Salem: Devilish Indians and Puritan Fantasies* (1996). See also John Demos, *Entertaining Satan* (1983).

On slavery see Hugh Thomas, *The Slave Trade* (1997). Standard works on the origins of slavery in the colonies are David Brion Davis, *The Problem of Slavery in Western Culture* (1966) and Winthrop Jordan, *White Over Black: American Attitudes towards the Negro, 1550–1815* (1968). A good overview is Betty Wood, *The Origins of American Slavery: Freedom and Bondage in the English Colonies* (1997). See also Peter Kolchin, *American Slavery 1619–1877* (1993).

Gender roles are the focus of Mary Beth Norton's *Founding Mothers and Fathers: Gendered Power and the Formation of American Society* (1996). Kathleen Brown examines gender issues in the South in *Good Wives, Nasty Wenches, and Anxious Patriarchs: Gender, Race, and Power in Colonial Virginia* (1996). This work should be set beside Julia Cherry Spruill's earlier pathbreaking *Women's Life and Work in the Southern Colonies* (1938). A rich collection of articles set in the southern colonies is Catherine Clinton's and Michelle Gillespie's *The Devil's Lane: Sex and Race in the Early South* (1997). On the northern colonies see Laurel Thatcher Ulrich, *Good Wives: Image and Reality in the Lives of Women in Northern New England, 1650–1750* (1982) and Lyle Koehler, *A Search for Power: "The Weaker Sex" in Seventeeth Century New England* (1980).

On the colonial economy, see Michael Kammen, *Empire and Interest: The American Colonies and the Politics of Mercantilism* (1970), Richard R. Johnson *Adjustment to Empire* (1981), and John J. McCusker and Russel R. Menard, *The Economy of British America 1607–1789* (1985).

The Devil in the Shape of a Woman?

Paul Boyer and Stephen Nissenbaum

More than a hundred years ago, Charles W. Upham, a public figure in Salem whose lifelong avocation was the study of the witch trials, published a map which located with some precision the home of nearly every Salem Village resident at the beginning of 1692. Using Upham's careful map as basis, it is possible to pinpoint the place of residence of every Villager who testified for or against any of the accused witches and also of those accused who themselves lived within the Village bounds. A pattern emerges from this exercise. . . .

There were fourteen accused witches who lived within the bounds of Salem Village. Twelve of these fourteen lived in the eastern section of the Village. There were thirty-two adult Villagers who testified against these accused witches. Only two of these lived in that eastern section. The other thirty lived on the western side. In other words, the alleged witches and those who accused them resided on opposite sides of the Village. . . .

What are we to make of this pattern? To begin an answer, we must take a close look at Salem Village before its moment of notoriety. . . . [T]he town of Salem, Massachusetts, began as a commercial venture. From the first its gaze was directed outward toward Europe, the West Indies, and the sea. . . . With the tide of Puritan immigrants to Massachusetts after 1630, Salem prospered, soon outgrowing the narrow neck of land that was its original site. Responding to these pressures the Town selectmen began to make grants of land several miles in the interior. . . . This was the beginning of what in time would be called Salem Village [as opposed to the more mercantile Salem Town].

At least some of these farmers . . . soon began to chafe beneath the power which Salem Town held over them. . . . Salem Village's uncertain status seems, too, to have contributed to a strikingly high level of internal bickering and disarray. . . . Given the ineffectiveness of the Village's institutional structures, private grievances and disputes escalated with a rapidity which must have startled even those embroiled in them. . . .

The witchcraft episode did not generate the divisions within the Village, nor did it shift them in any fundamental way, but it laid bare the intensity with which they were experienced and heightened the vindictiveness with which they were expressed. . . .

[Afterwards] a genuine effort was made by a chastened community to give voice to all factions in the search [for a replacement for Samuel Parris, a controversial minister]. . . . The long cycle of acrimony was at last winding down. . . . The nineteen bodies that swung on Witches' Hill in the summer of 1692 were part of the price Salem Village paid. . . .

By the end of the seventeenth century the sense that there was a dangerous conflict between private will and public good had become seriously eroded in many quarters by two generations of population growth, geographic dispersal, and economic opportunity. . . . New England towns of the 1700s conceded that they were made up of a diverse mixture of imperfect and self-seeking human beings, and they largely abandoned the effort to be anything more.

Paul Boyer and Stephen Nissenbaum, *Salem Possessed: The Social Origins of Witchcraft* (Cambridge, MA: Harvard University Press, 1974), pp. 35, 36, 37, 39, 44, 45, 69, 75, 105.

Carol P. Karlsen

The single most salient characteristic of witches was their sex. At least 344 persons were accused of witchcraft in New England between 1620 and 1725. Of the 342 who can be identified by sex, 267 (78 percent) were female. Roughly half of the seventy-five males accused (thirty-six), as the historian John Demos has pointed out, were "suspect by association": they were the husbands, sons, other kin, or public supporters of female witches. . . .

During severe outbreaks, the reaction of the authorities to witchcraft accusations presents a more complicated, if finally consistent, picture. Though proportionately more men found themselves under suspicion during outbreaks than at other times, officials seem to have been even more reluctant than usual to give credence to these suspicions. While they decided to try fifty-eight of the 156 women accused (37 percent), they indicted only eight of the forty-nine men (16 percent). . . .

Statistics can establish the extent to which New Englanders considered witchcraft the special province of women, but they cannot convey the vindictiveness that characterized the treatment of female suspects. This sexual double standard is perhaps most vividly seen in the different punishments meted out to confessed witches outside of the Salem outbreak.

Deeming voluntary confession one of the best "proofes sufficient for Conviccon," ministers and magistrates put considerable pressure on women to admit they had covenanted with the Devil. No comparable coercion was used with men.

Men who confessed to witchcraft outside of the Salem outbreak were punished, to be sure—but whereas most confessing women were taken at their word and executed, confessing men were almost all rebuked as liars. . . .

Some women who questioned the authority of their husbands were also considered witches. Colonial culture strongly discouraged the use of witchcraft accusations as a way of severing marital bonds. Nevertheless, a wife's insubordination to her husband is implicit in many of the sins that New Englanders saw as witchcraft, from adultery to the murder of one's own spouse and children to the pursuit of independent economic activities.

Witchcraft in colonial New England meant more than women's refusal to subordinate themselves to men with institutional authority over them: it suggested their refusal to subordinate themselves to all persons whom God had placed above them in the social hierarchy. In some cases, women came under suspicion for acting as if they were above other women whom society had defined as their betters. Most often, though, suspicion originated in women's interactions with men, whom society implicitly held to be superior to all women. While Puritans surely would have denied the principle that *all* women were subject to *all* men, the record shows the lack of deference for male neighbors to be a common thread running through the many sins of witches. It was not just pride that most fundamentally distinguished witches from other people; it was female pride in particular. . . .

By treating female [religious] dissent as evidence of witchcraft as well as heresy, the authorities may have effectively silenced Puritan women's opposition. Indeed, by 1660 the debate over women's participation in the church had all but ended—and women had lost many of the gains of the early years. After 1660 Puritan ministers increasingly found reasons to celebrate rather than vilify their most active female congregants, but women's religious activity had taken on a decidedly submissive character. Women continued to join the church in proportionately larger numbers than men for the rest of the century, but if the ministers can be believed, female congregants now listened more than they spoke.

Carol P. Karlsen, *The Devil in the Shape of a Women: Witchcraft in Colonial New England* (New York: W. W. Norton & Company, 1987). Reprinted with permission.

The Death of Wolfe, by Benjamin West. Though General James Wolfe was killed in action at Quebec, the British victory there marked a turning point in the French and Indian War. *(Courtesy, National Gallery of Canada)*

An Independent Spirit
1763–1776

THE PLAINS OF ABRAHAM

At 2:00 a.m. on September 13, 1759, Major General James Wolfe ordered two lanterns raised to the maintop shrouds of his British flagship, the *Sutherland,* anchored on the St. Lawrence River. It was the signal to attack the French fortress of Quebec. The city lay on the heights 175 feet above the dark river. Its high rock cliff made it the most formidable natural fortress in North America.

The attack had been long delayed. Wolfe and his army of redcoats, Scottish highlanders, and American rangers had arrived before the French stronghold the previous June, fighting a score of skirmishes with the French-Canadian militia, their Indian allies, and the crack French regulars of the Guyenne, Royal Roussillon, Bearn, La Reine, and La Sarre regiments. By now the brief Canadian summer was nearly spent, and the bitter northern winter would soon descend. The British naval commander, faced with the prospect of being trapped by ice, was threatening to sail home with his fleet.

Wolfe and his men were quite confident. They were fewer than the French, but what they lacked in numbers they made up in morale and experience. Also, they had been laying siege to the city for weeks. Yet in the boat taking him to the French side Wolfe himself, as though with some premonition of what was about to happen to him, recited Gray's "Elegy in a Country Churchyard." It contained the line "The paths of glory lead but to the grave."

As the small boats carrying the British troops edged along the

continued

HISTORICAL EVENTS

1689–97
War of the League of Augsburg

1702–13
War of the Spanish Succession
(Queen Anne's War)

1740–48
War of the Austrian Succession
(King George's War)

1756
French and Indian War begins

1760
Montreal surrenders to Britain

1763
France and Britain sign the Treaty of Paris • American settlers begin moving west of the Appalachians • Chief Pontiac attacks British at Detroit • Proclamation of 1763

1764
Revenue Act • Currency Act • Sugar Act

1765
Quartering Act • Stamp Act • Stamp Act Congress

darkened north bank of the St. Lawrence, a French sentry shouted: "what regiment?" "The Queen's," responded a highland officer in fluent French. The boats were allowed to pass. Soon after, they touched the bank close to where Wolfe some days before had spied a zigzag path up the steep cliff that separated the river from the plain stretching before Quebec city. Twenty-four volunteers leaped out and, grabbing trees and bushes, pulled themselves up the plateau. Hundreds more followed.

The invaders spied a small French encampment. They immediately attacked, captured two of the French soldiers, and put the rest to flight. Hearing the triumphant shouts of his men above, Wolfe and his remaining force disembarked and scaled the cliff by way of the path to join the advance party. As morning broke with clouds and threatening rain, 4,000 British troops drew themselves up in battle order on the Plains of Abraham a mile west of Quebec, the center of French power in America, where General Louis Montcalm commanded 14,000 troops.

In the walled city itself, news of Wolfe's surprise move provoked great alarm. For many weeks the *Quebeçois* had endured bombardment from the British fleet and army. Much of the city was in ruins, and it was packed with refugees from the countryside who jammed into every remaining dwelling and spilled over into the town's hospitals, convents, and public buildings. As news spread of the British success in scaling the heights, the French and Canadians poured out of the town to assemble on the plain outside the walls. Montcalm asked the city commander to send him big guns from the palace battery, but was given only three on the plea that the rest were needed to defend the town itself. Montcalm might have waited for more troops, but the local commander held back. As his men formed ranks, Montcalm rode back and forth along his lines brandishing his sword and urging his troops to show their mettle for France and for the King.

At 10:00 a.m. the French, with the white-clad regulars in the center and the Canadians at either end, started forward against the double-ranked British, firing and shouting. The redcoats and highlanders advanced a few yards and then stopped. When the two lines were within forty paces the British commander ordered his men to fire. Two precise volleys rang out like single shots, and then a ragged clatter as the men reloaded and fired at will. When the smoke lifted, it was clear that the battle was over. As far as the eye could see, the field was strewn with French dead and wounded, 1,400 in all. The French troops still on their feet had stopped short and were milling around in a confused mob. The British officers now gave the order to charge. The cheering redcoats ran forward with their bayonets poised. The highlanders dashed ahead yelling in Gaelic and brandishing their broadswords. Leading one force was Wolfe himself. At that moment of

French troops being reviewed in Quebec, an almost impregnable fortress commanded by Louis Joseph Montcalm. *(Courtesy, William H. Coverdale Collection, and the Canada Steamship Lines Limited, Montreal, Canada)*

triumph the British general was struck in the chest by a French bullet and taken to the rear. A few minutes later he died.

By now the French were fleeing pell-mell to the safety of Quebec's walls. Borne along with the human tide was Montcalm, still mounted. Close to the walls a British shot hit him in the thigh and passed along it to lodge in his stomach. The French commander was escorted through the city gate by three soldiers and brought to the military surgeon. But nothing could be done, and he died the next day. Montcalm's successor surrendered the city. The great war between France and Britain went on officially for three and a half more years before the negotiators at Paris signed a peace treaty in 1763. In reality, it had ended on the cloudy battlefield at Quebec, where both brave commanders surrendered their lives.

News of Wolfe's victory deeply affected the North American public. The young hero had given his life to save Protestant America from Catholic France and his sacrifice took on epic proportions.

The French and Indian War

A World War for Empire Though they had claimed and occupied much of North America for more than a hundred years, the French had by no means settled it. In the mid-eighteenth century there were only about 55,000 French settlers in North America, the overwhelming majority in the far northeast and along the St. Lawrence River and the remainder distributed in widely scattered trading posts on the Great Lakes and the Ohio and Mississippi rivers. Quebec and Montreal were the only towns of consequence on

As time went on it became apparent that the Iroquois tribes were more friendly to the French settlers of North America than they were to the English. In the eighteenth century Governor James DeLancey of New York stood before Iroquois chieftains and read a proclamation pledging to "brighten the Chain of Friendship . . . Inviolate and Free from Rust." As each part of the speech was translated, the Indians were presented with a decorative belt, to which they gave a ceremonial *"yo-heigh-eigh"* in unison. Normally the tribes voice their agreements individually, *yo-heigh-eigh*s coming one after another. By mixing them together, noted a member of the audience the Iroquois delegates "had a mind to disguise that all the nations did not give their hearty assent to the Covenant."

J. Hector St. John de Crèvecouer, a Frenchman who came to the colonies in 1759 and lived there until 1780, wrote Letters from an American Farmer. *Here he describes society in British North America.*

"Here are no aristocratical families, no courts, no kings, no bishops, no ecclesiastical dominion, no invisible power giving to a few a very visible one; no great manufacturers employing thousands, no great refinements of luxury. The rich and the poor are not so far removed from each other as they are in Europe. Some few towns excepted, we are all tillers of the earth, from Nova Scotia to West Florida. We are a people of cultivators, scattered over an immense territory, communicating with each other by means of good roads and navigable rivers, united by the silken bands of mild government, all respecting the laws, without dreading their power, because they are equitable. . . ."

the St. Lawrence, and New Orleans the only important town on the Mississippi. The vast area of New France, comprising most of present-day Canada, the Ohio Valley, the Mississippi, and lands to its west, constituted nonetheless a serious threat to the English colonies. France established a brisk fur trade with Algonquian-speaking Indian tribes and supplied guns to their Indian allies. As French traders moved along the St. Lawrence and into the Great Lakes region, they established Indian alliances that would later aid them in fighting the English.

Since the last years of the seventeenth century Britain and France had been rivals in Europe and wherever their empires clashed. The War of the League of Augsburg, waged from 1689 to 1697, had led to French and Indian raids on New England's frontier and attacks by New Englanders on the French in Canada. The British colonists called this conflict King William's War. The War of the Spanish Succession, from 1702 to 1713, again produced its small counterpart in America, Queen Anne's War. So far the colonial fighting had consisted of border raids between British and French colonists, sometimes employing their Indian allies. The American phase of the War of the Austrian Succession, which took place from 1740 to 1748, was called King George's War. New England troops won an important victory in the capture of Louisburg, which guarded the entrance to the St. Lawrence River. Colonists were disappointed when Britain returned Louisburg in the Treaty of Aix-la-Chapelle. Territory the British retained, now called Nova Scotia, the French had named l'Acadie. Many of the French colonists, the Acadians, remained hostile to British rule, and in 1749 the conquerors undertook a deportation of Acadians. Between six and seven thousand left, some to France, others later to return to Nova Scotia, still others going to Louisiana, where to this day their descendants are known as Cajuns, a variant of "Acadians." Then in 1756 Britain and France began their seven-year world war for empire. The fighting in North America became known as the French and Indian War.

Skirmishes in the Ohio Valley

A new governor of Virginia, Robert Dinwiddie, had instructions to promote the concerns of Britain in the Ohio Valley, but to do so without antagonizing the French. Accordingly he dispatched a seven-man mission, which included a twenty-one-year-old surveyor named George Washington, to urge the French to respect British rights in the area. The mission was politely received and, with equal politeness, informed that the construction of Fort Duquesne would begin in the spring. The place where the fort was to be located, the site of present-day Pittsburgh, was in territory then claimed by Virginia. Upon being told of the French intention, Governor Dinwiddie rushed a workforce to the area with instructions to build a British fort on the spot. To protect the workers young Washington followed with troops a little later, quite unaware that the French had expelled the workforce almost immediately upon its arrival. In May 1754 Washington was encamped on the Monongahela River when he learned of the existence of a small French contingent a few miles ahead. He ordered a night march and attacked the French, capturing twenty-one and killing ten. Then he pushed on until he learned that the French were about to attack him in force. He retreated and hastily threw up a stockade, imaginatively called Fort Necessity. In June his troops of 150 grew by 200 more men, and on July 3 he was attacked by 500 French and 400 Indians. After a nine-day siege Washington surrendered. The future commander of the American forces had gotten his first taste of battle. "I heard the bullets whistle," Washington wrote to his half-brother, and there was "something charming in the sound."

Albany Plan of Union   Even before Washington's abortive expedition, the Board of Trade had ordered a conference of colonial officials, and even as Washington was blundering in the wilderness a colonial congress was in session in Albany, New York. Schemes for uniting the colonies were afloat at the congress. The Pennsylvania delegation, led by Benjamin Franklin, proposed what is known as the Albany Plan of Union. The plan called for a president-general for the British colonies, to be chosen and supported by the Crown, and a grand council, representing the several colonies in proportion to their contributions to the colonial treasury. This agency was to have general legislative and taxing powers for defense costs and improving Indian relations. The delegates approved the plan with modifications, but the colonies rejected it. The first effort to establish an American union was stillborn. The colonial legislatures had been jealous above all of sharing their power to tax. That jealousy would later involve them in a revolution against Great Britain.

General Braddock's Defeat   As hostilities continued on the frontier it remained obvious that some sort of plan would have to be devised for coping with the French in America. Official British policy was to engage in what, at a later day, would be called limited warfare. Two British regiments at half strength, the rest to be made up of colonial militiamen, would march up from Virginia to attack Fort Duquesne. Another similar force, to be gathered in New England and New York, would seize Fort Niagara. General Edward Braddock, sixty years old with forty-five years' military experience, was put in charge of the campaign.

Braddock arrived in Virginia early in 1755, then delegated responsibility for raising troops for the multiple attack, and chose Washington as one of his aides-de-camp. In June he started over the mountains with a force of over 1,400 men and 150 wagons, cutting a road through the wilderness as he went. In an open space near Fort Duquesne on July 9 French and Indian forces fighting from behind cover surprised Braddock's troops. Some Virginia troops abandoned the close-ranked, conventional eighteenth-century military formation and tried to fight in the frontier manner, which meant using cover. Some of the British regulars attempted the same thing, but Braddock and his officers ordered them back into line, where they were slashed by enemy fire until they broke. Many ran, as George Washington said, "as sheep pursued by dogs." By the next evening Braddock's forces had been destroyed; Braddock himself was killed. Of 1,459 men, 977 were dead or wounded. In the

Virtual Representation

In the eighteenth century the popularly elected lower houses of the legislatures in the royal colonies protested against whatever they found to be heavy-handed in imperial policy or in the conduct of governors. In time the lower houses came to argue that since colonists were entitled to "the rights of Englishmen," they were entitled to representation in any body that governed them. The full implication of this argument, which it took a generation or more to realize, was that, since colonists were not properly represented in Parliament, only the lower colonial houses could legitimately pass laws for British America.

Some British defenders argued that the colonists were already "virtually" represented in Parliament and needed no other voice in the imperial government. A member of Parliament, so the concept of virtual representation argued, spoke not only for his own constituency but for other constituencies with similar interests. This reasoning would hold that a member of Parliament from a seaport town in England also represented Bostonians or New Yorkers. It made a certain sense to the English because the franchise in Britain was severely limited. But on the other side of the Atlantic, virtual representation made no sense.

North, the planned expedition on Fort Niagara, directed by the new Governor William Shirley of Massachusetts, got as far as Oswego, half the distance, before being defeated.

Attack on Canada

By the middle of 1756 the French had taken the offensive, and throughout 1757 French forces won victory after victory. Then a new expedition, commanded by General John Forbes, took the remains of Fort Duquesne, which the French, deserted by their Indian allies, had blown up before retreating. Forbes immediately began to reconstruct the fort, rechristened Fort Pitt after the great British statesman. In 1759 an expedition of 3,500 Americans, 2,500 British regulars, and 1,000 Indians under Sir William Johnson seized Fort Niagara, cutting off Montreal and Quebec from the Great Lakes region. A force commanded by Sir Jeffrey Amherst was directed to clear the French posts on Lake Champlain and lay siege to Quebec from the southwest. General James Wolfe was ordered to move with a combined army and naval force up the St. Lawrence and attack Quebec from the other side. Amherst's expedition took both Ticonderoga and Crown Point, but was so slow in the doing that it was forced to stop on Lake Champlain for the winter of 1759–60. That left Wolfe to attack Quebec alone. Montcalm remained inside the fortress, confident that high cliffs would prevent any attack on Quebec from the southwest by way of the Plains of Abraham. The ensuing battle and English victory were a momentous occasion for the future of North America.

Armies had to drag their artillery with them, sometimes through deep snow. (*Courtesy, Scribner's Archives*)

Imperial Reform

The Treaty of Paris (1763)

The French and Indian War was an invigorating experience for Americans. They had fought well in a score of battles from Canada to the Caribbean. After 1763 they would exhibit a new confidence and pride in what they, mere provincials before, could accomplish. For a century New France and then Louisiana, representing absolutism and clericalism, had hung like a sword over Anglo-America, forcing the colonists to acknowledge dependence on the British army and navy. The Treaty of Paris in 1763 changed all this. To Great Britain, which had already won Canada by the surrender of Montreal in 1760, France now relinquished all claims to America east of the Mississippi. Spain, an ally of France, turned over Florida to the British. In compensation for Spanish losses, the French gave Spain New Orleans and all their possessions west of the Mississippi. Now that the most dangerous foreign power had been removed, the colonists were free to reassess their relationship with the mother country.

The British were aware of the possibility of change in the colonial temperament. During the negotiations at Paris the Duke of Bedford spoke for returning Canada to France to prevent Americans from growing too mighty and asserting their independence. Bedford's views were overruled, but in later years there were those who believed that the conquest of New France had been a mistake.

During the fierce debate between the colonies and Britain that preceded independence, the loyalist governor of Massachusetts, Thomas Hutchinson, noted:

"Before the peace of 1763 I thought nothing so much to be desired as the cession of Canada. I am now convinced that if it had remained to the French none of the spirit of opposition to the Mother Country would have yet appeared and I think the effects of it worse than all we had to fear from the French or Indians."

Renewed Conflict with Indians

During the war American settlers and Indian traders had moved into the trans-Appalachian region in the wake of British victories over the French. The newcomers often plied the Indians with rum and then "bought" their lands for a few cheap goods and rifles and powder. Once the Americans poured across the mountains in force after 1763, the Indian frontier exploded. One of the Indian leaders was the Delaware Prophet, a visionary and seer who assured his followers that if they rejected the European's ways, they would regain their former strength and former lands. The other, the Ottawa chief Pontiac, led his warriors in May 1763 against the British fort at Detroit and came close to taking it. Pontiac's attack commenced a massive Indian uprising all along the northern frontier; by June only three major British military posts remained.

The British quickly struck back. Two columns went to the relief of the surviving posts. One, led by Colonel Henry Bouquet, forced Pontiac to accept a truce. Soon after, Pontiac's chief allies made peace with the English, and before long Pontiac himself came to terms with the British and Americans. On the Pennsylvania frontier in 1764 a band known as the Paxton Boys attacked some peaceful Indians and then marched on Philadelphia, "uttering hideous cries in imitation of the war whoop" and bent on killing the Indian refugees who had fled to the capital for protection. Benjamin Franklin persuaded them not to invade the city.

The End of Salutary Neglect

The French forced the British government to focus attention on American affairs as never before, and the experience was an eye-opener. As British officials saw it, the Americans had behaved badly. Their illegal trade with the enemy had profited them and made the war more costly in men and money. British officials argued that the easy and benign policy of governing the colonies by "salutary neglect," a policy of leaving the colonies alone, would have to be replaced by a tighter, more rational, and financially sounder system. Spokesmen for the Americans pointed out that heavy local taxation for the repayment of the colonial war debt already burdened British America. Colonists were also prepared to argue that the Navigation Acts pulled wealth from the colonies into Britain.

The chief advocate of the British position was George Grenville, Chancellor of the Exchequer and King George III's chief minister following the retirement of William Pitt, the great wartime leader. Grenville was a man of limited vision who treated the empire as if it were a business concern. As a contemporary noted, Grenville judged "a national saving of two inches of candle . . . a greater triumph than all Pitt's victories." He soon initiated measures to reduce British expenses and to generate income for the mother country.

Grenville first took aim at policy toward the West and the Indians. To generate orderly settlement and in an attempt to prevent further Indian wars caused by land-hungry settlers, the Proclamation of 1763 set the limit of colonial settlement at the crest of the Appalachians. All colonists west of that line must "forthwith . . . remove themselves." British military authorities would now be in charge of all Indian territory

King George III, at age thirty-three.
(Courtesy, Library of Congress)

west of the mountains; all traders in Indian territory would have to be licensed, and they could trade only at designated points under British military supervision. The Proclamation was soon followed by a flurry of measures designed to raise revenue in America whenever the colonists might refuse to provide for their own defense.

The intention of the Sugar Act of 1764, a revision of the Molasses Act of 1733, was to increase the scanty receipts of the British customs service in America. The law added a dozen items to the list of enumerated American exports that must go first to Britain to be taxed before they could be sent elsewhere. The law also established a new set of taxes for goods imported into the colonies and set up new admiralty courts with power to enforce their collection with the aid of general search warrants, called "writs of assistance." The most important change affected the trade between the mainland colonies and the West Indies. Molasses was the chief raw material in the making of rum, a major New England industry. For many years American merchants had relied on the French and Dutch Caribbean islands for this product, which was cheaper there than in the British Caribbean islands. By smuggling, the colonists had evaded the high tax Britain had imposed on foreign-produced molasses. Because the duty of sixpence a gallon had been

British Legislation Affecting the Colonies, 1764–74			
Legislation	*Date*	*Provisions*	*Colonial Reaction*
Sugar Act	April 5, 1764	Revised duties on sugar, coffee, tea, wine, other imports; expanded jurisdiction of vice-admiralty courts	Several colonial assemblies protest taxation for revenue
Stamp Act	March 22, 1765; repealed March 18, 1766	Printed documents issued only on stamped paper purchased from appointed distributors	Riots in some cities; collectors forced to resign; Stamp Act Congress (October 1765)
Quartering Act	May 1765	Colonists must supply British troops with housing, candles, firewood, and so on	Protest in assemblies; New York Assembly punished for failure to comply
Declaratory Act	March 18, 1766	Parliament declares its authority "in all cases whatsoever"	Ignored
Townshend Revenue Acts	June 26, 29, July 2, 1767; all repealed—except duty on tea, March 1770	New duties on glass, lead, paper, paints, tea; customs collections tightened	Nonimportation of British goods
Tea Act	May 10, 1773	Parliament gives East India Company the sole right to sell tea directly to Americans (some duties on tea reduced)	Tea destroyed in Boston (December 16, 1773)
Coercive Acts (Intolerable Acts)	March–June 1774	Closes port of Boston; restricts town meetings; troops quartered in Boston	Boycott of British goods; First Continental Congress convenes (September 1774)

uncollectable, the British now cut the duty in half—but determined to collect the money.

A second measure of 1764, the Currency Act, struck at the practice of issuing legal tender, or paper money. The colonials believed paper to be an indispensable medium of exchange in a chronically coin-poor community. British merchants had long complained, however, that the paper issued under the colonial legal-tender laws was a cheap and flimsy currency. Its use by Americans, especially southern planters, in payment of their debts to British creditors amounted to a scaling down of the debt. The right to issue legal tender had already been forbidden the New England colonies. Now, the prohibition would extend to the middle and southern colonies as well.

The Proclamation of 1763 threatened the ambitions of land speculators, Indian traders, and would-be settlers in the West alike. For the moment, Americans interested in western development simply ignored British policy and went ahead with their own plans. As George Washington wrote a fellow land speculator: "any person who . . . neglects the present opportunity of hunting out good Lands and in some measure marking and distinguishing them for his own . . . will never regain it." Reaction to the Revenue and Currency Acts was more vigorous. A Boston town meeting listened to James Otis's impassioned attack on writs of assistance and condemned the Revenue Act as taxation without representation. A group of Boston merchants, joined by the city's artisans, resolved to boycott several items imported from Britain. By the end of 1764 a limited boycott of British goods had spread to several other colonies.

The New York Gazette *reported that in New Haven, as a patriotic act,*

"the young Gentlemen of Yale have unanimously agreed not to make use of any foreign spiritous liquors. . . . This will not only greatly diminish the Expences of Education, but prove, as may be presumed, very favourable to the Health and Improvement of the Students."

The Stamp Act Crisis

Trouble awaited the Grenville program. But few people could have anticipated the full extent of American hostility to British policy. Then came the Stamp Act—the first attempt to impose an internal tax on American colonists, a tax on their activities within their own localities. Previous taxes had been external; they had applied to American commerce with the outside world.

Grenville must have realized the danger in the new policy, for when he asked for a tax that would apply directly to transactions in America rather than to overseas trade, he promised to consider other means of raising revenue in the colonies if Americans objected. But he gave the colonial legislatures little time to respond. When their London agents, including Benjamin Franklin, the agent for Pennsylvania, tried to induce Grenville to withdraw the stamp tax proposal, he refused.

In February 1765 the fatal measure came before a poorly attended session of the House of Commons. The debate, though brief, was significant as an expression of the differing views of the colonies that were then current among Englishmen.

Speaking for Grenville, Charles Townshend gave voice to a widespread condescension toward Americans that would poison relations between the two peoples. Townshend called Americans "children

Demonstrations erupted throughout the colonies in response to "taxation without representation." In New England, suspected supporters of the hated Stamp Act were hanged in effigy. *(Courtesy, Scribner's Archives)*

(Courtesy, Scribner's Archives)

planted by our care." They had been "nourished up" by British "indulgence" and protected by British arms. Would "they grudge to contribute their mite" to relieve the British people from "the heavy burdens" they suffered?

Townshend's remarks offended Colonel Isaac Barré, an officer who had fought under Wolfe and unlike other upper-class Englishmen argued for relaxing the bonds of empire. Townshend was seriously mistaken, Barré declared. The Americans had been planted not by British care, but rather by British oppression, which had driven refugees to the New World. Nor were they nurtured by British indulgence. Rather they "grew by your . . . neglect of 'em." These "sons of liberty," Barré said, had suffered under greedy British officials for many years. Nor had they been protected by British arms; they had nobly fought for themselves.

Americans would cheer Barré's words, and rebel organizations would soon adopt "Sons of Liberty" as their name. But Parliament was unmoved. On March 22, 1765, it passed the Stamp Act, taxing newspapers, almanacs, pamphlets, legal documents, insurance policies, dice, playing cards, and other items. These taxes would be paid in the form of a stamp, purchasable from officials to be chosen from among Americans residing in the colonies, and placed on the specified documents. England had a similar tax, and Grenville expected the law to raise £60,000 of the £300,000 needed to maintain the British military establishment in North America. Tax evaders could be tried in vice-admiralty courts, which had no juries.

News of the Stamp Act's passage reached America in mid-April. Although the act would not take effect until November 1, consternation was immediate.

In the Virginia House of Burgesses at Williamsburg the young lawyer Patrick Henry denounced the measure in a speech that has become famous. "Caesar had his Brutus; Charles the First his Cromwell; and George the Third—[here tradition has it that the House Speaker interrupted with a shout of "Treason!" whereupon Henry continued] may profit by their example. If this be treason, let us make the most of it." Although some doubt exists that the eloquent and ringing version well known to generations of American schoolchildren represents Henry's actual words, he apparently came close to suggesting rebellion. After this speech the delegates at Williamsburg adopted a set of resolutions proclaiming that the House of Burgesses possessed the "only and sole power to lay taxes . . . upon the inhabitants of this colony," and that Virginians were "not bound to yield obedience to any law" that Parliament might pass to tax them. Various of these Virginia Resolves appeared in colonial newspapers, serving as "an alarum bell to the disaffected." Soon almost all the other colonies had adopted similar resolutions. In June 1765, when the Massachusetts General Court proposed that representatives of all the colonies meet in New York in October to consider joint action against the detested measure, nine of the colonies quickly and enthusiastically accepted the invitation.

Long before the Stamp Act Congress assembled, Americans resorted to more than words to express their indignation.

Sons of Liberty

In August 1765 Boston's Sons of Liberty hanged in effigy the man who was to be the new tax commissioner, Andrew Oliver. Oliver was a brother-in-law of Lieutenant Governor Thomas Hutchinson, who was also chief justice of the Superior Court of Massachusetts. Later the mob tore down a house that Oliver had allegedly built to serve as his tax office. The crowd next marched on his home and broke all the windows. The following day Oliver resigned his tax commission. The Boston Sons of Liberty next attacked the house of William Story, deputy register of the admiralty court, smashed down the doors, and burned Story's public and private papers. Another contingent sacked the home of the comptroller of customs, carried away his records, and pillaged his wine cellar. On August 26 the mob targeted Hutchinson's three-story brick mansion. The swarm battered down the walls, burned the furniture, destroyed the library, tore windows and doors from their frames, drank all the liquor, and even cut down the trees in the Hutchinson yard. Individuals also stole £900 in cash and walked off with the family silver. Hutchinson, who escaped through his back garden, had actually opposed both the Revenue Act and the Stamp Act.

At the State House the morning after, a disheveled Thomas Hutchinson took his place in court without his chief justice's robes. It was the second time a member of the family had faced the wrath of Boston. Thomas Hutchinson was the great-great-grandson of Anne Hutchinson. She had stood up to the governmental and ministerial establishment of the colony. With an equally stubborn courage that he would display in the aftermath of the Boston Massacre of 1770, he was prepared to stand up to the mindless fury of the mob.

The violence appalled even some opponents of British policy. The Boston town meeting condemned the rioting, and the authorities issued a warrant for the arrest of Ebenezer McIntosh, the leader of the Sons of Liberty, but the damages were never repaid.

In Newport, Rhode Island, a crowd burned and sacked the homes of "Tories" (so called after the more conservative of Britain's political parties), who defended British authority. In Newport as in Boston, the mobs forced the Stamp Act collector to resign. In Connecticut, citizens conducted a mock trial of stamp distributors. New York Sons of Liberty vented their fury on the house of the British military commander who had sworn to "cram the Stamp Act down the people's throats." In Charleston, capital of South Carolina, a mob attacked the house of the prominent merchant Henry Laurens, suspected of being the future stamp distributor. Only Laurens's bold denials kept the crowd from doing harm to him and his property.

So it went from colony to colony. Everywhere Tories were intimidated, and collectors forced to surrender their commissions. When the stamps finally arrived, there was no one to sell them or to see that they were affixed to the designated documents.

Crowds like those that roamed the streets during the Stamp Act crisis would appear in later confrontations between colonists and the British government. They were, in fact, a feature of eighteenth-century politics. Across the Atlantic, the London mob was a menacing presence to the government. And before the end of the eighteenth century, the Paris mobs of the French Revolution would enter history.

The Stamp Act Congress — In the early fall of October 1765, twenty-seven delegates from nine colonies—all but New Hampshire, North Carolina, Virginia, and Georgia—convened in New York to consider united action against the detested law. This Stamp Act Congress was relatively conservative, but its Declaration of Rights and Grievances effectively summed up most of the colonists' complaints. Taxation, the Declaration asserted, could be imposed only by the people's consent, "given personally, or by their representatives." Trial by jury, ignored by the new admiralty courts, was an inherent right of Englishmen. The Stamp Act as well as the other recent measures restricting American commerce, the Congress declared, must be repealed.

Far more effective than the words of the Stamp Act Congress were the actions of businessmen in the major American port cities. Two hundred New York merchants agreed not to take new orders for British goods so long as the Stamp Act remained. They were joined by the traders of Philadelphia, Boston, Salem, and other ports. Meanwhile, November 1, the date when the Act was supposed to take effect, rolled around. For a while business was disrupted, since very little could be done legally without the stamps. Slowly it resumed without them. The law was dead.

The British government could not ignore the American response to the Stamp Act. Some Englishmen were outraged at American defiance. Dr. Samuel Johnson, the critic and lexicographer, called the opponents of the Act "incendiaries" and "fractious demagogues." But others, particularly merchants who found their American business dwindling, sympathized with the Americans and bombarded Parliament with petitions for repeal of the measure. In Manchester, Leeds, Nottingham,

THE STAMP ACT CRISIS

The Stamp Act crisis was in several senses the "prologue to the Revolution." What made it particularly so was that, as in later conflicts, the disgruntled colonists along with their opponents were stating the clash as a matter of absolute principle. It was a foretaste of the peculiarly intellectual flavor that characterized the American Revolution.

The colonists objected not simply to the particular exercise of power (which, however ill-advised, was anything but tyrannical), but to what it boded for the future. Americans of the revolutionary generation had a positive genius for searching out the farthermost implications of every British action. Hence they devoted their most vigorous condemnations not to the Stamp Act but to the principles it embodied. The British were equally sensitive to questions of principle. For them, too, the Stamp Act quickly ceased to be a mere means of raising revenue and became instead a test of parliamentary authority. Each party, believing that the other was aiming at the total overthrow of legitimate law and justice, assumed that it had to defend itself by the assertion of its absolute and inviolate rights.

Both sets of suspicions were initially mistaken. Parliament did not wish to enslave America. It wished merely to oblige the colonists to pay a larger share of the expenses of running the empire. The colonists did not wish to be independent. They wished simply not to be taxed internally without their consent. But the intense suspiciousness on both sides meant that their expectations, however wrong initially, quickly became self-fulfilling prophecies. Colonial intransigence provoked ever sterner measures from Parliament. The colonists in reaction advanced ever greater claims to home rule, culminating in the Declaration of Independence.

and other English industrial towns, thousands of workingmen lost their jobs as the workshops and mills dependent on the American market slowed and then stopped.

The man who now had to face the uproar was the Marquis of Rockingham, who had succeeded Grenville as prime minister in July 1765. Rockingham's group drew its support largely from the merchants and manufacturers and was particularly sensitive to their plight. Leading the battle for repeal in Parliament was William Pitt, the great wartime prime minister. Pitt eloquently defended the colonists' rights. "The Americans," he declared, "are the sons, not the bastards of England." The Stamp Act must "be REPEALED ABSOLUTELY, TOTALLY, IMMEDIATELY. . . ." In March 1766 Parliament complied. But at the same time it passed the so-called Declaratory Act, asserting its power to make laws binding the American colonies "in all cases whatsoever."

Amid general rejoicing at the end of the detested stamp tax, few Americans took note of the Declaratory Act. Merchants immediately abandoned their nonimportation agreements and placed large orders with British suppliers. New York City voted to erect statues to Pitt and George III. Other towns and villages put up monuments to Pitt, the "Great Commoner." The ordinary people rang church bells, put lighted candles in their windows, and fired off guns. The Boston Sons of Liberty built on Boston Common "a magnificent pyramid, illuminated with 280 Lamps." Crowning the pile was a box of fireworks that went off at dusk to splendid effect.

Whig Political Philosophy   By the 1760s many Americans were adhering to the Whig political theories popular among so many British citizens. Whig philosophy proceeded on the assumption that all human beings are vulnerable by nature to the seductions of money and power. Governments are necessary evils, needed for guaranteeing order and protecting basic liberties. But governments are tainted by the same human evils that make governments necessary. Government was synonymous with political and economic power. Individuals who hold public office, unless they are rigidly limited by constitutional restrictions, are virtually certain to abuse their power eventually. They will use the power of government to promote their own personal interests or to hurt their political opponents. Every institution and tradition that limits the arbitrary power of government deserves therefore the most careful preservation.

Naturally suspicious of politicians, Americans were always worried about government's using its authority in abusive and unconstitutional ways. Their own British heritage had given them strong beliefs in representative government, jury trials, and freedom from unreasonable searches and seizures. Both the Sugar Act of 1764 and the Stamp Act of 1765 had, in the opinion of many Americans, compromised those liberties. They were ready to resist any future violations.

Even angry colonists, then, still saw themselves as part of the empire, subjects of the King, sharing in the rights that belonged to the British nation and history. But recent events had made them touchy; they were developing a habit of asking large questions about the legitimacy of the actions of the British government. And in the Stamp Act

A popular song was written for the celebration in Boston of the repeal of the Stamp Act:

In spite of each parasite, each cringing slave,
Each cautious dastard, each oppressive knave,
Each gibing ass, that reptile of an hour,
The supercilious pimp of abject slaves in power,
We are met to celebrate in festive mirth,
The day that gave our freedom second birth,
That tells us, British Grenville never more
Shall dare usurp unjust, illegal power,
Or threaten America's free sons with chains,
While the least spark of ancient fire remains.

A teapot celebrating Parliament's repeal of the Stamp Act in March 1766. *(Courtesy, Essex Institute, Salem, Massachusetts)*

Congress they had gained experience in confronting Great Britain not as Virginians or people of Massachusetts but as united colonists, as Americans.

The British Blunder Again

**The
Quartering
Act Crisis**

In 1765 General Thomas Gage, the commander of all British forces in North America, asked Parliament to pass an act that would reduce the financial burdens associated with the defense of the colonies. In March Parliament passed the Quartering Act. It required colonial officials, for a two-year period, to provide barracks and supplies for the British troops. While the Stamp Act was lighting a political firestorm in the colonies, the new law was further stoking the flames.

The French and Indian War, by eliminating France as a North American power, appeared substantially to reduce the need for the permanent stationing of British troops in the thirteen colonies. The Indians had been driven far away into the western lands. Most British troops, however, were still billeted in or near the major American population centers. Were the troops really there to protect the colonies or to control them?

In December 1765 General Gage asked the New York legislature to obey the Quartering Act and provide the funds necessary to support his troops. The legislators refused, arguing that because so many British troops, as well as Gage's headquarters, were located in New York, the financial burden fell too heavily on them. Tensions mounted throughout 1766, aggravated when Parliament passed a second Quartering Act providing for the billeting of soldiers in inns, alehouses, and vacant buildings. Brief skirmishes occurred between New York citizens and British soldiers in August 1766, and in December the legislature refused to appropriate any money for the troops. In retaliation, Parliament suspended the New York assembly, an act many New Yorkers considered a violation of their constitutional rights. The controversy did not subside until October 1, 1767, when the New York assembly finally appropriated £3,000 for the support of Gage's troops.

**Townshend
Duties**

Many British leaders still wanted colonials to pay a larger share of their administrative and military costs. In early 1767, Charles Townshend, Chancellor of the Exchequer, unveiled his program. The colonies had successfully resisted the Stamp Act, which had taxed their internal business without their consent. But the colonials themselves had not yet challenged Parliament's right to tax their external commerce, which could be perceived as coming within Parliament's authority to regulate the affairs of the empire as a whole. It might therefore still impose an import tax. Capitalizing on the distinction between "internal" and "external" taxation, Townshend proposed taxing a wide range of colonial imports including glass, paper, lead, and tea. These duties, he argued, would raise badly needed funds and also teach the disruptive colonials that Parliament had the authority to tax them. He further proposed creation

Grant Wood, *Daughters of Revolution*. In this twentieth-century painting, the artist captured a later proud group of upper-class women who could trace their ancestry to the American Revolution. *(Courtesy, The Edwin and Virginia Irwin Memorial)*

of a new American customs service as well as a crackdown on New York's continually defiant assembly. After Parliament enacted all these potentially explosive measures, the ministry indicated its determination to enforce the trade laws. In the fall of 1767 when the Acts went into effect, Parliament appointed several unpopular officials to the new customs board and established the body's headquarters in Boston, the center of opposition to stricter commercial regulation.

In some areas, enforcement of commercial regulations broke down almost completely. A Boston ship's captain, Daniel Malcolm, drew a pistol on two revenue agents searching for illegal wine in his basement. Returning with the sheriff and a search warrant, the agents discovered the captain's house surrounded by a crowd of his friends, and the harried sheriff avoided a direct confrontation only by stalling for time until the search warrant expired. After the officials departed, Captain Malcolm treated his protectors to buckets of smuggled wine. Such cases were not infrequent.

Investigating previous cases of enforcement, Townshend's customs board discovered only six seizures and one smuggling conviction in all of New England during two and one half years. Mobs had rescued three of the seized ships, and colonial juries acquitted two other defendants. Initially the new customs officials fared little better, enforcing restrictions only enough to enrage colonial merchants. The same Captain Malcolm brought an entire load of illegal wine into Boston on small boats during the night and then boldly sailed his empty ship into port the next day. The vessel's water line revealed his subterfuge, but enraged customs officers could find no Bostonian who would testify against him. In June 1768 a British customs official was locked in the cabin of John Hancock's sloop *Liberty* while the crew unloaded untaxed madeira wine. When customs officials tried to seize the vessel, citizens forced them to flee to the British garrison at Castle William, where they appealed for British troops to help keep order.

Another Boycott
Conditioned by the Stamp Act, Americans were sensitive about any further extension of British power, and an outcry greeted the Townshend Duties. That the duties did not constitute an internal tax failed to impress the colonists. This time, though, leading merchants and lawyers kept

In Virginia "An Address to the Ladies" asked them to forswear imported finery:

And as one all agree that you'll not married be
To such as will wear London factory,
But at first sight refuse, tell them such you do choose
As encourage our own manufactory.
No more ribands wear, nor in rich dress appear,
Love your country much better than fine things,
Begin without passion, 'twill soon be the fashion
To grace your smooth locks with a twine string.

dissent under control. In each colony, the Sons of Liberty and the merchants adopted strict nonimportation agreements. In Massachusetts early in 1768 the popular Samuel Adams drew up a "circular letter" laying out British misdeeds and suggesting united colonial actions. The Massachusetts General Court approved it, and so did several other colonial assemblies. Governor Francis Bernard of Massachusetts did not approve, and dissolved the General Court. In South Carolina, the legislature resolved that until the colonies were restored to their former freedom by repeal of the Townshend Duties the people of the colony would refuse to import any of the manufactures of Great Britain. South Carolinians would practice the "utmost economy in our persons, houses, and furniture, particularly that we will give no mourning, or gloves, or scarves at funerals."

The Townshend Duties and the nonimportation movement encouraged a great deal of pamphleteering advocating a new imperial relationship with more freedom for the colonists—or, rather, with the liberties of Englishmen that they claimed already to possess. The most effective and eloquent of these arguments was John Dickinson's "Letters of a Pennsylvania Farmer to the Inhabitants of the British Colonies" (1768). Posing as a simple Pennsylvania yeoman, Dickinson cautioned against violence and expressed an affection for "mother Britain" that foreshadowed his later refusal to sign the Declaration of Independence. But on the question of British taxation he was adamant. And Dickinson meant all taxation, taxes on imports as well as on internal business.

Lord North   In the summer of 1768 Governor Bernard called on British authorities for troops to restore order in unruly Boston and prevent a repetition of the *Liberty* incident. In September the new British prime minister, Lord Frederick North, ordered two regiments of redcoats from Ireland to the rebellious Massachusetts capital despite threats of armed resistance by the Sons of Liberty.

North and his colleagues were having second thoughts about the Townshend Duties. Widely evaded, the taxes brought in virtually no revenue. Particularly galling was the smuggling of untaxed Dutch tea into the colonies. And nonimportation agreements had reduced annual exports to America. The British government was in a quandary: repealing the duties would end nonimportation, but it would also be the second time the British government had backed down.

In the end, the North ministry yielded to American pressure, but in a grudging and halfhearted way that only highlighted British weakness without calling forth American gratitude. In 1770 Parliament allowed the Quartering Act to expire and rescinded the taxes on glass, paper, and painters' colors; it also reduced the tea tax from twelve to three pence a pound, but did not repeal it.

This partial repeal ended the boycott. It did little to end resentment of Britain. As one American merchant remarked about the repeal: "Doing things by Halves of all others [is] the worst Method." Many fundamental disagreements with Britain persisted. The whole question of the constitutional relationship between mother country and colonies was still unsettled. What body, colonists asked, was the ultimate source of authority in America, the colonial legislatures or Parliament? By now some colonials were advocating an American relationship with Great Britain resembling that of the later British dominions within the British Commonwealth. The King of England would also be King of the colonies, but each American colony would be autonomous in all its domestic affairs. Few, if any, thought of complete independence. Americans remained proud of their British heritage and of the rights of "free-born Britons." Even the most ardent champions of colonial freedoms still insisted that they merely wished to preserve these rights from the arrogant usurpers who had gathered around the King.

The Boston Massacre

Quartering British Troops   In the months following repeal of the Townshend Duties, resentment toward Britain remained particularly strong in Boston. Aside from the long-standing grievances the Boston townspeople shared with other communities, there was the question of the recently arrived troops. If Massachusetts was not at war, what justified the sending of nearly 2,000 soldiers to Boston Common?

" 'The Bloody Massacre perpetrated in King Street, Boston on March 5th, 1770, by a party of the 29th Reg [iment].' Engrav'd, Printed and Sold by Paul Revere, Boston." *(Courtesy, Museum of Fine Arts, Boston)*

THE BOSTON MASSACRE

John Tudor, a Boston merchant, described the "Massacre" in his diary:

"On Monday Evening the 5th current, a few Minutes after 9 O'Clock a most horrid murder was committed in King Street before the Customhouse Door by 8 or 9 Soldiers under the Command of Capt Thos Preston drawn of from the Main Guard on the South side of the Townhouse.

This unhappy affair began by Some Boys & young fellows throwing Snow Balls at the sentry placed at the Customhouse Door. On which 8 or 9 Soldiers Came to his assistance. Soon after a Number of people colected, when the Capt commanded the Soldiers to fire, which they did and 3 Men were Kil'd on the Spot & several Mortaly Wounded, one of which died next morning. The Capt soon drew off his Soldiers up to the Main Guard, or the Consequencis mite have been terable, for on the Guns fiering the people were alarm'd & set the Bells a Ringing as if for Fire, which drew Multitudes to the place of action. Leu^t Governor Hutchinson, who was commander in Chefe, was sent for & Came to the Council Chamber, w[h]ere som of the Magistrates attended. The Governor desired the Multitude about 10 O'Clock to sepperat & go home peaceable & he would do all in his power that Justice shold be done &c. The 29 Rigiment being then under Arms on the south side of the Townhouse, but the people insisted that the Soldiers should be ordered to their Barracks 1st

Before the British regiments arrived in the fall of 1768, the Boston town meeting urged the people of the city to arm themselves and demanded that Governor Bernard call a meeting of the General Court, which he had dissolved in June. When he refused, spokesmen for Massachusetts called an assembly of the colony's towns as a substitute for the General Court. This "convention" helped to acquaint the citizens of smaller communities with the view of the radical leaders of the capital, and it demonstrated that John Hancock (Harvard '54), Boston's richest merchant, John Adams (Harvard '55) the prominent lawyer, his cousin Samuel Adams (Harvard '40), the failed brewery owner who found his true calling in political activism, and the rest spoke for a large number of the colony's people, not just for the merchants and artisans of the metropolis.

The day the convention adjourned, the British troops dispatched by North arrived in Boston harbor, protected by guns of British men-of-war. While the city's dubious citizens looked on, the soldiers debarked at the Long Wharf and marched up King Street to the music of drums and fifes. It was a moving sight, even for the most dedicated radicals. The men's red tunics, criss-crossed by white straps, and their black three-cornered hats were far more colorful than modern uniforms. Towering over the regular troops were the grenadiers, chosen for their height, a feature emphasized by their tall, mitre-shaped bearskin caps. The grenadier officers wore crimson sashes and carried swords at their sides.

Boston's pleasure at the bright display soon faded, however, and the troops found it no pleasure to be quartered among a hostile populace. While their officers had no difficulty finding good lodgings with wealthy Tories, the city council refused to assign barracks for the troops, and soldiers had to be scattered around the town at whatever empty buildings, generally workshops and warehouses, the British could rent. In a town of about 17,000 the redcoats were conspicuous.

before they would sepperat, Which being don the people sepperated about 1 O'Clock.—Capt Preston was taken up by a warrent given to the high Sherif by Justice Dania & Tudor and came under Examination about 2 O'clock & we sent him to Goal [jail] soon after 3, having Evidence sufficient, to committ him, on his ordering the soldiers to fire: So aboute 4 O'clock the Town became quiet. The next forenoon the 8 Soldiers that fired on the inhabitants was allso sent to Goal. Tuesday A.M. the inhabitants mett at Faneuil Hall & after some pertinant speches, chose a Committee of 15 Gentlem^n to waite on the Leu^t Governor in Council to request the immediate removeal of the Troops. . . .

(Thursday) Agreeable to a general request of the Inhabitants, were follow'd to the Grave (for they were all Buried in one) in succession the 4 Bodies of Mess^s Saml Gray Saml Maverick James Caldwell & Crispus Attucks, the unhappy Victims who fell in the Bloody Massacre. On this sorrowfull Occasion most of the shops & stores in Town were shut, all the Bells were order'd to toll a solom peal in Boston, Charleston, Cambridge & Roxbery. The several Hearses forming a junction in King Street, the Theatre of that inhuman Tradgedy, proceeded from thence thro' the main street, lengthened by an immence Concourse of people, So numerous as to be obliged to follow in Ranks of 4 & 6 abreast and brought up by a long Train of Carriages. The sorrow Visible in the Countenances, together with the peculiar solemnity, Surpass description, it was suppos'd that the Spectators & those that follow'd the corps amounted to 15,000, som supposed 20,000. Note Capt Preston was tried for his Life on the affare of the above Octob^r 24 1770. The Trial lasted 5 Days, but the Jury brought him in not Guilty."

Lobsterbacks   Before long, the bored troops turned for solace to Boston's cheap rum and loose women. To get money for their dissipations, many engaged in petty theft. Inevitably they got into fights, especially with sailors in the local taverns. When winter came many soldiers deserted. The citizens of the Massachusetts countryside had little love for the "lobsterbacks," as they termed the British troops with their long red coats. But they also refused to help the military authorities return deserters to duty. The colonists saw the redcoats as an army of occupation and both sides often traded insults.

On Friday, March 2, 1770, a civilian ropemaker, William Green, asked a soldier passing by, Patrick Walker of the Twenty-ninth Regiment, whether he wanted work. Such part-time jobs were permitted to off-duty soldiers, and Walker said yes. Green responded: "Then go clean my shithouse." Walker retorted in kind and left, threatening to come back with some friends. Soon afterward he appeared with forty of his mates, led by a tall, black regimental drummer. The soldiers, armed with clubs, sailed into Green and his friends, who defended themselves with sticks. When other civilians joined in, the soldiers retreated.

All that weekend rumors circulated that the soldiers intended revenge. And so they did. On the night of Monday the 5th, bands of soldiers and of citizens roved the icy streets of Boston looking for trouble. It came at Private White's sentry post adjacent to the Custom House, when a wigmaker's apprentice baited White until the sentry hit him with the butt of his gun. When the apprentice fled, a British sergeant pursued him, brandishing his musket.

News of the fight spread quickly, and a half-dozen young men descended on the sentry post screaming "Lousy rascal! Lobster son of a bitch!" Soon the swelling crowd pelted White with snowballs and jagged chunks of ice, crying "Kill him, kill him, knock him down." Finally Captain Thomas Preston, officer of the day, decided he must save White even at the risk of a serious confrontation. With six grenadiers he marched on the beleaguered sentry post and surrounded White. But with angry civilians pressing on him from every direction, Preston now found that he could not return to the safety of the barracks. He tried to persuade the crowd to disperse; its response was to dare the soldiers to shoot. At this point someone struck one of the redcoats with a club, knocking him off his feet. The soldier fired, and then another. A third pulled the trigger of his musket and hit Crispus Attucks, a black man, in the chest. By the time the shooting stopped, three Bostonians lay dead and two others were mortally wounded.

The whole city might have erupted in a bloody rebellion, but Lieutenant Governor Hutchinson intervened, and by promising a quick investigation and punishment of the guilty parties prevented a blow-up. Preston and his men were arrested and confined to jail pending trial. The silversmith Paul Revere quickly made an engraving of the "Bloody Massacre." The trial itself was conducted with propriety and fairness. Captain Preston hired as counsel two prominent Boston patriots, John Adams and Josiah Quincy, who took the case out of a combined concern for the colony's and their own good names. Bostonians wished to avoid any suspicion that the Massachusetts courts would not give the accused a fair trial. Adams demolished the charge that Preston had given the order to fire. He and Quincy appealed for fairness. "The eyes of all are upon you," Quincy told the jurors. The two defense lawyers called witnesses who demonstrated that the soldiers had been taunted and abused beyond bearing. Some soldiers were convicted of manslaughter but punishments were light. Massachusetts justice had been vindicated.

The trial eased angers in Boston and the colonies as a whole. It was followed by a period of relative calm in relations between Britain and the colonies. During these months the nonimportation agreements totally collapsed, despite the attempts of more radical colonials to continue them until tea too was exempted from duty. At Samuel Adams's suggestion the Boston town meeting organized a "committee of correspondence" to keep other towns informed of what the British were up to. "Let every town assemble" said Adams. "Let associations and combinations be everywhere set up, to consult and recover our just rights."

Phillis Wheatley, a seventeen-year-old slave girl who had published her first poem in Boston at age thirteen, wrote of the Boston Massacre, "AMERICANS were burden'd sore / When streets were crimson'd with their guiltless gore!"

Phillis Wheatley the poet.
(Courtesy, Library of Congress)

The *Gaspée* and the Boston Tea Party

The Burning of the *Gaspée*

Then in June 1772 came the *Gaspée* affair. Rhode Island, one of the two colonies whose charter did not require a governor appointed by the Crown (Connecticut was the other), had long been notorious for ignoring imperial trade laws. For years, Rhode Island's many coves and inlets had sheltered smugglers who defied the customs authorities with impunity. To stop the traffic, the British authorities finally dispatched the ship *Gaspée* to Narragansett Bay. Tricky tides ran the ship onto a sandbar near Providence. That night a band of Rhode Island Sons of Liberty boarded the stranded *Gaspée*, overwhelmed its captain and crew, and burned the vessel to the waterline.

The British were outraged. Civilians had attacked one of the King's naval vessels in performance of its lawful duties. British authorities immediately appointed a commission of inquiry, with power to send suspects to England for trial. Despite a £500 reward, the commission—stymied by the refusal of witnesses to testify against the suspects, many of them substantial citizens of the colony—adjourned without fulfilling its mission.

The *Gaspée* affair had important consequences. British officials concluded that colonists would stop at nothing, and resolved to take a harder line. Colonials themselves were angered by the authorities' intention to drag men off to England to stand trial for crimes committed in America. It violated one of the elementary "rights of Englishmen," and they determined to prevent it from taking place. British officialdom announced, moreover, that the salaries of both the governor and the judges of Massachusetts were now to be paid by the Crown, which would free them from dependence upon the good will of the colonists.

The East India Company   Another brief period of calm followed the *Gaspée* affair. Then came swift events that ripped apart the old empire. The shock came from an unexpected source.

In 1773 the East India Company was on the verge of financial collapse. Since the seventeenth century the company had traded in India as its private corporate enterprise. Many company officials had become rich through bribery and special privileges, but the company itself had suffered. One of its few remaining assets, seventeen million pounds of tea held in its London warehouses, remained unsold because of the American boycott, and also because heavy taxes made it too expensive in Britain itself. Why not, Lord North asked, drastically reduce the import tax on tea? With only three pence per pound to be paid on arrival in America, the tea would become so cheap that it would undersell smuggled Dutch tea. The tea would sell widely, its profit saving the East India Company from ruin and its tax bringing the government at last some much-needed revenue from the troublesome mainland colonies. This plan received legislative form in the Tea Act of 1773.

What North did not foresee was that Americans were opposed on principle to paying any tax, however cheap, to which they had not consented. To make matters worse, he consigned the East India Company tea exclusively to colonial merchants who favored British policies and obeyed the trade laws.

News of the new British affront enraged the radicals. In New York City, most of the merchants resolved that the tea would not be sold. Philadelphians adopted resolutions declaring that since "the duty imposed by Parliament upon tea landed in America is a tax on the Americans, or levying contributions on them without their consent, it is the duty of every American to oppose this attempt." Along the Delaware River, a "Committee of Tarring and Feathering" threatened captains of vessels carrying tea that their cargo would bring them "into hot water." In Charleston, patriot pressure also frightened off tea importers. As usual, Boston responded more violently than any other town.

Governor Hutchinson warned the British authorities soon after the Tea Act passed that "at and near Boston the people seem regardless of all consequences. To enforce the Act appears beyond all comparison more difficult than I ever before imagined." If Hutchinson had allowed this perception to guide him, disaster might have been avoided. But though he was American born, as governor of a British colony he felt bound to enforce the law, and when three cargo ships carrying tea arrived in Boston harbor he determined that they must unload.

The Tea Party On the evening of December 16, 1773, a gathering of perhaps 8,000 men, much of the town's contingent of able-bodied males, assembled at Old South Church. They were there to hold a town meeting, to ask that the hated tea not be landed. Their request was not granted, and at the end of the meeting Sam Adams rose from his seat and said "This meeting can do nothing to save the country." As if by prearranged signal, as soon as the meeting adjourned, a band of men disguised as Mohawk Indians rushed down Milk Street to Griffin's Wharf. Three companies of these instant Indians rowed out to the anchored tea ships, boarded them, split open the tea chests, and dumped their massive contents into the waters of the harbor. Their mission accomplished, the men quickly and quietly dispersed.

The British saw the Boston Tea Party as an outrage and they determined not to let it go unpunished. In Parliament William Pitt, now Earl of Chatham, and the eloquent Irish member Edmund Burke warned that punitive measures would lead to revolt. Burke urged the government to let Americans tax themselves, and not worry about whether they were legally required to obey Parliament. But the Burkes and the Pitts were a minority. Other politically influential Englishmen believed, as one expressed it, "that the town of Boston ought to be knocked about their ears and destroyed." Determined to prevent the Americans from ending all parliamentary control, North introduced the

George Hewes, one of the "Indians" involved in the tea party, recalled later that he had taken

"a small hatchet, which I and my associates denominated the tomahawk, with which, and a club, after having painted my face and hands with coal dust in the shop of a blacksmith, I repaired to Griffin's wharf, where the three ships lay that contained the tea. . . . [T]here appeared to be an understanding that each individual should volunteer his services, keep his own secret, and risk the consequences for himself. No disorder took place during that transaction, and it was observed at that time that the stillest night ensued that Boston had enjoyed for many months."

THE BOSTON TEA PARTY

Bostonian John Andrews described the tea controversy in a series of letters to his brother:

November 29th [1773]. Hall and Bruce arriv'd Saturday evening with each an hundred and odd chests of the detested Tea. What will be done with it, can't say: but I tremble for yͤ. consequences should yͤ. consignees still persist in their obstinacy and not consent to reship it. They have softened down so far as to offer it to the care of Council or the town, till such times as they hear from their friends in England, but am perswaded, from the present dispositions of yͤ. people, that no other alternative will do, than to have it immediately sent back to London again. . . . Yͤ. bells are ringing for a general muster, and a third vessel is now arriv'd in Nantasket road. Handbills are stuck up, calling upon Friends! Citizens! and Countrymen!

December 1st. Having just return'd from Fire Club, and am now, in company with the two Miss Masons and Mr. Williams of your place, at Sam. Eliot's,

who has been dining with him at Col°. Hancock's, and acquaints me that Mr. Palfrey sets off Express for New York and Philadelphia at five o'clock tomorrow morning, to communicate yͤ. transactions of this town respecting the tea. . . . The consignees have all taken their residence at the Castle, as they still persist in their refusal to take the tea back. Its not only yͤ. town, but the country are unanimous against the landing it, and at the Monday and Tuesday Meetings, they attended to the number of some hundreds from all the neighboring towns within a dozen miles. . . .

December 18th. However precarious our situation may be, yet *such* is the present calm composure of the people that a stranger would hardly think that ten thousand pounds sterling of the East Indian Company's *tea* was destroy'd the night, or rather evening before last, yet its a serious truth; The affair was transacted with the greatest regularity and despatch. . . . A general muster was assembled, from this and all yͤ. neighbouring towns, to the number of five or six thousand, at 10 o'clock

Boston Port Bill. Until Massachusetts had paid for the tea destroyed, a naval force would close Boston Harbor to shipping. Troops withdrawn from the town to Castle William following the Boston Massacre would reenter the city.

Fury in Boston itself was predictable. Messages of sympathy for Boston's plight poured in from every colony. George Washington urged his fellow Virginians to support the Bostonians. We must not "suffer ourselves to be sacrificed by piece meals," he wrote. The Virginia House of Burgesses convened in the Raleigh Tavern in Williamsburg after the Tory governor refused to let it sit at the capitol, and there it called for a continental congress to meet to consider united action. Similar calls came from New York, Providence, and Philadelphia. Everywhere Americans recognized that a crisis had been reached, and in North Carolina groups began to arm and drill in preparation for combat.

The closing of the port of Boston was the first in a series of parliamentary measures of 1774, known collectively as the Coercive or Intolerable Acts. The Administration of Justice Act declared that any royal official sued for carrying out his official duties could have his trial transferred out of unfriendly Massachusetts to Britain, where he would face a more favorable jury. The Massachusetts Government Act struck a severe blow at self-government by taking away from the provincial legislature many of its powers of appointment and giving them to the royal governor. Henceforth the governor, not the assembly, could appoint the council, and juries were to be summoned by sheriffs rather than elected by the town meetings, which only the governor could call.

Another measure passed in 1774, the Quebec Act, was not intended as punishment, but so offended the colonists that it is often included

Indignation over closing the Boston port swept the colonies. The Reverend Joseph Fish of Stonington, Connecticut, wrote to his daughter:

"I don't remember any time, since I lived, so alarming as these, on account of the tyrannical measures which the ministry at home have taken & are designing to take against the colonies. They seem (by accounts sent over) determined to distress us to the last degree, if not to destroy us, unless we submit to the yoke of slavery they have prepared for us."

The Boston town meeting sent a circular letter about the closing of the port to the other colonies, declaring that

"this attack, though made immediately upon us, is doubtless designed for every other colony who will not surrender their sacred rights and liberties into the hands of an infamous ministry. Now therefore is the time when all should be united in opposition to this violation of all the liberties of all."

Thursday morning in the Old South Meeting house, where they pass'd a *unanimous* vote that the *Tea* should go out of the *harbour* that afternoon, and sent a committee with Mr. Rotch to y^e. Custom house to *demand* a clearance, which the collector told 'em was not in his power to give, without the duties being first paid. They then sent Mr. Rotch to Milton, to ask a pass from y^e. Governor, who sent for answer, that "consistent with the rules of government and his duty to the King he could not grant one without they produc'd a previous clearance from the office."—By the time he return'd with this message the candles were light in [the] house, and upon reading it, such prodigious shouts were made, that induc'd me, while drinking tea at home, to go out and know the cause of it. The house was so crouded I could get no farther than y^e. porch, when I found the moderator was just declaring the meeting to be *dissolv'd*, which caused another general shout, out doors and in, and three cheers. What with that, and the consequent noise of breaking up the meeting, you'd thought that the inhabitants of the infernal regions had broke loose. For my part, I went contentedly home and finish'd my tea, but was soon inform'd what was going forward: but still not crediting it without ocular demonstration, I went and was *satisfied*. They muster'd, I'm told, upon Fort Hill, to the number of about two hundred, and proceeded, two by two, to Griffin's wharf, where Hall, Bruce, and Coffin lay, each with 114 chests of the *ill fated* article on board; the two former with *only* that article, but y^e. latter arriv'd at y^e. wharf only y^e. day before, was freighted with a large quantity of other goods, which they took the *greatest* care not to injure in the least, and before *nine* o'clock in y^e. evening, every chest from on board the three vessels was knock'd to pieces and flung over y^e. sides. They say the actors were *Indians* from *Narragansett*. Whether they were or not, to a transient observer they appear'd as *such*, being cloath'd in Blankets with the heads muffled, and copper color'd countenances, being each arm'd with a hatchet or axe, and pair pistols, nor was their *dialect* different from what I conceive these geniusses to speak, as their jargon was unintelligible to all but themselves.

among the Intolerable Acts. This law established a permanent government for the conquered province of Canada that provided few of the rights the English colonists enjoyed. It also extended toleration to the predominant religion of Quebec's inhabitants, Roman Catholicism. And the law extended the boundaries of Quebec south to the Ohio River into a region claimed by Virginia, Connecticut, and Massachusetts.

Resistance Turns to Armed Conflict

The First Continental Congress

In Carpenter's Hall, in Philadelphia, early in September 1774, the first Continental Congress assembled. Twelve colonies were represented. The popular royal governor had dissuaded Georgians who were trying to pass a resolution to send a delegation. Of the fifty-six delegates, twenty-two were lawyers, and most of the others were planters or merchants. Almost all had been prominent in the affairs of their individual colonies, and many had belonged to the committees of correspondence.

The delegates did not all agree on the best course. Some held it sufficient to petition the King informing him of wrongs done the colonists and asking that he intervene. The Massachusetts delegates, led by John and Sam Adams, along with Christopher Gadsden of South Carolina, and Patrick Henry and Richard Henry Lee of Virginia, favored retaliatory measures such as a new nonimportation agreement and a blunt refusal to pay for the tea dumped at Boston. Still, the delegates quickly demonstrated an emerging sense of continental unity and shared nationality. Patrick Henry, in a sample of his famous oratory, sounded the note. "The distinctions between Virginians, Pennsylvanians, New Yorkers, and New Englanders," he declared, "are no more. I am not a Virginian, but an American." All imperial government, he continued, was at an end. "All Distinctions are thrown down. All America is thrown into one mass." Henry was exaggerating, but the Congress would help to create a new feeling that Americans all shared a common destiny.

It was a radicals' convention. In the midst of the deliberations the delegates received a set of resolutions adopted by a convention recently held in Suffolk County, Massachusetts brought by Paul Revere. These declared that Americans should not obey any of the Coercive Acts, and declared the Quebec Act "dangerous in an extreme degree to the Protestant religion and to the civil rights and liberties of all America." Citizens should "use their utmost diligence to acquaint themselves with the art of war as soon as possible, and do, for that purpose, appear under arms at least once every week." Until redress was obtained, nonimportation of all British goods should be the rule. Over the strong objections of conservatives, the Congress endorsed the "Suffolk Resolves."

When it came to resolutions of their own, the delegates disagreed. On one side were the moderate Joseph Galloway of Pennsylvania and his supporters, who proposed a "Plan of Union" that would establish an overall government for the colonies with a president-general appointed by the King. This official would exercise authority over a grand council selected by the various colonial assemblies. Together the president-

John Singleton Copley's portrait of Paul Revere represents him as a silversmith and craftsman. Revere also cast cannon for the army and designed the state seal still used by Massachusetts.
(Courtesy, Museum of Fine Arts, Boston)

general and the grand council would constitute an "inferior branch" of the British Parliament. Radicals in the Congress, believing that this would freeze into law the colonies' political subordination to Britain, tabled it. The radicals' own plan, which was adopted, denounced the Coercive Acts as oppressive and unconstitutional and condemned the various revenue measures Parliament had passed since 1763, the enlargement of the vice-admiralty courts' jurisdiction, the maintaining of a British standing army in America, and the dissolution of colonial assemblies by British authorities. The Congress also adopted a plan known as the Continental Association, a stringent set of regulations virtually cutting off all commercial relations with Britain until American grievances had been redressed. A final resolution called for a second Congress to meet on May 10, 1775, if by that time Britain still refused to yield.

The work of the Congress pleased many colonists. Following adjournment the Pennsylvania Assembly gave the delegates a dinner at the City Tavern, where their work was toasted and praised. Radicals throughout British America congratulated Congress for its efforts. Tories were dismayed and depressed by what had transpired in Philadelphia. Governor William Franklin of New Jersey, Benjamin Franklin's Tory son, noted that the Congress had left Britain "no other alternative than either to consent to what must appear humiliating in the eyes of all Europe, or to compel obedience to her laws by a military force." The Franklins, father and son, became bitter political enemies.

In England itself, high officials were thunderstruck. British merchants once more became a voice for conciliation. So did Pitt and Burke.

Lexington and Concord In the fall of 1774 in Boston, events moved toward a showdown. For months the army commander there, General Thomas Gage, had been reinforcing the British garrison so that by the end of 1774 there were eleven battalions of redcoats, some 4,000 men, in the city and at nearby Castle William. Patriots, as opponents of parliamentary rule over the colonies were termed, armed and drilled. Outside the city, bands of militia calling themselves Minute Men, ready to "meet at one minute's warning equipped with arms and ammunition," patrolled the countryside and made it dangerous for British troops to leave the city even on official business. Before long, Gage began to feel as though he were under siege and fortified Boston Neck against the time when he might actually be attacked. The Massachusetts Provincial Congress had ordered the stockpiling of arms and ammunition at nearby Concord. Within a few months, the colonists secreted some twenty thousand pounds of musket balls and cartridges, besides a considerable number of tents, axes, spades, and supplies of beef, flour, rice, butter, and rum—all hidden in private houses and barns in Concord. The town's men and women helped to manufacture still more supplies: cartridge boxes, belts, and holsters. A fifteen-year-old girl supervised the young women of the town in manufacturing cartridges. As one Concord resident observed, "the people are ready and determine[d] to defend this Country Inch by Inch."

Relations between Boston patriots and British authorities reached the flash point early in 1775. There was a brawl between butchers and

The poet Ralph Waldo Emerson wrote these verses on the fiftieth anniversary of the Battle of Lexington and Concord:

By the rude bridge that arched the flood,
  Their flag to April's breeze unfurled,
Here once the embattled farmers stood,
  And fired the shot heard round the world.

Following the rout at Lexington, farmers and Minute Men surprised the British at the North Bridge in Concord and sent them into retreat to Boston. *(Courtesy, Scribner's Archives)*

redcoats at the public market. Then British troops tried to confiscate military supplies at Salem, but were turned back by Sons of Liberty. The Massachusetts legislature, in defiance of Gage's orders, was holding meetings at Concord. In mid-April Gage laid a plan to capture the arms that he had heard were stored there and perhaps seize some of the rebellious patriot leaders.

On the evening of April 18, 1775, a force of 700 redcoats set out for Concord. Patriots in Boston quickly learned of the move and dispatched William Dawes and Paul Revere to alert the Minute Men and the patriot leaders that the British were coming. Revere was captured and Dawes turned back, but another rider conveyed the news to the patriots at Concord in time. When the British reached nearby Lexington after marching most of the night, they discovered seventy armed Minute Men lined up on the town commons shivering in the early morning chill. The British commanding officer, Major John Pitcairn, immediately rode toward them shouting: "Ye villains, ye rebels, disperse! Lay down your arms!" At the same time the British light infantry began to run forward to intercept the Americans, who retreated to a stone wall at the edge of the field. Tradition has it that their commanding officer Captain John Parker, said, "Stand your guard. Don't fire unless fired upon. But if they mean to have a war, let it begin here." No one knows which side fired first, but at the wall the Minute Men stopped and fired off a ragged volley, wounding one redcoat and Major Pitcairn's horse. The British replied more effectively, killing eight of the Americans and wounding nine others.

As the British reassembled to move on Concord, the Massachusetts countryside rose in fury. By the time the redcoats arrived at their destination, a large force of armed and angry farmers had collected to intercept them. The British forces entered the town, and the militia took up a position beyond the town's center. In the meantime, Concord's women did their best to conceal the precious stores of military supplies. When the Americans began to advance on their enemy, the British tried to withdraw. At this point the Minute Men fired, killing three and wounding a dozen of the redcoats. Now began a long, dismal, and bloody British retreat from Concord all the way back to the safety of Boston.

The British arrived back in Charlestown in the evening and counted their losses. Despite their contempt for amateur soldiers they had to admit that the colonists' fire was often deadly. Of the 700 men sent to Concord, 73 had been killed, 174 wounded, and 26 reported missing. Only by the sheerest luck had the Americans been prevented from cutting off the whole force and capturing it. The Americans had won a victory against the finest troops of Europe.

The Loyalists   After April 19, 1775, there was no turning back. From that day until July 2, 1776, the Continental Congress, in its desperate efforts to resolve the crisis, was, as John Adams said, caught "between hawk and buzzard." General Gage warned the British government: "These people are now spirited up by a rage and enthusiasm as great as ever People were possessed of, and you must proceed in earnest or give the Business up." Yet in the ensuing months thousands of native-born Americans would become Tories, partisans of the King. Loyalism was to be especially strong among certain groups of Americans. Natives like Thomas Hutchinson who had close ties to the British government were natural loyalists. Anglican ministers who recognized the King as head of the Church of England also tended to take the British side, as did many Anglican laymen, especially in New England, where they formed an unpopular minority. Loyalists were not invariably rich with a large property stake in society. Besides loyalist merchants, officials, and planters, there were also loyalist mechanics, farmers, and small shopkeepers. They too were patriots, with as much right to the title as the rebels had. What claimed their patriotism was not Massachusetts or Rhode Island alone, or British America alone, but the whole British empire including the colonies. By tradition, however, the word "patriot" is reserved to the rebels.

Like the loyalists, the patriot rebels came in different shapes and sizes. Almost all Congregational and many other ministers outside the Church of England chose Congress. In the major port towns—Boston, Newport, New York, Philadelphia, and Charleston—artisans, apprentices, and laborers were rebels. But so were the merchants, especially those who felt threatened by the trade regulations that had been piled on top of the Navigation Acts since 1763. The landed gentry of New York split. Families such as the Delanceys took the King's side; the Schuylers and the Livingstons, equally wealthy and aristocratic, supported Congress. In Virginia and the Carolinas, the patriot leaders were almost all Anglican gentlemen. Many of them, such as George Washington, Henry Laurens, and Thomas Jefferson, were owners of large estates and scores of black slaves.

New England Rallies to Arms   The response of patriot leaders to the events in Massachusetts was prompt and vigorous. In Massachusetts the Provincial Congress, as the illegal colonial legislature was called, authorized the raising of troops and appealed to the other colonies for aid. Before long, several thousand militia from Rhode Island, Connecticut, and New Hampshire, along with contingents of Indians, were pouring into the colony and assembling in a ring around Boston, where Gage's troops were en-

A Philadelphia woman wrote to a British officer:

"I have retrenched every superfluous expense in my table and family. . . . Tea I have not drunk since last Christmas, nor bought a new cap or gown since your defeat at Lexington, and what I never did before, have learnt to knit, and am now making stockings of American wool for my servants, and this way do I throw in my mite to the public good. I know this, that as free I can die but once, but as a slave I shall not be worthy of life. . . . All ranks of men among us are in arms. Nothing is heard now in our streets but the trumpet and drum, and the universal cry is 'Americans, to arms!' "

camped. The American general in charge was Artemus Ward; his subordinates included the talented Nathanael Greene and Israel Putnam.

In some ways the besiegers of Boston were in worse shape than the besieged. The hastily-assembled colonial troops lived without sufficient tents and amidst filth. They were unused to the standards of hygiene necessary where men lived together in masses, and before long dysentery and other diseases invaded the American camp. The British in Boston, on the other hand, seemed to be living off the fat of the land, well housed and well supplied with food and necessities. At the end of May 1775, Gage was joined by three other high-ranking British officers, Sir William Howe, Sir Henry Clinton, and John ("Gentleman Johnny") Burgoyne. Howe took over command from Gage, who remained as civilian governor of the colony.

"Bunker Hill"   Sooner or later, Howe would have had to attack the troops surrounding Boston, but they forced his hand by fortifying Breed's Hill, across the Charles River from Boston and within cannon range of the city. On June 17, 1775, the British navy began to bombard the new fortifications. Confident that the untried amateur soldiers under Colonel William Prescott's command could not stand up against redcoats in a regular battle, Howe and his fellow officers decided to make a direct attack on the entrenched Americans. Troops of grenadiers and light infantry, with packs containing three days' rations, were ferried across the Charles to Charlestown peninsula.

As the British troops landed on the beach, the Americans waited silently. When the redcoats prepared to charge, Prescott gave the order to fire. There was a great crash and a cloud of smoke; scores of Welsh Fusiliers fell. In seconds the light infantry regiment was fleeing in panic, leaving behind its wounded, its dead, and most of its equipment. Meanwhile the tall grenadiers were advancing on Breed's Hill in well-dressed lines. When the redcoats were within twenty yards of the American position a volley rang out, knocking down scores. The grenadiers continued to advance, their bayonets fixed. The Americans, now almost within spitting range, continued to fire away. Finally the grenadiers too broke ranks and fled.

Howe was not finished. Once more he ordered his men against the American position. Once more they were mowed down and retreated. Again Howe ordered his men to attack, this time without their heavy packs. By now the Americans were low in ammunition. Assuming the battle was over, many had disobeyed their officers and had begun to leave for home. Despite heavy casualties, this time the redcoats drove the Americans off the hill and took possession of the Charlestown peninsula. The British had won, but at what a price! Over a thousand redcoat casualties, with over two hundred killed. Almost fifty percent of the British troops engaged were either dead or wounded. As Howe commented: "A dear bought victory, another such would have ruined us."

The battle, misnamed "Bunker Hill," was of vast symbolic importance. To Americans it was a great moral triumph. Combined with Lexington and Concord it had demonstrated that American militia were able to stand up to the best the British could throw against them. In reality, the Americans, with 15,000 men encamped around Boston,

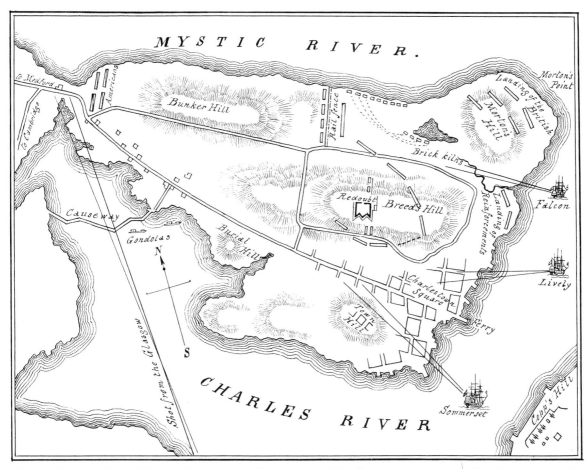

The Battle of Bunker Hill (actually Breed's Hill), June 17, 1775. The British won but suffered a great number of casualties. For the Americans it was a moral victory.

could have done much better with sufficient training. Far too many had been insubordinate. The Americans' staff work and supply services had been poor. American success had been due as much to British errors in using a frontal assault as to their own planning. Still, the Americans had reason to be proud and to look to the future with some hope.

A Continental Army Takes Shape

Washington Takes Command
In early May 1775, the Second Continental Congress had assembled in Philadelphia, as scheduled. Among its first acts was the choice of commander for the whole Continental army, who would take charge of the troops around Boston. Following the advice of John Adams to make a bid for unity by choosing a southerner, Congress on June 15, just days before Breed's Hill, appointed George Washington of Vir-

The Second Continental Congress appointed George Washington commander of the Continental army. A few years earlier he had hoped to get a commission as an officer in the British army. The portrait is by Charles Willson Peale. *(Courtesy, The Pennsylvania Academy of the Fine Arts)*

George Washington's appointment filled him with "inexpressible concern." Other Americans exulted in having a leader at last. By the fall of 1775, babies were being named after him. Phillis Wheatley wrote, "A crown, a mansion, and a throne that shine, / With gold unfading, WASHINGTON! be thine." She sent her poem to General Washington, and he wrote to thank her, adding, "If you should ever come to Cambridge, or near head-quarters, I shall be happy to see a person so favored by the Muses."

ginia. Congress also voted to raise six companies of riflemen from the middle colonies and the South to join the New Englanders at Boston and decided to issue bills of credit to support the accelerating rebellion.

Despite the outbreak of hostilities, Congress resisted a final political break with Britain. A few, among them Sam Adams, favored a bold declaration of American independence. His cousin John, however, urged the delegates to accept the advice of Massachusetts and endorse the formation of new constitutions for each colony to break the tie with England. These independent states, he believed, would ally themselves in a continental league that would be equivalent to a free nation. But even this oblique road to independence did not please most of the delegates, who still hoped for British conciliation.

Washington arrived in the Boston area after Breed's Hill to find the largely New England army a disappointment. They were, the Virginian complained, "an exceedingly nasty and dirty people," excessively concerned with money. Other observers found the troops enterprising, though highly individualistic, and unwilling to submit to discipline or even to call their officers by official titles. The new commander in chief had to turn this ragged collection of farmers and mechanics into an army and to combine it smoothly with the regiments of Virginians, Marylanders, and Pennsylvanians who began to arrive at Cambridge.

In these months of 1775, and virtually all through the war, one of the general's chief problems was simply to keep his force intact. Few Americans considered military service a full-time occupation. Farmers were willing to enlist for a few months, especially in the winter or after the crops had been planted. But when needed at home, or when confronted with long stretches of idleness, they grew restless. Some simply deserted. Others waited until their term of enlistment had ended and, regardless of the military situation, went home.

Early Fighting

Even before Washington arrived to construct a Continental army out of fifteen thousand individualists encamped outside Boston, the war was progressing elsewhere. In May 1775 a force of Massachusetts men and Vermonters under Ethan Allen and Benedict Arnold had attacked and captured the small British garrison at Fort Ticonderoga on Lake Champlain. The Americans acquired valuable military supplies, including a hundred cannon. In August the rebels launched from the captured British post an attack on Canada led by General Philip Schuyler of New York and Richard Montgomery, born in Britain. On November 13, 1775, Montgomery captured Montreal. Meanwhile, Arnold, with one thousand volunteers from Washington's force, set out across Maine heading toward Quebec City. He reached the British fortress in November and was joined by Montgomery and his men. The combined little army attacked the city in a howling snowstorm. In the battle Montgomery was killed and Arnold wounded. A hundred Americans were killed and four hundred captured. With his pitiful remnant Arnold continued to besiege the town all through the winter. In the spring he gave up the siege and returned home.

In Virginia the royal governor, the Earl of Dunmore, had gathered the colony's loyalists together at Norfolk, formed them into a small army, and set them to destroying plantations owned by patriots. In November, Dunmore issued a proclamation establishing martial law and calling on all citizens to support the King. He also offered freedom to all slaves who would desert their patriot masters and join his forces. This proved to be a mistake. Dunmore's little army did attract some runaway slaves, but white Virginians feared nothing more than a slave uprising, and Dunmore's proclamation may have pushed many of the undecided into the patriot camp. When he sallied out of Norfolk with his mixed band of loyalists and blacks, he was defeated. Soon after, he loaded his followers aboard ships and abandoned Norfolk to the Americans. He later returned and set fire to the city.

Peace Proposals   While Americans and Englishmen were sporadically killing one another in the fields and forests of North America, efforts were being made to bring the two sides together. In July 1775 Congress adopted the Olive Branch Petition announcing continued American attachment to the King and asking him to desist from further hostile acts until some scheme of reconciliation had been arranged. It also adopted a "Declaration of the Causes and Necessities of Taking Up Arms." This document did not proclaim independence, but pronounced American determination to refuse submission. Several weeks later, Congress rejected Lord North's proposals of February, by which the British government offered to forgo parliamentary taxes on any colony that would agree to tax itself for defense and to pay its own expenses.

Congress adjourned in August 1775, but reconvened in mid-September with a full representation from all thirteen colonies. In early November, members learned that the King had rejected the Olive Branch Petition and declared the colonies in open rebellion. On December 6 Congress responded to the King's declaration by disavowing American obedience to Parliament, but acknowledging continued allegiance to George III, perceived as the legitimate sovereign of all the British empire. If Congress had gotten its way, Parliament would have legislated for the inhabitants of Great Britain and American legislators for the colonies, both peoples giving homage to the Crown.

Wartime Government   As these proposals and counterproposals flew back and forth across the Atlantic, Americans were moving rapidly toward practical self-government. Congress had a Continental army. It appointed commissioners to deal with the Indian tribes and set up a post office department. It organized a navy. Its most momentous act was to appoint in November 1775 a five-man Committee of Secret Correspondence to negotiate with potential allies abroad. In December the Committee made contact with a French agent, who informed it that France would aid the colonists against the British. The French, of course, were delighted to see the British empire weaken. Soon after, the French Foreign Minister, Comte de Vergennes, consulted his Spanish counterpart regarding joint action to aid the Americans. When the Spanish gave their approval, Vergennes ordered a large amount of munitions to be shipped to the Americans through a "front" company, Hortalez et Companie. In April 1776 Congress opened American ports to the commerce of all nations except Britain.

Common Sense and
The Declaration of Independence

A final wrench to the remaining ties of empire came with the publication of *Common Sense*, a hundred-page pamphlet published early in 1776 by a recently arrived Englishman, Thomas Paine. Written with extraordinary passion and eloquence, *Common Sense* denounced the institution of hereditary kingship. "For all men being originally equals, no *one* by *birth* could have a right to set up his own family in perpetual preference to all others forever," Paine declared. George was a "royal brute," not the generous father of his people, and Americans had no reason to continue to obey him or remain his subjects. George III was in fact not a royal brute, but *Common Sense* was an important document in the modern rejection of the whole system of hereditary rule.

The pamphlet had an electrifying effect. Countless Americans read it as it passed from hand to hand, and were profoundly affected by its message. Washington noted that it was "working a powerful change in the minds of men." After reading it, he himself ceased to toast the King, as he had done till then.

The Declaration of Independence   On April 12, 1776, the North Carolina Convention authorized the colony's delegates in Congress to vote for independence. The Virginia legislature followed soon after. On June 7 Richard Henry Lee, responding to the House of Burgesses, offered a motion in Congress that "these United Colonies are, and of a right ought to be, free and independent states, and that all political connection between them and the state of Britain is, and ought to be, totally dissolved." Despite John Adams's earlier remark that "Every post and every Day rolls in upon Us, Independence like a Torrent," the delegates were not unanimous in support of such a bold move.

Congress responded by appointing to frame a statement of independence a five-man committee consisting of Thomas Jefferson, John Adams, Benjamin Franklin, Roger Sherman, and Robert Livingston. The group chose Jefferson to write a first draft. At thirty-three the tall Virginian was one of the youngest members of Congress. But he was also a man of great charm and eloquence, with a reputation for scholarship.

Jefferson's Declaration of Independence is one of the most eloquent and moving endorsements of human freedom and equality ever composed. With simplicity and directness the document, reprinted along with the Constitution at the end of this book, captures the essence of the ideas that numbers of European political philosophers had articulated, among them the seventeenth-century English Whigs who had overthrown James II and helped establish England's constitutional

COMMON SENSE
by Thomas Paine
Paine's rousing pamphlet circulated by the tens of thousands and galvanized sentiment against England in the spring of 1776.

"The sun never shined on a cause of greater worth. 'Tis not the affair of a city, a county, a province, or a kingdom; but of a continent—of at least one-eighth part of the habitable globe. 'Tis not the concern of a day, a year, or an age; posterity are virtually involved in the contest, and will be more or less affected even to the end of time by the proceedings now. Now is the seedtime of continental union, faith, and honor. The least fracture now will be like a name engraved with the point of a pin on the tender rind of a young oak; the wound would enlarge with the tree, and posterity read it in full grown characters. . . .

Small islands not capable of protecting themselves are the proper objects for government to take under their care; but there is something absurd in supposing a continent to be perpetually governed by an island. In no instance hath nature made the satellite larger than its primary planet; and as England and America, with respect to each other, reverse the common order of nature, it is evident that they belong to different systems. England to Europe: America to itself. . . .

O ye that love mankind! Ye that dare oppose not only the tyranny but the tyrant, stand forth! Every spot of the old world is overrun with oppression. Freedom hath been hunted round the globe. Asia and Africa have long expelled her. Europe regards her like a stranger, and England hath given her warning to depart. O receive the fugitive, and prepare in time an asylum for mankind."

monarchy. The document announces that "all men are created equal" and "endowed by their Creator with certain unalienable Rights," more especially to "Life, Liberty and the pursuit of Happiness." Governments exist only to "secure these rights." When a government becomes "destructive of these ends," it is "the Right of the People to alter or abolish it" and establish a new one that will respect them. The colonists' rights of Englishmen had now transformed themselves into the natural rights of peoples everywhere.

Americans today do not have to be reminded that the framers of the Declaration of Independence did not intend the reference to "the People" to imply that all inhabitants of a country should be active participants in the political life of the nation. The Congress was accustomed to institutions that defined a portion of the population as expressing the will of the whole. Masters were seen as speaking for servants; husbands for their wives. A few months prior to the signing of the Declaration, Abigail Adams had written to her husband, John Adams, that she longed "to hear that you have declared an independency." And, she added, for the new code of laws "which I suppose it will be necessary for you to make I desire you would Remember the Ladies, and be more generous and favourable to them than your ancestors." Abigail Adams was not claiming citizenship or equal political rights for women. She sought only that the lawmakers "not put such unlimited power into the hands of the Husbands." For, she reminded her husband, "all Men would be tyrants if they could." John Adams' wife marvelously adapted the revolutionary vocabulary of her day to women's situation as she understood it. She accepted women's domestic role, but sought to introduce greater freedom for women into that sphere. Should men fail to reduce their own domestic tyranny, she warned, the ladies would surely foment their own "Rebellion." And any notion of the Declaration as a democratic and egalitarian document will have to take account of

Windsor chair, reputed to be the sort used by Thomas Jefferson while he wrote the Declaration of Independence, probably made in New England, mid-eighteenth century. *(Courtesy, Index of American Design)*

The Declaration of Independence **by John Trumbull shows, standing at center, left to right, John Adams, Roger Sherman, Robert R. Livingston, Thomas Jefferson, and Benjamin Franklin.** *(Courtesy, Yale University Art Gallery)*

An angry New York crowd pulls down a statue of George III in 1776. Patriots had long accepted the conventional belief that the King could do no wrong and had attacked his ministers instead. The change in regard for the King was embodied in the Declaration of Independence, which repudiated George III, accusing him of plotting "an absolute tyranny." *(Courtesy, The New York Public Library, Astor, Lenox, Tilden Foundations)*

Twelve-year-old Jemmy Noyes of Connecticut, visiting New York City, wrote to his grandmother:

"I see four large ships there; one a seventy gun ship; and I saw the King's statue, and he sat on a great horse, both covered over with leaf gold; and the King had one bullet hole through his cheek, and another through his neck, and they talk of running his Majesty up into bullets for he and his horse are made of lead."

the existence of slavery, about which the members in their deliberations showed a flicker of conscience, but little more.

The rest of the Declaration was a detailed indictment of King George III, not the real culprit, which was Parliament. Here Jefferson marshaled virtually every American grievance, both immediate and of long standing, against Britain and defended the actions of the colonists during the years since 1763. All pointed toward one inescapable end: "these United Colonies are, and of Right ought to be, Free and Independent States." "With a firm reliance on the Protection of Divine Providence," the Declaration concluded, "we mutually pledge to each other our Lives, our Fortunes and our sacred Honor."

Adams, Franklin, and the rest of the committee suggested a number of changes, primarily stylistic. Congress as a body, when it received the draft, struck out several phrases and clauses, including an attack on the slave trade. On July 2 Congress voted to accept it. But it is July 4, when members of the Congress signed it, that Americans have chosen to commemorate. The Declaration was read to large gatherings of Americans throughout the self-proclaimed independent country. In Philadelphia John Nixon, head of the city guard, read the document to a large audience in the State House yard. When he finished, the crowd cheered. In New York, the officers of the Continental army, after hearing the Declaration read, all "went to a Publick House to testify to . . . their joy at the happy news of independence." The next day the statue of George III in New York City was "pulled down by the populace," and its 4000 pounds of lead were melted down for musket balls. Bostonians celebrated by removing from the State House wall the plaque bearing the King's coat of arms and burning it.

That the list of accusations in the Declaration of Independence largely exaggerates the actions of the British is to be expected of a document intended to justify a revolution. The document makes out the

King to be the villain. George III, to be sure, had been among the most eager advocates of a policy of forcing the colonists into submission, but it was Parliament that had been the effective agent of repression, and for some time the American rebels had professed their loyalty to the King, rejecting only parliamentary rule. Taken literally the attack on the King, foreshadowed in Paine's *Common Sense,* is absurd. But it is not to be taken literally. In effect, the King was serving as a symbol. In the earlier days of colonial resistance, he had been a symbol of the British nation and institutions, for which the rebels still felt affection. Now he was a symbol of arbitrary power, which the revolution claimed to be overthrowing in defense of liberty. The man George III, confused and muddling through like the rest of the human race, deserved better than to be appointed either symbolic role.

Now there could be no turning back. Victory would mean that the efforts at Philadelphia had not been in vain. Defeat might mean the surrender of lives, fortunes, and sacred honor.

John Adams wrote to his wife Abigail that the adopting of the Declaration would be

"celebrated by succeeding generations as the great anniversary festival. . . . It ought to be solemnized with pomp and parade, with shows, games, sports, guns, bells, bonfires and illuminations, from one end of the continent to the other, from this time forward forevermore."

Suggested Readings

Study of the American Revolution should begin with Bernard Bailyn's classic, *The Ideological Origins of the American Revolution* (1967) and Kenneth Lockridge, *Settlement and Unsettlement in Early America: The Crisis of Political Legitimacy before the Revolution* (1981). Kenneth Silverman, *The Cultural History of the American Revolution* (1976) is a detailed analysis of relationships between politics and the arts. On social history see Oscar and Lilian Handlin, *A Restless People: Americans in Rebellion, 1770–1787* (1982), and Stephanie Grauman Wolf, *As Various as their Land: The Everyday Lives of Eighteenth-Century Americans* (1993). Gary Nash studies the importance of cities in *The Urban Crucible: Social Change, Political Consciousness, and the Origins of the American Revolution* (1979).

Pauline Maier traces the rise of popular hostility of England in *From Resistance to Revolution* (1972). See also Peter Thomas, *Tea Party to Independence: The Third Phase of the American Revolution* (1991). More specialized works include Edmund and Helen Morgan, *The Stamp Act Crisis* (1953), Benjamin Labaree, *The Boston Tea Party* (1964), Hiller Zobel, *The Boston Massacre* (1970), and David Ammerman's *In Common Cause: The American Response to the Coercive Acts of 1774* (1974). David Hackett Fischer's *Paul Revere's Ride* (1994) examines the outbreak of hostilities at Lexington and Concord.

See also Robert Gross, *The Minute Men and Their World* (1976), Benjamin Quarles, *The Negro in the American Revolution* (1961), Philip Foner, *Blacks in the American Revolution* (1976), Ira Gruber, *The Howe Brothers and the American Revolution* (1972), Charles Royster, *A Revolutionary People at War* (1979), J. A. Henretta, *The Evolution of American Society* (1973), Michael Kammen, *Empire and Interest* (1974), Francis Jennings, *Empire of Fortune* (1988), Edward Countryman, *The American Revolution* (1985), and A. F. Young, ed., *The American Revolution* (1976).

On the Declaration of Independence see Pauline Maier's *American Scripture: Making the Declaration of Independence* (1997) and Gary Wills's *Inventing America: Jefferson's Declaration of Independence* (1978). Other studies include Marc Egnal, *A Mighty Empire: The Origins of the Revolution* (1988), Philip Lason, *George Grenville: A Political Life* (1984), John Phillip Reid, *Constitutional History of the American Revolution: The Authority of Rights* (1986), Peter D. G. Thomas, *The Townshend Duties Crisis: The Second Phase of the American Revolution, 1767–1773* (1987), Richard Bushman, *King and People in Provincial Massachusetts* (1985), Jerrilyn Greene Marston, *King and Congress: The Transfer of Political Legitimacy, 1774–1776* (1987), Fred Anderson, *A People's Army: Massachusetts Soldiers and Society in the Seven Years' War* (1984), Bernard Bailyn and Philip D. Morgan, eds., *Strangers Within the Realm: Cultural Margins of the First British Empire* (1991).

Why Did the Americans Rebel?

Bernard Bailyn

The primary goal of the American Revolution was not the overthrow or even the alteration of the existing social order but the preservation of political liberty, threatened by the apparent corruption of the [British] constitution. . . .

The colonists believed that they saw emerging from the welter of events during the decade after the Stamp Act a pattern whose meaning was unmistakable. They saw in the measures taken by the British government and in actions of officials in the colonies something for which their peculiar inheritance of thought had prepared them only too well, something they had long conceived to be a possibility in view of the known tendencies of history and of the present state of affairs in England. They saw about them, with increasing clarity, not merely mistaken, or even evil, policies violating the principles upon which freedom rested, but what appeared to be evidence of nothing less than a deliberate assault launched surreptitiously by players against liberty both in England and in America. The danger to America, it was believed, was in fact only the small, immediately visible part of the greater whole whose ultimate manifestation would be the destruction of the English constitution, with all the rights and privileges embedded in it.

This belief transformed the meaning of the colonists' struggle, and it added an inner accelerator to the movement of opposition. For once assumed, it could not be easily dispelled: denial only confirmed it, since what conspirators profess is not what they believe; the ostensible is not the real; and the real is deliberately malign.

It was this—the overwhelming evidence, as they saw it, that they were faced with conspirators against liberty determined at all costs to gain ends which their words dissembled—that was signaled to the colonies after 1763, and it was this above all else that in the end propelled them into Revolution.

It was an elevating, transforming vision: a new, fresh, vigorous, and above all morally regenerate people rising from obscurity to defend the battlements of liberty and then in triumph standing forth, heartening and sustaining the cause of freedom everywhere. In the light of such a conception everything about the colonies and their controversy with the mother country took on a new appearance. Provincialism was gone: Americans stood side by side with the heroes of historic battles for freedom and with the few remaining champions of liberty in the present. What were once felt to be defects—isolation, institutional simplicity, primitiveness of manners, multiplicity of religions, weakness in the authority of the state—could now be seen as virtues, not only by Americans themselves but by enlightened spokesmen of reform, renewal, and hope wherever they might be—in London coffeehouses, in Parisian *salons,* in the courts of German princes. The mere existence of the colonists suddenly became philosophy teaching by example.

Bernard Bailyn, *The Ideological Origins of the American Revolution* (Cambridge: Harvard University Press, 1967).

Gary B. Nash

Recent studies of the American Revolution have relied heavily on the role of ideas to explain the advent of the American rebellion against England. The gist of the ideological interpretation of the Revolution is that colonists, inheriting a tradition of protest against arbitrary rule, became convinced in the years after 1763 that the English government meant to impose in America "not merely misgovernment and not merely insensitivity to the reality of life in the British overseas provinces but a deliberate design to destroy the constitutional safeguards of liberty, which only concerted resistance—violent resistance if necessary—could effectively oppose." It was this conspiracy against liberty that "above all else . . . propelled [the colonists] into Revolution."

An important corollary to this argument, which stresses the colonial defense of constitutional rights and liberties, is the notion that the material conditions of life in America were so generally favorable that social and economic factors deserve little consideration as a part of the impetus to revolution. "The outbreak of the Revolution," writes Bernard Bailyn, a leading proponent of the ideological school, "was not the result of social discontent, or of economic disturbances, or of rising misery, or of those mysterious social strains that seem to beguile the imaginations of historians straining to find peculiar predispositions to upheaval." Nor, asserts Bailyn, was there a "transformation of mob behavior or of the lives of the 'inarticulate' in the pre-Revolutionary years that accounts for the disruption of Anglo-American politics."

I do not suggest that we replace an ideological construction with a mechanistic economic interpretation, but argue that a popular ideology, affected by rapidly changing economic conditions in American cities, dynamically interacted with the more abstract Whig ideology borrowed from England. These two ideologies had their primary appeal within different parts of the social structure, were derived from different sensibilities concerning social equity, and thus had somewhat different goals. The Whig ideology, about which we know a great deal through recent studies, was drawn from English sources, had its main appeal within upper levels of colonial society, was limited to a defense of constitutional rights and political liberties, and had little to say about changing social and economic conditions in America or the need for change in the future. The popular ideology, about which we know very little, also had deep roots in English culture, but it resonated most strongly within the middle and lower strata of society and went far beyond constitutional rights to a discussion of the proper distribution of wealth and power in the social system. It was this popular ideology that undergirded the politicization of the artisan and laboring classes in the cities and justified the dynamic role they assumed in the urban political process in the closing decades of the colonial period. . . .

The most generally recognized alteration in eighteenth-century urban social structures is the long-range trend toward a less even distribution of wealth. Tax lists for Boston, Philadelphia, and New York, ranging over nearly a century prior to the Revolution, make this clear. By the early 1770s the top 5 percent of Boston's taxpayers controlled 49 percent of the taxable assets of the community, whereas they had held only 30 percent in 1687. In Philadelphia the top twentieth increased its share of wealth from 33 to 55 percent between 1693 and 1774. . . .

Though city dwellers from the middle and lower ranks could not measure this redistribution of economic resources with statistical precision, they could readily discern the general trend. No one could doubt that upper-class merchants were amassing fortunes, when four wheeled coaches, manned by liveried Negro slaves, appeared in Boston's crooked streets, or when urban mansions, lavishly furnished in imitation of the English aristocracy, rose in Philadelphia and New York. Colonial probate records reveal that personal estates of £5000 sterling were rare in the northern cities before 1730, but by 1750 the wealthiest town dwellers were frequently leaving assets of £20,000 sterling, exclusive of real estate, and sometimes fortunes of more than £50,000 sterling—equivalent in purchasing power to about 2.5 million dollars today. Wealth of this magnitude was not disguised in cities with populations ranging from about 16,000 in Boston to about 25,000 in New York and Philadelphia. . . .

In the third quarter of the eighteenth century poverty struck even harder at Boston's population and then blighted the lives of the New York and Philadelphia laboring classes to a degree unparalleled in the first half of the century. . . . The data on poor relief leave little room for doubt that the third quarter of the eighteenth century was an era of severe economic and social dislocation in the cities, and that by the end of the colonial period a large number of urban dwellers were without property, without opportunity, and, except for public aid, without the means of obtaining the necessities of life.

Reprinted from "Social Change and the Growth of Prerevolutionary Urban Radicalism" by Gary B. Nash, in *The American Revolution: Explorations in the History of American Radicalism*, edited by Alfred F. Young. Copyright © 1976 by Northern Illinois University Press. Used by permission of the publisher.

Josiah Wedgwood (1730–1795), manufacturer of English ceramics, designed this medallion as an antislavery symbol. It appeared on the title page of the 1814 edition of Equiano's *Narrative* and remained the symbol for the abolition movement through the American Civil War. *(Courtesy, Smithsonian Institution)*

Revolution and Independence
1776–1787

LIBERTY AND SLAVERY

To those slaves who heard it, the rhetoric of liberty and equality that accompanied the American Revolution must have sounded hollow. What would African slaves have made of Patrick Henry's "Give me liberty, or give me death" or Thomas Jefferson's "All men are created equal"?

Slaves did not write letters to one another or set down their thoughts in diaries, but their actions give ample proof that the extreme irony of the patriot cause was not lost upon them. In 1765 slaves in Charleston, South Carolina, frightened whites by parading and shouting "liberty" in imitation of a recent patriot demonstration against the Stamp Act. In 1773 some slaves in Boston petitioned for their freedom. In 1774 in Georgia's St. Andrew Parish, a small band of slaves conspired to rebel and killed or wounded several whites before being apprehended.

The irony of cries for "liberty" in colonies that held some 500,000 individuals in bondage was not lost upon the British, who seriously debated offering freedom to slaves as a way to retaliate against colonial rebels. News of an emancipation proposal in the British House of Commons reached the colonies in January 1775. The proposal did not carry, but the news of it did—to both slaves and slaveholders. In April 1775 a group of Virginia slaves offered to join that colony's loyalist governor, John Murray, Earl of Dun-

continued

HISTORICAL EVENTS

1775
- First antislavery society formed
- Committee on Indian Affairs established

1776
British send fleet to New York
- Independence is declared
- Continental Congress sends Franklin to France to negotiate alliance

1777
British capture Fort Ticonderoga
- Battle of Saratoga • Articles of Confederation adopted

1778
Franco-American alliance

1779
War at stalemate

1780
Benedict Arnold commits treason
- "Tarleton's Quarter"
- Pennsylvania passes gradual emancipation law

147

more, in opposing local patriots. On that occasion he refused their offer and told them to "go about their business." A few months later he had second thoughts.

In November 1775 Lord Dunmore issued a proclamation promising freedom to all "indented servants, Negroes, and others . . . that are able and willing to bear arms," if they would desert their patriot masters and ally themselves with the British cause. By December Governor Dunmore had a regiment of about three hundred slave soldiers in uniforms that bore the slogan "Liberty to Slaves." Other slaves served the British as crewmen and pilots for the many small vessels that plied coastal waters. Slaves also conducted raids on plantations and farms along that coast, taking livestock and other provisions for use aboard British ships.

To American slaves Paul Revere's famous warning, "The British are coming!" carried a far different meaning. In Charleston, many slaves left their masters' households and fled to an island in Charleston Harbor to await the arrival of British ships. Sullivan's Island was not much frequented, since it was the site of the pest house, where diseased passengers off ships from the Caribbean and Africa were quarantined. Now it was a hopeful place, as more and more fugitives stealthily rowed their way to its beaches. In those chill December days, as they camped on the island, the runaways were heartened by the support of South Carolina's loyalist governor.

On December 7, 1775, the South Carolina Council of Safety ordered one of its officers to send two hundred men "this ensuing night" to "apprehend a number of negroes, who are said to have deserted to the enemy." An ominous postscript to this order, added that "The pest house is to be burned, and *every kind of live stock to be driven off or destroyed*." Within the next few days some of the Sullivan's Island blacks found safety aboard the British man-of-war *Scorpion* and other British vessels. Other slaves, assigned to work details in Charleston Harbor, refused to obey their masters, in open defiance of white authority. Finally, before daylight on the morning of December 18, a force of about fifty "patriots" referred to in a report as "Indian Rangers" attacked Sullivan's Island, burned a house, captured four blacks, and killed many others.

Henry Laurens, slave holder, fervent patriot, later president of the Continental Congress, wrote: "It is an awful business notwithstanding it has the sanction of Law, to put even fugitive & Rebellious Slaves to death." But Laurens blamed the British for the deaths, and justified the patriot actions as necessary for "the American Cause" and "the happiness of ages unborn."

The slaves who died at the hands of colonial patriots give a new poignant meaning to Henry's "Give me liberty or give me death." What happened there, moreover, confounds simple explanations of racial, ethnic, and political divisions in the colonies: Americans killing slaves, white soldiers behaving like Indians, British embracing slaves: In the words of a contemporary song, the American Revolution did indeed bring about a "World turned upside down."

The Armies

The King's and Patriot Armies

A soldier of the Revolution who overheard talk in the ranks of the King's troops might have caught the sound of various accents from the British Isles, or American accents, for there were several loyalist regiments among the Crown troops. And it is likely that he would have heard German. In the eighteenth century a nation might rent whole military units from such rulers as were willing to go into the business, and in the course of the war the British rented nearly 30,000 troops from German princes, including the Hessians from the principality of Hesse-Cassel. The regular British army also contained many Germans recruited by contractors. The patriot army, like the troops who were to fight for the Union in the Civil War nearly a century later, was itself a little congress of nations and ethnic groups, as were the colonies themselves. New Englanders, descendants of German and Scotch-Irish immigrants, and southerners of varied ancestry in the British Isles were prominent. The Continental army, like the loyalist forces in Virginia, contained black recruits. About 5,000 blacks, including many freemen from the New England states, fought for American independence.

In Virginia, South Carolina, and Georgia many slaves sided with the British, who promised them freedom. In the course of the war there were deserters from the patriot forces to the King's troops, and from the King's to the patriot, which added to the diversity in both armies.

In the American navy, which preyed on British commerce, the *Bonhomme Richard* can exemplify the diversity of the ethnic and national strains that could collect under a single flag. This ship, the conqueror in 1779 of the British warship *Serapis,* had been supplied by France. It was under the command of John Paul Jones, a Scotsman who had come to America not long before the war. Only a minority on board the *Bonhomme Richard* were clearly definable by residence as American. By their side were seamen from Scotland and Ireland, Scandinavia, Portugal, and France.

The patriot forces contained both local militias and Continental army troops. Congress had no power to conscript troops, and so it had to assign quotas to the states for the Continental army and let each state decide how to fill them. Congress, also lacking the authority to tax, even had to requisition money from the states and hope that they would fulfill their obligations. More effective, perhaps, were the bounties that states offered, which later in the war were supplemented with a draft. A state, in turn, might impose quotas on towns, and they could pay men to enlist. States also raised their own militias, in which discipline was likely to be light. After Washington took command outside Boston, he induced about 10,000 militiamen to join the Continental army. The army of the

A British sentry in full regalia; the colonists wore simpler uniforms or their ordinary clothes.
(Courtesy, The New York Public Library, Astor, Lenox and Tilden Foundations)

Midshipman Augustus Brine,
**1782. The American painter, John
Singleton Copley, painted this
young British seaman.** *(Courtesy,
The Metropolitan Museum of Art)*

Revolution was a foreshadowing of something more modern than the
King's troops: it represented the beginnings of a citizens' army, like
those that have fought in the major wars since the French Revolution.
And like citizens' armies since then, it had to find ways of dealing with
the reluctance of citizens to join.

The Rebel Way of Fighting As the patriot troops differed from the Crown forces
in their recruitment, they differed at least somewhat
in methods of fighting. At the beginning of the war
outside Boston, soldiers had been electing their own
officers, and it was some time before the practice was ended. The
Continental army had to instill discipline, which was difficult among
soldiers with no thought of becoming long-term military professionals.
In 1778 Washington put the Baron von Steuben, a former captain in the
Prussian army, in charge of training the troops. He made an army out of
the ragtag Continentals, commanded a division, and became an American citizen after the war. These forces did not remain consistent or
predictable in size. Citizen soldiers, committed more to their families

*General Nathanael Greene remarked of
the militiamen:*

"They are naturally brave and spirited, as the peasantry of any country,
but you cannot expect veterans of a raw
militia from only a few months' service."

and their crops than to army life, might decide to go home to plow, returning to the army if and when they felt like it.

Soldiers so averse to military discipline and the formalities of eighteenth-century battle not unexpectedly became known for fighting as individuals, firing from behind cover rather than in ranks, and taking aim. Some Americans were expert marksmen and used the Pennsylvania rifle, which was more accurate at longer distances than the smooth-bore musket. The colonists' method of fighting from cover had come from fighting the Indians, who also fought as individuals and had never read a military manual. These tactics infuriated the British, who thought the colonists unprofessional or cowardly. But as rifle fire became more deadly, supplemented by explosives, barbed wire, air bombardment, and the increasingly sophisticated weaponry of recent times, the eighteenth-century American practice of firing from cover along with a reliance on the skills of individual soldiers would become standards of warfare. Like the American Civil War of the 1860s, the American Revolution fore-shadowed the course of military practice.

The picture that comes down to us of the American always crouched behind a stone fence and picking off soldiers in the bewildered British ranks may owe much to the Massachusetts farmers at Lexington and Concord. During much of the war, Americans fought on the open field, managing as much of conventional warfare as training could teach them and their inclinations allowed. And in the course of the fighting, the Continental army developed a pride in itself as a seasoned and knowledgeable fighting force. If few of its troops wanted to become permanent professionals, if most of them like citizen soldiers in later wars wanted a quick return to their homes, they were nonetheless more than farmers or artisans who had picked up a gun for a scrap or two with the British. They were now real soldiers of a trained and national army. That meant that they were a major embodiment of the new nation itself.

Women and the Military   The women who accompanied the army in diverse capacities also contributed to its being a people's army, an incorporation of American society. Only officers were provided with quarters that could accommodate their wives, but other women accompanied the army as laundresses, nurses, cooks, provisioners, and camp-followers. Wives might also accompany husbands to the actual field of battle and assist them by such tasks as fetching the water required to keep the cannon functioning. It is not certain that the legendary Molly Pitcher actually existed, but many women did what has been attributed to her: they not only brought their husbands water for the cannon, but then also took over firing it themselves after their husbands had been wounded. Some women disguised themselves as men and fought undetected for long periods. Others capitalized on their femininity to serve successfully as spies and messengers.

Many American women who did not participate in battle or accompany the armies also provided important services that today would be the responsibility of the military authorities. They provided lodging for officers or allowed their homes to be turned into prisons and hospitals, and a vast network of women emerged to make shirts and knit stockings

A Connecticut man would remember:

"I was att my house in bed, between Brake of Day and Sunrise. I hard the Signel of an-larm by the fireing of thre Cannon . . . I turn'd Out and ask'd my wife to git Brakefast as soon as possabel for I must go off. I went Down on the hill . . . Whare the fleet was in fare Site in a line acrost the haber. There was 15 Sale of Ships an other Square rig'd Vesels, besides other Vesels. I came home. My brakefast was redy. After Brakefast . . . My hors Being redy I Slung my Musket & Cartrig Box and mounted with my littel Black Boy to bring the hors Back . . . After I got Under Way my wife Called to me pretty loud. I Stopt my hors and ask'd her What She wanted. Her answer was Not to let me hear that you are Shot in the Back."

A lament of one girl a soldier left behind is said to date from the American Revolution.

Here I sit on Buttermilk Hill,
Who could blame me cry me fill?
And every tear would turn a mill;
Johnny has gone for a soldier.

I'd sell my clock, I'd sell my reel,
Likewise I'd sell my spinning wheel
To buy my love a sword of steel;
Johnny has gone for a soldier.

Some women raised money for Washington's army.

Philadelphia, July 4th, 1780
Sir,
The subscription set on foot by the ladies of this City for the use of the soldiery is 200,580 dollars, and £625 6s.8d. in specie, which makes in the whole in paper money 300,634 dollars.

The ladies are anxious for the soldiers to receive the benefit of it, and wait your directions how it can best be disposed of. We expect some considerable additions from the country and have also wrote to the other States in hopes the ladies there will adopt similar plans, to render it more general and beneficial. . . .

E. Reed

for the soldiers. Nothing better illustrates the impact of the war on American society than the extensive participation of women. The war effort fully mobilized the nation.

The King's Way of Fighting The British were not scrupulous in their methods of recruitment. British prisons yielded some recruits for the army, and strict enforcement of the vagrancy laws helped, for enlistment was a way to avoid prison. But harsh British military discipline turned the recruits into a fighting machine that operated according to a set of prescribed rules for battle. Officers would march the troops as close to the enemy as possible. The soldiers, placed in several parallel ranks, one behind the other, would fire in unison, not taking careful aim, for the troops on the other side were also closely packed. The troops might thereupon have time to reload and fire at will, as the British had done on the Plains of Abraham against the French defending Quebec. But reloading was a lengthy process, and in place of a second volley the soldiers might charge with bayonets, which in the eighteenth century were a major weapon. What a European army needed from the bulk of its troops, then, was not literacy, technical or administrative skills, or initiative in the performance of a job. Required instead was the ability to go through the formal operations of an eighteenth-century manual of arms: to stand or kneel in rank and not break under fire, to shoot or to charge at the proper time. The disposition of troops in a battle, one rank behind another, had as one of its objects to prevent the front ranks from fleeing. European discipline produced an army that could endure much enemy fire without breaking. But under sufficiently heavy fire, the best of soldiers could break.

The Fortunes of War

The Critical Battles, 1776–1778 Against the rebels Britain massed an overwhelming force. Only days after Congress proclaimed independence in July 1776 a huge British fleet—a "forest of masts"—sailed into New York harbor: 32,000 soldiers with 11,000 sailors manning thirty major ships of the line and dozens of transports. The commanders, General William Howe and his brother Admiral Richard Howe, aimed at establishing a principal base in New York, isolating New England from the other states, and providing easy communication with Canada. One British force would descend from Canada by way of Lake Champlain and the Hudson River; the main force would strike New York City from the sea. The British fleet's blockade of the coastline was intended to deprive the Americans of both income and supplies from trade. The Howe brothers had brought with them instructions from Lord North to put out offers of peace. The "revolting colonies," said the prime minister, "cannot last long." But he was mistaken, and the peace overtures were ignored.

The Howes' upstate campaign was never effective. The brilliant tactics of Benedict Arnold in his courageous stand against a superior enemy fleet on Lake Champlain delayed a British thrust southward for

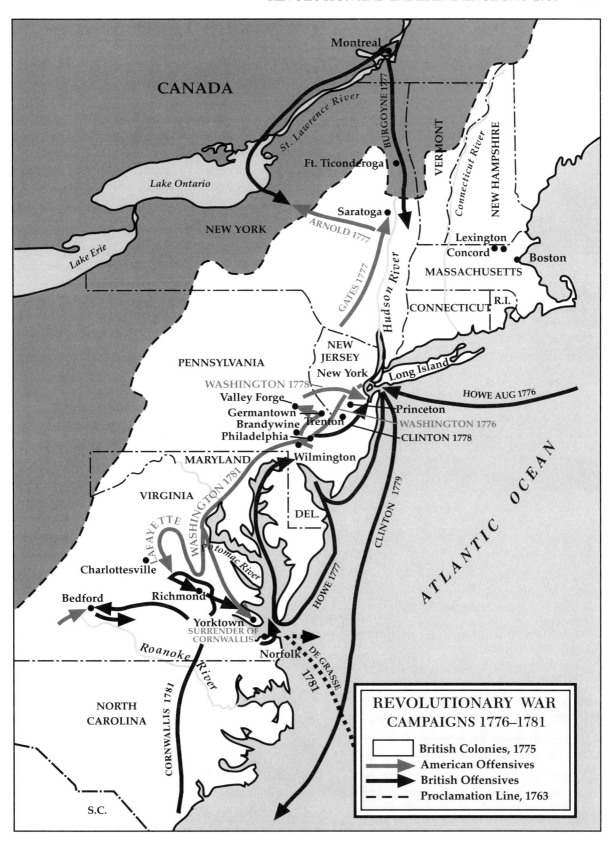

CANADA

St. Lawrence River

Montreal

Lake Ontario

BURGOYNE 1777

Ft. Ticonderoga

VERMONT

Connecticut River

NEW HAMPSHIRE

NEW YORK

Lake Erie

Saratoga

ARNOLD 1777

GATES 1777

Hudson River

Lexington
Concord
Boston

MASSACHUSETTS

CONNECTICUT   R.I.

PENNSYLVANIA

NEW JERSEY

New York

Long Island

HOWE AUG 1776

WASHINGTON 1778

Valley Forge
Germantown
Brandywine   Trenton
Philadelphia

Princeton
WASHINGTON 1776
CLINTON 1778

Wilmington

MARYLAND

WASHINGTON 1781

VIRGINIA

CLINTON 1779

DEL.

LAFAYETTE

Potomac River

HOWE 1777

ATLANTIC OCEAN

Charlottesville

Bedford

Richmond

Yorktown
SURRENDER OF
CORNWALLIS

Norfolk

DE GRASSE 1781

Roanoke River

CORNWALLIS 1781

NORTH
CAROLINA

S.C.

REVOLUTIONARY WAR
CAMPAIGNS 1776–1781

British Colonies, 1775
American Offensives
British Offensives
Proclamation Line, 1763

The Marquis de Lafayette wounded at the Battle of Brandywine Creek. *(Courtesy, Emmet Collection, New York Public Library)*

One of Washington's soldiers was to recall that the crossing of the Delaeare River took place on

"as severe a night as I ever saw—the frost was sharp, the current difficult to stem, the ice increasing, the wind high and at eleven it began to snow."

***Washington Crossing the Delaware**, by Emanuel Leutze. On Christmas night, 1776, General George Washington led his troops across the icy Delaware River, a maneuver that surprised the Hessian troops at Trenton and led to a much-needed American victory. This romantic mid-nineteenth-century painting is, however, filled with historical inaccuracies and unlikely poses: The crossing took place at night; Washington was not standing; the flag shown was not yet in use; and so on.* *(Courtesy, The Metropolitan Museum of Art)*

a year. The British strike against New York City, on the other hand, was child's play. Washington unwisely divided his makeshift army, sending about half of his troops to Long Island while the rest stayed on Manhattan. English ships slipped around both islands to block retreat, while Howe's soldiers attacked Brooklyn Heights, inflicting heavy losses. Realizing his mistake, Washington skillfully eluded the blockade, retreating across both islands into New Jersey. It was, Washington lamented, a "disgraceful and dastardly" flight. With the retreating army, now demoralized and in disarray, was volunteer aide-de-camp Thomas Paine, who had written in a widely-distributed pamphlet, "These are the times that try men's souls. The summer soldier and the sunshine patriot will, in this crisis, shrink from the service of his country; but he that stands by it now, deserves the love and thanks of man and woman."

Wishing to negotiate with the revolutionaries, not destroy them, Howe pursued them only as far as the Delaware River. Washington used this pause to regroup his armies, and on Christmas night of 1776 returned to the attack. After a daring military maneuver across the icy Delaware River, his army pounced on a camp of Hessian mercenaries at an outpost in Trenton, New Jersey. The Hessians, who had gone to bed drunk and confident that no army would attack on such a hallowed occasion, were quickly overwhelmed. Nearly 1,000 were captured. A week later Washington struck again, outmaneuvering a British force at Princeton and driving the enemy back to the Hudson before both armies went into hibernation. Washington took up winter quarters in the hills of western New Jersey; Howe diverted himself in New York "in feasting, banquetting, and in the arms of Mrs. Loving. . . ." He had fumbled a chance to end the war quickly.

In 1777 Britain's army renewed its efforts to occupy major coastal cities and isolate New England. In July General Howe embarked from New York with 15,000 men, sailed around to land at the head of Chesapeake Bay, and began fighting his way toward Philadelphia. Washington and his troops scurried overland to meet the British at Brandywine Creek, but could not turn them back and made an orderly retreat. By September 26 Washington had lost a fifth of his total force

and Howe had occupied Philadelphia, forcing Congress to flee to the Pennsylvania interior. On October 4, at the Battle of Germantown, Washington executed a series of intricate maneuvers that placed him in a position to destroy Howe's main encampment, but the American troops became lost in a heavy fog and at one point even fired on one another. Only General Nathanael Greene's skill prevented complete disorder. Humiliated, Washington's ill-clothed and underfed remnant of an army was forced to spend the winter near Valley Forge, Pennsylvania, one of the few iron foundries still in patriot hands.

Saratoga   Colonial leaders had long worried that the British might become "masters of the Hudson River," which would "divide our strength, and enfeeble every effort for our common preservation and security."

The campaign began with a signal British victory by General Burgoyne on July 6, 1777, the capture of Fort Ticonderoga, essential to the lake route to Albany. But then Burgoyne immediately blundered. Deciding that he now had ample time to move his army a mere seventy miles to Albany, he set out through the woods rather than follow Lake George. Hauling fifty-two cannon, his enormous wardrobe, his ample wine cellar, and a female entourage along a route obstructed by hundreds of trees that the Americans had felled, Burgoyne covered only twenty-three miles in twenty-four days. Meanwhile, at Oriskany and Fort Stanwix in the Mohawk Valley, in tough hand-to-hand fighting, the Americans soundly defeated the British army advancing from the west. Then the murder and scalping of a young New York woman, Jane McCrea, by Burgoyne's Indian allies sent the citizens of the upper Hudson Valley into a fury at the British, who had been paying Indians for the scalps of revolutionists.

Short of troops, hungry for supplies, and facing a large and capable Continental army well supported by local militia, Burgoyne was now in serious trouble. Crossing the Hudson he stood at Saratoga, New York, facing General Horatio Gates's army, which held a commanding position behind powerful fortifications built at the direction of a Polish engineer, Tadeusz Kósciuszko. On September 19, Burgoyne threw his troops into action against Gates at Freeman's Farm. The battle sapped British strength while Gates easily reinforced his army. With supplies running low, Burgoyne had to decide whether to fight again or retreat. He fought and on October 7, in the second battle of Saratoga, again suffered heavy losses. A popular topical verse said it all:

> Burgoyne, alas! unknowing future fates,
> Could force his way through woods,
> but not through GATES.

The French Alliance   As early as 1775, the Continental Congress had sent agents to France. Some, like Silas Deane and Arthur Lee, had arranged a trickle of loans and shipments of military supplies. The small Dutch island of St. Eustatius in the Caribbean served as a transit point: French ships unloaded munitions there, and patriots picked them up. Late in 1776, Congress sent Ben-

Private Joseph Martin wrote of eating nothing at Valley Forge for two days

"save half a small pumpkin, which I cooked by placing it upon a rock, the skin side uppermost, and making a fire upon it.... Had there fallen deep snows (and it was the time of year to expect them) or even heavy and long rainstorms, the whole army must inevitably have perished."

The Marquis de Lafayette, the Frenchman who had fought with Washington, observed that

"the unfortunate soldiers... had neither coats, nor hats, nor shirts, nor shoes; their feet and legs froze till they grew black, and it was often necessary to amputate them."

Franklin's unique combination of sophistication and homespun ways won him favor as a diplomat in Paris. *(Courtesy, Scribner's Archives)*

General Washington himself petitioned the Continental Congress in the fall of 1780 after he had been chided for inaction:

"Where are the Men—where are the Provisions—where are the Cloaths—the every thing necessary to warrant the attempt you propose, in an inclement Season? Our numbers, never equal to those of the enemy in new York—our state lines never half compleat in Men, but perfectly so in every species of want, were diminished in the Field so soon as the weather began to grow cold—near 2000 men, on account of Cloaths which I had not to give. . . . It would be well for the Troops if like Chameleons they cd. live upon air—or like the Bear suck their paws for sustenance during the rigour of the approaching season."

jamin Franklin to Paris to negotiate an alliance. But King Louis XVI hesitated. His government was nearly bankrupt; his Spanish allies feared that the example of the Revolution might encourage revolution among their own colonies; the armies of the United States appeared weak. It seemed enough to have the secret trade in military hardware supporting the patriot armies, accomplishing French objectives by tying Britain down in a protracted war. However much Franklin's republican wit and easy charm captivated courtiers at Versailles, diplomatic grace could not by itself gloss over hard realities. For two years, Franklin moved through France, winning many friends for the new nation and establishing his own formidable reputation. But for the moment the King avoided any overt alliance.

Nonetheless, France and Spain did see opportunities. King Louis yearned for revenge against an old enemy, while Spanish courtiers in Madrid feared the mushrooming British empire in the New World. After the Battle of Saratoga, opponents of the war in Britain persuaded Parliament to open peace negotiations, and by early spring 1778 a delegation under the Earl of Carlisle was on its way to the colonies with an offer of limited autonomy within the British empire. Fears that the Americans might accept such terms, along with the victory at Saratoga, finally prompted Louis XVI and his foreign minister to offer Congress a formal alliance. The patriots ratified the bargain on May 4, 1778, only weeks before the Carlisle commissioners arrived in Philadelphia. With the entry of France into the conflict, the American Revolution became a world war.

Dark and Drifting Times

By 1778, the United States could not find a winning strategy; neither could British generals defeat Washington's army or control the countryside. One major difficulty for the British was the sheer vastness of the country. The redcoats fought at the end of a 3,000-mile line of supply; slow-moving ships could not maintain large land armies. Americans, on the other hand, could attack like guerrillas and then easily escape across rivers into forests. Short of occupying the whole country—a physical impossibility—His Majesty's generals could find no way to strike some final blow that would crush the rebellion once and for all. Fighting to bring the rebels back into the empire, some of the British soldiers sympathized with the Americans' cause. As British strategy failed to divide the states or to quell the rebellion, Parliament grew increasingly restless with the war.

American strategy played upon British weakness. Unable to dislodge the redcoats from major seaport cities or confront their superior numbers in pitched battles, Washington adopted a policy of watchful waiting. Patriot forces sometimes conducted guerrilla warfare against isolated British units or their supply columns. Washington hoped to wear down the resolve of the British to continue the war or to force them into a situation in which he could make a decisive strike.

Washington needed time, and yet the new nation found even this passive strategy difficult to execute. Most men shunned enlistment in the Continental army, especially as patriotic fervor subsided after 1776.

Farming required the most work in spring and early fall, precisely those times most favorable for battle. The sense of a common nationhood was as yet half-formed, and state governors maintained tight control over their local militias, sometimes not letting them leave the state. Many Americans, fearful of military authority and centralized power, refused to pay taxes to support Washington's troops, and so the regular army lacked not only soldiers but also adequate arms and equipment. Unable to levy taxes, the Continental Congress printed millions of paper dollars popularly called "continentals." This flood of currency drove up prices mercilessly. After the French alliance Congress, hoping that the French would help pay its bills, printed still more paper money. By 1780 few merchants or farmers would accept "continentals" in payment for supplies. Washington had to resort to impressment—forced sales on credit—to provision his troops.

Stalemate   By 1779 the war had reached a stalemate. Both sides reduced the scale and intensity of the fighting in North America as skirmishes there simply became part of an international war. Now forced to defend as well their possessions in India and the Caribbean, the British withdrew ships and men from America. France, benefiting from England's distress, was slow to aid the patriot forces. For a year after the unsuccessful battle of Monmouth, New Jersey, in June 1778, Washington's beleaguered army had mounted no major offensive.

Civilian morale sagged; unrest mounted in the army. In 1780 General Benedict Arnold, reprimanded for misuse of his powers while he was commander of colonial troops at Philadelphia, began treasonable negotiations with the British to turn over West Point. When his activities were discovered he fled to the British, who made him a brigadier general. Bonuses paid to new recruits outraged some Pennsylvania troops in Washington's army, and on New Year's Day 1781, they mutinied and marched off to seek redress from Congress. Only promises of quick relief persuaded them to return to camp. Three weeks later some New Jersey troops mutinied, and two soldiers were executed.

In the winter of 1778–79 the new British commander in chief in America, General Henry Clinton, lacking sufficient troops to pacify the North, had shifted British operations to the South, where he anticipated aid from the large loyalist population. Events there gave the patriot cause little reason for encouragement. The British took Savannah and Charleston and encouraged the loyalists to make war on their patriot neighbors. In these circumstances the war in the backcountry became uncharacteristically savage. At Waxhaws Creek, South Carolina, in May 1780, Colonel Banastre Tarleton's loyalist troops massacred a Virginia regiment that had surrendered. The term "Tarleton's Quarter" became a rallying cry among southern patriots.

One boost to American morale in these bleak years had been the unexpected naval victory of John Paul Jones's *Bonhomme Richard* over the British warship *Serapis* in September 1779. The story has it that when asked whether he wished to surrender at one point during the battle, the intrepid Jones replied, "I have not yet begun to fight."

Colonel Banastre Tarleton.
(Courtesy, Hugh Cleland Collection)

According to an eyewitness to the Wax-haws Creek massacre:

"Not a man was spared . . . and for fifteen minutes after every man was prostrate [the Tories] went over the ground plunging their bayonets into everyone that exhibited any signs of life, and in some instances, where several had fallen one over the other, these monsters were seen to throw off on the point of the bayonet the uppermost, to come at those beneath."

"A successful cavalry charge exploited by a bayonet attack is bound to be messy," observes one scholar of Tarleton's Quarter.

An American at Yorktown wrote in his diary an account of the final days of the war:

17th.—Had the pleasure of seeing a drummer mount the enemy's parapet, and beat a parley, and immediately an officer, holding up a white handkerchief, made his appearance outside their works. . . . Our batteries ceased. An officer from our lines ran and met the other, and tied the handkerchief over his eyes. The British officer conducted to a house in rear of our lines. Firing ceased totally. . . .

19th.— . . . All is quiet. Articles of capitulation signed; detachments of French and Americans take possession of British forts. . . . I carried the standard of our regiment on this occasion. On entering the fort, Baron Steuben, who accompanied us, took the standard from me and planted it himself. The British army parade and march out with their colors furled; drums beat as if they did not care how. Grounded their arms and returned to town. Much confusion and riot among the British through the day; many of the soldiers were intoxicated . . . our patrols kept busy.

As the British formally surrendered at Yorktown, the band played, among other tunes, the British nursery rhyme "The World Turned Upside Down":

If buttercups buzzed
after the bee;
If boats were on land,
churches on sea;
If ponies rode men,
and grass ate the cow;
If cats should be chased,
into holes by the mouse;
If mammas sold their babies,
to gypsies for half a crown;
If summer were spring
and the other way round;
Then all the world would be
    upside down.

Victory   Then, in the summer of 1781, the war turned in favor of the rebels. Congress centralized the administrative departments and enacted a new financial program under the direction of Robert Morris. Supplies were soon flowing to the army again. Meanwhile French money and manpower finally began to arrive in significant amounts. And on the military front Washington in August 1781 received word that a French fleet was en route to Chesapeake Bay. Washington at last had a chance to strike.

In the Carolinas, harassed by guerrillas and "tired out marching about the country in quest of adventures," General Charles Cornwallis marched his army north toward Virginia for the purpose of cutting rebel communications between North and South. Counting on protection and supplies from the seemingly invincible Royal Navy, he violated one of the cardinal rules of warfare: never let your forces be backed up to terrain where retreat is impossible. In August 1781 Cornwallis made the fatal blunder: he moved his army onto a narrow peninsula between the York and James rivers near Yorktown and encamped there. Soon the French navy was at his back and a combined force of 9,000 Americans and 7,800 French began to besiege him by land. Hopelessly trapped, he surrendered his whole army on October 19, 1781.

Diplomacy and Independence

The defeat at Yorktown was by no means a complete military disaster for the British, since they still held America's major seaports. What Yorktown did accomplish was to dramatize how slender were the possibilities for eventual British victory against the combination of American armies and guerrillas and French power. Another vital consideration was that an end to the fighting in North America would free badly needed fleets and armies to fight against England's enemies in the West Indies and India. Early in 1782, Parliament forced Prime Minister North out of office and demanded negotiations with the United States. Although George III disagreed, many of his subjects thought that a generous peace might conciliate the former colonists, and even draw them back into the British orbit.

The Peacemaking   The Americans, too, were ready to end the war. In the Continental Congress one overworked member complained that "the little leisure we have is not sufficient for the common functions of life & exercise to keep us in health." The Continental Congress was near collapse, and local loyalties and interests were continuing to strain against the national purpose. In Congress, planters worried about "getting home to their plantations at a season in which planters in general have so very much to attend to." One lawyer complained, "I have lost my Clients the benefit of a Circuit and now despair of doing any thing the ensuing Term." Said another, "This trade of patriotism but ill agrees with the profession of a practising Lawyer." One member, however, enjoyed "the company of a number of very fine ladies." Another could talk of nothing but his speculation in western land.

The victory at Yorktown, however welcome, was more lucky circumstance than a triumph of superior military power or skill. Chances for a large territorial settlement and the prospect of better relations with Britain, a dangerous adversary for any nation so exposed to attack from the sea, understandably attracted many Americans. In fact, the Congress authorized its negotiating team, headed by Benjamin Franklin, to accept almost any treaty that included independence and a withdrawal of British troops. With their mutual interests so aligned, the two enemies seemed likely to conclude a quick agreement.

Yet negotiations in Paris dragged on for nearly two years. The Franco-American alliance of 1778 bound the United States not to make a separate peace. In turn, Louis XVI and his minister Vergennes, in order to gain Spanish support, had promised ministers in Madrid much British territory as booty, especially strategic Gibraltar. The Spanish, moreover, wanted to confine the United States to the area east of the Appalachian Mountains. Although the Spanish could expect few concessions from Great Britain, they might hold up indefinitely a settlement between Britain and the United States. America now had more to lose from its friends than from its enemies.

| **The Treaty of Paris** | At last, Franklin broke the diplomatic deadlock by violating the terms of the alliance with France and opening separate negotiations with English agents. |

The French, themselves weakened by a long and costly conflict, were not much upset. Once started, talks progressed steadily. The series of treaties that ended the war, collectively known as the Treaty of Paris, was signed on September 3, 1783. England granted independence and promised to withdraw all its troops from the colonies. The new nation acquired a huge grant of land: from the Atlantic seacoast to the Mississippi River. Its boundaries in the north with Canada remained vague, and redcoats still occupied forts south of the Great Lakes. The Gulf Coast was ceded to Spain, although both Americans and Englishmen were guaranteed navigation rights on the Mississippi. Britain successfully demanded that "no unlawful impediment" block the collection of prewar debts Americans owed to British merchants. The treaties also pledged the United States to make restitution to loyalists who had suffered financially during the Revolution. British merchants did succeed in closing the Americans out of imperial commerce, a serious loss for the young nation. Despite these concessions and the lack of adequate enforcement procedures, the Americans had benefited handsomely from European rivalries. War and diplomacy created a new nation with boundaries generous enough to ensure future growth and prosperity.

The War at Home

| **Prosperity and Inflation** | Eight years of warfare not only profited many individuals but also invigorated the whole economy. An immense amount of money in circulation raised the |

price of nearly everything. The Continental Congress and the state governments had spent on the war nearly $200 million in hard money, followed by many more millions in paper currency. British soldiers and

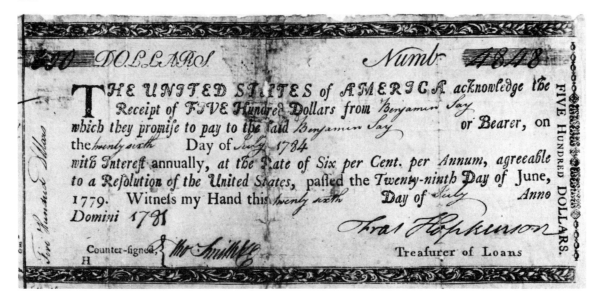

Bonds paying 6% per year were sold to finance the Revolution. The inflation rate was much higher.
(*Courtesy, Chase Bank Collection of Moneys of the World, New York*)

Head of a Negro, by John Singleton Copley. By 1780, some 500,000 slaves worked the lands of the South.
(*Copyright © 1983, Founders Society, Detroit Institute of Art*)

purchasing agents poured another $50 million into the economy. All this money created an extraordinary demand for commodities and, of course, persistent inflation resulted. Yet few Americans suffered economically. War stimulated production. The need for uniforms and arms, for example, produced rapid growth in the textile and iron industries. Merchants' inventories and farmers' crops grew in value. Bankers lent at high rates of interest to importers and privateers—goods brought through the British blockade commanded enormous profits. Many state and local governments imposed price and wage controls, a device used since the Middle Ages to control inflation. Congress regulated monopolies and prevented some exports of needed raw materials. More and more local economies were coming together into a broad national market. A nation was slowly unifying.

Despite occasionally rigorous efforts at regulation, the pressures of wartime inflation produced extensive black markets. Shopkeepers and small farmers preferred to deal with Englishmen and private citizens who spent silver and gold coin. An indignant Pennsylvanian angrily refused to sell his grain to one of Washington's agents, saying, "Your money's not worth a damn continental." The phrase caught on. Throughout most of the war, private citizens prospered while the government and army suffered penury and hardship. This paradox so angered Washington that he proposed hanging all profiteers.

Social Change   Major changes occurred in the pattern of land ownership. Probably a quarter of the population was loyal to the British Crown, either openly or secretly. By 1778 all thirteen states had confiscated the property of those who "took refuge with the British tyrant." Some 100,000 already had left the country, most for Canada or England, and their estates were sold for money to support the patriot cause. Much of the confiscated land was bought up by rich speculators or other large landowners, not by tenants and small farmers, who rarely had enough money to buy in places already settled. Instead, many of them and their children looked westward to the mountains and beyond. Even before the war ended, thousands had migrated, going into what were to be Tennessee and Kentucky, into northern New England and northern New York.

Religion   The Revolution also affected religion. Most states disestablished churches, ending the special privileges or civil functions of particular sects. Only Massachusetts and Connecticut still collected taxes to fund a state church; the other states viewed competing religions as equal in the eyes of the law. Tolerance did not extend to atheists, however, and most state legislatures established a religious test for holding public office. Blasphemy remained a crime punishable by imprisonment.

Documents like Thomas Jefferson's Statute of Religious Freedom in Virginia, finally enacted by the Virginia legislature in 1786, granted tolerance for the free practice of religion, not a guarantee of rights for nonbelievers. If narrow by twentieth-century standards, the statute was for its time a model, proclaiming to the rest of the world an example of the nation's new freedom.

Slaves   The Revolution also made for a rhetoric of liberty that stumbled against the reality of human bondage. "How is it," chided the crusty British writer Samuel Johnson, "that we hear the loudest yelps for liberty among the drivers of Negroes?" A group of blacks in Boston announced to the General Court that their race looked for "great things from men who have made such a noble stand against the designs of their *fellow-men* to enslave them." During the war over 5,000 blacks served in the American army and navy. Several states granted freedom to slaves who served in the military. Soon a voluble antislavery movement emerged. Philadelphia Quakers had formed the first antislavery society in 1775. In most northern states, slavery was not a large part of the economy, and patriot leaders struck decisively at the institution.

In 1780 the Pennsylvania legislature passed a gradual emancipation law freeing its slaves; and Massachusetts abolished slavery by court order in 1783. Connecticut and Rhode Island soon passed general abolition laws, and New York and New Jersey passed similar laws. In 1787 Congress passed the Northwest Ordinance, which prohibited slavery in the Ohio Valley, the region that would become Ohio, Indiana, Illinois, Michigan, and Wisconsin. After fierce debate in 1787 the Constitutional Convention permitted outlawing the importation of slaves after 1808. The American Revolution that brought freedom from England won, for northern African Americans, freedom from bondage.

Legal freedom did not mean equality. Most northern whites were racists, and they acted on their fears and convictions. In Ohio, Indiana, and Illinois white settlers from the South segregated free African Americans whenever possible, and black youths were often placed in long-term apprenticeships closely resembling slavery. African-American

In 1781 a Massachusetts judge declared:

"As to the doctrine of slavery and the right of Christians to hold Africans in perpetual servitude, and sell and treat them as we do our horses and cattle, nowhere is it expressly enacted or established. It has been a usage—a usage which took its origins from the practice of some of the European nations, and the regulations of British government respecting the then Colonies, for the benefit of trade and wealth. But whatever sentiments have formerly prevailed in this particular or slid in upon us by the example of others, a different idea has taken place with the people of America, more favorable to the natural rights of mankind, and to that natural, innate desire of Liberty, with which heaven (without regard to color, complexion, or shape of noses . . .) has inspired all the human race. And upon the ground our Constitution of Government, by which the people of this Commonwealth have solemnly bound themselves, sets out with declaring that all men are born free and equal—and that every subject is entitled to liberty and to have it guarded by the laws, as well as life and property—and in short is totally repugnant to the idea of being born slaves."

The inscription on the Concord grave-stone of John Jack, a slave who bought his freedom in the 1760s and died in 1773, reads:

God wills us free; man wills us slaves.
I will as God wills; God's will be done.
Here lies the body of
JOHN JACK
a native of Africa who died
March 1773 aged about 60 years
Tho' born in a land of slavery,
He was born free.
Tho' he lived in a land of liberty,
    he lived a slave. . . .

adults could not serve on juries or vote, and the immigration of blacks from other states was barred. Between 1807 and 1837 New Jersey, Connecticut, New York, Rhode Island, and Pennsylvania passed laws disfranchising African Americans. And throughout the North, black people were widely discriminated against in the job market.

Indians Conscience sharpened by the libertarian rhetoric of the Revolution moved white Americans to make some efforts toward the elimination of slavery. Neither conscience nor the language of the Declaration bestowed noticeable benefits on the Indians. Relations between the Indians and the new republic took their character not from the sensibility of the eastern educated gentry, but from the land greed, the fears, and the prejudice of western settlers.

During the war both Britain and the United States vied for Indian support. In 1775 the Continental Congress formed a Committee on Indian Affairs, and commissioners went to different tribes either to win their support or to persuade them to remain neutral during the conflict. Most tribes, however, joined the English cause. During the French and Indian War they had sided with the French instead of the English and subsequently paid a price for their decision. It was to be no different this time. When the war ended in 1783, England recognized the independence of the United States but neglected to put any provisions into the treaty protecting their former Indian allies. Under the Articles of Confederation, the new central government was too weak to control Indian affairs effectively, especially since the states had supreme authority to handle policy within their boundaries. When the Confederation government passed the Northwest Ordinance of 1787, establishing steps by which an area could achieve statehood, it included a clause urging the fair and just treatment of the Indians. But again, land speculators and settlers, now resentful of the aid Indians had given to the British during the Revolution, continued to ignore Indian rights.

For a brief period after the American Revolution many colonists, having defeated the British, could treat as conquered peoples the Indian allies of the redcoats. The government dictated several treaties. In the Treaty of Fort Stanwix of 1784, for example, the Iroquois had to cede lands in western New York and Pennsylvania. During the last decades of the eighteenth century, the Iroquois living in the United States quickly degenerated as a nation, losing most of their remaining lands. Witnessing the destruction of the Iroquois Confederacy, tribes such as the Shawnees, Miamis, Delawares, Ottawas, Wyandots, and Potawatomis formed their own confederacy and informed the United States that the Ohio River was the boundary between their lands and those of the settlers. It was only a matter of time before further hostilities ensued.

By 1790 the tens of thousands of settlers living in Kentucky and the Ohio Valley demanded that the United States send expeditions against the Indians who were attacking their settlements. In 1790 and again in 1792, American expeditionary forces were defeated in their attempts to subdue the confederacy. Finally, in August 1794, General "Mad" Anthony Wayne defeated the confederacy at Fallen Timbers. The Indians signed the Treaty of Greenville in 1795, surrendering to the United

States most of present-day Ohio and Indiana. Settlers poured into the newly available western lands.

The American Revolution had much to offer the world by way of example. But for most Indians, the Revolution and its aftermath were an unmitigated disaster.

**Women's
Lives**   The war also affected the lives, and perhaps the self-image, of women. Many had participated in the war effort, either at the front or on the home front. Many more had become accustomed to discussing politics and military news. Some few, like Mercy Otis Warren, who first wrote anti-British plays and then a history of the Revolution, engaged directly in propaganda. Others, like Abigail Adams, took over the management of farms and businesses about which they had previously known little. In this sense, the war years offered many women an education in independent action.

Few, if any, colonial women translated their revolutionary experience into a demand for political rights or equality with men. But many women must have emerged from those years with greatly increased confidence in their own abilities. Those who had worked together in the Ladies Association that organized a national fund drive to collect money for the American troops had also experienced the power and satisfaction of collective action. That experience would be multiplied in the many women's voluntary associations that emerged in the early nineteenth century.

By and large, women did not gain independence from the Revolution in the same sense that most free men gained it. During the final decades of the eighteenth century single, property-holding women were allowed to vote in New Jersey, but that state soon rescinded this limited suffrage. Few Americans of either gender seriously contemplated political rights for women. Certainly the Revolution did not noticeably improve married women's standing in law in general, or their right to hold property in particular. Yet in one respect the Revolution brought significant improvement in the status of women—the ideal of virtuous "republican motherhood." This suggested that women—republican mothers—deserved a special kind of independence and dignity within the domestic sphere. There they would contribute their special qualities of nurture to the raising of virtuous young republicans to ensure the future of the new nation.

No more in this respect than in any others did the slim advantages gained by free white women extend to black slave women, whose experience looked more like a grim caricature than like an extension of the sanctity and dignity of motherhood.

A version of the concept of republican motherhood was set forth in the commencement oration at Columbia College in 1795:

"Let us then figure to ourselves the accomplished woman, surrounded by a sprightly band, from the babe that imbibes the nutritive fluid, to the generous youth, just ripening into manhood, and the lovely virgin. . . . Let us contemplate the mother distributing the mental nourishment to the fond smiling circle . . . watching the gradual openings of their minds, and studying their various turns of temper. . . . the Genius of Liberty hovers triumphant over the glorious scene."

How Revolutionary?

Historians have argued about whether or not American society became more open, more fostering of upward mobility, during the Revolutionary era. Certainly some older marks of privilege did disappear. Since feudal

**"Hessian Soldier" andiron,
one of a pair; cast iron, painted;
late eighteenth century.**
(Index of American Design)

**Dress, imported brocaded silk,
made in Boston, about 1770.**
(Index of American Design)

times European law, seeking to keep intact the property of the upper classes, had enforced the principle of entail, that property could be passed on only within the same family, and the rule of primogeniture, that it could not be divided in inheritance but must go to the eldest son. Such rules had survived in some colonial laws, applying at least in cases in which a landowner had not provided otherwise in a will. These laws were now swept aside as relics of an age of artificial privilege and inequality. In addition, the emigration of thousands of loyalists left many local political offices vacant and created new opportunities.

Yet America remained firmly under the control of an elite that had never had a fixed membership. Revolutionary ardor hardly touched the traditional politics of deference south of Pennsylvania. There the local gentry kept control over tidewater society and government. In Philadelphia, New York, and Boston a coalition of lawyers, merchants, and landowners dominated the cities after the war, much as it had before. The rich held disproportionate power in the Continental Congress. Robert Morris, for example, a merchant and speculator who served in the early 1780s as the nation's chief treasury official, possessed a fortune of $8 million.

The American Revolution and its aftermath, then, presented no scenes of revolutionary crowds pitted against a besieged upper class. What happened instead was an application of the principle, pronounced in the Declaration of Independence, that governments derive "their just Powers from the consent of the governed." Under the new state constitutions drafted during the war, most legislatures welcomed representatives from backcountry areas; the middling ranks of society—small farmers, local businessmen, and artisans—came to occupy office in larger numbers; and bills of rights prefaced many constitutions. Everywhere governors lost power, and elected assemblies gained control of patronage and tax matters. Legislators stood for election each year. In Pennsylvania, a new constitution abolished altogether the legislature's upper house, traditionally the bastion of the wealthy. Pennsylvania's candidates for election were forbidden to give "meat, drink, money, or otherwise" as gifts to voters. New York experimented with the secret ballot instead of voice voting, claiming that the ballot "would tend more to preserve the liberty and equal freedom of the people."

Some less democratic practices lingered. In many states property ownership was still a requirement for voting; high political office might require the ownership of large amounts of land. Upper chambers of most state legislatures could block the demands of the majority, and in South Carolina, Virginia, and Georgia, unfairly apportioned assemblies mocked the popular will. In Georgia, for example, the piedmont—the inland region just east of the mountains—contained three-fourths of the population yet received only one-fourth of the seats in the assembly, which tidewater plantation owners still rigidly dominated. Nonetheless, in all the colonies government officials were elected, lower houses had most of the power, and state officials proved susceptible to public opinion. Many people never before interested in politics had discovered their voice. Individuals of every class now found themselves taking part in a democracy of public discussion and common action—a democratic activity more basic than the formal democracy of the vote.

Republicanism   The most radical implication of the American Revolution was a concept derived only in part from the Declaration of Independence and expressed only partially in the democratic reforms initiated by the states. This was the idea and creation of a republic.

Republicanism has much to do with liberty, but the meaning of the word should not be confused with popular notions of freedom. It does not mean the liberty to be private, to withdraw property and energies from uses that might serve the public good. That is a later corruption of what eighteenth-century philosophers were thinking. Liberty was perceived as the proud possession of republican citizens virtuous in habits, industrious, generous, quick to engage in public service. The word "republic" had to eighteenth-century revolutionists a noble ring. It recalled the austere city-states of Greece, the stern citizenry of Rome, the stately Roman senators. To be a citizen of a republic was to be an actor in a continuing history, a contributor to the common good. Yet liberty in the service of the public welfare does not mean surrender to the popular will. Free citizens, as republican theorists perceived them, have minds of their own and can stand against the mass emotions of the moment. Virtuous liberty is a necessity for the continuance of a republic. The republic, in turn, has as its purpose the cultivation of liberty and virtue.

Republicanism defined as the participation of free citizens in a collective enterprise was as much an accident as an ideological choice on the part of the leaders of the Revolution. The citizen Continental army that Congress projected and Washington led was a necessity of war. The participation of civilians, male and female, in the war effort seems to have been more the expression of individual conviction and social pressure than the product of some idea of republicanism. Yet the result suggests the deliberately, philosophically republican decree of the French revolutionary leaders of 1793 in the face of invasion of France: "Young men will go into combat. . . . Women will make tents and uniforms and serve in hospitals. . . . Old men will have themselves carried to public places to arouse the courage of warriors and to preach hatred of kings and the unity of the Republic."

A conflict between republican unity and republican liberty was foreshadowed even before the Revolution. The mobs that appeared periodically in resistance to British measures demanded unity and attacked whoever they believed to be in support of British oppression. Against popular passions stood libertarians: Lieutenant Governor Thomas Hutchinson of Massachusetts, the crusty descendant of the dissenter Anne Hutchinson and the opponent of the Revolution; Boston patriots John Adams and Josiah Quincy, who successfully defended in court the British officer accused of responsibility for the Boston Massacre. And in American history ever since, the claims of individual liberty and dissent have clashed with the clamors of conformist popular emotion.

Property and republicanism have had a similarly uneasy relationship. Early in American national history, republican theorists such as Thomas Jefferson expected a wide distribution of property ownership, made possible by the abundance of land, and assumed that holders of

Lantern of pierced tin called a "Paul Revere"; probably made in New England; eighteenth to nineteenth century. (*Index of American Design*)

Dowry chest, Pennsylvania German; inscribed with name of first owner, Jacob Rickert, dated 1782. (*Index of American Design*)

small property would make responsible, public-spirited citizens. Yet property, especially ownership of land, also drew Americans away from one another: physically so in the westward movement, socially in the unwillingness of the owning classes to put their property to public uses. Economic individualism and republican virtue would continue a quarrel that derived from their common grounding in American material, political, and ideological conditions.

Yet another dilemma for American republicanism lay in the belief that virtues most flourish in simple agricultural societies. Republics themselves, those of ancient Greece along with Rome and more recent polities, were city-states, and cities, most notably Boston, were breeding grounds for the American Revolution. Still, the idea persisted that living on the land and working it made for habits of diligence, honesty, and independence. But the energies released in part by the American Revolution would lead to the development of great cities and of industries severed from the land. In time it became necessary for American social critics to learn the ways in which these too can give shape to virtue.

The Articles of Confederation
and the Critical Period

The New Government   The Continental Congress that convened in May 1775 following the battles at Concord and Lexington sat in continuous session until 1787. Members came and went, but during this wrenching and momentous period Congress operated with remarkable effectiveness. While drafting a new form of government, the Articles of Confederation, Congress raised an army and appointed its commander in chief, negotiated with the enemy, authorized a navy, and sent agents and commissioners to France, Spain, Prussia, Austria, and Tuscany. It also issued millions of dollars of paper money.

In June 1776, almost simultaneously with the resolution that led to the Declaration of Independence, Richard Henry Lee proposed a permanent new government to represent all the states. In July, John Dickinson of Pennsylvania, chairman of the committee appointed to draw up the plan of government, submitted his proposals. Dickinson's scheme contained several controversial features. The new Congress was to have broad powers, including the right to establish state boundaries and to dispose of unoccupied western lands. Each state would have one vote, regardless of its population and the number of representatives it actually sent to Congress.

The Dickinson proposals came under immediate attack in open Congress. The large and influential state of Virginia, which claimed much of the trans-Appalachian West, opposed granting the new government sweeping powers over lands. Many of Virginia's most prominent leaders had for years anticipated selling western lands to the farmers whom they expected to spill over the mountains when peace returned. On the other hand, delegates from states such as Maryland and Pennsylvania, owning no western lands as far inland as Virginia claimed, wanted the United States as a whole to acquire the lands toward the Mississippi River. Only in this way, they insisted, could Americans from all parts of the new nation benefit from these millions of fertile acres. The delegates also fought over the voting provision. Large states wanted voting by size of population. The small states supported Dickinson's proposal. By their reasoning, allotting one vote to each state meant that the new government was a league of sovereign states. Apportioning representation to the states on the basis of their population would suggest that the power of the new government flowed directly from the American people, bypassing the states. Some members of Congress feared even the Dickinson document for giving too much power to the central government. This issue would arise again in the debates on the Constitution of 1787, and, in fact, the question of states' rights was to be a perennial problem in American politics.

The Articles of Confederation For almost a year and a half, amidst the smoke and flames of war, Congress debated the powers of the new government. One New Jersey man thought that "Congress have not reserved enough power for themselves." Opponents of the original proposal succeeded in adding to it a provision that Congress could exercise only those powers specifically delegated to it by the states. Another change was a victory for Virginia. Under strong pressure from that land-rich state, the delegates at Philadelphia agreed to drop the provision that Congress would control the new nation's western lands. With these modifications accepted, Congress in November 1777 adopted the Articles of Confederation and sent the new frame of national government to the states for ratification.

Twelve states swiftly ratified the Articles. Maryland, however, held out for the original proposal that Congress control western lands and refused to ratify until it was restored. A number of prominent Virginians, including Thomas Jefferson, had a grander vision of the West than merely as a mammoth, overgrown Virginia. The great interior valley of North America, they believed, should be carved into new, self-governing states, rather than remain colonies of the seaboard. For the good of the whole nation they were willing to surrender their own state's claims. Under their influence, Virginia ceded its western lands to Congress, and in 1781 Maryland relented and the Articles of Confederation finally went into effect. It pledged all the states to "a firm league of friendship" with one another, and committed them to mutual support against attack. It gave to Congress sole power over foreign affairs and over the issues of war and peace. Congress would also deal with the Indians, and the states agreed to surrender to one another all escaped criminals and to give "full faith and credit" to court orders, sentences, and other judicial decisions of sister states.

From the very first, the Articles proved inadequate as a basis for dealing with the difficulties of a new nation. The Confederation amounted to a league of virtually independent sovereign states, not a modern nation. The new government lacked one vital power—the power to tax or to force the states to levy taxes in its behalf. Congress had to depend on contributions from the states. Nor could it regulate trade and commerce among the states. Any attempt to change or modify

Article 2 of The Articles of Confederation and Perpetual Union Between the States *provided:*

"Each state retains its sovereignty, freedom, and independence, and every power, jurisdiction, and right which is not by this confederation expressly delegated to the United States in Congress assembled."

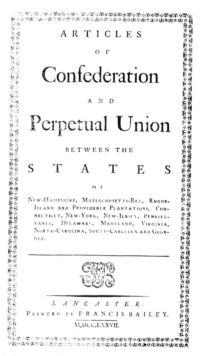

The Articles of Confederation pledged the thirteen states to "a firm league of friendship" with one another but failed to create a strong national government.

the Articles required the agreement of all the states. There were no executive and no national judiciary. Under this instrument of government, however weak, Americans did succeed in bringing the war to a successful conclusion. But the Confederation's authority would be too feeble to garner the fruits of victory and manage demobilization.

Debt Problems

During the months following Yorktown, the strains of nationhood, no longer obscured by military events, became painfully apparent. By early 1783 discontent plagued the army. Officers protested Congress's failure to establish a promised pension system for discharged veterans. In early March a group of officers at Newburgh, New York, threatened a military coup until Congress found the means to provide the officers with five years of full pay in lieu of the pensions.

The rank-and-file soldiers still had not received their pay. Congress simply could not raise the money. In the end, Congress discharged most of the troops without meeting their demands. Most of them rushed back to civilian life with little fuss, but several hundred marched to Philadelphia protesting their shabby treatment. Unable to meet the soldiers' demands and terrified by the angry troops, Congress fled first to Princeton, then to Annapolis, and finally came to rest in New York, which remained the national capital for several years.

Some patriots despaired over the pitiful state of the national government. Congress could pay neither its troops nor its creditors. The war had been financed by a combination of loans, paper money, and, in the case of several states, some taxes. The paper money had seriously depreciated; in 1781 Congress announced that it would not give in exchange to holders of paper currency the hard coin (specie) that in those days was considered to be the only reliable money. Other sizable obligations remained. Congress had borrowed directly from its own citizens, issuing IOU's in exchange for supplies, food, services, and cash. It had also borrowed from Dutch bankers. The states had similar problems. Massachusetts and a few others imposed high taxes to pay their debts; most were content to default like the Confederation government. These unpaid public debts cast a pall over the nation in the years after the war. How could such a country not be an object of scorn in the eyes of the whole world?

Creditors of the new government, whether original holders of the securities issued by Congress or speculators in them, had reason not to respect the new government. They had little hope of ever being paid. Farmers who had supplied commodities to the British West Indies and southern Europe, merchants who had traded with these regions, and all those in the port towns who had relied on this trade for a living saw their economic horizon shrink. Equally aggrieved were craftsmen and artisans in the towns whose businesses and jobs were washed out by a deluge of cheap British goods.

Debtors, too, found times hard and sought to offset the difficulties they encountered. One favorite scheme of debtor groups to counteract the postwar deflation was paper money issued by the states. When paper money is in circulation a unit of money tends to decline in value more

---

The story of Rachel Wells is particularly revealing of the problems faced by the impoverished states:

"To the Honnorabell Congress I rachel do make this Complaint Who am a Widow far advanced in years & Dearly have ocasion of ye Interst for that Cash I Lent the States. I was a Sitisen in ye jersey when I Lent ye State a considerable Sum of Moneys & had I justice dun me it mite be Suficant to suporte me in ye Contrey whear I am now, near burdentown. I Leved hear then . . . but Being . . . so Robd by the Britans & others i went to Phila to try to get a Living . . . & was There in the year 1783 when our assembley was pleasd to pas a Law that No one Should have aney Interst that Livd out of jearsey Stats . . .

Now gentelmen in this Liberty, had it bin advertised that he or She that Moved out of the Stat should Louse his or her Interest you mite have sum plea against me. But I am Innocent Suspected no Trick. I have Don as much to Carrey on the Warr as maney that Sett now at ye healm of government. . . . your asembly Borrowed £300 in gould of me jest as the Warr Comencd & Now I Can Nither git Intrust nor principall Nor Even Security. . . . My dr Sister . . . wrote to me to be thankfull that I had it in my Power to help on the Warr which is well enough but then this is to be Considered that others gits their Intrust & why then a poor old widow to be put of[f]. . . .

God has Spred a plentifull table for us & you gentelmen are ye Carvers for us pray forgit Not the Poor weaklings at the foot of the Tabel ye poor Sogers [soldiers] has got Sum Crumbs That fall from their masters tabel."

quickly than when the only currency is in hard money of gold or silver. That is because the quantity of gold and silver is limited while paper can be printed in any amount a government chooses. Even when the understanding is that the government will give gold or silver to any holder of paper money who demands the exchange, the government can print more paper than it possesses in gold and silver, hoping that it will never be asked to exchange all the paper for metallic coin. The more paper money a government prints, or the greater the public expectation that the government will flood the economy with paper, the less will be the value of any single unit of currency. A paper currency would therefore be to the advantage of debtors, for they would be able to pay their debts with units of money cheaper than those they had borrowed. In Maryland indebted planters supported paper-money schemes, and in Pennsylvania and South Carolina merchants endorsed them. Not only were planters and merchants often in debt themselves, but many believed that the lack of paper money made all business hard to conduct and contributed to the depressed state of the economy.

In a number of states, paper money became in effect a way of confiscating a part of creditors' property. In North Carolina, Georgia, and New Jersey the paper money issues authorized by the state legislatures quickly depreciated, yet creditors were forced to take it at face value. The most notorious case occurred in 1786 when Rhode Island issued an avalanche of paper money. These notes were legal tender, so if any creditor refused to accept them the bills could be deposited with a judge and the debt legally canceled. Many Rhode Island merchants closed their doors rather than accept the notes. Creditors fled the state to escape debtors anxious to pay them in depreciated paper.

Toleware coffee pot from Lebanon, Pennsylvania.
(Index of American Design)

| **Trouble with Spain** | Spain controlled both Florida and the lower reaches of the Mississippi, including the important port of New Orleans. By the end of the Revolution 50,000 |

American farmers lived on the "Western waters" in Kentucky and Tennessee, and many more Americans were eagerly awaiting the opportunity to cross the mountains to the fertile lands of the Mississippi Valley. If these people were not to remain subsistence farmers, they would need outlets for their wheat, pork, beef, corn, and forest products. The route east over the mountains was too difficult for the shipping of bulky products, but the great river that flowed to the Gulf of Mexico was a cheap and safe natural highway. Raft-like flatboats could be constructed of local lumber and loaded with barrels of pickled beef, pork, and grain to float with the current to New Orleans. There the rafts could be broken up and sold for lumber, and the barrels reloaded on oceangoing vessels to be carried to the Atlantic coast ports, the Caribbean islands, or Europe. The farmer could then buy some horses and return to Kentucky with some cash in his pocket and manufactured goods in his saddlebags. Control of New Orleans, then, gave Spain a strong hand in dealing with the United States.

In 1784 the Spanish government announced that it was closing the Mississippi to American commerce. Now only Spanish subjects could use the river and the port of New Orleans. All others would be arrested.

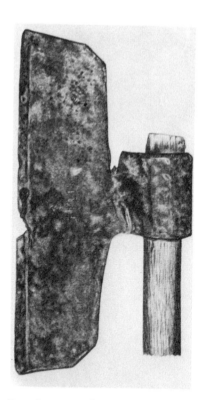

Broadax, wrought iron, oak handle, eighteenth century.
(Index of American Design)

Settler's wagon; length, over
14 feet; wagon bed, 10½ feet;
wheel diameters, 42 inches
and 33½ inches; about 1800.
(*Index of American Design*)

Westerners threatened to raise ten thousand troops to march on New Orleans. Some listened to British agents who promised protection if they would reunite with Great Britain. George Washington, seriously worried at the prospect of national dismemberment, reported after a long journey through the frontier that "the western settlers . . . stand as it were upon a pivot. The touch of a feather would turn them any way."

The nation's diplomatic weakness was soon confirmed. Negotiations began in 1785 between Spain and the United States over the "right of deposit" at New Orleans—in effect, the right to use the port there for foreign trade. Dour, tight-lipped John Jay, Congress's Secretary for Foreign Affairs, met with the suave and charming Don Diego de Gardoqui, Spain's negotiator. The Spanish emissary knew that the powerless Americans were in no position to threaten Spain, and refused to grant the major American demand, the right of deposit, although he was willing to make minor boundary adjustments along the West Florida border and allow some American trade within the Spanish empire. Congress refused to accept the treaty, and it died. New Orleans remained a locked gate at the mouth of the Mississippi.

Trouble with Britain   The British, who could make more trouble for the new nation than Spain, had no reason to wish the Americans well. In July 1783 the Privy Council issued an order that closed the British West Indies to most American commerce. This order dismayed farmers of the northern states, who had long sent their surplus provisions to Jamaica, Barbados, and the other British islands. It also hurt the New England fishing industry, which had supplied the sugar plantations with dried cod and mackerel, and the merchants of New York, Philadelphia, Salem, and Boston who had carried these goods. The shipping industry employed hundreds of seamen and thousands more in such related occupations as shipbuilding and the making of sail and rope. The British Caribbean planters connived at the smuggling of needed products, but this scarcely made up for the damage to American interests.

The Americans were in no position to retaliate. The British, of course, needed the American market for their manufactured goods, and in the immediate postwar period flooded the United States with cheap products to the distress of American artisans and manufacturers. Paying for imports from Britain also drained gold and silver coin from the nation. Several states, urged on by mass meetings of artisans and craftsmen, imposed duties on foreign goods. But the British found ways of sending their product through adjacent states that had no such taxes. Efforts to erect trade barriers among states created bad feeling between neighbors. Merchants of New London, Connecticut, boycotted New York; New Jersey taxed the New York lighthouse at Sandy Hook.

Under the peace treaty ending the war, the British had granted the United States the territory south of the Great Lakes and north of the Spanish possessions—all the way to the Mississippi River—and had promised to give up their military posts in the Northwest "with all convenient speed." For some time, however, they refused to remove the garrisons. The British did not wish to abandon their Indian allies and were reluctant to surrender the rich fur trade. They justified their delay by citing two provisions of the peace treaty: the promise that the Americans would do nothing to prevent British creditors from collecting millions of pounds in prewar debts, and the assurance that Congress would try to get the states to compensate loyalists for their wartime losses. The states had not yet fulfilled either of these promises, and Congress was powerless to compel compliance.

Barbary Pirates

One final confrontation came close to being the most humiliating of all. For many years the deys and pashas of the Barbary Coast states of North Africa, Algiers, Tunis, Tripoli, and Morocco had preyed on European commerce. Most European nations either paid blackmail to these corsairs or provided naval protection for their own commerce. So long as the Americans were dependents of Great Britain, the British navy and treasury had covered them as well as Englishmen. After independence this protection ceased. In 1785 the New England ship *Maria* was captured by Algerians, who stole its merchandise, stripped the crew of all their clothes and possessions, and then sold them into North African slavery. American merchants demanded that Congress respond to such ruthless attacks. But without a navy or the means to create one, the Confederation government could do nothing to overawe the Barbary Pirates. Congress did manage to raise $80,000 to buy exemption from the deys, but this was so little that only the Moroccan leader concluded a treaty. In a few years, under the administration of Thomas Jefferson, the American navy in one of the most assertive acts of the new nation would punish the pirates. Great Britain later crushed them for resuming their attacks.

The Period of the Confederation

Expanding Commerce

With the break from England, American merchants, no longer hindered by the Navigation Acts, began direct trade with parts of Europe from which they had been virtually excluded. Soon American vessels were showing up regularly in the harbors of Sweden, Holland, and Denmark, and even faraway Russia.

Still more interesting was the new trade with the Far East. In 1784 Robert Morris and some partners fitted out the 360-ton *Empress of China* with a cargo containing ginseng root, which the Chinese believed increased sexual potency. The vessel sailed for Canton around the Cape of Good Hope. It returned to New York the following year with tea, silk, chinaware, cotton cloth, and other goods that earned a profit for the promoters of almost $40,000. In a few years American ships were rounding Cape Horn, scudding up the Pacific coast to the region north of California, picking up otter skins in the Pacific Northwest, and sailing on to Canton. On one such voyage in 1792, Captain Robert Gray discovered the mighty Columbia River. These voyages provided a much-

Tribute to the Barbary States, 1785–1802

The United States, as a newborn maritime nation, faced the age-old problem of securing safe passage for its merchant ships, and paid tribute to the Barbary States:

Morocco 1786: £5,000 for a treaty guaranteeing "no future presents or tributes"; 1795: the same sum for renewal of the treaty plus consular presents, field-pieces, small arms, and gunpowder; 1802: top gun carriages.

Algeria 1793: $10,000 for relief of prisoners; 1796: nearly $1,000,000 for a treaty—$612,500 in cash, $21,000 annual tribute in naval stores, and $300 in gifts to the Dey. A long delay in payment called for an additional $53,000 in presents and bribes and the promise of a 36-gun ship; 1797: frigate *Crescent* delivered; 1798: the *Hamdullah* and $8,000 in lieu of stores; 1799: the brig *Sophia* and two schooners in lieu of stores.

Tunis 1798: $107,000 for a treaty and one barrel of gunpowder for every salute requested by an American ship; private presents (jewels, small arms, cloth) for the Bey; and public gifts suitable to the occasion; 1800: additional presents amounting to £7,000; 1802: special jewels and clothes for the Bey.

Tripoli 1787: demand (unpaid) for $100,000 yearly for peace or 30,000 guineas for perpetual peace; 1796: $56,486 for a treaty; 1799: $24,000 for presents and other items, in lieu of stores; 1802: $6,500 to ransom the crew of the *Franklin*.

(Courtesy, American Heritage)

needed outlet for American commodities, and at the same time created a taste for Chinese furniture, housewares, and textile patterns, as well as an interest in Chinese civilization.

The Public Lands   The peace treaty of 1783 had left the United States with a princely landed domain. Between the Appalachians and the Mississippi, stretching from Canada in the North to Florida in the South, lay enough unoccupied real estate to provide every free American family with a tract of 750 acres, or over one square mile of land. The Indians, especially the Shawnee, Wyandot, Iroquois, and Miami in the North, and the Cherokee, Choctaw, and Chickasaw to the south, claimed millions of acres as their hunting grounds. Most stood ready to resist any white settlers who would come to occupy their lands. Isolated settlements of French farmers and merchants were still scattered through the region.

The legal rights to this magnificent region were ambiguous. Virginia, with the broadest claims, had ceded its lands to the Confederation government. But other states tried to hold substantial portions of the West, a number of them awarding some of this land to their war veterans. Bit by bit, the states gave up their claims in favor of the nation, retaining in most cases only small parcels. For many years, however, state and federal claims overlapped.

Some easterners who feared the political eclipse of their own part of the country wanted the new region to remain secondary to the older states, with new settlers denied full representation in Congress. Others hoped to see equal states carved out of the region. It was in the interest of the older states to use the public domain as a source of federal revenue. One obvious maneuver was to sell the land at high prices for immediate returns. Large wholesale parcels could be sold to land speculators, who in turn could profit by retail sales to settlers. Against this notion of the uses of the federal lands was a vision of a West of small or moderate farms made easily available to settlers of modest financial means.

The Land Ordinance of 1785 was one of two measures in which the Confederation government laid down its basic policy toward the West and the public domain. It provided first for a careful survey of the land and then its division into townships six miles square, these to be divided into thirty-six sections, each one square mile, or 640 acres. Half the township might be sold as a unit; the other half would be offered on the market only in single sections. Actual sales at auction to the highest bidder started with a minimum price of a dollar an acre. Congress reserved four sections of each 36-section township for later use and kept one to sell for revenue to maintain local schools.

The Land Ordinance did not please everyone. Its minimum price and prescribed plot size meant that a pioneer farmer needed at least $640 to acquire a farm—in those days, a hefty sum. At the same time, the ordinance favored the establishment of family farms over speculation. Congress soon violated its own principles, however, by also selling almost two million acres of land to a group of speculators organized under the name of the Ohio Company, granting them an option on an additional five million—all for well under a dollar an acre.

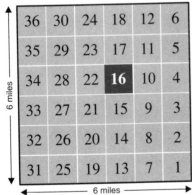

6 miles

Grid pattern of a township
36 sections of 640 acres (1 square mile each)

16 Income of one section reserved for the support of public education

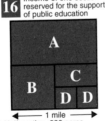

1 mile

A Half-section 320 acres
B Quarter-section 160 acres
C Half-quarter section 80 acres
D Quarter-quarter section 40 acres

Land Ordinance of 1785

The Northwest Ordinance

Before long, Congress also reached a decision on the political organization of part of the trans-Appalachian area—the region bounded by Pennsylvania on the east, the Great Lakes to the north, the Mississippi on the west, and on the south the Ohio River. The Northwest Ordinance of 1787 was a milestone in the progress of Americans across the continent. This law, along with the Land Ordinance, was a triumph of statesmanship for the Confederation Congress. Borrowing from an earlier plan proposed by Jefferson, the Ordinance laid out the process by which the Northwest might eventually become a group of self-governing states, equal in all respects to the original thirteen.

The area would be carved into between three and five territories, governed initially by officials appointed by Congress. When a territory acquired a population of 5,000 adult males, it would be allowed to elect an assembly and could send a nonvoting delegate to Congress. Attaining a population of 60,000 free inhabitants would make the territory eligible to apply for admission as a fully equal, self-governing state. The final section of the Ordinance of 1787 reflected the most liberal spirit of the Revolutionary era. All residents of a territory were to enjoy complete freedom of worship, trial by jury, full representation in the territorial assembly in proportion to their numbers, and other fundamental protections to both persons and property. In the whole of the vast region slavery was forbidden.

There remained an important western problem that the Confederation government could not solve: what to do with the Indians. In 1784 Congress had sent five commissioners to meet with the tribes of the Northwest in an effort to open the eastern portion of the region to white settlement. At Fort Stanwix the commissioners got the Iroquois to surrender their claims for a few trinkets. Next, they coerced the Chippewa, Ottawa, Wyandot, Shawnee, and Delaware into giving up most of their Ohio lands. The resentful tribesmen quickly repudiated these agreements and were soon trading blows with the frontiersmen now

Primitive conditions on the American frontier enforced a life of simplicity. The woman in this engraving stands proudly at the door of a hut, described by another pioneer as "a barbarous rectangle of unhewed and unbarked logs." The menacing pine trees hint at the artist's reservations about isolation and difficulties of life in the wilderness. *(Courtesy, Newberry Library)*

pouring into the Ohio country. The government sought to pacify the irate Indians by promising them additional gifts, while at the same time it strengthened the army garrisons in the West.

Daily Life

A lady's dressing table of the era, made in Baltimore. Patriotic touches, like the eagle that surmounts the mirror, are characteristic of post-Revolutionary times. *(Index of American Design)*

Farmers and Planters   Despite the problems of government in the "Critical Period," in the summer of 1787 most ordinary Americans went about their daily affairs without giving too much thought to the concerns of the new nation. The vast majority of the 2.5 million Americans of 1780—say, ninety percent—made their living from the soil. They were by no means all alike. Some 600,000, virtually all living south of Pennsylvania, were black slaves. Another considerable group was made up of white tenants or white servants. A few thousand Americans, most of them in the South, some in the Hudson Valley and a few other spots as well, were owners of great estates or plantations. The largest group, perhaps sixty percent, was made up of free farmers who owned their own land.

Yeoman farmers who owned their hundred to two hundred acres of land outright were especially numerous in New England, Pennsylvania, New Jersey, and the backcountry and mountain areas of the southern states. Those who lived close to cities or were connected to them by good roads or navigable rivers produced crops not only for themselves and their families, but also perhaps for distant markets in the West Indies, the Mediterranean, or Newfoundland. These farmers were by no means rich; the trade provided the means to buy a few luxuries and goods they could not themselves produce. Families were large, and children helped. Their labors created modest comfort and a rough abundance of food, clothing, and shelter.

A few got rich cultivating the soil: successful tobacco growers in Maryland and Virginia, some rice planters in South Carolina and Georgia, New York landlords who grew grain and raised livestock. Along the streams and inlets of the Chesapeake region, in the Carolina and Georgia sea islands and coastal lowlands, and in the Hudson Valley, a traveler could encounter many fine houses. Most of these houses built since the 1740s were of brick with plaster trim, designed in the gracious Georgian style with evenly spaced windows and classical cornices and moldings over windows and doors. With large ballrooms, imported English furniture, and many bedrooms, these structures attested to growing affluence and sophistication.

Merchants and Townspeople   Maritime merchants of the port cities constituted another wealthy class. In Boston the average merchant left $5,000 in real estate and personal property to his heirs at a time when few laborers earned more than fifty cents a day. A few merchants were fabulously rich. Sharing in the prosperity in about equal measure were lawyers and doctors, especially those who practiced in the larger communities. Instead of country homes the urban rich had large townhouses surrounded by gardens. These men and women, like their counterparts in the country, ate elaborate meals, dressed in silk and fine broadcloth, wore wigs or powdered their hair, and traveled by coach or on horseback.

The towns were busy with the work of shopkeepers, innkeepers, clerks, seamen, laborers, and artisans. A day laborer's wages could keep a young man in modest comfort, but not a married man with a family. Porters, pick-and-shovel workers, and the like could make ends meet only if their wives worked as seamstresses, laundresses, or servants. Skilled craftsmen, on the other hand, had little trouble earning a good living. Many carpenters, blacksmiths, shipwrights, tailors, cordwainers, barrelmakers, masons, printers, and other artisans owned their own shops. Some craftsmen became fairly prosperous. One tailor, for example, had a house and land worth $1,130, a silver pocket watch, silver buckles for his shoes, two gold rings, six silver spoons, and furniture and household goods worth $375.

Pat Lyon at the Forge, a painting by John Neagle. Many skilled craftsmen owned their shops and had little difficulty earning a good living. Lyon, at the time a prosperous man, had once been jailed for debt in the building shown behind him. *(Courtesy, Museum of Fine Arts, Boston)*

Churches   Sunday was a day of rest not only in Congregational New England, but also in the middle states and the South, where there were many Baptists, Methodists, and Presbyterians, as well as Episcopalians. Religious observances were more than a quest for solace in an uncertain world, or traditional rites imposed by community pressure. They were also social events. People dressed up not only for the minister but for one another. And church was one of the few meeting places for young men and women. Many a courtship began in church under the watchful eyes of parents and older brothers and sisters.

Members of the evangelical sects, such as the Baptists, Methodists, and "new light" Presbyterians, found deep emotions in church attendance and did not confine their religious participation to Sundays. Beginning in the 1780s, great revivals periodically swept the backcountry, especially in the South. Many of these were held in churches; others took place at temporary encampments in open places where hundreds of pious people came for several days to listen to eloquent preachers exhort sinners to repent their evil ways, turn to God, and find everlasting salvation. More sedate people despised these camp meetings; they sneered at the "ranting" preachers and expressed horror at the shrieks, jerks, and groans of the listeners caught up in the emotions of the event. Critics also claimed that these camp meetings were opportunities for the nubile young to indulge their awakening sexual appetites. However unseemly or disreputable, the camp meeting provided an important emotional release for rural Americans whose lives otherwise were largely bound up in rounds of monotonous toil.

Urban Amusements   The ten percent of Americans who dwelt in substantial towns or cities enjoyed more varied lives. Cities were centers of culture. Boston, New York, Philadelphia, and Charleston had theaters where traveling companies performed the works of Shakespeare and other English playwrights. There were subscription concerts in several cities, and in Charleston the St. Cecilia Society, founded in 1762, the oldest musical society in America, imported musicians from Philadelphia and New York. In Boston in 1786 a "Concert of Sacred Music" with seventy performers played to an audience of 2,000. There were no art galleries or museums, but a handful of distinguished painters—Charles Peale, John Singleton Copley, John Trumbull, and Gilbert Stuart—were the equals of Britain's artists. Battle scenes and portraits by American artists captured the Revolution for posterity. Benjamin West, another outstanding painter American in birth, had lived in England since before the Revolution.

In addition to concerts and plays in the cities, there were dances, horse races, and celebrations of public events. During and after the war the anniversary of the signing of the Declaration of Independence became a general occasion for bonfires, fireworks, and noisy parades. In Philadelphia, news of the treaty of peace set off a surge of revelry so boisterous that prudent citizens feared for the safety of their property.

Then, as today, Americans were susceptible to fads and crazes. A peculiar one of the Confederation period was for balloons, the first of which, inflated with hot air, had recently been launched in France. The

The Constitution, mural by Barry Faulkner, showing James Madison presenting the Constitution to George Washington and the Convention. *(Courtesy, The National Archives, Washington, D.C.)*

idea that the human race could free itself from the force of gravity seized the public's imagination. By midsummer 1784 it was said that nothing attracted attention unless it had the word "balloon" attached to it. Fashionable people wore "balloon" ornaments and a farmer hawking his vegetables in town sold them as "fine balloon string beans."

Prelude to the Constitution

The move to convert the Confederation government into a more effective political instrument had begun when the war ended. In 1783 nationalists devised a scheme to grant Congress the right to collect duties on imported liquors, sugar, tea, coffee, cocoa, molasses, and pepper; each state would collect the duties at its own ports and then

remit them to the Confederation treasury. This plan was submitted as an amendment to the Articles, and so required the agreement of all the states. New York, however, refused to accept it.

As Congress declined to little more than a sleepy debating society, the future of national affairs passed into the hands of men who thought, as Alexander Hamilton of New York put it, "continentally." In early 1785, commissioners from Virginia and Maryland met at Washington's home, Mount Vernon, to discuss common problems concerning navigation of the Potomac River, which separated the two states. So successful was this meeting that it led to calls by Virginia for a larger conference on commercial cooperation to meet at Annapolis the following year. Only twelve delegates from five states turned up at Annapolis, and so consideration of the planned agenda was postponed. Instead the delegates, led by Hamilton, drew up a proposal for a new convention, to meet at Philadelphia in May 1787, to discuss every issue necessary "to render the constitution of the Federal Government adequate to the exigencies of the Union." Congress received this proposal and cautiously endorsed it.

By the time of the Philadelphia meeting, all doubts moderate Americans may have entertained about the need for a stronger central government had been shattered by the farmers of western Massachusetts. One state that took its wartime debt seriously, Massachusetts had imposed heavy taxation on its citizens to meet this obligation. At the same time, farm prices declined. There were efforts to relieve by issues of paper money the distress of farmers who had gotten into debt. But in Massachusetts creditor groups defeated the attempts to issue paper currency. In the Berkshire hills of western Massachusetts, where few farmers had ready cash, many lost their land for non-payment of debts or taxes. The troubles that followed made it look as though anarchy threatened at least a portion of the new republic.

Suggested Readings

A recent study by a master historian is Edmund Morgan's *Inventing the People: The Rise of Popular Sovereignty in England and America* (1988). Also provocative are Michael Kammen, *A Machine that Would Go of Itself: The Constitution in American Culture* (1986) and John P. Diggins, *The Lost Soul of American Politics: Virtue, Self-Interest, and the Foundations of Liberalism* (1984). See also Robert M. Calhoon, *Dominion and Liberty: Ideology in the Anglo-American World, 1660–1801* (1994), and Jack N. Rakove's *Original Meanings: Politics and Ideas in the Making of the Constitution* (1996).

Garry Wills's, *Explaining America: The Federalists* (1981) offers a fresh reading of the work of devising the Constitution. Gordon Wood explores the relationship between political ideology and society in two works, *The Creation of the American Republic* (1969) and *The Radicalism of the American Revolution* (1992). See also Christopher Duncan, *The Anti-Federalists and Early American Political Thought* (1995), Stanley Elkins and Eric McKitrick, *The Age of Federalism* (1993), and Thornton Anderson, *Creating the Constitution: The Convention of 1787 and the First Congress* (1993). In *We the People: The Economic Origins of the Constitution* (1958) and *E Pluribus Unum: The Formation of the American Republic, 1776–1789* (rev., 1979), Forrest McDonald presents the Founding Fathers as statesmen committed to the founding of a secure republic. On the Anti-Federalists see Stephen Boyd, *The Politics of Opposition: Anti-Federalists and the Adoption of the Constitution* (1979).

Jackson Turner Main stresses class and sectional differences in *The Social Structure of Revolutionary America* (1966) and subsequent studies. Other important works are Mary Beth Norton, *Liberty's Daughters: The Revolutionary Experience of American Women* (1980) and Linda Kerber, *Women of the Republic: Intellect and Ideology in Revolutionary America* (1980). A nationalist account of the confederation era is Jack N. Rakove, *The Beginnings of National Politics: An Interpretive History of the Continental Congress* (1979).

See also Robert A. Becker, *Revolution, Reform, and the Politics of American Taxation, 1763–1783* (1980), Ira Berlin and Ronald Hoffman, eds., *Slavery and Freedom in the Age of the American Revolution* (1983), Joy Day Buel and Richard Buel, Jr., *The Way of Duty: A Woman and Her Family in Revolutionary America* (1984), Laurel Thatcher Ulrich's prizewinning *Midwife's Tale* (1990), Jan Lewis, *The Pursuit of Happiness: Family Values in Jefferson's Virginia* (1983), and Michael Kammen, *A Season of Youth: The American Revolution and the Historical Imagination* (1978). Sylvia Frey examines the effects of the American Revolution on African Americans in *Water from the Rock: Black Resistance in a Revolutionary Age* (1991). Indian attitudes are explored in Gregory Dowd, *A Spirited Resistance: The North American Indian Struggle for Unity, 1745–1815* (1992).

How Radical Was the American Revolution?

Forrest McDonald

Revolutions, we customarily think, are born amidst the poor and oppressed. The crowds call for bread and for release of political prisoners whose bodies are broken with torture. In the American Revolution the colonists were indeed reacting in anger, an anger that seems to come from a people brutally abused by vicious masters. The King, wrote Thomas Jefferson in the Declaration of Independence, has "sent hither swarms of Officers to harass our People, and eat out their substance. . . . He has plundered our seas, ravaged our Coasts, burnt our towns, and destroyed the lives of our people." But the slaveholders and merchants who led the American Revolution were in no way the victims either of poverty or of British oppression, nor were the common folk who lived in comfortable and prosperous North America.

It is also customary to expect revolutions to make for violent change: the destruction of a ruling class, the overthrow of political institutions, and even the coming of a revolutionary style of dress and behavior. The French Revolution favored mustaches and for men the trousers (in place of stockings and knee breeches) and short hair that have been standard ever since, and revolutionists addressed one another as Citizen, as Communists would later call one another Comrade. By such measures as these, the American Revolution was no revolution at all. It was instead an attempt by Americans to preserve what they already had.

What the leaders of the Revolution had to preserve was their substance and position. Neither was seriously threatened by the attempts the British government had begun making to rule the colonies more closely, but the taxes and the trade regulations passed by Parliament could make a dent in their fortunes, and they did not care for this. The wealthy revolutionary families talked much about the rights of the people, and they even meant it, but they were not intent on making a revolution that would redistribute land and power downward to the common folk.

Nor did those common folk demand any such thing. The small farmers, the craftsmen, and the frontiersmen who supported the Revolution did not resent the leadership of the powerful, or at any rate not enough to turn against them. As conservatives, well satisfied with their basic condition, common people joined with the wealthy in resisting the efforts of the British to impose change on the colonies.

Britain, the ideological leadership of the Revolution believed, had once been a virtuous agricultural nation, with a balanced government, honest labor on the land and craftsmanship in the cities, and direct honest trade among individuals. It had been, in effect, a society much like that in the British colonies. But Britain, so the argument held, had now sunk into corruption, enslaved to money that brought monopolies, standing armies, and vicious government hungry for tax revenues. Britain had actually given birth to a modern, dynamic, expanding economy that would greatly improve the well-being of its inhabitants. In this sense the American Revolution was a conservative rebellion against the forces of modernism.

The American Revolution, then, was culturally, politically, socially, and economically a conservative movement. But the revolutionists' successful defense of their established ways had an ironic outcome. Their victory brought great change. The new states found themselves unable to deal with their problems, and soon they had to create a central government with far greater powers than any that Parliament had dared to exercise.

Precisely because the impulses to revolution in eighteenth-century America bear little or no resemblance to the impulses that presumably account for modern social protests and revolutions, we have tended to think of the American Revolution as having no social character, as having virtually nothing to do with the society, as having no social causes and no social consequences. . . . Consequently, we have generally described the Revolution as an unusually conservative affair, concerned almost exclusively with politics and constitutional rights, and, in comparison with the social radicalism of the other great revolutions of history, hardly a revolution at all.

If we measure the radicalism of revolutions by the degree of social misery or economic deprivation suffered, or by the number of people killed or manor houses burned, then this conventional emphasis on the conservatism of the American Revolution becomes true enough. But if we measure the radicalism by the amount of social change that actually took place—by transformations in the relationships that bound people to each other—then the American Revolution was not conservative at all; on the contrary: it was as radical and as revolutionary as any in history. . . .

That revolution did more than legally create the United States; it transformed American society. Because the story of America has turned out the way it has, because the United States in the twentieth century has become the great power that it is, it is difficult, if not impossible, to appreciate and recover fully the insignificant and puny origins of the country. In 1760 America was only a collection of disparate colonies huddled along a narrow strip of the Atlantic coast—economically underdeveloped outposts existing on the very edges of the civilized world. The less than two million monarchical subjects who lived in these colonies still took for granted that society was and ought to be a hierarchy of ranks and degrees of dependency and that most people were bound together by personal ties of one sort or another. Yet scarcely fifty years later these insignificant borderland provinces had become a giant, almost continent-wide republic of nearly ten million egalitarian-minded bustling citizens who not only had thrust themselves into the vanguard of history but had fundamentally altered their society and their social relationships. Far from remaining monarchical, hierarchy-ridden subjects on the margin of civilization, Americans had become, almost overnight, the most liberal, the most democratic, the most commercially minded, and the most modern people in the world.

And this astonishing transformation took place without industrialization, without urbanization, without railroads, without the aid of any of the great forces we usually invoke to explain "modernization." It was the Revolution that was crucial to this transformation. It was the Revolution, more than any other single event, that made America into the most liberal, democratic, and modern nation in the world. . . .

The Revolution not only radically changed the personal and social relationships of people, including the position of women, but also destroyed aristocracy as it had been understood in the Western world for at least two millennia. The Revolution brought respectability and even dominance to ordinary people long held in contempt and gave dignity to their menial labor in a manner unprecedented in history and to a degree not equaled elsewhere in the world. The Revolution did not just eliminate monarchy and create republics; it actually reconstituted what Americans meant by public or state power and brought about an entirely new kind of popular politics and a new kind of democratic officeholder. The Revolution not only changed the culture of Americans—making over their art, architecture, and iconography—but even altered their understanding of history, knowledge, and truth. Most important, it made the interests and prosperity of ordinary people—their pursuits of happiness—the goal of society and government. The Revolution did not merely create a political and legal environment conducive to economic expansion; it also released powerful popular entrepreneurial and commercial energies that few realized existed and transformed the economic landscape of the country. In short, the Revolution was the most radical and most far-reaching event in American history.

Reprinted from Gordon S. Wood, *The Radicalism of the American Revolution* (New York: Alfred A. Knopf, 1992).

In the fall of 1786, debt-ridden farmers in New Hampshire, Vermont, and Massachusetts staged protests at courthouses demanding tax relief. One of these confrontations in Massachusetts led to an episode that goes by the name of Shays's Rebellion. *(Drawing by Howard Pyle, Courtesy, The Library of Congress)*

We the People
1787–1800

SHAYS'S REBELLION (1786–87)

On a snowy January afternoon in 1787 at Springfield, Massachusetts, a ragtag army of 1,200 farmers advanced toward the federal arsenal building. They were angry because the state legislature had ignored the petitions of hundreds of debt-ridden farmers whose farms and homes were in danger of foreclosure for failure to pay taxes. At their head was Daniel Shays, a former captain in the Continental army, now a destitute farmer. Near the arsenal, some 600 militiamen under General William Shepard waited, their cannons trained on Shays and his men. When the farmers came within a hundred yards of the arsenal, the cannons belched fire and smoke, the attackers faltered, and four fell dead. The rest broke ranks and retreated in disarray.

On January 27 General Benjamin Lincoln and a hastily-recruited force of over 4,000 men joined the militia at Springfield and pursued the embattled farmers across western Massachusetts to the village of Petersham. On February 4, this little army surprised the rebels and captured 150 of them. The rest fled, and Shays escaped across the snow-covered hills to Vermont.

Ever after, this episode was known as Shays's Rebellion. Some politicians made much of the unrest in Massachusetts as proof of the weakness of the Articles of Confederation government. If Daniel Shays had not been an "ill-fated Chief," one argued, he might have caused the downfall of Massachusetts. As another observer noted, "What if a greater than Shays, a CROMWELL or a CAESAR should arise?" Thomas Jefferson, on the other

continued

hand, thought the Massachusetts uprising "honourably conducted." "It has," Jefferson said, "given more alarm than I think it should have done." Many Americans were nonetheless alarmed by what happened in Massachusetts. They feared the government was too weak, and that the country was on the verge of anarchy.

How did it happen that less than a decade after the Revolution, former comrades in arms were aiming guns at each other, and some people feared that the fragile young republic was about to disintegrate? In 1782 the Massachusetts state government, in order to pay off its Revolutionary War debts, had required all taxes to be paid in specie—hard money—instead of depreciating paper money, so that the state could afford to pay off its notes and bonds at their full face value. But for many people, coin was hard to come by. Especially in the four westernmost counties was the tax burdensome. Foreclosures were growing each year with no relief in view and little chance of redress from the legislature, which was controlled by the maritime and mercantile interests of the eastern part of the state.

In the best tradition of revolutionaries the farmers held protest meetings, drafted petitions, and organized committees of correspondence, using the methods perfected in the struggle against Great Britain a decade before. Conservatives in Boston, however, condemned acts outside normal political conduct: "Let the majority [of the legislature] be ever so much in the wrong," legislative action was still the only course "compatible with the ideas of society and government." One of the loudest voices raised against the rebels was that of Sam Adams, who in the colonial political conflicts with the British government had been notable for his radical rhetoric.

The farmers were not disposed to listen. Their wrath focused on the county courts, where judges were busily ordering forced sales of land to pay taxes and reimburse creditors. In August 1786, fifteen hundred farmers of Hampshire County had prevented the

Paul Revere, the patriot silversmith, made this silver punch bowl to honor the militia for defeating the Massachusetts farmers' rebellion led by Daniel Shays. (*Courtesy, Yale University Art Gallery*)

meeting of its Court of Common Pleas. A few weeks later, at Worcester, a hundred men armed with swords, muskets, and clubs blocked the judge from entering the courthouse.

In the spring, annual elections replaced Governor James Bowdoin with John Hancock, and a new slate of legislators who were mostly sympathetic to the farmers' plight took control. With a "total change of men," said Noah Webster, "there will be, therefore, no further insurrection, because the Legislature will represent the sentiments of the people." Hancock pardoned Shays; the legislature passed laws offering tax relief and exempting clothing, household items, and tools from seizure for debt. The rebellion was over, but concerns about the stability and order of the young republic remained.

The uprising alarmed many Americans outside Massachusetts. In a letter to a friend George Washington could have been speaking for many who had fought to form a nation. "I am mortified beyond expression," he wrote, "that in the moment of our independence we should by our conduct render ourselves ridiculous and contemptible in the eyes of all Europe." Richard Henry Lee of Virginia declared: "We are all in dire apprehension that a beginning of anarchy with all its calamitys has approached, and have no means to stop the dreadful work." The rebellion was an argument for Washington's conviction: "I do not conceive we can exist long as a nation without lodging, somewhere, a power which will pervade the whole Union in as energetic a manner as the authority of the state governments extends over the several states."

The Constitutional Convention

The scene now shifted to Philadelphia and the coming conference to write a constitution. With its 40,000 inhabitants, the city was the largest in the United States. During the postwar period it had suffered like other ports from the decline of foreign trade. Nonetheless, it remained a bustling community whose neat, tree-lined streets reflected the original orderly plan of its founder, William Penn, and the sobriety as well as the prosperity of its Quaker elite. The delegates from the thirteen states who gathered in 1787 in Independence Hall were a mixed lot. Several men were prominent national leaders; others disappeared from history after their brief day at the Convention. Together this group from a settlement on the edge of a wilderness were to produce one of the most remarkable political arrangements in the history of Western civilization.

The Founding Fathers   The presiding officer, George Washington, richly honored as the commander in chief of the Continental forces that had defeated the British and made independence possible, enjoyed enormous prestige throughout the nation. His opening appeal to "raise a standard to which

"I am a plain man, and I get my living by the plow," wrote Jonathan Smith, a farmer unsympathetic to Shays. He spoke to his fellow "plow-joggers": "I have lived in a part of the country where I have known the worth of good government by the want of it. The black cloud of Shays rebellion rose last winter in my area. It brought on a state of anarchy that led to tyranny. . . . People, I say, took up arms, and then, if you went to speak to them, you had the musket of death presented to your breast. They would rob you of your property, threaten to burn your houses. . . .

When I saw this Constitution [of the United States] I found that it was a cure for these disorders. I got a copy of it and read it over and over. I had been a member of the convention to form our own state constitution, and had learnt something of the checks and balances of power; and I found them all here. . . .

I don't think the worse of the Constitution because lawyers, and men of learning, and moneyed men are fond of it. [They] are all embarked in the same cause with us, and we must all swim or sink together."

The American Star, by Frederick Kemmelmeyer. (*Courtesy, The Metropolitan Museum of Art*)

the wise and the honest can repair" set the tone for the solemn deliberations that followed. Nearly as eminent was Benjamin Franklin, fresh from the triumphs he had won as minister to France and chief negotiator of the peace treaty. Though now eighty-one and somewhat infirm, Franklin could still inspire confidence and rally support. Both men favored a stronger central government. Yet a short and lively Virginian, the thirty-six-year-old James Madison, proved more important at the Convention than either of these two commanding figures. A close friend of Jefferson, a man of wide reading and deep reflection, Madison would be the major architect of the Constitution.

A few of the more able men present at Philadelphia during the spring and summer of 1787—Robert Yates of New York, Luther Martin of Maryland, and George Mason of Virginia, for example—remained defenders of local power against expanded federal authority. Most of the delegates, however, were strong nationalists who wished and expected to remake the federal government into an effective instrument of the national will. Perhaps the Convention's most extreme nationalist was also one of the youngest: New York's Alexander Hamilton, at the age of thirty, had scant use for the states at all and would prefer to see them reduced to little more than administrative units.

All through the Philadelphia summer the fifty-five delegates in Independence Hall argued, negotiated, maneuvered, and deliberated. Nearly all of them lawyers and educated men, they drew on their knowledge of history, especially the experience of the ancient Roman republic. They also culled ideas from the political thinkers of their time, most notably Montesquieu, Harrington, and Blackstone. But ultimately their own common sense, their experience of government, and the interests of their states and their sections guided their decisions. Said John Dickinson, "Experience must be our only guide. Reason may mislead us."

All agreed that the new government must be strong without being oppressive, and the delegates kept striving to balance liberty and order. The Constitution they finally produced reflects a series of compromises between strong government and government limited in the interests of freedom, between national and local authority, and between the interests of the large states and the concerns of the smaller ones. Their debates produced a document that in both strenghtening and limiting the powers of government has served the country to this day.

Virginia and New Jersey Plans

As debate opened Edmund Randolph of Virginia presented a proposal by his friend Madison. The Virginia Plan, as it would come to be called, recommended a new national legislature representing not the states, as the Confederation Congress did, but the people. The new body was to have two houses. The numbers that each state would have in both houses was to be proportionate either to its population or to its wealth. The voters of each state would choose directly their representatives to the lower house, and that state's delegation would select its delegates to the upper house. On other matters delegates in both houses were to vote as individuals, not as members of separate delegations. The new Congress could define the powers of the federal government and overrule the states, appoint a national executive, and choose a new national judiciary.

The Virginia Plan came under immediate attack. Many delegates believed that it veered too far toward nationalism, practically obliterating the states as governing units. It also smacked of favoritism: the largest and richest states such as Virginia, Massachusetts, or Pennsylvania would have many more delegates in the new Congress than the smaller or poorer ones such as New Hampshire, Georgia, and Rhode Island.

Opponents of the Virginia Plan countered with a scheme submitted by William Paterson of New Jersey. This New Jersey Plan provided for all the states to have equal representation in a single-chamber legislature. This new Congress would regulate foreign and interstate commerce, levy tariffs on imports, and impose various internal taxes. It would also choose the officers of the executive and judicial branches. All those powers not specified were to remain with the states.

For many weeks, debate swirled around these two proposals. Against Paterson's proposal was the consideration that it would be unjust to allow, say, the voice of a few thousand New Jerseyites to equal the voice of many more Virginians. Randolph's scheme raised another difficulty: who were to be counted as "population"? Should slaves, who could not vote, be considered the equals of free men for purposes of representation? If so, the southern states, with their many slaves, would have many more delegates in proportion to their voting population than the northern states.

A Balanced Government

In a committee charged with seeking a way out of the impasse over representation, the delegates from Connecticut took the lead in proposing what became known as the Connecticut Plan. This compromise that the Convention finally hammered out established today's two-house national legislature. In the lower, the House of Representatives, the people of each state would be directly represented in proportion to population. In the upper, the Senate, each state legislature would elect two members regardless of population. A later arrangement determined that a slave would be treated as three-fifths of a person for the purpose of calculating representation in the House of Representatives. The new Congress was given broad powers over foreign and interstate commerce, permitted to levy taxes directly on citizens, and awarded the sole right to coin money and regulate its value.

The Constitution borrowed from the British model of mixed government. In Great Britain that meant a government of monarch, aristocracy embodied in the House of Lords, and democracy (actually expressed in the votes of a small portion of the British public) represented in the House of Commons. In the American scheme the President was no monarch, but he was supposed to provide the unifying force that in Britain was assigned to the Crown. The Senate would supply, not quite an aristocracy, but at least the wisdom and stability that supposedly resided in an upper class of wealth and social standing. The House of Representatives was intended to convey the will of the democracy.

Political Parties

Students of government have credited American political parties with making the constitutional system work. It is therefore no small irony that the Founding Fathers detested the very idea of political parties and hoped to create a political system in which the "spirit of party" would wither away. Their feelings go back to pre-revolutionary days. As colonists, Americans had come to associate British parties with corruption. Eighteenth-century British parties, in fact, often were corrupt. They were organized by means of family ties and patronage. And the Crown, because it had at its disposal a vast number of political offices, was frequently able to use the "spirit of party" to control Parliament. Colonists, in turn, often blamed their own troubles on these same corrupt parties.

In *The Federalist*, Number 10, Madison wrote that the great diversity of interest groups in the new country would prevent the formation of large parties. In fact, it did not. Diversity did, however, help determine the character of the parties that arose. The need to achieve a majority in the electoral college forced American parties to become broad coalitions that could then appeal to a broad range of interests. So the United States got parties, but they were very different from both the small clusters of individuals that had formed in the eighteenth-century British Parliament and the large but ideologically cohesive parties that developed in nineteenth-century Europe.

Baron de Montesquieu (1689–1775), author of *Spirit of Laws*, was a French philosopher who, distrustful of republics, advocated dividing powers among the executive, legislative, and judicial branches of government.
(Courtesy, Scribner's Archives)

Along with this arrangement went another that partly overlapped with it, a scheme of checks and balances ensuring that no one part of government would be able to wield unrestrained power. To this purpose the Constitution projected another triad: the executive; Congress as a whole, embracing both senators and representatives; and the judiciary. The President, or executive, would be chosen by a group of "electors" in each state, the electors being in turn selected by any method each state legislature deemed best. The judicial branch, headed by a Supreme Court, would be selected by the President with the approval of the Senate. To ensure the judges' independence from political pressure, the Convention provided that they would serve for life and could not have their salaries reduced. The President, too, was to be independent of Congress. His term of office would last four years regardless of what Congress thought of him, and he could be reelected. Each branch of government—executive, legislative, and judiciary—was empowered to check the others.

Among these was the President's power of veto over laws enacted by Congress. This veto could be overridden by a two-thirds vote in both houses. The President would choose all federal judges, ambassadors, and high officials of executive departments, including what would later come to be called his cabinet. But most of these appointments had to be confirmed by the Senate. The Supreme Court, having jurisdiction over violation of federal laws and over suits between citizens of different states, was also going to exercise its own important brake on the other two branches. Though the Constitution contains no clause giving the Supreme Court and the lower federal courts the power to declare a federal law to be in violation of the Constitution, the Court soon after its establishment was to conclude that by implication it possessed that authority, and it has exercised that implicit power ever since. Congress, in its turn, could put on trial and remove from office for bad conduct both the President and members of the judiciary. The model of mixed government gave Congress its own built-in check.

The Senate, the upper house, its members chosen by state legislatures rather than by the people at large, would supposedly be above the public whim that might sway the House of Representatives. That lower chamber, which by custom has come to be called simply "the House" or "Congress," would in turn be able to resist the aristocratic arrogance that might infect the Senate. Since any measure would have to pass both chambers to become law, each would check the other. To assure protection against excessive taxation, the Convention provided that all money bills would have to originate in the House.

By September 1787 the new Constitution had assumed its essential form. A substantial number of delegates continued to complain that the Constitution conferred too much power on the federal government. At least one delegate, Alexander Hamilton, believed it created too weak a government for the nation's needs. Gouverneur Morris of Pennsylvania wrote a preamble to the document, and, with only three members abstaining (George Mason of Virginia said that he would rather cut off his right hand than sign the new document), the delegates affixed their signatures to the Constitution. Now it awaited the approval of the Confederation Congress—and the people.

Ratification

On September 20, 1787, the Confederation Congress in New York received the Constitution composed in Philadelphia. One of its sharpest critics was the man who had first proposed independence in 1776: Richard Henry Lee of Virginia. Favoring the new strengthened Union was his cousin "Light Horse Harry" Lee, a young ex-cavalry officer and the future father of Robert E. Lee, who in the 1860s would lead an army against that Union. Article 7 of the proposed Constitution provided for a ratification process in which the document was submitted to special state conventions. For over a year, national political discussion would revolve about whether to accept the new Constitution or continue with the Articles.

The Anti-Federalists, the opponents of the Constitution, have been called "men of little faith." Beneath their specific objections to one or another provision of the new constitution lay a deep-seated distrust of all government no matter what form it might take. Governments are dangerous, said the Anti-Federalists, because they are composed of men, and men are corrupted by the exercise of power.

Federalists were themselves men of little faith. They shared with their political opponents the same dour view of human nature. The difference was that they feared government less and people more. Hence they were eager to shield much of the government from direct popular control. Only the House of Representatives would be directly answerable to the people, and then only once every two years. The Senate was to be elected by the state legislatures, the President by an electoral college. The judiciary would be appointed, and would hold office indefinitely. Each branch of the government would balance the others so that no one individual or party could long work its will.

By early 1788, five states, either unanimously or by overwhelming majorities, had ratified the Constitution. Elsewhere, especially in Massachusetts, Virginia, and New York, there was a strong opposition. The *Massachusetts Gazette* observed: "It is impossible for one code of laws to suit Georgia and Massachusetts." In March 1788 the Federalists received a modest setback when Rhode Island rejected the Constitution. Since Rhode Island had refused even to send delegates to the Constitutional Convention in 1787, Federalists did not expect much support there; but the nature of the political struggle was significant. Rhode Island politics during the 1770s and 1780s had been known for its battles between debtors and creditors. The state represented a clear-cut division along economic lines. The merchants and professional men, smelling certain defeat, boycotted the state ratifying convention, and their absence gave the Anti-Federalists a margin of ten to one. But Federalist victories by large margins soon followed in Maryland and South Carolina. On June 21, New Hampshire became the ninth state to ratify and, by the terms of its own ratification provision, the new Constitution was now technically in effect, for nine states had accepted it. Yet two very important states, New York and Virginia, had not yet acted.

In Virginia the formidable Patrick Henry, James Monroe, and George Mason led the Anti-Federalists. Favoring the Constitution were

Amos Singletary, a self-described "poor" person of Massachusetts, put his case against the new Constitution:

"We fought Great Britain—some said for a three-penny tax on tea; but it was not that. It was because they claimed a right to tax us and bind us in all cases whatever. And does not this Constitution do the same?

These lawyers and men of learning and moneyed men, that talk so finely and gloss over matters so smoothly, to make us poor illiterate people swallow down the pill, expect to get into Congress themselves. They expect to be the managers of this Constitution, and get all the power and money into their own hands. And then they will swallow up all us little folks, just as the whale swallowed up Jonah!"

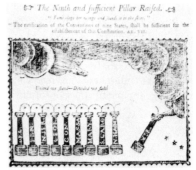

The votes of nine states were needed to ratify the Constitution of the United States. *(Courtesy, American Antiquarian Society)*

Ratification of the Constitution Votes at State Ratifying Conventions		
State	Date	Vote Y/N
Delaware	Dec. 1787	30– 0
Pennsylvania	Dec. 1787	46– 23
New Jersey	Dec. 1787	38– 0
Georgia	Jan. 1788	26– 0
Connecticut	Jan. 1788	128– 40
Massachusetts	Feb. 1788	187–168
Maryland	April 1788	63– 11
South Carolina	May 1788	149– 73
New Hampshire	June 1788	57– 47
Virginia	June 1788	89– 79
New York	July 1788	30– 27
North Carolina	Nov. 1789	194– 77
Rhode Island	May 1790	34– 32

When a president-to-be of another era, John F. Kennedy, was growing up, his father made him and his brothers take the parts of Hamilton, Jefferson, and others, and argue at the dinner table over whether to ratify the Constitution.

James Madison, Edmund Randolph, and, above all, George Washington. The expectation that the state's most revered statesman would be the first President of the Republic made the Federalists difficult to stop. In the end Virginia ratified, but like Massachusetts requested a bill of rights.

The Federalist Papers and The Bill of Rights

Now the struggle shifted to New York. The inclusion of that state, with its great port and strategic mid-continental location, was essential if the Union was to work. But for a while it seemed as if New York would refuse to ratify. The convention that assembled in Poughkeepsie was under the control of the state's stalwart Anti-Federalist governor, George Clinton. Arrayed against Clinton and his supporters, however, were John Jay and the strong-willed Hamilton. Soon these two New York Federalists, joined by James Madison, were engaged in a war of words with their Anti-Federalist opponents. Day after day the *Independent Journal* carried the closely-argued essays in which the three men, writing under the common name "Publius," explained the virtues and necessity of the new Constitution. Dealing both with immediate concerns and universal political values, these eighty-five pieces—in 1788 published under the collective title *The Federalist*—constitute a classic commentary on the nature and purposes of government. Publius's articles, however, did little to change the minds of the Poughkeepsie delegates, most of whom were Anti-Federalists. More important was pressure from New York City, where merchants and artisans threatened that if New York State did not join the Union, New York City would. On July 25, 1788, after an impassioned personal address to the delegates by Hamilton, the state ratified the new frame of government.

Rhode Island and North Carolina were still outside the new Union, but they did not seem essential. One North Carolinian grumbled, "We see plainly that men who come from New England are different from us. They are ignorant of our situation, they do not know the state of our country. They cannot with safety legislate for us." Yet in November 1789 North Carolina officially ratified the Constitution and entered the Union. Reluctant Rhode Island joined at last in 1790.

After setting up electoral procedures, the old Congress operating under the Articles of Confederation quietly passed out of existence. When the body of electors—called the "electoral college"—voted on February 4, 1789, every presidential vote cast went for Washington, with John Adams of Massachusetts receiving the vice presidency. Newly-elected representatives and senators set out for the nation's temporary capital, and on March 4, 1789, the first Congress under the new Constitution assembled in New York City. Federal Hall, the former city hall, was still being remodeled and the new senators and representatives took their seats amidst the carpenters' noise and flying sawdust. The confusion and disorder caused little harm. Only eight senators and thirteen representatives had slogged their way through the muddy roads of spring to take their oaths of office that opening day.

On April 14, 1789, Washington received formal notice of his election. Two days later he wrote in his diary, "About ten o'clock I bade farewell to Mount Vernon . . . and with a mind oppressed with more anxious and painful sensations than I have words to express, set out for New York." There, in the nation's temporary capital, on April 30, he was sworn into office and delivered his first inaugural address. The celebration in New York when Washington came to the city for his presidential inauguration exceeded anything previously held in the young nation. The barge that brought the President-elect across New York harbor from New Jersey was surrounded by large and small vessels of every sort, full of cheering passengers. Washington made his way through streets lined with exuberant citizens. At night the city was illuminated with bonfires, and celebrants crowded the thoroughfares.

The next few months were busy ones. In the fall, Congress drafted a Bill of Rights, the first ten amendments to the Constitution, which the prescribed three-fourths of the states quickly ratified. The first eight amendments placed certain fundamental restraints on the power of the federal government over ordinary citizens. Congress could not limit free speech, interfere with religion, deny to the people the right to keep and bear arms, require the quartering of troops in private homes, or allow homes to be searched by federal authorities without search warrants. Persons accused of federal crimes could not be made to testify against themselves, nor could the federal government deny the citizens trial by jury or deprive them of life, liberty, or property "without due process of law." The central government could not impose excessive bail or "cruel and unusual punishments." Amendment IX ordained that the rights included in the earlier list did not exclude others; Amendment X provided that those powers not given to the federal government or denied the states should belong solely to the states or the people.

Never before had any single document enumerated so clearly and emphatically the rights of private citizens. The Bill of Rights became, accordingly, a landmark in the history of human liberty. But the Bill applied to the federal government only. Most of the states had similar provisions in their own constitutions. But what if a state chose to violate fundamental human rights; would a citizen have any official or agency to turn to? The Thirteenth, Fourteenth, and Fifteenth Amendments, adopted after the Civil War, would begin to address that question, but it was not really to be answered until the civil rights movement of the 1960s, if then.

The Newly Formed Regime

The New Government Friends of the Constitution composed most of Congress. Many members had been present at Philadelphia during the momentous summer of 1787 to write the new frame of government, and the majority hoped to carry out the purposes of the nationalists: to make the United States a going concern and create respect for the republic among the older nations of the world. The framing of the Bill of Rights was in itself one of the most momentous actions of any Congress in the nation's history.

Yet the first deliberations had been nearly farcical. For three weeks the members debated the proper title of address for the President. Vice

President John Adams insisted that without some such title as "His Elective Highness" or "His Excellency," the President might be mistaken for the head of a volunteer fire company. Adams' opponents believed any such title would be "aristocratical," unrepublican. They mocked the pudgy Vice President's serious concern, and took to calling him "His Rotundity."

Washington himself settled the momentous issue of his title. Though protective of his dignity on all occasions, he preferred to avoid "monarchical" trappings. He did travel through the streets in a gilded coach and held "levees," formal receptions for visitors and guests, but he would not accept a title of any sort. He wished to be addressed as "Mr. President"—the same as when he had presided over the Convention of 1787. From the beginning, Washington's commanding presence lent the new government some badly needed stateliness. Besides his title, the first chief executive set other less impressive precedents for the conduct of the presidency. Early in his administration Washington, taking literally his power to "make treaties" with "the advice and consent of the Senate," appeared before the senators to explain an Indian treaty. After an awkward debate a senator proposed referring the treaty to committee. The President, offended by this snub, stormed out, saying that he would "be damned" if he would ever come back. He did return once, but no other President has attempted to discuss treaties personally with the entire Senate.

Meanwhile, Congress had set up three major executive departments, State, War, and Treasury, and appointed a postmaster general. It also passed the Federal Judiciary Act, which specified that the Supreme Court was to consist of a chief justice with five associates. John Jay, the first chief justice, resigned to run for governor of New York in 1795, saying that under "a system so defective, the court would not obtain the energy, weight and dignity which are essential. . . ." At Jefferson's urging the justices discarded the English practice of wearing wigs, which he said made "the English Judges look like rats peeping through bunches of oakum." Congress also established a system of federal courts and created the office of attorney general for the government's chief law officer.

Alexander Hamilton and the Nation's Debts

In response to one of the new government's most pressing concerns, that of providing itself with revenues, Congress passed the nation's first tariff, setting low duties on a host of imported goods. Congress now had the means to pay the army and official salaries, and to begin to meet its debts. By 1789 those debts amounted to about $52 million—$40 million owed to Americans, and $12 million due foreigners. In addition to these obligations of the federal government, there were the state debts still unpaid, amounting to about $25 million.

Few people doubted that the foreign debt must be paid in full. Otherwise, the United States would not earn the respect of foreign powers or be able to borrow abroad again. But what about the domestic debt? Speculators had bought Continental IOU's for a song from those who had actually given the wartime Congress money or supplies to fight

Alexander Hamilton advocated a strong central government. The artist is John Trumbull. *(Courtesy, Yale University Art Gallery)*

the British. Should these speculators alone benefit by the improved credit of the national government, or should the original holders also get something? And what about the state debts? Some southern states had paid portions of these obligations while many northern states had not. If the government were to "assume" or take over these obligations, the residents of the middle states and New England would benefit at the expense of those south of Pennsylvania. Congress turned over to Alexander Hamilton, Washington's secretary of the treasury, the problem of how to handle the debt as well as other pending financial questions.

A young man of thirty-five, Hamilton was a former aide-de-camp to Washington who had married into the prominent Schuyler family of New York. Able, handsome, and well-connected, he had risen high in New York political life after his army service despite his West Indian origin and his illegitimate birth.

Hamilton was a nationalist, lacking the emotional attachment that men like Jefferson and Madison felt for the local community. Like many other veterans of the Continental Army, he recalled bitterly the petty jealousies and selfishness of the states during the Revolutionary War. He had so little respect for the states that at the Constitutional Convention he had proposed their virtual elimination. He prized banking, trade, and manufacturing, and believed that the United States could not afford to remain an agricultural nation, producing raw materials for Europe. Britain, rapidly becoming the industrial workshop of the world, must be the country's example, he claimed. This required a vigorous central government commanding its citizens' loyalty. Hamilton was skeptical of human nature. A branch of the eighteenth-century Enlightenment that included Jefferson believed that human beings were inherently more good than evil, social and political evil being the result largely of evil institutions. Freed of these, mankind would undoubtedly flourish. But Hamilton believed that the people tended to be "ambitious, vindictive, and rapacious."

Congress's problem was Hamilton's opportunity. The new secretary of the treasury seized the occasion to advance some of his fondest political and economic hopes. In three great *Reports* he incorporated into larger plans for American society his solution to several immediate problems.

Hamilton's Reports   The *Report Relative to Public Credit* boldly proposed that the national debt be paid in full through a complicated process known as "funding." Current holders would exchange their IOU's at par for interest-bearing bonds. Hamilton asserted that the public debt would prove a "national blessing." His *Report on a National Bank* early in 1791 explained why. The nation's economic development required stronger currency and banking facilities. Hamilton proposed a new federally chartered banking corporation, drawing its capital both from the Treasury and from private investors. The new "Bank of the United States," governed by privately elected directors and others chosen by the government, would serve both public and private needs. It would stimulate commerce and manufactures by lending money to private businessmen. The bank would as well hold the government's deposits, pay its bills, and accept its receipts. The institu-

Alexander Hamilton wrote:

"A national debt, if it is not excessive, will be to us a national blessing."

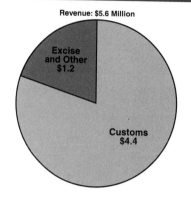

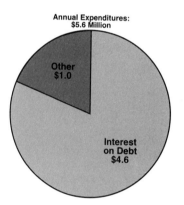

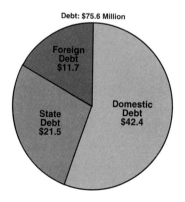

Under Hamilton's plan, over 80 percent of federal revenues went to pay the interest on the national debt. In the 1990s, interest payments consumed less than thirty percent of the federal budget.

James Goodwyn, *American Sleigh Ride.* (*Courtesy, Museum of Fine Arts, Boston*)

Alexander Hamilton had clear ideas and expressed them forcefully:

"All communities divide themselves into the few and the many. The first are the rich and wellborn, the other the mass of the people. . . . The people are turbulent and changing; they seldom judge or determine right. Give therefore to the first class a distinct, permanent share in the government. They will check the unsteadiness of the second. . . ."

tion's most important service was to issue the paper money of the nation. In itself, paper money was considered a cheap, untrustworthy currency, but the Bank's paper would have something solid to back it up. Its holders could, if they so wished, have the government give them in place of it an equivalent amount in the securities that were part of the new funding scheme. And the public's knowledge that the currency would be so exchanged would make for willingness to use it. Hamilton was planning to convert the national debt of a gold-poor country into a powerful engine for mobilizing its economy.

Later in 1791 Hamilton issued the last of the major *Reports,* on manufactures. The secretary acknowledged that agriculture was currently the most important single economic activity, but he saw no conflict between agriculture and industry. The two complemented each other; both together would benefit the nation. Noting the beginnings of the factory system in Britain, Hamilton observed that the new system of manufacture employed every class of people in productive labor, even women and children. Hamilton especially favored the employment of women in factories, believing that in a predominantly agricultural society men would be needed, and would prefer, to work the land. He viewed women as the most readily available pool of wage labor. The United States with its magnificent resources was potentially a great industrial nation, but to compete with other nations would require government aid. To protect "infant industries" until they could compete successfully, the government must impose high tariffs that would raise the price of foreign manufactures. It should also offer premiums for the production of needed goods and for inventions. Above all, the proposed bank must lend capital to entrepreneurs.

Hamilton's *Reports* together outlined an economic revolution. Through the energetic use of the national government, the country might be transformed: bustling cities, humming factories, and busy arteries of communication and transport would erupt from the quiet American landscape of prosperous farms and trackless forests.

Opposition to Hamilton's Nationalism

The Hamiltonian program, so bold in its projections, aroused fierce opposition. Said one observer, "Faction glows within like a coalpit." Hamilton's vision threatened to violate the character of the nation as some Americans saw it, a land of small farms and the simple social relations of the countryside. Many also feared the expansion of federal powers his program required. They imagined that Hamilton's schemes would create an all-powerful centralized government breeding graft and corruption. In the new nation, as in Britain, liberty and republican virtue would then degenerate into tyranny and licentiousness. Especially fearful were the Virginia leaders—James Madison, now a leading member of the House of Representatives, and Thomas Jefferson, Washington's secretary of state. The two Virginians believed that Hamilton and his supporters wanted to create a plutocracy, a government of the rich. Jefferson feared both the rich and the mob; the Hamiltonians, it seemed, feared only the mob.

Hamilton's bill to fund the public debt aroused Madison, who quickly became the leader of the forces arrayed against him. Madison spoke as a southerner, aware that four-fifths of the unpaid securities and state debts were northern. Yet his attack was a principled one. He did not oppose funding in itself, he declared; rather, he believed that Hamilton's scheme unduly benefited speculators. Under Hamilton's plan these people would receive the full face value of their holdings, while original possessors would get nothing. Even now, Madison and his supporters asserted, advance news that the government would assume the state debts had been leaked by people in high places, and speculators were traveling through the South buying up securities from gullible farmers.

For many weeks the funding bill remained blocked. The particular sticking point was the provision that the federal government would assume the payment of the states' debts. Then one morning in July, Jefferson bumped into Hamilton on the steps of the President's house. The secretary of the treasury told the secretary of state that the deadlock in Congress was endangering the Union. Could Jefferson do anything to help? The next day the two cabinet officers met with Madison, and a deal was arranged. The national capital would be moved from New York to Philadelphia. Then, in ten years, it would be permanently located in the South between Virginia and Maryland. ("It is the opinion of all the Eastern states," one northerner protested, "that the climate of the Potomac is not only unhealthy, but destructive to northern constitutions.") In return, Madison and his friends would cease to oppose assumption. The following month the funding measure passed Congress.

The Bank of the United States

Next on the agenda was a national bank. The bill would charter a Bank of the United States for twenty years with a capital of $10 million, one-fifth to be subscribed by the federal government and the remainder by private investors. Philadelphia was to be the bank's home office, but it might establish branches in other cities.

Over the opposition of Madison, Congress passed the bill charter-

Despite Hamilton's grand plans, most American pioneers settled into subsistence farming. One recounted:

"In the early years, there was none but a home market and that was mostly barter—it was so many bushels of wheat for a cow; so many bushels for a yoke of oxen. The price of a common pair of cowhide boots would be $7, payable in wheat at 62 cents per bushel."

ing the Bank and sent it to the President for his signature. Washington was stumped. His fellow Virginian, Madison, had raised doubts about whether the Constitution allowed Congress to charter such a bank. The President asked for the opinions of his cabinet. Both Jefferson and Attorney General Edmund Randolph replied that by no stretch of its meaning did the Constitution authorize a federally chartered bank. Hamilton took the opposite view. In a masterly application of what came to be called the principle of "broad construction" of the Constitution, he argued that since a bank was necessary to the collecting of taxes, the regulating of trade, and other functions explicitly conferred on Congress in that great document, its constitutionality was "implied," even though not specified. Convinced by Hamilton's logic, Washington signed the bill into law.

The Whiskey Rebellion (1794)

Although the federal government now possessed augmented powers under the new Constitution and the prestige that the national hero, George Washington, brought as its President, it was nonetheless a most fragile polity beset by enormous pressures. No one was certain what to expect from a republic. Different American regions, political factions, and ethnic groups had their own interests, and looming over all were the diverging concerns of the rich and the poor, the agrarians and the developing commercial elites, the varying class and economic groups of a sprawling new nation.

The tarring and feathering of an excise officer during the Whiskey Rebellion. *(Courtesy, Brown Brothers)*

The new government's great initiative to unite this variegated republic was Hamilton's financial plan. One cornerstone of that policy was an excise tax on alcoholic beverages. This would provide revenues to fund the national debt and to finance the government—including, many feared, its military capacity.

Whiskey was the cash crop of western Pennsylvania. Readily transportable and salable, corn liquor stored much better than the grain whence it came. Some of it no doubt gurgled and jostled in jugs and barrels swaying across the mountains on the backs of pack animals to slake the thirst of easterners. Westerners, even when they hungered for the word of God, continued to thirst for the "old Monongahela rye," and most of it was consumed in the West. The evangelical religion so strong in western Pennsylvania had not yet come out against drinking.

Though the farmer with a small still paid very little excise tax, westerners did not like it. They objected, as one petition phrased it, to "a duty for drinking our grain more than eating it." They objected to the appointment of excisemen with their right of entering private property and inspecting stills. And they especially objected to the federal court's trying cases against those who refused to pay the exciseman's levy. These trials required expensive and disruptive jaunts across the mountains to federal court at Philadelphia. The West, in 1794 still cut off from the Mississippi trade by the Spanish, and from most trade other than in alcohol by the expense of carrying goods over the mountains, was desperately short of currency. The drain of excise payments, though comparatively slight, was a burden on the region's economy.

The backcountry was not strong on being governed. These western farmers had little faith in anyone's governance but their own. They were soon passing resolutions not merely calling for an end to the tax, but overtly threatening excisemen and even those who cooperated with them by paying the tax. Soon barns began to be fired, gristmills damaged, excisemen attacked. "Tom the Tinker's men," it was claimed, were everywhere "mending" stills. This became the local expression for shooting holes in stills whose owners had paid the tax.

The West was not united on the issue. Battle spread between the small and the large whiskey producers, as the more prosperous distillers began to realize that this specie-draining tax would eventually drive the small producers out of business, leaving the more substantial men with a lucrative monopoly. Wealthy men feared as well that this excise rebellion could ignite into a war against property. In 1794 this almost came true, as the backwoods farmers marched on Pittsburgh, threatening to burn to the ground that symbol of the advance of commercial capitalism. Only adroit maneuverings by several Pittsburgh leaders persuaded the farmers that they ran too large a risk of retribution if they fired the city.

Something had to be done about the sporadic rioting in the West. A finding that the courts had been obstructed in carrying out the excise law provided the federal government with grounds for intervention. Hamilton, eager for a show of force that would establish the authority of the federal government, led the administration in a vast overreaction. Washington himself for a time directed a larger force than he had ever at one time commanded during the Revolution. Disorganized militia,

A local observer wrote of the backcountry habits:

"The use of whiskey was universal. The quality was good, the taste pleasant, its effect agreeable. Storekeepers kept liquor on their counters and sold it in their stores, and the women customers used it as well as the men. Farmers kept barrels of it in their cellars. . . . It was good for fevers, it was good for a decline, it was good for ague, it was good for snake-bites. It made one warm in winter and cool in summer. It was used at all gatherings. Bottles of it were set out on the table at christenings and wakes. . . . Ministers drank it. . . . Rev. Father McGirr's drink was whiskey-punch, of which it is said he could drink with any of his day without giving scandal."

about 13,000 strong, slogged through endless mud during a rainy November in search of a rebellion. Hamilton marched with the army from start to finish but was not away from his desk overly long; the army remained in the West about three weeks before arresting a few men and marching back to Philadelphia for heroes' welcomes. A grand jury in 1795 indicted over thirty men for treason. All of these but two were let free. Both of the others were mentally incompetent, and Washington pardoned them.

Despite the element of comedy within the rebellion, a sense that it had perhaps resulted from a bit too much of the spirits at issue, the episode possesses considerable importance for the political and constitutional development of the United States. A direct result of the insurrection was the forcing out of the last Jeffersonian, Edmund Randolph, who had succeeded Jefferson as secretary of state. Never again, except in moments of wartime emergency and then as a deliberate departure from the norm, would any President strive for a nonpartisan rather than a party government. The events of the rebellion had brought successes for both sides in the quarrel. The precedent of national power that Hamilton and Washington considered necessary for the future success of the American experiment was firmly established: without an armed clash, they had won something they had succeeded in defining as a war. What the farmers failed to achieve by rioting they got from the political activity that followed: in 1802 the new Jeffersonian government repealed the hated excise tax. Americans remained by all accounts one of the hardest-drinking people in the world for two more generations until a new wave of evangelism from the West brought fundamental changes in American values, and popular sentiment for the "old Monongahela rye" gave way to denunciation of Demon rum.

Hamiltonians vs. Jeffersonians   As Congress and the American people debated the Hamiltonian program, two distinct and conflicting positions began to emerge. One had as its principal spokesmen Jefferson and his chief congressional lieutenant, Madison. On the other side were Hamilton and his followers, John Adams, and, increasingly, President Washington himself.

The Jeffersonians favored state over national power and agriculture over industry, trade, and banking. They advocated a limited government and "strict construction" of the Constitution, a refusal to believe that the Constitution granted to any branch of government the slightest particle of power beyond what the words of the document specifically stated. They claimed to have faith in the people and to distrust the rich and powerful. Many were southerners, deeply attached to their local communities, which they did not want to come under the domination of a powerful central government. But the Jeffersonian party would also win support among the farmers of the middle and New England states and the artisans of the towns. Many Baptists and Methodists were of like opinion. Increasingly these citizens called themselves the Democratic Republicans, a label they adopted to contrast their political views with the supposedly more "monarchical" ideas of their Federalist opponents.

The Hamiltonians favored an ever stronger federal government, if necessary at the expense of the states. They believed that the nation's future lay in industry, not in agriculture alone. Generally speaking, they accepted republicanism as best suited to the American genius, but they did not trust majority rule as much as did their opponents, and they hoped to attract the support of the rich and the powerful to the new national government by making their interests coincide with those of the government. The Federalists could count on strong support within the major commercial towns, including such southern ports as Charleston. As defenders of order and stability they could also count on those people who were by temperament conservative. One group that contained many Federalists was the Congregational church in New England, which for a time enjoyed the support of state governments in the region.

The Government Seeks a Foreign Policy

The French Revolution (1789)
No sooner had the new government under the Constitution begun its work in New York than Europe went into a colossal political convulsion. In France, the colonies' ally in the war for independence, the American struggle for liberty had been deeply influential. "Enlightened" men and women recognized a larger significance in the event, and it strengthened their resolve to reform the Bourbon monarchy, custodian of the privilege and inequality that for centuries had shackled the French people. In August 1788 King Louis XVI, faced with a severe financial crisis induced partly by France's recent aid to the American revolutionaries, called into session the Estates General, representative of the clergy, nobility, and middle class, expecting that body to give him the taxes he needed, and then adjourn. But instead groups of reformers quickly took over. In a matter of a few months they had converted the Estates General into a revolutionary body that began to replace the entire old regime and convert the nation into a constitutional monarchy based on respect for human rights and on wide popular political participation. On July 14, 1789, a Paris mob attacked the Bastille, the prison that had become a notorious symbol of oppression, tore down the walls, and freed the prisoners.

The early response in the United States to the electrifying events in France was almost universally favorable. When the Marquis de Lafayette, who had helped lead the early stages of the Revolution, sent Washington the key to the Bastille, the President hung it prominently in the presidential mansion. He later wrote Gouverneur Morris that he hoped the disorders in France would "terminate very much in favor of the rights of man." If such a reserved and inherently conservative man as Washington could applaud the French uprising, the followers of Jefferson were sure to be still more enthusiastic. Some Republicans, in imitation of French egalitarianism, adopted the title "Citizen" or "Citizeness" in place of "Mister" or "Mistress." Others began to abandon knee breeches and adopt the long trousers worn by the Paris artisans and the French radicals. Within a few decades, trousers along with the short hair favored among revolutionary men in France were to become the standard among male Europeans and Americans, whatever their politics.

At first, Republicans considered the French Revolution the beginning of an age. As Jefferson wrote, "the liberty of the whole earth" depended on the contest in France. In time the initial consensus among Americans disintegrated. Increasingly the French radical leaders, called Jacobins, denounced the church and organized religion. In 1791 Louis XVI fled Paris with his family, but was caught and thrown into prison. By this time many enemies of the Revolution, including a large part of the French clergy and nobility, had been either driven from the country or hustled off to jail. Soon after, the revolutionary leaders began a reign of terror against all opponents of their policies, even the moderate reformers. In 1793 a revolutionary tribunal proclaimed a "war of all peoples against all kings." The tribunal then pronounced the death sentence on Louis XVI, and the sentence was promptly carried out. In October his Queen, Marie Antoinette, was also sent to the guillotine. As time passed the excesses of the French revolutionaries shocked many Americans.

France Seeks Aid   Before long, France was at war with Austria, England, Prussia, and Spain. Surrounded as it was with enemies, France sought aid from its friend, the United States. Jefferson thought France's struggle "the most sacred cause that ever man was engaged in" but did not want to go to war. Under the alliance of 1778 the Americans were bound to protect France's West Indies colonies against any enemy. England was certain to use her powerful fleet to blockade and, if possible, take these possessions. The United States now faced the serious prospect of war with Great Britain.

Many Americans would have welcomed such a war. Britain still limited American commerce with her own West Indies possessions. She still occupied western forts on United States soil. She still stirred up the Indians of the Northwest to discourage American settlement west of the mountains. Now that Britain was locked in combat with revolutionary France, she seemed the special enemy of liberty and freedom. And in 1793 the British began to seize American vessels engaged in trade with the French West Indies and to throw their crews into foul dungeons.

Among the followers of Hamilton, however, France represented all that was chaotic, disorderly, irreligious. That country, exclaimed Fisher Ames, was "an open hell, still ringing with agonies and blasphemies, still smoking with sufferings and crimes." Britain the Hamiltonians perceived as a bulwark of sanity and moderation, and they thought her victory in the struggle to be essential for world order. Another consideration weighed heavily in Federalist calculations. The whole Hamiltonian fiscal program depended on international trade, and in 1793 the United States, like the colonies for over a century before, traded primarily with Britain. Any wartime disruption of this trade would dry up revenues, injure the new national government, and thwart the Federalist economic program.

Citizen Genet   Meanwhile, the French Republic had dispatched Citizen Edmond Genet as diplomatic minister to the United States to do what he could to make trouble for Great Britain. Arriving on April 8, 1793, Genet immediately set to work recruiting Americans in his nation's cause. Even before presenting his formal credentials to Washington and Secretary of State Jefferson in Philadelphia, he had commissioned Americans as privateers to prey on British commerce, and opened negotiations with several American frontier leaders to attack Spanish Florida and Louisiana. Despite these high-handed actions, American friends of France cheered Genet as he made a triumphal procession to the capital. "I live in a round of parties," he wrote, "Old Man Washington can't forgive my success."

But Washington, supported by Hamilton and Jefferson, had decided to proclaim American neutrality. On April 22, 1793, the President issued a proclamation declaring the intent of the United States "to pursue a conduct friendly and impartial toward the French and British." Genet learned of this seeming repudiation of the 1778 treaty but, convinced by his recent experience that Americans were fervent partisans of the French, he determined to ignore it. Hinting that the United States might acquire Canada by aiding the French cause, Genet commissioned several land speculators as officers in the French army. Though at first a hero to Jeffersonians, Genet finally offended even the friends of the French Republic. So outrageous were his actions that Jefferson wrote Madison that the French minister would "sink the Republican interest" if the Republicans did not "abandon him." Reprimanded by President Washington and informed that his acts infringed upon American sovereignty, Genet promised to cease his activities, but then he immediately set about arming yet another vessel as a privateer. Warned not to continue, he threatened to appeal to the American people over the head of Washington. The administration decided it had had enough. In August the United States government demanded Genet's recall. Washington informed the Congress that the French envoy's conduct threatened "war abroad and discord and anarchy at home." But in France the Jacobins were in power, and Genet, who did not belong to this group, most certainly would have been beheaded had he been forced to return to France. The administration allowed him to stay in the United States, but refused to deal with him any further. He soon married the daughter of a member of the politically prominent Clinton family and settled into the quiet life of a country gentleman.

Citizen Genet, who came to America to stir up controversy against Britain, remained to live as a country gentleman in Orange County, New York. *(From the Emmet Collection, Manuscript Division, New York Public Library)*

Reconciliation with Great Britain   While Americans rioted in the streets for or against Genet, the United States was moving toward a settlement of sorts with Great Britain. Late in 1793 Jefferson resigned as secretary of state. Edmund Randolph, another Virginian, succeeded him. Early in 1794 after learning that the British were building a new fort south of Lake Erie and were attacking United States ships in the West Indies, Washington sent Chief Justice John Jay to England as special envoy. John Adams wrote to Jefferson: "The President has sent Mr. Jay to try if he can to find a way to reconcile our honour with Peace. I have no great Faith in very brilliant

Success; but hope he may have enough to keep us out of war." Jay, a staunch Federalist, knew that it would be difficult to get an agreement with Great Britain that would be popular. He was right. But Alexander Hamilton, in threatening war against Britain, had prepared the way.

One journalist wrote:

"John Jay, ah, the arch traitor—seize him, drown him, hang him, burn him, flay him alive! Men of America, he betrayed you with a kiss! As soon as he set foot on the soil of England he kissed the Queen's hand . . . and with this kiss betrayed away the rights of man and the liberty of America."

***John Jay,* by Gilbert Stuart. Jay's Treaty of 1795 settled most of the disputes with Britain left over from the Confederation period, but was very unpopular at home.** (*Courtesy, National Gallery of Art, Washington, D.C. Lent by Mrs. Peter Jay*)

The Jay Treaty (1795) The British made much of the American emissary. He in turn bowed to the Queen and kissed her hand, an act that outraged ardent Republicans. The British, who feared French attacks in Canada, drove a hard bargain. In the agreement that Jay carried back from London, the British promised finally to surrender the military posts they had illegally occupied since 1783. Other disagreements, including disputes over the pre-Revolutionary debts owed Englishmen, a boundary dispute with Canada in the Northwest, and the recent British ship seizures, were referred to arbitration commissions composed of British and American representatives. This device of an arbitration commission was an important diplomatic innovation, and in future years the two countries would make much use of it. Left unsettled were such long-standing American complaints as British incitements of Indians in the West and restrictive trade practices in the British West Indies colonies. On the question of British right to limit neutral trade in wartime, Jay retreated from the original American principle "free ships make free goods"—that a nation at war could not seize the goods carried in a neutral ship trading with the enemy nation—and agreed that the British could seize French or other enemy property found aboard American ships. Jay returned to the United States to find his fellow Americans in no mood to swallow this agreement.

In 1795 Jay's negotiations were greeted everywhere with outrage. One ardent Republican, unable to contain his feelings, inscribed on his fence: "Damn John Jay! damn every one that won't damn John Jay!! damn every one that won't put lights in his windows and sit up all night damning John Jay!!!" When Republicans met in taverns they toasted "A perpetual harvest to America; but clip't wings, lame legs, the pip, and an empty crop to all Jays." Jay himself ruefully remarked that he could have traveled across the nation by the light of his burning effigies.

Hamilton and other Federalists nonetheless marshaled their forces and wrote articles supporting the agreement as the best that could be obtained. Federalist Congressman Fisher Ames argued that if it were not approved the British and Indians would attack the frontier settlements. Washington put his prestige behind the treaty, earning for his efforts the contempt of the Republicans. Jefferson remarked: "Curse on his virtues; they have undone the country." But in June 1795 the Senate by a close vote confirmed the treaty, and the public reelected a Federalist Congress in 1796.

Whatever its inadequacies, the Jay Treaty settled most of the disputes with Britain left over from the Confederation period. But difficulties with Spain remained. Then, in 1795, the Spanish government and the United States signed the Pinckney Treaty. This agreement, coming after Jay's Treaty had neutralized the British, granted the Americans rights of access to the Mississippi River, imposed restraints on the Florida Indians, and provided Americans the right to take their goods through New Orleans for a period of three years. Spain also recognized American boundary claims under the Treaty of 1783, which consisted of the Mississippi River to the west and the 31st parallel to the south. Although the three-year provision implied possible trouble for the future, the nation greeted the Pinckney Treaty with great enthusiasm and the Senate ratified it unanimously. The treaty ended temporarily the threat that western regions of the United States, dependent on unimpeded use of the Mississippi River, might secede from the Union.

The Presidency of John Adams

Political Parties
In 1796 the nation faced its first contested presidential election. By this time American voters had a choice between two distinct parties. As yet, little of the machinery of party politics or campaigns had appeared, but throughout the nation people had begun to call themselves either Federalists or Republicans and their opponents by ruder names. Public men, Jefferson wrote a friend, no longer seemed "to separate political and personal differences. Men who have been intimate all their lives, cross the street to avoid meeting, and turn their heads another way, lest they should be obliged to touch their hats." Name-calling and violence became commonplace, especially in the newly emerging party press. The extreme Federalist William Cobbett described Republicans as "cut-throats who walk in rags and sleep amidst filth and vermin." Some New Yorkers threw stones at Alexander Hamilton. Even Washington himself became the target of vicious remarks: in Virginia his opponents toasted "a speedy death to President Washington."

By the mid-1790s the two political parties possessed distinct characteristics. The Federalists were centered in the Northeast, where business and commerce were concentrated. Many were well-to-do businessmen who wanted to use the federal government to strengthen the industrial sector of the economy. Federalists favored high tariffs and the national bank. Republicans clustered in the South and West. There were also substantial numbers of working-class Republicans living in the eastern cities. The Republican persuasion favored a weak central government, opposed high tariffs and the national bank, and championed states' rights.

The division of the country into these two opposing political camps disturbed many Americans. The founders of the republic, including the authors of the Constitution, had not envisioned political parties. The voters, they believed, should choose for office the best, most public-spirited men. Partisan organizations appeared to be dangerous instruments of selfish men that impeded, rather than advanced, expression of the general will. Many Americans of the 1790s regarded parties as symptomatic of a disease within the body politic. Even the ambitious men engaged in creating the factions thought that they were, at best, necessary evils. "If I could not go to heaven but with a party," Jefferson once wrote, "I would not go there at all." Such fears were, in part, the legacy of revolutionary thought, particularly the tendency to see an embattled republic surrounded by foreign foes and beset with domestic dangers. These beliefs actually contributed to the party spirit and the

President John Adams, by E. F. Andrews. Washington's Vice President won a close election in 1796 to become America's second President. *(Courtesy, The New-York Historical Society, New York City)*

frenzied political temper of the 1790s. The distrust of party, the belief that party politics expressed corruption and conspiracy, made Americans of each faction look on the other side as polluting the virtuous republic: and so each faction deepened its own partisan emotion.

Washington's official family felt the strains. Even before his resignation from the Cabinet, Jefferson, the arch-Republican, ceased to talk to Hamilton, the arch-Federalist. In 1795 Hamilton, too, left official life, going back to the practice of law in New York. Neither man, however, abandoned politics. From Monticello, the classical mansion he designed for a hill with a view of the Blue Ridge Mountains, Jefferson continued to advise by letter his friends and political allies in Philadelphia and around the nation. Hamilton also remained active politically and would exert great influence in the administration that followed Washington's.

Washington, no doubt, could have held the presidency for life had he so desired. But he was weary of politics and anxious to return to Mount Vernon; he looked forward, he said, to sitting down to dinner alone with his wife, Martha. He refused to accept a third term, and with the help of Madison and Hamilton he prepared a final address to his fellow citizens. Washington's Farewell Address (never presented orally but printed in a Philadelphia newspaper) devoted more attention to domestic than to foreign matters. The retiring President deplored the state of political conflict that had arisen and warned Americans against disunity, whether sectional or political. He also cautioned the nation to be wary of permanent alliances with foreign nations. He did not advocate isolation from international affairs; he merely recommended that the country be guided by its own essentially modest interests and not become too closely tied to the grander designs of other nations.

As Washington prepared to return to Virginia, political conflict remained fierce. As yet there were no national nominating conventions as we now know them. Instead, both Federalist and Republican leaders merely agreed among themselves on who should run.

The Election of 1796   The choice of the Federalist Party was Vice President John Adams. Less extreme than the "high Federalists" such as Hamilton, he was nevertheless peppery and opinionated as well as learned and public-spirited. Ever since the 1770s Adams had been in the forefront of the struggle for nationhood. Now he considered France the chief threat to his country's peace and order. The Republicans turned to their acknowledged chief, Jefferson. Tall, loose-jointed, red-haired, the former secretary of state was as hostile to the British and as friendly to the French as ever. Britain, he believed, was determined to subjugate the United States economically and he thought that under Hamilton's auspices the British had come to dominate the American government.

Intrigues, maneuverings, libels, and attacks flourished. The Republican press assailed Adams as a monarchist who, if elected, would enslave the American people. The Federalist press accused Jefferson of being a lackey of the French and claimed that as governor of Virginia during the Revolution he had fled his capital in a "cowardly" escape from the British.

In his Farewell Address of September 1796 President Washington denounced partisanship, pleading for the republican ideal of disinterested, independent statesmen as the only safe guide for the nation. He also warned against permanent foreign alliances and cautioned that the Union would be endangered if political parties continued to be characterized "by geographical discriminations—*Northern* and *Southern, Atlantic* and *Western*—whence designing men may endeavor to excite a belief that there is a real difference of local interests and views."

Meanwhile, the new French Minister in the United States, Citizen Adet, was angry at the Federalist administration for coming to terms with the British and he joined the fracas. In November 1796 he published in the American newspapers a set of proclamations announcing that France would suspend diplomatic relations with the United States and come down hard on neutral shipping. The blame for this new policy, he declared, lay with the Federalists' friendship with Britain.

Adams gained seventy-one electoral ballots to Jefferson's sixty-eight, with Thomas Pinckney—an ally of Hamilton—coming in third. Under the then existing provisions of the Constitution, John Adams became the second President of the United States, and Jefferson the Vice President. Two political enemies—a Federalist and a Democratic Republican—were now yoked together. Besides partisan politics President Adams would face a complex set of problems, especially in foreign relations.

Renewed Trouble with Britain   The United States by now had become a major international trader, its ships calling in virtually every port in the world. The reason for this growth was the great European war. As the British Royal Navy swept French and Spanish vessels off the high seas, France and her allies depended increasingly on the most important maritime neutral, the United States, to carry goods to and from their colonies. By 1796 American merchants were bringing in millions of dollars' worth of molasses, rum, sugar, and other products from French and Spanish possessions in the New World, landing them at New York, Baltimore, Charleston, or Philadelphia and then sending them, marked as American exports, to France, Spain, or some other part of continental Europe. They were also pouring into the French and Spanish colonies European goods that Britain's enemies feared to carry on their own vessels.

This wartime trade rained dollars, pounds, doubloons, and gilders on American merchants. Great mansions arose in Salem, Boston, Newburyport, Charleston, and the other centers of foreign trade. Every harbor along the Atlantic coast was dotted with the white sails and black hulls of the brigs, sloops, barges, and full-rigged ships engaged in world trade, while on the shore the streets were crowded with clerks, stevedores, porters, teamsters, and jack-tars hurrying about their business of moving the world's goods and making money.

The British were angry. The good fortune of the United States came at their expense. Not only were the Americans helping their enemies evade the British blockade of Europe and of French and Spanish America, but they were also taking over business formerly handled by British merchants. And the expanding American merchant marine was luring many of Britain's best seamen. Experienced British merchant seamen preferred the high wages and clean ships of the Americans, and were deserting.

For a while after the Jay Treaty, the British left American ships and seamen alone. But then, in 1796, when marine manpower shortages began to hurt, they resorted to impressment. Whenever a British man-of-war stopped an American merchant vessel to inspect her cargo for goods going to France, a British naval officer lined the men up on deck. Back and forth he went, asking each to speak up and identify himself. Anyone with an English, Irish, or Scottish accent could be assumed to be a British subject and removed to serve in the Royal Navy. The *American Daily Advertiser* fumed: "Are our sailors to be maltreated, our ships plundered and our flag defied with impunity?" Some of the sailors taken by the British, wrote one ship captain, "are American born, and have wives and children, whose existence, perhaps, depends on the welfare of a husband in slavery—a father in chains!"

The XYZ Affair   The French were no better. The French Directory, as the ruling body was called between 1795 and 1799, considered the victory of Adams, a sympathizer with Britain, to be an unfriendly act on the part of the American people. In 1797 the French government ordered that every United States citizen captured aboard a British vessel be hanged; if any single item of British make was found aboard an American ship, the vessel was to be confiscated. The French gave the United States minister his walking papers, in effect cutting off diplomatic relations.

Knowing that the United States was ill prepared to go to war, Adams decided to negotiate and appointed three commissioners, Elbridge Gerry, Charles Cotesworth Pinckney, and John Marshall, to go to Paris to seek a settlement. At the same time, the administration asked Congress for money to build naval vessels and expand the army. In October 1797 the three American emissaries arrived in Paris prepared to negotiate with the French foreign minister, Talleyrand. Over several weeks they were forced to talk to three French officials whom they later identified only as X, Y, and Z. The Americans, these gentlemen informed Marshall, Gerry, and Pinckney, would have to apologize for some recent anti-French statements of President Adams; they would need to promise a loan to France; and they must privately pay money to Talleyrand and members of the Directory. The American envoys were not naive about how diplomacy was conducted in Europe, but they refused to pay bribes before the French agreed to a settlement, and broke off the talks. Said Pinckney, "No, no, not a sixpence!" Soon after, the emissaries reported to Adams on what had transpired during their mission.

In 1798 the American government published the entire "XYZ" correspondence. "Millions for defense but not a cent for tribute"—a famous toast to Justice John Marshall on his return from a trip to France in 1795—became a popular slogan. Whatever the worldly American emissaries felt, the American people were shocked by France's seeming contempt for the United States. Overnight all but the most ardent Republicans became anti-French. Congress appropriated money for forty naval vessels, and for trebling the size of the army. Congress also ended commerce with France and ordered the suspension of the Franco-American alliance of 1778. Shortly thereafter, a full though undeclared naval war broke out on the Atlantic, American frigates and French vessels exchanging broadside volleys and French privateers attacking United States merchant vessels within sight of the American coast.

A cartoon indicating the anti-French feeling generated by the XYZ Affair. The three American ministers at left reject the "Paris Monster's" demand for money.

In the undeclared naval war with France, the American frigate *Constellation* captured the French ship *L'Insurgent*, February, 1799. *(Courtesy, The Peabody Museum of Salem)*

Alien and Sedition Acts (1798)

In this time of intense political excitement, Federalists found it impossible to regard their opponents' views as legitimate expressions of dissent. As yet, few Americans fully accepted the legitimacy of a party system and so Federalists (like Republicans) found the opposing party to be treacherous by its very existence. And the French Revolution went so far beyond the American Revolution in attacking traditional social institutions that conservatives saw in it chaos, anarchy, and atheism. In this mood a Congress dominated by the Federalists passed in 1798 four measures, called collectively the Alien and Sedition Acts, designed to curb opposition and prevent internal subversion.

The Naturalization Act extended from five to fourteen years the period of residence required for citizenship. The Alien Act gave the President the power to deport any alien suspected of "treasonable or secret" intentions. The Alien Enemies Act gave him the authority in time of war to arrest or banish from the country any citizen of an enemy power. These three measures were all aimed at foreigners. The Sedition Act was directed at Americans, and especially at opponents of the administration. Under its terms any resident of the United States who sought to prevent the execution of federal law, to stop a federal official from performing his duties, or to start any riot, "insurrection," or "unlawful assembly" could be fined or imprisoned. Anyone convicted of publishing "any false, scandalous and malicious writing" against Congress, the President, or the government could be fined or sentenced to prison for two years. A New Jersey man, watching a salute fired to honor President Adams on a visit there, remarked that he would have liked to see the cannon wadding "lodged in the President's backsides." For that observation he was fined $100.

Using his powers under the Alien and Sedition Acts, Secretary of State Timothy Pickering began a series of prosecutions of Republican newspaper editors and political leaders. The owners of four leading Republican newspapers were indicted and three Republican editors were convicted of violating the Sedition Act. Pickering also charged Matthew Lyon, a Vermont congressman, with libel against President Adams. Lyon is immortalized in American history for spitting in the eye of a Federalist Representative from Connecticut and then being drawn into a brawl with his enemy. The Irish-born Lyon—once an indentured servant and later one of Ethan Allen's Green Mountain Boys who captured Fort Ticonderoga during the Revolution—was convicted, fined a thousand dollars, and hustled off to jail for four months. He was, however, reelected to Congress from his jail cell.

The prosecutions under the Sedition Act damaged Adams and the Federalists badly. Many fair-minded Americans considered the acts violations of the freedom of speech and press guaranteed by the Bill of Rights. Before long, opponents of the measures and the prosecutions were holding meetings throughout the middle states, the South, and the West and sending petitions of protest to Congress. Great rolls of paper containing thousands of names were soon deposited on the desks of the House and Senate clerks.

Kentucky and Virginia Resolutions

No Americans were more disturbed by the Federalist repressions than the leaders of the Republican Party, Jefferson and Madison. Both regarded the Alien and Sedition Acts not only as a violation of freedom, but also as granting excessive power to the federal government over the states. Jefferson and Madison each secretly drafted a set of resolutions against the Federalist laws; friends steered Jefferson's through the Kentucky legislature, and allies took Madison's through Virginia's.

The Kentucky Resolution argued that "when the federal government exercises powers not specifically delegated by the Constitution, each state has equal right to judge for itself . . . of the mode of redress." The Virginia Resolution claimed that when the federal government acts contrary to the Constitution the states "have the right and are in duty bound to interpose for arresting the progress of the evil." Together the Kentucky and Virginia Resolutions stated that the federal government was a compact of states for certain limited purposes. Under the Constitution the national government did not possess the sort of powers it was seeking to exercise under the Alien and Sedition Acts. The two Republican leaders then attacked the Sedition Act as contrary to the Bill of Rights. Neither Kentucky nor Virginia went so far as to nullify the Alien and Sedition Acts, but in 1832 South Carolina would draw on this precedent to nullify a federal tariff.

Adams Compromises with France

Despite his lack of personal popularity, Adams and his party remained in firm control, and the President could have gotten Congress to declare war on France. Instead, in 1799, without consulting the cabinet, Adams announced that he intended to send another mission to France to resume negotiations of outstanding differences.

When the American delegates arrived in Paris, they encountered a changed situation. The leader of France now was First Consul Napoleon Bonaparte. Flushed with new victories, the French were reluctant to grant the Americans the indemnities they wanted for "spoliations" of their commerce. But Napoleon was not entirely unreasonable. He agreed to end the naval war and attacks on American commerce; he also consented to release the United States from its obligations to France under the Treaty of 1778. The American envoys were disappointed but seeing no possibility of better terms accepted this convention of 1800. Many Federalists thought it a cowardly surrender. The President disagreed—the negotiations, he believed, were "the most disinterested, the most determined, and the most successful" of his whole career. But they cost him a second term.

John Adams wrote:

"I desire no other inscription over my gravestone than: 'Here lies John Adams, who took upon himself the responsibility of the peace with France in the year 1800.'"

The Election of 1800

The political campaign of 1800 was one of the most momentous in the nation's history and in the evolution of modern political democracy. For the first time power passed peaceably and constitutionally from one political party to another.

The rhetoric was by no means peaceable. The Republicans attacked the President once again as a friend to Britain, a monarchist, a spendthrift who had burdened the country with enormous debts. Jefferson, the Federalist press charged, was an atheist who placed scientific reason above the teachings of the Bible. Elect him President, Federalists said, and religion would vanish and infidelity flourish. The man was a "voluptuary" who, it was alleged, had fathered children by a slave.

The New Capital

One item in the Republicans' indictment of their opponents was the extravagant cost of the new national capital under construction on the Potomac River. Actually, by the time the government moved from Philadelphia, the federal city was still more a plan than a reality. The scheme drawn up by a Frenchman, Major Pierre L'Enfant, was magnificent in its broad streets, its malls, plazas, and circles; but for the moment it had given place to a more modest and achievable plan. The government had begun construction of the President's house in 1792, and shortly thereafter the Capitol began to rise. The third building to appear was a tavern.

The first government officials arrived from Philadelphia in June 1800. On November 1, President Adams and his family moved into the president's house. The new city was little more than a paper community. Besides the Capitol, the tavern, and the President's house (it would not be called the White House until the early 1900s), Washington consisted of some boarding houses, a few huts for construction workers, and not

Abigail Adams confided to a friend her impressions of her journey in 1800 to the new capital in Washington, D.C.:

"I arrived here on Sunday last, and without meeting with any accident worth noticing, except losing ourselves when we left Baltimore, and going eight or nine miles on the Frederick road, by which means we were obliged to go the other eight through woods, where we wandered two hours without finding a guide, or the path. Fortunately, a straggling black came up with us, and we engaged him as a guide, to extricate us out of our difficulty; but woods are all you see, from Baltimore until you reach [Washington]. . . ."

Pierre L'Enfant's plan for the city of Washington. The basic plan with its circles and broad converging streets was retained. (*Courtesy, Stokes Collection, The New York Public Library*)

John and Abigail Adams were the first presidential couple to occupy the new "President's Palace," as the executive mansion was called. In late 1800, just three months before Adams would vacate it for Jefferson, they moved in. Only six rooms in the mansion were finished, but they had to move in because a 1790 law stated that Philadelphia would be the seat of government for only ten years. In a letter to her daughter, Abigail described her feelings about the new lodgings:

"The house is on a grand and superb scale, requiring about 30 servants to attend and keep the apartments in proper order, and perform the ordinary business of the house and stables. . . .

The lighting of the apartments from the kitchen to parlors and chambers is a tax indeed and the fires we are obliged to secure us from daily agues is another cheerful comfort. To assist us in this great castle, and render less assistance necessary, bells are wholly wanting, not one single one being hung in the whole house, and promises are all you can obtain. This is so great an inconvenience that I know not what to do. . . .

If they will put me up some bells, and let me have wood enough to keep the fires, I deign to be pleased. I could content myself almost anywhere for three months; but surrounded with forests, can you believe that wood is not to be had. . . . We have not the least fence, yard or other convenience without; and the great unfurnished audience room I make a drying-room of to hang up the clothes in."

much else. Streets had been laid out, but these muddy or dusty tracks were lined, not with residences or stores, but with virgin forest. Even the President's new home was only half complete.

Aaron Burr   Under the existing provisions of the Constitution, the electors who would place a President and Vice President in this raw new city did not vote separately for each office. Every elector cast two ballots, and the person with the highest vote total was declared President while the runner-up became Vice President. The Republican caucus in Congress had designated Jefferson as the party's presidential and Aaron Burr as its vice-presidential candidate, but in the actual voting all the Republican electors voted for both equally. When the votes were counted, therefore, Jefferson and Burr were tied for first place. This situation threw the choice of President into the House of Representatives, where the members of each state would cast a single collective vote and for election a candidate needed the vote of a majority of states.

The Federalists did not control enough states to reelect President Adams, but they could deny the presidency to anyone else. It was not likely that they would block a choice, since that would paralyze the nation, but they were capable of excluding Jefferson and substituting Burr. And the Federalists found Burr preferable to Jefferson. The New Yorker was an aristocrat, a friend of banks and Hamiltonian funding, and a believer in a strong executive. He also had the reputation of being corrupt, ambitious, cynical, and unscrupulous, but under the circumstances that was to the good: he could be counted on to make whatever arrangements with the Federalists they desired. The choice of Burr would also be sure to upset and confound the Republicans.

Some Federalist leaders nonetheless recoiled from this choice. Hamilton despised Burr, who he believed would "employ the rogues of all parties to overrule the good men of all parties." Jefferson, though in Hamilton's view "tinctured with fanaticism nor even mindful of truth," had some "pretension to character." Hamilton advised voting for the Virginian if he would give the Federalists guarantees that he would uphold the Federalist fiscal system, remove no Federalist from office except those of Cabinet rank, sustain the army and navy intact, and maintain the principles of neutrality in foreign affairs established by the two Federalist Presidents. Burr was meanwhile refusing to treat directly with the Federalists, since that would have outraged his fellow Republicans and lost him any scrap of their support.

In the end, Jefferson gave the Federalists some indirect assurances and he was declared elected. The nation could now resume as a going political concern.

The Revolution of 1800	Jefferson's election has been called the "revolution of 1800." The apprehensive Federalists would not have disagreed. Not only had they lost the presidency; they had also been swept from power in Con-

gress. There was still hope: the judiciary might be saved. Hours before leaving office President Adams appointed a flock of Federalists to new judgeships and other legal posts created by the Judiciary Act of 1801. These "midnight judges" might be able to stop the Republicans from upsetting the economic and political arrangements of the country. Adams separately appointed John Marshall to be chief justice of the United States. The President did not rank this appointment as one of the great contributions of his administration, yet it would turn out to be the most significant of all.

A Slave Plot

While Federalists and Democratic Republicans fought their political battles in the election of 1800, in Jefferson's own Virginia another kind of battle was almost joined. In Richmond a slave blacksmith named Gabriel Prosser and his brother, Martin, a slave preacher, organized a slave uprising that came to be known as Gabriel's Rebellion. Inspired by the rhetoric of the American and French revolutions and the ongoing political discourse in the United States about rights and liberty, Gabriel plotted with slaves in outlying plantations to march on Richmond and kill all the whites except some Quakers and Methodists who were known to harbor anti-slavery views. But the uprising never took place: on the designated night a fierce rainstorm washed out the unpaved roads leading into Richmond, and the would-be rebels scattered, their momentum gone.

Suggested Readings

On George Washington see Richard Brookhiser's *Reinventing George Washington* (1996). See also James Thomas Flexner, *Washington: The Indispensable Man* (1974) and Marcus Cunliffe's *George Washington: Man and Monument* (1958). Forrest McDonald's *Alexander Hamilton* (1979) and Richard Beeman's *Patrick Henry* (1982) offer views of a staunch Federalist and an equally adamant Anti-Federalist. On the background of the Constitution see David Szatmary's *Shays's Rebellion: The Making of an Agrarian Insurrection* (1980), Jay Fliegalman, *Prodigals and Pilgrims: The American Revolution Against Patriarchal Authority, 1750–1800* (1982), and Richard Beeman, Stephen Botein, and Edward C. Carter, eds., *Beyond Confederation: Origins of the Constitution and American National Identity* (1987).

Lance Banning, *The Jeffersonian Persuasion* (1978) traces Republican thought in the 1790s. Banning explores James Madison's role in the shaping of the new nation in *The Sacred Fire of Liberty: James Madison and the Founding of the Federal Republic* (1995). Morton J. Horowitz in *The Transformation of American Law, 1780–1860* (1977) examines the process by which law, having been rigid in the eighteenth century, became more flexible in the nineteenth.

Alexander DeConde is standard on *The Quasi-War: Politics and Diplomacy of the Undeclared War with France, 1797–1802* (1966). Like everything else that Richard Hofstadter wrote, *The Idea of a Party System* (1973) is illuminating and graceful. On the slave uprising in Virginia see Douglas Egerton, *Gabriel's Rebellion: The Virginia Slave Conspiracies of 1800 and 1802* (1993).

See also Joseph J. Ellis, *After the Revolution: Profiles of Early American Culture* (1979), Reginald Horsman, *The Frontier in the Formative Years, 1783–1815* (1970), Ralph Adams Brown, *The Presidency of John Adams* (1975), Richard H. Kohn, *Eagle and Sword: The Federalists and the Creation of a Military Establishment in America, 1783–1802* (1975), and John F. Hoadley, *Origins of American Political Parties, 1789–1803* (1986). Lorraine Smith Payle and Thomas L. Payle, *The Learning of Liberty: The Educational Ideas of the Founding Fathers* (1993), explores early efforts to promote civic virtue in a democratic republic. Jack P. Greene, *The Intellectual Construction of America, Exceptionalism and Identity from 1492 to 1800* (1993) examines European and American views of America's unique role as a land of opportunity and democracy.

What Did Women Gain from the Revolution?

Elizabeth Fox-Genovese

Was the American Revolution, whether conservative or radical for men, a revolution at all for women?

When Abigail Adams wrote to her husband that he should "remember the ladies," she was asking that the domestic powers of husbands be reduced and, above all, that they cease behaving like tyrants within the household. But she was not asking that women be allowed to participate in government. During the second half of the eighteenth century advanced advocates of women's rights were insisting on women's capacity for an essentially female excellence, not asking that women be recognized as functionally interchangeable with men.

In effect, the American Revolution strengthened gender as a form of social classification. Previously women had been able to relate to the polity, or at least the public area, as delegates of families on occasion when family and class membership superseded gender membership. After the Revolution they related to the polity as women first and members of families or classes second. This intensification of gender as a form of social classification has led historians to argue that women actually lost opportunities as a result of the Revolution. Others contend that women gained through their heightened identification with other women, through the emergence of a recognizable "woman's sphere" within which they forged tight bonds of sisterhood. But the question remains: if the Revolution did not result in women's inclusion in the polity, if the new republic did not welcome women as citizens, what did the revolutionary times specifically offer women?

The change amounted to an improvement in the view of women specifically as women: the view of what it meant to be a woman. Earlier seen as potentially dangerous and deviant, as possible witches or probable shrews, women were suddenly seen as the mothers of citizens of the republic. Previously obliged to labor under the direction of the male heads of their households, they now were granted governance of the home. The ties that bound women to their gender tightened, but their gender gained status. The belief that women had a particular feminine sensibility legitimated their demands for education, though an education different from that for men. The conviction that they were capable of superior moral purity and had special insights into the human condition legitimated their concern with social problems, as long as they did not take those concerns into the political sphere. The respect and self-respect that they had won legitimated their quest for excellence within their own sphere.

The record then leaves us with a paradox. The most important results of the Revolution were political and resolutely excluded women. The indirect results were social and ideological and attempted to circumscribe and control women. But in contributing to a clearer definition of women as women, these results also undercut the time-honored vision of women as inferior or lesser men. By proposing that women should aspire to excellence in their own sphere, they allowed that women *could* be excellent. Once that possibility had been granted, it remained only a matter of time until women would begin to claim that they could be excellent in roles previously ascribed to men.

Joan Hoff

Before, during, and after the Revolution, American women were experiencing important demographic changes that ultimately contributed to their socioeconomic subordination in the modern world. These demographic factors were of such an evolutionary nature, however, that few seem to have been directly affected by the Revolution itself, save for the temporary disruption of the nuclearity of family life, as men left home to participate in political or military activities, and for the lowering of sexual and moral standards that normally accompany wars. . . .

By 1750, at least northern colonial America could no longer be considered a "paradise on earth for women," where every free, white female could marry and where a stable, parental dominated marriage system or family of orientation (birth) prevailed. It was in the throes of a "demographic crisis. . . ." In addition to facing the possibility of not being able to marry, or remarry, in the case of widows, by the time of the Revolution women had been gradually adjusting to changing courtship and marriage patterns, loosened sexual mores, smaller family size, and (among the wealthier, better educated) to more permissive theories from foreign authors about child raising, romantic love, and sex-stereotyped definitions of feminity. All of these demographic alterations were part of the process of family modernization—that is, the evolution from the family of orientation to the family of procreation. This transition was most pronounced in the late eighteenth and early nineteenth centuries, and is therefore coincidentally connected but not substantially affected by the Revolution.

[E]xcept for the actual years in which the war was fought, colonial women found more and more of their traditional familial duties and responsibilities syphoned off as the economy became more commercially specialized and as other social institutions such as schools became more commonplace. Only women living in the most isolated frontier areas escaped this experience of declining importance and function within the family unit, and their position was far from enviable because of the physical and mental harshness of frontier life. . . .

Even the best educated women could not realize that they were demographically on their way toward modernization within the family of procreation that offered them the "cult of true womanhood" in place of collective validation and a sense of individual worth. Nor could they be expected to have anticipated other "double standard" limitations associated with this new family pattern, such as increased vicarious fulfillment through their husbands or male children and the psychic burden of the permissive child-centered household that epitomized individualism.

Reprinted from *The American Revolution: Explorations in the History of American Radicalism,* ed. Alfred F. Young (De Kalb: Northern Illinois University Press, 1976), 82, 83, 84, 88.

Lewis and Clark holding a council with the Indians. Their expedition was prompted by President Jefferson's vision of an America stretching from "the Western ocean . . . to the Atlantic." This drawing is from the 1812 edition of Patrick Gass's *Journal*, one of the first authentic accounts of the expedition. *(Courtesy, Scribner's Archives)*

Independence Confirmed
1800–1816

THE LEWIS AND CLARK EXPEDITION

Thomas Jefferson wrote eloquently of independence, religious liberty, the education of a free people. So had others; but Jefferson's words inspired a new nation, a bill of rights, a system of education. The expedition of Meriwether Lewis and William Clark from 1804 to 1806, exploring the Missouri River, the Rocky Mountains, and the Columbia River basin, was a bold Jeffersonian vision become a great historical event.

Like Christopher Columbus, he saw the westward passage as a way to the riches of the East. Commerce might move "possibly with single portage, from the Western ocean . . . to the Atlantic." To this ancient dream Jefferson added the prospect of more immediate riches: the "great supplies of furs and pelts" that were then flowing chiefly into English, not American, coffers. It meant even more to Jefferson that much of the West could become a vast, peaceful garden filling with the sturdy yeomen he expected to be the embodiments of republican virtue. The West could also be a garden for Indians weaned from their hunting ways by the advance of trade that would "place within their reach those things which will contribute more to their domestic comfort than the possession of extensive, but uncultivated wilds." The more rugged West of the great rivers and mountains would exhibit treasures of natural history. Mammoths, Jefferson suspected, might still roam the lands farther west. Perhaps the llama ranged this far north. For years, Jefferson had encouraged all who would listen to explore the great West for science, for country, for riches.

HISTORICAL EVENTS

1801
Spain cedes Louisiana to France
• Barbary Pirates declare war

1803
Marbury v. Madison
• Louisiana Purchase

1804
Lewis and Clark expedition begins
• American navy blockades coast
of Tripoli (Algeria)

1806
Berlin Decree

1807
Embargo Act

1809
Embargo Act repealed
• Non-Intercourse Act

1810
Macon's Bill No. 2

1811
Battle at Tippecanoe Creek

1812
War of 1812 • campaigns against
Canada fail

continued

Of the Shoshone Indians, Lewis wrote in his diary:

"They seldom correct their children particularly the boys who soon become masters of their own acts. They give as a reason that it cows and breaks the spirit of the boy to whip him, and that he never recovers his independence of mind after he is grown. They treat their women but with little respect, and compel them to perform every species of drudgery. they collect the wild fruits and roots, attend to the horses or assist in that duty, cook, dress the skins and make all their apparel, collect wood and make their fires, arrange and form their lodges, and when they travel pack the horses and take charge of all the baggage; in short the man does little else except attend his horses hunt and fish. The man considers himself degraded if he is compelled to walk any distance; and if he is so unfortunately poor as only to possess two horses he rides the best himself and leavs the woman or women if he has more than one, to transport their baggage and children on the other, and to walk if the horse is unable to carry the additional weight of their persons. The chastity of their women is not held in high estimation, and the husband will for a trifle barter the companion of his bed for a night or longer if he conceives the reward adequate."

Except for slightly underestimating the number of men who would be needed (thirty to fifty in various stages of the expedition), and with no idea that an Indian woman, her infant son, and a giant Newfoundland dog named Scammon would go along as well, Jefferson got exactly the expedition and the results he had envisioned. Seven men kept diaries; almost every moment when they were not exploring, negotiating, or being ill the two leaders spent taking detailed field notes and reworking them into coherent accounts, complete with drawings, maps, and lexicons for Thomas Jefferson and the world.

Meriwether Lewis and William Clark, like Jefferson, were amateurs. Though both were soldiers, neither had been a professional military man, Lewis being on leave from the army to serve as Jefferson's secretary and Clark having resigned some time before. Nor were they professional scientists or explorers: once Jefferson appointed them, they had to scramble for a rapid education in geography and mapmaking, celestial navigation, mineralogy, and medicine to keep an expedition alive for two years. Lewis sought the counsel of the nation's most distinguished physician, Dr. Benjamin Rush of Philadelphia, who supplied him with a little information and a large supply of "Rush's Thunderbolts," his famous, violently purgative pills, which Lewis and Clark used for all ailments.

The expedition went from St. Louis to the mouth of the Columbia River and back, through incredibly difficult country, with elementary equipment. The first leg, up the Missouri with a winter's stop in an Indian village, was brutally hard work: poling, pulling, and portaging a string of boats up a huge river whose powerful current undermined banks at each bend, created mudslides, and sent vast jams of tree trunks cascading downriver to knock over the expedition's boats. The second leg, over the mountaintops through high barren badlands, was the hardest part of all. The trip down the Columbia River system was least eventful. The explorers eventually realized that they had gone the long way around and correctly plotted the shortest and fastest route home through the mountains. But on the return trip they proved that there was no route, even with portages, where small boats could practically be carried over the continental divide and relaunched on the western rivers. Rather, there was a set of mountains and valleys between. The way west would not be direct or easy: the three-century-old hope of finding a direct northwest passage had to be forgotten, at least for a time.

Lewis and Clark studied dozens of Indian tribes, arranging trade agreements, asserting the government's influence, presenting gifts, recording manners and customs, seeking geographical information. Lewis and Clark also identified 300 new plant and animal species or subspecies, collecting bones, fossils, and seeds.

The homely names they gave the new species—since neither man knew Latin—have not survived in the naturalist literature; but creatures like *Salmo clarkii*, the beautiful cutthroat trout named for Clark, and *Asyndesmus lesis*, Lewis's woodpecker, attest to the ichthyologists' and ornithologists' appreciation of their works. The *Notebooks* and *Journals* of the expedition became fundamental early sources for naturalists, geographers, anthropologists, and historians.

Lewis and Clark filled their journals with drawings and descriptions of plants, and animals, such as this report on the white salmon trout. *(Courtesy, Library of Congress)*

The rigors of the journey produced much illness and hardship, yet only one man lost his life—from a ruptured appendix that in those days would have killed him even had he been in Philadelphia. The only serious injury was to Lewis himself, when one of his own men accidentally shot him in the backside. (Lewis made few mistakes: going hunting for food with a one-eyed sergeant was one of them.) There were only one or two small scrapes with Indians, although it took firm diplomacy and carefully manned swivel guns, small portable cannons, to prevent a few rough encounters from becoming dangerous. Clark's slave, York, the one black member of the expedition, was the wonder of dozens of Indian tribes. The Indians would pay to touch his hair or run their fingers over his skin to see whether the dark color would come off. One of the interpreters persuaded Lewis to allow him to take his Indian wife, Sacajawea, and their two-month-old baby on the roughest part of the trip from the upper Missouri over the mountains to the Pacific. Apparently, her knowledge of the Shoshonean dialects led the captain to agree. When they first met up with the mountain Indians, the first party of braves they encountered had as its chief her brother, whom she had not seen since she had been abducted from her hunting party as a small child. No novelist could have gotten away with such an unlikely plot.

Jefferson had made to Congress his proposal for the expedition before Talleyrand offered to sell the United States the Louisiana Territory; the President had planned to grasp the trade of the West with stations on territory both unknown and unowned. By the time the expedition set out from St. Louis, Louisiana was United States territory. But the Oregon country beyond the Great Divide was not. It belonged perhaps to Great Britain or maybe to Spain. Yet Lewis, once back at St. Louis, wrote of "possessions" west of the mountains, and Jefferson himself by January 1807 was referring to "our country, from the Missisipi [sic] to the Pacific." He supported John Jacob Astor's efforts to create a fur empire that would crowd the British out of the market. In the ensuing race for the strategic mouth of the Columbia River, Astor moved his men across the trail that Lewis and Clark had blazed, while the British pushed southwest from Canada. In July 1811, when the great British explorer and entrepreneur David Thompson pushed his way to the Columbia and canoed to its mouth, he beheld the flag of the republic flying from the parapets of four-month-old Fort Astoria. Lewis and Clark's expedition would, in the end, make Jefferson's largest vision—a continental United States—the future.

The Dawn of a Century

The People   In the twenty-five years since the opening gun of the Revolution the country's population had grown from about 2.5 to 5.3 million. The nation's white population remained overwhelmingly British in origin and Protestant in religion. Germans were found in eastern Pennsylvania, in the Shenandoah Valley, and along the Mohawk River in New York. The Hudson Valley contained many Dutchmen, and the guttural sound of Dutch could still be heard in Albany. Scattered here and there, primarily in the towns, were small enclaves of Jews and Huguenot French, as well as a handful of Irish Catholics. The largest non-British group by far was the blacks, who numbered over a million, almost all south of Pennsylvania and the overwhelming majority slaves. But the Revolution and difficulties of postwar readjustment had discouraged the slave trade as well as immigration. The vast majority of the slaves were native-born Americans.

Americans were a young people. Half the population was under seventeen years old. Households were large; almost one-fourth of all families had seven or more people living under one roof. This placed a heavy burden on families, and especially on women, who spent many of their best, most vigorous years bearing and rearing children.

The United States in 1801 was a nation of farms and villages. Only 300,000 Americans lived in communities of even 2,500 people—fewer than seven percent of the total.

The Cities   Of these the largest, most cosmopolitan, and most gracious was Philadelphia, with almost 70,000 inhabitants. Penn's town was also the most modern in the nation. Most American city dwellers drew their water from wells or cisterns or bought it from vendors. They relied on hogs to consume the garbage dumped on the street. They were forced to tramp roads usually ankle deep in either dust or mud, depending on the season. Not so Philadelphians: the city of Brotherly Love, after cholera and yellow fever epidemics in the 1790s, piped its water from the Schuylkill River and its streets, paved with cobblestones, were regularly cleaned.

Boston, with 25,000 inhabitants, had fallen behind New York and Baltimore in population since colonial days. Nevertheless, it remained the commercial, financial, and intellectual capital of New England. With its narrow streets and crowded wharves, it had not much changed since the 1770s. The city government was still the same as in the seventeenth century: its affairs were in the hands of "selectmen" chosen at the town meeting. Although Boston's elite was no longer composed of stern Puritan gentlemen, the Federalist merchants, ministers, and lawyers who now formed the town's upper crust retained much of the old Puritan granite character and respect for learning.

Two hundred miles to the south and west of Boston was New York, on Manhattan Island. Even more than Boston and Philadelphia, New York thrived on commerce; most of its 60,000 inhabitants were crowded into the southeastern corner of the island, adjacent to the docks and warehouses. The rich resources of New York port—its accessibility in winter, its many landing spots, its deep water—would soon catapult the city into becoming the nation's most populous.

Baltimore was a comparatively new city. The outlet for much of the Chesapeake tobacco crop, it also tapped the farm produce of the Pennsylvania backcountry through the Susquehanna River. Charleston, the capital of South Carolina, may have been the most colorful of all. It was both a major port and a summer resort where rice planters from the malaria-ridden coastal lowlands went during the fever season to protect their health. Built in brick and stone, the city was ruled by a planter and merchant elite who combined republican principles with the aristocratic arts of good living, polite letters, fine manners, and elegant hospitality. These avowed republicans could not live without slaves. Of the 18,000 people who packed the little port, 6,000 were blacks; they helped keep its streets clean, its markets stocked, and its wharves busy.

Any observer of Charleston between 1790 and 1800 would have noticed a particularly promising development: a new crop, cotton, was being loaded aboard ships in the harbor by black stevedores. With the perfection of the cotton gin by the Connecticut Yankee Eli Whitney, green-seed cotton had become a profitable crop in the interior of the Carolinas and Georgia. The South's one major Atlantic port was feeling the invigorating economic effects of the thousands of bales it shipped to Liverpool and Glasgow to feed the new textile factories of Great Britain.

The small town of Pittsburgh was situated where the Allegheny and Monongahela rivers join to form the great Ohio River. With about two thousand inhabitants in 1800, it had become a supplier of manufactured goods to the burgeoning West, producing iron, glass, and textiles, along with vessels for the river trade. As early as 1800 an English visitor reported the town covered with a pall of smoke from the numerous coal fires that fueled the iron foundries and glassworks.

Outside the new United States other settlements that would eventually become cities in the new nation were slowly gaining population. St. Augustine, Florida, founded by the Spanish in 1585, would be an American town by 1819. New Orleans, settled by the French in 1718, had 10,000 people when Jefferson purchased Louisiana in 1803. In Texas, San Antonio, also dating back to 1718, had over 1,200 people by 1800, and Santa Fe, New Mexico, along with San Diego and San Francisco in California, were small trading villages.

The Farms   A typical American yeoman and his family worked hard for what they had. Animals had to be fed and watered, their stables cleaned. Plowing in the spring, weeding and cultivating in summer, and harvesting in fall all required heavy labor. The women cooked, cleaned, spun, made preserves, and took care of flocks of young children. Clearing new land on the frontier required the

One country boy remembered the period:

"My father was A Farmer and by the help of his trusty rifle Kept the family in wild meat such as bear, Elk, Deer, and wild Turkey.

How well I Remember the old Hunting stories he used to tell us boys. I will give you a sketch of a hunting expedition my father and three other men took on one of the head branches of the licking River. They killed 16 Bear and A Number Deer. They took their horses with them and they would tye one horse and the others wouldn't leave him they would then dig out troughs and pack the meat their horses couldn't carry home in Pack saddles. They would pack the Meat in them troughs and split out puncheons and cover the meat with them and pin them down to keep the wolves from eating their meat till they took their first loads home and go back after it. They used the fat bear meat to cook the Deer meat with."

backbreaking labor of girdling trees, clearing underbrush, and breaking virgin sod. The pioneer farmer of Vermont, western New York, or the newly opened Ohio or Alabama country was lucky if he could add more than four or five usable acres to his farm a year. Even then it took many years before the frontier farmer's land was fully cleared of stumps and he could plow a straight furrow. Meanwhile, his family lived in a primitive one-room log house with a sleeping attic above. Techniques of planting and harvesting had not advanced much beyond medieval practices. American plows in 1800 were heavy wooden contraptions pulled by oxen or mules. Farmers still used the scythe to harvest grain and threshed it with a hand flail made of two sticks joined by a leather thong. *Yeah.*

Yet the yeoman family enjoyed a rough abundance. Since the soil was rich, the American farm family ate well and produced more than it consumed. Travelers through the nation's rural regions remarked on signs of prosperity. One Englishman reported of the Connecticut countryside during Jefferson's presidency that it "had the appearance of wealth, numerous broods of poultry straying about, with sheep and cattle grazing in great numbers in the fields." Travelers who accepted the hospitality of local yeomen, rather than brave the fare of notoriously bad country inns, reported on the abundance of everything served. Breakfast tables were loaded down with boiled fish, beefsteak, ham sausages, hot breads, and cheese.

Isolation   The typical farm family was an isolated social unit. Except in southern New England, where the imprint of the old town system of colonial days remained, the rural American lived in a house widely separated by fields and virgin forest from his nearest neighbor. Communication benefited from an improvement in postal service and roads. In the 1790s there were seventy-five post offices in the entire nation, connected by 1,875 miles of post roads. But by the War of 1812 the nation had 2,610 post offices and over 39,000 miles of roads. The steepness of postal rates (8 cents per letter, 12½ cents for a letter sent over 100 miles) still worked to isolate much of the rural population.

Farm women suffered acutely from the isolation of their lives. Many lacked the close network of female kin and friends from which New England women drew comfort and companionship. One lonely woman in Ohio lamented: "Tis strange to us to see company. I expect the sun may rise and set a hundred times before I shall see another human that does not belong to the family." Ribbons and mirrors remained rare; cookstoves and shoes might have to be ordered from New England. And although husbands and wives frequently worked as close collaborators in daily life—bringing in the harvest, or even delivering children—the lines between male and female spheres remained tightly drawn. When men would get together to raise a house, the women cooked for the large throng.

A way out of the desolateness was newspapers. One traveler noted how a small New Hampshire town hungered for news: "It was entertaining to see the eagerness of the people on our arrival to get a sight of the last newspaper from Boston. They flocked to the post-office and the

---

His farm, said a Maryland yeoman of Jeffersonian times,

"gave me and my family a good living on the produce of it; and left me, one year with another, one hundred and fifty dollars, for I have never spent more than ten dollars a year, which was for salt, nails, and the like. Nothing to wear, eat, or drink was purchased, as my farm provided all. With this saving, I put money to interest, bought cattle, fatted and sold them, and made great profit."

inn, and formed a variety of groups round those who were fortunate to possess themselves of a paper." But in rural New England a traveler in the early 1800s observed that "there is scarcely a poor owner of a miserable log hut, who lives on the border of the stage road, but has a newspaper left at his door." In 1801 there were 200 newspapers in the nation; by the 1830s there would be more than 1,200.

For a portion of the rural population, relief might come by way of books. Almanacs, a staple of the farm homestead, urged farmers to buy and read books. The farmer, one author claimed, sees "his barns, granaries, and cellars, all well filled by his own industry and frugality; his farm affording him all the comforts and necessaries of life, enables him to spend the long and tedious winter evenings with his family round a good fire and a clean hearth, where he may read THEOLOGY, GEOGRAPHY, HISTORY, &C. and edify and entertain them. . . ." The *Farmer's Almanack* paid tribute to another almanac-writer, Benjamin Franklin, recommending "The Life of Dr. Franklin" (published in 1794) "for the amusement of winter evenings."

When rural Americans did gather with neighbors and friends, it was often to engage in rough-and-tumble sports that could turn brutal. Wrestling included kicking, biting, punching, and eye-gouging. "I saw more than one man who wanted an eye," noted an easterner as he crossed the border into Kentucky. Country people, especially on the frontier, "baited" bulls and bears—that is, set large dogs to attack them while rooting for either attacker or defender—or they bet on the outcome of cockfights. Whether at taverns or at religious camp meetings, at dances and hoedowns or in the home, Americans consumed vast quantities of whiskey, rum, and brandy. Women drank punch or toddies made of these.

It would take years of steady cultivation of the land, good roads, and growth of towns before the rudeness of the country lessened along with its isolation.

This symbol of the Philadelphia Society for Promoting Agriculture illustrates Republican agrarianism. The yeoman farmer is shown ploughing his field under the approving gaze of the figure of Columbia.

Some young men left the farm to attend school. A student in Philadelphia wrote a letter to his parents in Allegheny County:

"I now take up my pen to write, but what to say I know not, sinking into debt and no prospect of making any thing to relieve myself. I continue to teach a gentleman's sons the Greek and Latin languages, for which I receive one hundred dollars per year, but this is far from being sufficient to answer my demands. . . . Last summer I bought two pair of nanking pantaloons and a light vest, the whole amounting to $7.60, and this is all I have got since I left home. If I should leave this place, one thing will be in my favour, that is I shall not be burthened with clothes. . . ."

President Thomas Jefferson

The Inauguration At noon on a blustery March day in 1801, Jefferson took the oath of office and became the third President of the United States. He had come to Washington the previous November and had spent the winter at Conrad and McMunn's boardinghouse, where for $15 a week he dined and roomed unostentatiously. The inauguration ceremonies were brief and austere, as befitted a party that made a point of republican simplicity. Jefferson's expensive velvet suit failed to arrive, and he walked in plain garb to the still uncompleted Capitol.

In the crowded Senate chamber, Jefferson swore to defend the Constitution and faithfully discharge the duties of his office. Then he delivered his inaugural address, pledging freedom of religion and the press. He endorsed the encouragement of agriculture, and of commerce as its handmaid. The federal government, the new President declared, must conduct its business economically and attempt to pay off its debts. The state governments were "the surest bulwarks against anti-republi-

"I have this morning witnessed one of the most interesting scenes a free people can ever witness," a Philadelphia woman wrote to her sister-in-law. "The changes of administration, which in every government and in every age have most generally been epochs of confusion, villainy and bloodshed, in this our happy country take place without any species of distraction, or disorder."

Thomas Jefferson struck a strong note of conciliation in his First Inaugural Address:

"We are all Republicans—we are all Federalists. If there be any among us who would wish to dissolve this Union or to change its republican form, let them stand undisturbed as monuments of the safety with which error of opinion may be tolerated where reason is left free to combat it."

Thomas Jefferson, inaugurated as third President of the United States in March 1801. *(Portrait by Rembrandt Peale, 1800, White House Collection)*

can tendencies." But besides making these predictable Republican pronouncements, Jefferson sought to calm the fears of Federalists. The nation, he declared, must avoid "entangling alliances": this was a signal that the Republicans would accept the recent termination of the 1778 French alliance. They would also avoid extreme partisanship. Now that the great contest of 1800 was over, all Americans "will, of course, arrange themselves under the will of the law, and unite in common efforts for the common good." Minority rights would be protected, and no one would suffer persecution: "We are all Republicans, we are all Federalists. . . . Let us, then, with courage and confidence pursue our own Federal and Republican principles, our attachment to union and representative government."

So softly did the fresh-minted chief executive speak that few in the crowded room could hear what he said. But printed copies of the speech were available, and ushers distributed these to the assembled dignitaries. That evening, the President returned to Conrad and McMunn's to dine as usual. When he entered the dining room, a lady among the paying guests offered him a chair. Jefferson declined and went to his usual place at the foot of the table, far from the warming fire. A simpler age of American manners had begun.

Yet republican plainness, as Jefferson understood it, meant something quite opposite to the affected bluntness and democracy of style, and the crude appeals to popular emotions, that have been a temptation among American politicians. Jefferson was a gentleman. Graciousness, an unwillingness to draw attention to himself, a refusal to make overly much of his social and governmental rank belonged to a sophisticated gentleman's deportment. The republic Jefferson sought was not a mobocracy but a nation of citizens raised upward in learning, independence, and virtue. Reflective of what a republican citizen—an extraordinary one, to be sure—might do in private life was Jefferson's most striking achievement: his Monticello.

Monticello   The Lewis and Clark expedition illustrates the mind of the new President putting scientific curiosity and political vision to a large project. In Monticello, his country estate, his restless intelligence applied itself to specific problems in invention. Monticello is an early instance of the tinkering and practical science that Americans were to think of as a mark of the American character.

Jefferson had begun building his "little mountain" home near Charlottesville in 1768 on land that his father had owned. The site overlooks the Blue Ridge Mountains in the west and the Virginia plains to the east, vistas that had intrigued Jefferson since childhood. Unable to find a competent architect in the colonies, the resourceful Virginian studied a few books, drew his own plans, and supervised most of the forty-one years of construction. Laid out as an Italian villa, Monticello also has a Greek portico, a Roman dome, and colonial detail. But Jefferson relied principally upon Andrea Palladio, the architect who had created the Georgian style in England. Taken together, Monticello's diverse design did much to launch the classical revival in architecture, which swept the United States during the early nineteenth century.

Graceful use, not merely symmetrical display, dictated the general

Thomas Jefferson's home, Monticello, near Charlottesville, Virginia. (*Courtesy, Virginia State Travel Service*)

layout of the thirty-five room manor. Most colonial estates grouped carriage house, kitchen, stable, laundry, and smokehouse in separate buildings removed from the main house. For convenience and efficiency, Jefferson moved these functional areas indoors, connected to the living quarters. He built them under terraces that flank Monticello on either side and open away from the inside. This innovation was soon copied throughout the South. Between the two basements were separate storage rooms for wine, beer, hard cider, and rum.

Monticello is noted for its gadgetry. A pair of glass doors between the main hall and a drawing room opens simultaneously when only one is pushed—Jefferson had installed a series of gears under the floor, much like a modern bicycle-pedal system. Jefferson connected the weathervane on the roof of Monticello to a dial on the ceiling of the portico so he could read the wind without going outside. A pulley arrangement carried a used bottle of wine to the cellar and retrieved a cooled one. His kitchen drew from a pond stocked with fish to be caught fresh for the dinner table.

Style, contraptions, and even its history mark Monticello as uniquely American. In 1781 a platoon of British soldiers raided the house in hopes of capturing its owner, then governor of Virginia; Jefferson narrowly escaped up the mountainside. After a life of political and diplomatic service to the nation, he would retire from the presidency in 1809 and return to the just-completed house. Despite spiraling debts, aggravated by the costs of Monticello's upkeep, loans from friends enabled Jefferson to live in the house until his death on July 4, 1826.

Thomas Jefferson wrote:

"There is a natural aristocracy among men. The grounds of these are virtue and talents."

"The selfish spirit of commerce . . . knows no country, and feels no passion or principle but that of gain."

"Government, even in its best state, is a necessary evil; in its worst state, an intolerable one."

"I have sworn upon the altar of God eternal hostility against every tyranny over the mind of man."

Limited Government

Jefferson simplified the government. He and his treasury secretary Albert Gallatin opposed any rise in the federal debt, and they managed to cut military spending to a third of what it had been under the Federalists. The army was reduced to just 3,000 regulars and 172 officers. The five frigates built during Adams's administration were all rendered inactive; in their place the Jeffersonians created a navy of gunboats fit only for coastal service. The President also closed the American legations in Holland and Prussia. The new administration could not abolish the Bank of the United States before its charter expired in 1811, but under Gallatin the government sold its Bank stock at a profit and ceased to take on any further banking role.

If government as Jefferson conceived of it had little business regulating finances, and little use for a large military establishment, it certainly had no taste for enforcing political loyalty. He allowed the Sedition Act to lapse; there would be no more criminal prosecutions for attacking the government.

Jefferson's republic would have a virtuous simplicity. He would have shuddered at the size and scope of twentieth-century governments; but he would have shuddered also at twentieth-century business or twentieth-century cities. He advocated the very sort of limited government that Hamilton in *The Federalist* had warned against: "a government at a distance and out of sight." The national government, Jefferson declared in his first message to Congress, was "charged with the external and mutual relations only of these states." It was the states that had "principal care of our persons, our property, and our reputation." The national government had become "too complicated, too expensive"; offices and officers had "multiplied unnecessarily and sometimes injuriously to the service they were meant to promote." As means to his goal, Jefferson's administration sought economy, a limit to federal powers, and decentralization. It is curious that the Federalists, less egalitarian than Jefferson, actually had a concept that comes closer to the reality of modern democratic societies. They had planned for a more active economy than Jefferson seems to have envisioned, and their government policies would draw the country's labor and resources more closely together and put them more vigorously to work for the increase of prosperity.

More immediately Jefferson sought to weed out of the federal bureaucracy those Federalists who had taken too partisan a role in the political battles preceding 1801. Most of these were officeholders whom the President could remove at will; but at least one, Supreme Court Justice Chase, had life tenure and could be gotten rid of only by a House impeachment followed by trial and conviction by the Senate. In 1805 a

Republican House of Representatives did impeach Chase on charges of high crimes and misdemeanors, but the Senate failed to remove him from office.

Marbury v. Madison (1803) Far more significant in its ultimate result was the Jefferson Administration's attempt to undo the effects of the 1801 Judiciary Act. Under that measure Adams, just before leaving office, had appointed a flock of Federalist judges and law officials with lifetime tenure; his purpose had clearly been to retain Federalist control in at least one branch of government and, as the Republicans saw it, prevent the new administration from carrying out the will of the people. Hoping to frustrate this goal, Jefferson's secretary of state Madison refused to deliver several newly appointed officials their commissions. William Marbury sued the secretary, charging that his action was illegal under the Judiciary Act of 1789. By the provisions of that measure, Marbury's lawyers argued, the Supreme Court could compel a federal official to issue a commission whether he wished to or not.

In 1803 the case came before the United States Supreme Court, Chief Justice John Marshall presiding. Marshall was a Virginian, but not of the political stamp of his fellow Virginians Jefferson and Madison. A Federalist, he deplored the Republican preference for a small national government. He also wanted a strong Supreme Court. Yet Marshall and the Court held, in *Marbury v. Madison*, that the Court could not compel Madison to deliver a commission to Marbury, since that portion of the Judiciary Act of 1789 that would have made Madison issue the commission was unconstitutional and therefore unenforceable. The Supreme Court, it seems, was surrendering a little power that it might have claimed and exercised. But it was doing so at great gain. *Marbury v. Madison* immeasurably strengthened the Supreme Court, for it announced and won wide acceptance of the principle of judicial review: that the Court could decide whether a piece of federal legislation was constitutional. Although the idea of judicial review had been asserted before *Marbury v. Madison*, that case provided the first occasion for the Supreme Court to define and exercise the right.

The Louisiana Purchase (1803) In 1803 the United States acquired the province of Louisiana from France and thereby almost doubled its size. Louisiana was a gigantic wedge of territory stretching from the Gulf of Mexico in the South to somewhere in the present-day Dakotas in the North, and from the Mississippi in the East to the Rocky Mountains in the West. Its exact boundaries were unclear, its richness and strategic value unquestioned.

Spain had owned the province until ceding it to France in 1801 with the promise that it not be given to a third party. Tentative reports of the transfer alarmed Jefferson. The President looked forward to an "empire for liberty" consisting of American farmlands stretching over much of North America. So long as weak Spain controlled the sparsely settled province, Jefferson could afford to wait until it dropped into the American lap. But if powerful France now possessed it, who knew

The decision the Supreme Court issued in *Marbury v. Madison* (1803) contained this sentence "It is a proposition too plain to be contested that the Court Controls any legislative act repugnant to it: A legislative act contrary to the Constitution is not law"

As Chief Justice of the United States, John Marshall wrote decisions that helped strengthen the federal government. *(Portrait by J. W. Jarvis, Courtesy, Richard Coke Marshall Collection, Frick Art Reference Library)*

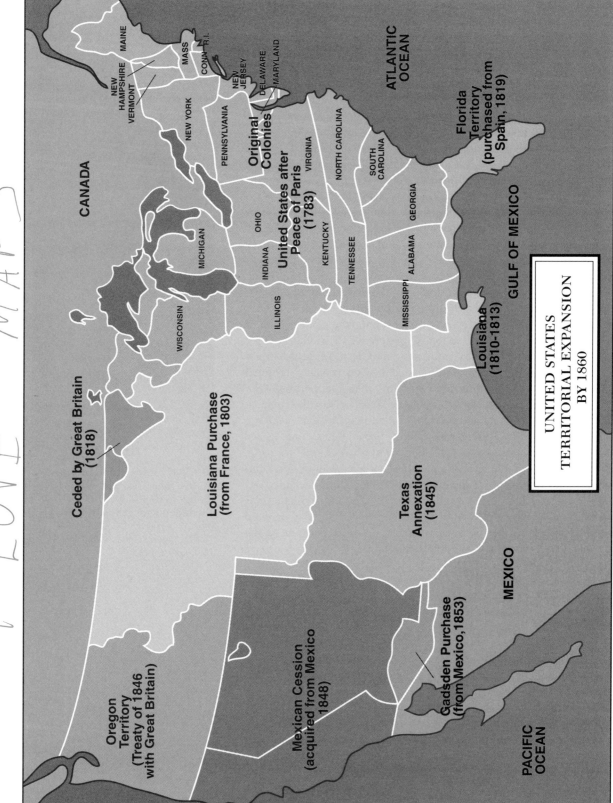

I LOVE MAPS

UNITED STATES
TERRITORIAL EXPANSION
BY 1860

CANADA

ATLANTIC OCEAN

GULF OF MEXICO

MEXICO

PACIFIC OCEAN

Ceded by Great Britain (1818)

Oregon Territory (Treaty of 1846 with Great Britain)

Louisiana Purchase (from France, 1803)

Mexican Cession (acquired from Mexico 1848)

Texas Annexation (1845)

Gadsden Purchase (from Mexico, 1853)

Louisiana (1810-1813)

Florida Territory (purchased from Spain, 1819)

United States after Peace of Paris (1783)

Original Colonies

MAINE
NEW HAMPSHIRE
VERMONT
MASS
CONN
R.I.
NEW YORK
PENNSYLVANIA
NEW JERSEY
DELAWARE
MARYLAND
OHIO
INDIANA
ILLINOIS
MICHIGAN
WISCONSIN
VIRGINIA
NORTH CAROLINA
SOUTH CAROLINA
GEORGIA
KENTUCKY
TENNESSEE
ALABAMA
MISSISSIPPI

whether the United States would ever be able to acquire it? Besides, Louisiana included the port of New Orleans. Whoever controlled this port controlled the trade and commercial outlet for much of the western United States. Hoping to prevent final consummation of the arrangement between Spain and France or at least to acquire some port on the Gulf Coast, Jefferson dispatched Robert Livingston to Paris.

The French meanwhile were beginning to lose interest in the territory. For a time Napoleon had hoped to fit Louisiana into a great French colonial empire that would also include the valuable Caribbean sugar island of Hispaniola. He first had to recapture the western part of Hispaniola from the blacks who in the 1790s had risen up against French masters there and established the Republic of Haiti. Napoleon sent an army of thirty thousand men, headed by his brother-in-law, to subdue the Haitians under their brilliant leader Toussaint L'Ouverture. The task was impossible. Eventually the French captured L'Ouverture by treachery, but not before their army had been virtually wiped out by a combination of enemy action and tropical disease. Napoleon decided to abandon his dream of a restored French empire in the New World.

When he arrived in Paris, Livingston confronted this new situation. France no longer cared much about Louisiana; and Napoleon, now

William Wordsworth, the English poet, wrote of Toussaint L'Ouverture's consignment to a dungeon by the French:

There's not a breathing of the common
  wind
That will forget thee; thou has great
  allies;
Thy friends are exhultations, agonies,
And love, and man's unconquerable
  mind.

Toussaint L'Ouverture proclaims the constitution for the republic of Haiti. *(Courtesy, Library of Congress)*

rearming to invade archenemy Britain, was certain that he could not keep it from falling into British hands. On the American side, the situation had also changed. In October 1802 Spain, still in legal possession of New Orleans, decided to deny once more to citizens of the United States the access to the port that the Pinckney Treaty of 1795 had temporarily granted.

Jefferson now dispatched James Monroe to France with new orders. He should try to get New Orleans from the French, or at least to acquire from Spain part of the Gulf Coast panhandle of West Florida. Either would give the United States an outlet for southern trade. Two days after Monroe joined Livingston in the French capital, they learned a prodigious piece of news: Napoleon would sell not only New Orleans but all of Louisiana. The price: 60 million francs, and up to 20 million francs in settlement of all American claims against France for the "spoliations" of the 1790s. The offer flabbergasted the envoys. They were not authorized to negotiate such an arrangement, but it was far too good to turn down, and they eagerly accepted. In short order, the signed document was on its way to Washington for Congress and the President to confirm.

It may seem surprising that any American should have questioned such an extraordinary bargain, but many did. One prominent Federalist denounced the purchase as "a miserable calamitous business"—the new nation would now be so gigantic that it would fall apart. Some Federalists were unhappy that the United States had promised to grant citizenship to all the French and Spanish inhabitants of Louisiana. Federalists like Timothy Pickering were sincere opponents of slavery, concerned that the new territory would allow for extension of slaveholding. Even Jefferson worried that by buying Louisiana he had exceeded the authority of the federal government under the Constitution, and for a while he supported a constitutional amendment authorizing the purchase. In the end neither side's scruples could compete with the reality of the most successful land deal in history. On October 20, 1803, the Senate confirmed the treaty, and two months later the United States took formal possession of the province. For a total of $15 million the United States had acquired a region almost equal in area to the whole of western Europe.

To the west and the north the vast domain touched Spanish and British territory, but exactly where nobody really knew. The Spaniards suspected that the United States had designs on their possessions in New Mexico and Texas. Years before, they had secretly entered into a financial arrangement with James Wilkinson, a Kentucky adventurer, to act as their spy and agent in the American camp. Wilkinson remained in their pay while rising to brigadier general in the United States Army and to the post of military commander of the new Louisiana Territory. Another prominent American, Vice President Aaron Burr, was fishing in the same troubled western waters.

Aaron Burr's schemes to detach the West from the United States led to indictments for treason, charges which he managed to escape. (*Courtesy, The New-York Historical Society*)

Burr Again   Burr was a complex man. Witty, charming, and intelligent, he was also ambitious and devious. This son of a Presbyterian minister, this grandson of Jonathan Edwards, this former theology student became a notorious womanizer. In 1804 at

Weehawken, New Jersey, he killed Alexander Hamilton in a duel that was the culmination of long-standing animosity between the two men.

A year later, Burr, according to Wilkinson, was deeply involved in a scheme to detach Louisiana from the United States, join it together with Texas and other parts of Spanish Mexico, and create a new nation. But Wilkinson decided in the end that it was more profitable to stay in Spain's employ than to continue with this chancy venture. In November 1806 he wrote to Jefferson, warning that Burr intended to detach the West from the United States.

Jefferson ordered the arrest of Burr, who quickly set out for Pensacola in Spanish Florida, probably intending to escape to Europe. But he was captured and brought to Richmond, Virginia, and tried for treason, Wilkinson serving as an important witness against him. The prosecution produced much damaging evidence against Burr. But the former Vice President had the support of the presiding judge, Chief Justice Marshall; when the jury returned the verdict of "not proved," Marshall changed it to "not guilty."

The government refused to drop the matter. Soon after, it obtained Burr's indictment on another treason charge. This time Marshall granted him bail pending trial and rather than face another legal battle, Burr fled to Europe. He remained abroad for four years, and then returned to live a scandalous life in New York City. In his seventies he fathered two illegitimate children, and at the age of eighty he was sued for divorce on the grounds of adultery.

No viagra   here.

France and England Once More

Foreign Entanglements   Thomas Jefferson had been in office for only a few months when foreign policy demanded his attention.

Ever since 1789 the United States had followed the British practice of paying tribute to the Barbary States: Algiers, Morocco, Tripoli, and Tunis. In return, the Barbary Pirates, as many Americans preferred to call them, agreed to allow American merchant vessels to have free access to the Mediterranean ports of North Africa. But in May 1801 the Pasha of Tripoli substantially increased his tribute demands and unilaterally declared war on the United States. Jefferson decided to take a stand. He sent a small naval fleet to the Mediterranean late in 1803, and early in 1804 the fleet destroyed an American ship that Tripoli had captured and converted to its own use. The American navy then blockaded the Tripoli coast. After more than a year, Tripoli acquiesced and signed a treaty ending the war.

In the early 1800s England and France ended their long, exhausting war. It now looked as if the American people would be spared the ordeal they had faced ever since war between the world's two most powerful nations erupted in 1793. No longer would American commerce be the defenseless prey both of the Royal Navy and of French revenue cutters and port officials. But peace lasted only fourteen months. By May 1803 Britain was once more at war with France. Once again, the United States found itself caught between the British hammer and the French anvil.

The Royal Navy immediately resumed its practice of impressing seamen aboard American vessels, claiming that they were deserters from the British fleet. Outside American harbors, British ships waited for American merchant vessels, stopped them, sent an officer aboard, and took crewmen. Britain also reversed its former policy and refused any longer to allow Americans the "broken voyage," a practice by which they had transported French goods under the protection of American neutrality by shipping them through American ports. Britain's primary purpose was not to injure United States commerce but to frustrate the French war effort.

Responding to the British blockade of the continent of Europe, dominated by France, Napoleon issued in 1806 the Berlin Decree, ordering the seizure of any vessel carrying British goods. The following year he directed French privateers to stop all ships, including neutral ones, suspected of carrying enemy cargo. The Berlin Decree set off a round of British countermeasures, followed by still further French retaliation. It began to seem that no American ship would be able to leave port or approach European shores without facing confiscation.

The American response to these indignities and harassments was mixed. Since Britain was now violating American sovereign rights even more flagrantly than France, Britain was the object of an enraged American patriotism. Continuing problems with the Indian tribes in the Northwest increased anger against the British. Not all Americans, however, agreed that strong measures were called for. Especially in the Atlantic ports, many citizens were willing to accept harassment. For despite it, American commerce was flourishing in a war-stricken world. So pressing was the need for shipping space that ocean freight rates shot upward. Insurance costs were also high and there was always the risk of confiscation, but profits were unprecedented. Between 1803 and 1807 American exports, much of them in tropical goods from the French and Spanish New World colonies, leaped from $56 million to $108 million, and the American merchant marine grew from 950,000 tons to almost 1.3 million. Why not accept the situation, asked the merchants of Boston, Salem, Providence, New York, Philadelphia, and other ports.

Pressures for War   Still, even the most materialistic citizens could forget their immediate interests in the heat of anger at some indignity committed by the British or French. One such incident took place in the early summer of 1807.

On June 22, the *Chesapeake*, a brand-new Navy frigate commanded by Commodore James Barron, left Norfolk, Virginia, for a Mediterranean cruise. Aboard were several deserters from the Royal Navy. When the *Chesapeake* was only a few miles at sea, it was overtaken by H.M.S. *Leopard*, part of the British squadron patrolling off Hampton Roads. The British captain ordered Barron to heave to and allow a naval party to board to look for deserters. This was the first time the British had attempted impressment of an American man-of-war, and Barron refused. But most of the *Chesapeake*'s guns were not yet mounted, and the ship could not defend itself. After repeated murderous broadsides from the *Leopard*, Barron struck his colors; the British removed four

The attack on the U.S.S. *Chesapeake* by H.M.S. *Leopard* on June 22, 1807, set off a furor among Americans, but Jefferson avoided armed conflict through diplomacy and passage of the Embargo Act. *(Courtesy, The Mariners Museum, Newport News, Virginia)*

deserters and departed. The *Chesapeake* limped back to port with three dead, eighteen wounded, and a tale certain to inflame every American patriot.

Americans demanded war against Britain. "The country," Jefferson noted, "had never been in such a state of excitement since the battle of Lexington." But the President, although he could undoubtedly have obtained a declaration of war from Congress, wished to avoid armed conflict. He was not a pacifist, but he deplored the expensive armies and navies war required. In accordance with his distaste for a large military, Jefferson had so reduced American forces that war was virtually out of the question. And the United States, he believed, still had at its disposal some powerful unused weapons short of war.

Diplomatic pressure was one of these, and Jefferson immediately dispatched a message to Britain demanding disavowal of the attack, reparations for lives lost and damage inflicted, and an end to the impressment policy. He also ordered all British ships out of United States territorial waters and stepped up preparations for defense in case the British forced the nation's hand. The British response to American diplomatic demands was unsatisfactory. Jefferson now invoked his last peaceable weapon. American trade, the President believed, was essential to both the major belligerents. Both needed American wheat, provisions, and lumber, and the French relied on the United States to carry their Caribbean products. During the imperial crisis before 1775, Americans had forced Britain to back down by boycotting British goods. In all likelihood, Jefferson thought, they would yield to commercial pressure if it were applied firmly.

The Embargo and Non-Intercourse Acts

Under the President's prodding, Congress passed the Embargo Act of 1807. The law prohibited American commercial ships from sailing for foreign ports. The Embargo Act was temporarily popular in the South and the West. But to the trading centers of the Northeast it seemed a disaster. Almost overnight the glittering

John Lambert, a stevedore, wrote of the effects of the embargo on the wharves of New York City:

"When I arrived at New York in November [1807], the port was filled with shipping, and the wharfs were crowded with commodities of every description. Bales of cotton, wool, and merchandise; barrels of potash, rice, flour, and salt provisions; hogsheads of sugar, chests of tea, puncheons of rum, and pipes of wine. . . . All was noise and bustle . . . But on my return . . . the following April, what a contrast was presented to my view! . . . The coffee-house slip, the wharfs and quays along South street, presented no longer the bustle and activity that had prevailed there five months before. The port, indeed, was full of shipping; but they were dismantled and laid up. Their decks were cleared, their hatches fastened down, and scarcely a sailor was to be found on board. Not a box, bale, cask, barrel or package, was to be seen upon the wharfs."

trade bubble that had lasted since 1793 burst. Ships rode at anchor, their sails furled, while worms riddled their wooden hulls. Waterfront streets once busy stood emptied of their milling crowds of seamen, teamsters, tavern-keepers, and stevedores.

Overall, the embargo did not have much effect on the European belligerents. It hurt British workingmen and French colonists, but the ruling classes in both Britain and France were scarcely affected. British manufacturers, meanwhile, could continue to send their goods in their own vessels to compete with American products in the United States. "It was," wrote a critic, "as if a flea had tried to stop a dogfight by threatening suicide."

In demanding the subordination of economic self-interest to peace, Jefferson had overestimated the patience and patriotism of his fellow citizens. So loud became the domestic outcry against the Embargo Act that Congress in 1809 replaced it with the Non-Intercourse Act, permitting exports to every nation except England and France. These two offenders could now neither buy from the United States nor sell to her. If either of the two powers reversed its hostile policies toward the United States, this country could resume trade with it. The man who would administer the new law was not Jefferson but his successor, James Madison.

James Madison Takes Over

No one else had been so instrumental as Madison in fostering and shaping the federal Constitution. After the inauguration of the national government, it had been Madison who led the forces against Hamilton and, in alliance with his good friend Jefferson, helped to create the Republican Party. In 1801 Jefferson selected him as his secretary of state and he served with distinction in that office.

Many Republicans viewed Madison as Jefferson's natural successor—but not all. Opposed to him was a group of militant Republicans called the "Tertium Quids," who considered both Jefferson and Madison to be too friendly to Federalist principles. The leading voice of the Quids was John Randolph of Roanoke, an eloquent defender of lost causes and an irresponsible verbal brawler. The Quids tried to deny Madison the nomination, but with Jefferson's support the party caucus in Congress endorsed him. The Federalists were now the minority party, and Madison in 1808 easily defeated their candidate, Charles Cotesworth Pinckney of XYZ fame.

Physically, the new President was not a commanding figure. Small and wizened, he spoke in a barely audible voice and often seemed bored. The First Lady, the former Dolley Todd, helped to offset her husband's dour demeanor. Buxom, pink-cheeked, and charming, Mrs. Madison was a vivacious hostess whose parties and receptions seemed to the social set a vast improvement over the widowed Jefferson's bachelor dinners. Washington was still a city of magnificent intentions, as an early observer of its raw, unfilled spaces called it; the presidential mansion was still not complete. But at least the capital now had a social focus it had lacked before.

James Madison, inaugurated as President in 1809, faced growing pressure from the "War Hawks" and others to act against Britain and finally declared war in June 1812. *(Portrait by Gilbert Stuart, Courtesy, Bowdoin College Museum of Fine Arts, Brunswick, Maine)*

John Randolph of Roanoke. *(Courtesy, Scribner's Archives)*

The new Non-Intercourse Act created difficulties for Madison. Ships leaving American ports were not supposed to touch at French or British ports, but it quickly became clear that there was no way of guaranteeing they would obey the law. The British, in particular, scorned it; it promised to cause them little harm, and they could see little reason to settle the pending *Chesapeake* claims or satisfy American commercial demands. The British minister in Washington, David Erskine, was friendly to the United States and wanted to placate the Americans. He told Madison that the British intended to modify their harsh policy toward American trade. On this basis, the President issued a proclamation reopening trade with Great Britain while retaining the restrictions on France. Soon after, British Foreign Secretary Canning learned of his minister's indiscretion and disavowed it. The President thereupon reimposed the Non-Intercourse arrangement on Britain.

Macon's Bill No. 2   Dissatisfaction with the Non-Intercourse Act forced Congress into a new tack against the belligerents. In May 1810 it passed Macon's Bill No. 2. This measure was one of the most devious in American history. It allowed the President to reopen trade immediately with both Britain and France. In the event that either of the two warring powers modified its trade policies toward the United States before March 1811, the President might reimpose the trade prohibition upon the other. In effect, the United States was offering to ally itself economically against whichever nation was the slower in according it its commercial rights.

An embarrassing and costly blunder was soon forthcoming. In August 1810, when Napoleon learned of the terms of Macon's Bill, he instructed his foreign minister, Duc de Cadore, to inform the Americans that his commercial decrees would be revoked as of November 1, provided that the United States invoke nonintercourse against the British. (Napoleon had larceny in his heart: even as he issued these instructions he prepared to seize any American vessels that might appear near France.) Cadore took the liberty of informing the United States that the French decrees had actually been canceled. Once again, as in his optimistic reaction to Erskine's assurances, Madison responded without checking. He reopened trade with France and declared that trade with Britain would be closed the following February, unless Britain should revoke its Orders in Council before that time. The British replied by once again stationing their warships outside New York harbor and stepping up their campaign of impressing seamen on American ships. Vessels that eluded British capture were confiscated by Napoleon as soon as they reached France.

The War Hawks   Among the victors in the 1810 elections to Congress was a group of young men, most of them from the West and South, who were unwilling to temporize. Labeled War Hawks, the aggressive youngsters were led by Henry Clay of Kentucky, a young congressman with a rare eloquence and an unusual charm. Although this was his first term in the House of Representatives, the magnetic Clay was elected Speaker. He quickly placed young men of like mind in key House posts. Peter Porter of western New York became chairman of the Foreign Relations Committee, where he had the support of such fellow War Hawks as John C. Calhoun of South Carolina, Felix Grundy of Tennessee, and Joseph Desha of Kentucky.

The War Hawks thundered against the indignities inflicted by the British. England's "aggression, and her injuries and insults to us," proclaimed Henry Clay, were "atrocious"—far more so than those of France. Besides, British assaults on American shipping were responsible for the weakness of crop prices in the West since they interfered with sales of these crops abroad. The British practice of taking seamen from American ships and impressing them into the service of the Royal Navy constituted a violation of national sovereignty. The War Hawks also blamed British agents for instigating Indian uprisings. The Kentucky *Gazette* complained that the British could wield "greater influence with [the Indians] of late than American justice and benevolence."

Western Indians   For some time, in fact, the government had been carrying on military campaigns against western Indians. The real explanation for the renewed violence on the western frontier, however, was the increase in white settlement. By 1810 there were approximately 875,000 settlers in Ohio, Kentucky, Tennessee, Indiana, Illinois, and Missouri. Tecumseh, the Shawnee chief, and his brother The Prophet were concerned about the rising tide of settlement and forged an alliance of several regional tribes. The Indians wanted to present a united force to block the expansion of American settlement. Aware that relations between Great Britain and the United States were reaching the breaking point, Tecumseh also hoped to secure British support.

In 1811 Governor William Henry Harrison led a strong militia force against the Indians and defeated a multitribe force at Tippecanoe Creek. At the time Tecumseh was working his way through several southern tribes, attempting to recruit them into the coalition. Harrison went on to attack and destroy Tecumseh's main camp at Prophetstown. When

To his braves, Tecumseh said:

"Since the days when the white race first came in contact with the red men, there has been a continual series of aggressions. The hunting grounds are fast disappearing, and they are driving the red men farther and farther to the west. The mere presence of the white men is a source of evil. . . . The only hope . . . is a war of extermination against the paleface. They seize your land; they corrupt your women. . . . Back whence they came, upon a trail of blood, they must be driven!"

Tecumseh saving white prisoners. Despite his martial intentions, he was known for his revulsion at senseless cruelty. *(Courtesy, Henry E. Huntington Library and Art Gallery)*

Harrison discovered a cache of British weapons at Prophetstown, and released the news to government officials and the press, protest swept throughout the United States. Feelings were most intense, however, in the West. The War Hawks were especially vocal in denouncing the British. When the War of 1812 broke out, General Harrison was determined to kill Tecumseh and destroy his confederacy. In October 1813 at the Battle of the Thames, he succeeded in both goals.

Land Hunger   The War Hawks had even more than the common American appetite for land. For years the United States had disputed with Spain the boundary of West Florida. That narrow province stretched westward along the Gulf coast from the main Florida peninsula, cutting off much of the American Southwest from the sea. Spain, now an ally of England, held the province loosely. If war broke out, it could certainly be wrenched easily from her feeble hands. And there was Canada. One congressman declared that "the Author of Nature has marked our limits in the south, by the Gulf of Mexico; and on the north, by the regions of eternal frost."

While the War Hawks and their supporters naturally thought of attacking and taking the exposed colonies of both Spain and England, conquest was not their chief purpose. They were nationalists and patriots who remembered the Revolution and hated British arrogance, yearning to avenge the humiliations Britain had recently inflicted. For twenty years, they argued, Britain had refused to treat the United States as a sovereign nation. The effort to preserve peace at any price was making the American republic once more a British colony.

The Coming of War   Madison, concerned especially with maintaining American agricultural markets in Europe, was soon adopting a tougher policy toward England. In 1811 he asked Congress to vote money to build up the army and navy. In the spring of that year, the U.S.S. *President* encountered the British sloop of war *Little Belt*. Although the results were actually inconclusive—the powerful *President* gave the *Little Belt* a drubbing, but failed to sink the weaker British vessel—Americans considered the results ample revenge for the *Chesapeake* attack of four years before.

For months in early 1812 the prospect of war hovered while both the chief executive and Congress dithered. The Republicans had by now come to assume that war was inevitable, but when it came to voting money in preparation for it, their fear of extravagance got in the way of their common sense. Little had been done to authorize the building of new ships, and appropriations for the army remained inadequate. How the country intended to defend its commerce, and pursue an aggressive policy toward Florida and Canada, nobody made clear.

In the end, war came by mistake. Early in 1812, the British government finally decided to modify its commercial policies. On June 23 it announced that the notorious Orders in Council that had so offended the United States would be lifted. It was too late. Before the news arrived, Madison impatiently had asked for a declaration of war. On June 4, the House voted in favor by 79 to 49; two weeks later the Senate followed, 19 to 13. The vote revealed a disunited nation. If the

"What are we not to lose by peace?" Clay asked. His answer: "Commerce, character, a nation's best treasure, honor! I prefer," orated Clay, "the troubled ocean of war, demanded by the honor and independence of this country, with all its calamities and desolation, to the tranquil and putrescent pool of ignominious peace."

Henry Clay. *(Courtesy, Scribner's Archives)*

way congressmen voted is taken as indicative, southern New England, as well as much of New York, New Jersey, and Maryland, opposed the war. Would they continue to resist once the fighting had begun?

The War of 1812

A New York clergyman tried to rally support for the war:

"Suppose that one man should presume to enjoin his will upon another equally free,—suppose he should say to him, You shall neither buy nor sell at such or such a market; . . . or suppose that, seeing him in the pursuit of some profitable business, he should tell him, You shall pursue that business no longer; perhaps because he is in it himself and wishes to monopolize the profits. . . . Can you then for a moment hesitate as to the duty of the citizen thus insulted!—thus injured! . . . The application to nations is perfectly convenient. . . .

—Either she must tamely and dastardly submit to the dictates and oppressions of imperious Britain, and so make, at once, a surrender of her rights, and an acknowledgment that she is no longer free; or, in the noble spirit of '76, call together her patriotic sons—vest them with authority—furnish them with arms, and say to them, Go,—go by sea and land,—go vindicate my rights, avenge my wrongs, and maintain my liberty, the bounteous gift of heaven, and the invaluable price of your fathers' blood."

One young Maine man explained to his mother upon enlisting:

"I know I sacrifice my time, and my ease, and expose my morals to be corrupted by the licentiousness of a camp, my health to be impaired by fatiguing marches and the chilly cold of a more northern clime, and my life to danger . . . [but] I am satisfied that the essential rights of my country have been trampled on and are at stake and that the war in consequence thereof is a righteous and necessary war, and that it ought to be spiritedly supported by every man in America."

"Mr. Madison's War"
By almost any measure, the War of 1812 was mismanaged, and for three years the Americans lumbered from one encounter to another.

The country presented a logistical nightmare. To move troops and supplies over such enormous distances would be next to impossible. Roads were few and poor. The steamboat had been introduced on the Hudson in 1807, but steamboat travel on the Mississippi and the Great Lakes was in its infancy. The armed forces were unready. Only 7,000 men were immediately available for service, and most of these were scattered in small frontier posts. The state militias were a potential pool of manpower, but most militiamen were poorly trained and led. The best of the state forces were those of New England. But the Yankee governors refused to allow their soldiers to be called into federal service unless their own states were threatened with invasion.

And the country was disunited. Many Federalists thought the war a mistake. It was "Mr. Madison's war," a Republican venture, not a national one. Particularly in New England, the bastion of Federalism, the war seemed likely to produce a commercial disaster. Inevitably, Yankees said, theirs would be the commerce swept off the seas by the Royal Navy. Strong leadership might have overcome many of these difficulties, but Madison was a better philosopher and congressional manager than war leader. And almost all the high military officers were elderly gentlemen who had not commanded troops against a trained European army since the Revolution.

Canadian Campaigns
Oblivious to these weaknesses, the United States began the fighting with an invasion of Canada led by General William Hull, commanding 2,000 regulars. Launched from Detroit, far to the west of Canada's chief population centers, the invasion was seriously misconceived. It required extended supply lines, and to protect these long lines the troops of the United States had to control Lake Erie. But without much of a naval force on the lake they could not do so.

Nevertheless, the campaign at first seemed to be succeeding. Hull crossed the Detroit River into Canada unopposed. He immediately issued a proclamation that if the Canadian militia remained at home they had nothing to fear from the American republic. In a matter of days half of them had deserted the British and returned to their farms. The British now expected an immediate attack across the river from Detroit on Fort Malden, which was garrisoned by only a few hundred regulars, some Indians, and the remaining militia. But the invaders delayed. By the time Hull's forces mounted their guns against the British, the United States garrison at Michilimackinac to the east had surrendered. Certain that his supply lines were now endangered, Hull withdrew across the river

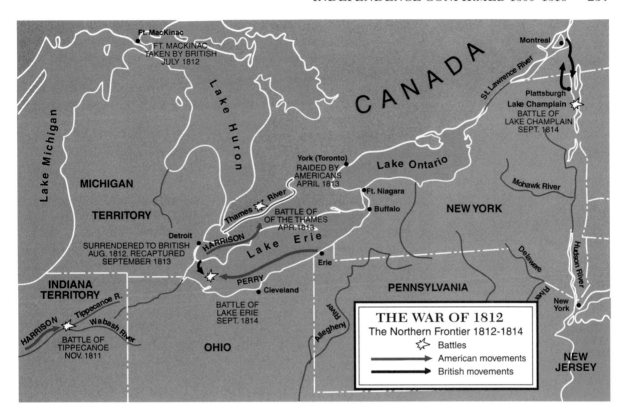

and locked himself up in Detroit. On August 17 he surrendered to the British commander. Prospects of taking Canada now appeared bleak. If the invasion prong in the West, where the people were enthusiastic supporters of the war, had failed, what could be expected in the hostile East?

From New York, a part of that state's militia crossed the Niagara River to attack the British and Canadian forces. They scored some early successes, but then were pinned down. They could have been rescued and the operation saved, but the remaining New York militia refused to cross the Niagara. Without reinforcements, 900 United States troops were captured at Queenston Heights.

The third prong of the invasion was no more successful than the first two. This attack, aimed at Montreal, was at least strategically sound. That city was the heart of British power in North America, and its capture would have been a disaster to England. But the United States delayed its operations and gave the British many months to prepare. By the time the militia moved northward against a well-entrenched enemy, the autumn was far advanced. The ill-equipped troops slogged their way through mud and drenching cold rain, sleeping without tents on the soggy ground with dripping blankets. When the troops reached the Canadian border, many refused to cross. After fighting a few skirmishes, their commander ordered a retreat to Plattsburgh, New York. There the militia made camp amid mud and snow; many contracted pneumonia. "The very woods," an army surgeon reported, "[ring] with coughing and

A sailor related the fate of one American privateer, cruising the ocean for prey:

"On the 25th of January, 1814, being just one month after we sailed from Portsmouth, at 5 o'clock in the morning, the word was passed from the lookout above, 'Sail, oh!' We bore away, and made sail for the strange vessel. She was a large man-of-war brig, and by her model and rig, we judged her to be an English one. We speedily hauled upon the wind and made all sail, endeavoring to show the enemy a clear pair of heels; . . . . We felicitated ourselves for some time with the hope of escape, but it was a delusive hope. . . . The chaser still gained upon us. We were in the neighborhood of Porto Rico, and we still hoped to keep clear of the brig until darkness came on, and under its cover to escape into the harbor. We lightened our schooner by throwing overboard all our guns, most of our provisions and water, all our small arms, irons, caboose, &c. We sawed down our plank shires, started out the wedges of our masts, and kept our sails continually wet. But all would not do, for at 5 P.M. the brig had neared us sufficiently to commence firing on us with her bow-guns. The brig kept up a steady fire upon us till 7 o'clock; but as we were low in the water, they did not often strike us. At 7 o'clock, all hope of escape departed from the captain. He mounted up into the main rigging, and hailing the brig, announced our surrender."

groaning." Shortly afterward the invasion force dispersed. Eighteen-twelve ended with Canada still firmly in British hands and the morale of the United States in the cellar.

The Naval War

The naval war on the Atlantic Ocean was going better. Although the British far outmanned and outgunned the Americans at sea, they were also stretched thin, and suffered from overconfidence. The Americans, they were certain, could not match the Royal Navy in battle or do serious damage to their merchant shipping. They were wrong. Many American merchant captains had secured letters of marque commissioning their vessels as privateers. Over the next two and a half years, these ships attacked British commerce in the West Indies, off the east coast of the United States, and even in the waters around the British Isles. While many privateers were captured, others took rich prizes. The success of the small American navy, though less significant in material terms, was important for national morale. The American frigates proved to be remarkably effective in single-ship combat.

In August 1812 the U.S.S. *Constitution*, commanded by Isaac Hull, sighted the British frigate *Guerrière* in the mid-North Atlantic. The *Guerrière* was a slightly smaller vessel with a lighter broadside; part of her crew, moreover, consisted of impressed Americans who had to be allowed to go below rather than fight their own countrymen. The British captain tried evasive maneuvers, but Hull was able to bring his ship within fifty yards of the enemy. For two hours he poured deadly broadsides into the British ship, leaving it a wreck. The *Guerrière* struck her colors. Both sides had fought well and bravely, but the performance of the inexperienced Americans was exceptional. American sailors had fought with greater spirit than American infantry. This victory was the first of several such single-ship combats that helped redeem the honor of American arms. Several weeks later the *United States*, under Stephen Decatur, encountered H.M.S. *Macedonian* and in a bloody battle sank her. At the end of the year the *Constitution* defeated H.M.S. *Java* in a two-hour engagement. Chagrined by their losses, the British began to

Constitution and ***Java.*** *(Courtesy, New-York Historical Society)*

reinforce their squadron off North America. Bit by bit its blockade of the American Atlantic coast became tighter and more effective, confirming all the fears of Northeasterners that war would destroy American commerce. The Americans soon lost control of their own coasts and shortly would be unable to repel British troop landings when they came.

Further Defeats in Canada
Another major attack on Canada came in 1813. In April, 8,500 troops gathered at the eastern end of Lake Ontario under the command of Henry Dearborn. On April 25, 1,700 men of this force sailed off to attack the Canadians at the western end of the lake, and two days later they arrived before York (now Toronto). The town was defended by only 800 soldiers and some Indians. The British had prepared a surprise in the form of a giant underground mine jammed with high explosives, but the mine went off at the wrong time, killing as many British as United States troops. Dismayed and outnumbered, the British commander now withdrew. After occupying York for four days, the invaders from the south looted it and burned the parliament buildings—acts for which their country would pay dearly the following year. They then departed for the mouth of the Niagara to attack Fort George. This time the aging Dearborn was too exhausted to lead the expedition, and he turned his command over to the vigorous Winfield Scott. Soon to join the expedition was an equally aggressive young naval officer, twenty-seven-year-old Oliver Hazard Perry.

The strengthened naval force was transported across Lake Ontario, and completed a difficult amphibious landing before Fort George. The troops, led by Scott and Perry, scrambled ashore with their heavy equipment and secured a foothold while still more men followed. Supported by the guns of the flotilla, the invasion force drove off the British counterattack. The British commander now withdrew from Fort George and retreated. Scott was all for pursuing the enemy and destroying his army completely, but was overruled by his superior in the Niagara theater of operations. When the troops of the United States were finally allowed to set off after the defeated British, Scott remained behind. The results were disastrous. The British commander surprised the invaders in their sleep, captured their leaders, and drove them back.

The British had now regained the initiative, and advanced with a supplement of Indians. The Indian auxiliaries fell upon a number of soldiers from the broken invasion force, who held them off until a party of British regulars approached under a flag of truce. Lieutenant James Fitzgibbon, the young British officer in charge, told the commander of the beleaguered unit that he was being closely followed by the main British army of 1,500 regulars and 700 Indians. The defenders, Fitzgibbon argued, could not possibly withstand the attack of this force, and in all likelihood the British would not then be able to restrain the bloodthirsty Indians; the wise course would be to surrender now and prevent a massacre. The defenders laid down their arms and waited for the main British party to arrive. It never did. A unit of 500 men had surrendered to a force only half its size. The setback on the Niagara frontier was matched by a major defeat before Montreal. Advancing on the Canadian city, the forces from the United States ran into stiff opposition and abandoned the invasion. Soon afterward, the British captured Fort Niagara. They also took Buffalo and burned the city to the ground.

The Battle of Lake Erie   In July 1813 six British warships arrived by way of the Saint Lawrence River at Lake Erie, and Captain Perry, commanding the hastily-built American fleet there, sent an urgent plea for men: "Think of my situation: the enemy in sight, the vessels under my command more than sufficient, and ready to make sail. . . ." But when the men came, he complained that they were "a motley set, blacks, soldiers, and boys. . . ." His commanding officer wrote back: "I regret that you are not pleased with the men sent you . . . , a part of them are not surpassed by any men we have in the fleet; and I have yet to learn that the color of the skin, or the cut and trimmings of the coat, can affect a man's qualifications or usefulness." On September 10, 1813, Perry and his crew, about one-fourth of whom were black, defeated the British fleet in a bloody three-hour battle. On the back of an envelope, Perry scrawled a now-famous message to General Harrison: "We have met the enemy and they are ours." Lake Erie was now in the hands of the United States, and the British were forced to abandon Detroit. A month later, Harrison overtook a retreating party of British and Indians and at the Battle of the Thames in Canada defeated them decisively. The chieftain Tecumseh was one of those who fell on the British side. Soon afterward, Tecumseh's federation of tribes collapsed and most of Britain's Indian allies deserted her cause.

These victories and the notable performance of the American navy notwithstanding, the British established a clear superiority in the Atlantic and in American coastal waters. The Royal Navy could with impunity sail up the Chesapeake Bay, attack merchant ships, and bombard strategic towns and military positions, amplifying the desperate plight of the United States and the Madison Administration's blunders. Hardpressed New England was riddled with disloyalty. Yankees had not wanted war and felt little inducement to support it now that it was proving so expensive. Hoping to rescue something from the calamity, they became the chief suppliers of commodities to the British army in Canada. Madison sought to cut off this dangerous trade and induced Congress to pass an embargo bill in December 1813 restricting all exports from the United States. The effects were disastrous. American

Oliver Hazard Perry's dispatch to General Harrison on his victory at Lake Erie reflected the pride of the Americans on finally winning a naval battle.

exports plummeted and prices increased sharply. The Treasury found that it could not borrow the money it needed for military operations, and was forced to the edge of bankruptcy. In April 1814 Congress repealed this embargo.

Meanwhile the gloomy military situation promised to get worse. In the spring of 1814, Napoleon's empire collapsed and the conqueror of Europe went into exile on the island of Elba. Until then, the British had been conducting a series of holding operations in America on both land and sea. Now, with France out of the war, all the vast resources of the Royal Navy and the seasoned veterans of the European fighting would be free to teach the pesky Americans a lesson. In early May, the first detachments of British troops began to arrive in Quebec from Europe. Their mission, as explained in orders to the British commandant in Canada, Sir George Prevost, would be to drive the troops of the American republic out of Canada and recover the American Northwest, and thereby to secure Canada's safety. Winfield Scott leading the United States troops attacked first. At Chippewa and Lundy's Lane, his troops fought gallantly against many of the same seasoned British and Canadian forces who had earlier won at Detroit. The campaign ended in a draw if not a British victory, but temporarily British goals in the Northwest had been frustrated.

British Offensives The British soon resumed the offensive. In late summer they set out for Plattsburgh, New York, near Lake Champlain. The British plan, as during the Revolution, was to split the United States in two along the line of Lake Champlain and the Hudson Valley. By September Prevost's army was at Plattsburgh's gates. There the American commander was the scrappy John Wool. Though outnumbered almost three to one, Wool put up such a fight along the approaches to Plattsburgh that Prevost paused and called on Captain George Downie, in command of the British fleet on the lake, to come to his aid. Together the navy and army would pound the Americans into submission and advance on New York City to complete their mission.

It was not to be. Standing between Prevost and the fulfillment of his scheme was the United States naval squadron commanded by Captain Thomas Macdonough. Macdonough's little fleet on Lake Champlain consisted of four moderate-sized vessels and ten tiny gunboats, but in firepower it just about matched Downie's squadron.

Downie attacked the Americans. His first shot hit the deck of Macdonough's flagship, the *Saratoga*, and destroyed the coop of the sailors' champion gamecock. The bird was unhurt and immediately flew to a gun carriage where, its feathers ruffled, it crowed defiance at the enemy. The men laughed and cheered; it seemed a good omen. For over two hours the opposing fleets poured ammunition into each other. Macdonough himself was knocked unconscious three times. At last the British surrendered. Macdonough brought the defeated British officers aboard the *Saratoga*, complimented them on their bravery, and refused to accept their swords. And a signal victory it was. When Prevost learned of Macdonough's triumph, he decided he could not continue; with the enemy in command on the water, his flanks were exposed. Instead of resuming the assault, he marched his men back to Canada. Another invasion threat was over.

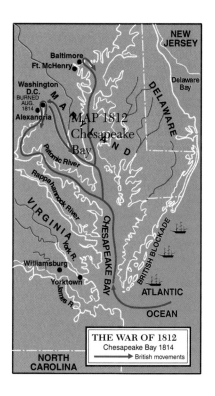

The Burning of Washington

A second British invasion prong was meeting with greater success. On August 19, 1814, Sir George Cockburn landed with 4,000 men between Baltimore and Washington, and set out for the nation's capital. A hastily organized defense force of militia, sailors, and a few regulars sought to stop the British just outside the capital at Bladensburg, but the inexperienced Americans could not hold against seasoned veterans and many fell into British hands. Later that afternoon, after learning of the defeat, Madison and his Cabinet left the city to avoid capture. His wife, the resourceful Dolley, had already removed the sterling silver and other valuables from the presidential mansion. At 8 p.m. the British entered the city. At the President's house British officers ate the formal dinner Madison had abandoned. The next morning British soldiers burned the public buildings, including the President's house, the Capitol, the Treasury, and the War Office. The following day they left the smoldering capital, having avenged the burning of York.

In early September the British, arriving by land and sea, moved on Baltimore. They broke through the Americans' first line of defense and drew to within a mile and a half of the city. At this point the British commander decided to call on the British flotilla offshore to bombard the city, to help soften it up for his final assault. All through the day and night of September 13 the British fired rockets, big guns, and mortars at Forts McHenry and Covington, but could not silence them. At daybreak the American flag still flew over Fort McHenry. Watching the attack was a Baltimore lawyer, Francis Scott Key. Deeply moved by the sight of the flag, he wrote a poem, "The Star Spangled Banner." Soon set to the melody of a popular English drinking song, the piece was to be adapted as the national anthem in 1931, well over a century later. The British failure to reduce the harbor defenses discouraged further action, and they withdrew. The city was safe.

Baltimore's escape was, of course, a welcome event, but it could not wipe out the memory of Washington's capture and the general

---

A British soldier recalled the "beautiful spectacle" of the burning of Washington:

The blazing of houses, ships, and stores, the report of exploding magazines, and the crash of falling roofs [informed him and his troops] as they proceeded, of what was going forward. You can conceive nothing finer than the sight which met them as they drew near to the town.

The sky was brilliantly illumined by the different conflagrations; and a dark red light was thrown upon the road, sufficient to permit each man to view distinctly his comrade's face. A storm began and the flashes of lightning seemed to vie in brilliancy, with the flames which burst from the roofs of burning houses, while the thunder drowned the noise of crumbling walls, and was only interrupted by the occasional roar of cannon, and of large depots of gunpowder, as they one by one exploded.

The President [James Madison] had hurried back to his own house, that he might prepare a feast for the entertainment of his officers, when they should return victorious. For the truth of these details, I will not be answerable; but this much I know, that the feast was actually prepared, though, instead of being devoured by American officers, it went to satisfy the less delicate appetites of a party of English soldiers. When the detachment, sent out to destroy Mr. Madison's house, entered his dining parlour, they found a dinner-table spread, and

In August 1814, the British captured and burned the city of Washington, including the President's house, the Capitol, the Treasury, and the War Office. *(Courtesy, The New-York Historical Society)*

ineptness of the American war effort. In the wake of the Chesapeake invasions defeatism swept the nation.

The fall and winter of 1814–15 was also a time of political crisis. Massachusetts elected representatives to meet with delegates from other New England states at Hartford, Connecticut, to consider defense problems and to discuss the possibility of revising the federal Constitution. Behind this action were the profound disgust of New Englanders with the war and their feeling that their section was suffering unduly. At Hartford the militants intended to consider either seceding from the war or seceding from the Union itself, but by the time the convention met in December they were outnumbered. New Hampshire and Vermont refused to send delegations at all; and the delegates from Connecticut and Rhode Island proved to be more moderate than anyone

covers laid for forty guests. Several kinds of wine, in handsome cut-glass decanters, were cooling on the sideboard; plate holders stood by the fire-place, filled with dishes and plates; knives, forks, and spoons, were arranged for immediate use; in short, every thing was ready for the entertainment of a ceremonious party. Such were the arrangements in the dining room; whilst in the kitchen were others answerable to them in every respect. Spits, loaded with joints of various sorts, turned before the fire; pots, sauce-pans, and other culinary utensils, stood upon the grate; and all other requisites for an elegant and substantial repast, were exactly in a state which indicated that they had been lately and precipitately abandoned.

You will readily imagine, that these preparations were beheld, by a party of hungry soldiers, with no indifferent eye. An elegant dinner, even though considerably overdressed, was a luxury to which few of them, at least for some time back, had been accustomed; and which, after the dangers and fatigues of the day, appeared peculiarly inviting. They sat down to it, therefore, not indeed in the most orderly manner, but with countenances which would not have disgraced a party of aldermen at a civic feast; and having satisfied their appetites with fewer complaints than would have probably escaped their rival *gourmands,* and partaken pretty freely of the wines, they finished by setting fire to the house which had so liberally entertained them.

O say can you see, ~~through~~ by the dawn's early light,
what so proudly we hail'd at the twilight's last gleaming,
whose broad stripes & bright stars through the perilous fight
O'er the ramparts we watch'd, were so gallantly streaming?
And the rocket's red glare, the bomb bursting in air,
gave proof through the night that our flag was still there,
O say does that star spangled banner yet wave
O'er the land of the free & the home of the brave?

Francis Scott Key's "The Star-Spangled Banner": detail written during the War of 1812.

had expected. The Convention did not call for dissolution of the Union. It urged amendments to the Constitution that would reduce the power of the West and the South and require that non-intercourse acts, admission of new states, and declarations of war all receive a two-thirds vote of Congress. But the resolutions in the end amounted to little more than a protest.

The Treaty of Ghent

As early as November 1813 the British and American governments, partly at the urging of the Russian Tsar, had agreed to meet to discuss peace terms. Neither government was happy about the war both had sought to avoid; now, even while fighting continued, they began to arrange for its end.

Negotiations conducted at Ghent in Belgium moved slowly. The British hoped that before long their armies would occupy large stretches of the United States and they could use this territory as leverage for extracting favorable terms. Perhaps they might even get their long-held wish to create an Indian state in the Northwest, cutting off the United States from the interior of the continent. The American negotiators, Henry Clay, John Quincy Adams, and Albert Gallatin, rejected any scheme to slice up their country and insisted on the abandonment of the impressment of sailors from American ships. At first, neither side would budge.

During the last half of 1814, however, the British began to realize that, though they could win victories, they could not count on totally defeating the stubborn Americans. Then, too, Britain and Russia began to clash at the Congress of Vienna called to sort out the complex affairs of Europe after Napoleon's defeat. Under the circumstances, war with the United States now seemed an unimportant sideshow that should be ended as soon as possible. The Americans, too, were anxious to bring matters to a conclusion, and they abandoned their demand for an explicit condemnation of impressment.

On Christmas eve, 1814, the commissioners at Ghent finally signed a peace treaty. This agreement merely restored the situation as it had existed before the war. Commissioners from both nations would meet to settle a dispute over the boundary between the United States and Canada, a dispute that had resulted from imperfections in the geographical knowledge available in 1783. The war had been nearly pointless. It would not be the last such in American history.

The Battle of New Orleans

Yet the war went on. News of the Treaty of Ghent did not reach the United States for many weeks, and by that time hundreds of men had died in unnecessary battles. The greatest of these was the Battle of New Orleans, which created a national hero, helped destroy what remained of the Federalist Party, and restored the nation's battered self-respect. The hero was General Andrew Jackson of Tennessee, a roughhewn, self-made planter, lawyer, and soldier.

General Andrew Jackson
Born in South Carolina, Jackson had gone to Tennessee when that future state was still the western district of North Carolina. He had served his adopted state in Congress and as a judge. In 1813–14 he led the Tennessee militia against the Creek Indians in Mississippi Territory following the massacre of 250 whites at Fort Mims. At Horseshoe Bend, Jackson surprised the Creeks and defeated them in a fierce battle. For his services the government made him a major general in the army and commander of the Seventh Military District with headquarters at Mobile.

While at Mobile, Jackson learned that the British, as part of their final push to crush the Americans, intended to attack New Orleans with another army of European veterans. Though weak with fatigue and dysentery, Jackson hurried to the city to prepare its defenses. A flood of directives—to obstruct the roads and bayous leading to the city, to build fortifications, and to strengthen the existing ones—flowed from his headquarters. Militia and volunteers from Kentucky, Tennessee, and Mississippi made up the core of Jackson's army, and he recruited additional troops from among the people of French or Spanish origin and black freemen of New Orleans. To the army paymaster who questioned equal pay for the black troops Jackson wrote: "Be pleased to keep to yourself your opinions upon the policy of making payments of the troops with the necessary muster rolls without inquiring whether the troops are white, black or tea." Jackson also agreed to accept the services of a group of river pirates led by Jean Laffite, a colorful rogue in trouble with the governor of Louisiana.

On the morning of December 23, 1814, British troops newly arrived from the West Indies began to disembark fifteen miles southeast of New Orleans, after a cold trip across Lake Borgne in open boats. Jackson quickly learned of the landings. A more cautious general might have waited to see whether this was the main attack or a mere feint. But Jackson immediately turned to his officers and declared: "Gentlemen, the British are below; we must fight them tonight!" With 2,000 men he advanced on the British force of some 1,600 that was waiting for further reinforcements before advancing against the city. Jackson achieved

To the governor of Louisiana General Jackson wrote:

"Our country has been invaded. . . . She wants Soldiers to fight her battles. The free men of colour in yur city are inured to the Southern climate and would make excellent Soldiers. They will not remain quiet spectators of the interesting contest. They must be for, or against us—distrust them, and you make them your enemies, place confidence in them, and you engage them by every dear and honorable tie to the interest of the country who extends to them equal rights and priviledges with white men."

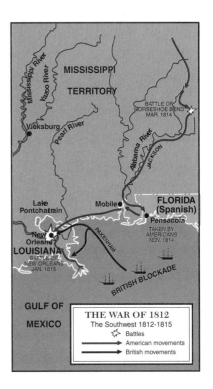

THE WAR OF 1812
The Southwest 1812-1815
☆ Battles
→ American movements
➤ British movements

An ecstatic American newspaper writer
could hardly contain himself in his dispatch describing the Battle of New Orleans:

"Glory be to GOD, that the barbarians have been defeated and that at
Orleans the intended plunderers have
found their grave!—Glory to *Jackson*,
Carroll and *Coffee*, and the hardy and
gallant *Tennesseeans*, *Kentuckians* and
Louisianians who 'seized opportunity
by the forelock' to 'demonstrate' what
freemen can do in defence of their altars
and firesides. Glory to the *militia*, that
the 'soldiers of *Wellington*,' the boastful
conquerors of the legions of *France*,
have shrunk from the *liberty-directed*
bullets of the high-souled sons of the
west! Sons of freedom—saviors of *Orleans*—benefactors of your country and
avengers of its wrongs, all hail! Hail glorious people—worthy, thrice worthy, to
enjoy the blessings which heaven in
bounteous profusion has heaped on
your country! Never may its luxuriant
soil be trodden unrevenged by insolent
foreigners in arms!

*Who would not be an American?
Long live the republic! All hail! last asylum of oppressed humanity! Peace is
signed in the arms of victory!"*

complete surprise and gave the enemy a serious shellacking. The British
line held, however, and Jackson withdrew to a position between the river
and a swamp.

Here, just as the commissioners were signing the peace treaty at
Ghent, Jackson and his men prepared to face the British assault behind
breastworks of cotton bales and earth. Both sides were being reinforced.
All night long, American raiders made sorties against the British, doing
little harm, but keeping their opponents from getting any sleep. The
next morning, with the battlefield enveloped in ground fog, the British
advanced on Jackson's men hidden behind their breastworks. For a
while they made headway against the firearms and artillery to their front,
but shelling on their flank by the U.S.S. *Louisiana* from the river proved
more than flesh could bear, and the advance stopped.

For the next three days the two armies confronted each other across
a field strewn with dead and dying. On the morning of December 31,
the British attacked again and the battle became an artillery duel,
Laffite's pirates with their big guns doing especially effective work. For
almost five hours the cannon boomed, until the discouraged British
suspended their attack. Once more both sides brought up reinforcements. When the British commander, Sir Edward Pakenham, was ready
to resume the attempt to reach New Orleans, he had close to 10,000
men to Jackson's 5,000.

On the morning of January 8, 1815, Pakenham asked his veterans
for the last time to brave the American defenses. Once more, the attack
failed. As the redcoats trudged across the ground in front of the American position, their ranks were shredded by grapeshot and arms fire.
Some reached the American lines, but then a counterattack threw them
back. Many British officers were hit, and Pakenham himself died on the
field.

**Victory after
Defeat**   The victory was astounding. Over 2,000 British
troops had died or been wounded against American casualties of twenty-one. Soon after the smoke
cleared, Jackson and his jubilant staff passed along the lines of cheering
troops to the stirring strains of "Hail Columbia" played by the army
band. It was a glorious moment for the young nation.

A mismanaged war that had humiliated Americans now became a
matter of great national pride. Overnight new confidence suffused the
nation. Americans had taken on the greatest power in the world, and in
the end had defeated the best it could throw at them. No longer would
the nations of Europe treat the United States with the contempt they
had been showing. American nationalists managed the incredible feat
of puffing a disastrous war into an epic victory.

The war had momentous political consequences. The Federalists
had bet on the wrong side. If not for New Orleans and the exhilaration
that made a bungled national enterprise seem a triumph, Federalist
opposition to the war might have been rewarded with public favor, but
Jackson's victory made suspect the patriotism of every Federalist who
had praised England and attacked the administration. In the presidential contest of 1816, the Republican James Monroe overwhelmed the
Federalist candidate, Rufus King of New York, carrying every state in

the Union except Massachusetts, Connecticut, and Delaware. Thereafter, although they continued to muster some isolated support, the Federalists were finished.

Meanwhile, a strange thing happened: the Republicans became Federalists. In his annual message in 1815, Madison asked Congress to pass a protective tariff, charter a second Bank of the United States, and appropriate funds for the construction of roads and canals—"internal improvements," as they came to be known. Led by Clay, Calhoun, and other nationalists, Congress obliged. In 1816 it passed a tariff affording at least modest protection to American industry, and established the Second Bank of the United States with an even larger capitalization than that of the first. Madison, having changed his mind, vetoed the bill for internal improvements on the grounds that federal funding of them was of dubious constitutionality; but his successors thought differently and thereafter federal subsidies would help the nation overcome its vast distances.

Finally, there was Andrew Jackson. New Orleans had created the nation's first folk hero since George Washington. Congress struck a gold medal in Jackson's honor and confirmed his rank of major general with the munificent salary of $2,400 a year. Before long, a biographer was busy writing a life of the general for an eager public. At this point Jackson might have chosen a life of ease at the Hermitage, his plantation near Nashville, amidst the plaudits of his fellow citizens. His future took a different course. Before many months had passed, Americans would hear from him again.

Suggested Readings

Studies of the years 1800 to 1816 includes Joyce Appleby, *Liberalism and Republicanism in the Historical Imagination* (1992), Drew McCoy, *The Last of the Fathers: James Madison and the Republican Legacy* (1989), Pierre Berton, *The Invasion of Canada* (1980), (1987), J. C. A. Stagg, *Mr. Madison's War: Politics, Diplomacy, and Warfare in the Early Republic, 1783–1830* (1983), and James P. Ronda, *Lewis and Clark Among the Indians* (1984). See also John Logan Allen, *Passage Through the Garden: Lewis and Clark and the Image of the American Northwest* (1968). Alexander DeConde surveys *This Affair of The War of 1812* (1969). On the War of 1812 see also Donald R. Hickey, *The War of 1812: A Forgotten Conflict* (1989), Clifford L. Egan, *Neither Peace nor War: Franco-American Relations, 1803–1812* (1983), Burton Spivak, *Jefferson's English Crisis: Commerce, the Embargo, and the Republican Revolution* (1979), and Robert A. Rutland, *Madison's Alternatives, Jeffersonian Republicans and the Coming of War, 1805–1812* (1975).

Dumas Malone presents *Jefferson and His Times* (1948–1981) in six volumes. Merrill Peterson's is a one-volume biography, *Thomas Jefferson and the New Nation* (1970). Forrest McDonald's *The Presidency of Thomas Jefferson* (1976) complements Fawn M. Brodie's *Thomas*

Jefferson: An Intimate History (1974). Gore Vidal's *Burr: A Novel* (1973) presents the controversial Aaron as a gentleman and portrays the vulgarities and hypocrisies of the society that surrounded him. Also sympathetic is Milton Lomask's biography, *Aaron Burr* (1983).

Useful on politics are Noble E. Cunningham, Jr., *The Process of Government under Jefferson* (1978), Marshall Smelser, *The Democratic Republic, 1800–1815* (1968), David Hackett Fischer, *The Evolution of American Conservatism* (1965), and James M. Banner, *To The Hartford Convention: The Federalists and the Origins of Party Politics in Massachusetts, 1789–1815* (1970).

On the women at the Lowell Mills see Thomas Dublin, *Women at Work: The Transformation of Work and Community in Lowell, Massachusetts, 1826–1860* (1979). Two rewarding studies of other women's experiences in this period are Nancy Cott's *The Bonds of Womanhood: "Woman's Sphere" in New England, 1780–1835* (1977) and Suzanne Lebsock's *The Free Women of St. Petersburg: Status and Culture in a Southern Town, 1784–1860* (1984). For an interpretation of child-rearing practices see Philip Greven, *The Protestant Temperament: Patterns of Child-Rearing, Religious Experience, and the Self in Early America* (1

How Republican Were the Jeffersonian Republicans?

Drew McCoy

Many years after his first election to the presidency, Thomas Jefferson commented that "the revolution of 1800" was "as real a revolution in the principles of our government as that of 1776 was in its form." Jefferson was undoubtedly using the term "revolution" not in the modern sense of a radical creation of a new order, but in the traditional sense of a return to first principles, of a restoration of original values and ideals that had been overturned or repudiated. For him, the election of 1800 was a revolution because it marked a turning back to the true republican spirit of 1776. Jefferson was excited by the prospect of the first implementation of the principles of America's republican revolution in the national government created by the Constitution of 1787, since in his eyes a minority faction . . . had captured control of that government almost immediately after its establishment. From Jefferson's perspective, indeed, the Federalists had done more than threaten to corrupt American government by mimicking the English "court" model. Just as frightening was their apparent desire to mold the young republic's political economy along English lines, a desire reflected both in their call for the extensive development of government-subsidized manufacturing enterprises and in their attempt to stimulate a highly commercialized economy anchored to such premature and speculative ventures as an overextended carrying trade. Jefferson's fundamental goal in 1801 was to end this threatened "Anglicization" of both American government and society. In so doing he would restore the basis for the development of a truly republican political economy, one that would be patterned after Benjamin Franklin's vision of a predominantly agricultural empire that would expand across space, rather than develop through time.

Within the Jeffersonian framework of assumptions and beliefs, three essential conditions were necessary to create and sustain such a republican political economy: a national government free from any taint of corruption, an unobstructed access to an ample supply of open land, and a relatively liberal international commercial order that would offer adequate foreign markets for America's flourishing agricultural surplus. The history of the 1790s had demonstrated all too well to the Jeffersonians the predominant danger to a republican political economy of corruption emanating from the federal government. They were especially troubled by the deleterious political, social, and moral repercussions of the Federalists' financial system, which they regarded as the primary vehicle of corruption both in the political system and in the country at large. Although Jefferson concluded rather soon after his election that his administration could not safely dismantle Hamilton's entire system with a few swift strokes, he was committed to doing everything possible to control that system's effects and gradually reduce its pernicious influence. Extinguishing the national debt as rapidly as possible, reducing government expenditures (especially on the military), and repealing the Federalist battery of direct and excise taxes became primary goals of the Jeffersonians in power. . . .

In itself, the electoral revolution of 1800 promised to remove the primary threat to a republican political economy posed by the machinations of a corrupt administration. But the Jeffersonians also had to secure the other necessary guarantors of republicanism: landed and commercial expansion. Although the pressure of population growth on the supply of land in the United States had never been a problem of the same immediate magnitude as political corruption, the social and economic dislocations of the 1780s had prompted some concern with this matter. Through the Louisiana Purchase of 1803, undoubtedly the greatest achievement of his presidency, Jefferson appeared to eliminate this problem for generations, if not for centuries, to come. But the third and thorniest problem, in the form of long-standing restrictions on American commerce, proved far more frustrating. . . .

Elusive Republic: Political Economy in Jeffersonian America (Chapel Hill: The University of North Carolina

Joyce Appleby

I believe that the new European demand for American grains—the crops produced by most farm families from Virginia through Maryland, Pennsylvania, Delaware, New Jersey, New York, and up the Connecticut River Valley—created an unusually favorable opportunity for ordinary men to produce for the Atlantic trade world. Far from being viewed apprehensively, this prospect during the thirty years following the adoption of the Constitution undergirded Jefferson's optimism about America's future as a progressive, prosperous, democratic nation. Indeed, this anticipated participation in an expanding international commerce in foodstuffs created the material base for a new social vision owing little conceptually or practically to antiquity, the Renaissance, or the mercantilists of eighteenth-century England. From this perspective, the battle between the Jeffersonians and Federalists appears not as a conflict between the patrons of agrarian self-sufficiency and the proponents of modern commerce, but rather as a struggle between two different elaborations of capitalistic development in America. Jefferson becomes, not the heroic loser in a battle against modernity, but the conspicuous winner in a contest over how the government should serve its citizens in the first generation of the nation's territorial expansion.

Anyone searching for the word *yeoman* in the writings of the 1790s will be disappointed. The absence of the word *yeoman* is negative evidence only. The error in current scholarly usage, however, is not lexical, but conceptual; it points Jefferson and his party in the wrong direction. Despite Jefferson's repeated assertions that his party was animated by bold new expectations for the human condition, the agrarian myth makes him a traditional, republican visionary, socially radical perhaps, but economically conservative. The assumed contradiction between democratic aspirations and economic romanticism explains why his plans were doomed to failure in competition with the hard-headed realism of an Alexander Hamilton. . . .

Viewed retrospectively by historians living in an industrial age, Jefferson's enthusiasm for agriculture has long been misinterpreted as an attachment to the past. So dazzling were the technological triumphs of railroad building and steam power that the age of the marvelous machines came to appear as the great divide in human history. . . .

Two interpretative tendencies have followed from this point of view. One has been to treat proponents of agricultural development as conservative and to construe as progressive those who favored manufacturing and banking. The contrast between Jefferson cast as an agrarian romantic and Hamilton as the far-seeing capitalist comes readily to mind. The other retrospective bias has been the characterization of industrialization as an end toward which prior economic changes were inexorably moving. Both classical economic and Marxist theory have contributed to this determinism, which recasts historical events as parts of a process, as stages in a sequential morphology. Under this influence the actual human encounter with time is reversed; instead of interpreting social change as the result of particular responses to a knowable past, the decisions men and women made are examined in relation to future developments unknown to them. The situation in America at the end of the eighteenth century is exemplary.

Joyce Appleby, *Liberalism and Republicanism in the Historical Imagination* (Cambridge, MA: Harvard University Press, 1992), pp. 257–58, 259, 260–61.

The Erie Canal at Rochester, New York. Cities prospered all along the canal, which extended from Buffalo on Lake Erie, to Albany on the Hudson, opening an economical transportation system from the Great Lakes to the Atlantic. *(Courtesy, New-York Historical Society, New York City)*

8
Sinews of Nationhood

THE ERIE CANAL

Pushed through the New York legislature in 1817 by Governor De Witt Clinton's powerful political machine, the Erie Canal project has been called "the most decisive single event in the history of American transportation." Beginning at Albany on the Hudson, the finished canal wound 363 miles through the Mohawk River Valley to Buffalo, on Lake Erie. Along the way eighty-three locks lifted the boats up and down the 650-foot elevation, and eighteen stone aqueducts carried the canal over rivers and streams. The Great Western Canal—one of its more formal names—was but four feet deep and forty feet wide, later deepened to seven feet and widened to seventy.

The Erie Canal was an immediate success. Before its opening, the cost of hauling grain across the Appalachian foothills to New York City had been three times the market value of wheat, six times that of corn, ten times that of oats. Overnight these stifling transportation costs disappeared, as horses pulled hundred-ton barges loaded with freight along "Clinton's Big Ditch" at rates as low as a cent a ton-mile. At the canal's Albany terminus steamboats took over for the comparatively swift and economical trip down the Hudson to New York City. By 1825, when the Erie was completed, toll revenues already exceeded a half million dollars a year. Soon the canal's entire $7 million cost had been recovered, and state officials ordered the canal widened to accommodate the increased traffic. Towns all along the route from Buffalo to New York City prospered, none more than New York, which became the transportation gateway to the West and the nation's largest port.

HISTORICAL EVENTS

1807
Fulton invents the steamboat

1810
Fletcher v. Peck

1811
Charter of the first Bank of the United States expires

1814–15
Hartford Convention

1816
James Monroe elected President • Tariff of 1816 • Second Bank of the United States is chartered

1819
Panic of 1819 • *Dartmouth College v. Woodward* • *McCulloch v. Maryland*

1820
James Monroe reelected President

1821
Cohens v. Virginia

1823
Biddle becomes president of the Bank of the United States

1824
Gibbons v. Ogden

Governor De Witt Clinton of New York predicted:

"As an organ of communication between the Hudson, the Mississippi, the St. Lawrence, the great lakes of the north and west, and their tributary rivers, [the canal] will create the greatest inland trade ever witnessed. The most fertile and extensive regions of America will avail themselves of its facilities for a market. All their surplus . . . will concentrate in the city of New York. . . That city will, in the course of time, become the granary of the world, the emporium of commerce, the seat of manufactures, the focus of great moneyed operations. . . . And before the revolution of a century, the whole island of Manhattan, covered with habitations and replenished with a dense population, will constitute one vast city."

Once opened in 1825, the Erie became an essential part of a tourist's itinerary: "The canal is in everybody's mouth," one traveler rather awkwardly expressed it. The bustle and activity, the remarkable circumstances of its construction, its overwhelming success and national importance made it an eighth wonder of the world. Mule teams on the towpath zipped the fast passenger boats (called packets) along at the canal speed limit of four miles an hour, while freighters made but one and a half to two miles per hour, and log rafts annoyed everyone with their slowness.

"Commending my soul to God," remarked a first-time rider boarding at Rochester, "and asking His defense from danger, I stepped on board the canalboat and was soon flying towards Utica." Long trips by water had always been dangerous, and the idea of taking a trip of over 300 miles in complete safety was fascinating. Mock-heroic epics of the dangers of a storm at sea became a standard bit of Erie folklore: the ship pitching, the captain barking orders, the endless verses celebrating each maritime danger.

Buffalo was the tame end of the canal. At the other end, in Watervliet near Albany, the notorious "side-cut" area with its twenty-nine saloons in two blocks with names like The Black Rag and The Tub of Blood, its fights, its large-scale vice, and an occasional body floating in the canal gained the district the title "The Barbary Coast of the East."

The Erie traveler saw a splendid microcosm of a young nation.

SHOOTING PIGEONS

by James Fenimore Cooper

Not too many miles south of the route of the Erie Canal the environmental splendors of the United States were already under attack. James Fenimore Cooper (1789– 1851), born in upstate New York, wrote the Leatherstocking Tales, *a series of five novels about life on the American frontier. The series takes its name from its hero, a woodsman who is variously called Natty Bumppo, Deerslayer, Hawkeye, Pathfinder, Leather-stocking, and the "trapper."*

This excerpt, taken from Pioneers *(1823), describes a pigeon hunt. The passage furnishes one of the earliest lessons in environmentalism to be found in American literature. Cooper perceived the limits of the seemingly inexhaustible American landscape.*

If the heavens were alive with pigeons, the whole village seemed equally in motion with men, women, and children. Every species of fire-arms, from the French ducking-gun with a barrel near six feet in length, to the common horseman's pistol, was to be seen in the hands of the men and boys; while bows and arrows, some made of the simple stick of a walnut sapling, and others in a rude imitation of the ancient cross-bows, were carried by many of the latter.

The houses and the signs of life apparent in the village, drove the alarmed birds from the direct line of their flight, toward the mountains, along the sides and near the bases of which they were glancing in dense masses, equally wonderful by the rapidity of their motion, and their incredible numbers. . . .

Across the inclined plane which fell from the steep ascent of the mountain to the banks of the Susquehanna, ran the highway, on either side of which a clearing of many acres had been made at a very early day. Over those clearings, and up the eastern mountain, and along the dangerous path that was cut into its side, the different individuals posted themselves, and in a few moments that attack commenced.

The men and women who made the canal work, "part water, part sand, part wind . . . but all canawler," were a colorful lot. The tough Irish workers who had dug the ditch now crewed the boats. The pompous captains, the fierce lock-keepers in endless battle with the crews, the floating showboats, saloons, general stores, and vice dens were famous among travelers, as were the legendary cooks: one "with a bosom like a boxcar," another who "stood six feet in her socks; her hand was like an elephant's ear, her breath would open locks."

These boats to Buffalo allowed remarkable freedom for travelers to see the countryside when they were not ducking under the famous low bridges. Even on the packets, a passenger could walk the towpath alongside the boat for exercise. On the slower boats, poor travelers could step ashore and forage for their food, picking berries and hunting rabbits. And the scenes were grand: bustling ports, ingenious locks and romantic swamps, rivers, and streams, and magnificent aqueducts; curious bridges of water allowed ships to pass over such picturesque obstacles. Sometimes the canal cut straight through primeval forests with no hint of man's work but the calm swath of canal and towpath. Charles Dickens has left a vivid recollection. The "exquisite beauty of the opening day, when light came glancing off from everything; the gliding on at night so noiselessly, past frowning hills sullen with dark trees and sometimes angry in one red, burning spot high up, where unseen men lay crouching round a fire; the shining out of the

The Erie as an Engineering Project

The canals were the first projects that required modern engineering skills. If their walls were not of a needed thickness, for example, they would leak, the water level would fall, and the boats would be unable to move. This is, in fact, what happened with several of the country's early canals.

The Erie presented enormous technical challenges. Gratings had to be measured exactly, new kinds of locks designed and built, and all constructed to last for generations. The rule of thumb would not suffice. So the first generation of American engineers learned their profession on the job. For the next thirty years, the graduates of the Erie Canal would build the nation's canals, railroads, and machines.

In this sense the Erie had an enormous impact on American economic and cultural development quite apart from the improvement in transportation and shipping it brought. The Erie not only opened the West, but also provided the opportunity for Americans to learn the skills that rapid industrialization would require.

Among the sportsmen was the tall, gaunt form of Leather-stocking, walking over the field, with his rifle hanging on his arm, his dogs at his heels; the latter now scenting the dead or wounded birds, that were beginning to tumble from the flocks, and then crouching under the legs of their master, as if they participated in his feelings at this wasteful and unsportsmanlike execution.

The reports of the fire-arms became rapid, whole volleys rising from the plain, as flocks of more than ordinary numbers darted over the opening, shadowing the field like a cloud; and then the light smoke of a single piece would issue from among the leafless bushes on the mountain, as death was hurled on the retreat of the affrighted birds, who were rising from a volley, in a vain effort to escape. Arrows, and missiles of every kind, were in the midst of the flocks; and so numerous were the birds, and so low did they take their flight, that even long poles, in the hands of those on the sides of the mountain, were used to strike them to the earth. . . .

Among the relics of the old military excursions, that occasionally are discovered throughout the different districts of the western part of New-York, there had

been found . . . a small swivel, which would carry a ball of a pound weight. . . . This miniature cannon had been released from the rust, and being mounted on little wheels, was now in a state for actual service. For several years it was the sole organ for extraordinary rejoicings used in those mountains. On the mornings of the Fourths of July, it would be heard ringing among the hills. . . .

"An't the woods his work as well as the pigeons? Use, but don't waste. Wasn't the woods made for the beasts and birds to harbor in? And when man wanted their flesh, their skins, or their feathers, there's the place to seek them. But I'll go to the hut with my own game, for I wouldn't touch one of the harmless things that cover the ground here, looking up with their eyes on me, as if they only wanted tongues to say their thoughts."

With this sentiment in his mouth, Leather-stocking threw his rifle over his arm, and followed by his dogs, stepped across the clearing with great caution, taking care not to tread on one of the wounded birds in his path. He soon entered the bushes on the margin of the lake, and was hid from view.

bright stars undisturbed by any noise of wheels or steam or any other sound than the limpid rippling of the water as the boat went on; all these were pure delights."

A New Society

Tocqueville observes in his optimistic Democracy in America:

"No novelty in the United States struck me more vividly during my stay there than the equality of conditions. In America men are nearer equality than in any other country in the world. . . . Wealth . . . is within reach of all. . . . In Europe to say of someone that he rose from nothing is a disgrace and a reproach. It is the opposite here. . . . The whole society seems to have turned into one middle class."

When the French nobleman Alexis de Tocqueville began his tour of the United States in 1831, he imagined that he was looking into the very face of the modern democratic future. His *Democracy in America,* published here in translation in the late 1830s, described a nation of exploding energies, of individualists throwing lifetimes of force and work into the pursuit of achievement. Certainly many immigrants complained about the "go along steam-boat" pace of life in the United States. James Dawson Burn, a British immigrant, wrote that "work, work, work is the everlasting routine of everyday life." Americans were "savagely wild in devouring their work."

At first skeptical about democracy, Tocqueville nevertheless liked much of what he saw. He was respectfully surprised that American society had managed to enjoy so much liberty amid an equality that he had thought to be an enemy to liberty. And yet he found American individualism flawed. The haste to succeed prevented the slow cultivation of excellence, and the individual American, lacking smaller communities and classes with which to identify, was pitifully submissive to public opinion.

Tocqueville's analysis of early nineteenth-century American individualism does not take adequate account of powerful elements of community and cooperation in neighborhoods, in churches, in voluntary associations and activities. And in describing the American mentality as one of submission to public opinion, he was writing too early to see the full flowering of an American literature of private visions and of brooding inquiry into the depths of the soul. Nathaniel Hawthorne, Edgar Allan Poe, Herman Melville, and other seers into the secret heart might have revealed to Tocqueville a side of the American mind that was not bustlingly aggressive but darkly introspective. Tocqueville's portrayal of the energetic American, free to chase after wealth, did not fit the case of Americans condemned to drudgery, struggle, and isolation on farms, or pressed down into the poverty of the growing cities. And of course, as he knew, it did not apply to the black slaves. But Tocqueville offers a starting point for understanding a society that was, by and large, bursting with energy and hope, and committed to democracy, with its conflicting urges toward freedom and toward conformity.

The Transportation Revolution

In 1808, when Secretary of the Treasury Albert Gallatin proposed his ambitious system of internal improvements at federal expense, it took a New Yorker three days to travel to Boston, ten days to reach Charleston, and nearly six weeks to journey west to St. Louis. The movement of bulky or heavy goods over long distances by land was prohibitively expensive:

it cost more to drag a ton of iron overland a few miles than to bring it across the ocean. Farmers and merchants still depended mainly on waterways to move their crops and merchandise. Coastwise shipping was inexpensive but slow. Inland areas were peculiarly dependent upon river transportation. But this was strictly a one-way affair—downstream. The flatboats that floated down to New Orleans with western produce had to be broken up for lumber, and the boatmen left to get home as best they could. Sectional jealousies and constitutional squabbles prevented the passage of Gallatin's and Clay's plans for internal improvements. Transportation remained haphazard and wasteful. Nonetheless, the fragmented American republic slowly linked itself into a connected whole.

Turnpikes   Early American roads were little more than broad, stump-filled paths through the forest. Impassable in wet weather, they were adequate only for local needs. A system of through routes, bringing together the chief commercial centers, was desperately needed. In the 1790s private corporations had begun building turnpikes along the most important routes of travel. These companies financed construction mainly by the sale of stock to investors, and sought profits by collecting tolls from people using the roads. The best turnpikes had a firm stone foundation overlaid with gravel, drainage ditches for run-off, and substantial stone or wooden bridges. The extreme difficulty of moving men and material during the War of 1812 stimulated a boom in turnpike construction. By 1825 these roads crisscrossed New England and the mid-Atlantic states; Pennsylvania alone had about 2,400 miles of toll road. In the West and South, where private capital was scarce, state and local governments often financed the turnpikes. The greatest of them all, the National Road, was built by the federal government. Begun in 1811, it ultimately stretched from Cum-

Leila T. Bahmah, *Geese in Flight* (ca. 1850). **The absorbing theme of this painting is movement both man-made and in nature: the geese, the smoke and steam of the riverboat and locomotive, the galloping horse.** *(Courtesy, National Gallery of Art)*

Robert Fulton. *(Courtesy, Library of Congress)*

Steamboats were also hazardous. One account of 1851 noted:

"Our steamboats very far exceed in number those of any other country, and the navigation of most of our rivers is dangerous in the extreme. The frequency of explosions upon our Western boats is owing in a great measure to their employing high pressure boilers and engines. The steam is generated with great rapidity by this mode, yet as long as the boat is in motion all is safe, but let a boat under a full head stop suddenly and there is always a danger of explosion; so much so indeed, that old stagers will generally be seen hurrying to the stern as soon as the engineer's bell is heard to command 'stop her. . . .' With regard to the frequent losses of boats by fire, these are too often the result of the manner in which they are built and freighted. The cabin is entirely above the deck, built of the lightest material, and always as dry as tinder, from the constant heat beneath. It only wants a full load of cotton to complete the danger. When a boat is fully freighted with

(continued on p. 257)

berland, Maryland, to Vandalia, Illinois. Travelers on this great western highway encountered a stream of people on foot, on horseback, in stagecoaches, on one-horse wagons, and driving lumbering teamster wagons.

Few of these turnpikes ever showed a profit to their owners. Maintenance was a constant drain. The public devoted considerable ingenuity to outwitting toll collectors: short roads popularly known as "shunpikes" frequently circled around the toll gates. The turnpikes, although popular with travelers, failed to provide economical long-distance freight transportation. Even where tolls were low, it was not profitable for heavy wagons with six- and eight-horse teams to make long hauls over them. Many of the turnpike companies had failed even before the emergence of competition from canals and railroads.

Steamboats   Men had been experimenting worldwide for years with the application of steam power to water transportation, but it remained for Robert Fulton, a young American engineer, to perfect an efficient design. His steamboat, the *North River* (or *Clermont*), equipped with an English-built engine and paddle wheels, averaged five miles per hour on its first voyage up New York's Hudson River in 1807. Spectators on shore watched in astonishment as it overtook the sluggish sailing vessels and "passed them as if they had been at anchor." Fulton and his partner, Robert R. Livingston, tried to keep exclusive control over their invention, but steam navigation was too important to be monopolized. By the time the Supreme Court, in *Gibbons v. Ogden* (1824), formally annulled the Fulton-Livingston monopoly in New York, steamboats had been introduced on every major river in the country.

The years from 1820 to 1850 were the age of the steamboat, the first economical inland transportation for both freight and people. On eastern rivers, harbors, and bays, steamboats served primarily as passenger vessels. They were designed for speed and comfort, with razor bows, long narrow hulls, giant paddle wheels amidships, and elegantly furnished cabins. Even larger boats plied the Great Lakes, carrying thousands of immigrants west to Detroit and Chicago. But it was in the fertile valley of the Mississippi that steamboats had their greatest importance. Ingenious shipbuilders quickly adapted them to navigate the western rivers even at low water. Hulls were made broad and shallow, engines and cabins placed on deck, and paddle wheels moved to the stern. Western rivermen boasted that all they needed for successful navigation was a heavy dew. Some of their boats could operate in water as shallow as thirty inches. These ungainly boats brought the West firmly into the national economy.

The new steamboats at last made it economical to ship the bulky exports of the interior to market. Receipts of produce at New Orleans jumped from $12 million in 1820–21 to $197 million in 1850–51. There larger ships took on the grain and cotton for destinations on the east coast or in Europe. On their return upstream the steamboats carried consumer goods formerly hauled overland at enormous cost.

The boats were not what Americans of the 1990s would consider fast. One helmsman wrote home to his family: "They can run from New

Steamboats loaded with bales of cotton were tinderboxes. (*Courtesy, Library of Congress*)

(*continued from p. 256*)

this article she appears like a moving mass of cotton bales, no part of her hull being visible except the paddle-boxes.

Around the bows and upon the guards the bales are piled as high as the 'hurricane deck.' They almost touch the boilers, which are exposed and unprotected upon the forward deck, and generally surrounded by huge piles of wood, not unfrequently in absolute contact with them. A tier of cotton often adorns the hurricane deck itself, and needs but a spark from the smoke-pipe to convert the boat into a fiery furnace, from which the chance of escape is small indeed."

Orleans to Pitsburgh in 16 and 18 days which is 25 hundred miles. They can go down in 8 and 10 days. They can carry 200 passengers each." The correspondent added: "Thare are a grate many fish caught in this river. Catfish which way from 10 to 100 pound. Thare are steam packets that carry from 100 to 700 tuns burden each."

Canals   Knowing the success of the early English canals, landlocked Americans had talked for years of linking the nation's navigable rivers and lakes with artificial waterways. A major obstacle was the inability of private capital to supply the large sums—$25,000 a mile or more—necessary for canal construction. By 1816 only about a hundred miles of canals had been constructed in the United States, most less than two miles long. None had returned a profit to their owners. Then came the Erie Canal.

The success of the Erie touched off a nationwide boom in canal building. Several eastern states, jealous of New York's position, tried to tap the western market with canals of their own. Pennsylvania's Main Line system over the Allegheny Mountains required a portage railroad—a stairstep of inclined planes by which cable cars carried the canal boats up one side of the highest ridges and down the other. In the West, Ohio and Indiana raced to link the waters of Lake Erie and the Ohio River. Indiana's contribution, the Wabash and Erie Canal, was over 450 miles long. By 1840, when the boom collapsed, the American people had constructed over 3,300 miles of canals, at a total cost of $125 million. State governments provided most of this huge capitalization, selling bonds against anticipated revenues. Few states or bondholders recovered even a fraction of their investment. Many of the canals were poorly planned and constructed; maintenance costs were high; ice or low water closed them at certain seasons. Nevertheless, these costly ditches greatly stimulated the economy. They offered the first economical means of transferring eastward the bulky products of the West.

Peter Cooper's "Tom Thumb," the first locomotive made in America, racing with a horse-car on the Baltimore and Ohio line, 1830. *(Courtesy, New York Public Library)*

Railroads   The nation soon had cheaper, faster, more dependable and profitable overland transportation. Americans had taken an early interest in another English development, the railroad. Construction of a few small tramways began in the United States during the 1820s, and in 1828 the first major railroad, the Baltimore and Ohio, was chartered. Many early railroads ran only short distances, being designed to serve mainly as feeders into nearby rivers and canals, but major eastern cities like Boston and Baltimore, which lacked adequate water connections, promoted longer lines. Merchants of Charleston, South Carolina, anxious to divert upcountry cotton shipments to their wharves, built a railroad to Hamburg on the lower Savannah River. When completed in 1833, it extended 136 miles and was the longest railroad in the world. In these years ingenious American inventors made a number of important technical improvements in the design of locomotives and roadbeds. By 1840 the nation's total railway mileage equaled that of canals, and many lines were competing successfully with canal companies for business.

Railroads, like other forms of transportation, received public aid. Between 1830 and 1843 the national government lowered tariff duties on railroad iron. State legislatures—once again taking the lead in public assistance—granted tax incentives, required newly chartered banks to invest in railroad stock, extended large grants, and sometimes operated lines directly. Added to the foreign capital that American railroads attracted, government help provided strong impetus to private companies. Almost 9,000 miles of track were laid in the 1840s and 22,000 more in the next decade. At the beginning of the Civil War railroads overshadowed all other forms of long-distance transportation in the country.

Corporations

To finance the more extensive of the manufacturing and transportation enterprises of the astonishing economy that was emerging early in the nineteenth century, society had a ready and time-honored institution, the corporation. The word comes from the Latin *corpus*, for "body," and corporations or bodies of various sorts had been a major form of organization in the European past. The members of the company that colonized Massachusetts Bay and later governed it constituted a corporation. An economic corporation was a body of investors chartered in Britain by the Crown and in the United States by a state—there was no federal equivalent—to engage in an undertaking that the chartering authority held to be at least in part for the common good. The grant would set the terms of the project, which might be as small as a bridge or as large as a railroad, and it would give the investors certain rights and protections.

Corporations so construed were entirely in accord with the original concept of a republic. The members of the corporations aimed, of course, to get money, power, or both. But they were also bringing their initiative and intelligence to an enterprise for the public welfare, and acting under directions set by the state. Yet as corporations in the course of the nineteenth century became increasingly an instrument of quick and big money, even the concept of a stockholder as being, in a sense, a quasi-public official as well as a public benefactor was to fade. Here was one of many ways in which a republic of virtue came into danger of becoming a republic of acquisition.

Sources of Northern Labor

The transportation revolution, making the movement of goods vastly easier and cheaper, opened up a large new potential market for manufactured products. Corporations made possible the bigger manufacturing concerns along with large transportation projects. But where would the workers come from to produce these goods?

Since colonial times, labor had been in short supply. Cheap land was so available that people could work their own land instead of hiring out their labor. In 1800 only ten percent of the white labor force were people who sold their services. The rest of the workforce were farmers, self-employed artisans and mechanics, and independent tradesmen.

Early manufacturers experimented with various ways of overcoming this acute labor scarcity. One was the "domestic" or "putting-out" system. Entrepreneurs furnished raw materials to people who worked in their own homes, making cloth, shoes, and wearing apparel; the entrepreneurs then collected and marketed the finished product. At a time when most people lived in the countryside, this system, though cumbersome, allowed manufacturers to tap a tremendous pool of part-time labor, especially women and children. Other businessmen tried to centralize production, hiring whole families whom they housed in tenements adjacent to their mills. But as factories grew larger, requiring a labor force of hundreds, even thousands, factory owners turned increasingly to the Waltham system.

The Waltham System   This system was the brainchild of Francis Cabot Lowell, an early textile manufacturer in Waltham, Massachusetts. Eager to recruit young women from New England farms to work in his mill at East Chelmsford, Massachu-

"Susan," a Lowell worker, wrote home of the difficulties of the work itself:

"It makes my feet ache and swell to stand so much. . . . The girls almost all say that when they have worked here a year or two they have to procure shoes a size or two larger than before they came. The right hand, which is the one used in starting and stopping the loom, becomes larger than the left; but in other respects the factory is not detrimental to a young girl's appearance."

setts. Lowell built dormitories nearby to house them. In order to counteract the widespread reputation of mills as places of loose morals, he placed these dormitories in charge of respectable widows who maintained rigid rules of conduct. The factory girls typically had to be in their rooms by 10 p.m., to attend church regularly, and to save part of their earnings. A few mills sponsored evening classes and libraries for their workers.

Lowell's plan was an immediate success and East Chelmsford was renamed Lowell in his honor. Many young women welcomed the chance to get away from the farm for a few years and to earn a little money of their own. In the 1820s and 1830s they flocked by the thousands to New England mill towns like Lowell, Chicopee, and Manchester. Visitors to the textile factories usually praised the Waltham system. After a tour in 1834, Davy Crockett described Lowell's "mile of gals" as "well-dressed, lively, and genteel" and happy in their work.

In time, though, the economics of profit took over. The workers

TIME TABLE OF THE LOWELL MILLS,

Arranged to make the working time throughout the year average 11 hours per day.

TO TAKE EFFECT SEPTEMBER 21st., 1853,

The Standard time being that of the meridian of Lowell, as shown by the Regulator Clock of AMOS SANBORN, Post Office Corner, Central Street.

From March 20th to September 19th, inclusive.

COMMENCE WORK, at 6.30 A. M. LEAVE OFF WORK, at 6.30 P. M., except on Saturday Evenings.
BREAKFAST at 6 A. M. DINNER, at 12 M. Commence Work, after dinner, 12.45 P. M.

From September 20th to March 19th, inclusive.

COMMENCE WORK at 7.00 A. M. LEAVE OFF WORK, at 7.00 P. M., except on Saturday Evenings.
BREAKFAST at 6.30 A. M. DINNER, at 12.30 P.M. Commence Work, after dinner, 1.15 P. M.

BELLS.

From March 20th to September 19th, inclusive.

Morning Bells.	Dinner Bells.	Evening Bells.
First bell,..........4.30 A. M.	Ring out,..............12.00 M.	Ring out,............6.30 P. M.
Second, 5.30 A. M. ; Third, 6.20.	Ring in,...........12 35 P. M.	Except on Saturday Evenings.

From September 20th to March 19th, inclusive.

Morning Bells.	Dinner Bells.	Evening Bells.
First bell,..........5.00 A. M.	Ring out,...........12.30 P. M.	Ring out at...........7.00 P. M.
Second, 6.00 A. M. ; Third, 6.50.	Ring in,.............1.05 P. M.	Except on Saturday Evenings.

SATURDAY EVENING BELLS.

During APRIL, MAY, JUNE, JULY, and AUGUST, Ring Out, at 6.00 P. M.
The remaining Saturday Evenings in the year, ring out as follows :

SEPTEMBER.	NOVEMBER.	JANUARY.
First Saturday, ring out 6.00 P. M.	Third Saturday ring out 4.00 P. M.	Third Saturday, ring out 4.25 P. M.
Second " " 5.45 "	Fourth " " 3.55 "	Fourth " " 4.35 "
Third " " 5.30 "		
Fourth " " 5.20 "	DECEMBER.	FEBRUARY.
	First Saturday, ring out 3.50 P. M.	First Saturday, ring out 4.45 P. M.
OCTOBER.	Second " " 3.55 "	Second " " 4.55 "
First Saturday, ring out 5.05 P. M.	Third " " 3.55 "	Third " " 5.00 "
Second " " 4.55 "	Fourth " " 4.00 "	Fourth " " 5.10 "
Third " " 4.45 "	Fifth " " 4.00 "	
Fourth " " 4.35 "		MARCH.
Fifth " " 4.25 "	JANUARY.	First Saturday, ring out 5.25 P. M.
	First Saturday, ring out 4.10 P. M.	Second " " 5.30 "
NOVEMBER.	Second " " 4.15 "	Third " " 5.35 "
First Saturday, ring out 4.15 P. M.		Fourth " " 5.45 "
Second ". " 4.05 "		

YARD GATES will be opened at the first stroke of the bells for entering or leaving the Mills.

SPEED GATES commence hoisting three minutes before commencing work.

Penhallow, Printer, Wyman's Exchange, 28 Merrimack St.

opposed a series of attempts by the mill owners to increase the amount of work—"speed up" and "stretch out"—and reduce the pay. A group of the more experienced workers founded the Lowell Female Reform Association, essentially one of the first labor unions in the United States. Ultimately, their two large strikes and their appeal to the Massachusetts state legislature failed to accomplish their goals. The rapid increase in the immigration of destitute Irish during the 1840s permitted the owners to turn to a new and more dependent supply of labor.

Lowell himself, as befitted an upper-class New Englander, had intended his plan to be not merely a moneymaker for himself but a contribution to the social good. In this sense, the Lowell mills were a forerunner of the reformist schemes in education, care of the mentally ill, abolition of slavery, and other goals that Yankees of social station would later be sponsoring. That Lowell was concerned for the financial independence and the intellectual development of young women makes him something of a deviant among early nineteenth-century American men as they have often been portrayed. Lowell's approach, to be sure, was paternalistic; but genteel reformers could be equally paternalistic toward the male recipients of their benevolence. And in their own way, the Lowell mill girls constituted something of an elite labor force. When they struck they claimed the rights of direct heiresses of the Revolution, daughters of the Sons of Liberty. The events at Lowell in fact had much to do with the status of women in the early nineteenth century.

Inventions   Improved transportation unified the national economy, mass immigration provided the necessary labor force, and corporations nurtured its larger undertakings. Only one additional ingredient was yet required for the American economy to take off—a native technology capable of sustaining mass production.

Here again, the nation was at first heavily dependent on Britain. When Robert Fulton designed his steamboat, he had the engine made in England, for no one in the United States could produce such a complex piece of machinery. Why did Americans turn to technological innovation? It has been suggested that Britain's restriction on the export of textile machinery and on the emigration of skilled mechanics unwittingly forced Americans to become inventive. Or that the shortage of labor compelled Americans to devise labor-saving machinery. But in colonial times, Britain had not exported textile machines, and later Americans borrowed some British technology shaping it to their needs.

Neither the absence of machinery nor the absence of a large labor force compelled Americans to become technologically progressive. Certain facts of American society and culture, however, may explain why modern technology, once Americans did begin to take to it, grew so much more rapidly here than elsewhere. The new nation had a sense of its newness, an awareness of itself as an invention, and this self-image could have invited Americans to engage in technical experimentation. Perhaps also the nation's natural wealth and the spread of prosperity among its citizens enticed Americans to see how the bounty at their disposal could be made even richer through technology. And the inventiveness that flowered amid this freedom and this promise was not for the sake of material gain alone: intellectual curiosity and an urge to

One very articulate worker at Lowell, Harriet Robinson, remembered:

"At this date woman had no property rights. A widow could be left without her share of her husband's property. . . . A woman was not supposed to be capable of spending her own or of using other people's money. In Massachusetts, before 1840, a woman could not legally be treasurer of her own sewing-society, unless some man were responsible for her.

The law took no cognizance of woman as a money-spender. She was a ward, an appendage, a relict. Thus it happened, that if a woman did not choose to marry, or, when left a widow, to re-marry, she had no choice but to enter one of the few employments open to her, or to become a burden on the charity of some relative.

In almost every New England home could be found one or more of these women, sometimes welcome, more often unwelcome, and leading joyless, and in many instances unsatisfactory, lives. The cotton-factory was a great opening to these lonely and dependent women. From a condition approaching pauperism they were at once placed above want; they could earn money, and spend it as they pleased; and could gratify their tastes and desires without restraint, and without rendering an account to anybody. . . ."

invent were then powerful motives, as they have been in other times of technological and scientific experimentation.

During the first half of the nineteenth century, inventions for manufacturing and agriculture multiplied. Besides developing the automated grist mill, Oliver Evans pioneered in the design of the high-pressure steam engine, a distinct improvement over the British engines of Newcomen and Watt. Norbert Rillieux, a free black, invented a multiple-effect evaporator to process the sugar cane grown in his native Louisiana. The endless fields stimulated significant improvements in farm machinery. Before Cyrus McCormick invented his reaper in 1831 a man with a sickle could cut approximately one acre of wheat in a day; with a reaper he could harvest ten to twelve. In 1837 John Deere perfected a steel plow capable of turning the tough prairie sod of Iowa and Illinois. In 1860 the United States Patent Office issued 4,589 new patents, a five hundred percent increase over patents granted in 1820.

While inventions transformed basic industries and with them much of American life, other ingenious tinkerers sought to increase the comforts of the home: the steam radiator for home heating; an immensely important ice-making machine; condensed milk and concentrated coffee (which came in a cube, light, and with sugar), both invented by Gail Borden in the 1850s; the paper window shade; hundreds of different kinds of new stoves and lamps; thousands of household gadgets. A comfortable, efficient home sheltering a happy and sturdy family was an implicit part of the American democratic ideal, and technology rushed to further it.

Eli Whitney. *(Courtesy, Library of Congress)*

Interchangeable Parts   Along with inventions came a specifically American development: mass production employing interchangeable parts. This concept had originated in Europe, but Eli Whitney, an American son of a three-hundred-pound Scots peddler, first put it into practice. An outstanding inventor best known for his cotton gin, a device for extracting seeds from raw cotton that transformed southern agriculture, Whitney struck upon an idea for producing great numbers of muskets quickly. A factory making muskets would not make each one separately from parts constructed for it alone, but would make every component part in great quantity and then assemble the parts into identical muskets. "In short," Whitney wrote federal officials in 1798, "the tools which I contemplate are similar to an engraving on copper plate from which may be taken a great number of impressions exactly alike."

This was a bold proposal at a time when gunsmiths still made muskets one at a time, filing and fitting the individual pieces to mate them into a working mechanism. The government, then fearful of war with France, and highly respectful of Whitney's talents, accepted his audacious offer to manufacture ten thousand muskets in twenty-eight months. Whitney badly underestimated the difficulties of tooling up for this kind of operation; he was several years late in delivering the promised muskets. Gradually, however, his uniformity system gained acceptance, and it was applied in dozens of industries. The spread of interchangeable parts made it possible for owners of damaged objects

Technological Developments, 1790–1860			
(Dates refer to patent or first successful use)			
Year	*Inventor*	*Contribution*	*Importance / Description*
1793	Eli Whitney	Cotton gin	Simplified process of separating fiber from seeds; made cotton a profitable staple of southern agriculture
1798	Eli Whitney	Jig for guiding tools	Facilitated manufacture of interchangeable parts
1802	Oliver Evans	Steam engine	First American steam engine
1807	Robert Fulton	Steamboat	*North River* (or *Clermont*), first successful American steamboat based on earlier invention of John Fiten
1813	Richard B. Chenaworth	Cast-iron plow	First iron plow made in three separate pieces, making possible replacement of parts
1830	Peter Cooper	Railroad locomotive	First steam locomotive built in United States
1831	Cyrus McCormick	Reaper	Mechanized harvesting
1836	Samuel Colt	Revolver	First repeating pistol
1837	John Deere	Steel plow	Steel surface made farming easier on rich prairies
1839	Charles Goodyear	Vulcanization of rubber	Made rubber free of sticking and melting in hot weather
1842	Crawford W. Long	First administered ether in surgery	Reduced pain and risk of shock during operations
1844	Samuel F. B. Morse	Telegraph	Long-distance communication made instantaneous
1846	Elias Howe	Sewing machine	Practical machine for automatic sewing
1846	Norbert Rillieux	Vacuum evaporator	Improved method of removing water from sugar cane; revolutionized sugar industry and later other industrial processes
1847	Richard M. Hoe	Rotary press	Printed an entire sheet in one motion
1851	William Kelly	"Air-boiling process"	Improved method of converting iron into steel; similar to later Bessemer process
1853	Elisha G. Otis	Passenger elevator	When electrified, stimulated development of skyscrapers
1859	Edwin L. Drake	First American oil well	Initiated United States oil industry
1859	George M. Pullman	Pullman car	First sleeping car for long-distance travel

to send away to a factory for the needed part, confident that the new one would precisely substitute for the old. Americans proved especially adept at designing and building the lathes, borers, and calipers necessary for the precision manufacture of parts for clocks, watches, and sewing machines.

Industrialism and the Republic

Manufacturing on a mass scale altered American expectations. From colonial days the material environment had been permanent. Most people lived in the same houses, used the same furniture, employed the same implements, wore the same clothes, and viewed the same scene from youth to old age. Variety was the privilege of the rich. With the growth of manufactures all this changed. The material surroundings of the average American became diversified in ways undreamed of before. Americans were learning to live in a perpetually changing environment. Their surroundings increasingly taught them that the physical world of buildings, vehicles, implements of work could change again and again, as the older, stable, agricultural environments had once taught people that the world never changes much.

The industrial order that began with Whitney and Lowell, with steamboats and the Erie Canal, was in spirit both the extension and the overturning of the republic of Washington and Jefferson. What occurred, in essence if not in words, was the transformation of the republican concept of virtue.

For all the radical newness of the early republic, Americans who thought of such matters were likely to equate proper conduct with the maintenance of good and established republican practices. These would include well-ordered families, intelligently tended crops, proud and independent crafts, honest businesses and professions, dignified governance. The yeoman doubtless wished to learn how to increase the yield of his land, the craftsman to perfect his skill. But the point of a good life was conscientiously to work the land or the shop, to train children in citizenship, and otherwise to ensure the continuance of the good life that settlers and revolutionists had planted in the new continent. The very idea of a republic was backward-looking, to the ancient polities of Greece and Rome.

Perhaps the forward-looking ways first clearly revealed themselves in Methodism and the revival movements that preceded by some years the flourishing of the new inventions and industries. These invited a moment of radical conversion, a receptivity to divine grace that could involve overwhelming emotions of repentance and joy and, if it occurred at a revival meeting, violent motions of the body. The outcome, however, as at least some evangelical Christians conceived it was to be a lifetime of attention to work and the other virtues. Methodists, freewill Baptists, and other nineteenth-century sectarians expected more than their Puritan ancestors that the redeemed human will can achieve greater and greater goodness, an increasing conquest of sinful impulses. An extension of this was to assume that society can improve in response to reformist programs. The physical world itself, it was meanwhile becoming apparent, could be increasingly subdued by industrious individuals, coaxing greater productive efficiency from it as they achieved victories over their wayward urges.

Evangelical religion, though countless Americans remained outside it, contributed to supplementing the original republican idea of virtue with strenuous mastery of self. Of comparable importance was the effect of invention itself. The demonstration that steam engines and textile machines could order the physical world made some Americans perceive that achievement as an important continuing task for the nation. Others saw it as a means to quick wealth.

At the same time that industrialization progressed in company with a revised view of morality, it threatened the whole republican project of good citizenship. The individual, set free to seek moral self-improvement or to corner some portion of the growing material wealth of the country, was at increased liberty to pursue personal aggrandizement. And so that fine old institution the corporation, understood to be a band of respectable gentlemen taking on a project in the public interest, came to be quite unashamedly an instrument of swift personal profit. Even in that form, to be sure, corporations would do a great amount of good, along with much harm, in their financing and organizing of invention and productivity. But that very fact reinforced the belief, which early in the nineteenth century had become economic orthodoxy, that self-interest is the best engine of economic progress.

The effect of industrialization on the common American varied, of course, from one individual to another. Through much of the nineteenth century, a great amount of production and maintenance remained in the hands of individual artisans and craftsmen: blacksmiths, cobblers, carpenters. Many such labors continue today, in shops aided by machinery on a small scale or undertaken by skilled hired hands. Probably most Americans of English, Scottish, or other old American lineage continued to live out as much of the old republican existence as could survive. As for those Americans, a very large portion of them immigrants or second-generation citizens, who worked in factories, debate continues over whether industrialization degraded them and robbed them of skills or required new kinds of thinking and adaptation. Yet industrialization seemed to require the spread of one particular skill, that of literacy. That became essential as old sedate ways of passing on practical knowledge gave way to the necessity of reading instructions, job advertisements, and whatever other information the individual might need to negotiate increasingly mechanized surroundings.

A Resurgent Nationalism

At the end of the War of 1812, no federal official would have foreseen the enormous role that national and state government was going to take in the process of industrialization. Political events, however, were taking the federal government in a direction eventually beneficial to industry and innovation. In essence, the federal establishment was learning to do what Hamilton had wished of it: to become an active partner in economic growth. It was to provide further sinews of nationhood.

What happened to the Federalists once their party disintegrated?

Some remained in office, especially in Connecticut and Massachusetts. Others, like John Quincy Adams, went to the Republicans and continued in public life. Still others folded their tents and stole away, a few reappearing in sulky memoirs.

Among the most interesting of the Federalists are those who sought nongovernmental means of furthering their social and political goals. Clyde Griffen has written a fascinating account of this last group who became *Their Brother's Keeper* by establishing a series of benevolent societies. Their societies, like the American Bible Society, the American Tract Society, and the American Anti-Slavery Society, formed a "benevolent empire." The goal was to shore up the social order, temper the excesses of democracy, and raise the moral tone of the nation. The societies, which quickly became very large, encouraged people to observe the Sabbath, avoid drunkenness and unseemly language, attend church regularly, and practice the other traditional Christian virtues. They organized Sunday Schools, financed ministers in the developing West, distributed millions of pamphlets and tracts, and otherwise sought to raise the moral tone of society.

The Decline of the Federalist Party

By the end of the War of 1812 the Federalist Party of George Washington, Alexander Hamilton, and John Adams had crumbled before the assaults of Jeffersonian Republicans who championed the yeoman farmers and denounced the monied interests of the Northeast. But it was not their look of elitism that doomed the Federalists. During the war, many Federalists openly opposed the military effort, and their opposition resulted in the Hartford Convention of 1814–15, when Federalist delegates from the New England states protested the war and even hinted at secession. The Hartford Convention was held in secret, and when news of the meetings reached the press, Democrats roundly criticized Federalists for disloyalty and conspiracy. Andrew Jackson's great victory at New Orleans occurred during the deliberations of the Hartford Convention, which embarrassed the Federalists. In the election of 1816, James Monroe defeated Rufus King by 183 electoral votes to 34. The Federalist Party then disappeared.

Era of Good Feelings

After many years of political bickering, an interlude of one-party politics followed the war. However divisive the War of 1812 had been, its ending brought a general sentiment of patriotism along with an awareness of weaknesses that had made the conduct of the war so difficult. A consensus grew in favor of some unified political solution to the nation's problems. For a time it was common for voters to call themselves Jeffersonian Republicans, and politics became no more than a contest of personalities within a politics of national harmony. To a people brought up with an eighteenth-century view of political parties as self-serving, divisive instruments, this actually seemed healthy. The "demon of party," a newspaper editor noted in 1817, had been exorcised for good.

Like his Virginia predecessors, James Monroe had spent his life serving his country. At eighteen he had been wounded in the Revolutionary War. He later served as minister to France, governor of Virginia, minister to England, and secretary of state. (From 1813 to 1815 he frequently doubled as secretary of war.) Monroe when he became President was nearing sixty years. Dignified in appearance, cautious in manner, he provided a link with the heroic past. At a time when most men wore trousers, he still dressed in old-fashioned knee breeches and silk stockings. On ceremonial occasions he wore a faded Revolutionary uniform—fitting garb for the last Revolutionary War veteran in the White House.

President Monroe's Grand Tour

As President, Monroe sought to create "a union of parties in support of our republican government." His choice of Cabinet members reflected this goal: he tried to pick Republicans from every section of the country. Secretary of State John Quincy Adams was a New Englander. Georgian William H. Crawford stayed on in the Treasury Department. Unable to find a westerner for secretary of war, Monroe finally picked young John C. Calhoun of South Carolina. Restrained by their loyalty to the President, these political rivals served Monroe well. He also worked hard to gain the confidence of prominent Federalists. Harrison Gray Otis was deeply touched when the "Old Sachem" not only invited him to the White House for dinner, but "drank a glass of wine with me to make friends."

In pursuit of national unity, Monroe set out shortly after his election on a tour of the northern and eastern states. Paying his own travel costs, he followed the seaboard north to Portland, Maine, then headed westward, going as far as Detroit—a three-and-one-half month journey by carriage and steamboat. It was a triumphal procession. Everywhere crowds gathered to honor this "last of the Revolutionary farmers." The high point came at Boston, where over forty thousand turned out to welcome the President. At a public dinner, local Federalists and Republicans sat down together for the first time in years. Monroe's visit, a staunch Federalist editor reported, had established an "Era of Good Feelings." Newspapers throughout the country soon picked up the phrase. For a time, despite bickering on the state and local levels, it seemed appropriate. In 1820 Monroe was reelected without opposition; only one negative vote in the electoral college prevented his election from being, like Washington's, unanimous.

James Monroe, elected in 1816, sought to unify the states and parties, and establish an "Era of Good Feelings." *(Portrait by Gilbert Stuart, Courtesy, The Metropolitan Museum of Art, Bequest of Seth Low, 1929)*

Government and the Economy

Monroe's presidency was also a time of economic nationalism. Instructed perhaps by the War of 1812 that the country could not get by with the limited central government that the Jeffersonian Republicans had once favored, President Madison in 1815 had recommended an energetic governmental program for the nurturing of the economy. Congress responded by rechartering a national bank, voting funds for internal improvements, and enacting a protective tariff. "Our two great parties," said the retired President John Adams, "have crossed over the valley and taken possession of each other's mountain."

Transportation—"Let us conquer space"   During the War of 1812, the nation's transportation network had proved no more adequate to wartime demands than its banking system. With coastal shipping choked off by the British blockade and canals still in their infancy, the burden fell almost entirely on the roads. In a few places in the East turnpikes had been built, but they deteriorated quickly under heavy use. Most roads were hardly more than broad country paths through the forest, filled with ruts and stumps, turning to mud during rain.

Recognition that the country needed a better transportation system was one element in the governmental and economic nationalism to which President Madison turned from his earlier philosophy of limited government. He called for a system of roads and canals "executed under national authority." He recommended a constitutional amendment that would eliminate continuing doubts over the federal government's authority to finance such projects. Representative John C. Calhoun of South Carolina, then a vigorous young nationalist, brushed aside constitutional objections. Sheer size and poor communication, he warned the House—in words that would later haunt him—exposed the country to that "greatest of all calamities," disunion. "Let us, then, bind the Republic together with a perfect system of roads and canals. Let us conquer space." Calhoun proposed setting aside, as a fund for internal improvements, the government's share of the profits from the new Bank of the United States. In 1817 Congress narrowly approved Calhoun's plan, only to have Madison, then about to leave the White House, veto it on constitutional grounds. The states and private enterprise would have to finance most internal improvements. That very year New York began construction of the Erie Canal.

The Tariff of 1816   Before 1807 Americans had imported most manufactured goods from Europe, but Jefferson's embargo and the war had stimulated the growth of domestic industries. In New England and the Carolinas, mills were spinning and weaving cotton; a new iron industry flourished at Pittsburgh; Kentuckians began making local hemp into bagging. But when the war ended, British manufacturers moved quickly to crush these new rivals. In 1816 they dumped vast quantities of goods on the American market at cut-rate prices, in order, a spokesman explained, "to stifle in the cradle those rising manufacturers in the United States, which war had forced into existence, contrary to the natural course of things." To protect these new industries, President Madison proposed increased tariff duties on competing imports, which would push up their price. Congress was receptive, since nearly every section of the country had an interest to be protected. Southerners, who had the least to gain, supported higher duties on political and patriotic grounds. The Tariff of 1816 placed a duty of twenty-five percent on woolen, iron, and cotton products coming into the United States. Congress imposed rates as high as thirty percent on a variety of paper, leather, and textile products. A

The American Economy		
	1815 (1820*)	**1860**
U.S. Population	8,419,000*	31,513,000
Northeast	50.4 percent*	36.5
South	30.4	25.6
West	19.2	37.8
Annual Immigration	8,385	153,640
Miles of Railroads	23	30,626
Cotton Production (bales)	209,000	3,841,000
Lumber Production (board feet)	600,000,000	8,000,000,000
Soft Coal Production (tons)	253,000	9,057,000
Comparative GNP per capita	67.6	137.0

subsequent Tariff of 1818 increased the tariff rate on iron and extended the duty on cotton until 1826. Within a few years, a series of threatening events would cause many southerners to reexamine their jubilant support of economic nationalism.

The Second Bank of the United States When the charter of the first Bank of the United States expired in 1811, the state banks had gone wild. The number increased from eighty-eight to over two hundred. In making loans and paying debts, they issued huge quantities of banknotes, which thereupon circulated as regular currency. A banknote was, in effect, a piece of paper carrying a bank's promise that upon request the bank would give to the bearer of the note an amount of money in specie (gold or silver) equal in value to the sum printed on the note. A holder of a banknote for, say, $1.00 could believe that while the note was not itself a real dollar, it was virtually an equivalent since it could be exchanged for a specie dollar: and so storekeepers and other merchants were willing to accept banknotes from customers.

As long as there was plenty of reliable specie in the banks—enough to cover a comfortable portion if not all of the banknotes in circulation in case many holders of notes got hungry for metallic money—the notes were a useful currency. A bank's ability to issue them allowed it to make more loans, pay more debts, and in general nourish more business than it could have done if its activities had been restricted to what its holdings in specie alone could accomplish. But if the banknotes got far out of proportion to the specie on which they were supposed to be based, the public would cease to trust them as currency, they would depreciate in value, and business would suffer from the uncertainty. And that is what happened as the state banks multiplied and carried out their transactions with no national bank to steady them. The mass of confusing, depreciated paper money worried businessmen and pleased counterfeiters. The lack of a national currency such as a Bank of the United States could have issued made it difficult to carry on business among different parts of the country.

Then wartime borrowing overwhelmed this shaky system. By the summer of 1814 every bank outside of New England had suspended the practice of paying specie to holders of notes who demanded it. The country's credit practically vanished. And after the war the federal government, to accommodate settlers in the West, offered for sale vast tracts of public land. The government's terms were generous: the minimum purchase was 160 acres, and the purchaser had four years to complete payment. Much of the land was purchased with credit supplied by state banks. Land sales, then, were inviting more bad currency into circulation.

In response to the crisis in banking, Congress in 1816 chartered a second Bank of the United States, with headquarters at Philadelphia. It was capitalized at $35 million, of which the government put up $5 million. The President was to appoint five "government directors," and the domestic stockholders would elect the other members of the twenty-five member board: foreign stockholders were not allowed to vote. The Bank was to serve as a repository of government funds and could

"I know towns, yea cities," charged one westerner: "where this bank already appears as an engrossing proprietor. All the flourishing cities of the West are mortgaged to this money power . . . they are in the jaws of a monster! A lump of butter in the mouth of a dog! One gulp, one swallow, and all is gone!"

allow people who had purchased public lands on credit additional time to pay. Real debtor relief came mainly from the states. Several passed stay laws delaying foreclosure for debt. Cities set up soup kitchens, and churches collected funds for the relief of paupers.

Out of the confused debate on the depression, the Bank of the United States emerged as the chief scapegoat. Charges of fraud and mismanagement abounded. The old southern agrarians, Thomas Jefferson among them, condemned the Bank and the federal government for creating a "paper bubble" and hoped the shock of depression would restore the country to its sound, paper-free past. These critics likened the Bank to a monster, foreclosing everything in its path.

Many of these accusations were unfair. Fraud and mismanagement there had been, but the Bank was not responsible for fluctuations in the world market or for the public's compulsion for speculation. If the Bank had been inconsistent in dealing with the state banks, so had politicians and the public. But these considerations made little impression on a people mired in debt and depression. The economy recovered in the early 1820s, but by this time the reputation of the Bank among some constituencies had deteriorated beyond repair. Yet the recovery would owe much to the Bank and its new president, Nicholas Biddle.

Nicholas Biddle, president, beginning in 1823, of the Second Bank of the United States. *(Courtesy, The National Portrait Gallery)*

Nicholas Biddle Brings Order   Biddle, a wealthy Philadelphian, took over the Bank in 1823 and immediately set about putting its affairs in order. Born into a wealthy Philadelphia family, Biddle had displayed a precocious versatility from the start. After graduation from Princeton at the age of fifteen, he traveled widely, served in the diplomatic corps, and wrote a classic account of the Lewis and Clark expedition. Impressed with his knowledge of banking, President Monroe appointed him a director of the Bank; four years later, at the age of thirty-seven, he became its president. The choice was a good one. Biddle understood banking and the function of the Bank in the American economy at a time when few others did. One reform was to increase the BUS's specie reserve, the amount of hard currency it kept on hand. This policy effectively meant that the paper money issued by the Bank was "as good as gold." Biddle also reformed the BUS's policies with respect to the notes issued by other banks. Most state-chartered banks had little specie reserve for their notes. When those notes were presented to the BUS for redemption, as they routinely were, Biddle could either demand payment in specie from the bank of issue or refrain from doing so. This was an enormously important power because it enabled Biddle and the other BUS directors to control how much currency was in circulation. That was critical for the simple reason that there was far too little gold and silver available to support a growing economy. The nation's gross national product, the total amount of goods and services produced, was perhaps fifty times greater than the amount of gold and silver. Without paper money the economy would have come to a halt. Too much of it, of course, would further weaken the economy. And it was Biddle's bank that largely determined how much money would circulate.

For the most part Biddle exercised these enormous powers wisely, and after a shaky start the bank prospered. But the Bank's private ownership remained a source of suspicion. Another potential problem was Biddle's practice of making loans on especially favorable terms to important politicians and newspaper editors. The Bank had many enemies, and charges of corruption would dog its career throughout Biddle's tenure in office.

Nationalism and the Supreme Court

Between 1810 and 1824, the Supreme Court, in a series of important cases decided under Chief Justice John Marshall, provided a legal and judicial equivalent to the political and economic nationalism that swept the country during and after the War of 1812. The decisions expanded the constitutional authority of the federal government in ways that complemented its increasing political and economic power. The Court declared the primacy of the federal government over the states and strengthened federal control over interstate commerce. It also reduced the power of state governments over corporations, and protected private contracts against state regulation. These rulings, in weakening the authority of the states, indirectly added to that of the nation.

Leading Constitutional Decisions   Marshall's commitment to the sanctity of contracts was revealed in 1810 when the court handed down its decision in *Fletcher v. Peck*. In 1795 the Georgia legislature had sold thirty-five million acres along the Yazoo River to four land companies for $500,000. The deal was riddled with corruption complete with bribes and kickbacks to the legislators, and during the next legislative session, a new group of legislators rescinded the land grants, claiming that they were corrupt, fraudulent, and therefore invalid. When the case reached the Supreme Court, Marshall wrote the majority opinion, declaring unconstitutional the law to rescind the sales. Marshall argued that the law violated the section of the Constitution prohibiting the states from invalidating contracts.

In *Dartmouth College v. Woodward* (1819) the Court ruled that the Constitution protected charters of incorporation from legislative interference. Dartmouth College had been granted a charter in 1769 by King George III. In 1816 the New Hampshire legislature, in an effort to make the college more democratic, tried to replace the self-governing trustees with a board appointed by the state governor. The trustees retained Daniel Webster, a Dartmouth alumnus and eloquent orator, to fight their case. Webster's theatrics ("It is . . . a small school," he plaintively told the Justices, "and yet there are those who love it.") and his arguments proved effective. Dartmouth's charter, wrote Marshall, was a contractual relationship between the Crown and the College. The state of New Hampshire was a continuation of the Crown; the obligations of contract remained unchanged. So long as the trustees did not abuse their powers, the state could not interfere without violating the contract clause of the Constitution. Coming at a time when private corporations were rapidly gaining favor in transportation, finance, and manufacturing, this defense of contracts made it more difficult for the states to control corporate activity.

The act of the New Hampshire legislature put the Dartmouth campus in an uproar. One student wrote:

"Such a state of [affairs] necessarily discomposes the mind, and unfits it for steady and quiet reflection. . . . You may easily suppose that it is impossible to sit down cooly & composedly [to] books, when you are alarmed every minute by a report, that the library is in danger or that a mob is about collecting or that we are all about to [be] fined & imprisoned."

"Let the end be legitimate," wrote Chief Justice Marshall enunciating the doctrine of implied powers in *McCullough v. Maryland* (1899): "let it be within the scope of the Constitution, and all means which are appropriate, which are plainly adapted to that end, which are not prohibited, but consistent with the letter and spirit of the Constitution, are constitutional."

In *McCulloch v. Maryland* (1819) the Court confirmed the broad construction of the Constitution that Alexander Hamilton had defended thirty years before during arguments over the first Bank of the United States. Several states, Maryland among them, had placed high taxes on the Bank's branches within their borders. The cashier of the Baltimore branch, James McCulloch, refused to pay the tax and Maryland brought suit. In his opinion, Marshall upheld the constitutionality of the Bank. The creation of such an institution, he admitted, was not among the powers listed in the Constitution. But Congress also possessed "incidental or implied powers." He found that the financial powers of the national legislature gave it the implied power to charter a national bank that would aid Congress in exercising its authority over finance. Maryland's tax, which attempted to destroy a lawful agency of the federal government, was therefore unconstitutional: "the power to tax . . . is the power to destroy." Champions of states' rights denounced this opinion, which would stretch the Constitution beyond its literal statements and have it implicitly grant large powers to the federal government.

Marshall's opinion two years later in *Cohens v. Virginia* further distressed states' rights advocates. At issue here was the right of a state to limit appeals to the United States Supreme Court from its own courts. The Cohens had been convicted of selling lottery tickets under a Virginia law that prohibited appeals from such a conviction. Asserting that the case involved a "federal question," they turned to the Supreme Court for relief. Counsel for Virginia denied the Court's right of judicial review, claiming that the state's legitimate authority was under attack. The Chief Justice disagreed. He maintained that Virginia had surrendered some of her powers when she joined the Union. The right of the Supreme Court to review cases involving "federal questions" was absolutely essential if the operation of the Constitution was to be uniform throughout the country. Otherwise, the federal government would be prostrate "at the feet of every state in the Union." This opinion, added to that in *Marbury v. Madison,* solidly fixed the Supreme Court as the final arbiter of all constitutional questions.

Gibbons v. Ogden (1824), Marshall's last great decision, gave force to the clause of the Constitution that had empowered Congress "to regulate commerce with foreign nations, and among the several states." Early in the nineteenth century a number of states had begun awarding monopolies to the operators of the new steamboats. In 1808 New York gave Robert Fulton and Robert Livingston an exclusive right to operate steamboats on the state's waters. It also awarded Aaron Ogden an exclusive franchise to run steamboats on the Hudson River between New York and New Jersey. When Thomas Gibbons began a rival service on this route, Ogden brought suit to restrain his competitor. The New York courts upheld the monopoly. Gibbons appealed to the Supreme Court. Once again Marshall championed federal supremacy. A narrow construction of the Constitution, he declared at the outset, "would cripple the government, and render it unequal to the objects for which it is declared to be instituted, and to which the powers given, as fairly understood, render it competent." New York's law was unconstitutional because it conflicted with a 1793 act of Congress regulating the coastwise trade. Congress's power to regulate commerce, "like all others vested in Congress, is complete in itself, may be exercised to its utmost extent, and acknowledges no limitations, other than those prescribed in the Constitution."

A few years later Marshall could not prevent the removal of the Cherokee Indians from Georgia. He also ducked a case involving the rights of free blacks. Yet his nationalism ultimately helped to free the slaves. For over thirty years Marshall had argued that the United States was a consolidated nation rather than merely a compact of sovereign states. In 1861, when Abraham Lincoln called for troops, thousands of young men took up arms to defend the national Union Marshall's decisions had done so much to define. And consigning slavery to economic and social obsolescence was the industrial system that, under the protection of the federal government, had both extended and transformed the classical republicanism of the Jeffersonians.

Suggested Readings

On the transportation revolution see David Hawke, *Nuts and Bolts of the Past: History of American Technology, 1776–1860* (1988), David J. Jeremy, *Transatlantic Industrial Revolution: The Diffusion of Textile Technology Between Britain and America, 1790–1830* (1981), Thomas Dublin, *Farm to Factory: Women's Letters, 1830–1860* (1981), Barbara Tucker, *Samuel Slater and the Origins of the American Textile Industry, 1790–1860* (1984), and Thomas C. Cochran, *Frontiers of Change: Early Industrialism in America* (1981). On canals see Peter Way, *Common Labour: Workers and the Digging of North American Canals, 1780–1860* (1993) and Ronald E. Shaw, *Canals for a Nation: The Canal Era in the United States, 1790–1860* (1990).

Other studies of economic development are Charles Sellers, *The Market Revolution: Jacksonian America, 1815–1846* (1991), Stuart Bruchey's *Roots of Economic Growth, 1607–1861: An Essay in Social Causation* (1968), Thomas C. Cochran's *200 Years of American Business* (1977), and George Rogers Taylor's *The Transportation Revolution, 1815–1860* (1951). The economic changes under way in the pre–Civil War era are covered in Cochran's *Frontiers of Change* (1981) and Paul Gates's *The Farmer's Age: Agriculture, 1815–1860* (1960). A recent study is Stuart Bruchey, *Enterprise: The Dynamic Economy of a Free People* (1990).

See also David A. Hounshell, *From the American System to Mass Production, 1800–1932: The Development of Manufacturing Technology in the United States* (1984). Anthony Wallace's *Rockdale: The Growth of an American Village in the Early Industrial Revolution* (1977) is an important study of an early textile community near Philadelphia.

The classic work on the United States of the 1830s is Alexis de Tocqueville's *Democracy in America* (1835), which remains one of the most perceptive studies of American society. Bray Hammand's *Banks and Politics in America from the Revolution to the Civil War* (1957) admires the Bank of the United States, and admiring of Biddle is T. P. Govan, *Nicholas Biddle* (1959). See also Peter Temin, *The Jacksonian Economy* (1969) and J. M. McFaul, *The Politics of Jacksonian Finance* (1972).

On John Marshall's Supreme Court decisions, see G. Edward White, *The Marshall Court and Cultural Change, 1815–1860* (1991), R. K. Nemya, *The Supreme Court Under Marshall and Taney* (1968), Richard E. Ellis, *The Jeffersonian Crisis: Courts and Politics in the Early Republic* (1971), F. M. Stites, *John Marshall: Defender of the Constitution* (1981), and John A. Garraty, *Quarrels that Have Shaped the Constitution* (1987).

American Living Standards in an Industrializing Economy

Sean Wilentz

In 1845, the New York *Daily Tribune* prepared a series of reports on the condition of labor in New York. What the *Tribune* reporters found shocked them, and they groped for explanations—especially to account for the outrageous underbidding and exploitation that riddled the city's largest trades. A few years later, after he had read the works of the greatest urban journalists of the age, a *Tribune* correspondent named George Foster had found the right term: it was "sweating," "the accursed system. . . ." It arose in its purest forms in the consumer finishing trades, and most notoriously in the production of clothing.

From the cutting rooms (out of sight of the customers), the head cutter or piece master distributed the cut cloth to the outworkers and contractors, and it was here that the worst depredations of sweating began. A variety of outwork schemes existed. While most contractors were small masters unable to maintain their own shops, or journeymen looking for the surest road to independence, some cutters and in-shop journeymen also managed to subcontract a portion of their work on the sly. Some firms dealt directly with outworkers. In all cases, the system invited brutal competition and a successive lowering of outwork piece rates. At every level of the contracting network, profits came from the difference between the rates the contractors and subcontractors received and the money they paid out for overhead and labor. Two factors turned these arrangements into a matrix of unremitting exploitation: first, the successive bidding by the contractors for manufacturers' orders (as well as the competition between manufacturers) depressed the contractors' income; second, the reliance of the entire trade on credit buying by retailers and country dealers prompted postponement of payment to contractors until finished work was done—and, hence, chronic shortages of cash. The result: contractors steadily reduced the rates they paid their hands and often avoided paying them at all for as long as possible. To middle-class reformers, the great villain of the system was the contractor himself, the "sweater," the "remorseless sharper and shaver," who in his endless search for profits fed greedily on the labor of poor women and degraded journeymen. But the contractors and garret bosses had little choice in the matter, as they tried to underbid their competitors and survive on a wafer-thin margin of credit. "If they were all the purest of philanthropists," the *Tribune* admitted in 1845, "they could not raise the wages of their seamstresses to anything like a living price." Hounded by their creditors, haunted by the specter of late payment and bankruptcy, the contractors and garret masters lived an existence in which concern for one's workers was a liability and in which callousness (and, in some recorded cases, outright cruelty) became a way of life. . . .

The sufferings of the outwork and garret-shop hands—the vast majority of clothing-trade workers— taxed the imaginations of even the most sentimental American Victorians; if the reformers' accounts sometimes reduced a complex situation to a moral fable, they in no way falsified the clothing workers' conditions. All pretensions to craft vanished in the outwork system; with the availability of so much cheap wage labor, formal apprenticing and a regular price book had disappeared by 1845. At any given moment in the 1830s and 1840s, the underbidding in the contracting network could depress outwork and garret-shop piece rates so low that stitchers had to work up to sixteen hours a day to maintain the meanest of living standards: in 1850, some of the largest southern-trade clothing firms in the Second Ward paid their *male* workers, on the average, well below subsistence wages. Housing was difficult to come by and could amount to no more than a cellar dwelling or a two-room flat, shared with two or more families; single men crammed into outwork boardinghouses. During slack seasons or a bad turn in trade, the clothing workers struggled harder to make ends meet, with a combination of odd jobs, charity relief, and the starchiest kinds of cheap food.

Sean Wilentz, *Chants Democratic: New York City and the Rise of the American Working Class, 1788–1850* (New York: Oxford University Press, 1984).

[A] prosperous American economy was a precondition for large-scale immigration. Henry Price, a cabinetmaker, recalled in his diary his reasons for leaving England: "I never had enough to spend on to supply what I conceve to be sufficient for the supply of the legitimate Wants of My family." . . .

Although the tight labor market kept wages high, the true cost of labor was low because the pace of work was so fast and regular. American manufacturers were aware of this. "The French weaver," the *United States Economist and Dry Goods Reporter* told its readers, "lives very cheap, but he works very slowly. American labor costs more, but is more productive." . . .

The compensation for such hard work was the ability to live at a standard higher than in Europe. Indeed, male and supplementary female workers, both native and foreign, discovered for one of the first times in history that common people might live comfortably. . . .

Even more remarkable was the American *diet*. Its quality and availability had an impact on the standard of living of the common people that can only be called revolutionary. . . .

The prospect of improved diet seems to have been the most important factor in encouraging immigration. "Hunger brought me . . . here [and] hunger is the cause of European immigration to this country," wrote Henry Brokmeyer, a German immigrant who worked in New York in the 1850s as a tanner and shoemaker. Ole Helland wrote back to Norway in 1836, "I have such good service with board and bed that you would not believe it. Yes, I often think of you when I go to a prepared table with much expensive food before me." In 1844 Robert Williams wrote, "the chief farmers of Wales would be amazed to see the tables of the poor spread with dishes at every meal."

Grain was the staple food in Europe and meat a luxury rarely indulged in. By contrast, meat was virtually the staple of the American workingman's diet: of the $12 million in sales of produce in the city in 1841, 39 percent was spent on meat, 25 percent on grain, 22 percent on dairy products, and 10 percent on vegetables. Of the meat sold, 53 percent was beef, 22 percent pork. The huge amount of uncleared land in the Midwest suitable for grazing kept beef and pork prices low, and high wages made meat easily affordable. In New York meat was "beef-steaks (cut from the ribs), mutton chops, fish, fried potatoes, boiled potatoes, huckleberries and sugar . . . fresh butter, [and] new bread" three times a day. . . . Bread in the New World was almost always wheaten. "Not one in a hundred" New Yorkers had even heard of eating oat bread. In addition, it was always first-class wheat bread.

John Harold recorded in his diary his astonishment at New York boardinghouse fare. The day began with "Beef Steaks, fish, hash, ginger cakes, buckwheat cakes etc such a profusion as I never saw before at the breakfast tables," and dinner was "a greater profusion than breakfast." . . .

Generally, physicians were impressed with the health of city residents. The physician Benjamin McCready, though warning of overcrowded housing, was relieved that in 1837 the city was free of the "disease and deformity which . . . could only be found in the over-grown towns of Europe. . . ."

Workers did not live luxuriously, but most workers' apartments were decently furnished. Many homes had frame beds, comfortable chairs, and bookcases. William Thomson, a Scottish weaver, noted that American workers "have rocking arm chairs that are a real luxury." Most amazing to immigrants was the presence of rugs in workingmen's apartments. Burn noted in 1865 that the floors "even [of] the poor classes of the people are covered with bits of carpet." Large carpet factories, such as the Higgins Company in Ward 22, produced rugs at modest prices. . . .

William McLurg no doubt spoke for many when he wrote to his parents, "there is nothing I regret so much as not coming here . . . sooner."

Richard B. Stott, *Workers in the Metropolis: Class, Ethnicity, and Youth in Antebellum New York City* (Ithaca: Cornell University Press, 1990).

John Gast's rendition of Manifest Destiny shows Indians and wild animals skulking off before the advance of westward expansion embodied in Columbia's stringing telegraph wires across the continent. (*Courtesy, Library of Congress, ca. 1862*)

Sectionalism and Party 1816–1828

9

THE WESTWARD MOVEMENT

For almost 200 years American society had grown in the corridor between the Atlantic Ocean and the Appalachian range. Mountains, Indian tribes, and conflict among European powers had discouraged Americans from pushing into the West. Even those who crossed some of the eastern mountains found the inviting valleys angling south through Pennsylvania, Virginia, and the Carolinas far more tempting than scaling the next ridges toward an uncertain domicile in the western plains. Then, after about 1795, with the Revolution won, the Indian tribes dispersed, and the price of good eastern land mounting, a vast folk migration began. Only briefly interrupted by wars and depressions, it relentlessly populated the continent. The land seemed suddenly and permanently to have tilted, shaking its human burden westward in a long rough tumble toward the Pacific.

The return of peace on the frontier after the War of 1812 and rising prices worldwide for agricultural products quickened the migration. In 1810 only one American in seven lived west of the Appalachians; in 1820 it was one in four. Before the land fever subsided, five new states had entered the Union—Indiana in 1816, Mississippi in 1817, Illinois in 1818, Alabama in 1819, and in 1821 Missouri—and they made the West a new force to be reckoned with in national affairs.

Settlers traveled by wagon, flatboat, horse, even on foot. The road west was often scarcely a road at all, but a slightly widened

continued

HISTORICAL EVENTS

1787
Northwest Ordinance prohibits slavery in the Northwest Territory

1793
Whitney perfects the cotton gin

1803
South Carolina reopens its foreign slave trade

1808
Constitution ban on importation of slaves takes effect

1811
Astor establishes fur-trading post in Oregon • Henry Clay becomes Speaker of the House

1814
Revolutions begin in Central and South America

1816
Monroe elected President

1817
John Quincy Adams becomes secretary of state • Rush-Bagot agreement

HISTORICAL EVENTS

1818
Treaty of 1818 with Britain • Jackson advances with his troops into Florida

1819
The Tallmadge Amendment is debated • Adams-Onis Treaty

1820
Missouri Compromise

1822
Monroe vetoes funds for the Cumberland Road • Vesey Conspiracy • U.S. formally recognizes Mexico, Colombia, Chile, Peru, and the provinces of Río de la Plata

1823
Monroe Doctrine

1824
John Quincy Adams elected President • Bolívar proposes Pan-American conference

1828
Andrew Jackson elected President

New Englanders traveled west singing:

Come all ye Yankee farmers who wish to
    change your lot,
Who've spunk enough to travel beyond
    your native spot,
And leave behind the village where Ma
    and Pa do stay,
Come follow me and settle in Michi-
    gania.

But others who had been there chanted:

Don't go to Michigan, that land of ills;
The word means ague, fever, and chills.

trail full of ruts and stumps so that for a passenger in the unsprung wagons "the pain of riding exceeded the fatigue of walking." Americans of the early nineteenth century were hungry for internal improvements, for turnpikes, canals, and finally railroads.

Often, in the stretches that were to be one day a land of motels, fast-food stands, and gas stations, the travelers perceived all around them nothing but a forest of tall hardwood trees, dark, sinister, and gloomy. Settlers gloated over the mighty fires that followed a boisterous log-rolling, when perhaps hundreds of trees, felled after backbreaking labor, vanished into smoke, fire, and ash.

Yet the farmers preferred the forests to the prairies, endless meadows of tall grass sweeping across northern Indiana and Illinois and beyond. Settlers, much as they might curse the trees they had to girdle, cut, and burn, hard as they might work to let in sunshine so that crops could grow, believed that hardwood forests indicated fertile soil. The prairies (actually richer soil where thick grass strangled other vegetation) evoked, as one traveler noted, "a certain indescribable sensation of loneliness." Rich as prairie soil was, settlers discovered that to farm this land meant first to break the thick, heavy sod. In the early part of the century, when plows were still small and primitive, it was muscle-wrenching labor.

In addition to doing backbreaking agricultural labor, a man with implements no more sophisticated than an axe and chisel would make "gates, carts, barrows, plow frames, ox yokes, wooden shovels, hay forks, troughs, benches, woodhorses, tool handles, stirring paddles, rakes, mortars, flails, cradles for mowing, swingling knives, flax brakes, and many other articles." More talented woodworkers could make their own wagons and furniture as well. And of course everyone, with neighbors helping to raise the logs, built his own house. Women worked equally hard or harder, raising vegetables and herbs, making soap, butter, and other household articles, and carrying out every step of the manufacture of clothing, from spinning to sewing. This labor, combined with housekeeping and childbearing, tolled heavily. Many women appeared old at thirty, and men widowed two and three times were common. Clouds of flies and mosquitoes, drafty walls, primitive sanitation, and animal waste around cabins were more hazardous to life than the better-known dangers of hostile Indians and prairie fires.

The reward was often worth the travail. At the end of the journey and the settlement lay independence and wealth as nineteenth-century Americans understood it: the ownership of productive agricultural land. The true pioneer stage passed rapidly; mills, towns, canals, newspapers, churches, cloth imported from the East, hardware, glass, even pianos eased and elevated the crude life of the frontier, and families rapidly moved from the backwoods to the front pews.

But for a moment, and only for a moment, the frontier was just what legend says it was. A vivid frontier imagination spoke in words attributed to Davy Crockett of western Tennessee. "I'm fresh from the backwoods," he is said to have boasted, "half alligator, a little touched with the snapping turtle; can wade the Mississippi, leap the Ohio, ride upon a streak of lightning . . . hug a bear too close for comfort. . . ."

A Resurgent Sectionalism

The expansion of the country and its economy made for clashing interests among regions. These soon expressed themselves in disputes over the tariff, internal improvements, and land policy.

The Tariff The South produced cotton for export, obtaining manufactured goods from the North and West as well as from Europe. The tariff pushed up the retail price of European products in this country and thereby allowed northern manufacturers to raise their prices, too, or forced foreign products out of the American market. Compelled to purchase at higher prices, southern planters feared also that Europe would retaliate against American tariffs by putting high duties on southern agricultural goods. Southerners quickly regretted their support for the Tariff of 1816. The disastrous decline in cotton prices after 1819, which cut the planters' purchasing power, made the tariff still more burdensome. In 1820 southerners in Congress barely defeated a bid to raise import duties again.

Internal Improvements Sharp sectional jealousies thwarted plans for a national system of internal improvements. New England did not favor building roads that, by connecting rival ports with the West, would injure Boston. New York and Pennsylvania longed for the national government to construct such routes; but finally, having lost extravagant sums put into their own roads and canals, they abandoned their enthusiasm for federal projects. Southern support for federal improvements faded rapidly. Such expenditures, increasing the need for revenue, would justify the hated tariff, and federal internal improvements implied a broad construction of the Constitution that could ultimately interfere with sectional interests. Only the West consistently demanded a federal system of internal improvements. A shortage of capital and a vast expanse of territory made that section perpetually hungry for government assistance.

Several times Congress responded by appropriating funds for western roads, but a series of presidential vetoes blocked these expenditures. The most prominent of those vetoes came from President James Monroe in 1822. Congress had passed legislation to pay for completion of the Cumberland Road, also known as the National Road, to link Cum-

Timothy Flint, a missionary in the Ohio Valley in the 1820s, wrote:

"The backwoodsman of the West, as I have seen him, is generally an amiable and virtuous man. His general motive for coming here is to . . . have plenty of rich land. . . . His manners are rough. He wears, it may be, a long beard. He carries a knife or a dirk in his bosom and when in the woods has a rifle on his back and a pack of dogs at his heels. An Atlantic stranger would recoil from an encounter with him. But his rifle and his dogs are among his chief means of support and profit. Remember that he still . . . meets bears and panthers."

One observer caught the flavor of raw western politics:

"I have just witnessed a strange thing—a Kentucky election—and am disposed to give you an account of it. An election in Kentucky lasts three days, and during that period whisky and apple toddy flow through our cities and villages like the Euphrates through ancient Babylon. I must do Lexington the justice to say that matters were conducted here with tolerable propriety; but in Frankfort, a place which I had the curiosity to visit on the last day of the election, Jacksonism and drunkenness stalked triumphant—'an unclean pair of lubberly giants.' A number of runners, each with a whisky bottle poking its long neck from his pocket, were busily employed bribing voters, and each party kept half a dozen bullies under pay, genuine specimens of Kentucky alligatorism, to flog every poor fellow who should attempt to vote illegally. A half a hundred of mortar would scarcely fill up the chinks of the skulls that were broken on that occasion. I barely escaped myself."

berland, Maryland, with Wheeling on the Ohio River in present-day West Virginia. Monroe believed that the bill was unconstitutional, that Congress did not have the authority to finance such a road. He claimed that a national system of internal improvements could not be undertaken until an appropriate constitutional amendment had been ratified. His veto forced state governments and private corporations in the Northwest to join in financing an extensive network of turnpikes and canals.

Public Land Policy   Public land policy also divided the sections. The West craved cheap land but land sales were a major source of federal revenues, and the seaboard states favored high prices. Northern manufacturers also hoped that such prices would discourage their workingmen from going west. Though the worn-out cotton lands of the older slave states could not compete with the virgin soil of the Southwest, southeasterners usually voted for cheap land, perhaps seeing the West as a field for the expansion of a slave system to which they were becoming culturally and politically loyal. In

A PIRATE SLAVE SHIP IS BOARDED

The conditions described aboard this slaver are typical. The importation of slaves from outside the United States had ended in 1808, but slave traders continued to sell their human cargoes in the Caribbean and Latin America until the 1830s.

On Friday, May 22, [1829] . . . a midshipman entered the cabin and said in a hurried manner that a sail was visible to the northwest on the larboard quarter. We immediately all rushed on deck, glasses were called for and set, and we distinctly saw a large ship of three masts, apparently crossing our course. It was the general opinion that she was either a large slaver or a pirate, or probably both. . . .

At twelve o'clock we were entirely within gunshot, and one of our long bow guns was again fired at her. It struck the water alongside, and then, for the first time, she showed a disposition to stop. While we were preparing a second she hove to, and in a short time we were alongside her.

The first object that struck us was an enormous gun, turning on a swivel, on deck—the constant appendage of a pirate; and the next were large kettles for cooking, on the bows—the usual apparatus of a slaver. Our boat was now hoisted out, and I went on board with the officers. When we mounted her decks we found her full of slaves. She was called the *Veloz*, commanded by Captain José Barbosa, bound to Bahia. She was a very broad-decked ship, with a mainmast, schooner rigged, and behind her foremast was that large, formidable gun, which turned on a broad circle of iron, on deck, and which enabled her to act as a pirate if her slaving speculation failed. She had taken in, on the coast of Africa, 336 males and 226 females, making in all 562, and had been out seventeen days, during which she had thrown overboard 55. The slaves were all inclosed under grated hatchways between decks. The space was so low that they sat between each other's legs and [were] stowed so close together that there was no possibility of their lying down or at all changing their position by night or day. As they belonged to and were shipped on account of different individuals, they were all branded like sheep with the owner's marks of different forms. These were impressed under their breasts or on their arms, and, as the mate informed me with perfect indifference "burnt with the red-hot iron." Over the hatchway stood a ferocious-looking fellow with a scourge of many twisted thongs in his hand, who was the slave driver of the ship, and whenever he heard the slightest noise below, he shook it over them and seemed eager to exercise it. . . .

But the circumstance which struck us most forcibly was how it was possible for such a number of human beings to exist, packed up and wedged together as tight as they could cram, in low cells three feet high, the greater part of which, except that immediately under the grated hatchways, was shut out from light or air, and this when the thermometer, exposed to the open sky, was standing in the shade, on our deck, at 89dg. The space

1820 Congress reduced the minimum purchasable tract from 160 to 80 acres and the price from $2 to $1.25 an acre. An act of 1830 gave special rights to the squatter who occupied public land he did not own; he could later purchase his tract prior to public sale at the minimum price, regardless of its market value.

The Revival of Slavery   In the North the libertarian ideology of the American Revolution, along with the larger drift of the eighteenth century toward rationalism and humanitarianism, had led numbers of people to believe slavery was in decline. Beginning with Pennsylvania in 1780, the northern states provided for the abolition of slavery. Federal legislation ended the importation of slaves as of 1808. The South's depressed economy in the years after the American Revolution reinforced the moral objection to slavery. Soil exhaustion and a glutted world market injured Virginia's and Maryland's tobacco economy. Many planters switched to wheat, a crop that required fewer slaves to cultivate.

---

between decks was divided into two compartments 3 feet 3 inches high; the size of one was 16 feet by 18 and of the other 40 by 21; into the first were crammed the women and girls, into the second the men and boys: 226 fellow creatures were thus thrust into one space 288 feet square and 336 into another space 800 feet square, giving to the whole an average of 23 inches and to each of the women not more than 13 inches. We also found manacles and fetters of different kinds, but it appears that they had all been taken off before we boarded.

The heat of these horrid places was so great and the odor so offensive that it was quite impossible to enter them, even had there been room. They were measured as above when the slaves had left them. The officers insisted that the poor suffering creatures should be admitted on deck to get air and water. This was opposed by the mate of the slaver, who, from a feeling that they deserved it, declared they would murder them all. The officers, however, persisted, and the poor beings were all turned up together. It is possible to conceive the effect of this eruption—517 fellow creatures of all ages and sexes, some children, some adults, some old men and women, all in a state of total nudity, scrambling out together to taste the luxury of a little fresh air and water. They came swarming up like bees from the aperture of a hive till the whole deck was crowded to suffocation from stem to stern, so that it was impossible to imagine where they could all have come from or how they could have been stowed away. On looking into the places where they had been crammed, there were found some children next the sides of the ship, in the places most remote from light and air; they were lying nearly in a torpid state after the rest had turned out. The little creatures seemed indifferent as to life or death, and when they were carried on deck, many of them could not stand.

After enjoying for a short time the unusual luxury of air, some water was brought; it was then that the extent of their sufferings was exposed in a fearful manner. They all rushed like maniacs towards it. No entreaties or threats or blows could restrain them; they shrieked and struggled and fought with one another for a drop of this precious liquid, as if they grew rabid at the sight of it.

It was not surprising that they should have endured much sickness and loss of life in their short passage. They had sailed from the coast of Africa on the 7th of May and had been out but seventeen days, and they had thrown overboard no less than fifty-five, who had died of dysentery and other complaints in that space of time, though they had left the coast in good health. Indeed, many of the survivors were seen lying about the decks in the last stage of emaciation and in a state of filth and misery not to be looked at. . . .

While expressing my horror at what I saw and exclaiming against the state of this vessel for conveying human beings. I was informed by my friends, who had passed so long a time on the coast of Africa and visited so many ships, that this was one of the best they had seen. The height sometimes between decks was only eighteen inches, so that the unfortunate beings could not turn round or even on their sides, the elevation being less than the breadth of their shoulders; and here they are usually chained to the decks by the neck and legs. . . .

Cotton Gins

But southern planters were anxiously experimenting with new crops, especially cotton. Samuel Crompton's spinning-mule, James Hargreave's spinning-jenny, and Richard Arkwright's spinning-frame and water-frame, as well as other innovations in manufacturing, had dramatically lowered the cost of spinning and weaving cotton fiber into cloth, stimulating a worldwide demand for cotton goods. The appetites of English manufacturers for raw cotton became insatiable. As early as 1786 planters in lowland South Carolina and Georgia began to experiment with growing the silky, long-fibered sea-island cotton. It proved much superior to the short-staple upland variety that had been produced in small quantities for many years. When the cotton bolls were passed between two close-set rollers, the smooth black seeds of the sea-island variety popped right out; the same roller gin crushed the sticky green seeds of the upland variety, making it unmarketable. But sea-island cotton would grow only in the warm, humid lowlands of the coast. Large-scale cotton cultivation awaited a successful process to remove the seeds from short-staple cotton.

Eli Whitney

A Connecticut Yankee came to the South's rescue. In 1793 young Eli Whitney, fresh out of Yale and unemployed, came South to work as a tutor. On the way he stopped to see his friend Phineas Miller, the overseer at Mulberry Grove near Savannah, the plantation of Catherine Greene, widow of General Nathanael Greene. There he turned to inventing a machine to clean the cotton of its seed. In just six months he had perfected his "absurdly simple contrivance." The cotton was fed into a hopper. A toothed roller caught the fibers of the cotton boll and pulled them through a slotted iron guard, its slits wide enough to admit the teeth and the cotton fibers caught on them, but too narrow to let the seeds through. A revolving brush then swept the cotton from the roller's teeth. One man could operate a small gin; larger ones could operate by horse or water power. Whitney and his friend quickly formed a partnership to manufacture their gins. "It makes the labor fifty times less," the inventor observed proudly, "without throwing any class of people out of business."

Whitney's statement hid a cruel fact. The agricultural depression, by throwing slaves out of work, might ultimately have ended slavery. The cotton gin fastened slavery on the South. Rival manufacturers and local artisans quickly copied Whitney's design. Cotton cultivation spread rapidly through upland South Carolina and Georgia. By 1820 the United States was producing 335,000 bales of cotton (a bale weighed about 500 pounds), as opposed to 10,000 bales in 1793. The opening of the rich Black Belt of Alabama and Mississippi after the War of 1812 pushed the crop above one million bales by 1835. The cotton boom created an unprecedented demand for slaves. In 1803 South Carolina reopened its foreign slave trade. Before the federal ban went into effect in 1808, nearly 40,000 Africans had entered Charleston. Between 1790 and 1820 the slave population of the South more than doubled, from 657,000 to more than 1,509,000. Such a massive growth would have enormous political and social repercussions.

The career of Eli Whitney held another irony for the South. This imaginative inventor went from the cotton gin to the manufacture of

Eli Whitney's cotton gin created a cotton boom in the South—and a doubling of the number of slaves by 1820. *(Courtesy, The Smithsonian Institute)*

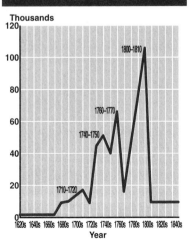

arms, and in that line he was instrumental in developing the principle of interchangeable parts. The principle was a major contribution to the industrial revolution. And industrialism, so it can be argued, met the South on the battlefields of the Civil War, defeating the slavery that the cotton gin had revived.

The Question of Slavery: The Tallmadge Amendment

Saturday, February 13, 1819, was a dull day in Washington. The Senate was not meeting and the House was occupied with a proposal to reduce the number of officers in the army. Late in the day the representatives took up a routine bill for Missouri statehood. Without warning, James Tallmadge, Jr., of New York offered an amendment to prohibit the further introduction of slavery into Missouri and gradually to emancipate slave children born there. An "interesting and pretty wide debate" on Tallmadge's amendment began at once. For the next two and a half years the question of slavery in Missouri—which Thomas Jefferson likened to "a fire bell in the night"—paralyzed Congress. "This momentous question, . . ." the seventy-six-year-old ex-President wrote, "awakened and filled me with terror. I considered it at once as the knell of the Union."

Prior to 1819 new states had entered the Union without much controversy over slavery. The Northwest Ordinance had prohibited slavery in the territory north of the Ohio River. North Carolina and Georgia ceded to the federal government most of the area south of the Ohio, with the stipulation that slavery should be permitted. Before 1820 new slave and free states entered in equal numbers: Louisiana, Mississippi, and Alabama balanced Ohio, Indiana, and Illinois. In 1819 there were eleven slave and eleven free states. The admission of Missouri threatened to upset this delicate balance.

New Englanders had watched with dismay the march of settlement westward; some hoped to preserve their section's influence by checking the expansion of slavery into new territory, and thereby making it their economic and political ally. Federalists had long attributed the triumph of Jefferson's Republican Party to "slave representation." They charged that the Constitution's "three-fifths" clause, allowing three-fifths of the slave population of a state to be counted in granting it House seats, gave the South a disproportionate influence in national politics. Advocates of the tariff and internal improvements looked increasingly on slaveholders as the opponents of their special interests. But at bottom the opposition of slavery was before long to join two quite differing ideas: the conviction that human bondage violated the ethos of the Revolution and the republic; and, especially as time passed, the nineteenth-century humanitarian impulse to abolish or mitigate suffering by means of social reform.

Federalist leaders such as Senator Rufus King of New York aimed at reinvigorating their party with an appeal against slavery's expansion. They allied with a faction of northern Republicans under Governor De Witt Clinton of New York, who resented the southern leadership of the party. Antislavery activists like former Chief Justice John Jay added their support. The House passed Tallmadge's amendment during 1819, but the Senate rejected it. Congress adjourned without reaching an agree-

Soon northerners would spread accounts, many of them true, of cruel slave owners. Stories like this one gradually awakened the moral sense of the nation:

"I now entered on my fifteenth year—a sad epoch in the life of a slave girl. My master began to whisper foul words in my ear. Young as I was, I could not remain ignorant of their import. I tried to treat them with indifference or contempt. . . . He was a crafty man, and resorted to many means to accomplish his purposes. . . . He peopled my young mind with unclean images, such as only a vile monster could think of. I turned from him with disgust and hatred. But he was my master. I was compelled to live under the same roof with him—where I saw a man forty years my senior daily violating the most sacred commandments of nature. He told me I was his property; that I must be subject to his will in all things. My soul revolted against the mean tyranny. But where could I turn for protection? No matter whether the slave girl be as black as ebony or as fair as her mistress. In either case, there is no shadow of law to protect her from insult, from violence, or even from death; all these are inflicted by fiends who bear the shape of men. The mistress, who ought to protect the helpless victim, has no other feelings towards her but those of jealousy and rage. The degradation, the wrongs, the vices, that grow out of slavery, are more than I can describe."

One northerner observed:

"I believe some years ago there was an openness in the minds of the people, in which they saw the iniquity of slavery, but I believe since the discussion of the Missouri question in Congress, the prejudices of slaveholders have increased against the advocates of liberty. . . ."

ment, and Missouri remained a territory. For the time, congressional politics was taking on a distinct sectional alignment, pitting North against South as morality, politics, and self-interest intersected.

The Missouri Compromise   In due course a compromise emerged. Massachusetts had agreed to the creation of a new state, Maine, out of her northern counties, provided Congress acted by March 4, 1820. The free states hoped to admit Maine before the deadline. The Senate decided to tie Maine to Missouri. It added to the Maine statehood bill then before Congress a section admitting Missouri without restrictions on slavery. In order to make this bill more acceptable to the northern-dominated House, Senator Jesse B. Thomas of Illinois offered his famous amendment prohibiting slavery "forever" in the rest of the Louisiana Purchase territory north of latitude 36° 30′—the southern boundary of Missouri. In this form the Maine-Missouri bill went to the House, where, after much wrangling, Speaker Henry Clay secured its passage on March 2. On the key question of excluding slavery in Missouri the vote was extremely close—the motion lost by 90 to 87, with four northern congressmen absent. The vote was traumatic for southerners, who increasingly drew into themselves and lived in a closed society.

Denmark Vesey   In the summer of 1822 the white South was shaken by the discovery of an apparent conspiracy led by Denmark Vesey, a free black carpenter who had closely followed the Missouri debates. It was said that he had recruited hundreds of slaves in Charleston, South Carolina, to rise up at midnight, kill whites, and fire the city. A slave revealed the plot to authorities only a few days before the apparent time of the uprising, and a special court sentenced thirty-five blacks to death. The executions were a public spectacle: at a mass hanging on July 26 several of the condemned twisted in an "agony of strangulation." Afterward, the authorities left the bodies dangling for hours as an example to other blacks.

Slaves and slaveholders everywhere trembled. The court report noted Vesey's careful reading of the Missouri debates. The involvement of so many trusted family servants was especially disturbing to whites. The South Carolina governor had often left his family in the care of Rolla, his beloved personal slave. Yet Rolla was listed among the arch-conspirators.

Southern lawmakers moved at once to prevent a repetition of the Denmark Vesey slave conspiracy. They tightened their slave codes and outlawed the distribution of antislavery propaganda. Southerners resisted all further discussion of slavery in the federal Congress. The South Carolina legislature forbade the entry of free blacks into the state. Free black seamen who violated the law were jailed until their ships left port. When the British government protested these detentions and a federal judge ruled the law unconstitutional, the South Carolina Senate defiantly replied that "the duty of the state to guard against insubordination or insurrection" was "paramount to all *laws*, all *treaties*, all *constitutions*. It arises from the supreme and permanent law of nature, the law of self-preservation; and will never by this state be renounced, compromised, controlled or participated with any power whatever." Neighboring states quickly passed similar statutes. Henceforth, the South bristled at every criticism of what came to be called its "peculiar institution."

In the period that followed the angry arguments over Missouri, and in reaction to the Vesey conspiracy, criticism of slavery virtually ceased in the South. Proslavery theorists—South Carolina's John C. Calhoun among them—who might earlier have labeled slavery a "necessary evil," began to defend it as a "positive good." Blacks, they contended, could not prosper as freedmen, and the South would be abandoned without black labor to work the cotton fields and rice swamps. Protected by benevolent masters from the burdens of sickness, unemployment, and old age, the slaves, they claimed, were better off than industrial workers in the North or in Europe.

Viewing the growing intransigence of the South on slavery as well as the hardening antislavery feeling in the North, politicians resolved to mute the slavery issue in the future. For a time they succeeded. The division of the Louisiana Purchase territory into slave and free soil removed the question of slavery expansion from national politics for twenty-five years. But beginning in 1846, with the acquisition of new territory, the furious political struggle over slavery was to revive. Just as John Quincy Adams had predicted, the Missouri Controversy turned out to be "a mere preamble—a title-page to a great tragic volume."

John Quincy Adams and American Continentalism

For the United States, a fortunate feature of the Louisiana Purchase was that no one knew the exact boundaries. When Robert Livingston, one of the American negotiators, pressed the French minister Talleyrand on this point, he replied: "I can give you no direction; you have made a noble bargain for yourselves, and I suppose you will make the most of it." John Quincy Adams, President Monroe's secretary of state, did just that. In important boundary treaties Adams expanded the nation's frontiers into a continental realm.

Few men have been better equipped to guide American diplomacy than John Quincy Adams. In 1778, at age eleven, he had accompanied his father, John Adams, to France. By the time he was thirty he had served as American minister to the Netherlands and to Prussia. Then, in 1801, Massachusetts elected him to the United States Senate as a Federalist. To the distress of his party, Adams proceeded to side frequently with the rival Jeffersonians. When he voted for the hated Embargo, the state legislature, dominated by the Federalists, evicted the "scoundrel" from his seat. Under President Madison he acted as American minister to Russia and to England, and helped negotiate the Treaty of Ghent. In 1817 Monroe named him secretary of state.

Adams took great pride in his country's military and diplomatic victories during these years. The law of nature had intended "our proper dominion to be the continent of North America." It was our national mission to expand westward to the Pacific and north and south as well.

As secretary of state under Monroe, John Quincy Adams negotiated treaties in seeking to build an "American Continental Empire." This photograph, suggesting his bulldog tenacity and moral commitment, is an interesting daguerreotype of Adams taken when he served in the House of Representatives later in his life. (*Stuart and Sully Portrait, Courtesy, Fogg Art Museum, Harvard University*)

Adams disliked European colonialism, with its commercial monopolies and its pretentious claims to "fragments of territory . . . fifteen hundred miles beyond the sea, worthless and burdensome to their owners. . . ." As secretary of state, Adams deliberately sought to make an "American Continental Empire."

One step toward it was taken in 1817. By a mutual agreement between the United States and Great Britain, both nations signed notes limiting their naval forces on the Great Lakes. This arrangement, known as the Rush-Bagot agreement, was formalized by acting Secretary of State Richard Rush and the British minister Charles Bagot.

The Treaty of 1818 with Britain
But controversy still lingered with Britain over the northwest boundary. The treaty of 1783 had described the boundary line as running from the northwesternmost point of the Lake of the Woods due west to the Mississippi River—an impossible line, since the Mississippi actually arises 150 miles south of the Lake of the Woods. The Louisiana Purchase had compounded the error by creating a northern boundary running all the way to the Rocky Mountains. Britain had repeatedly sought to set the boundary far enough south for Canadian access to the Mississippi.

West of the Louisiana Purchase was land inviting territorial dispute. In 1792, when he discovered the Columbia River, Captain Robert Gray had first claimed the Oregon country for the United States. The explorations of Lewis and Clark fired American interest in the area; John Jacob Astor's company established a fur-trading post there in 1811. The United States, Great Britain, Spain, and Russia each had claims in this region. During the War of 1812 British forces seized Astor's post, which they renamed Fort George. Britain retained this fort until 1818, when Lord Castlereagh, the foreign secretary, ordered it returned to the United States. Castlereagh intended this gesture as looking to a reconciliation between Britain and the United States. Britain, absorbed by events in Europe, dared not risk a further quarrel with the United States. The War of 1812, moreover, had shown how exposed was Canada's position—only military blundering on the part of the United States had saved it. Canada had become a hostage for Anglo-American peace.

Castlereagh next invited the United States to send commissioners to London for the purpose of settling all the differences between the two countries. At these negotiations the American envoys, acting under Adams's instructions, secured important gains for the United States. The Treaty of 1818—which one expert has called the most important treaty in the history of relations between Canada and the United States— granted the republic permanent rights to fish off the coasts of Newfoundland and Labrador. On the northwest boundary the United States refused to budge, and Britain agreed to draw it at 49° north latitude as far as the Rocky Mountains. Adams's stubbornness had saved for the United States a strip of land more valuable than he could have realized: it contains the rich Mesabi iron range of northern Michigan and Minnesota. West of the Rockies, neither side would yield its claim. As a stopgap, both agreed to joint occupation of the Oregon country, a compromise that lasted until the 1840s.

The Treaty of 1819 with Spain   Adams inherited another set of problems with Spain. The Spanish government had never accepted the American claim that west Florida was part of the Louisiana Purchase, nor had the border between Louisiana and Texas ever been determined. Beyond Texas, the western boundary of the Louisiana Purchase remained undefined. Spain still hoped to salvage part of this vast area, and to retain its own claim to the Oregon country.

The United States had tried for years to acquire the strategic area of West Florida, which stood out on the map like a pistol barrel pointing at New Orleans, the vital outlet for the Mississippi River. Spain's grasp on the whole of Florida gradually loosened after the War of 1812. The Napoleonic conflict in Europe and revolutions in Spanish America had exhausted its strength. When President Monroe ordered troops to occupy Amelia Island, Spain in 1817 decided to offer Florida to the United States in return for a favorable boundary west of the Mississippi and a pledge not to recognize the provinces of Spanish America that had revolted.

The two sides were still far apart in negotiations at Washington

William Sidney Mount, *Early American Farmhouse.* (*Courtesy, Metropolitan Museum of Art*)

when General Andrew Jackson took matters into his own hands. Old Hickory had been sent to the Florida frontier with orders to adopt all "necessary measures" to halt Indian raids into the United States. Jackson, interpreting his orders broadly, advanced into Florida in 1818 with 3,000 soldiers, pushed back the Seminole Indians, and seized the towns of St. Marks and Pensacola. For good measure, he tried and executed two British subjects who had been inciting the Indians. Jackson's acts embarrassed the Monroe Administration. Secretary of War John Calhoun wanted Jackson court-martialed, but Adams defended Jackson's conduct. The secretary of state urged that the occupation of the towns continue until Spain should send a force sufficient to pacify the Indians. Monroe agreed, and Spain received an ultimatum: either place a force in Florida adequate to maintain order or cede it to the United States.

These bold strokes got the negotiations moving. After weeks of hard bargaining, the two sides agreed, and Adams and the Spanish minister, Luis de Onis, signed the Adams-Onis treaty of 1819. Spain ceded Florida to the United States. Nothing was said about the recognition of the rebellious Spanish colonies. In return for fixing the Texas boundary at the Sabine River, Adams secured a magnificent transcontinental settlement from Spain, including title to all Spanish territory north of latitude 42° between the Continental Divide and the Pacific Ocean, which would include much of the present Northwest. Adams reckoned that the four nay votes on the treaty in the Senate included two Clay men, one enemy of Jackson, and one suffering from "some maggot in his brain." With this treaty Adams had at last achieved his "Continental Empire" and a place in history as a brilliant secretary of state.

The Monroe Doctrine

A French newspaper derided President Monroe for assuming in the Monroe Doctrine

"the tone of a powerful monarch, whose armies and fleets are ready to march. . . . Mr. Monroe is the temporary President of a Republic situated on the east coast of North America. This republic is bounded on the south by the possessions of the King of Spain, and on the north by those of the King of England. Its independence was only recognized forty years ago; by what right then would the two Americas today be under its immediate sway from Hudson's Bay to Cape Horn?"

The boldest assertion of nationalism in this period came from President James Monroe. His annual message in December 1823 laid down two important principles: that "the American continents, by the free and independent condition which they have assumed and maintain, are henceforth not to be considered as subjects for future colonization by any European power"; and that the United States would consider any attempt by the European powers "to extend their political system to any portion of this hemisphere as dangerous to our peace and safety." In later years these two maxims, known as "non-colonization" and "non-interference," came to be called together the Monroe Doctrine. No other presidential statement, with the possible exception of Washington's Farewell Address warning against "entangling alliances," has won such acceptance from the American people. On the hundredth anniversary of Monroe's message, Mary Baker Eddy, the founder of Christian Science, spoke for millions when she said: "I believe in the Monroe Doctrine, in our Constitution, and in the laws of God."

From the first, Americans had sought refuge in the New World in order to escape the Old. Out of the Revolutionary experience inevitably flowed the belief that the New World should where possible and in its self-interest try to isolate itself from the alliances, the quarrels, and the colonizing schemes of the European powers. Washington gave this idea its classic expression in his Farewell Address, and Jefferson echoed it in his warning against subordinating American affairs to those of Europe. In 1823 Monroe and Secretary of State John Quincy Adams shaped these broad beliefs into an official statement.

Russia and Spain   Adams had for years sought an excuse to forbid further European colonization in the Western Hemisphere. Russia unexpectedly gave him the opportunity. Russian explorers had long before laid claim to the northwest coast of America. By 1812 the Russian-American Company extended its trading operations southward to within only a few miles of San Francisco. Suddenly, in 1821, Tsar Alexander I issued an imperial decree conferring upon this company exclusive trading rights down to 51° north latitude and forbidding all foreign vessels to come near the coast. In July 1823 Adams flatly told the Russian minister at Washington that the United States would assert the principle "that the American continents are no longer subjects for *any* new European colonial establishments." Here was the genesis of the Monroe Doctrine; President Monroe inserted almost these very words into his annual message six months later.

The warning against European interference within the hemisphere attacked a fundamental threat to interests of the United States. Spain's colonies in Central and South America had been struggling for independence for some time. When Spain tried to regain her American provinces by force, full-scale war broke out. For six years, beginning in 1814, the revolutionists, led by Simón Bolívar and José de San Martín, liberated one colony after another. The United States sympathized with these heroic struggles and granted belligerent status to the rebellious colonies, enabling them to buy supplies in this country. But Monroe, and especially Adams, hesitated to recognize the new revolutionary governments until Britain did. The British government twice refused invitations from the Monroe Administration to do this jointly. Finally, the United States decided to act alone, extending formal recognition in 1822 to Mexico, Colombia, Chile, Peru, and the provinces of Río de la Plata, present-day Argentina. Having taken this bold step, the administration was alarmed at the prospect of intervention.

Great Britain shared this concern, for the Spanish-American revolts had opened a whole continent to British trade. When in 1823 rumors of possible intervention by other European powers reached George Canning, the British foreign secretary, he decided to seek the cooperation of the United States in opposing such a scheme. Canning proposed a treaty or exchange of notes between the two countries expressing joint opposition to any attempt to restore Spain's lost colonies by force; he still refused, however, to agree to immediate British recognition of the former colonies.

Monroe almost accepted Canning's offer. Former Presidents Jefferson and Madison both advised acceptance, as did all the Cabinet— except the secretary of state. "It would be more candid as well as more dignified," Adams argued, "to avow our principles explicitly . . . , than to come in as a cock-boat in the wake of the British man-of-war." At this point in 1823 Monroe drafted the famous declaration in his annual message opposing further intervention by the European powers in the Western Hemisphere. At Adams's insistence Monroe inserted a statement claiming that his country had no intention to interfere "in the wars of the European powers in matters relating to themselves." And Adams publicly admitted that it was the power of the British navy that had enabled the United States to throw down its audacious challenge to the rest of Europe.

Americans cheered the President's message. Europeans labeled it "blustering," "haughty," "arrogant." It had little effect on the actions of the continental powers. Russia, a major object of the non-colonization clause, had already decided to limit its territorial claims in North America to the area north of latitude 54° 40′. Late in 1823 Canning, tired of waiting for American agreement on a joint statement, had served an ultimatum on France. During the next twenty years Britain and France both violated the Doctrine with impunity. Not until the late nineteenth century, when the United States had become a major power, did the Old World respect the new hemisphere. Yet Monroe's message had an important future. Against an Old World order founded on a doctrine asserting the absolute rights of sovereigns and empires, Monroe championed a new order founded on the right of peoples to determine their own destiny. Only later, by a series of corollaries, did Monroe's successors turn his Doctrine into an instrument for meddling by the United States in Latin American affairs.

The Election of 1824

From 1796 to 1816 meetings of the congressional members of each party had nominated their own presidential candidates. In 1820, when President Monroe ran unopposed, the Republicans did not even bother with a caucus nomination. By 1824 that party, lacking an organized opposition, had dissolved into a series of warring factions.

The "Old Republicans," of the caucus devoted to states' rights and economy, pushed William H. Crawford of Georgia as their candidate for President. Others attacked the caucus as undemocratic. Crawford is an obscure figure today, but to his contemporaries he was a "plain *giant* of a man." Like many young men of his day, he had turned a successful law practice into a distinguished career. He married a wealthy heiress, spent a few years in the state legislature, and then went to Washington as a senator. Crawford later served as minister to France and secretary of war, and had, since 1816, been secretary of the treasury. He used this last post to pack government offices with his supporters. In 1823, just when his position seemed impregnable, illness struck him. Medical experts bled him twenty-three times within three weeks. Crawford never fully recovered, but his partisans continued to put his name forward.

As an alternative to the congressional caucus, the other candidates accepted nominations from state legislatures and public meetings. Several New England states endorsed John Quincy Adams, Monroe's capable secretary of state. South Carolina had supported John C. Calhoun, but he dropped out when Pennsylvania Republicans failed to

William H. Crawford of Georgia, who might have become President. *(Courtesy, Scribners Archives)*

nominate him. The young Carolinian would instead accept the vice-presidential spot. Besides these candidates were Henry Clay, one of the most dynamic politicians in American history, and Andrew Jackson, among the most charismatic.

Henry Clay and Andrew Jackson   Henry Clay had been charting a course toward the White House for a decade. Born in Virginia, he had migrated to Kentucky, where he became a highly successful criminal lawyer—so successful, according to legend, that no person who hired Clay to defend him was ever hanged. After a stint in the state legislature he went on to Congress, a perfect environment then for a man with his quick mind, engaging personality, and fondness for drinking and gambling. In 1811 his colleagues made him Speaker of the House. After the war Clay became a vigorous advocate of internal improvements, a national bank, and a protective tariff. He hoped that this program, which he called the American System, would win support in every part of the country. This was, for practical purposes, the nation's first campaign platform. Clay had anticipated rising sectional jealousies. "I will be opposed," he wrote before the election, "because I think that the interests of all parts of the Union should be taken care of. . . ."

Clay's rival for the western vote was Andrew Jackson, a latecomer to the race. Jackson's victories over the Creek Indians at Horseshoe Bend and the British at New Orleans had made him a national hero. "I cannot believe that killing 2,500 Englishmen at New Orleans qualifies for the various, difficult and complicated duties of the Chief Magistracy," said Clay. Jackson's arrogant conduct during the Seminole campaign in 1818 only increased his popularity. In spite of brief terms in both houses of Congress, Old Hickory was not associated in the public mind with the grimy politics of Washington; he was a "plain farmer," his backers claimed, fresh from the people. In the uncertain politics of the time, his lack of experience in public affairs probably worked to his advantage. While the other candidates discussed the tariff or internal improvements, the Jackson people, observed John Quincy Adams resentfully, had only to shout "8th of January and the Battle of New Orleans" to win votes.

The Questioned Election of 1824   The Constitution had granted to the legislature of each state the authority to decide on a method for selecting presidential electors, the small group of people who actually vote for the President. By 1824 it had become common for states to choose these electors by popular vote. That November, the popular ballots cast for electors committed to Jackson added to 43 percent of the nationwide total. Electors for Adams, his nearest rival, garnered 31 percent. But none of the candidates had a clear majority in the electoral college; there were 99 votes for Jackson, 84 for Adams, 41 for Crawford, and 37 for Clay. As the Constitution provides, the House of Representatives was required to select the chief executive from among the three men with the largest number of electoral votes. Each state would cast one ballot, determined by majority vote of its delegation.

Everyone now looked to Clay, whose fourth-place finish had eliminated him from the contest. As Speaker he had enormous influence in the House, and the managers and friends of the three candidates besieged him with arguments and deals. Clay carefully considered their words and his own political fortunes before making up his mind. He easily eliminated Crawford; the Georgian was physically unfit to assume the burden of the presidency. Clay was inclined to dismiss Jackson as a "military chieftain" with no moral, intellectual, or other attributes worth the name. And the general was a dangerous rival for the western vote; it was to Clay's future political advantage to exclude him from the contest. This left John Quincy Adams. The two men had quarreled in the past, but Adams was unquestionably qualified for the presidency, and he shared Clay's faith in a strong national government. After consulting with friends, Clay threw all his support behind the secretary of state. By a bare majority, John Quincy Adams was elected President.

At first Jackson took the news of his defeat gracefully. Then, three days after the election, Adams announced his intention to appoint Clay to be secretary of state. The warm and impulsive Clay contrasted to the dour Adams. Working together in Belgium on the treaty to end the War of 1812, Adams had written in his diary: "Just before rising I heard Mr. Clay's company retiring. . . . I had left him . . . at cards. They parted as I was about to rise." But the appointment was made, and the cry of "corrupt bargain" went up at once. "So you see," wrote Jackson bitterly, "the *Judas* of the West has closed the contract and will receive the thirty pieces of silver." Had there been a deal? No evidence, then or later, has clarified the matter. Adams insisted that the Kentuckian was the best man for the job. Politically, the appointment drove the Jacksonians and the Calhoun men into immediate opposition to the newly elected administration. Jackson, heretofore a hesitant candidate, set out for Tennessee in full cry: "The people have been cheated," he charged. "The corruptions and intrigues at Washington [have] defeated the will of the people." The campaign of 1828 was under way before John Quincy Adams had settled into the President's house in 1824.

The Second President Adams

John Quincy Adams, a biographer once remarked, "was not among America's more lovable figures." By his own description, he was reserved, stubborn, and independent. "It is a question," an observer wondered, "whether he ever laughed in his life." A reporter at the Ghent peace conference termed him "a bulldog among spaniels." When he was secretary of state, these qualities served Adams well; once he was President, they quickly became his undoing.

Instead of seeking to overcome his liabilities by building a political machine in the federal bureaucracy and developing a popular program, Adams in the interest of conciliation appointed to his Cabinet political opponents and retained outspoken critics in government offices. Above all, he scorned public opinion. The great object of government, Adams believed, was to improve the condition of mankind. It was the President's duty to give direction to the national government, and the peo-

The House of Representatives, 1821. As provided in the Constitution, the House elected John Quincy Adams President in 1824 after none of the four candidates had received a majority in the electoral college. *(Courtesy, Library of Congress)*

ple's to follow. Even when proposing a popular measure, Adams made no effort to dramatize it. Rather than make a straightforward statement urging Congress to pass a federal bankruptcy law, he recommended "the amelioration in some form or modification of the diversified and often oppressive codes relating to insolvency." In 1828 the Jacksonians would revive a withering popular campaign slogan: "John Quincy Adams who can write and Andrew Jackson who can fight."

Adams had an articulate nationalistic program. Now that the nation's independence had been secured and her borders enlarged, he would strengthen the country internally with a nationally planned and financed system of roads and canals, a national university, a naval academy, astronomical observatories along with expeditions to map the country, both supported by the government, and a department of the interior to regulate the use of natural resources. Adams expected to finance this program by selling public lands. But it was not the right time for a nationalist President, particularly one lacking the political skill to rally support. Westerners wanted free or cheap public land, not sales at high prices for revenue. Southerners increasingly feared that a powerful federal government would interfere with slavery. The Old Republicans accused the President of trying to revive the Federalist policies of his father. "The cub," John Randolph remarked, "is a greater bear than the old one." The Jacksonian press derided Adams's proposals: his reference to astronomical observatories as "light-houses of the skies" became a national joke. Congress rejected every one of the President's recommendations.

At every turn, Adams's integrity and his belief in national authority landed him in trouble. In 1825, for example, he refused to enforce a fraudulent treaty dispossessing the Creek Indians of their tribal lands in Georgia. Governor George Troup of Georgia, anxious to open these rich cotton lands to settlement, sent surveyors into the Indian country anyway. A confrontation between the United States and Georgia threatened. A new treaty averted a clash: the Creeks agreed to cede all their lands and move west. Adams's stand had been honorable, the more so in being unpopular. Southerners condemned his challenge to state authority; westerners objected to it for defending Indians.

The failure of Adams's domestic program had profound consequences for the country. A vast system of roads and canals, coming at a time when the forces of sectionalism were gaining strength, might have tied the nation together and in such manner as to resist the later disintegration of the Union. Instead, as Adams predicted, "the clanking chain of the slave" was riveted "into perpetuity," and "the invaluable inheritance of the public lands" was wasted "in boundless bribery to the West."

Bolívar, who won independence for much of South America from Spain, wrote,

"A state too extensive in itself . . . ultimately falls into decay. Its free government is transformed into a tyranny; it . . . finally degenerates into despotism."

The Panama Congress   Adams's presidency was never to reward with success the skills and brilliance he brought to it. His chief effort in foreign policy went no farther than his domestic programs.

In 1824, Simón Bolívar, the "Liberator" of Spanish America, proposed a conference to be held in Panama. He hoped to bind the former Spanish colonies into a confederation to protect the hemisphere against Europe's Quadruple Alliance. Mexico and Colombia, rebuffed in earlier efforts to obtain individual treaties of alliance with the United States, added the republic of the North to the list of participants. All hoped to bring the United States into a hemispheric alliance that would make the Monroe Doctrine Pan-American. Their invitations reached Washington early in 1825, just as John Quincy Adams was entering the White House.

Secretary of State Henry Clay welcomed the idea of an inter-American conference. He had ardently supported the cause of Latin American independence. Clay envisioned a cooperative system of republics, led by the United States, standing against the despotism of the Old World. Adams himself, as Monroe's secretary of state, had rejected all proposals for collective security with the Latin American republics. At Clay's urging, however, he asked Congress to confirm the appointment of two delegates to the Panama meeting. It was the time, he decided, to extend "the most cordial feelings of fraternal friendship" to our sister republics. Adams hoped to advance throughout the hemisphere fundamental principles of commercial reciprocity, neutral rights, freedom of the seas, and resistance to European colonization.

The President's request met unexpected opposition in Congress. Led by Vice President Calhoun and supporters of Andrew Jackson, the faction within the Republican Party that was to call itself the Democrats attacked the administration. It accused Adams and Clay of seeking to fasten the United States to a hemispheric alliance. Southerners had a further objection to the Panama meeting. Delegates from Haiti were expected, and the question might arise of recognizing the black republic, whose slaves under the leadership of Toussaint L'Ouverture had won their indepedence from France and their colonial masters. Haiti was the second republic in the western hemisphere, founded in 1804. Recognition warned a Georgia senator, would "strengthen and invigorate" the determination of black revolutionaries, whose hands still reeked "in the blood" of their murdered masters, "to spread the doctrines of insurrection" to the United States.

Adams defended his proposal. Times and circumstances, he argued, had changed since Washington's day; the United States had trebled its territory, population, and wealth and must act with a breadth of vision befitting a great nation, said this devoted nationalist. After months of debate and delay, Congress finally approved the President's choice of delegates and appropriated funds for the mission. Adams had scored a major triumph—the only one of his presidency.

But the triumph was empty. One of the delegates from the United States died on his way to the conference; the other arrived too late. The meeting itself was a fiasco. Only four Latin American nations sent representatives. They signed a treaty of mutual defense and alliance, and quickly adjourned from fever-ridden Panama City, planning to meet again in Mexico early in 1827. By that time Bolívar had lost interest in the idea of a hemispheric confederation, and the conference never reconvened.

At home, the issue of Haiti quickened the sectional controversy that had flared in the debates over the Missouri Compromise. Southerners once again envisioned the federal government as moving against their "peculiar institution." Adams's proposal gave his political enemies their first opportunity to attack the President and his secretary of state. Once again John Quincy Adams was ahead of his time; the American people in 1826 were looking west, not south. Not for another fifty years would the United States take an interest in the concept of Pan-Americanism.

His administration a failure in both domestic and foreign affairs, Adams gave up all hope of reelection. His subsequent career was notable of an American President. In 1830 he was elected to the House of Representatives. "No election or appointment conferred upon me ever gave me so much pleasure," said Congressman Adams. A spokesman for the antislavery forces and a model of integrity, he served until his death in 1848 at the age of eighty-one.

Andrew Jackson and the Election of 1828

A national hero since the Battle of New Orleans in 1815, Andrew Jackson would put his stamp on American politics and give his name to an age. Jackson had been born in 1767 in the Waxhaws, a wooded frontier area on the border between North and South Carolina. During the Revolution he lost both brothers and his widowed mother. For a time he seemed destined to be "the most roaring, rollicking, game-cocking, horse-racing, card-playing, mischievous fellow" in the neigh-

In 1804 Jackson repeatedly published a cruel advertisement for the return of a runaway slave:

FIFTY DOLLARS REWARD

Eloped from the subscriber, living near Nashville, on the 25th of June last, a Mulatto Man Slave, about thirty years old, six feet and an inch high, stout made and active, talks sensible, stops in his walk, and have a remarkable large foot. . . . The above reward will be given any person that will take him, and deliver him to me, or secure him to jail, so that I can get him. If taken out of the state, the above reward, and all reasonable expenses paid—and ten dollars extra, for every hundred lashes any person will give him, to the amount of three hundred.

ANDREW JACKSON
Near Nashville
State of Tennessee

borhood. Then, fired with ambition, he began reading law. In 1788, after completing his studies, he moved to Tennessee to take a position of public prosecutor.

This developing country was the ideal place for an eager young attorney. Jackson speculated avidly in land, slaves, and horses. As a public prosecutor, he usually sided with the creditors, executing numerous writs against debtors. In 1796 he was elected to Congress from Tennessee. Albert Gallatin would remember him as "a tall, lanky, uncouth-looking personage . . . [hair] down his back tied with an eel skin . . . manners of a rough backwoodsman." After three years in Washington he returned to Tennessee, where he served as a superior court judge, once again siding with the land barons. Near Nashville he acquired a fine plantation, the Hermitage, and many slaves. Although success had polished his rough edges, Jackson never lost his "roaring, rollicking" character; he was wounded three times in duels.

When in 1814 the theater of war with the British shifted south, a desperate national government called on this victor against the Creeks to save New Orleans. His famous victory over "the conquerors of Europe" electrified the country. He was the nation's savior, its greatest hero since George Washington. His rough handling of the Florida Indians and their British allies in 1818 was wildly popular on the frontier.

Jackson lost heavily in the Panic of 1819. In its wake a group of his wealthy friends, alarmed by the growing demand for debtor relief in Tennessee, decided to use Jackson's immense popularity to protect their assets. They began touting him as the "people's candidate" for President—this man who had recently brought suit against 129 people who owed him money. His candidacy caught fire. For what people believed about Jackson was perhaps more important than the facts.

Though Jackson was a large landowner and by some standards an aristocrat, he did have perhaps more democratic sentiments than any previous President. He had a westerner's inherent distrust of entrenched status and dictatorial government. In his youth he had been of fairly moderate means. And so if Jackson did not come to the presidency with any clearly articulated beliefs, he did have styles and tastes that accorded with popular policies other politicians devised.

The Second Party System   In the 1820's a second two-party system was forming, in which each of the parties would appeal more directly for wide popular support than had the old Federalists and Republicans. They would in time set up extensive local organizations for winning an electorate and holding its loyalty. The new party system rested in part on legal changes that broadened the popular base of government: the gradual removal of qualifications for voting, and the trend among the states toward popular election of public officials and presidential electors in place of the earlier practice of leaving the choice to state legislatures. The new party system was a way of capturing this larger voting public.

In choosing John Quincy Adams over Jackson in 1824, the House of Representatives had unwittingly ushered in the new era of partisan politics. In the next four years the followers of Adams and Clay, working for federal policies that would actively promote the nation's economy, began to call themselves National Republicans; their opponents went by the name Democratic Republicans, soon shortened to Democrats. Because the House had selected Adams over General Jackson—recipient of the greater number of popular and electoral votes—under circumstances that suggested to many people the existence of a "corrupt bargain," Jackson became an even stronger political figure than before. He captured the imagination of the public and infused new glamour into national politics.

After his defeat, Jackson allied with Senator Martin Van Buren of New York, a highly skilled political manager, to create the new Democratic Party. At its core were the original Jackson men, those who had supported him in 1824. They were joined after the election by the followers of John C. Calhoun, whose own path to the presidency the alliance between Adams and Clay had blocked. Between 1826 and 1828, Van Buren brought into the party the southern Republicans who had formerly supported Crawford. United in their opposition to the policies of Adams and Clay that gave the federal government a larger role in organizing the economy, the new coalition worked in Congress to block the administration's programs.

Election of 1828

The election of 1828 was a landmark in American politics. For the first time in nearly twenty years two vigorous parties contested for the presidency. Responding to this stimulus, the voters turned out in unprecedented numbers to elect Andrew Jackson President of the United States.

Jackson had begun by building the necessary organization to boost him into the presidency. Most states had adopted the system, still in use today, that gives all the state's electoral votes to the presidential candidate who wins the state's popular vote. Since winning a majority of the popular vote brought so rich a reward, parties wanted a state machinery that could mobilize voters throughout the state. Van Buren thoroughly organized the Democratic Party, establishing central committees in Washington and Nashville. These committees worked closely with influential state leaders, who in turn organized Hickory Clubs at the local level. A string of newspapers favorable to Old Hickory appeared across the country. Jackson remained at home in Tennessee, posing as the innocent victim of a "corrupt bargain." Yet he supervised every detail of the campaign. In order to hold together his fragile coalition, he avoided taking a stand on issues. When asked for his position on the tariff, Jackson replied ambiguously that he favored a "middle and just course." When Van Buren quoted Jackson's comment on the tariff at a New York rally, one man in the audience cheered the remark and then asked his neighbor: "On which side of the tariff question was it?" Meantime, Adams steadfastly refused to electioneer in his own behalf. Too late, his friends tried to erect an organization similar to that of the Democrats.

In 1828, as in 1824, more was made of personalities than of issues. The campaign itself was unbelievably dirty. No charge was too base. Jackson was portrayed as a frontier ruffian, a gambler, the son of "a

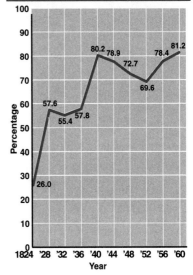

COMMON PROSTITUTE." A "coffin hand-bill" charged the general with the cold-blooded murder of six militiamen during the Creek Campaign of 1814. A rhymester wrote:

> All six militia men were shot;
> And O! it seems to me
> A dreadful deed—a bloody act
> of needless cruelty.

Jacksonians replied that the six were deserters who had been executed after a proper court-martial. Jackson's wife Rachel was not spared. The two had met while Rachel was separated from her first husband. In 1791, believing that her husband had obtained a divorce, she married Jackson. Not until some time later did the couple learn that the divorce had not become final. The earlier marriage was formally dissolved in September 1793, after which Rachel and Andrew recited their wedding vows a second time. Rumors of this technical adultery circulated for years. But when his beloved Rachel, sick and shamed by

The Verdict of the People, by George Caleb Bingham. Americans of the 1830s widely linked Andrew Jackson with the rise of the common man, though the number of elective offices had been increasing for decades. *(Courtesy, Collection of the Boatmen's National Bank of St. Louis)*

the "wormwood and gall" of ugly publicity, died suddenly in December 1828, Jackson blamed his political opponents. "May God Almighty forgive her murderers," he cried at her funeral, "as I know she forgave them. I never can." And he never did.

Jacksonians countered with some mudslinging of their own. It was said that President Adams, while minister to Russia, had procured an American girl for Tsar Alexander I. Adams's wife was reported to have had premarital relations with her husband. Stories of the president's "aristocratic" receptions at the White House and his use of public funds to buy "gambling devices" (actually a chess set and a billiard table) circulated widely.

Jackson's victory in November 1828 was a triumph both for the Old Hero and for the Democrats' fresh style of political appeal. Over three times as many voters turned out as in 1824. The general received fifty-six percent of the popular vote, a margin unequaled in any other presidential election during the nineteenth century. Jackson the southwesterner, to all appearances a reflection of the democratic way of the West and a spokesman for inland interests however ill-defined, swept the South and West. Adams carried his native New England along with Delaware and New Jersey, and shared with his rival New York and Maryland, which had not instituted the system of awarding the state's entire electoral vote to the popular winner. Exuberant Jacksonians hailed the election results as a revolution, a triumph of "democracy" over "aristocracy." The following January, after burying his wife, a broken-hearted Andrew Jackson set out for Washington.

The Spoils System   Arriving in Washington, Jackson found the government offices filled with bureaucrats, many of them supporters of the men who had slandered his beloved Rachel. As an astute politician, Jackson recognized the value of rewarding his partisans with government jobs. He agreed with his New York lieutenant, William Marcy, that "to the victors belong the spoils." And Jackson firmly believed that no one had "any more intrinsic right to official station than another." Men who held office too long were "apt to acquire a habit of looking with indifference upon the public interests, and of tolerating conduct from which an unpracticed man would revolt." In his first annual message, Jackson therefore recommended that appointments be limited to four years. Congress balked, but Jackson "rotated" officeholders anyway, insisting: "The duties of all public officers are, or at least admit of being made, so plain and simple that men of intelligence may readily qualify themselves for their performance." In eight years Jackson replaced about twenty percent of the government's employees, sometimes with due cause. Jefferson had removed roughly the same proportion. But it was the Jacksonians who fixed firmly upon American politics the spoils system and rotation in office as expressions of a system of parties shaped to capture and represent popular wishes. For example, when the Jacksonian Democrats lost to a new party, the Whigs, in the election of 1840, Democrats lost their government jobs, which were filled by members of the new party. The process would become an American political tradition through most of the nineteenth century.

The Rise of the Common Man?

For years many history books pictured Jackson as the champion of frontier democracy, battling the forces of privilege and corruption. During his presidency the common man won the right to vote and took politics out of the hands of the elite. Socially and economically, too, the Jacksonian era brought greater equality. With Jackson's election, according to one historian, "a new day dawned in American history. The democratic philosophy of Thomas Jefferson became a reality."

Recent studies have substantially modified this view. Historians now realize that the political power of the common man had been increasing for decades. Even in colonial times, the franchise had been quite open in some places. The Revolutionary ideology and the fierce political contests of the Jeffersonian era brought still greater participation in politics. The new western states adopted constitutions that gave the vote to all adult white males and made most public offices elective. Many of the older states, concerned about the loss of population to the West, followed their example. By Jackson's time only two states, Delaware and South Carolina, still left to their legislatures the selection of presidential electors. The Jacksonians shrewdly developed techniques to win this broader electorate. But the most notable political innovation of the Jackson period, the national convention, initially a democratic way of capturing popular sentiment, was invented not by Democrats but by the Anti-Masonic Party in 1831. The Anti-Masons were a short-lived party opposing the fraternal order of Freemasonry, which had aroused suspicion with its secrets and its tight loyalties.

Foreign visitors such as the French writer Alexis de Tocqueville and the English writers Frances Trollope and Charles Dickens wrote with amazement of America's egalitarian social conditions. Recent historians have thought differently. Two million blacks were held as slaves. For most women, free blacks, Irish-Catholic immigrants, and many others, social and economic equality did not exist. Such important economic developments as the rise of the factory system and the transportation revolution were not affected much by Jackson's presidency. Many studies of social mobility indicate an increasingly less egalitarian society, urban elites growing in wealth while industrialism and mass immigration created new lower classes.

And yet people at the time believed that Jackson's eminence was linked to the "rise of the common man." Millions of Americans—for diverse and often conflicting reasons—could readily identify with him. It was a "Go Ahead" era, remarked one observer; "the whole continent presents a scene of *scrambling* and roars with greedy hurry." And some saw in Jackson the egalitarian spirit of the nation; he was a child of the frontier, self-made, independent, and democratic. They gloried in his success and hoped to imitate it. As a big loser in the Panic of 1819, this pursuer of his own debtors appealed to hard-pressed debtors in the West and South. His opposition to the older entrenched banking system got him support from businessmen who wanted banks that would extend credit more freely. Others, looking back romantically to what they thought of as a simpler agrarian society, perceived Jackson as a simple and noble embodiment of that earlier time.

Parties and the Republic

In their opposition to political parties, what the first republicans had feared were not the nationwide institutions that today go by the name. In the eighteenth century, these did not exist, though the Federalists and the Jeffersonian Republicans foreshadowed them. "Party," in the thinking of early Americans, referred to groups of politicians in pursuit of some narrow objective. The parties that took form in the 1820s under the superintendence of such political artisans as Martin Van Buren were essentially new. Both in sustaining eighteenth-century republicanism and departing from it, that new party system was equivalent to what was also happening in economics, industry, and civic life.

The contribution that the new structured parties made to the republican principles of an earlier time is simply stated. It drew to the polls a larger percentage of the population than had before voted. Neither the possession nor the exercise of the vote had been so important to traditional republicans as has sometimes been thought. The practice of farming or a trade, the raising of a family, perhaps even the public expression of an opinion: these were more solid expressions of republican civic responsibility than the mere casting of a ballot. But voting is at least the simplest gesture of citizenship. To that extent the new party politics, which presented issues to voters, mobilized them, and got them to the polls, extending the implications of the republic of 1776.

The parties emergent during the 1820s, however, also had a place in the alteration of the old republican concept of personal and civic virtue. They signified what in reality had been the case from the beginning: that American politics were to be not a stately, ritualistic maintainance of a status quo but a ceaseless forging and winning of reformist programs. In this they resembled the industrial enterprises intended to transform the physical world, and the reform movements, soon to appear in abundance, that aimed to transform social relations and, in some cases, the human soul.

Suggested Readings

On politics, see Mary M. W. Hargreaves, *The Presidency of John Quincy Adams* (1985) and Ralph Ketcham, *Presidents Above Party: The First American Presidency, 1789–1829* (1984). On the fateful beginnings of slavery as a political issue see Randolph B. Campbell, *An Empire for Slavery: The Peculiar Institution in Texas, 1821–1825* (1989) and Robert McColley, *Slavery and Jeffersonian Virginia* (1964).

On the changing history of the American West see Richard White, *"It's Your Misfortune and None of My Own": A History of the American West* (1991), Patricia Nelson Limerick, *The Legacy of Conquest: The Unbroken Past of the American West* (1987), Julie R. Jeffrey, *Frontier Women: The Trans-Mississippi West, 1840–1880* (1979), Annette Kolodny's *The Land Before Her: Fantasy and Experience on the American Frontiers* (1984), and June Nmias, *White Captives: Gender and Ethnicity on the American Frontier* (1993). See also *The History of the Westward Movement* (1978) by Frederick W. Merk and Ray Allen Billington's *Westward Expansion* (rev. 1974). See also Malcolm J.

Rohrbough, *The Land Office Business: The Settlement and Administration of American Public Lands, 1789–1837* (1968) and John Mack Faragher, *Sugar Creek: Life on the Illinois Prairie* (1986).

On population shifts, there are Richard H. Easterlin, *Population, Labor Force, and Long Swings in Economic Growth* (1968) and Robert Riegal and R. G. Athearn, *America Moves West* (1964).

On other issues of this period see Ernest R. May, *The Making of the Monroe Doctrine* (1975), Harry Ammon, *James Monroe: The Quest for National Identity* (1971), George Dangerfield, *The Awakening of American Nationalism* (1965), Glover Moore, *The Missouri Compromise* (1953), Richard Wade, *The Urban Frontier* (1964), Stuart Blumin, *The Emergence of the Middle Class: Social Experience in the American City* (1989), and David Roediger, *The Wages of Whiteness: Race and the Making of the American Working Class* (1991).

North vs. South: A Clash of Cultures?

Edward Pessen

Several historians have recently argued that the Old South, though influenced by modern capitalism, belonged (as do early modern India and Saudi Arabia, among others) to the category of "premodern" societies that have been the economic and political dependencies of the dynamic industrial world that exploits them. The antebellum South's banking, commercial, and credit institutions did not in this view manifest the section's own capitalistic development so much as they served to facilitate the South's exploitation by the "capitalistic world market." . . .

[But] capitalism is not a rigid system governed by uniform economic practices, let alone inflexible definitions. The economy of the antebellum United States, like capitalistic economies in Victorian England and other nations, was composed of diverse elements, each playing a part in a geographical and functional division of labor within the larger society. Southern planters had the attitudes and goals and were guided by the classic practices of capitalistic businessmen. The antiurbanism and antimaterialism that [Eugene D.] Genovese has attributed to the great planters is unconvincing because they are thinly documented and contradicted by much other evidence. Some people, including planters themselves, may have likened the planter class to a seigneurial aristocracy. Unlike the lords of the textbook manor, however, Southern planters depended heavily on outside trade, participated enthusiastically in a money economy, and sought continuously to expand their operations and their capital. . . .

The Southern economy did differ in important respects from the Northern, developing special interests of its own. Yet, far from being in any sense members of a colony or dependency of the North, the Southern upper classes enjoyed close ties with the Northern capitalists who were, in a sense, their business partners. The South was an integral component of a wealthy and dynamic national economy, no part of which conformed perfectly to a textbook definition of pure capitalism. In part because of the central place in that economy of its great export crop, cotton, the South from the 1820s to the 1860s exerted a degree of influence over the nation's domestic and foreign policies that was barely equalled by the antebellum North. The South's political system of republicanism and limited democracy, like its hierarchical social structure, conformed closely to the prevailing arrangements in the North, as they also did to the classic features of a capitalistic order.

The antebellum North and South were far more alike than the conventional scholarly wisdom has led us to believe. Beguiled by the charming version of Northern society and politics composed by Tocqueville, the young Marx, and other influential antebellum commentators, historians have until recently believed that the Northern social structure was far more egalitarian and offered far greater opportunity for upward social movement than did its Southern counterpart and that white men of humble position had far more power in the Old North than they did in the Old South. In disclosing that the reality of the antebellum North fell far short of the egalitarian ideal, modern studies of social structure sharply narrow the gulf between the antebellum North and South. Without being replicas of one another, both sections were relatively rich, powerful, aggressive, and assertive communities, socially stratified and governed by equally—and disconcertingly—oligarchic internal arrangements. That they were drawn into the most terrible of all American wars may have been due, as is often the case when great powers fight, as much to their similarities as to their differences. The war owed more, I believe, to the inevitably opposed but similarly selfish interests—or perceived interests—of North and South than to differences in their cultures and institutions.

Late in the Civil War, William King of Cobb County, Georgia, reported that invading Union officers had told him, "We are one people, [with] the same language, habits, and religion, and ought to be one people." The officers might have added that on the spiritual plane Southerners shared with Northerners many ideals and aspirations and had contributed heavily to those historical experiences the memory and symbols of which tie a people together as a nation. For all of their distinctiveness, the Old South and North were complementary elements in an American society that was everywhere primarily rural, capitalistic, materialistic, and socially stratified, racially, ethnically, and religiously heterogeneous, and stridently chauvinistic and expansionist—a society whose practice fell far short of, when it was not totally in conflict with, its lofty theory.

Reprinted by permission from "How Different from Each Other Were the Antebellum North and South?" *American Historical Review,* 86 (December 1980).

The South was not just another society that tolerated slavery as an expression of its traditions. It was a slave society. The distinctive features of southern culture were the products of slavery—more precisely, of the relationship between master and slave. The slaveholders were very much a breed apart, with contradictory qualities rooted in the condition of being outright owners of human flesh. They had their virtues, which even some of their harshest critics admired: graciousness, generosity, tolerance of human foibles, physical courage, a commitment to personal and family honor. These were the proud virtues of a people who, as masters, could afford and were expected to show a certain confident kindness toward others, and as masters shunned any conduct suggestive of weakness or smallness. And the slaveholders had their vices, which their warmest admirers conceded: hot tempers, a frightening penchant for violence, an inability to allow contradiction on any matter that touched their honor, and a fearful habit of defining their honor to include everything and anything. These were the proud vices of masters. If slaveholders despised the virtues northern culture admired and practiced, it was precisely because they were slaveholders. The diligent money-making of the North seemed to them mean, beneath the dignity of masters.

Most southern whites owned no slaves. The South was nonetheless a slave society. A much smaller percentage of citizens of the United States today owns capital; yet few if any would argue that the United States is therefore not capitalist. Capitalism, like slavery and all other systems in which one class dominates another, defines itself by its ruling classes.

One reason why people who did not own slaves supported the slave owners' regime was their fear of what the black population might do if it were free. But this fear has been exaggerated. That small farmers in the plantation areas were related to slaveholders by blood was additional reason for their good will toward the slave system. Then, too, they suffered no direct exploitation by the slaveholders, and only the most knowledgeable could glimpse the ways in which slavery as a whole oppressed them. Their small surpluses of food or cotton had to be sold to the wealthy planters or marketed through them: the planters were able to offer friendship and services. These and other relationships strengthened the ties between planters and other whites and lessened the antagonisms. Probably, too, people who did not own slaves shared a little of the pride of the planters. If they were not masters, they could at least see themselves as participating in the masters' domination of the slaves.

Southern society was a system of fixed status, while the North expected individuals to make their own lives. Certainly slavery fixed the status of black southerners, and to a lesser extent the status of whites. But the northern economy was establishing itself as another system of domination, collecting power not in institutions of slavery but in institutions of wealth. Workers in the United States in the nineteenth century could speak of what it was to be victims of this domination. So could the poor today in regions of the world where capitalism based in this country has established itself. So could people all over the globe who are shut out from the power and wealth of the more affluent classes. The abolition of southern slavery was but a beginning to the work of bringing about a genuinely just and democratic distribution of power.

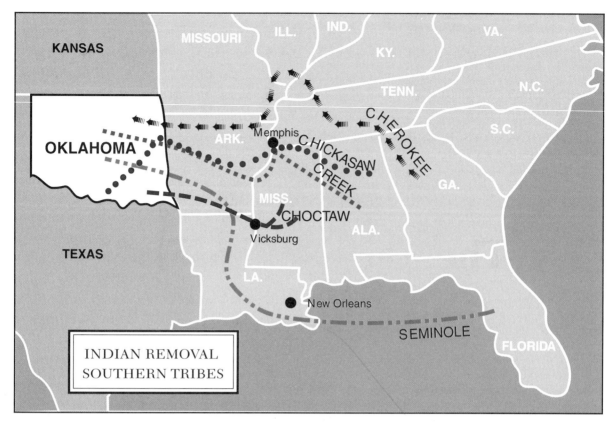

The Trail of Tears, by Robert Lindneux. Jackson disregarded the Supreme Court ruling that the Cherokees of Georgia had a right to their land. Many perished when they moved west on "the trail of tears." (*Courtesy, Woolaroc Museum*)

10

The Jacksonian Era
1828–1840

THE TRAIL OF TEARS

Early in 1837 about six hundred Cherokee Indians were removed by United States government policy from their home in the southeastern United States to land in present-day Oklahoma under the Treaty of New Echota (1836). Along with them on their journey through Kentucky, Illinois, Missouri, and Arkansas went oxen, horses, and slaves. Had this been the general story of the Cherokee migration, its path would not be known today as the Trail of Tears. But it is not the whole story.

The second wave of Indians had a wretched time of it. Traveling much of the way by water, they were subject to a range of sicknesses. The mass of the Cherokee population in the East, preferring to remain in old Cherokee country, was meanwhile victimized by a policy so harsh that even some of the soldiers assigned to carrying it out were unhappy at their task. General Winfield Scott, whose historical misfortune it is to have been associated with the removal itself, showed in various kindnesses to his charges his own discomfort at their plight.

Soldiers, some of them acting with a brutality that Scott had warned them against, seized some thirteen thousand Indians, plucking families from their cabins, and put them in stockades where for months they endured overcrowding, illness, and the psychological pains of uprooting. Then in separate groups army escorts accompanied them westward in 1838. They had scarcely

HISTORICAL EVENTS

1828
Tariff of 1828 • Calhoun writes *Exposition and Protest*

1829
Senator Foote proposes limiting sale of public lands

1830
Jackson vetoes bill for interstate turnpike • Indian Removal Act

1831
Cherokee Nation v. Georgia • first nationwide presidential nominating convention

1832
Tariff of 1832 • Bad Axe Massacre • *Worcester v. Georgia* • Charter of the Second Bank of the United States • Jackson reelected

1833
Force Bill • Compromise Tariff

1836
Specie Circular • government deposits in state banks • Martin Van Buren elected President

continued

One survivor remembered of "The Trail of Tears":

"One each day, and all are gone. Looks like maybe all be dead before we get to new Indian country, but always we keep marching on. Women cry and make sad wails. Children cry, and many men cry, and all look sad when friends die, but they say nothing and just put heads down and keep on go toward west. . . . She [his mother] speak no more; we bury her and go on."

One spokesman argued in the Indians' behalf:

"Do the obligations of justice change with the color of the skin? As the tide of our population has rolled on, we have added purchase to purchase [of Indian lands]. The confiding Indian listened to our professions of friendship: we called him brother, and he believed us. Millions after millions he has yielded to our importunity, until we have acquired more than can be cultivated in centuries—and yet we crave more. We have crowded the tribes upon a few miserable acres on our southern frontier; it is all that is left to them of their once boundless forests: and still, like the horse-leech, our cupidity cries, 'give! give!' "

enough supplies to carry them through. Sickness followed the migrants during a brutally cold winter. Of all the Cherokee who were subject to removal, about three to four thousand died in stockades or on the trail.

How did such inequalities in conditions come to the Cherokee people? The Cherokee had originally lived in a roughly egalitarian society. Law and coercion in a European sense were entirely absent, and women were not excluded from positions of leadership, including war councils. The Cherokee lived for war. A white account reports that when the English in 1730 urged them to make peace with the Tuscarora, the Cherokee replied that then they would merely have to make war on someone else. Frontiersmen found the Cherokee prone to savagery and bloodlust; the Indians found the frontiersmen insatiably land-hungry. Both judgments got it right.

The new American government faced genuine dilemmas after winning independence. Committed to a respect for the individual and communal rights of everyone except slaves, and recognizing that frontiersmen were no better for the welfare of Indians than Indians had been for the safety of the white frontier, the government reasoned that removal to a land of their own might be good for the tribes. Besides, whites kept encroaching on Cherokee and other Indian lands, and the government had to recognize that for practical purposes the old tribal territories were shrinking. Americans of that age believed that land and other resources should be so worked as to support as many people as possible. Southern states, moreover, were not eager to accept Indians as citizens. From Jefferson's time onward the government had been urging the Indian tribes to sell their lands and migrate westward.

In a string of dealings, Washington won land cessions from the Cherokee Nation, typically in exchange for relief from debts. Thereafter the government urged the Cherokee and other Indians to move west. At the same time it was contradictorily advocating that they adopt in their present locations the ways of white agriculture and industry. Missionaries would set up schools for young people of both genders, teaching them farming and industrial techniques. The Cherokee Nation made major progress against illiteracy, aided by the Indian alphabet devised by the famous Sequoyah.

In 1829 Andrew Jackson, who had commanded Cherokee troops during the War of 1812 but was known to be no friend to their claims, became President. At the end of the year Georgia passed a series of laws seizing part of Cherokee territory. Much of American public sentiment was now recoiling from the policy of Jackson and Georgia. In *Worcester v. Georgia*, the Supreme Court in 1832 in effect found Georgia to be illegally superseding federal jurisdiction over the Cherokee. The case seemed to be a victory for the Nation, but President Jackson's unwillingness to force Georgia to cease interfering with Cherokee affairs made it irrelevant. A well-known but unverifiable story is that the President remarked, "John Marshall has made his decision. Now let him enforce it."

In the next few years, unanimity within the Nation shattered. What happened is that the transformation from a simple tribal existence to a more energetic pursuit of farming, the crafts, and lawmaking brought with it the visions, the arguments, and the divisions of modern society. In its past already distant by the 1830s, the tribe had relied on a single activity, that of making war. Now the Cherokee had a class structure based in wealth and indirectly in race: mixed bloods, whose white ancestors had passed on their property and education, had the best opportunities. A number of prosperous mixed bloods were declaring their support of emigration. The simplest explanation is that the Indian supporters of removal believed it was in the interest of all Cherokee to submit to inevitability and get the best possible deal from the government. One point is certain: Whatever their larger motives, the advocates of removal brought about a fraudulent arrangement. Presenting themselves—without tribal wish or authorization—as the representatives of the Cherokee Nation, they effected with the federal government the agreement for removal.

Sequoyah (1770?–1843) devised the Cherokee written alphabet in the early nineteenth century.
(Courtesy, Library of Congress)

Removal of Indians

The Indian Removal Act (1830)

For some time, white Americans had been considering the idea of removing eastern Indians to the West. President Thomas Jefferson had supported such a scheme, and the establishment of an "Indian country" beyond the Mississippi River was one reason for the Louisiana Purchase of 1803. While greed for land was a primary consideration, "removal" was not merely a malicious assault on Indian land titles. Many people, including President Andrew Jackson himself, believed that the removal policy was the only way of saving Indians from extermination. As long as they remained on land coveted by white settlers, their lives were in danger, and as long as they even lived in relatively close proximity to white communities, they would be ravaged by disease, alcoholism, and poverty. Removal would insulate them from the worst features of white civilization. An assimilationist rhetoric also supported the idea of removal. Protestant missionary groups interested in proselytizing and "civilizing" the Indians believed that if the Indians were living in relatively secure places, the opportunities to teach them the virtues of Christianity, agriculture, and the ~~nuclear~~ family life would improve greatly. So while white settlers were clamoring for removal in order to

General Scott threatened:

"The full moon of May is already on the wane, and before another has passed away, every Cherokee man, woman, and child must be in motion to join their brethren in the far west. . . . My troops already occupy many positions in the country that you are to abandon; thousands and thousands are approaching from every quarter, to render resistance and escape alike hopeless. Will you, then, by resistance, compel us to resort to arms? God forbid! Or will you, by flight, seek to hide yourselves in mountains and forests, and thus oblige us to hunt you down? I am an old warrior, and have been present at many a scene of slaughter; but spare me, I beseech you, the horror of witnessing the destruction of the Cherokees."

free up valuable land for settlement, Protestant churches were supporting those demands for humane reasons. Still other whites opposed removal altogether.

Since Jefferson's time the government had been forcing the Indian tribes to sell their lands and migrate westward. In 1830 the President urged Congress to set apart "an ample district west of the Mississippi" for their permanent use. Here the "aborigines" might learn "the arts of civilization" and form "an interesting commonwealth, destined to perpetuate the race and to attest the humanity and justice of this government." Senators such as Theodore Frelinghuysen of New Jersey courageously defended the right that Indians possessed by "immemorial possession, as the original tenants of the soil," but the Indian Removal Act passed anyway. The Act provided for the relocation of most tribes in the eastern United States to reservations west of the Mississippi River. Some tribes, particularly the remnants of the Iroquois Confederacy, were allowed to remain on reservations in the East. But the rest of the Indians were not so fortunate. In the following years many Indian nations, recognizing the futility of resistance, signed over their lands and moved west, some of them prodded by the federal army.

Resistance and Resignation

Although disunited and demoralized by defeat, some Indians did not passively acquiesce in the march westward. In Illinois portions of the Sauk and Fox tribes, led by Chief Black Hawk, refused to leave their rich ancestral lands. Black Hawk initially hoped that, if his people remained peaceful, they would be permitted to keep their farming communities and live alongside the incoming whites. But land hunger on the part of whites and incessant military pressure finally forced Black Hawk into war. It was a one-sided fight. In the final battle of the Black Hawk War, the Bad Axe Massacre of 1832, regular troops and militiamen killed between 400 and 500 Indian men, women, and children. In the South, the Seminole War that lasted from 1835 to 1838 was even bloodier. Many Seminole tribesmen, led by Chief Osceola, refused to leave Florida. Accompanied by runaway blacks, they retreated into the swamps. Jackson sent troops, but the Indians conducted a skillful guerrilla war in the impenetrable Everglades. It took several years and $14 million even partially to subdue Osceola's warriors.

Other Trails of Tears

The Choctaws, who like the Chickasaws and the Cherokees were a settled people skilled in agriculture, were forced out of Mississippi in the dead of winter, "thinly clad and without moccasins." In 1838 the government forcibly removed the Potawatomis from Indiana. They began the trek west "under a blazing noonday sun, amidst clouds of dust, marching in a line, surrounded by soldiers who were hurrying their steps. Next came the baggage wagons, in which numerous invalids, children, and women, too weak to walk, were crammed." Dozens died along this "Trail of Death." The resettlement of these farming Indians west of the Mississippi River created bitter resentment among the Plains tribes who hunted there. The government was soon forced to send troops to the West to separate the warring peoples.

Andrew Jackson's Inaugural

In the winter of 1828–29 Washington, D.C., was a cheerless place. The weather was dreadful: "snow storm after snow storm—the river frozen up, and the poor suffering the extremity of cold and hunger," wrote Margaret Bayard Smith, a resident who has left us the most vivid account of Washington in the winter of Jackson's inauguration. Even the supporters of the victorious Andrew Jackson were subdued. With their leader in mourning over the recent death of his wife, Rachel, Democrats avoided putting on too boisterous a display of pleasure over their triumph.

Jackson decreed a sober and dignified inauguration: he would have no military parades, no pre-inaugural festivities. Like Jefferson, he would walk to the Capitol to take the oath, then proceed to the presidential mansion on horseback. Margaret Smith approved Jackson's "avoidance of all parade—it is *true* greatness, which needs not the aid of ornament and pomp," but wished that "the good old gentleman might indulge himself with a carriage." But some 20,000 people of every class and from every section of the country flooded into the capital to witness the inauguration of the "people's President." It was "like the inundation of the northern barbarians into Rome," wrote one haughty Washingtonian, "save that the tumultuous tide came in from [all points] of the compass."

The sun finally shone on March 4, and tens of thousands of citizens gathered for the oath-taking. The spectacle reflected the fondest hopes of ardent Democrats. People "without distinction of rank" stood "silent, orderly and tranquil" to glimpse Jackson—who could be picked out from the crowd around him because he alone wore no hat—a servant of the sovereign people: "There, there, that is he." "Which?" "He with the white head." "Ah, there is the old man and his gray hair, there is the old veteran, there is Jackson."

Jackson, in a low voice that only a handful of the massed thousands could have heard, delivered his inaugural address, which John Quincy Adams described as "short, written with some eloquence, and remarkable chiefly for a significant threat of reform." Then, in a scramble of people that suggested to some the mobs of the French Revolution, but to a modern observer would seem reasonably orderly, farmers, politicians, women, children, carts, wagons, horses, and carriages followed the silver-haired hero down Pennsylvania Avenue to the official reception. Once there they jammed inside hoping to pump the President's hand and share his offering of ice cream, cake, lemonade, and orange punch that had been intended only for the eligible social elite of Washington.

It was a physical impossibility. Ladies fainted from the press; in the grab for refreshments glasses and china broke, people's clothing got ripped, fights broke out; strong men had to cordon off the frail President to prevent injury by exuberant well-wishers. To thin the crowd inside the house, alert servants began carrying tubs of rum punch onto the lawn. The event passed off with nothing worse than mudprints on the furniture (anything to catch a glimpse of Old Hickory) and broken plates and cups. It was not a party anyone would want to repeat, but neither

Asher Durand conveys Andrew Jackson's willfulness by giving attention to his angular nose and jaw; even his swept-back hair stands at attention. (*Courtesy, Historical Pictures Service, Chicago*)

A Washingtonian wrote this account of Jackson's inaugural party:

"The *Majesty of the People* had disappeared, and a rabble, a mob, of boys, negros, women, children, scrambling, fighting, romping. What a pity, what a pity! No arrangements had been made, no police officers placed on duty and the whole house had been inundated by the rabble mob. We came too late. The President, after having been *literally* nearly pressed to death and almost suffocated and torn to pieces by the people in their eagerness to shake hands with Old Hickory, had retreated through the back way or south front and had escaped to his lodgings at Gadsby's. Cut glass and china to the amount of several thousand dollars had been broken in the struggle to get the refreshments, punch and other articles carried out in tubs and buckets, but had it been in hogsheads it would have been insufficient. . . . Ladies fainted, men were seen with bloody noses and such a scene of confusion took place as is impossible to describe,— those who got in could not get out by the door again, but had to scramble out of windows."

was it the opening scene of a social revolution. The product of happenstance, of poor planning, the inaugural party spoke as much of the American people's instinctive good-natured sense of order as it did of their new sense that the President's home and the President now belonged to them.

The character of the newly elected representative of the people illustrates the elusive nature of American democracy. Of humble origins, Jackson was nonetheless by this time clearly a member of the patrician class: a slaveholder, a commander of troops, the master of a large and gracious estate. Even his simple manners, which had the politically useful look of democracy, could as easily present itself as the plain direct demeanor appropriate to a military aristocracy. Americans have thought themselves committed to democracy. They have also wisely or absentmindedly neglected to establish any rigorous test of what properly constitutes a democracy or its leadership.

Van Buren vs. Calhoun

The coalition that elected Andrew Jackson in 1828 was a makeshft. Immediately after the election a struggle broke out between two of its major figures, Martin Van Buren and John C. Calhoun. The clash between these two intensely ambitious men was inevitable.

Usually dressed in black, Calhoun with his great eyes glowing looked as though his face were consumed by inner fires. Having already suffered one setback in his quest for the presidency, Calhoun accepted another vice-presidential term in 1828, with the firm expectation of succeeding Jackson in 1832.

In Martin Van Buren, Calhoun met his equal. This shrewd New Yorker was one of the nation's first professional politicians. Starting as a lawyer in his hometown of Kinderhook, Van Buren had climbed the political ladder rung by rung: county surrogate, state senator, state attorney general, United States senator. He fashioned a powerful political machine in New York, known as the Albany Regency, which dispensed patronage, subsidized friendly newspapers, ran campaigns, and set the party line. Van Buren usually worked invisibly, trying to mold a consensus toward his own ends. Whenever possible, he avoided controversial commitments. He had managed "to be on circuit" in 1820 when a meeting was called at Albany to endorse the prohibition of slavery in Missouri; he was accompanying "a friend on a visit to the Congressional Cemetery" during a key vote on the tariff in 1827. Enemies considered Van Buren devious, opportunistic, hypocritical; admirers nicknamed him the Red Fox and the Little Magician.

In 1828 Van Buren helped to bring the Old Republicans into the Jackson camp and worked tirelessly for the general's election. Jackson rewarded Van Buren's efforts by making him secretary of state. Otherwise, the new Cabinet was undistinguished. Jackson had no intention of calling on it for advice or of allowing powerful figures like Calhoun to undermine his own power. Instead, he relied on an informal circle of political cronies, who came to be called the Kitchen Cabinet. Besides

John C. Calhoun. As Vice President, Calhoun worked against Jackson, especially during the controversy over a state's right to nullify a federal law that infringed on its sovereignty.
(Courtesy, Collection of the Corcoran Gallery of Art)

old Tennessee friends like Major William B. Lewis, who actually roomed at the White House, this group included several newspaper editors and, before long, even Van Buren, who took up horsemanship in order to accompany the President on his morning rides.

The Peggy Eaton Affair   Calhoun fretted over these signs of Van Buren's growing influence. The Vice President had hoped to control the Cabinet appointments, and especially to make a South Carolinian secretary of war. But Jackson appointed to that position another old Tennessee friend, John H. Eaton. Calhoun was humiliated, and to reassert his power, he set out to force Eaton from the Cabinet. An opportunity soon appeared. The secretary of war had recently married the notorious Peggy O'Neale Timberlake, a Washington tavern-keeper's daughter with a dubious reputation. Eaton had lived with her while she was married to John Timberlake, a navy officer, and it was said that he even used his influence to have Timberlake sent to sea. After Timberlake's death, Eaton married Peggy with Jackson's blessing. Washington society hummed with scandal. An English diplomat described one of Mrs. Eaton's antagonists in the "Ladies' War" as having "worn the enamel off of her teeth by the slander of her tongue." The other Cabinet wives, led by the aristocratic Mrs. Calhoun, refused to receive Peggy socially.

The President, recalling the slander heaped on his own wife, was sympathetic to the Eatons. "I tell you," roared the Old General, "I had rather have live vermin on my back than the tongue of one of these Washington women on my reputation." Jackson had a tendency to personalize issues, to make them death struggles with a hated foe. Calhoun, he announced, was trying "to weaken me . . . and open the way to his preferment on my ruin." He summoned a special Cabinet meeting to examine the evidence, then pronounced Peggy "chaste as a virgin," and demanded that she be treated with respect. When most of the Cabinet refused, further meetings were suspended. Only Van Buren, long a widower, accepted Mrs. Eaton as a respectable lady.

This petty struggle dragged on into 1831. Finally, to break the deadlock, Van Buren and Eaton offered their resignations. This calculated gesture gave Jackson a chance to reorganize his Cabinet. He asked the other secretaries to resign and replaced them with loyal followers. As a reward, Jackson nominated the faithful Van Buren to be minister to Great Britain. In December, when Congress reconvened, Calhoun plotted revenge. A tie vote in the Senate allowed him, as Vice President, to cast the deciding vote, and he gleefully spiked Van Buren's nomination. "It will kill him dead, sir, kill him dead," Calhoun gloated. "He will never kick, sir, never kick." But others agreed with Missouri Senator Thomas Hart Benton, who replied, "You have broken a minister, and elected a vice-president."

Benton was right. The President had suspected for some time that it was Calhoun who had urged Monroe's Cabinet in 1818 to censure Jackson's Florida raid. During the Peggy Eaton controversy Calhoun's old enemy, William H. Crawford, provided proof of Calhoun's complicity. Hastily, the Vice President published a pamphlet disclosing the feuds within the administration. When Jackson saw it, his well-known

The British traveler Harriet Martineau would describe the gaunt Calhoun as

"the cast-iron man, who looks as if he had never been born and never could be extinguished. . . . His mind has long since lost all power of communicating with any other. I know of no man who lives in such utter intellectual solitude. He meets men, and harangues them by the fireside as in the Senate; he is wrought like a piece of machinery."

temper flared. "They have cut their own throats," he said of Calhoun and his allies. Van Buren's triumph was complete. He would be Jackson's successor.

Jackson and States' Rights

For years Van Buren had worked to build a political alliance between North and South, stressing principles of laissez-faire and states' rights. He sought particularly to avoid conflicts over the slavery issue, fearing the rise of an antislavery party in the North, and to find a compromise on the tariff. Pennsylvania Democrats desired a protective tariff—a tariff high enough that it would protect American manufactured goods by pushing the price of imported goods beyond the level at which they could compete—while southern party voters demanded free trade. Van Buren's efforts to reconcile the two sections marked his early career, as opposition to southern slavery would define him later.

Calhoun, who also advocated states' rights and limited government, had as much taste for confrontation as did Van Buren for compromise. The South Carolinian, increasingly the champion of southern rights, believed that only a party dominated by southerners could protect the South. During Jackson's first term, he and his followers worked in Congress to create an alliance between South and West based on a program of cheap land for the West and a tariff kept low in the interest of the South. The political maneuvering soon provoked a great national debate on the nature of the federal Union.

Those who argued for states' rights denounced Jackson as "King Andrew" who stomped on the rights of the states. *(Courtesy, Hugh Cleland Collection)*

Public Lands   Late in 1829 Senator Samuel A. Foote of Connecticut proposed a resolution of inquiry into limiting the sale of public lands. Senator Benton of Missouri promptly denounced Foote's resolution as a plot by eastern manufacturers to prevent their workers from migrating to the West. Robert Y. Hayne, a debonair young senator from South Carolina, supported Benton and spoke vigorously in favor of a cheap land policy. Continued large revenues from land sales, he warned, would be used to create a powerful and tyrannical government; they would be "a fund for corruption—fatal to the sovereignty and independence of the states. . . ."

Webster vs.   Daniel Webster of Massachusetts rose to answer
Hayne   both Benton and Hayne. The New Englander was one of the great orators and constitutional lawyers of the day. Deliberately goading Hayne, Webster claimed that the South Carolinian's appeals to state sovereignty were equivalent to preaching disunion. In January 1830 Hayne, with Calhoun's coaching, rose to the challenge. He vigorously defended the right of a state to nullify a federal law that violated "the sovereignty and independence of the states." New Englanders, he reminded Webster pointedly, had been "not unwilling to adopt" this same doctrine at Hartford in 1814, "when they believed themselves to be the victims of unconstitutional legislation."

The next day, before a packed gallery, Webster answered Hayne. The people, Webster contended, and not the states, had formed the

Constitution. They, and not the individual states, were sovereign. If each of the states could defy the laws of Congress at will, the Union would be a mere "rope of sand." The Union was "a copious fountain of national, social, and personal happiness," and the individual states and sections should subordinate their selfish interests to the common good. Webster closed with a moving appeal, memorized by later generations of school children: "Liberty *and* Union, now and forever, one and inseparable!"

Jackson vs. Calhoun

Webster had voiced the feelings of a generation of Americans who believed that "while the Union lasts we have high, exciting, gratifying prospects spread out before us—for us and our children." Did Andrew Jackson share this vision? The President's answer came a few weeks later, at a Jefferson Day dinner. The exponents of nullification planned to use the celebration to advertise their views. Jackson, forewarned of their intentions, had prepared his toast in advance. When his turn came, the President, glaring at Calhoun, raised his glass and declared: "Our Federal Union—it must and shall be preserved." The boisterous crowd stood in deathly silence. The diminutive Van Buren had climbed onto a chair so as not to miss a moment of his triumph. Calhoun, his hand trembling so "that a little of the amber fluid trickled down the side" of his glass, replied: "The Union—next to our liberties most dear." There was no mistaking the President's words; despite his sympathy for states' rights, he would not countenance nullification. Calhoun was further discredited. Westerners scurried to the banner of Jackson and Van Buren.

Jackson, the most politically powerful champion of the federal Union, tried to balance the powers of the federal government and the rights of the states. In 1830, anxious to reassure the strict constructionists in the party, he vetoed a bill providing federal aid for the construction of a turnpike from Maysville to Lexington, Kentucky. This road lay entirely within a single state, and Jackson doubted the constitutionality of federally funding projects of a "purely local character." But well-publicized vetoes like this were the exception; at other times Jackson approved substantial amounts of federal aid for building roads and canals. During his presidency, appropriations for this purpose averaged over $1.3 million annually, nearly double that under Adams.

A Conflict of Interests

South Carolina and Nullification

South Carolina had once been rich. The mucky swamps of its low country were ideally suited for growing rice. After the invention of Whitney's gin, the Carolina upcountry became a major cultivator of cotton and for a time the little state produced half the nation's crop. Rejoicing in prosperity, South Carolinians shared fully in the nationalistic fervor of the early republic. Native sons like the Pinckneys, Calhoun, and Cheves served ably in the nation's councils.

Abruptly in 1819, the state's economic fortunes slid into decline. Falling world prices for cotton, coupled with increased competition from the newer states to the Southwest that could produce it more cheaply, wrecked the South Carolina cotton planters' economy. Their worn-out soils could not stand against the fertile lands of Alabama and Mississippi. Facing ruin, South Carolinians migrated westward by the thousands.

The Tariff   Those who remained increasingly fixed their frustration and anger on the protective tariff. When Congress began raising duties to protective levels, they objected angrily. Resentful at being deprived of the cheaper prices that foreign manufactured goods would have carried without the tariffs, South Carolinians also warned that foreign governments might retaliate by imposing high tariffs on American exports, such as cotton. In 1830 Congressman George McDuffie of South Carolina charged that higher prices ultimately cost the southern planter the equivalent of forty out of every one hundred bales of cotton produced. McDuffie and others exaggerated the tariff's pernicious effect on their economy, but protective duties were not in the interest of South Carolina.

In 1824 representatives from the manufacturing, grain, and wool states had pushed through a bill increasing duties on a wide variety of items. Flushed with victory, protectionists held a grand convention at Harrisburg, Pennsylvania, to map out a campaign for still higher duties. In the 1828 session of Congress, northern protectionists resorted to a trading of votes and programs that goes by the term logrolling. They persuaded members representing Missouri lead miners, Kentucky hemp raisers, Vermont wool growers, and Louisiana sugar planters to support higher rates on manufactured articles in exchange for protective duties on their own constituents' products.

Nullification   Recoiling from this "Tariff of Abominations," southerners threatened to boycott goods from the tariff states. Some began dressing in clothes of homespun, scorning northern broadcloth. Immediately after the tariff bill passed, the South Carolina delegation in Congress met at the home of Senator Robert Y. Hayne to plot resistance. In the fall of 1828 Vice President Calhoun set to work writing his famous *Exposition and Protest* developing the doctrine of nullification, which held that a state could prevent the exercise of a federal law within its borders.

By now Calhoun was revealing himself to be a relentlessly combative political philosopher, single-minded in his commitment to the doctrine of state sovereignty. Must South Carolina submit to the federal government? No, Calhoun insisted, and here, rather than on the tariff issue itself, his argument had its most ominous implications.

Prior to the formation of the Constitution, Calhoun observed, the states had been independent and sovereign. They had created the federal government and endowed it with strictly limited powers. A state therefore had the "right" to "interpose" its original sovereignty against the "despotism of the many," the sheer weight of a national majority. Thus a state could call a state convention and nullify any act of Congress that exceeded the authority granted by the Constitution.

Under the Constitution, Calhoun argued, Congress might tax for

By 1832 nullifiers like George McDuffie were spoiling for a fight. "South Carolina," he told Congress in a typical speech

"is oppressed (a thump). A tyrant majority sucks her life blood from her (a dreadful thump). Yes sir (a pause), yes, sir, a tyrant (a thump) majority unappeasable (horrid scream), has persecuted and persecutes us (a stamp on the floor). We appeal to them (low and quick), but we appeal in vain (loud and quick). We turn to our brethren of the North (low, with a shaking of the head), and pray them to protect us (a thump), but we t-u-r-n in v-a-i-n (prolonged, and a thump). They heap coals of fire on our heads (with immense rapidity)— they give us burden on burden; they tax us more and more (very rapid, slam-bang, slam—a hideous noise). We turn to our brethren of the South (slow with a solemn, thoughtful air). We work with them; we fight with them; we vote with them; we petition with them (common voice and manner); but the tyrant majority has no ears, no eyes, no form (quick), deaf (long pause), sightless (pause), inexorable (slow, slow). Despairing (a thump), we resort to the rights (a pause) which God (a pause) and nature [have] given us (thump, thump, thump). . . ."

purposes of raising revenue, but not to protect domestic industry against foreign competition. The Tariff of 1828 was therefore "unconstitutional, unequal, and oppressive." It made southerners "the serfs of the system—out of whose labor is raised, not only the money paid into the Treasury, but the funds out of which are drawn the rich rewards of the manufacturer and his associates in interest." A state, said Calhoun, could legitimately nullify the tariff.

Racial Fears   In 1828 Calhoun's remedy seemed too drastic for many Carolinians who still turned hopefully to Jackson. In the meantime, the nullifiers worked to strengthen their cause. They were aided by a deepening of racial fear in South Carolina, a state where in some areas slaves outnumbered whites by a ratio of eight to one. Denmark Vesey's revolt in their own state in 1822 and a rebellion in Virginia led by Nat Turner in 1831 left white southerners fearful for their property and lives. They blamed these events on the small but noisy antislavery movement. The bitter Missouri controversy had awakened slaveholders everywhere to the potential threat that the federal government posed to their peculiar institution. And so even those whites who had not suffered by the fall in cotton prices embraced the doctrine of nullification as offering a constitutional protection against the growing antislavery movement.

The Ordinance of Nullification   By 1832 Jackson and his party, faced with an impending election, were determined to reform the Tariff of Abominations. John Quincy Adams, newly elected to the House of Representatives and already the chair of the Committee on Manufacturing, would help. Adams realized that the tariff was a sectional rather than a party issue and accepted the political necessity of moderating the rates. So he cooperated with the administration in framing a bill that essentially repealed the increases of 1828 and restored the rates of the tariff of 1824. Jackson happily signed a lower tariff that provided a real measure of protection to northern manufacturers and also met the legitimate complaints of the South, or so he thought. John C. Calhoun did not agree. He had resigned as Vice President to lead the anti-protection battle in the Senate and was determined to press the issue even after the tariff of 1832 was passed.

In October, after a hard-fought contest, the nullification party elected an overwhelming majority to the South Carolina legislature. The governor immediately called the legislature into session, whereupon it authorized a state convention and a special election of delegates. On November 19, 1832, 136 nullifiers and 26 unionists met at Columbia, the state capital. The convention passed an Ordinance of Nullification declaring the tariffs of 1828 and 1832 unconstitutional, and null and void in South Carolina. The collection of duties by the federal government after February 1, 1833, was forbidden, unless Congress lowered the tariff to twelve percent. Any attempt by Washington to coerce the state, warned the Ordinance, would be "inconsistent with the longer continuance of South Carolina in the Union." The legislature, at its regular session in December, took steps to implement the Ordinance and appropriated money to buy arms and raise an army.

John C. Calhoun wrote:

"I never use the word 'nation' in speaking of the United States. I always use the word 'union' or 'confederacy.' We are not a nation, but a union, a confederacy of equal and sovereign states. . . ."

The Nullification Crisis threatened to tear the Union apart. This 1833 cartoon supporting Jackson portrays the South Carolina resolution as leading to civil war and despotism. *(Courtesy, The New York Public Library, Astor, Lenox and Tilden Foundations)*

The nullifiers soon discovered that they had penned themselves in. At home, a band of unionists prepared to resist their fellow Carolinians by force: both sides were soon drilling volunteers across the state. Neighboring slave states sympathized with South Carolina, but condemned her "reckless precipitancy." President Jackson was determined to uphold national authority. He reinforced federal installations in Charleston harbor and ordered General Winfield Scott to take charge of military preparations. The President's famous Nullification Proclamation of December 10, 1832—written by a southerner, Edward Livingston, of Louisiana—squarely repudiated the doctrine. American nationhood, Jackson asserted, had existed before the states; the Constitution only made more workable a preexisting Union. Under these circumstances, "to say that any state may at pleasure secede from the Union is to say that the United States is not a nation." The power of nullification was *"incompatible with the existence of the Union, contradicted expressly by the letter of the Constitution, unauthorized by its spirit, inconsistent with every principle on which it was founded, and destructive of the great object for which it was formed."* Disunion by armed force, Jackson concluded, was *"treason,"* in the face of which he, as President, could not "avoid the performance of his duty." On a trip to New York City, greeted enthusiastically by a corps of state militia, Jackson announced *"Nullification will never take root* HERE."

The Compromise Tariff of 1833   At the same time that he confronted the nullifiers, Jackson reached out to them. He urged Congress further to lower the tariff, limiting protection to articles essential to the nation's defense. In order to avoid a premature clash of arms, he removed federal troops from the Charleston Citadel to the forts in the harbor. Yet he also secured a Force Bill from Congress early in 1833, authorizing the collection of import duties from ships offshore and reaffirming his power to call up the state militias and to use the army and navy. Old Hickory had completely outmaneuvered the Carolina radicals. As the "Fatal First" of February approached, they prudently decided to delay enforcing nullification until Congress completed its deliberations on the tariff. Early in March 1833, Congress passed a compromise tariff, which provided that rates on protected articles would be lowered in gradual stages to twenty percent in mid-1842. Even though the new rates were eight percent higher than what the nullification ordinance had demanded, South Carolinians accepted the compromise figure with relief. The convention promptly rescinded the Ordinance of Nullification; then, as a symbolic gesture, it declared the Force Bill null and void.

South Carolina had lost. The passage of the compromise tariff was a signal triumph for nationalism. Nullification as a principle had been thoroughly discredited. In the process, South Carolinians had learned an unforgettable lesson: successful resistance to northern "tyranny" demanded the cooperation of the other slave states.

The Second Bank of the United States

Andrew Jackson brought with him to the White House a westerner's instinctive dislike of monopolies and entrenched privilege, and a vague distrust of banks and paper money. Beyond this, however, he had few ideas about economics; political needs shaped his tariff and internal improvement policies. But in his first message to Congress he sharply criticized the Bank of the United States for its failure to establish "a uniform and sound currency." He urged the lawmakers to consider carefully "the constitutionality and expediency" of renewing the Bank's charter at its expiration in 1836. Though his direct responsibility was to private stockholders, Nicholas Biddle's chief concern as the head of the Second Bank of the United States seemed to be the welfare of the country as a whole. He liked to boast that the institution was "the balance wheel of the banking system."

Troubles of the Bank

Biddle's very success proved his undoing. Some people sincerely questioned the constitutionality or the wisdom of making an essentially private bank the depository of the public funds. Many still blamed the Bank for the Panic of 1819. Advocates of cheap money, most of them state bankers and speculators, objected to the Bank because it restrained the state banks from issuing notes as freely as they wished. At the other extreme partisans of hard money, believing that specie was the only safe currency, condemned all note-issuing banks—the National Bank among them—as instruments of speculation. Advocates of hard money were now employing the populistic rhetoric, spiced with denunciations of privileged wealth, that more often in American history, as in the case of Shays's Rebellion, has been the rhetoric of champions of cheap or paper currency. Banknotes, wrote one critic, formed "the foundation of *artificial* inequality of wealth, and, thereby, of *artificial* inequality of power."

The source of Jackson's own hostility to the Bank remains uncertain. He did not act in response to popular demand or on behalf of state banks. In spite of his well-known suspicion of banks and paper money, Old Hickory had kept his own money in the Bank's Washington and Nashville branches for years. Most likely, his antagonism stemmed from the uncontrolled political power of the Bank and its identification with unfriendly eastern interests. He readily believed the reports that some of the branches had worked against his election in 1828, and reached the conclusion that the Bank was a "hydra of corruption—dangerous to our liberties by its corrupting influence everywhere." He must, he decided, strip the "Monster" of its malign power. Once engaged in the contest, Jackson quickly turned the dispute into another death struggle between himself and a loathsome foe.

For a time Biddle tried to placate Jackson, but with no success. He then turned to the President's enemies for support. He extended generous loans to Clay, Webster, and other influential politicians and newspaper editors. In 1832 he reluctantly acquiesced in their plan to seek a recharter well in advance of the expiration date. It was an election year, and the Bank's friends reasoned that Jackson would hesitate before vetoing a recharter bill. If he did veto it, they would have a good issue in the presidential campaign.

The Bank War

The bill renewing the Bank's charter cleared Congress in July 1832, with nearly a third of the Democratic representatives voting in favor. Jackson was enraged. "The Bank," he told Van Buren, "is trying to kill me, *but I will kill it!*" Jackson was, he said, "as firm as the Rocky Mountain. . . . Providence has a power over me, but frail mortals . . . can have none." He sent the bill back to Congress with a blistering veto message in which he denounced the Bank as "not only unnecessary, but dangerous to the government and country." It enjoyed a virtual "monopoly of foreign and domestic exchange"; it threatened the rights of the states and the liberties of the people; it discriminated against the West. Refusing to be guided by the opinion of the Supreme Court in the *McCulloch* case,

Jackson declared the Bank unconstitutional: "The opinion of the judges has no more authority over Congress than the opinion of Congress has over the judges, and on that point the President is independent of both." One fourth of the Bank's stock was held by foreigners, the veto message observed; the country needed a *"purely American"* institution. Jackson closed with an impassioned attack on the renewal bill as an attempt by "the rich and powerful" to "bend the acts of government to their selfish purposes" and pledged to resist "the advancement of the few at the expense of the many."

Jackson vs. the Bank   The veto message was superb propaganda but poor economics. A developing country like the United States needed a stable currency to encourage foreign investment, not wildcat banking to drive it away. The Bank was not a monopoly. In 1830 it made about one-fifth of the nation's bank loans and had barely one-third of the total bank deposits and specie reserves held by American banks. In his message Jackson completely ignored the important services the Bank provided and offered no effective substitute for them.

At first, Jackson's enemies rejoiced over the message. Biddle compared the President to "a chained panther biting the bars of his cage" and called the veto "a manifesto of anarchy." But in November 1832 Jackson, with Van Buren as his running mate, overwhelmed the National Republican candidate, Henry Clay, by a margin of five to one in the electoral college.

Jackson took his decisive victory as a mandate to destroy the Bank even before its charter expired. As soon as the nullification crisis passed,

Anonymous, *Stage Coach*, nineteenth century. *(Courtesy, Museum of Fine Arts, Boston)*

he set out to remove the government deposits from the bank and place them in selected state banks. By law, it was the secretary of the treasury who had to give the actual order for removing them. When he refused, Jackson "promoted" him to the State Department and named a new treasury secretary. This official, too, refused to do Jackson's bidding, citing the "irresponsible" policies of the state banks. The President then replaced him with Roger B. Taney, formerly the attorney general. The faithful Taney continued drawing on the government's funds in the Bank to meet current expenses, but he began depositing the incoming receipts in certain state banks. These banks were supposedly chosen for their fiscal soundness, but political considerations were not overlooked. Prior to 1836 over seventy-five percent of the officers in these banks were Democrats. The administration's critics nicknamed them "pet banks."

As the government's deposits dwindled, Biddle began calling in loans and curtailing the issuing of new notes. In the beginning this contraction was thoroughly justifiable, since the federal deposits had given the notes much of their reliability. But Biddle soon succumbed to opportunistic motives. He continued the contraction into the spring of 1834, in the hope of producing a short recession that would force a recharter of the Bank. "Nothing but the evidence of suffering," he reasoned, would "produce any effect in Congress." As interest rates climbed and credit dried up, the business community begged for relief. All over the country supporters of the Bank organized meetings and flooded Congress with petitions. A Cincinnati man tried a more direct approach: "Damn your—soul," he wrote Jackson, "remove them deposits back again, and recharter the bank or you will certainly be shot in less than two weeks and that by myself!!!"

The Bank Closes Its Doors

Old Hickory refused to budge. Told of rumors that a mob threatened to "lay siege to the Capitol until the deposits were restored," he promised to hang the ringleaders "as high as Haman." When a delegation of businessmen visited him seeking relief, he replied coldly: "Go to the Monster, go to Biddle. . . . Biddle has all the money!" In the end Jackson had his way. Biddle was forced to let credit flow more freely, and the economy quickly recovered.

The chief result of the so-called "Biddle depression" was a marked decrease in the Bank's popularity. In 1836, when the old federal charter expired, the Bank received a new one from the state of Pennsylvania. In 1841, after a series of financial reverses, it closed its doors forever. Biddle died three years later, a broken man. Jackson had destroyed the Bank in the name of sound money and "those habits of economy and simplicity which are so congenial to the character of republicans." But in so doing he removed the most effective restraint on "the stock-jobbers, brokers, and gamblers" he professed to despise. Aided by the government deposits, the "pets" flooded the country with paper banknotes. An orgy of speculation and inflation followed. Belatedly, between 1834 and 1836, Jackson tried to drive paper money from circulation. He directed the deposit banks not to issue or receive notes worth less than $10. Land officers were instructed not to take small notes in payment for public lands. Jackson secured a law preventing deposit banks from issuing bills valued at under $20. Finally, in 1836, Jackson issued the Specie Circular, which prohibited the purchase of public lands in anything but coin. He acted too late. In 1837 bad money helped to plunge the country into its worst depression to date. Jackson had accused the Second Bank of being beyond federal control, but so were the state banks in which he had deposited federal revenues.

Boom and Bust

On March 4, 1837, Andrew Jackson turned over the presidency to Martin Van Buren. As the Old Hero left the Capitol, the crowds cheered him lustily. For once, remarked Thomas Hart Benton, "the rising was eclipsed by the setting sun." Even as Van Buren delivered his inaugural message, depression was clouding the country again.

Since the early 1820s the American economy had grown steadily. Demand for American agricultural products seemed insatiable: exports of cotton alone increased from 92 million pounds in 1818 to 300 million pounds in 1830. Moving these bulky products to market required the expenditure of immense sums on transportation projects of all kinds. Construction of turnpikes and bridges continued in most parts of the country, and steamboat building became an important industry. The success of the Erie Canal in New York State brought a time of canal building, even while more than three thousand miles of railroad were completed in the same period. And the construction boom went far beyond internal improvements: the rapid settlement of the West and the growth of urban areas created a great demand for new homes, barns, stores, and public buildings. Manufacturing industries, particularly cotton textiles, iron, and machinery, also grew rapidly.

The United States had long had a vigorous entrepreneurial tradition. Fathers in Boston during Jacksonian times guided sons on daily walks to the wharves, banks, and counting houses a few blocks from home. Eight-year-old Frank Appleton reported to his bank-president father that he had "laid out 1 cent for 8 marbles and one cent for 2 allies." As teenagers, William and Amos Lawrence kept strict accounts, heeding their parents' advice to record "*every cent* you receive, and *every cent you expend.*" Western farms were now becoming more intent on making money by selling part of their crops than on raising produce for their own consumption. And westerners and southerners often opposed entrenched financial interests that prevented them from getting ahead.

Martin Van Buren of New York was one of the country's first professional politicians. His loyalty to the President won him the chance to succeed Jackson in that office. *(Courtesy, Scribner's Archives)*

Speculative Fever
But by the middle 1830s healthy growth was giving way to feverish speculation. Investors, most of them British, bought enormous quantities of stock in state-owned canal companies and other public works of increasingly doubtful utility and profitability. With labor and materials in short supply, these new construction projects merely drove up wages and prices. Sales of public land—mainly to speculators—rose from only $2,300,000 in 1830 to almost $25,000,000 in 1836. As speculators snapped up everything in sight, urban land values also soared. When Chicago was incorporated in 1833, optimists were already buying and selling lots twenty miles from

One traveler commented on the deluge of paper:

"The greatest annoyance I was subjected to in travelling was in exchanging money. It is impossible to describe the wretched state of the currency—which is all bills issued by private individuals; companies; cities and states; almost all of which are bankrupt; or what amounts to the same thing, they cannot redeem their issues. All the bills are at a discount, varying from ten percent to fifty percent; and such rags of bills, too! And these do not pass out of the state, or frequently, out of the city in which they are issued. . . ."

Lake Michigan. All over the West and South, farmers and planters plunged heavily into debt for land and slaves, sometimes borrowing at rates as high as thirty percent. The number of state banks rose from 330 in 1830 to 788 in 1837. Many were purely speculative ventures, deliberately located "out where the wildcats howled" on the assumption that there they could avoid holders of their notes seeking redemption in specie. Lax state laws permitted these "wildcat banks," as they were called, to issue banknotes without maintaining adequate specie reserves to back them up. The note circulation of state banks soared from $61 million in 1830 to $149 million in 1837.

The Panic of 1837

In 1837 the boom collapsed. The Specie Circular requiring all payments for public lands in gold or silver led banks in the West to draw heavily on eastern banks for coin. In the midst of this specie drain a recession in Britain depressed cotton prices, and British investors called in their loans. On May 10 New York banks suspended specie payments. Other banks followed. Prices fell and credit tightened: for speculators the only question, an observer wrote, "was as to the means of escape, and nearest and best route to Texas."

The depression that stretched from 1839 to 1843 was one of the severest in American history. Prices fell by as much as one-half in some places; real estate values and stocks declined even more drastically. The collapse of prices set off a wave of bankruptcies. Under the federal Bankruptcy Act of 1841, some 28,000 debtors freed themselves of nearly a half-billion dollars of debt. Rural areas were hardest hit, but they at least were self-sustaining. In the cities unemployment brought widespread distress.

Mobs in New York looted the flour stores in 1837 and similar violence flared elsewhere. Once again municipalities and charitable agencies set up soup kitchens and unemployment offices. Casting about for a more permanent solution to urban unemployment, the journalist Horace Greeley advised the unemployed to "go to the Great West, anything rather than remain here." Public land sales had plunged by 1842 to less than six percent of their 1836 peak. With land sales and tariff receipts declining, the federal government, which had been out of debt since 1835, began running a new deficit. The states, which had contracted nearly $200 million of debts, were especially hard-pressed. By 1842 eight of them had defaulted, and three had even repudiated part of their debt, thereby ruining American credit with European investors for years to come.

One faction in the Democratic Party favored banks and paper money, wanting the federal government to maintain some active role in managing the economy. Radicals, on the other hand, clung resolutely to hard money and would have the government do little in the economy except discourage banks from issuing paper notes. Van Buren decided to stick with Jackson's policies. He refused to repeal the Specie Circular. Calling Congress into special session, he blamed the depression on "excessive issues of bank paper" and "reckless speculation." Concerned about the growing strain on the federal Treasury, he asked Congress to authorize the borrowing of $10 million for current expenses. And he specifically recommended passage of a law permitting the federal government to keep its receipts in its own Treasury vaults, which would sever all connections with the nation's banks. Beyond this Van Buren refused to go. It was not the place of government, he insisted, to relieve economic distress. The framers of the Constitution had "wisely judged that the less government interfered with private pursuits the better for the general prosperity." Many of the states made at least some effort to relieve hunger and unemployment.

In spite of protests against leaving the people to survive on their own, most of Van Buren's program became law in 1837. The President's opponents concentrated their fire on the Independent Treasury Bill. This proposal would require customs collectors, postmasters, and other government receivers of funds to hold their receipts until ordered to pay them out. It would also direct the secretary of the treasury to withdraw the government's deposits from the "pet" banks and to place them in special subtreasuries. Opponents charged that the bill would curtail loans and credit, thereby stifling recovery. Van Buren's supporters countered that it would keep the government independent and the currency safe and check unwise expansion of bank notes. A coalition blocked the scheme until 1840, when it finally passed Congress. But the Democratic Party was now presiding over a depression, and that is never a good position for a party in power to occupy.

The Democrats vs. the Whigs

By the end of Andrew Jackson's second term in 1837, the Democratic Party had changed significantly. Gone was the diverse political coalition that had elected the Old Hero in 1828; its leadership now adhered to a fairly definite body of ideas. Government, the Jacksonians believed, should restrict its intervention in the economy to eliminating special privilege and monopoly, leaving a fair field for individual competition. Like Adam Smith, whose *Wealth of Nations* (1776) many of them had read, they believed that the power of the marketplace would best regulate the economy and distribute wealth equitably. Fearing that the rich would use the government for personal advantage, the Jacksonians advocated universal political freedom (for white men) and majority rule. Although recognizing the supremacy of the Union, Jacksonians respected states' rights, holding that federal authority should be kept within narrow bounds.

The party in the late 1830s and 1840s was much influenced by the Locofocos, a powerful Democratic splinter group in New York. These dissidents—who took their name from a type of friction match they had used to light candles when rival Democrats tried to disrupt one of their meetings by turning off the gas lights—opposed monopoly in any form. They denounced banks and corporations, demanding a return to hard money and the abolition of laws allowing limited liability for stockholders. They advocated free trade, labor unions, free public education, and abolition of imprisonment for debt.

Chief Justice Roger Taney. A former secretary of the treasury under Jackson, Taney succeeded John Marshall in 1836. (*Courtesy, Library of Congress*)

Chief Justice Roger Taney

The decisions of the Supreme Court in the late 1830s reflected Democratic thinking. During his two terms, Jackson appointed seven associate justices. And when Chief Justice John Marshall died in 1835, the President named Roger B. Taney (pronounced "tawny") to succeed him. Under Taney's leadership the Court showed a less rigid respect for private property rights as against the rights of popular majorities, and had more regard for states' rights.

In the *Charles River Bridge* case of 1837 the Court again took up the question posed in the 1819 *Dartmouth College* case of whether a state could alter an agreement with a private corporation. The Massachusetts legislature had incorporated the Charles River Bridge Company to operate a toll bridge under a long-term contract. Later it authorized another corporation to build a bridge over the Charles River at a point nearby that would in twenty years become toll free. The older company sought an injunction, contending that the second charter constituted a breach of contract. Taney sided with Massachusetts. The great object of government, he declared, was "to promote the happiness and prosperity of the community." In a collision between the rights of private property and those of the community, the rights of the people came first. The Court could not consent, Taney said, to take away from the states "any portion of that power over their own internal police and improvement, which is so necessary to their well being and prosperity." Denounced by conservatives as a blow to business and the sanctity of contract, the decision was in fact liberating. The young American economy would have been greatly handicapped if established companies had been able to maintain monopolies and choke off competition. Taney's opinion opened the way for a host of developments in industry and transportation.

Two years later, in *Bank of Augusta v. Earle,* the Court enlarged state powers again. Here Taney rejected the claim of a Georgia bank that under the federal Constitution a corporation, like a citizen, could automatically enter another state and engage in business there. Though in the absence of positive legislation a company might do business in another state, said Taney, that state had the power to exclude the corporation if it wished. In the wake of this decision, many states enacted regulatory laws for outside corporations. On the whole, they were socially beneficial, since there was as yet virtually no federal regulation of interstate commerce.

Rising Opposition to the Jacksonians

The Democratic appeals for strict economy, equal rights, and the abolition of government favors appealed to popular sentiments. By the late 1830s there was some truth in Jackson's claim that his party represented the "farmers, mechanics, and laborers." It especially attracted people who resented the privileges that established bankers and tariff-protected businessmen enjoyed; people who had been affected adversely by changing patterns of transportation and trade; ordinary people who had been hurt by currency fluctuations and unstable commodity prices. Others supported the Democrats for special reasons. Many southern planters looked to them to protect slavery and southern rights from government interference. Businessmen engaged in international trade favored Jackson's call for a lower tariff. The Democratic Party early recognized and encouraged the aspirations of immigrants, particularly Irish Catholics, who flocked to the party. Opponents of evangelical Protestantism, with its righteous moralizing and aggressive crusading, found refreshing the rough-and-tumble egalitarianism of the Democrats. The party attracted freethinkers and intellectuals. Many Democratic voters just plain liked Jackson.

Yet Jackson's policies and political success provoked growing opposition. Initially, Old Hickory's opponents lacked cohesion, and political alliances were unsettled. In time they would gather into a party that could compete with the Democrats in the tapping of popular emotions.

One of the first of the forces to oppose Jackson was the Anti-Masonic Party, which after 1826 had gained strong support in New England, New York, and Pennsylvania. Originally a protest movement against the supposedly despotic political and economic power of Masonry, it soon turned into a general protest against inequality and immorality. As a powerful religious and democratic movement, it attracted ambitious young politicians—William Seward, Thaddeus Stevens, Horace Greeley, and Millard Fillmore—who welded it into an effective political party. Because Andrew Jackson was a Mason, and because his party was in power, these leaders made the Democrats the chief target of attack. In 1831 the Anti-Masons held at Baltimore the first nationwide presidential nominating convention in the country, choosing William Wirt as their presidential candidate. He won just seven electoral votes in 1832, splitting the anti-Jackson vote with Henry Clay, the National Republican candidate. After that election, leaders of these two groups began organizing a political force alternative to the Democrats.

The Anti-Masons were joined by a motley assortment of former Jacksonians. Jackson's firm rebuke to nullification drove many southern states' righters into opposition. Then the bank war caused many to desert the President. The selection of the New Yorker Martin Van Buren as Jackson's successor awakened hostility in the South and West. Even John C. Calhoun cooperated for a time with nationalists like Clay and Webster in opposing administration measures in Congress.

The Whigs   In 1834 a newspaper gave the anti-Jackson coalition the title "Whigs." That name had been in use for earlier British opponents of policies of the monarchy, and for rebel colonists in the period of the American Revolution; it was now supposed to define the opponents of the tyrannical "King Andrew."

Use of the name "Whig" by opponents of Jackson and Jacksonianism became widespread in 1834, but the actual formation of a Whig Party varied in time from state to state. It was organized first in the New England and mid-Atlantic states, later in the West and South. The lack of an effective national organization and conflicts in ideology among the coalitionists hindered the Whigs in 1836. Unable to agree on a common platform or a single presidential candidate, they adopted the strategy of running strong regional candidates in the hope of throwing the election into the House of Representatives. In the South, the Whigs' choice was

Hugh Lawson White, a Tennesseean who, like many southern Jacksonians, distrusted Van Buren on the tariff and slavery. In the East, they ran Daniel Webster. The candidate in the West was General William Henry Harrison of Ohio, a former governor of Indiana Territory and the hero of the Battle of Tippecanoe. Among them the three Whigs piled up 124 electoral votes, but Van Buren, with Jackson's prestige behind him, had 170, enough to win the election.

The Nature of the Growing Whig Party   During the next four years the Whigs slowly gathered strength and developed a more coherent political philosophy. As the Panic of 1837 worsened, people throughout the country flocked to the new banner, convinced that Van Buren's hard-money policies were somehow responsible for their woes. The Whigs' ambitious economic nationalism attracted new adherents in the South, even while it drove Calhoun and the extreme states' righters back to the Democrats.

The Whigs brought democratic manners and sentiments to an essentially Hamiltonian concept of government and economics. They believed that it was a chief function of government to promote, actively and positively, the national economy. They advocated a national banking system, internal improvements at federal expense, and a protective tariff for industry. As they saw it, a wise government working alongside capital and labor would harmonize the interests of every class and section.

There was also a strong strain of evangelical Protestantism in Whiggery, which gave rise to moral and humanitarian reform. Many Whigs still hoped "to Christianize America through politics." They frequently criticized Jackson's Indian policy; and numbers of northern Whigs opposed slavery. Reformist activities among Whigs came in part from the more well-to-do element in the party, who like upper-class federalists before them took seriously the responsibility of the favored class to give moral direction to society.

The Whigs attracted a substantial following among all classes of society. Many northern merchants, bankers, and industrialists found the Whig philosophy appealing; so did large cotton, tobacco, and sugar planters and their urban business associates in the South. Many farmers, hungry for internal improvements, voted Whig. The party was popular among Protestants and native-born Americans concerned about the influx of immigrants, particularly Irish and German Catholics. Workingmen in industries hurt by foreign imports, or fearful of immigrant competition for jobs, supported the Whig ticket. With broad support throughout the country, the Whigs looked forward eagerly to the election of 1840.

The Election of 1840

In 1840 the second national party system came of age. The Democratic organization now faced a Whig Party just as skillfully devised for the winning of a large electorate. The Whigs now proceeded to beat the party of Jackson at its own game.

The Democratic convention had little choice but to renominate

Van Buren. The Democratic platform endorsed the Independent Treasury and condemned federally sponsored internal improvements, a national bank, and protective tariffs.

The early front runner for the Whig nomination was Henry Clay. The veteran senator from Kentucky had been the chief spokesman for Whiggery and master of the opposition to Jackson in Congress. The new professional politicians in the Whig Party, however, had a different strategy in mind. Men like Thurlow Weed of New York wanted a candidate with "availability"—someone inoffensive who could appeal to a broad spectrum of the electorate. Clay was too closely identified with the Bank of the United States, and had too many enemies. The Whigs especially wanted a military hero. Their convention passed over Clay and chose William Henry Harrison, whose rout of Tecumseh's outnumbered Indians at Tippecanoe in 1811 had made him a national figure. In an attempt to balance the ticket geographically, the Whigs selected as Harrison's running mate John Tyler of Virginia, a states' rights strict constructionist. Because there were divergent views within the party on national issues, the Whigs adjourned without drafting a platform.

The Log Cabin Campaign   Born on a Virginia plantation in 1773, the son of a signer of the Declaration of Independence, Harrison had begun his career in the Old Northwest, first as an army officer, then as governor of Indiana Territory. Later, "Tippecanoe," as commander in the Northwest during the War of 1812, had won the important Battle of the Thames, finally driving the British and their Indian allies off the soil of the United States. Following the war, Harrison spent much time on his farm in Ohio, and also served briefly as a United States senator and as minister to Colombia. Thereafter, however, his career languished and he was serving as a county clerk in 1836 when the Whigs tapped him as one of their presidential candidates. His strong showing at the polls—he got over half the Whig vote—kept him in public view until 1840.

At first, the Democrats professed joy at the Whigs's decision to run "Granny" Harrison (he was sixty-seven) instead of Clay. But when a Democratic newspaper, sneering at Harrison's presumed lack of sophistication, suggested that he would be content with a barrel of hard cider, a log cabin, and a pension of $2,000 a year, the Whigs seized on the remark. Mounting an elaborate campaign, they cast Harrison in Jackson's image and portrayed the Whigs as the friends of the people.

In their songs and speeches Whig orators glorified Harrison as a plain, virtuous farmer whose cabin door (he actually owned three thousand acres and lived in a substantial home) was always open to strangers. "Matty" Van Buren, by contrast, was pictured as a bloated aristocrat, squandering the public funds on lavish White House entertainments in the midst of a depression. Why, thundered one Whig orator, this "democratic peacock" had even installed a bathtub at a cost of "thousands of the people's dollars." Davy Crockett observed that "it would be difficult to say, from personal appearance, whether he was man or woman. . . . Aunt Matty was the perlitest cretur among the wimmen."

The Whigs held parades and rallies, with floats, flags, bands, and endless replicas of log cabins. They paraded fake Indians, to remind the

One gem from the musical political campaign of 1840 purported to give a biography of Van Buren:

Who never did a noble deed?
Who of the people took no heed?
Who is the worst of tyrant's breed?
    Van Buren!

Who, while but a little boy,
Was counted crafty, cunning, sly,
Who with the wily fox could vie?
    Van Buren!

Who, when an urchin, young at school,
Would of each classmate make a tool,
In cheating, who the roost would rule?
    Van Buren!

Who like the wily serpent clings,
Who like the pois'nous adder stings,
Who is more base than basest Kings?
    Van Buren!

Who rules us with an iron rod,
Who moves at Satan's beck and nod,
Who heeds not man, who heeds not God?
    Van Buren!

Who would his friend, his country sell,
Do other deeds too base to tell,
Deserves the lowest place in Hell?
    Van Buren!

A political cartoon captured the colorful nature of the 1840 presidential campaign.
(Courtesy, Hugh Cleland Collection)

A Democrat, after witnessing the spectacle of 10,000 Whigs celebrating Harrison Day in Cleveland on September 10, 1840, recoiled with disgust:

"I have seen vast assemblages collected together at great labor and cost, not to respond to any principle, or listen to any argument but to drown the voice of reason in shouts of revelry, and lead captive the feelings of the people in a senseless excitement. Hurrah for the newly found hero, annunciations of his poverty or his residence in a Log Cabin and love of hard cider, the hauling of miniature log hen coops and canoes, gourds, shells, and cider barrels through the streets, the rolling of balls, and a display of different colored banners with unmeaning mottos, doggerel, rhymes, and vulgar pictures.

The drinking of hard cider . . . and imitating the cries of birds and the howl of wild beasts with other mummery and mockery, are disgraceful to the country. It is saying to the people, you are too ignorent for self government, and is a down right insult to the good understanding of the American freeman."

voters of Harrison's record of Indian fighting. Another reminder was their catchy campaign slogan, "Tippecanoe and Tyler Too!" Barrels of cider were everywhere, with sweet cider for the drys and hard for the wets. The E.C. Booz Company of Philadelphia packaged its Old Cabin whiskey in log-cabin-shaped bottles, and "booze" entered the language as a synonym for hard liquor. Wealthy Whigs dressed in homespun and boasted of their humble upbringing. The party distributed a campaign newspaper, the *Log Cabin,* and countless songbooks in the first musical campaign of American history.

The Whig campaign theme, then, made use of the democratic, populistic posturing that had served the Democrats so well. But it was not merely posturing and strategy. The Hamiltonian program for economic development, a clear antecedent to the program of the Whigs, had seemed aristocratic, but that was partly because of the character of its Federalist architects. The idea of a federal government actively managing a single national economy in the interest of the common good is at bottom entirely democratic, and to that the politics of the twentieth century will attest. The economic nationalism and the populism of the Whigs went together genuinely as well as strategically, and foreshadowed a continuing if rocky alliance of Hamiltonianism and democracy.

The Democrats tried to counter hard cider with hard money, commending the virtues of the newly established Independent Treasury. No one listened. Attracted by the ballyhoo and angry over the depression, voters swarmed to the vigorous young party. Nearly eighty percent of the eligible electorate went to the polls. Harrison won a clear-cut victory, carrying nineteen out of twenty-six states and fifty-three percent of the two-party vote. Nearly unnoticed in the hullabaloo was the Liberty Party, whose meager 6,225 votes represented an early stirring of antislavery politics in the North.

The election of 1840 established a new pattern in American politics. For the first time a President had been saddled with responsibility for hard times and turned out of office. The carnival atmosphere of the campaign inaugurated a tradition that has to some extent persisted in American presidential elections. The public had adopted politics as its favorite spectator sport, and the presidential campaign as its most important national ritual. For the rest of the nineteenth century, about eighty percent of the electorate turned out to vote in most presidential contests.

World Affairs in the Jacksonian Era

During the age of Jackson, Americans were preoccupied with redefining their political philosophies, coming to terms with the meaning of democracy and realigning their political parties. Presidents Andrew Jackson and Martin Van Buren had little to think about in foreign policy. But the nation did face some delicate situations.

French Affairs During the Napoleonic era, French naval vessels had periodically boarded and seized American merchant ships carrying goods to and from Great Britain. The United States at the time demanded compensation, but when the War of 1812 broke out and France was in effect an American ally, those demands receded. In the years afterward the United States raised the issue, reminding France of the claims, but in turn the French began arguing that the United States had violated the rights of some French citizens in Louisiana. Diplomatic teams from both countries negotiated the differences, and in July 1830 a treaty was signed. France agreed to pay twenty-five million francs in six annual installments, beginning in 1834, and the United States agreed to a payment of 1.5 million francs to compensate French citizens in Louisiana.

In 1834, France over the vehement protests of the Jackson Administration unilaterally decided to postpone the payments. In December 1834 the President threatened to seize property under French ownership in the United States in lieu of the payments, and he spoke threateningly of naval action. Eventually, Great Britain took the role of mediator in the dispute. France made in the spring of 1836 a single payment of seventeen million francs and completed the compensation during the next two years.

Amistad Incident One diplomatic incident during Van Buren's presidency involved slavery, the issue that would not lie still. In 1839 off the coast of Cuba a Spanish ship carrying slaves from Africa and bearing the ill-fitting name *Amistad*—"friendship"—fell to a mutiny by its black captives, who were suffering under vile conditions. When it entered the territory of the United States, the navy in Long Island Sound seized their brave leader Cinqué along

Cinqué was an African chief who aboard a slave ship organized a mutiny that killed most of the Spanish crew. Spain had signed a treaty, however, agreeing not to take part in the slave trade. Cinqué and his cohorts wound up in a Connecticut jail after entering Long Island Sound. Defended by seventy-three-year-old John Quincy Adams, then a congressman, Cinqué was released in 1841. *(Courtesy, National Portrait Galley).*

with the mutineers and took them to New Haven, Connecticut. The Spanish insisted on their return, and Van Buren's administration wished to send them back. Their case went through the court system, finally reaching the Supreme Court. Before that body Congressman John Quincy Adams pled their cause, and in 1841 they were freed. They went home to Africa.

In the *Amistad* affair and throughout the later years of his life, Adams was a major opponent of the institution of slavery. In 1848, he fell sick on the floor of the House of Representatives while protesting an honor to be paid to officers in the Mexican War, dying soon after. Antislavery forces had detested that war for its injustice to Mexico and its possible opening of conquered territory to plantation slavery. Conscience soon put Van Buren in the antislavery ranks. In 1848 he ran for the presidency as the candidate of the Free Soil Party, which argued for banning slavery from the western tertitories, governed directly by the federal government.

The Jacksonian Legacy The Jacksonian era, which includes the campaigning of the Whigs who were victorious in 1840, firmly established the political system that has prevailed ever since. The significance of the change does not lie primarily in the extended importance of the popular vote or in the increased rowdiness of popular politics. Of greater moment was the

George Caleb Bingham, ***Raftsmen Playing Cards,*** **1847.** *(Courtesy, The Saint Louis Art Museum)*

appearance of parties that, far more broadly than the old Federalists and Jeffersonians, could articulate fairly complex national policies and present them to the public. In 1840, to be sure, the Whigs did little explaining: cider and log cabins are not issues that bear largely on the future of the republic. But the emergence of nationwide parties that, however divided internally, represented clear interests and beliefs went parallel to the industrial revolution in marking the demise of the staid old republicanism of the Founders. Together with the inventions, the factories and railways, the westward expansion of one-crop commercial agriculture, and the other quickened activities of the time, they signified that from then onward the country was to be a project worked and reworked by the restless will of its people.

Suggested Readings

On the Jacksonian Era see Daniel Feller, *The Jacksonian Promise: America, 1815–1840* (1995), Harry Watson, *Liberty and Power: The Politics of Jacksonian America* (1990), and Arthur Schlesinger, Jr.'s classic on Jacksonian democracy, *The Age of Jackson* (1945). See also Lawrence Kohl, *The Politics of Individualism: Parties and the American Character in the Jackson Era* (1989), Merrill D. Peterson, *The Great Triumvirate: Webster, Clay, and Calhoun* (1987), Richard E. Ellis, *The Union at Risk: Jacksonian Democracy, States' Rights, and the Nullification Crisis* (1987), Daniel B. Cole, *Martin Van Buren and the American Political System* (1984), and Edward Pessen, *Riches, Class, and Power before the Civil War* (1973). See also Pessen's *Jacksonian America* (rev. 1978) and Marvin Meyer's *The Jacksonian Persuasion* (1957). Richard P. McCormick describes *The Second Party System* (1966). On Jackson, Robert V. Remini's three-volume biography of *Andrew Jackson* (1977, 1984, and 1987) is definitive. David B. Cole, *The Presidency of Andrew Jackson* (1993) is a fine one-volume biography. Michael Paul

Rogin's *Fathers and Children: Andrew Jackson and the Subjugation of the American Indian* (1975) is intriguing and debatable history and psychohistory. Compare William G. McLaughlin, *Cherokee Renascence in the New Republic* (1980) and Michael D. Green, *The Politics of Indian Removal* (1982). Lee Benson's *The Concept of Jacksonian Democracy: New York as a Test Case* (1961) remains provocative.

See also John Niven, *John C. Calhoun and the Price of Union* (1988), Richard Hofstadter, *The Idea of a Party System: The Rise of Legitimate Opposition in the United States, 1780–1840* (1970), Harry L. Watson, *Liberty and Power: The Politics of Jacksonian America* (1990), John Niven, *Martin Van Buren: The Romantic Age of American Politics* (1983), Daniel W. Howe, *The Political Culture of the American Whigs* (1979), Thomas Brown, *Politics and Statesmanship: Essays on the American Whig Party* (1985), and Irving H. Bartlett, *John Calhoun: A Biography* (1993).

Why Did Jackson Remove the Indians?

Michael Paul Rogin

America clearly began not with primal innocence and consent but with acts of force and fraud. Indians were here first, and it was their land upon which Americans contracted, squabbled, and reasoned with one another. Stripping away history did not permit beginning without sin; it simply exposed the sin at the beginning of it all. The dispossession of the Indians, moreover, did not happen once and for all in the beginning. America was continually beginning again on the frontier, and as it expanded across the continent, it killed, removed, and drove into extinction one tribe after another.

The years spanned by Andrew Jackson's life were the great years of American expansion. Born on the frontier, Jackson joined the movement west as a young man. In the years of his maturity and old age, from Jefferson's Presidency to the Mexican War, expansion across the continent was the central fact of American politics. Two-thirds of the American population of 3.9 million lived within fifty miles of the ocean in 1790. In the next half-century 4.5 million Americans crossed the Appalachians, one of the great migrations in world history. The western states contained less than three percent of the U.S. population in 1790, twenty-eight percent in 1830. In two decades the west would become the most populous region of the country.

Indians inhabited in 1790 almost all the territory west of the original thirteen states. If America were to expand and take possession of the continent, they would have to be dispossessed. Indians had not mattered so much, in the history of Europeans in the English new world, since the colonial settlements. They would never matter so much again. Indian removal was Andrew Jackson's major policy aim in the quarter-century before he became President. His Indian wars and treaties were principally responsible for dispossessing the southern Indians during those years. His presidential Indian removal finished the job. . . . Historians, however, have failed to place Indians at the center of Jackson's life. They have interpreted the Age of Jackson from every perspective but Indian destruction, the one from which it actually developed historically.

Indian dispossession, as experienced by the whites who justified it and carried it out, belongs to the pathology of human development. Indians remained, in the white fantasy, in the earliest period of childhood, unseparated from "the exuberant bosom of the common mother." They were at once symbols of a lost childhood bliss and, as bad children, repositories of murderous, negative fantasies. . . . Replacing Indians upon the land, whites reunited themselves with nature. The rhetoric of Manifest Destiny pictured America as a "young and growing country"; it expanded through "swallowing territory," "just as an animal eats to grow." Savagery would inevitably "be swallowed by" civilization. . . .

Expansion, whites agreed, inevitably devoured Indians; only paternal governmental supervision could save the tribes from extinction. Paternalism, however, met white needs better than Indian ones. . . . In their paternalism toward Indians, white policy-makers indulged primitive longings to wield total power.

Indian dispossession is part of the history of American capitalism. Jackson and other political figures, freeing Indian land for the commodity economy, initiated a market revolution. They cleared the obstacles to free market relations, politically and by force, before the market could act on its own. The state and private instruments of violence massively assaulted tribal structures. They acquired the resources under Indian control for capitalist development. Force and fraud characterize American-Indian relations throughout our history, but their scope and timing give the Age of Jackson its significance.

Paul Rogin, *Fathers and Children: Andrew Jackson and the Subjugation of the American Indian* (New York: Alfred A.), 3–4, 9, 10, 12, 13. Reprinted by permission.

The draft treaty [of 1835] provided that the Nation cede and relinquish to the United States their rights and titles "to all lands owned, claimed and possessed" by the Cherokees, including lands reserved for a school fund, east of the Mississippi River, in return for which they would receive $5 million. This amount, in the opinion of one modern historian, represented "unprecedented federal generosity." A program of removal was also provided, along with scheduled payments for subsistence, claims and spoliations, blankets, kettles, rifles, and the like. After due notice, the treaty was to be submitted to the Cherokee National Council assembled at New Echota, Georgia, for their approval, and for the approval of the President with the advice and consent of the Senate. . . .

The treaty plucked from the Cherokees an enormous domain of choice land in western North Carolina, northern Georgia, northeastern Alabama, and eastern Tennessee, comprising approximately 7 million acres. It was an acquisition of staggering proportions. Small wonder American newspapermen gloated over it and reckoned the spectacular benefits for the country. Cherokees were aghast at the loss of their country and pledged to fight it at New Echota. Some of them appealed to Jackson for better terms. They assured him that the treaty could never win approval. They predicted death for those who had signed the document in the name of the Cherokee Nation, and they reminded Jackson of the many services they had provided him personally, going back to the Creek War in 1813. They said they were sure he would heed their supplications and do justice to his "red children."

As always, Jackson accorded Cherokee delegations marked deference when they visited him at the White House to make this appeal. He treated them as dignitaries of a foreign nation, although he would never acknowledge anything remotely resembling independence or sovereignty. And, as usual, he gave them one of his famous "talks," a talk usually distributed among the Cherokee people and published in the newspapers. . . . "Most of your people are uneducated, and are liable to be brought into collision at all times with your white neighbors. Your young men are acquiring habits of intoxication. With strong passions, and without those habits of restraint which our laws inculcate and render necessary, they are frequently driven to excesses which must eventually terminate in their ruin. The game has disappeared among you, and you must depend upon agriculture, and the mechanic arts, for support. And, yet, a large portion of your people have acquired little or no property in the soil itself, or in any article of personal property which can be useful to them. How, under these circumstances, can you live in the country you now occupy? Your condition must become worse and worse, and you will ultimately disappear, as so many tribes have done before you."

On December 28, what came to be called the Treaty of New Echota—it basically repeated the provisions of the "draft treaty" approved in March—was brought to the assembled Cherokees. The committee of twenty announced its acceptance of the terms of the treaty. A vote was taken and the treaty approved by the count of 79 to 7. This incredibly low number represented few Cherokees, certainly not the elected government of the Nation and certainly not the thousands of Indians who should have participated in the ratifying process. No matter. The treaty was approved and signed.

It was chicanery, pure and simple. The ratifying process was a fraud, an act approaching highway robbery. Nonetheless, it produced a removal treaty, and the power of the Cherokee Nation was broken at last.

The removal of the American Indian was one of the most significant and tragic acts of the Jackson administration. It was accomplished in total violation not only of American principles of justice and law but of Jackson's own strict code of honor. . . .

Andrew Jackson left office bowed down by the stupefying misery involved in removal, but he left knowing he had accomplished his goal and that thousands of Indians had found what he considered a safe haven west of the Mississippi River. He left believing he had saved the Indians from inevitable doom. And, indeed, he had.

Robert V. Remini, *Andrew Jackson and the Course of American Democracy, 1833–1845,* III (New York: Harper & Row, 1984), 296–7, 298, 300, 314. Reprinted by permission.

Elizabeth Cady Stanton. *(Courtesy, American Antiquarian Society)*

Lucretia Mott. *(Courtesy, Library of Congress)*

Stanton and Amelia Bloomer shown wearing the daring loose "bloomers"—long full Turkish trousers of black broadcloth with a short skirt and Spanish cloak. *(Seneca Falls Lily)*

An Age of Reform

THE WOMEN'S DECLARATION OF SENTIMENTS, 1848

The World Anti-Slavery Convention, held in London in 1840, was an important event in the women's rights movement as well as in the antislavery movement. American women, who had gained their first access to public platforms in antislavery activity, were horrified when their idols, the heroes of Great Britain's successful abolition of slavery in the empire, refused to allow them to be seated as delegates to the conference. Lucretia Mott, who had long exercised a public role both in Quaker and in antislavery affairs, was particularly incensed. Her straightforward anger, her willingness to argue with the men, and especially her preaching in a Unitarian Church in London "opened to me a new world of thoughts," Elizabeth Cady Stanton would recall. "As Mrs. Mott and I walked away arm in arm, commenting on the incidents of the day, we resolved to hold a convention as soon as we returned home, and form a society to advocate the rights of women."

Eight years elapsed before this resolve bore fruit in the Seneca Falls Woman's Rights Convention. The barriers had been many. Elizabeth Cady Stanton was newly married in 1840, and in the subsequent eight years she settled in three different locations, bore three children, and assumed all the other cares of a busy middle-class household. She needed further maturation and confidence to move on to a public stage. Lucretia Mott was unusual in having had so many opportunities, largely because of her Quaker environment, to speak in public and organize meetings. Her more cautious friend worked for a New York State law that would give married women control of their inherited wealth, but

HISTORICAL EVENTS

1817
American Colonization Society founded

1820
Washington Irving publishes "Rip Van Winkle" and "The Legend of Sleepy Hollow"

1821
Prison built in Auburn, New York, featuring solitary confinement at night and group labor by day

1823
James Fenimore Cooper begins the "Leatherstocking Tales"

1830
Joseph Smith publishes *Book of Mormon*

1831
The *Liberator* established in Boston
• Nat Turner revolt in Virginia

1833
Legal emancipation of British West Indian slaves

1839
Mormons migrate to Illinois and establish city of Nauvoo
• Theodore Weld, Angelina Weld, and Sarah Grimké publish *American Slavery as It Is*

continued

she remained quite timid, fearing the social disapproval that might befall women who spoke in public on any subject, more particularly women's rights. Finally in 1848, Lucretia Mott having planned a visit to relatives in the Seneca Falls area, the two women made a last minute decision to hold a small local convention on July 19–20, which they advertised only in the Seneca Falls newspaper.

The results were a surprise to the organizers, the participants, and particularly the press and pulpit whose subsequent attacks gave the conference much of its historical importance. Three hundred people—including forty men—attended this meeting. Overwhelmed by the response, the women had Lucretia's husband James preside. In two days of orderly meetings, the Convention heard a series of well-prepared speeches, adopted a Declaration of Sentiments and a set of resolutions, and planned a set of further meetings that flowered into one of the major reform movements of American history.

What made the Seneca Falls Convention special and powerful was its Declaration of Sentiments. Written by Elizabeth Cady Stanton and modeled after Jefferson's Declaration of Independence, the document aligned women's rights with American ideology, challenging the nation to be true to its tradition.

DECLARATION OF SENTIMENTS (1848)

When, in the course of human events, it becomes necessary for one portion of the family of man to assume among the people of the earth a position different from that which they have hitherto occupied, but one to which the laws of nature and of nature's God entitle them, a decent respect to the opinions of mankind requires that they should declare the causes that impel them to such a course.

We hold these truths to be self-evident: that all men and women are created equal; that they are endowed by their Creator with certain inalienable rights; that among these are life, liberty, and the pursuit of happiness; that to secure these rights governments are instituted, deriving their just powers from the consent of the governed. Whenever any form of government becomes destructive of these ends, it is the right of those who suffer from it to refuse allegiance to it, and to insist upon the institution of a new government, laying its foundation on such principles, and organizing its powers in such form, as to them shall seem most likely to effect their happiness. Prudence, indeed, will dictate that governments long established should not be changed for light and transient causes; and accordingly all experience hath shown that mankind are more disposed to suffer, while evils are sufferable, than to right themselves by abolishing the forms to which they were accustomed. But when a long train of abuses and usurpations, pursuing invariably the same object evinces a design to reduce them under absolute despotism, it is their duty to throw off such government, and to provide new guards for their future security. Such has been the patient sufferance of the women under this government, and such is now the necessity which constrains them to demand the equal station to which they are entitled.

The history of mankind is a history of repeated injuries and usurpations on the part of man toward woman, having in direct object the establishment of an absolute tyranny over her. To prove this, let facts be submitted to a candid world.

He has compelled her to submit to laws, in the formation of which she had no voice.

He has withheld from her rights which are given to the most ignorant and degraded men—both natives and foreigners.

Having deprived her of this first right of a citizen, the elective franchise, thereby leaving her without repre-

In the 1840s farmers and craftsmen, inventors and factory workers, were pressing form and efficiency upon the physical world. Evangelical Protestantism and the growing public school system were working to bring greater order to American minds and souls. A new party system was claiming to design programs for the better management of the American economy. Amidst these efforts, the women's rights movement along with innumerable other reform efforts of its time represented a large determination to perfect the republic of the Founders and, if possible, the world beyond the nation's borders.

Political and Economic Radicalism

During the second quarter of the nineteenth century, new social forces broke in upon the American villages, farms, and regions that had once existed in near isolation, practicing slow, traditional ways of work and life. Poverty, disease, and illiteracy became more concentrated and apparent as cities grew. The transportation revolution broke down barriers of distance and isolation, uprooting established communities and existing markets. Increasing reliance on machines turned independent craftsmen and sturdy farmers into wage earners. The tempo of life had speeded up. An English watchmaker who emigrated to New

sentation in the halls of legislation, he has oppressed her on all sides.

He has made her, if married, in the eye of the law, civilly dead.

He has taken from her all right in property, even to the wages she earns.

He has made her, morally, an irresponsible being, as she can commit many crimes with impunity, provided they be done in the presence of her husband. In the covenant of marriage, she is compelled to promise obedience to her husband, he becoming, to all intents and purposes, her master—the law giving him power to deprive her of her liberty, and to administer chastisement.

He has so framed the laws of divorce, as to what shall be the proper causes, and in case of separation, to whom the guardianship of the children shall be given, as to be wholly regardless of the happiness of women—the law, in all cases, going upon a false supposition of the supremacy of man, and giving all power into his hands.

After depriving her of all rights as a married woman, if single, and the owner of property, he has taxed her to support a government which recognizes her only when her property can be made profitable to it.

He has monopolized nearly all the profitable employ-

ments, and from those she is permitted to follow, she receives but a scanty remuneration. He closes against her all the avenues to wealth and distinction which he considers most honorable to himself. As a teacher of theology, medicine, or law, she is not known.

He has denied her the facilities for obtaining a thorough education, all colleges being closed against her.

He allows her in Church, as well as State, but a subordinate position, claiming Apostolic authority for her exclusion from the ministry, and, with some exceptions, from any public participation in the affairs of the Church.

He has created a false public sentiment by giving to the world a different code of morals for men and women, by which moral delinquencies which exclude women from society, are not only tolerated, but deemed of little account in man.

He has usurped the prerogative of Jehovah himself, claiming it as his right to assign for her a sphere of action, when that belongs to her conscience and to her God.

He has endeavored, in every way that he could, to destroy her confidence in her own powers, to lessen her self-respect, and to make her willing to lead a dependent and abject life.

A British mechanic wrote of his obser-
vations in the United States during the
late 1830s:

"Mechanics work harder, and labour in most occupations is greater, generally speaking, than in any other part of the world. Everything, in fact, connected with trade or business seems to proceed at a sort of railroad pace; all move at the very top speed—at a kind of high pressure rate: 'go along steam-boat' is the familiar expression of one to the other; sex and age offer no difference—the impulse is common to all."

York in 1832 wrote in his diary: "My employers have brought me so much work that I have scarce anytime for reading." An Irish moulder was shocked by his first visit to an American foundry: "I peered into the semi-darkness and saw men, bare-headed and almost nude racing back and forth, handling between trips small wooden hammers most dextrously. I asked . . . a bystander what was going on inside, and was told it was a foundry. The information made me gasp. I had never seen a foundry like it. Mechanics, and for that matter all others in the old country never worked so exhausting a way as these men did. . . . The American moulders seemed desirous of doing all the work required as if it were the last day of their lives."

During the first half of the nineteenth century a few Americans questioned the very foundations of capitalism. Some turned to religious or social experiments designed to reform society. A large number aimed at correcting specific problems. Reformers disagreed on goals and methods. But they shared frustration at disorder in society, apprehension about loss of consensus and community, and fear that morality was declining. These pessimistic motives for reform combined with an optimistic motive: a faith in the ultimate perfectibility of the world in general and American society in particular. A vigorous and many-sided movement for reform gained energy in the 1830s and continued to the Civil War.

The Early Labor Movement   The American labor movement had its origins in the economic upheavals of the Jacksonian era. In dozens of cities, craftsmen and artisans organized associations and sponsored strikes for better hours and wages. A few citywide federated unions and one national federation—the National Trades' Union—existed until hostile judges and the economic cataclysm of 1837 dragged them under. Labor also entered politics. In the early 1830s, for example, New York City workingmen organized politically to seek improved working conditions, free public education, abolition of imprisonment for debt, and an end to chartered banks and other monopolies. Most of their demands were eminently practical; some of their leaders were not.

The writer and social critic George Henry Evans had another remedy for unemployment and poverty: "Let us . . . emancipate the white laborer, *by restoring his natural right to the soil.*" As early as 1834, Evans advocated free land grants to actual settlers and a limitation on the holdings of any one person. Adopting the motto "Vote yourself a farm," he tried for years to convince eastern workingmen that their happiness and independence could be found only in agriculture. In 1862, six years after Evans's death, Congress passed the Homestead Act, offering free grants of western land. Workingmen did not have the capital, the knowledge, or the desire to go west and take up farming; and so the Homestead Act did not succeed in making independence and prosperity available to the whole nation. But the Act, an important component of the new Republican Party's scheme for nurturing the economy under governmental leadership, was a nineteenth-century foreshadowing of more daring twentieth-century social reforms.

Labor agitation and similar efforts were addressing, without quite recognizing the fact, a problem inherent in the American political, social, and economic system. Freeing work and property of traditional restrictions allowed for accumulations of land and other property. Unrestricted freedom also invited a competitiveness that militated against the cooperative civic ethic that had been another component of traditional republicanism and mocked the spirit of charity preached by American religion. Ever since, American reformers have striven to resolve the contradictions.

Voting Rights   Among the powerful social and political forces that the spirit of Jacksonian democracy unleashed in the United States, none was more compelling than the question of voting rights. Real democracy, of course, was still a long way in the future. The debates over voting rights during the Jacksonian era included no serious discussion of extending political rights to women or minorities. At the time of the Civil War, free African Americans would have the vote only in New Hampshire, Maine, Massachusetts, and Vermont. The only issue at hand was whether all adult white males should be able to vote. In 1800, only Vermont, New Hampshire, and Kentucky allowed all adult white men to vote. Every other state had either property or taxpaying requirements.

But as the rhetoric of democracy became increasingly popular in the early 1800s, the property and taxpaying requirements for voting began to fall. Conservatives still made their arguments, and some farmers worried that extending the right to vote to urban workers would only give more power to their employers. But other people were arguing that voting was a God-given right and should not be confined to elites. Between 1800 and 1840 state after state dropped the property requirement for voting. By 1840 only Louisiana, Rhode Island, and Virginia still had restrictive requirements.

The Rhode Island restrictions led to Dorr's Rebellion in 1841. At the time less than half of Rhode Island's white males could vote. Thomas W. Dorr, a Democrat and a lawyer, campaigned for relaxation of the property requirements, and when the governor and legislature refused to respond, he organized his own convention to write a new state constitution and abolish the property requirements. The governor called out the state militia to break up the convention, and in response Dorr and some of his followers attacked the militia's arsenal in Providence. Dorr was arrested, convicted of treason, and sentenced to life in prison. But by that time he was a folk hero to many people in the state, and in 1842 the governor gave him a pardon. In 1843 Rhode Island adopted a new state constitution that substantially broadened the right to vote.

Thomas W. Dorr led a popular rebellion in Rhode Island in 1841 to extend the franchise. (*Courtesy, Library of Congress*)

An Egalitarian Culture   The growing faith in the common people, the suspicion of political, social, and economic elites, had its reflection in the dress and demeanor of politicians. Earlier in the century, for example, national politicians had proudly worn powdered wigs, silk suits and stockings with knee breeches, polished shoes with buckles, and ruffled shirts, while other American men, even of conservative persuasion, were adopting the long trousers and short hair popularized by the French Revolution. Even after the disappearance of details of prerevolutionary dress, politicians continued to cultivate a look not of equality but of wealth, breeding, and refinement. All that changed with Andrew Jackson. Politicians began to brag about their common roots, about making it by their own effort. Silk was out, and cotton and woolen fibers were in. The Whig campaign of 1840 marked how far the styles of democracy had gone.

European travelers in the United States were quick to point out how the spirit of democracy was affecting other American institutions. By the late 1830s, most hotels in the United States had abandoned first-class accommodations and room service. All rooms were the same size with the same appointments, and guests ate their meals in family style around a large table. Some hotels refused to take advance reservations by mail, advertising themselves as first-come, first-serve establishments. Many domestic steamships, stagecoaches, and railroads also abandoned services that divided people into classes, catering to the well-to-do.

During the 1830s and 1840s a reaction also took place against professionalism. By that time the nation was well into the beginnings of the industrial revolution, and the importance of job skills, education, and technical expertise was increasingly clear. As society and the economy became more complicated, the educational requirements for engineers, accountants, physicians, and attorneys also became more complex. But those changes came at a time when it was a fashion to be suspicious of any elites—political, economic, or professional. When doctors tried to secure legislation in the 1840s requiring minimal educational requirements before an individual could practice medicine, they encountered stiff resistance in state legislatures where faith healers, naturopaths, and herbal practitioners joined with Jacksonians to defeat the measures. When the representatives of large banks tried to secure legislation requiring new state banks to have at least a defined amount of capital, they encountered similar resistance.

Religious Movements

The Second Great Awakening   In the 1820s and 1830s Americans experienced a second Great Awakening of religious enthusiasm. This religious resurgence reflected distinctly American values and attitudes. Its intensely democratic message stressed individual free will and immediate salvation; it breathed optimism; it brought religion to the people in language they could understand. Relying on the excitement of revival meetings, a wide variety of evangelical sects sought to turn the masses toward spiritual regeneration. Evangelists like Charles Grandison Finney rejected the harsh traditional Calvinist view of original sin and predestination and preached that any good Christian could attain eternal salvation. Their teachings generally involved a literal interpretation of the Bible. Many emphasized the Second Coming of Christ and believed that God's Kingdom would establish itself on earth. The common people appreciated sermons devoid of "literary quibbles and philosophical speculations." As one hymn put it to music, every person wanted to "see bright angels stand waiting to receive me."

The Second Great Awakening has been called "a women's awakening." Men certainly responded to the religious enthusiasm, but women far outnumbered them among converts and played a decisive part in leading men either back to established churches, or into new ones. Historians have shown that male conversions frequently followed the conversion of one or more female members of the family. Mothers often proved especially influential in converting their sons and husbands. But the most characteristic converts were adolescent girls. An affirmation, or reaffirmation, of religious belief and commitment seems to have offered young women a powerful sense of identity and purpose.

A belief distinctive to some participants in the Second Great Awakening was perfectionism, the idea that human beings could not merely achieve salvation, but overcome sin altogether. Perfectionism's scriptural basis lay in the New Testament account of Jesus' telling his disciples that they are to "be perfect, even as your Heavenly Father is perfect." Charles Finney, the most successful of the revivalists of the day, read this text literally. Jesus does not tell his followers to try to be perfect, Finney reasoned. He tells them to be perfect. Since he does so, Finney argued, he must have also supplied the means for them to do so. Like the first Great Awakening of a century before, the new evangelicalism was more than a religious movement. And the spirit of perfectionism animated the many reform movements of the era.

Religious enthusiasm rapidly increased the membership of most Protestant denominations, Methodists and Baptists increasing the fastest. But new sects also arose. Each new prophet, interpreter, or mystic found followers willing to join in anticipating the literal fulfillment of even the most outlandish prophecies. For a time the poor farming district of upstate New York burned with religious emotions. "Enthusiastic" sects, sects cultivating emotion, flourished in this "burned-over district," as it was called: whatever the original derivation of the phrase, it came to signify a region seared by fires of religious enthusiasm.

The Shakers and the Mormons   The Shaker faith, brought to this country by Ann Lee in 1774, received that name from one of its most distinctive practices, a sacred dance during which the members "shook" their bodies free of sin through their fingertips. "Mother Ann," as she was called, believed that she had received direct revelations from God and, since she preached millennialism—that is, the imminent coming of the millennium, the period of Christ's rule on earth—she saw no need for the Shakers to have children. The members therefore practiced celibacy. After reaching a membership of some six thousand in the 1830s, the Shakers gradually died out. Their furniture and housing arrangements, which were simplicity itself, are their best-remembered achievements.

By far the most important of the religious communitarians were the Mormons. Mormonism strikingly elaborated the new theology of free will, direct revelation, universal salvation, the expectation of Christ's imminent return, and the establishment of a millennial Kingdom.

In 1830, at the age of twenty-five, Joseph Smith of Palmyra, New

The Age of Finney

Historians, long preoccupied with politics, have characterized the period between the "Era of Good Feelings" and the onset of the Civil War as the Age of Jackson. An equally strong case can be made for calling it the Age of Finney—after the leading revivalist of the day, Charles Grandison Finney. Finney was the George Whitefield of the nineteenth century. His revivals had the same spectacular success. And his methods were equally sensational. Finney, for example, often prayed for sinners by name.

Finney's preaching reflected the general concern for order. Like the upper-class reformers who generously supported his work, he saw religion as a bulwark of the social order. And he encouraged his converts to join established churches. But Finney also preached the primacy of the individual conscience. He told his listeners that conversion would mark a radical change in their lives. They should, he urged, reexamine the whole pattern of their lives. Finney always left it for his converts to determine the direction of their new lives for themselves. He did not attempt to channel the enthusiasm he unleashed. And so Finney's revivals, despite the conservative cast of much of his preaching, could produce radicals of various stripes.

Shaker Society Meeting.
During worship members
were sometimes "seized with a
mighty trembling, with violent
agitations of the body, running
and walking on the floor, with
singing, shouting, and leaping
for joy." (*Courtesy, American
Antiquarian Society*)

The Mormon monument, a forty-
foot shaft capped by a statue of
the angel Moroni, stands atop
Hill Gumorah, a glacial rise in
northwestern New York State.
Here, in 1823, Joseph Smith
said he found the golden plates
he translated into the *Book of
Mormon.* (*Courtesy, American
Heritage*)

York, published the *Book of Mormon*. He had transcribed it, he claimed, from gold plates that had lain undisturbed in a nearby hillside for more than a thousand years. The angel Moroni directed him to the spot where the plates were buried. Using two magic "seeing stones" fixed in silver bows, Smith translated the ancient script into a readable text. The book was a curious mixture of Old Testament theology, popular history, and social beliefs of the times.

Although Mormonism borrowed freely from the convictions and practices of evangelical Protestantism, it offered a simple alternative to the confusing proliferation of Christian sects. By extending salvation to all adherents and clerical status to each adult white male, and by stressing the sanctity of secular accomplishments and the need for a community of "saints" (the church's official name was and is "The Church of Jesus Christ of Latter-day Saints"), the new faith tapped the energies and talents of the unsuccessful and the neglected. In Joseph Smith, a prophet who was believed to receive revelations directly from God, Mormonism provided theological truths and authoritarian leadership to whoever craved practical and spiritual guidance.

After converting a small group of relatives and friends, Smith moved his flock to Ohio and then to Missouri in an attempt to establish a commonwealth of believers. In each place, nonbelievers persecuted the Mormons and drove them from their lands. In 1839 Smith led his followers to Illinois. After securing political authority from state officials, he founded a city, called Nauvoo, which became a self-sufficient religious community. The success of Nauvoo, which grew to fifteen thousand inhabitants by 1844, as well as its voting power in state elections, brought the envy and hostility of outsiders. Smith's increasingly eccentric behavior (he declared himself a candidate for President in 1844) also generated unfavorable publicity. When a disgruntled Mormon confirmed that Smith and other members of the church's elite practiced polygamy, state officials arrested him and his brother. Soon after their confinement at Carthage, a mob of disbanded militia murdered them both.

"A New Zion"   When the harassment and violence continued, Brigham Young, Smith's successor to the presidency of the church, led the Mormons on the long difficult exodus from Illinois to uninhabited Mexican territory beyond the Rocky Mountains. Under Young's stern but effective leadership, the Mormons established a thriving agricultural community near the Great Salt Lake. By 1877, the year of Young's death, the commonwealth numbered some 350 settlements with a total population of 140,000.

Organized like a medieval kingdom, the church collected from each individual an annual tithe in goods, labor, or money, and channeled this surplus into projects that benefited everyone. Banning or discouraging the use of tea, coffee, tobacco, liquor, fashionable clothing, and elegant furniture, the church curtailed wasteful spending and assured the development of an industrious community. This mixture of collectivism and private enterprise saved the community from the worst evils of uncontrolled capitalism and prevented Utah from becoming dependent on imports from the industrial East.

Although the Mormons wished to be self-sufficient and independent, they also considered themselves Americans and asked for Utah's admission to the Union. Congress, however, balked at the Mormon practice of polygamy, which the new Republican Party of Abraham Lincoln had linked to slavery. In fact, only a small percentage of the community participated in this patriarchal institution; but the American public thought that Brigham Young's twenty-seven wives and fifty-six children were typical. In 1890 the church formally renounced polygamy, and Congress admitted Utah to the Union in 1896.

Millennialism   Some Americans looked to the fulfillment in their own time of the New Testament prophecy of Christ's Second Coming. The foremost exponent of millennialism was William Miller, a hardworking farmer in upstate New York who became caught up in a revival shortly after the War of 1812 and spent the rest of his life pondering religious questions. A literal interpretation of the Bible led him to a graphic belief in the Second Coming or Advent, which he calculated would occur in about 1843.

Aided by the widespread economic distress of the late 1830s, Miller made crowds of converts throughout New England with his vivid sermons depicting the glory of the Advent, the joy of those who would be saved, the suffering of the unrepentant. In a single year he gave 627 hour-and-a-half lectures before eager audiences, often of a thousand or more. Ministerial disciples with a knack for publicity spread Miller's views over an even wider area.

Miller hesitated to give his frantic followers a definite date, promising only that deliverance would come soon, in God's appointed time. As 1843—the Last Year—passed, March of 1844 came to be accepted as the crucial month. Finally, when nothing happened, a weary and discouraged Miller frankly admitted his mistake, explaining that he had done his best. But his lieutenants were not yet ready to quit. They chose October 22, 1844, as the new "Advent Day" and talked Miller into accepting it. Excitement mounted higher than before as extensive preparations were made to enter God's Kingdom. The faithful made

Priscilla Evans, though pregnant, walked with a handcart made of hickory from Iowa to Utah. Her account reveals the religious and economic motives that drove the Mormons across the continent to the Great Salt Lake.

"We began our journey [from Iowa City to Utah] of one thousand miles on foot with a handcart for each family, some families consisting of man and wife, and some quite large families. There were five mule teams to haul the tents and surplus flour. Each handcart had one hundred pounds of flour, that was to be divided and [more got] from the wagons as required. At first we had a little coffee and bacon, but that was soon gone and we had no use for any cooking utensils but a frying pan. The flour was self-raising and we took water and baked a little cake; that was all we had to eat.

After months of travelling we were put on half rations and at one time, before help came, we were out of flour for two days. We washed out the flour sacks to make a little gravy. . . .

No one rode in the wagons. Strong men would help the weaker ones, until they themselves were worn out, and some died from the struggle and want of food, and were buried along the wayside. It was heart rending for parents to move on and leave their loved ones to such a fate, as they were so helpless, and had no material for coffins. Children and young folks, too, had to move on and leave father or mother or both. . . .

We were much more fortunate than those who came later, as they had snow and freezing weather. Many lost limbs, and many froze to death. . . .

We reached Salt Lake City on October 2, 1856, tired, weary, with bleeding feet, our clothing worn out and so weak we were nearly starved, but thankful to our Heavenly Father for bringing us to Zion. . . ."

William Miller spoke lines like these throughout the 1830s:

"Ah! what means that noise? Can it be thunder? Too long—too loud and shrill—more like a thousand trumpets sounding an onset. It shakes the earth. . . . See how it reels. How dreadful! How strange! The very clouds are bright with glory. . . . See, the heavens do shake, the vivid clouds, so full of fire, are driven apart by this last blast, and rolling up themselves, stand back aghast—And O, my soul, what do I see? A great white throne, and One upon it. . . . Before him are thousands and thousands and thousands of wingèd seraphim, ready to do his will. The last trumpet sounds—the earth now heaves a throb for the last time, and in this last great throe her bowels burst, and from her sprang a thousand thousand, and ten thousand times ten thousand immortal beings into active life. . . . I saw them pass through the long vista of the parted cloud, and stand before the throne. . . . The air now became stagnated with heat; while the dismal howlings of those human beings who were left upon the earth, and the horrid yells of the damned spirits . . . filled my soul with horror not easily described."

themselves white "ascension robes" and neglected nearly all secular business. Voting in the fall elections was very light in some districts. On the night of October 21, Millerites gathered on hilltops to meet the new world together. No provisions were made for eating or sleeping, and many suffered as the night and the next day and then another night passed; thunderstorms added to their terror. Some claimed to have seen a jeweled crown in the sky, and there were meteor showers that night. In western New York, an earthquake intensified the expectation. A few Adventists committed suicide—one man leaped over Niagara Falls. The day of the "Great Delusion" effectively ended that movement, although Adventist sects continue to flourish.

The Fox Sisters

Various forms of spiritualism, or attempts to contact the spirit world, were another manifestation of the desire to break down all barriers between this world and the next. Mesmerism, electro-biology, clairvoyance, phrenology, magnetism—each had its following.

New York farmer John Fox had two remarkable young daughters, Maggie and Katie. Wherever they went in their home, mysterious rapping sounds were heard. Eventually the girls and their mother worked out a system of communication with the presumably otherworldly source of the rappings. Soon the neighbors flocked in to observe these conversations with the spirit world. The Fox home in the year 1848 set off a mania of spiritualist excitement. With an older sister acting as manager, the Fox girls began holding exhibitions—at the insistence of the spirits, of course—and quickly developed into professional fee-charging media.

With the wide publicity given the Fox sisters, media rapidly appeared all over the country, and spiritualist circles developed in nearly every town and village. They refined their techniques as they went along; the Foxes' managing sister, for instance, discovered that total darkness could produce many more manifestations of the spirits' presence. Table-moving, spirit-writing, and cold, ghostly hands soon supplemented the mystic rappings, and within a few years all the now-familiar paraphernalia of spiritualism were in use. The spiritualist excitement filled for thousands of people a need to become more comfortable with the mysteries of death and immortality. A number of intellectuals saw in spiritualism a replacement for traditional Christianity—a proof of the existence of a supernatural world for a scientific age that could not accept revelation resting only on faith. Even when the Fox sisters some years later admitted that their whole career had been a fraud (the rappings had from the first been produced by the joints of their toes), many spiritualists remained undeterred.

Methodism

The most powerful evangelical movement, more orthodox than these other religions of excitement, had begun in the eighteenth century. John Wesley had led within the Church of England a revival movement that after his death produced a separate denomination, the Methodist church. Methodists believed in free will. In its early days especially, Methodism had a strong element of emotional revivalism; but it also preached a rigorous piety and a morality of self-discipline, industry, thrift, and good works. Methodism was powerfully attractive, in Great Britain to the working classes and to the poor, and in this country to people on the frontier. In both nations it had something to do with the bringing of an ordered moral life to previously disordered sections of society. While the Methodist church did have an organization, in its first period it did not stress the role of bishops or of a highly trained ministry. That made it possible for Methodism here to develop a distinctive and effective system in which preachers, many with little, if any, formal religious education, would travel about on the frontier, bringing a sustaining Methodism to the families and communities at which they stopped.

Each preacher worked a "circuit" or route that covered a particular area. Francis Asbury, who had come to this country in 1771 and was influential in the beginnings of Methodism here, was an early and influential traveling preacher. The typical circuit rider went by horseback, depended on friendly settlers for food and shelter, and was much a part of the frontier environment: the evangelist Peter Cartwright could thrash a rowdy who tried to disrupt a Methodist meeting. Cartwright would hold his revivals outside in a grove because the local church could not hold the crowds he attracted.

The Methodists divided their territory into regions, each holding an annual conference that heard reports, appointed new preachers, and assigned circuits. As the frontier became heavily populated, large circuits—some had been hundreds of miles long—were replaced by smaller ones, and by about the middle of the nineteenth century these had given way to settled parishes. By that time the Methodist church was one of the largest Protestant denominations in the country.

Secular Communitarianism

Dozens of experimental communities built upon a trust in human perfectibility sprouted up in the nineteenth century. Some of them later succumbed to selfishness, quarrels, or loss of interest.

New Harmony   Robert Owen was a famous English socialist whose model factory town at New Lanark, Scotland, inspired many American utopians. In 1824 he organized his own communal experiment at New Harmony, Indiana, collecting a mixed group of followers whom he intended to transform into a prosperous, self-governing community. Practicing cooperation and common ownership of property, Owen hoped to eliminate selfishness and want. Quarrels and dissatisfaction finally forced Owen to abandon his misnamed experiment. Such experiments, his son Robert Dale Owen later concluded, were bound to fail in a country where cheap land and high wages fostered individualism and discouraged cooperative action.

Nashoba   The Owens's friend, feminist reformer Fanny Wright, tried her own utopian experiment in 1824 in Tennessee. Spending her inheritance, she established a community

Of his own conversion at a camp meeting, the Methodist minister Peter Cartwright recalled:

"The people crowded to this meeting from far and near. They came in their large wagons, with victuals mostly prepared. The women slept in the wagons, and the men under them. Many stayed on the ground night and day for a number of nights and days together. Others were provided for among the neighbors around. The power of God was wonderfully displayed; scores of sinners fell under the preaching, like men slain in mighty battle; Christians shouted aloud for joy.

To this meeting I repaired, a guilty, wretched sinner. On the Saturday evening of said meeting, I went, with weeping multitudes, and bowed before the stand, and earnestly prayed for mercy. In the midst of a solemn struggle of soul, an impression was made on my mind, as though a voice said to me, 'Thy sins are all forgiven thee.' Divine light flashed all round me, unspeakable joy sprung up in my soul. I rose to my feet, opened my eyes, and it really seemed as if I was in heaven; the trees, the leaves on them, and everything seemed, and I really thought were, praising God."

called Nashoba, where selected slaves would work the land, earn enough money to buy their freedom, and then be relocated outside the United States. But Fanny Wright also advocated free love and sexual equality in Nashoba, and her project had few outside supporters. She finally settled a few of the slaves in Haiti, but financial problems and public disapproval ended Wright's dream of emancipating America's blacks. She later moved to New York and took up the cause of urban working-men. Working with Robert Dale Owen, she edited a newspaper and recommended such radical notions as state guardianship of all children. In the 1840s she became an enthusiastic supporter of the women's rights movement.

Brook Farm   Brook Farm, a New England community, existed for a few years in the 1840s. Most of its members, such as Margaret Fuller, Nathaniel Hawthorne, and its founder George Ripley, were New England intellectuals; and it was influenced by Transcendentalism, a moral and spiritual doctrine to which numbers of New England writers and social critics adhered. Transcendentalism was an American variant of the idealist philosophy which teaches that the world of material objects as we see them is really no more than an expression of mind or consciousness. Transcendentalists believed that since it is mind rather than the objective and physical world that is the ultimate reality, the mind ought to draw into itself and cultivate its own powers. Transcendentalist intellectuals such as Ralph Waldo Emerson opposed slavery and other institutions that they perceived as getting in the way of individual and collective perfection. Emerson's *Essays* (1844) emphasized self-reliance and originality, perhaps a semi-solitary life close to nature. Brook Farm aimed at combining manual and intellectual work; this, its members hoped, would develop and enrich the inner self. Brook Farm—much of it destroyed by a major fire—is remembered for the high and not always practical intellectuality of its life, though residents did operate a successful experimental school.

The Oneida Community   John Humphrey Noyes, whose social ideas rested on perfectionism, founded a community at Oneida in upstate New York. Residents operated thriving manufactures, but the community was better known for its sexual arrangements. Wishing to substitute cooperativeness for competitive individualism, Noyes prohibited "special love" and instead established "complex marriage," a system in which every member resident was considered married to every other of the opposite sex. Like the Shakers, the communitarians at Oneida were seeking to control sexuality. They wished to break down the idea that any woman "belonged" to any man or that any child was the exclusive "property" of the biological parents. So while the Shakers practiced strict abstinence, Noyes and his followers engaged in what they called "sexual communion." This involved sexual intercourse in which the male refrained from climax, unless the community had previously decided on the desirability of the woman's becoming pregnant.

Sexual communion involved the regular rotation of sexual partners.

The sharp line between men's and women's spheres did not exist at the Oneida community, as this photo of a pea-shelling bee in the 1850s shows. *(Courtesy, Oneida Ltd. Silversmiths)*

And it entailed the use of communal nurseries to raise children. Women had sexual equality with the men and shared in the work; the entire community had responsibility for the children. The community had a prosperous and successful existence, derived from making Oneida silverplate and carrying on other successful business enterprises. Later in the century it abandoned complex marriage in the face of attacks from moral critics.

Social Reform

Some shared an optimistic conviction that the United States was still a growing society, not yet set in its ways, and therefore malleable to the reformers' efforts. Some prison reformers, for example, thought that new penitentiaries would all but eradicate crime. Others came to reform out of a deep pessimism. They believed that American society was in an advanced state of collapse and that only the most radical reform could halt the decay they saw all about them.

At the top of their list of danger signals was the decline, as pessimistic reformers saw it, of religion in American public life. Actually, Americans in the Jacksonian era were much more likely to belong to a church and to attend it faithfully than their parents and grandparents of the Revolutionary era had been. But as people followed the frontier westward, they left their churches behind and many feared that the Ohio and Mississippi Valleys would develop as pagan enclaves. Or worse. Protestants worried that the Catholic presence in St. Louis, a holdover from the French exploration of the Mississippi, might presage the loss of the interior of the continent to Romanism, as Catholicism was often called. Many Americans were leaving their homes not for the frontier but for the rapidly growing cities. Some, like Rochester, New York, were brand new boom towns. Others, like New York City, were already well established. No longer was the church the essential institution it had been, and still was, in village life. No longer did the pastor exert personal influence over everyone's public behavior. In the cities houses of prostitution operated seven days a week. Taverns served all comers. And the city's anonymity weakened old forms of social control, such as neighbors' disapproval of certain kinds of behavior. Large-scale immigration, especially of Irish and German Catholics, seemed further to endanger the old reign of Protestant morality.

Still another danger sign was the crime that accompanied urban growth. Packs of young toughs roamed the streets and made travel after dark a risky undertaking. As disturbing as crime was the growth of a highly visible underclass of the propertyless and homeless. Middle- and upper-class Americans were horrified to discover young children, often called street arabs, sleeping in alleyways, begging for food, and selling themselves into prostitution.

In the first half of the nineteenth century, reformers of all sorts set themselves the task of shoring up the social order, as pessimists thought, or to perfect what optimists believed to be an already progressive society. Such organizations as the Bible Society, the American Tract

Society, and the Home Missionary Society worked to instill religious principles in the population or portions of it; meanwhile, revivalists like Charles G. Finney preached to crowds. Other reformers worked for education, women's rights, improvement of prisons, care of the insane, temperance in drinking, total abstinence from drink, or the abolition of war. The best known of the reform movements, of course, were those opposed to slavery. Some opponents of slavery wished to colonize former slaves in Africa; some wanted to keep slavery from being permitted in the western territory; others, the most militant, called for abolition of slavery in the South. For all its varieties and conflicts of objectives, much of the reformist activity in the United States was of a single mind in its restless morality, its conviction that the world can be improved.

Personal experience motivated such reformers as southern abolitionists Angelina and Sarah Grimké, of a South Carolina slaveholding family, and the black abolitionist Frederick Douglass. Thomas Gallaudet's work for the deaf led to the founding of the American Asylum, a free school for the deaf in Hartford, Connecticut. Numbers of reformers, especially members of the Bible societies and the American Tract Society, came from a social elite. Fearing that disorder would grow worse unless the masses were inculcated with proper values, they took it upon themselves to serve as the moral stewards of the nation. "The gospel is the most economical police on earth," said a leader of the Home Missionary Society. The religious enthusiasm of the 1830s inspired such men as the antislavery activist Theodore Dwight Weld and the temperance advocate Neal Dow. And the prevalent belief in moral perfectionism sharpened the conviction of many reformers. Samuel Gridley Howe, a doctor, toured the country with a blind and deaf girl, Laura Bridgman, in order to prove that such people were not mentally deficient. The abolitionist editor William Lloyd Garrison, for example, became so committed to moral purity that he publicly burned a copy of the Constitution, symbolically dissociating himself from a document contaminated by slavery.

One former drinker confessed:

"I began Backsliding to the drinking of Eggnog. I went to a house-raising never thinking Satan would tempt me But they had the curse of the nation there and they took sugar, milk, and Eggs and stirred into the whiskey and begged me to Drink of it and I was green enough to submit and drank too much I crawled away and lay down, trying to hide the Disgrace. Poor old mother wept bitter tears when she heard of my Downfall and begged me to repent But all to no purpose for I was young and stubborn. I kept going on from bad to worse. Drinking fighting gambling playing the fiddle for dances and a great many other things."

Temperance   From colonial days Americans had been heavy drinkers. When Thomas Jefferson returned from France in 1789, he brought back over three hundred bottles of wine. New Englanders settled for rum, which the Puritans and later generations distilled from West Indian molasses. Before the advent of canals and railroads, farmers often sent their corn to market distilled in a jug or barrel: whiskey cost less than corn to ship over long distances and found a ready market. In many places it was safer to drink than water. An early nineteenth-century traveler in Ohio found the use of ardent spirits near universal: "A house could not be raised, a field of wheat cut down, nor could there be a log rolling, a husking, a quilting, a wedding, a sheepwashing, or a funeral without the aid of alcohol." Concerned particularly over the harm that drink could do to the family, reformers mounted a determined attack on it.

The temperance crusade was one of the most successful reforms. Using techniques borrowed from religious revivals and mass politics, temperance workers distributed leaflets, held "cold water parades," and

The DRUNKARD'S PROGRESS,

OR THE DIRECT ROAD TO POVERTY WRETCHEDNESS & RUIN.

Designed and Published by J.W.Barber, *New Haven. Com. Sept. 1826.*

Woe unto them that rise up early in the morning that they may follow Strong Drink . . . Isa. 5 C. 11v.

Woe unto them that are mighty to drink wine, and men of strength to mingle Strong Drink . . . Isaiah 5 C.22v.

Who hath woe? Who hath sorrow? Who hath contentions? Who hath wounds without cause? . . . They that tarry long at the wine. Prov. 23

The drunkard shall come to poverty. Proverbs. 23. Chap. 21 v. The wages of Sin is Death Romans. 6. Chap. 23 v

The MORNING DRAM.

The Beginning of Sorrow, Neglect of Business, Idleness, Languor, Loss of Appetite, Dulness and Heaviness, a love of Strong Drink increasing.

The GROG SHOP.

Bad Company, Profaneness, Cursing and Swearing, Quarreling & Fighting, Gambling, Obscenity, Ridicule and Hatred of Religion. The Gate of Hell.

The CONFIRMED DRUNKARD.

Beastly Intoxication, Loss of Character, Loss of Natural Affection, Family Suffering, Brutality, Misery, Disease, Mortgages, Sheriffs, Writs &c.

CONCLUDING SCENE.

Poverty, Wretchedness, a Curse and Burden upon Society, Want, Beggary, Pauperism, Death.

An 1826 caricature depicting the evils of drink. *(Courtesy, The New-York Historical Society)*

organized lecture circuits of reformed drunkards who made emotional appeals for converts to sign temperance pledges.

In the late 1830s a million people belonged to temperance societies. Timothy Shay Arthur's lurid account of the evils of drink, *Ten Nights in a Bar-room, and What I Saw There* (1845), ranked just behind *Uncle Tom's Cabin* as a best-seller of the 1850s. A book of etiquette of the period instructed a lady to write to a young man fond of liquor: "Under ordinary circumstances, I would be delighted to go to the opera with you. I regret to add, however, that I have undoubted evidence that you are becoming addicted to the use of the wine-cup. With an earnest prayer for your reformation, ere it be too late, I beg you to consider our intimacy at an end." The growing numbers of immigrants, the Germans bringing their tradition of beer and the Irish their taste for hard liquor, gave temperance crusaders further concern, and gave to the temperance cause an element of anti-Catholicism and hostility to immigrants. Many women's rights activists also joined the cause. Feminists argued that women, as the victims of the behavior of drunken men, were the chief sufferers.

Slowly, moral appeals gave way to political action. Under the leadership of Neal Dow, Maine in 1851 passed the nation's first statewide prohibition statute. In the next decade over a dozen states followed Maine's lead, although not all of these measures remained on the books.

The temperance agitation of those times and later is remembered

"Signing the Pledge."
A temperance society lithograph of
1846. (*Courtesy, Library of Congress*)

Alcohol Consumption per Capita, 1820–1850

Whatever the underlying causes for the dramatic fall in alcohol consumption during the 1830s, the untiring efforts of temperance reformers must have had some effect.

for its passion and its moral absolutism. Yet within the temperance movement were advocates not of total abstinence from alcohol but of moderation in its use, accompanied perhaps by a decision to refrain from hard liquor. Some of the evils they denounced were real. Drunkenness on the frontier, and in the growing cities with their individuals uprooted from traditional communities and thrown into urban crowds and poverty, was a destroyer of families and lives. In the course of the nineteenth century, restraint in the use of alcohol appears to have spread. That may be attributable to orderly conduct inculcated by public schooling, and to the diffusion throughout society of middle-class modes of behavior. But surely some credit should go to the temperance crusade itself.

Public Education For much of American history, formal education had been the province of families who could afford to pay for it. The Puritans, of course, had been exceptions to that rule, but for the most part, until the early nineteenth century, education was a private affair. Jacksonians wanted to remove education from the control of social and economic elites.

Like temperance, educational reform appealed both to Americans who believed that moral decay was spreading throughout the land and to others who more cheerfully thought that their age was a time of universal progress. Horace Mann, the first Massachusetts superintendent of education, warned that "the unrestrained passions of men are not only homicidal, but suicidal; and a community without a conscience would soon extinguish itself." Universal education, entailing moral guidance and firm discipline, must become the responsibility of the state and receive public financing. Mann and his supporters in the common school movement argued that leaving education in the hands of families, or preserving it as a luxury of the elite, threatened the nation's political and economic stability. The schools would also prepare Americans for the exercise of intelligent, informed citizenship.

In 1800 there were no public school systems outside New England; by 1850 every state had at least some public elementary and secondary schools. Northern states surpassed southern in the percentage of white children enrolled. Several states made appropriations for schools to educate the deaf and the blind. Public schools required a new, more practical curriculum in place of the traditional, classical learning designed for an elite. The study of Greek and Latin along with classical authors would be of limited value for future generations of farmers and mechanics. McGuffey's *Reader* and Webster's *Speller,* whose short lessons simultaneously taught useful skills and proper moral habits, became standard classroom texts, and teachers added exercises in geography, American history, and science. Gradually, the look of the classroom changed—maps, globes, and blackboards all made their first appearance.

Institutions of higher education also proliferated. New kinds of schools opened: technical schools such as Rensselaer Polytechnic Institute in New York; state universities in most western states; hundreds of denominational colleges; and some "colleges"—more correctly, advanced academies and seminaries—for women. Women's education presented a special problem and challenge to the reform movement. Since the end of the eighteenth century, sentiment had grown among both men and women in favor of education for women. But few of those who sought to educate women wanted to train them for the professions or otherwise give them a schooling identical to men's. Women were to be educated for enlightened republican motherhood, and to be suitable companions to educated husbands. Female educators such as Emma Willard, founder of Troy Seminary, and Mary Lyon, who founded Mount Holyoke Seminary, justified women's schooling with the claim that educated women would enhance the home. But increasingly, some female educators, notably Catharine Beecher—daughter of Lyman Beecher and sister of Harriet Beecher Stowe—also stressed the importance of educating women as primary school teachers, especially single women who would have to earn their livings. The teaching profession, by the middle of the century distinctly moving toward feminization, was viewed as an appropriate extension of women's primary domestic role.

Throughout higher education the content of schooling changed. Older universities modified their curricula, reducing the heavy dose of theology and the classics in favor of modern languages, political economy, and the sciences. Several added professional programs in law, medicine, or engineering. A number of western colleges adopted the unusual concept of student self-help through manual labor. Founded by radical reformers, these schools, such as Oberlin in Ohio (also, in 1837, the first to be coeducational) and Knox in Illinois, became centers of both educational experimentation and antislavery activism.

In taking over from the family the primary obligation for schooling, the state was doing what it was coming to do also for other dependent members of society. Formerly, responsibility for them, too, had gone to the family or to local authorities; but as an increasing density of popula-

In a republic," Horace Mann wrote "ignorance is a crime."

"If we do not prepare children to become good citizens—if we do not develop their capacities, if we do not enrich their minds with knowledge, imbue their hearts with the love of truth and duty, and a reverence for all things sacred and holy, then our republic must go down to destruction, as others have gone before it; and mankind must sweep through another vast cycle of sin and suffering, before the dawn of a better era. . . ."

tion intensified social problems, reformers began seeking better solutions. To the Christian cult of perfectionism these humanitarians added a growing belief in the power of environment to shape human character. The result, in the words of one historian, was "the discovery of the asylum."

Reform of Prisons and Asylums   At the urging of reformers, most states rewrote their colonial penal codes, abolishing imprisonment for debt and restricting the application of the death penalty to murderers. For lesser offenses, imprisonment took the place of such brutal corporal punishments as whipping, dunking, and branding. To house and rehabilitate prisoners, the states began to build modern prisons. (Connecticut had formerly housed felons in an abandoned copper mine.) New York, with the construction of its prison at Auburn in 1821, inaugurated the system of individual confinement by night and group labor by day. Under the theory that isolation would promote moral reflection (in fact it often promoted suicide), Pennsylvania in 1829 established a penitentiary that provided for strict solitary confinement of prisoners at all times. Alexis de Tocqueville concluded that while the Pennsylvania system made "the deepest impression on the soul of the convict," the Auburn system was "more conformable to the habits of man in society, and on this account effects a greater number of reformations." States also created special correctional facilities for juveniles, and for minor criminals such as drunks and vagrants.

Before 1840, victims of mental illness had been cared for privately—in locked rooms, cages, or outhouses—or else confined to jails and poorhouses. A Massachusetts schoolteacher, Dorothea Dix, undertook an investigation of the problem in her native state. Armed with the facts, she prepared a memorial to the legislature. Pledging to "tell what I have seen," she described graphically "the *present* state of insane persons confined within the Commonwealth, in *cages, closets, cellars, stalls, pens! chained, naked, beaten with rods, and lashed into obedience!*" The lawmakers, shocked by her descriptions, voted funds in 1843 to enlarge the state hospital for the insane. During the next decade Miss Dix traveled over thirty thousand miles in behalf of her cause. As a result, nearly every state made some provision for the care and treatment of the indigent insane. Some members of the health care services were also coming to believe that asylums, besides easing the suffering of the mentally ill, could provide an environment in which patients could regain their sanity.

Dorothea Dix's crusade on behalf of victims of mental illness led most states to make provisions for the indigent insane. *(Courtesy, Library of Congress)*

The Science of Reform   The concept of the penitentiary and the asylum, along with the extension of the public school system, shared half explicit assumptions. One of them, reflected also in religious perfectionism and those temperance advocates who called for voluntary abstinence or moderation, was that human will and intelligence can be brought to master the rest of the wayward personality. Criminals can be conditioned to overcome their deviant impulses, the insane to recover lucidity, schoolchildren to acquire orderly thought and conduct. Beyond this was a notion that there is a right method for improving the state of individuals and society. Even as assertive democrats were denying that scientific professions have the right to establish standards for admission, fields of social expertise were beginning to emerge. A people increasingly aware that method could trap steam and command threads to weave themselves into fabrics could scarcely doubt that method might also bring health to society and its members.

Women's Sphere

The career of Dorothea Dix illustrates nicely the general plight of free women in the mid-nineteenth century. Intelligent, educated, and an expert in her field, she was obliged, in the interests of maintaining a "womanly dignity," to work quietly, rarely speaking in public herself. The only professions open to upper-class and middle-class women at that time were those of teacher, missionary, and writer; women of other classes worked in factories or as laundresses, seamstresses, or servants.

In other ways, society was defining for middle-class women a life of privacy and domesticity. From the beginning of the nineteenth century, but especially following 1820 and particularly in the Northeast, home was becoming separate from income-earning work. A major reason was that the development of commerce and cities, along with the march of modern industry, created workplaces physically as well as socially distant from dwellings. Men went out to work; women, or a large proportion of them, stayed home. This separation of home from "work" reinforced the nineteenth-century ideals of domesticity and true womanhood, which suggested that human life is divided into a public male sphere of labor and a private female sphere of nurture and morality. In the home under a woman's governance a "man . . . seeks refuge . . . where some of his finest sympathies, tastes, and moral and religious feelings are formed and nourished," so declared a New Hampshire minister in 1827.

Public opinion and economic circumstance were embodied in the law, which regarded women as perpetual minors. Married women had almost no rights over their property or children and could not sue in their own name. They could not even sign contracts. Divorces were rarely granted. The Civil War diarist Mary Chesnut wrote: "there is no slave . . . like a wife."

Women and Reform

After the Seneca Falls Convention of 1848, all this could have discouraged women from joining reform movements, which aggressively entered the public sphere that tradition claimed to be the domain of males; and many women undoubtedly drew that lesson. But the idea central to the nineteenth-century exclusion of women from public life, the belief that they possessed a superior intuition into morality and a superior urge to nurture the sick and helpless, was to provide in time an argument for their entrance into the public sphere. If morality is the special province of women, they must have important things to say about issues that were

This letter of 1837 expresses the Congregationalist clergy's reaction to speeches in favor of abolitionism. The document indicates the degree of authority felt and exercised by the clergy at that time, and their concern over the public role of women who were making speeches at antislavery conventions.

"We invite your attention to the dangers which at present seem to threaten the female character with wide-spread and permanent injury.

The appropriate duties and influence of woman are clearly stated in the New Testament. Those duties and that influence are unobtrusive and private, but the source of mighty power. When the mild, dependent, softening influence of woman upon the sternness of man's opinions is fully exercised, society feels the effects of it in a thousand forms. The power of woman is in her dependence, flowing from the consciousness of that weakness which God has given her for her protection, and which keeps her in those departments of life that form the character of individuals and of the nation. We appreciate the unostentatious prayers and efforts of woman in advancing the cause of religion at home and abroad; in Sabbath-schools; in leading religious inquirers to the pastors for instruction; and in all such associated effort as becomes the modesty of her sex. . . .

But when she assumes the place and tone of man as a public reformer. . . , we put ourselves in self-defence against her; she yields the power which God has given her for protection, and her character becomes unnatural. We cannot, therefore, but regret the mistaken conduct of those who encourage females to bear an obtrusive and ostentatious part in measures of reform, and countenance any of that sex who so far forget themselves as to itinerate in the character of public lecturers and teachers."

ELIZABETH BLACKWELL

Elizabeth Blackwell was the first woman in the United States to receive a medical degree, awarded to her by Geneva Medical College in 1849. She had applied for admission to Harvard, Yale, and other schools only to be rejected. Then she was accepted by a little known institution in upstate New York. She was overjoyed to receive a letter stating:

"Resolved that one of the radical principles of a Republican Government is the universal education of both sexes; that to every branch of scientific education the door should be open equally to all; that the application of Elizabeth Blackwell to become a member of our class meets with our entire approbation."

Classmates gave these accounts:

"Elizabeth Blackwell was a determined young lady and took the train and stage to the village on Seneca Lake. Her first step was to find a room in a boarding house, but many landladies were afraid to rent a room to a female planning to become a doctor. What would the other boarders say? Finally Elizabeth persuaded a tough-minded Scotswoman to accept her. Her fellow boarders were shocked. Some ignored her; others gave her a frozen glance.

She then went to the college where the dean was astonished to see her; he had never expected that she would actually appear. He told her that in order to matriculate she needed the approval of the faculty and student body. Furthermore she would need the unanimous approval of the students who had never voted unanimously in the history of the college.

Great was the excitement and hilarity of the students who treated the matter as a joke. Some shouted: 'Down with the men.' Others called for trousers for all students. When the student chairman put the motion to admit Elizabeth to the college, the assembly shouted 'Yes.' One weak voice in the corner said 'No.' At once his neighbors surrounded him, shoved him to the floor, and pounded on his shoulders. He finally whispered 'Yes.'

The dean wrote a letter to Miss Blackwell welcoming

This portrait, by Elizabeth Glaser of Maryland in about 1830, epitomizes the "cult of true womanhood." The doll-like woman seems unsuited for anything more demanding than fanning herself. *(Courtesy, Scribner's Archives)*

at once public and moral, such as the dangers of alcohol, or matters concerning the protection of the weak and the ill.

Women engaged in a long struggle to assert their right to speak in public, to organize, and eventually to vote on behalf of moral issues. They made slow but solid progress. In their effort they relied particularly upon the bonds and networks that they had established with other women—the bonds of sisterhood. These female networks supported a wide variety of female associations providing charity to the needy, raising funds for the education of ministers, combating slavery, working for various moral reforms that included temperance and the elimination of prostitution, and giving support to mothers seeking to set their children on the right path. Although many reform associations, such as those contributing to the abolitionist and the temperance movements, remained firmly under male leadership throughout the first half of the nineteenth century, female reformers supplied much of the dedication.

Women's Rights
The cause of women's rights soon became a movement in itself. Lucy Stone, an antislavery and women's rights activist who retained her maiden name after marriage, refused to pay taxes since she was not represented in the government. Some women rejected their long, immobilizing skirts in favor of the less constricting "Bloomer" costume. It consisted of a tunic that fell to mid-calf worn over a pair of ample bloomers that covered the legs and were gathered tightly at the ankle. In its time and place, it earned the women who wore it ridicule, hostility, and a show-

her to the student body. The students signed it with mixed feelings. Many thought that she would not accept or would never stay because of the hostile greeting. Dean James Hadley, however, offered to conduct her to her first class and he urged the students to treat her with respect. Although she had to suffer some pranks and horseplay, she soon showed her ability. In 1849 she graduated at the head of her class."

Another observer described the commencement exercises to a friend:

"We sat in the Second tier [the gallery]. About half past ten or eleven the procession entered the building. The Lioness of the day, Miss Blackwell, met them at the door and entered with the Medical Students—*without* hat or shawl. She wore a black silk dress and cape-lace collar and cuffs and her reddishly inclined hair was very nicely braided. She sat in the front side pew with old Mrs. Waller until she received her Diploma. . . . Take it altogether—*the ladies* carried the day! There was scarcely a coat—excepting the Students'—visible! Noth-

ing but a vast expanse of woman's [sic] bonnets and curious eyes. The noise on the 'Singers' bench' completed, President Hale made a brief Address to the graduating class, then donned the velvet cap and seated himself in the large chair. . . . He called up the graduates. Four at a time they came on the stage. The Doctor spoke. They *looked* Knowing. One of them grasped the bundle of sheepskins, all four bowed and vanished. Last of all came 'Domina Blackwell'. She ascended the steps. The President touched his cap and rose. You might have heard a pin drop. He handed her the diploma and bowed, evidently expecting she would bow also and retreat. Not so, however! She seemed embarrassed and after an effort, said to the Dr.—'I thank you Sir. It shall be the effort of my life, by God's blessing, to shed honor on this Diploma'—then bowed, blushed scarlet, left the stage and took her seat in the front pew among the Graduates amid the Enthusiastic applause of all present. . . ."

Dr. Elizabeth Blackwell founded the New York Infirmary for Women and Children where she trained women to become doctors.

ering of rotten eggs and tomatoes. Even those most determined advocates of women's rights, Susan B. Anthony and Elizabeth Cady Stanton, eventually gave up the mode of dress with heartfelt relief. The Bloomer costume was an attempt to break through social convention and constriction. Other reforms aimed at protecting women against the harms to which they were distinctively subject.

Woman reformers proved especially active in defense of the personal rights of other women whom they perceived as oppressed or exploited by the familial and sexual demands of men. Susan B. Anthony helped a woman kidnap her child from her husband's custody—idealization of motherhood notwithstanding, fathers usually got custody of children. Other women worked for temperance to protect women from the beatings and domestic violence of drunken husbands. Objecting to the double standard that allowed men to have sex outside marriage while denying it to women, a group of New York women started a society to reform the city's prostitutes.

Numbers of middle-class women who took up feminist causes had begun by becoming involved in other social reforms. As women extended their interests outside the home, met together, assumed leadership, and became adept at public speaking, they soon came to recognize the status in which women were kept. "In striving to strike the [black man's] irons off, we found most surely, that *we* were manacled ourselves," wrote Abby Kelley, a women's rights leader. But if the antislavery cause helped launch the women's rights movement, it also contributed to a temporary demise. Even many sympathetic men aban-

Angelina Emily Grimké, originally from South Carolina, was both an abolitionist and a crusader for women's rights. She wrote succinctly that

"[I]t is a woman's right to have a voice in all the laws and regulations by which she is governed, whether in Church or State. . . . The present arrangements of society, on these points are a *violation of human rights, a rank usurpation of power,* a violent seizure and confiscation of what is sacredly and inalienably hers."

Sojourner Truth. In her bag she often carried copies of the narrative of her life to sell. *(Courtesy, State University College, New Paltz, N.Y.)*

doned feminist causes when they threatened to divert or divide the antislavery crusade.

One especially striking feminist was a former slave, Sojourner Truth. Born Isabella in New York in 1797, she stood at a stunning six feet. A domestic servant for many years following New York's emancipation law of 1827 and illiterate until her death, she was a commanding orator in the cause of both abolition and women's rights.

Reaction   Women's rights advocates encountered stiff resistance from conservative groups. Industrialization, the reform movements, and the rise of a democratic political culture were rapidly altering American society, and most people wanted to preserve at least some of the old ways. They decided to keep their homes as they supposedly had always been, and that meant confining women to domestic careers as wives and mothers. The "Cult of Domesticity," or "True Womanhood," was a powerful force. Popular magazines talked incessantly about the elevated status of women: they raised the sons who would become the next generation's leaders, they kept men's sexual passions in line, and their purity, chastity, and compassion preserved virtue and gentility in a rapidly changing world. A popular poem of the 1840s, very much in the spirit of "True Womanhood," is a repudiation of the women's rights movement. The only "rights" that women embrace, the poet explains, are

> The right to love whom others scorn,
> The right to comfort and to mourn,
> The right to shed new joy on earth,
> The right to feel the soul's high birth.

Many years after the event, an Ohio feminist, who had presided over the 1851 women's rights convention, recorded this inspiring talk of Sojourner Truth:

Every eye was fixed on this almost Amazon form, which stood nearly six feet high, head erect, and eyes piercing the upper air like one in a dream. At her first word there was a profound hush. She spoke in deep tones, which, though not loud, reached every ear in the house, and away through the throng at the doors and windows.

"Wall, chilern, whar dar is so much racket dar must be somethin' out o' kilter. I tink dat 'twixt de niggers of de Souf and de womin at de Norf, all talkin' 'bout rights, de white men will be in a fix pretty soon. But what's all dis here talkin' 'bout?

Dat man ober dar say dat womin needs to be helped into carriages, and lifted ober ditches, and to hab de best place everywhar. Nobody eber helps me into carriages, or ober mud-puddles, or gibs me any best place!" And raising herself to her full height, and her voice to a pitch like rolling thunder, she asked, "And a'n't I a woman? Look at me! Look at my arm! (and she bared her right arm to the shoulder, showing her tremendous muscular power). I have ploughed, and planted, and gathered into barns, and no man could head me! And a'n't I a woman? I could work as much and eat as much as a man—when I could get it—and bear de lash as well! And a'n't I a woman? I have borne thirteen chilern, and seen 'em mos' all sold off to slavery, and when I cried out with my mother's grief, none but Jesus heard me! And a'n't I a woman? . . .

Den dat little man in black dar, he say women can't have as much rights as men, 'cause Christ wan't a woman! Whar did your Christ come from?" Rolling thunder couldn't have stilled that crowd, as did those deep, wonderful tones, as she stood there with outstretched arms and eyes of fire. Raising her voice still louder, she repeated, "Whar did your Christ come from? From God and a woman! Man had nothin' to do wid Him." Oh, what a rebuke that was to that little man.

The Dark Side of Reform

The reform movements were not unmixed blessings for the United States. The reformers, in their passion for eliminating evil, sometimes defined evil in a way that had vicious consequences.

Hostility to Catholicism and Mormonism   The conviction that American society has special democratic and moral traditions to preserve and protect has led more than once to movements to rid the country of something or somebody. A case in point is the rapid growth of anti-Catholic sentiment after 1830. Before then American Catholics had been too few in number to attract much attention. Over the next thirty years, mass immigration, especially from Ireland and Germany, swelled the Catholic proportion of the total population from one in fifty to one in ten. Many native-born Protestants believed that the newcomers posed a direct threat to the nation's democratic heritage. In part this conviction grew out of their understanding of history.

The American Revolution, in their eyes, was an extension of the Protestant Reformation, particularly of Luther's doctrine of the primacy of individual conscience. The Reformation, many thought, had been a struggle for liberty against an oppressive, autocratic perversion of true

Some native-born Protestant Americans despised immigrant Catholics, as illustrated in this lithograph of a Philadelphia riot in 1844 between Catholics and non-Catholics. This sentiment led to the founding of the American Party in the 1850s. (*Courtesy, Library of Congress*)

Christianity. Their own Revolution had carried the struggle into the political domain. So the rapid increase in the Catholic population caused many to worry for the nation's commitment to a republican form of government. Such prominent men as Lyman Beecher, the celebrated preacher, and the inventor Samuel F. B. Morse warned against "papal puppets working to inflame and divide the nation, break the bond of our union, and throw down our free institutions." American bishops and other Catholic clergy aggressively campaigned in New York City and Lowell, Massachusetts, and elsewhere for public funds for parochial schools, an issue that especially inflamed Protestants. Militant Protestants formed societies aimed at converting "Papists" to Christianity (these had little success) and stoutly resisted all attempts at suggestions of public aid to parochial schools (sometimes with success, sometimes not). Some antislavery activists were hostile to Catholicism, holding it to be, like slavery, an affront to republican freedom.

Anti-Catholicism, however, did not spring simply from devoted concern for the purity of the Revolutionary tradition. It also sprang from distaste for the immigrants themselves. The Irish were stereotyped as drunken brutes. One woman recalled seeing the "poor fellows, strung along the canal, stupid from drink . . . they are for the most part covered with mud, where they have rolled when drunk." The German-American practice of bringing beer even to such innocent activities as Sunday picnics affronted Protestant sensibilities. Protestant nativists also drew upon centuries of anti-Catholic propaganda. Zealots composed and circulated fictitious stories of convent life replete with sex orgies among nuns and priests.

Mormons, like Catholics, came into conflict with many traditional Protestants. Wherever they had settled, Mormons voted as a bloc, following the dictates of their leaders, Joseph Smith and later Brigham Young. In their loyalty to their community and its leaders, the Mormons closed ranks and often enjoyed political power far greater than numbers alone would provide. The practice of polygamy was also an outrage to nineteenth-century Protestantism. It contradicted the Bible, the laws of the land, and the cult of true womanhood. In the 1840s Mormons were victims of harassment and violence.

The Anti-Immigrant Crusade

The attacks on Catholics and Mormons were part of a larger, ethnocentric fear of immigrants. While the influx of millions of Irish immigrants in the 1830s and 1840s swelled the numbers of Catholics in the United States, the Mormon Church had attracted thousands of immigrant converts from the British Isles and Scandinavia. The fear on the part of native-born Protestants was not only of alien religions, but also of immigration in itself as a threat to democratic values and the fundamentals of Anglo-American culture.

For some time, a nativist movement had been prominent in American society and politics. In 1843 the American Republican Party called for limiting the right to vote to native-born American Protestants. In April 1844 nativists established the American Republican Association at Philadelphia. Its anti-immigrant rhetoric led to rioting in Philadelphia and the deaths of twenty people. The next year the group became known as the American Party. By the early 1850s it would be known as the "Know-Nothing Party," after a popular perception of its members as secretive, refusing to acknowledge that they knew anything about the movement.

The Arts

During Jacksonian times and just after, the United States at last achieved cultural independence of Europe in literature, painting, and architecture. The newly popular lyceums and public lectures furnished native talent with an audience. In 1860 knowledgeable Europeans would no longer ask, as one English literary wit had in 1820, "In the four quarters of the globe, who reads an American book? Or goes to an American play? Or looks at an American picture or statue?"

Speaking at Harvard in 1837, the transcendentalist philosopher Ralph Waldo Emerson attacked "the timid, imitative, and tame" in American creative life. Americans, he asserted, must learn to work with their own hands and speak with their own minds. And they were doing so.

American painters abandoned the formal, classical style of the eighteenth century. Influenced by the romantic movement and nationalism, they experimented with more individualistic, democratic, emotional styles of painting. Genre painters like William Sidney Mount and George Caleb Bingham took their studios outdoors to capture revealing incidents of American life. Bingham's "Stump Speaker" and "Country Elections" are miniature essays on Jacksonian politics. Nature painters like Thomas Cole glorified the spectacular qualities of the American landscape. Cole was a leader of the so-called Hudson River School, those painters who captured especially the magnificent Hudson River Valley with its deep woods, its jagged rocks, its sweeping vistas.

American architects also turned from eighteenth-century styles of European origin. Their search for a pure, simple, democratic architecture led naturally to the Greek Revival, inspired by the buildings of ancient Greece. Among the best examples of this style are Benjamin Latrobe's Bank of the United States at Philadelphia and Robert Mills's Treasury Building at Washington. Responding to the individualistic and romantic impulses of the age, American architects later adopted a variety of styles. By 1850 Philadelphia had an Egyptian jail, a Greek bank, medieval cottages, and Moorish churches, while New York boasted a synagogue with a Gothic tower.

American Literature   American writers and poets too were influenced by the forces of nationalism. Breaking with the rigid neoclassical writing of the eighteenth century, they sought a literature that was expressive, imaginative, intuitive.

Much of American literature made use of native settings. Washington Irving drew on the history of his native New York in stories such as "Rip Van Winkle" and "The Legend of Sleepy Hollow" (1820). In a series of novels known as the "Leatherstocking Tales" (1823–41), James Fenimore Cooper's frontiersman is a noble figure. Not at all so are the

William Sidney Mount, *The Banjo Player.* *(Courtesy, Museums at Stony Brook)*

William Sidney Mount, *Dancing On the Barn Floor.* *(Courtesy, Museums at Stony Brook)*

vulgar common folks whom the patrician Cooper censured for their translation of democracy into pushy assertiveness.

Yet American literature, born of a nation that appeared so boisterously cheerful, was distinguishable for a character of brooding introspection, an exploration into the deepest human motives and the mind's most wayward fantasies. This surely was owing in part to the American religious preoccupation with the inner life. It may also be that American republicanism, in cutting the individual loose from the political and social institutions of older cultures, made novelists curious about the private, inward experience of the individual adrift. Edgar Allan Poe, examining the resources of the imagination with something of the experimental care that other Americans were addressing to the workings of the physical world, labored to awaken in his readers sensations of mystery and eeriness. Ralph Waldo Emerson composed carefully wrought essays and was a great orator. Nathaniel Hawthorne brought intensity, depth, and craftsmanship to the American novel. In works like *The Scarlet Letter* (1850) and *The House of the Seven Gables* (1851) he probed the souls of American Puritans. Hawthorne looked into dark

---

Ralph Waldo Emerson's most famous essay was "Self Reliance":

Trust thyself; every heart vibrates to that iron string. To believe your own thought, to believe that what is true for you in your private heart is true for all men—that is genius. In every work of genius we recognize our own rejected thoughts; they come back to us with a certain alienated majesty. Great works of art have no more affecting lesson for us than this. They teach us to abide by our spontaneous impression with good-humored inflexibility, then most when the whole cry of voices is on the other side. Else tomorrow a stranger will say with masterly good sense precisely what we have thought and felt all the time, and we shall be forced to take with shame our own opinion from another.

Whoso would be a man, must be a nonconformist. He who would gather immortal palms must not be hindered by the name of goodness, but must explore if it be goodness. Nothing is at last sacred but the integrity of our own mind. Absolve you to yourself, and you shall have the suffrage of the world.

What I must do is all that concerns me, not what the people think. This rule, equally arduous in actual and in intellectual life, may serve for the whole distinction between greatness and meanness. It is the harder because you will always find those who think they know what is your duty better than you know it. It is easy in the world to live after the world's opinion; it is easy in solitude to live after our own; but the great man is he who in the midst of the crowd keeps with perfect sweetness the independence of solitude.

The other terror that scares us from self-trust is our consistency. A foolish consistency is the hobgoblin of little minds, adored by little statesmen and philosophers and divines. With consistency a great soul has simply nothing to do. If you would be a man speak what you think today in words as hard as cannon balls, and tomorrow speak what tomorrow thinks in hard words again. . . .

Ralph Waldo Emerson. *(Library of Congress)*

motives and somber emotions, but looked as well for the innocence and freshness that human nature could contain. Herman Melville aspired to be a "thought-diver." His *Moby Dick* (1851), with its driven Captain Ahab searching for the great white whale, symbolized the human quest for the mysterious forces of the universe.

Walt Whitman celebrated every democratic American impulse. He called for a poetry that was one with the spirit of the times and with the country's culture, incarnating its "geography and national life and rivers and lakes." Whitman's *Leaves of Grass* (1855) sings of American labor, land, place names, and crowds.

Popular Writing and Diversions   Then, as now, the mass of Americans preferred a different sort of literature. The development of more efficient printing techniques sent inexpensive books and newspapers into wide circulation. The most prolific type of fiction was the sentimental domestic novel. Filled with scenes of domestic joy and sorrow, these novels preached conventional morality and pictured church, home, and family as anchors against life's trials. Novels like Mrs. E. D. E. N. Southworth's *Retribution* and Mary Jane Holmes's *Tempest and Sunshine* were best-sellers for years. Another form of popular culture was the humorous essay, which dated from Benjamin Franklin's *Poor Richard*. It gained new popularity in the 1830s with Seba Smith's *Jack Downing Papers*. Downing was a cracker-box philosopher who commented on current events and poked gentle fun at American foibles. Smith soon had dozens of imitators, among them James Russell Lowell's Hosea Bigelow, Charles F. Browne's Artemus Ward, and Johnson Hooper's Simon Slugs. Plays, minstrel shows, lectures, and public speaking also provided entertainment and education.

The cult of patriotism grew in the early nineteenth century. Holidays were increasingly devoted to skyrocketing oratory, parades, and patriotic enthusiasms. Monuments and statues appeared by the hundreds, and biographies of American heroes sold by the tens of thousands. And along with the cult of patriotism flourished a variety of popular symbols.

Americans had already adopted a native bird, the eagle. For holidays they chose Washington's Birthday and the Fourth of July. "Uncle Sam," a creation of the War of 1812, soon displaced "Yankee Doodle" as the national prototype. Although not adopted officially as the national anthem until 1931, Francis Scott Key's "Star-Spangled Banner" gradually replaced "My Country 'Tis of Thee." No token of nationalism became more important than the American flag. Originally created in 1777, the stars and stripes had remained chiefly a naval flag until 1834, when the army adopted it as well.

Along with symbols, Americans needed heroes. They turned to the Revolutionary War for material. By Jackson's day the important figures in the war—Ethan Allen and his Green Mountain Boys, the martyred Nathan Hale, and Generals Anthony Wayne and Nathanael Greene—were celebrated in song and prose. After the Battle of New Orleans, Andrew Jackson himself became an instant hero. Above all other national heroes was George Washington. Even before his death

Nathaniel Hawthorne. He and the other writers of the period— Poe, Emerson, Melville, Whitman, Thoreau—created a literature that was uniquely American and attracted international attention. *(Courtesy, Essex Institute, Salem, Massachusetts)*

Herman Melville wrote of Hawthorne:

"This great power of blackness in him derives its force from its appeal to that Calvinistic sense of innate depravity and original sin from whose visitation, in some shape or other, no deeply thinking mind is always and wholly free."

Abolitionism: Religious Movement or Psychic Aberration?

Abolitionism was a remarkably dangerous trade. Elijah Lovejoy had his printing press thrown in a river, and subsequently lost his life as a mob sought to seize a second. Other abolitionists also confronted angry mobs. Most escaped with their lives, but not without suffering harrowing ordeals. Terrifying as they were, some abolitionists seemed to court these dangers. Theodore Dwight Weld was wont to ride into hostile towns, announce an abolitionist meeting, and then attempt to convert the angry crowd.

This seeking of danger has led some historians to suspect that many abolitionists suffered from a martyr complex. This explanation may hold for one or another individual, but it is hazardous to psychoanalyze historical figures. And psychoanalysis deals with the individual psyche. It is misleading to speak of whole groups such as the abolitionists as if they shared a single mental life.

We still need to explain the extraordinary fortitude of the abolitionists. One explanation concentrates on the element of religious revivalism in the antislavery movement. Weld was a convert of the evangelist Charles Finney, as were many other abolitionists. They adopted the movement against slavery as a vocation, a form of ministry; it was their calling, the work they were intended to do. And, like the early Christians they so often modeled themselves after, they were even willing to suffer martyrdom. Not all abolitionists, of course, were evangelical converts; some, like William Lloyd Garrison, had no formal connection with any church. Yet Garrison too was an intensely religious person. He too regarded slavery as a sin. There is, in brief, much evidence to suggest that abolitionism is better understood as a religious movement than as a psychic aberration.

Washington had attained in the estimation of his countrymen a place above politics and above criticism. Much of the responsibility for the adulation of Washington should go to Mason Locke Weems. In 1800 this itinerant book salesman and evangelist published his *Life of Washington*. Partly fabricated (the cherry tree story started here), the book fulfilled the American public's need for heroes.

"We were taught every day and in every way," according to the recollections of one nineteenth-century American, "that ours was the freest, the happiest, and soon to be the greatest and most powerful country in the world. . . . We read it in our books and newspapers, heard it in sermons, speeches, and orations, thanked God for it in our prayers, and devoutly believed it always." Not even the cult of patriotism, however, could quiet the issue of slavery, the great contradiction to American patriotic pride in freedom.

The Antislavery Crusade

The roots of the antislavery movement in the United States stretched back to the eighteenth century. Confronted by the powerful forces of rationalism and revolution, many Americans had condemned slavery as incompatible with the egalitarianism of the Declaration of Independence. In 1787 Congress excluded slavery from the area it was organizing north of the Ohio River as the Northwest Territory. That same year the delegates to the Constitutional Convention agreed to a compromise permitting Congress to abolish the African slave trade in 1808. In the meantime, a number of northern states abolished slavery within their own borders, and abolition societies multiplied even in a few southern states.

Many Americans opposed to slavery rejected the idea of its immediate eradication in the South, fearing serious constitutional, economic, and social difficulties. Some favored a policy of gradual emancipation, to be followed by deportation. With the support of such influential men as Henry Clay and John Marshall, these gradualists in 1817 founded the American Colonization Society. The Society worked to resettle emancipated American blacks in Africa, particularly in the new country of Liberia on the coast of West Africa. "We are *natives* of this country," one protested; "we only ask that we be treated as well as *foreigners*." Their opposition gradually undermined the Society's efforts. In 1829 a free black named David Walker published "An Appeal to Blacks," calling for emancipation. The year after this work was published, Walker died under mysterious circumstances.

The Abolition Movement

During the early 1830s a small but vocal band of activists began calling for the total and immediate abolition of slavery. Abolitionism became an integral part of the reform ferment of the Jackson era. Slavery, abolitionists believed, was both a national and an individual sin; Americans could not wait for time or circumstance to eradicate it. These abolitionists viewed gradual emancipation and colonization as dead ends. Any large-scale

An 1850 lithograph of Henry "Box" Brown. He escaped from slavery in Richmond, Virginia, by mailing himself north in a box 3 feet long, 2½ feet deep, and 2 feet wide. *(Courtesy, Library of Congress)*

Accounts of slaves sold and families broken made a powerful argument for abolition. Elwood Harvey, an observer at a sale of slaves, recounted the event:

"[In 1846] we attended a sale of land and other property, near Petersburg, Virginia, and unexpectedly saw slaves sold at public auction. The slaves were told they would not be sold, and were collected in front of the quarters, gazing on the assembled multitude. The land being sold, the auctioneer's loud voice was heard, 'Bring up the *niggers!*' A shade of astonishment and affright passed over their faces, as they stared first at each other, and then at the crowd of purchasers, whose attention was now directed to them. . . .

During the sale, the quarters resounded with cries and lamentations that made my heart ache. A woman was next called by name. She gave her infant one wild embrace before leaving it with an old woman, and hastened mechanically to obey the call; but stopped, threw her arms aloft, screamed, and was unable to move.

One of my companions touched my shoulder and said, 'Come, let us leave here; I can bear no more.' We left the ground. The man who drove our carriage from Petersburg had two sons who belonged to the estate—small boys. He obtained a promise that they should not be sold. Asked if they were his only children, he answered: 'All that's left of eight.' Three others had been sold to the South, and he would never see or hear from them again."

deportation of blacks would have raised both enormous practical obstacles and grave moral difficulties. And southern opposition to gradual emancipation, which stiffened after the invention of the cotton gin, indicated that the opponents of slavery had little to lose by adopting a more radical stance. The British abolitionist movement in winning in 1833 legal emancipation of British West Indian slaves gave new hope to advocates of immediate emancipation in the United States. The president of Harvard, Edward Everett, registered the intensity of these militants' feelings when he responded to criticism of his having allowed a black student to take the entrance test: "If this boy passes the examination he will be admitted; and if the white students choose to withdraw, all the income of the college will be devoted to his education."

Everett was a good representative of the eastern intellectual wing of the antislavery movement. Very many abolitionists were of a different character, drawing their inspiration from revivalistic religion. Their religion put the matter as bluntly as Everett but in a different vocabulary. Slavery is wrong; being a good Christian means rejecting and resisting it. When enough individuals embrace God's way, the larger society can be purged of evils such as slavery. Slaveholders meanwhile had only to recognize their complicity in sin and renounce it. It was by using the techniques of moral suasion—appealing to the American conscience rather than employing legal coercion—that abolitionists, so they thought, would end human bondage in the United States.

Garrison and Weld   One person led to abolitionism by perfectionist beliefs was the young William Lloyd Garrison. He had embraced a number of reform causes in the 1820s and worked with the famous Quaker abolitionist Benjamin Lundy before establishing his own antislavery newspaper, the *Liberator,* at Boston in 1831. Garrison preached the cause of immediate abolition with no compensation to slaveholders: "I *will be* as harsh as truth, and as uncompromising as justice. . . . I will not equivocate—I will not excuse—I will not retreat a single inch—AND I WILL BE HEARD." In his moral purity, he denounced the churches as "cages of unclean birds" for tolerating slavery. Northerners at first dismissed Garrison as a fanatic. But the Nat Turner revolt of 1831 made his name familiar throughout the nation, as nervous slaveholders connected the "incendiary publications" of Garrison, and others with the bloody events in Southampton County, Virginia, in which fifty-seven whites were killed. The Georgia Senate offered a $1,000 reward for Garrison's arrest and conviction. Newspapers throughout the country began reprinting his fiery editorials, and the stern Massachusetts editor soon became the very personification of abolition. On July 4, 1854, Garrison burned a copy of the Constitution, proclaiming "So perish all compromises with tyranny."

Some of Garrison's contemporaries, and a few later historians, considered Theodore Dwight Weld an even more important figure. Intense religious convictions about the evils of slavery had driven Weld, like Garrison, into the movement. After being converted by the evangelist Finney, he devoted his life to the cause of moral reform. In 1834, while a student at Cincinnati's Lane Theological Seminary, he organized debates on the slavery question. After eighteen nights of discussion, the students endorsed immediatism—immediate abolition—and rejected colonization. When their antislavery activities aroused opposition among Lane's trustees, Weld and forty others left to attend Oberlin College near Cleveland. Securing funds from two wealthy New York City reformers, Arthur and Lewis Tappan, the Lane rebels made Oberlin a center of abolitionist activity. By employing the techniques and rhetoric of the religious revival, they converted to abolitionism thousands throughout the Old Northwest and nearby areas of New York and Pennsylvania. Weld also joined with his southern wife, Angelina, and her sister, Sarah Grimké, to write *American Slavery as It Is* (1839). This popular tract, a compilation of southern newspaper accounts revealing the cruelties of slavery, offered documentary evidence to support the abolitionists' moral outrage. "Slaves," it declared,

> are often hunted with bloodhounds and shot down like beasts, or torn in pieces by dogs . . . they are often suspended by the arms and whipped and beaten till they faint, . . . and sometimes till they die; . . . they are maimed, mutilated and burned to death over slow fires. All these things, and more, and worse, we shall PROVE.

The treatment of slaves of course reflected the qualities of their masters. Some were kind. Frederick Douglass was "astonished" at the "goodness" of his mistress, Sophia Auld, "a woman of the kindest heart and finest feelings," who taught him how to read. Others were cruel. But that was not the point. The details of slave life were incidental to the violence that the institution of slavery in itself did to the nation's boast of freedom. So in time, the country's reformist energies converged upon the great, divisive, threatening question of slavery.

Suggested Readings

On the women's movement a good beginning is Elizabeth Cady Stanton's autobiography, *Eighty Years and More, Reminiscences, 1815–1897* (1898). Other studies are Barbara J. Berg, *The Remembered Gates: Origins of Feminism—Women and the City, 1800–1860* (1977). See also Blanche Glassman Hersh, *The Slavery of Sex: Feminists and Abolitionists in America* (1978), Ellen Carol DuBois, *Feminism and Suffrage* (1979), Donna Dickson, *Margaret Fuller: Writing a Woman's Life* (1993), Nancy Woloch, *Women and the American Experience* (1984), Mary P. Ryan, *Cradle of the Middle Class, The Family in Oneida County, New York, 1790–1865* (1981), Barbara Welter, *Godey's Lady's Book: The Women Who Wrote It and the Women Who Read It* (1989), and Christine Stansell, *City of Women: Sex and Class in New York, 1789–1860* (1980). On Sojourner Truth see Carlton Mabee, *Sojourner Truth: Slave, Prophet, Legend* (1993) and Nell Irvin Painter, *Sojourner Truth: A Life, A Symbol* (1996). See also Shirley Yee, *Black Women Abolitionists: A Study in Activism* (1992).

On antebellum reforms see Steven Mintz, *Moralists and Modernizers: American Pre–Civil War Reformers* (1995) and B. G. Walter's *American Reformers, 1815–1860* (1978). See also *The Discovery of the Asylum: Social Order and Disorder in the New Republic* (1971) by David S. Rothman. On religion see William G. McLoughlin, *Revivals, Awakenings, and Reform* (1978) and *Modern Revivalism: Charles Grandison Finney to Billy Graham* (1959), Lawrence Foster, *Woman, Family and Utopia: Communal Experiments of the Shakers, the Oneida Community and the Mormons* (1991), Michael Barkun, *Crucible of the Millenium: The Burned-over District of New York in the 1840s* (1966), Marvin S. Hill, *Quest for Refuge: The Mormon Flight from American Pluralism* (1989), Kenneth H. Winn, *Exiles in a Land of Liberty, 1830–1946* (1989), and Richard Rabinowitz, *The Spiritual Self in Everyday Life: The Transformation of Personal Religious Experience in Nineteenth-Century New England* (1989). See also Paul E. Johnson, *A Shopkeeper's Millennium: Society and Revivals in Rochester, New York, 1815–1837* (1978) and John Boles, *The Great Revival in the South* (1972). Herbert Hovenkamp, *Science and Religion in America, 1800–1860* (1978) is a useful survey of the relation of religious to scientific thought in the early republic.

A recent study of alternative lifestyles is Richard Francis, *Transcendental Utopias: Individual and Community at Brook Farm, Fruitlands, and Walden* (1997). See also Louis J. Kern, *An Ordered Love: Sex Roles and Sexuality: Three American Communal Experiments of the Nineteenth Century* (1981).

On the antislavery movement, there are James B. Stewart's *Holy Warriors: The Abolitionists and American Slavery* (1976), Robert H. Abzug, *Passionate Liberator, Theodore Dwight Weld and the Dilemna of Reform* (1980), Benjamin Quarles, *Black Abolitionists: The Negro in the Free States 1790* (1969), John L. Thomas, *The Liberator: William Lloyd Garrison* (1963), and Leonard L. Richards, *"Gentlemen of Property and Standing": Anti-Abolition Mobs in Jacksonian America* (1970).

See also Louis Gerteis, *Morality and Unity in American Antislavery Reform* (1987), Bertram Wyatt-Brown, *Lewis Tappan and the Evangelical War Against Slavery* (1959), Gerda Lerner, *The Grimké Sisters from South Carolina: Pioneers for Women's Rights and Abolition* (1967), and Blanche Hersh, *The Slavery of Sex: Female Abolitionists in Nineteenth-Century America* (1978).

Women in the Antebellum South: Plantation vs. City

Catherine Clinton

Rachel O'Conner of Louisiana was a woman planter of indefatigable energy. She chronicled her activities in a steady stream of correspondence to relatives. In November of 1823, she reported to her brother: "I have seventy bales of Cotton Prep'd and hauling them as fast as possible to the river to ship for N. Orleans—I answered my dear little Niece's last letter on saturday which I am afraid she cannot read easily. It rained and they were preparing cotton and I had to stop very often to get whatever they wanted which put me out of sorts." When her sister-in-law requested directions for planting leeks, Rachel O'Conner sent her a detailed set of instructions testifying to her planting expertise. She wrote to her brother David frequently about the trials of plantation business, bemoaning faulty machinery and the falling price of cotton. Many women kept detailed business records to safeguard themselves in the complex process of plantation management.

Such management, either in a husband's absence or during widowhood, was problematic for reasons that had nothing to do with a woman's personal experience or expertise. Wives who took little or no interest in farming accounts often regretted their neglect after their husband's death, and were forced to call upon male relatives for assistance. But even a mistress who demonstrated a clear ability to manage her plantation as a discrete economic unit and make it pay was not permitted by law to handle personal or business affairs in the public sphere. Women's inadequacies, real or perceived, were a direct result of the "sheltering" system that designated women as dependents, under the protection—and at the mercy—of men. While this sytem failed to keep women from exercising authority and demonstrating capability in daily routines, it effectively shackled them in any external dealing beyond plantation boundaries. Ready to make full use of her talents as household manager and domestic laborer, the society—ruled by males in the legislature and in the courts—deprived the plantation mistress of her own legal identity.

As a result, women rightly felt vulnerable in the world of legal finance. They held no power before the law, which provided for man's total control over woman: her property, her behavior, her very person. This was a logical development in an extended patriarchy, built upon racial and sexual differentiation and bolstered by a hierarchy of fixed roles and duties.

Moral and legal arguments quickly developed to guarantee a husband's domination of his wife, including, of course, the critical issue of reproduction. Women often referred to a girl's marrying as "resigning her liberty." One Virginia matron confessed to her journal: "Our mother Eve when she transgress'd was told her husband should rule over her—then how dare any of her daughters to dispute the point. . . ."

All women in southern society recognized the important financial and legal handicap under which they lived, and most accepted the limitations imposed by society as unalterable. Women did not resist as much as resent dependency. The psychological tensions—exacerbated by the enormous strain of physical chores—created depression, melancholy, and a whole range of debilities for women. . . . These women did not inhabit mythical estates, but rather productive working plantations: the routine was grueling, life was harsh. No wonder they complained of being themselves enslaved. The plantation mistress found herself trapped within a system over which she had no control, one from which she had no means of escape. Cotton was King, white men ruled, and both white women and slaves served the same master.

Catherine Clinton, *The Plantation Mistress: Woman's World in the Old South* (New York: Pantheon Books, 1982), pp. 33–4, 35. Reprinted with permission.

Suzanne Lebsock

Women in Petersburg [a Virginia city, in the early nineteenth century] experienced increasing autonomy, autonomy in the sense of freedom from utter dependence on particular men. Relatively speaking, fewer women were married, more women found work for wages, and more married women acquired separate estates, that is, property that their husbands could not touch.

When we explore how this new autonomy was acquired and what changes it inspired in turn, the line curves in intriguing ways. To cite the clearest example, women acquired separate estates, not because anyone thought women deserved more independence, but because of the nineteenth century's sudden panics and severe economic depressions. A separate estate was a means of keeping property in the family when times were hard and families stood to lose everything because of the husband's indebtedness. It did not take organized feminism to bring about positive change in the status of women. . . .

In the new century . . . the more prominent form of public activity by far was organization, initially for the benefit of the female poor and subsequently for the spread of the gospel. Such organizations were mushrooming all over the country, of course, and historians have rightly identified them as essential to the changing status and developing consciousness of nineteenth-century women. To what ends they were essential, however, is the subject of some controversy, a controversy that is part of the larger argument over the value of women's separate "sphere." Most scholars would agree that the growth of organized benevolence brought women a number of short-term benefits—an area for activity outside the home, a heightened sense of personal usefulness, a deeper appreciation of the needs and abilities of other women, and a chance to develop leadership and organizing skills and to participate in democratic decision making. . . .

"Woman's sphere" was never a fixed space. True enough, the nineteenth century's basic ideology of male and female spheres was already ossified by 1820; women were endlessly told that they belonged in the home while their men braved the crueler worlds of commerce, politics, and war. But this left a considerable quantity of social space unaccounted for. Rigid as nineteenth-century Americans were in defining sex roles, with voluntary associations they left themselves room for invention, maneuver, and experimentation.

Was it coincidence that men took over so many of women's causes in the 1850s? The assumption of voluntary poor relief as a male responsibility, the take-over of the female orphan asylum, the formation of women's auxiliaries, the injunction against women speaking in public, the use of the husband's name to identify the married woman—the motives behind these new moves cannot be assigned with any confidence. . . . The effect was to erase, in symbol and in organizational structure, the appearance of autonomous action by women in the public sphere. This did not entail crushing female assertiveness or achievement wherever it arose. Rather it meant that women's roles were to be relational, that women were to act and achieve through men.

For the women of Petersburg, the story of the antebellum period was not one of linear progress or decline; in organizational terms, it was neither a permanent retreat into a separate sphere nor a steady march from the confines of the home to the riskier and more varied regions the nineteenth century called "the world." Instead, there was a trade of sorts. Women were experiencing growing autonomy in their personal lives. For this, they apparently paid a price; in their public lives, they lost both the symbols and structure of autonomy. The consolation, if there was one, was that the men who co-opted their causes had no choice but to adopt some of their values.

Suzanne Lebsock, *The Free Women of Petersburg: Status and Culture in a Southern Town, 1784–1860* (New York: W. W. Norton & Company, 1984), pp. xv–xvi, 196, 198–99, 236. Reprinted with permission.

Caricature of Davy Crockett. The celebrated Tennessee frontiersman fought for Texas independence.
(Courtesy, American Antiquarian Society)

12

Westward Expansion: The 1840s

THE BATTLE OF THE ALAMO

In the 1830s, no place in North America had a larger reputation for wild living than Texas. Men tired of society could move to the edges of settlement in their states or go west to the territories, or they could go to Texas. The history of Texas justified this reputation. For nearly three centuries it had belonged to Spain, but hundreds of miles of deserts and mountains separated Texas from the other Spanish lands in Mexico and California, and fierce Plains Indians—mainly Comanches and Apaches—did not take kindly to life at Spanish missions. The land Mexico inherited with its independence from Spain lay long ungoverned.

When Mexico became independent in 1821, Texas was joined to its state of Coahuila, with a promise that when its population was large enough, it would become a separate Mexican state. The newly-established Mexican government planned to develop Texas by encouraging settlers from the United States, provided they became at least nominal Catholics and Mexican citizens. The plan worked too well. By 1831 approximately 20,000 settlers had poured in. Heads of families could, for a modest fee, have 4,428 acres for grazing land and 177 acres for farming. Soon the Mexicans began to fear this potentially rich province slipping from them. So they banned further immigration, raised tariffs, restricted trade, and reinforced their military presence. They did so with reason. Numbers of immigrants from the United States swearing loyalty to their new Mexican country apparently did not mean it, or meant it only indifferently.

continued

HISTORICAL EVENTS

1821
Mexico wins independence from Spain

1833
American Antislavery Society is formed

1834
Santa Anna declares himself president of Mexico

1835
"Gag" rule approved by the House of Representatives

1836
Santa Anna begins his siege of the Alamo (February) • the Alamo falls to Santa Anna (March) • Texans declare independence from Mexico • General Sam Houston defeats Santa Anna

1842
Commonwealth v. Hunt • *Prigg v. Pennsylvania* • Tyler proposes annexation of Texas

1844
James Knox Polk elected President

The situation was further complicated by unstable Mexican politics. Antonio López de Santa Anna, a Mexican general, was challenging his own government. The Texans, led by Stephen F. Austin, who had brought 300 families in 1825, petitioned for separate statehood. Then in 1834 Santa Anna proclaimed himself president of Mexico forever and sent its Congress home. Said Austin: "War is our only recourse." Once Santa Anna took control in Mexico City and moved to garrison his northern province, the Texans were ready to fight.

Jim Bowie, a legendary figure of the tough southwest frontier, having recently turned from land speculation, slave trading, and brawling with the aid of his famous eight-and-one-half-inch-long knife, is said to have declared: "We will rather die in these ditches than give up [the mission known as the Alamo] to the enemy." Located in present-day San Antonio, the Alamo desperately needed reinforcements. It got a few, powerful in legend. William Barret Travis, an advocate of war and now a colonel in the rag-tag Texas army, arrived with thirty of his soldiers to add to Bowie's volunteers. When Bowie fell ill with pneumonia, Travis took command of the beleaguered fort. Davy Crockett arrived from Tennessee with twelve men. Then as now he was the epitome of the American frontiersman, the teller and subject of tall tales. Following his legend right into the West, by some instinct he wound up at the place that would transform his essentially comic career into real and towering heroism. Eventually thirty-two more volunteers arrived from the nearby town of Gonzales. And so it was that, all told, 187 men including nine Tejanos, or Hispanic Texans, garrisoned the old mission, when on February 23, 1836, Santa Anna's army of 4,000 began its siege.

On February 24 Travis wrote a letter addressed "To the People of Texas and All Americans in the world." The enemy, he declared, "has demanded a surrender at discretion, otherwise, the garrison are to be put to the sword, if the fort is taken—I have answered the demand with a cannon shot, & our flag still waves proudly from the walls—*I shall never surrender or retreat.*"

With Mexican guns tightly ringing the fort, the Alamo's defenders finally abandoned their hopes of further reinforcements. Tradition has it that Travis called the men together, explained their probable fate, and offered a chance to leave to those who wished it. Drawing a line in the dust with his sword, he stepped across it and asked who would join him and who would leave. All but one man—who got through the Mexican lines and lived to tell the tale—crossed the line. Bowie, from his sickbed, asked to be carried across. On March 3 Travis wrote a final letter, correctly predicting that "The victory will cost the enemy so dear that it will be worse for him than defeat." Unknown to Travis and the others inside the Alamo, a convention meeting March 2 at a tiny settlement called Washington-on-the-Brazos had declared independence from Mexico. Texas had become a nation.

As the Mexican troops advanced on the Alamo, Santa Anna's buglers played the dreaded "El Degüello," a tune that everyone knew. It meant "no quarter: death to all enemies."

The first assault with scaling ladders was repulsed with dreadful carnage. A second wave was more successful, actually getting ladders onto the walls, only to be driven off by rifle butts, tomahawks, and Bowie knives. Then came the third assault, and there were simply not enough Texans, enough cannon, or enough wall left. Taking astonishing losses—one regiment lost 670 of 800 men—the Mexican soldiers advanced with a courage to match that of their adversaries. Abandoning the central plaza of the Alamo, the defenders retreated to the smaller rooms, to kill and then to die in hand-to-hand battle. Among the few survivors of the Alamo were some Tejano women and children, family members of men who had joined the Anglo-Texans to fight for Texas, and a black man who was Travis's slave. A handful of the Alamo's defenders were taken prisoner and executed, though the exact circumstances of their deaths are disputed.

There is no question about the result of the battle: Santa Anna's "victory" cost him the war. He had lost at least 1,600 of his best troops, with many more wounded. He had lost not only the weeks it took to besiege the fortress, but the weeks his army needed afterward to recover. That delay gave General Sam Houston a chance to build an army.

Santa Anna and Houston met April 21 at the San Jacinto River where it forms an elbow at an intersection with a bayou. Houston burned his bridges behind him so that neither his army nor Santa Anna's could retreat. The Texans, shouting as their battlecry

General Sam Houston. (*Courtesy, Hugh Cleland Collection*)

The Battle at the Alamo, 1836. The Mexican "victory" cost Santa Anna 1,600 of his best troops and helped Texas win its war of independence. (*Courtesy, Scribner's Archives*)

"Remember the Alamo!" destroyed the Mexican army in an afternoon and captured the general, ending the threat of further hostilities. Texas was an independent nation, the Lone Star Republic, until 1845, when it was admitted to the Union as the twenty-eighth state.

The Nation in 1840

In 1840 the future of the young American republic seemed rich with promise. In fifty years the population had increased by over four hundred percent, while the land area had more than doubled. As each region found what it could best manufacture or grow and as transportation improved, the different sections became more interdependent in the making of a richer economy. With two national parties competing for office in every part of the country, the political system worked not to divide the country but to bind it together, which would have puzzled the nation's earliest leaders in their fear of party. The vast majority of Americans remained English in speech, Protestant in religion, lower middle-class in social status, agricultural in occupation. This common ground, together with the experience of two wars against Britain, made for a shared national loyalty. Each July 4, Americans in every part of the country gathered for elaborate ceremonies glorifying the Union. Alexis de Tocqueville was deeply impressed by one such celebration at Albany, with its dramatic reading of the Declaration of Independence and its parade of Revolutionary veterans "preserved like precious relics, and whom all the citizens honor. . . ."

And yet, even as patriotism and economic interdependence strengthened the Union, the slavery question was becoming entangled with the issue of territorial expansion, and that combination gradually eclipsed all other issues. Unable to settle the question peacefully, by 1861 Americans would resort to arms.

Immigration

Immigration is the single most consistent public event in United States history. During the colonial period, settlers poured in from England, Scotland, Northern Ireland, Germany, and Holland, and after the American Revolution and the Napoleonic wars that stream of settlers became a flood. Nothing had prepared the country for the mass immigration that took place in the first half of the nineteenth century. After 1815, especially beginning in the 1840s, newcomers came in endless waves for a variety of economic and political reasons. Between 1815 and 1860 nearly five million immigrants entered the country—more than the entire population of the United States in 1790. Over ninety percent of the immigrants came from England, Scotland, Wales, Ireland, Germany, Norway, Sweden, and Denmark. Their arrival transformed the political, social, and economic landscape of the United States, as waves of immigration later in the century from eastern and southern Europe would again alter the country's character.

European Background

The primary reason so many Europeans came to the United States was economic. The smallpox vaccine, the introduction of the American potato into the diets of poor people throughout Europe, and the lack of protracted warfare all combined to reduce death rates in Europe. Europe's population increased from 140 million people in 1750 to more than 260 million in 1850. The pressure of population, combined with technological changes in Europe and prosperity in the land beyond the ocean, made for one of the greatest migrations in history.

As population grew in Europe, farm sizes dwindled and many younger sons and laborers realized they would never be able to own their own land. At the same time, improvements in American wheat production, combined with faster and more reliable ocean transportation, made cheap American wheat competitive in European markets. World grain prices and the incomes of millions of small European farmers fell. These changes took place gradually over the course of many years, and just as gradually increasing numbers of European farmers began to travel during the winter months to such cities as Bergen, Amsterdam, Christiana, Copenhagen, Hamburg, Bremen, Antwerp, Vienna, or Prague in search of work. Many immigrants had been migrant workers long before they made the move to the United States. Just as opportunities in agriculture were eroding, factory production in Europe was displacing many independent artisans. They found themselves working longer hours for less money in order to compete with mass-produced goods from American, English, and German factories. Worried about their economic futures, they were intrigued by the advertisements of American railroads hungry for workers, steamship companies seeking passengers, and new states and territories eager to attract settlers.

In considerable part, this immigration was not of the most impoverished Europeans. Few chronically unemployed workers and peasants laboring on large landed estates emigrated. Imagination and at least some economic resources were necessary prerequisites to the risky and difficult act of migrating to a new continent. It was status-conscious workers and small farmers, poor but not the poorest of Europe's poor, who came to live in the new lands.

The Migration from the British Isles

People from the British Isles had constituted the vast majority of immigrants during the colonial period, and that continued to be true during the years before the Civil War. Between 1815 and 1860, approximately 2,775,000 people from Great Britain settled in the United States. More than 750,000 were from England, Scotland, and Wales, while about two million were from Ireland. Another 350,000 Canadians crossed the border into the United States before the Civil War.

Most of the immigrants from England, Scotland, and Wales were Protestant—Anglican, Methodist, Baptist, and Presbyterian. By 1830 Great Britain was the most advanced industrial nation in the world, and perhaps half of these immigrants were skilled workers. They carried their skills with them and settled where they could earn high wages—textile mills, blast furnaces, forges, factories, and iron, coal, copper, and

Immigration, 1840–1860	
Belgium	20,000
England	420,000
France	180,000
Germany	1,500,000
Ireland	2,900,000
Italy	15,000
Netherlands	20,000
Poland	5,000
Scandinavia	30,000
Scotland	40,000
Switzerland	30,000
Wales	15,000

tin mines. Many of the British immigrants who did not get skilled jobs in the new industries of the United States found farms of their own. One English immigrant writing home said: "I *own* here a far better estate than I *rented* in England, and am already more attached to the soil . . . We are in a good country, are in no danger of perishing for want of society, and have abundant means of supplying every other want." The British Protestants were welcome. They shared culture, religion, and language with Americans, and they brought skills with them. The Irish Catholic immigrant received quite another reception.

Irish Immigrants   Ireland was poor, and in 1845 that poverty assumed cataclysmic proportions when a mysterious fungus destroyed most of the Irish potato crop. The potato, carried several centuries earlier from the New World to Europe, was the staple of the peasant masses, and they could not survive without it. Similar famines struck the island in 1846 and again in 1847, and in the process more than one million Irish peasants died of starvation. Another two million between 1845 and 1860 escaped by heading for the United States. Most of the Irish arrived here poor, illiterate, and unskilled.

Unlike large numbers of the other immigrants, the Irish stayed in the urban centers of the industrial Northeast. Irish ghettos appeared in Boston, New York, Philadelphia, and Baltimore because the immigrants picked the cheapest housing available and took the first jobs they could find. In the cities they were highly visible. The Irish immigrants were Roman Catholics—devout Catholics who, in spite of their poverty, managed to build churches, parochial schools, monasteries, and convents. The influx of so many Catholics frightened many American Protestants. Religious animosities were intense in the nineteenth century, and more than a few Americans worried about rumors of Catholic conspiracies, led by popes and priests, to take over the country. During the late 1840s and throughout the 1850s, a wave of antagonism to Irish and to Catholics swept through the United States, and Irish Catholics often found themselves victims of discrimination and violence.

It was not uncommon for Irish workers to find themselves trapped in the lowest-paying factory jobs, victimized by their lack of skills and the greed of their employers. During the 1840s they rapidly began to replace native farmers' daughters in New England textile and shoe factories. By now whatever paternalism on the Lowell model might have made factory employment more humane was clearly and permanently absent.

German and Scandinavian Immigrants   More than 1,500,000 German-speaking immigrants settled in the United States between 1815 and 1860. Most came from the Lutheran regions of what is today northwestern Germany. During the colonial period, most Germans had settled in Pennsylvania and Maryland, but beginning in the 1830s Germans headed for the upper Midwest. So many German immigrants settled there that the region became known as the "German triangle"—the region bounded by Cincinnati, Ohio, to the east, St. Louis, Missouri, to the west, and Milwaukee, Wisconsin, to the north. The Germans were not treated as well as the British immi-

"I regard people just as I regard my machinery," a manufacturer explained in 1855:

"So long as they can do my work for what I choose to pay them, I keep them, getting out of them all I can. What they do or how they fare outside my wall I don't know, nor do I consider it my business to know. They must look out for themselves as I do for myself. When my machines get old and useless, I reject them and get new, and these people are part of my machinery."

grants or as badly as the Irish Catholics. The Lutheran religion that at least a plurality of them professed did not pose much of a threat to other Protestants, but they seemed insulated and clannish. They spoke a strange language and were extremely loyal to it, and they tended to vote in ethnic blocs, a practice that would give them political power disproportionate to their numbers. During the 1850s anti-immigrant propaganda and political action victimized the Germans. The presence among them of substantial numbers of Roman Catholics added to the hostility.

Approximately 400,000 immigrants came to the United States from Sweden, Norway, and Denmark. The predominant religion among them as among the Germans was Lutheran, and they too headed to the Midwest, settling to the north and west of the German triangle. Most of the Scandinavian immigrants became farmers in Illinois, Wisconsin, Iowa, or Minnesota. Because they were white Protestants and because they settled in rural areas far from population centers, the Scandinavians did not become the victims of sustained anti-immigrant prejudice in the United States. By the second generation they were marrying outside their own ethnic group and rapidly assimilating.

Chinese Immigrants One of the smallest group of immigrants in numbers, but among the most visible, were the more than 300,000 Chinese who came to the United States between 1849 and 1880. Like the European immigrants, they faced population pressures at home, and when news reached China of the discovery of gold in California in 1848, thousands came across the Pacific Ocean to make their fortune. Most of them were from the coastal area

---

The German immigrant John Sturm, in an autobiographical fragment, recounts his family's crossing of the Atlantic in 1847. It was an easier voyage than was typical for the time. Usually there were several deaths on a crossing.

When we set out from home, we went to Mannheim in a wagon, then to Mainz and Koln on the Rhine in a steamboat and then to Antwerp, a seaport, where we lay over several days until a ship was ready.

Our baggage was supposed to be in Koln when we got there, but it was not there. My father looked around for it for several days, but he did not find it. We were told it must have been sent to Antwerp and we would find it there. But to our misfortune and almost to our utter despair, everything was lost.

In Antwerp we waited several days until our ship was ready to go to sea. My father bought food again for use on the ship, because what we had brought from home was all lost. Before we boarded ship, my father hunted for our baggage again, but in vain. So we had nothing but the clothes on our backs. When the ship was ready to go, we had to go along.

The ship was a three-master, the "Carolina." We had many a stormy day. There were many of us on the ship. There was only one kitchen for all the people to cook in, for the passengers had to cook, each family for itself. So it happened that each family had a chance to cook only once in two or three days. We had little interest in eating, anyway, as most of the people were sea-sick and had no appetite.

The ship heaved and rolled almost all the time so that we had to hold on to something. Many people never came up on deck at all during the entire journey. The trunks and boxes had to be tied fast so they wouldn't be thrown about. Some of the children were happy and gay, but most of them were not.

One day a pirate ship came toward us and everyone had to come on deck, no doubt to show how many able-bodied men we had.

The sailors had their own kitchen and their own cook. Peas cooked with bacon and beans were their main foods. We also had bacon and black bread, which we almost had to split with an ax. Here a dog would hardly eat it. Some had white bread, which was more appetizing than the black. But in spite of all this, we survived. One child died on the ship. It was buried at sea.

of southwestern China, and most of them settled along the Pacific coast, especially in California. The Chinese panned for gold until the easiest finds played out, and then they went to work for commercial mines, construction companies, and railroads.

The Chinese immigrants were unlike the other people coming to the United States. They were racially different from Europeans, and they were Buddhists and Confucians. Unlike most of the other immigrants, the Chinese were known as "birds of passage"—immigrants who did not intend to stay in the United States. The vast majority of them were men who simply wanted to earn a reasonable sum of money, return to China, and purchase land for their families. They were willing to live and work in the United States for many years in order to achieve that objective. They worked hard and lived on a shoestring; it was the only way of making the money they needed to return home in style. Their ethnic distinctiveness and the competition they posed to American workers destined the Chinese immigrants to have a hard time. Discrimination against the Chinese increased steadily in the 1850s and after the Civil War exploded into full racism.

The Land and the People: The Northeast and Mid–Atlantic

Between 1820 and 1860 manufacturing grew rapidly in the New England and mid-Atlantic states. Both sections boasted readily available capital and labor and superior transportation. Turnpikes, rivers, the Erie Canal, and safe harbors provided good access to raw materials and markets. Commerce and agriculture, particularly dairy and truck farming, remained important in the region, but southern New England and the Hudson and Delaware river valleys began to resemble the most industrialized areas of Great Britain in their economy and social structure.

White southerners could be as shocked at the condition of northern "free" labor as some northerners were at slavery. Free labor, wrote George Fitzhugh of Virginia,

"is more cruel, in leaving the laborer to take care of himself and family out of the pittance which skill or capital have allowed him to retain. When the day's labor is ended, he is free, but he is overburdened with the cares of family and household, which make his freedom an empty and delusive mockery. . . . The Negro slave is free, too, when the labors of the day are over, and free in mind as well as body; for the master provides food, raiment, house, fuel, and everything else necessary for the physical well-being of himself and family."

Factory Life The conditions of labor changed fundamentally after 1820, as independent craftsmen, many men, women, and children from farms, and masses of immigrants became wage earners. The widespread adoption of steam power in the 1840s freed factories from their dependence on rural free-flowing streams for their power, and allowed them to be placed near cities. Henceforth workers were completely divorced from the land. The influx of immigrant labor worsened wages and working conditions in many industries. Most workers had no protection against long hours, occupational hazards, illness, or unemployment. Apprentice girls could have particularly trying assignments; the best that Lydia Noyes could say to her friend Mary was "we are not required to work before light or after nine at night." The limited attempts at unionization in this period failed in the face of public hostility and periodic panics that so depressed the economy as to make it impossible for workers on strike to survive. Not until 1842, in the case of *Commonwealth v. Hunt*, did the Massachusetts Supreme Court uphold the legality of trade unions.

Cities Industrialism, immigration, and the expanding transportation system brought a more rapid growth of cities than has occurred at any other time in American history, before or since. In 1820 only 6.1 percent of the population lived in urban areas, places, as the census bureau would define them, of 2,500 or more inhabitants. On the other hand, Pittsburgh in the same year was so heavily industrialized that, according to one traveler, "It is surrounded . . . with a dense black smoke which, bursting forth in volume from the foundries, forges, glasshouses, and the chimneys of all the factories and houses, falls in flakes of soot upon the dwellings and persons of the inhabitants. It is, therefore, the dirtiest town in the United States." By 1860 close to 20 percent of the people were city dwellers. On the eve of the Civil War there were fifteen cities (nine of them in the Northeast) with populations in excess of 50,000. Philadelphia exceeded 500,000 and New York passed 1,000,000.

The cities were hopelessly ill-equipped to deal with these numbers of people. Municipal water and sewage systems were in their infancy. Pigs roamed city streets, the only effective street cleaners. Housing was always in short supply. Many people lived in tiny apartments; often a whole family, and perhaps a few boarders, were crowded into the same room. The poorest lived in unfinished cellars. In 1849 a Boston doctor found "one cellar . . . occupied nightly as a sleeping-apartment for thirty-nine persons. In another, the tide had risen so high that it was necessary to approach the bedside of a patient by means of a plank which was laid from one stool to another; while the dead body of an infant was actually sailing about the room in its coffin."

Cities festered in filth, overcrowding, and poverty. Cholera epidemics in 1832 and 1849 killed thousands. Fires were an everyday occurrence, sometimes leveling whole sections of cities. Crime, ranging from prostitution to burglary and murder, flourished everywhere, even on New York City's Broadway, where according to one contemporary "whores and blackguards made up about two-thirds of the throng." In response the business and middle classes created or expanded such institutions as the police force. Slowly, grudgingly, but inevitably cities ran up debts to finance water and sewer systems, street lights, schools, and parks.

Cities alternately repelled and fascinated Americans. Moralists condemned them as sinful. Native Protestants shuddered at the rapid growth of ethnic ghettos, where immigrants retained their old customs, languages, and Catholic religion. Americans now confronted contrasts between wealth and poverty that their republic in its origins had never imagined. Still, people came to the cities in ever-increasing numbers—to visit, to work, to seek their fortunes.

The Land and the People: The West

Farming Between 1820 and 1860 the American economy grew more and more specialized regionally. While manufacturing expanded in the Northeast and the South continued to cultivate staple crops for agriculture, the West turned increasingly to commercial agriculture. The growth of industry, and the resulting rise

A canal boat helmsman wrote in 1834:

"I am at present stearing the canal boat 'Emigrant' which runs from Cincinnati to Dayton which is 65 mils. I went to Santlewes [St. Louis] last sumer and staed thare one month. The collary [cholera] was thare very bad and in Cincinnati. Thare was not many cases on the canal but in town thare ware 80 and 100 of a day."

At the beginning of the nineteenth century eastern and European travelers were amazed at the fertility of western farms. One visitor to the Ohio River Valley in 1818 wrote:

"I believe I saw more peaches and apples rotting on the ground than would sink the British fleet. I was at plantations in Ohio where they no more knew the number of their hogs than myself. . . . And they have such flocks of turkies, geese, ducks, and hens, as would surprise you. . . . The poorest family has a cow or two and some sheep . . . and adorns the table three times a day like a wedding dinner—tea, coffee, beef, fowls, pigs, eggs, pickles, good bread; and their favorite beverage is whiskey, or peach brandy."

of cities in the Northeast and in Europe, created a steadily expanding market for farm products. The upper Mississippi and Ohio valleys, with their fertile soil and vast tracts of public land, were in an ideal position to meet this need, especially after canals and railroads made it possible to ship directly eastward large quantities of meat and grain.

With every decade the centers of production for wheat, corn, cattle, hogs, and sheep shifted westward, as settlers opened the prairies to cultivation. Many of these newcomers had abandoned the thin soils of New England for places like Indiana and Michigan, where wheat yields were several times greater per acre. Farmers from the upper South flocked into the southern counties of Ohio, Illinois, and Indiana and gave that region a distinctively southern character. Sizable numbers of English, German, and Scandinavian immigrants migrated west, fanning out through the rich farmlands of Iowa, Illinois, Minnesota, and Wisconsin. On the eve of the Civil War the population of the West, which had numbered less than one million in 1820, exceeded nine million.

Farms were small—about 200 acres on the average. Most farmers owned their own land, relying for labor on their families, on hired help, and increasingly on machines. Wheat was the cash crop; and mechanical drills, harvesters, and threshers permitted an enormous increase in production throughout the period.

In the 1840s and 1850s wheat dominated farming in the upper Mississippi Valley almost as completely as cotton dominated agriculture in the lower South. Wheat and flour became important export items in the fifties. Western farmers also grew much corn and oats, but primarily as feed for livestock. The demands of eastern cities and southern planters assured a ready market and good prices for the beef, pork, and mutton of the prairies. Before railroads came to the Ohio Valley, cattle were driven overland to market; most hogs were slaughtered and packed locally. Frequently they were "stuck," or cut in the throat—often the pioneer woman's job. Then women and children took out and washed the various innards, saving the bladder to inflate and use as a football. So much pork was processed at Cincinnati that the city became known for a time as "Porkopolis." Later, increasing numbers of livestock were shipped east by rail to city markets for slaughter.

Europeans were shocked that Americans bolted their food or gorged themselves on anything within reach, as this English drawing indicates. Such habits reflected both the indifferent preparation of food and the frenetic tempo of American life. *(Courtesy, Scribner's Archives)*

Cities   While the Midwest remained primarily agrarian, the region's cities grew swiftly. Older communities like St. Louis, Cincinnati, and Louisville all expanded rapidly. Even more spectacular was the progress of new cities like Milwaukee, Indianapolis, and especially Chicago. In 1833 Chicago consisted "of about 150 wood houses . . . ," wrote one resident. "This is already a place of considerable trade, supplying salt, tea, coffee, sugar, and clothing to a large tract of country to the south and west." The Windy City had barely 17,000 people when Cyrus McCormick moved his farm machinery factory there in 1847: thirteen years later the population numbered 109,000. Yet the city remained a raw and uncomfortable place. Its mud was the subject for endless tales. Signs read "No Bottom," "Road to China," or "Man Lost." A story told of a man who sees a hat in the mud. Picking it up, he discovers a man's face underneath. "Say, stranger, you're stuck in the mud! Can I give you a hand to pull you out?" "Oh, no, thanks," replies the face, "I'm riding a good horse. He's got me out of the worst spots." These western cities served principally as extensions of the rural economy, processing, shipping, and marketing agricultural products. Their mills and packing houses led the country in 1850 in the production of lumber, flour and meal, liquor and meat. Factories in these cities made ever more complex machines that made farming more efficient.

The expansion of urban markets had a powerful effect on sectional alignments. Between 1820 and 1860, western farmers came increasingly to depend on eastern cities to purchase their produce, while the industrial Northeast, in turn, found a growing market for its manufactures in the western states. An economic bond was being forged between the two sections that would undermine the old alliance between the West and the South.

The Farther West   The Indian Removal Act of 1830 made for the eventual settlement west of the Mississippi River of almost 100,000 Indians. Life there was hard for them. The land and climate were unfamiliar. They found farming more difficult and were not as adept at hunting the buffalo as the Plains Indians, who resented the newcomers and resisted their settlement. Comanches, Pawnees, Osages, and other western tribes, aware that government protection of the new tribes was minimal, regularly raided them and stole their livestock. Poverty, disease, and despair became the heritage of the relocated Indians in the 1840s and 1850s.

And no sooner had the Indians been relocated west of the Mississippi River than new waves of white settlers began arriving there as well. By the 1850s settlers were pouring into the Far West, even into land west of the Mississippi River that had so recently been reserved "forever" for the Indians. The mining frontier in California and the intermountain West, the Mormon colonies in the Great Basin, and the glowing reports of excellent farmland attracted hundreds of thousands of settlers into the western territories.

By the end of the 1850s, Governor Isaac I. Stevens of Washington Territory had negotiated fraudulent treaties with such tribes as the Nez Percé, Cayuse, Yakima, Spokane, and Walla Walla. The tribes ceded millions of acres of land and moved to reservations. On the west side of

One visitor to South Carolina observed that the state's inland people were no match for Yankee peddlers:

"As the value of the lands and the wealth of the inhabitants decrease, while you journey toward the back country, so also does the intelligence of the people. I never met in my whole life with so many white persons who could not read nor write, who had never taken a newspaper, who had never travelled fifty miles from home, or who had never been to the house of God, or heard a sentence read from his Holy Word, as I found in a single season in South Carolina. Many of them could not discern between the right hand and the left.

What wonder then that the hosts of Yankee peddlers until driven out by the sumptuary laws, fattened upon the land! 'What do you think I gave for that?' asked an ignorant planter in Sumpter district, while pointing to a Connecticut wooden clock which stood upon a shelf in the corner of the room. 'I don't know,' was my answer, 'twenty dollars, or very likely twenty-five!' The man was astonished. 'Stranger' said he, 'I gave one hundred and forty-four dollars for that clock, and thought I got it cheap at that! Let me tell you how it was. We had always used sun-dials hereabout, till twelve or fourteen years ago, when a man came along with clocks to sell. I thought at first I wouldn't buy one, but after haggling about the price for a while, he agreed to take sixteen dollars less than what he asked, for his selling price was one hundred and sixty dollars. I concluded to strike a bargain.'

In fact, during those years when wealth flowed in an uninterrupted stream through every channel of industry, the farms and plantations of the South became the legitimate plunder of Yankee shrewdness. It was no meeting of Greek with Greek in the contest of wits, but a perfect inrush of shrewd, disciplined tacticians in the art of knavery."

the Mississippi River, government agents in the 1850s had to make way for new hordes of settlers coming into Kansas, Nebraska, and Iowa. They developed a policy of moving tribes to new reservations, including Indians recently arrived from the East. In California, the gold rush brought tens of thousands of miners who, when the gold became more difficult to find, settled on Indian land and became farmers. Between 1849 and 1860, the Indian population of California declined from more than 100,000 to less than 30,000. By 1860 there were only 15,000 Indians still alive in California.

The Land and the People: The South

The antebellum southern economy was surprisingly diverse. Cotton was the most prominent yield, but corn was actually the South's most widely grown crop. Many planters in Virginia and Maryland, their soil exhausted after prolonged tobacco cultivation, shifted to raising wheat or cattle. Rice grew in the swampy low country of South Carolina and Georgia. Southern Louisiana produced another exotic crop, sugar.

Cotton, the South's major cash crop, was cultivated throughout the lower South. The center of cotton production moved steadily westward after 1820, the inevitable result of overplanting and soil exhaustion. Just before the Civil War over a fourth of the 4.3 million bales grown in the United States came from Arkansas, Louisiana, and Texas, all states west of the Mississippi River.

In Texas, or the Lone Star Republic as it was known from 1836 until it entered the Union in 1845, the towns of Galveston, on the Gulf Coast, and Houston, on the banks of Buffalo Bayou, became major ports and trading centers. San Antonio was a center for stagecoaches and freight wagon trains heading westward for California. Texas towns were small—Galveston, the largest in 1850, had a population of five thousand—and rough-hewn, with few urban amenities until after the Civil War. Cattle ranching was widespread, and would eventually give rise to the cowboy culture that set Texas apart from other states. Texas was also different in its cultural diversity. Only about half of its people in 1850 were Anglo-Americans. The rest were Mexican, other Europeans, Indians, and African Americans. Slaves made up over twenty-seven percent of the population.

Contrary to popular myth, the South was not inhabited solely by rich planters, poor whites, and enslaved blacks. In 1860 the bulk of the South's 5.5 million whites lived on small farms not unlike those in the North. These yeoman farmers raised most of the same crops as did the planters: only rice and sugar were confined to the larger growers. Even families living far in the backlands might be living in a rough plenty, keeping unfenced cattle and raising their own subsistence crops.

The Whites   The actual number of planters was small. The federal census of 1860—defining a planter as a person owning at least twenty slaves—counted 46,274. Most of these owned up to fifty slaves and 500 to 800 acres. They were hardworking businessmen with field work to supervise, laborers to oversee, books to balance. And their wives seldom conformed to the southern-belle stereotype. Managing a large household required energy and intelligence, not merely graceful manners. Home was more likely to be a modest frame cottage than a Tara or a Mount Vernon. At the apex of southern society were the large planters. Although few in number—only 1,700 people owned as many as a hundred slaves in 1850—these planter aristocrats cast a giant shadow over the region. Their wealth gave them considerable social and political influence. Living in palatial mansions or elegant townhouses, surrounded by vast fields and liveried servants, they were the few authentic representatives of the South of myth and romance.

Plantation kitchen. (*Courtesy, Hugh Cleland Collection*)

In spite of this diversity, the white South possessed a distinctive flavor. The great majority of southern whites were Protestant and of British ancestry. The economy was colonial: southerners raised staple crops for export and imported finished goods. Before the Revolution the South had traded mainly with England, but in the first half of the nineteenth century southern trade, lacking local capital for financing merchant shipping, came increasingly under the control of northerners, and particularly under the dominance of the port of New York. Above all, there was slavery, a uniquely southern institution that exerted a powerful influence over the region.

Although the number of great planters was small, slaveholding was remarkably widespread throughout the white South. According to one estimate, fewer than forty percent of the farmers in the Cotton South in 1850 owned no slaves. By 1860 this number increased to almost half, largely because the rapidly increasing cost of purchasing a slave priced many small farmers out of the market. But the important point is that on the eve of the Civil War a large proportion of white farmers in the cotton-growing portions of the region were themselves slaveholders. And this understates the whites' stake in the South's peculiar institution. Some who did not own slaves rented them. Others served as overseers on plantations, usually in the hope that several successive good harvests would earn them enough to buy a small farm and slaves of their own. Still other white southerners had sold their own slaves, prompted to do so by the windfall profits they could realize. All of these non-slaveholders had as pervasive ties to the institution of slavery as did the planters themselves. Further, the presence of millions of blacks gave whites of all classes a common determination to keep the white race dominant, and an unearned pride in race gave the whites a psychological bond.

The Slaves   Slaves worked everywhere in the antebellum South: as common laborers, skilled craftsmen, and servants; in factories, mines, and foundries; on riverboats, wharves, and railroads; in hotels, stores, and private homes. A Charleston census of 1848 listed forty-six occupations that employed slaves. Most, of course, worked as field hands. Over half belonged to planters who owned twenty or more slaves. These large units were especially common in the newer states of the lower South, where the work was harder and the conditions more brutal than in the older slave states.

On farms of less than ten slaves, the slaves usually worked alongside their masters, who directly supervised their labor. Male slaves frequently performed the same tasks as the farmer and female slaves the same tasks as his wife, though in the busiest seasons all slaves were likely

A slave family in the cotton fields of Georgia. *(Courtesy, New-York Historical Society)*

to work in the fields together. On plantations slaves were organized in two ways. Rice planters preferred the task system, allotting individual slaves a particular task for the day. Cotton and tobacco planters favored the gang system, dividing the slaves into work parties under the supervision of an overseer or trusted black driver. The plantation routine followed the seasons in a monotonous cycle. Both men and women worked in the fields, plowing and planting in the spring, weeding in the summer, harvesting in the fall. In winter and in slack times, they dug ditches, repaired fences, and sawed wood. Although masters of large plantations usually worked their female slaves as hard as their male slaves, and assigned them to most tasks in the fields, they frequently observed gender distinctions in the organization of labor. Masters rarely assigned supervisory positions in field work to female slaves. The young and the elderly tended livestock or cared for the small children. Field hands labored from sunrise to sunset, with a rest at midday. Most had Sunday off and received a week's vacation at Christmas. For many slaves these holidays, with their occasional feasts, dances, and visits to neighboring plantations, provided relief from the hardship of their daily lives. And in religious meetings the slaves created an invisible church. On Sunday nights they would go into the woods to sing and pray.

Most slaves lived in rude cabins. Some masters encouraged their bondsmen to marry and live as families; others left the matter to the slaves or assigned them arbitrarily to a mate. The owner provided food, clothing, and medical care. The typical slave's ration consisted of cornmeal, fatback, and molasses; but many slaves varied this boring and unhealthful diet by raising their own vegetables or fishing.

Was Slavery Profitable?   Household servants and city slaves enjoyed a somewhat easier life than field hands. And many slaveholders hired out their bondsmen as servants, laborers, and mechanics, sometimes for extended periods. This practice of hiring out was especially common in the upper South and in the cities, where there was frequently a surplus of slaves. Many hired slaves became quasi-free, but the practice of hiring out normally brought more advantages to male than to female slaves. Female slaves might be hired out as house servants, especially as cooks, cleaners, or nursemaids. Their position did not give them much excuse for free movement in society. Slave women, much like free white women, tended to be confined within households. Masters almost never offered slave women training in such skilled crafts as carpentry or blacksmithing. But the slave men who held those positions received an unusual opportunity to learn to read, to accumulate some money of their own, and, above all, to have an excuse to circulate fairly freely in society. The pool of slave craftsmen provided runaways and participants in revolts in disproportionate numbers. Women were less likely than men to run away or to engage directly in revolts.

Slaves had little motivation to work hard. Although some worked willingly for kindly masters, others delighted in "first-rate tricks to dodge work." In an attempt to make their slaves work efficiently, planters combined close supervision with a system of incentives: praise, additional rations, extra holidays. But many masters found it necessary to resort to whipping, deprivation of privileges, and other punishments. "The only principle that can maintain slavery," one comment went, "is the principle of fear." Those who found distasteful the employment of a lash—and there were many—might see their plantation go to ruin. Yet punishment too severe could bring the injury or loss of a prime male or fertile female, and no owner would want that. And of course there were cases of affection or respect. Some owners allowed their slaves to acquire property or taught them to read and write.

Slave men lacked many of the powers that free men could draw upon to maintain their control of women, notably the legal powers assigned to husbands and property owners. Yet slave women, as women, remained vulnerable to particular hardships such as sexual exploitation on the part of white men and separation from their children. Slave women's ability to bear children also afforded them some marginal advantages. Since masters were eager to increase the numbers of their slaves through reproduction, they were likely to accord women who claimed to be pregnant some release from work. But overall, slave women benefited not at all from the idealization of womanhood that whites cultivated for themselves.

Was slavery profitable to the planters? Not all the evidence is in. Investments in new plantations in the lower South consistently yielded

A former slave, Moses Roper, wrote in the 1840s to a sympathetic white man about the brutal treatment suffered by some slaves.

"It happened where I was then living, at Greenville, in the county of the same name, in South Carolina. This slave was a preacher in the state of Georgia. His master told him if he continued his preaching to his fellow-slaves, he would for the next offense give him 500 lashes. George (for that was the name of the slave) disregarded his master's threat, and continued to preach to them. Upon his master having discovered the fact, George, being dreadfully alarmed lest the threatened punishment should be carried into effect, fled across the Savannah River, and took shelter in the barn of a Mr. Garrison, about seven miles from Greenville. There he was discovered by Mr. G., who shot at him with a rifle, on his attempting to run away, without effect. He was then pursued by Mr. G., who endeavoured to knock him down with the butt end of the piece, unsuccessfully. George wrenched the rifle out of his hands, and struck his pursuer with it. By this time several persons were collected, George was secured, and put into Greenville jail. The facts having transpired, through the newspaper, his master came to Greenville to claim him as his property, but consented, upon being required to do so, to receive 550 dollars as his value, with which he returned home. Shortly after this, George was burnt alive within one mile of the court-house at Greenville, in the presence of an immense assemblage of slaves, which had been gathered together to witness the horrid spectacle from a district of twenty miles in extent.

Take another case in the Village of Liberty Hill . . . Henry, failing to accomplish the task given to him to do on a Saturday, and fearing the punishment of a hundred lashes, with which he had been threatened, finished it on Sunday morning. His labour on the Sabbath was discovered by his master, and on the following day his master, as he said, "for violating the Sabbath," tied him to a tree, and flogged him with his own hand, at intervals from eight in the morning until five o'clock in the evening. About six o'clock two white men, in the employ of Mr. Bell, pitying his wretched condition, untied him, and assisted him home on a horse, a distance of about a mile. He was at this time in a state of great suffering and exhaustion. A short time after they had place him in the kitchen they heard him groan heavily; Bell also heard him, and said, "I will go out and see what is the matter with the nigger." He went, and found him breathing his last, the victim of his brutal treatment.

This case was brought to trial; my then master, Mr. Gooch, was on the jury. The evidence of the two white men was taken, and Bell was adjudged to pay the value of the slave he had destroyed. This he was unable to do, and a Mr. Connighim, a wealthy and extensive planter in the neighbourhood, paid it for him, on condition of Bell's becoming a drive on one of his estates. To this arrangement he consented, and the matter was settled."

A southern senator later asserted:

"You dare not make war on cotton. Cotton is King."

a return upon capital sufficient to attract outside funds, an indication that a well-managed cotton plantation on good soil was at least as profitable as alternative forms of investment. Slaveholders in the less productive regions of the upper South exported their surplus slaves profitably to the Cotton Belt. None of this, however, demonstrates that the slave system itself added to the efficiency and productivity of cotton planting. In the United States and abroad, masses of workers clothed themselves in this strong but comfortable fiber, and textile mills hungered for it. In those early days of large-scale cotton production, a free black labor force might have moved as swiftly as marketed slaves in response to the regional fortunes of cotton production. Still, slavery allowed plantation owners to keep their workers at lowest subsistence level, and thereby to benefit as individuals. For the South as a whole slavery was probably an economic liability. Four million blacks were kept in the strictest poverty, when as free property owners they could have provided a rich market for the products of southern agriculture and industry, and as free workers they could have constituted a versatile and energetic workforce. Slavery caused white southerners to concentrate their resources in staple agriculture at the expense of industry and transportation. And, of course, it stifled the intellectual and creative energies of generations of black Americans.

Race Control   Slavery was more than a labor system; it was also a means of race control. The southern states enacted elaborate slave codes touching virtually all of black life. Slave marriages and divorces had no legal validity. Slaves were forbidden to leave their plantations without a pass, to be out after curfew, to congregate in groups unless a white man was present, to carry arms, or to strike a white person. They could not own property or testify in court against whites. Punishment for most crimes was left to the master, who was given immunity from prosecution should a slave die under "moderate" correction. Death was the penalty for rebellion or plotting to rebel. To enforce these codes, the white males mounted regular patrols, which traveled the neighborhood at night in search of arms or runaways. Members were chosen at militia muster and all members of the community—slaveholders and non-slaveholders alike—were supposed to take their turn.

Enslaved blacks faced the constant task of adjusting to the condition of bondage. Rebellion was rare; outright resistance was suicidal. When Nat Turner, a slave preacher, led a band of armed followers through Southampton County, Virginia, in 1831, killing fifty-seven men, women, and children, terrified whites retaliated by slaughtering at least one hundred blacks. The South was on edge for months afterward. No one knew when this black fury, like some smoldering volcano, would erupt again. Individual acts of resistance, such as arson, running away, or even suicide, were not uncommon. Instead of confronting their masters directly, blacks developed various stratagems of accommodation and subtle resistance. They became particularly adept at malingering, breaking tools, and otherwise obstructing the workings of a system in which they were not free participants.

The black family may have been a more cohesive unit than historians and sociologists once believed. If plantation records contain instances of the breakup of families through sale, these same sources reveal many others in which they remained intact over several generations. And even when spouses and children were sent to other areas, black people retained a powerful sense of family. After emancipation, thousands of blacks wandered across the South in search of relatives and loved ones.

A treasury of folklore demonstrates the extent to which slaves retained a sense of identity. Slaves blended African and New World materials into their own culture. Black spirituals were a form of religious music unique in sound and feeling but expressive of profoundly Christian themes of sorrow and hope. Spirituals could also be a commentary on the system in which the slave was imprisoned. One song, ostensibly about Biblical Samson, expressed the wish that "if I had my way, I'd tear this building down."

And in their quarters, conducting prayer meetings of their own, often in defiance of the law, the slaves created forms of preaching, of worship, of social union that would give structure to black society not only under slavery but in the dangerous century of freedom that followed emancipation. The participation of black southern churches in the great civil rights movement of the 1950s and 60s is in its way the culmination and triumph of those humble and at times furtive gatherings.

"Field hollers" and work songs combated the boredom of mindless field labor and provided the coordination and timing essential to people working under close and difficult conditions:

Massa in the great house, counting out
 his money,
Oh, shuck that corn and throw it in the
 barn.
Mistis in the parlor, eating bread and
 honey.
Oh, shuck that corn and throw it in the
 barn.

The South Closes Ranks

The rise of militant abolitionism, coupled with the Nat Turner uprising, stimulated another round of soul-searching among southern whites. In 1831–32 the Virginia House of Delegates began a lengthy debate on a plan for the gradual emancipation and deportation of all slaves. The proposal was at last defeated, and this defeat marked a turning point. Thereafter, few white southerners would deny that slavery was sanctioned by the Bible and the laws of nature, or that it provided a harmonious solution to the South's racial dilemma and offered beneficent schooling to the black race.

To shore up their "peculiar institution," as it was often called, southern legislatures enacted tougher slave codes and further curtailed the liberties of free blacks. In many states it was illegal to teach slaves to read and write, and in some they were not allowed to work as typesetters or printers. The repression touched whites as well. Slave-state lawmakers forbade the publication or distribution of antislavery propaganda—sometimes under penalty of death. Public pressure silenced other critics of slavery: several prominent university professors left the South. The antislavery societies that had existed throughout the region quickly disappeared.

The increasingly insistent abolitionist rhetoric of the 1830s and 1840s convinced many southerners that the North was really trying to destroy slavery outright. The debate between gradual and immediate abolition meant nothing to southerners, because the end of slavery in any fashion would doom their way of life. In response to northern attacks on slavery, southerners stopped apologizing for the institution, and

CASH!

All persons that have SLAVES to dispose of, will do well by giving me a call, as I will give the

HIGHEST PRICE FOR

Men, Women, &

CHILDREN.

Any person that wishes to sell, will call at Hill's tavern, or at Shannon Hill for me, and any information they want will be promptly attended to.

Thomas Griggs.

Charlestown, May 7, 1835.

PRINTED AT THE FREE PRESS OFFICE, CHARLESTOWN.

southern writers like William Harper, Thomas R. Drew, and James H. Hammond launched an assertive argument for it.

One line of defense claimed to find evidence from the Old Testament that black people were descendents of Ham, the cursed son of Noah, destined for the role of servants. A secular version of that argument held that Africans were biologically different from Europeans, designed for lives of servitude under white owners whose biology dictated responsible and benevolent mastery. Pseudoscientific investigations in aid of this thesis were popular among spokesmen for slavery.

Southern polemicists argued that slavery provided the economic prosperity of the South and the economic foundation for the rise of southern civilization. Many people in the southern planter class came to view themselves as aristocratic. Some claimed descent from the Cavalier aristocracy of Great Britain. Southern society, as they perceived it, was genteel, cultured, and paternalistic.

Finally, the defenders of slavery offered a scathing critique of northern society. They blasted the hypocrisy of northerners who criticized slavery while ignoring the poverty and suffering of their own working classes. Southerners argued that capitalism in the North was a brutal institution that exploited poor people in the name of profits, and they pointed to the plight of factory workers and the urban homeless. Slavery, on the other hand, was an institution in which the slave owners took care of their workers from the cradle to the grave. Slave owners, so southern authors contended, provided their slaves with the blessings of living in a cultured, Christian civilization, and the slaves lived lives of loyalty and tranquility. George Fitzhugh held the organic bond between slaves and owners to be an expression of the harmony and oneness that prevails throughout biological nature. Freedom, by this argument, severs workers from employers and sends cracks and ruptures throughout the human community that should be an instance of the unity of nature.

| The "Gag" Rule | Southerners also sought to stifle criticism from outside. Backed by a war chest of over $30,000, abolitionists embarked in 1835 on a campaign to send |

hundreds of thousands of antislavery pamphlets to all parts of the country. A mob of South Carolinians seized the materials from the Charleston post office and in a huge bonfire burned them, along with effigies of Arthur Tappan and William Lloyd Garrison. Afterward, Postmaster General Amos Kendall, with President Jackson's approval, authorized southern postmasters to censor the mails and stop the flow of antislavery material into the South. Southern politicians urged the House of Representatives not to receive petitions demanding the abolition of slavery in the states or the District of Columbia. Formerly Congress had accepted such memorials and then rejected them as "inexpedient." Following angry debate, the House now approved a modified "gag" rule; henceforth it would receive antislavery petitions but automatically table them without formal consideration. Whatever might be the technical status of the gag rule, it looked very much like a violation of the First Amendment right of the people to petition the government. Former President John Quincy Adams, now a Massachusetts congressman, led the battle to vindicate the historic right of

In January 1848 one new resident in Kentucky observed an increasingly closed society:

"The man with whom I board (a slave holder) says that all questions that involve the subject of slavery ought not to be discussed in Ky. And I have heard him say that slavery was an evil, yet he says it ought not to be debated in Ky. for it makes the Negroes uneasy & has a tendency to make them try to escape (which by the way) a great many do. . . . A minister to go into the pulpit and preach Anti slavery doctrine, as some do in the East, would be in danger of his life, it would not be allowed—Aye, in our boasted land of *Liberty* one has not the privelege of expressing his opinions—Shame on such actions! Call not this the land where Liberty's broad shield shines over all, while one sixth of her sons & daughters toil & bleed beneath the lash, 'tis a disgrace to the Union—Our Eagle is no longer an emblem of protection, but of Despotism, Tyranny, & Oppression. It lives by plunder, it feasts on innocence—& drinks the life blood of its victims. Does not the present war with Mexico show it. It tears her *limbs* from her body & then because she writhes & offers some resistance, she strikes her beak to its very vitals. I have said more than I intended but not half what I feel."

petition. Year after year "Old Man Eloquent," though never an advocate of immediatism, fought to get petitions discussed before the House of Representatives, winning thousands to the antislavery cause in the process. In 1844 Adams finally secured repeal of the gag rule. He served in Congress until 1848 when he suffered a stroke in the House and died two days later at the age of eighty-one.

Repressive tactics rebounded against slaveholders. The gag rules, mob attacks, the censorship of mails, and other violations of civil liberties created a reaction that broadened the antislavery movement's appeal. Abolitionists charged that a vast slave power conspiracy was threatening the liberty of northern whites as well as southern blacks. Slaveholders and their northern allies, those "gentlemen of property and standing," despised freedom in general, for whites as for blacks. That claim, speaking to the pride of white Americans in their own freedom, would become in time a main component of the antislavery movement.

The Antislavery Spectrum

The place of black people in American life became the central political issue in the United States during the 1840s and 1850s. The question of whether, and if so how, the slaves should be freed was only part of the controversy. Free blacks in the North and the South also wanted to know whether they would ever be accepted as equals and enjoy the same civil liberties given to whites under the Constitution.

Northern Blacks The quarter of a million blacks who lived in the free states had only a threadbare kind of freedom. In most places they could not vote, hold office, or testify in court. They were confined to menial jobs and wretched housing. Everywhere law and public opinion combined to exclude or segregate them: in railroad coaches, schools, restaurants, theaters, churches, even cemeteries. Most northerners, including some who condemned slavery, viewed this not as a departure from democratic principles, but as a natural and legitimate response to the black presence.

Excluded from the dominant political and social institutions, northern blacks found in the abolitionist crusade their first opportunity to have a major role in American public life. Their subscriptions kept Garrison's newspaper alive, and Boston blacks protected him from violence. Escaped slaves like Frederick Douglass lectured and wrote of their experiences. Harriet Tubman, an escapee who made nineteen trips into slave country to bring out runaways, had a price of $40,000 on her head. Initially the protégés of white abolitionists, blacks gradually asserted their independence. They founded newspapers and rights organizations of their own and established vigilance committees in northern cities that protected black fugitives from slave-catchers.

As they struggled to influence popular opinion, abolitionists promoted one broad organization: the American Antislavery Society, founded in 1833. Garrison, Weld, the Tappan brothers, and the Grimké sisters all belonged to the Society, which claimed as many as thirteen hundred local chapters. Under Weld's direction, the Society's members

Illustrations of the American Anti-Slavery Almanac for **1840**.

"*Our Peculiar Domestic Institutions.*"

Northern Hospitality—New-York nine months law. [The Slave steps out of the Slave State, and his chains fall. A Free State, with another chain, stands ready to re-enslave him.]

Burning of McIntosh at St. Louis, in April, 1836.

Showing how slavery improves the condition of the female sex.

The Negro Pew, or "Free" Seats for black Christians.   *Mayor of New-York refusing a Carman's license to a colored Man.*

Servility of the Northern States in arresting and returning fugitive Slaves.

Selling a Mother from her Child.

Hunting Slaves with dogs and guns.   A Slave drowned by the dogs.

"*Poor things, 'they can't take care of themselves.'*"

Mothers with young Children at work in the field.

A Woman chained to a Girl, and a Man in irons at work in the field.

Branding Slaves.

Cutting up a Slave in Kentucky.

Paid.   Unpaid.

One of the publications of the abolitionist crusade. An integral part of the reform sentiment that began in the 1830s, the movement emphasized moral suasion rather than legal coercion.
(Courtesy, Library of Congress)

bombarded Congress with petitions opposing slavery in the District of Columbia and urging an end to the interstate slave trade. The petition campaign attracted widespread support after southern congressmen obtained their "gag" rule. American abolitionists also sought closer ties with British reformers, and in 1840 many attended the World Anti-Slavery Convention in London. Yet the antislavery movement had deep internal divisions. Personality clashes, doctrinal conflicts among different religious denominations, and fundamental differences over strategy splintered the movement.

Tactical Disagreements The split over strategy and tactics involved conflicting interpretations of American society and the role of abolitionism in American life. Shocked by mob violence against abolitionists, Garrisonians concluded that American society was sick. Slavery was one of the symptoms of moral decay, but there were others—militarism, expansionism, the oppression of women and the poor. Only a total reformation of the nation's ethical values would suffice. Abolitionists, Garrison maintained, must "revolutionize the public sentiment" by an expanded campaign of moral suasion; having done this, they would accomplish the overthrow of slavery. Garrison's opponents in the antislavery movement believed that efforts to link the movement too closely with other causes risked alienating people who had been converted by the campaign against postal censorship or angered by southern violations of the civil liberties of whites. "Garrisonian fanaticism," so they feared, endangered the future of abolitionism.

Slavery in the Territories

Although Americans had been debating the issue of slavery ever since the Missouri controversy stretching from 1818 to 1820, the debate did not begin to destabilize the political system until the 1840s. The issue that eventually disrupted the Union and brought on the Civil War was the question of whether slavery should be permitted to expand out of its base in the South to the new territories of the West. For a variety of deeply-held political, economic, and social reasons, most southerners supported expansion of slavery westward. A great many northerners, though shunning abolitionism as radical and impractical, opposed that expansion.

The Liberty Party The "Log Cabin and Hard Cider" campaign of 1840 expressed the nation's new fascination with mass politics, and many antislavery leaders wanted to get involved. Even in these times before the conflict with Mexico and the consequent acquisition of land heated the controversy, the success of the petition drives and other quasi-political activities offered some hope that electoral politics would be responsive to antislavery sentiment. A group of abolitionists formed the Liberty Party in 1840. As their presidential candidate, they selected James G. Birney, a slaveholder turned abolitionist, and they framed a platform attacking slavery. Lost in the hoopla of the contest between the Whig Harrison and the Democrat Van Buren, the Liberty Party attracted little attention. Birney, in London for the World Anti-Slavery Convention, did not even campaign. In the next presidential election Birney polled about 65,000 votes. An improvement over 1840, this still represented only 32 out of every 1,000 votes cast in the North. Garrison and his followers consistently opposed the Liberty Party experiment. Political organizations, they argued, implied acceptance of the legitimacy of the existing system, which they held to be morally diseased at its root. Retaining his faith in perfectionism and therefore rejecting participation in the unclean institutions of law and politics, Garrison refused even to vote.

But abolitionists, even Garrison, were more than simple idealists or frustrated politicians. Most were hard-headed reformers who recognized the need for many types of nonviolent action. They tried unsuccessfully to organize a boycott of the products of slave labor. They worked to impel churches to denounce slavery. A few helped slaves escape on the celebrated "underground railroad."

Slavery in the West In 1840, the antislavery movement was still struggling for a foothold in American politics. Abolitionist sentiment was vague, sporadic, and moralistic; the slavery interest was concentrated, practical, and testily defensive. Moral suasion had utterly failed to convert southerners, who feared not only a loss of property but a loss of racial mastery. Countless northerners found the abolition movement radical and disruptive. The vast majority of northern whites discriminated against free blacks and were content to leave slavery alone where it existed. Most northerners probably opposed, or sooner or later would come to oppose, slavery in the abstract, but few favored immediate emancipation. They feared that the free states would be overrun with emancipated blacks. Slavery also had powerful allies among northern businessmen dependent on the success of southern crops. The churches, too, wrestled with the problem of slavery. By the end of the 1840s the Presbyterians, the Methodists, and the Baptists, unable to reach a consensus on slavery at their national meetings, had split into northern and southern organizations.

The Constitution itself discouraged abolitionists. Both sides in the slavery controversy recognized that the Constitution perceived slaves as property and that the federal government could not abolish slavery in the states. This was a decision for the people of the states themselves to make. The southern states were happy to uphold a Constitution and a Union that protected slavery. For decades, moreover, Americans had agreed to an informal division of territory into free and slave soil. The Northwest Ordinance of 1787 had prohibited slavery north of the Ohio River. South of the Ohio, North Carolina and Georgia had ceded western lands to the national government on the specific condition that slavery should be permitted in the states that would eventually be formed from these lands. The Missouri Compromise line of 1820 divided the vast Louisiana Purchase into slave and free soil. These arrangements covered all the existing United States territory, leaving nothing after 1820 for argument in Congress. Abolitionists were left to battle over such narrow issues as the gag rule and the status of slavery

One Quaker recalled the workings of the underground railroad:

"In the winter of 1826–27 fugitives began to come to our house. The roads were always in running order, and the connections were good, the conductors active and zealous, and there was no lack of passengers. Seldom a week passed without our receiving passengers by this mysterious road. We knew not what night or what hour of the night we would be roused from slumber by a gentle rap at the door. Outside in the cold or rain there would be a two-horse wagon loaded with fugitives, perhaps the greater part of them women and children. When they were all safely inside and the door fastened, I would cover the windows, strike a light, and build a good fire. By this time my wife would be up and preparing victuals. The companies varied in number, from two or three fugitives to seventeen.

The pursuit was often very close, and we had to resort to various stratagems in order to elude the pursuers. Sometimes a company of fugitives were scattered and secreted in the neighborhood until the hunters had given up the chase. At other times their route was changed and they were hurried forward with all speed. It was a continual excitement and anxiety to us, but the work was its own reward."

Newspapers commonly ran notices like this one:

THIRTY DOLLARS
REWARD

Ran away last night, from the subscriber, living on the waters of Little Pipe-Creek, near Westminster Town, Maryland, a tall, well-made, and active country born Negro Man, named PETER, about 30 years of age, 5 feet 8 or 10 inches high, wears the wool on the top of his head commonly platted, and when loose is very long and bushy, but will likely have it cut short; there remains the mark of a burn near the wrist, on the back part of one of his hands, believed to be the right, which he received when young, has a down look when spoken to, but is a handsome erect figure with smaller features, than is common for a Negro of his age, and speaks German nearly as well as English. He was brought up by me to plantation work chiefly, of which he is very capable, but can do a little at blacksmith, shoemaking and carpenters work, and has some knowledge of making gun barrels—he had on and took with him a fur hat about half worn; a home made soili'd lincey doublet of a yellowish color, a swansdown jacket, with yellow flannel backs and lining, a pair of torn linnen trousers, which he wears very high, and a pair of common half worn shoes, but as he is an artful and active fellow, and has money, it is expected that he will soon exchange them. He also plays on the fiddle and fife tolerably well. Whoever takes up said Negro, and brings him home, shall receive if 15 miles from home 5 dollars; if 30 miles 10 dollars; if 60 miles 20 dollars: if 100 miles or upward, the above reward and 10 dollars if lodged in any goal and notice given me thereof by a letter, directed to the Post Office, at Westminster, Frederick County, Maryland.

DAVID SHRIVER

in the District of Columbia, issues over which Congress had undisputed authority.

In one vast area, however, the federal government did hold power over slavery. The Constitution authorized the Congress to make "all needful rules and regulations" respecting the territories. Suddenly in the late 1840s the issue of slavery in the territories came alive. Congress had to deal with slavery in the regions acquired after the Mexican War. The government, which could not constitutionally interfere with slavery in the states, could determine the status of slavery in the territories. Abolitionists, therefore, now had an issue on which they could make a concrete demand of Congress: keep slavery out of the new territories. And because many northerners had economic or political reasons for wanting slavery kept out of the new domain, abolitionists could appeal to self-interest as well as to conscience. Beginning in the late 1840s the antislavery movement fixed upon the territorial issue, and for the next fifteen years this question dominated national politics as no issue before or since.

For a variety of reasons, northerners opposed the expansion of slavery into the territories. Some northerners fought it because they believed that slavery was evil; others opposed it because they had some thought of moving into the new territories and did not want the land monopolized by a slave economy. Many northern businessmen feared that senators and representatives from new slave states would vote in Congress against tariffs, banking, legislation, and internal improvements. Northern workers believed that the expansion of slavery would eliminate jobs and depress wages.

Most southerners, on the other hand, were passionately committed to the expansion of slavery into the western territories. Cotton and tobacco cultivation eventually exhausted the land, forcing slave owners to move to new land farther west. If Congress passed legislation confining slavery to the South, slave owners believed, they would face eventual bankruptcy and, worse yet, would have to free their slaves. Southerners also argued that it was their right to take their slaves out west. The right to possess and keep private property, they claimed as conservatives have claimed ever since, is fundamental; and they considered their slaves to be their property. Finally, many southerners believed it imperative for new slave states to come into the Union. Only then could they maintain their dominance of the United States Senate and protect themselves from legislation in Congress hostile to the South.

Fugitive Slaves

Late in 1841 an American slave ship, the *Creole*, set out from Hampton Roads, Virginia, planning to carry a large cargo of slaves to New Orleans. Off the Atlantic coast of Florida, the slaves mutinied and took control of the ship. They killed one crew member in the process and then sailed the ship to Nassau in the Bahama Islands. The Bahamas were a British colony, and Great Britain had legally abolished slavery in 1833. The United States demanded the return of the ship and all of the slaves, but Great Britain refused. Instead, the British freed all of the slaves except those directly responsible for killing the crew member. In the midst of the controversy, Congressman Joshua Giddings, a Whig from Ohio, introduced a series of antislavery resolutions in March 1842. The resolutions condemned slavery and the slave trade. They did not pass in the House of Representatives, but their introduction inspired dozens of southerners to praise the virtues of slavery on the floor of Congress. Meanwhile, another issue involving fugitives from slavery was further inflaming southern feelings.

The Fugitive Slave Act of 1793 had provided for the use of federal marshals to assist in the capture of slaves who had escaped into free states. But as the slavery issue became more and more controversial in the early nineteenth century, some of the free states refused to provide any assistance in arresting, detaining, and extraditing escaped slaves. Beginning in 1820, a number of northern states, including Pennsylvania, New York, Connecticut, Massachusetts, Vermont, and Ohio, passed what they called "personal liberty laws" to protect the former slaves and impede the enforcement of the Fugitive Slave Act of 1793.

The passage of the personal liberty laws outraged southern slave owners. The matter, to be sure, did pose a constitutional dilemma for them. Ever since Thomas Jefferson and James Madison wrote the Virginia and Kentucky Resolutions in 1799, the South had insisted on the supremacy of states' rights as opposed to the authority of the federal government. That had been the position of Calhoun and South Carolina during the nullification crises. But on the question of runaway slaves, southerners found themselves calling for the federal government to interfere with state prerogatives. They demanded enforcement of the Fugitive Slave Act of 1793 and repeal of the personal liberty laws. Pennsylvania in 1826 had passed its personal liberty law, which banned the seizure and extradition of fugitive slaves. The Pennsylvania statute was challenged by an owner who demanded the return of his escaped slave. Although the Supreme Court in *Prigg v. Pennsylvania* (1842) held the state law unconstitutional, it also proclaimed that enforcement of the Fugitive Slave Act of 1793 was exclusively a federal responsibility and that state governments were not obliged to provide any assistance. The decision led to a series of new personal liberty laws in northern states. The legislation prohibited the use of any state resources—personnel, jails, or courts—in assisting federal authorities in the return of escaped slaves. Without at least some state assistance, the national government was unable to return the vast majority of escaped slaves. The conviction deepened in the South that much of the North was prepared to express its contempt of the slave system legislatively.

Whigs, Democrats, and Westward Expansion

John Tyler: Another Southern President

In March 1841 jubilant Whigs flooded Washington, hungry for government offices. The crush of office-seekers proved tiring for the elderly and infirm William Henry Harrison. A cold contracted while he was doing the presidential grocery shopping soon developed into pneumonia, and on April 4—just a month after the inauguration—he died. Two days later Vice President John Tyler, summoned

President John Tyler. *(Courtesy, Hugh Cleland Collection)*

hastily from his Virginia plantation, took the presidential oath. Since Harrison was the first President to die in office, questions arose over whether Tyler was actually President or merely the Vice President assuming the duties and responsibilities of the presidency. Tyler simply took on the title of President and thereby settled the matter.

Lean and hawk-nosed, with a Virginian's pride and a streak of obstinacy, the fifty-one-year-old Tyler entered the White House with a distinguished career in Virginia politics behind him. He had started in politics as a states' rights Democrat, and he and the Whigs were mismatched from the start. The new President resisted domination by Clay and Webster, the acknowledged leaders of the party. He had no sympathy for the Whigs' economic nationalism. In September, when he vetoed Clay's bill to reestablish a national bank, the entire Harrison Cabinet resigned except Secretary of State Webster. He stayed on to conduct negotiations with Great Britain over various problems, especially the disputed northeastern boundary between Maine and New Brunswick.

Tempers had flared between the United States and Great Britain in 1837 when a small steamer, the *Caroline*, was burned by the British when it was caught ferrying supplies to a group of Canadian nationalists on the Niagara River. Two years later Alexander McLeod, a Canadian deputy sheriff, was arrested in New York State for murder in connection with the *Caroline* incident. McLeod was released only after border skirmishes and talk of war with Britain filled the newspapers. In 1842, the secretary of state managed to conclude the Webster-Ashburton Treaty, which settled the bloodless "Aroostook War" over lumbering rights along the Maine boundary and other problems by compromise, and set an example for the friendly resolution of future disputes between Britain and the United States and between this country and Canada. Shortly after the treaty was signed, Webster too left the Cabinet. That resignation completed the break between Tyler and the Whigs, who henceforth referred to the President as "His Accidency."

Tyler appointed a new Cabinet heavy with southern Democrats, and began searching for issues that would win him reelection. For the North he signed the Tariff of 1842, restoring protective duties to roughly the level of 1832. To soothe southern resentment over the tariff, Tyler offered a daring proposal—the annexation of Texas, an area that since 1836 had been an independent nation known as the Lone Star Republic. Annexation was a policy sure to anger the Mexican republic, which was losing its control over the whole of its vast western lands.

Annexation of Texas   During the Texan war of independence, the United States had adopted a distinctly unneutral attitude. Money was raised for supplies, and many volunteers swelled the ranks of the Texan army. After independence, much of the public on both sides of the border between Texas and the United States favored annexation. But since Mexico refused to acknowledge Texan independence, annexation might provoke war. Politicians also feared that incorporating new slave territory into the Union would aggravate the rising antislavery sentiment in the North. President Jackson waited until his last day in office before recognizing the new Texan republic. His successor, Martin Van Buren, carefully avoided the question of annexation. Texas drifted for several years, developing ever closer ties with Great Britain.

The movement for annexation revived in 1842. Facing an empty treasury and renewed hostilities with Mexico, Sam Houston as President of Texas made overtures to Washington and found an enthusiastic ally in John Tyler. Annexation was politically expedient, and, like other slaveholders, Tyler was convinced that continued expansion was vital to the slave economy and the southern way of life. After the unsympathetic Webster resigned as secretary of state, Tyler appointed a fellow Virginian, Abel P. Upshur, and ordered him to seek a treaty of annexation.

The move was well timed: the country dreamed of continental empire. Southerners feared that Britain, which had abolished slavery in its possessions in 1833, was working to abolish slavery in Texas. Northern commercial interests sought control by the United States of valuable Pacific coast ports as trading centers, and annexation of Texas would shorten the distance to the Pacific. Secretary Upshur, confident that the Senate would approve a treaty, negotiated with Texan representatives. After Upshur's death the new secretary of state, John C. Calhoun, completed the arrangements for annexation and submitted the treaty to the Senate.

James Polk: Expansionist   The Senate, however, delayed action until after the 1844 party nominating conventions, at which Texas suddenly emerged as a major political issue. Both leading candidates, Henry Clay and Martin Van Buren, came out against annexation. The Whigs, passing over President Tyler, nominated Clay; the Democrats bypassed Van Buren in favor of an avowed expansionist, James Knox Polk. This political maneuvering and Calhoun's defense of annexation as a proslavery measure doomed the treaty. A combination of Whigs and disappointed Van Buren Democrats killed it. Tyler refused to surrender; he sent a message to the House of Representatives three days later proposing to annex Texas by other means.

Tyler, before leaving the White House, had forced the issue of expansion to the center of American politics. Democrats hoped to preserve sectional harmony within their party by promising both the "re-annexation" of Texas and the "re-occupation" of Oregon to the very northerly latitude of 54° 40′. Whigs and Democrats again clamored for votes. In Lowell, Massachusetts: "The Whig Party of this city have got a large flag stretched across one of our streets. The Democratic Party not to be outdone [obtained] a large hickory tree surmounted with a flag staff, making the whole length upwards of 100 feet." The Oregon occupation slogan "Fifty-four forty or fight" became popular among expansionists.

Too late, Clay sensed the public mood and endorsed annexation of Texas "upon just and fair terms." That November, Polk won a narrow victory in the presidential election. President Tyler interpreted Polk's victory as a mandate for annexation of Texas. Just before he left office in March 1845, the President got Congress to admit Texas to the Union by a joint resolution, which required only a majority vote in each house, while a treaty would have required approval by two-thirds of the Senate. When Polk entered the White House, annexation was a settled question.

"Give up Oregon?" asked one senator:

"History, speaking from the sepulchre of the sainted dead, forbids it. The shades of Washington, of Adams, of Henry, and of their immortal compeers, forbid it. The still small voice of Camden and Concord forbids it. The holy blood that fell in torrents in the parched fields of Monmouth, and Camden, and the Brandywine, forbids it. . . . In the name of the past, in the name of the unborn millions whose proud fortune it will be to direct the destinies of free America— I protest here, in the face of Heaven and all men, against any dismemberment of our territory—the surrender of our principle—the sacrifice of our honor! "

The Oregon Question   Another of Polk's major objectives was the solution of the Oregon boundary question. Formidable mountain barriers had retarded settlement in the Pacific Northwest until the 1830s, when traders and missionaries began publicizing the area. By 1845 some 5,000 Americans had migrated there, settling mainly in the fertile Willamette Valley in Oregon. Throughout his campaign, Polk promised to assert American control over all the Oregon Territory, which the United States and Great Britain had occupied jointly since 1818. Once in power, however, Polk began a search for compromise with Britain.

The British government at first rejected the American idea of putting the line at the 49th parallel, which would place the Columbia River wholly in the hands of the United States. Polk then called upon Congress for authority to give the required one year's notice terminating joint occupation. The United States, he announced, would look John Bull "straight in the eye." Congress consented. Polk served the expected notice in April 1846; on both sides of the Atlantic, people talked of war. One newspaper declared: *"Oregon is ours,* and we will keep it, at the price, if need be, of every drop of the nation's blood."

Neither country really wanted a fight. Britain had all but abandoned to the advancing wave of settlers the land between the Columbia River and the 49th parallel. Polk, anticipating war with Mexico at any moment, could no longer afford a quarrel with Britain. He therefore welcomed a British offer to divide Oregon at the 49th parallel. The Senate approved this arrangement. Northwestern Democrats charged that Polk and his southern Democratic allies, having acquired Texas, had reneged on their promise to acquire "all of Oregon or none." Their residual bitterness combined with antislavery sentiment to strengthen opposition to Polk's conduct of the Mexican War.

Polk's other objective, acquiring California, was not so easily accomplished. Mexico had no intention of selling the province. In March 1845, in protest over the decision of the United States to annex Texas, the proud Latin republic had broken diplomatic relations with the United States. And a controversy had arisen over the question of just what had been annexed. Texans asserted that their republic stretched as far south as the Rio Grande; Mexico insisted that the province's boundary stopped at the Nueces River. Mexico probably had the better case. Polk nevertheless claimed all the disputed area for the United States and used his nation's demands on the Texas boundary to press Mexico to a settlement on California.

The Mexican Settlements   After Mexico won its independence in 1821, the Spanish outposts to the North remained in their customary isolation from the South. They enjoyed much self-sufficiency, and they were receptive to the manufactures that traders from the United States were able to furnish. By 1824 wagons and pack animals were hauling tools, textiles, and weapons over the Santa Fe Trail, forged by William Becknell in the early 1820s. In the 1830s English-speaking Americans and even Europeans began to drift into California. Some traversed the California trail and competed as successful ranchers alongside the Spanish. The Swiss John Sutter, who would discover gold in California in 1849, settled in Monterey.

Young America   As the United States pressed westward, the expansionist urge acquired an explicit ideology. It was associated with the phrase "manifest destiny." In 1845 John L. O'Sullivan, editor of an expansionist newspaper entitled *The United States Magazine and Democratic Review,* spoke of "our manifest destiny to overspread the continent allotted by Providence for the free development of our yearly multiplying millions." Late in 1845 during the debate over the Oregon Treaty, the New York *Morning News* picked up on the phrase, and by 1846 newspapers made "Manifest Destiny" familiar throughout the United States. Manifest Destiny came to mean that the institutions and values of the United States were destined to spread across the continent, from the Atlantic to the Pacific. Nature and God intended this to take place, and the government should assist in bringing it about, even if it meant war.

Closely associated with Manifest Destiny was the Young America movement. Its leading exponent was George N. Sanders, who wrote regularly for the *Democratic Review.* The advocates of Young America believed that the United States had a special mission that would eventually envelop the entire world. Young America was a global extension of Jacksonian democracy and Manifest Destiny. Its adherents called for the United States to embrace all of North America, not only from the Atlantic to the Pacific but from the Isthmus of Panama to the Arctic. They also wanted the United States to provide assistance to revolutionary movements everywhere. When the revolutions of 1848 erupted throughout Europe, the advocates of Young America wished for the United States to get involved and provide political and economic support to the insurgents. As it turned out, the Young America movement was ahead of its time, but it did generate at least some of the energy that fueled politics during the 1840s and led to expansion into the Spanish Southwest and the British Northwest.

Of the annexation of Texas, the expansionist editor John L. O'Sullivan wrote:

"Texas has been absorbed into the Union in the inevitable fulfillment of the general law which is rolling our population westward; the connexion of which with that ratio of growth in population which is destined within a hundred years to swell our numbers to the enormous population of *two hundred and fifty millions* (if not more), is too evident to leave us in doubt of the manifest design of Providence in regard to the occupation of this continent. It was disintegrated from Mexico in the natural course of events, by a process perfectly legitimate on its own part, blameless on ours; and in which all the censures due to wrong, perfidy, and folly, rest on Mexico alone. And possessed as it was by a population which was in truth but a colonial detachment from our own, . . . their incorporation into the Union was not only inevitable, but the most natural, right and proper thing in the world—and it is only astonishing that there should be any among ourselves to say it nay."

The Mexican War

The Coming of War   In July 1845, Polk ordered General Zachary Taylor, with nearly 4,000 troops, to take up a position south of the Nueces River. Taylor halted at Corpus Christi, where he remained for several months. At about the same time, the President issued secret orders to naval officers in the Pacific to occupy the California ports in the event of war with Mexico. He worked actively to encourage a revolution among settlers in the manner of the Texas uprising. Just in case the dissatisfied settlers from the United States needed any help, the President sent Colonel John C. Frémont and a scientific expedition to California, on which the engineering equipment included a heavy stock of arms.

His weapons now primed and ready, Polk sent John Slidell, a Louisiana politician, to Mexico in November 1845 to negotiate. The

President, refusing to compromise on the Rio Grande River boundary that would bite into territory claimed by Mexico, offered only to assume payment of claims by citizens of the United States against the Mexican government in return for accepting that river as marking the frontier between the two republics. He also authorized Slidell to purchase all or part of Upper California and New Mexico. When two successive Mexican governments refused to risk public disfavor by receiving him, Slidell withdrew. "Be assured," he wrote to the secretary of state, "that nothing is to be done with these people until they shall have been chastised." Polk had reached the same conclusion. In January 1846 he sent General Taylor's army to the Rio Grande. In late March Taylor and his men took up a fortified position opposite the Mexican city of Matamoros; naval units then blockaded the mouth of the river. For several weeks, nothing happened.

On May 9 Polk decided to ask Congress for a declaration of war against Mexico for failing to pay the claims due citizens of the United States and refusing to receive Slidell. News arrived that very evening of a skirmish with Mexican forces on the north bank of the Rio Grande. Polk at once revised his war message. Mexico, he told Congress, had "invaded our territory and shed American blood upon American soil." Congress, not fully aware of the President's maneuvering, voted overwhelmingly for war. Thousands of volunteers enthusiastically answered the call.

Polk and his Cabinet agreed at the outset that the United States must acquire both New Mexico and Upper California (the present state, as distinct from Lower California, still part of Mexico) and secure the Rio Grande boundary. New Mexico and California took but six months to conquer. During the summer of 1846 Colonel Stephen W. Kearny's

One soldier stationed near Matamoros wrote home:

"We had just moved our camp into a corn field newly ploughed, the soil an adhesive clay, and by the time I had in some measure secured my baggage . . . the water was some inches deep, or rather there was a soft adhesive mortar bed, about ankle deep, over the whole camp. The rain and gale were still at their worst, when I began looking about to see the state of the nation. In every direction the tents were overthrown and their contents scattered in the mud. My own company had almost entirely disappeared, a few despairing wretches, groping about in the mud for their arms, were all that were left. The fires were extinguished and desolation reigned throughout the camp."

ESSAY ON CIVIL DISOBEDIENCE (1846)

by Henry David Thoreau

Thoreau was ardently opposed to both slavery and the Mexican War.

How does it become a man to behave toward this American government to-day? I answer, that he cannot without disgrace be associated with it. I cannot for an instant recognize that political organization as my government which is the slave's government also.

All men recognize the right of revolution: that is, the right to refuse allegiance to, and to resist, the government, when its tyranny or its inefficiency are great and unendurable. But almost all say that such is not the case now. But such was the case, they think, in the Revolution of '75. If one were to tell me that this was a bad government because it taxed certain foreign commodities brought to its ports, it is most probable that I should not make an ado about it, for I can do without them.

When a sixth of the population of a nation which has undertaken to be the refuge of liberty are slaves, and a whole country is unjustly overrun and conquered by a foreign army, and subjected to military law, I think that it is not too soon for honest men to rebel and revolutionize. What makes this duty the more urgent is the fact that the country so overrun is not our own, but ours is the invading army.

If the injustice is part of the necessary friction of the machine of government, let it go, let it go, perchance it will wear smooth,—certainly the machine will wear out; if the injustice has a spring, or a pulley, or a rope, or a crank, exclusively for itself, then perhaps you may consider whether the remedy will not be worse than the evil; but if it is of such a nature that it requires you to be the agent of injustice to another, then, I say, break the law. Let your life be a counter friction to stop the machine. What I have to do is to see, at any rate, that I do not lend myself to the wrong which I condemn.

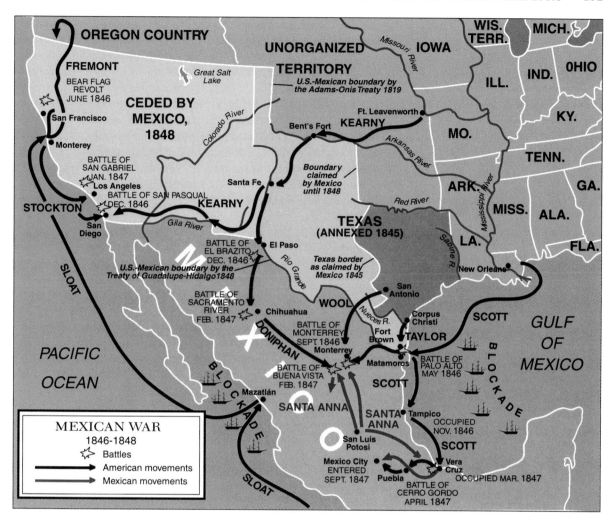

Army of the West (actually just sixteen hundred men) marched from Fort Leavenworth, Kansas, to Santa Fe, and occupied it without opposition. Kearny then proceeded with part of his force to aid the navy in the conquest of California. A column of Missouri volunteers under Colonel A. W. Doniphan descended the Rio Grande to El Paso, marched from there into the interior, and in March 1847 occupied Chihuahua.

Beyond the capture of Upper California and New Mexico, Polk's objectives were unclear. Apparently he hoped that an advance into Mexico would force General Santa Anna into a quick settlement. So Taylor at once pushed the Mexicans back across the Rio Grande and occupied Matamoros. In September, Taylor captured the Mexican stronghold of Monterrey and moved on to Saltillo and Victoria. The following February he repulsed Santa Anna at Buena Vista. Old Rough and Ready's victories and Doniphan's occupation of Chihuahua secured their country's possession of Mexico's northern territories. In the meantime, Polk had decided to bring the stubborn Santa Anna to terms with a strike at Mexico City itself.

At another camp, on the Rio Grande, a volunteer in the Mexican War reported:

"The water here unless well-qualified with brandy has a very peculiar effect on one . . . it opens the bowels. . . . Gen. Scott came to see us the other day. He complimented Major Sumner very warmly on our improvement and especially on the extraordinary vigilance of our scouts—who, as he said, were peering at him from behind every bush as he approached the camp. To those aware of the disease prevalent here, the mistake of the General is ludicrous."

Senator Thomas Corwin of Ohio, a Whig, also spoke out against the war:

"How is it that my country is involved in this war? I looked to the President's account of it, and he tells me it was a war for the defense of territory of the United States. . . . I know that the people of the United States neither sought nor forced Mexico into this war, and I know that the President of the United States . . . did seek that war, and that he forced war upon Mexico."

Polk, hating the Whigs even more than the Mexicans, picked General Winfield Scott to lead the campaign instead of Zachary Taylor, who was already being pushed as a Whig presidential candidate. Landing at Vera Cruz in March 1847, Scott took the city with few casualties on his side. The loss of life among Mexicans at Vera Cruz, by their own report, was 1,100, mostly by the explosion of shells, while only thirteen United States soldiers died. Scott then pushed inland through the mountains, routing Santa Anna at the pass of Cerro Gordo, after a party of engineers under Captain Robert E. Lee had hacked a path through ravines and underbrush to surround the Mexicans. On September 13, Scott's army stormed the fortress of Chapultepec guarding Mexico City. The capital fell the next day.

The Treaty of Guadalupe Hidalgo (1848)

Whigs meanwhile were capturing a widespread domestic opposition to "Mr. Polk's War." Whig politicians—among them a young Illinois congressman named Abraham Lincoln—accused the President of provoking Mexico into war as an excuse for expansion.

In December 1847 Lincoln introduced resolutions requesting Polk to inform Congress as to the "exact spot" where the first "blood of our *citizens* was shed." He declared "that the war with Mexico was unnecessarily and unconstitutionally commenced by the President." Later Lincoln praised a speech by Congressman Alexander Stephens of Georgia, who said that "the principle of waging war against a neighboring people to compel them to sell their country, is not only dishonorable, but disgraceful and infamous." In the Senate, Illinois Democrat Stephen Douglas spoke up for the President, quoting Frederick the Great's maxim, "Take possession first and negotiate afterward." A new senator from Mississippi, Jefferson Davis, who had fought at Buena Vista, said that Mexico was held "by title of conquest." If the United States could not agree, said Davis, then "let the sections part."

Outside Congress, other voices of opposition were heard. James Russell Lowell accused the President of wanting "bigger pens to cram with slaves." The American Peace Society grew in membership. Henry David Thoreau counseled civil disobedience and spent a night in jail for refusing to pay taxes to a government that supported the war. Some critics of the war even longed for the defeat of the United States. As Scott's army approached Mexico City, William Lloyd Garrison thundered in the *Liberator:* "We only hope that, if blood has had to flow, that it has been that of the Americans, and that the next news we shall hear will be that General Scott and his army are in the hands of the Mexicans. . . ."

Especially in the West and in the border states feelings about slavery and the Mexican War were smouldering on both sides of the issue. At the same time "Continental Democrats," party members of extreme expansionist persuasion, were urging the President to take all of Mexico. Polk had previously dispatched Nicholas P. Trist to Mexico as a peace negotiator, and although in late 1847 he called Trist home, the emissary ignored Polk's order and stayed to sign the Treaty of Guadalupe Hidalgo on February 2, 1848. The United States gained the

Rio Grande boundary, New Mexico, and California in return for an agreement to assume the claims of its citizens against the Mexican government, and to pay $15 million to Mexico.

The ratification in 1848 of the Treaty of Guadalupe Hidalgo turned over to the United States approximately 80,000 Mexicans whose citizenship and property rights the treaty supposedly guaranteed along with their religious freedom. Mexicans residing within the United States gradually saw their property and influence dwindle as they faced increasing pressure from the flood of Anglo Americans. The California Land Law of 1851 required that they submit proof of their land ownership. The cost of doing so in taxes, legal fees, and battles with squatters, in combination with the rainfall conditions that made incomes uncertain, gradually took away their land. Violence broke out in northern California in the 1850s and 1860s, and some Mexican Americans, called *Californios,* resorted to banditry. *Bandidos* who roamed California spawned legends. In southern California, in the 1870s and 1880s, the *Californios* lost more land to the railroads, which nonetheless provided jobs for Hispanics. In New Mexico, the *ricos,* wealthy Mexican landowners and merchants, took an important part in the creation of the territorial government. While remaining largely separate from the Anglo Americans, they retained substantial influence after the Civil War. In Texas, as the cattle industry grew enormously in response to the demand for beef that increased with the country's population, the Spanish and Anglo cultures would blend after the war into now familiar cowboy traditions. But many inhabitants of Mexican birth or ancestry continued to experience discrimination.

A Mexican historian has observed: "To explain then in a few words the true origin of the war, it is sufficient to say that the insatiable ambition of the United States, favored by our weakness, caused it." For an apparently small price the United States had rounded out its continental domain, acquiring the present states of California, Nevada, Utah, New Mexico, and Arizona. Soon, however, the cost would prove enormous: the problem of organizing this vast new territory reopened the explosive issue of slavery expansion, ultimately splitting in two the new transcontinental republic.

Crisis at Midcentury   When Congress adopted the Missouri Compromise in 1820 it had also adopted the rule that all territories above 36° 30′ would be closed to slavery while all below this line would be open to it. This formula had worked for a quarter of a century, in large measure because both northerners and southerners believed it fairly divided the national domain. The war with Mexico changed this. Most of the land acquired fell below the line. And California, easily the most valuable of the new territories even before the discovery of gold triggered the famous rush of 1849, would have been divided into two with the compromise line. Meanwhile the Polk Administration's diplomatic settlement of the Oregon boundary with Britain, although probably the best arrangement the United States could have gotten short of war, also rankled northerners who saw the Mexican War as a conspiracy to advance the power of the slave states.

With this in mind a member of President Polk's own party, a

In 1859 Juan Cortina, the "Robin Hood of Texas," launched an armed rebellion to protest the wholesale loss of land by native Tejano farmers to Anglos. He battled United States soldiers and Texas Rangers until the summer of 1860, when he escaped across the border into Mexico. He issued a manifesto to all Mexican Americans in South Texas on November 23, 1859:

"Mexicans! Many of you have been robbed of your property, incarcerated, chased, murdered, and hunted like wild beasts. . . . [J]ustice had fled from this world, leaving you to the caprice of your oppressors, who become each day more furious toward you. . . . Mexicans! My part is taken; the voice of revelation whispers to me that to me is entrusted the work of breaking the chains of your slavery, and that the Lord will enable me, with powerful arm, to fight against our enemies. . . . On my part, I am ready to offer myself as a sacrifice."

first-term congressman from Pennsylvania named David Wilmot, introduced his famous proviso in August of 1846 to a military appropriations bill. The Wilmot Proviso would have prohibited slavery from ever being introduced into lands acquired from Mexico. The House, with both northern Whigs and northern Democrats voting in favor, adopted the Proviso. The Senate, where southerners were more powerful, rejected it. Congress was now splitting not so much between Whigs and Democrats as between northerners and southerners. The question of slavery was taking over politics. Senator Thomas Hart Benton compared it to the Biblical plague of frogs: "You could not look upon the table but there were frogs, you could not sit down at the banquet but there were frogs, you could not go to the bridal couch and lift the sheets but there were frogs!" So it was with the slavery question, "forever on the table, on the nuptial couch, everywhere!"

Sooner or later, Congress would have to act to organize the new territories. And each time a bill concerning them came up in the House, that chamber attached the Wilmot Proviso to it guaranteeing its defeat in the Senate. Calhoun, leader of the militant proslavery forces, determined to force an outcome satisfactory to the South and drew up his own set of resolutions that not only rejected the Wilmot Proviso but declared that Congress had no power to bar slavery in any territory. This meant that, in Calhoun's view, even the Missouri Compromise line was an unconstitutional measure although he was willing to continue to abide by it as a practical matter. Calhoun's resolutions rallied the South. In the midst of this acrimonious and inconclusive struggle the election of 1848 was fought.

James Buchanan, a Pennsylvanian with strong southern ties, sought to settle the debate by extending the Missouri Compromise line to the Pacific. Buchanan's main Democratic challenger, Michigan Senator Lewis Cass, had originally supported the Wilmot Proviso, but quickly realized that he could never hope for any southern support unless he took a more conciliatory line. This he found in a concept he called popular sovereignty. Instead of Congress's deciding the question of slavery in the territories, Cass declared, the voters living there should choose for themselves whether they wanted slavery. This proposal had the merit, from Cass's point of view, of appearing to favor both sections. Southerners could take heart that it did not bar slavery from any of the territories while northerners could find comfort that few slaveholders would be foolish enough to move into the territories and risk their valuable property until slavery had already been adopted.

The Democrats decided on Cass and popular sovereignty. A group of disgruntled New York Democrats, angry over Cass's role in preventing the nomination of their own Martin Van Buren in 1844, formed the Free Soil Party with the Little Magician as their standard bearer. They demanded "free soil, free speech, free labor and free men." They were joined by the so-called "Conscience Whigs," northerners who could not support their own party's nominee, Zachary Taylor, the hero of the Mexican War they had opposed and the owner of a Louisiana plantation. Also joining the Free Soilers were the remnants of the old Liberty Party. The key to Taylor's victory may have been that his position on slavery in the territories was even vaguer than Cass's. If the Michigan sena-

James Buchanan. *(Courtesy, Library of Congress)*

tor's popular sovereignty doctrine blurred the question, Taylor simply ducked it altogether. His southern supporters used the fact of his being a slaveholder to reassure that section that he was safe on the issue. At the same time his northern backers, including such stalwarts as Abraham Lincoln, were promising that, if elected, Taylor would accept the Wilmot Proviso. Taylor himself said nothing. So the election of 1848 ended without any clear resolution of the slavery question.

The Gold Rush and the 49'ers vastly sped up settlement and contributed to the reputation nearby San Francisco was acquiring for gambling, drinking, and prostitution. Most claims soon petered out, and miners either became wage workers or chased the get-rich-quick rainbow to another site. Others coming to California established trading enterprises in San Diego and elsewhere.

One letter sent home measured the gold fever in California in 1849:

"People are arriving and departing daily and hourly. I have no doubt 400 people have already arrived from Oregon. They usually camp for a day or so near us, look about, swear at the high prices and disappear in the grand vortex. . . . It is impossible to get at anything like truth, but that the amount of gold in these mountains exceeds any previous calculation I have no doubt. . . ."

A miner complained to his wife:

"I do not like to be apacking a thousand dollars about in my coat pockets for it has toar my pockets and puld the Coat to peaces."

Suggested Readings

William H. Freehling's *The Road to Disunion: Secessionists at Bay, 1776–1854* (1991) is a good overview of the developing political tensions in the antebellum years. Sectionalism is the theme of William Brock's *Parties and Political Conscience: America Dilemmas, 1840–1850* (1979). Other political works are Paul Bergeron, *The Presidency of James K. Polk* (1987), Steve Stowe, *Intimacy and Power in the Old South: Rituals in the Lives of the Planters* (1987), Norma Peterson, *The Presidencies of William Henry Harrison and John Tyler* (1989), Daniel W. Howe, *The Political Culture of the American Whigs* (1980), Jack Bauer, *Zachary Taylor* (1985), and Gavin Wright, *The Political Economy of the Cotton South* (1978). See also Holman Hamilton, *Prologue to Conflict: The Crisis and Compromise of 1850* (1964) and Merrill Peterson, *The Great Triumvirate: Webster, Clay, and Calhoun* (1987).

Eugene D. Genovese's *Roll, Jordan, Roll: The World the Slaves Made* (1974) has become a classic. Genovese's *The World the Slaveholders Made* (1969) elaborates on the class structure of southern society. Herbert G. Gutman in *The Black Family in Slavery and Freedom, 1750–1925* (1976) challenges theories that speak of the disorganization of the black slave family. Other studies of the domestic side of slavery are Drew Gilpin Faust's *Mothers of Invention:*

Women of the Slaveholding South in the Civil War (1996), Janet Cornelius, *When I Can Read My Title Clear: Literacy, Slavery, and Religion in the Antebellum South* (1991), Elizabeth Fox-Genovese's *Within the Plantation Household: Black and White Women of the Old South* (1989), and Catherine Clinton's *The Plantation Mistress: Women's Work in the Old South* (1982). George M. Fredrickson examines the sources of racist ideas in *The Black Image in the White Mind* (1971).

On the Mexican War see John S. D. Eisenhower, *So Far From God: The U.S. War with Mexico 1846–1848* (1989), Jack Bauer's *The Mexican American War* (1974), David Pletcher, *The Diplomacy of Annexation: Texas, Oregon, and the Mexican War* (1973), and Robert W. Johannsen, *To the Halls of Montezuma: The Mexican War in the American Imagination* (1985). Gene M. Brack's *Mexico Views Manifest Destiny, 1821–1846* (1975) presents the Mexican viewpoint. See also Richard Griswold del Castillo, *The Treaty of Guadaloupe Hidalgo: A Legacy of Conflict* (1990) and *Occupied America: A History of Chicanos* (1988) by Rudolfo Acuna. Andrew Rolle's *John Charles Frémont: Character As Destiny* (1991) is a study of a soldier's position on the West. Frederick Merk, *Manifest Destiny and Mission in American History* (1965) is the classic account of westward expansion.

What Caused the Mexican War?

John S. D. Eisenhower

Overshadowed by the cataclysmic Civil War only thirteen years later, the Mexican War has been practically forgotten in the United States. Through the years, despite our growing interest in Mexico, it is rarely mentioned. And when the subject comes up, it nearly always deals with the questionable manner in which it came about. More specifically, was the United States right in sending Zachary Taylor to the Rio Grande in early 1846, thus provoking war with Mexico? Opinions vary.

Ulysses S. Grant, for one, was certain that the United States was wrong. He did, in fact, call the Mexican War "the most unjust war ever waged by a stronger against a weaker nation. . . . an instance of a republic following the bad example of European monarchies. . . ." And without a doubt, the preponderance of American opinion has agreed with Grant that the United States treated Mexico unjustly.

Actually, the issue is not simple, and opinions on it are colored by its role in accelerating the growth of animosity between the Northern and Southern states of the Union which eventually led to the Civil War. The North feared the expansion of slave territory. Thus the facts regarding the conflict that extended the borders of the continental United States from the Rio Grande to the Pacific have been submerged in the slavery issue. . . .

Contrary to common understanding, the war with Mexico was supported with enthusiasm by most of the population for at least the first year, by the end of which the necessary armies were recruited and supplied. Volunteers flocked to the colors to rescue "Old Rough and Ready," Zachary Taylor, from the menace of the Mexicans on the Rio Grande. And as the result of his remarkable series of victories, that same "Zack" Taylor was later elected president, an honor rendered only to victorious generals in popular wars. Boredom and impatience set in among the American population toward the end of the war, but moral disapproval was confined largely to a few New Englanders and some New England settlers in the Midwest.

The fact is that Mexico stood in the way of the American dream of Manifest Destiny. Although that dramatic, pious term was of relatively recent coinage in 1845, the idea of expansion westward to the Pacific had long been in the American mind. As far back as his first inaugural address in 1801, President Thomas Jefferson referred to a vast territory that would provide "room enough for our descendents to the thousandth and ten thousandth generation." And Jefferson did much to make that dream a reality by purchasing the great Louisiana territory from Emperor Napoleon of France and sending exploratory expeditions to the West, first under Zebulon Pike, later under Lewis and Clark.

To the student of today the fate of Mexico is sad, for the Mexicans were victims of both their history and Yankee expansionism. But that sadness need not be exacerbated by excessive shame for the conduct of the United States, because Mexico's disorganization, corruption, and weakness created a power vacuum that would inevitably have been filled by some predator—if not the United States, then Britain, less likely France, and even, remotely, Russia. American haste to occupy California, for example, was prompted more by fear of British action than by concern of what Mexico would do. After all, the United States and Britain were threatening war over the Oregon territory just north of California. Mexico's weakness stemmed from nearly three centuries of autocratic Spanish rule and from its own devastating war of independence, not from the actions of the United States.

John S. D. Eisenhower, *So Far From God: The U.S. War with Mexico, 1846–1848* (New York: Random House, 1989), pp. xvii–xi. Reprinted by permission.

Mexicans realized . . . that American expansion threatened their territorial integrity. Ambivalence gave way to outright, near-unanimous hostility after 1836, for the struggle over Texas appeared to be nothing but thinly veiled American aggression. . . .

It was as though the United States had set out, purposefully and diabolically, to become an object of hatred in Mexico. Three hundred years of Anglo-Spanish rivalry virtually guaranteed tense relations between the two countries. From Spain, Mexico also inherited fear that the ambitious and rapidly expanding United States threatened the territorial possessions of all who stood in the way of its aggrandizement. Relations nevertheless began rather smoothly, due in large part to prompt American recognition of Mexican independence. And the selection of the able Joel Poinsett as first American minister to Mexico seemed to promise further amity. But Poinsett carried instructions to seek a treaty of limits that would recover Texas, its claim to which the United States had surrendered to Spain in 1819, and to obtain a reciprocal agreement concerning fugitive slaves. Poinsett failed at both, succeeding only in establishing in Mexican minds a direct relationship between American expansion and the institution of slavery, toward which Mexicans felt a genuine loathing. . . .

Given the deportment of American diplomats and the expansionist policies of the American government and people, it did not take long for Mexicans to discern the similarity of American attitudes toward blacks, Indians, and Mexicans. The American, they knew, justified the despoliation of Indians by insisting that the Anglo-Saxon race could make better use of their lands. Americans used precisely the same argument in justifying their craving for Mexican territory. Perhaps the most volatile single issue in the conflict of cultures that divided the two nations was religion. Mexicans were as scornful of American Protestantism as Americans were of Mexican Catholicism. But American Protestantism nurtured also the "work ethic," which exaggerated the supercilious attitudes of Americans toward Mexico and her people. Americans in Mexico frequently observed that Mexicans did not realize that time was money; that Texas under Mexican rule was worthless, but American enterprise caused it to flourish; that Mexican mines produced a fraction of what Americans would take from them; and that Mexicans were simply lazy. The Mexican, then, was no more entitled to his territorial possessions than was the Indian. Over the years Mexicans had become increasingly aware that many Americans, especially those who most vociferously advocated Southwestern expansion, looked upon Mexicans as inferior beings. This had frightening implications, for Americans had respect for neither the rights nor the culture of those whom they considered inferior. They had been merciless in their treatment of the Indian and had reduced blacks to a brutal form of servitude. Mexicans were perceptive enough to recognize that a similar fate threatened them should they fall under American domination.

American racism alone did not cause the Mexican War, of course. Mexico after all did not provide a model of enlightened humanitarianism toward her own Indians, and in their attitudes toward the United States Mexicans appeared in their own way ethnocentric. With the exception of liberals, who tended to be anticlerical, Mexicans scorned American Protestantism. The American frontiersman, viewed in the United States then as now as a noble precursor of civilization, was regarded by Mexicans as a barbaric, shiftless wretch who smoothed the way for the more sophisticated, but shrewdly manipulative, land-hungry, profit-seeking, and more dangerous Americans who followed. Such additional factors as domestic political conditions, the extended incitement of opinion over Texas, and genuine concern for the national honor help to explain Mexican attitudes on the eve of war. Still, without advocating Mexican fear of American racism as a substitute for other causes of the war, many Mexicans seemed genuinely to fear cultural extinction at the hands of Americans, and that fear helps explain why "Manifest Destiny" appeared so threatening to Mexico that she fought a war for which she was dubiously prepared rather than accede peacefully to American territorial ambitions. "Manifest Destiny" was itself an ethnocentric notion.

Reprinted from Gene M. Brack, *Mexico Views Manifest Destiny, 1821–1846* (Albuquerque: University of New Mexico Press, 1975), 169, 170, 181, 182.

This frontispiece of an edition of *Uncle Tom's Cabin* pictures the slave Eliza escaping to freedom over the ice floes in the Ohio River. *(Courtesy, The New-York Historical Society)*

Impending Crisis: The 1850s

UNCLE TOM'S CABIN (1852)

In 1826, when Harriet Beecher was fifteen years old, she had already read much of her father's theological library. She would recall with fondness her pious childhood in Massachusetts and Cincinnati and her admiration for her "God-like" father, Lyman Beecher. In Harriet's youth her father became president of Lane Theological Seminary, and she married a young teacher there, Calvin Stowe. Stowe encouraged his wife's first writings for literary magazines, and she supported him during his long encounter with hallucinations and an inability to work. In 1850, Bowdoin College offered her husband a professorship. Within a few months of Harriet's arrival in Maine she began to turn her moral attention to matters of a worldly nature. After a chance reading of a southern slave-dealing newspaper, American black slavery arrested her with "an icy hand." Mrs. Stowe began a considerable research into the institution of chattel labor, reading southern defenses of slavery as well as the attacks on it by Theodore Weld and Frederick Douglass.

The Fugitive Slave Law of 1850 angered her into action, and she wrote *Uncle Tom's Cabin* in serial form in 1851. Mrs. Stowe later described the novel as having been "dictated" to her from a source outside of herself. One measure of the novel's power was the number of imitations it generated. More than fifty novels about slavery appeared after *Uncle Tom's Cabin* was published, some thirty of which were intent on portraying the institution as

HISTORICAL EVENTS

1846
Treaty with Colombia

1849
Harriet Tubman escapes from slavery

1850
Compromise of 1850 • Fugitive Slave Law • Clayton-Bulwer Treaty

1852
Harriet Beecher Stowe publishes *Uncle Tom's Cabin* • Whig Convention splits over slavery

1853
Gadsden Treaty

1854
Ostend Manifesto • Kansas-Nebraska Act • the Republican and "Know-Nothing" Parties are formed

1855
Kansas has two rival governments and internal fighting begins

1856
James Buchanan elected President

continued

One southern reviewer wrote in ardent denial:

"We have said that Uncle Tom's Cabin is a fiction. It is a fiction throughout; a fiction in form; a fiction in its facts; a fiction in its representations and coloring; a fiction in its statements; a fiction in its sentiments; a fiction in its morals; a fiction in its religion; a fiction in its inferences; a fiction equally with regard to the subjects it is designed to expound, and with respect to the manner of their exposition. It is a fiction, not for the sake of more effectually communicating truth; but for the purpose of more effectually disseminating a slander. It is a fictitious or fanciful representation for the sake of producing fictitious or false impressions. Fiction is its form and falsehood is its end."

beneficial. None of these captured Mrs. Stowe's great audience. Sales in book form set publishing records: 300,000 copies the first year, a million in seven years. Adapted for the stage, the story quickly became the nation's most popular play. By 1861, millions of northerners had thrilled over Eliza's dramatic escape and wept for Tom's fortitude under the lash.

The first part of the story is about George Harris and Eliza, his wife, slaves so near white that they can pass while escaping from slavery. Mistreated by his master, George disguises himself as a gentleman traveler and quits Kentucky with the help of a sympathetic white southerner. Eliza overhears that the slave foreman, a robust, kindly figure named Tom, is to be sold by his master, and she and her son Harry take flight to join George in Canada. With Harry in her arms Eliza escapes from the slave traders—the stage versions have her leaping melodramatically from ice floe to ice floe—across the Ohio River, to the northern underground railroad. Tom the slave is sold to a New Orleans family and makes friends with the saintly Little Eva, who dies of tuberculosis in a scene that has wrung tears from generations of readers. In the end Tom is sold to Simon Legree, a savage drunk who flogs him. Tom dies, like Christ, forgiving his killers.

Mrs. Stowe cut right to the heart of the matter: it was not fundamentally people who were evil, but the system under which they lived. Given absolute power over their slaves, few masters could resist the temptation to use it. Slavery often dragged down even good masters when circumstances occurred beyond their control. At its worst (Simon Legree's domain) the peculiar institution brutalized everyone—black and white. It is difficult to measure the exact impact of *Uncle Tom's Cabin,* but after its appearance the northern attitude toward slavery would never be quite the same. There was truth in the remark with which President Lincoln allegedly greeted Mrs. Stowe when she visited the White House during the Civil War: "So you're the little lady who wrote the book that made the great war."

Mrs. Stowe was not pursuing slavery with a bludgeon. Her instrument was as delicate as a surgeon's knife, and she operated on the national psyche. The slave was commercial property, and the business of slavery passed through northern as well as southern hands. The trade in human beings, a constant assault on the black family, tore against the fabric of a society woven of Christianity and the family. Mrs. Stowe possessed a firm sense of the uneasiness that many Americans felt over the disrupting tendencies of commerce. Instead of making the slaveowning South a direct contrast with the "free" society of the North, she made it a grotesque extension and intensification of that world. Men "alive to nothing but trade and profit—cool, and unhesitating, and unrelenting as death and the grave roamed the American earth, building things and disrupting and destroying lives." Under slavery, men of commerce could take their avarice to its final meaning: trade in human flesh. Mrs. Stowe originally and correctly subtitled her book *The Man That Was a Thing*, a commodity to be traded on the market. Northerners understood her picture of slavery because it reached the guilt they felt about their own society.

Southerners knew this too: their many replies to *Uncle Tom's Cabin* aimed ineffectual blows at northern commercial society.

The Compromise of 1850

It was a warring Congress that met in December 1849. It took three weeks and fifty-nine ballots to elect a Speaker of the House. Californians, tired of waiting for Congress, held a convention at Monterey and drafted a state constitution prohibiting slavery: some of them simply did not want whites to have to compete with black labor. Without waiting for congressional approval, California chose a governor and legislature. California now had to seek formal admission to statehood.

On this Congress could not agree. The new President, Zachary Taylor, decided to intervene in the imbroglio. Although a southerner, Taylor opposed the expansion of slave territory. Like Polk, he considered California and the Southwest unsuitable for slavery. The President therefore recommended to Congress that California and New Mexico be admitted directly to statehood, bypassing the territorial stage. The residents could then decide the slavery question for themselves without embarrassment to Congress. Southerners, seeing that California had already prohibited slavery and expecting New Mexico to do the same, realized that Taylor's plan was as effective as Wilmot's Proviso in keeping slavery out of this area. When they protested, the old soldier drew a firm line, threatening to use force if necessary to preserve the Union.

Taylor, southerners decided, had betrayed them. California would be the first in what they feared were to be many new free states admitted to the Union. Free and slave states had been equal in number, and therefore North and South had enjoyed equal representation in the Senate. Now the South was about to lose that precarious equality. Northerners would make war upon slavery—an institution, southern spokesmen insisted, "upon which is staked our property, our social organization and our peace and safety." When a call went out in October 1849 for the southern states to send delegates to a convention at Nashville the following June to consider secession, most of these states accepted.

The intensity of southern sentiments revealed itself late in 1849 when sixty-nine congressmen and senators from the South convened a special caucus in Washington, D.C. Calhoun, who emerged as leader of the caucus, accused the North of committing numerous "acts of aggression" against the South. According to Calhoun, and the forty-eight congressmen who eventually signed the caucus petition, the North was out to destroy the southern way of life. As proof he cited the individual

Senator Daniel Webster of New Hampshire, urged both North and South to avoid extreme positions on slavery. *(Courtesy, Scribner's Archives)*

AKA "Death"

Daniel Webster made this memorable plea for Union:

"When my eyes shall be turned to behold for the last time the sun in heaven, may I not see him shining on the broken and dishonored fragments of a once glorious Union; on States disevered, discordant, belligerent; on a land rent with civil feuds, or drenched, it may be, in fraternal blood. . . . Liberty and Union, now and forever, one and inseparable."

laws prohibiting slavery in various territories and the problems southerners were having in recapturing fugitive slaves living in the North. Calhoun insisted that the only way out of the impasse was to restore to southerners their Fifth Amendment property rights, which he interpreted as meaning that slave owners should be able to take their slaves anywhere in the United States and should be afforded adequate legal assistance in repossessing escaped slaves.

Clay, Calhoun, and Webster

At this moment, with disunion threatening, an aged Senator Henry Clay offered a compromise that he hoped would settle for good the territorial crisis and other disputed issues between the sections. Clay's plan, introduced in Congress in January 1850, contained five key provisions: immediate admission of free California; organization of the rest of the area acquired from Mexico into two territories, Utah and New Mexico, without restriction on slavery, the matter to be decided by their own constitutions; assumption of the Texan national debt by the federal government; abolition of the slave trade in the District of Columbia; and a tough new fugitive slave law.

The debate on Clay's compromise was the grand twilight for the generation of statesmen who had guided the nation's destinies since 1812. Twice before, in 1820 and 1833, stirring appeals to love of Union, flag, and Constitution had soothed sectional tensions. During the winter and spring of 1850, Senate veterans tried to revive this tested formula. Day after day, packed galleries followed their speeches.

Clay took the floor first, urging the North not to demand the principle of the Wilmot Proviso—nature would as effectively exclude slavery—and to honor the constitutional obligation to return fugitive slaves. He reminded the South of the many benefits she enjoyed in the Union. The Great Pacificator closed his two-day oration with an appeal to both sides to pause at the edge of the cliff, before leaping "into the yawning abyss below." Clay expressed the hope that, should disunion occur, he would not live to see it.

Clay's compromises did not go far enough to satisfy John C. Calhoun. The Old Nullifier, his body wracked by tuberculosis, sat defiantly wrapped in a black shawl while his speech was read for him. Northern agitation on the slavery issue, he said, had "snapped" many of the "cords which bind these states together in one common Union. . . ." The North, moreover, had taken advantage of tariffs and other federal favors to outstrip the South in population and power. Without an equality of votes in the Senate, the fragile equilibrium between the sections was doomed. Without such equality the South was defenseless and could not stay in the Union. Calhoun demanded that the North not only grant slaveholders equal rights in the territories but pass constitutional guarantees giving the South equal power in the government. The only alternative for the South was to secede from the Union. Calhoun would die in less than a month. After his speech, the state of Mississippi called for a convention of southern states "to devise and adopt some mode of resistance to northern aggression."

Daniel Webster spoke on March 7, displaying an eloquence remi-

New Englanders severely criticized Senator Daniel Webster for his support of the fugitive slave bill that became part of the Compromise of 1850. In this lithograph he is the central figure. "He exceeds my most sanguine expectation," cries the slave catcher running beside him. (*Courtesy, Scribner's Archives*)

niscent of his brilliant reply to Hayne two decades before. He pleaded with both sections to show tolerance for the sake of Union. He criticized the abolitionists' ethical absolutism and deplored the agitation over slavery in the territories. The law of nature precluded a slave economy there, he asserted, and no legislation was needed to reenact God's will. He took sharp issue with Calhoun's talk of "peaceable secession": "There can be no such thing as a peaceable secession. Peaceable secession is an utter impossibility." A thousand physical and social ties bound the sections together. Disunion, Webster warned the South pointedly, "must produce such a war as I will not describe, *in its twofold character*"—a

As a northern Democrat and senator from Illinois, Stephen A. Douglas skillfully engineered the Compromise of 1850. *(Courtesy, Scribner's Archives)*

hint at the prospect of slave revolts. Much to the anger of abolitionists, who criticized it savagely, Webster's Seventh of March speech did much to rally northern support for compromise.

For all his skill, Clay had miscalculated. Patriotic appeals for Union could not overcome sectional bitterness in 1850. When Clay's package of compromise measures came to a vote, opponents of the individual measures defeated it. His bill and his health in ruins, Clay withdrew into retirement.

Stephen A. Douglas   Five feet four and thirty-four years old, Stephen A. Douglas assumed Clay's place in steering the compromise through Congress. This brash, hard-driving senator from Illinois devised a new strategy. He introduced Clay's measures separately, relying on sectional blocs and a few swing votes to form majorities for each. Two events immeasurably aided his efforts that hot summer. The unexpected death on July 9 of President Taylor put in the presidency Millard Fillmore, who supported the compromise measures. And Texas bondholders—who, along with New England bankers they owed money, stood to gain handsomely if the federal government purchased their depreciated securities for giving up some territory to New Mexico—lobbied for the legislation.

Douglas's strategy worked. The individual bills, one observer remarked, resembled "cats and dogs that had been tied together by their tails for months, scratching and biting." Upon being released "every one of them ran off to his own hole and was quiet." The North won admission of free California and a ban on the slave trade in Washington. The South had a more stringent fugitive slave law and a promise that there would be no congressional prohibition of slavery in the New Mexico and Utah territories. The federal government assumed the Texas debt.

The Compromise of 1850 was only a short-lived armistice. The South had lost its majority in the Senate: this was a major defeat. The abolitionists found the Fugitive Slave Act appalling, and it was. But attempts to enforce it only inflamed northerners, giving the antislavery movement splendid propaganda and greater public support. Yet the compromise received an enthusiastic welcome. Celebrations were held in many cities. In Washington, word went out that it was the duty of every patriot to get drunk. Before the next morning dawned, many citizens, including Senators Foote, Douglas, and Webster, had proved their patriotism. To many Americans, it now seemed that the slavery question had at last been settled. But in the South there were still 3,204,000 slaves worth over one and one half billion dollars—a property many southerners were determined to protect at any cost.

Events soon revealed that the Compromise had settled nothing at all. Deliberate ambiguities embedded in it raised questions instead of comfortably obscuring them. The Utah and New Mexico territories had been organized without congressional restriction on slavery. The Compromise said only that they would be admitted to statehood with or without slavery, as their constitutions prescribed "at the time of their admission." But could the people of these territories now restrict slavery as long as the new lands remained in a territorial status? Opponents of slavery believed that even in the period before they attained statehood, the people of Utah and New Mexico would have the right to decide whether to exclude the practice. Southerners, convinced that slaveholding like any other conventional form of property should be permitted unless prohibited by a state of the Union, insisted that as long as the new lands remained territories, slavery must not be restricted. The critical question of slavery in the territories had merely been evaded. There had been no compromise in 1850, only a fragile truce.

The Fugitive Slave Law

President Fillmore, in signing the Compromise of 1850, called it the "final settlement." But its weakest link, the Fugitive Slave Law, soon caused the slavery issue to flare anew. The Constitution itself had contained a clause providing for the return of "any person held to service or labor in one state" who escaped to another. The new legislation had been passed in response to southern complaints that a law passed by Congress in 1793 lacked the strength to be enforced, putting slaveholders to great personal expense and failing to provide for assistance from federal officers. The new law of 1850 remedied these defects, and did

FUGITIVE
SLAVE BILL!

HON. HENRY WILSON
Will address the citizens on
Thursday Evening, April 3,

At the

At 7 o'clock, on the all-engrossing topics of the day—the FUGITIVE SLAVE BILL, the pro-slavery action of the National Government and the general aspect of the Slavery question.

Let every man and woman, without distinction of sect or party, attend the meeting and bear a testimony against the system which fills the prisons of a free republic with men whose only crime is a love of freedom—which strikes down the habeas corpus and trial by jury, and converts the free soil of Massachusetts into hunting ground for the Southern kidnappers.

Ashby, March 29, 1851.

White & Potter's Steam Press—4000 Impressions per hour—Spring Lane, Boston.

more. It created special commissioners to deal with fugitive-slave cases. These commissioners had only to be convinced of a fugitive slave's identity before granting the owner authority to seize the runaway. They were empowered to call on federal marshals to enforce the law, and to compensate slaveholders who had incurred undue expense. Anyone who aided fugitives or obstructed their arrest was subject to fine and imprisonment. The new law even required that all citizens were expected to assist officials in apprehending runaways. That cast northerners as slave catchers. Here was a slaveholder's dream. But to many northerners it was an outrage. Especially offensive were the sections denying accused fugitive slaves the right to a jury trial, or even to testify in their own behalf.

Here was not a complicated, constitutional issue pitting federal against local rule in the territories. Here was concrete oppression on northern soil before northern eyes. Northerners had before them the spectacle of fugitive slaves, handcuffed and guarded, and read of cases of mistaken identity in the kidnapping of free blacks. The fugitive slave question drew together the splintered antislavery movement. Garrisonians, free-soilers, Whigs, Democrats, blacks: all could agree on it.

Enforcement of the Fugitive Slave Law sparked several well-publicized acts of resistance. In 1851 a mob of blacks in Boston burst into a courtroom during the extradition hearing of a fugitive slave named Shadrach. While the crowd struggled with the police, two husky blacks grabbed the startled Shadrach and carried him out of the building. Shadrach was soon spirited off to Canada. Later that same year, black and white abolitionists successfully resisted enforcement of the law at Syracuse, New York, and Christiana, Pennsylvania. In Indiana, agents tore one man away from his wife and children and returned him to a slave owner who showed that the former slave had run away nineteen years before.

In over eighty percent of the cases brought under the law, slaveholders successfully recovered their property. But spectacular rescues like that of Shadrach confirmed southerners in their conviction that the Fugitive Slave Law could not be enforced north of the Mason-Dixon Line. As a result, few southerners made use of the new law. Instead the South nursed its feeling that the North had failed to fulfill an essential part of the compromise. A Tennessee man warned that if the new legislation were not enforced, southern moderates would be overwhelmed by *"fire-eaters."*

Harriet Tubman

No one recorded the birthday of Harriet Ross, one of eleven children born to a slave family on the eastern shore of Maryland. But the child who would become Harriet Tubman was probably born in 1820 or 1821. She never spent a day in school and never learned to read or write. Her childhood in any sense that we would understand the term ended at the age of five or six. Then her master attempted unsuccessfully to apprentice her to a weaver. Various efforts to make her useful about the master's house also proved unsuccessful, and Harriet became a runaway for the

An antislavery writer, Thomas Wentworth Higginson, boasted of Harriet Tubman in 1859:

"We have had the greatest heroine of the age here, Harriet Tubman, a black woman, and a fugitive slave, who had been back eight times secretly and brought out in all sixty slaves with her, including all her own family, besides aiding many more in other ways to escape. Her tales of adventure are beyond anything in fiction and her ingenuity and generalship are extraordinary. . . . The Slaves call her Moses. She has had a reward of twelve thousand dollars offered for her in Maryland and will probably be burned alive whenever she is caught, which she probably will be, first or last, as she is going again."

Herself an escaped slave, Harriet Tubman returned to the South and, risking great danger, repeatedly led groups like the one pictured here north to freedom. *(Courtesy, Sophia Smith Collection, Smith College)*

first time at age seven. She stayed away four days, hiding in a pigsty and scrapping with the pigs for garbage to eat, until hunger drove her back to the inevitable whipping. Eventually she was sent to the fields, where she became a powerful worker, a match for most of the men. A serious head injury in her early teens left her with a permanent disability which caused her to fall asleep involuntarily for brief periods, even at the height of danger. Her rebellious temperament, combined with this odd malady, set her apart from others in her youth, and she absorbed a brand of millennial slave Christianity. Marriage to a free black, John Tubman, further aroused her questionings about slavery and freedom, but the difficulty of escape and concern for her parents and husband held her back until 1849, when the death of her owner led her to fear being sold into the deep South. Harriet headed north, traveling by night, and with help from some sympathetic whites made her way to Pennsylvania.

And so she did, earning money as best she could to finance such desperate ventures. Joining with the loose network of free blacks and Quakers—out of whose limited activities post-Civil War legend created the "Underground Railroad," complete with "switching station," "conductors," and "brakemen"—and traveling without benefit of maps or signs, she brought back from Maryland first her relatives, then other slaves, and finally her aged parents. Even in December 1860, with political turmoil over slavery at its height, Harriet made her last trip south before the war, returning with seven slaves, one of them an infant

"I had crossed the line [into northern territory]," Harriet Tubman recalled.

"I was free; but there was no one to welcome me to the land of freedom. . . . My home, after all, was down in Maryland; because my father, my mother, my brothers, my sisters, and friends were there. But I was free and they should be free! I would make a home in the North and bring them there!"

Other former slaves, such as John P. Parker, worked as "conductors" on the Underground Railroad. Parker dedicated his life to helping slaves cross the Ohio River from Kentucky to Ohio. He remembered:

"I heard the cry of hounds. The patrol had worked faster than I thought. Leaping into the boat to tear up a seat to use as a paddle, I stumbled over the oars, which I had found missing in the dark. With a halloo, I piled the crowd in the boat, only to find it so small it would not carry all of us. Two men were left on the bank."

child who had to be drugged with paregoric to keep its cries from giving away their hiding places. Accounts credit her with aiding in the escape of more than five hundred slaves.

Harriet headed south again during wartime, now to serve as a nurse, a scout, and even a spy for the Union army in South Carolina.

Harriet Tubman outlived the entire generation of antislavery heroes with whom she had worked, becoming a legendary reminder of the age of runaway slaves and abolitionists. Her home in Auburn, New York, became a place of pilgrimage. Black leaders like Booker T. Washington would visit Harriet and then view John Brown's grave in the Adirondacks. Woman suffrage leaders came as well; this had become one of her causes in the postwar years. She founded a Home for the Aged and Indigent in Auburn on land abutting her house, moving to it herself in 1911 when she became too infirm to live alone. She died in 1913 and received, fittingly enough, a soldier's burial, with the local post of the Union army veterans' association, the Grand Army of the Republic, presenting the honors.

Manifest Destiny Revisited

In his inaugural address a new President, Franklin Pierce, would call for further expansion. "My administration," he boldly proclaimed in 1853, "will not be controlled by any timid forebodings of evil from expansion." The direction of any more expansion, of course, would have to be to the south. After the Oregon Treaty of 1846, most policymakers in the United States knew that dreams of expanding north into Canada were unrealistic. Canada was a stable country that Great Britain had no intention of surrendering without a fight. Territories to the south, in the Caribbean, Central America, and Mexico, were more likely candidates for annexation. Mexico, Spain, and the tiny countries there would be hardpressed to defend their territory.

But expansion into Mexico and the Caribbean raised the hostility of abolitionists, free-soilers, businessmen, and workers in the North. Slavery was deeply ensconced in the sugar plantations of Cuba, Hispaniola, and Puerto Rico, and few people doubted the ability of southerners to transplant cotton cultivation to Mexico. Opponents realized that plantation production of crops like coffee, indigo, cacao, and a variety of fruit products was possible in Central America. President Franklin Pierce's ambitious attempts to push the spirit of Manifest Destiny south toward the equator encountered stiff opposition in the North.

The Gadsden Purchase True to his word, Pierce dispatched James Gadsden of South Carolina to Mexico with instructions to purchase additional territory. At the very least, Gadsden was to acquire the Gila River region, which lay along the proposed southern railroad route to the Pacific. In addition, he might offer up to $50 million for the northern provinces of Mexico. The Mexican government refused to sell anything more than the Gila River region. Even this small triumph for Gadsden was too much for the

IMPENDING CRISIS: THE 1850S

Senate; northern senators, suspecting a southern plot to expand the domain of slavery, accepted the Gadsden Treaty only after 9,000 square miles, one-sixth of the total, had been cut from the purchase. For the first time in its history, the United States had refused to accept land ceded to it. Despite this minor setback, the hapless Pierce embarked upon a new imperialist venture. This time the object was Cuba, owned by the Spanish.

The Ostend Manifesto   For a time in the 1850s, some Cubans flirted with the notion of annexation by the United States. During the early part of the century the social and economic relationship between Cuba and the mainland had grown stronger. By the 1840s Cuba's foreign trade with the United States exceeded its trade with Spain, and increasing numbers of Cubans were travelling to the United States on business and vacations. Cuban slave-owners worried that independence from Spain would deprive them of the military means to defend themselves against a slave uprising. They were also concerned that the increasingly powerful antislavery movement in Great Britain might eventually force Spain to abolish slavery in Cuba. Annexation by the United States, where slavery was firmly entrenched, would solve both problems. Cuban slaveowners would be rid of Spain but they would still have a powerful military force capable of maintaining the existing social order. The annexationists tried unsuccessfully to sponsor uprisings in Cuba against the Spanish.

Cuban annexationists were encouraged by expansionist sentiments in the United States. When the Mexican War ended in 1848, President James K. Polk offered to pay Spain $100 million for Cuba, but the offer was refused. Many Cubans living in the United States tried to promote annexation. Cristobal Madán, a prominent Cuban sugar planter, founded the *Consejo de Gobierno Cubano* in New York. Madán's wife was the sister of John O'Sullivan, the New York journalist who originated the phrase "Manifest Destiny." The *Consejo* published its own newspaper, *La Verdad,* and lobbied throughout the United States for annexation. The advocates of territorial expansion had joined hands with the champions of Cuban annexation. Some of the more vociferous advocates of annexation added violence to their campaign. Late in the 1840s and early in the 1850s, Narciso López launched against Cuba a series of "filibustering" expeditions, referring to small-scale private military operations. He enjoyed the financial support of the *Consejo,* and, with small armies composed mostly of southerners, he invaded Cuba in 1848, 1849, and 1851 and tried to inspire insurrection. The expeditions all failed to bring the desired uprising, and at Bahía Honda in 1851 López was captured and executed.

During 1853 the Pierce Administration lent support to John A. Quitman of Mississippi and others who proposed to "liberate" Cuba by force. When Quitman backed off, Pierce instructed the American minister in Madrid, Pierre Soulé, to offer Spain as much as $130 million for Cuba. But Spain indignantly rejected the American offer. Soulé then arranged a meeting at Ostend, Belgium, in October 1854, with the American ministers to London and Paris, to consider further action regarding Cuba. Their recommendations to Washington, known as the

A New Orleans newspaper reflected popular feeling:

"The North Americans *will* spread out far beyond their present bounds. They *will* encroach again and again upon their neighbors. New territories *will* be planted, declare their independence, and be annexed! We have New Mexico and California! We *will* have old Mexico and Cuba! The isthmus cannot arrest—nor even the Saint Lawrence!! Time has all of this in her womb."

"Ostend Manifesto," soon found their way into print, to the great embarrassment of the Pierce Administration. Particularly damaging was the statement that, should Spain refuse renewed offers to purchase Cuba, the United States would "by every law, human and Divine, be . . . justified in wresting it from Spain." Both American and European critics denounced the Manifesto. It was "a robber doctrine," "a highwayman's plea." The administration promptly repudiated the Manifesto, whereupon Soulé resigned amidst bitter recriminations. Manifest Destiny had suffered by its association with slavery. Renewed expansion would have to await the return of sectional peace.

The Filibusterers
The filibusterers against Cuba were among a number of paramilitary expeditions coming out of the United States in the 1850s. The most notorious of the filibusterers was William Walker, who had grandiose dreams for himself. In 1853 he led a private army in an unsuccessful invasion of Lower California and barely escaped with his life. Two years later he learned of the desire of the Accessory Transit Company of New York to secure territory in Central America for construction of a transoceanic canal. With the company's financial backing, and with a civil war under way in Nicaragua, Walker launched a new filibustering expedition in 1855. He succeeded temporarily in setting himself up as dictator of Nicaragua. When President Franklin Pierce agreed to receive Walker's diplomatic representative, Walker interpreted it as official recognition, and a few weeks later he issued a proclamation opening up Nicaragua to slavery. Antislavery forces denounced this as one more act of the expansionist slaveocracy. Walker remained in power for another year until Cornelius Vanderbilt, the new head of the Accessory Transit Company, decided he was unstable and ousted him. Walker attacked Nicaragua with a new expedition in 1857 but failed. The United States Navy captured him but let him go with a warning to cease his filibustering campaigns. In 1860 Walker attacked Honduras with a private army, but this time he was captured and executed.

Although most southerners had little to do with the filibustering escapades against Cuba, Mexico, and Nicaragua in the 1850s, northerners accurately saw in them the hand of the enemy. That President Franklin Pierce had tried to purchase Cuba and the originally huge Gadsden region, combined with his initial reception of Walker as head of state in Nicaragua, confirmed northern suspicions that the federal government was trying to expand the base of slave operations.

Paths to the Pacific
The settlement of the Oregon boundary controversy and the acquisition of California made the United States a Pacific power. American commerce quickly expanded across the great ocean. In 1844 Caleb Cushing, the first American minister to China, negotiated a treaty granting Americans special trade privileges in that country. A decade later, Commodore Matthew Perry gained a diplomatic and commercial toehold in Japan. The United States sought unsuccessfully in 1854 to annex the Hawaiian Islands, already a cultural outpost of the United States. Forward-looking Americans proclaimed the dawn of a great commercial era in the Pacific.

HUCKLEBERRY FINN

by Samuel Clemens (Mark Twain). Huck talks about his feelings towards the slave Jim.

. . . I about made up my mind to pray, and see if I couldn't try to quit being the kind of a boy I was and be better. So I kneeled down. But the words wouldn't come. Why wouldn't they? . . . I was trying to make my mouth say I would do the right thing and the clean thing, and go and write to that nigger's owner and tell where he was; but deep down in me I knowed it was a lie, and He knowed it. You can't pray a lie—I found out.

So I was full of trouble, full as I could be; and didn't know what to do. At last I had an idea; and I says, I'll go and write the letter—and then see if I can pray. Why, it was astonishing, the way I felt as light as a feather right straight off, and my troubles all gone. So I got a piece of paper and a pencil, all glad and excited, and set down and wrote:

Miss Watson, your runaway nigger Jim is down here two mile below Pikesville, and Mr. Phelps had got him and he will give him up for the reward if you send.

I felt good and all washed clean of sin for the first time I had ever felt so in my life, and I knowed I could pray now. But I didn't do it straight off, but laid the paper down and set there thinking— thinking how good it was all this happened so, and how near I come to being lost and going to hell. And went on thinking. And got to thinking over our trip down the river; and I see Jim before me all the time: in the day and in the night-time, sometimes moonlight, sometimes storms, and we a-floating along, talking and singing and laughing. But somehow I couldn't seem to strike no places to harden me against him, but only the other kind. I'd see him standing my watch on top of his'n, 'stead of calling me, so I could go on sleeping. . . . and at last I struck the time I saved him by telling the men we had small-pox aboard, and he was so grateful, and said I was the best friend old Jim ever had in the world, and the only one he's got now; and then I happened to look around and see that paper.

It was a close place. I took it up, and held it in my hand. I was a-trembling, because I's got to decide, forever, betwixt two things, and I knowed it. I studied a minute, sort of holding my breath, and then says to myself: "All right, then, I'll go to hell"—and tore it up.

For shortening the route from Atlantic ports to the Orient and improving communications between the two American coasts, the United States began considering a canal that would link the two oceans. An 1846 treaty with Colombia granted citizens of the United States the right of transit across the Isthmus of Panama, in return for recognition of Colombian sovereignty there. Efforts to control the alternative canal route through Nicaragua aroused protests from Britain, which had bases of its own in the vicinity. In 1850 the two sides compromised their differences in the Clayton-Bulwer Treaty. Each party agreed not to seek exclusive control over the proposed isthmian canal or to colonize the surrounding area. In spite of this official enthusiasm, capitalists showed little interest in the idea of building a canal. Travel across the isthmus remained a primitive affair until 1855, when a railroad replaced muleback and coach as the chief means of transportation.

More attractive was the idea of a transcontinental railroad. Asa Whitney, a New York merchant who had made a fortune in the China trade, labored throughout the 1840s to persuade Congress to finance construction of a railroad from Lake Michigan to the mouth of the Columbia River. This route, although mountainous, had the advantage of passing north of Mexican California. The Treaty of Guadalupe-Hidalgo brought California into the United States, but a new obstacle— sectional rivalry—soon appeared. The South favored a southern route for the railroad, running from New Orleans to California via Texas and the Gila River Valley. The North preferred either Whitney's northern route or a central way, extending from Chicago or St. Louis by way of

Samuel Clemens (*Courtesy, Scribner's Archives*)

South Pass to San Francisco. Unable to agree on any one route, Congress in 1853 authorized surveys of all three.

This delay was intolerable to Stephen A. Douglas of Illinois, the foremost advocate of a central route. As chairman of the Senate Committee on Territories, Douglas had pioneered in opening the Mississippi Valley to settlement. A Pacific railroad would help his concept of a great West become a reality. Personal considerations also motivated Douglas. His home town of Chicago, where he had heavy real estate investments, would be the probable eastern terminus of a central railroad. But the land known as Nebraska west of Iowa and Missouri was still unorganized Indian country. Until the region had territorial government, it could not be surveyed and opened for settlement. In this respect, advocates of a southern route had a real advantage: all the area along their route had already been made into states or territories.

The Kansas-Nebraska Act

Senator Douglas late in 1853 had to find some way to induce southerners in Congress to vote for a bill organizing Nebraska. Southerners had no motive to support a measure that cleared the path for a rival railroad route to the Pacific. And they had absolutely no reason to vote to create what would become another free territory. As part of the Louisiana Purchase, Nebraska had been made "forever" free by the Missouri Compromise of 1820. Senator David Atchison of Missouri spoke for many southerners when he vowed that he would "sink in hell" before handing Nebraska over to the free-soilers. Douglas therefore decided that he would have to make a concession to the South.

Popular Sovereignty The Illinois Senator offered the repeal of the Missouri Compromise line excluding slavery north of 36° 30′ latitude. His territorial bill, introduced in Congress in January 1854, would create two territories—Kansas and Nebraska. It would specifically repeal the Missouri Compromise restriction on slavery. In its place, Douglas substituted the principle of popular sovereignty, as it was called. The people of the two territories were free "to form and regulate their domestic institutions in their own way." Thus, to enlist southern support for his railroad, Douglas held out the bait of making Kansas and Nebraska slave states by the operation of popular sovereignty.

As Douglas himself had predicted, the idea of repealing the Missouri Compromise line raised "a hell of a storm." Northerners regarded the Act of 1820 as an inviolable pledge of freedom. Repeal was part of a slaveholder's plot to make free territory into "a dreary region of despotism, inhabited by masters and slaves." In Congress, many northern Democrats joined their Whig colleagues in opposition. Objections came not only from abolitionists but from moderates who, having accepted the Compromise of 1850, had now lost all confidence in the good faith of the South. Douglas and his co-conspirators, wrote Horace Greeley in the *New York Tribune,* had made "more abolitionists than Garrison . . . could have made in half a century." Slavery, Douglas insisted in response, was an outmoded institution, unsuited by climate and geography to the plains of Kansas. Popular sovereignty would just as effectively bar slavery as would exclusion. After three months of fierce debate Douglas, with the support of President Franklin Pierce, carried his bill.

Passage of the Kansas-Nebraska Act shredded what little had remained of the uneasy truce of 1850. It turned Kansas into a battle-ground and ruptured the Democratic Party. By using the scheme of popular sovereignty to open free soil to slavery, Douglas discredited what until then had been an effective instrument for compromise. Rarely in American history had so much been risked for so little. The next year—1855—when Douglas introduced his long-awaited Pacific Railroad bill in Congress, his enemies had their revenge by killing it. At Douglas's death in 1861 his great Pacific railroad, on which he had expended so much energy and prestige, was still bottled up in Congress, a victim of the sectional conflict he had helped to revive.

"Bleeding Kansas"

With the passage of the Kansas-Nebraska Act, the slavery contest moved from the halls of Congress to the plains of Kansas. Both sections attached great importance to the decision over slavery there. Southerners hoped to make Kansas a slave state and thereby to restore to the South the equality of representation in the Senate that the region had lost when California was admitted as a free state. Slavery expansion also had great symbolic importance to southerners. By denying the South's right to expand, the North seemed to be denying southern equality. Southerners reasoned that if they could not take their slaves into the common territories, they would no longer be the equal of northern citizens. Opponents of slavery of course wished to prevent its extension into Kansas. Resistance to the expansion of slavery also had a more unsavory side. Many northerners, especially in the Midwest, were determined to preserve the rich prairie soils for the white race. Here, said David Wilmot, "the sons of toil, of my own race and color, can live without the disgrace which association with Negro slavery brings upon free labor." Such attitudes increasingly entered the antislavery movement, and conditioned the public views even of moral opponents of slavery like Abraham Lincoln. The demand for free soil, then, greatly broadened the antislavery movement's appeal at the same time that it diluted the morality of the movement.

Border War   From the beginning, the contest in Kansas over slavery was mainly the work of outsiders. In the North, groups like the New England Emigrant Aid Company, founded in 1854, subsidized the migration of free-state settlers to Kansas. To protect them, the Company sent new breech-loading rifles known popularly as "Beecher's Bibles," after Harriet's ministerial brother, Henry Ward Beecher, who proclaimed them a greater moral agency in Kansas than the Bible. Bands of Missouri border ruffians regularly

A southerner first observed in letters written home to his sister:

"The Missourians . . . are very sanguine about Kansas being a slave state & I have heard some of them say it *shall* be. Everyone seems bent on the Almighty Dollar, and as a general thing that seems to be their only thought."

Later he wrote:

"I fear, Sister, that coming here will do no good at last, as I begin to think that this will be made a Free State at last. 'Tis true we have elected Proslavery men to draft a state constitution, but I feel pretty certain, if it is put to the vote of the people, it will be rejected, as I feel pretty confident they have a majority here at this time. The South has ceased all efforts, while the North is redoubling her exertions."

Thomas Henry Tibbles was sixteen years old when he fought briefly with John Brown in "Bleeding Kansas."

This Platte County, into which John Brown had invited me, was thickly settled. Though most of the houses were built of logs, there were a few fine frame residences. Also, behind these residences, there were always "nigger quarters," ramshackle stables, and loom-houses where Negro women wove the jeans and linsey-woolsey which formed the outer clothing of the whole population. The planters' wealth was made up of fine horses, "likely niggers," and a rich soil which produced immense crops of corn and hemp. Though many of the owners of this countryside could neither read nor write, they were proud and rich. How long John Brown had been secretly lingering there near his chosen rendezvous, or how many men he had with him, I never knew.

Night settled down dark and moonless. Clouds hung low in the west. I had difficulty in making my way to the appointed place, but there I found Brown. . . . [He] directed our group to go to a certain cabin belonging to a certain house and get the slaves who were expecting us. We all were to take them to the [Missouri] River by

a road he described. Then the rest of our group were to take these Negroes over the river in skiffs that would be found at a designated place. . . . Brown said there was a regular road in front of the house where we were to get the Negroes, but that, as it was guarded by the planters' patrol, our party was to enter the farm from the rear and approach the slave quarters through a cornfield. He bade me go alone a mile up the direct front road to watch for the patrol and keep our main party informed of any danger from that source.

When I objected to dismounting and separating myself from my horse, Brown told me with a metallic ring in his voice: "You will obey orders." Doubtless if there had been more light, I should have seen a peculiar gleam in his eye. Anyone who had anything to do with Brown in Kansas learned that it was death, after one joined his band, to disobey any order he issued.

I went with his men as he had ordered. Because the night was so very dark, we had difficulty in finding the right place. I took my post in the bend, while the other men crept up through the cornfield. Just then the wind blew furiously and the rain poured down. I could see nothing except when lightning flashed now and then.

crossed into neighboring Kansas to aid the proslavery cause. In March 1855, at the first election for a territorial legislature, their votes helped to give the proslavery party a majority. This assembly immediately enacted a slave code for the territory. Free-state settlers, refusing to recognize this legislature, elected one of their own. By late 1855, Kansas had two rival governments, neither of which would recognize the other's laws or participate in its elections.

Orderly government was impossible, and militants on both sides of the slavery question carried on a private war of their own. After proslavery men raided the free-state stronghold of Lawrence, the fanatical John Brown and seven followers (four of them his sons) retaliated at Pottawatomie Creek by bursting in on five sympathizers with slavery, slashing and hacking them to death with broadswords. When one of his men urged caution, Brown responded that it was "nothing but the word of cowardice." Many settlers had to take sides in self-defense. The recently established telegraph system, which now made possible swift reports of faraway events, brought the warfare in Kansas extensive press coverage. The antislavery press pictured the sack of Lawrence as an orgy of destruction and killing. In reality, it was a rather tame affair; only one person was killed, and he was a proslavery man struck on the head by a falling brick.

Early in 1857 federal troops restored order to Kansas, and the free- and slave-state parties each promptly fell to internal quarreling. Before the year was out, a visitor to Kansas reported that "speculations run high

Without warning someone threw his arms around me from behind, pinioning my elbows to my sides. Instantly two more men leaped upon me, but before they could clap a hand over my mouth, I uttered the loudest yell that had ever come of me. It was the only warning I could give my associates.

My captors tied my hands and feet; they put a rope around my neck and dragged me along the ground by it for some distance. Then they lifted me to my feet, threw the rope end over the limb of a tree. Just at that moment pistols flashed. Two of the men who had been holding the rope dropped to the ground; the other ran away. My "gang," who had succeeded in creeping up through the cornfield and bringing away two Negro men and one woman, had then overheard the rather loud talk of the patrol at my "hanging bee." Thanks to the black night and the rain, they had stolen up to us unnoticed.

They soon had me on my feet and helped me to find Old Titus and mount him.

Long before daylight it became obvious that the entire district was on the warpath. Certainly John Brown's "nigger stealing" raid into Platte County had started a tremendous uproar. By now, however, probably all the rest of Brown's men were safely back across the river, and here was I, at sixteen, left alone to fight the whole county.

Just as day broke, I reached a dim lane that led toward the river. From sounds behind me I knew that not much over a mile away a large party was on my trail. . . . I leaped a fence into a cornfield—but they had seen me. I have never heard a more fiendish yell than they loosed then and there.

I plunged across the cornfield and finally reached the bottom lands of the river, which were covered in some places with grass as high as a man on horseback and in others with a dense growth of willows. My pursuers evidently had wholly lost my trail. My only way of escape was to swim to Missouri River with its rapid current, its rushing, mud-colored water, and its treacherous quicksands. After much thought I decided to take the risk. I led Old Titus down to the bank. I took hold of his tail and swam behind him; thus I not only relieved him of my weight, but was able to steer him wherever I wished. We landed [safely in Illinois] in a wild and desolate spot.

[here], politics seldom named, *money* now seems to be the question." The territory remained deeply divided, with each side retaining its own government.

The struggle in Kansas forced the slavery issue back into Congress. (The intent of instituting popular sovereignty had been to get the slavery question out of that body.) In 1856 the House of Representatives sent a fact-finding committee to Kansas. Meantime, Congress endlessly debated the Kansas question amid steadily rising tempers. Passion spilled into violence on the floor of the Senate. Senator Charles Sumner of Massachusetts delivered a violent antislavery speech entitled "The Crime Against Kansas." In it he made several personal references to Senator Andrew P. Butler of South Carolina. Butler's nephew, Representative Preston S. Brooks of South Carolina, decided to avenge these insults to an elderly kinsman. Brooks stole up behind Sumner at his Senate desk during a recess and beat him severely over the head with a cane.

The attack, northerners believed, was another example of the domineering insolence of slaveholders. The injured Sumner became a martyr of the antislavery cause. Southerners, although many privately disapproved, publicly applauded Brooks's action and showered him with canes inscribed with slogans like "Use Knock-down Arguments." When Brooks resigned from Congress, his Carolina constituents reelected him. This incident, and the controversy over Bleeding Kansas, further polarized a country already divided.

Political Cataclysm

Before 1850 the country's political system had been a bond of union. In both the Whig and the Democratic parties, strong northern and southern wings had worked together in their mutual interest, especially in presidential elections. The dependence of each wing on the other served to override the potentially divisive effect of issues like slavery. Party loyalty was intense. William Pitt Fessenden, a Whig stalwart, declared that he "would vote for a dog, if he was the candidate of my party." The Compromise of 1850 and the Kansas-Nebraska Act drastically altered the system, destroyed one party, disrupted another, and created a new one. A once unifying political system had become sectionalized.

FILLING IN THE CONTINENT

These excerpts from a letter of Lucia Loraine Williams show that parts of the United States were far removed from the slavery controversy of the 1850s:

September 16, 1851

Dear Mother,

We have been living in Oregon about two weeks, all of us except little John, and him we left twelve miles this side of Green River. He was killed instantly by falling from a wagon and the wheels running over his head.

After passing the desert and Green River [in present-day Wyoming] we came to a place of feed and laid by a day for the purpose of recruiting [resting] our teams. On the morning of 29 June we started on. John rode on the wagon driven by Edwin Fellows. We had not proceeded more than 2 miles before word came for us to turn back—we did so but found him dead. The oxen had taken fright from a horse that had been tied behind the wagon preceding this, owned by a young man that Mr. Williams had told a few minutes before to leave, and [the runaway team had] turned off the road. Two other teams ran also.

John was sitting in the back of the wagon, but as soon as the cattle commenced to run he went to the front and caught hold of the driver who held him as long as he could, but he was frightened and did not possess presence of mind enough to give him a little send which perhaps would have saved him.

Poor little fellow! We could do nothing for him, he was beyond our reach and O! How suddenly!

One half hour before we had left him in health as lively as a lark, and then to find him so breathless so soon was awful. I cannot describe to you our feelings.

We buried him there by the roadside, on the right side of the road, about 1/2 mile before we crossed the Fon-tonelle, a little stream. We had his grave covered with stones to protect it from wild beasts, and a board with his name and age. If any of our friends come through I wish that they would find his grave and if it needs, repair it.

[The letter proceeds to give excerpts from a diary of the trip.]

NEBRASKA

21 May—We had one of the worst storms that I ever read of. It beggars all description—thunder, lightning, hail, rain and wind. Hailstones so large that they knocked a horse onto his knees. The driver got out and held the oxen by the heads for they showed a disposition to run. Most of our things were completely soaked, so the next day we stopped and dried up.

On the 23rd we came to a creek that overflowed its banks, Elm Creek. The water was some 20 feet deep but not very wide. They fell a tree over the creek and packed the loading [across on foot], put our wagons into the water with a rope attached to the tongue, and swam them across.

June 1—Passed the Sioux village. Their wigwams are made of buffalo skins (the Pawnees' were mud). They seemed to be a much wealthier tribe than any that we [had] yet seen. The squaws were in antelope skins ornamented with beads; the men were also clothed with skins or blankets. They owned a great many ponies. On one of the wigwams were several scalps hung out to dry—taken from the Pawnees. They were friendly.

I saw some beautiful bluffs, apparently not more than 1/2 mile off, and wished to visit them. W consented to go with me but said that it was further than I anticipated. We walked 4 miles, I should judge, crossing chasms and

The Decline of the Whig Party

It was the Whigs who felt the strain of slavery first. They had never been as strong organizationally as the Democrats, and they drew their strength in the North from Yankee Protestants whose sense of moral stewardship made them especially sympathetic to the antislavery cause. The abolitionist and Free Soil movements made many converts among these "conscience Whigs." At the 1852 Whig Convention the dispute over slavery broke wide open. The two sides even disagreed over the choice of a minister to lead the opening prayer. President Fillmore, the favorite of southern Whigs, had supported the Compromise of 1850, and so northern Whigs opposed him. The northerners backed instead another Mexican War hero, the Virginian General Winfield Scott, and Scott was finally chosen after fifty-three ballots: a southerner whose

---

bluffs before we reached the road and after all did not ascend the one we set out for. Camped by the Platte. No wood [to burn], but buffalo chips, which we have used for a long time.

WYOMING

On the 7th we arrived at Fort Laramie, and on the 8th commenced crossing the black hills. Some of them were steep. Laramie Peak to the left covered with snow. 9 June—Crossed the red hills and camped by a lake.

17 June—Traveled over 20 miles and camped by the Devils Hole, or Gate. In the morning two young ladies and myself visited it. The rocks on each side were perpendicular, 400 feet high, and the narrowest place was about 3 feet, where [the] Sweetwater came tumbling through. The road leading to it was crooked and thorny, but we found all kinds of beautiful flowers blooming beside the rocks; it was the most sublime spectacle that I ever witnessed

19 June—[Could] see the Rocky Mountains [at] a distance of some 60 miles. The tops were covered with snow, and from there they looked like fleecy clouds. Camped near two snowbanks in a beautiful valley.

IDAHO

2 July—[During the] night we were awakened by serenaders—five horsemen circled around the carriage singing "Araby's Daughter." It was a beautiful starlight night. We were surrounded by bluffs in a little valley, and on being awakened by their song, seeing their panting steeds and looking around upon the wild country, it seemed as tho we were transported into Arabia. They were beautiful singers from Oregon; said they were exiles from home. They sang "Sweet Home" and several others. Invited us to stay and celebrate the 4th. Said they would make us a barbecue, but we were anxious to get

on and the affliction that we had just suffered unfitted us for such a scene.

31 July—Camped on the Snake. Indians came with salmon to sell. I let them have Helen's apron with a needle and thread and bought salmon enough for several meals. I wish you could [have eaten] with us. I certainly never tasted any fowl or fish half so delicious.

OREGON

3 September—Arrived at Milwaukie, and went into a house to live again, the first one that I had been in since we crossed the Missouri....

If a nearby family's dinner in Oregon was typical, the journey was worth it:

Well We had Rosted Ducks . . . And Fat Chickens And Rosted pig and Sausages And green Apl pie And Mince pies and Custard pies And Cakes of difrent kindes [and] Inglish goosburyes And Plums Blue And green gages And Siberian crab Apples And oregon Apples. . . . Like wise Buter And Sturson pikles and Beet pickles And Sauce And Bread and Mashed potatoes and Oister pie And Coffe And Tea to be shore. Now I Must tel you What other preserves that I have. I have peaches And citrons And Sweet Aples, Crab Aples Jelley And Tomatoes And Mince And pairs and Aple Butter. And now I will Tel you of the Rest of My Winter Suplies. I have A plenty of Butter And Milk And a Thousand poundes of Salman And plentey Cabage And Turnips And A Bout A Hundred and Fiftey Bushel of potatoes And plentey of dried fruits—Aples and Black Buryes the Best that I evr saw. . . . I never Saw Sutch Black Buryes And Ras Bryes As There Is in this Countrey in All My Life Time. . . . O yes I Have plentey Shougar Laid in For Winter This Year Two. And Salt   (new year's day, 1852)

A wayside grave on the route west. *(Courtesy, Library of Congress)*

political strength was in the North. In retaliation, southern Whigs rammed through a platform endorsing the Compromise, including the Fugitive Slave Law.

Saddled with a candidate unpopular in the South and a platform unpopular in the North, the Whigs lost disastrously in 1852. Franklin Pierce of New Hampshire, the Democratic candidate, carried twenty-seven of thirty-one states—the most lopsided election victory since 1820. Surveying the ruins, antislavery Whigs began to seek a new alliance.

Not long afterward, it was the Democrats whom the slavery issue divided. The Kansas-Nebraska Act bitterly antagonized northern anti-slavery Democrats, and their frustration found expression in the "Appeal of the Independent Democrats," composed in 1854 by Charles Sumner, Salmon P. Chase, and other antislavery Democratic congressmen. The appeal invited all opponents of slavery expansion to form a common front "to rescue the country from the domination of slavery."

This rebellion among antislavery Democrats made for a dramatic restructuring of northern politics. Antislavery politicians—former Whigs, breakaway Democrats, some of the more moderate abolitionists—struggled to create the coalition called for in the appeal. The new organization came formally into existence at a convention held in Ripon, Wisconsin, in February 1854; the delegates adopted a statement of principles proclaiming their opposition to the extension of slavery in the territories. The new party officially adopted the name "Republican" a few months later.

The "Know-Nothing" Party

For a time another party, the "Know-Nothings," was also in the field. The flood of Irish and German immigrants after 1840 had alarmed lower-class, old-stock Protestants, who feared that this predominantly Catholic immigration would undermine republican institutions. Those "governed by a head in a foreign land," exclaimed one nativist editor in reference to the Pope, where *"no genuine liberty, either civil or religious"* exists, must not "control the American Ballot Box." One nativist blamed "the vast influx of immigrants" for lowering wages, raising the price of food and rent, and bringing "a thousand evils . . . [on] the working class." The newcomers were also charged with corrupting the nation's morals. According to another nativist, they brought "grog shops like the frogs of Egypt upon us." The visit of a special papal envoy to the United States in 1853 triggered a series of riots in Cincinnati, Pittsburgh, and elsewhere. A mob in Charlestown, Massachusetts, burned a Catholic convent to the ground. In 1849 Charles B. Allen of New York had formed a secret "patriotic" society, the Order of the Star-Spangled Banner, anti-Catholic and anti-foreign. Party members, when questioned by outsiders, customarily answered, "I know nothing." For a few years the society remained an obscure local organization, but in 1854, hoping to capitalize on the breakup of the old party alignments, nativists went political and formed the American or "Know-Nothing" Party.

For a time the Know-Nothings demonstrated much political strength, capturing several state governorships and seventy-five seats in Congress. They were strongest in the Northeast and the border states. The Know-Nothings soon discovered, however, that as a bisectional party, they enjoyed no more immunity from the disruptive influence of the slavery question than the other parties. After a quarrel at the 1855 national convention, the party disintegrated. Most northern Know-Nothings went into the new Republican Party, which had been actively soliciting the nativists with pledges of "No Popery and Slavery."

The Republican Party

The 1856 Republican Convention resembled a revival meeting. "There is but a slight quantity of liquor consumed," a journalist reported, "very little profane swearing is heard, and everything is managed with excessive and intense propriety." The platform condemned slavery as a "relic of barbarism" and reaffirmed the "right and duty" of Congress to prohibit it in the territories. For President the Republicans nominated forty-three-year-old John C. Frémont, the dashing "Pathfinder" of western exploration. The Democrats bypassed President Pierce and Stephen A. Douglas, who were too closely identified with the Kansas-Nebraska Act, in favor of sixty-five-year-old James Buchanan of Pennsylvania. Buchanan was a veteran politician and diplomat who, happily, had been out of the country during the Kansas-Nebraska struggle. A third candidate, ex-President Millard Fillmore, was nominated by the still-existing southern wing of the Know-Nothing Party.

The election itself was not a three-cornered affair, but rather two separate contests—one between Buchanan and Frémont in the North, the other between Buchanan and Fillmore in the South. As the only

A Frémont campaign song demonstrated the feelings of the Republican Party toward the slave South:

The Freemont Train has got along,
Just jump aboard ye foes of wrong,
Our train is bound for Washington
It carries Freedom's bravest son.

CHORUS:

Clear the track, filibusters,
Now's no time for threats and blusters
Clear the track (or) ere you dream on't,
You'll be 'neath the car of Frémont.

Now don't you see we've just the man
To meet the foe?—for he who can
Brave torrents wild and mountain snows
Will fear no Brooks nor Southern blows.

So jump aboard the Frémont train
And soon the Capital we'll gain;
Then we'll rejoice there's one in power
Who never will to slavery cower.

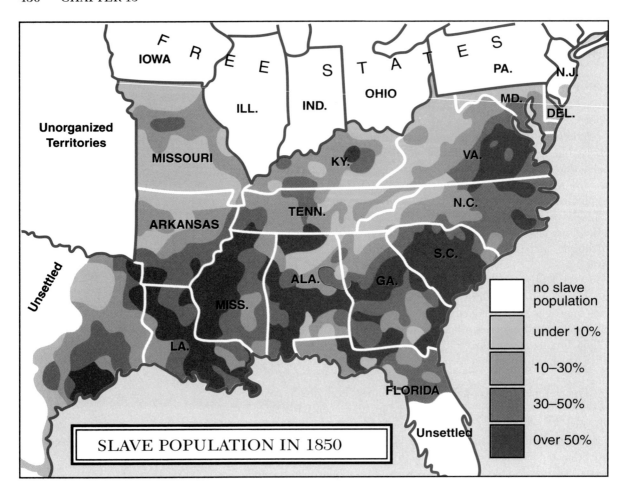

SLAVE POPULATION IN 1850

really national candidate, Buchanan benefited from the fear that a clear-cut sectional victory would split the Union. In November he won, carrying all the slave states but one, and gaining Pennsylvania, New Jersey, Indiana, Illinois, and California. In the other eleven free states, Frémont made a clean sweep—an impressive showing for a new party.

The real winner in 1856 was sectionalism: with the exception of Ohio, all eleven Frémont states were farther north than any of the twenty Buchanan states. No longer was the national political system a bond of union. Another of the cords holding the country together had snapped.

Sectionalism Ascendant

The year 1857 was auspicious, and ominous, for the United States. The Dred Scott decision by the United States Supreme Court undermined any hopes for future compromise on the issue of the expansion of slavery, the debate over the Lecompton Constitution in Kansas destroyed the northern branch of the Democratic Party, the Panic of 1857 convinced southerners of the superiority of the plantation economy, and the writings of Hinton Rowan Helper predicted the demise of slavery. The events of 1857 made political compromise between the North and the South all but impossible.

Dred Scott   After 1848 the slavery question, like some curse, transformed everything it touched. It divided churches, shattered political parties, turned Congress into a battleground, and ruined presidential careers. Only one institution—the Supreme Court—had remained unchanged. Pressure had been building on the Court for a definitive judgment regarding slavery in the territories. In 1857, in the case of *Dred Scott v. Sanford,* the Court's majority, sympathetic to the South, abandoned judicial impartiality in the hope of settling this nagging question once and for all. The justices assumed that respect for the Court would insure acceptance of its decision by all sides. Rarely had American public figures so misgauged the popular temper: rather than settling the slavery question, the *Dred Scott* decision pushed the country forward on the road to civil war.

The case involved a Missouri slave, Dred Scott, who had sojourned with his master for several years in Illinois and in Minnesota Territory. Upon returning to Missouri, Scott and his wife sued for their freedom, contending that they had been emancipated by virtue of their residence on free soil. Chief Justice Roger B. Taney, speaking for a majority of the Supreme Court, rejected the Scotts's claim on three grounds: as black people they could not be citizens and therefore had no right to bring suit in the federal courts; as residents of Missouri they did not fall within the law of Illinois prohibiting slavery; and their sojourn in the Minnesota Territory had not emancipated them, for the provision of the Missouri Compromise prohibiting slavery north of 36° 30' was unconstitutional. Congress, Taney declared, had no right to deprive citizens of their property in the territories without "due process of law," and he was defining slaves as property.

On nearly every point the Chief Justice's opinion was either plainly wrong or open to serious dispute. To declare that black people in general, and hence even free blacks, were non-citizens who, as Taney said, had "no rights [that whites] were bound to respect" defied American history. Free blacks had always been recognized as citizens in at least some northern states, and therefore did have the right to sue in the federal courts. In rejecting the principle that the status one state granted to an individual held for that person in another state, Taney ignored several earlier decisions in which Missouri courts had recognized the claim to freedom of slaves who had sojourned in free territory. The supreme authority of Congress over the territories had previously been upheld no less than three times by the Taney Court itself.

Taney's pronouncement that it was unconstitutional for Congress to exclude slavery in the territories provoked a storm of criticism in the North. Republicans dismissed the decision as part of the "slavepower conspiracy." According to Horace Greeley's *New York Tribune,* it was entitled "to just so much moral weight as would be the judgment of a majority of those congregated in any Washington bar-room." The decision also embarrassed northern Democrats such as Stephen A. Douglas. They had fixed their hopes on the doctrine of popular sover-

Dred Scott. The Supreme Court's decision in the Scott case—denying both the right of a slave to sue for freedom and the right of a territory to exclude slavery within its boundaries—further inflamed the antislavery factions. *(Courtesy, The Missouri Historical Society)*

eignty. But if Congress could not exclude slavery in the territories, then neither could it bestow on the people of a territory the authority to do so. Southerners, of course, hailed the *Dred Scott* decision as a vindication of their claim that slavery could not be excluded from the territories prior to statehood. By striking down popular sovereignty, the Supreme Court had destroyed just about the last device for sectional compromise. Meanwhile, events in Kansas deepened sectional division still further.

The Lecompton Constitution   In 1857 the proslavery faction in Kansas held a convention at Lecompton, drafted a constitution recognizing slavery, and applied for statehood. Although a clear majority of the territory's residents opposed the Lecompton Constitution, President Buchanan accepted it and asked Congress to admit Kansas to statehood. The President took this fateful step out of fear that a rejection of Lecompton would antagonize southern Democrats.

Buchanan's action outraged Stephen Douglas, who had proposed popular sovereignty as a democratic solution to the question of slavery in Kansas. Bucking the administration, he denounced the "Lecompton fraud" as a travesty on popular sovereignty and joined with Republican congressmen in opposing it. Douglas's opposition to Lecompton offended southerners and probably ruined his presidential prospects. After a struggle, Congress in 1858 sent the Lecompton Constitution back to the people of Kansas to be voted on again. This time a fair election was held, and Kansas rejected the "Lecompton fraud" by a margin of 11,300 to 1,788. Kansas remained a territory until after the Civil War had begun.

Buchanan's attempt to ram the Lecompton Constitution through Congress, coming so soon after the Kansas-Nebraska Act, broke the northern wing of the Democratic Party. Few northern Democrats who supported him on Kansas survived the 1858 mid-term elections. From this point on and for about a century thereafter, the white South was to identify with the Democratic Party.

In the North and West, meanwhile, within the Republican party antislavery sentiment was coalescing with economic nationalism.

Numbers of American statesmen, among them Hamilton, John Quincy Adams, and Henry Clay, had wished to make the national government an active partner in the shaping and strengthening of a unified American economy. But economic nationalist programs differed in detail. Adams would have kept a high price on public lands in the West and applied the revenues to his ambitious governmental programs for the enriching of the economy and culture. For a time, northeastern business interests also had wanted the price of public lands to remain high, for they feared that cheap land would drain away eastern labor to the West. But now industrialists could think differently: immigration was supplying labor for northern industry and a prosperous West could be a customer for northeastern manufactured goods. So northerners of varying economic condition, landhungry farmers along with ambitious businessmen, could unite behind a nationalist program that would have the government nurture northern industry, turn government land over to western settlers, and finance transportation connecting the Northeast to the West.

This economic nationalism had much common ground with the antislavery movement. Northerners wishing to settle in the West did not want the new lands dominated by the slave powers. Northern industrialists were at war politically with southern slaveholders who opposed protective tariffs. The Republican conviction that Congress had the authority to prohibit slavery in the territories blended with a larger belief in strong federal government, the kind that could legislate an active and continental economic program. Perhaps northerners who championed a vigorous program of economic development could even detect a cultural identity between their economic and their antislavery convictions, believing that industriousness and progress were the way of the free-labor North while indolence was the way of the southern slaveholding class.

In any event, Republicans sponsored legislation in Congress favoring free homesteads for settlers, agricultural colleges financed by grants of land, internal improvements aided by the federal government, and a protective tariff. Southern Democrats blocked each of these measures. By obstructing the dynamic economic forces then at work in the North and Midwest, the South pressed these two sections to work together.

Northern politics, like the northern economy, was now moving along an east-west axis. And the Republican program for the economy, like the Republican opposition to slavery, had the more generous view of how the republic could conduct its life, for the party was really looking beyond the localism of states' rights and proposing a cooperative commonwealth in which the resources of the entire nation would be put to the common welfare.

The Panic of 1857

In the midst of the civil war in Kansas and the debates over the Dred Scott case, the Ohio Life Insurance and Trust Company of New York City declared bankruptcy and triggered a financial panic throughout the major cities of the North and upper Midwest. A wide range of smaller financial institutions went under, as did dozens of brokerage firms and larger industrial concerns that could no longer secure credit. Unemployment spread. But the southern economy remained prosperous. Between 1836 and 1840 cotton producers had exported a total of $321 million of cotton, and that volume jumped to nearly $750 million between 1856 and 1860. The plantation South not only survived the panic of 1857; it experienced unprecedented prosperity.

The Panic of 1857 convinced southerners that their way of life was superior to that of the North. While northern businesses went broke or at best barely survived, southern plantations thrived. While northern workers lost their jobs and their homes, southern slaves were housed, fed, and clothed better than before. Southerners elevated their rhetoric once again, praising slavery as a moral good and an essential feature of the American economy. The Southern Commercial Convention, meeting in Vicksburg, Mississippi, in May 1859, went beyond even that and called for restoration of the Atlantic slave trade as a means of strengthening the southern economy.

Lydia M. Child had called attention to the mistreatment of blacks in the North:

"While we bestow our earnest disapprobation on the system of slavery, let us not flatter ourselves that we are in reality any better than our brethren of the South. Thanks to our soil and climate and the early exertions of Quakers, the *form* of slavery does not exist among us; but the very *spirit* of the hateful and mischievous thing is here in all its strength. . . .

Of the attempt to establish a school for African girls at Canterbury, Connecticut, Child wrote:

"Had the pope himself attempted to establish his supremacy over that commonwealth, he could hardly have been repelled with more determined and angry resistence. A colored girl who availed herself of this opportunity to gain instruction was warned out of town, and fined for not complying; and the instructress was imprisoned for persevering in her benevolent plan."

Hinton Rowan Helper

Hinton Rowan Helper, a native of the upper South, was not so sure about the virtues of the southern economy. Using statistics gleaned from the Census of 1850, Helper concluded that plantation slavery had actually impoverished the vast majority of southern whites. In New York in 1857 he published *The Impending Crisis of the South*. By implying that most southern whites would be better off in a free economy, Helper became *persona non grata* in the South. Southern state legislatures declared the book to be treasonous and provocative, and they prohibited its sale in bookstores and its distribution through federal post offices. A host of northern congressmen endorsed the book and even had more than 100,000 copies printed for distribution to their constituents. The stage was set for another confrontation between North and South.

Abe Lincoln of Illinois

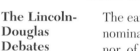

The Lincoln-Douglas Debates

The earliest principal contender for the Republican nomination in 1860 was William Seward. As governor of New York for four years and senator for twelve, he enjoyed a national reputation. But suddenly, in 1858, a new potential candidate appeared. Throughout that summer, newspapers carried reports of a series of debates between Stephen A. Douglas and a little-known Illinois lawyer and former congressman named Abraham Lincoln. The occasion was the contest for Douglas's seat in the Senate. Political feelings in the 1850s ran so strong that one debate, at Galesburg, drew many horse drawn floats; one carried thirty-two young women, one for each state, dressed in white, and a thirty-third in black labeled "Kansas" carrying a banner, "THEY WON'T LET ME IN." One woman who lived into the 1930s would remember the "electricity crackling in the air" and Douglas' remark that if Lincoln thought so much of the Negro he imagined Abe would like one for a wife. Replied Lincoln in his slow drawl: "No, I do not want a negro for a wife, neither do I want one for my slave." When the debates were over, Lincoln had lost the election but had become a figure to be reckoned with in the Republican Party. "You are like Byron," a friend wrote, "who woke up one morning and found himself famous."

Young Abraham Lincoln lost the 1858 election for senator of Illinois to Stephen A. Douglas, but beat Douglas and two other candidates to become President of the increasingly divided nation in 1860.

The Supreme Court's *Dred Scott* decision, which in effect denied to the people of a territory the right to exclude slavery within its boundaries, had placed Douglas in a difficult situation. The "Little Giant" was the foremost advocate of popular sovereignty. If he accepted the Court's decision, he would probably lose the election in Illinois, where free-soil sentiment was strong. But if he reaffirmed the right of settlers to decide the slavery question for themselves, he would lose the support of southerners, which he desperately needed if he hoped to win the Democratic presidential nomination in 1860.

According to legend, Lincoln took advantage of Douglas's predicament to further his own political ends. At Freeport he asked Douglas whether, in light of Taney's opinion, the people could still exclude slavery from a territory. Douglas replied that they could, merely by withholding the police regulations and local laws that slavery needed in order to exist. The Freeport formula, summed up in the phrase "unfriendly legislation," supposedly assured Douglas's reelection to the Senate, but would cost him the support of southerners in 1860. Lincoln, so the legend goes, had thus with superhuman foresight sacrificed the short-run of a Senate seat in the interests of winning the big prize in 1860.

This story, like so many pieces of Lincoln lore, is more fiction than fact. In reality Douglas had announced his doctrine of "unfriendly legislation" months before the Freeport debate. And by the time of his confrontation with Lincoln, popular sovereignty was no longer a major issue. The real issue between the two men—and the one Lincoln strove to develop—was the ultimate one of the morality of slavery. Here Lincoln and Douglas differed fundamentally.

Douglas did not regard the question of slavery in the territories as a moral issue. He believed that blacks, whatever their status, would never achieve equality with whites. Whether they were subordinated as slaves, therefore, or merely as second-class citizens was not a matter of great concern for him, certainly not an issue worth breaking up the country over. Douglas disliked slavery; but what to do about it, he thought, should remain a local decision. Southerners had chosen to keep it. Northerners had decided to get rid of it. In the territories Douglas would let the local residents decide by popular sovereignty. He would never try to impose a single national policy on the slavery question. This position accorded with his friendly way with the voters: "I live with constituents," he once proudly asserted, "drink with them, lodge with them, pray with them, laugh, hunt, dance, and work with them. I eat their corn dodgers and fried bacon." He wanted them all to like him and, like Henry Clay before, wanted desperately to be President, thinking a middle ground the safest route to victory in national politics. But by temporizing in an era of polarization, he would lose both poles of the electorate.

For Lincoln slavery was a moral wrong. Although political considerations and respect for constitutional guarantees to slaveholders often impelled Lincoln to compromise his moral views in public, he never deserted them. Lincoln could never say, as Douglas said, that he did not care whether slavery was "voted up or voted down."

Lincoln differed from Douglas on another point: he insisted that slavery, as a national problem, required a national policy. Lincoln would not interfere with slavery where it existed; but he would not allow it to expand. Lincoln believed that the Founding Fathers, recognizing slavery as a wrong, had placed restrictions on it designed to produce its eventual extinction. Douglas and the Democrats, by refusing to recognize the moral wrong, had provided constitutional sanctions for slavery and made possible its expansion.

In 1858, Douglas narrowly won reelection to the Senate. But it was Lincoln who had sensed and shared the growing moral and emotional concern over the slavery issue in the North. This would be critical in the election of 1860.

As the election year approached, North and South ceased even to pretend to any interest in compromise. In 1859 Senator Jefferson Davis

A popular song of the time, referring both to the Compromise of 1850 and to popular sovereignty, pointed to the difficulty of Douglas' position:

Once we had a Compromise,
A check to Slavery's wrong,
Douglas crushed the golden prize,
To help himself along,
Then the North and then the West,
Arose with giant power,
Pierce succumbed to the South's behest,
But Douglas had to cower.
　Hi! Douglas! Sly Douglas!
　A Senator would be.

of Mississippi introduced resolutions in Congress designed to get the Democratic Party to support the extreme southern position on slavery in the territories. These upheld the constitutional right of slaveholders to go into territories and called for the creation of a federal slave code for those areas. Senate Democrats finally adopted the Davis resolutions, over the vigorous objections of Stephen Douglas. At about the same time some southerners launched a movement to revive the African slave trade. This proposal had no chance of success, even among southerners; its main purpose, successfully achieved, was to irritate northern sensibilities. During the 1850s several northern state legislatures had defied the Fugitive Slave Act by passing "personal liberty" laws. Most of these prohibited state officers from aiding federal officials in their efforts to reclaim fugitives. In 1854 the Wisconsin supreme court had carried defiance of the federal government a step farther by declaring the Fugitive Slave Act of 1850 unconstitutional. Eventually the United States Supreme Court overturned this judgment, whereupon the Wisconsin legislature, taking a line from the Kentucky Resolution of 1798, declared the Court's action to be "an act of undelegated power, void, and of no force." But going beyond these acts of North and South in prefiguring sectional war was John Brown's raid at Harpers Ferry, Virginia.

The Election of 1860

The Democrats Meet in Charleston

Four months after John Brown's execution, the Democrats began their national convention at Charleston, South Carolina. The choice of the convention site was unfortunate; Charleston was a tinderbox of southern radicalism. For the Democrats, 1860 was the climax of the intra-party struggle between the dominant southern faction and the northerners, whose spokesman was Stephen Douglas. Ever since the split over Lecompton, both sides had been spoiling for a confrontation over the question of slavery in the territories. Most southern delegates came to Charleston pledged to the adoption of the Davis Resolutions opposing any limitation on slavery in the territories. When the convention rejected their inclusion on the platform, delegates from eight southern states left. The convention then adjourned for several weeks, reassembling at Baltimore on June 18, where the fight immediately resumed. This time delegates from eleven southern states (all the future states of the Confederacy) walked out. The remaining delegates nominated Douglas for president on a platform endorsing popular sovereignty. The bolters met in another hall and nominated John Breckinridge of Kentucky for President. Their platform upheld the Davis Resolutions. The split between the Democrats was complete.

A number of factors brought this fatal action by the southern Democrats, which virtually assured a Republican victory in November. A few hotheads sought deliberately to split the party, precisely in order to produce the Republican victory that would, they anticipated, precipitate secession. Some delegates hoped merely to force the election into the House of Representatives. The Democrats had met amidst extreme excitement, and many delegates were simply swept away by the violent speeches of "fire-eaters," a term applied to agitators like William Yancey of Alabama. They bolted without fully considering the consequences. Right up to November, many of the bolters assumed that somehow the party would come back together.

Between the two Democratic conventions another party had met at Baltimore. This was the Constitutional Union Party, composed mainly of old Whigs from both sections and of southern Know-Nothings. These conservatives joined in their general concern for the safety of the Union. For President, they nominated John Bell of Tennessee, a Whig and a large slaveholder, although not an extreme advocate of southern rights. As their platform, the Constitutional Unionists settled for a vague pledge to uphold the Constitution and the Union.

John Bell. *(Courtesy, Library of Congress)*

The Republicans Convene in Chicago

The Republican convention opened at Chicago on May 16. The Republican strategy in 1860 was simple: to win the presidency the party had only to win the same states Frémont had carried in 1856, and just 34 additional electoral votes. This meant carrying Pennsylvania (27 votes) and either Illinois (11), Indiana (13), or New Jersey (7). All these states adjoined the South and were less hostile to slavery than was the upper North. And each of these four states had reason to desire such Republican measures as the tariff and internal improvements.

The Republican platform had these states in mind. It treated the slavery question cautiously. The delegates reaffirmed Republican opposition to the expansion of slavery, but promised to leave slavery alone where it existed. The platform pledged support for a protective tariff, a Pacific railroad, and a homestead law.

This same concern for the swing states governed the choice of a candidate. William Seward was considered extreme on the slavery question, and the party's congressional and local candidates in the states in question did not want to run with him. After reviewing the other contenders, the party pros settled on Abraham Lincoln as the man most "available": he resided in the important state of Illinois, was a moderate on slavery, had never been identified with nativism, and had made fewer enemies than his rivals. Lincoln also benefited from the shrewd tactics of his managers, who packed the galleries at the convention hall by distributing counterfeit tickets, and stationed men around the floor to begin noisy demonstrations on a prearranged signal.

In 1860 the national political system effectively failed to operate. There were two campaigns that year. In the North the contest was between Lincoln and Douglas: Bell and Breckinridge were also on the ballot, but neither had much support. In the South Breckinridge divided votes with Bell, though Douglas was also on the ballot. Lincoln, Bell, and Breckinridge adhered to the tradition of staying close to home and letting supporters do the campaigning. On the real issue of the campaign, the possible dissolution of the Union, Lincoln and Breckinridge remained silent. Stephen Douglas campaigned hard and heroically

John Breckinridge. *(Courtesy, Library of Congress)*

This cartoon employs a setting from the new game of baseball to argue that Lincoln won the 1860 election because he stood for equal rights and free territory. *(Courtesy, The New-York Historical Society, New York City)*

throughout the country—at some risk to his personal safety in the South—attempting to break down the barriers between the two sections.

On election day each of the hard-line candidates won in his own section. Lincoln carried all the northern states except New Jersey; Breckinridge captured eleven slave states. Douglas ran well in the North, but carried only Missouri and three electoral votes in New Jersey. Bell, whose popular vote was the smallest, took Virginia, Kentucky, and Tennessee. In the country as a whole Lincoln won only thirty-nine per cent of the popular vote, but his votes were concentrated in the populous North. As a result, he had a clear victory in the electoral college—180 votes against a total of 112 for his three opponents. He would have won even if the opposition to him had been united. The Republican victory in November might not alone have ruptured the Union. Conservatives within the Republican Party hoped to appease the upper South with a policy of popular sovereignty instead of outright opposition to admission of any of the territories as slave states. But a single event of 1859 stuck in the craw of southerners, the act of a madman or a saint—John Brown's nightmare attack at Harpers Ferry.

Suggested Readings

Books on the 1850s include William E. Gienapp, *The Origins of the Republican Party, 1852–1856* (1987), Deborah White, *Ar'n't I a Woman? Female Slaves in the Plantation South* (1985), Eugene D. Genovese, *Freedom and Progress in Southern Conservative Thought, 1820–1860* (1991), Michael F. Holt, *The Political Crisis of the 1850s* (1976), David M. Potter, *The Impending Crisis: 1848–1861* (1976), Gerald W. Wolf, *The Kansas-Nebraska Bill: Party, Section, and the Coming of the Civil War* (1977), Don E. Fehrenbacher, *The Dred Scott Case* (1978), and Eric Foner, *Free Soil, Free Labor, Free Men: The Ideology of the Republican Party Before the Civil War* (1970).

Other important studies are Mitchell Snay, *Gospel of Disunion: Religion and Separatism in the Antebellum South* (1993), Richard J. Carwardine, *Evangelicals and Politics in Antebellum America* (1993), George B. Forgie, *Patricide in the House Divided: A Psychological Interpretation of Lincoln and His Age* (1979), and Drew Gilpin Faust, *A Sacred Circle: The Dilemma of the Intellectual in the Old South, 1840–1860* (1978). Stephen B. Oates's biography of John Brown is entitled *To Purge This Land With Blood* (1970). The best discussion of *Uncle Tom's Cabin* appears in the opening pages of Edmund Wilson's *Patriotic Gore* (1961). Milton Rugoff's family history is entitled *The Beechers* (1981). See also Joan Hedrick, *Harriet Beecher Stowe: A Life* (1993).

Don E. Fehrenbacher, *The Dred Scott Case: Its Significance in American Law and Politics* (1978) is the definitive work. See also Philip Paludan, *A People's Contest: The Union and the Civil War* (1988), Kenneth M. Stampp, *America in 1857: A Nation on the Brink*, Leon F. Litwack, *North of Slavery: The Negro and the Free States, 1798–1860* (1961), and James Oakes, *Slavery and Freedom: An Interpretation of the Old South* (1990).

What Caused the Civil War?

Kenneth M. Stampp

During the 1850s the proslavery South had won a series of striking political victories. In the Compromise of 1850, it had obtained a new and more stringent Fugitive Slave Act, which gave slaveholders the assistance of federal commissioners in their efforts to recover runaways. In 1854 southern Senators forced [Illinois Senator Stephen A.] Douglas to agree to the repeal of the Missouri Compromise before giving their support to the Kansas-Nebraska Act. In 1857 the Supreme Court's Dred Scott decision affirmed the right of slaveholders to carry their property into all the territories of the United States. The year 1857, in fact, marked the high tide of the proslavery South's national political power. It had the sympathy of the Buchanan administration. It controlled the Supreme Court. It dominated the Democratic majority in both houses of Congress. Pressing on, aggressive proslavery leaders ignored the advice of more cautious proslavery spokesmen, such as the *Richmond Enquirer,* not to force their northern allies to support policies that would destroy them—in short, not to endanger the survival of the Democratic party as a national organization. Instead, they disregarded election frauds and the clear will of the Kansas majority and, with the wholehearted support of the administration, demanded congressional approval of the [pro-slavery] Lecompton constitution.

[The president] had concluded that it would be folly to oppose the Lecompton constitution simply because it protected the owners of a few hundred slaves! Looking back, knowing the ultimate consequences of Buchanan's policy decision, it stands as one of the most tragic miscalculations any President has ever made. . . . The Buchanan administration was discredited; southern control of the House of Representatives was lost in the elections [of 1858]; and the Democratic party was split. The Republican victory in the presidential election of 1860 was the logical result. . . .

Would all this have been avoided—would the course of the sectional conflict have been significantly altered—if Buchanan had remained true to his pledge and demanded the submission of the whole Lecompton constitution of the voters of Kansas? This is a question no historian can answer. It is doubtful that a firm stand by Buchanan would have resulted in southern secession, because the provocation would not have been sufficient to unite even the Deep South behind so drastic a response. Nor would it have been sufficient to produce a major split in the national Democratic party. Accordingly, without a divided and demoralized national Democracy, Republican successes in the elections of 1858 and the presidential election of 1860 would have been a good deal more problematic. . . .

How Buchanan, a shrewd and experienced politician, one of the best trained Presidents the country has ever had, could have been responsible for a political disaster of such magnitude has been variously explained by hostile contemporaries and by historians. According to his modern biographer, Buchanan was a legalist and accepted the constitution because the Lecompton convention was a legal body, and no law required it to provide for full ratification. . . . [Another] explanation for Buchanan's Lecompton policy is that there was no significant difference between his outlook and that of the Southerners in his Cabinet. They shared an extreme dislike of abolitionists and Republicans, and they saw no great wrong in the existence of black slavery.

Kenneth M. Stampp, *America in 1857: A Nation on the Brink* (New York: Oxford University Press, 1990), pp. 329–30.

Richard H. Sewell

[This account] of what Abraham Lincoln called the American Union's "fiery trial" seeks to refocus attention on slavery as the taproot of sectional discord and civil war. It represents, that is, a modest challenge to those historians who see slavery as a largely artificial or symbolic issue. Of course, slavery was not the only item on the political agenda in the troubled 1850s, but it was, I think, the most important. The North and South may not have *been* distinct cultures, but by mid-century each section *thought* of itself as possessing a distinct and superior way of life, one shaped most profoundly by the absence or presence of human bondage. The debate over slavery's right to expand not only aroused feelings of jealousy, honor, and regional pride, but raised fundamental questions about the future direction of American society. Unable to find common ground with such vital issues at stake, the Union broke asunder. . . .

The slaveholding South had good reason to take alarm at Lincoln's victory. Its perception of the Republican party as first and foremost an antislavery instrument was fundamentally correct. Even conservative Republicans, who stressed the danger of Slave Power aggression and showed scant concern for those in chains, damned slavery as a "blighting institution" and sought a congressional barrier against its spread. The events of the 1850s—Kansas-Nebraska, Dred Scott, Lecompton and "Bleeding Kansas," proslavery designs on Cuba, and talk of reopening the African slave trade—had progressively radicalized party moderates, producing a heightened sensitivity to the immorality of slavery and a determination, in Lincoln's words, to pursue its "ultimate extinction" throughout the land.

There were limits, of course, to the antislavery steps Republicans might take. . . . Still, Lincoln's triumph was a palpable menace to the South. Quite aside from the long-range damage to be expected once Congress and the Supreme Court also came under Republican control (namely, exclusion of slavery from all territories, abolition in the District of Columbia, an end to the interstate slave trade, repeal or drastic modification of the Fugitive Slave Law), the new president, acting solely on his executive authority, might make no end of mischief. By appointing Republicans to judgeships, collectorships, postmasterships, and other positions in the South he could foster an antislavery influence dangerous not only to the peculiar institution but, once it reached the slave quarters, to the very lives of Southern whites. Such patronage, moreover, might spawn Republican organizations in the South destructive to the unity on which the region's special culture depended.

In fact, Lincoln's election itself, independent of the policies he and his party might be expected to pursue, represented an assault on the honor and well-being of the South. By electing a candidate pledged to slavery's destruction, the Northern majority had grossly insulted the South and proclaimed its determination to make vassals—slaves—of Southern whites. To prideful Southerners, the voters' verdict amounted to "a declaration of war against our property and the supremacy of the white race," a slap in the face that demanded retribution. More practical considerations also fueled Southern indignation at Lincoln's victory. Many fretted that slave property, its value dependent upon an expectation of future returns, "must be greatly depreciated" under a "black Republican" administration. The *Charleston Mercury* estimated that "the submission of the South to the administration of the Federal Government under Messrs. Lincoln and Hamlin, must reduce the value of slaves in the South, one hundred dollars each," a loss to the region of more than $400 million. Worse yet, as slave prices skidded, planters in the upper South (where slavery was deemed a marginal investment) would feel pressure to sell off their chattels. Then, worried the *Mercury*, "the Frontier States [will] *enter on the policy of making themselves Free States.*" Meanwhile, word of the election of an antislavery president seemed in itself sufficient to promote bloody insurrections against the "master race." Finally, magnifying all such fears was the fear of the unknown. Abraham Lincoln would be the *first* Republican president and history offered no reassurances concerning his probable behavior in office.

Richard H. Sewell, *A House Divided: Sectionalism and Civil War, 1848–1865* (Baltimore: The Johns Hopkins University Press, 1988), pp. 11, 76–78.

John Brown. *(Courtesy, Library of Congress)*

442

14

A Great Civil War
1861–1865

JOHN BROWN'S RAID

In the summer of 1859, the nation seemed still capable of veering off the collision course on which its sections were hurtling. Then John Brown, his bloody work in Kansas still fresh in memory, shocked the country with a bold desperate stroke in the slave south.

Brown, whom William Lloyd Garrison described as a "tall, spare, farmer-like man, with head disproportionately small, and that inflexible mouth," had gone in July 1859 to Harpers Ferry in Virginia, about sixty miles northwest of Washington, D.C., at the confluence of the Potomac and Shenandoah rivers. He rented a farm near the town and, using funds supplied by several abolitionists, accumulated 198 rifles and 950 cast-iron pikes with which to arm slaves. He also had an army of sixteen whites and five blacks. On the evening of October 16, Brown's little band set out to capture the town and its federal arsenal. No slaves voluntarily joined the raiders, and the townspeople, along with militia from the county and then United States marines led by Robert E. Lee, besieged them. Within thirty-six hours, Brown and the remnant of his army were captured. Ten of the party had been killed, including two of Brown's own sons. The raid was a total failure, a demonstration of the impossibility of starting a vast slave insurrection.

That was all there was to the raid, but not all there was to John Brown. "He is the gamest man I ever saw," admitted the governor

continued

HISTORICAL EVENTS

1860
South Carolina secedes
from the Union

1861
Confederate States of America
formed • Jefferson Davis becomes
provisional President of the Confederacy • Morrill Tariff • Fort Sumter
attacked by Confederate forces
(April 12) and the Civil War begins
• Battle of Bull Run

1862
Homestead Act of 1862 • Morrill
Land Grant Act of 1862 • Lincoln
suspends some civil liberties • Union
begins recruiting blacks for military
service • Battle at Shiloh • Union
Army captures New Orleans • the
Merrimac vs. the *Monitor* • Battles of
Antietam • Emancipation
Proclamation

1863
National Banking Act of 1863
• General Hooker defeated at
Chancellorsville • Union victories at
Gettysburg and Vicksburg
• antidraft riot in New York City

In his impassioned religious imagery, Brown was very much a part of his nineteenth-century American culture. Yet his Christianity differed from the perfectionist Protestantism that had spread with the evangelical movements of the age. That Protestantism, committed to the perfection of the individual, went with an energetic American belief in the moral conquest of social evil. John Brown's strategy for overthrowing slavery worked instead with primal theological materials—sin, sacrifice, retribution, redemption. But a vocabulary of retribution and redemption would also mark President Lincoln's solemn and magnificent second inaugural address. Given just weeks before the victory of the Union, and just weeks before his own death, it speculated that the war might continue "until every drop of blood drawn with the lash shall be paid by another drawn with the sword."

of Virginia, upon questioning the wounded captive. Brown replied to every questioner at his interrogation and at his trial with crisp assurance born of clarity of purpose. His many letters after his conviction breathed saintly dedication to the biblical injunction to remember them that are in bonds as bound with them. Brown never wavered, showed no fear, no vindictiveness toward his captors, no selfish purposes at all. He awed his enemies and captured the respect of much of the North for a deed that few could actually condone.

John Brown's favorite saying was that "without the shedding of blood there is no remission of sin." When his eldest son, John, Jr., was less than ten years old, he had kept a record of the son's sins. One day the elder Brown removed his own shirt, handed the boy the whip and ordered him to "lay it on." "I dared not refuse to obey," John, Jr., would remember, "but at first I did not strike hard. 'Harder!' he said, 'harder, harder!' until he *received the balance of the account*." It was only years later that John, Jr., began to think that he understood this bizarre event. It was, he decided, a "practical illustration" of the doctrine of atonement. "I was then too obtuse to perceive how Justice could be satisfied by inflicting penalty upon the back of the innocent instead of the guilty."

In 1856 on Pottawatomie Creek in Kansas, and in 1859 at Harpers Ferry, John Brown offered an entire nation a "practical illustration" of the doctrine of atonement that he had derived from his family heritage and from "the ponderous volumes of Jonathan Edwards' sermons which father owned." John Brown, a lifelong failure, a bankrupt, sometime thief, eccentric, fanatic, liar, perhaps insane, would take upon his own back the nation's giant sin, would remove the debt that a society gone morally and politically bankrupt with slavery could not discharge.

Brown's acts struck terror in the South, aroused many fears and uncertainties in the North, yet played upon the deepest chords of the Puritan conscience. Herman Melville later called Brown the "meteor" of the Civil War. Brown's behavior in the face of execution, which impressed even his captors, caught the imagination of Americans who accepted the doctrine of atonement, voiced most eloquently in Lincoln's Second Inaugural Address. Ralph Waldo Emerson predicted that Brown "will make the gallows as glorious as the cross."

The South Secedes

As soon as Lincoln's election was certain, the South Carolina legislature called for a state convention. On December 20, 1860, the convention met at Charleston and unanimously declared "that the Union now subsisting between South Carolina and other States of America is hereby dissolved." Similar declarations followed in rapid succession in Alabama, Georgia, Florida, Mississippi, and Louisiana. The smooth course of secession was upset only in Texas, where crusty old Governor Sam Houston, a staunch Unionist, refused to summon a special session of the legislature. The lawmakers met anyway, and called a convention without Houston's authorization.

Up to this point, the secession process had moved forward with electrifying speed. Moderates tried to avert the catastrophe. But too much blood had been shed in Kansas, too much noble madness displayed at Harpers Ferry. In the space of forty-two days, seven states, stretching from South Carolina to Texas, seceded from the Union. On February 4, 1861, however, the secessionist tide broke momentarily when the voters of Virginia elected a majority of convention delegates opposed to immediate secession. Subsequently the electorate in four other upper South states—Tennessee, North Carolina, Arkansas, and Missouri—voted in effect against secession. The three remaining slave states—Kentucky, Maryland, and Delaware—did not even call conventions. Having stronger ties to the North and smaller ratios of blacks in its population, the upper South was hesitant to secede. For the moment, the lower South was isolated.

Nonetheless, at Montgomery, Alabama, on February 7, 1861, delegates from the seven states proceeded to adopt a provisional constitution for the Confederate States of America. It was modeled closely on the United States Constitution, but several modifications safeguarded state sovereignty and slavery. The Confederate Constitution reserved to the states the power of amendment and even permitted them to impeach Confederate officials under certain circumstances. It guaranteed the property rights of slaveholders both in the existing states and in any future territory the Confederacy might acquire. To lead the new government the delegates chose Jefferson Davis of Mississippi as provisional President and Alexander H. Stephens of Georgia as Vice President.

President and Mrs. Jefferson Davis. In February 1861, the first seven Confederate States of America—there were to be eleven in all—elected Davis as President. (*Courtesy, Confederate Museum, Richmond, Virginia*)

A Compact of States   Declarations issued by the various state conventions spelled out the reasons for secession. South Carolina's was typical. The United States Constitution, the declaration begins, was a compact among sovereign states for the purpose of establishing "a government with defined objects and powers." Like all compacts, this one bound the contracting parties to certain mutual obligations. The failure of one of the parties to perform these obligations, in whole or in part, released the other from its bond. The northern states, continues the South Carolina declaration, had refused to fulfill their constitutional obligation to return fugitive slaves. They had tolerated abolition societies "designed to disturb the peace and steal the property of the citizens of other states." They had encouraged "servile insurrection"—a reference to John Brown. At last, a sectional party "hostile to slavery" had captured control of the federal government. This party, the declaration concludes, was dedicated not merely to excluding slavery from the "common territory," but to slavery's ultimate extinction.

Southerners might associate the case for slavery with the case for secession, claiming that both slaveholding and states' rights were old institutions strongly founded in law. But the two issues were in fact quite separate. In previous years northern opponents of slavery had proposed that free states refuse cooperation with a national government that protected slavery; and in 1860 some sympathizers with slavery were also supporters of the Union.

Earlier in the century political and constitutional quarrels had taken place over whether it was the Union or the states that possessed sovereignty. The argument looked back to the process of ratification, in which each state had held a convention to decide whether that state should adhere to the Constitution.

Nineteenth-century champions of state sovereignty concluded from this that ratification had been by individual states, each state retaining sovereignty and the right of independence. They believed that sovereignty belonged also to the states formed after ratification.   The opposite argument started with the proposition that at the time of the American Revolution it had been the whole people who asserted sovereignty, rebelling against the false claim of the British throne to be sovereign over British America. Thereafter that same whole and undivided sovereign people, following the Confederation period, voted for the Constitution, the states providing no more than convenient administrative units for the conduct of the vote. If the states at the time of ratification had been that—administrative units within the nation—they could not later present themselves as being sovereign and having been so in the eighteenth century. Americans who thought this way could believe that in opposing southern secession they were opposing an illegal rebellion by a part of the people against the whole people.

The Union Responds By early winter 1861 Lincoln was on his way to Washington. The seven states of the deep South had seceded and formed the Confederate States of America, with Montgomery, Alabama, as their first capital. The crisis was the greatest since the Revolution. Washington was astir with worry and excitement.

The nation's capital, tucked between the slave states of Virginia and Maryland, was a largely southern city. For decades southern politicians, or "northern men with southern principles," had dominated the political, business, and social life of the capital. The city still had slaves in its population, although since the 1850 Compromise the slave pens and auction blocks had gone. Now, in the country's greatest crisis, the southern sympathies of many Washingtonians were visible everywhere. At the city's many bars the imbibers of toddies and flips announced that Lincoln would never be inaugurated: proud "southrons" would not allow it. At the government executive departments young clerks wore secession cockades to show their support of the South.

Unionists who found themselves in the capital during the secession winter were apprehensive. The young Henry Adams, who had come to Washington as private secretary to his father, Congressman Charles Francis Adams of Massachusetts, thought the southerners "demented," so confident of independence that they were already cultivating the good will of their future Yankee customers. Senator Stephen Douglas,

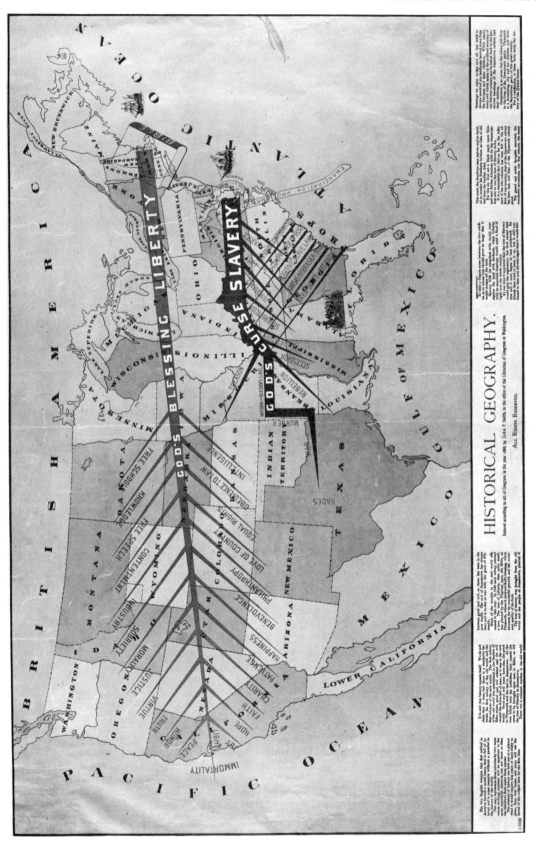

An old northern textbook map depicting the tree of Slavery (God's curse) branching out across the South and into Missouri; and the tree of Liberty (God's blessing) branching out across the rest of the nation. The traditional dividing line between North and South was the Mason-Dixon line, a 1769 survey of the Pennsylvania-Maryland border by Charles Mason and Jeremiah Dixon.

waiting for Congress to begin its session, talked darkly of the "slave power" conspiracy that had connived at defeating him for President and was now intent on breaking up the Union. Unionists charged that the conspirators could be found in President Buchanan's cabinet itself. Cabinet members Howell Cobb of Georgia, Jacob Thompson of Mississippi, and John B. Floyd of Virginia, they said, were providing the Confederacy with guns and ammunition from federal arsenals and threatening the weak-willed Buchanan that if he tried to move against the secessionists he would be either assassinated or impeached.

Indeed, from the Unionist view it looked at first as if the seventy-year-old James Buchanan had been terrified into inaction. The Democratic President had proclaimed secession illegal and declared the Union "perpetual." But he apparently doubted that the federal government had any constitutional authority to force the return of seceded states, and he feared that any attempt at coercion would make the situation worse. Buchanan attributed the whole trouble to fanatical abolitionists and to the menace the free-soil movement posed for the South. The President hoped for some new compromise that would still the issue of slavery as had the arrangements of 1820 and 1850.

Efforts at compromise were not wanting. The issue needing resolution was that of slavery in the territories. Early in 1861 the Washington Peace Convention, a gathering of statesmen under the chairmanship of former President John Tyler, looked for a solution. Congress also debated. A plan pressed by Senator John J. Crittenden of Kentucky would extend the Missouri Compromise line to the Pacific and add a constitutional amendment protecting slavery wherever it existed. But the extremists dominating politics in the cotton states would probably have turned down the plan, and it is doubtful that the Republican Party would have abandoned its principle of opposing an unrestricted right to slavery in the territories.

While attempts at compromise were unsuccessful, neither secession nor war appeared certain. Republican and Democratic upholders of the sovereignty of the United States perceived secession as an impulsive and irrational act that the South could decide to reverse. War, or at any rate a prolonged one, must have been almost unthinkable. While Unionists argued with assurance that secession was unconstitutional, it was not clear that the federal government had the constitutional right to prevent it by force. Nor could supporters of the Union have any confidence that the northern people would summon the will to march against the seceded states. For President-elect Lincoln and prospective members of his cabinet, the problem was to find a political solution to the crisis.

The Problem of the Forts

Lincoln in his inaugural address told the South that he would enforce the Fugitive Slave Law and support a constitutional amendment protecting slavery where it already existed. But he did not modify his position on free soil in the territories; and he condemned secession, pledging to "hold, occupy and possess" all Union property within the regions that had announced their secession.

By February 1861 federal forts, customs houses, and post offices throughout the lower South had fallen into the hands of the Confederate or state authorities. But two key posts held out, Fort Pickens at Pensacola, Florida, and Fort Sumter in Charleston harbor. For the secessionists to concede these to the United States meant accepting the intolerable presence of a foreign power in the new southern nation's domain. For the Union to surrender them would be acquiescence in southern independence. The situation of Fort Pickens was not acute, since Florida authorities had not challenged the presence there of federal troops. Fiery Charleston was a different story.

As the citizens of the southern port went about their business, they were aware of the drama at their doorsteps. Across the harbor they could see the Stars and Stripes flying defiantly over Sumter, while on Morris Island and at the city's main fortifications uniformed men loyal to the new Confederacy rushed here and there moving big guns, ammunition, and powder.

For weeks South Carolina officials had been negotiating with both the Washington authorities and Major Robert Anderson, the garrison commander, for evacuation of the fort. Anderson had holed up at Sumter when he concluded that his small force was inadequate to occupy all three federal strong points in the harbor, but from that grim, gray bastion he refused to depart. Soon after the new year Buchanan, his resolve stiffened by four new Unionist cabinet members, dispatched the *Star of the West,* an unarmed steamer, to reinforce Anderson with men and supplies. The Charleston authorities ordered their guns to fire at the vessel. Anderson came within an eyelash of returning the fire to protect the ship, but before he did, it turned back.

Upon his inauguration in March 1861, Lincoln had to confront the problem of Sumter. He sought advice from his cabinet members and other statesmen. William Seward of New York, his secretary of state, startled him with the suggestion that the administration bring the country together by getting into a war with Europe. On April 4, 1861, the President announced that he was sending a squadron for the relief of Fort Sumter. The ships would carry only food. If the secessionists allowed them through, the federal government would make no attempt to send men or ammunitions to Anderson.

News of Lincoln's intentions infuriated the Confederate authorities in Montgomery, who believed that the Republican President had assured them he would evacuate Sumter. Convinced that they could not avoid a clash without seeming to be weak, they reluctantly ordered an attack on Sumter before the promised reinforcement could arrive.

Charleston rejoiced. Happiest of all, perhaps, was the venerable Edmund Ruffin, a leading writer on southern agronomy. Now a silver-haired man of sixty-seven, Ruffin had been among the staunchest defenders of southern rights, long advocating secession. When his own state of Virginia proved slow to take up the northern challenge he came to fire-eating Charleston and, despite his age, joined the South Carolina infantry. When the order to attack Sumter was given early on the morning of April 12, the elderly gentleman was positioned at the great

A reconstruction by the lithography firm of Currier and Ives of the bombardment of Fort Sumter in Charleston Harbor, the attack that launched the Civil War. *(Courtesy, Hugh Cleland Collection)*

Columbiad cannon pointing at the federal fort. In reality his shot was preceded by a mortar barrage, but history has accorded him the symbolic honor of opening the war.

The bombardment lasted for a respectable several hours for the outnumbered Union force. Anderson, his food and gunpowder low, finally sent word that he was ready to surrender. The next day the flag of the Union was lowered and the Palmetto banner of South Carolina raised. No soldier was killed or seriously injured. But by seceding and then firing the first shot, the Confederacy brought together in defense of the Union a North that surely would not have chosen to fight the South on the question of slavery alone.

War Strategies

Immigrants or citizens in the Union army celebrated their experiences in their native languages:

Viva Grant! Viva Grant! ciudadanos,
que cinco años la guerra sostuvo,
y un ejército enorme mantuvo
en defensa de la libertad.

  Y después de sangrientos combates,
do murieron valientes soldados;
fueron libres aquellos estados
que jamás pretendían la igualdad.
Dios te salve, caudillo del Norte!
Yo saludo tu sacra bandera,
que en el mundo flamea por doquiera,
ofreciendo la paz y la unión.

  También México ensalza tu nombre
porque fuiste con el indulgente,
fuiste siempre y serás el valiente
que defiende la Constitución.

Ich in Gettysburg mit schlug,
Half erringen jenen Sieg,
Und die Kosten auch mit trug,
Wenn ich auch keinen Nickel krieg.
Hancock führte an, du sagst,
Im Gefecht ein grosser Mann,
Ob ich für ihn stimm', du fragst?
Nein, o nein, das geht nicht an.
Damals trug er Union Blau,
Jetzt liebt er Rebellen Grau.

Northern Strategy

The attack on the fort began the Civil War. In the absence of Congress, which was not yet in session, President Lincoln issued a proclamation requesting 75,000 volunteers for putting down "combinations too powerful to be suppressed by the ordinary course of judicial proceedings." When Congress assembled, it gave its support to this proclamation along with other actions that Lincoln had taken in the military emergency.

Lincoln's call for troops confronted the upper South states with an unwelcome choice: either fight against the South or fight against the Union. Virginia, North Carolina. Tennessee, and Arkansas joined the Confederacy. Four slave states remained in the Union: Delaware, Maryland, Kentucky, and Missouri. Of these, only Delaware did so peaceably. In the other three states opinion was divided. President Lincoln used force to aid the Union cause in strategic Maryland. When a mob favoring the South attacked federal soldiers in Baltimore and cut the rail line between that city and Washington, he sent troops to subdue the disorder and arrest potential secessionists. Kentucky, birthplace of both Lincoln and Jefferson Davis, declared its neutrality, but within months both Union and Confederate troops had entered the state. Kentucky and Missouri were torn by guerrilla warfare, as supporters of both sides fought for control of the state governments. Although the Confederacy claimed these two states, both remained in the Union. In 1863, the federal government arranged to make into a separate state West Virginia, the northwestern region of Virginia where slaves were few and Unionist sentiment was strong.

For the North, the basic strategy was clear: use its advantage of vast material and human resources to subdue the South. Its population in 1860 numbered over twenty million, while the South had barely nine million, forty percent of whom were slaves. Nine-tenths of the country's manufacturing capacity was situated in the North, which also had two-thirds of the railroad mileage. Most of the nation's merchant shipping and financial resources were in northern hands.

General Winfield Scott, one of several southerners who was a high-ranking Union officer during the Civil War, was the first commander of the federal forces under Lincoln, who as President was Commander-in-Chief. At the war's beginning the ailing Scott in his short remaining tenure in office mapped out the basic northern strategy. He proposed blockading southern ports, dividing the Confederacy by an occupation of the Mississippi River, and sending in armies of invasion that would break the southern nation into bits. Northerners expected a short war, but once the reality of a long war sank in, they closely followed Scott's strategy, soon named after the anaconda, the snake that squeezes its prey. The anaconda policy was ultimately to conquer the Confederacy.

Southern Strategy The Confederacy's crucial disadvantage was economic, though it also suffered from a deep moral isolation in a world that increasingly repudiated slavery as a loathsome and retrograde remnant of a benighted past. Having few mills, factories, and foundries, the South began the war with little more than a stockpile of captured or imported equipment. In spite of heroic efforts toward industrial self-sufficiency, the South could never replace equipment as rapidly as it wore out. Since the naval coils of the northern anaconda were meanwhile stifling southern commerce with the outside world, the Confederacy had no way of supplying itself with the means of waging a multi-sided, fully aggressive conflict.

Yet the South at the beginning of the war was not in a weak position. For while the Confederacy could not win a head-on conflict with the North, it did not have to do so. Against the North's enormous task of conquering a vast territory, the rebels needed to do no more than demonstrate to the northern people and to Europe, by one military strategy or another, that the old Union was no longer a single, workable nation.

On at least one count, the South made a major mistake. It invested a naive faith in the power of "King Cotton." Convinced that British industry could not long do without southern cotton, the new Confederate government in 1861 forbade all exports of this, the South's only major source of foreign credit. Starving British textile makers, Richmond thought, would force Britain to intervene in the Confederacy's behalf. But British manufacturers, expecting war in America, had stockpiled cotton. By the time the South realized its error, the northern blockade had closed tight. For the rest of the war the South's "white gold" rotted

Resources of the Union and the Confederacy, 1861		
	Union	*Confederacy*
Population	23,000,000	8,700,000*
Real and personal property	$11,000,000,000	$5,370,000,000
Banking capital	$330,000,000	$27,000,000
Capital investment	$850,000,000	$95,000,000
Manufacturing establishments	110,000	18,000
Value of production (annual)	$1,500,000,000	$155,000,000
Industrial workers	1,300,000	110,000
Railroad mileage	22,000	9,000
		*40 percent were slaves (3,500,000)

on the wharves while southerners lacked military supplies and civilian goods.

Wartime Legislation   In 1861, just before Lincoln's inauguration, Congress passed the Morrill Tariff, a protectionist measure putting duties to the levels they had been at in 1846; and later the national legislature raised duties even higher. The war put a strain on the system of banking and currency. In response, Congress reformed the system in a way that agreed with the Republican concept of strong government in the service of a national economy. The National Banking Acts of 1863 and 1864 provided that, in return for investing one-third of their capital in federal banks, private banks could issue national bank notes that would serve as paper money: these could be in amounts up to ninety percent of the market value of the securities the banks had purchased from the government. The notes of state banks, which had circulated as a form of money, were unstable and injured the economy. In order to suppress them, Congress later placed a ten percent tax on the notes of all institutions that did not take part in the national bank system.

The Republican idea of supplying federal lands for settlers triumphed in the Homestead Act of 1862. A settler who filed a claim to a quarter-section of one hundred and sixty acres of federal land and lived on it for five years would get ownership of it after payment of a small fee. The act permitted single women as well as men to file a claim. In practice, women alone, or even women with children, had great difficulty in sustaining their claims. Men needed the assistance of a woman as much as women needed the assistance of a man, but when men and women settled together in a family unit, the man invariably held title to the claim and officially directed its operation. Nor did the law permit married couples to file claims. Later in the century considerable amounts of the land went to timber and mining companies that had employees put in claims for homesteads. But at the time of the adoption of the act, there was some expectation that it would pull labor from the East to the free lands. And because of the labor shortage that the war was bringing about, Congress authorized immigration of contract workers from Europe and the Orient, permitting employers who paid the laborers' passage to deduct that cost from the pay.

In another use of federal lands, the Morrill Land Grant Act of 1862 offered lands to states that in return would finance colleges offering schooling in agriculture, engineering, and military science. It was a less dramatic measure than others of these wartime years, but significant in making the national government a partner to modern technical education.

The absence of legislators from the deep South made it easier for Congress during the war to adopt a scheme for a transcontinental railway running through the middle of the country, from Omaha to California. Southerners would have fought for a more southerly road. During the 1860s the national legislature granted to railroad developers thirty million acres of federal land and made them millions in loans to see the project through. It was one of the first of many extensive projects in which the government has joined with business.

***Harper's Weekly* published this drawing of a "long" Lincoln, by which it meant length in character and ability.** *(Courtesy, Library of Congress)*

Civil Liberties   In the extraordinary danger that the nation faced at the time of the war, free civil institutions continued in the North and for the most part in the border states. Lincoln's government did not attempt in any major and consistent way to put those institutions aside. But it was conscious that disruption or demoralization among the people in the regions loyal to the Union could upset the entire conduct of the war.

Lincoln suspended the writ of *habeas corpus*—the power of a court to have a prisoner brought before it—in cases in which individuals were suspected of disrupting the war effort. The suspension meant that the federal government could hold people for long periods without trial. Despite protests, Lincoln in the autumn of 1862 issued a proclamation subjecting to martial law and to trial in military tribunals anyone who discouraged others from enlisting or committed any disloyal act. The War Department in the course of the conflict arrested at least thirteen thousand people, most of whom never came to trial.

The chief northern political opponents of the conduct of the war were the Peace Democrats, or Copperheads, as supporters of the war called them. The most prominent among those was Clement Vallandigham of Ohio, who insisted that the war was strengthening the central government at the expense of civil liberties. Vallandigham called for "the Constitution as it is, the Union as it was." In 1862 he was defeated for reelection to Congress. He continued his attacks on the war and a military tribunal finally sentenced him to prison for its duration. The affair was an assault on the constitutional right of free speech. Protest was so widespread as to become a political danger to the administration. To deflect the issue, Lincoln by use of his executive power banished Vallandigham to the Confederacy. But the Ohioan returned to the North and kept up his criticisms. The administration now left him alone. Vallandigham tried to get the Supreme Court to consider his claim that the government had been acting unconstitutionally. The Court in 1864 ruled in *ex parte Vallandigham* that it had no jurisdiction over the proceedings of military tribunals. In 1866, however, the Supreme Court did find the methods of the war administration to have been unconstitutional. In *ex parte Milligan* the Court held that martial law and the subjection of civilians to military trials were illegal when the civil courts were open and in full operation.

Stalemate: The Early Campaigns, 1861–1862

The American Civil War, like other wars, was shaped as much by geography as by generals. The removal of the Confederate capital from Montgomery to Richmond, only one hundred miles from Washington, focused the fighting in the East in a narrow theater between and around the capitals. Here rival armies marched and countermarched for four years, as each side sought to protect its capital and threaten that of its rival. The dramatic battles fought here—such as at Chancellorsville and, just north of Maryland, at Gettysburg—constitute the classic war so celebrated in Civil War legend.

Robert E. Lee, native son of Virginia, brilliant military strategist, and leader of the Confederate forces. *(Courtesy, Library of Congress)*

Robert E. Lee wrote of the Confederate Congress:

"been up to see the Congress and they do not seem to be able to do anything except to eat peanuts and chew tobacco, while my army is starving."

Robert E. Lee, who led the Confederacy's northern Virginia troops and would become the South's most prominent general, had been no enthusiast for secession. Family tradition opposed it: his father, "Lighthorse Harry" Lee, had been a Revolutionary War hero, and his mother's family had also played an honorable role in the founding of the United States. His wife was the great granddaughter of Martha Washington, and Lee had grown up in Alexandria, Virginia, surrounded by mementos of George Washington, upon whom he modeled himself. Educated at West Point, Lee before the Civil War spent all his adult life in the United States Army, distinguishing himself in the Mexican War, serving as the superintendent of West Point, and achieving some eminence as an army engineer. When secession came, the Lincoln Administration sounded him out about taking command of the Union army. Lee saw no choice but to resign his commission rather than to face the prospect of leading troops against his native state. In the end he was a Virginian first. When after 1865 the Confederacy was no more, he could find it relatively easy to resume his loyalty to the Union and to urge other southerners to follow his lead.

While the two warring governments were preoccupied with the territory between their capitals, the decisive theater of the Civil War was in the West. Here nature had formed a series of southerly-flowing rivers—the Cumberland, the Tennessee, the Mississippi—that thrust into the heart of the Confederacy. Union strategists recognized early the value of these rivers for rapid movement of men and supplies, and acted to control them. It was here, and in Sherman's later invasion of the deep South from the West, that the North won and the South lost the Civil War.

In April 1861 both governments were unprepared for war. Guns and ammunition were in short supply. Few officers on either side had commanded large bodies of men. The hastily-formed volunteer regiments lacked even the rudiments of military training. Some such units wore gaudy, impractical uniforms and adopted flamboyant names.

These amateur armies had their first taste of war in July 1861. Pressured by a public demand to take Richmond at once, Union General Irvin McDowell led his ill-trained army into northern Virginia, followed by carriages full of Washingtonians out to see the show. At Bull Run (or Manassas Junction), the Union troops met an equally ill-prepared army under General P.G.T. Beauregard. For some time the two armies fought with a courage beyond their experience. After early reverses, Confederate troops rallied behind General Thomas Jackson—"Stonewall," as he would soon be known for a moment at Bull Run when he and his troops stood against an enemy attack "like a stone wall." Retreat became chaos as green troops struggled with panic-stricken civilians along the roads to Washington. McDowell's army simply fell apart; soldiers threw down their guns, canteens, and coats, and ran. "One Southerner is equal to five Yankees," pronounced a southern newspaper. But the Confederate soldiers, nearly as disorganized, did not pursue; Jackson boasted that with 5,000 men he could have finished the job.

Bull Run awakened the North to reality. Lincoln gave the command to General George B. McClellan, a cautious soldier but brilliant

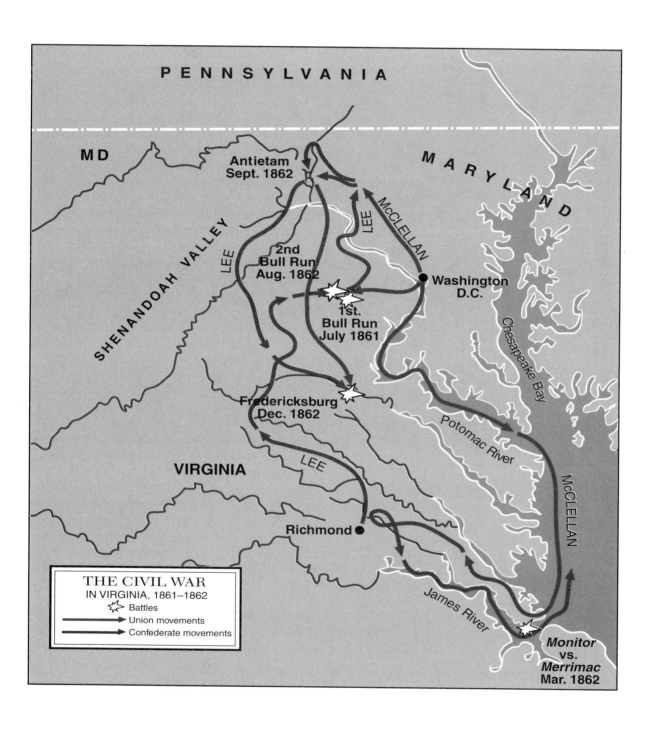

PENNSYLVANIA

MD

MARYLAND

Antietam
Sept. 1862

LEE

McCLELLAN

SHENANDOAH VALLEY

LEE

2nd
Bull Run
Aug. 1862

Washington
D.C.

1st.
Bull Run
July 1861

Chesapeake Bay

Fredericksburg
Dec. 1862

Potomac River

VIRGINIA

LEE

McCLELLAN

Richmond

James River

THE CIVIL WAR
IN VIRGINIA, 1861–1862

☆ Battles
→ Union movements
→ Confederate movements

Monitor
vs.
Merrimac
Mar. 1862

organizer. As McClellan trained his troops in the East, critical events were taking place in the West. Union attention here focused on the rivers, where Confederate strong points barred an advance southward.

Western Campaigns

In February 1862 an army under General Ulysses S. Grant, supported by a fleet of iron-clad gunboats, pushed up the Tennessee River and captured Fort Henry. Union forces also besieged Fort Donelson on the Cumberland. Grant took this fort, too, firing the North's imagination with his demand for "immediate and unconditional surrender."

Confederate troops struck back hard at Grant's army in April at Shiloh, on the Tennessee River near the northern border of Mississippi. Catching Grant off guard, they nearly pushed his troops back into the river. All day long the battle raged. "From right to left, everywhere," an Illinois soldier wrote, "it was one never ending, terrible roar, with no prospect of stopping." Grant's second in command, General William Tecumseh Sherman, was wounded twice, once in his hand and once in his shoulder, and a ball of shot passed through his hat; he also had several horses shot from under him during the day. At nightfall Union reinforcements turned the battle. Shiloh cost nearly 23,000 casualties.

At Shiloh the Confederacy lost its supreme bid to regain western

A New York soldier stationed in Louisiana wrote of the insensitivity the carnage had wrought:

"What hardened wretches we have become. The word came, 'Eph. Hammond is dead, hurry up and make a box for him.' He was one of the best-liked men in the regiment. Yet not a tear was shed, and before his body was cold he was buried in the ground. We will talk about him more or less for a day or two and then forget all about him. That is what less than a year has done to us."

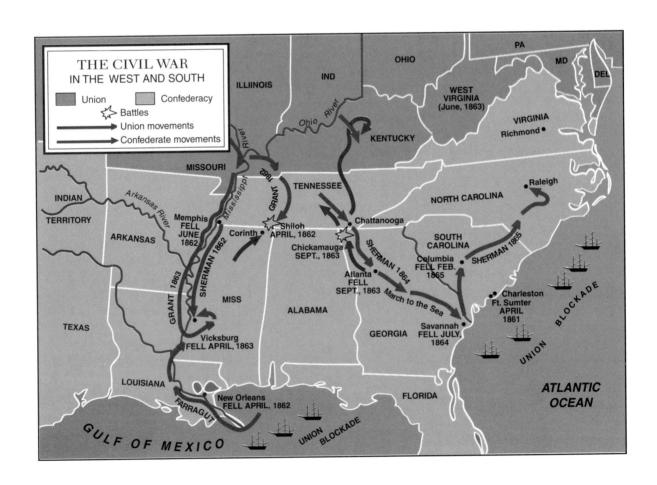

Tennessee. Other Union forces opened the upper Mississippi as far south as Memphis. That same April of 1862 the Confederacy suffered one of its greatest losses when Admiral David Farragut of Tennessee, one of the distinguished southerners who had remained with the Union, captured New Orleans, the South's biggest seaport. By midsummer the South's hold on the Mississippi was limited to a narrow stretch of river between Vicksburg, Mississippi, and Port Hudson, Louisiana.

Diplomacy and the Blockade   Late in 1861, the Union got for a moment into a dangerously confrontational situation with Britain. A federal ship stopped the British steamer *Trent* outside United States waters and seized two southern diplomats, James Mason, who was seeking to represent the Confederacy in Britain, and John Slidell, aiming to do the same in France. Anger flared in the British government and public. Lincoln quickly made amends of a sort by releasing the two. But the incident indicated the delicacy and the riskiness of relations between the United States and European countries as it patrolled the waters in pursuit of victory.

A particular point of risk was the blockade. While the North was pressing in on the Confederacy in the West, it was also pushing in from the sea. The blockade aimed at stopping foreign merchant ships and confiscating even nonmilitary goods that they were carrying to the Confederacy. Such seizures were questionable under international law, and France and Britain complained.

For a time the Union had to face the possibility that Great Britain or France, not displeased at a weakening of the United States and eager to resume full trade with the cotton South, might recognize the Confederacy as a separate nation. British recognition would give a tremendous lift to southern morale and injure that of the North, France might recognize the Confederacy in return for southern support of Napoleon III's plan to install a French puppet, Austrian Archduke Maximilian, on a specially created Mexican throne. But when federal troops in September 1862 stopped the rebel invasion at the Battle of Antietam (or Sharpsburg, as southerners called it), Great Britain decided to put off recognition of the Confederacy. The blockade remained safe from direct foreign interference.

The small Confederate navy was no match for the formidable Union fleet. For one day in 1862 in a battle off Hampton Roads, Virginia, however, the Confederate vessel *Merrimac* did much damage to Union naval forces. In a great technological innovation, the ship had been covered with iron plates, and against them northern naval guns had little effect. The next day the North set its own ironclad *Monitor* against the *Merrimac,* rendering it harmless. Later in the war northern commerce suffered from the raids of the Confederate ship *Alabama,* built in Britain by a private company. Charles Francis Adams, the United States minister to Britain, protested to the British government for its failure to stop the construction of the ship, and after the war the United States would win compensation from Britain for losses the ship had inflicted. The Union navy finally sank the *Alabama.*

Merrimac **and** *Monitor.* (*Courtesy, R. Burnes*)

The port of Norfolk, Virginia, a southerner confided to his diary on May 20,

"has been evacuated by the Confederate troops and the Merrimack has been destroyed. There ends for the present all hope of a southern navy. The loss of Norfolk involves that of the Navy yard at Portsmouth with its dry dock and ship building facilities. Yet, I believe, the destruction of the Merrimack produced a deeper mortification in the South than all the other losses that attended it. There had been among the people the most exaggerated expectations."

Confederate privateers could attack merchant ships, but were no threat to the northern navy. While the blockade could not keep the Confederacy from the sea trade, it was effective enough to deprive Confederate society of much that it needed to function smoothly.

Eastern Campaigns   In the East, General McClellan in 1862 drilled his Army of the Potomac for months, all the while ignoring the public clamor for action. (An exasperated Lincoln once said he would like to borrow McClellan's army if the general did not intend to use it.) Prodded by the President, McClellan finally proposed in the spring of 1862 a bold plan to take Richmond from the rear. Instead of fighting his way overland, he would make an amphibious landing on the James River Peninsula; from there he could march up the Peninsula and seize the Confederate capital. Lincoln approved, provided McClellan left enough men behind to protect Washington.

When McClellan embarked in March 1862, he did not leave behind the force intended for the defense of the capital. Lincoln thereupon recalled part of the Army of the Potomac. This nearly immobilized the cautious McClellan, who consistently overestimated Confederate strength: he in fact still had 90,000 men to the enemy's 70,000. The slowness of his progress up the Peninsula gave the Confederate troops, commanded by Lee, time to organize. In a series of battles known as the Seven Days, Lee hammered at McClellan's army and threw it back. In August McClellan began a slow withdrawal from the Peninsula. Command of the Army of the Potomac passed to General John Pope.

Sensing an opportunity to strike before the federal army could regroup, Lee took the offensive. On August 30 he smashed Pope's army at the second battle of Bull Run, then swung north into Maryland. But a copy of his battle plans fell into the hands of McClellan, whom Lincoln had hurriedly recalled to command. On September 17, McClellan engaged the invading Confederate troops at Antietam Creek. After the bloodiest single day's battle of the entire war—24,000 dead and wounded—Lee withdrew unpursued. Tactically the battle had been a draw, but measured against Confederate expectations it was a crushing defeat.

Although Lee had failed at Antietam, he was still unbeatable on his home ground. Twice during the winter of 1862–63, federal generals renewed the offensive against Richmond, each time with disastrous results. In December General Ambrose Burnside, a handsome West Pointer remembered for his legendary growth of side whiskers, and now in command in place of McClellan, was soundly defeated at Fredericksburg. At Chancellorsville in the spring of 1863, Lee and Jackson caught the army of Burnside's successor, General Joseph Hooker, straddling the Rappahannock River, and cut it to pieces. Lee paid a fearful price—"Stonewall" Jackson was mortally wounded, shot down by his own men in the confusion of battle as they waged hopeless frontal assaults against entrenched Union forces. After two years the northern drive on Richmond was back where it had started—on the Potomac.

The northern nurse Clara Barton evoked the sorrow and scope of battle:

"Antietam! With its eight miles of camping armies, face to face; 160,000 men to spring up at dawn like the old Scot from the heather! Its miles of artillery shaking the earth like a chain of Etnas! Its ten hours of uninterrupted battle! Its thunder and its fire! The sharp unflinching order—'Hold the Bridge, boys—always the Bridge.' At length, the quiet! The pale moonlight on its cooling guns! The weary men—the dying and the dead!"

War Fortunes Turn, 1863–1864

The victory at Antietam provided Lincoln with the political momentum he needed to move ahead with legally liberating the slaves in the rebellious states of the Confederacy. The President was looking to the election of 1864, and he was worried about his prospects. One group of Republicans, coming to be known as Radical Republicans, from whom Lincoln needed at least some support if he was to be renominated, was pushing hard for emancipation. He was also sincerely if cautiously committed to the principle of freeing the slaves. But if he liberated them in too bold a manner, he might lose valuable support in the slaveholding states still loyal to the Union. Lincoln would have to strike a fine balance.

Northern soldiers. *(Courtesy, Library of Congrss)*

Emancipation   At the beginning of the war the federal government was careful to insist that it was fighting only to preserve the Union and not to free the slaves. The war, said a resolution adopted by Congress, was not for "overthrowing or interfering with the rights or established institutions" of the seceded states. The government wanted to convince those proslavery southerners who were prepared to be sympathetic to the Unionist cause that the institution of slavery was not in danger. But it is reasonable to suppose that something beyond mere political strategy lay behind the caution of the President and Congress about interfering with slavery. Neither Lincoln nor most of the national legislators had been abolitionists. However distasteful slavery was to much of the government, the slave system was so firmly established, and so hedged with legal protections, that even opponents might have had doubts about the sudden military abolition of slavery. Politicians and statesmen, like the rest of humankind, are hesitant to imagine any workable society that is far different from whatever one they are accustomed to. It took time and the events of the war to make the government see the tangible possibility of wiping out slavery at a stroke.

Confederates soldiers. *(Courtesy, Library of Congrss)*

General John C. Frémont jumped ahead of the government when he issued a military order freeing the slaves in Missouri. Lincoln modified Frémont's order, but he did ask Congress in 1862 to grant federal funds to any state adopting a scheme of emancipation. Congress did not respond, but in the Second Confiscation Act of 1862, authorizing the seizure of all rebel property, it declared that slaves who come into Union lines were to be free. It also empowered the President to recruit blacks into the army. The Act was both a substantial measure and a somewhat limited one. It did not apply to slaves held by southern Unionists. But the Second Confiscation Act signified that Union politicians were losing their timidity about abolishing slavery, and the very existence of the Act provided a certain momentum toward abolition. Abolitionists meanwhile were urging a wider policy of emancipation. Such a policy, moreover, could have desirable diplomatic effects. The apparent success of the South in maintaining its independence, and the advantage that European countries could gain from a division of the United States, raised the danger that they might recognize the Confederacy as a sovereign nation. That would greatly weaken the Union effort. Lincoln believed that if European nations could see the war as a struggle not merely between Union and secession but between freedom and slavery, they would be less likely to recognize the slave republic. And while Lincoln had not been an abolitionist, he had been a free soiler and a moral opponent of slavery. Surely his conscience welcomed the decision toward which political considerations were pushing him.

The Emancipation Proclamation   The Confederate failure at Antietam gave Lincoln the opportunity to issue in September 1862 a preliminary Emancipation Proclamation, announcing that as of January 1, 1863, all slaves in those regions still in rebellion on that date would be free. Lincoln was offering to secessionists an alternative to loss of their slaves: if they voluntarily brought their communities back into the Union quickly enough, they might maintain the institution. The Emancipation Proclamation itself, issued on January 1, carried out the terms of the preliminary proclamation: it declared that all slaves in areas still in rebellion were "then, thenceforward, and forever free." Lincoln was drawing on the power he possessed as Commander-in-Chief; the Proclamation was essentially a military order, on somewhat the same principle as the instructions an officer might give his troops for the treatment of citizens and property. The Emancipation Proclamation, like the Second Confiscation Act, was of sharply limited scope; it freed no slaves immediately because it did not apply to the border states or to regions already under Union control. But it was understood at the time, as it has been understood ever since, as the great symbolic moral action of the war, a public statement that the war was now being fought for freedom. After the preliminary Proclamation the military had begun seriously taking in black volunteers.

Congress contained a variety of opinions on racial matters. At one extreme were several Democrats reluctant to make changes in existing institutions. At the other extreme, as the war progressed, was a small but important group of Republicans who wanted the strongest possible policy of abolition and protection of the rights of the freed slaves. Within this faction ideas emerged for going beyond emancipation and bringing about changes in the social and economic condition of black Americans. Congress in the course of the war repealed a law prohibiting blacks from carrying the mail and a ban on testimony of black witnesses in federal court. It outlawed slavery in the territories, and established a scheme for emancipation in the District of Columbia that would provide compensation to the slaveholders. Blacks were allowed in places from which they had once been excluded: the congressional visitor's gallery, lectures at the Smithsonian Institution. Some states got rid of a number of discriminating laws. The country was taking some halting steps beyond emancipation and toward equality or at least a concept of justice. When Congress passed and in 1865 the necessary number of states approved the Thirteenth Amendment outlawing slavery, the nation was confirming the policy to which events had been leading it.

Vicksburg and Gettysburg   In the summer of 1863, Ulysses S. Grant won one of two battles that put the North on the way to final victory. For months his troops had besieged Vicksburg, the last Confederate stronghold on the Mississippi River. Situated high on a bluff above the river, with bayous

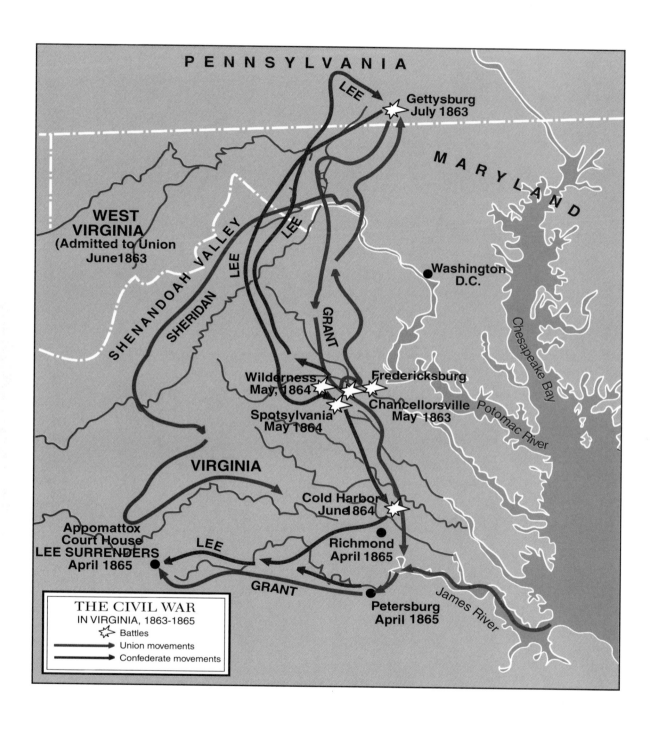

PENNSYLVANIA

LEE

★ Gettysburg
July 1863

MARYLAND

WEST
VIRGINIA
(Admitted to Union
June1863

LEE

LEE

SHENANDOAH VALLEY

SHERIDAN

GRANT

Washington
D.C.

Chesapeake Bay

Wilderness
May, 1864

Fredericksburg

Chancellorsville
May 1863

Spotsylvania
May 1864

Potomac River

VIRGINIA

Cold Harbor
June 1864

Appomattox
Court House
LEE SURRENDERS
April 1865

LEE

Richmond
April 1865

GRANT

Petersburg
April 1865

James River

THE CIVIL WAR
IN VIRGINIA, 1863-1865
★ Battles
→ Union movements
→ Confederate movements

A Civil War Gallery

Confederate prisoner James Washington and union officer George A. Custer. They had been West Point classmates. *(Courtesy, Library of Congress)*

Union soldiers at Manasses, Virginia, July 1862. *(Courtesy, Library of Congress)*

Union nurses in the Civil War. *(Courtesy, Library of Congress)*

A Civil War volunteer soldier. *(Courtesy, Library of Congress)*

Black cooks during the Civil War. *(Courtesy, Library of Congress)*

A cockfight in a southern camp, 1864. *(Courtesy, Library of Congress)*

Overturned Confederate train. Similar problems plagued Confederate transportation. *(Courtesy, Library of Congress)*

Dead soldiers after a battle. *(Courtesy, Library of Congress)*

Armory Square Hospital (Union). *(Courtesy, Library of Congress)*

Union quartermasters camp. 1st Division, 9th Army Corps. *(Courtesy, Library of Congress)*

A public hanging for treason in Washington, D.C. *(Courtesy, Library of Congress)*

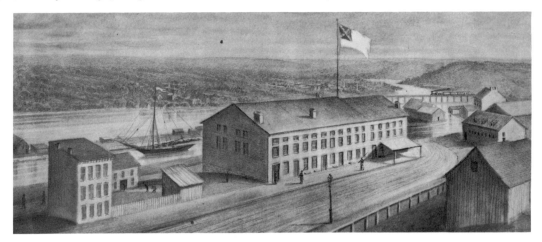

Libby Prison, Richmond, Virginia. *(Courtesy, Museum of Fine Arts, Boston)*

Trenches at Fredericksburg, Virginia. *(Courtesy, Library of Congress)*

Confederate camp, Warrington Navy Yard, Pensacola, Florida, 1861. *(Courtesy, Library of Congress)*

ABRAHAM LINCOLN

and his

Emancipation Proclamation

Whereas, On the Twenty-second day of September, in the year of our Lord one thousand eight hundred and sixty-two, a Proclamation was issued by the President of the United States, containing among other things the following, to-wit:

"That on the first day of January, in the year of our Lord one thousand eight hundred and sixty-three, all persons held as slaves within any State, or designated part of a State, the people whereof shall then be in rebellion against the United States, shall be then, thenceforward and forever free, and the executive government of the United States, including the military and naval authority thereof, will recognize and maintain the freedom of such persons, and will do no act or acts to repress such persons, or any of them, in any efforts they may make for their actual freedom.

"That the executive will, on the first day of January aforesaid, by proclamation, designate the States and parts of States, if any, in which the people thereof respectively shall then be in rebellion against the United States, and the fact that any State, or the people thereof, shall on that day be in good faith represented in the Congress of the United States by members chosen thereto at elections wherein a majority of the qualified voters of such State shall have participated, shall, in the absence of strong countervailing testimony, be deemed conclusive evidence that such State and the people thereof are not then in rebellion against the United States."

Now, therefore, I, ABRAHAM LINCOLN, President of the United States, by virtue of the power in me vested as Commander-in-Chief of the Army and Navy of the United States in time of actual armed rebellion against the authority and government of the United States, and as a fit and necessary war measure for suppressing said rebellion, do, on this first day of January, in the year of our Lord one thousand eight hundred and sixty-three, and in accordance with my purpose so to do, publicly proclaim for the full period of one hundred days from the day first above mentioned order, and designate as the States and parts of States wherein the people thereof respectively are this day in rebellion against the United States, the following, to-wit: ARKANSAS, TEXAS, LOUISIANA (except the parishes of St. Bernard, Plaquemines, Jefferson, St. John, St. Charles, St. James, Ascension, Assumption, Terre Bonne, Lafourche, St. Mary, St. Martin, and Orleans, including the city of New Orleans), MISSISSIPPI, ALABAMA, FLORIDA, GEORGIA, SOUTH CAROLINA, NORTH CAROLINA and VIRGINIA (except the forty-eight counties designated as West Virginia, and also the counties of Berkley, Accomac, Northampton, Elizabeth City, York, Princess Ann and Norfolk, including the cities of Norfolk and Portsmouth), and which excepted parts are, for the present, left precisely as if this Proclamation were not issued.

And by virtue of the power and for the purpose aforesaid, I do order and declare that all persons held as slaves within said designated States and parts of States are and henceforward shall be free; and that the executive government of the United States, including the military and naval authorities thereof, will recognize and maintain the freedom of said persons.

And I hereby enjoin upon the people so declared to be free, to abstain from all violence, unless in necessary self-defence, and I recommend to them that in all cases, when allowed, they labor faithfully for reasonable wages.

And I further declare and make known that such persons of suitable condition, will be received into the armed service of the United States to garrison forts, positions, stations and other places, and to man vessels of all sorts in said service.

And upon this act, sincerely believed to be an act of justice, warranted by the Constitution, upon military necessity, I invoke the considerate judgment of mankind, and the gracious favor of Almighty God.

In testimony whereof, I have hereunto set my name, and caused the seal of the United States to be affixed.

Done at the City of Washington, this first day of January, in the year of our Lord one thousand eight hundred and sixty-three, and of the Independence of the United States the eighty-Seventh.

By the President:

ABRAHAM LINCOLN.

WILLIAM H. SEWARD, Secretary of State.

NOTE.—The rest of the slaves were afterwards freed by Legislation and Constitutional Amendments.

Lee surrenders to Grant at Appomattox Court House in Virginia. *(Courtesy, Library of Congress)*

Drawing by J. A. Arthur of Washington welcoming Lincoln to Heaven with a crown of laurels, 1865.
(Courtesy, Library of Congress)

General Grant's victories come at a great expense in lives.

"He is a butcher and is not fit to be at the head of army, 'declared Mary Lincoln.' He loses two men to the enemy's one. . . . He would depopulate the North." "But he has been very successful in the Field," quietly observed the President.

"Where the line stood the ground was covered in blue," a Georgia soldier recalled, speaking of the corpses of Union soldiers at Gettysburg. "I could have walked on them without putting my feet on the ground."

General Ulysses S. Grant.
(Courtesy, Library of Congrss)

on both flanks, the city seemed impregnable. After repeated failures to dislodge the Confederate defenders, Grant hit on a bold plan. Abandoning his supply base, he slipped around the city on the Louisiana side, marched downstream, and crossed below Vicksburg. With dazzling speed, he moved inland to Jackson, cutting Vicksburg's rail link with the Confederacy, then turned west to lock up the city from the land side. Cut off, Vicksburg surrendered on July 4, 1863. Grant had reopened the Mississippi and split the Confederacy in two, leaving the trans-Mississippi region isolated.

In the East, just a day before Grant's victory at Vicksburg, the Union army at Gettysburg had won what was to become the most famous battle of the war. Gettysburg was the devastating outcome of a daring Confederate attempt begun in June, when Lee marched his army north again in search of a decisive victory.

The South needed one. It was in trouble in the West, and the Union blockade was withering the southern economy.

In the first stage of the campaign that was to end at Gettysburg, Lee's army moved quickly out of the Blue Ridge Mountains into Maryland. Hooker followed, keeping to the east in order to protect Washington. As Lee drove into Pennsylvania, Lincoln replaced the timid Hooker with George G. Meade. Respectful of General Meade's abilities, Lee concentrated his forces at Gettysburg. Rushing forward, Meade collided with him at that Pennsylvania town, and on July 1, 2, and 3 they fought the greatest single battle of the war.

Lee struck first, before Meade could concentrate his army, and on July 1 nearly drove the federal army from the field. During the night Union troops arrived in strength and dug in. On the next two days Lee attacked at both flanks and the center of the Union line in a total effort to crush the Army of the Potomac. But nothing quite worked. The climax came on July 3 when 15,000 Confederate troops under General George Pickett made a gallant frontal assault on the Union center on—appropriately—Cemetery Ridge. On Pickett's men came, "an ocean of armed men . . . magnificent, grim, irresistible," as Union gunners fired triple loads of iron shot into their ranks. A few Confederate soldiers reached

The blood-soaked battlefield at Gettysburg after the fighting of July 1, 1863. *(Courtesy, Scribner's Archives)*

the Ridge; then suddenly Union reinforcements poured into the breach. The surviving Confederate troops retreated, leaving many of their number dead. The battle was over. On July 4, while a rainstorm washed the blood from the grass, the Confederate army withdrew. Meade, as paralyzed as his predecessors, did not pursue. Lee had lost 20,000 men—a third of his army. The Confederacy's offensive power was broken forever.

Life in the Confederacy

During the rush of enthusiasm following Sumter many southerners rejoiced at the prospect of glory and independence. "I feel as tho' I could live poetry," exclaimed Mrs. Catherine Edmonston, mistress of a North Carolina plantation. But within the South's white population some wondered whether their section had not made a colossal mistake.

Even slaveholders had their doubts. One Mississippi planter anticipated the defeat of the Confederacy and feared a time "when the northern soldier would tread her cotton fields, when the slave should be made *free* and the proud southerner stricken to the dust in his presence." And in the mountain backbone that split the older from the newer South, Unionist sentiment smoldered. There slaveholding was not extensive. Virginia's western counties would carry their dissent so far as to secede from Secessia and form the state of West Virginia. In eastern Tennessee, western North Carolina, and Kentucky—that state never seceded anyway—thousands of young men joined the Union army. In region upon region where small farmers tilled their acres with the sole help of their families or a few hired hands, the Union found some degree of favor. In places like northern Louisiana, Alabama, and Mississippi, however, Unionist sentiment was more difficult to act on than in the mountains.

Economic Problems   After the early months of enthusiasm passed, life in the Confederacy was difficult for everybody. The southern economy was not suited for swift adaptation to war production. The rail network could not efficiently transport troops and supplies. Most southern railroads were short lines. The rail system consisted of eleven different gauges, which meant that a railroad car fitted for one gauge would have to confine itself to some portion of the tracks. Nor was there enough railway equipment. The South in 1861 did only a fifth of the whole nation's manufacturing, and it lacked the knowledge and technology necessary for quick growth. By the award of generous contracts, the Confederate and state governments gave their encouragement to industries such as textiles and iron, and by the end of the war Atlanta had become a considerable industrial center. But some manufacturers had to be satisfied with makeshifts, such as lard in place of grease and cloths soaked in linseed oil as a substitute for machine belts. The Confederacy had to import much of its arms and civilian goods, slipping a large portion of them through the Union blockade. To support itself the Confederate government turned to "tithing in kind," collecting from farmers one-tenth of their produce in certain crops, and

A southerner's diary entries, for 1861 and 1865, tell the course of war:

Saturday, July 13, 1861. Events transcending in importance anything that has ever happened within the recollection of any living person in *our* country, have occurred since I have written last in my Journal. Since then *War* has been declared. Our ministers sent North to negotiate terms of peace have been treated with cool indifference. Our forts are still retained with the exception of Sumter. *There* the ever memorable victory was achieved which added fresh laurels to the glory of the gallant little state of South Carolina. Never shall I forget the state of intense excitement which pervaded the city of Augusta when it was announced that the fight was going on down at Sumter. Pa went down to Charleston just in time to witness from the top of the Charleston Hotel, the whole proceeding of the bombardment. It is needless to account the gallant achievement of Wigfall and others or to note the additional honour acquired by Gen Beauregard. . . .

Wednesday, March 29, 1865. I know I will regret hereafter that I have made no record of time and events which are fraught with so much interest, record of events which are hourly making history—but I cannot. I shrink from the task. At times I feel as if I was drifting on, on, ever onward to be at last dashed against some rock and I shut my eyes and almost wish it was over, the shock encountered and I prepared to know what destiny awaits me. I am tired, oh so tired of this war. I want to breathe free. I feel the restraint of the blockade and as port after port becomes blockaded, I feel shut up, pent up and am irresistibly reminded of the old story of the iron shroud contracting more and more each hour, each moment. I live too fast. A strange contradiction, yet true. A life of emotion, quick rapid succession of startling events will wear upon the constitution and weaken the physical nature. I may perhaps be glad hereafter that I have lived through this war but now the height of my ambition is to be *quiet*. . . .

One southern woman, Margaret Preston, wrote in her diary:

April 3d, 1862: . . .

"Darkness seems gathering over the southern land; disaster follows disaster; where is it all to end? My very soul is sick of carnage. I loathe the word —*War.* It is destroying and paralyzing all before it. Our schools are closed—all the able-bodied men gone—stores shut up, or only here and there one open; goods not to be bought, or so exorbitant that we are obliged to do without.

Sept. 4th: The worst has happened— our fearful suspense is over: Willy, the gentle, tender-hearted, brave boy, lies in a soldier's grave on the Plains of Manassas! This has been a day of weeping and of woe to this household. I did not know how I loved the dear boy. My heart is wrung with grief to think that his sweet face, his genial smile, his sympathetic heart are gone. My eyes ache with weeping. . . . Oh! his precious stricken Father! God support him to bear the blow! . . . Alas! the beloved son has been five days in his grave. My poor husband! Oh! if he were only here, to groan out his anguish on my bosom. I can't write more."

printed great amounts of paper money that worsened inflation. Shortages, invasion, and a sense of defeat were the lot of the rebel population as the war dragged on.

The price of flour in Richmond more than doubled in the first year of the war. Soap, made from scarce animal fat, went up a thousand percent in price. Imported coffee, selling for twelve cents a pound before the war, went to five dollars by 1863. In late December of that year, apples went in Richmond for $65 or $75 a barrel in Confederate money, while onions were $30 a barrel, Irish potatoes, $6 to $9 a bushel, sugar, $3.50 a pound, and eggs, $3 a dozen. Worst of all to one young soldier stationed at the Confederate capital was the price of whiskey. "It would cost about fifty Dollars to get tight here," he wrote his family in 1863.

At times essential commodities were unavailable at any price. Shortages were more common in the cities, swollen with war refugees and soldiers, than in the countryside. In the spring of 1863, three hundred Richmond women, some brandishing revolvers and others bowie knives, attacked the city's business district demanding affordable food. The riot soon got out of hand and the women looted the jewelry and clothing stores before they were stopped. And even in the country districts food and clothing shortages provoked direct action. In 1863 fourteen women armed with "guns, pistols, knives, and tongues" attacked a mill near Thomasville, Georgia, and seized a large supply of flour.

Changes in the South   War transformed the lives of southern white women. Many were fiery Confederate patriots. It has been said that southern belles, by favoring army volunteers and shunning young men who avoided the war, were the most effective recruiters for the Confederate army. Southern women of the middle and upper classes had always managed large households. As the war progressed, their administrative skills were put to running the plantations and businesses their husbands had left behind. Wives of ordinary farmers, too, took over managerial duties. The Confederate Treasury hired hundreds of women clerks. Some women found jobs in the South's factories or worked in Confederate hospitals. The visible presence of these women in the public sphere faded after the war.

States' rights, the doctrine upon which the Confederacy had been founded, was no help in wartime. Several governors, notably Joseph E. Brown of Georgia and Zebulon Vance of North Carolina, showed a narrow jealousy of every exercise of Confederate power. They developed revenue programs of their own and obstructed Confederate tax collections in their states. They retained control of state troops and even prevented them from leaving the state. In Georgia, men who wished to escape Confederate service could do so by enlisting in the state militia. Governor Vance hoarded food and supplies for North Carolina troops that Lee's starving army at Richmond desperately needed.

Ultimately the Confederate government resorted to measures of centralization that amounted to a revolution within a revolution. Davis declared martial law in "disloyal" areas. The Confederate Congress authorized the first thorough military draft on the North American

Slaves planting sweet potatoes on James Hopkinson's plantation, Edisto Island, South Carolina, 1862. Though there were no major uprisings, the old slave system began to disintegrate by late 1863 as blacks refused to work for their old masters or simply left the plantations. *(Courtesy, The New-York Historical Society)*

continent. Richmond took an increasingly active role in the southern economy, impressing food supplies from farmers, building factories to produce critical war materials, commandeering space on blockade runners for essential imports. In 1865 the Confederate government reached the ultimate measure of centralization when it authorized the military to take black men into the army.

For many years after the Civil War southerners with a nostalgic affection for the Confederacy would speak of how loyal slaves had been to their southern masters. When southern white men were off fighting Yankees and blacks had a chance to revolt, they remained at their jobs, providing the Confederacy with its food and manufactured goods. This romantic image of contented and loyal slaves is only partly accurate. The experience of the Pryor family of Georgia furnishes an example. In 1861 Shepard G. Pryor went off to fight, leaving his wife in charge of his farm and his thirteen slaves. Mrs. Pryor chose as her overseer a white man who had no control over the slaves. Eventually she made a crucial decision to appoint one of her slaves, Will, as overseer. The choice was fateful for the Pryors' corner of the slave system. For a while Will performed as his mistress wished, and he successfully managed the 1862 crop harvest. But soon Will was hiding slave runaways and in general refusing to cooperate with the slave system. The authorities finally arrested him for sheltering slave fugitives. By late 1863 the slave system was disintegrating in many parts of the South. Nowhere was there a major slave uprising, but black people were helping to pull the system apart in other ways. Whenever rumors spread of Yankee troops nearby the slaves of the neighborhood would desert the plantations in droves. Many of those who remained became disobedient and refused to work. One elderly slave was overjoyed when freedom came. She "dropped her hoe" and shouted at her mistress: "I'm free! Ain't got to work for you no more! You can't [sell me] now!"

Life in the Union

Initially the northern economy faltered as businessmen, fearful of disruption and disorder, sought to call in debts. In many northern cities, especially New York, Chicago, and Cincinnati, the loss of southern customers disrupted the economy. Some economic historians claim that on the whole the Civil War slowed economic growth. Yet the newspapers of the day suggest that, after the middle of 1862, the Union experienced an economic boom. The draining of men into the military left shortages of labor. On some farms women filled in. The North, however, had more machines than the South that could replace manpower; from 1860 to 1865 the McCormick Reaper Company received more orders for its harvesting machines than it could fill. The continuing influx of immigrants, almost half a million during the war years, relieved labor shortages in the cities. The demand for war supplies invigorated the northern economy, already fitted for manufacturing. Factories hummed and wages rose. Farmers benefited from the increase in demand for food. The effect of the war on the economy of the North was quite the opposite from the effect in the South, where invasion unsettled the normal pattern of production and trade and the blockade broke commerce with Europe.

Still, the Union had an inflation rate only slightly less staggering than that of the Confederacy. One reason for that was the policy of financing the war by a combination of heavy borrowing and paper money. Another was the scarcity of labor that machines and immigrants only partially offset. And the wartime prosperity bestowed itself unevenly. While consumer prices had risen by 1865 between seventy-five and a hundred percent, the wages of skilled workers went up during the same period about sixty percent, and those of common laborers rose just under fifty percent. Meanwhile the business and professional classes crowded Broadway in New York, Michigan Avenue in Chicago and Pennsylvania Avenue in Cincinnati, buying at the fashionable shops, attending the theaters, and dining at the fancy restaurants. Some of these people were profiteers who had made a good thing out of the swelling orders from the War and Navy Departments and the flow of greenback currency. Charging the government high prices for desperately needed supplies, some profiteers also provided uniforms and shoes that disintegrated at the first heavy rain, powder that would not explode, and beef, pork, and flour that were inedible.

Army Life

The Civil War sorely tested the American traditions of individualism and provincialism. In the beginning men on both sides enlisted in local regiments raised by the state governors. Each regiment wore its own uniform and many elected their own officers, a practice that discouraged strict discipline. Gradually all this changed. The Union and Confederate governments took over many duties of recruitment and the appointment of officers. Standardized uniforms were introduced. Drill and discipline tightened. The sons of a rawboned democracy slowly adjusted to become cogs in a larger machine. At the same time they accustomed themselves to a world beyond their own communities. Their care and feeding became increasingly the responsibility of central governments or national organizations like the United States Sanitary Commission.

Along with the Union victory, the experience of army life must have contributed to the nationalist element in American civilization that has struggled to maintain itself against the pull of loyalty to region, state, or locality.

At the same time that the armies were taking American farmboys and town dwellers away from their familiar surroundings, they were pulling in thousands of immigrants. The Union army especially spoke with many tongues, and in that sense represented what American cities were and would increasingly become in the years after the victory of the Union.

In the Field   Of about two million federal troops, 360,000 died. Among the more than one million who at some time served in the Confederate military, some 250,000 never came back. Only one in three of these died of battle wounds; the others succumbed to disease or accident. There were also about a half million wounded, many of them severely maimed.

During the Civil War, infantry weapons became highly destructive while infantry tactics continued to follow older concepts. Many soldiers carried rifles rather than smooth-bore muskets. These hurled a bullet for hundreds of yards with deadly accuracy. Yet until the very end of the war commanders on both sides frequently ordered their men to charge the enemy across open fields as if only the older, less accurate musket opposed them. Toward the end of the war attackers had to face the fast-firing breech-loaders with which more and more soldiers were being equipped.

If a man was wounded his chance for survival was precarious. Little was known about infections, and military surgeons performed operations without sanitary precautions. Soldiers contracted gangrene and other deadly infections. Though anesthetics were known, doctors did not always have them on hand, and shock, followed by death, was often the consequence of major surgery. Long delays occurred in getting the casualties to medical aid stations or hospitals.

Pests such as mosquitoes, lice, and biting flies infested the battlefront, spreading diseases that included malaria and yellow fever. Heat in the deep South and cold, particularly in the mountain areas and the upper South, afflicted the soldiers. Wool uniforms were standard year-round issue and soldiers of both armies simply shed as much as they could during the summer. Northern troops were often overdressed; rebels were often half naked. As the Union blockade took hold and internal transport broke down, Confederate soldiers found it difficult to get replacements for worn or torn uniforms. Many ended up wearing homemade garments sent by relatives and friends. Others relied on captured Yankee shoes and other clothes. Especially serious was the shortage of boots and shoes. In the last winter of the war many of the troops accompanying General J. B. Hood on his campaign through Tennessee marched barefoot through snow and sleet. The path of Hood's army, it was said, was marked by a trail of blood.

Few Union soldiers went hungry, but the diet of salt pork, bread, and coffee undermined health. The Confederate soldier's standard diet consisted of bacon, cornmeal, and coffee—when he could get them.

One experience of northern troops was firsthand observation of slaves whom they had known only through newspaper accounts and antislavery literature. One northerner wrote in his diary:

"Some of them were scarred from head to foot where they had been whipped. One man's back was nearly all one scar, as if the skin had been chopped up and left to heal in ridges. Another had scars on the back of his neck, and from that all the way to his heels every little ways; but that was not such a sight as the one with the great solid mass of ridges, from his shoulders to his hips. That beat all the antislavery sermons ever yet preached."

Following the battle of Seven Pines in mid-1862, wounded federal soldiers were carried to the rear for shipment to the hospitals around Washington. The trains were slow to arrive, a sensitive observer noted, and the men sometimes

"lay by the hundreds on either side of the railway track . . . exposed to the drenching rain . . . shivering from the cold, calling for water, food, and dressings . . . the most heart-rending spectacle. Many died from exposure, others prayed for death to release them from their anguish."

Soldiers soon lost their sense of the romance of war. A North Carolina volunteer wrote home in 1862:

"The dirt of a camp life knocks all its poetry into a cocked hat. . . . We had no tents after the 6th of August, but slept on the ground, in the woods or open fields, without regard to the weather. . . . I learned to eat fat bacon raw, and to like it. . . . Without time to wash our clothes or our persons, and sleeping on the ground all huddled together, the whole army became lousy more or less with body lice."

Coffee, an imported item that had to get through the Union blockade, went quickly; the bacon lasted longer, but it, too, was often in short supply and southern troops occasionally supplemented their meat rations with cuts of mule, horse, raccoon, and bear. Sometimes Confederate troops were reduced to consuming little more than parched corn. Chewing the grains, reported one southern soldier, was "hard work"; it made "the jaws ache and the gums so sore as to cause unendurable pain."

War Mobilization   During the Civil War, as during the Revolution, both sides required the mobilization of society as a whole in the service of the war effort. But the Civil War reflected social and economic changes that would also influence the nature of the civilian contribution. The nursing of soldiers acquired a far more organized and professional character. Under the auspices of the United States Sanitary Commission, Dorothea Dix organized nursing services for the Union side. In the early months of the war, Ladies Aid Societies sprang up throughout the North to provide volunteer services for soldiers, including sewing, assembling food, clothing, and supplies, and providing communication between soldiers and their families. These societies eventually joined in a unified national institution. In the South, comparable societies remained local, volunteer efforts. Southern women nursed the wounded soldiers of the Confederacy in what were frequently makeshift hospitals.

At the beginning of the war, both the North and the South had relied on volunteers and militia. In time, both sides resorted to a draft, the Union conscription law permitted a draftee to find a substitute. He could also make a payment in place of service; that feature drew charges that the law favored the wealthy. In neither North nor South was conscription popular. In 1863 an antidraft riot broke out among the Irish in New York City. Before federal troops could restore order, the rioters lynched several blacks and burned a black orphanage. But the Union military continued to attract volunteers. The large bounty the Union offered was an inducement, as was the lurking presence of the draft. Patriotism and in some cases hostiltiy to slavery also drew volunteers.

While it was not until the South was badly in need of additional troops at almost the end of the war that the Confederacy contemplated the recruitment of blacks, the Union was accepting them as early as 1862. Earlier Lincoln's government had held back, fearing that the presence of black soldiers would seem to indicate that the war was not only for restoration of the Union but for the abolition of slavery. The acceptance of black volunteers, from both the North and the South, came at the urging of black leaders and white abolitionists, and by the end of the war, blacks composed about a tenth of the federal army and a fourth of the navy. For most of the war, black privates got three dollars a month less than whites. Some were relegated to labor units. Some Confederate commanders declared a policy of putting black prisoners into slavery. Confederate General Bedford Forrest promised to kill any blacks in uniform. But in combat the black soldiers won the respect of their officers and helped to discredit further the remnants of the slave system.

In time, as blacks themselves went to war, attitudes in New York City changed, or so one account indicates:

"Eight months ago the African race in this City were literally hunted down like wild beasts. They were shot down in cold blood, or stoned to death, or hung to the trees or to the lamp-posts. . . . How astonishingly has all this been changed! The same men now march in solid platoons, with shouldered muskets, slung knapsacks, and buckled cartridge boxes down through the gayest avenues and busiest thoroughfares to the pealing strains of martial music, and everywhere are saluted with waving handkerchiefs, with descending flowers, and with the acclamations and plaudits of countless beholders."

One officer wrote of his black comrades:

"No officer in this regiment now doubts that the key to the successful prosecution of this war lies in the unlimited employment of black troops. Their superiority lies in that they have peculiarities of temperament, position, and motive which belong to them alone. Instead of leaving their homes and families to fight they are fighting for their homes and families. . . ."

The End Stage, 1864–1865

Generals Grant and Sheridan

In 1864 the Union organized for final victory. Lincoln called Grant to Washington and put him in overall command of federal armies. Grant outlined a coordinated Union campaign. In the East he would lead an army against Lee. From the West, which the victory at Vicksburg had placed firmly under northern control, Grant's trusted subordinate Sherman would press into Georgia.

In May Grant pushed south. In a region of Virginia known as the Wilderness, his army, larger than Lee's, drove relentlessly forward. Repeatedly Lee checked Grant's advance, but the northern troops did not retreat. After each battle Grant went around the Confederate right flank and continued south, never giving Lee the initiative. The brilliant Virginian had no chance to organize a counterstroke of the kind that had disrupted previous federal offensives. By the end of June the Confederate troops were bottled up around Richmond. There followed months of siege warfare suggestive of World War I, as Grant gradually squeezed Lee's troops.

In September and October of the same year, the Union won an important victory when forces under General Philip Sheridan of the cavalry drove the rebels out of Virginia's Shenandoah Valley. That combat produced one of the best remembered incidents of the war. On October 19, Confederate soldiers commanded by Jubal Early sent the federal troops into a confused retreat from Cedar Creek. Sheridan, away at the time, rode on horseback to rejoin his men and by skill and force of personality turned them to a counter attack. The rebels, victorious earlier in the day, were crushed, and the Shenandoah Valley belonged to the Union.

To the south of both Sheridan and Grant, further disaster was befalling the Confederacy. Sherman was hacking his way through the lower South, slashing to bits much of what remained of the rebel heartland.

Making possible Sherman's march had been hard fighting nearly a year earlier in eastern Tennessee, a region containing much Unionist sentiment. On September 19, 1863, at Chickamauga Creek, the intervention of the Virginia Unionist General George H. Thomas—henceforth known as the Rock of Chickamauga—kept a federal defeat from turning into a rout. But afterward, Union troops in east Tennessee, now under the command of Grant, had better fortunes, and in late November they won a major victory at Chattanooga, crowned by a heroic and successful assault up the steep slope of nearby Missionary Ridge. Thenceforth, eastern Tennessee was available to federal forces as a launching point for an invasion of the deeper South. It was after this triumph that Grant received command of all federal armies and initiated his campaign in Virginia. Simultaneously with that Virginia offensive, Sherman began an advance from Tennessee into Georgia. Joseph E. Johnston conducted a skillful retreat, and the invaders did not reach Atlanta until September. At this point Sherman changed the rules. Leaving sufficient troops behind to deal with Johnston, he marched off across Georgia, allowing his men to burn and loot as they went. Sher-

General William Tecumseh Sherman, second to Ulysses S. Grant among northern generals, marched through Georgia in 1864. His army, burning and looting, left a wide path of destruction in its wake. *(Courtesy, Library of Congress)*

A Union soldier describes Sherman's march through Georgia:

"You can form no idea of the amount of property destroyed by us on this raid. All the Roads in the state are torn up and the whole tract or country over which we passed is little better than a wilderness. I can't for the life of me think what the people that are left there are to live on. We have all their Cattle, Horses, Mules, Sheep, Hogs, Sweet Potatoes, and Molasses and nearly everything else. We burnt all the Cotton we met which was millions of pounds. Our teams with all their hard driving are better today by about 200 percent than they were when we started because we have more than 2/3 new mules, besides all the old ones we could bring with us. Those that couldn't travel we killed and the road is lined with those that died. A tornado 60 miles in width from Chattanooga to this place 290 miles could not have done half the damage we did."

—W.F. Saylor

man's army reached Savannah in December, leaving a fifty-mile-wide path of destruction in its wake. From there, Sherman slashed northward through the Carolinas, while Johnston tailed him, powerless to intervene.

The Election of 1864   To wage the war successfully, Lincoln needed as much popular support as he could get. In his 1864 reelection campaign he ran not as a Republican but as the candidate of a coalition of Republicans and Democratic supporters of the war, which called itself the Union Party. The vice-presidential candidate of the party was Andrew Johnson, a Tennessee Democrat who had remained loyal to the Union. The presidential candidate of the regular Democratic Party was General McClellan, who had been commander of the Union armies. McClellan was loyal to the war effort, and in effect he rejected the claim by some northern Democrats that the war was a failure. By the time of the campaign and election the war had been going so successfully for the North that Lincoln's victory was assured.

While winning the war was the most important objective for the Republicans, they were committed also to an entire political, social, and economic policy within which the emancipation of the slaves and the preservation of the Union were elements. Before the Civil War much of the antislavery movement had also wanted a more vigorous national government working for the achievement of an advanced industrial and agricultural economy. Some Americans had possessed a vision of what a powerful American economy and society might be: an industrialized Northeast trading its manufactured goods for the produce of a great agricultural West. The federal government, these people believed, should stimulate eastern manufactures through a protective tariff, populate the agrarian West by giving government lands to settlers, and tie together the two regions by a railroad system built with federal aid. Northern politicians who thought this way could wish to exclude slavery from the territories not only because they genuinely disliked slavery on moral grounds, but also because they desired that the western lands be reserved for free American farmers. And in the years before the Civil War they had clashed with the South on other political issues: the southern cotton interest opposed a protective tariff, wanting instead to bring manufactured goods more cheaply from Europe, and resisted the construction of a northern railroad from East to West, holding out for a southern route. It is fitting that political circumstances put the Republicans in command of the war to save the the Union; for the Union came to mean strong central government presiding over a vast and economically progressive nation, while secession would have broken the country into weaker republics. It is fitting also that the Republicans became the champions of federally enforced emancipation.

For decades after the Civil War, the Republicans would continue to be the party favoring a cooperative society and economy, centrally planned and nourished by the federal government. Not until the twentieth century, and especially the coming of the New Deal, did the Democratic Party assume that role, while the Republicans became the party favoring a shrinkage in government.

Appomattox Court House　　The Confederacy's end came swiftly in the spring of 1865. The Union blockade had a stranglehold on the southern economy, while the Union occupation of large sections of the South badly disrupted agricultural production. Confederate troops were suffering for lack of food and clothing, and desertion rates skyrocketed. Between January and March 1865, General William Sherman's army moved through South and North Carolina, laying waste to farms, plantations, towns, and cities along the way. Farther to the north, in Virginia, the army of Ulysses S. Grant met the army of Robert E. Lee for a final confrontation. Late in March, Lee made a desperate attempt to break through the siege Grant had imposed, but the southern forces had neither the manpower nor the resources to succeed. On April 2, Lee abandoned Petersburg and Richmond and scrambled toward the south, hoping to get his troops into North Carolina.

It was not to be. Within a week Lee's army, now down to only 30,000 men, was surrounded by the armies of Grant and William T. Sherman. Grant caught up with Lee near Appomattox Court House. On April 9, 1865, Lee surrendered his proud but exhausted Army of Northern Virginia. General Joseph Johnston surrendered to General Sherman a few days later. Some rebel troops in the West held out a little longer. But the Civil War was over.

Civil War drum, Ninth Regiment, Vermont Volunteers, U.S. infantry, made about 1860. *(Index of American Design)*

Suggested Readings

On the Civil War era see Philip Paludan, *"A People's Contest": The Union and the Civil War* (1988), Frederick Blue, *Salmon P. Chase* (1987), Gerard Linderman, *Embattled Courage: The Experience of Combat in the American Civil War* (1987), John M. Priest, *Antietam* (1989), and Drew Gilpin Faust, *The Creation of Confederate Nationalism* (1988). See also Eugene Genovese's perceptive study, *The Slaveholders' Dilemma: Freedom and Progress in Southern Conservative Thought, 1820–1860* (1992).

A standard work is James G. Randall and David Donald, *The Civil War and Reconstruction* (revised 1973). James McPherson presents an excellent guide to the period in *Ordeal by Fire: The Civil War and Reconstruction* (1982); all of Bruce Catton's books make beautiful reading. See also Frank Vandiver, *Blood Brothers: A Short History of the Civil War* (1990). Emory L. Thomas analyzes *The Confederate Nation* (1979), and studies its greatest military leader in *Robert E. Lee: A Biography* (1995).

For biographies of Union and Confederate leaders see David Donald's *Lincoln* (1995) and William C. Davis's *Jefferson Davis: The Man and His Hour* (1991). See also Stephen B. Oates, *With Malice Toward None* (1978) and Clement Eaton's *Jefferson Davis* (1977). Two major books on the response of intellectuals to the war are George Fredrickson, *The Inner Civil War: Northern Intellectuals and the Crisis of the Union* (1965) and Daniel Aaron, *The Unwritten War: American Writers and the Civil War* (1973).

Other studies include Richard E. Beringer and others, *The Elements of Confederate Defeat: Nationalism, War Aims, and Religion* (1989), James M. McPherson, *What They Fought For, 1861–1865* (1994) and two older works, *Abraham Lincoln and the Second American Revolution* (1990) and *Battle Cry of Freedom* (1988). See also Paul D. Scott, *After Secession: Jefferson Davis and the Failure of Confederate Nationalism* (1978), Herman Hathaway and Archer Jones, *How the North Won: A Military History of the Civil War* (1983), Burke Davis, *Sherman's March* (1980), James L. Roark, *Masters Without Slaves: Southern Planters in the Civil War and Reconstruction* (1977), Adrian Cook, *The Armies of the Streets: The New York City Draft Riots of 1863* (1974), and Harold M. Hyman, *A More Perfect Union: The Impact of the Civil War and Reconstruction on the Constitution* (1973).

Military tactics are treated in *Lincoln and His Generals* by T. Harry Williams, Reid Mitchell, *Civil War Soldiers* (1988), Joseph T. Glatthaar, *The March to the Sea and Beyond: Sherman's Troops in the Savannah and Carolinas Campaign* (1985), Grady McWhiney and Perry D. Jamieson, *Attack and Die: Civil War Military Tactics and the Southern Heritage* (1982), Charles Royster, *The Destructive War: William Tecumseh Sherman, Stonewall Jackson, and the Americans* (1991), and Stephen W. Sears, *Landscape Turned Red: The Battle of Antietam* (1983).

Who Freed the Slaves?

James M. McPherson

After the battle of Antietam, Lincoln issued the preliminary Proclamation warning that on January 1, 1863, he would proclaim freedom for slaves in all states or portions of states then in rebellion against the United States. January 1 came, and with it the Proclamation applying to all or parts of ten southern states in which, by virtue of his war powers as commander in chief, Lincoln declared all slaves "forever free" as "a fit and necessary measure for suppressing said rebellion." . . .

Emancipation, then, became a crucial part of northern military strategy, an important means of winning the war. But if it remained merely a *means* it would not be a part of national strategy—that is, of the *purpose* for which the war was being fought. Nor would it meet the criterion that military strategy should be consistent with national strategy, for it would be inconsistent to fight a war using the weapon of emancipation to restore a Union that still contained slaves. Lincoln recognized this. Although restoration of the Union remained his first priority, the abolition of slavery became an end as well as a means, a war aim virtually inseparable from Union itself. The first step in making it so came in the Emancipation Proclamation, which Lincoln pronounced "an act of justice" as well as a military necessity. Of course the border states, along with Tennessee and small enclaves elsewhere in the Confederate states, were not covered by the Proclamation because they were under Union control and not at war with the United States and thus exempt from an executive action that could legally be based only on the president's war powers. But Lincoln kept up his pressure on the border states to adopt emancipation themselves. With his support, leaders committed to the abolition of slavery gained political power in Maryland and Missouri. They pushed through constitutional reforms that abolished slavery in those states before the end of the war.

Lincoln's presidential reconstruction policy, announced in December 1863, offered pardon and amnesty to southerners who took an oath of allegiance to the Union *and* to all wartime policies concerning slavery and emancipation. Reconstructed governments sponsored by Lincoln in Louisiana, Arkansas, and Tennessee abolished slavery in those states—at least in the portions of them controlled by Union troops—before the war ended. West Virginia came in as a new state in 1863 with a constitution pledged to abolish slavery. And in 1864, Lincoln took the lead in getting the Republican national convention that renominated him to adopt a platform calling for a Thirteenth Amendment to the Constitution prohibiting slavery everywhere in the United States. Because slavery was "hostile to the principles of republican government, justice, and national safety," declared the platform, Republicans vowed to accomplish its "utter and complete extirpation from the soil of the republic." Emancipation had thus become an end as well as a means of Union victory. As Lincoln stated in the Gettysburg Address, the North fought from 1863 on for "a new birth of freedom." . . .

Emancipation and the enlistment of slaves as soldiers tremendously increased the stakes in this war, for the South as well as the North. Southerners vowed to fight "to the last ditch" before yielding to a Yankee nation that could commit such execrable deeds. Gone was any hope of an armistice or a negotiated peace so long as the Lincoln administration was in power. The alternatives were reduced starkly to southern independence on the one hand or unconditional surrender of the South on the other.

Reprinted from James M. McPherson, *Abraham Lincoln and the Second American Revolution* (New York: Oxford University Press, 1990).

On Jan. 1, 1863, Abraham Lincoln promulgated his Emancipation Proclamation. A document whose grand title promised so much but whose bland words delivered so little, the Emancipation Proclamation has been an enigma ever since. Like contemporaries, historians have been unsure whether to condemn it as a failure of idealism or applaud it as a triumph of *real-politik*.

Lincoln's proclamation, as has often been noted, freed not a single slave. It applied only to the slaves in territories then beyond the reach of federal authority. It specifically exempted Tennessee and Union-occupied portions of Louisiana and Virginia, and it left slavery in the loyal border states—Delaware, Maryland, Kentucky and Missouri—untouched. Indeed, the Proclamation went no further than the Second Confiscation Act of July 1862, which freed all slaves who entered Union lines professing that their owners were disloyal, as well as slaves who fell under federal control as Union troops occupied Confederate territory. . . .

What then was the point of the Proclamation? It spoke in muffled tones that heralded not the dawn of universal liberty but the compromised and piece-meal arrival of an undefined freedom. Indeed, the Proclamation's flat prose, ridiculed by abolitionists as having the moral grandeur of a bill of lading, suggests that the true authorship of Afro-American freedom lies elsewhere—not at the top of American society but at the bottom.

From the first guns at Sumter, the strongest advocates of emancipation were the slaves themselves. . . . Steadily, as opportunities arose, slaves risked all for freedom by abandoning their owners, coming uninvited into Union lines and offering their help as laborers, pioneers, guides and spies.

Slaves forced federal soldiers at the lowest level to recognize their importance to the Union's success. That understanding traveled quickly up the chain of command. In time, it became evident even to the most obtuse federal commanders that every slave who crossed into Union lines was a double gain: one subtracted from the Confederacy and one added to the Union. The slaves' resolute determination converted many white Americans to the view that the security of the Union depended upon the destruction of slavery. Eventually, it tipped the balance in favor of freedom, even among those who had little interest in the question of slavery and no love for black people. . . .

As black laborers became essential to the Union war effort and as demands to enlist black men in the federal army mounted, the pressure for emancipation became inexorable. On Jan. 1, Lincoln fulfilled his promise to free all slaves in the states still in rebellion. Had another Republican been in Lincoln's place, that person doubtless would have done the same. Without question, some would have acted more expeditiously and with greater bravado. Without question, some would have acted more cautiously with lesser resolve. In the end, Lincoln did what needed to be done. His claim to greatness rests upon his reading of the moment.

The Emancipation Proclamation's place in the drama of emancipation is thus secure. To deny it is to ignore the deep struggle by which freedom arrived. It is to ignore the soldiers who sheltered slaves, the abolitionists who stumped for emancipation and the thousands of men and women who—like Lincoln—changed their minds as slaves made the case for universal liberty. In this sense, slaves were right in celebrating Jan. 1 as the Day of Jubilee. The Emancipation Proclamation reminds us that real change derives only from the actions of the people and that political leadership finds its truest moment when it acts upon the authentic will of the people.

Ira Berlin, "How the Slaves Freed Themselves," *Washington Post*, December 27, 1992. Reprinted by permission.

Ku Klux Klansmen in the South, ca. 1870. *(Courtesy, Hugh Cleland)*

15

"Been in the Storm So Long": Emancipation and Reconstruction

THE KLAN'S LYNCHING OF JIM WILLIAMS

On the night of March 6, 1871, a group of men mounted on horses gathered near Yorkville, South Carolina. Most wore black gowns with black face masks, and some had decorated themselves with horns. Meeting up with another party, they rode to the cabin of a black man, Jim Williams. There they demanded guns that they claimed were hidden. Then they took Williams away. The next day he was found hanged from a tree.

For its time and place the story is not unusual. What makes it noteworthy is that Williams had been captain of a militia unit organized by the Republican Reconstruction government of South Carolina. His murderers, of course, belonged to one of the innumerable local bands in the South that went under the general heading of the Ku Klux Klan. The killing was a moment in a paramilitary conflict that followed the formal end of the Civil War.

The war itself had not been merely a regional battle. In the mountains especially, many southern whites remained loyal to the Union. By the time of General Robert E. Lee's surrender, blacks had enlisted in large numbers in the Union army. After the war, its social character became clearer. White Unionists along with black southerners found themselves pitted against white former rebels of all social classes.

HISTORICAL EVENTS

1863
Lincoln presents "ten percent plan" of Reconstruction

1864
Lincoln vetoes Congress's Wade-Davis Reconstruction Bill

1865
Civil War ends (April) • Thirteenth Amendment • Freedmen's Bureau established • Lincoln assassinated • Andrew Johnson becomes President • all-white southern legislatures begin to pass Black Codes

1866
Civil Rights Act passed over Johnson's veto • first Ku Klux Klan is organized

1867
Tenure of Office Act • Johnson suspends Secretary of War Edwin Stanton • Freedmen's Bureau ends

1868
Fourteenth Amendment • Johnson impeached by House, acquitted by Senate • Ulysses S. Grant elected President

continued

"I have vowed," declared a Virginian toward the end of the war, "that if I should have children—the first ingredient of the first principle of their education shall be uncompromising hatred & contempt of the Yankee."

A North Carolinian—his sons killed and his home burned by Yankees—"hate[d] 'em. I git up a half-past four in the morning, and sit up till twelve at night, to hate 'em."

The origins of the Klan seem fairly clear—as clear as can be expected of a phenomenon that enforced secrecy. It began in 1866 as a fraternal society. A year later in Nashville, the Klan reorganized on more ideological lines. "Dens" of Klansmen appeared throughout the former Confederacy. All this suggests a central structure, but no general regional Klan existed. And even within the local dens, the ability of leaders to keep discipline was slight. Had it been greater, the brutality of the Ku Klux might have been somewhat lessened.

The Klan became quickly known for flamboyant costumes. For these there were two clear motives: secrecy—for the activities of Klans could bring trouble to their perpetrators—and the belief that freed blacks were gullible and could be made to think that ghosts, specifically of the Confederate dead, were abroad in the night. Robes of various colors Klansmen supplemented with simple cloth masks or hideous faces, horns, tall conical hats, and sometimes coverings for their horses. The announcement that a Klan had organized in a locality would go to a newspaper in declarations with references to "Serpent's Den," "Hollow Tomb," "dark and dismal hour," "Great High Giant," "Shrouded-Knight," or whatever else could convey a sense of dread mystery. Warnings could take the form of gallows or miniature coffins at the houses of victims.

As confrontation mounted between the Klan and its black and white Unionist Republican enemies and as the ranks of armed whites swelled, the Reconstruction governor of South Carolina disarmed the county militias, which left Republicans at the mercy of the Klan. Estimates have it that in about a year from September 1870 eleven murders occurred in York County alone, including that of Jim Williams. In 1871 more than three-fourths of the county's white adult males were Klansmen. In some districts almost all the black population slept in the woods for much of the year.

Soon the national government began implementing legislation imposing control over Klan activity. By the end of 1871 violence finally had subsided.

The South after the Civil War

Hatred crackled and seared among white southerners in the first postwar days, amidst other emotions: sadness, resignation, relief, doubtless in a few cases a renascent loyalty to the Union. The feelings of the freed slaves are easy to imagine: their joy at the dizzying prospect of freedom has been documented. "I'm free as a frog!" one exultant former slave exclaimed. The southern land, meanwhile, was in a physical disruption to match the broiling emotions of the more irreconciled of its inhabitants.

Wherever travelers went in the months following Appomattox they saw abandoned fields, twisted rails, and burned structures. People in creaking wagons drove their gaunt mules for miles to find fords across bridgeless streams. For decades to come, men hobbling on one leg or dangling an empty sleeve were to be common sights throughout Dixie. In 1866 the state of Mississippi would spend a fifth of its revenues on artificial arms and legs for Confederate veterans. The defeat of the Confederacy had also wiped out millions of dollars of bank capital and made all Confederate money worthless. But most unsettling of all the changes the war had brought was the end of slavery. For generations it had been the foundation on which the entire southern economy rested. Now that it was gone, what would take its place?

Some former slaves remained on farms and plantations, but many others had departed. Some had gone to the towns, where life seemed more interesting than in the sleepy countryside. Others took to the road to test their new freedom. Many went traveling to seek out lost relatives and friends separated years ago by the migration of white masters or by the domestic slave trade. Eventually most would return to the land somewhere in the South.

Lincoln and most other northerners had entered the Civil War determined only to preserve the Union. Southerners, believing they saw larger and more menacing aims on the part of the North, had been as determined to protect their independence. The Emancipation Proclamation gave the Union a moral purpose and confirmed the fears of many white southerners that victory for the Union would mean social revolution. It was the leveling of the southern social and racial hierarchy as much as it was the leveling of Atlanta that caused bitterness among southerners after General Robert E. Lee surrendered at Appomattox Court House.

Together, the ending of slavery and the social dislocations of defeat prepared the South for the very thing that white southerners had dreaded and most northern Unionists had not wanted. The South was ripe for social revolution. That revolution, in fact, had already come in the sheer numbers of black southerners free and in motion across the countryside. What form that revolution would take, how long it might endure: all this in 1865 was a matter of endless and unpredictable possibility.

Would liberty fulfill itself, as black southerners wanted, in the independence that comes of owning a plot of land? Would liberty amount to the freedom defined by northern capital: freedom on the part of workers, black and white, to sell their labor to the highest bidder? What form would black family life take on: the patriarchy of the white family or the community of affection that had developed in slave quarters? Would blacks achieve social equality and integration with whites? What were white southerners going to think about black freedom, now that they had to think about it?

Such questions would have been unimaginable two or three years earlier as immediate practical considerations. New conditions now made them inescapable. There could be no retreat.

"Right off colored folks started on the move," one ex-slave was to recall. "They seemed to want to get closer to freedom, so they'd know what it was—like it was a place or a city."

In northern Florida, a black preacher advocated testing freedom by moving. He told a large crowd of former slaves:

"You ain't, none o' you, gwinter feel rale free till you shakes de dus' ob de Ole Plantashun offen yore feet an' goes ter a new place whey you kin live out o' sight o' de gret house. So long ez de shadder ob de gret house falls acrost you, you ain't gwine ter feel lak no free man, an' you ain't gwine ter feel lak no free 'oman. You mus' all move—you mus' move clar away from de ole places what you knows, ter de new places what you don't know, whey you kin raise up yore head douten no fear o' Marse Dis ur Marse Tudder. Go whey you please—do what you please."

In the end, social revolution was not to endure. That failure has defined the character of American social and political life ever since.

Reconstruction

Reorganizing the Union

The Confederate surrender opened a difficult constitutional question about the status of the defeated states. Did the former rebel states have the right, as members of the Union, to come straight back to Congress and resume their old political life under the Constitution? Would the government have no authority to set conditions that they would have to meet before they resumed their seats in the House and Senate? If so, Congress would lack the power to force on the South whatever reforms might be necessary for the protection of the freed slaves and the prevention of any future disloyalty. Republicans who favored a coercive policy toward the South argued that by the act of secession the Confederate states had forfeited their status of statehood and reverted to the condition of territories. If they were no longer states, they were not entitled to the rights of states and could therefore be directly subject to the will of the federal government.

Some fundamental reform of the South, at any rate, was necessary, especially since the southern states were imposing oppressive codes of conduct on the freed slave. In the absence of reform, the Union victory might actually give the South a stronger presence in the House of Representatives than the region had enjoyed before the war, and with no consequences to the white majority. For the Constitution had provided that in counting the population of a state to determine how many members it was to have in the House, three-fifths of the slaves in the state were to be counted in. But if slavery no longer existed and the blacks were legally free, the whole black population would be counted within the population of the state, and the South would gain about twenty House seats. And if former Confederate states should succeed in finding methods for denying full freedom for the black populace, the South would be getting extra seats without even having to give up its oppression of the black race.

Overshadowing all these issues was the question of the future status of the black people. By eradicating slavery, the country unwittingly confronted questions regarding the civil and political status of blacks. Would the ballot and citizenship be conferred on them?

Such questions had to be worked out amid a legacy of bitterness and frustration created by the war. White southerners found themselves in the unique position of being the only Americans to know defeat in wartime, their region burned and bare, their economy a shambles. The North had not suffered the physical and economic devastation experienced by the South. Even its human losses were proportionally less. But northerners had sacrificed to preserve the Union. They needed to know that their expenditures had gone for something, that their principles had been vindicated. They expected a measure of symbolic satisfaction from the South as well as physical surrender.

Blacks recalling slavery decades later had a wide spectrum of memories.

"Might as well tell the truth. Had just as good a time when I was a slave as when I was free. Had all the hog meat and milk and everything else to eat."

—HARDY MILLER

"De white folks wuz good ter us, an' we loved 'em. But we wanted ter be free 'cause de Lawd done make us all free."

—TOM WILCOX

"There was no such thing as being good to slaves. Many white people were better than others, but a slave belonged to his master, and there was no way to get out of it."

—THOMAS LEWIS

"I thought slavery wuz right. I felt that this wuz the way things had to go—the way they were fixed to go. I wuz satisfied. The white folks treated me all right. My young missus loved me, and I loved her. She whupped me sometimes—I think, just for fun, sometimes."

—JOE HIGH

"Some colored people say slavery was better, because they had no responsibility. It is true, they were fed, clothed, and sheltered, but I'm like the man that said, 'Give me freedom or give me death!'"

—BELLE CARUTHERS

Lincoln's Reconstruction Plan

In the efforts during the war to settle on some scheme for restoration of the rebel states to the Union, President Lincoln generally favored policies that would make few demands on the South. He had originally hoped for a speedy end to the war and a rapid resumption of antebellum political ties. Although the prolonged struggle on the battlefield made that impossible, the President continued to advocate a moderate postwar Reconstruction. Lincoln had not been an advocate of black equality. He always approached racial issues cautiously. He had hoped that the process of emancipation would be gradual and under the direction of officials of the former slave states. Believing that the colonization of blacks outside the United States was the ideal solution, Lincoln's administration sponsored efforts to resettle blacks in the Caribbean and Central America. And Lincoln was a cagey politician. An ex-Whig himself, he may have had it in mind that moderate policies attractive to southern former Whigs might draw them to the Republican Party.

In December 1863 Lincoln outlined a formal plan for Confederate areas coming under Union control. It contemplated swift restoration, with no penalties for ex-rebels beyond loss of their slaves. It did not anticipate black participation in Reconstruction. Under Lincoln's "ten percent plan," whenever a total of whites equal to one-tenth the number who had voted in 1860 took an oath of future loyalty to the United States and its laws—which included the abolition of slavery—they could form a new state government. Before the war ended Lincoln had recognized "ten percent" governments in Arkansas, Tennessee,

---

WHAT WOULD LINCOLN HAVE DONE?

Historians have long speculated over how Lincoln would have approached the problem of postwar reconstruction had he not been assassinated. And in so doing they are merely following the lead of his contemporaries, most of whom claimed their own proposals reflected Lincoln's plans. The real question may be: did Lincoln have any plans?

It seems probable that he did, but Lincoln confided them to no one. In this matter, as in most others, he kept his own counsel. The result is that, following the assassination, people have tried to infer his postwar plans from his wartime programs. This is a very dubious enterprise. The reason is that Lincoln sought throughout the war to shorten it by enticing the seceding states back into the Union. The generous terms he offered were contingent on their willingness to lay down their arms. And so those terms should be seen as the carrot Lincoln used alongside the military stick. That they should not be seen as likely precedents for his postwar plans is suggested by this logic. Leniency was held out as a reward for volun-

tarily returning to the Union. None of the Confederate states earned that reward. That means that Lincoln, by his own terms, was free to deal with them as harshly as circumstances might demand. All this is technically true, and indicates Lincoln's essential conservatism. Yet there is a contrary truth to the Emancipation Proclamation. Lincoln knew what it implied, and so did the white South in its angry public reaction to the Proclamation. It was, by implication and beneath its limited surface, a declaration of war against slavery. We also have Lincoln's reaction to the Wade-Davis Bill to go by. He objected not so much to its rigor as that it would tie his hands in advance. Lincoln wanted to be free to deal with a defeated South as circumstances might suggest.

All in all it seems that we will never know what Lincoln would have proposed, much as we might like to think he would have striven for Negro equality. But the disastrous course of Johnson's attempts at reconstruction will always invite speculation on what Lincoln might have done had he lived.

Abraham Lincoln toward the beginning of the Civil War.
(*Courtesy, Library of Congress*)

Lincoln's second inaugural address described his postwar plans in humane but unspecific terms:

"With malice toward none; with charity for all, with firmness in the right, as God give us to see the right, let us strive on to finish the work we are in: to bind up the nation's wounds. . . ."

and Louisiana. But Congress refused to admit representatives from these states, and their votes were not counted in the 1864 presidential election. Lincoln agreed that Congress should take some role in the reconciliation process, but he always sought to keep restoration under presidential leadership.

The national legislators were looking for a plan more firmly ensuring that the new southern governments would remain loyal. The Wade-Davis Bill of 1864 required that before a formerly seceded state could form a government, fifty percent of the adult white males in that state would have to take an oath of loyalty to the Union. The state could then hold a constitutional convention to make a new government for itself. But voting for delegates to that convention would be limited to people who had taken an oath that they had never supported secession. The bill included legal equality for blacks, but did not provide them with the vote. Thinking the Wade-Davis Bill too severe and an invasion of presidential responsibility, Lincoln pocket vetoed it.

Neither Lincoln's plan nor the Wade-Davis Bill provided for blacks to be given the vote. But some Republicans in Congress wished to grant a wide range of rights to the freedmen. Legislators of this kind wanted the national government to have strong control over former rebel states, so that their legal and social systems could be thoroughly reshaped and white southerners would not get the chance to bring back the old slavery system in a new form.

During the final year of the war President Lincoln appeared to be moving somewhat toward a more active and progressive solution to the race question. In March 1864 he came out in favor of granting the vote to "very intelligent" black people and black Union soldiers. He pressed for the Thirteenth Amendment outlawing slavery. A month before his death Lincoln signed the bill creating a Freedmen's Bureau to aid the ex-slaves in their transition to freedom.

In the end, Reconstruction was to be in hands other than Lincoln's. But in the spring of 1865 the President and the Union public did have a brief period to savor victory.

Lincoln's Last Days   On April 4 Lincoln went to Richmond to view the Confederate capital now evacuated by the government of Jefferson Davis. Accompanied by his son and a military escort, he walked up Main Street to the Confederate executive mansion. Black men and women crowded around the presidential party and sang and shouted. When he entered the Confederate President's house and took a seat in Davis's chair, the Union troops, black and white, cheered. Later the President toured the captured city that for four bloody years had been the supreme goal of Union armies. Like many other large southern towns Richmond was in ruins: it was blackened by a fire set accidentally by the Confederate authorities before they withdrew.

Lincoln returned to Washington on April 9, the day Lee surrendered to Grant at Appomattox. The news reached Washington the next day and the government declared a holiday for its employees. On the tenth, throngs gathered on the streets of the capital. The crowds eventually converged on the White House, where Lincoln was working at his desk. They interrupted him several times by their shouts for a speech until he finally made an appearance. He would deliver some appropriate remarks the following evening, he said, but for the moment he would just order the bands to play "Dixie." The Confederate anthem, he noted, was now the lawful property of the Union.

The next evening the President came to the upper window of the White House as he had promised. He delivered a thoughtful address, his last, on the problems to come. If the crowd had wanted a rousing cock-crow of triumph, it was disappointed. At least one man in the audience, however, found himself deeply moved, but to rage and anger. John Wilkes Booth was a Marylander, an actor from a distinguished theatrical family. The defeat of the South had sent him into despair.

On the evening of April 14 the President, accompanied by his wife and several friends, went to see the comedy *Our American Cousin* at Ford's Theater. The President's party arrived late but quickly settled down to enjoy the story of a shrewd comic American visiting his English relatives. During the third act the sounds of a muffled shot and a scuffle came from the President's box. Suddenly a tall figure leaped from the box to the stage and shouted *Sic semper tyrannis!* (thus ever to tyrants), the motto of Virginia. Before he could be stopped Booth escaped into the night.

They carried the unconscious President to a house across the street. While high officials and family members gathered around, the doctors examined him. The bullet had entered the rear of his head and lodged near his eye. Nothing could be done. He died at 7:22 a.m.

Robert E. Lee at first would not believe the news of Lincoln's death. Then he told a visitor that he had "surrendered as much to [Lincoln's] goodness as to Grant's artillery."

Andrew Johnson

Like other Vice Presidents in American history, Andrew Johnson was selected without much consideration that he might become President. A self-educated tailor from east Tennessee and a strong Jacksonian Democrat, Johnson had been in 1861 the only senator from a secessionist state to support the Union. After Tennessee fell to Union troops, Lincoln made him war governor, a task he performed with vigor and fortitude. In 1864 the Republican Party, seeking to broaden itself into a Union party, turned naturally to Johnson, an ex-Democrat and a southern Unionist, to be Lincoln's running mate. Then suddenly, on April 14, 1865, he was the President.

Johnson, a President without a party, had to deal with a Republican Congress. And Johnson was a southern white supremacist, willing and perhaps happy to accept emancipation and some rights for black Americans but close in his thinking to southerners who wished to place strict controls over the black population. This brought him into conflict not only with the increasingly strong band of Radical Republicans in Congress but with moderates as well. Courageous and stubborn but belligerent and lacking in political tact, Johnson had one of the most troubled presidential administrations in American history.

Johnson wanted an easy restoration of the seceded states. There was not yet any clearly defined program that would instruct a rebel

Andrew Johnson's attempt to assume primary responsibility for Reconstruction after Lincoln's death alienated Congress, while his leniency toward the South increasingly angered northern voters. *(Courtesy, Library of Congress)*

state in how it must go about reorganizing itself so as to be accepted back into the Union, and Johnson did not wait for Congress to reconvene (it was out of session until December) before dealing with the problem. Like Lincoln, Johnson offered pardon to ex-rebels pledging future loyalty. He asked only that the reorganized state governments nullify their ordinances of secession, repudiate their Confederate debts, and ratify the Thirteenth Amendment.

Assuming primary responsibility for Reconstruction, Johnson chiseled a policy bound to alienate Republicans in Congress. His leniency toward the South angered Radicals. Southerners, moreover, took a course that aroused northern resentment. They elected to state office and to Congress prominent ex-rebels, including Confederate Vice President Alexander Stephens and numerous generals. Some of the reorganized state governments refused to repudiate their Confederate debts or nullify their secession ordinances. A number of them passed "Black Codes" defining the rights of emancipated slaves in ways that severely restricted their freedom.

A typical code might bar blacks from jury duty and from testifying in court against whites; it might forbid them to take up any occupation except agriculture or to rent land on their own; some subjected unemployed blacks to arrest and forced labor. The character of the "restored" governments and the "Black Codes" seemed to indicate that southerners remained rebels at heart. Mississippi's version of the Black Codes contained a section levying fines and possible imprisonment for former slaves "committing riots, routs, affrays, trespasses, malicious mischief, cruel treatment to animals, seditious speeches, insulting gestures, language, or acts, or assaults on any person, disturbance of the peace, exercising the function of a minister of the Gospel without a license . . . vending spiritous or intoxicating liquors, or committing any other misdemeanor, the punishment of which is not specifically provided for by law."

Early Reconstruction

When Congress met in December 1865, it refused to seat newly elected southern representatives, but disagreed on what to do next. Radical Republicans demanded a thoroughgoing political and economic shake-up of the South. Congressman Thaddeus Stevens of Pennsylvania and Senator Charles Sumner of Massachusetts led the Radicals. Many southerners thought the Republican Congress wanted to punish the South by providing numerous political and economic rights for the freedman. Stevens in fact wanted Confederate lands appropriated by Washington and given to blacks. At this point, however, moderates still dominated Republican policy. But they too wanted to ensure the civil rights of black southerners. In 1865 Congress passed a bill giving to a Freedmen's Bureau the power to try by military commission anyone charged with depriving freedmen of their civil rights. It also put through a bill that gave the freedmen citizenship and civil rights. Johnson vetoed both bills as unconstitutional extensions of fed-

Edffe Murphy

eral power. Congress thereupon enacted the civil rights measure over his veto, passed a revised bill for a Freedmen's Bureau, and overrode Johnson's veto of it.

Congress's establishment of the Freedmen's Bureau departed from normal government policy by addressing various aspects of people's lives that had normally been left to private initiative. The Bureau, empowered also to care for white refugees, was essentially responsible for protecting blacks against reenslavement in the unsettled conditions of the southern states. Under its commissioner, Union veteran and general Oliver O. Howard, it provided direct aid to blacks, found them employment, supervised labor contracts, set up schools and courts, gave public recognition to marriages among black southerners, attempted to provide them with abandoned land and in general worked to ensure that freedom would be a reality.

The Fourteenth Amendment

Congress soon offered Johnson and the South another chance. It framed an elaborate Fourteenth Amendment covering a range of issues and gave each of the state governments favored by Johnson the opportunity to return to Congress if it should ratify.

The Fourteenth Amendment declared that "All persons"—the lawmakers were thinking particularly of black Americans—"born or naturalized in the United States, and subject to the jurisdiction thereof, are citizens of the United States and of the State wherein they reside." The Amendment prohibited the states from violating the "privileges or immunities of citizens of the United States," depriving "any person of life, liberty, or property, without due process of law," or denying "to any person within its jurisdiction the equal protection of the laws." The Amendment did not directly extend the right to vote. It attempted instead to entice the states to give the vote to blacks. It provided that a state would lose seats in the House of Representatives in proportion to the number of its adult males denied the right to vote.

Miss M. A. Parker, a white schoolteacher, observed the hunger for education on the part of some black parents for their children:

Raleigh, N.C., Feb. 22, 1869

It is surprising to me to see the amount of suffering which many of the people endure for the sake of sending their children to school. There is one woman who supports three children and keeps them at school; she says, "I don't care how hard I has to work, if I can only sen[d] Sallie and the boys to school." . . . One may go into their cabins on cold, windy days, and see daylight between every two boards, or feel the rain dropping through the roof; but a word of complaint is rarely heard. They are anxious to have the children "get on" in their books, and do not seem to feel impatient if they lack comforts themselves. A pile of books is seen in almost every cabin, though there be no furniture except a poor bed, a table and two or three broken chairs.

—Miss M. A. Parker

The Freedmen's Bureau Commissioner in Mississippi and Louisiana wrote:

"I hear the people talk in such a way as to indicate that they are yet unable to conceive of the negro as possessing any rights at all. . . . To kill a negro they do not deem murder; to debauch a negro woman they do not think fornication; to take the property away from a negro they do not consider robbery. The people boast that when they get freedmen affairs in their own hands, to use the classic expression, 'the niggers will catch hell.' "

A state ratifying the Amendment could expect to be granted readmission without further reform. Implicit in the offer was a penalty for rejection: the process of restoring the state to the Union would begin anew, with Congress dictating terms. Had it not been for Johnson, the South might have ratified. But Johnson refused to bend. On his advice all the southern states except his Tennessee rejected the Amendment. Tennessee ratified and was readmitted to the Union. The other ten, said James A. Garfield, had "flung back into our teeth the magnanimous offer of a generous nation."

The break between the President and Congress was now complete. In the fall of 1866 Johnson stumped the North encouraging the defeat at the polls of leading Republican congressmen. The tour was a disaster for the President personally and politically. Forgetting that he was no longer a Tennessee stump-speaker, Johnson engaged in undignified arguments with hecklers and even suggested hanging leading Radicals. In November the Republicans swept the elections, winning over a two-thirds majority in both houses of Congress. That gave the Republicans in each house the ability, if they stood together, to muster the votes necessary to override a presidential veto of a bill. Reconstruction would begin anew, under the leadership of such Radicals as the Massachusetts Senator Charles Sumner and Representative Thaddeus Stevens of Pennsylvania.

Radical Reconstruction

The situation when Congress met in December 1866 was very different from that a year earlier. Events during 1866 had conspired to bring together moderate and Radical Republicans, at least temporarily. A majority in Congress now agreed on the necessity of creating new southern state governments on the basis of black suffrage and exclusion of the former rebel leadership from participating in the drawing up of state constitutions. Arming blacks with the ballot, Republicans hoped, would give them a weapon against white Democratic oppression and build a strong Republican Party in the South.

The Military Reconstruction Act of 1867 set the terms of the congressional program. It divided the South into five military districts. Military governors in each were to register voters, including blacks but not whites who had held public office before the Civil War and then supported the Confederacy. The governors would thereupon call elections for new constitutional conventions. These conventions had to write black suffrage into the new state constitutions. Once the voters had approved these constitutions and the Fourteenth Amendment, the states might apply to Congress for readmission. If the constitution met approval, the state would be readmitted to the Union and its representatives seated. Three other Reconstruction Acts followed the first. In 1868 the necessary number of states ratified the Fourteenth Amendment, and it became part of the federal Constitution.

Reconstruction had something in common with the economic policy of the Republican Party and with the party's defense of the

Union during the Civil War. It represented that commitment to strong and active central government toward which Republicans then tended. In the enforcement of civil rights, the effort to establish universal male suffrage, and the work of the Freedmen's Bureau, the federal government for the first time in its history was lending its resources to a political and social revolution.

To southern whites haunted by the old antebellum fear of slave insurrection, Radical Reconstruction seemed a nightmare come true. With their traditional leaders barred from office and illiterate ex-slaves enfranchised, they predicted a grim era of black rule.

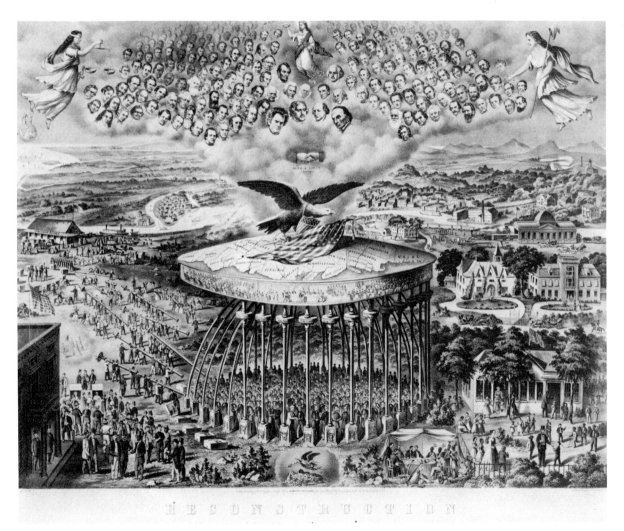

The artist of this 1867 glorification of Reconstruction focuses on raising the missing pillars (the returning southern states) to form a rotunda of the reunited Republic. Clasped hands above the American eagle carry the words "Union and Liberty Forever." From heaven, the country's great leaders look down approvingly— Washington, Lincoln, Jefferson, Webster, Calhoun, and many more. Black and white babies (bottom, center), sleeping innocently in baskets, remind the viewer that "All men are born free and equal." Black and white children play together—a nation's noblest dream. *(Courtesy, Library of Congress)*

Massachusetts Senator Charles Sumner (top) and Pennsylvania Representative Thaddeus Stevens, leaders of Radical Reconstruction.
(Courtesy, Library of Congress)

Who Were the Radicals?

The earliest historians of Radical Reconstruction condemned it as a rape of southern society. Political opportunism and hatred of the South, so such critics argued, had motivated the Radical Republican policies: military rule and black suffrage violated the spirit, if not the letter, of the Constitution. Accounts sympathetic to the white South stressed the corruption of Reconstruction state regimes and the unruliness—by which some of them may have meant the claims to equality—of former slaves. Scholars denounced northern "carpetbaggers," who according to folklore had gone southward carrying carpetbag luggage and intending to profit from the helplessness of the ex-Confederacy. Their partners in evil, so the same version of history claimed, were southern "scalawags" who in greed turned against their own region and people and entered the Reconstruction state governments. Reconstruction was a "blackout of honest government." In this view, the political triumph on the state level of the "redeemers," some of whom were of the old planter class, rescued the South from the work of Radical Reconstruction and brought back constitutional government and proper race relations.

By the 1930s historians were becoming increasingly interested in explaining events by economic causes. That brought a new way of interpreting Reconstruction. Now writers looked back to the days before the Civil War when southerners had opposed such measures favorable to northern business as the protective tariff, which would force the South to buy its manufactured goods from the North rather than at cheaper European prices. Those scholars perceived the Radical Republicans as representatives of northeastern business interests. These interests had feared that a speedily reconstructed South might regain its political power and overturn the control of the national government acquired by northern business during the war years. It was for that reason, this interpretation would hold, that Republicans in Congress gave the vote to southern blacks, who were sure to vote for the Republican Party.

More recently, a generation influenced by the civil rights struggles of the 1950s and 1960s has begun describing Reconstruction as another phase in the black American search for justice. Radical Republicans, this analysis insists, represented the last moment of abolitionist idealism. The Radicals tried to provide national protection for the rights of the freed people and to extend some measure of social and economic assistance. Not particularly vindictive and not the tools of a capitalist conspiracy, congressional Republicans, moderates as well as Radicals, undertook their actions only after they realized the extent of white southern stubbornness and presidential obstructionism. And their measures were not especially severe, particularly when compared to the postwar policies of other victorious nations. The national government committed only a small number of troops to military Reconstruction, and the whole process lasted only a few years. This recent idea of Reconstruction would hold that if any fault is to be found with the policy, it is not for being too severe toward the defeated South but for not being thorough enough to win the black race full and permanent equality and justice. The very word "Radical" has been questioned, since most measures passed were compromises unsatisfactory to true radicals.

Impeachment of Johnson

Although his policies had clearly been rejected and Republicans now held two out of three seats in both houses, enough to pass legislation over his veto, President Johnson continued to resist Radical Reconstruction by every possible means. Using the authority he possessed as commander-in-chief, he issued orders curtailing the powers of the military commanders in the South. He also removed from office people friendly to Radical policies. Congress responded in 1867 and 1868 by trying to trim the President's powers so as to reduce his capacity for harm. In particular it passed the Tenure of Office Act, which forbade him to dismiss federal officials without the consent of the Senate. Another law required him to issue all orders to the army through its commanding general, U. S. Grant.

There had been talk among Radicals for some time of removing Johnson from office. Under the Constitution a President could be removed for "Treason, Bribery, or other high Crimes and Misdemeanors." Johnson had committed none of these. His only real offense was to refuse to cooperate in legislative policies that Congress and the public had approved. This might indicate bad political judgment. But bad judgment is not a high crime or misdemeanor.

Then Johnson, always his own worst enemy, made a major political blunder. In August 1867 he suspended Secretary of War Edwin M. Stanton, a close ally of the Radicals. There followed a comic opera in which Stanton barricaded himself in his office for two months while his successor periodically stood outside begging him to vacate. Outraged at Johnson's defiance, and convinced that he intended to destroy Radical Reconstruction, the House of Representatives in February 1868 impeached the President—that is, charged him with misconduct. Johnson stood accused of a number of doubtful offenses such as delivering "inflammatory and scandalous" speeches, but especially the offense of

Facsimile of a ticket to Andrew Johnson's impeachment trial. Though Johnson was guilty of no crime other than continued resistance to Radical Reconstruction, a switch of a single Senate vote would have removed him from office. *(Courtesy, Library of Congress)*

dismissing Stanton in violation of the Tenure of Office Act. Impeachment meant that Johnson now had to go on trial before the Senate, which would decide whether to remove him from the presidency. For three months the Senate sat as a court, listening to arguments from attorneys for both sides. Johnson's lawyers argued that a President could be removed only for violation of criminal law; counsel for the House contended that Johnson had exceeded his presidential authority and therefore provided adequate grounds for removal. Suspense mounted as it became clear that Republican senators were divided over the question of Johnson's guilt. In the end, seven Republicans broke with their colleagues and voted with Democrats against conviction. As a result the Senate fell one vote short of the required two-thirds needed to remove the President from office.

Johnson's impeachment and trial were the product of nerves stretched to the limit after three years of feuding. So convinced were many northerners that Johnson had joined with unrepentant rebels to undo the results of the war that they sanctioned any means to drive him from office. Johnson's conviction—especially on such flimsy grounds—might have damaged permanently the role of the President in the American political system.

Blacks and the Land

Advertisements, angry or despairing, were placed in newspapers by blacks following the war:

"Information Wanted, of Caroline Dodson, who was sold from Nashville, Nov. 1st, 1862, by James Lumsden to Warwick, (a trader then in human beings), who carried her to Atlanta, Georgia, and she was last heard of in the sale pen of Robert Clarke, (human trader in that place), from which she was sold. Any information of her whereabouts will be thankfully received and rewarded by her mother. Lucinda Lowery, Nashville."

The Black Family

The country roads in the early days after Appomattox, crowded with newly freed slaves seeking lost loved ones, speak of the violence the slave system had done to the black family. Protecting their absolute right to their property, slaveholders had refused to give formal and legal recognition to slave marriages. Masters had often found it in their interest, however, to encourage slave unions: children were future laborers, and family responsibility would restrain rebelliousness. Yet when the economics of plantation life demanded it, husbands would be separated from wives, wives sold away from husbands, and children torn from mothers and fathers.

It is logical to suppose that in the absence of socially protected marriage, the mother would assume the primary parental role. Historians have described the slave family as matriarchal. That view is under question. Evidence indicates the presence within the slave community of males who performed the tasks of husband and father: providing their families with game or fish as dietary supplements, fashioning articles of furniture, passing along to a child some memory from an earlier time and a different land, and, when possible, protecting a wife or child against an abusive overseer or master.

But beyond these elements of similarity between black and white fatherhood, little division of responsibilities along gender lines existed within slave quarters. The necessities of plantation agriculture assured, for example, that the great majority of slave men and women worked alongside one another in the fields. Slave parents, faced with the problem of bringing children to maturity, rarely observed Victorian distinctions in sex roles. Both parents taught their children survival, the subtle art of accommodation to the plantation system. Yet whites might accept from a slave woman a degree of aggressiveness in defense of her children that they would not tolerate from black fathers.

Unable under the conditions of slavery to enjoy a secure and stable nuclear family life, blacks established an enlarged community of relations, stretching from one plantation to the next, of "brothers" and "sisters," "aunts" and "uncles" who took up family responsibilities. When the opportunity presented itself after the war, the freed slaves rejoined their immediate biological families and sought legitimacy and protection in legally recognized marriages. The Freedmen's Bureau presided over many of these unions and made them a matter of public record.

For blacks, gaining control of their own families was perhaps the most important immediate consequence of freedom. But emancipation also worked to alter relations within the black family. Slavery had flattened, though not entirely, the differences between men's and women's roles; emancipation made possible a differentiation between roles that the larger society endorsed. Black males most often went to work for whites in various jobs as they had done before the war, but now for hire. They generally preferred, however, that their wives not work for the white man, and many black females wished to create a conventional household and give their energies to raising children. In the years immediately following the war, white southern landowners complained of the scarcity of black women and children available for field work or domestic employment. For black men and women emancipation was supposed to mean at least the freedom whites enjoyed to organize a household.

Freed women when they stepped out from their homes encountered barriers already set up for the rest of their sex. Black women who had to seek employment complained to Freedmen's Bureau officials that they received wages lower than men were getting for the same work. Bureau policy required husbands to sign contracts for the labor of their wives. Though black men—for the most part temporarily— acquired more and more political liberty throughout the Reconstruction era, especially the right to vote and hold office, black women like their white sisters remained outside the political system. The experience of sexual equality that had belonged to slavery was being swallowed in theories of male primacy that came with freedom.

The black family, meanwhile, thrived in freedom. By 1870 a large majority of black children were growing up in households of two parents. Relations between the sexes, while not so nearly equal as under slavery, were not so sharply defined and as hierarchical as conventional morality might have demanded. Blacks, in any event, now had a stable home foundation on which to build wider forms of community and political organization.

Building the Black Community

From the earliest days of Reconstruction, there emerged into full public view an institution that had maintained a powerful place in slave society and among antebellum free blacks. Evangelical Protestantism spoke to the condition of American blacks. Most slave states

One freedman observed:

"Perhaps some will get an education in a little while. I *knows de next generation will.* But . . . we has been kep down *a hundred years* and *I* think it will take *a hundred years to get us back again.*"

Another ex-slave would recall sending his children to school:

"We had no idea that we should see them return home alive in the evening. Big white boys and half-grown men used to pelt them with stones and run them down with open knives, both to and from school. Sometimes they come home bruised, stabbed, beaten half to death, and sometimes quite dead. My own son himself was often thus beaten. He has on his forehead today a scar over his right eye which sadly tells the story of his trying experience in those days in his efforts to get an education. I was wounded in the war, trying to get my freedom, and he over his eye, trying to get an education."

had made it illegal to educate slaves. But the incomparable vocabulary of the King James Bible was available. Illiterate blacks could learn the cadences by ear; free blacks with schooling could read it, like slaves who had learned to read despite the prohibitions. A story of ancient Jews whose lot seemed close to that of the slaves; a language of bondage, flight, and deliverance, of suffering endured, rendered into prayer and devotion and in time ended: all was magnificent material for preaching and for hymns. With religion came a ministry of slaves and free blacks. During Reconstruction, blacks pressed for separate churches, nurturing their own congregations already established. The black ministry gained political leadership to supplement its spiritual role, taking a place within the black community that it would still occupy during the civil rights struggles of the 1950s and 1960s.

Side by side with the ministers in a position of leadership stood the teachers, now at liberty openly to instruct other blacks and to enlarge their own education. Ex-slaves and black southerners who had been free even in slavery times now joined with black and white teachers who had come from the North to serve in the new time of emancipation. Schools flourished: vast numbers of tiny schools ran on a shoestring; most received the countenance and aid, however meager, of the Freedmen's Bureau. The teachers might be passing on the fragments of learning they had snatched and hoarded in the days of slavery; pupils, eager for a schooling that Americans in general have traditionally prized as a means of success and a good in itself, might have the ambition to become teachers. The halting eloquence to be found among the papers of newly schooled Reconstruction blacks has its counterpart in the letters of immigrants, trying in their freshly acquired English to explain their place and hopes in their adopted country.

Community Voices   Even before the end of the war, black southerners in regions under control of federal troops were meeting to provide a voice for their community. The main insistence in the gatherings was on political and legal rights. More generally, they appear to have had as their objective the establishment of an organized and articulate presence in American society. Underlying this purpose was a fear that even the more enlightened of white Americans were likely to treat the freed slaves as no more than recipients of white benevolence. That was not going to be to the liking especially of blacks who had won for themselves an education, whether pieced together in defiance of laws forbidding literacy schooling for slaves or acquired in the precarious margins of southern society allowed to free blacks before the war. Blacks made more particular demands during the early days of Reconstruction for the right to vote, to serve on juries, to exercise the other freedoms of Americans. These demands too can perhaps best be understood as reflecting the determination to be an active rather than a passive component of the nation. The plan of Reconstruction imposed by Congress later in the decade would succeed, if only briefly, because there existed among southern blacks a roughly hewn political structure, a stratum of educated leaders, and a political will. These could respond to the congressional program for bringing the freed slaves into the nation's public life.

Humanitarian Efforts

During the Reconstruction years, the national government provided some assistance to the freed people in the South. The Freedmen's Bureau coordinated relief activities and tried to ease the difficult transition from slavery to freedom. Critics at the time generally indicted the Bureau for doing too much to assist blacks. Later historians have found quite the opposite. Many of the well-meaning officials were overly paternalistic; others displayed outright prejudice toward black people; some encouraged freedmen to enter into exploitive labor contracts; the agency did too little to enlarge opportunities for the former slaves. Yet the Bureau represented a notable though mild and temporary expansion of the social role of the federal government. In 1869, with its work still only a beginning, Congress cut its appropriation. This was a sign of northern retreat from Reconstruction. By 1872 the Freedmen's Bureau was defunct.

Private philanthropic and religious groups tried to aid freed people. Various churches, especially the Congregationalists and the Quakers, sent both money and volunteers to the South. Educational institutions related to the churches gave many black children and adults their first opportunity to learn to read and write. Blacks rushed to make use of the new schools, where northern female schoolteachers took an especially important role. Their devotion to the people they were teaching mingled with their commitment to inculcating them with northern, middle-class values. Church groups also helped establish black colleges and industrial schools, and the Freedmen's Bureau extended some financial assistance to missionary schools, including Howard University in Washington, D.C.

Many northern black churchmen and educators journeyed south to spread the Gospel and the schoolbook among the ex-slaves. Former slaves themselves put up schoolhouses and paid for teachers, established churches, organized conventions to lobby for equal rights and the ballot, and opened savings banks.

The Fifteenth Amendment

By the Fifteenth Amendment, ratified in 1870 by the necessary number of states, Congress brought the right to vote under federal control. The Amendment declared that a citizen's right to vote "shall not be denied or abridged . . . on account of race, color, or previous condition of servitude." The Amendment applied to black males in the North—much of the North had not allowed black Americans to vote—as well as to former slaves in the South. Most of the black vote went to Republicans, and some northern supporters of the Amendment may have been mainly concerned with strengthening the Republican Party. But others risked a white backlash to guarantee suffrage to the black man.

The vote that was granted to black males was denied to both black and white females. White leaders of the movement for women's rights were incensed. Before the war, they had worked within the abolitionist movement and then supported the Republican cause. In 1866, Susan B. Anthony, Elizabeth Cady Stanton, Lucy Stone, and Lucretia Mott organized the American Equal Rights Association to support suffrage for both white women and blacks. Some even asserted that white

---

Sarah Jane Foster, a Quaker volunteer teacher from Maine, wrote to her home town newspaper about her experiences during Reconstruction:

Letter from Martinsburg, West Va., Feb. 11th 1866

"My day school is growing larger. Its list is now seventy, while the night list approaches fifty. . . . I spoke of good spelling in my last letter. Week before last a boy of sixteen, named Willoughby Fairfax, who chanced to recite alone, spelled seventy-five long words and only missed *two*. At the beginning of the year he was in words of four letters. He is one of my best pupils. . . . I daily become more and more interested in the school, and in all that concerns the welfare of the colored people here."

Febr- 28

"The cognomen of 'nigger teacher' seems to have died out, and I occasionally hear my own name as I pass in the street, or, more frequently some person is notified that 'there goes the Freedmen's Bureau.' I have not met with any annoyance on the street but once, and then a white man addressed an insolent remark to me as I was going into the schoolroom door. I don't mind such things at all. Report has married or engaged me several times to men connected with the school, and, Mrs. Vosburgh was actually asked by a neighbor the day I was there 'if I was not part nigger.' I hope they will believe it, for then surely they could not complain of my teaching the people of my own race."

Harper's Ferry, April 20th, 1866 [May 9]

"The colored people here are scattered, and many of them in very destitute circumstances. They do not now come into school so well as they did last term. The older ones are gone out at service, and smaller ones, who have long distances to come, fear to do so without protection; for the white boys will molest them when they find an opportunity. . . ."

Susan B. Anthony (1820–1906) and Elizabeth Cady Stanton (1815–1902), the two most influential leaders of the woman suffrage movement, ca. 1870. Both broke with their longtime abolitionist allies after the Civil War when they opposed the Fifteenth Amendment. They argued that the doctrine of universal manhood suffrage it embodied would give constitutional authority to the claim that men were the social and political superiors of women. *(Courtesy, Schlesinger Library, Radcliffe College)*

women were better fitted to vote than black men. In the ensuing dispute about priorities, the Equal Rights Association split into two groups. Lucy Stone and Henry Blackwell formed the American Woman Suffrage Association, which in order not to jeopardize the vote for black men accepted the refusal to grant women the vote. Susan B. Anthony and Elizabeth Cady Stanton organized the more militant National Woman Suffrage Association. Bitter about what they took to be betrayal by male Republican leaders, they warned that women could not trust men, refused to support the freedmen's right to the vote, and even used racist arguments to explain that it was of greater importance to give the vote to white women. Although their racism declined after the passage of the Fifteenth Amendment, it left a disturbing legacy to the women's movement.

Reconstruction Governments   In most southern states, Reconstruction lasted for only a few years. In states with large white majorities, conservatives regained political control rather quickly. Virginia was "redeemed" in 1869, Tennessee and North Carolina in 1870. Georgia fell under conservative rule in 1872, Alabama, Texas, and Arkansas in 1874, and Mississippi in 1875. In only three states—Louisiana, Florida, and South Carolina—did Radical Republican government last a full decade, and they were all "redeemed" in 1877.

Even in those states where blacks made up a majority of the voters, they did not dominate the reconstructed state governments. They formed a majority in one state constitutional convention, that of South Carolina, exactly one half the membership in the Louisiana convention, and a minority in eight others. After the new governments were formed, blacks never held a majority in both houses of a state legislature. No state had an elected black governor; only two black senators and fourteen black representatives were elected to the national Congress. At the local level, blacks never enjoyed a proportionate share of offices. In the constitutional conventions and in legislatures, blacks rarely pressed for equal access to public facilities. Still, during the Reconstruction era blacks were a significant force in southern politics.

The Reconstruction governments were far from being the corrupt and mischief-making institutions that an early generation of historians of the Reconstruction period were to describe. Much of the leadership of Republican regimes fell to native whites or to northerners who had resettled in the South after the war. Most of the local whites who supported or entered Reconstruction governments and became known derisively as "scalawags" were ex-Whigs seeking to reenter politics. These were not mere opportunists; as Whigs they had supported a vigorous federal government, and their beliefs accorded with the policies of congressional Reconstruction. The northerners whom their opponents labeled "carpetbaggers" defy easy characterization. On the average, they were well-educated middle-class professionals: physicians, lawyers, teachers. Many were former Union soldiers attracted by the South's climate and cheap land. Some undoubtedly were profiteers;

others, like Governor Adelbert Ames of Mississippi and Governor Daniel Chamberlain of South Carolina, were idealists. Any discussion of corruption must be measured against the records of previous white southern administrations and against the sorry performance of several northern governments during this era. On the whole, Reconstruction governments made substantial progress toward postwar recovery and social reform. They drafted progressive new constitutions, reapportioned legislatures to give backcountry districts equitable representation, expanded social services, improved roads, encouraged railroad construction, and established the South's first substantial public school system. Much of the so-called extravagance of Reconstruction legislatures merely represented expenditures for public services that previous regimes had neglected.

The Land Question

The blacks were legally free and had the vote. But they lacked the one essential basis of independence and equality: land or an equivalent property. Both races in the postwar South recognized the importance of the land question. "The way we can best take care of ourselves is to have land and turn it and till it by our labor," contended a delegation of freed people in 1865. This is exactly what former slaveholders feared, and they determined early on to prevent blacks from owning land. Without access to employment except on land owned by whites, all the ballots and education in the world would be worthless. "They who own the real estate of a country control its vote," warned one observer. It is this as much as anything else that explains the successful overthrow of Reconstruction in the South.

A few antislavery activists had wanted to provide land for emancipated slaves. As early as 1862 Congress passed legislation confiscating plantations of Confederate sympathizers, and it was proposed to resettle blacks on them. But the Lincoln Administration showed little interest. In 1865 General William T. Sherman temporarily allotted to thousands of homeless ex-slaves small tracts of confiscated land along the South Atlantic coast. "Forty acres and a mule" became a byword among landless ex-slaves. The Freedman's Bureau attempted a scheme of renting abandoned land to blacks, who were to own it after three years.

This was as close as anyone came to providing a new life for blacks to move into when they moved out of slavery. Andrew Johnson restored confiscated lands to their previous owners and evicted the black tenants. Few northerners supported Stevens' plan to seize private property, even from slaveholders. Congress soundly defeated his watered-down confiscation plan in 1866. It did set aside certain public lands in the South for purchase by freed people. This scheme failed badly, however, because the land available was inferior, and because few ex-slaves had the capital to buy land and farm equipment.

In many areas, the first system to develop in the absence of slavery was that of wage labor. Guided and prodded by agents of the Freedmen's Bureau, blacks signed contracts to work for so much a month and were provided with cabins, often in the former plantation slave quar-

They were free, but the economic condition of most black tenant farmers and sharecroppers was not dramatically better than that of slaves. Redistribution of some confiscated plantation lands might have improved their lot, but the government undertook no such sizable programs.
(Courtesy, Library of Congress)

ters, and sometimes with food. Yet work in the fields at the white man's bidding, on the white man's land, under the immediate supervision of a white overseer seemed far too much like old slavery in a new guise. Many blacks would have none of it and sabotaged the arrangement. One way was to collect wages during the planting and cultivating months and then decamp just before the crucial harvest, which left the owner with the problem of gathering in the cotton or tobacco without a workforce.

Sharecropping   The specific reason for the rejection of the gang labor system was that it suggested the organization of field work under slavery. But in looking for some alternative, the freed slaves were acting in keeping with an American tradition that identified personal independence with the possession of property. One estimate has a fifth of black farm workers owning land by the 1880s. For most, conventional ownership was not an immediate option. Sporadic attempts, soon after the defeat of the rebels, to seize the land of planters met with resistance by the federal government. An alternative, however inadequate, gave the black family an opportunity to work independently on a plot of ground. This land and labor system finally devised in the postwar South was sharecropping. In this form of tenancy the black worker contributed labor and perhaps the use of some tools and a mule, and received from the landlord some land to farm. At harvest time the cropper got to keep from one-half to two-thirds of the crop, the remaining portion going to the landowner.

The system had some advantages. Blacks now had some personal freedom; there was no overseer to supervise their work. Instead of living in the old slave quarters, moreover, each black family could reside apart on its own rented piece of land. Some blacks simply took their slave cabin from the old quarters to their own farm. Blacks could now decide how to spend their money. And they could arrange their own family division of labor.

The sharecropper system was nevertheless a poor substitute for landowning. Sharecroppers, like other tenants, had little incentive to improve the land they farmed since they did not own it. The credit system that grew up alongside sharecropping was its worst element. Tenants often could not wait until harvest to buy the things they needed during the year. Storekeepers sold them cloth, tools, knick-knacks, and even food on credit, taking out a lien, a kind of mortgage, on the crop as security until harvest time in the fall. Then, when the crop was sold, the storekeeper subtracted the debt from the cropper's share. Those caught in this crop-lien process might not ever see any cash once the storekeeper and the landlord had taken their shares. Goods bought on credit were far more expensive than those bought with cash. The system also allowed many opportunities for fraud. Storekeepers, themselves under considerable economic pressure, kept the accounts and sometimes juggled the books to make sure that the sharecropper remained permanently in debt. Such a tenant remained tied to the storekeeper as a perpetual customer, unable legally to deal with any other merchant until the debt was discharged. Some scholars have seen this debt peonage as the virtual reenslavement of the South's black population. It certainly weakened the possibility that sharecropping might become for any sizable number of former slaves a way station to land ownership.

As pursuers of the nineteenth-century American ideal of small property ownership, the ex-slaves had been from the beginning cousins to the middling and poor whites of the South. In Reconstruction days as before, landowning was common among whites who had possessed no slaves or few. In this respect much better off than the newly freed black population, the white plain folk in this time of uncertainty and open possibility had reason for antagonism to the planters who had led them on a fruitless war for the maintenance of a slaveholding system in which they had largely not shared. But no politics of cooperation materialized between blacks and whites. Racist psychology dominated, and instead of seeing blacks as fellow victims of planter hegemony, poor whites would soon come to view them as upstart competitors for the scraps and tatters of poverty. This gave added cause for the violence that blacks even a century later have suffered from their white neighbors.

As regional impoverishment continued throughout the remainder of the nineteenth century, increasing numbers of rural whites and blacks were ground down into sharecropping. All in all, racial animosity never gave way to a politics of class, but by the late 1880s there were to be some feeble beginnings of just such a politics. Tentative alliances between a few poor blacks and poor whites form a remarkable though faltering episode of late nineteenth-century southern history.

A SHARECROPPING CONTRACT

This contract made and entered into between A. T. Mial of one part and Fenner Powell of the other part both of the County of Wake and State of North Carolina—

Witnesseth—That the Said Fenner Powell hath bargained and agreed with the Said Mial to work as a cropper for the year 1886 on Said Mial's land on the land now occupied by Said Powell on the west Side of Poplar Creek and a point on the east Side of Said Creek and both South and North of the Mial road, leading to Raleigh, That the Said Fenner Powell agrees to work faithfully and dilligently without any unnecessary loss of time, to do all manner of work on Said farm as may be directed by Said Mial, And to be respectful in manners and deportment to Said Mial. And the Said Mial agrees on his part to furnish mule and feed for the same and all plantation tools and Seed to plant the crop free of charge, and to give the Said Powell One half of all crops raised and housed by Said Powell on Said land except the cotton seed. The Said Mial agrees to advance as provision to Said Powell fifty pound of bacon and two sacks of meal pr month and occasionally Some flour to be paid out of his the Said Powell's part of the crop or from any other advance that may be made to Said Powell by Said Mial. As witness our hands and seals this the 16th day of January A.D. 1886

Witness

     A. T. Mial [signed]   [Seal]

         his

     Fenner X Powell   [Seal]

         mark

W. S. Mial [signed]

A black newspaper in New Orleans predicted about sharecropping:

"A kind of general serfdom and humiliation is about to take the place of slavery."

The End of Racial Progress and the Compromise of 1877

Reconstruction remained, at least in fragments, into the 1870s. After white organizations, among them the Ku Klux Klan, began threatening and committing violence on black citizens for exercising their newly acquired rights, the national legislature in the early 1870s put through several Force Acts that aimed at restraining the terrorist groups. A law in 1870 made it a felony to interfere with the exercise of the right to vote. The administration of Ulysses S. Grant, elected President in 1868 as the candidate of the Republican Party, broke the Klan by the end of 1871. Grant had easily won reelection in 1872 against Horace Greeley, publisher of the *New York Tribune*, but his administration suffered from a number of political scandals that suggested widespread corruption. Crédit Mobilier, a dummy corporation formed by a circle of Union Pacific Railroad shareholders, extorted wealth from the company and distributed bribes to prominent congressmen. For a while into the 1870s, some southern states had Reconstruction governments that represented black as well as white voters. And in 1876 there were still a few federal soldiers in the South whose object was to defend the rights of the black community. But the era of Reconstruction was coming to an end.

Finally, in the events that followed the presidential contest of 1876 between the Republican candidate Rutherford B. Hayes of Ohio and

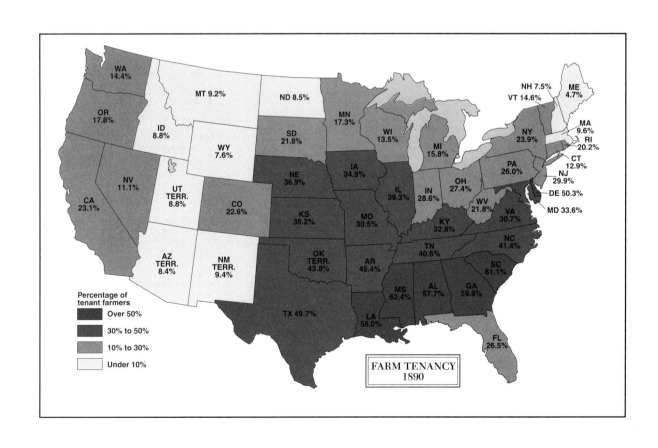

Percentage of tenant farmers

- Over 50%
- 30% to 50%
- 10% to 30%
- Under 10%

FARM TENANCY
1890

Democrat Samuel J. Tilden of New York, the Republican Party abandoned black southerners and their rights. After the general election, which chose the presidential electors who were to cast the actual vote for President, charges of irregularities had arisen concerning procedures in three southern states, South Carolina, Florida, and Louisiana. There the election boards that had counted the popular presidential vote, giving it in each case to the Republicans, were under the control of Republican Reconstruction forces; Democrats suggested that the vote in each state had actually gone for the Democrats. Both parties also claimed one disputed electoral vote in Oregon. Unless the Republican claims could stand in each of the four states, the majority in the whole electoral college would be Democratic and Tilden would be the next President. Democrats and Republicans worked out a scheme for a commission that was to decide among the disputed electors. It was supposed to be balanced between Democratic and Republican members, with one other member, Justice David Davis of the Supreme Court, who was a Republican but was expected to be independent of either party in his decisions. But in a twist of political events Davis resigned, Republican Justice Joseph P. Bradley was appointed in his stead, and the commission by a divided vote chose all the disputed Hayes electors. Democrats believed that they were about to have the election taken away from them. After the dispute had lasted for months, during which there was talk of renewed civil war, the parties came to a solution. In return for a Democratic agreement not to oppose the selection of Hayes electors, Republicans agreed that a Republican presidential administration would not only remove the remaining federal troops from the South but also give political patronage to white southerners and be friendly to economic legislation beneficial to southern states. Hayes, who had expressed concern for the rights of black southerners, presided over the end of a policy that by 1877 no longer had political support. The Republican effort to protect civil rights in the South had ceased.

Suggested Readings

Readings on Reconstruction could start with Eric Foner's volume of that title (1988). Kenneth Stampp's *The Era of Reconstruction, 1865–1877* (1965) is also thorough on the Reconstruction years. An important study of the consequences of freedom for blacks is Leon F. Litwack's *"Been in the Storm So Long:" The Aftermath of Slavery* (1979). Harold M. Hyman analyzes the constitutional issues of the era in *A More Perfect Union* (1973). Michael Les Benedict, *The Impeachment and Trial of Andrew Johnson* (1973) is a superior analysis of the divisions and alignments within the Radical Reconstruction Congress and its relationships with the President, whom the author depicts unfavorably. See also Benedict's *A Compromise of Principle: Congressional Republicans and Reconstruction* (1974), which argues that the Radical Republicans found the Reconstruction measures mere compromises. C. Vann Woodward's *Reunion and Reaction* (1951) is about the Compromise of 1877; Keith Polakoff, *The Politics of Inertia* (1977), gives a differing interpretation.

See also John Hope Franklin, *Reconstruction After the Civil War* (1961), William Gillette, *Retreat from Reconstruction, 1869–1879* (1980), Eric McKitrick, *Andrew Johnson and Reconstruction* (1965), and Allen W. Trelease, *White Terror: The Ku Klux Klan Conspiracy and Southern Reconstruction* (1971). And see William E. Nelson, *The Fourteenth Amendment* (1988), and Richard Current, *Those Terrible Carpetbaggers* (1988).

On the Freedmen's Bureau there are George R. Bentley, *A History of the Freedmen's Bureau* (1965) and William S. McFeely, *Yankee Step-Father: General O. O. Howard and the Freedmen's Bureau* (1965). A good state study is Joe Gray Taylor's *Louisiana Reconstructed, 1863–1877* (1974).

Herbert Gutman in *The Black Family in Slavery and Freedom* (1976) argues that even under slavery there was often a strong nuclear family with the father in charge. See also Hans Trefousse's *Andrew Johnson: A Biography* (1989), and William S. McFeely's *Grant: A Biography* (1981).

☆ ☆ ☆ **POINTS OF VIEW** ☆ ☆ ☆

Should Andrew Johnson Have Been Impeached?

Michael Les Benedict

As Americans for the first time seriously discussed the possibility of impeaching a president, they arrived at two opposing concepts of the law of impeachment. . . .

Democrats, Republicans who opposed impeachment, and most lawyers argued that a government officer could be impeached only for an act actually criminal, a violation of a criminal statute. Many historians have accepted this view as embodying the proper law of impeachment, accusing those who insisted on a broader interpretation of using impeachment wrongly in a purely political vendetta. But those who espoused the narrow view had an extremely difficult task in sustaining it, because in fact it was a novel argument, running counter to precedent, the overwhelming weight of American legal authority, and logic. . . .

Since legal authorities had almost unanimously adopted the broad view of impeachment, conservatives proceeded to the lawyerlike task of citing their testimony on questions not quite in point. They argued that the power of impeachment should be determined primarily by the words of the Constitution. The framers had authorized the House of Representatives to impeach government officers for "treason, bribery, or other high crimes and misdemeanors." Arguing that the language raised the presumption that impeachment lay only for actual crimes, despite the number of impeachments that seemed to imply the opposite, conservatives cited the great English constitutional commentators Blackstone, Wooddeson, and Hale to the effect that a crime was a violation of law and that laws must be known to the people. . . .

Radicals argued that the "misdemeanors" the Constitution referred to as grounds for impeachment included misfeasance and malfeasance in office as well as crimes indictable before criminal courts. . . .

The radicals' greatest strength resided in the unanimity with which the great American constitutional commentators had upheld the broad view of the impeachment power. . . .

As a practical matter, American constitutional commentators—[Supreme Court Justice Joseph] Story, [William A.] Duer, [James] Kent, [William] Rawle, and the authors of *The Federalist*—recognized that the maintenance of proper checks and balances in government, which they believed guaranteed liberty, depended upon the good faith and restraint of those entrusted with power. They recognized that the danger to liberty and the efficient workings of government lay not in the possibility that the president or lesser executive officers might act illegally, but rather that they might abuse the powers the Constitution *had* delegated to them. . . . The abuses commentators feared were precisely those "too artful to be anticipated by positive law, and sometimes too subtle and mysterious to be fully detected in the limited period of an ordinary investigation. . . ."

Had Republicans acted upon these doctrines, there can be no doubt that Andrew Johnson could have been impeached, tried, convicted, and removed at any time after December 1865, for his activities fitted precisely into the pattern Pomeroy, Rawle, and others had outlined. . . .

Historians have often interpreted the impeachment movement as part of a drive for congressional supremacy. Had it succeeded, some suggest, the government of the United States might have evolved into a parliamentary system. But in fact it had not been Congress but the President who had been claiming broad new powers. It was Andrew Johnson who had appointed provisional governors of vast territories without the advice and consent of the Senate, who had nullified congressional legislation, who claimed inherent quasi-legislative powers over Reconstruction. In many ways, Johnson was a very modern president, holding a view of presidential authority that has only recently been established. Impeachment was Congress's defensive weapon; it proved a dull blade, and the end result is that the only effective recourse against a president who ignores the will of Congress or exceeds his powers is democratic removal at the polls.

Michael Les Benedict, *The Impeachment and Trial of Andrew Johnson* (New York: W. W. Norton and Co., 1973). Reprinted by permission.

So Johnson had won. . . . To find the reasons for his victory, the political situation and the circumstances of the trial must be kept in mind. True, the Republicans enjoyed an overwhelming majority in both houses, the president had forfeited much of his popularity, and the country was anxious to proceed with Reconstruction, but it proved impossible to convict the executive on the charges presented. In the first place, they were dubious. From the very beginning, Thaddeus Stevens himself realized their weakness. "As the Committee are likely to present no articles having any real vigor in them," he wrote [Representative Benjamin F.] Butler on February 28, "I submit to you if it is not worth our while to attempt to add at least two other articles." The result was the addition of the last two charges [one accusing Johnson of having brought Congress into disrepute and the other summarizing the previous charges], which even radical newspapers and editors criticized as a mere afterthought. . . .

The House should have waited a few days before acting, Representative Thomas A. Jenckes heard from his home in Rhode Island. "Johnson would then have been mad enough to commit some further misdemeanor upon which you could have prosecuted him with the certainty of convicting him." The charges added up to a "penny whistle affair," thought Benjamin B. French, and Senator John B. Henderson characterized them as counts of "narrow bounds in offense both in act and intent."

If the case was weak, the managers' conduct did not help. "The managers of the House of Representatives have been poor judges of human nature and poor readers of human motives," wrote the Chicago *Tribune* on May 9. One could hardly call Johnson a "great" criminal as they had done. Butler, who had vowed to try the case as he would a horse case, appeared aggressive and offensive. Because the managers had a poor case, they took refuge in various legal devices, a tactic seen as a confession of weakness.

Constitutional considerations also played a role in Johnson's acquittal. The genius of the American system was widely believed to be founded on the tripartite division of government. The legislative, executive, and judicial branches operated each in its proper sphere, and as the impeachment trial coincided with attacks on the Supreme Court, there was widespread fear of the danger of legislative supremacy. Assessing the case many years later, Edmund Ross came to the conclusion that "the impeachment of the President was an assault upon the principle of coordination that underlies our political system and thus a menace to our established political forms, as, if successful, it would, logically, have been the practical destruction of the Executive Department." And [Senator Lyman] Trumbull, in justifying his vote for acquittal, stated: "Once set the example of impeaching the President for what, when the excitement of the hour shall have subsided, will be regarded as insufficient causes . . . no future President will be safe who happens to differ with a majority of the House and two-thirds of the Senate on any measure deemed by them important, particularly if of political character. . . . What then becomes of the checks and balances of the Constitution, so carefully devised and so vital to its perpetuity? They are all gone."

The short time left of Johnson's term was also a factor. "To convict and depose a Chief Magistrate of a great country while his guilt was not made palpable by the record, and for insufficient cause, would be fraught with greater danger to the future of the country than can arise from leaving Mr. Johnson in office for the remaining months of his term," Trumbull wrote in his opinion. Conviction would not have benefited Grant, and the Republicans were now determined to elect him president. Thus Republicans failed to find Johnson guilty, as he had gambled they would.

And what had the President accomplished by his victory? Above all, he had succeeded in preserving the Constitution that he admired so much. No other President would ever again be impeached for political differences with Congress; the separation of powers was preserved, and the United States retained its presidential form of government, which set it apart from the cabinet systems of European countries.

Hans L. Trefousse, *Andrew Johnson: A Biography* (New York: W. W. Norton and Co., 1989). Reprinted by permission.

President Grant starting the Corliss steam engine at the opening of the Centennial Exposition, Philadelphia, 1876.

Industrialism and Labor Strife 1865–1900

THE CENTENNIAL EXPOSITION

The hundredth anniversary of the signing of the Declaration of Independence, 1876, had as its centerpiece the Centennial Exposition in Philadelphia. About one in five Americans would visit the dozens of exhibition halls, the restaurants, the galleries, the train ride through the grounds, able to savor the excitement of a great world's fair and the pride of a nation at its hundredth birthday. The Civil War was a recent memory, and the celebrants were mindful both that the Union had barely survived destruction and that its people were just becoming reunited. Nevertheless, centennial mania dominated the summer of '76. People wore centennial hats and scarves, attended centennial balls, drank centennial coffee, listened to centennial songs. Some dressed in the fashion of 1776 or contributed artifacts from the nation's history, including a pair of George Washington's false teeth. Temperance organizations at the Exposition provided visitors with free ice water from a giant fountain they had built in the form of a Greek temple, with twenty-six spigots.

On opening day, May 10, 1876, over 100,000 people came to see the "greatest spectacle ever presented to the vision of the Western World." Banners, flags, and streamers festooned the usually staid city. Before a vast platform filled with dignitaries from all over the world, a 150-piece orchestra played national songs of all the countries represented at the fair. As the maestro called for the Brazilian national hymn, Emperor Dom Pedro of

HISTORICAL EVENTS

Late 1860s
Bessemer and open-hearth methods revolutionize steelmaking

1871
Knights of Labor formed • Charles Darwin's *Descent of Man* (*Origin of Species* was published in 1859)

1873
"Crime of '73": Congress stops issuing silver dollars

1876
Centennial Exposition in Philadelphia

1877
Railroad and other strikes

1878
Bland-Allison Silver Purchase Act

1879
Thomas A. Edison invents incandescent electric lightbulb

1886
American Federation of Labor (AFL) founded

continued

Inside the Art Hall, the statue of George Washington perched on an eagle. *(Courtesy, Free Library of Philadelphia)*

Brazil appeared on the platform, the first reigning monarch ever to appear in the United States. The republican crowd made him the hero of the day, wildly cheering this plainly dressed "true Yankee emperor with go-ahead American traits." Dom Pedro, whose travels the press had closely attended, endeared himself to Americans with his interest in translating the "Star-Spangled Banner" into Portuguese. He had also ordered the abolition of slavery in Brazil. The arrival of President Grant signaled the orchestra to begin the "Centennial March," a piece that the Women's Centennial Committee had purchased from the great German composer Richard Wagner for $5,000.

The exhibit, with its galleries, its statues (the hand and torch of the unfinished Statue of Liberty were a major attraction), its displays of inventions, machinery, furniture, publications (the Newspaper Pavilion had 10,000 up-to-date newspapers, each in its own pigeonhole, for visitors to read), its commercial displays, was a microcosm of American achievements—gaudy, good-natured, diverse, never accepting the limitations of the present. The chief symbol of the centennial was in the great Machinery Hall. When President Grant and Dom Pedro entered it, silent machines were spread over fourteen acres—machines to saw logs, to spin cotton, to print newspapers—hundreds of different kinds waiting to drive the nation into a glorious commercial future. At the center of the hall stood the giant Corliss engine: forty feet high, 700 tons, capable of generating 2,500 horse-power. The Emperor and the President each turned a lever at the bottom of the vast machine, a hiss of steam escaped, the giant beams of the engine began to rise and fall, and as this power was transmitted over thousands of shafts, belts, pulleys, and gears, all fourteen acres of machinery leaped into life. Foreign visitors recognized that the United States now led the world in machinery and invention.

A few determined women recognized that replacing muscle with steam should open the workplace to females. The Women's Centennial Committee, headed by Mrs. Elizabeth Duane Gillespie, an energetic great-granddaughter of Benjamin Franklin, organized subcommittees in every state that raised money for a Women's Pavilion showing female achievements. On May 10 the Empress Teresa, Dom Pedro's wife, opened the Women's Pavilion. She pulled a golden cord that started a six-horsepower steam engine to run spinning frames and looms on which were displayed the work of female artisans, as well as a printing press that turned out a magazine, *The New Century for Women*, written, edited, printed, and published by women. Americans did not consider the operating of machinery to be female work, and Mrs. Gillespie had scoured the country in search of a woman who knew how to run a steam engine, finally importing from Canada Emma Allison, "an educated and accomplished lady" who became one of the stars of the fair. Operating a steam engine, she assured countless audiences, was far less complicated than caring for a child. The Women's Pavilion was one of the great successes of the Exposition.

The competition among inventions for Exposition awards in June produced perhaps the most lasting legacy of the Centennial Exposition. A reluctant Alexander Graham Bell, thinking that he should stay in Boston where he had examinations to grade and a speech course to finish teaching, took the train to Philadelphia to display his recent "invention in embryo," the "speaking telephone." On a Sunday, June 25, when the exhibits were closed and sounds could therefore be carefully tested, the ubiquitous Dom Pedro and nearly fifty scientists trudged from exhibit to exhibit, while out west at the Little Big Horn River in Montana, Chief Sitting Bull and 5,000 braves were destroying Custer's army. Late in the afternoon, the scientists lingered over the display of one of Bell's competitors in the race to perfect the electronic transmission of sound. They would have ceased their labors for the day, so Bell would later recall, if it had not been for the personal interest of the Emperor, who had met Bell in Boston and was impressed by his work with the deaf. Dom Pedro and the other judges listened to Bell's voice over the wires from across the long gallery asking, "Do you understand what I say?" "I hear, I hear!" shouted the excited Emperor, who then raced across the gallery at a very un-emperor-like gait to congratulate the inventor.

Our Five-Magnet Compact Bridging Telephone.

By 1897 Sears, Roebuck and Co. was selling Alexander Graham Bell's invention to Iowa farmers. The text below gives their sales pitch.

A FARMER'S EXPERIENCE.

"Last Spring the farmers around this neighborhood decided to build a telephone line and wanted me to go in on the line. I didn't see any use for a telephone and told them I didn't believe I would need one just then. Everything went along all right till about two months ago, when I drove to town one day with the boys and left the women folks alone. We didn't start back from town till about dark, and when we got to the farm we found there was a big crowd there and most of our household goods were setting out in the yard. When I finally found the women folks I learned that one of the girls had dropped a coal oil lamp and it had started a blaze in a minute. Before they could hitch up and drive to the neighbors for any help the fire had got such headway that when the men arrived from the next farm it was almost impossible to check the flames, but they finally succeeded in getting the fire under control, but not until it had destroyed most of the house and a good part of our furniture, besides injuring some of the people who were trying to fight the fire. Well, after we got the house repaired and bought a lot of new furniture, paid all the doctor's bills, bought the women folks new dresses and borrowed some money from the bank to get things fixed up, I decided that it might be cheaper to put in a telephone after all, and you bet I did so mighty quick."

IF AN ACCIDENT SHOULD HAPPEN

This farmer's story illustrates only one of the many reasons why every farmer should have a telephone in his home. If anyone should take sick the doctor can always be called immediately by the telephone.

The Great Surge

Economic Growth

By the Civil War the United States was already among the very richest of nations. Its prosperity largely depended on its bounteous fields, forests, and mines. Many of the manufactured items Americans used came from abroad, paid for by cotton from the South, gold from California, and the shipping that the efficient American merchant marine provided for European commerce. The textile industry of the Northeast, iron manufacturing in Pennsylvania and Ohio, flour mills along the Delaware and on the Chesapeake, and shipbuilding along the New England and Middle Atlantic coast also contributed to American incomes. But as of 1860, the United States was still primarily a producer of food and raw materials for its own people and for consumers elsewhere in the Atlantic world. In the half century that followed, the United States became the world's largest industrial power.

Much of the surge in production of wealth came in agriculture. In 1860 the total value of all farm products had been about $1.5 billion. In 1919 it reached $7.5 billion. American agriculture was meeting

Iron and Steel Firms, 1870 and 1900	
1870	
No. of Employees	78,000
Output (tons)	3,200,000
Capital invested	$121,000,000
1900	
No. of Employees	272,000
Output (tons)	29,500,000
Capital invested	$590,000,000

the needs of expanding populations at home and abroad. Yet other branches of the economy had grown so much faster that as a proportion of all economic output agriculture was now about seventeen percent, down from well over a quarter. Manufacturing and mining now dominated the American economy.

In the half century following the Civil War the growth of industry was spectacular. From about 20 million tons in 1860, coal production attained 500 million in 1910. Lumber output, at 12.7 billion board feet in 1869, reached over 40 billion by 1910. Petroleum, having yielded half a million barrels in 1860, was at 209 million in 1910.

Americans who lived through the half century of growth did not need to see figures and graphs to understand what had taken place. Everywhere the country displayed change. Lying over the Lehigh Valley of eastern Pennsylvania, the Mahoning Valley of eastern Ohio, the Ohio Valley at Pittsburgh, layers of smog covered steel and glass mills. Everywhere new cities and towns appeared to shelter people at the newly opened mines and mills. Outside the most rural and isolated areas, time in communities throughout the country was marked off by the blast of factory whistles summoning employees to work early in the morning and signaling an end to the day.

Intrinsic to industrialization were the settlement and use of the country's vast lands, providing coal and minerals, timber, food for cities and factory workers, and a market for the farm machinery and other goods that the new technologies were turning out. The eastern countryside and the western wilds alike came to bear the scars of the mammoth labors of workers and machines. Loggers nearly destroyed forests of the Pacific Northwest, mining scratched and gouged the landscape, industrial wastes fouled waterways, rainstorms turned trees, houses, and much of the landscape a sooty gray near steel mill smokestacks.

Economic Infrastructure   A necessary basis of industrialization is the development of a modern economic infrastructure, as economists name the network of institutions that makes for the efficient distribution of products and information. Mass production can occur only if a country has the capacity for the large-scale distribution of manufactured goods.

The most significant improvement by far in the American infrastructure was the construction by 1910 of 240,000 miles of main railroad trackage. Major cities as well as farms and small towns were linked together in a vast transportation system that permitted the efficient mass distribution of raw materials, farm produce, and products of manufacture. George Westinghouse's invention of the air brake late in the nineteenth century had improved the safety of railroads, and in making possible the attachment of a greater number of cars to a single locomotive increased the volume of rail traffic.

In the decades after the Civil War, new technologies made the instantaneous exchange of information a reality. Samuel Morse had earlier invented the telegraph, a mechanism providing for the electromagnetic transmission of coded messages. In 1844 a completed telegraph line connected Washington, D.C., with Baltimore. During the rest of the nineteenth century, contractors built telegraph lines simultaneously with the construction of railroad trackage. Alexander Graham Bell received a patent on the telephone in 1876, and by 1900 there were nearly 1,500,000 operating telephones in the United States, providing voice transmission among the major towns and cities of the eastern United States. A number of other inventions meanwhile greatly improved the efficiency of producing written documents. In 1873 the Remington Company began selling large numbers of the recently invented typewriter, and by 1875 the development of the rotary printing press made it possible to print on both sides of a sheet of paper simultaneously. Edmund Barbour invented a calculating machine in 1872 that provided for printed totals and subtotals. By the end of the nineteenth century, businesses had the capacity to produce large volumes of information efficiently and to distribute that information quickly.

The end of the nineteenth century would be incomprehensible without Thomas A. Edison, inventor in 1877 of the phonograph and in 1879 of the incandescent electric lightbulb, and a pioneer in the motion picture. Well known, but worth repeating, is his method of inquiry, which he described as one percent inspiration and ninety-nine percent perspiration. Legend, at any rate, says that he shunned theory. If Edison had been set to finding the needle in the haystack, so the story goes, he would not have stood back and considered where the needle had fallen and where, therefore, it must be; he would instead have looked at one haystraw after another, until he found the elusive object. Although the description is no doubt somewhat exaggerated, Edison represented the American of his time, hardworking, suspicious—perhaps overly so—of abstraction. Whether because the process of sifting through things one by one came most naturally to him or because there was no other way of doing the task, he tested 6,000 materials in the course of seeking a filament that would glow indefinitely in a vacuum within a translucent glass ball. It was also in the spirit of his time that one of his first uses of electricity was to light up Wall Street. The financier J. P. Morgan glowered and shouted at the telephone but in illuminating his house and bank with electricity was one of the earliest to light up structures with the new technology. In 1888 the inventor formed the Edison General Electric Company.

While new transportation and information facilities were creating a single national market, that market was thriving on the products of the nation's burgeoning factories, along with the produce of its farms. In 1859 there were 140,000 establishments that had any claim to the label "factory." Most of these were tiny undertakings with one owner and four or five workers. In 1914 there were 268,000 factories, many of them large firms with vast numbers of employees. Electricity was lighting them, while electrical currents (Edison had also invented a method of transmission) supplied them with power. This freed mechanical enterprises from the necessity of being close to a source of natural power. It also liberated cities from the darkness, allowing for a brightly lit nightlife such as had never happened before.

Thomas Edison, unkempt and wrinkled in his research lab. *(Courtesy, Bettmann Archives, New York City)*

The growth of the steel industry in the years following the Civil War illustrates the role of the railroad in American economic development. The railroad played an important part in shipping the iron ore and coke to the mills, and the finished steel to the ultimate users. It was also the largest single customer for steel. Rail construction meant steel—for the rails, for the rolling stock, for bridges, trestles, and terminals. Hence the growth of the railroads stimulated the steel industry. Economists refer to this kind of stimulation as the "multiplier effect."

Furtunately for the steel industry, the automobile and trucking industries that so weakened the railroads were also huge consumers of steel. That steel is an essential ingredient in so many products is what leads economists to label it a basic industry.

Industry

Steel   Before the Civil War, steel, an alloy composed primarily of iron and carbon, had been an expensive material, produced in small amounts by hand labor and used largely for knives, razors, swords, and springs. It was far more common not to work iron into steel. Iron itself came in two forms. Cast iron could be poured into molds, but the large amounts of dissolved carbon it contained made it brittle; wrought iron, containing little carbon, was soft and ductile, and used largely for ornamental shapes, nails, and horseshoes. Neither of these forms was very useful in construction, where great strength and the ability to take shock were vital. Americans built their bridges, public buildings, and ships of stone, brick, or wood. Even machinery in these years used much wood.

After the Civil War two new processes appeared—the Bessemer and the open-hearth—that revolutionized the production of steel. Both removed the right amount of dissolved carbon in cast iron to create a form of steel with great strength. Unlike previous steelmaking techniques the new methods used little labor in producing large quantities and thereby brought down the price. Suddenly steel became usable in place of wood, brick, or tensility iron, with tremendous gains in strength, durability, and cost. The first great use of the new cheap steel

Steelmaking furnaces, Braddock, Pennsylvania. (*Courtesy, Library of Congress*)

was in rails, where it resulted in increases in safety and load-carrying capacity. Before long, the use of steel spread widely. The first steel bridges came in the 1870s. Steel soon became common for ocean-going vessels, and was the foundation for the giant passenger liners of 20,000 tons or more that plied the Atlantic by the end of the century. Steel made possible the skyscraper, a building constructed around a light but strong metal frame that could soar many stories from the street without the thick, space-wasting walls formerly necessary for tall structures.

The steel industry's expansion was phenomenal. In 1860 the United States produced 13,000 tons of steel. By 1879 American furnaces were turning out over a million tons a year. By 1910 the United States was making over twenty-eight million tons, and was by far the largest producer of steel in the world.

Andrew Carnegie   No one individual can be given credit for this extraordinary transformation. But the most prominent of the steel industrialists was Andrew Carnegie.

Carnegie was not a typical business leader of this period. Historians who have looked into the social origins of late nineteenth-century businessmen have concluded that most of them came from native-born elite backgrounds and had received excellent educations for the day. Carnegie, however, was born of working-class parents in Scotland and

Andrew Carnegie, self-styled "distributor of wealth for the improvement of mankind," devoted to public causes ninety percent of the fortune he made in the steel industry. *(Courtesy of the Carnegie Corporation)*

came to the United States with his family as a thirteen-year-old in 1848. Near Pittsburgh, where the Carnegies settled, Andrew started at the bottom as a $1.20 a week helper in a textile factory, doing piecework. He very quickly moved on to a telegraph office and then, during the Civil War, became a manager with the Pennsylvania Railroad. Wherever he worked the sprightly lad impressed his employers with his energy, intelligence, and enterprise, and they consistently pushed him ahead and let him in on opportunities. Gradually, as he accumulated money, he invested it in various new enterprises including oil refining, Pullman cars, and a company that built iron bridges. In 1872, Carnegie, by now thoroughly familiar with the processes of business and finance, organized the Union Mills to manufacture Bessemer steel.

Neither an inventor nor a gifted financier, Carnegie never really understood the chemistry of iron and steel. Nor did he ever engage in any of those elaborate stock deals that helped enrich speculators such as Jay Gould and James Fisk. Carnegie's chief talents in steelmaking were in choosing competent subordinates who knew their jobs well and in ruthlessly cutting costs by the elimination of bottlenecks and by the running of all equipment full blast, even if this meant replacing it early. While others were cutting back on costs during the depression that began in 1873, Carnegie was taking advantage of the cheapness of equipment and improving his plant. His business skill consisted above all of examining every expense to see whether it was needed.

Of course Carnegie was riding the wave of economic expansion that each year created ever greater need for cheap steel. Still, he forged far ahead of all other steel producers. By the beginning of the twentieth century the Carnegie works in the Pittsburgh area were producing

ANDREW CARNEGIE

Andrew Carnegie was once quite an ordinary man. While most business leaders of his and future times came from wealth, Carnegie was free to give this inspirational address, based partially on his own career, to Curry Commercial College in Pittsburgh during 1885.

THE ROAD TO BUSINESS SUCCESS:
A TALK TO YOUNG MEN

It is well that young men should begin at the beginning and occupy the most subordinate positions. Many of the leading business men of Pittsburgh had a serious responsibility thrust upon them at the very threshold of their career. They were introduced to the broom, and spent the first hours of their business lives sweeping out the office. . . . I was one of those sweepers myself, and who do you suppose were my fellow sweepers? David McCargo, now superintendent of the Alleghany Valley Railroad; Robert Pitcairn, Superintendent of the Pennsylvania Railroad, and Mr. Moreland, City Attorney. . . .

Assuming that you have all obtained employment and are fairly started, my advice to you is "aim high." I would not give a fig for the young man who does not already see himself the partner or the head of an important firm. Do not rest content for a moment in your thoughts as head clerk, or foreman, or general manager in any concern, no matter how extensive. Say each to yourself. "My place is at the top." *Be King in your dreams. . . .*

The first and most seductive, and the destroyer of most young men, is the drinking of liquor. I say to you that you are more likely to fail in your career from acquiring the habit of drinking liquor than from any, or all, the other temptations likely to assail you. . . .

Assuming you are safe in regard to these your gravest dangers, the question now is how to rise from the subordinate position we have imagined you in, through the successive grades to the position for which you are, in my opinion, and, I trust, in your own, evidently intended. I can give you the secret. It lies mainly in this.

700,000 tons of steel a year, more than all of Great Britain. In 1895 the Carnegie Company earned a profit of $5 million; in 1900 it made $40 million. Since Carnegie owned by far the largest share of the firm, most of this went into his own pocket—in an era with no income tax.

Carnegie's Charitable Work   By the early 1890s, Andrew Carnegie's powerful steel firm was both efficient and immensely profitable. Meanwhile, other steel men were creating parallel firms that unlike the Carnegie Company turned out various finished steel shapes and products. When Carnegie threatened to undertake this kind of work, he frightened his competitors badly. They turned to J. P. Morgan and asked him to organize a merger that would stop this impending war.

At first Carnegie was reluctant to join the merger, but then he yielded. The "star-spangled Scotsman" had long dreamed of withdrawing from business and devoting his time to culture and his money to good causes. Here was his chance, and when Morgan offered him the equivalent of almost half a billion dollars, he agreed to the deal. Most of what he received was in the form of bonds and stock in the United States Steel Company, a firm organized out of the Carnegie firm and a dozen others with a total capitalization of $1.4 billion. United States Steel at its moment of birth controlled sixty percent of the country's steel business as well as vast reserves of ore and coal and over a thousand miles of railroad. It was the largest corporation in the world. Carnegie himself enjoyed his money to the full. But not in the usual way. He founded 3,000 public libraries and provided over 4,000 churches with organs. He founded the Carnegie Institute of Technol-

---

Instead of the question "What must I do for my employer?" substitute "What can I do?" Faithful and conscientious discharge of the duties assigned you is all very well, but the verdict in such cases generally is that you perform your present duties so well that you had better continue performing them. Now, young gentlemen, this will not do. The rising man must do something exceptional, and beyond the range of his special department. *He must attract attention.* . . . Some day, in your own department, you will be directed to do or say something which you know will prove disadvantageous to the interest of the firm. Here is your chance. Stand up like a man and say so. Say it boldly, and give your reasons, and thus prove to your employer that, while his thoughts have been engaged upon other matters, you have been studying during hours when perhaps he thought you asleep, how to advance his interests. You may be right or you may be wrong, but in either case you have gained the first condition of success. You have attracted attention.

Always break orders to save owners. There never was a great character who did not sometimes smash the routine regulations and make new ones for himself. The rule is only suitable for such as have no aspirations, and you have not forgotten that you are destined to be owners and to make orders and break orders. . . .

And here is the prime condition of success, the great secret: concentrate your energy, thought, and capital exclusively upon the business in which you are engaged. Having begun in one line, resolve to fight it out on that line, to lead in it; adopt every improvement, have the best machinery, and know the most about it.

The concerns which fail are those which have scattered their capital, which means that they have scattered their brains also. They have investments in this, or that, or the other, here, there and everywhere. "Don't put all your eggs in one basket" is all wrong. I tell you "put all your eggs in one basket, and then watch that basket." It is trying to carry too many baskets that breaks most eggs in this country. He who carries three baskets must put one on his head, which is apt to tumble and trip him up. One fault of the American business man is lack of concentration.

ogy, built the Peace Palace at the Hague for the International Court of Arbitration, and constructed Carnegie Hall in New York as a showcase for concerts and cultural events. He set aside $125 million for the Carnegie Foundation. When he died he had given away virtually all his Morgan money.

Meatpacking   The making of steel is an example of a producer goods industry—one that manufactures a product used by other businessmen rather than by the public directly. Many other fast-growing industries in these years belong in the same category: coal mining, copper smelting, cement manufacture. Other great industries supplied consumers with goods or commodities. An outstanding instance was meatpacking.

Before the railroad age Americans got their meat from their own livestock or from animals slaughtered in the immediate neighborhood. Gustavus Swift saw that the railroads offered an opportunity to center slaughtering operations in one place, preferably close to cheap corn and grass, and distribute meat nationally. For years live cattle had been sent to eastern consumers from western grasslands and the corn belt, but live animals did not travel well. Swift's idea was to slaughter cattle and hogs in Chicago and ship the trimmed carcasses to eastern distributors. Freight costs would be lower, the slaughtering process would be cheapened, and the disposing of vast herds in one spot provided for the convenient gathering of byproducts such as bristle, bone, hides, and fertilizer. For a while the scheme worked only in the winter months, when the cold reduced spoilage. But by 1880 the refrigerator made it possible to ship beef and hog carcasses all year round. By 1890 the Chicago packers were shipping a million trimmed sides of beef a year.

Vertical and   American entrepreneurs found two basic ways to
Horizontal   transform the small enterprises characteristic of
Integration   pre-Civil War manufacturing into giant corporations able to dominate national and even international markets. Economists define two structures of consolidation: vertical and horizontal integration.

Of vertical integration Carnegie was the chief exemplar. Carnegie determined to control every stage in the steelmaking process from the mining of the iron ore to the manufacture of steel rails and other finished products. So he purchased iron mines on the Mesabi Range, and he took on Henry Clay Frick as a partner because Frick owned soft coal that Carnegie needed to heat his blast furnaces. He also acquired huge fleets of ships to bring his iron ore to his mills and rail lines to transport his coal. Bringing all the elements in the production process under the control of a single company allowed Carnegie to produce his steel much more cheaply than his competitors could, and his ability to undersell them enabled him to crush those firms that stood in the way of his monopolizing the manufacture of steel. Most of his competitors realized that they could not withstand Carnegie's ability to cut prices below the level at which they could remain in business and so accepted his offers to buy them out.

The other form of consolidation is known as horizontal. In horizontal integration the business does not attempt to control several stages in an industrial process. The objective instead is to control as much as possible of one stage, buying up enterprises performing the same tasks. The large railway companies are an illustration. They did not choose to control the whole transportation process: the manufacture, for example, of locomotives and rails. They were content to the contrary to absorb other railways all doing the same single thing: moving freight and passengers from place to place.

Money, Banking, and Finance

All the business of the nation, whether manufacturing, wholesaling, or retailing, rode on a sea of money and credit supplied either by the federal government or by the private banking system. Money and credit aroused controversy not only among businessmen and financial experts, but also among politicians and ordinary citizens. At times it became the focus of fierce and raucous political debate.

Greenbacks   Many of the financial issues of the late nineteenth century were related to the Civil War. The war had forced the Union government to issue almost a half-billion dollars worth of greenbacks, paper money that the government made legal tender, a currency that creditors must accept in payment of all debts. The government had also sold many hundreds of millions of dollars worth of bonds. Linked to the bonds was a new banking system. Private financial promoters of any bank intended to be designated a national bank had to deposit bonds with the federal Comptroller of the Currency, who would then issue banknotes to the extent of ninety percent of the value of the bonds. These banknotes entered general circulation when the banks lent money to borrowers, and, along with the greenbacks, they became the paper money that Americans used until 1913. The system, though an improvement over the chaotic banking structure prevailing from 1836 to 1863, had many drawbacks.

One of its failings was that the supply of currency did not grow fast enough to meet the needs of the nation's expanding economy. The system also failed to establish a central bank that could come to the rescue of hard-pressed financial institutions in time of panic, when money went into hiding. Agrarians particularly objected to the provision of the national banking acts that forbade the federally chartered banks to accept mortgages as security for loans. There was a parallel state banking system, and during these years it expanded primarily to fill rural needs, but it never could fully meet the farmers' demands for abundant cheap credit on the security of their lands.

The very existence of the bonds and greenbacks made for controversy. It was generally thought that a hard currency—a currency made of metal—would hold more firmly to its value than soft or paper currency: that since the government could easily print more and more paper money, a paper dollar would be distrusted and tend to fall in value. A hard currency would keep prices from becoming inflated, and

The Greenback Party flourished in 1874–84 following the hard times that resulted from the Panic of 1873. Under the name Greenback Labor, the party polled more than 1,000,000 popular votes in 1878, electing 14 congressmen. When in 1879 the national government successfully resumed specie payments (*i.e.*, greenbacks became redeemable in gold), silver replaced greenbacks as the most popular medium for advocates of currency expansion. The party steadily declined thereafter, holding its last convention in 1888.

Greenbackers gradually joined the Free Silver Movement, which had similar objectives but advocated the use of silver instead of paper currency. Meanwhile, the Greenback Movement had supplied the precedent for agrarian political action and provided much of the leadership for the Populist movement of the late nineteenth century.

it benefited creditors, who of course wanted repayment in dollars as valuable as possible. Paper money would benefit debtors, for they would be paying in relatively cheap dollars, perhaps less valuable than those they had borrowed.

In the late nineteenth century, the prosperous favored hard dollars while spokesmen for debtors demanded paper. Among the advocates of "sound money," as partisans of metallic currency called it, were many bankers and merchants, along with conservatives who believed that paper money cheated creditors and would disrupt the economy. Defenders of sound money called for the withdrawal from circulation of greenbacks, issued during the Civil War, and insisted that the government would redeem this currency in gold. Soft money partisans—identified immediately after the war with some manufacturers, farmers, and other groups whose work was in production rather than finance—feared that the removal of all paper dollars from the currency would drive down prices and therefore lessen profits. They also argued that it would injure debtors, forcing them to pay back in hard dollars more valuable than the dollars they had borrowed.

Some partisans of soft currency insisted that even more greenbacks be printed. This scheme, called the "Ohio Idea" and championed by Ohio Democratic Senator George Pendleton, became a major issue between the parties shortly after 1865. In later years the idea of increasing greenbacks became the basis of a political movement to expand the country's money supply. During the 1870s and 1880s various greenback parties fought for soft money as relief to debtors and advocated general programs of aid to wage earners. In the South blacks formed a significant part of the greenback parties.

Silver   A second battle between soft and hard currency began in the mid-1870s. Radicals made a sharp distinction between "producers"—the farmers and workers who actually made some useful commodity—and the financiers who manipulated the market without producing a single steel girder or a single sack of grain. The producers had been victimized when Congress in 1873 stopped issuing the old silver dollar. Because silver is a less precious metal than gold, a silver currency is considered softer, its dollars more likely than gold dollars to shrivel in value. Silver coin, then, was one kind of metal currency that had something of the financial softness of greenbacks. So champions of paper currency found it easy to become champions of silver. Silver advocates insisted that the "Crime of '73," as they called the action of Congress, had been the result of a plot by bankers and other capitalists. Then in 1879 the Treasury redeemed greenbacks in gold. This meant that holders of paper money could now have the government give them gold money in exchange for it. Since the supply of gold was limited, the supply of paper money would be limited also. Unless the nation restored silver to the money supply at the ratio of sixteen ounces of silver to one ounce of gold, argued the soft-money people, the country would be at the mercy of the bankers, especially those whose resources were strengthened by connections abroad. Debtors injured by the obligation to repay in relatively valuable dollars would have to go to the banks for further loans.

Mining interests in the western states strongly supported the farmers, debtors, and soft-money economists who were calling for the expansion of the money supply by remonetizing silver. The huge discoveries of silver in Nevada, Colorado, and Utah in the 1870s increased silver production and undermined its price. The profits of mine owners declined, as did the wages of miners and the number of jobs in the industry. Congressmen from those states, anxious to raise silver prices to satisfy their constituents, joined with farm and labor groups who wanted soft money. They became a powerful political coalition in Congress.

In 1878 the silverites got Congress to pass the Bland-Allison Silver Purchase Act requiring the Treasury to buy monthly not less than $2 million and not more than $4 million of silver on the open market and coin this bullion into dollars. The adding of silver to greenbacks and national banknotes, the advocates of this measure hoped, would not only give the country some needed immediate monetary relief, but make it impossible to uphold the gold standard, since the amount of currency would be too great to be exchangeable for the government's gold. But the Treasury had a large enough gold reserve to treat the new silver dollars as just another kind of paper money. Anyone who wished might come to the banks and get a gold dollar for a silver one in the same manner as a banknote was exchangeable for gold. In 1890 came the Sherman Silver Purchase Act ordering the Treasury to purchase 4.5 million ounces of silver each month and to issue new paper money against it redeemable in either gold or silver. There the issue rested until the Panic of 1893 produced a great monetary crisis by undermining public confidence in the Treasury's reserve and sending thousands to convert their silver and paper into gold coin.

Investment Bankers

The national and state banks had their failings, but they successfully performed business for the nation. In the cities the national banks handled thousands of daily transactions, making business loans and transferring funds from place to place. In the small towns and country communities the state banks helped local feed-and-grain merchants and advanced cash to carry farmers over until the time for selling their crops. And farmers could mortgage their property to banks in return for loans with which to buy machinery or to build a barn or house.

Far removed from the farm communities, standing above even the big-city banks, were the investment bankers. These businessmen did not accept deposits and make loans to merchants. Rather, they marketed securities for large private corporations as well as for cities, states, counties, and even the federal government.

Wall Street   The investment bankers put much of their funds into the stock market, the institution identified with Wall Street in lower Manhattan, where securities of all sorts—government and private corporation bonds and corporation stocks—were

Systems of finance and communications intersected at Wall Street, New York, where the nation's most important investment banks and markets were located. The Great Blizzard of 1888 buried the district with snow and also shadowed in white the crisscrossing "blizzard" of wires needed for the communications networks.
(Courtesy, Culver Pictures)

bought and sold. The New York Stock Exchange was a private body of brokers who managed their affairs like a club, a loosely run club with scant regard for the public. The enormous expansion of industry after 1865 created a need for billions in capital. The Exchange provided the means for that capital to be distributed.

During the Gilded Age (in 1878 Mark Twain coined this phrase for his times: dazzling on the surface, base metal underneath) buying and selling securities on the Exchange, especially trading in common stock, resembled the operations of a gambling casino. "Bull" speculators bet, as they do today, on a rise in stock prices and "bear" speculators bet on a fall. Few conservative investors cared to buy the common stock traded on Wall Street. The competition of bulls and bears made for wild fluctuation in prices, and ownership seldom brought substantial dividends. Too much of the common stock was "water," issue in excess of the bedrock assets of the companies putting it out, and even the most profitable firm could seldom pay much return on a share. On the other hand, the stock market provided an indirect investment to banks and other financial institutions with some excess funds to invest for short periods. Brokers and stock gamblers could use such money and were willing to pay good rates of interest for it. This created a call loan market where money could be lent on a day-to-day basis, subject to instant recall by the lender.

The call loan market introduced another element of instability into the country's financial structure. Every fall when money was needed for marketing the country's crops, money left Wall Street to return to the farm areas. The flight of money from the stock market for whatever reason sometimes turned into a financial panic, as in 1873, 1884, 1893, and 1907.

Capital needed safer outlets than all this for investment. Steadier if less exciting than stock trading was the bond market. Investors were willing to buy corporate bonds since these represented a debt of the firm and had to be paid, interest and principal, before any other obligation, even if the firm made no profit in a given year. Useful in marketing these securities were special investment bankers who agreed to sell large blocks of bonds, taking a commission for their work. Slowly the public also developed an interest in common stock, especially if it was sold by one of the large investment houses like Kidder, Peabody of Boston; Kuhn, Loeb of New York; and J. P. Morgan and Company. These firms not only stood behind the issues in a general way but also often insisted on putting one of their partners on the corporation's board of directors as insurance to purchasers that the corporation's affairs would be well managed.

J. Pierpont Morgan, banker and financier whose investments in railroads and steel made his company one of the most powerful banking houses in the world. *(Courtesy, Morgan Guaranty Trust Co.)*

Mergers

Pools, Trusts, and Holding Companies

During the last decades of the century firms battled furiously for customers. To keep their share of a business, manufacturers and railroad operators had to cut their prices and costs. This was fine for consumers; in the course of a price war among the trunk railroads connecting New York to Chicago, the rate for a carload of cattle, normally costing the shipper $110, dropped to one dollar. But competition was hard on businessmen, and numbers of them sought in every way possible to reduce it. Often firms in a particular business would arrange informal "gentlemen's agreements" assigning each company a fixed share of the market. This ended any need to cut price in pursuit of keeping customers. Pools were similar arrangements but involved an actual written contract among the participants. Both were difficult to enforce. When the agreements fell through, businessmen created other devices for achieving an end to competition.

One of these, the trust, required stockholders of several firms to turn over their voting rights to trustees who thereafter ran the businesses as a unit, paying dividends to the original shareholders. John D. Rockefeller, in his effort to reduce the competition in the oil refining business during the early 1880s, was the first to employ the trust scheme. When state and federal courts declared trusts illegal, ingenious businessmen turned to the holding company. Taking advantage of a New Jersey law of 1889 allowing one corporation to hold stock in others, corporation lawyers arranged for a single large firm, a holding company, to acquire stock in companies that had been competing with one another. The holding company executives, of course, could then decide to limit competition in any way they chose among the firms they controlled. Some of their buyouts were generous. But they could ruthlessly drive independent firms out of business. Trusts and their ilk were real enough and led to a concentration of wealth. At the same time, the existence of mergers awakened suspicions that much of the country was in the hands of conspiratorial, unseen interests.

During the 1870s and 1880s consolidations took place on a wide scale in many consumer goods industries: leather products, salt, sugar, biscuits, starch, kerosene, rubber boots, and gloves. During the depression of the early 1890s the movement toward consolidation stopped. After 1897 it resumed with a rush, primarily in the producer or capital goods industries, but also in a few newer consumer goods industries, such as meat and cigarettes, that catered primarily to city people.

In the eight years from 1898 through 1905 more than 3,000 important business mergers occurred in industries that included steel, machinery, tobacco, copper, and cans. In this second wave the role of investment bankers was prominent. The holding company that was to control the formerly competing firms had to raise capital to buy up their stock and this required the services of bankers. The investment bankers were also useful for reassuring stockholders of the individual companies and those with savings to invest that the new firm would be reliable. One of the classic instances of mergers in this era was the formation of the United States Steel Company in 1901.

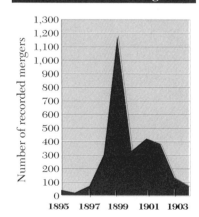

Mergers in Mining and Manufacturing

Retailing

By late in the nineteenth century, mass production by large corporations for a national market was increasing spectacularly the volume of goods available to consumers and, as this new technique lowered the price of goods, handling the flood of consumer commodities required new methods of retailing them.

The General Store   In the early nineteenth century, when most Americans lived in villages and on farms, they bought either from traveling peddlers or from general stores those goods they did not produce for themselves. The general store, in turn, received agricultural commodities from the surrounding farmers, often in exchange for other goods. A farmer's wife, for example, who wanted a bolt of cloth would pay the merchant with a few dozen eggs or several wheels of cheese if she did not have the cash. Most of the local merchant's goods, especially tropical products and manufactured items, came from the merchants of the big coastal cities, who imported them from the Caribbean or from England and France. To stock their shelves, the more ambitious country merchants trekked annually to the big port towns—New York, Boston, Charleston, Philadelphia, Baltimore, or New Orleans—to visit the warehouses of the large importers and buy on credit. The general store sold almost everything: silk ribbon, needles, hammers, nails, gunpowder and lead shot, flour, tea and coffee, yarn and cloth, candy, pickled fish, books, and whiskey. These items were seldom packaged; they were placed in barrels or bins and sold by weight or volume. Generally they were carried away in the customer's own container. Prices were not necessarily uniform. Customers bargained with the storekeeper and often received credit.

As manufacturing grew and more and more of the finished goods that consumers bought were produced in the United States, local retailers became less dependent on importers, turning instead to wholesalers who bought up the output of home factories. Located in the larger inland cities as well as on the East Coast, these wholesalers dealt either in a number of items or in some full line such as hardware or dry goods. In the growing cities and towns more and more general merchants began to specialize in selling specific products such as hats, or shoes, or books. General stores continued in smaller communities until the twentieth century.

The Department Store   During the years following the Civil War new kinds of retail outlets—the chain store, the mail-order house, and the department store—revolutionized the merchandizing of goods to consumers. Actually the department store had first made its appearance in the United States in the 1840s, when a few American merchants began to imitate a Paris institution, the Bon Marché, which combined a number of distinct specialty shops under one roof. The first great American department store magnate, A. T. Stewart of New York, was followed soon after by John Wanamaker of Philadelphia. As these stores grew in size it became impossible for owners to bargain with customers over prices. An owner did not care to delegate the responsibility to a clerk, and so the policy of charging one consistent price for an item, first adopted by R.H. Macy's in New York, quickly came to be standard for department stores and then for other retail establishments.

The first 5 & 10¢ store in the United States, opened by the F. W. Woolworth Company in Lancaster, Pennsylvania, 1879. *(Courtesy, the F. W. Woolworth Company, New York City)*

Selling goods on such a large scale, the big stores could exert an enormous amount of market leverage. Rather than deal with wholesalers, they could go directly to the manufacturers and so were able to bypass a whole layer of middlemen. Promising large volume orders, they could also compel manufacturers to give them good prices for their products, and they generally passed on the savings to consumers. Another advantage of the department store was its range of services. It delivered purchases to customers and it guaranteed quality, accepting returns from dissatisfied customers. "Your money back if . . ." became one of the Chicago store's mottoes. Another new marketing device was recommended by an Ohio retailer: "Give store arrangement greater consideration, and create in the mind of the customer a desire for other things she sees, as well as the article she asks for. People used to buy what they needed, now it's what they want; and that want is created by store display or advertisement."

In major cities all over the country department stores soon became prominent landmarks. New York had A. T. Stewart as well as Macy's, the largest store in the world under one roof, and a flock of others. Philadelphia had Wanamaker's and Gimbel's. In Boston there were Jordan Marsh and Filene's. Chicagoans shopped at Marshall Field's and Carson, Pierce, Scott. In Columbus the big store was Lazarus; in Dallas, Neiman-Marcus; in Los Angeles, Bullock's; in Brooklyn, Abraham and Straus. Many of the department-store owners were either New England Yankees or German-Jewish merchants who had begun as peddlers or small shopkeepers before the Civil War and carried their marketing skills over to the new form when it appeared.

Department stores were especially designed to catch the attention of urban, middle-class women with money to spend and time to shop, and encouraged such women to raise shopping to an important pastime. By the 1880s *The New York Times* deplored the "awful prevalence of the vice of shopping among women," claiming that it was "every bit as bad as male smoking or drinking." The stores made increasing use of decorations, many of them evoking other cultures, exotic countries, and something of a dream world. They provided a protected space in which women could forget their daily cares and imagine themselves transformed by possession of alluringly packaged commodities. Eventually, the department stores provided special corners in which women could enjoy lunch or tea, for middle-class women a novel kind of freedom from domestic confinement.

Chain Stores and Mail-Order Houses   Along with the department store came the chain store. These establishments flourished especially in the grocery and variety trades, of which the A & P (the Great Atlantic and Pacific Tea Company) and the Woolworth Five and Ten were the prototypes. Each store in a chain was expected to make a profit by itself, but management and accounting tied them together. Still more significant for the consumers was that the chains, like the department stores, could buy cheaply from suppliers. They refused credit, selling for cash only on a one-price basis. The effect was to cut prices to the consumer. This made customers happy but displeased small storekeepers, who charged

Shoppers crowd the aisles to hunt for bargains in New York City's Siegel Cooper department store in 1897. *(Courtesy, Museum of the City of New York, Byron Collection)*

The department stores attempted to make women dependent on buying things that promised to realize their fantasies. The variety of consumer goods and the nurture of a consumer mentality can be seen in this young girl's diary:

"I got three pieces of Dutch silver from Momma and Grandma, a windmill, a mandolin and a little sleigh. A set of little leather box books for odds and ends. Packs of cards in black leather with silver cornered case. Silver gilt needle case from Miss Smith. Two bottles with silver all over them from Momma and Mrs. Yznaga. Pin cushion from Alfred P. Sewing box with initials from Josie, quilt basket filled with candy lined with blue silk and a beautiful black leather book for my photos with G.E.M. in the corner from Poppa, a present from Fraulein and a $5 gold piece from Mom."

These mail-order advertisements are for one of Montgomery Ward's earliest washing machines (top) and one from the 1897 Sears, Roebuck catalog (below).

that the chains engaged in unfair competition. Store owners also protested that the chain outlets were owned by absentees, not the local people who operated the small, familiar store. But by World War I the chain store had become an established feature of the American economy.

So had the mail-order house. Unlike chain stores and department stores, the mail-order or catalog house catered largely to a rural or small-town clientele. But it too sought to replace the middleman, in this case by selling goods the customers ordered from a catalog. Aaron Montgomery Ward's success owed to his shrewd judgment of customers and the hostility of farmers to middlemen. He and his arch rival, the firm of R. W. Sears and A. C. Roebuck, also benefited from the quickening of railroad traffic, which by the end of the century had improved postal services immensely. Within a few years rural free delivery was bringing letters and packages to the farmer's front door.

A Business Civilization

Big businessmen despised trade unionism and believed that they alone were the proper judges of labor's well-being. When John Mitchell, leader of the anthracite coal strike of 1902, asked George Baer of the Philadelphia and Reading Coal Company to submit the dispute to arbitration, Baer allegedly responded: "The rights and interests of the laboring man will be protected and cared for, not by the labor agitators, but by the Christian men to whom God in His infinite wisdom has given control of the property interests of the country, and upon the successful Management on which so much depends." Many businessmen fought to retain control of wages, hours, and working conditions, and refused to share their power with anyone else, whether politicians or labor leaders. The only arrangement they recognized as legitimate was the individual bargain struck with the worker.

The attitude of employers toward unions was at bottom a matter of simple self-interest. It also had to do with a more general notion about economics that much of society, and even workers themselves, shared in some measure.

Laissez-faire and Social Darwinism That notion had as one of its components the principle of laissez-faire that came from the teachings of many British thinkers, among them Adam Smith and David Ricardo. The principle held that the way to get the greatest and cheapest possible productivity was to leave the individual employer and the individual worker to the free market. Any attempt to interfere through unions or through govermental action would distort the market and reduce total production, to the injury of laborers, employers, and consumers. At times laissez-faire thinkers invoked divine sanction for their theories. One economist believed that free markets were governed by "God's laws," and claimed that observing these laws would not only benefit individuals in this life, but prepare them "for the life that is to come."

Ideas such as these had long circulated in the United States.

Laissez-faire was the basic economic doctrine of college courses and enjoyed enormous prestige among educated Americans. After about 1870 it had reinforcement from another set of principles, often called Social Darwinism, derived in part from the ideas of Charles Darwin, the English naturalist. Just as Darwin, according to his earliest interpreters, had shown that in the biological world progress from the lowliest creature to man depended on a fierce struggle for survival, so Social Darwinists argued that social progress depended on competition among human beings. To interfere with this struggle in any way would result in the collapse of civilization or, at the very least, in stagnation. When one small businessman was asked what he would do to alleviate the economic evils of the day, he replied: "Nothing! You and I can do nothing at all. It's all a matter of evolution. We can only wait for evolution. Perhaps in four or five thousand years evolution may have carried man beyond this state of things. But we can do nothing."

The concrete applications of laissez-faire could be heartless. Sometimes factory owners acknowledged that the wages they paid did not cover workers' basic needs.

Social Darwinism, in fact, had scant approval, if any, from biologists in its use of theories of evolution; it was a mistaken effort to find similarities between biological and economic events. Darwin himself had nothing to do with it. Social Darwinism was promoted most notably in the United States by the Yale sociologist, William Graham Sumner. Recent scholarship has indicated that not many businessmen took much serious account of the idea, or perceived of a sound economy as being as brutally competitive as Social Darwinists would seem to insist. But Social Darwinism, along with the free market doctrines that colleges had been teaching for many years, did represent the dominance in American thinking of the principle of laissez-faire. It had further support from a moral and constitutional conviction that individuals should be free to manage their property as they please and to enter into contracts of their own choosing, and that any major interference on the part of the government in relations between labor and management would violate both the employer's property rights and the right of employer and worker to make a contract.

Whatever sense this concept of free contract might make in a small-town or rural economy, it was nonsense in an era of giant corporations and great disparities in property. There was no equality between the bargaining position of a coal miner and that of Baer's coal company over the terms of employment, no free contractual agreement between equals; the individual worker was free only to accept the employer's terms or to accept hunger in place of them. The use that conservatives and businessmen made of doctrines of laissez-faire involved other contradictions as well. Critics pointed out that businessmen actually detested competition when it threatened profits. Cut-throat domestic competition had fueled the merger movement. Afraid to compete with foreign manufacturers, the iron producers, the textile mill owners, the woolen manufacturers, and many others fought for ever higher protective tariffs, tariffs on foreign goods high enough to raise their price greatly and thereby protect American manufacturers from competition with them. In these years Congress gave in to the pressures of Ameri-

Charles Darwin's theory of evolution and natural selection challenged traditional thinking in America. Many traditionalists felt that his views were a blatant rejection of biblical teachings. *(Courtesy, Library of Congress)*

can industrialists and raised tariffs far beyond where they had been before the Civil War. Nor were businessmen averse to direct government subsidies when they could be had.

This dialogue from Alger's Ragged Dick *is not untypical:*

"I wish you'd tell me a little about yourself. Have you got any father or mother?"

"I aint got no mother. She died when I wasn't but three years old. My father went to sea; but he went off before mother died, and nothin' was ever heard of him. I expect he got wrecked, or died at sea."

"And what became of you when your mother died?"

"The folks she boarded with took care of me, but they was poor, and they couldn't do much. When I was seven the woman died, and her husband went out West, and then I had to scratch for myself."

"At seven years old!" exclaimed Frank, in amazement.

"Yes," said Dick, "I was a little feller to take care of myself, but," he continued with pardonable pride, "I did it. . . ."

"I went into the match business," said Dick; "but it was small sales and small profits. Most of the people I called on had just laid in a stock, and didn't want to buy. So one cold night, when I hadn't money enough to pay for a lodgin', I burned the last of my matches to keep me from freezin'. But it cost too much to get warm that way, and I couldn't keep it up."

"There's one thing I never could do," he added, proudly.

"What's that?"

"I never stole," said Dick. "It's mean and I wouldn't do it."

The Horatio Alger Hero

Despite the inconsistencies, it would be a mistake to dismiss the laissez-faire principle as a rationalization and a sham. People are capable of believing two conflicting ideas simultaneously. Ideas, moreover, are not merely rationalizations. They frequently take on a life of their own and become powerful forces. Americans deeply believed in private property and economic freedom. It was assumed that society was open and allowed for movement upward of the hardworking, the sober, and the able, and that no one need settle permanently for a place in the economic cellar.

The story of a boy's odyssey from poverty to riches became an influential genre in the skilled hands of Horatio Alger, a prolific writer who pounded out scores of novels with such titles as *Work and Win, Strive and Succeed, Do and Dare, Sink or Swim, Risen from the Ranks,* and *Facing the World.* Alger's typical hero is a boy of about fifteen, often the age for starting adult life in this period. He possesses all the virtues of honesty, sobriety, willingness to work hard. The Alger hero, however, makes his fortune not by these virtues alone but by a stroke of good fortune. He is always on hand when a child of a rich industrialist falls off the Staten Island ferry or a rich girl trips into the path of a runaway horse or slips into the Niagara River just above the falls. The heroic lad is rewarded by a job, marriage to the daughter, and eventually the wealth of the grateful father-in-law. It is to be understood, though, that he is rewarded also for his integrity, determination, and work. But along the way the young male reader was made aware of the great possibilities open to him in the United States.

The myth of success remained exclusively a male myth; women were not encouraged to move upward by their own effort. Among the middle and upper working classes, in fact, one test of a man's success was his ability to support a wife who would devote herself exclusively to providing for his comfort and their children's. The scholar Thorstein Veblen perceived and identified an extreme version of this attitude when he described women's fashions as nothing but embodiments of male success. Most women were not fashionable women, but even a woman's reserved domesticity could indicate that a man had become successful.

Many ordinary Americans had some reason to believe the success story. A common experience among Americans in the years from 1859 to the early part of the twentieth century was the accumulation of some property over an entire working life. Many did rise occupationally either in level of skill or from manual to white-collar status. Others saw their children move upward.

Another reason the nation gave business a considerable acceptance on its own terms was that so many Americans were themselves businessmen of one sort or another. An enormous number of American family heads in this era were farm owners who raised crops for sale. In 1890 there were about 3.3 million of these out of about 13 million families in the country. Add to this another million business concerns, mostly small firms, and the result is a figure that suggests that about a third of all American families of 1890 made their incomes from selling commodities or services. By 1890 many farmers were becoming skeptical of big business, but on two points they certainly agreed with it: private property deserved protection from those who would attack it; and there was nothing intrinsically wrong with the profit system. Agrarian radicals wanted, in fact, a nation of holders of small private property, and they attacked the capitalist classes for depriving the poor of property and robbing the farmers of legitimate profit.

Labor 1865–1900

The United States in the late nineteenth century was for many the land of opportunity it has always been. Yet it had its outsiders, people excluded from enjoyment of the nation's prosperity or excluded by social custom or law from participation in its politics. Most obvious among the oppressed were the southern freedmen and blacks in the North. But other groups, among them women workers and mine and factory workers, and the most recent immigrants, were outsiders as well if their condition is compared with that of the solid, propertied Americans whose images appeared in popular art and literature as representative of American society.

The nation at its founding and then in its defeat of slavery had pledged itself, in rhetoric and in law, to the attainment of equality and justice. Yet it had never been quite clear what that should ultimately mean. Most of the world, of course, had its full share of poor people, or victims of ethnic or racial bigotry, or workers at low wages for wealthy or distant employers. But in the United States such conditions were not only disturbing in themselves but scandalous: they seemed to contradict the country's origins, as only a few years earlier slavery had contradicted it. The nation's commitment to equality provided a continuing and troubling judgment on the condition of the outsiders.

The Wage Earner
In 1870 relatively few Americans worked for wages. Those who did got along relatively well with shop owners. One brass worker would recall that labor and management worked closely together after the Civil War. Most adults of working age, housewives aside, were still farm owners or, in the case of the South, belonged to the new class of sharecroppers that the breakdown of slavery had created. Many city artisans still worked in jobs like that of silversmith; cobblers made shoes by hand. Individuals often took enormous pride in their work. By 1900, however, a very large proportion consisted of wage earners rather than self-employed people. Of the twenty-seven million in the labor force in this later year, about nineteen million, or roughly two-thirds, were people who primarily sold their labor or skills to others for a daily or weekly wage. In the intervening years, conditions between workers and owners had deteriorated. The same brass worker who described shop relations as

THE WAY TO GROW POOR

THE WAY TO GROW RICH

These Currier and Ives prints preached that the way to grow rich was through hard work and thrift; in reality, a little shrewdness was also needed.

A Joliet, Illinois, railroad brakeman supported his wife and eight children on $360 a year in 1883. All ten people in his family were crammed into a three-room house where they ate chiefly bread and potatoes. The reporting investigator noted:

"Clothes ragged, children half-dressed and dirty. . . . They all sleep in one room regardless of sex. The house is devoid of furniture, and the entire concern is as wretched as could be imagined."

Many other workers gave honest testimony to their pathetic plight. One testified in 1888,

"A coal miner . . . has to work so hard to make wages that he is an old man when he should be in his prime."

having been in 1869 that of "one happy family" wrote in 1883 that "now the boss is superior" and the "average hand" would not think of addressing him. Another laborer observed, "The employer has pretty much the same feeling toward the men that he has toward his machinery."

Few wage earners were the sole support of their families. Many working families had several wage earners besides the male head. Most were sons but, increasingly, daughters and sometimes even the mother of the family worked outside the home for wages. When all went well these earners, even the unskilled, all combined could provide a family with a more than adequate living. But sickness, lack of skill, the needs of young dependents could bring down living standards to a pitiful level. During the 1880s people put aside twenty-five percent of their incomes for savings: morality, an American morality that combined virtue for its own sake with the practical advantages of virtue, instructed them to save, and there was no other way to provide for sickness, accident, or old age. In the late nineteenth century 35,000 Americans a year died of industrial accidents, far more than Europe in proportion to population. Railroads alone accounted for a shocking 6,000 fatalities a year.

Without unions, wage workers for big companies were the creatures of their employers, to be hired or dismissed at will, and when they tried to form unions other Americans looked at them as radicals or hoodlums. Against labor organization, management had an array of schemes. In yellow-dog contracts, prospective employees had to agree not to join unions. Blacklists were circulated among employers giving the names of labor activists. Spies infiltrated unions. Lockouts kept strikers from plants. Strikebreakers were available. "I can hire one half the working class to kill the other half," remarked the robber baron Jay Gould. The struggle to unionize the mines and the factories was ultimately a struggle to give wage earners a place, a community, a definition within American society.

Labor Mobility   Average real wages rose, probably by about twenty-five percent, between 1860 and 1900. Many American workers were able to advance in their jobs and in economic standing. Especially in larger communities such as Boston, many Jewish and north European along with native-born workers advanced remarkably. And in middle-sized communities, too, those workers who remained in the city for a long time usually could look forward at least to some property or savings at the end of a long working life.

Yet for every male worker who stayed put and advanced in his job or accumulated some property, several failed and departed to seek their fortune in some other place. The geographical mobility of the average working-class family in this era was astonishing. During the six decades from 1830 to 1890, Boston increased its population by about 387,000, while over 3.3 million had at one time or another arrived in the city to live. For the vast majority of new arrivals, then, Boston was a revolving door, and it is to be assumed that most of those who departed had been disappointed in their economic hopes.

The Workplace

Jobs were insecure. Without strong unions to worry about, an employer could let any worker go for union activity or for refusal to accept a speed-up. Corporations worked hard to instill habits of subordination. In the periods 1873–79, 1884–86, and 1893–97, severe business slumps forced many thousands of men and women to lose their jobs. In the last of these, as many as 4.5 million wage earners were out of work—over eighteen percent of the labor force.

Men, women, and children worked amid the smoke, flame, and din of furnaces and exposed machinery. Boiler explosions, mine cave-ins, train wrecks, uncontrollable fires, and other accidents were grim events in the lives of industrial workers. Thousands were maimed or killed, and few workers or bereaved families collected anything in compensation for loss, pain, or suffering. Some workers fell victim to the slower processes of industrial disease. Maladies that we today would recognize as black lung or some form of industrial poisoning generally went undetected. The most serious disease of all that working people regularly contracted was the "white plague," tuberculosis, a product in most cases of crowding, overwork, and poor nutrition that afflicted thousands, especially in the big cities.

The workday in American mines, mills, factories, and construction sites was long throughout the half century following the Civil War. In 1890 factory workers typically labored some sixty hours a week at their machines. Bituminous coal miners had an equally long workweek. Bakers and steelworkers averaged sixty-five hours or more. Only postal employees and other government workers, with their forty-eight-hour week, approached modern standards. A British immigrant observed, "Labour in most occupations is greater, generally speaking, than in any other part of the world. Everything, in fact, connected with trade or business seems to proceed at a sort of railroad pace; all move at the very top speed." An immigrant hatter in Newark complained that Americans "are savagely wild in devouring their work." Whatever its overall achievements, the American industrial economy provided ample cause for unrest among wage earners. In the era after the Civil War discontent would erupt in spasms of violence that shocked middle-class public opinion profoundly and sometimes injured the cause of labor.

Labor Unions Following the Civil War

For many years after the Civil War American workingmen had not been able to sustain an effective labor movement and did not support radical political action in substantial numbers. Labor organizations had a way of growing in times of prosperity and declining when times were bad, precisely when they were needed most.

During the years immediately following Appomattox, the National Labor Union was formed. It demanded an eight-hour day and wished to establish cooperatives among workers. In 1872 the group turned to politics and supported a labor party. With the panic of 1873 and the depression that followed, the National Labor Union collapsed, along with a number of other unions that had confined their work to particular trades.

Unemployment Rates, 1870–1899			
Period	Average Percent Unemployed	Peak Year	Percent Unemployed in Peak Year
1870–79	10	1876	12–14
1880–89	4	1885	6–8
1890–99	10	1894	15+

The International Harvester Corporation published this in a brochure for its Polish workers:

I hear the whistle. I must hurry.
I hear the five minute whistle.
It is time to go into the shop.
I take my check from the gate board and hang it on the department board.
I change my clothes and get ready to work.
The starting whistle blows.
I eat my lunch.
It is forbidden to eat until then.
The whistle blows at five minutes of starting time.
I get ready to go to work.
I work until the whistle blows to quit.
I leave my place nice and clean.
I put all my clothes in the locker.
I must go home.

The historian Herbert Gutman writes of the cultural shock of moving from an agrarian society with its seasonal patterns of work and leisure to an industrial society, which aims to organize all activities by the clock. Factory work required new forms of discipline that workers, accustomed to setting their own work pace, resisted. Labor and management confronted each other with mutually exclusive notions of what constituted a fair day's work for a fair day's pay.

All industrializing nations experienced these clashes to some degree, but in the United States the constant immigration of workers with no previous industrial experience prolonged the cultural dislocations. In most other modernizing societies they disappeared with the coming of a second generation of industrial workers, used to the new social patterns of work. Here the constant infusion of inexperienced immigrant workers retarded the growth of labor unions.

Samuel Gompers, leader of the American Federation of Labor, the first successful federation of trade unions, formed in 1886.
(Courtesy, U. S. Signal Corps, National Archives)

Knights of Labor, American Federation of Labor

With the economic revival of the late 1870s, the Knights of Labor, established in 1871, began to gain adherents in large numbers. Headed by Terence V. Powderly from 1878 to 1893, the organization was open to almost every variety of working person. The Knights in 1878 advocated equal pay for women and one year later permitted them to become members. At the height of the Knights' strength, women constituted about ten percent of the membership. It would be a long time before women again did so well in the organized labor movement.

The "true Knight," the order proclaimed, was "sober, respectable, conservative, modest, non-opportunistic, lawful, respectful, educated." During the years of its prosperity the organization seldom supported strikes for the sake of raising wages and improving working conditions. Rather, it concentrated on political agitation for the eight-hour day, a graduated income tax, consumer and producer cooperatives, and, in labor disputes, the use of boycotts and arbitration. The Knights were never clear as to what they wanted to be: union, reform association, or fraternal society.

Despite its professed reluctance to strike, the Knights went out against several railroads in the mid-1880s. Its initial success brought a wave of supporters who pushed the membership list to over 700,000. But thereafter, as a result of specific defeats in strikes, the Knights precipitously declined. During the 1890s the organization survived as a shadow of its earlier self, largely with agrarian support.

Meanwhile, the Knights had been eclipsed by the American Federation of Labor (AFL), founded in 1886 by Peter McGuire, Samuel Gompers, and Adolph Strasser. Gompers and Strasser were cigar makers. In 1879 they had organized the skilled cigar workers who, following introduction of the cigar mold, had lost their status of independent self-employed craftsmen. As leaders of the AFL, Gompers and Strasser elevated the techniques they had earlier learned into a set of principles that enabled the new federation of unions to weather depressions and become the first successful national organization in American labor history.

Under Gompers, the AFL avoided politics. A former socialist, he concluded that capitalism was in the United States to stay. Whatever benefits wage earners gained they would have to get within the capitalist system. Taking up with radical movements would only alienate the middle class. Even engaging in middle-of-the-road politics was a mistake. Better to stick to simple trade unionism. As Strasser stated the AFL case in a famous observation: "Our organization does not consist of idealists. . . . We have no ultimate ends. We are going on from day to day. We are fighting only for immediate objects—objects that can be realized in a few years."

The AFL formula worked. Skilled workers, most of them of native background, swelled the ranks of AFL affiliates. Since they could not easily be replaced, their threats to strike were often effective and they were able to maintain a privileged position as an American labor elite. By 1902 over a million wage earners were in unions, three quarters of them in affiliates of the Federation.

Violence Between Employers and Workers

The murder and intimidation that swept the Pennsylvania anthracite coal regions during the 1860s and 1870s is an early instance of violence between management and labor. The Pennsylvania unrest has traditionally been ascribed to a secret society called the Molly Maguires, an outgrowth, supposedly, of an Irish-American benevolent society. The Mollies flourished amid low wages, physical danger, and repression, to which they responded by violence against coal company officials and miners who threatened to reveal their secrets. The Mollies probably did not exist as an organized conspiratorial body, but violence against unfriendly mine operators was common in the east Pennsylvania coal fields, and that intimidation was used to reinforce the more conventional labor weapons of strikes and boycotts.

In 1873 Frank B. Gowen, the tough, anti-union president of the Philadelphia and Reading Railroad, an owner of coal mines, hired an agent of the Pinkerton private detective agency to infiltrate the union supporters. At enormous risk, James McParlan over the next months gained the confidence of the workers by treating liberally at the local saloons and by his happy-go-lucky demeanor.

By this time a major strike had broken out in the coal fields, a dispute marked by violence on both sides as the operators brought in vicious strikebreakers and company police and the miners attacked the scabs. After five months of threats, arson, and murder, the miners surrendered and went back to work. With the strike over, McParlan surfaced with evidence naming union leaders who had been directly involved in the murder of company officials.

During the Molly Maguire trials that followed, McParlan was the state's chief witness. At least one of the accused turned state's evidence and testified against his fellow workers. On dubious evidence twenty-four men were convicted, ten of whom were hanged and fourteen sent to jail. It was many years before the anthracite coal miners were in a position to challenge the mine owners again.

The trials of the Molly Maguires, if that elusive term is to be applied to them, had scarcely concluded before the country experienced an eruption of violence that went far beyond the coal field outburst. In 1873 a sharp stock market panic set off a severe depression. In an economy still marked by fierce business competition, employers found themselves forced to cut back or face bankruptcy. As the economy flattened out, they imposed wage cuts on their men. The response was widespread.

The Strikes

Few actions by management are as appalling to workers as wage cuts. When, in 1877, the Baltimore and Ohio Railroad announced the second ten-percent reduction for its workers in eight months, the men became enraged. First at Baltimore and then at Martinsburg to the west, they uncoupled cars from locomotives and stopped passage of trains. Urged on by railroad management, the governor of Maryland called for federal troops and himself sent in state militia to force the men to let the trains through. The militia clashed with the workers and before the week was out, the strike had

One coal miner described his working life:

"Day in and day out, from Monday morning to Saturday evening, between the rising and the setting of the sun, I am in the underground workings of the coal mines. From the seams water trickles into the ditches along the gangways; if not water, it is the gas which hurls us to eternity and the props and timbers to a chaos.

Our daily life is not a pleasant one. When we put on our oil soaked suit in the morning we can't guess all the dangers which threaten our lives. We walk sometimes miles to the place—to the main way or traveling way, or to the mouth of the shaft on top of the slope. And then we enter the darkened chambers of the mines. On our right and on our left we see the logs that keep up the top and support the sides which may crush us into shapeless masses, as they have done to many of our comrades.

We get old quickly. Powder, smoke, after-damp, bad air—all combine to bring furrows to our faces and asthma to our lungs."

THE PREACHER AND
THE SLAVE

*Joe Hill, songwriter for the IWW, paro-
died the popular Salvation Army gospel
hymn, "In the Sweet Bye and Bye."*

Long-haired preachers come out every
   night,
Try to tell you what's wrong and what's
   right;
But when asked how 'bout something
   to eat
They will answer with voices so sweet:

Chorus

You will eat, bye and bye,
In that glorious land above the sky;
Work and pray, live on hay,
You'll get pie in the sky when you die.

And the starvation army they play,
And they sing and they clap and they
   pray,
Till they get all your coin on the drum,
Then they'll tell you when you're on the
   bum:

Holy Rollers and jumpers come out,
And they holler, they jump and they
   shout.
"Give your money to Jesus," they say,
"He will cure all diseases today."

If you fight hard for children and
   wife—
Try to get something good in this life—
You're a sinner and bad man, they tell,
When you die you will sure go to hell.

Workingmen of all countries, unite,
Side by side we for freedom will fight:
When the world and its wealth we have
   gained
To the grafters we'll sing this refrain:

Last Chorus

You will eat, bye and bye,
When you've learned how to cook and
   to fry.
Chop some wood, 'twill do you good,
And you'll eat in the sweet bye and bye.

spread to all parts of the B&O and to other roads coast to coast. By the time it ended it had affected fourteen states and produced a casualty list of over a hundred killed, including strikers, militia, and bystanders. Millions of dollars in railroad property went up in smoke. In this and other strikes in 1877, one observer noted the strong participation of women "boldly urging the men on to acts of outrage and bloodshed."

The 1877 strikes shook the confidence of the middle class in the stability of the economic system. The *Philadelphia Inquirer* charged that the railroad workers, particularly the woman members of mobs, had "practically raised the standard of the Paris commune," while the president of the Pennsylvania Railroad noted that what had begun as a riot had grown into an "insurrection." Allan Pinkerton, the head of the strike-breaking detective agency, claimed that the strikes were "the direct result of the communist spirit spread through the ranks of rail-road employees by communistic leaders and their teachings." In the wake of the upheavals, many states passed laws making it a criminal offense to conspire among workers to injure employers.

With the return of good times in 1879, relative quiet descended over labor. But during the next twenty years, workers confronted with wage cuts responded angrily or violently. In May 1886 workers at McCormick International Harvester, the world's largest maker of farm machinery, were on strike. The Chicago police, openly on the side of the employers, killed four workers. On May 4, at a rally at Haymarket Square called by anarchists in support of the strikers, someone threw a bomb. The explosion killed seven policemen and injured sixty-seven. Gunshots by police killed four demonstrators. The ensuing wave of anti-labor feeling turned otherwise sensible people slightly mad with fear of anarchism and led to the hanging of four anarchists and the

**The Haymarket Riot, May 4, 1886. A bomb tossed among policemen
trying to disperse a crowd killed or wounded over seventy people.
Contemporary line drawing.** *(Courtesy, Scribner's Archives)*

imprisoning of four others, although there was no valid proof that any of the convicted men had been directly involved in the crime.

In 1892 members of the American Railway Union, acting in support of a strike in the company town of Pullman, Illinois, declined to handle Pullman cars. John Altgeld, governor of Illinois and for his time a radical, was sympathetic. But Democratic President Grover Cleveland and his attorney general Richard Olney, a former railroad lawyer, claiming that the disruptions were a federal matter since they threatened the federal mails, sent troops to Chicago, and a federal court put the ARU under an injunction. The strikers, in fact, had allowed mail to go through if it was not connected to Pullman cars.

Homestead Steel Strike

At Homestead, Pennsylvania, there had occurred a strike that took on the character of military confrontation. Homestead in 1892 was a town of about 12,000 inhabitants. Seven miles east of Pittsburgh, Pennsylvania, on the left bank of the Monongahela River, the town was dominated by a Carnegie plant that made steel boiler plates, structural steel, armor plate, and beams. The workforce of the plant—3,800 people—and their families made up the town. Most of this force was unskilled labor working for very low wages and belonging to no union. Many were recent immigrants, predominantly eastern European. But 800 of the skilled workers, numbers of them earning about $200 per month, belonged to the Amalgamated Association of Iron and Steel Workers. This union, with about 25,000 members, was probably the strongest in the country, as the Carnegie Corporation, forerunner of the United States Steel Corporation, was among the most powerful and successful corporations in the nation. Since 1889 the union had worked under an agreement by which wages would rise and fall with the market price of steel, but never below a fixed minimum. The agreement was set to expire on June 30, 1892.

In the spring of 1892, Andrew Carnegie, a former proponent of trade unions who no longer actively managed the business, decided along with his chief manager Henry Clay Frick that they would destroy the union at Homestead and henceforth run all their plants on a nonunion basis. Frick negotiated with the union in the most cursory way while literally preparing for battle. He turned the steel plant into an armed fortress, with solid board fencing complete with gun holes and topped with barbed wire and high platforms with electric search lights. He arranged with the Pinkerton Detective Agency for 300 armed men to guard the plant so that he could bring in nonunion workers, then announced the new terms: no union, and wage reductions that averaged over twenty percent.

The workers were confident they could beat the corporation. They were not a downtrodden desperate proletariat. Rather, the Amalgamated members were part of the local elite. They assumed, correctly, that the unskilled workers would follow their leadership, and that the merchants and professionals of the town would be on their side, extending credit to the men and using their influence to settle the strike to the union's advantage. Most of all, these skilled men, proud to be rollers, or heaters, or shearers, or cutters, did not believe that the plant

The factory town at Pullman, Illinois, provided for the employees' needs in a paternalistic way. One worker commented:

"We are born in a Pullman house, fed from the Pullman shop, taught in the Pullman school, catechized in the Pullman church, and when we die, we shall be buried in the Pullman cemetery and go to the Pullman hell."

Andrew Carnegie's change of heart about unionism, signaled by his decision to break the Amalgamated Association of Iron and Steel Workers during the Homestead Strike of 1892, brought him into line with the great majority of large employers of the late nineteenth century. A variety of economic, political, legal, and even demographic factors all played into these employers' hands. The result was that trade unionism developed more slowly in the United States than in any other industrial country. How did the willingness of governments to use their powers to break strikes, the attitudes of the courts toward strikes and boycotts, and the increasing number of immigrants come together to weaken unionism? What sorts of differences would a stronger union movement have brought to American history?

This contemporary scene shows the Carnegie Homestead works in Pennsylvania as they appeared at the time of the great strike of 1892. In each corner of this pro-strike engraving are scenes showing the "defeat and capture of the Pinkerton invaders." *(Courtesy, Library of Congress)*

could be run without them. In the face of national union support, other men with their skills would never become "black sheep" and work for Carnegie as strikebreakers.

The great Homestead strike was technically not a strike but a lockout, since Frick initiated it by shutting the mill hours before the contract was scheduled to expire. The company placed ads for fresh labor in newspapers around the country. The workers, virtually one with the local government anyhow, took over the town, arranging patrols to prevent the influx of strikebreakers, consulting with the saloon-keepers to prevent drunkenness, and generally securing order.

Victory and Defeat   In the early hours of July 6, 1892, the news spread that two barges filled with men were being towed up the river. A huge crowd of workers with their families assembled at the landing. The Pinkertons in the barges attempted to land, a shot rang out—no one knows from where—and Homestead was at war. All that day, the workers besieged the 300 men in the barges. At 5:00 p.m., after nine of the workers and three of the Pinkertons had been killed, the "Pinks" surrendered. The workers marched their captors to a temporary prison in a skating rink and set fire to the barges.

Despite the peace that now appeared to prevail in Homestead, the governor of Pennsylvania called out the National Guard on July 10. The strikers and town government planned a great reception with bands and speeches of welcome, but General Snowden, the Guard commander, had come to put down "revolution, treason, and anarchy." Under the protection of the troops, Frick reopened the plant with nonunion men and began legal prosecutions of a number of the leaders. Frick hoped to break the strike by convincing the men that the plant could operate without them and by tying up their leadership in court battles. Frick's plans probably would have succeeded in any case, but the strategy of identifying the strikers with ambitions more sinister than union recognition and the maintenance of their pay scales received unexpected assistance. On July 23, a Russian emigré anarchist, Alexander Berkman, bursting into the corporation's office in Pittsburgh, shot and then stabbed Frick, seriously wounding him. The unions instantly dissociated themselves from this episode, but it robbed the strikers of much public support.

The union fought almost 200 separate charges, exhausting its resources and its leadership. One leader urged the strikers to continue: "The battle is with you; see that you win it. If you lose such conditions as never confronted the slaves in the South will be yours." But with the strike over five months old and the winter approaching, the entire town, not simply the strikers, was at the point of desperation. The union surrendered and the men began trickling back to the plant. Low wages and for many workers a twelve-hour day with a twenty-four-hour stretch every other week when the shifts changed soon became the norm. True to its promise, the Carnegie Company, and its successor, the United States Steel Corporation, maintained nonunion plants, and led national efforts to retain the open shop until the Congress of Industrial Organizations (CIO) succeeded in organizing steel in the waning years of the Great Depression of the 1930s.

1F YOU DON'T COME IN SUNDAY DON'T COME IN MONDAY.

THE
MANAGEMENT

Women Wage Earners

Much of the work of white adult male wage earners of the Gilded Age was by present standards uncertain and repugnant. But it was enviable beside most of the work of blacks of both genders as well as that of white women and children.

In 1880 women accounted for 2.6 million, or about one-seventh, of the paid labor force of 17.4 million. Although working-class and even many middle-class women worked throughout their adult lives, they did not, like most men, participate in the labor force on a regular basis. Men were expected to work for a wage whenever work was available. Most women who worked outside the home for a wage did so only for a few years during their lives, the majority when they were in their teens, twenties, or early thirties, still single, and still living with their

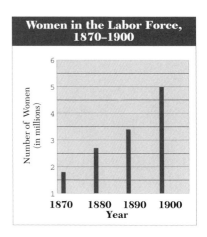

Women in the Labor Force, 1870–1900

Shop girls and women at Westinghouse Electric Corporation, 1894. The majority of the 2.6 million women working outside the home in the 1880s and 1890s were young and single. *(Courtesy, Westinghouse Photo)*

families of origin. Of the 3.7 million women in the publicly defined labor force in 1890, only 500,000 were married. But the labor of a married woman could be necessary to the survival of a family.

Much of that labor escaped the attention of census takers, especially when it was work done in the home, such as piecework, or taking in laundry or boarders. Normally the statisticians and economists did not classify as productive labor the duties of farm women. Since all groups preferred to have married women work for their own families within their own households, we can assume that a married woman's participation in the labor force resulted from need rather than choice, from her husband's inability to support the family by his own efforts. Only after the beginning of the twentieth century did the notion of a "family wage" as a wage large enough to support an entire family, but paid to the male wage earner, become an accepted priority for workers and management. And even then, only the most skilled and successful male wage earners received it.

The preference of both capital and labor for a male workforce subjected women to systematic discrimination in the job market. They were virtually excluded from the learned professions. By 1900 a few hundred women were doctors, largely because of the efforts of a few pioneers. Among them was Elizabeth Blackwell, who had, in 1849, become the first American woman to earn an M.D. degree. But there were next to no women in the legal profession. The Supreme Court declined to review Myra Colby Bradwell's suit against the Illinois Bar, which had refused to admit her. The Protestant ministry similarly attempted to exclude women, and the natural and social sciences included only a few such as the astronomer Maria Mitchell and the anthropologist Erminnie Smith. Male prejudice and the male monopoly of professionalization explains much of women's exclusion; the opposition of traditionalist women to careers for other females contributed as well.

After the Civil War, the founding of the coeducational land-grant colleges and the eastern women's colleges considerably improved women's opportunities for education. But the curricula deemed appropriate to women still included a heavy dose of "feminine" subjects, with a minimal offering in the sciences and pre-professional training. And the graduate schools in all fields still largely excluded women. In the 1890s, the new University of Chicago became the first graduate school to train significant numbers of women, especially in sociology and the other social sciences.

Teachers and Nurses   During the last half of the nineteenth century teaching jobs opened for well-educated middle-class women. Earlier in the century many women had taught, but mainly at the very lowest levels of informal "dame schools" where young children learned their ABCs. With the advent of the publicly supported common school, women began to replace men in the better elementary school jobs. Upon the arrival of the public high school, largely after the Civil War, they also displaced men in the secondary schools. In 1860 about twenty-five percent of the country's public school teachers were women; by 1880, sixty percent; by 1910, eighty percent. Men usually occupied the supervisory jobs of principals, commissioners, and superintendents at every level of training and grade, and were paid better. Indeed, one reason why school systems hired so many women was that their lower pay placed less of a burden on taxpayers. Yet however imperfect the system, the development of the teaching profession was a great boon to many women.

Nursing, a new profession, was another breakthrough. Before the Civil War, hospitals had employed only male attendants. The work of the attendant was considered dirty, harrowing, and hard, and therefore unsuitable for ladies. During the Civil War, the need for nurses with the armed forces, combined with the earlier example of the Englishwoman Florence Nightingale during the Crimean War of 1853–56, broke down resistance. After 1865 several major hospitals established training schools for female nurses, and gradually these raised their standards of admission and training. By the end of the century the new profession and vocation of trained or registered nurse had come into being, providing a decent occupation for thousands of ambitious young women.

Social Work   A final professional opportunity for women, appearing at the end of the century, was that of social worker. Until the post-Civil War period, charity of various kinds had been distributed primarily on an informal, emergency basis by churches, benevolent societies, and local governments. Most of those who administered the dispensing of funds were volunteers, predominantly middle-class women, who considered their efforts simply a matter of social responsibility. Toward the end of the century, various reformers, in an attempt to deal more systematically with the brutalities of city life, established citywide charity organizations to provide welfare on a scientific basis. Along with these agencies grew a professional class of social workers trained in techniques for making charity a means of

Jane Addams, the founder of Hull House in Chicago, defines the Social-Settlement Movement, 1892:

"I believe that there is a distinct turning among many young men and women toward this simple acceptance of Christ's message. They resent the assumption that Christianity is a set of ideas which belong to the religious consciousness, whatever that may be. They insist that it cannot be proclaimed and instituted apart from the social life of the community and that it must seek a simple and natural expression in the social organism itself. . . .

Certain it is that spiritual force is found in the Settlement movement, and it is also true that this force must be evoked and must be called into play before the success of any Settlement is assured. There must be the overmastering belief that all that is noblest in life is common to men as men, in order to accentuate the likenesses and ignore the differences which are found among the people whom the Settlement constantly brings into juxtaposition. . . .

The Settlement, then, is an experimental effort to aid in the solution of the social and industrial problems which are engendered by the modern conditions of life in a great city. It is an attempt to relieve, at the same time, the overaccumulation at one end of society and the destitution at the other; but it assumes that this overaccumulation and destitution is most sorely felt in the things that pertain to social and educational advantages."

giving the poor skills and ambitions that would lift them out of poverty. Many of these professionals were women. Much of the growth of social work as a profession would come in the early twentieth century, but by 1900 this new opportunity for educated, middle-class women had already presented itself. Some, however, could not shed their social biases. One wrote of an Italian family that they were not yet Americanized: they were "still eating spaghetti."

Women also took an active role from the beginning in the American Social Science Association, founded in 1865 by an influential group of Boston reformers. It included women, such as Caroline Dall, who were devoted to the rational reform of social problems. During the 1870s and 1880s, the organization spawned affiliates and associated organizations in various cities. Many of these groups soon outgrew the parent association, but perfectly captured its spirit of rational, institutional reform with which more and more women were associated. Such participation did not offer women professional careers in the strict sense, but did draw them into reform activities, institutional politics, and advanced currents of thought. Women's interest in social science and rational reform would in many cases merge with their commitment to "social housekeeping" as a particularly female response to the problems of urban society. This doctrine advocated extending to society the methods of efficient and caring management and the standards of purity, such as sobriety and sexual purity, whose enforcement within the family and household was the woman's task.

The openings that came to women in the later nineteenth century expressed those technological and social forces that had swept Welshmen and Irishmen to Pennsylvania coal mines, pulled Americans and Europeans to the western frontiers, and swelled the commercial and industrial cities of the Old and the New World. Social work, nursing, even public education represented, each in its own way, the replacement of traditional skills with scientific technologies. There was to be a technology of social work, a professionalization of caring for the sick, an

Young boys, some of them barefoot, clamber among the great textile machines in a Georgia cotton mill adjusting spindles. Many of them were the children of women who worked in the plants. The photograph is by Lewis Hine. (*Courtesy, Bettmann*)

A federal investigating committee in 1890 examined the superintendent of the Enterprise Manufacturing Company:

Q: How much help do you employ?
A: We have, I think, 485 on our pay-roll.
Q: How many of those are men?
A: I cannot answer that exactly; about one-seventh.
Q: The rest are women and children, I suppose?
A: Yes, sir.
Q: How many of them would you class as women and how many as children?
A: I think about one-third of the remainder would be children and two-thirds women. That is about the proportion.
Q: What is the average wages that you pay?
A: Eighty-two cents a day for the last six months, or in that neighborhood.
Q: What do the women make a day?

A: About $1.
Q: And the men?
A: Do you mean common laborers?
Q: Yes; the average wages of your laborers.
A: About $1 a day.
Q: What do the children make on an average?
A: About from 35 to 75 cents a day.
Q: You employ children of ten years and upward?
A: Yes, sir.
Q: Do you employ any below the age of ten?
A: No.

Eva Lunsky, an employee, testified at a later hearing:

Q: When were you born?
A: I don't know.

efficient, regular, and universal education of the young, just as there was a new technology of steelmaking and a mass production of clothing. Like the factories and the mines, the new professions destroyed slow, customary ways of life. As an Irish peasant, who a century ago would have tended an ancestral plot of ground, now traveled across an ocean and joined the rushing crowds of an industrial city, a woman who might earlier have spent her life at ancient tasks on a farm now entered the ranks of an army of teachers or hospital workers. And the professionalization of teaching, nursing, and charity that was changing the lives of at least a small number of women represented, like the industrialization of the rest of life, a force for social equality of a sort. Once the individual had been defined as a member of a distinct family, or an inhabitant of a particular town, or the practitioner of a family craft. These definitions had put the individual into a structure of social classes: an upper class of landholders, a middling class of merchants, a city class of artisans, a lower class of peasants. Now some women, like very many men, were definable not by the class and community they had been born into but by the skills they had acquired and the work they were ready to do.

Domestics   Although these gains were impressive, they were restricted to a relatively small percentage of working women. Most still had to be content with menial, low-paying jobs. One of the largest categories of women workers was that of servants or domestics. Of the five million gainfully employed women workers of 1900, 1.5 million were listed as "private household workers." About a fifth of these were laundresses, the rest "housekeepers" of one sort or another. The conditions under which these women lived and labored varied a good deal. Many, especially among the older women, were married and came into their employers' households to work for the day. They had their own homes, and generally their wages were supplements to their husbands' incomes. Wages for laundresses, maids, cooks,

Women and children in a food processing plant with foreman watching over them. *(Courtesy, George Eastman House, Inc.)*

Q: Nobody has ever told you?
A: No, sir.
Q: Did you mamma ever tell you when you were born?
A: She told me, but I have forgotten.
Q: You don't know whether you ever had a birthday party or not?
A: Yes, sir; I have had a birthday party.
Q: When?
A: Last year.
Q: How old were you last year?
A: I was 15.
Q: Was it in the winter time?
A: It was in the summer time.
Q: And you don't know the month?
A: No, sir.
Q: Do you know when the Fourth of July is?

A: No, sir.
Q: Do you know when the summer time is when they fire off fire crackers; don't they have any down your way? (The witness gave no answer.)
Q: Did you ever go to school in this country?
A: I went only three months.
Q: When was that, Eva?
A: That was last summer.
Q: What time in the summer was it that you went there; what months, do you know?
A: No.
Q: Do you know the names of the summer months?
A: No, sir.
Q: What month is this; do you know what month this is?
A: No.

Though the Supreme Court did not often look with favor upon laws regulating economic activity, more and more states toward the end of the 1800s began limiting the working hours of children and women. *(Courtesy, International Museum of Photography)*

and other domestics were not good—less than a dollar a day—but women had lives of their own after hours. The situation of the "widow-lady" who had to support herself by her wages as a servant, or even herself and young children, was far less tolerable. Equally unhappy was that of the live-in servant girl who was at the beck and call of her middle-class mistress or master for long hours and, living in her employer's household, seldom had much privacy. No doubt some young women found kindly friends and protectors in their employers; no doubt some servant girls became loyal and cherished family retainers within middle-class families. But the circumstances of the live-in maid were inherently unenviable.

Generally speaking, by the late nineteenth century domestic service was not—outside the South—a job that native-born women performed. It seemed far too menial for them. In farm regions, many of the hired girls called in to assist the farmer's wife during the harvest season, when there were many extra hands to feed, were the daughters of a neighbor. They considered their job to be merely helping out, and therefore without stigma. Long-term domestic service was largely confined to Irish and German women in the North and to black women in the South. After 1880 newer immigrants began to take their places. Without skills, these young women had few alternatives.

Another large category of female workers consisted of factory operatives. Like servant girls, most of these were young and unmarried; like their sisters in domestic service, they were underpaid, especially relative to men. The job of the factory girl seldom had anything to recommend it except a modest return that helped to supplement her family's income. Factory work was often a harsh and squalid life for young women.

Child Labor

One southerner described the cotton-mill children of the Tennessee Valley early in the twentieth century:

"They were children only in age . . . little, solemn pygmy people, whom poverty had canned up and compressed into concentrated extracts of humanity . . . the juices of childhood had been pressed out . . . no talking in the mill . . . [no] singing. . . . They were flung into an arena for a long day's fight against a thing of steam and steel. . . . They were more dead than alive when, at seven o'clock, the Steam Beast uttered the last volcanic howl which said they might go home . . . in a speechless, haggard, over-worked procession."

The census of 1900 showed that as many as four out of every hundred nonagricultural jobs were still held by youths between the ages of 10 and 15, a total of about 700,000. In the big cities many were messengers and errand boys. Others were newsboys or shoeshine boys. In the Pennsylvania coal fields, hundreds of lads labored for ten hours a day over rushing belts of coal, picking out slate and stones while breathing in dangerous, dust-laden air. Both boys and girls worked in city loft cigar factories, rolling tobacco to make cheap "cheroots." In the southern piedmont, young girls worked from sunup to sundown in the newly established cotton mills.

Children had worked for time out of mind on the farms of the Western world. But there child labor had been part of a family enterprise with mothers and fathers as supervisors and employers. In the new Gilded Age, however, it largely ceased to be part of a family system.

At first, the influence of traditional farm habits stilled the outcry against child labor. But toward the end of the century, as the rural experience receded and as childhood came more to be considered a

Coal miners picking slate at a coal chute; their clothes and faces black with coal dust, these boys earned $2.50 for a sixty-hour work week. (*Courtesy, George Eastman House, International Museum of Photography*)

time for careful nurturing and extended education, protests against the system grew. In the 1890s the National Consumers' League, organized by New York and Chicago women, began to demand the abolition of child labor. Educators too attacked it for interfering with schooling. Yet the practice had its defenders: employers anxious to keep down labor costs and many working-class parents who either saw nothing wrong with supplementing the family income out of child labor or found they had no choice.

The Supreme Court

The attitudes of the Supreme Court in these years reflected and reinforced values favorable to business. The Court in a number of important decisions resisted governmental regulation of economic life.

The Supreme Court played a vital role in shoring up a business civilization during the later portion of the nineteenth century. The Court's decision to extend the "due process" clause of the Fourteenth Amendment to corporations had the effect of seriously weakening legislative restraints on corporate behavior. This decision was revolutionary, at least in the sense that it reversed several centuries of judicial practice.

"I give you," a New York banker toasted in 1895, "the Supreme Court of the United States—guardian of the dollar, defender of private property, enemy of spoliation, sheet anchor of the republic."

State Regulations Upheld and Denied

Such views did not at first prevail. Louisiana had granted to a slaughterhouse company a monopoly of that business. In 1873 the Supreme Court heard arguments that it declare the monopoly invalid. The opponents of the monopoly claimed that in favoring one slaughterhouse company over others Louisiana had violated the provisions of the Fourteenth Amendment that states must offer equal protection of the law. The purpose of the Amendment, the Court declared in upholding the state in the "Slaughterhouse" cases, was to protect black people, not to place the federal government in the position of protecting citizens' property rights against a state legislature. In the case of *Munn v. Illinois* (1877) the Supreme Court upheld a law the Illinois legislature had passed to regulate the price charged by grain elevator companies for storing grain. This was one of a flood of laws passed during the 1870s by midwestern states at the behest of the farmer groups called Grangers and designed to regulate railroads and middlemen. An elevator company claimed that it was being deprived of its property in a way that violated the Fourteenth Amendment. Chief Justice Morrison Waite, speaking for the Court, declared that in the case of a business "clothed with a public interest," a business that affected the well-being of the public, it was the right of a legislature to protect that public interest.

Then business had its triumphs. In two cases in the mid-1880s the Court drastically restricted the power of states to regulate business. In *Santa Clara Co. v. Southern Pacific Railroad* (1886) the Court accepted the view that corporations were legal "persons" and so, like black people, protected by the Fourteenth Amendment against being arbitrarily deprived of property. That same year, in *Wabash, St. Louis & Pacific Railroad Company v. Illinois*, the Court struck down an Illinois law regulating railroads. Here it stressed not the Fourteenth Amendment but the section of the Constitution giving the national Congress the authority to regulate interstate commerce. The Illinois law, the Court declared, was an unconstitutional assumption by that state of a power granted only to Congress. The Court also prevented the government from acting in matters of child labor. These conservative Supreme Court decisions, however, by no means ended state efforts to exercise their police powers over corporations. Between 1887 and 1897 the states and territories passed over 1,600 laws dealing with working conditions.

The Supreme Court meanwhile was restricting on constitutional grounds the scope of federal legislation. The Wilson-Gorman Tariff Act of 1894 had established the first income tax in United States history. It imposed a tax on income from personal property and from municipal bonds and raised a storm of protest from business groups and the well-to-do. The Supreme Court heard the case—*Pollock v. Farmers' Loan and Trust Company*—in 1895 and overturned the income tax, arguing that the legislation was unconstitutional because it amounted to a direct tax on personal property. In subsequent years, reformers launched an income tax movement that eventually added the Sixteenth Amendment to the Constitution, permitting the federal government to impose on each income a tax commensurate with its size.

Interstate Commerce Commission Congress, under pressure from farmer and merchant groups who complained about excessive charges for the hauling of their goods, rushed to fill the gap created by the *Wabash* case. Whether the Supreme Court had been correct in denying to states the right to regulate commerce that flowed across state boundaries, there was no doubt that Congress possessed that authority. In 1887 the national legislature passed the Interstate Commerce Act. This measure declared illegal all rebates—portions of rates returned to the payers—that a railroad might make to its more extensive users; all customers must be charged alike for services. The law made it illegal for railroads to engage in the practice, common at the time, of charging higher rates per ton mile for short hauls than for long ones. It outlawed the forming of railroad pools. The Act required that "all charges . . . be reasonable and just." It established a five-member Interstate Commerce Commission (ICC) that could examine complaints or investigate railroad practices on its own initiative. If the Commission found that a railroad had violated the Act, it could bring the violation before the federal courts and compel the railroad to comply with its ruling.

On the face of it the law seemed an effective assertion of federal power to regulate interstate transportation in the public interest. It was not. Thomas M. Cooley, the first chairman of the ICC, was a leading constitutional lawyer who deplored "hostility to railroad management," and believed "antagonism to acquired wealth" to be "dangerous." Under Cooley the ICC favored the railroads and allowed them more or less to charge what the traffic would bear. It even warned against freight and passenger rates that were too low. When the Commission did attempt to limit what the railroads might charge, the Supreme Court in 1897 in the *Maximum Freight Rate* case declared, despite the intent of Congress, that the ICC had "no power to prescribe the tariff or rates which shall control in the future."

Sherman Antitrust Act Trusts were widely seen as squeezing out financially smaller competitors and thereby injuring both small business and the public. In response to widespread anger at trusts, Congress in 1890 passed the Sherman Antitrust Act. The national legislature was acting under its power to regulate foreign and interstate commerce. The measure declared that "every contract, combination in the form of trust or otherwise, or conspiracy, in restraint of trade or commerce among the several States or with foreign nations, is hereby declared to be illegal." A person who violated the Act would be committing a misdemeanor. An actual person found guilty would be subject to fine or imprisonment. "Person" within the meaning contemplated by the Act referred also, and more importantly, to corporations, which by law are definable for some purposes as persons. A guilty corporation might pay a fine and receive an order for the dissolution of the illegal combination. Federal district attorneys could prosecute suspected violators and those wronged by their actions could sue for triple damages.

The act was not especially effective. The legislators who drafted it had not foreseen loopholes that the lawyers hired by the corporations could find. In the first important antitrust case brought before the Sherman Act, *United States v. E.C. Knight* (1895), the Supreme Court gutted it. The *Knight* case involved purchases by the American Sugar Refining Company of several refineries in Philadelphia that when added to its existing capacity gave American Sugar control of 98 percent of all American refining. Few monopolies could have been more inclusive. Yet in a decision that dismayed even many lawyers who were partisans of business, the Court declared that sugar refining was manufacturing, not trade or commerce, and was therefore not subject to the Sherman Act. Thereupon, until Theodore Roosevelt and the progressives invoked it in the new century, the law was made inactive as a regulation of business. Meanwhile it was applied vigorously against labor unions on the grounds that strikes were devices to restrain trade. Under this interpretation the courts issued several injunctions to keep labor unions from interfering with business. In the *Danbury Hatters Case* (1905), the Supreme Court also decided that under the Sherman Act, a labor union could not initiate a secondary boycott—could not boycott one business to force it to put pressure on another engaged in a labor dispute.

Toward the end of the century an increasing number of state legislatures began to pass laws limiting the working hours of women and children, and of men in unhealthy or dangerous occupations. This represented a new social concern that in the early twentieth century would culminate in a mass of social legislation that contemporaries gave the label "Progressivism." To defenders of laissez-faire, these laws seemed yet another violation of fundamental economic law; and doctrinaire champions of private property thought them an invasion of the rights of employers to control their business. In *Lochner v. New York* (1905) the Supreme Court declared unconstitutional a New York law limiting the hours at which employees in the baking industry could be kept at work. In a famous dissent Associate Justice Oliver Wendell Holmes, Jr., attacked the basis of the majority opinion. The Constitution was "not intended to embody a particular economic theory, whether of paternalism . . . or of *Laissez-faire*."

The Supreme Court drew on the legal doctrine that the act of entering into a contract concerning the conditions of work is a fundamental right—a right that in this case, so the Court believed, the Fourteenth Amendment protected against certain kinds of interference on the part of state governments. Often in the real economic world, however, no actual equality of bargaining power exists between employer and employee, and poverty may force people into unhealthy occupations. That reality can make a mockery of such philosophical and constitutional abstractions as the rights of property and the rights of free contract. The Supreme Court had to learn to allow legislatures considerable freedom to look for the real and particular facts of economic life and to make laws accordingly.

In a series of decisions from 1904 onward the Court did allow the Sherman Act to be a weapon against combinations in restraint of trade. And in 1908, in *Muller v. Oregon,* it refused to strike down an Oregon law limiting the working hours of women. Yet despite this moderate change of heart the Supreme Court was to remain skeptical of the constitutionality of laws regulating economic activity. Not until well into the 1930s would it come down with some consistency on the side of the public interest as defined by Congress against the private interest of property holders and business firms.

Suggested Readings

Recent scholarship on late nineteenth-century industrial America includes Maury Klein, *The Life and Legend of Jay Gould* (1986), Vincent P. Carosso and Rose C. Carosso, *The Morgans, 1853–1913* (1987), David F. Hawkes, *John D: The Founding Father of the Rockefellers* (1980), Susan P. Benson, *Counter Cultures: Saleswomen, Managers, and Customers in American Department Stores, 1890–1940* (1986), Walter Licht, *Working for the Railroad* (1983), James Ward, *Railroads and the Character of America, 1820–1887* (1986), and Alan Trachtenberg, *The Incorporation of America* (1982).

Anthony F. C. Wallace, in *Rockdale: The Growth of an American Village in the Early Industrial Revolution* (1978), analyzes, from the standpoint of a cultural anthropologist, the social and ethnic composition of a nineteenth-century community as it became industrialized. He also considers the religious and moral ideology that the social and business elite fashioned for conditioning the population to the disciplines of industrialism. Alfred D. Chandler, Jr., *The Visible Hand: The Managerial Revolution in American Business* (1977) follows the development of a managerial structure in American business and the reasons for it. The work argues that it was not the "invisible hand" of unregulated economic forces but the conscious decisions of managers that have given shape to the American economy. See also Glenn Porter, *The Rise of Big Business* (1973) and Stuart Bruchey, *Growth of the Modern Economy* (1974). Irwin Unger won a Pulitzer Prize for *The Greenback Era: A Social and Political History of American Finance, 1865–1879* (1964). Albro Martin, *James J. Hill and the Opening of the Northwest* (1976) is superb on development of railroads. Samuel Hays, *The Response to Industrialism* (1957) is a classic study. Robert W. Fogel uses a quantitative approach in *Railroads and American Economic Growth: Essays in Econometric History* (1964). *Andrew Carnegie and the Rise of Big Business* (1975) by Harold C. Livesay supplements Carnegie's *Autobiography* (1920). See Robert C.

Bannister, Jr.'s careful *Social Darwinism: Science and Myth in Anglo-American Social Thought* (1979).

Other good books on the period include Peter Temin, *Iron and Steel in Nineteenth-Century America* (1964), Sidney Fine, *Laissez Faire and the General-Welfare State* (1956), John Brooks, *Telephone* (1976), W. P. Strassmann, *Risk and Technological Innovation* (1959), H. B. Thorelli, *The Federal Antitrust Policy* (1954), Carl Solberg, *Oil Power* (1976), H. J. Habakkuk, *American and British Technology in the Nineteenth Century* (1962), Leon Wolff, *Lockout* (1965), G. W. Miller, *Railroads and the Granger Laws* (1971), A. D. Chandler, Jr., *Railroads: The Nation's First Big Business* (1965), Almont Lindsey, *The Pullman Strike* (1942), H. C. Passer, *The Electrical Manufacturers* (1953), Julius Grodinsky, *Transcontinental Railway Strategy* (1962), and Gabriel Kolko, *Railroads and Regulation* (1965).

On labor there are Leon Fink, *Workingmen's Democracy: The Knights of Labor and American Politics* (1983), Bruce Laurie, *Artisans Into Workers: Labor in Nineteenth-Century America* (1989), David A. Hannsell, *From the American System to Mass Production* (1984), David Montgomery, *Workers' Control in America* (1979) and *The Fall of the House of Labor: The Workplace, the State, and American Labor Activism, 1865–1925* (1987), Michael S. Frisch and Daniel J. Walkowitz, eds., *Working-Class America: Essays on Labor, Community, and American Society* (1983), David M. Gordon et al., *Segmented Work, Divided Workers: The Historical Transformation of Labor in the United States* (1982), John Bodnar, *Immigration and Industrialization: Ethnicity in an American Mill Town* (1977).

See also among older books Robert V. Bruce, *1877: Year of Violence* (1959), Stanley Buder, *Pullman: An Experiment in Industrial Order and Community Planning, 1880–1930* (1960), and, on the IWW, Melvyn Dubofsky, *We Shall Be All* (1969).

Jay Gould: Robber Baron or Industrial Statesman?

Maury Klein

[Jay] Gould emerged as the foremost villain of the [Gilded Age] not merely by piling up a fortune; that was acceptable, even desirable, so long as one did it in the proper way with appropriate gestures toward convention. His rise to success followed the classic pattern of the rags-to-riches myth except in the crucial area of method. He did not display the probity and purity of conscience so prominent in Horatio Alger heroes, but neither did the vast majority of businessmen. Elsewhere, however, Gould snubbed convention at every turn. In business he was ruthless and devious, clever and unpredictable, secretive and evasive. Above all he was imaginative, not only brilliant but thoroughly original. In an age that relished flourish, he possessed a stunning economy of motion. . . .

Critics condemned him for his deceit and treachery. Yet the impression lingers that many of them actually loathed Gould because he was too honest for minds used to dealing with reality under wraps. Gould knew what he wanted, went after it, and did not mouth pieties to justify his course. Nor did he ever try to disguise himself in airs of respectability. By keeping his numerous acts of charity behind the scenes he deprived himself of the standard act of atonement expected from men of vast wealth. . . .

There was an intellectuality in his approach to business, the joy of a lawyer handed a juicy brief to write or a Gordian knot to unravel. All these aspects set Gould apart from other men. The role of unsparing realist was not easy in an age that preferred to cushion the harshness of social and economic change with bloated sentimentalism.

Even before Gould's death he had become the symbol for an era tarnished and embarrassing to its children. The writers known loosely as muckrakers and debunkers shrank in horror from the excesses and iniquities of industrial society. Unable to put the larger experience into perspective, tormented by the contradictions and paradoxes of what Twain dubbed the Gilded Age, they seized upon its dominant business personalities as sufficient explanation for its aberrations. They were not the first to cope with a revolution by personalizing the vast forces that impelled it, and their chosen targets were certainly vivid and inviting enough. . . .

"Robber Baron" must surely be the most overused and least useful label in all American history. It is not surprising that the popular notion of the industrial era continues to be shaped by the phrase and portrait made famous by Matthew Josephson half a century ago.

Reprinted from Maury Klein, *The Life and Legend of Jay Gould* (Baltimore: The Johns Hopkins University Press, 1986).

The history of American industry in the late nineteenth century is a story of the financial empire building of Jay Gould and his many contemporaries and successors. But it is far more importantly a story of great crude productive endeavors, rails flung across empty stretches of the continent, smokestacks spewing embers over the roofs of factories where immigrant laborers wrestled at clanking machinery. Twisted steel and smashed boxcars meanwhile left their testimony that the country had the worst railroad safety record of any industrialized nation. Accidentally ignited gases in turn-of-the-century mines could send a path of flame through the tunnels, or hurl as far as a mile the massive door at a mine's entrance. Industry did not grow in response to human need or the advice of socially responsible technicians. It grew in ways that serviced the money and power hunger of its financial leaders or their smaller likenesses; and that ensured the continuance of the accidents, the machinery run wastefully to ruin.

The beneficiaries of the system of ownership and finance did not for the most part make anything, except money. They did not dig for coal, or pour molten ore, or design a machine, or conduct a laboratory experiment that might advance any of these things. Finance aimed only at profits, and that meant driving the course of industry in whatever direction profits were greatest; and that, in turn, made for the twisted steel along railway lines, the gas flames streaking through mining tunnels. It is true that in the absence of some more sophisticated form of investment, Wall Street and the corporations did bring together the resources under which genuine production took place. But it was not for the purposes of production that they did so. To attribute to the corporation and financial system the preeminent credit for the magnificent productivity of industry is to disgrace industry along with the anonymous workers and technicians who strained it into existence, and wrought ever closer perfection into it.

In short: the system disgraced work itself.

From the time of the American Revolution, citizens had perceived their country, in one form or another, as a republic of workers. But also from that beginning, a corruption had crept into the idea of work: the notion that the aim and the evidence of work are wealth. The belief that wealth can ever be the measure of hard and careful work is nonsense. Good workmanship reveals itself in the conduct of the craftsman and the excellence of the product, and nowhere else. It certainly does not reveal itself in the twists and flips of a market that makes a financial con artist fifty times more affluent than the janitors who do the useful labor of cleaning his floor. The belief that wealth is the prize and ornament of work, elusively present in the American mind from the time of the nation's origins, won wide credence in the age of the financiers. The vision of a republic of honest workers suffered, and has continued to suffer.

Yet there were honest laborers, machinists, and technicians who could take pride in what they did, and know that they were perfecting the nature of work and its instruments. The growing precision and sophistication of machines, the exactitude that modern technology demanded of its skilled operatives and its engineers: all this expressed workmanship of the highest order. The social commentator Thorstein Veblen was soon to note the contrast between the rigor of modern technology and the shoddiness of the financial and business ownership that presided over that technology. A businessman might calculate only the profits of a quick sale; a technician had to calculate to a fraction of an inch the fittings of gear to gear. Industry, even as avarice and competition drove its owners, was also requiring in its actual productive capacity a closer and more widespread cooperation of functions nationwide, and internationally, than any previous form of production had needed. A Minnesota iron miner's yield traveled east to be turned into the steel rails that carried farm machinery to the West, and that region's wheat eastward to the tables of steel workers. But none of this could be adequately recognized and respected so long as the slash-and-burn greediness of the market drew more attention than the quiet skills and the expert knowledge of the age.

Driving the Golden Spike on May 10, 1869, at Promontory Point, Utah, joining the Union Pacific and Central Pacific lines and completing the first transcontinental railroad. Chinese workers had furnished much of the labor for the Central Pacific. Note the absence of Chinese faces in this photograph. *(Courtesy, Union Pacific Railroad Museum Collection, Omaha, Nebraska)*

17
The West and South
1865–1900

THE GOLDEN SPIKE: MAY 10, 1869

"What do we want with . . . this region of savages and wild beasts, of deserts of shifting sands and whirlwinds of dust, of cactus and prairie dogs?" asked Daniel Webster in 1845. "To what use could we ever put those endless mountain ranges, impenetrable and covered to their bases with eternal snow? What could we do with the western coast three thousand miles away, rockbound, cheerless and uninviting?" When Webster made this estimate of the value of California, the four hundred immigrants from the East who lived there knew nothing of the gold beneath their feet. To get there they had traveled for months over waterless plains and forbidding mountains, or sailed completely around the Americas, or made the dangerous crossing of the Panamanian isthmus. In 1855, the U.S. Army Engineers pointed out that California, its riches by then well known, could be conquered by a foreign power before military assistance would arrive from the East. With the coming of the Civil War, which revealed further the fragility of the Union, a federally subsidized transcontinental rail connection became a political and military necessity.

On July 1, 1862, Congress granted charters to two companies: the Union Pacific, to build westward from Omaha, and the Central Pacific, to construct eastward from San Francisco, across the Sierras and through Nevada. Government aid, in the form of alternate sections of land along the right-of-way and government bonds for each mile of completed track, induced each company

HISTORICAL EVENTS

1849
Gold discovered in California

1862
Homestead Act encourages western settlement (gave 160 acres to anyone who would pay $10 registration fee and pledge to live on and cultivate the land for five years)

1864
Chivington massacre of Cheyennes at Sand Creek, Colorado

1865–67
Great Sioux War

1866
Sioux massacre of 81 of Fetterman's forces on Bozeman Trail
• Texas cattle drive begins

1869
Golden spike completes transcontinental railroad • Board of Indian Commissioners created to eradicate corruption • Wyoming gives women the right to vote

1872
Yellowstone National Park created

continued

Proud Americans who crossed the continent on the silver rails added their descriptions in diaries and letters:

"My boyish dreams were realized," one man recorded: "For hours, at the school desk, have I pondered over the map and wandered, in imagination, with Lewis and Clark, the hunters and trappers and early emigrants, away off to these Rocky Mountains, about which such a mystery seemed to hang,—dreaming, wishing and hoping against hope, that my eyes might, some day, behold their snow-crowned heights. And here lay the first great range in the pureness of white; distant, to be sure, but there it lay, enshrined in beauty."

to race ahead so as to move the final meeting point as far into its competitor's territory as possible. The race was on.

The Union Pacific rolled steadily across the plains on the strength of black and Irish labor. In this flat country, nature was easy to subdue. Not so the Indians seeing their land about to be permanently split by steel rails. The Union Pacific organized its crews—which after the war swelled with ex-soldiers—in military fashion in order to be ready to fight off any trouble.

Meanwhile, the Central Pacific brutally shouldered its way up the Sierra Nevada, blasting and tunneling, indifferent to expense, winter storms, or workers' lives, hoping to reach the profitable flat plains where the government subsidies would be worth much more. Charles Crocker, relentless boss of the construction crews, had solved by hiring Chinese immigrants the problem of where to find tens of thousands of railroad workers in labor-scarce California. An associate had at first objected because the Chinese workers "were not masons," but Crocker lightly countered that the Chinese had built the greatest piece of masonry in the world—the Great Wall. They quickly proved their worth in breaching the great wall of the Sierra. In 1866–67, under white foremen, Crocker's work gangs crossed the mountain summit at the famous Donner Pass. Working furiously to get tunnel headings constructed before they were locked in snowdrifts, the crews continued throughout the winter, gouging out the insides of hill after hill.

The great "iron horse race" aroused extraordinary feats in 1868–69 as the two roads pushed ever closer. On a single day the Union Pacific crews, after elaborate preparation of men and teams and materials, laid over seven miles of track. Not to be outdone, Crocker boasted that his men would top ten miles in a day. On April 27, 1869, after the Central Pacific had spent days hauling material into place and rehearsing 4,000 men in their duties, an engine ran off the track, ending the day's proceedings. But the next morning at 7:00 a.m., railroad cars, small hand cars, horse teams, and disciplined crews began dropping rails and spikes along the prepared grade and eight Irish rail handlers started moving rails into place. As the rails were bolted by Chinese gangs, fresh rails were hauled along the new track and the process was repeated. Maintaining a frantic pace, this collective John Henry advanced six miles before the foremen called a halt for lunch. Working more slowly through the afternoon, the crews by seven in the evening had added ten miles and fifty-six feet of new track. The rail handlers, heroes of the day, had each lifted 125 tons of iron in that one long march.

The two lines met reluctantly, on May 10, 1869, at Promontory Point, Utah, on the northern shore of the Great Salt Lake. The meeting had in fact been scheduled for May 8, and then delayed by rain. In San Francisco and Sacramento, plans for festivities for the 8th had advanced too far to be canceled, and those two points on the new transcontinental route were forced to celebrate the momentous event for three days. Elaborate national preparations included wiring the final spike, made of pure gold, to the Western Union telegraph system so that the blows of the hammer could register throughout the nation. In several cities, cannon were wired to the telegraph to detonate from the blow thousands of miles away. The man given the honor of striking the blow—Leland Stanford, ex-governor of California and president of the Central Pacific—was not up to the occasion: he missed the spike. The local telegraph operator closed the circuit anyhow, so that the cannons, bells, and whistles blasted across the nation on schedule. Stanford, a practical man even if not adept with a hammer, talked more plainly of transporting "coarse, heavy and cheap products for all distances at living rates to the trade." The golden spike was a fit symbol for a nation that had endured four bloody years to remain indivisible.

Railroads nourished the West, carrying settlers, bringing the manufactured goods that the East made in exchange for western wheat and minerals. Lifelines other than the Union Pacific and the Central Pacific quickened the development of the region. The Southern Pacific reached from San Francisco to Los Angeles and then on through the Southwest to New Orleans. The Atchison, Topeka and Santa Fe got to the Pacific in 1887 by way of a southerly route. The privately financed Great Northern stretched from St. Paul, Minnesota to Puget Sound in Washington State.

Landholding in the West and South

Since the early days of settlement, Americans had looked to small landholding as a promise of the young country. Most Americans did not move westward for land, but many did, and for others the West was a vision, to be cherished if only in romantic fantasy. As cities grew and the industrial revolution progressed, more and more nineteenth-century Americans either sought or had to settle for some other form of ownership or sustenance. Beyond the Mississippi, though, lay vast empty spaces. Through the nineteenth century and into the twentieth, the old hunger for farmland remained strong enough to fill much of what remained of the vacant West.

The West, however, was much a part of the industrial future. There too, towns and cities appeared and expanded; the proportion of urban to rural dwellers actually became higher in the West than in any other part of the nation. The West supplied not only food for industry

Rain and snow were exciting events. The train on which Harvey Rice was journeying in 1869 ran through a violent Great Plains thunderstorm:

"The heavens became, suddenly, as black as starless midnight. The lightning flashed in every direction, and electric balls of fire rolled over the plains. It seemed as if the artillery of heaven had made the valley a target and that we were doomed to instant destruction. But happily our fears were soon dissipated. The storm was succeeded by a brilliant rainbow."

Engineer Cy Warman would tell of bucking an eighteen-foot snowdrift with double engines. His locomotive trembled and shook as if it were about to be crushed to pieces:

"Often when we came to a stop only the top of the stack of the front engine would be visible. . . . All this time the snow kept coming down, day and night, until the only signs of a railroad across the range were the tops of the telegraph poles."

Passengers recorded the resounding names: Castle Rock, Hanging Rock, Pulpit Rock, Devil's Gate, Devil's Slide, Horsethief Trail. Along the way lay reminders of the pioneers: solitary grave markers, the bones of long-dead horses or oxen, broken wagon wheels, relics of a time that the railroad was consigning to history.

but a good deal of its mined raw materials, and there was some local iron-making. Industry in the form of railroads reciprocated by taking settlers west and keeping the region in commercial contact with the East. Farming itself, in the West as elsewhere, was becoming mechanized, industrialism taken to producing food as it produced concrete and steel. Mechanization along with the filtering down of scientific ideas of soil nurture taught small farmers new skills and a new way of thinking about their work, even as much of the country was losing the old skills of agriculture. It also put relatively small commercial farmers at competitive risk: they could go into debt to buy machinery or lose out to more affluent growers who could produce at volume. The story of the last frontiers, then, is of the interaction between the old ideal of independent farming and the newer forces of the times.

For people still craving property in land, at any rate, the West seemed the most promising place. The South, meanwhile, was the least promising. Black southerners, denied the property that a few Radicals during Reconstruction had contemplated, were forced into tenancy or sharecropping. That was better than slavery, offering a family the freedom to work the same plot of ground year after year; but it put the family at the precarious will of the owner. Whites as well as blacks became tenants or croppers. In the South as well as the rest of the country, cities expanded and industry turned workers into wage earners. In landholding, the South represented the end of a long era that the West seemed, for a moment, to continue.

The Railroads

Old Mac, the station master on the Chesapeake and Ohio line, ca. 1874, is an interesting face and figure out of the past. Imagine what his various duties were.
(*Courtesy, Cook Collection, Valentine Museum*)

The Rail Network   In 1860 the railroad network was already extensive, measuring over 30,000 miles. But it did not constitute the complete system that would later knit the nation together. Little mileage stretched beyond the Mississippi River, and none beyond the Missouri. The South had a decent amount of track, but it was in short stretches, not tied up with major through routes, and connected at only a few points with northern lines. The country had hundreds of different railroad companies and several distinct rail gauges that required unloading of freight and reloading on different boxcars. In 1860 movement of freight and people was still slow, difficult, and relatively expensive. Around each local population center there remained a ring of small producers providing goods for the neighborhood on a small scale, and often at a high price.

Many Americans were conscious of the deficiencies of the country's rail network and sought to overcome them. In the better settled parts of the country it was only a matter of time. There, traffic was potentially heavy and private capital was readily forthcoming. Yet even in the populous Northeast many promoters seeking funds for railroad building resorted to the tactic of promising local communities rail connections if they would lend the promoters money or provide other bonuses. In newer areas the hurdles were greater. Railroads across empty country could be justified on the ground of the needs of

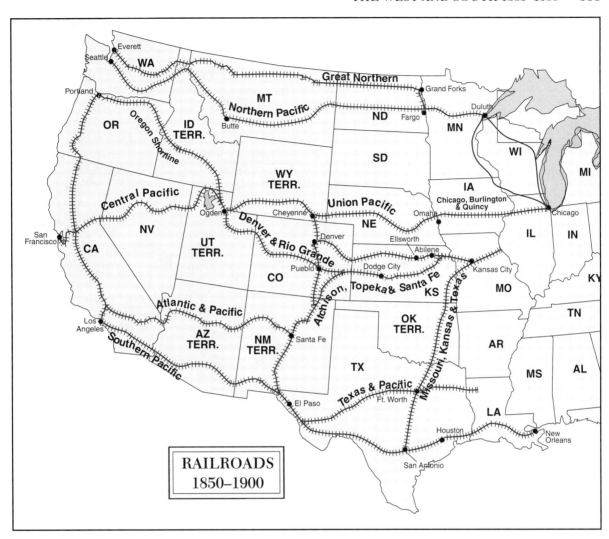

RAILROADS
1850–1900

society in general, but not on the basis of immediate profit to investors. Eventually, no doubt, the transcontinental railroad would create its own business by opening up the country. But that might take years and meanwhile what would the investors do for dividends? It seemed clear to many Americans that if the country was to have railroads connecting the settled portions of the East with the West Coast it would have to be willing to pay for them in some fashion; private capital alone would not do the job.

Land Grants to Railroads   For a decade or more before 1860, businessmen, journalists, and politicians had debated how to finance a Pacific railroad. Following a practice of land grants that went back as far as the Land Ordinance of 1785, the federal government in 1850 transferred several million acres of the vast public domain to promoters who promised to build a railroad connecting the Great Lakes with the Pacific Coast. Northerners and southerners agreed on the need for such a road, but they fought furiously over whether the route should be a southern, a central, or a northern one. Not until the South left the Union was the issue settled by the Pacific Railroad bill of 1862.

The Union Pacific–Central Pacific was the first of the transcontinentals subsidized by federal land grants. In 1864 Congress chartered the Northern Pacific Railroad and gave it an even larger land grant. Another road, later to become the Atchison, Topeka, and Santa Fe, also received a land grant, as did a far southern route that eventually came to be called the Southern Pacific. In all, Congress handed out over 131 million acres of federal land to railroad promoters, while the states gave an additional 49 million acres. The total was finally as large an area as the state of Texas.

Railroad promoters often bribed legislators who would be instrumental in the granting of government lands. And some promoters made large profits out of the land they had received. But building railroads across wildernesses in advance of settlement meant taking a serious risk. In most cases the federal government was given cheap rates for shipping its own freight over the transcontinentals, and thereby saved itself millions of dollars. The government also gained by the rise in value of federal lands adjacent to the railroad. It is a mistake to assume that the land that went to the roads was thereby lost to farmers. The railroads were anxious to fill the land with settlers who could provide the commerce the roads needed. Each of the Pacific railroads set up a department that sold land to settlers at from two to eight dollars an acre, often arranging credit and providing free transportation for prospective customers. Each also maintained a bureau of immigration that advertised in Europe and the eastern United States promoting the western lands.

The policy of land grants to railroads has been taken, correctly, to represent the friendliness of the American government to big business. But it also meant that the government was willing to put itself boldly into the economy in a way that went against nineteenth-century doctrines of competitive private enterprise. Between the end of the Civil War and 1910, the country increased its main railroad trackage to 240,000 miles, eight times the mileage of 1865. Railway roadbeds were improved, steel rails substituted for iron, and iron locomotives made larger and more efficient.

Freight and Passenger Travel In 1886 the last company shifted to the standard gauge of 4′ 8½″. Freight and passengers could be sent long distances over several companies' trackage without interruption. The completion of the railroad network helped to create a national market. Innumerable crossroad hamlets had spurs connecting them to the major commercial trading and manufacturing centers of the nation and the major ports of the world. By 1910 almost every American farm was within convenient wagon distance of some railroad depot and thence connected to the world's markets. Now for the first time manufacturers could locate their plants almost anywhere and be assured that they could bring in raw materials cheaply and send their finished products wherever they could find customers. Every region of the country could specialize in crops best suited to its climate and supply consumers with food at lower prices than their own neighborhoods could. Such changes help to explain the rising gross national product of these years.

By present-day standards, train travel was rough. In much of the country dust had to be kept out and ventilation was spare. Passenger cars going west were coupled and recoupled to freight cars going in the same direction. Locomotives, which bore at their front a frame called a cowcatcher designed for pushing obstructions away, did hit cattle and passengers were jolted. The powerful machines made for thousands of horrible industrial accidents. A brakeman describes his in 1888: "It was four or five months before I 'got it.' I was making a coupling one afternoon. . . . Just before the two cars were come together, the one behind me left the track. . . . Hearing the racket, I sprang to one side, but my toe caught the top of the rail. I was pinned between the corners of the cars as they came together. I heard my ribs cave in like an old box smashed with an ax." Between 1890 and 1917, some 72,000 railroad workers died on the job and nearly two million were injured.

Filling in the Continent

Between the Civil War and 1900 Americans enormously increased the lands they effectively occupied. In 1865 the continental United States had already reached its present three million square miles, but vast expanses remained virtually empty of people. In the next thirty-five years the population swept across the sparsely settled plains. The term "West," which had once referred frequently to what is now called the Middle West, could now more appropriately apply to the whole of the land from the Mississippi to the Pacific. By the beginning of the twentieth century the United States had not only filled in its continental limits; it had expanded its land area to 3.6 million square miles by acquiring nonadjacent territory, such as Alaska and Hawaii. Besides this, it had extended its influence and economic power far beyond the borders of the parochial nation that had renewed its bonds at Appomattox Court House. The settlement came at a good time for the West as well. The growth of population in the East increased the demand for livestock and other agricultural products along with timber and minerals, and better transportation increased markets abroad.

"Down the Sierra Nevadas," 1865, etching. *(Courtesy, Scribner's Archives)*

The Plains and the Great Basin The Great Plains are an enormous flat plateau rising gradually from the Mississippi River to about 5,000 feet above sea level, where it reaches the edge of the Rocky Mountains. The Great Basin to the west of the Plains is a vast shallow bowl dotted with a few mountainous regions between the eastern Rockies and the Sierra-Cascade ranges of California, Oregon, and Washington. Both regions are deficient in rainfall; the Basin approaches true desert in places. And both are treeless, except along stream banks or in other especially moist spots. The Plains are covered with short grass; the Basin is sprinkled with sagebrush, cacti, and creosote brushes. The Plains rivers are shallow,

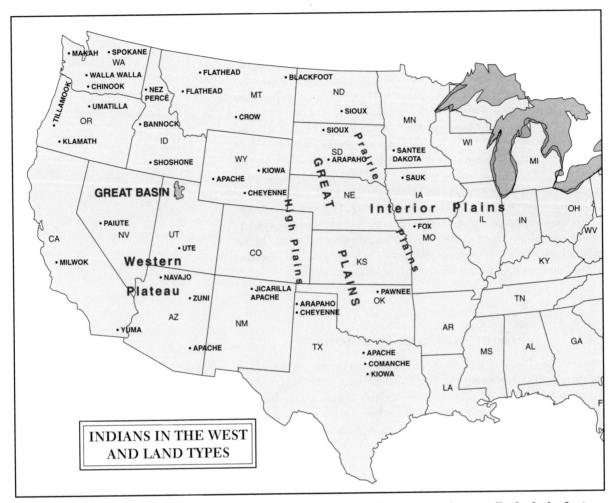

INDIANS IN THE WEST
AND LAND TYPES

In the Great Plains and Great Basin, the topography, climate, altitudes, crops, and especially the lack of rain led to changes in a mode of settlement that had been essentially uniform through Kentucky and Ohio and on to Missouri. The rectangular land surveys and quarter-section lots that were traditional in woods and fertile, watered prairie could not accommodate Great Plains or Great Basin conditions.

especially in the fall. In the Basin, the few streams have water only in the spring, when melt-off from mountain snows fills their banks. None of these has any ocean connection. They simply die in some sink hole where the water gives out.

The weather of the Plains and Great Basin is of the type geographers call "continental." Winters are often fiercely cold, with temperatures plunging to as low as forty degrees below zero. On the Plains, the frost comes with roaring blizzards covering the land with a white layer that sometimes drifts roof-high. Springs are frequently balmy, with the ground covered by a carpet of wildflowers brought forth by melting snow or brief rains; they are usually short, however, followed by brutally hot summers when temperatures climb into the nineties and the sun beats down remorselessly from cloudless skies. Among the more disturbing characteristics of the region's climate and weather is its inconsistency. In the arid Basin, where rainfall seldom exceeds one or two inches per year, a sudden cloudburst can pour down the average yearly allotment in an hour or two. The Plains do not usually experience such deluges, but rainfall can vary sharply from year to year and decade to decade. Some periods are quite dry and drought-afflicted. These will be followed by extended periods of abundant rainfall, when the grass remains green and lush for much of the year.

The Plains and Basin have sheltered a profusion of animals. Antelope, rabbits, gophers, squirrels, wolves, and coyotes were once found everywhere. Along many streams, especially at the mountain edges, were beaver with thick, soft pelts prized as raw material for felt hats. The most visible and abundant of all the Plains animals were the bison or American buffalo.

For the native peoples of the region, the buffalo were an extraordinary asset. Fresh buffalo meat was a staple of their diet. Dried meat, sliced thin, was carried on long trips, along with pemmican—dried meat mixed with berries, fat, and marrow and stuffed into a buffalo-gut bag. Buffalo skins served as clothing and as the walls of tents, or tepees, and were used to make containers of various kinds. Buffalo sinews became rope and bowstrings. Even buffalo droppings, or chips, were valuable: when dried, they made an excellent fuel on the treeless Plains. It was "a rather hard matter," wrote one pioneer woman, "that the Buffalo should furnish the meat and then the fuel to cook it."

Although only thinning herds of buffalo remained near the Union Pacific right-of-way after train travel began, the iron horses of the Kansas Pacific occasionally were surrounded by buffalo and had to slow down or wait until the herd passed. In its early days, the Kansas Pacific engineers willingly stopped trains to permit the passengers to leave the cars and shoot at passing buffalo.

To encourage buffalo hunting as a sport, railroads crossing the Great Plains had the animal heads mounted by their own taxidermists for display at ticket stations. (*Courtesy, Kansas Pacific Railroad, DeGolyer Library, Southern Methodist University*)

E. N. Andrews gives this firsthand account of shooting buffalo from a passenger train:

"Our excursion party, organized for the benefit of a church in that place, and numbering about three hundred, left Lawrence, Kansas, Tuesday, A. M., at 10 o'clock, October 6, 1868, by the Kansas Pacific Railway. . . . The all-important question, revealing very plainly the thought and desire of all, was: 'Where shall we see the buffalo?'... [W]hat a sight was gradually unfolded to our vision! In estimating the number, the only fitting word was 'innumerable,' one hundred thousand was too small a number, a million would be more correct. Besides, who could tell how many miles those herds, or the herd, extended beyond the visible horizon? Powder and ball were brought into requisition. Shots enough were fired to rout a regiment of men. Ah! see that bull in advance there; he has stopped a second; he turns a kind of reproachful look toward the train; he starts again on the lope a step or two; he hesitates; poises on the right legs; a pail-full of blood gushes warm from his nostrils; he falls flat upon the right side, dead. . . . The pleasure and excitement were all the greater because so unexpected. The engineer was kind enough to shut off the steam; the train stopped, and such a scrambling and screeching was never before heard on the Plains, except among the red men, as we rushed forth to see our first game lying in his gore . . . the cornet band gathered around, and, as if to tantalize the spirits of all departed buffalo, as well as Indians, played Yankee Doodle. . . . 'Glory enough for one day,' thought we; 'now what shall the morrow reveal?' "

Developing the West

Visions of land had brought the first European colonists to America in the seventeenth century, and that same dream pushed their descendants across the continent in the eighteenth and nineteenth centuries. In pursuit of Manifest Destiny, the United States in the 1840s acquired title to Texas, the Far West, and the Southwest. After the Civil War those areas began to fill with settlers. Millions of Americans wanted land out west, and it became the express purpose of federal and state governments to assist and finance them.

**Government
Policy**   Because railroad building required enormous capital investment, those governments donated land to help finance construction. The subsidies began in 1830 with the first state land grants, and in 1871 the federal government issued its final grant to the Texas and Pacific Railroad. During those years seventy railroads received title to 130 million acres of public domain land. The railroads stood to gain far more from a flourishing commerce along their routes than from the short-term profits of selling plots at high prices. Eager to encourage settlement and economic growth, they provided reasonable terms to purchasers of their landholdings.

The federal government also made it progressively easier for settlers to acquire land. The Homestead Act of 1862 provided 160 acres of free public domain land to a settler paying a registration fee and working the land for five years. The act was part of the Republican policy of vigorous federal promotion of the nation's economy. The Timber Culture Act of 1873 granted 160 acres to whoever would plant trees on a portion of it. The Desert Land Act of 1877 allowed settlers to acquire 640 acres at $1.25 an acre in more arid regions, the proviso being that the occupant irrigate the land. Speculators, using such devices as hiring stand-ins to file claims, managed to acquire much of the land that the federal government had intended to go directly to independent farmers. The land grabbers would thereupon sell to genuine settlers. Agricultural machinery and worldwide demand for food made for a trend toward large-scale farming. By 1900 farms of a thousand acres accounted for two-thirds of California's arable soil. The 160-acre tracts provided by the Homestead Act and subsequent legislation, at any rate, were too small for the commercial farming that came to dominate western agriculture.

Water Policy   The dry climate of the Great Plains, Great Basin, and Southwest posed formidable obstacles to land development, since possession of water rights determined who throve and who perished. Water use had initially been determined by what has become known as the "prior appropriation doctrine." The individual who first put water to beneficial use retained rights to that water for as long as the use continued. During periods of water shortages, these senior users were allowed to consume all of their appropriation before junior users received any water.

Water development, then, became a priority of public policy. If

Canyon de Chelly, Arizona, where the canyon walls project upward about 1,200 feet. (*Courtesy, Scribner's Archives*)

the arid West was going to fill up with large numbers of small farmers, they had to have water. Without some type of federal legislation, most of the water would end up in the hands of a privileged few. One strategy of the federal government was to set aside national forests that were to act as watersheds, protected from lumbering and overgrazing. President Benjamin Harrison set aside sixteen million acres and President Grover Cleveland twenty-one million. The Carey Act of 1894 ceded millions of acres of public domain lands to the states. With the proceeds from the sale of those lands, the state governments were supposed to embark on ambitious water development projects. When the states failed to establish workable programs, Congress passed the Newlands Act of 1902, which set up the Reclamation Service and committed it to seeing to the construction of flood control, irrigation, and river development projects throughout the West.

The results of the land and water development legislation were dramatic. In 1840 only one percent of the non-Indian population of the United States—perhaps 175,000 people—had lived west of the Mississippi River, but forty years later there were more than ten million people there, approximately twenty percent of the population. The pioneers, convinced like other Americans of their right to property, were determined to acquire a chunk of it in the West. They were also relatively indifferent to the possibility that any race or people unlike themselves might have a prior claim to it. Relatively few of them set out for the frontier hoping to injure the Indians or Mexicans living there. They simply wanted to better themselves—to leave something behind for their children. But the collective impact of millions of well-meaning settlers moving across the landscape with the backing of the government was a political and economic catastrophe for the original inhabitants of the American West.

The Native Peoples

Before the coming of the whites, 250 to 300 thousand Indians had inhabited the region, divided into many major tribes and dozens of bands.

"Digger Indians" The major tribes of the Great Basin included the Bannock, Shoshone, Paiute, Ute, and Snake. Theirs was a harsh environment where agriculture was impossible without a highly developed social order to promote irrigation.

Among these peoples, tribes existed as linguistic entities, but they were not usually joined politically. The only true social unit was the extended family of about twenty-five to thirty individuals. There were no chiefs, only talkers, influential men considered wise and worthy of being consulted. Each winter a group of families might gather together to take shelter in some especially warm spot. During these months they formed loose personal and group connections. But in the spring these villages would break up. The Basin peoples lived almost entirely by food-gathering supplemented by a little hunting. In the spring they collected edible plants in the valleys. Later they would wander to higher land where they gathered berries, nuts, seeds, and roots. They also ate lizards, mice, birds, and grasshoppers. Their use of sticks to extract roots got them the name "Digger Indians."

The Basin peoples lived in brush huts and even in hollowed-out depressions in the earth. Their clothing was rudimentary. The men wore breechcloths; the women, an apron of milkweed fiber. Often both wore nothing at all. They had baskets, but no pottery. They lacked any sort of domesticated animals.

He is "awkward on the ground," a painter wrote of the Plains Indian, but "the moment he lays his hand upon a horse, his face . . . becomes handsome, and he gracefully flies away like a different being."

Plains Indians At the eastern fringes of the region, the Great Basin tribes merged with the more numerous Indians of the Plains. Originally an agricultural people, the Plains Indians, except in the more humid eastern parts, had become by around 1500, overwhelmingly nomadic hunter-gatherers whose chief source of sustenance was the buffalo. About 1700 this nomadic pattern was reinforced by the arrival of horses, strays from the Spanish lands at the northern edges of Mexico.

The Plains Indians are the classic natives of American legend. Tall, bronzed, well-muscled, hawk-nosed, wearing fringed leather clothing and feathered war bonnets, living in colorfully decorated tepees, magnificent horsemen, renowned as marksmen with the bow and arrow, they have entered our folk history as the worthy opponents of the cavalry or the cowboy.

There were many Plains tribes. To the north, spilling over into Canada, were the Blackfeet, a confederation of several tribes. Adjacent were the Crows. In western South Dakota and Nebraska, as well as parts of Montana and Wyoming, were the various bands of the Sioux. South of these were the Cheyenne, while on the southern Plains lived the Comanches, Kiowas, and Kiowa-Apaches.

At the opening of the nineteenth century the Plains culture, as white Americans came to know it, had fully emerged. The Plains tribes decorated their leather clothing with beads, quills, eagle feathers, and pictures; they recorded important occurrences and drew calendars with paint on leather. Many of their tepees were large structures with abundant room for a whole family. They took much of the technology of white culture: horses, cloth, metal tools, firearms, though their bows were capable of driving an arrow through a bull buffalo. They made superb cavalry, adept at ambushes, and if pursued able to disappear into the brush.

Social organization was more complex than that of the Basin peoples. Tribes, many of them large, were guided by chiefs, though ruled by councils of leading men. The typical social unit was the band of a few hundred, rather than the tribe. Within the bands there was often a multitude of male societies that resembled white men's lodges, with regalia, ceremonies, officers, and songs. The societies were also charged with the authority to police behavior.

Unlike the Indians farther west, the Plains people gave scope to the full tribe. Periodically there were gatherings of whole tribal groups where people visited, gambled, played games, raced, met in councils, and shared in religious ceremonies. Many of the Plains tribes performed a ritual called the Sun Dance, usually held in the summer. Sun Dance performers gathered near a painted pole and danced for days without food and water until they fell down exhausted. The purpose of the dance was to produce a trance and visions. Some tribes sought to produce trances or religious ecstasy by self-torture that included suspension from a sacred tree by skewers inserted through slits in the chest.

A Sioux chief, Spotted Tail, later remarked: "We do not like to live like the white man. . . . The Great Spirit gave us hunting grounds, gave us the buffalo, the elk, the deer, and the antelope. Our fathers have taught us to hunt and live on the plains and we are contented."

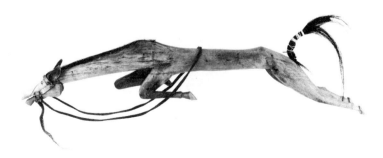

This Sioux horse effigy conveys powerfully the central place that the horse occupied in the life of the Plains Indians. (*Courtesy, South Dakota State Historical Society*)

Red Armed Panther, Cheyenne scout. Efforts to force Cheyennes and Arapahos into smaller land areas than promised sparked an Indian war in 1861. *(Courtesy, The Huffman Pictures, Coffrin's Old West Gallery, Miles City, Montana)*

Relations Between Indians and Whites

The first white intrusion came well before the Civil War. During the war itself, the railroads began to penetrate the region, stimulating wide bands of settlement along their rights-of-way. To protect the railroads and then the settlers, the federal government established numerous army posts that became centers of white culture and points of contact between white and red peoples.

The Indians both feared whites and admired them. Many Indians could see that the future belonged to the whites, and many wanted to acquire some of their ways. The horse, a contribution of European whites, was, of course, a splendid animal for enabling the tribes to travel and bring along heavy loads. Acquiring food became less of a problem. Sometimes Indians took the white man's vices. Ever since the colonial period, rum and brandy had been used in the Indian trade, and by the end of the nineteenth century drinking had become a chronic problem among some tribes.

In general, Anglo-Saxons unlike the French, Spanish, and other Latins did not sexually mingle with Indians. In this American Protestants were acting in accord with their general cultural provincialism. More compelling as a reason for antagonism was greed. The Indians had what the whites wanted—land, millions of acres of some of the finest land on earth. To the western farmer or the land speculator, the presence of the original inhabitants was an obstacle in the way of livelihood and profit. But even many people not directly involved in western development asked whether a few thousand "primitives" should be allowed to retain so much of the nation's rich resources while each year the white population grew at an explosive rate. Undoubtedly there was a large element of cultural chauvinism in this. Yet by white standards, the retention of so much of the West by a few thousand hunter-gatherer nomads seemed a criminal waste of resources.

Greed and contempt were not the sole white responses to the Indians. Generally the most aggressive opponents of Indian claims were westerners. Easterners could afford to be more generous and philosophical, and by the mid-nineteenth century many sincerely regretted the way the Indians had been treated. Few of these people actually wanted to leave the great West permanently in the hands of the tribes, but they did wish to guarantee fair treatment. Many also hoped that the Indians could be weaned away from their traditional nomadism, "civilized," and confined to settled compact agricultural communities where they could support themselves as small farmers like other Americans. Yet earlier in the century Cherokees who actually conformed to this prescription had been swept aside from their Georgia lands anyway.

The Plains Indians Subdued

Indian Policy

Before the Civil War, the government's Indian policy had at first been based on the idea of a permanent Indian domain west of the Mississippi into which whites would not intrude. In the late 1840s, after thousands of whites began to cross the Plains on their way to Oregon and California, the policy gave way to a plan of establishing Indian reservations, the land between being made available to settlers. Meanwhile, the migrants to California and Oregon pushed through the tribal territories, altering the environment and economy of the Indians. In the Treaty of Fort Laramie (1851), the Plains tribes, in exchange for a promised long-term federal subsidy, agreed to move to reservations. The new arrangement did not preserve peace. Whites took over many Indian lands; Indians found the reservations too confining after their free roaming life.

During the Civil War General John Pope, the failed commander of the Union Army of Virginia, set about to subdue the Sioux of the northern Plains, an Indian group not yet brought under the reservation policy. After Sioux attacks on several Minnesota towns, Pope ordered his deputy, Colonel Henry Sibley, to make an example of them. "They are," he ordered, "to be treated as maniacs or wild beasts, and by no means as people with whom treaties or compromises can be made." Sibley attacked the Indians in September 1862 and captured 1,800 warriors, more than 300 of whom he condemned to death. President Lincoln reprieved all but thirty-eight, to the disgust of Minnesota settlers.

War Other troubles soon followed. Efforts to force the Cheyenne and Arapaho into smaller land areas than those promised sparked an Indian war throughout Colorado Territory in 1861.

In late November 1864 the Colorado militia under Colonel John Chivington, a former preacher, surrounded a friendly band of Cheyenne at Sand Creek in eastern Colorado Territory, and attacked them without provocation. The militia fired volleys at the men. Women and children who fled to nearby caves were dragged out to be knifed or shot. Only fifty escaped the bestial Chivington massacre. For the next three years many of the Plains tribes went to war.

In 1867 President Johnson appointed a commission that patched up a peace. During the next thirty years the military commanders at the Plains army posts had to deal frequently with hostile tribesmen who found the reservations confining and longed to return to their old ways. A few of the commanders were insensitive or cruel men; officers like General Oliver O. Howard and George Crook, however, were men of their word whom many Indians respected. But they had the thankless task of defending every renegade white man, however brutal he had been toward the Indians, and of enforcing the basically harsh reservation policy.

In this period, as in preceding centuries, white Americans disgraced themselves in their treatment of the Indians. But lest we romanticize the beleaguered Indian, driven from his ancestral home by greed and bigotry, remember also the tales of Indian cruelty and of sudden violence inexplicable to whites. The history of relations between Indians and settlers in this country reflects badly, not solely on the white race or on the red, but on the human race.

A series of Indian depredations, raids, and pitched battles lasted

An Indian trader at the scene of the Chivington massacre later testified:

"They were scalped, the brains knocked out; the men used their knives, ripped open women, clubbed little children, knocked them in the head with their guns, beat their brains out, mutilated their body in every sense of the word."

Colonel J. M. Chivington defended his actions in 1865:

"My reason for making the attack on the Indian camp was, that I believed the Indians in the camp were hostile to the whites. That they were of the same tribes with those who had murdered many persons and destroyed much valuable property on the Platte and Arkansas rivers during the previous spring, summer and fall was beyond a doubt. When a tribe of Indians is at war with the whites it is impossible to determine what party or band of the tribe or the name of the Indian or Indians belonging to the tribe so at war are guilty of the acts of hostility. . . ."

Colonel George Armstrong Custer, whose bravado exceeded his wisdom, did not hesitate to attack a much larger force of Sioux Indians at the Little Big Horn River. It was his last stand. *(Courtesy, Anheuser-Busch, Inc.)*

"The more we can kill this year," said one Civil War general in 1869, "the less will have to be killed the next war, for the more I see of these Indians the more I am convinced that all have to be killed or [sent] away into the emptiness of the surrounding grasslands." Yet when he observed that a mere fifty Indians could often "checkmate" 3,000 soldiers, he also said, "We took away their country and their means of support, broke up their mode of living, their habits of life, introduced disease and decay among them, and it was for this and against this that they made war. Could anyone expect less?"

until the 1890s. Indians inflicted heavy casualties on the United States Army. In 1866 they had wiped out Captain William Fetterman's detachment of eighty men on the Bozeman Trail. In 1876 Colonel George Custer's troop of 265 men set out after Sitting Bull's Sioux warriors, who had left their reservations in protest against the government's allowing gold prospectors to trespass on their reservation in the Black Hills. The megalomaniacal Custer encountered the Sioux at the Little Big Horn River and foolishly attacked the much larger force of Indians. Custer and his band were wiped out to a man. In White Bull's recounting of the engagement: "The fight lasted only a short time. All of us were crazy. We had killed many soldiers. They had attacked us and meant to wipe us out. We were fighting for our lives and homeland. Cries of victory went up. Our women came through the timber by the river and began to strip the dead soldiers. Some of the sisters and wives and mothers of slain warriors cut the bodies of the soldiers to pieces. They were crazy with sorrow."

Cruelties and brutalities were committed on both sides. One scholar maintains that between 1798 and 1898 whites killed 4,000 Indians, while the Indians themselves killed some 7,000 soldiers and civilians. These figures, however, do not include the many Indians who died by starvation and disease as a result of federal policy. Nor do they take it into account that the white killers were the advance forces of a culture that perceived itself as advanced and humane.

The Nez Percé One case involved the Nez Percé of the far Northwest, who contradicted almost every stereotype of the Indian. Ensconced in the narrow valleys between the Cascade and

Bitterroot mountains (lands now parts of Idaho, Washington, and Oregon), they apparently never attacked settlers before their great war with the whites in 1877. Their forebears had aided Lewis and Clark in 1805. They welcomed outsiders and were quick to learn from them. The tribe even survived a gold rush into its lands in the 1860s, remaining at peace despite numerous outrages by the miners. Nonetheless, friction sharpened in the 1860s as cattle ranchers eyed lands on which Indian horses grazed. In 1863 the federal government negotiated a treaty to delimit Indian land titles, but a group of braves, loosely led by Old Joseph, the father of a more famous Joseph, rejected it. Turning away from the Christianity they had learned from missionaries, they began a peaceful but determined resistance to the white man's designs on their ancestral lands.

Although Chief Joseph struggled to avoid conflict, his people's fate was all too typical: rapacious settlers pressing for land, unfeeling Indian agents, bungling governmental departments, an unsympathetic general, a forced and hurried evacuation of their lands, and finally young braves driven to fury and terrible violence. Once at war, Joseph and his tribe enacted one of the great feats of military prowess and human endurance: for this army traveled with its women and children, its sick and aged. A United States Army ROTC instruction manual describes Joseph's achievement: "In 11 weeks, he had moved his tribe 1600 miles, engaged 10 separate U.S. commands in 13 battles and skirmishes, and in nearly every instance had either defeated them or fought them to a stand-still." Joseph and fewer than two hundred braves withstood an army. The effort, of course, was doomed, and with its failure, the Nez Percé would no longer exist as an independent people.

For all the fame of Chief Joseph as a guerrilla leader, he was essentially a diplomat. When the United States government immediately reneged on the terms under which he had surrendered, shipping the tribe to Indian Territory in the present state of Oklahoma, Joseph began a careful and patient campaign to return his people to their mountain home. While he never succeeded in regaining his beloved Wallowa Valley—Old Joseph's gravesite—after five years of direct interviews with the President, the secretary of the interior, and numerous congressmen, and by enlisting the editorial support of several eastern journals, he did get his dispirited and rapidly decreasing tribe back to the mountains where they could thrive again. In his new home in western Washington, Joseph became an Indian elder statesman, a national symbol of courage and resistance and freedom. He returned to the Wallowa Valley but once, in 1900, an old man. There he found only the consolation that a settler—a man with, as he said, "a spirit too rare among his kind"—had enclosed and cared for his father's grave.

| **The Decline of the Buffalo** | In the end, it was not the army that subdued the Plains Indians. It was the destruction of the buffalo. So long as the tribes could hunt the great shaggy |

beasts, they could survive off the reservations. Once the buffalo were killed off, the dependence of the Indians on white largesse became almost complete.

"My son," Old Joseph whispered as he lay dying, "you are the chief. . . . You must stop your ears whenever you are asked to sign a treaty selling your home. . . . This country holds your father's body. Never sell the bones of your father and your mother."

Chief Joseph surrendered on October 5, 1877. His memorable speech gave all the reasons:

"I am tired of fighting. Our chiefs are killed. Looking Glass is dead. The old men are all killed. It is the young men who say yes or no. He who led the young men is dead. It is cold and we have no blankets. The little children are freezing to death. My people, some of them, have run away to the hills and have no blankets, no food; no one knows where they are, perhaps freezing to death. I want time to look for my children and see how many of them I can find. Maybe I shall find them among the dead. Hear me, my chiefs, I am tired; my heart is sick and sad. From where the sun now stands. I will fight no more forever."

A Sioux educated in New England wrote of what he saw on a bright New Year's Day in 1891:

"On the day following the Wounded Knee massacre, there was a blizzard. On the third day it cleared, and the ground was covered with fresh snow. We had feared that some of the wounded Indians had been left on the field, and a number of us volunteered to go and see.

Fully three miles from the scene of the massacre, we found the body of a woman completely covered with a blanket of snow, and from this point we found them scattered along as they had been hunted down and slaughtered. When we reached the spot where the Indian camp had stood, among the fragments of burned tents and other belongings, we saw the frozen bodies lying close together or piled one upon another. I counted eighty bodies of men, who were almost as helpless as the women and babes when the deadly [gun] fire began, for nearly all their guns had been taken from them.

Although they had been lying in the snow and cold for two days and nights, a number had survived. Among them I found a baby of about a year old, warmly wrapped and entirely unhurt. Under a wagon, I discovered an old woman, totally blind and helpless. . . ."

Black Elk said of Wounded Knee that

"something . . . died there in the bloody mud, and was buried in the blizzard. A people's dream died there. It was a beautiful dream. . . . There is no center any longer, and the sacred tree is dead."

Indians, often sentimentalized as a race living in unbroken harmony with the land and its animals, might better be respected as human beings possessed of all the virtues and vices of the species. Once Europeans had equipped them with horses and guns, they began doing what whites would soon be doing: killing the buffalo. But because Indians continued to hunt buffalo for subsistence rather than for commercial gain, it is doubtful that the numbers slaughtered approached those killed by the white man. Then during the building of the great western railroads, tens of thousands of buffalo were killed for food and sport. In 1871 a Pennsylvania tanner discovered that buffalo skins made good leather. With hides selling at two to three dollars apiece, a hunter could make a fine profit slaughtering the beasts. Soon groups of hunters accompanied by wagons were swarming over the Plains, often killing fifty or more a day, skinning them, and leaving the carcasses to rot. Between 1872 and 1874 alone, some nine million animals were killed. By 1878 the southern herd was no more; by 1883 the northern herd was gone. In 1903, in the place of all the millions that had once thundered across the Plains, there survived a known total of thirty-four bison.

Without the buffalo the Indians were tied down to the reservation. Yet even now they were not completely subjugated. In 1890 the Teton Sioux of South Dakota faced hunger as a result of drought and congressional stinginess. They came under the spell of a prophet, Wovoka, who told them that if they performed certain dances the dead would be resurrected, white men driven out, and Indian lands restored. The Ghost Dancers alarmed the local whites, who called for troops. The soldiers, in turn, frightened the Indians, who came under the influence of aggressive Sioux warriors. "If the soldiers surround you," one warrior promised, "three of you, on whom I have put holy shirts, will sing a song around them, then some of them will drop dead. Then the rest will start to run, but their horses will sink into the earth." The upshot of all this was the massacre at Wounded Knee, when soldiers armed with repeat-firing Gatling guns mowed down nearly 200 Indians of both sexes, young and old.

Indian Reform   Although Wounded Knee was the last actual Indian battle, the Indian issue did not go away. For nearly three centuries American economic interests—farmers and later railroads and timber and mining companies—were relentless at seizing land from the Indians. They preferred taking the land peacefully, but if violence was necessary, the settlers and the companies were usually more than willing to resort to it. But many Americans hated the rapacity of the economic interest groups and wanted to end the violence by assimilating Indians into the larger society—converting them to Christianity, awarding them citizenship, and helping them make the transition to the ways of a modern economy. Congress took the first step toward assimilation by passing legislation transferring Indian affairs from the Department of State to the Department of the Interior. No longer would Indian tribes be treated as sovereign nations. Nor would the United States government ever again sign treaties with them. The reformers worked through the Board of Indian Commissioners, nominated by major Protestant denominations including Quakers. They also organized the Indian Rights Association and the Women's National Indian Association. Missionaries went west to eradicate tribal customs such as the consignment of hunting to men and farming to women. Indians would abandon many communal practices, turning instead to individually owned homesteads; children, their hair trimmed short, would be in boarding schools, shedding traditional values, learning to celebrate the Fourth of July. The reformers gathered 100,000 signatures calling for phasing out the reservation system, providing universal education to Indian children, and giving a title to 160 acres to anyone willing to accept it. Particularly effective in behalf of Indian reform was *A Century of Dishonor* (1881), by the novelist Helen Hunt Jackson.

In the late nineteenth century, the reform panacea was known as "allotment." To bring about assimilation, Congress passed the Dawes Severalty Act of 1887, dividing reservations into smaller allotments—usually 160 acres—which would be awarded to each Indian family. With their allotments of land, Indians would also receive United States citizenship. Reformers hoped the Indians would become small farmers like millions of whites.

The Dawes Severalty Act received widespread support from reformers committed to protecting Indians from economic interest groups. A provision of the act was for distributing "excess" reservation land to whites. In 1887, for example, the Sisseton Sioux of South Dakota owned 918,000 acres of rich virgin farmland on their reservation. But since there were only 2,000 members of the tribe, the Dawes Act left about 600,000 acres available for white families. In short order the Department of the Interior opened the surplus Sisseton land to white farmers, who moved in among the Indians. In 1887, when the federal government launched the allotment program, American Indians controlled more than 138 million acres of land on their reservations. The Indian Reorganization Act of 1934, affirming the integrity of Indian cultural institutions and returning land to tribal ownerships ended the allotment program. By then the Indians had 48 million acres left, most of that in the arid deserts of the Southwest. Tribes disappeared or existed in remnants. The Navaho survived by making rugs; the Hopi, by crafting dolls. The northwestern tribes remained longest, living on salmon.

Besides setting up the allotment program, Congress appropriated money for establishing special schools where Indian youths could learn the white man's agricultural and mechanical trades. Frequently finding it difficult to lead Indian men out of their customary ways, reformers put considerable effort into the education of Indian women. Members of the Bureau of Indian Affairs in Washington insisted that the best way to bring the Indians into the modern world was to transform the women into proper domestic beings who could raise the next generation acting in accord with white society's values. The women were to be trained in the white American way of performing such domestic work as spinning, sewing, housekeeping, and child rearing. This approach essentially embodied the attitude of the social workers who

HELEN HUNT JACKSON
from A Century of Dishonor

"There is not among these three hundred bands of Indians one which has not suffered cruelly at the hands either of the Government or of white settlers. The poorer, the more insignificant, the more helpless the band, the more certain the cruelty and outrage to which they have been subjected. . . .

It makes little difference . . . where one opens the record of the history of the Indians; every page and every year has its dark stain. The story of one tribe is the story of all, varied only by differences of time and place. . . . Colorado is as greedy and unjust in 1880 as was Georgia in 1830, and Ohio in 1795; and the United States Government breaks promises now as deftly as then, and with an added ingenuity from long practice. . . .

To assume that it would be easy . . . to undo the mischief and hurt of the long past . . . is the blunder of a hasty and uninformed judgment. The notion which seems to be growing more prevalent, that simply to make all Indians at once citizens of the United States would be a . . . panacea for all their ills . . . is a very inconsiderate one. . . . Nevertheless, it is true, as was well stated by one of the superintendents of Indian Affairs in 1857, that, 'so long as they are not citizens of the United States, their rights of property must remain insecure against invasion. The doors of the federal tribunals being barred against them. . . . The utter absence of individual title to particular lands deprives every one among them of the chief incentive to labor and exertion. . . .'

Cheating, robbing, breaking promises—these three are clearly things which must cease to be done. One more thing, also, and that is the refusal of the protection of the law to the Indian's right of property. . . .

When these four things have ceased to be done, time, statesmanship, philanthropy, and Christianity can slowly and surely do the rest."

also would try to teach immigrant women to be proper American wives and mothers.

Hispanics

In addition to confronting several hundred thousand American Indians on the frontier, the pioneers encountered around 90,000 to 100,000 Mexican Americans living in the Southwest. Beginning in the late seventeenth century, Hispanic pioneers had moved north out of New Spain and then Mexico. When the Treaty of Guadalupe Hidalgo ended the Mexican War in 1848, approximately 50,000 of them lived in and around Santa Fe, New Mexico, while another 30,000 were split evenly between south Texas and the coast of California. The vast majority of Mexican Americans were small farmers, although there were large estates and business communities in cities like San Antonio, Santa Fe, and San Francisco. The Treaty of Guadalupe Hidalgo guaranteed them citizenship in the United States, freedom of religion, and protection of their land titles. But guarantees of citizenship and property were little protection when millions of Anglo pioneers settled in the West later in the century.

Anglos had migrated in peak numbers during the first years of the Gold Rush, and the Mexican inhabitants of California, who were known as *californios*, were soon greatly outnumbered. When the gold rush played out, tens of thousands of Anglo immigrants squatted on *californio* land. To resolve the question of title, the state legislature passed the Land Act of 1851, creating a Board of Land Commissioners to mediate conflicting claims. The board was hopelessly biased. The commissioners were all Anglos, the hearings were conducted in English, and the burden of proof rested on the *californio* owners, not the Anglo squatters. By 1860 the board had turned over more than four million acres of land to the Anglo squatters. When the board decided in favor of the *californio* owners, the squatters often resorted to the federal court system, where cases took an average of seventeen years to resolve. During the litigation, the squatters were allowed to remain on the land.

Ethnic relations were even worse in Texas. The state legislature and local townships imposed heavy taxes on land owned by Mexican Americans, and when they failed to pay and went into default, county sheriffs auctioned their land to Anglo owners. Intimidation was common. During the second half of the nineteenth century the Texas Rangers may have killed nearly 5,000 *tejanos,* as the Mexicans in Texas were called. In hundreds of cases the Rangers simply helped Anglos dislodge *tejanos* from the land. Richard King was one of the Texas robber barons who used the Rangers to secure his land claims. The son of poor Irish immigrants, King moved to South Texas and founded the King Ranch, eventually increasing his holdings to more than 600,000 acres. Similar events occurred throughout South Texas, and by 1880 only two of the wealthiest 300 landowners in the state were *tejanos.* The transfer of land was nearly complete.

In New Mexico, the Santa Fe Ring seized control of much *nuevo mexicano* land between 1860 and 1890. The Ring was a small clique of Anglo bankers, merchants, and lawyers who were closely tied to the wealthiest twenty *nuevo mexicano* landowners and controlled the territorial legislature. Like their Hispanic counterparts in California and Texas, many *nuevo mexicanos* found themselves facing heavy property taxes, high interest rates, tax auctions, and land losses. To deal with the controversy, Congress created the Court of Private Land Claims for New Mexico, Colorado, and Arizona in 1891, but the proceedings were conducted in English and the burden of proof rested on *nuevo mexicano* owners, not the Anglo claimants. Between 1892 and 1905 the court evaluated 301 claims and found for the Anglo 226 times.

When New Mexico became a state in 1912, its constitution guaranteed the equality of the Spanish and the English languages.

The Mining Frontiers

The departure of the Indians and the buffalo opened the trans-Mississippi West to white exploitation. First to arrive had been the miners and prospectors who streamed to Colorado when gold was discovered there in 1849 and then moved on to western Nevada, Idaho's Snake River Valley, and western Montana when further deposits were discovered in those areas. Many of these men came to the Great Basin and the Plains from the diggings in California, having failed to find wealth there or having found and lost it. Other adventurers departed from Missouri River towns. Each of these river towns did a land-office business outfitting and supplying the gold-seekers. An observer reported of one: "The streets are full of people buying flour, bacon, groceries, with wagons and outfits, and all around the town are little camps preparing to go west."

Mining Towns   Few who joined in these rushes and later ones— Black Hills in 1874, Coeur d'Alene in 1883—ever saw many golden flakes in their pans. "The stories you hear frequently," one gold-seeker wrote home, "are the most extravagant lies imaginable—the mines are humbug . . . the almost universal feeling is to get home." Another wrote more joyfully: "It would astonish you to see a town grow up out here. You old fashioned people in the States would go crazy. . . . Some of the most desirable lots [in California] sold at first for $250, now command from $10–$15,000. I saw a hole 20 ft. deep out of which $50,000 has been taken. I am worth now about $10,000." Some of the unlucky drifted on to the next strike. Those who did get rich—and some of those who did not—stayed on and became the founders of Denver, Boise, Helena, and other flourishing cities that grew up around the mining camps.

One notable feature of the mining towns was the absence of women. At first, generally, there were no women at all, and when one put in an appearance, miners would come to gape at her. Soon, contingents of "fancy women" arrived—dance-hall girls and prostitutes—to help relieve the miners of their newly-gained wealth. Eventually, when and if the mining camp became a permanent community, respectable

Mexican Immigrants

In the late nineteenth century economic activity bustled along the southwest border. After the railroads were built, farming developed in south Texas, copper mines opened in Arizona, and irrigated fruit farms sprang up in southern California. The border with Mexico remained open until 1917, and Mexicans had been coming to the United States to work in substantial numbers since the 1880s. One educated guess puts the figure of those who arrived in the year 1900 at somewhere between 60,000 and 100,000. Almost all were low paid and physically overworked.

Nevada's Virginia City

Virginia City began as a flimsy mining camp after the Comstock lode was discovered in 1859. By the 1870s it was a boom town with a stock exchange, five newspapers, a hundred saloons, and many houses of prostitution (in 1870 twice as many men as women lived there). By 1880, however, there were church picnics, small houses being erected for families, and even an opera house. Most of the men gambled their lives underground for about $4 a day, too often victims of the enormous hazards of hard-rock mining.

Result of a Miss Deal, by **Frederic Remington**.

women appeared: wives, sisters, and mothers, as well as a few school-teachers, seamstresses, and shopkeepers. The arrival of such women usually marked the end of the initial disorderly and unstructured phase of a mining town's existence.

In their early years the towns were cosmopolitan places where professional men and scholars mingled with roughnecks. The gold-seekers were of every race and nationality. Most were whites from the Midwest and South, but there were many Europeans along with blacks, Indians, and a substantial number of Mexicans. The presence of easily portable wealth in the shape of gold dust or nuggets encouraged theft and gambling. Claim-jumping, the stealing of someone else's strike, was a frequent occurrence in the mining camps and a constant source of violence. And men without families and with money in their pockets often took to heavy drink and general hell-raising. At times despera-does virtually took over whole communities, terrorizing the decent folk.

Vigilantes   At this point the forces of law and order might rally and organize a vigilance committee. The term "vigilante" is now in bad repute—it has come to suggest mob passions and the repression of dissent. In mining camps after the Civil War, however, it was sometimes an intelligent and a moderately democratic response to lawlessness. The vigilance committee might draw up a set of rules under which the members agreed to function until order could be restored. Then, confident of their strength, they would make examples of the worst rogues by sudden arrest, quick trial, and at times prompt hanging from the nearest tree. A few of these swift executions were generally enough to end the reign of violence and establish civilization.

Vigilante justice was in part a response to the federal government's slowness in providing government for the mining frontier. It often was many months before Congress took note of the political needs of the mining population and established a territorial government with a governor, courts, and federal law-enforcement officials. In several cases, the people of a region established a provisional regime well before Congress acted, and began to pass laws for dealing with the normal problems of any civilized community. Eventually, the laggard Congress responded, and in a few years had arranged the Great Basin region into organized territories, repeating the process of state-making that had begun farther east back in the 1790s.

The Other Extractions The most excitement accompanied the mining of gold. The production of silver, the other most precious of metals in popular estimation, increased with the discovery of deposits in Nevada, Colorado, and Utah. By the 1890s, the question of whether silver should be freely coined had become a major political question. Meanwhile, however, the West was contributing other riches that had much more of substance to give to the growth of industrialism (the major industrial uses of gold and silver had yet to be exploited). In the second half of the century, iron was mined in Michigan, Minnesota, and Colorado. The importance of iron magnified when innovations in technology made possible its efficient conversion into steel. In Michigan, Minnesota, Arizona, and Montana, industry gained deposits of copper. By the turn of the twentieth century, the West was supplying coal from Iowa, Kansas, Missouri, Indian Territory (soon to be part of Oklahoma state), Texas, New Mexico Territory, Utah, Colorado, and Montana. A significant partner in the nation's industrial expansion, furnishing not only food for the cities and workers of the East but coal and metals for factories, the West participated as well in the labor mobilization that attended industrial progress. The militant Western Federation of Miners, for example, organizing workers in mining other than coal, was a major force in the formation in 1905 of the radical Industrial Workers of the World.

Mining was hard, dangerous work, but it paid fairly well. The owners of mines often imported champagne and oysters until the lodes gave out. *(Courtesy, Scribner's Archives)*

The Cattleman's Frontier

The level Plains east of the Rockies followed a different course of development from that of the Great Basin. The vast grasslands of the Plains were ideally suited to grazing and quickly became a stock-raiser's frontier. "Cotton was once crowned king," exulted one westerner, "but grass is now." The process was gradual, a slow spread from south to north.

Texas Cattle   The original focus of the Plains cattle industry had been south Texas where, before the Civil War, ranchers raised thousands of cattle. The Texas longhorn was of Spanish ancestry, a hardy beast that could fend for itself on the open range without shelter or fodder. It was not a particularly good beef animal, but that made little difference: in the absence of modern transportation, the markets for beef were too far from Texas. Hides were another matter. In the 1850s thousands of Texas cattle were slaughtered for the tanneries of the Northeast.

During the Civil War, Texas was cut off from its chief customers and the cattle multiplied rapidly. Soon after Appomattox some ranchers conceived the idea of herding the cattle north to Sedalia, Missouri, for shipment east over the Missouri Pacific railroad. The farmers along the way objected to Texas cattle as disease-carriers and as a danger to standing crops, and did not allow the ranchers to pass through. But the idea of the long drive had been born and became practical when the drives went farther west through unsettled country.

In its full development between the end of the 1860s and 1880 the long drive became an annual overland expedition northward from Texas to the nearest east-running railroad. The drives set out when the grass was green so that the cattle could graze along the way. Each group consisted of as many as one thousand cattle driven by cowboys who kept the herd moving and prevented strays from wandering off and stampeding frightened animals. Leading the band was a cook and his

Cowboys round up a herd near Cheyenne, Wyoming, during one of the great cattle drives that briefly characterized the ranching economy of the West. *(Courtesy, American Heritage Center, University of Wyoming)*

chuck wagon, carrying food and supplies, followed by the wrangler with the spare horses, both followed by the herd itself.

The cowboys driving the herds north were a mixed group. Most of them were whites, a large portion of these from the South; between a fifth and a third were African Americans, Mexicans, or Indians. After the Civil War, almost ten thousand black men made their way from the plantations of the South to jobs on ranches and cattle trails in the West. They worked as cooks, wranglers, ordinary hands, and top hands, but they were usually unable to move all the way to the top of the cowboy hierarchy and become ranch or trail bosses. Pushing a herd across a flooded river was dangerous. Just as railroad construction foremen frequently used Chinese workers to set explosive charges, cowboy trail bosses often made sure that black, Mexican, or Indian cowboys tested the depth of a river and the strength of its current. It "was the Negro hand," a white cowboy would remember, "who usually tried out the swimming water when a trailing herd came to a swollen stream."

Cattle Towns and Cowboys   Soon many of the drives were rerouted along the Chisholm Trail, due north to Abilene in central Kansas. There, on the Kansas Pacific railroad, an Illinois cattle dealer, Joseph McCoy, had in 1867 constructed stock-yards, cattle pens, loading ramps, and a hotel. McCoy chose the hamlet of Abilene because, as he wrote, "the country was entirely unsettled, well watered, excellent grass, and nearly the entire area of country was adapted to holding cattle." Once arrived in town, the drivers sold their herds to McCoy or some other dealer and departed with money in their pockets. The cattle were loaded on freight cars and sent east.

Abilene was only the first of a number of cattle towns. As the region around this small city became settled farming country, the Texas drives were deflected farther west to Ellsworth, Newton, and Dodge City. Like the mining camps, the cattle towns were at first almost all-male communities. Cowboys with money were just as wild as miners in the same lucky situation. Their average age was only twenty-four.

Hollywood movies have correctly portrayed the cowboy's life as hard, but they miss the drudgery of the labor that made it unromantic. The baking of the summer sun, the cutting cold of January, the relent-less nerve-scraping groan of the prairie wind accompanied the cowboy's work; not gunplay but pneumonia and riding accidents threatened his life. Instead, the western film celebrates the West of Wyatt Earp and Jesse James and the shootout at the OK Corral, making it difficult to distinguish reality from myth. Westerns reflect above all Americans' dislike of authority and aim to distill primal virtues and redeem us from a decayed present. Films, such as *High Noon* (1952) with Gary Cooper, are to a considerable extent about the era when they were made, offering reassurance in hard or worrisome times.

The great annual cattle drives belonged to an era that began in the late 1860s and lasted less than two decades. In that period there were about 40,000 cowboys. Most typical of a cowboy's work then and later was riding endlessly, sometimes in wind and rain, to mend fences or look for lost cattle. The animals he had to tend to were signally incapable

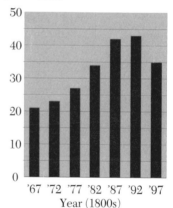

Beef Cattle Consumption in the United States 1867–1897

Numbers of Beef Cattle
(in millions)

Year (1800s)

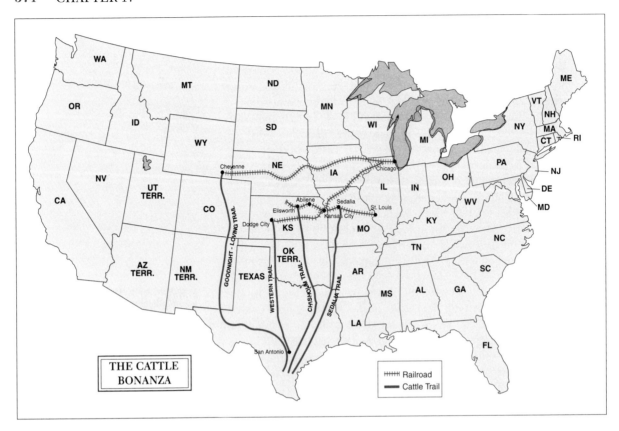

THE CATTLE BONANZA

of looking after themselves. In a blizzard they might be discovered with their eyelids frozen shut and their muzzles dripping icicles. Cowboys had to chop through snow crusts and ice so cattle could drink, for the animals lacked the instinct to eat snow for moisture. Driven through the desert and arriving at a river, numerous steer would drink too much and die. Through luck or biological sense, others did manage to wade in, moan for a half hour or so, drink a little, stand for another interval, drink some more, and survive.

The gear and style of the cowboy were colorful enough but determined by utility. Included in the working equipment were a horse, a rope for subduing the thousand-pound animals, and a pistol or rifle. The Colt revolver was highly inaccurate: the kind of quick-draw precision shooting from the hip once ascribed to gunfighters would have been quite a surprise. Cowboys spent two months' wages, about $50, on their boots. They were at least seventeen inches high: this was to prevent twigs or pebbles from getting inside. The high heels were to hold the stirrup. Cooks often prepared sonofabitch stew made of cattle hearts, bull testicles (sometimes called prairie oysters), tongues, liver, marrow, gut, and semidigested food found inside dead cattle. For whatever reason—the nature of the work, the starkness of the environment, or the absence of anything interesting to talk about—cowboys became known for being reserved in speech.

Ranching   The annual long drive lasted until about 1880. During the years it prospered, about four million cattle were driven north from Texas to Kansas railroads for shipment east. By 1880, the fate that had overtaken Abilene also claimed the other cow towns: an ever-denser farm population increasingly interfered with the drive. In addition, new railroads through the Texas plains made it possible to ship cattle directly from the local ranches of the Texas panhandle. By this time, too, the northern plains—the Dakotas, Wyoming, Montana, and Colorado—were stocked with cattle, hybrids with the hardiness of longhorns and the beef of Angus and Herefords. These animals became the major source of beef for the thriving cities of the East.

For a decade and a half the northern Plains range cattle industry flourished. Young cattle could be bought for a few dollars and put out to pasture on government land. The rancher did not have to invest in barns or other buildings. All he needed was a cabin by a streambank from which he and his hands could ride out occasionally to inspect the stock. The cattle wintered out and gained weight on the nutritious grass. Twice each year—spring and fall—the rancher and his hands conducted a roundup, separating out the mingled herds of neighbors and branding calves with their owner's mark. When shipped to market after four or five years, a calf had increased in value by about ten times.

So long as winters were moderately mild and the range not overstocked, the system worked. But its very success became a pitfall. Attracted by dazzling profits, investors went into the cattle industry by the hundreds. For a while, London investors were in a dither over enormous potential profits in western cattle. "Drawing rooms buzzed with stories of this last of the bonanzas; staid old gentlemen, who scarcely knew the difference between a steer and a heifer, discussed it over their port and nuts." The romance of the open range drew easterners such as the New York aristocrat Theodore Roosevelt, who became a rancher in the South Dakota Badlands. In the cattle kingdom itself, the ranchers tried through various livestock associations to limit the number of cattle, but they were unable to prevent overstocking. By the mid-eighties so many cattle were tumbling into the eastern markets that prices began to decline.

Natural   Then disaster fell. The hard winter of 1885–86 was
Disasters   followed by a hot, dry summer that withered the grass and dried up waterholes. Prices of steers dropped from $30 each to $8. The winter of 1886–87 was a catastrophe. By November the snow on the northern Plains was so deep that cattle could not dig down to the grass. In late January the worst blizzard on record roared across the Plains from the Canadian border to Texas. This was followed by a cold snap that sent temperatures plummeting to 45 below zero. On the open plains, cattle froze upright in their tracks. Many thousands crowded into gullies and stream valleys for shelter and were buried in drifts. In the spring, the freshets from melting snow washed thousands of steer carcasses into the tributaries of the Missouri. The melting also revealed stacks of carcasses piled up

Spectacular were the dust storms, the wind driving dry topsoil against newly planted crops. A settler recorded one of them in the 1870s.

"The corn I had planted was looking fine, and the potato patch was getting green when on the tenth of May at about 11:30 a.m. we saw a cloud coming across the plain very low, and which sounded like wind. I put the horses under the wagon cover where we kept our grain, and we all rushed for the house. As the cloud approached, the noise increased until we could not hear each other speak, and the light from the sun faded as though night was coming. It was the most awesome and terrifying thing we had ever seen. Then it fell, and for a while we were in almost total darkness. As the light gradually came back, and with it the realization that we were safe in the house, we felt thankful, until we looked outside. There we saw a writhing black blanket that seemed to be crawling toward us from every direction. We each grabbed a child and held it to protect it. Soon the sun came out, but the blanket kept rolling, and the stench was so appalling it left us trembling. . . . Gradually the blanket lifted, and we could see the damage. Not a stalk of corn was left, nor a blade of grass; even the leaves on the trees were gone."

The productivity of the land was magnificent. "You have no idea, Beulah," a Dakota farmer wrote to his wife, "of what [large wheat farms] are like until you see them. For mile after mile there is not a sign of a tree or stone and just as level as the floor of our house. . . . Wheat never looked better and it is nothing but wheat, wheat, wheat."

against barbed wire, then a recent addition to the western landscape. Invented in 1874 by Joseph F. Glidden, barbed wire was significant in the ending of the open range.

Over the next few years, the cattle industry painfully reorganized. Many of the more speculative enterprises, including large cattle corporations representing eastern and European investors, went bankrupt. Thereafter the ranchers turned to smaller and better herds on fenced land and grew hay to provide fodder. Some cattlemen, especially on the dryer margins of the plains, turned to raising a hardier species of animal—sheep. Others resisted the sheepmen, and for a while open warfare raged between the ranchers and the herders in parts of the former cattle kingdom.

Specialized Farming   Equipped with barbed wire to fence off the timberless grasslands, with well-digging machinery and windmill pumps to provide drinking water for stock and human beings, and with new techniques of dry farming to offset sparse rainfall, farmers poured into the more humid portions of the Plains from the East. By the 1890s vast areas of the Dakotas, eastern Montana, and Colorado were covered with wheat fields. In the fall, great bonanza farms were crisscrossed by great harvesters pulled by six horses cutting enormous swaths through the yellow sea of grain.

In return for her generous yields, nature compensated: blizzards and droughts; prairie fires; and grasshoppers, flying in crowds so large they shut out the sun, eating clothing, mosquito netting, tree bark, plow handles, and of course crops. In one summer alone grasshoppers devastated the Plains from Texas to the Dakotas, eating everything "but the mortgage," in the words of one farmer.

To the trials that nature posed for the farmer was added constant financial stress. "Watch and study the markets and the ways of the marketman . . . learn the art of 'selling well,' " one country editor advised his readers in 1887. Farming particularly depended increasingly on machinery. "It is no longer necessary for the farmer to cut his wheat with sickle or cradle, nor to rake it and bind it by hand; to cut his cornstalks with a knife and shock the stalks by hand; to thresh his grain with a flail," noted one westerner. Farmers had to invest heavily in machinery, such as harvesters and binders. That forced them into burdensome mortgages and made them increasingly vulnerable to the wayward shiftings of the market and the will of eastern commercial interests. All this would sharpen the political conciousness of farmers.

The Cherokee Strip   An instance of the farming frontier was the Cherokee strip of two million acres in the present-day state of Oklahoma. Its fortunes illustrate both the genuine promise of the West and the hard life of farming. The region roughly equivalent to Oklahoma had been reserved in the 1830s for the five civilized tribes, the Seminoles, Cherokees, Choctaws, Chickasaws, and Creeks, which were removed from the East. Asserting that these tribes had sided with the Confederacy, the authorities later reneged on that promise but settled thousands of other Indians in the area, reducing their reservations so that the region could be opened to more white settlers. On April 22, 1899, the government officially opened the unoc-cupied Cherokee strip to settlement. On that April day near the dawn of the twentieth century, the original idea of the Homestead Act, that the West was to be a region of small independent farmers, seemed very much alive. Within two months, two thousand claims would be made.

The Strip was settled along with the rest of Oklahoma, which in 1907 became a state. Yet Oklahoma was no more a region of virtuously comfortable farmers than the rest of the open land that romanticists had dreamed of since the European discovery of the American conti-nent. In the absence of steady rain, countless farmers had to settle for being sharecroppers to more prosperous landholders. Farming dam-aged grasslands that had conserved water and made for soil erosion. Then in the Great Depression of the 1930s, drought turned the region into the Dust Bowl. Okies went to California—somewhere to the west, it still seemed, must lie prosperity and security—there to subsist in migrant camps, subject to the prejudice of Californians who feared that the newcomers would become an economic burden. As has been so often the case in American history, anger was directed not upward, toward the most affluent, but downward to the poorer.

Sang a folksong from an Oklahoma county:

Hurrah for Greer County! The land of
the free,
The land of the bedbug, grasshoper,
and flea;
I'll sing of its praises, I'll tell of its fame,
While starving to death on my government claim.

Frontier Women   Women went west for a variety of reasons. Most of them, of course, were farming women who wanted, like their husbands, to acquire more land and build a better life for their children and grandchildren. Some women mi-grated for religious reasons: Baptists, Methodists, Presbyterians, and Congregationalists went west as missionaries to bring Christianity to Indians and Protestantism to Spanish-speaking Roman Catholics. Other women, converted to Mormonism in the cities of the East or abroad in Great Britain and Scandinavia, went to Salt Lake City and from there to smaller towns and villages throughout the Great Basin to help build Zion in the wilderness. And tens of thousands of seam-stresses, laundresses, cooks, waitresses, maids, and teachers tried to make a living on the frontier.

Ada McCall gathering buffalo chips near Lakin, Kansas.
(Courtesy, The Kansas State Historical Society)

Women making the covered wagon crossing of the plains and deserts, or later going by train, and then trying to survive after finding a place to settle might live for years in dugouts or sod houses on the Great Plains or in lean-tos, small shacks, or cabins in the Far West. On the frontier, gentility was a luxury. Women fought a constant war against mud and wind and dust. All day long, summer and winter, they kept stoves hot for cooking, bottling, canning, washing clothes and dishes, and heating bathwater. And they often engaged in heavy farm labor alongside their husbands. The rigid divisions of labor so common back east tended to break down on the frontier.

It was a lonely existence. Farms were widely scattered and opportunities to interact with friends were rare. Men frequently left home to pan for gold, deliver cattle or sheep to market, engage in business and politics, or work for wages on ranches or in towns in order to buy the goods their farms needed. They could be gone for months at a time. Women stayed behind to watch after the farm and take care of the children. With their men gone, they might worry about bandits. Worst of all, however, was the excruciating, stifling loneliness.

Some historians have argued that the harshness of the frontier and its tendency to blur divisions of labor and social roles helped liberate women. Wyoming gave women the right to vote in 1869, Utah in 1870. But the harshest frontier living conditions only lasted a few years in most areas, and as soon as any semblance of community appeared in the frontier West, traditional sexual roles reasserted themselves. The cult of domesticity, the belief that women were to be the keepers of homes, the tenders of children, and the preservers of virtue against the cruder impulses of men, became as

EMMA MITCHELL NEW

remembers her pioneer days, beginning in 1877, on the Kansas prairie. She and her husband were homesteaders, settling public land that became theirs for a small fee after they had lived on it a number of years.

"We landed in Russell [on the prairie of central Kansas] forepart of December, 1877, with our car-load of goods, consisting of a few household goods, team of horses, a few chickens, a wagon and plow, enough lumber to build a small house, and a fairly good supply of provisions. We boarded at a hotel for two weeks and by that time the house was finished enough that we could move in out on a claim two miles northwest of Russell. Many a homesick day I saw, many a tear was shed. I couldn't bear to go to the window and look out. All I could see everywhere was prairie and not a house to be seen. . . .

I thought I was going to have a good garden, but the rain failed to come and we got nothing. In the meantime we were hunting water and hauling it in barrels. We dug a deep well and got nothing. Many a time I walked a quarter of a mile down into a deep draw with pails and carried water to wash with.

My husband broke prairie as fast as he could with the old team. One time he broke a fire guard around some grass that was quite tall and then set fire to it. The wind carried the sparks across the guards and set the prairie on fire. We worked hard to put it out to save our home and buildings, until we were completely exhausted. And many a time afterward I fought fires until I was all in, for we had so many in those days.

Years came along one after the other and also droughts. Times looked perilous to us. We finally got a cow, which helped us to live. Then there came along the Indian scare. All the people around about flocked to town for safety except me. I was all alone with my two children and knew nothing of it, as my husband was a good many miles from home trying to earn a little something. He worked out many a day for fifty cents and was glad to get it. Grasshoppers were very plentiful in those days. At times, swarms of them would shade the sun.

strong in the cities, towns, and villages of the West as it had ever been in the East. In Wyoming, the all-male territorial legislature gave women the right to vote because it hoped that feminine virtues would help tame the more lawless elements of the frontier and attract respectable settlers. In Utah, Mormon leaders gave women the right to vote once the completion of the transcontinental railroad threatened to bring large numbers of non-Mormons to the territory. Giving Mormon women the franchise was a way of preserving church control of territorial politics.

Frontier Thesis In the West, farming communities were dispersed thinly throughout the landscape, and by 1880 a greater percentage of the population was concentrated in cities and towns than in any other part of the nation. Yet by 1890 enough people were living across the region that, according to the Superintendent of the Census "at present the unsettled areas have been so broken into by isolated bodies of settlement that there can hardly be said to be a frontier line. In the discussion of its extent, its westward movement, etc., it can not, therefore, any longer have a place in the census reports." Frederick Jackson Turner, in a paper read before the American Historical Association in 1893, made this bulletin the starting point for the formulation of his famous frontier thesis. He ascribed many of the nation's social and political characteristics, particularly democracy and individualism, to the presence of a western frontier throughout American history. Turner neglected the New England town meetings and various important elements of the European heritage. The thesis also ignored frontiers of New Spain, which

THE HISTORIAN
FREDERICK JACKSON TURNER
ON THE FRONTIER
from "The Significance of the Frontier in American History," 1893:

"To the frontier the American intellect owes its striking characteristics. That coarseness and strength combined with acuteness and inquisitiveness; that practical, inventive turn of mind, quick to find expedients; that masterful grasp of material things, lacking in the artistic but powerful to effect great ends; that restless, nervous energy; that dominant individualism, working for good and for evil, and withal that buoyancy and exuberance which comes with freedom—these are traits of the frontier, or traits called out elsewhere because of the existence of the frontier. Since the days when the fleet of Columbus sailed into the waters of the New World, America has been another name for opportunity, and the people of the United States have taken their tone from incessant expansion which has not only been open but has even been forced upon them. . . . But never again [after 1890] will such gifts of free land offer themselves."

Our house was very poor, so my husband in a few spare minutes would saw soft rocks into bricks and lay them between the studding to make it firm, as the Kansas wind rocked it so bad. I helped carry all the bricks. We picked up and burned "cow chips" for fuel. . . .

Hardships and trials came along in their turn. Got a young team to deliver our milk to town. A baby girl came to us, making the second that came to us in Kansas without doctor or nurses and practically no help except the two older children.

We got along very well when a terrible storm and cloudburst came upon us and we lost almost everything, except the cows and an old team in the pasture. We had a nice cow barn put up and that day they put up a stack of millet the whole length of the barn. It commenced to rain in the afternoon, but in due time we started the children to town with the milk. It was a general downpour and the creeks were commencing to rise. . . .

The creek was up to the house and still pouring down. My husband investigated and found that the underpinning of the house was going and that we had to get out. We took a lantern and matches and some blankets, and started for the side hills. When we opened the door to get out, the water came up to our necks. We had a struggle to get out and I can't tell to this day how we ever made it, but the Lord must have been with us. My husband carried the baby girl in his arms as high as his head. We soon got out of the deepest water, as there was a turn in the creek. We went by way of the horse stable and found we would be safe in it. Still the water was up and it was pitch dark. The matches were wet, so we couldn't light the lantern.

We stayed there until the storm abated and the water went down. Then we started out to see if we had a home left and to our delight, even in such a mess, we found it still standing. It was still dark and we couldn't see what havoc the storm had made for us. We found some dry matches and lit the lamp. Such a deplorable sight words can't express. There was an inch of mud all over the carpets and floors. . . ."

had developed along more authoritarian lines. And scholars have since pointed out how premature the census announcement actually was: much land remained to be settled. Yet many Americans thought the frontier experience to be at an end, and with it the expansionist phase of the nation's history. Others believed that only the first chapter had ended. Now the vigorous people who had conquered the North American continent must look outward toward the larger world across the seas. There, expansionists said, lay the country's new destiny.

The South

Henry Grady's South   In 1886 Henry Grady, an *Atlanta Constitution* editor, spoke in New York to a group of industrialists. In his talk entitled "The New South" Grady lamented, of a southerner who had been buried amid solid marble in a pine forest, that his marble tombstone was made in Vermont and his pine casket in Ohio. Both should have come from his native South. Grady looked forward to an era of industrial prosperity in "the glorious sunny South" built by the safe investments of northern financiers. Another newspaper predicted that the South would be El Dorado of the next century. Financing did come from the North, particularly for the railroads whose tracks, formerly narrow gauged, were brought into conformity with northern trackage. In the rolling Piedmont growth came particularly in textile mills, which often exploited working children; in Birmingham an iron and steel industry came to thrive; in Richmond 100,000 cigarettes a day issued from the mechanized factories of James Buchanan Duke's American Tobacco Company. The pine woods yielded turpentine and lumber, and later refining of the Gulf Coast's sugar became a large industry.

No development so buoyed the hopes of New South proponents as the success of the region's textile industry. After 1877, new mills sprang up in South Carolina, North Carolina, and Georgia. This 1887 engraving of a model mill at Augusta, Georgia, conveys the South's pride in its new industrial prowess. —*Harper's Weekly*, 1887, pp. 158–9. (*Courtesy, Newberry Library, Chicago*)

Booker T. Washington The conviction that the South must diversify its agriculture, must expand its industrial plant, must learn the skills and the workwise mentality of the North continued as an alternative way of thinking about the future of the region. It would have upset white southerners of the late nineteenth and early twentieth century to know that today a black leader is that era's most honored advocate of agricultural and industrial training.

Born in 1856 in Virginia, the son of a slave woman, Booker T. Washington never knew the identity of his white father. At first he mined salt and coal. Then Mrs. Lewis Ruffner, a well-to-do white woman in whose home he worked, encouraged and helped him to attend Hampton Institute in Virginia which stressed vocational skills for its black student body. Washington arrived at Hampton footsore, dirty, and penniless; on his graduation three years later, he was endowed with a basic education and a high moral commitment. Washington taught school, becoming increasingly convinced of the necessity of teaching young black men and women practical skills and a belief in self-help and the dignity of labor.

In 1881 Washington became the founder and principal of Tuskegee Institute in Alabama. He acquired the land, built buildings, raised money for books, equipment, and salaries. For fifteen years Washington worked tirelessly to establish an all-black teachers' college with goals similar to those of Hampton. Graduates of Tuskegee went on to be teachers throughout the South and in Africa. The director of agricultural research at Tuskegee was George Washington Carver, an agricultural chemist born of slave parents. Educated at Iowa State, he became director of agricultural research at Tuskegee Institute in Alabama. His experiments with peanuts, sweet potatoes, and soybeans amounted to an argument for shifting the southern economy from its single crops, cotton and tobacco, to a healthier, more diversified production. More militant members of Washington's race were to complain that he was telling blacks to be content with the manual crafts to which whites wished to confine them. Washington did indeed argue for at least temporary accommodation to the racial customs of the times. But seen from another perspective, he was among the most progressive of southern educators, wishing to introduce a portion of the populace to the knowledge and work habits of the country's more technologically and scientifically advanced regions. Carver's agricultural research at Tuskegee was scientific and experimental, yet addressed to the uses of sweet potatoes and the South's other plain, common, and available vegetables.

Booker T. Washington, founder of Tuskegee Institute in Alabama in 1881. Some criticized his gradualist, conciliatory approach to race relations, but he was very much a man of action who often defied traditional racial conventions. *(Courtesy, Library of Congress)*

Cotton Despite an impressive showing in iron and steel, and despite the best efforts of its supporters of change, the South accounted for only a small part of the nation's industrial product and its mills employed but a fraction of the southern workforce. Much of the region's industry hired only whites, or took on blacks for the lowest jobs. Hired labor in general was poorly paid, and at its most brutalized was made up of convicts supplied by southern prison systems. Capital for the South's industrial enterprise came from the North, and southern banks, indebted to northern investors, had to pass on the debts to southern merchants, who in turn were required to squeeze small landowners, tenants, and sharecroppers by means of crop liens, the holding of crops as collatoral for debts. These the farmers never seemed able to repay. The farm machinery and the interest in scientific soil management that represented the advance of the industrial revolution into a portion of western and northeastern agriculture had no or little equivalent in the rural South.

The effect and cause of the South's misery, and the only way of living with it, was cotton. The South had for a long time been modern in one way: much of its agriculture, rather than being given merely to growing food for the sustenance of the small farmer, was dedicated to mass production of a commercial crop, the kind of production that has come to be the way of twentieth-century agriculture in the United States. That crop, moreover, went directly into a modern industry, that of factory-made textiles. In the South, however, single-crop agriculture was a force not for progress but for retardation. The North wanted cotton for mills—even much of the South's textile production was owned by northern capital; and as is customary, manufacturers have the advantage over the producers of raw materials. Cotton put the region into a chain of indebtedness that went up to the North as creditor. Cotton was the only kind of collatoral that creditors trusted; and so poor farmers had to keep growing it. Besides, cotton growing and picking were the skills and customs that the region's poor knew. So year after year, croppers, tenants, and large as well as small landowners kept growing the cotton that creditors demanded and northern capital wanted. Toward the end of the century, as the price of cotton fell, independent farmers had to sell out. By 1900 over half of white and a large majority of black farmers were sharecroppers or rent-payers. While even in the West tenancy was becoming frequent, the increase was not nearly so great.

Black Labor in the New South

Beginning in the 1880s, only a few years after retaking control of southern state governments, white Democrats created a series of legal institutions designed to keep black workers tied to the plantations. Laws were passed making it difficult for them to relocate outside the county. Southern bankers and lawyers often refused to allow them to purchase land of their own or to finance those purchases. When black people tried, they often encountered severe racism and threats of violence. A typical example occurred in Faulkner County, Arkansas, in 1883 when an African-American man attempted to buy fertile land. An armed mob delivered him a message in writing: "Mr. Nigger, just as shore as you locate yourself here—death is your potion." It was difficult for black farmers to secure reasonably long leases on a piece of land. Whites did not want African Americans working a piece of land independently; they wanted them out in the plantation fields. Many southern state practices in effect prohibited them from becoming apprentices in the skilled trades. In the South, the cotton mills that sprang up during the 1880s refused to accept black operatives; the new jobs were reserved for rural whites straight off the farm. By 1900 more than

For most blacks there was not much change in the kind of labor they had performed during the days of slavery. Edisto Island, South Carolina. *(Courtesy, New-York Historical Society)*

ninety percent of blacks in the South worked as field hands, sharecroppers, maids, or longshoremen.

If the North had presented a more equitable relationship between the races, the South might have been on the defensive. But north of the defeated Confederacy, things were not much better. Northern employers preferred white European immigrants to native American blacks. Black workers seeking jobs in industry met with threats or violence on the part of bigoted white workers. White employers aggravated the hostility, using black strikebreakers when their usual labor force refused to work. Few local unions would admit skilled black workers into their ranks. Among the national unions organized after the Civil War, only the ineffectual Knights of Labor actively sought black members. When it declined in the late 1880s and 1890s, black workers found themselves without protection. The American Federation of Labor (AFL), much of its membership an elite of skilled craft-workers, at first welcomed black members. An 1890 resolution of the AFL declared that the Federation looked "with disfavor upon trade unions having provisions which exclude from membership persons on account of race and color." But then Federation officials began to yield to the prejudices of the workers who made up its constituent unions. Efforts to organize all-black unions proved feeble, and in the end few black workers benefited from the AFL. As the craft unions that made up the Federation increased their control over jobs, their bias reinforced the exclusion of blacks from all but the most menial jobs.

Jim Crow   In many ways the lot of black Americans deteriorated in these years. Poverty and economic stagnation had afflicted them as sharecroppers in the post-Civil War South, and they had lost the fight to retain the political rights granted them during Reconstruction. Southern novelists often depicted blacks negatively. To Thomas Nelson Page they were "wild beasts." Joel Chandler Harris, in his Uncle Remus stories written for children, had a black man utter this pronouncement: "Put a spellin-book in a nigger's han's, en right den en dar' you loozes a plowhand. I kin take a bar'l stave an fling mo' sense inter a nigger in one minnit dan all de schoolhouses betwixt dis en de state er Midgigin." Southern blacks were economically better off under freedom, or what passed for it, than under slavery but not by much.

By the 1880s they had also begun to be surrounded by rising walls of legal segregation that excluded them from a wide range of public facilities, including good schools, colleges, and universities, and from decent housing in the towns and cities. Black Americans fought back as best they could against this policy of Jim Crow, but with few allies they could accomplish little. In 1883 the Supreme Court, reviewing a suit brought by five black Americans under the 1875 Civil Rights Act, declared that the law limited only the right of states to discriminate, not the right of private individuals. Most of the modest federal protection left was eliminated when, in *Plessy v. Ferguson* (1896), the Court upheld a Louisiana law requiring segregation of blacks on the state's trains. So long as equal facilities were provided, the Court declared, they could be separate without violating the equal-protection clause of the Fourteenth Amendment.

Essential to Jim Crow was the denial of the vote to blacks. The poll tax, a tax on voting, discouraged them from exercising the franchise. Another device for turning blacks away from the polls was the "grandfather clause." A state might impose certain requirements stiff enough to exclude from the polls both blacks and a substantial portion of the white population; at the same time it would set aside those requirements for anyone whose grandfather would have possessed the right to vote—and that waiver meant, of course, that whites could vote.

Black southerners had reason to fear the courts. Georgia and other states leased prisoners to road building contractors. One survivor of that system called it "hell itself." As late as 1931–32 the "Scottsboro boys" were imprisoned in Alabama for rape on the testimony of two white prostitutes, one of whom later recanted her testimony. The last Scottsboro boy, Andrew Wright, got free at the age of thirty-nine, remarking then of Alabama justice: "I am just like a rabbit in a strange wood, an the dogs is after him and no place to hide."

Reinforcing Jim Crow was a growing regime of terror. As a means of keeping blacks in their place, the less reputable elements in southern

Segregation

Racial segregation became an accepted way of life throughout the South late in the nineteenth century. At that time came the largest number of lynchings in the region, and vicious political rhetoric was directed against Negroes. Governor Ben Tillman of North Carolina, for example, called the black people "an ignorant and debased and debauched race."

Lynchings in the South, 1891–1907	
Year	No.
1891	192
1892	235
1893	200
1894	190
1895	171
1896	131
1897	166
1898	127
1899	107
1900	116
1901	135
1902	96
1903	104
1904	87
1905	66
1906	73
1907	56

white society turned more and more to vigilante action. In 1882 forty-nine blacks were lynched in the South. Ten years later there were 161 victims of white mobs. In the new century the number of lynchings declined, but race riots increased in frequency. In 1906 a wave of rioting broke out in Atlanta that left four dead and millions of dollars' worth of property destroyed. Nor were northern communities exempt from anti-black violence. A 1908 racial incident in Springfield, Illinois, set off several days of lynching and rioting. Six died and seventy were injured. These riots, like the one that broke out in Atlanta in 1906, involved bands of armed whites invading African-American neighborhoods. They set fire to churches, stores, and homes. They attacked bystanders on the street. And they sometimes lynched black males, especially those reputed to be proud or ambitious.

Even within the South an emerging black middle class was slowly building institutions that would provide coherence and train leaders for blacks. Religion and education drew the principal efforts of black people who were denied access to politics. Blacks founded their own schools and colleges, such as Spelman in Atlanta, to train both men and women to be ministers and teachers for their people. The black Baptist Church developed as an important and many-faceted institution.

Although blacks opposed women's entry into the ministry and their leadership of mixed groups as firmly as did whites, black women developed their own large network within the church that raised money for such church needs as training ministers, and gathered other women much as white women's organizations did in the North. A significant number of black women received higher education and pursued careers in teaching. Members of black women's clubs in cities such as Atlanta sought to improve urban conditions for black families by establishing playgrounds and other services. What these women did to build a cohesive and self-conscious black community laid the groundwork for the progress southern blacks would make during the twentieth century.

As the twentieth century opened, a new group of black leaders emerged. Over the next two generations, these men—Booker T. Washington, W. E. B. DuBois, and Marcus Garvey—would help transform race relations in the United States in fundamental ways.

The Atlanta Compromise   In 1895 at the opening of the Cotton States and International Exposition in Atlanta, Booker T. Washington stood before blacks and whites and, to the cheers of his audience and the acclaim of the nation, enunciated his doctrine of accommodation between the races. The relationship would be practical, working, and peaceful, blacks accepting those tasks that their training at the time fitted them for, and bettering their lot by their own effort in harmony with the white majority. Washington believed that the black community could progress only by careful and laborious accumulation of skills, education, and property. The address was not the submissive speech that legend has made it out to be, and quite possibly it reflected not Washington's idea of race relations in themselves so much as his more general respect for the virtues of work, education, and self-improvement. But the address—it came to be

BOOKER T. WASHINGTON

from "The Atlanta Compromise" address, 1895:

A ship lost at sea for many days suddenly sighted a friendly vessel. From the mast of the unfortunate vessel was seen a signal, "Water, water; we die of thirst!" The answer from the friendly vessel at once came back, "Cast down your bucket where you are." A second time the signal, "Water, water; send us water!" ran up from the distressed vessel, and was answered, "Cast down your bucket where you are." And a third and fourth signal for water was answered, "Cast down your bucket where you are." The captain of the distressed vessel, at last heeding the injunction, cast down his bucket, and it came up full of fresh, sparkling water from the mouth of the Amazon River. To those of my race who depend on bettering their condition in a foreign land or who underestimate the importance of cultivating friendly relations with the Southern white man, who is their next-door neighbour, I would say: "Cast down your bucket where you are"—cast it down in making friends in every manly way of the people of all races by whom we are surrounded.

Cast it down in agriculture, mechanics, in commerce, in domestic service, and in the professions. . . . Our greatest danger is that in the great leap from slavery to freedom we may overlook the fact that the masses of us are to live by the productions of our hands, and fail to keep in mind that we shall prosper in proportion as we learn to dignify and glorify common labour and put brains and skill into the common occupations of life. No race can prosper till it learns that there is as much dignity in tilling a field as in writing a poem. It is at the bottom of life we must begin, and not at the top. Nor should we permit our grievances to overshadow our opportunities.

---

called the Atlanta Compromise, and the title was not meant to be complimentary—became best known for its apparent dismissal of larger questions of injustice and white supremacy: that was what white conservatives liked about it, and what militant blacks scorned.

In 1901 Washington's autobiography *Up From Slavery* became a best-seller. A political incident of that year, Theodore Roosevelt's rather casual invitation to him to sit down to lunch, may be taken as a symbolic climax of Washington's career. This incident of social mingling between a President and a black man offended southern whites as had President Cleveland's meeting with Frederick Douglass a few years before. The larger implication of the meeting was the political power it implied. Washington acted as a presence behind the scenes in American political life, influencing both Roosevelt's and Taft's appointments and racial policies. He also enjoyed the acquaintance of industrialists and financiers and could tap them for powerful philanthropic support for black projects. Washington had gained his influence among the wealthy and politically powerful through much the same strategies of care and discretion that he had urged black Americans to adopt in their daily life and work. He consolidated power in the black community, offered political favors to Republicans, and cultivated friendships among whites.

Black opposition to Washington is represented by William Monroe Trotter and his militant newspaper, *The Guardian;* W. E. B. Du Bois's Niagara Movement; and the NAACP and its publication *The Crisis.* Trotter bitterly reproached Washington for obstructing black opportunity in the South, and Du Bois complained that Washington "practically accepts the alleged inferiority of the Negro races." Northern whites, however, regarded him as a "genius" (Teddy Roosevelt) and "wonderful" (Andrew Carnegie). Few contemporaries were willing to look behind his optimistic, conciliatory demeanor. Washington, in fact, was not averse to applying whatever tactic was necessary to stifle critics. He was a powerful figure constantly seeking to strengthen the Tuskegee Machine, a network of black political and business organizations throughout the country.

By the beginning of the twentieth century, the South had little by which to define itself except for a romantic myth of its gracious and aristocratic past: that and a racial system that defied reason and morality and gave white southerners a meaningless pride in whiteness. The West meanwhile had become something other than the open place of free and independent farmers that was its own romantic image. In both regions, politics had come to reflect the newer realities.

Suggested Readings

The most recent scholarship on the American West includes William Cronon, George Miles, and Jay Gitlin, *Under an Open Sky: Rethinking America's Western Past* (1992), Terry G. Jordan, *Trails to Texas: Southern Roots of Western Cattle Ranching* (1981), Roger D. McGrath, *Gunfighters, Highwaymen, and Vigilantes: Violence on the Frontier* (1984), Patricia Nelson Limerick, *Desert Passages: Encounters with the American Deserts* (1985), Robert M. Utley, *The Indian Frontier of the American West* (1984), Sandra L. Myres, *Westering Women* (1982), Polly Kaufman, *Women Teachers on the Frontier* (1984), Michael P. Malone, *Historians and the American West* (1983), Harry Drago, *The Great Range Wars* (1985), Joanna L. Stratton, *Pioneer Women: Voices from the Kansas Frontier* (1981), Annette Kolodny, *The Land Before Her* (1984), James S. Olson and Raymond Wilson, *Native Americans in the Twentieth Century* (1984), Julie Roy Jeffrey, *Frontier Women* (1979), Daniel McGood, *Command of the Waters: Iron Triangles, Federal Water Development, and Indian Water* (1987), Patricia Limerick, *The Legacy of Conquest—The Unbroken Past of the American West* (1990), James A. McDonnell, *The Dispossession of the American Indian, 1887–1934* (1991), Donald Worster, *Rivers of Empire: Water, Aridity, and the Growth of the American West* (1985), Elliott West, *Growing Up With the Country: Childhood on the Far Western Frontier* (1989), Lillian Schlitsel, Bud Gibbens, and Elizabeth Hampsten, *Far from Home: Families of the Westward Journey* (1989), Glenda Riley, *The Female Frontier: A Comparative View of Women on the Prairie and the Plains* (1988), and Robert Hine, *The American West* (2nd ed., 1984).

On that mythic hero see Joe B. Frantz and J. E. Cheate, *The American Cowboy: The Myth and the Reality* (1955), and David Dary, *Cowboy Culture: A Saga of Five Centuries* (1981). Mari Sandoz describes the destruction of the herds in *The Buffalo Hunters* (1945). Henry Nash Smith's masterful study of the impact of the West on the American imagination is *Virgin Land: The American West as Symbol and Myth* (1950). Other fine older books are Ray Allen Billington, *Westward Expansion* (1967), Bernard DeVoto, *Across the Wide Missouri* (1947) and Walter Prescott Webb, *The Great Plains* (1931). See also V. W. Paul, *Mining Frontiers of the Far West, 1848–1880* (1963), Lewis Atherton, *The Cattle Kings* (1961), and Frederick Merk, *History of the Westward Movement* (1978).

Robert M. Utley details the collapse of Sioux society in *The Last Days of the Sioux Nation* (1963). R. K. Andrist chronicles *The Long Death: The Last Days of the Plains Indians* (1964). See also Wilcomb E. Washburn, *The Indian in America* (1975). Dee Brown's *Bury My Heart at Wounded Knee* (1979) is a moving treatment.

Other good books on the West include Robert F. Berkhofer's *The White Man's Indian: Images of the American Indian from Columbus to the Present* (1978), Duane A. Smith's *Rocky Mountain Mining Camps* (1967), Rodman W. Paul's *The Far West and the Great Plains in Transition, 1859–1908* (1988), Richard W. Slatta's *Cowboys of the Americas* (1990), Francis Paul Prucha's *American Indian Policy in Crisis: Christian Reformers and the Indians* (1976), Paula Petrik's *No Step Backward: Women and Family on the Rocky Mountain Mining Frontier, 1865–1900* (1987), and William Cronon, *Nature's Metropolis: Chicago and the Great West* (1991).

The New South is the focus of the traditional account by C. Vann Woodward, *Origins of the New South* (1951) and the reinterpretation by Gavin Wright, *Old South, New South: Revolutions in the Southern Economy Since the Civil War* (1986). See also the ancient but interesting Wilbur J. Cash, *The Mind of the South* (1941) and Paul M. Gaston, *The New South Creed: A Study in Southern Mythmaking* (1970). Other studies include John W. Graves, *Town and Country: Race Relations in an Urban Rural Context, Arkansas, 1865–1905* (1990), Jacquelyn D. Hall et al., *Like a Family: The Making of a Southern Cotton Mill World* (1987), Robert Higgs, *Competition and Coercion: Blacks in the American Economy, 1865–1904* (1977), and Jacqueline Jones, *Labor of Love, Labor of Sorrow: Black Women, Work, and the Family from Slavery to the Present* (1985). C. Vann Woodward's *The Strange Career of Jim Crow* (2nd ed., 1974) is a minor classic. Nell I. Painter covers an interesting subject: *Exodusters: Black Migration in Kansas after Reconstruction* (1977).

The 'Old' vs. the 'New' West

Martin Ridge

Turner's followers studied and wrote about the internal history of the United States in the context of American uniqueness and its causes. Their "West" was an ever advancing frontier of opportunity and revitalization; it was a triumphant national experience that culminated in an individualist democracy that only reached a crisis as the frontier itself—with all the opportunity that it represented—came to a close in the final decades of the nineteenth century. For Turner, the nineteenth century was an era of abundance and success; the twentieth, a century when the institutions formed in the past would be tested in a society of closed space with diminished opportunity.

These views had a profound impact on historical writing. For one thing, they gave new relevance to local and state history. Local historians could now look not only to events in their own communities to show how they demonstrated national trends but also to the lives of persons still remembered to explain their roles in the making of a region.

Although there had been a persistent drumbeat of criticism of the Turnerian thesis beginning in the mid-1920s, it reached a flood tide in the 1930s. During the Great Depression, many American historians suffered a crisis in confidence and doubted the future of their nation, looked askance on a theory that rooted American free institutions in individualism or praised capitalist democracy. The rise of fascism and the onset of the Second World War, however, enforced a renewed respect for American institutions.

[A]n entirely new set of interests among western historians was challenging, broadening, and deepening the Turner paradigm. Although the intellectual and cultural origins of these interests may be debatable, what they are is quite clear. The current historical focus is on race, class, gender, and the environment. Although in itself scarcely new, it has not only reopened old arguments about the significance of the frontier as a liberating economic and political force but also allowed for the examination of previously ignored themes. The polemicists among this new group of historians find it self-gratifying to denounce Turnerians for their male-oriented (Turner did not mention women per se) and triumphalist view of the frontier, which, they insist, praises the economic and political success of white males in the establishment of an individualistic, capitalist democracy at the expense of the frontier's failures, the oppression and exploitation of minorities and women, and a degraded environment.

Turner's critics have their difficulties. In denying the utility of his paradigm, denouncing him for remaining unspoken on issues of class, gender, and the environment, anti-Turnerians are strangely haunted by his silent scholarly ghost, for they deny the usefulness of his historical vision but often unwittingly work within it.

Historians who prefer to continue to analyze the advancing frontier (either as a place or a process) and its consequences are comfortable with the freedom Turner offered. For them, like many artists, novelists, poets, and playwrights, the frontier still beckons. Moreover, there is now the chance to look at race, class, gender, and the environment within the Turnerian context and test its applicability. This strips those issues of the preconceptions of the polemicists who have their own scholarly agenda.

The new western historians, Turner's recent critics, must explain what is new about their work other than their personal assumptions and value judgments, unless they focus on the twentieth century, a period Turner did not treat. They must explain the merit of what they have substituted for the overarching and imaginative work of Turner. They may find that it is exceedingly difficult to bury his ghost.

Excerpted from Martin Ridge, "Frederick Jackson Turner and His Ghost: The Writing of Western History," *Proceedings of the American Antiquarian Society*, 101 (April 1991): 65-76. Reprinted by permission.

Donald Worster

The first historian to undertake serious study of the westward movement, Turner never stopped believing that the old story was literally true. Returning to the wilderness, men could be restored to the innocence of their youth, sloughing off the blemishes of age. He handed on his faith to his disciples, and so western history was born. . . . They would not have to pass foreign language exams, read works from abroad, or keep up with the Paris savants. They were excused from examining radical defects in the West, for there were none to be found. . . .

Around the year 1970 [the] untold side of the western past began to find its tellers. A younger generation, shaken by Vietnam and other national disgraces—poverty, racism, environmental degradation—could not pretend that the only story that mattered in the West was one of stagecoach lines, treasure hunts, cattle brands, and wildcatters, nor for that matter aircraft plants, opera companies, bank deposits, or middle-class whites learning how to ski. What was missing was a frank, hard look at the violent imperialistic process by which the West was wrested from its original owners and the violence by which it had been secured against the continuing claims of minorities, women, and the forces of nature. . . .

[I]t is the younger generation of the 1970s and 1980s who have made this new multicultural perspective their own. They have discovered not only that minorities have not always shared in the rising power and affluence of the West but also that they have in some ways thought differently about the ends of that power and affluence. As part of the reevaluation, we are increasingly asked to reexamine the process by which native peoples were dispossessed in the first place, to remind ourselves of the manner in which whites went about accumulating land and resources for themselves, and to uncover the contradictions in a majority, male-dominated culture that can in the same breath trumpet the idea of its own liberty and deny other peoples the right of self-determination. Further, we have learned to pay more attention to the substantial numbers of nonnative people of color, people from Africa, the Pacific islands, and Asia, who have come into the garden of agrarian myth to live alongside the European settlers, making the West in fact a far more racially diverse place than the myth envisioned—more diverse indeed than either the North or South has been. . . .

The drive for the economic development of the West was often a ruthless assault on nature and has left behind it much death, depletion, and ruin. Astonishing as it now seems, the old agrarian myth of Turner's day suggested that the West offered an opportunity of getting back in touch with nature, of recovering good health and a sense of harmony with the nonhuman far from the shrieking disharmonies of factories, technology, urban slums, and poverty that were making life in Europe and the East a burden to the spirit. . . .

Here again truth is breaking in, driving out myth and self-deception, as we face unblinkingly the fact that from its earliest days the fate of the western region has been one of furnishing raw materials for industrialism's development; consequently, the region was from the beginning in the forefront of America's endless economic revolution. Far from being a child of nature, the West was actually given birth by modern technology and bears all the scars of that fierce gestation, like a baby born of an addict. . . .

Over the past decade or two the neglect of industrial capitalism's impact on the western environment has begun to be repaired, due to the fact that the study of the West, more than of other regions, has come to be allied with the emerging field of environmental history. This alliance has encouraged doubts about the role of capitalism, industrialism, population growth, military expenditures, and aimless economic expansion in the region and has questioned whether they really have blazed a trail to progress. . . .

[W]estern elites have followed the old familiar tendency of those in power, to become corrupt, exploitative, and cynical toward those they dominate. Power can also degrade itself, as it degrades others and the land, yet it commonly tries to conceal that fact by laying claim to the dominant myths and symbols of its time—in the case of the American West, by putting on cowboy boots and snapbutton shirts, waving the American flag, and calling a toxic dump the land of freedom.

Reprinted from Donald Worster, "Beyond the Agrarian Myth," in Patricia Nelson Limerick, Clyde A. Milner, and Charles E. Rankin, eds., *Trails: Toward A New Western History* (Lawrence, KS: University Press of Kansas, 1991).

Trinity Church, New York City. *(Courtesy, New York Public Library)*

City and Farm
1865–1900

TRINITY CHURCH:
"GUARDIANS OF A HOLY TRUST"

Trinity Church, Episcopal, located on Broadway facing Wall Street in lower Manhattan, was by the nineteenth century the richest church in the United States. The historian and journalist James Parton described it in 1868 as "a richly furnished, quietly adorned, dimly illuminated, ecclesiastical parlor, in which a few hundred ladies and gentlemen, attired in kindred taste, may sit perfectly at their ease, and see no object not in harmony with the scene around them."

In 1910, when Trinity's vestrymen issued their first public account of church finances, they listed its expenditures for the previous year at $340,870. This included more than $60,000 for music alone. The rector's salary was $15,000, which made him the highest paid clergyman in the country, and the vicars of the nine other churches Trinity operated each received $8,000 a year, or more than what United States senators earned at that time. Yet contributions from churchgoers totaled only $18,210. The bulk of the rest of the money came from the church's real estate holdings, for Trinity owned over $16 million of tenement housing on Manhattan's West Side. This made it the largest slum landlord in the city if not the whole country. As the city's largest landlord Trinity, moreover, was the leading opponent of housing reform in the late nineteenth and early twentieth centuries.

In 1887, for example, New York City passed a tenement ordi-

HISTORICAL EVENTS

1860s
Rural Americans begin massive migration to the cities

1862
Congress creates U.S. Bureau of Agriculture • Morrill Land-Grant College Act

1867
First steam railroad ("el") • National Association of Farmers formed

1870
Brooklyn Bridge begun

1877
Granger laws upheld by Supreme Court

1883
Brooklyn Bridge completed

1887
New York City tenement ordinance

1888
First electric streetcar system

1890
First People's Party Convention

continued

HISTORICAL EVENTS

1894
Immigration Restriction League
formed

1895
First subway, in Boston

1898
Immigration tops more than
a million per year

nance requiring running water on every floor. Trinity's vestry challenged the law and, for the next eight years, until the Federal Court of Appeals upheld the city's power to regulate housing, Trinity's tenants had to continue using a single pump located in the courtyard of each of its buildings. A few years later, in 1901, New York State passed a model tenement house law. This legislation abolished open toilets in back yards and required indoor plumbing on each floor. The law also made it illegal to rent apartments with no windows opening onto the outside, largely because such dark and damp rooms had been linked to the spread of tuberculosis. For three years Trinity through court challenges delayed compliance.

How had a church come to be the foremost enemy of tenement reform? The answer goes back to how Trinity acquired title to all that real estate in the first place. The English crown granted the church a "bonus" in 1705 of the land known as "Queen's farm" along the Hudson River on Manhattan's West Side. Originally the grant had been to all "of the inhabitants of our said city of New York" in communion with the Church of England, but in 1814 Trinity's vestrymen successfully petitioned the New York State legislature to limit control over the land to "members of the congregation of Trinity Church or of any of the chapels belonging to Trinity Corporation." The right to decide who among the members would be entitled to vote for vestryman, the most important office, rested with the vestrymen themselves. As a result, control of the church's enormous real estate holdings passed into the hands of the members of what Parton called an "exclusive ecclesiastical club." Its members sought what they believed would be best for the church, a vision longtime Trinity Rector Morgan Dix defined as "ritual observance," "musical culture," and "ecclesiastical art." Dix dismissed the claims of Protestant reformers associated with the "Social Gospel" that low wages or dangerous working conditions or substandard housing were matters of pressing concern.

The American City

Besides transforming the incomes and political attitudes of Americans, the rapid growth of industry changed where many of them lived and worked. Between 1860 and 1910 millions of newcomers flocked to the cities. In 1860 over twenty-five million Americans had lived in rural areas and only 6.2 million in what the Bureau of the Census defined as "urban territory": the bureau set the puzzlingly low figure of 2,500 as the base for defining an urban center. Nevertheless, the country was urbanizing. In 1910, forty-two out of ninety-two million Americans resided in communities that were urban by the government's definition. In 1860 there had been no cities of a million, and only two, New

York and Philadelphia, with over half a million. By 1910, three American cities had a million people or more, and five additional ones had over half a million each.

Two Pathways to the City   Numbers of northern and western Europeans from Britain, Germany, and Scandinavia came to the United States before about 1880 and settled in rural communities. The Irish did not, but they were in some ways exceptional. The newcomers of the last two decades of the nineteenth century and the early part of the twentieth differed from their predecessors. These new immigrants came largely from southern and eastern Europe. Many were from Italy's depressed south or from Sicily. Others were from lands controlled by Austria or Russia. The new immigrants included thousands of Slavic Poles, Croatians, Czechs, and Serbs, as well as non-Slavic Greeks and Jews. By 1900 about fifteen percent of the population of the United States had come from abroad, and immigrants along with their children were giving distinctive cultural flavors to cities, as Irish and Germans had already been doing. Besides the crowds crossing the Atlantic were the tens of thousands who crossed the continental borders from Canada and Mexico. Many of the new arrivals were peasants, who might be expected to settle on the land. But since the Civil War land prices had risen and farm commodity prices fallen. After 1880, more and more of the immigrants settled in cities to work as wage earners in factories.

Native-born Americans from the nation's farms also were going to the towns and cities. Some Americans in these years sentimentalized farm life, but to young people particularly the farmer's lot seemed a hard one and farm life drab and cramped. When the parents of Hamlin Garland, the novelist, returned from an Iowa village to live again on a farm, their two sons were bitterly disappointed. They despised the "ugly little farmhouse" and the "filthy drudgery of the farmyard" and yearned for the "care-free companionable existence" of town. The Sears, Roebuck catalogue might be a farm family's only contact with the outside world. Writing in *Good Housekeeping* just before World War I, a journalist remarked on how many young women "were pining for neighbors, for domestic help, for pretty clothes, for schools, music, art, and the things tasted when the magazines came in."

These two human streams, one from abroad, one from the rural areas of the nation, belonged to a century marked by migration throughout the Western world. Growth in population, the result in part of a more varied and healthier diet, squeezed people out of the European countryside. And job opportunities brought by industrialization drew them to the cities of the Old World as well as the New. Open land in the United States, Canada, and elsewhere on the American continent enticed other migrants, some from Europe, some from settled areas in the hemisphere. Movement to America, of course, had gone on for several centuries. In the seventeenth century, meanwhile, Russians had heavily colonized Siberia. In the nineteenth century numbers of Russians were still moving into that great rich region, which the Russian Empire tapped with the Trans-Siberian Railway, a parallel to the American transcontinental railway system. Still another population

The United States needed laborers, and for varying motives some organizations were willing to sponsor newcomers. A Polish peasant wrote seeking assistance to emigrate:

"I want to get to America, but I have no means at all because I am poor and have nothing but the ten fingers of my hands, a wife and 9 children. I have no work at all, although I am strong and healthy and only 45 years old. I cannot earn for my family. I have been already in Dombrowa, Sosnowiec, Zawiercie and Lodz, wherever I could go, and nowhere could I earn well. And here they (the children) call for food and clothing and more or less education. I wish to work, not easily only but even hard, but what can I do? I will not go to steal and I have no work."

shift was to Australia and New Zealand. In the United States late in the century, restless Americans from the farms and migrants from Europe along with a relatively small but significant number from Asia converged on the towns and cities. There they were joined by the natural increase of the city population itself. The urban centers swelled.

Conditions in the Cities

By the standards of the great European capitals, the American cities of this period were disappointing. Few places, not even Washington until the twentieth century, could boast the monuments, the boulevards, the imperial buildings of Berlin, Paris, Vienna, St. Petersburg, or London. Too many American cities were dominated by commercial structures. Their streets were jammed with horse-drawn wagons and carriages, and with people pushing carts and wheelbarrows. Overhead a tangle of wires for the city's telephone and telegraph messages often obscured the sky. There were few trees or parks. The needs of commerce had won out over beauty and amenities, and almost all public land had been sold off for housing or commercial blocks. A few cities, including New York, Boston, Washington, San Francisco, and New Orleans, had some individuality, but others seemed to be built on a uniform monotonous plan of right-angle streets, with dreary stores and shops and utilitarian hotels.

By the 1870s a few of the largest American cities had installed underground sewers. But many still used privies and cesspools that periodically had to be cleaned out. In 1877 Philadelphia had 82,000 of these, and Washington, D.C., was not far behind. In some cities, among them Baltimore, New Orleans, and Mobile, sewage was actually allowed to run through open gutters. And even communities with better sewage collection facilities spilled their waste in the surrounding waters. Boston Harbor was "one vast cesspool, a threat to all the towns it washed." Nor were garbage disposal arrangements much better. Port cities usually dumped their garbage at sea, hoping it would not return at the next tide. Inland communities sold local farmers organic garbage for feeding to hogs. The result was a high incidence of trichinosis among swine and also among human beings who ate undercooked pork.

During the 1860s and 1870s Louis Pasteur in France, Robert Koch in Germany, and Joseph Lister in Britain were learning about the connection between bacteria and disease, and by the next decade their discoveries were influencing the planning of sewage disposal facilities and water supplies. Even before the Civil War, New York, Philadelphia, and a number of other communities had developed aqueducts to collect pure water from distant streams or lakes and pipe it into homes. Now, with the new knowledge at hand, the authorities began to clean up the water supply. Some cities resorted to the piping of clean water. Others adopted filtration or, after 1908, chlorination. By 1910 over ten million city people drank filtered water; that innovation contributed to the sharp decline in death rates from typhoid fever and cholera. This change was accompanied by the appearance of sanitary bathrooms and running water, improvements that owed much to rising

Pittsburgh, described here by a visitor in 1868, suffered worse pollution conditions than any other American city:

"There is one evening scene in Pittsburg which no visitor should miss. Owing to the abruptness of the hill behind the town, there is a street along the edge of a bluff, from which you can look directly down upon all that part of the city which lies low, near the level of the rivers. On the evening of this dark day, we were conducted to the edge of the abyss, and looked over the iron railing upon the most striking spectacle we ever beheld. The entire space lying between the hills was filled with blackest smoke, from out of which the hidden chimneys sent forth tongues of flame, while from the depths of the abyss came up the noise of hundreds of steam-hammers. There would be moments when no flames were visible; but soon the wind would force the smoky curtains aside, and the whole black expanse would be dimly lighted with dull wreaths of fire. It is an unprofitable business, view-hunting; but if anyone would enjoy a spectacle as striking as Niagara, he may do so by simply walking up a long hill to Cliff Street in Pittsburg, and looking over into—hell with the lid taken off."

living standards as well as to the growing awareness of infectious organisms.

Tenements

All over the world, wherever and whenever cities have grown rapidly, housing for the poor has been wretched. American cities of the late nineteenth century were more successful than Third World cities of the present in solving their housing problems, but not by a great deal. Some of the urban poor crowded into shantytowns at the edges of the cities where they illegally built shacks on land they did not own. In 1870 New York City's West Side north of Fifty-ninth Street looked like the outskirts of a Third World city today. The cast-off houses of the middle class now departing for newer residential sections also became tenements for the poor. These structures were cut up into small apartments that the newcomers could afford. Landlords threw up flimsy buildings for the poor in what had been spacious backyards. Few of the more substantial dwellings put up in response to the growth in the numbers of the poor were adequate in space, comfort, safety, or sanitation.

A letter of 1885 to a Little Rock, Arkansas, newspaper described a

"presence—right in the heart of the city—one of the most malignant, pestiferous disease breeders in the land. The town branch, or whatever poetic title you may apply to the muddy, filthy stream that penetrates directly through the city . . . is the root of evil. Open to the rays of the burning sun in the summer, great holes dug in its bottom by sand diggers . . . the reeking filth from barnyard, cesspool and worse, lie festering and tainting the atmosphere with diseases, death and odors. . . . Covered in places with boards, right in our business streets, hiding the reeking stench beneath, the death dealing gasses escape and little innocents wither and die, and strong men sicken and gasp. . . . Stop this eternal clamor about paved streets; go to work and convert this great natural artery into a magnificent sewer . . . and then children may thrive; strong men will grow stronger, and our city will be blessed with . . . health."

Hester and Clinton streets, New York City, ca. 1896. Immigrant neighborhoods often suffered from overcrowding and poor sanitary conditions. *(Courtesy, The New-York Historical Society, New York City)*

New York had appalling slums. Many others, like Philadelphia, had more single family homes and so their poor neighborhoods did not look quite so crowded as New York's. But the wooden row houses characteristic of Philadelphia or Cleveland were just as cheaply constructed and even more likely to catch fire than New York's tenements. Sanitary conditions, on the other hand, were somewhat better. New York's "old law" tenements had four or five stories, without hot water and proper bathrooms. After 1879 the city fathers required that all new tenements have at least one window in every room and two water closets to a floor. But the resulting "dumbbell" apartment with narrow air shafts on each side of the building was not appreciably better. In the absence of other means of disposal, air shafts became receptacles for garbage. Inadequacies in construction and in bathing and cooking facilities subjected everyone to noise, disorder, and bad smells. "How is it possible to preserve purity amid such homes, or to bring up children to be moral or decent?" asked one reformer.

The Children   The reform writer Jacob Riis takes readers on a tour of a tenement: "Be a little careful, please! The hall is dark and you might stumble. You can feel your way, if you cannot see it. Close? Yes! What would you have? All the fresh air that enters these stairs comes from the hall-door that is forever slamming." The tour guide pauses at the entrance to a windowless apartment. "Listen! That short, hacking cough, that tiny, helpless wail. . . . The child is dying of measles. With half a chance it might have lived; but it had none. That dark bedroom killed it." Riis was confusing his readers with an overdose of sentiment. He also posed photographs of newsboys sleeping at night outside in alleyways or over steel grates on city streets. But on the substance of what was happening he was right. The nation was neglecting its children.

Courts and overcrowded orphan asylums deposited thousands of such children annually at the Children's Aid Society in the late nineteenth century. A group of forty orphaned boys and girls was sent from eastern cities to a small midwestern town.

Urban Transportation   Much of the congestion of New York and the nation's other large cities might have disappeared if transportation had been adequate between outlying neighborhoods and the downtowns, where the stores, shops, small factories, and wholesale establishments were located and working people earned their livings. When men and women had to rely on their own legs or some equally inefficient means of transport, they had no choice but to take nearby housing, no matter how dilapidated or congested.

Before the Civil War a few of the country's largest cities had begun to develop public transportation systems. Horse-drawn omnibuses—essentially elongated carriages—ran over regular routes in New York, Philadelphia, and Boston by 1860. These were slow. The horse-drawn streetcar, pulled on rails, was somewhat better and became almost universal after 1865 in the larger towns and cities. But still

The Children's Aid Society took a protesting fourteen-year-old named Willie, along with some other children, to a local grange hall, where a group of farmers and their wives waited to look them over. According to the society's annual reports, only one couple wanted Willie. In a heavy German accent the farmer's wife explained:

"Because he please my old man." And Willie was carried away, struggling and protesting, in her thick arms. A few months later the agent of the Society returned to check on how his former charges were doing. When the German farmer saw who had come to call, he bridled:

"Mr. Agent," he said, "if you come to dake dot boy away, if you don't got de biggest yob on your hants what you ever had, den I don't know how it is. I wouldn't dake de whole United States for dot boy."

"I haven't come to take him away," the agent hastened to explain. "But how in the world do you manage him?"

"Oh, dot's easy," the farmer's wife said. "You see, we all luff him."

By the early 1890s New York City teemed with streetcars hauled by cables and elevated trains powered by steam locomotives. *(Courtesy, The H. N. Tiemann Company, New York)*

the system was inadequate and reformers demanded some means of rapid transit that would help end the congestion on city streets.

A breakthrough came in 1867 when the nation's largest city built the first "el," a steam railroad placed on high pillars above the traffic. New York's elevated system darkened the streets below, scattered ashes on pedestrians, made noise, and constituted an eyesore. But it did move people quickly. It was soon widely imitated. By the opening of the new century, Chicago, Boston, Kansas City, and Brooklyn had all built els. Meanwhile the horsecars had been replaced at street level by electric trolley cars drawing their power from overhead wires. In 1888 Frank Julian Sprague, a former employee of Edison, installed in Richmond, Virginia, the first electric streetcar system. By about 1900 there were 15,000 miles of electric streetcar lines in American cities under the control of some 900 companies.

The final innovation was the subway. Following London and Budapest, Boston in 1895 began construction of an underground railway that would avoid the street level congestion of downtown. New York, with an even greater congestion, embarked on a still more ambitious scheme and in 1904 completed the first leg of what would become the largest subway system in the world.

The new transit systems, especially the electric streetcar, opened up the cities. Now, usually for a fare of five cents, a wage earner who lived beyond easy walking distance of the job could get to work on time. Builders and developers laid out streets and lots on what had been open fields and put up small houses for city people to buy. Many thousands would put the whole family to work and devote all savings to the single goal of purchasing a home. Before long streetcar suburbs ringed cities, housing families happy to escape the noise, dirt, conges-

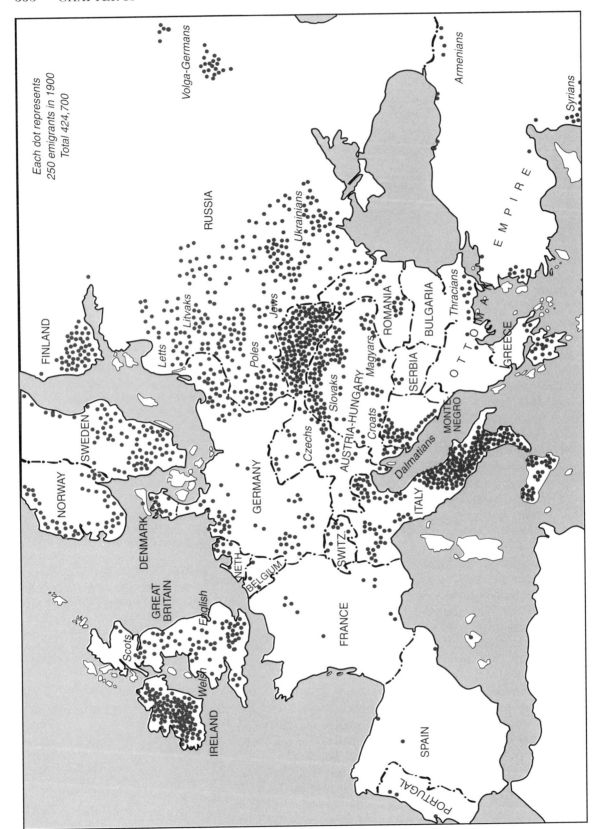

*Each dot represents
250 emigrants in 1900
Total 424,700*

Immigration from Europe to the United States in 1900.

tion, and other ills of the city centers. A common pattern, in fact, was for a slum to be surrounded by better neighborhoods, while outside these lay better housing still, each layer representing a higher income among its dwellers. A skilled mechanic or laborer, for example, would be able to live outside of the slum. The outer layer, the suburb, was the realm of the more affluent of the white-collar classes. Moving from one neighborhood to another could mark the growing success of an individual over a lifetime. The one group to violate the pattern was the wealthy, many of whom continued to live in city mansions, though the suburbs as well began to draw the rich.

Immigrants

The New Immigrants

Many Americans recoiled from the new immigration of Slavs, Italians, Jews, and Greeks that became noticeable during the 1880s. They held, for example, that a disproportionate number of new immigrants were men who came not to stay, but merely to make money and return home. Transatlantic passage having become cheaper and quicker, some of the newer immigrants were indeed mere sojourners; but many others came to stay and did so. Americans also perceived the newer arrivals as illiterate and unskilled. Again, this was only a partial truth: Jews, northern Italians, and Czechs were more skilled and literate than most of those who had come earlier.

The common American estimate of the newcomers, then, made little allowance for individual and group differences. Nevertheless, there are valid distinctions between new and older immigrant stock. Most of the countries of origin of the newcomers were autocracies, and they had little experience with democratic government. They were poorer than most of the earlier immigrants. A far lower percentage was Protestant. The country they came to, moreover, was notably different from the one their predecessors had entered. In 1850 the United States had still been overwhelmingly agricultural, and many of the new arrivals became farmers. By the 1880s, however, much of the best land was gone, and a giant American industry was beginning to pull into factories former peasants from Poland, Ukraine, Serbia, Greece, Romania, and the south of Italy. After 1895 immigration from eastern and southern Europe greatly accelerated.

As in the past, most of the Europeans settled in the Northeast or Midwest; few went to the South. The large African-American population in the rural South kept wage levels down, and in the Far West the available land was either too expensive or too dry to attract the immigrants. Instead, they headed for the industrial cities in what historians now call "chain migrations." Once a small contingent of immigrants had settled in a particular area, they tended to attract to their new communities their own relatives and friends from the Old World.

Many of the Italian immigrants, most of whom were from southern Italy or Sicily, sought out construction jobs in booming northeastern cities like Boston, New York, or Philadelphia. Most Italian immigrants lived with their relatives in the new country, or, if the immigrant was the

An observer commented on the importance of previous immigrants in drawing new ones:

"The workers on the hills of Galicia, in the vineyards of Italy, and the factories of Kiev, earn from 25 to 50 cents in a day. When the American immigrant writes home that he earns from $1.50 to $2.00, the able-bodied wage-earner in the fatherland who hears this will not be satisfied until he also stands where the higher wages govern. It is these homegoing letters more than all else which recruit the labor force. They are efficient promoters of immigration. Said Big Sam to me, in his broken English, 'There are no able-bodied men between the ages of sixteen and fifty years left in my native town in Servia; they have all come to America.' "

first member of the family to come, he would usually seek out companions from his own region of Italy. Among the chains that connected the New World cities with Italian villages, Mott Street in New York City between East Houston and Prince held Neopolitans, as did Mulberry Street. On the opposite side of Mott Street were the Basilicati. Calabrians settled Mott Street between Broome and Grand, Sicilians lived on Prince Street, and the Genoese on Baxter Street. Many Italians even settled along village lines. In Chicago western Sicilians congregated together, with immigrants from Altavilla on Larrabee Street; people from Alimenia and Shiusa Sclafani on Cambridge Street; immigrants from Bagheria on Townsend Street; and people from Sambuca-Zabut on Milton Street.

Jewish immigrants from Austria-Hungary and Russia found jobs in the needle trades and sweatshops of New York City, and like the Italians they tended to settle together in familiar clusters. The Slavic immigrants—Poles, Czechs, Slovaks, Ukrainians, Serbs, and Croatians—did not stop in Boston, New York City, Philadelphia, or Baltimore. They were more likely to move inland to the mills, mines, and stockyards of Pennsylvania, Ohio, Indiana, and Illinois. Cities like Chicago, Detroit, Cleveland, and Buffalo had heavy concentrations of Slavic immigrants.

Wherever they put down roots, the immigrants planted their Old World customs and traditions. Fundamental among these was religion, which for most of these newer groups was a part of daily life. A majority were Roman Catholic. By the 1880s the Catholic Church had been firmly established in the United States. Catholic Italians and Slavs, then, were not deposited in the midst of an alien religion. Yet the American Catholic Church was largely English-speaking and dominated by the Irish, and for many years the newcomers would battle with the earlier arrivals over such issues as the language of sermons and the dominance of the Irish among the clergy and hierarchy. In the Jewish community, too, the newly-arrived clashed with their coreligionists. Many of the German Jews of the antebellum period were by now thoroughly Americanized, and their religious practices had become more closely aligned with prevailing American modes of religious practice. Between 1880 and 1914, a third of eastern Europe's Jews left their homes, and in these years they made up ten percent of immigration to the United States. To these newcomers, their German-Jewish predecessors seemed scarcely Jews at all. The German Jews, in turn, found their Polish, Russian, and Romanian brethren outlandish folk, alien to the modern world.

Immigrant Women   The transition from one culture to another weighed especially heavily on immigrant women. Invariably, the different immigrant groups accepted—although for their own reasons—the dominant American belief that women belonged at home. But survival frequently dictated that married women and unmarried daughters contribute to the family income. First-generation immigrant women characteristically worked in the sweat trades, or did piecework at home, or took in boarders. Daughters

The editor of the Jewish Daily Forward, *a Yiddish-language paper in New York City, gave its new-immigrant readers advice on how to live in the United States. One reader, signing herself "Discontented Wife," wrote this letter:*

Dear Editor,

Since I do not want my conscience to bother me, I ask you to decide whether a married woman has the right to go to school two evenings a week. My husband thinks I have no right to do this.

I admit that I cannot be satisfied to be just a wife and mother. I am still young and I want to learn and enjoy life. My children and my house are not neglected, but I go to evening high school twice a week. My husband is not pleased and when I come home at night and ring the bell, he lets me stand outside a long time intentionally, and doesn't hurry to open the door.

Now he has announced a new decision. Because I send out the laundry to be done, it seems to him that I have too much time for myself, even enough to go to school. So from now on he will count out every penny for anything I have to buy for the house, so I will not be able to send out the laundry any more. And when I have to do the work myself there won't be any time left for such 'foolishness' as going to school. I told him that I'm willing to do my own washing but that I would still be able to find time for study.

When I am alone with my thoughts, I feel I may not be right. Perhaps I should not go to school. I want to say that my husband is an intelligent man and he wanted to marry a woman who was educated. The fact that he is intelligent makes me more annoyed with him. He is in favor of the emancipation of women, yet in real life he acts contrary to his beliefs.

Awaiting your opinion on this. . . .

Answer:

Since this man is intelligent and an adherent of the women's emancipation movement, he is scolded severely in the answer for wanting to keep his wife so enslaved. Also the opinion is expressed that the wife absolutely has the right to go to school two evenings a week.

were more likely to work in factories. Married women had to cope with providing food and clothing for their families under conditions of excruciating poverty in an unfamiliar environment. In his novel *Call It Sleep*, Henry Roth poignantly evokes the relation between a mother and her son whom she believes she is losing to a foreign language. Immigrants could frequently resent social workers and especially the school system, which they thought was robbing them of their children by pulling the young into a foreign culture. One mother born in Sicily made a common complaint: "When girls at thirteen and fourteen wasted good time in school, it simply made us regret our coming to America."

Prejudice   In the years of Irish Catholic immigration before the Civil War, there had been a flourishing of nativism, a word applicable to Americans who have feared immigration as threatening to change the country's distinctive character. In the later nineteenth century, when the nation was swelling with immigrants, nativism again became public and vocal. Hostility to immigrants had a basis in feelings of xenophobia, hatred of things foreign.

Anti-Catholicism ran high within sections of the Protestant population, leading to demands for immigration restrictions and for laws to prevent the Catholic Church from intruding into what the critics conceived of as secular affairs. This movement culminated in the formation of the American Protective Association in 1887; its members were pledged to work to exclude Catholics from political office, to seek to keep Catholic workers from taking jobs of Protestants, and to refuse to join Catholics in strikes. In the 1890s the group allied itself with Republicans in the Midwest in battles over the funding of parochial schools, and some members boycotted Catholic merchants.

Violence against Italian immigrants began as early as the 1870s. In 1874 four Italian strikebreakers were killed by union mine workers in Buena Vista, Pennsylvania, and in 1886 a mob in Vicksburg, Mississippi, lynched an Italian American. The worst incident occurred in 1891. Since the mid-1880s New Orleans newspapers had speculated about the existence of a Black Hand conspiracy, and the Irish police chief of New Orleans, David Hennessey, had built a political reputation investigating Sicilian crime. In 1891 he was murdered, and an outraged public decided the Mafia was responsible. Nine Italians were arrested, but a jury acquitted six of them and the court declared mistrials for the others. A mob entered the parish jail and lynched eleven Italian inmates, three of whom were Italian nationals. The Italian government lodged a protest. From 1880 to 1910 there were dozens of lynchings of Italians in the United States.

The most notorious case of anti-Semitism occurred in Georgia in 1915. Leo Frank was a Jewish businessman living in Atlanta. He managed a pencil factory. In 1914 Mary Phagan, a young female worker, was found murdered in the plant. Frank was arrested, tried, and convicted of the crime, even though the evidence against him was flimsy at best. The case attracted international attention, and in 1915 the governor of Georgia commuted Frank's sentence from the death penalty to life imprisonment. The decision enraged many Georgia whites, and a mob entered the state prison, took Frank from his cell, transported him 175 miles away, and lynched him in the middle of the night.

"The schools," one Chinese recalls, "were segregated—Chinese were separated from the Caucasians and so on. . . . The old people could only work maintaining white people's gardens, or picking weeds."

Economic competition also awakened hatred of immigrants, many of whom were willing to work for less and so drove down the wages of native Americans. In these years many unions were nativist, and in California, with its large Chinese population, white workers in 1877 organized an anti-Chinese Workingmen's Party, led by an Irish-American agitator, Dennis Kearney.

In 1882 Congress responded to strong anti-Chinese sentiment by excluding Chinese laborers from the United States for ten years in the Chinese Exclusion Act. Later this was extended. The effects of prejudice on Chinese Americans was devastating. Chinese were commonly refused service in West Coast restaurants until the post-World War II era.

Immigration Restriction   Within weeks of passing the restrictive legislation against the Chinese, Congress prohibited the immigration of people with criminal records or signs of mental instability. To keep paupers out of the United States, that same law imposed a fifty cent head tax on each incoming immigrant. Responding to the demands of organized labor, Congress prohibited the importation of contract laborers in 1885. Polygamists and people with communicable diseases were excluded in 1891.

In 1894 a group of upper-class Bostonians organized the Immigration Restriction League, which called for a literacy test that the League thought would exclude Slavic, Italian, and Hispanic immigrants while permitting the continued immigration of people from northern and western Europe. In 1897 Congress responded to the League's pressure by imposing a literacy test on immigrants, but President Grover Cleveland vetoed the bill. The League continued to agitate for restrictive legislation. In 1903 Congress raised the immigrant head tax to $2 (it doubled to $4 in 1907) and prohibited the immigration of prostitutes, anarchists, and epileptics. The mentally retarded were excluded in 1907.

Immigrants themselves fought against measures to exclude their countrymen. Since many urban politicians now relied on their votes, they wielded considerable power. There was also the American tradition of free immigration to reckon with: the nation had always served as a refuge for Europe's impoverished and oppressed millions. Many Americans believed in the endless ability of American society to take the foreigner, strip him of his outlandish clothes, language, and folkways and make him over into a "true" American. According to this way of thinking, the hope for a successful solution of the immigration problem rested with the schools, especially the urban public schools. In these immigrant children would study American history and traditions, and learn to read and write English. In a few years, it was assumed, they would be indistinguishable from the children of the Pilgrim fathers. Such notions were far more friendly to immigrants, of course, than was nativism. But another idea went further, welcoming immigrants not as potential Anglo Americans with east European names but as people with distinctive cultures who could enrich the British American traditions with new diverse folkways.

If some native workers feared the foreigners' "coolie wages," others recognized that they benefited from the cheap labor pool that the immigrant represented. Immigrant workers often needed native American foremen and managers, and their arrival in vast numbers thrust up literate old-stock workers into white-collar or managerial ranks. Middle-class people also relied on immigrants as servants. Employers valued the cheap and willing labor of eastern and southern Europeans. Their well-financed campaigns against laws to limit the number of immigrants were probably the most formidable opposition the restrictionists faced.

Immigrant Life   In the communities where they settled, immigrants found a rich life among their countrymen. The neighborhoods eased the adjustment to American life. There the immigrants could attend their own churches and hear their own languages spoken. Their friends, relatives, and countrymen were nearby. The buildings and shops had the flavor of home. Italian immigrants on Mulberry Street in New York saw the cheeses and sausages and pasta in the stores, the opera posters, or the ubiquitous pictures of the Madonna; Greeks, Syrians, and Armenians frequented such coffeehouses as the Acropolis, the Parthenon, or the Beirut House; Jews sat in cafes along Hester Street and talked business or debated religion and politics; Germans in St. Louis or Cincinnati had their beer gardens, bowling alleys, and shooting galleries; Japanese could purchase the fish and vegetables they liked in the shops of Little Tokyo in Los Angeles, and Chinese could do the same in San Fran-

That economics could be a force against the restriction of immigration is demonstrated in a newspaper comment:

"When prosperity is at flood, the men in charge of furnaces, foundries, forges, and mills in the Pittsburgh District cannot get the help they need. The cry everywhere is: 'Give us men.' A foreman, therefore, will assure Pietro and Melukas that if brothers or cousins or friends are sent for, they will get work as soon as they arrive. More than that, the Slav and Italian are no longer dependent upon the English boss in the matter of finding work for their countrymen. The inflow from southeastern Europe has assumed such proportions in the industries of the cities that superintendents have, in some instances, appointed Italian and Polish and Lithuanian foremen; and with these, as with German and Irish, blood is thicker than water. They employ their fellow-countrymen. They know the condition of the labor market and can by suggestion stimulate or retard immigration."

Native-born Americans of an open turn of mind found the immigrant ghettos of the big cities to be fascinating places. One reported of New York's Little Italy:

"The sons of Italy . . . are fond of music and outdoor life; and in New York they enjoy both of these luxuries when the band plays in Mulberry Bend Park. Then they pour forth from a hundred tenements . . . and stand listening in rapt delight by the hour to the strains of 'Il Trovatore.' . . . Nearly all the Italian societies give festivals annually, and these have been accompanied . . . by . . . a racket of fireworks. . . . Frequently great wooden and pasteboard shrines are erected on the sidewalk and the streets are arched with lines of Chinese lanterns. In a recent Elizabeth Street fiesta great wire brackets arched the street at intervals of one hundred feet for a quarter of a mile, and huge painted candles, eight to ten feet in height . . . were presented by the wealthier families to the Madonna. . . ."

Not like the brazen giant of Greek fame,
With conquering limbs astride from land to land;
Here at our sea-washed, sunset gates shall stand
A mighty woman with a torch, whose flame
Is the imprisoned lightning, and her name
Mother of Exiles. From her beacon-hand
Glows world-wide welcome; her mild eyes command
The air-bridged harbor that twin cities frame.
"Keep, ancient lands, your storied pomp!" cries she
With silent lips. "Give me your tired, your poor,
Your huddled masses yearning to breathe free,
The wretched refuse of your teeming shore.
Send these, the homeless, tempest-tost to me,
I lift my lamp beside the golden door!"

The New Colossus by Emma Lazarus

A gift from the Franco-American Union commemorating the nation's independence, the Statue of Liberty, unveiled in 1884, came to symbolize a nation of immigrants. *(Courtesy, J. Clarence Davies Collection, Museum of the City of New York)*

The novelist Edna Ferber, in an affirmation of ethnic identity, wrote affectionately of Poles:

"The Polish farmers spread over the Housatonic River Valley [of New England] and the region bloomed like a garden. . . . Fields thick with tobacco, barns bursting with hay, silos oozing, cattle in the meadows; children and chickens and geese and dogs shouting, cackling, barking, squawking in the yard—that was a Polish farm."

cisco's Chinatown; Irish and Slavic immigrants gathered in local taverns. The neighborhoods were rich in ethnic foods, ethnic newspapers, and ethnic holidays, all of which were familiar to the immigrants.

Nor were the immigrants invariably poor and downtrodden. Most no doubt started at or near the bottom. Poles and other Slavic people manned the coal mines and the iron mills. French Canadians replaced the Yankees and Irish in the New England cotton mills. In the Southwest, Mexicans worked on the railroads as laborers. Italians pushed wheelbarrows and wielded picks and shovels in the construction industry. Jews cut and sewed in the garment industry in Chicago, New York, and Rochester. Most groups, however, had their small contingent of professionals and intellectuals who served as doctors, lawyers, priests, teachers, newspaper editors, shopkeepers, and small manufacturers. More significant was the speed of upward movement. Some scholars believe that it was relatively slow for immigrants to advance up the economic ladder; others are impressed by their swiftness. The most convincing formula holds that it varied from place to place and from group to group. Boston's Italians, for example, improved their occupational positions more slowly than the city's Jews and people of British origin. On the other hand, one scholar finds that between 1880 and 1915 many Italians as well as Jews of New York City moved upward from the wage class into self-employment.

Complicating matters further is that occupational mobility was not the only source of striving and satisfaction to immigrants. Some, such as the Poles, marked their success by home ownership. Almost all groups gradually did eventually assimilate into the mainstream, though they retained distinctive national characteristics.

Most immigrants did find the United States a land of opportunity, a place where they could improve their lives and those of their children. And this conclusion only stands to reason. Why would immigrants have continued to come in such enormous numbers over so long a period unless the experience of friends and relatives here demonstrated that in the New World things were indeed better?

Crime

Slums and Crime
Cities in this era, as in others, were places where the broken as well as the successful congregated. Crime was by no means exclusively an urban affliction, of course. On the frontier, a few gangs like the James and the Dalton boys roamed the countryside attacking trains and stagecoaches, and made forays into town to rob banks. Yet the West was on the whole peaceable. It was in cities, in this era and others, that criminals most thickly congregated. Crime increased as cities grew. At the very end of the century, the *Chicago Tribune* estimated that murders and homicides nationally had climbed from 1,266 in 1881 to 7,340 in 1898, or from about 25 per million people to over 107 per million. Statistics on other, lesser crimes are not available, but contemporaries believed that all felonies had skyrocketed, a view seemingly confirmed by the startling increase of fifty percent reported for the national prison population between 1880 and 1890.

Urban crime flourished in the slums. Chicago's crime-ridden West Side in the 1890s was, according to a social worker, a place of "filthy and rotten tenements, . . . dingy courts, and tumble-down sheds . . . foul stables and dilapidated outhouses . . . broken sewer pipes [and] . . . piles of garbage fairly alive with diseased odors. . . ." In the Five Points area of New York City, criminal gangs such as the Whyos, the Dutch Mob, and the Molasses Gang preyed on pedestrians and householders, when they were not fighting one another. San Francisco's Barbary Coast, with streets carrying such labels as Murderers' Corner and Deadman's Alley, was the haunt of hundreds of thieves and murderers.

Prostitution
To the mind of the late nineteenth century, crime was closely associated with "vice." The term often meant prostitution. Always a profitable and widespread occupation except in tight-knit, small communities, it achieved in the Gilded Age city a special flamboyance. In New York the trade centered in the Tenderloin area given over to saloons, music halls, and beer parlors. Chicago's "sporting houses" were concentrated in the area between Harrison and Polk and Clark and Dearborn streets. In New Orleans, Storyville in the French Quarter was a semi-official red-light district, as well as the birthplace of a music ancestral to present-day jazz. These districts and their denizens were the objects of any number of crusades

Sickness, like crime, ravaged urban slums. Jacob Riis wrote in 1890 of one such epidemic.

"Under the most favorable circumstances, an epidemic, which the well-to-do can afford to make light of as a thing to be got over or avoided by reasonable care, is excessively fatal among the children of the poor, by reason of the practical impossibility of isolating the patient in a tenement. . . . Such an epidemic ravaged three crowded blocks in Elizabeth Street on the heels of the grippe last winter, and, when it had spent its fury, the death-maps in the Bureau of Vital Statistics looked as if a black hand had been laid across those blocks. . . . The track of the epidemic through these teeming barracks was as clearly defined as the track of a tornado through a forest district. There were houses in which as many as eight little children had died in five months. . . .

That ignorance plays its part, as well as poverty and bad hygienic surroundings, in the sacrifice of life is of course inevitable. They go usually hand in hand. A message came one day last spring summoning me to a Mott Street tenement in which lay a child dying from some unknown disease. With the 'charity doctor' I found the patient on the top floor, stretched upon two chairs in a dreadfully stifling room. She was gasping in the agony of peritonitis that had already written its death-sentence on her wan and pinched face. The whole family, father, mother, and four ragged children, sat around looking on with the stony resignation of helpless despair that had long since given up the fight against fate as useless. A glance around the wretched room left no doubt as to the cause of the child's condition. 'Improper nourishment,' said the doctor, which, translated to suit the place, meant starvation."

"The use of ardent spirits is a prominent cause. Stimulus of every kind tends to inflame the passions. . . . The saloon-keeper is largely responsible for the existence of vile dens of infamy, where impurity reaches its climax and exhausts its vitality in the early deaths of its withered victims. Banish strong drinks, and thousands will be saved from this fearful destiny. Many who are unsuspecting, through the use of stimulants, sometimes drugged, have been led on to commit the adulterous act.

The influence of alcohol on the social morals of our people can not easily be overestimated. A drunken person has neither conscience nor reason left; but the flame of passion burns all the brighter in the drunkard's heart when thus kindled by alcohol. The saloon is the strong ally of the brothel, and constantly feeds it. It corrupts husbands, and degrades the wife and children and forces them into the ranks of the vicious. The sin of intemperance sooner or later leads to social impurity. If the saloons were blotted out of existence to-day, a long stride would be taken toward the rescue of the masses from social ruin. . . ."

In St. Louis, Lincoln Steffens reported:

"Franchises worth millions were granted without one cent of cash to the city, and with provision for only the smallest future payment; several companies which refused to pay blackmail had to leave; citizens were robbed more and more boldly; pay-rolls were padded with the names of non-existent persons; work on public improvements was neglected, while money for them went to the boodlers."

against vice, usually conducted by middle-class, civic-minded women and ministers.

During the last third of the nineteenth century, public attention to prostitution divided into two camps. A group known as the regulationists and led by medical authorities and police officials sought to have all prostitutes registered by the state, closely supervised by the authorities, regularly examined for venereal disease, and subject to compulsory hospitalization if they were infected. On the other hand, women's groups, in alliance with ministers and some social reformers, sought to stamp out vice altogether. This movement has been appropriately called the purity crusade. And, on the whole, it advocated extending to men the standards of purity that custom had imposed on women. It increasingly rejected the notion that prostitution was a necessary evil and condemned it as a social wrong—for which men were responsible. The most enlightened women opponents of mere regulation, besides demanding a direct war on prostitution, gradually came to defend the rights and dignity of the women engaged in it. They blamed the practice on social ills—especially economic need—rather than on moral failings. But for the most part the fight against legalized regulation, which was interpreted as a de facto endorsement of prostitution, reflected a determination to impose a higher female morality on society.

The crusaders often discovered that the madams enjoyed police protection. The problem persisted because society was ambivalent about it as about so many other violations of social conventions. Middle-class Americans were shocked. Yet many people believed that there was no way of denying men access to sex for sale, and numbers of men, especially bachelors, saw nothing wrong with using the services of prostitutes. The willingness on the part of many men to pay for a service that in numbers of localities was now illegal created a gray area where graft and payoffs could flourish. New legislation that moral reformers had succeeded in winning against Sunday sports, cockfights, boxing, gambling, and drinking beyond certain specified hours opened similar opportunities for entrepreneurs to make money by bribes to police and officials. Reformers could do little to stop vice or prevent it from becoming a fertile source of political corruption.

City Political Machines

The beneficiary of much of this corruption was the city machine. Machines were political organizations that ran parallel to the legal government of the city. At their head was a boss. Few were mayors, but bosses came close to running city government. Below the boss were lieutenants, ward captains or, to critics, ward heelers, whose responsibilities and duties were confined to the city wards. Surrounding the ward leaders were crowds of hangers-on and underlings who served the machine at the neighborhood level. The local political clubhouse was the place where the captain and his underlings conducted their business. Most machines were affiliated with the Democrats; in Philadelphia and a few other cities they were Republican.

The successful machine ruled the city. The boss not only controlled the board of aldermen or the city council but also owned the county board of assessment along with the local water and police commissioners, and some exerted strong influence in the state legislature, where much authority over the city actually was lodged. To get something done, businessmen, civic leaders, and ethnic groups usually needed only to go to the boss. Decisions regarding conduct of city affairs and appointments to office were made in the clubhouses or by the boss and merely confirmed by the legal city officials. Machines and their bosses could have a direct and effective way with elections. In some cities, five dollars was the going price of a vote; sometimes it was as little as a shot of whiskey. "Doc" Ames in Minneapolis was willing to sell exemptions from arrest to any criminal who was willing to pay the price. New York's Tweed Ring collected millions of dollars from builders and contractors who built the municipal courthouse at wildly inflated costs and then kicked back part of the money to boss William Marcy Tweed and his Tammany Hall henchmen.

The boss, then, was an urban ruler. But he was more.

Newcomers to the city faced poverty, disease, congestion, unemployment, and trouble with the law. Cities had their charity societies, counties their poorhouses. The Chicagoan, Philadelphian, or New Yorker could turn to the minister, priest, or rabbi. Toward the end of the century, moreover, groups of middle-class philanthropists were establishing settlement houses in city slum neighborhoods to provide the urban poor with educational services, meeting halls, and places where they could get help and advice. But all these were not enough. Too often the middle-class charity and settlement workers had inadequate resources; and some of them patronized the poor or imposed harsh conditions for dispensing aid. Not so the boss and the ward captain. Few were prudes, and they refused to judge the morals or

"Let Us Prey"

Another devastating assault on the Tweed Ring, by Thomas Nast, printed in *Harper's Weekly*, helped bring about the ring's demise. In this cartoon Tweed and his fellow vultures cower under the storm against them. Tweed offered Nast $500,000 to stop the cartoon.

PLUNKITT OF TAMMANY HALL

George Washington Plunkitt's reflections on his political experience were recorded, and perhaps embroidered upon, by the journalist William L. Riordon.

Honest Graft and Dishonest Graft

Everybody is talkin' these days about Tammany men growin' rich on graft, but nobody thinks of drawin' the distinction between honest graft and dishonest graft. There's all the difference in the world between the two. Yes, many of our men have grown rich in politics. I have myself. I've made a big fortune out of the game, and I'm gettin' richer every day, but I've not gone in for dishonest graft—blackmailin' gamblers, saloonkeepers, disorderly people, etc.—and neither has any of the men who have made big fortunes in politics.

There's an honest graft, and I'm an example of how it works. I might sum up the whole thing by sayin': "I seen my opportunities and I took 'em."

Just let me explain by examples. My party's in power in the city, and it's goin' to undertake a lot of public improvements. Well, I'm tipped off, say, that they're going to lay out a new park at a certain place.

I see my opportunity and I take it. I go to that place and I buy up all the land I can in the neighborhood. Then the board of this or that makes its plan public, and there is a rush to get my land, which nobody cared particular for before.

Ain't it perfectly honest to charge a good price and make a profit on my investment and foresight? Of course, it is. Well, that's honest graft. . . .

The Curse of Civil Service Reform

This civil service law is the biggest fraud of the age. It is the curse of the nation. There can't be no real patriotism while it lasts. How are you goin' to interest our young men in their country if you have no offices to give them when they work for their party? Just look at things in this city today. There are ten thousand good

---

The historian James Mooney argues against bossism. Mooney observes that the urban political machine, in assuming that the poor and the immigrants were for sale, degraded them. The reformers at the turn of the twentieth century who attacked bossism showed far more respect for city dwellers by schooling them in civic responsibility.

customs of the local people. Many of them were Irish Catholics, yet they were tolerant of ethnic, religious, and racial differences. Gregarious glad-handers, they mixed easily with the city poor and shared their ceremonies, social events, joys, and sorrows.

Among their services was the dispensing of jobs. In the absence of effective municipal civil service procedures, they could hand out jobs at will in the police and sanitation departments, in laboring occupations, even in schoolteaching. Many a poor family owed its regular income to the precinct captain's generosity toward the family breadwinner. There was also the temporary help of a Christmas dinner or some coal to a destitute family in winter. Boss Tweed, as a member of the New York State legislature, got the state to contribute money to Catholic charities, though such action was widely thought to violate the principle of separation of church and state. The machine, through its control of municipal judges and courts, also got minor violations of the law dismissed.

The city's "better element" objected to these favors as expensive, inefficient, or corrupt. The boss did not care. As Martin Lomasney of Boston's Thomas Hendricks Club remarked: "I think there's got to be in every ward a guy that any bloke can go to when he's in trouble and get help—not justice and the law, but help, no matter what he's done."

The New Urban Architecture

Another side remained to the city that was remaking itself in the late nineteenth century and the early twentieth. Amidst the clutter of tenements, the richly strange customs and tongues of immigrant communi-

offices, but we can't get at more than a few hundred of them. How are we goin' to provide for the thousands of men who worked for the Tammany ticket? It can't be done. These men were full of patriotism a short time ago. They expected to be servin' their city, but when we tell them that we can't place them do you think their patriotism is goin' to last? Not much. They say: "What's the use of workin' for your country anyhow? There's nothin' in the game." And what can they do? I don't know, but I'll tell you what I do know. I know more than one young man in past years who worked for the ticket and was just overflowin' with patriotism, but when he was knocked out by the civil service humbug he got to hate his country and became an Anarchist.

This ain't no exaggeration. I have good reason for sayin' that most of the Anarchists in this city today are men who ran up against civil service examinations. Isn't it enough to make a man sour on his country when he wants to serve it and won't be allowed unless he answers a lot of fool questions about the number of cubic inches of water in the Atlantic and the quality of sand in the Sahara desert? There was once a bright young man in my district who tackled one of these examinations. The next I heard of him he had settled down in Herr Most's saloon smokin' and drinkin' beer and talkin' socialism all day. Before that time he had never drank anything but whisky. I knew what was comin' when a young Irishman drops whisky and takes to beer and long pipes in a German saloon. That young man is today one of the wildest Anarchists in town. And just to think! He might be a patriot but for that cussed civil service. . . . Nothin' doin', unless you can answer a list of questions about Egyptian mummies and how many years it will take for a bird to wear out a mass of iron as big as the earth by steppin' on it once in a century.

---

ties, the brawling politics of machine bossism, architects were building a more formal expression of the forces of their age. The Brooklyn Bridge, the skyscraper, the urban architecture making use of the steel that the Bessemer and open-hearth processes had liberated for mass production: all these embodied the mind of the machine technician bringing a new kind of order to the world.

The Brooklyn Bridge, in its time the longest suspension bridge in existence, had as its designer John Roebling. It was begun in 1870 and completed in 1883, President Chester A. Arthur officiating at its opening. Twenty men, including Roebling, died in the course of completing it. It had two double carriage lanes, two railway lines, and a footpath. It was one of the most impressive structures of its generation. Soon buildings even more representative of technological advance would appear. The skyscrapers were a way of conserving the spaces that the crowded new cities needed. They also demonstrated what steel can do in holding up buildings that wooden or stone or iron supports could not sustain. In their clear and economical surfaces, moreover, the skyscrapers were a statement of the intelligence behind the modern technology that had constructed them.

Louis Sullivan was a central figure in the new architecture, which did not make an office building or railway station look like a Greek temple or Renaissance palace but instead let the construction be efficiently and visibly appropriate to the building's intended use. Yet Sullivan, spokesman for the young technology of steel and glass, also represented a nineteenth-century feeling, deepened by Darwinism and the biological sciences, for the organic nature of plants and animals. An architecture demanding that the shape of a building be honestly expressive of what it is meant for, Sullivan believed, is in accordance with

After his father's death, Washington Roebling took over as chief engineer of the Brooklyn Bridge. Crippled by the "bends," he observes the construction work from his home in Brooklyn Heights. (*Courtesy, Culver Pictures*)

The Flatiron Building, New York City. *(Courtesy, National Archives, Rudolph Vetter/Interpretive Photography)*

nature, in which every part of a tree or shrub is simply fitted to what the whole organism is doing.

American cities were forming a new cultural life out of immigrant communities, a raucous politics, and the fact of sudden growth itself. The rural peoples who still composed most of the nation's population and appeared to hold more closely to its traditional ways were meanwhile transforming themselves just as notably in response to technological innovation and to the cities they fed. Amidst urban sprawl and confusion sprang up the practical, invented, day-to-day governance provided by the political machines, along with some effort at more systematic treatment of the cities' ills. In the countryside, the effort was to formulate an articulate ideology and national program for economic security and progress and for coming to terms with machinery, railroads, credit, and advances in methods of agriculture. Folk tradition associates cities with sophistication and the backcountry with narrow-mindedness. Yet in the late nineteenth century, it was from the regions of agrarian unrest that the more continental vision of remaking the nation arose. Only in the impressive though unsuccessful run of Henry George for the New York City mayoralty in 1886 did an urban center appear to show any large interest in an idea looking beyond the city limits. In truth, western farmers could not afford to confine their sight to their own community, and they knew it. Economically dependent on markets and industry in the East, to which they were connected by railroads, and at the mercy of a credit system housed on the Atlantic coast, they had to think continentally. An ordinary New Yorker was not obliged to look beyond his Irish or German neighborhood. So provinciality came more easily to the big cities than to the agricultural West. A politics fully embracing the two was not to come until early in the next century.

Agriculture

Agricultural Education   In agriculture as in transportation, the Civil War propelled the government into the economy. In 1862 Congress created the United States Bureau of Agriculture as a separate division within the federal government, below Cabinet rank: not until 1889 was the commissioner of agriculture to become a regular member of the Cabinet. Also in 1862, Congress passed the Morrill Land Grant College Act, donating thirty thousand acres of federal land to every state for each senator and representative it had in Congress. This land was to support at least one agricultural college in the state: in time the new schools also taught engineering and a multitude of other subjects. The act mandated that all the colleges established on the basis of its grants be coeducational. It thus represented an important gain for women's education, although decades would pass before the public came to expect women to use their education as a passport into an extensive range of occupations and professions.

Under the Morrill Act some sixty-nine land-grant colleges were established. By the 1890s, a flock of state agricultural and mechanical

Harvey Dunn, *Dakota Woman.*
(Courtesy, Friends of the Middle Border Museum)

colleges taught animal husbandry, horticulture, agricultural chemistry, entomology, and other courses designed to train farmers in scientific techniques. Many of these institutions maintained laboratories and experimental farms where their faculties sought to develop new fertilizers, new plant and animal strains, and new ways of dealing with plant and animal diseases.

This agricultural research and development had further encouragement from the Hatch Act of 1887. This law appropriated to each state $15,000 a year from public land sales for the establishment of an experimental station. By 1899 there were fifty-six such stations, in every state and territory, receiving overall more than $1 million a year to try out crops, fertilizers, and plowing, harvesting, and tillage techniques.

Inventions   Federal aid was one of a number of contributors to the marvelous growth of American agriculture in the later part of the century. The railroads opened up vast tracts of land. From nineteenth-century inventors and manufacturers farmers received a wealth of farm equipment: the harvester, the product of Cyrus McCormick and the Marsh brothers; James Oliver's chilled-iron plow; James Buchanan's threshing machine; Manly Miles's silo; S. M. Babcock's cream tester. State and regional agricultural journals encouraged farmers to be good businessmen, bold innovators, and careful cultivators. And there was the farmer: eager to produce in quantity for the market, quick to adopt new methods. American agriculture was very much a branch of modern technology. It was so in its use of new machines and even more in working the land by innovative methods, for it is not machines but the will to innovation itself that has distinguished the technological revolution of recent centuries.

Between 1866 and 1900 the number of American farms increased from 2.6 to 5.4 million, and total farm acreage between 1870 and 1900 rose from 493 million acres to 839. Cattle on American farms increased from 24 million head in 1870 to 52 in 1900. Cotton output, some 2.1 million bales in 1866, reached 11.2 in 1898; wheat, at 152 million bushels in 1866, went to 675 in 1898; corn production shot up from

Bad weather was one of the farmer's worst enemies. The results are best expressed in the words of individual farmers. Sarah Orcutt of Kansas wrote to a friend:

"I take my Pen In hand to let you know that we are Starving to death It is Pretty hard to do without any thing to Eat hear in this God for saken country we would of had Plenty to Eat if the hail hadent cut our rye down and ruined our corn and Potatoes I had the Prettiest Garden that you Ever seen and the hail ruined."

W. M. Taylor of Nebraska wrote to the editor of a farm journal:

"The hot winds burned up the entire crop, leaving thousands of families wholly destitute, many of whom might have been able to run through this crisis had it not been for the galling yoke put on them by the money loaners and sharks—not by charging 7 per cent. per annum, which is the lawful rate of interest, or even 10 per cent., but the unlawful and inhuman country destroying rate of 3 per cent. a month, some going still farther and charging 50 per cent per annum."

And W. R. Christy of Kansas wrote:

"We are worried over what our Poor People of our country are to do for fuel to keep them warm this winter. . . . there are at least 2/3 of the People that have to depend on Cow chips for fuel & as the cattle had to be Sold off verry close that its been difficult to get them. Some have went as far as 13 miles to get them. the thermometer this morning was 16 below zero & 4 or 5 inches of snow on the ground, under those circumstances what are the People to do. at this time our coal dealers have not all told more than 100 bushels of coal on hand & it cant be bought for less than 40¢ per hundred in Less than ton lots."

731 million bushels in 1866 to 2.6 billion bushels in 1900. By the end of the nineteenth century, the United States was an agricultural powerhouse, producing vast amounts of grain, meat, fiber, and other farm products for its own growing population and a large part of the Atlantic world. American economic growth after the Civil War is more visibly and imposingly an industrial event. But without the corresponding boom in agriculture the economic achievements of this period would have been far more modest, for the country could have fed only a small labor force.

Agrarian Discontent

American agriculture was as much a success story as American industry in the Gilded Age. It advanced in every index of productivity, and helped supply the food needed by the nation's growing urban population, besides providing large surpluses for export to other industrial lands. Yet the generation following 1865 was a trying period.

Northeastern farmers, ever since the transportation revolution before the Civil War opened up the fertile Middle West, had been forced to adjust to the stiff competition of the newer region. This competition continued after 1865 and pushed many people off the land in New England and the mid-Atlantic states. Many farms were simply abandoned. Others shifted to the production of fruits, vegetables, dairy products, and other perishables, where closeness to city consumers gave an advantage. By the 1870s farmers of the Midwest were also being forced to make painful adjustments. As the wheat belt moved further west into the Plains, some wheat farmers in the Old Northwest found they could no longer compete. And so along the Great Lakes and in Wisconsin they turned to dairying to supply the large midwestern cities. Farther south farmers shifted to corn for feeding hogs and cattle. By the 1880s fields of maize covered the prairie lands of Illinois, Iowa, Indiana, and eastern Kansas and Nebraska. In the barns and pens, hundreds of hogs grew fat from eating the previous year's crop. And whatever were the tribulations and the successes that came with the transformations of agriculture, farmers in the West, the Midwest, and the East faced the uncertainties of the yearly market. Bad weather and a scanty crop could ruin them; an abundant harvest, driving down prices, could be nearly as bad. Transportation costs or interest rates on loans could upset the delicate balance between expenses and income that some farmers precariously maintained from year to year. Eastern moneylenders were notorious for charging high interest and demanding a great deal of collateral for making loans. Banks, railroads, the merchants who sold agricultural implements to farmers and those who brought their crop for sale to the cities: all these were the targets of farm protest.

Granger Laws   Western and midwestern farmers expressed their discontent through the Patrons of Husbandry, popularly called the Grange. In 1867 Oliver Kelley, an employee of the

United States Bureau of Agriculture, undertook the task of organizing the first national association of farmers. Kelley's objective was primarily social. Farming on the Great Plains and out west where much of the population was widely scattered was a lonely existence. Farmers, particularly farm women, were desperate for more social contact, and Kelley created the Grange to sponsor lectures, dances, and picnics. The organization became extremely popular, and by 1875 its membership consisted of some 800,000 people. Whenever farmers gathered together for its entertainments, they talked about their problems— falling commodity prices, high interest rates, and exorbitant shipping costs. The Grange was soon a militant political organization.

The Grange analysis of the farmer's plight centered on the middlemen, the various business dealers who stood between the farmers and the consumer and added so much to the price the consumer would pay for food, or charged such a high price for supplying machinery and other items the farmer needed. To get around these middlemen the Grange, which included many small-town merchants, organized cooperative buying schemes for farmers and sought to establish businesses run by farmers that could produce what they needed at moderate expense. Grangers also tried to reduce middlemen's costs by imposing fixed rates on what railroads and grain elevator companies could charge for their shipping and storage services. This effort brought the Grangers into politics, and by the mid-1870s farmers' parties had been organized in eleven states, mostly in the Midwest. In at least four of these—Illinois, Wisconsin, Iowa, and Minnesota—the Grangers gained control of the state legislatures and enacted legislation authorizing the setting of rates for railroad freight and grain elevator storage. In 1877 the Supreme Court in *Munn v. Illinois* upheld these "Granger Laws."

In a definition of its purpose, the Farmers Alliance declared:

"Co-operation is the distinctive feature of the Farmers' Alliance. Its principles are founded upon equity and justice. It has entered the conflict against monopoly. . . . Nothing but an aggressive warfare will win. Monopoly and privileged classes are intrenched behind fortifications which the farmers have builded for them. The fight on the one side is waged to retain the privilege to rob and plunder. On the other hand it is made to regain constitutional rights. The fight on the part of the farmer is being made, not only for himself but for generations yet unborn. It is a fight for liberty, equality and a just reward for his labor. To lose is to be dependent, poor and miserable. To win is to be free, comfortable and happy. To banish monopoly of every description is to give new vitality to every industry, and strengthen the foundations of government. To fail, is to drift into centralization, where money and aristocracy will rule and land monopoly be the prevailing system. . . . It is the final struggle for the peaceful solution of the great issue between the people and Shylock. If this effort, this last hope, more sweet than the grapes of Eschol, fail; if it burn to ashes upon fallen altars, nothing short of a desperate revolution will ever save the Republic."

Later the Court reversed itself on regulation and embraced laissez-faire.

The Granger era lasted until about 1880. Thereafter, a successful readjustment to corn-and-hog and other specialty agriculture suited to domestic urban markets pacified the Midwest. In the next two decades it would be from other agricultural regions that political protest came.

The Farmers' Alliances

Wheat and Cotton Farmers   To the farm population of the Plains and the South, the 1880s and 1890s brought deep discontent. The wheat of the Plains and the cotton of the South depended on overseas markets far more than did the pork, beef, fruits, vegetables, and dairy products of the Northeast and Midwest. This meant that the chain of middlemen between producer and consumer was even longer for wheat and cotton than for the perishables of those other regions. In addition, the prices of wheat and cotton fell sharply beginning in the 1870s, dropping to about half of their initial level by the early 1890s. It is true that all other prices fell as well in the quarter-century between 1870 and the mid-1890s—interest rates and railroad freight rates declined, as did the price of farm machinery and of many of the manufactured goods that farm families consumed. But the prices of the great staples of the Plains and the deep South fell faster than those of other goods and services.

Grain and cotton farmers could offset the drop of staple prices by cutting costs and getting a larger production. In pursuit of increased production, wheat farmers bought much machinery during these years, and cotton farmers made heavy purchases of fertilizers; both promised increases in crops more than compensating for the initial investment. Careful attention to the best practices might yield a profit from wheat or cotton. But many farmers lacked the means to achieve that constant vigilance. And while it was of immediate advantage to any one farmer to grow more grain or wheat, the decision on the part of farmers collectively to do so meant flooding of the market and further declines in prices of produce. In the South and the Plains farm leaders sought other answers to the relentless battle against insolvency, and fastened on middlemen and financiers as scapegoats.

In both the South and the trans-Missouri West, railroad rates were higher than in the Northeast. So were credit costs, a condition that was particularly galling when the dollar was growing in value and so making debtors pay back with dollars more valuable than those they had borrowed. Whether or not this was an accurate assessment of the workings of money, farmers in debt had a hard time of it. Rates of interest on farm loans went into double digits. It was concern over debt that led to the free silver movement demanding coinage of that cheaper metal, which would make for a drop in the value of each dollar that a debtor had to pay. Manufacturers, too, seemed to take advantage of farmers. The farm machinery monopoly appeared to be a particularly effective agency for gouging them. Financiers, farm radicals believed, were conspiring to reduce the money supply of the nation in order to raise interest rates and push up the value of the dollars their debtors would have to pay them.

The Alliances   At the end of the 1870s, various new farmers' groups began to appear. Texas farmers organized an Alliance to keep up prices for their crops, to bring down prices of goods in country stores, and to resist the crop liens by which a creditor could seize part of a crop in payment of a debt. Over the next few years the Texans linked up with various other groups. By 1890 the Southern Alliance, led since 1886 by the farmer, lawyer, and physician Charles W. Macune, had a membership of a million. The Southern Alliance, at least in North Carolina and probably elsewhere, offered a more important role to women than did most of the northern labor organizations. Their programs included demands for education and rights for women and they admitted women as members. The all-white Southern Alliance had its parallel in the Colored Farmers' National Alliance and Cooperative Union. In the Northwest appeared the National Farmers' Alliance, or Northwestern Alliance. On a platform demanding federal regulation of railroads and free coinage of silver, the Northwest Alliance expanded rapidly in the wheat belt. By 1890 there were 130,000 Northwest Alliance members in Kansas. Nebraska, the Dakotas, and Minnesota were not far behind.

Before long, Alliance leaders moved to merge the two regional groups into one nationwide organization; this, however, proved slow, for each group refused to abandon its own special interests and concerns. By the 1880s the Alliances also began to enter state politics, usually by associating themselves with one or the other of the two major parties. A substantial group of farm leaders from the West and South decided that the mainstream parties were abysmally failing to come to grips with the plight of the rural regions and, beginning in the early 1890s, they came together to organize a new party, the People's Party.

In this political cartoon the railroad, represented here by an iron horse bolted together and breathing steam, is raiding the farmer's corncrib. *(Courtesy, Scribner's Archives)*

Populism

The People's   In 1889 farm Alliance leaders met at St. Louis to
Party   forge a political bond with the Knights of Labor.
                     Adopting a national platform endorsing greenbacks and free silver (both of them cheap currency favoring debtors), economy in government, confiscation of excess railroad lands, and public ownership of "the means of communication and transportation," the meeting recommended that all farmers and laboring men support candidates who were willing to pledge themselves to these principles. The following year, the Southern Alliance and the Colored Farmers' Alliance adopted a similar platform. Resistance to a third party collapsed and at St. Louis in 1889, the People's Party—the Populists, they would come to be labeled—was formally established. In July 1890 the first People's Party convention assembled in Omaha to select candidates and a platform for the 1892 election.

The Omaha meeting was a colorful assemblage. Most American

males had by now given up the Civil War era practice of wearing beards. Not so the delegates at Omaha. It seemed that there must be some connection between political dissent and abundant facial hair. Also noticeable was the number of women activists. Mary Elizabeth Lease—Mary Ellen to her friends, "Mary Yellin" to her critics—was the most prominent of these. Eloquent, courageous, mother of four, and member of the Kansas bar, she had made hundreds of speeches for the agrarian cause. The "West and South," one of her speeches reported, "are bound and prostrate before the manufacturing East. . . . The parties lie to us. . . . We were told . . . to go to work and raise a big crop . . . and what came of it? Eight-cent corn, ten-cent oats, two-cent beef and no price at all for butter and eggs." There were four black delegates, one each from Kansas and Virginia, and two from Texas. Amid roars of approval that impressed a reporter as having the "likeness of the enthusiastic Bastille demonstration in France," the convention adopted a platform that summed up the outlook of the agrarian dissenters.

Ignatius Donnelly, James B. Weaver   Written by the romantic and flamboyant Minnesota editor and politician Ignatius Donnelly, the platform preamble sounded the note of emergency that Populists felt. The nation was on "the verge of moral, political, and material ruin." Donnelly, who as a good agrarian prized silver coinage, declared that "silver . . . has been demonetized to add to the purchasing power of gold. . . . A vast conspiracy against mankind [has been] organized on two continents" by the money power, and "if not met and overthrown at once [will produce] terrible social convulsions, the destruction of civilization, or the establishment of an absolute despotism."

After this overwrought invocation, there were specific platform planks: demands for free and unlimited coinage of silver, a graduated income tax, government ownership of the railroads and the telephone and telegraph systems, a postal savings bank run by the government and designed for people of limited means, the secret ballot, direct election of United States senators, and restraints on immigration. The platform called for devices on the state level favoring direct democracy: the initiative, whereby a number of citizens can petition that a particular law be considered; the referendum, submitting a proposed law to a popular vote. Planks designed to attract wage earners attacked the Pinkertons, favored reduced working hours, and endorsed the Knights of Labor in their current battle with Rochester clothing manufacturers. Among the most imaginative of the ideas in the document was that for federal warehouses in which farmers could deposit crops as collateral for governmental loans at low interest, also leaving the crops stored until the price for them went up. The moment the platform was adopted, "the convention broke over all restraint and went wild" in a demonstration that lasted a full twenty minutes. With the nomination of General James B. Weaver of Iowa for President, the convention adjourned.

In the election that followed, the Populists won a million popular votes out of about seventeen million cast and twenty-two electoral votes. This was the best showing by far of any third party since the Republicans in 1856, and seemed to promise much. Close analysis, however, would have suggested that something was wrong. The Weaver-Field ticket had done very well in three small Rocky Mountain states—Idaho, Nevada, and Colorado; it had also run strongly in the wheat states of Kansas, North Dakota, South Dakota, and Nebraska. Except for Alabama, the South largely rejected the Populists. Worst of all was the showing in the industrial Northeast and older Midwest. A notable but short-lived phenomenon of the campaign preceding the election had been a real though small outreach on the part of southern white Populism toward black southerners. Tom Watson of Georgia was a Populist who in the early days of the movement made an appeal to black voters. He was later to become a virulent white supremacist.

By the early 1890s, the new cities had evolved folkways and a politics compounded of immigrant customs and Anglo-American traditions. They were also suffering from poverty and disorderly growth for which their dominant politics had no solution beyond the informal charity dispensed by political machines and whatever in the way of rational city planning the bosses and other influential forces saw fit to endorse. Out of agricultural regions were coming more articulate ideas for the mastery of the technological and financial energies of the era, and these ideas included at least some gestures of solidarity with labor that the city machine showed no inclination to reciprocate. In urban areas, socialists and anarchists too were thinking far beyond the limits set by machine politics; but these had little serious notice within the public at large. For many years, both politics and culture were to be in part a matter of divergence and coalescence as cities, labor, and farming interests defined on the national and the local level their troubles and their hopes.

Suggested Readings

The most recent scholarship on American cities includes Alan M. Kraut, *The Huddled Masses: The Immigrant in American Society, 1880–1921* (1982), Thomas J. Archdeacon, *Becoming American: An Ethnic History* (1983), Alan Trachtenberg, *The Incorporation of America* (1982), Jack Chen, *The Chinese of America* (1980), Gunther Barth, *City People* (1980), John M. Allswang, *Bosses, Machines and Urban Voters* (rev. ed., 1986), Gwendolyn Mink, *Old Labor and New Immigrants in American Political Development* (1986), Cindy Aron, *Ladies and Gentlemen of the Civil Service: Middle Class Workers in Victorian America* (1987), and Zane Miller and Patricia Melvin, *The Urbanization of Modern America* (1987).

Sam B. Warner, Jr., *The Urban Wilderness* (1972) describes the physical development of American cities. Warner has also written a model study of urban spread, *Streetcar Suburbs: The Process of Growth in Boston, 1870–1900* (1971). Stephan Thernstrom's *The Other Bostonians* (1973) and *Poverty and Progress* (1967) test for up-ward mobility in Boston and Newburyport, Massachusetts. Howard Chudacoff, *The Evolution of American Urban Society* (revised, 1981) is also valuable.

Philip Taylor, *The Distant Magnet: European Immigration to the United States* (1971) is a good introduction to the subject. John Higham, *Strangers in the Land: Patterns of Nativism, 1860–1925* (1955) is standard, and James Olson, *The Ethnic Dimension in American History* (1979) is a fine survey. See also David Ward's *Cities and Immigrants* (1971).

For farmers' problems toward the end of the century see Lawrence Goodwyn, *Democratic Promise: The Populist Movement in America* (1976) as well as subsequent works by the same author, R. W. Cherny, *A Righteous Cause: William Jennings Bryan* (1985), Robert V. Hine, *The American West* (1984), and Paul Kleppner, *The Cross of Culture: A Social Analysis of Midwestern Politics, 1850–1900* (1970).

Were Immigrants Psychologically Scarred or Dynamically Renewed?

Oscar Handlin

Immigration had transformed the entire economic world within which the [European] peasants had formerly lived. From surface forms to inmost functionings, the change was complete. A new setting, new activities, and new meanings forced the newcomers into radically new roles as producers and consumers of goods. In the process, they became, in their own eyes, less worthy as men. They felt a sense of degradation that raised a most insistent question: Why had this happened?

More troubling, the change was not confined to economic matters. The whole American universe was different. Strangers, the immigrants could not locate themselves; they had lost the polestar that gave them their bearings. They would not regain an awareness of direction until they could visualize themselves in their new context, see a picture of the world as it appeared from this perspective. At home, in the wide frame of the village, their eyes had taken in the whole of life, had brought to their perceptions a clearly defined view of the universe. Here the frame narrowed down, seemed to reveal only fragmentary distorted glimpses that were hardly reminiscent of the old outlines. . . .

This they knew, though, and could not mistake it: they were lonely. In the midst of teeming cities, in the crowded tenements and the factories full of bustling men, they were lonely.

Their loneliness had more than one dimension. It had the breadth of unfamiliarity. Strange people walked about them; strange sounds assailed their inattentive ears. Hard pavements cut them off from nature in all its accustomed manifestations. Look how far they could, at the end of no street was a familiar horizon. Hemmed in by the tall buildings, they were fenced off from the realm of growing things. They had lost the world they knew of beasts and birds, of blades of grass, of sprays of idle flowers. They had acquired instead surroundings of a most outlandish aspect. That unfamiliarity was one aspect of their loneliness.

In the new country, all these were gone; that was hard enough. Harder still was the fact that nothing replaced them. In America, the peasant was a transient without meaningful connections in time and space. He lived now with inanimate objects, cut off from his surroundings. His dwelling and his place of work had no relationship to him as a man. The scores of established routines that went with a life of the soil had disappeared and with them the sense of being one of a company. Therefore the peasant felt isolated and isolation added to his loneliness. . . .

To find a job or not, to hold it or to be fired, in these matters laborers' wills were of slight importance. Inscrutable, distant persons determined matters on the basis of remote, unknown conditions. The most fortunate of immigrants, the farmers, knew well what little power they had to influence the state of the climate, the yield of the earth, or the fluctuations of the market, all the elements that determined their lot. Success or failure, incomprehensible in terms of peasant values, seemed altogether fortuitous. Time and again, the analogy occurred to them: man was helpless like the driven cog in a great machine.

Loneliness, separation from the community of the village, and despair at the insignificance of their own human abilities, these were the elements that, in America, colored the peasants' view of their world. From the depths of a dark pessimism, they looked up at a frustrating universe ruled by haphazard, capricious forces. Without the capacity to control or influence these forces men could but rarely gratify their hopes or wills. Their most passionate desires were doomed to failure; their lives were those of the feeble little birds which hawks attack, which lose strength from want of food, and which, at last surrendering to the savage blasts of the careless elements, flutter unnoticed to the waiting earth.

Reprinted from Oscar Handlin, *The Uprooted: The Epic Story of the Great Migrations That Made the American People,* 2nd ed. (Boston: Little, Brown & Co., 1973).

Alan M. Kraut

The immigrants who came to the United States in such numbers between 1880 and 1921 dramatically affected the shaping of the American population. By their very presence, these newcomers altered the economy, politics, and culture of the country. In turn, the immigrants were changed, in varying degrees, by the society they entered. The history of immigration to America can only be understood in light of "what was done" to a newcomer and native alike by this massive migratory movement. Immigrants were confronted with a series of options not even primarily of their own making, options not entirely to their taste. But it was the immigrants themselves who chose how to react; they were not simply the passive victims of large social forces. To portray the newcomers as hapless wayfarers not only robs them of their dignity, but obscures the part they played in creating a new character for America reflective of values, attitudes, and beliefs imported from around the world. . . .

The contribution of so many varied immigrant cultures to the shape of the American national character is incalculable. Incalculable if only because that contribution is so elusive; often the influence of particular groups did not become apparent for a generation or so after arrival. As the immigrants learned English, they often left the imprint of their native tongue upon local linguistic patterns. In New York, Chicago, and Philadelphia, the English spoken in Polish, Italian, or Jewish enclaves filtered into the speech of nonimmigrant residents and of other ethnic groups. Similarly, the delicacies of Greece, southern Italy, Mexico, and China found their way onto menus throughout the country. More subtly, but even more importantly, the new immigrant groups left a legacy of social, moral, and religious values which their descendants have scattered throughout the population. The fierce loyalty of Italians to family, the yearning of east European Jews for scholarship and intellectual inquiry, the Asian emphasis on family and personal honor—all of these cultural imperatives have been woven into the American consciousness.

At times, cultural differences have promoted the creation of ethnic stereotypes and rivalries damaging to America's social harmony. Ancient antagonisms imported from the Old World have occasionally found their way into national politics, and foreign policy—especially as it relates to the countries of eastern Europe—rouses the slumbering loyalties of second- and third-generation immigrants. Sociologist Orlando Patterson has charged that these loyalties, camouflaged as ethnic pluralism, make a virtue of tribalism and segregation. He and others argue that only a new universalism can counteract the primitive parochialism of those who seek to preserve their old world customs in America at the cost of social cohesiveness and justice for the individual. However, others disagree. Sociologist Richard Gambino uses the term "creative ethnicity" to describe the predominately constructive rather than divisive role that new immigrant values contributed to American culture. According to Gambino, the varied heritages of new immigrants have been and can continue to be the inspiration for creative solutions to social problems which result from life in an affluent, geographically mobile, highly secular society in which individuality, material progress, and change often take precedence over community responsibility, order, and stability. . . .

A standard greeting among Chinese immigrants was, "When are you going back to China?" recalls historian Betty Lee Sung. "As a young child, I remembered the adult conversation invariably revolved around going back to China. I gained a deep impression that China must be some sort of fairyland paradise." Years later, however, the conversation changed, according to Sung. "Nowadays, when I go to visit my mother's good friend, I hear no more talk about going back to China. This woman's children are grown and married, living in their own homes near her. Her life, her roots are deeply imbedded in American soil. . . . She barely speaks a word of English, but her mind is now oriented to the thought that she is going to spend the rest of her days in the United States."

The Huddled Masses: The Immigrant in American Society, 1880–1921, by Alan M. Kraut, from pp. 180, 182, 184, 185, 188. The American History Series, © 1982 by Harlan Davidson, Inc. Reprinted with permission.

Jacob S. Coxey led his army of unemployed workers into Washington, DC, where Coxey was arrested and his army dispersed by club-wielding police. *(Courtesy, Culver Pictures)*

Culture and Political Thought in an Industrializing Nation

COXEY'S ARMY

"Coxey's army is no longer a joke," wrote a Washington newspaper as the Commonwealth of Christ marched over the Pennsylvania mountains. "The growth and progress of this horde of desperate characters are most serious matters for Washington to contemplate." The Secret Service feared that Coxey's band of unemployed workmen marching on the District of Columbia in 1894 might raid the United States Treasury.

The depression of the mid-nineties was a blockbuster. Most of the nation's railroads went into bankruptcy; banks closed by the hundreds, businesses by the tens of thousands; millions of workers lost their jobs. Thousands of workers, especially in the Far West, banded together into so-called armies of the unemployed to seek work. Jacob S. Coxey's inspiration was to transform these aimless unfortunates into a "petition with boots on."

Coxey was a successful businessman, a pillar of the community of Massillon, Ohio. In rimless glasses and a well-cut business suit, this forty-year-old man of medium height and build, brown hair, small mustache and earnest but undramatic speech hardly seemed a terrifying figure. Coxey offered his followers a program: "Good Roads and Non-Interest Bearing Bonds." Both would have authorized the secretary of the treasury to issue legal tender notes. Under the Good Roads Bill, the federal government would use the notes to hire workmen. Under the Bonds Bill, local and state governments could employ men on municipal improvement projects. Something like this plan, condemned as madness in the nineties, would become government policy in

HISTORICAL EVENTS

1868
Ulysses S. Grant elected President

1872
Grant reelected President

1874
Women's Christian Temperance
Union formed

1876
Rutherford B. Hayes elected
President • National Baseball
League formed

1878
New York Symphony formed

1879
Henry George's *Progress
and Poverty,* the century's
nonfiction best-seller

1880
James A. Garfield elected President

1881
Garfield assassinated • Chester A.
Arthur becomes President • Boston
Symphony formed

1883
Metropolitan Opera House opens

1884
Grover Cleveland elected President

continued

the next great depression of the 1930s. Coxey illustrated the sincerity of his belief in this panacea by christening his son Legal Tender Coxey and bringing him and his mother on the great march to Washington, D.C.

Coxey laid the groundwork for his enterprise with some care. He secured the cooperation of leading Populists and of numerous labor groups. Although most of the marchers were genuinely unemployed workmen, the charlatans and publicity seekers of the age did not pass up this opportunity. One, in fact, was at Coxey's right hand: Carl Browne, known familiarly as "Old Greasy" for his presumed hostility to bathwater. Huge, bearded, and unkempt, Browne was always dressed in a Wild West costume, complete with Mexican silver half-dollars for buttons. Soon to join them was a man quickly dubbed "the great unknown." A born leader who rapidly gained an important place in the army, he refused to reveal his identity, giving reporters a running story with which to flummox their readers. He was "Captain Livingstone, late of the British army" by one account; "Jensen, a Swede employed by the Pinkerton detective agency" according to another. A woman—the wife of the Great Unknown?—swarthed in heavy veils would appear and disappear. Then there was Cyclone Kirtland, the Pittsburgh astrologer; Honore Jaxon, half-breed Indian dressed in feathers and hired by the Chicago *Times* to make the march while eating nothing but oatmeal; and snappily dressed Douglas McCallum, author of "Dogs and Fleas, by one of the Dogs."

Coxey's daughter by an earlier marriage ran away from home to join him in Washington and led the hosts as the "Goddess of Peace" dressed in white with flowing blonde hair on a prancing stallion. In Washington only twelve hundred others converged with Coxey's group of a mere five hundred, and instead of Congress enacting his program under the pressure of soul force, police arrested Coxey and Browne for stepping "upon certain plants, shrubs, and turf then and there being and growing" on the Capitol grounds—in short, for disobeying a Keep Off the Grass sign.

There were points that almost no one got. The age of media politics had arrived. Coxey's real achievement was in forcing the newspapers to do his work for him. The charlatanism, the comedies, the sensations had performed a function: While publicizing the trivial, the newspapers had carried the serious message of want and need as well. Eventually, the nation would learn that media exposure, the manufacture of events, could have serious political meaning. Coxey's march was a beginning for an important strain in twentieth-century public life. And Coxey never changed: in 1928, shortly before his death, he was still good copy, as he again urged a march of the unemployed on Washington. Few took such unemployment seriously in 1928, but they would soon see their error. Before long, men would be marching again, and for the same reason that Coxey had led his Commonwealers.

Education

The cities that brought slums, smells, bad housing, and political corruption were also places where people learned and enjoyed themselves. The wealthy, of course, had the best opportunities for enjoyment. But more serious means of expanding minds and imaginations presented themselves in the cities. There talent from all over the country congregated in pursuit of training and self-cultivation, audiences and fame. In cities the newest and most interesting ideas got displayed, argued over, and exchanged. There millions of immigrants learned about American life and acquired the skills needed for a living.

Public Schools   Those of us used to the failings of big city schools today may be startled to discover that during the late nineteenth century and early twentieth, the city public school systems were at the forefront of American education. Before the Civil War most of the northern and western states had created free public school systems. The South lagged behind.

The typical rural school in 1890 was a small building with a single teacher and students of all ages and levels. These little red schoolhouses were generally not the cozy institutions that a later generation would recall with nostalgia. Some were drafty and cold in winter and stifling and airless in spring. Many of them had only a single class. Few teachers stayed for more than a year or two. Sessions were usually short, seldom lasting more than a hundred days a year. Compulsory attendance laws notwithstanding, parents often kept their children out of school for household or farm chores.

City schools enforced attendance laws. Each level of pupils had its own classrooms. Teachers were relatively well paid and trained. City schools also had money for laboratories, auditoriums, indoor gyms. Many city school systems toward the end of the century adopted kindergartens, borrowing the idea from Germany. Free secondary education first appeared in the cities. Fewer than 100,000 attended public high schools in 1878; in 1898 there were over half a million, most of them located in large or middle-sized urban centers.

City school curricula consisted of reading, writing, and arithmetic, with some history, geography, literature, and civics. Public high schools included Latin and geometry, and had begun to provide science, some commercial courses, and even some modern foreign languages. Nowhere as yet was a public school pupil exposed to the wide range of "practical" courses that, for good or ill, are available to students today. Much learning was still by memorization from a text and students who were slow might receive punishment by ridicule or paddling.

Assimilation   The greatest task, and triumph, of city school systems in this era was in adapting to American society the foreign-born children or second-generation offspring of recent immigrants. In many big-city neighborhoods these pupils were virtually

In 1870 a former resident of Hancock County, Maine, urged his daughter Mary to learn "to kep school" and not go to the "facters" [factories]. He added from personal experience:

"If I had good lerning I wood not be so hard up all the time. I wos oferd the sherff ofes but I dasent take it for I did not know a nof to do the bissness."

Only a limited number of immigrant parents eagerly attended night schools. Those who did, such as this woman, could gain much from the experience:

"For the last two winters I have been going to night school. I have learned reading, writing and arithmetic. I can read quite well in English now and I look at the newspapers every day. I read English books, too, sometimes. . . .

I am going back to night school again this winter. Plenty of my friends go there. Some of the women in my class are more than forty years of age. Like me, they did not have a chance to learn anything in the old country. It is good to have an education; it makes you feel higher."

the entire school population. Almost all of their teachers were young women either of native stock or of assimilated immigrant backgrounds. Some of these teachers regarded their pupils as strange and difficult to communicate with. Some found distasteful the religion or ethnic backgrounds of those they taught. It is a wonder, then, that the schools did remarkably well. In 1900 the American-born children of European parents were more literate than most children of American-born parents. The schools also tried to imbue their charges with American middle-class values, the work ethic, and knowledge of history and institutions.

In all this the schools also did some injury. Learning to be Americans meant for some children learning to despise their own early culture. Aside from doing emotional damage to the children themselves, the assimilation process often made for conflict between children and their families, and between children deeply affected by their school experience and their peers who failed to accept Americanization as thoroughly. Most sons and daughters of immigrants had a double identity: they were both Americans and offspring of the old country.

Universities and Colleges   Most of the state universities and the land-grant colleges that contributed so much to the American achievement in scholarship and learning were located in small communities such as Urbana, Ann Arbor, Madison, and Berkeley. Yet many of the leading institutions in this era were urban. Beginning with Johns Hopkins of Baltimore and joined soon after by the University of Chicago, Columbia, Harvard, Yale, and other city universities, the urban institutions led the movement into graduate

A geology field trip in the 1880s set out from the administration building of Smith College.
(Courtesy, Smith College Archives)

Edward Clarke argued that higher education destroyed the health and reproductive capacities of young women. Clarke gave as an example a young Vassar College student:

"Miss D——— went to college in good physical condition. During the four years of her college life, her parents and the college faculty required her to get what is popularly called an education. Nature required her, during the same period, to build and put in working-order a large and complicated reproductive mechanism, a matter that is popularly ignored,—shoved out of sight like a disgrace. She naturally obeyed the requirements of the faculty, which she could see, rather than the requirements of the mechanism within her, that she could not see. Subjected to the college regimen, she worked four years in getting a liberal education. Her way of work was sustained and continuous, and out of harmony with the rhythmical periodicity of the female organization. The stream of vital and constructive force evolved within her was turned steadily to the brain, and away from the ovaries and their accessories. The result of this sort of education was, that these last-mentioned organs, deprived of sufficient opportunity and nutriment, first began to perform their functions with pain, a warning of error that was unheeded; then, to cease to grow; next, to set up once a month a grumbling torture that made life miserable; and, lastly, the brain and the whole nervous system, disturbed, in obedience to the law, that, if one member suffers, all the members suffer, became neuralgic and hysterical. And so Miss D——— spent the few years next succeeding her graduation in conflict with dysmenorrhœa, headache, neuralgia, and hysteria. Her parents marvelled at her ill-health, and she furnished another text for the often-repeated sermon on the delicacy of American girls."

education and research that converted the college into the university and brought American higher education to the level of Europe's best.

Starting with Mount Holyoke and Vassar, Smith, Bryn Mawr, and other women's colleges were founded before the end of the century. The movement to provide higher education for women confronted male hostility as well as occasional support. Leading male educators argued that women's physiology in general, and menstrual cycles in particular, made them too weak to support the mental and physical strain of higher education.

Questions about what education was best suited for women persisted throughout the century. While some women frankly sought to provide themselves with an education that would permit them to take their place in the public world beside their brothers and enjoy economic independence, other advocates of women's higher education contended that it would make them better companions for middle-class men and better mothers for middle-class children.

Sports

Children have played games wherever they have been. But rural adults, already engaged in strenuous physical activities in the open air, had relatively little need for sports. The amusements we associate with them were dances, socials, house-raisings, and "bees" designed to bring isolated people together. But city dwellers, confined to monotonous work in factories or sedentary work in offices and stores, craved recreation in the open air. As one observer noted in 1902, "the disappearance of the backwoods and the growth of large centres of population have created the demand for an artificial outlet, and . . . games are the

A woman wrote in a Minneapolis newspaper:

"I can't see but that a wheel is just as good company as most husbands. . . . I would as lief talk to one inanimate object as another. . . . Another great superiority of the bicycle lies in the fact that you can always get rid of it when you wish."

A musical tribute to the team, 1869. *(Courtesy, American Antiquarian Society, Worcester, Massachusetts)*

natural successors of the youthful activities of a pioneer period." Often the facilities did not match the craving. Open space was hard to find. City folk flocked to the parks on weekend afternoons to play baseball, or picnic, or stroll. But until well into the new century there simply were not enough open spaces, and at some risk even in those days of horse-drawn vehicles, children played tag, hide-and-seek, and stickball on the city streets.

Bicycling   One sport that city people could take up was basketball, invented by James Naismith in 1891, which could be played indoors. Another was the bicycle. Until the 1890s bicycles had enormous front wheels and tiny rear ones, and it was difficult for anyone but trained athletes to use them. Then came the "safety" bicycle with two wheels of equal size. Bicycling soon became a virtual craze. Thousands, including many women, took it up. Frances E. Willard, the prominent temperance advocate, wrote *A Wheel Within a Wheel: How I Learned to Ride the Bicycle* to advertise the pleasures of "wheeling."

Many American cities and towns had ordinances against Sunday spectacles of any sort, whether games or theatrical performances. These blue laws sought to keep Sundays as a day of worship and religious contemplation. Largely the work of evangelical Protestants, the Sabbath laws often met resistance from Roman Catholics and others. Toward the end of the century the strict keeping of the Sabbath began to give way. "Where is the city in which the Sabbath is not losing ground?" lamented one rock-ribbed gentleman in 1887. "To the mass of the workingmen Sunday is no more than a holiday . . . it is a day for labor meetings, for excursions, for saloons, beergardens, games and carousels."

Baseball   On those liberated Sundays baseball flourished. Descended from several children's games, baseball in its modern form had appeared during the 1840s in the New York area as a gentleman's game. A decade later it began to attract artisans and laborers, some of them forced to play at dawn before going to work. Soon people were coming to watch as well as play, and teams charged admission to their fenced fields. During the Civil War, informal soldier teams spread interest in the sport, and that led to a proliferation of teams in the years following. In 1869 the Cincinnati Red Stockings began to hire players for paid admission exhibition games, and soon afterwards William A. Hulbert organized the National League of Professional Baseball Clubs, with teams in New York, Philadelphia, Hartford, Boston, Chicago, Louisville, Cincinnati, and St. Louis. Baseball got still greater attention from the next generation as city crowds reached out for things to keep themselves amused. By the late 1880s annual attendance at the National League games had reached eight million a year. Semi-professional groups and small-town clubs drew their own crowds. The American League was formed in 1899. For a while each league fought to supersede the other. But then they settled their dispute and in 1903 joined in the first world series. Baseball had become the national game.

The New York Polo Grounds, ca. 1900, where larger and larger crowds turned out to watch the country's national sport of baseball. *(Courtesy, The New-York Historical Society)*

Boxing and Football

Among the sports that city people were paying to see was boxing. During the 1880s and 1890s some Irish Americans—Paddy Ryan, Jake Kilrain, Robert Fitzsimmons, and, above all, John L. Sullivan—dominated the heavyweight lists. Like other sports, boxing was a ladder up for the talented of all races, most notably for Germans and blacks. In 1908 Jack Johnson, a black man, won the heavyweight championship.

The first college football game was probably played in New Brunswick, New Jersey, between Rutgers and Princeton in 1869, four years after the Civil War. As James Weeks has written, football was frequently described in the metaphor of war; it was played, one observer wrote, on "the field of battle." A survivor of Richmond's grim Libby prison noted that "the blood of the whole community is stirred by physical contests among the picked youth of the land, as once it was only stirred by tales of battle." During the reform era of the early twentieth century the sport was denounced as brutal. But on the gridiron even death was worthwhile, *The New York Times* said, "if it educated boys in those characteristics that had made the Anglo-Saxon race pre-eminent in history." By the last decade of the nineteenth century at several major universities scandals and sleaze marked the continued popularity of the sport.

Sports and Social History   During most of this period sports remained primarily a male interest. Women bicycled, played such genteel games as croquet, and practiced archery. They also became baseball enthusiasts in fair numbers. But girls, though many did heavy farm labor or relentless factory work, were supposed to be fragile, and custom forbade their participation in strenuous body contact sports. It would take another generation before women's interest in sports came to seem perfectly normal, and until almost our own day before professional woman athletes came into their own.

While both participation in sports and observance of them had ancient precedents, and both could take place in rural as well as in urban cultures, they are strongly expressive of modern urban civilization. Sports as an activity not only serve in the absence of the daily physical routines of agriculture, but also represent in some degree the modern bent for turning the process of living into rational, purposeful projects. Just as for several centuries the Western world, according to some social historians, has made of work something more specific, more conscious and deliberate, more clearly timed than it once was, so in the last century we have pursued sports as specific activities, instead of merely letting exercise happen in the course of the day. Spectator sports are modern in another way. They are events that engage large numbers of strangers in similar acts of observing and judging, so that people at opposite ends of a city in the late nineteenth century had opinions of the same baseball player on the home team. This bringing together of strangers who observe and think about the same event gives sports something in common with the plays and the musical performances that flourished in late nineteenth-century urban culture. What is happening in all these instances is the shaping of a modern urban public.

Amusements

Until the 1880s most American playwrights produced comic pieces or sentimental melodramas. In the eighties Bronson Howard began to write plays with believable characters and situations. James Herne's *Shore Acres* (1892) was the first prominent American play to embody the artistic style commonly known as realism: a style that in literature and drama presents without sentimental or heroic illusions the facts and troubles of real life. Between 1890 and 1910, David Belasco and Charles Hoyt wrote witty comedies rather than the broad farces of earlier decades.

Music   Many cities established major orchestras. New York's symphony, begun in 1878, the Boston symphony, initiated in 1881, and the Chicago symphony, which dates from

The newly invented Ferris wheel, designed by George W. G. Ferris, was a major attraction at the World's Columbian Exposition, Chicago, 1893. *(Courtesy, Chicago Historical Society)*

1891, soon rivaled the best in Europe. In 1883 a group of wealthy New Yorkers built the Metropolitan Opera House for the first resident American opera company.

Music, to countless Americans of the day, meant the sentimental, catchy products of Tin Pan Alley. New York's music publishing district turned out reams of sheet music to be played on the family piano while mother, father, and the children warbled out the words. Much of this music was saccharine, but some of it entered into the folk heritage of the American people. Tunes such as "After the Ball" (1892), "The Sidewalks of New York" (1894), "On the Banks of the Wabash" (1896), and "O Promise Me" (1889) are sung today.

A considerably zestier brand of popular music had appeared in the "darktowns," the black ghettos of American cities. Ragtime was syncopated, with the emphasis on the upbeat. Much of it was instrumental, to be played on the piano or on wind instruments. When vocal, it was often fitted with risqué words that offended prim and proper people.

Attacked by critics as "vulgar, filthy, and suggestive music," it attracted the young as well as those Americans who had had their fill of sentimental ballads. In the hands of Scott Joplin, a black musician from Texas, it reached a level of sophistication much appreciated today. By 1914 the ragtime craze was over, but it had left its permanent mark. The jazz that became nationally popular in the years after World War I borrowed from ragtime.

Vaudeville was open to black performers, who brought to it influences of the minstrel shows they had earlier played to exclusively black audiences. A few minstrel singers, including the popular Al Jolson, were whites in "blackface" makeup, but most were black. The music drew from jazz, gospel, and folk music. Both white and black performers played to the racial prejudices of white audiences.

Vaudeville In the dissemination of popular songs, sheet music took its place beside the vaudeville performance, the stage revue, the minstrel show, and the musical comedy.

In 1907 the impresario Florenz Ziegfeld began to present his reviews, which would feature comedians such as Bert Williams, Eddie Cantor, and Fannie Brice, along with scantily clad showgirls and tuneful songs. More widespread was vaudeville. Composed of comic skits, acrobatic acts, animal performances, dancing, and music both serious and comic, vaudeville achieved immense popularity with city audiences between 1890 and 1920. At one time New York had thirty-seven vaudeville houses, Philadelphia thirty, and Chicago twenty-two. Hundreds of performers made excellent money touring one of the better circuits that took them to scores of American cities. During its heyday, about one in seven Americans attended the vaudeville show at least once a week.

In the working-class neighborhoods and ethnic ghettos of the great cities lived thousands who could not afford the fifty cents of a vaudeville seat or spoke no English and could not follow the skits and comedy routines. By the opening years of the new century a medium had arrived that would appeal to these people, and attract millions of others as well.

Motion Pictures Motion pictures had awaited the development of electric or arc lights, photography, flexible celluloid film, and electric motors as well as lenses. The whole complex of inventions came of the fertile brain of Thomas Edison, though not at first as a projected film. Edison's kinetoscope of 1889 was a black box with a light. The viewer looked through an eyepiece at a backlighted moving film strip recording a brief story, or bit of moving scenery, or some action. Edison made these peep shows in a tarpaper shack at his laboratory in New Jersey. He rented these to arcade operators, who quickly learned that the public would pay a penny or two for the novelty of seeing lifelike miniature figures moving before their eyes.

Edison's peep shows could handle only one paying viewer at a time. By 1895, however, the projector that showed a large picture on a screen had appeared. All the operator needed was an empty store where he could place some chairs and his projector. But the new, large audience also called for something more ambitious than a one- or two-minute sketch, and as audiences increased it also became commercially feasible to provide these features. Before long Edison and a dozen other entrepreneurs were producing full-reel films running for twenty minutes or half an hour, with a wide range of stories and themes. These featured chases, comic sketches, dancing, travel scenes, and even early trick photography showing fantastic happenings. Among the early titles were "Umbrella Dance," "Venice," "A Narrow Escape on the Baltimore and Ohio Railroad," "The Ups and Downs of Army Life," and "The Kiss." Probably the first fully realized film with a story that provided a beginning, development, and denouement was *The Great Train Robbery* (1903).

By the opening years of the twentieth century the movies had become a major form of big-city entertainment. Enjoyment of a film did not require literacy or even an understanding of English; since films were silent it was essential for producers to make them understandable by visual means alone. By 1905 three thousand primitive movie theaters were in operation, most charging only a nickel—hence the name "nickelodeon." Soon afterward a few operators began to design halls exclusively for movie viewing and these became ever more elaborate. By the eve of the First World War there were 13,000 movie houses together catering to from five to seven million viewers a day. Audiences belonged to all ranks of society, but much of the popularity was among the poor. As one magazine noted, "in the tenement districts" the movies had "well nigh driven other forms of entertainment from the field."

The building of movie palaces in well-to-do neighborhoods made moviegoing respectable for middle-class families and inaugurated an important transformation in the kinds of movies produced. Throughout the early twentieth century, and especially after the advent of talking pictures, more and more attention would be given to middle-class women as the chosen movie audience. Plots accommodated the new clientele, and the whole cult of the movie star grew up around personalities such as Mary Pickford. Stars like her offered one of the few models of female success that corresponded to dominant ideas of women's roles, and girls would begin to dream of becoming stars themselves. But studio publicity departments also forced stars to share details of their own lives and to encourage ordinary middle- and lower-class women to identify with them.

Some stars of the silent screen were real ranchmen, among them steely-eyed William S. Hart. *(Courtesy, Museum of Modern Art)*

Chautauqua   The movies and the radio were two of the most extensive means of opening up the small towns and the countryside to the manners and doings of the cities and the rest of the world—though newspapers and other publications had been doing that since colonial times. Before the movies was the Sears, Roebuck catalog. From 1874 into the twentieth century existed an institution so exciting, and so answering to the hungers of rural Americans, that into the age of television older people would be speaking of it with nostalgia. The Chautauqua was something of a traveling show, with a difference: it aimed at educating, and at educating seriously. It might spend weeks in a town, presenting major political speakers, economists, and scholars in diverse fields; and in its later years it was holding seminars attended by backcountry folk whom city dwellers were supposed to scorn for their mental sluggishness. The Chautauqua brought not only impersonal knowledge but controversial beliefs. Villagers were

Rose Stokes, who worked in a sweat-shop making cigars, wrote of her attraction to socialism:

"Within the limited franchise for women I voted for socialist candidates (for school offices) when I became of voting age and went about with the vague notion that some day, in some way, we workers would abolish wage-slavery. When the local political boss, who had a saloon on Orange Street, asked me to 'vote Democrat,' I proudly announced that I was a socialist and would vote for socialist candidates only. Although friends had warned me that 'without this man's good-will no good can come to anybody in the entire neighborhood.'

Once a worker named Morris loaned me a copy of a [socialist] magazine published in Chicago. I remember only one thing in it . . . The Factory Whistle, four lines. I never forgot them:

'Across the flats, at dawn, the monster screams;
Its bulk blots the low sun. Ah, god of truth!
To wake from night's swift mockery of dreams,
To hear that hoarse throat clamoring for my youth!'

An attempt was made to organize several of the stogie factories. We hired a little hall, got the workers to attend several times; speeches were made; the group held together. But when we applied for membership in the Cigar Makers Union, we were told by the American Federation of Labor that there was no room in the union for unskilled workers."

hearing of socialism, woman suffrage, the justice of the labor movement. Along with public libraries that by the end of the century were opening in small towns as well as cities, the Chautauqua represented a popular belief in the good of knowledge and the world of ideas.

And so, by the second decade of the twentieth century, the lives of millions of Americans had been transformed by the forces of industrialization. In 1860 most adult Americans had worked as farmers or tillers of the soil of some kind, living in isolated farmsteads, cut off from much of the world around them. By 1910 far fewer than half were farmers. For millions in the cities life was congested, noisy, hectic, and often unhealthy. But it was also richer, more colorful, more interesting, and more aware than rural living had been. And many of the city problems, it soon became apparent, were not intractable. By the opening years of the new century there would be those who called the American city "the hope of democracy."

Radical Thought

Socialism   In the nineteenth century a number of social critics in Britain, continental Europe, and the United States came to fix their attention on the nature of work in modern society. Part of their concern was in reaction to modern technology itself. Many observers were convinced that modern factories and machines degrade the status of the workers, denying them the creativity that craftsmen once enjoyed. Others perceived a modern economy as offering especially sophisticated forms of work, replacing crude labor with verbal, mechanical, or mathematical forms of thought. But both sets of critics agreed that capitalism debases work by depriving the productive classes of control over the means of production and by reducing economic activities to their commercial values. The object, then, should be to put individuals and small groups of workers in control of the tools, machines, mines, and other instruments of productivity. That meant taking property out of the hands of capitalist and other privileged classes. Such ideas became grouped under the name socialism.

The ideas of the German theorist Karl Marx became so prominent by the late nineteenth century that the terms "socialist" and "Marxist" have often been used synonymously, to the displeasure of non-Marxist socialists. Marx described history as moving in definable stages, in each of which a laboring class had been subject to an oppressor class. In the most recent stage, according to Marx, workers came under the domination of industrial capitalism. In the end workers, made class conscious and militant by their experience, were to rise up against the now-rotten system and overthrow it. Thereafter, mankind would be free of economic exploitation and injustice and would finally advance to a new stage of steady progress, equality of wealth and power, and an end to class struggle.

Some socialists have rejected Marxism for describing history as a set of rigidly formal stages rather than as events that can change as a result of human decisions. Anti-Marxist radicals of this kind have wanted socialism to be not a scheme for mapping out history but a flexible and continuing method of criticizing social inequities. These include the inequities of the Soviet Union and other twentieth-century nations ruled by Communist parties that called themselves socialist. How the final overthrow of capitalism could be brought about has been in contention among socialists, Marxist and non-Marxist. Some believe that it could be done through peaceful means: a socialist party in a democracy can win a majority and legislate capitalism out of existence. Others hold that only violence can oust the capitalists from the seats of power.

Socialist Parties The first Marxist socialists in the United States were Germans who brought their new theories with them, some democratic and peaceful, some violent. During the 1870s the Marxist Workingmen's Party and the Social Democratic Party attracted a few foreign-born workers and a still smaller group of native-born Americans. Daniel De Leon's Socialist Labor Party, founded in the late 1870s, had fewer than 1,500 members in the early 1880s. At the very end of the century Eugene V. Debs, former leader of the American Railway Union who was sent to jail for defying a federal injunction during the Pullman strike, helped organize the Socialist Party of America. In 1904 the party, with Debs as its presidential candidate, won about 400,000 votes. In the next decade, after the arrival of many thousands of additional eastern Europe immigrants and an awakening of interest among American workers, the Socialist Party vote and membership rose sharply. In 1912 its growth would peak with the achievement of almost one million votes for Debs in that year's presidential election, about six percent of the total votes cast.

Conservatives saw socialism as an extreme danger and were not averse to discrediting all reform or indeed all attempts to improve the lot of wage earners as being the work of violent revolutionaries. In 1886, during a labor rally in Chicago's Haymarket Square a lethal bomb was thrown, and under questionable legal procedures a number of anarchists were convicted of the crime. In response, conservative journalists and opinion-makers were quick to attack all labor union leaders as agitators and dangerous radicals. In later years, many who dissented from the social and economic status quo would suffer similar attacks. These assaults were to be a heavy burden for both reformers and revolutionaries.

The basic structure of American life doomed the socialists to a peripheral political status. Some intellectual historians argue that to have a truly revolutionary tradition, the United States would have needed an aristocracy or a permanent peasant class, both conspiciously absent here. Even the American Revolution of 1776 was more of a rebellion against British political authority than a genuine revolutionary upheaval against the upper classes. Millions of immigrants came to the

Eugene V. Debs.

Eugene Debs thrilled audiences with his grand oratory. He once proclaimed:

"While there is a lower class, I am in it; while there is a criminal element, I am of it; while there is a soul in prison, I am not free."

new country hoping to better themselves, and they often defined success as the ownership of private property—a farm or a house or a small business of their own. And socialists, many Americans somewhat incorrectly believed, aimed to expropriate all private property.

Anarchism   Anarchism, which also had a following in late nineteenth-century American radical circles, carries to its farthest point the socialist hostility to institutions that are seen as enslaving workers or degrading the act of work. But while socialists have been willing to make use of government as an instrument of justice and equality, anarchists insist on the total abolition of government along with all but the smallest and most intimate forms of property. They hold that property gives its owners power over the propertyless. Anarchists desire the liberty and fulfillment of every human being. Some anarchists have argued for individual acts of violent rebellion or for popular revolution. But others have been pacifist, believing violence to be, like government, an unjust act of control by one person over another.

The two most visible anarchists in the United States in the later nineteenth century, both of them anarcho-communists, were Emma Goldman and Alexander Berkman, part of the wave of Jewish immigrants from the Russian empire. During the Homestead strike of 1892 Berkman wounded the Homestead manager Henry Clay Frick with gun and knife. He spent fourteen years in prison for his crime. Emma Goldman became the best-known advocate of anarchism as well as a leading advocate of free speech and women's rights. In 1919, during a popular wave of antiradical anger following the First World War and known as the Red Scare, she and Berkman were deported.

Other Visions   A late nineteenth-century alternative to socialism, anarchism, and the capitalist system of the time was the social philosophy of Henry George. His *Progress and Poverty* of 1879 became the century's nonfiction best-seller. Every individual has the same right to the life-sustaining land as to the air we breathe and the water we drink, argued George; private monopoly of land, then, violates life itself. The worker should have possession of whatever each has made, but all human beings should jointly control the land. While practical concerns may dictate that individuals possess and work specific portions of the land, justice demands that the government tax all value that comes of that private possession and use the revenue for the good of the whole community. This is to be the only tax. George's ideas, which ever since has been identified by the label "single-tax," won wide acclaim here and in Britain, Ireland, and Australia and continue to have advocates.

Also appealing was the pleasant future Edward Bellamy presented in his 1888 utopian novel, *Looking Backward,* describing a society carefully and humanely planned to serve human need and provide great freedom for every individual. During the 1890s writers, artists, editors, and ordinary middle-class men and women joined Nationalist clubs dedicated to Bellamy's "principle of association": cooperation in place of competition as the basic mode of social and economic conduct.

Alexander Berkman (top), and Emma Goldman (bottom).
(Courtesy, Library of Congress)

The Mainstream Parties

It was a brash, energetic, at times flamboyantly vulgar period, the staid old rural ways receding in face of the society and culture of the burgeoning cities and an agriculture increasingly enmeshed in the industrial forces of the day. Politics in the Gilded Age did not so much direct the course of things. For a time, national politics had a brilliantly roguish figure in the floridly dressed, witty Roscoe Conkling, a New York Republican who played Washington patronage games quite openly. The two major parties were remarkably well matched. From the 1870s onward, control of the national government seesawed back and forth between them. From the end of the Civil War to the mid-1890s there were more Republican than Democratic Presidents, but Democrats Tilden in 1876 and Cleveland in 1892 received more popular votes than their Republican opponents, though fewer votes in the electoral college. Dominance in Congress shifted from one party to the other. There were very few years between the end of Reconstruction and 1896 when one party simultaneously controlled the presidency and both houses of Congress.

President Ulysses Simpson Grant. *(Courtesy, Library of Congress)*

From Grant to Harrison   In 1868 Ulysses S. Grant, the final field commander of the Union forces in the Civil War, defeated his Democratic opponent, former governor Horatio Seymour of New York, on a platform endorsing Radical Reconstruction but also promising sectional peace. Grant's electoral college victory was decisive, but his popular margin was only 300,000 out of almost six million ballots cast. In 1872 Grant badly beat the Democratic candidate, *New York Tribune* editor Horace Greeley. In 1876 compromise between the alleged winner, Republican Rutherford B. Hayes, and Democrat Samuel J. Tilden eliminated Republican control of South Carolina, Florida, and Louisiana, and ended Reconstruction. In 1880 the Republican Party pitted Congressman James A. Garfield of Ohio against Winfield Scott Hancock of Pennsylvania. Both had been Union generals. Garfield won with a solid electoral college majority of 214 to 155, but his popular majority was under 10,000 votes.

Garfield's presidency was no great pleasure to him, and it had a cruel ending. He spent much of his time dealing with clamoring seekers of public office. After four months in the White House, he was shot by a disappointed claimant for a federal job. His Vice President and successor was Chester A. Arthur, a former abolitionist and during the Civil War quartermaster general of New York State. Arthur made an effective and dignified President. He helped pass the Pendleton Act of 1883, which set examinations for hiring in about a tenth of federal civil service jobs. The act lessened the prevalence of the spoils system, whereby an incoming party got to fire employees of its defeated opponent and replace them with party loyalists. That the Pendleton Act had the support of Arthur, widely perceived to be no more than a political hack, was a surprise. In the Republican convention of 1884 the party regulars passed over him and turned to the charismatic James G. Blaine of Maine. The Democrats chose the reform governor of New York, Grover Cleveland. The campaign was a dirty one. Blaine was accused,

President Garfield (middle), assassinated four months after taking office in March, 1881, was succeeded by Chester A. Arthur (bottom). *(Courtesy, The New-York Historical Society, New York City)*

Grover Cleveland campaign badge from the election of 1892, in which Cleveland defeated the incumbent Republican, Benjamin Harrison, and the Populist James B. Weaver to become the only President in American history to serve nonconsecutive terms of office. *(Courtesy, The New-York Historical Society, New York City)*

President Benjamin Harrison. *(Courtesy, Library of Congress)*

with good reason, of having taken bribes from a southern railroad for his support while he was a United States congressman. Some held it against Cleveland that he had fathered an illegitimate child. The Mugwumps, a group of Republican reformers offended by Blaine, rallied to the Democratic New Yorker. The name Mugwumps, from a northeastern Indian term for a great man, was apparently given them by enemies who saw them as self-importantly moral. Blaine inadvertently offended Catholic voters when he failed to reprove a bigoted Protestant supporter who, in his hearing, declared the Democrats the party of "rum, Romanism, and rebellion." Cleveland won by a hair: the electoral vote, 219 to 182; the popular vote, 4.9 million to 4.8. Here is a good example of the even balance between political parties of the times.

Cleveland was the first Democratic President since James Buchanan, and his administration was marked by controversy with Union veterans unused to a man who had not served in the Union Army. (Every President from Grant through Arthur had held the rank of general during the war.) Veterans resented deeply Cleveland's vetoes of pension bills and his effort to have the War Department return to the southern states captured Confederate battle flags. Honest government men, however, admired his principled stands in favor of civil service, a reduction in the protective tariff, and what they called sound money, meaning the gold standard.

In 1888 Cleveland, renominated as the Democratic candidate, emphasized tariff reduction during the campaign. The Republicans nominated the aloof but eloquent Benjamin Harrison of Indiana, still another Union general, on a platform supporting pensions and a high tariff. The election turned on the foolish statement of the British minister to the United States that he would like to be able to vote for Cleveland. This "Murchison letter" was published, and many Irish Americans defected to Harrison to give him the election. But the results again were close. Cleveland actually won 100,000 more popular votes than his rival, but lost the key states of New York and Indiana and received an electoral minority.

As President, Harrison rewarded his business supporters by signing the McKinley tariff of 1890, pushing rates to the highest level up to that time. The huge federal revenues that the tariff brought in gave the government large surpluses, with which it awarded generous pensions to Union veterans. So spendthrift was Harrison's first Congress that critics labeled it the "billion dollar Congress." In the 1890 congressional elections the Democrats won a large majority, gaining control of the House of Representatives.

The election of 1892 again pitted Cleveland against Harrison. This time a strong Democratic current was running and Cleveland, emphasizing his support for sound money and a tariff for revenue only, defeated his former opponent by a popular vote of 5.5 to 5.2 million and an electoral count of 277 to 145.

The Parties in Balance The disputes that informed these elections may not greatly interest a twentieth-century American, accustomed to arguments over poverty, social justice, and war. In considerable measure it was party loyalty itself, a loyalty that by now has much lessened, that drew voters to either of the two stolidly nineteenth-century candidates.

Relatively equal nationally, the two parties differed in strength from region to region. New England tended to be strongly Republican, and areas where people of New England descent lived, in northern New York and the older Midwest, also voted heavily for what had become known as the Grand Old Party. The South, on the other hand, was overwhelmingly Democratic, except in a few areas where, during the Civil War, sentiment for the Union had been strong. In the Midwest, areas settled by southerners before the Civil War—"Copperhead" or peace Democrat country—also voted for the Democrats.

These sectional patterns were an extension of the old antislavery battles of the 1850s: those Americans proud that slavery had been struck down and the Union preserved voted for the party of Lincoln; southerners continued to vote against it. Republican voters remembered the Civil War and, if they did not, Republican politicians quickly reminded them of it.

Republican politicians went out of their way to cultivate the Union veteran vote and to woo the Union veteran organization, the powerful Grand Army of the Republic (GAR). Former Union soldiers were urged to "vote as you shot." Whenever they could muster majorities in both branches of government, the Republicans appropriated money for Union veterans and widows. The billions paid out as pensions were meant, no doubt, as expressions of a nation's gratitude to those who had served it well. But they also held the veterans more firmly to the Grand Old Party.

Black voters, too, remembered the antislavery battles of the Civil War. In the years following "redemption" in the South, unfriendly southern state governments excluded many blacks from the franchise. In the North, black Americans voted Republican, in gratitude to the party of Lincoln for emancipation and as protest against the party of slavery and rebellion. Not until Franklin D. Roosevelt's New Deal of the 1930s were blacks to enter the Democratic Party in overwhelming numbers.

Party Differences   In contrast to the present-day party, the Republicans were more inclined than the Democrats to support a strong and active federal government. They endorsed a protective tariff, and they were the more strenuous of the two parties in turning federal lands over to the railroads. At the turn of the twentieth century, numbers of Republicans would call for setting the powers of the government to regulating and restraining industry for the sake of the public. That was another but not opposite concept of how an active Washington could serve the nation.

The wish on the part of Republicans to support railroads and manufacturers—a wish that Democrats shared—and later the determination of Republican progressives to impose federal regulation on business practices expressed for the most part their judgments and practical alliances from issue to issue. But the earlier history of the Republican Party as well predisposed it to be comfortable with federal power. Before the Civil War, the antislavery partisans who went into the

For many decades Civil War loyalties strongly influenced Americans' voting, and Republicans made the most of it:

"Every unregenerate rebel . . . calls himself a Democrat," shouted Republican Senator Oliver Morton in one typically fiery speech. "Every bounty jumper, every deserter, every sneak who ran away from the draft. . . . Every man . . . who murdered Union prisoners . . . calls himself a Democrat. . . . In short, the Democratic party may be described as a common sewer . . . into which is emptied every element of treason North and South . . . which has dishonored the age."

new party had asserted the right of the federal legislature to keep slavery out of the territories, and Republicans spoke for northern interests that saw the backwater slaveholding South as a drag on industry and progress. Then they presided over a war to preserve the Union against rebels who proclaimed the superiority of states' rights to federal authority. During Reconstruction, Republicans followed policies, however inadequate, to change fundamental patterns of race relations in the South, adopting into the Constitution itself measures to ensure justice to black Americans. The Republicans were therefore conditioned, especially more so than southern Democrats, to favor energetic federal government. In the later years of the nineteenth century, this meant putting Washington at the service of the leading commercial and industrial forces of the age; and then it meant imposing order and restraint on them for the sake of social health. It should also be remembered that though the North by the end of the nineteenth century had abandoned the cause of racial justice, Massachusetts Senator Henry Cabot Lodge and other Republicans as late as 1890 fought unsuccessfully for a bill protecting the right of southern blacks to vote.

Currency   The question of money made for divisions between the two parties and among classes and regions. Democrats were more likely than Republicans to advocate paper money and free silver. This gave the Democratic Party a considerable following among farmers. But much of the agrarian support for silver currency was among western farmers, joined by the western silver-mining interest. The election of 1896 revealed that New Jersey vegetable gardeners, midwestern dairy, corn, and hog farmers, and citrus growers in California doubted that inflating the currency with silver would be to their advantage. Financiers had a stake in gold: as creditors, they wanted to receive dollars backed by that most valuable of metals. Urban workers too could prefer the gold standard for ensuring the solidity of their wage and preventing inflation of the prices of consumer goods. Nor were Republicans neatly separated from Democrats on the issue. Many western Republicans supported silver. A wing of the Democratic Party, and notably President Grover Cleveland, favored gold.

Religious Differences in Politics   Within the Republican Party was a strong strain of moral and moralistic evangelical Protestantism. Many Republicans were supporters on the local level of blue laws—outlawing business and public recreation on Sunday—and laws against the sale of liquor. It was common among Americans of older stock to identify immigrant cultures with alcohol as well as Catholicism or other supposedly foreign persuasions or to fear that the new immigrants from southern and eastern Europe were fundamentally inferior. The American Protective Association, formed in 1887 and Republican by inclination, aimed to guard the nation's politics against the influence of Catholicism and immigrants. Organized in 1894, the more genteel Immigration Restriction League demanded that newcomers be screened by literacy tests. Many urban political machines appealing to groups of immigrant extraction were Democratic, a notable exception being that in Philadelphia.

The moralistic Protestantism of Republicans, like the party's taste for strong national government, had based itself in evangelical Protestants who defined slavery as a sin. To Protestants the Roman Catholic Church looked to be a force alien like slavery to free American institutions, and to reinforce this idea they need only observe the hostility of many Irish immigrants to blacks and to abolitionism. Among evangelical Protestants, Republicanism passed from parents to their evangelical offspring. There the preoccupation with sin, earlier fixed on slavery, could turn to banning liquor or Sunday baseball.

Doubtless the moral fabric of the republic could survive Sunday baseball. But alcoholism was a real problem. In rural regions, heavy drinking was common; amidst the brutal poverty and disorder of the crowded cities it was widespread. Not only petty moralism but a concern for the social good was involved in the effort to control the effects of drinking, an effort that eventually coalesced with movements opposing child labor or exploitation of workers.

Few eligible American voters in this era failed to exercise their franchise. Elections were exciting events. A resident of Burnside, Connecticut, in 1876 wrote of "two torchlight processions here one Republican and one Democrat." Turnouts often reached ninety percent of those eligible, and almost all strongly favored one of the two major parties. At least one group of upper-class, well-educated gentlemen refused to pledge loyalty to either party. The Mugwumps favored civil service reform, efficient and honest government, sound money, and free trade, and were willing to use either party to achieve their goals. But the Mugwumps were not typical of their time. As one observer noted, "What theatre is to the French, or the bull fight . . . to the Spanish, the hustings [electoral campaigning] are to *our* people."

Politics after 1892

The Populists in the election of 1892 had brought to national politics a clarity of principle that had been lacking for many years. The restlessness that Populism expressed was to remain through the election of 1896. Within months of Cleveland's victory, the country's economy faltered. In early 1893 a severe panic swept the nation, bringing five full years of depression. Hard times would alter the political perceptions of the American people and intensify the mood of political and social dissent.

Coxey's Army   The economy sank lower and lower. In the industrial regions, factories closed, and thousands of men were thrown out of work, many to tramp the streets, others to ride the rails from town to town looking for jobs or handouts and clashing with local police. One expression of the general breakdown was a march on Washington organized by Jacob Coxey of Ohio to demand that Congress appropriate $500 million in greenbacks to finance a public-works program. The program, it was argued, would create jobs, and the

A Pittsburgh union member wrote of Coxey's army:

"The movement is a *glorious* one. Long live *Coxey*. All recruits from here will be provided with rations for two days. One mammoth chicken pie. . . . I am satisfied that this is the turning point in the history of the United States. The results will be far reaching, and the name of Coxey will go thundering down the ages relegating to oblivion that of Washington and Lincoln. Many dropped out of the line of march or were detained by the authorities, who feared that the 'petition in boots' represented a dangerous radicalism. In late April 1894, about four hundred soldiers of the army straggled into Washington led by Coxey's seventeen-year-old daughter dressed as the goddess of peace. Coxey announced 'We're going to camp right on our own property.' Their leaders were arrested for trespassing on the Capitol lawn. Coxey observed to reporters: 'Of course, I appreciate as well as anyone else the fact that the preservation of the grass around the Capitol is of more importance than saving thousands from starvation.' "

greenbacks would inflate the economy, bringing high prices to business and agriculture.

Starting from various parts of the country, including the Far West where some followers seized a train, several thousand men in "Coxey's Army" set off for the nation's capital. At first enthusiasm was unrestrained. But once the marchers arrived in Washington many were arrested for trespassing, and the movement petered out.

Silver vs. Gold   President Grover Cleveland blamed the economic distress on the Sherman Silver Purchase Act (1890). Ever since its passage, he believed, business had been jittery. As the amount of silver coming into the Treasury's vaults grew larger and larger, it had become increasingly difficult to uphold the gold standard. Speculators and ordinary citizens, worried about the government's ability to redeem silver coin or paper money in gold on demand as the gold standard required, were coming to the Treasury to demand gold in exchange for their paper. With each passing month gold reserves diminished, and speculators and citizens became still more nervous. This uncertainty had knocked the economy off balance. Panic withdrawals of Treasury gold had become a flood, and it looked as if the country would have to go off the gold standard. To "gold bugs" like Cleveland and other eastern conservatives, such a prospect was terrifying. The fall of gold, some were certain, would bring the collapse of civilization.

One of Cleveland's first responses to the depression was to demand the repeal of the Silver Purchase Act. The Populists in Congress resisted fiercely. So did many southern and western Democrats and a few mountain state Republicans. By this time Populist ideas, especially

---

THE BIG SQUEEZE

An important part of American history is the story of the entrepreneur. For this businessman, James Kymer, the depression of 1893 was a shock:

"I went to work in Ohio with the rosiest expectations, only to find that there were many things about railroads that I did not know. The financing of such ventures was *terra incognita* to me. The Lancaster and Hamden [Railroad], however, was being built at a time such as I had never before experienced. Without my knowing it, the depression of 1893 was on the way. Some stock in the line had been sold, and a bond issue was to be floated. From these two sources the expense of building was to be met.

I was to do all the work, and things looked bright, but presently I was told that the money that had been raised by the sale of stock had been exhausted, while the bond issue had been delayed. I paid my men and bought my supplies, therefore, out of my own pocket. I could af-

ford to, and thought but little of it. The following month the same thing happened, and the month after that. I was low on funds but had no trouble in borrowing what I needed. . . .

I borrowed more and more, but property values were falling, and my holdings were soon mortgaged to the very hilt. Being told that the bond issue still had not been floated, I myself went to New York to force it through. It was not until then that I realized just what had happened. Bond issues were impossible. Money could not be had.

I returned badly frightened. I pounded tables and argued. I fought and swore and fought again. But it was hopeless. I gathered up my last remaining assets—selling, mortgaging. I raised enough to pay my bills in Ohio. And finally, seeing at last the hopelessness of it all, I took a train for Omaha with barely money enough left in all the world to get me home. I could not even afford a Pullman berth. I did not buy a meal along the way, but

regarding finance, had deeply penetrated the western and southern Democracy, and Democratic congressmen from these sections were willing to break with the eastern wing of their own party over the issue. Despite the opposition, Cleveland was able to muster enough votes to get the measure repealed; but the administration's position alienated many southern and western Democrats.

The repeal did little to rescue gold. As the depression tightened its grip, imports declined, and with them government gold revenues. At the same time, a nervous public further depleted the Treasury. By December 30, 1893, reserves had fallen to $80 million. To save the gold standard, Cleveland began to borrow gold from bankers in exchange for government bonds. But continued public fears promptly drew out of the Treasury the gold that had come into it. By early 1895 the reserve was down to $45 million, and it looked as if the silverites and other inflationists would finally realize their ambition of seeing the nation pulled off the gold standard.

At this point, Cleveland's secretary of the treasury approached the international banking house of J. P. Morgan and Company and August Belmont, a representative of the European Rothschilds. They promised the government 3.5 million ounces of gold on demand in exchange for $62 million in federal bonds. This stemmed the withdrawals temporarily, but led to angry charges by the silverites that the government had sold out the nation to the money power. Finally, after another $100 million gold purchase in 1896 the public became convinced of the Treasury's ability to maintain the gold standard, and the threat to the reserve ended. Cleveland had saved the gold standard, but only at the cost of worsening the split within his party.

---

existed instead on cheese and crackers that I had bought before I started.

I stepped onto the station platform in Omaha a tired, discouraged man. My wife had preceded me by a month or so, and when I reached home she put her arm about me and I cried.

What a tower of strength she was to me! For a time I could not bring myself to do a thing, thinking that the worst of calamities had befallen me—not knowing that what had happened was a trifle beside what was still to come.

I got about at last, trying to make a little money, but none was to be made. That year of 1893 had come, and with it every opportunity was lost.

I fought with every artifice I knew to keep my home. I traded horses when I could, but a year went past and what few dollars had been left had grown still fewer. At the stockyards in Omaha sheep were offered at fifty cents a head, with few buyers. Farmers were burning their corn because they could not sell it for enough to buy fuel. The whole nation was laboring under an eco-

nomic collapse of such severity as to seem to us almost unbelievable.

Horses at the stockyards were selling at such ridiculous prices that even I could buy some. I bought a carload and took them east, selling them in Pennsylvania and doubling my money. Still it amounted to nothing, and a letter from my wife telling me that she was ill brought me home as fast as I could come. . . .

She went to the hospital while holders of mortgages were hounding both of us. I fought them off—with nothing. I held them back in every way I could. To Hell with mortgages! How could I pay for the treatment my wife required?

A month passed. My wife grew weaker. The holders of those mortgages were constantly insistent. I fought with all my strength, my back against the wall. On the thirtieth of March, 1895, my wife died. . . .

I was left with two boys—one eighteen and one sixteen years of age. I had nothing. I owed the doctors, owed the undertaker, owed even for the cemetery plot where now my wife was lying."

William McKinley (top) decisively defeated "the boy orator of the Platte," William Jennings Bryan (bottom), and the Silver Democrats in 1896 to become the 24th President. *(Top, Courtesy, the New York Public Library Picture Collection; bottom, Courtesy, Mrs. Ruth Bryan Rohde, Ossining, New York)*

The Bryan Campaign of 1896

Circumstances promised that 1896 would be an exciting election year. Both parties had their silver wings, and it appeared that there would be major internal battles in each over both platforms and candidates.

In June 1896, the Republicans met at St. Louis to choose their candidates. Supported by his close friend and financial backer, the industrialist Mark Hanna, Ohio Governor William McKinley won the nomination. As a congressman, McKinley had introduced the high-tariff bill of 1890 that bore his name. McKinley's protectionist principles had long identified him with the industrialists, and his choice was a victory for the Northeast: a victory confirmed by the convention's adoption of a high-tariff platform, with only a nod to silver. In reaction, Senator Henry Teller of Colorado and a number of other western Republicans bolted the Convention and soon afterward organized the National Silver Republicans.

The Boy Orator of the Platte

In July, the Democrats met in Chicago. There the battle was far more bitter and divisive.

In March 1895, two western Democrats, congressmen Richard Bland of Missouri and William Jennings Bryan of Nebraska, had thrown the challenge to the eastern leaders by demanding the immediate adoption of free and unlimited coinage of silver. "Silver Dick" Bland was the front-runner as the delegates gathered, but coming up fast was ex-congressman Bryan.

Young, dynamic, handsome, eloquent, Bryan was in many ways a politician's dream. Born in Illinois in 1860, he had attended a small Protestant college where he absorbed a moralistic view of society and the oratorical rhythms of the Bible. In 1887 he moved to Lincoln, Nebraska. There he practiced law and joined the Democratic Party. He was elected to Congress in 1890 and served until March 1895.

Bryan was a sincere and simple Christian who accepted the literal truth of the Bible and interpreted human history as a titanic struggle between good and evil. To a Nebraska Democrat at that time, this meant perceiving gold as an agent of the dark forces and silver as an agent of truth and light. Bryan believed that humanity was being oppressed by the money power. In preparation for the struggle in Chicago he honed and polished a memorable address.

Battle was first joined over the platform, the eastern gold bugs insisting on support of the gold standard and the western and southern bloc along with Bryan demanding "the free and unlimited coinage of both gold and silver at the present legal ratio of 16 to 1: sixteen ounces of silver to one of gold." Speakers for the West and South, including Senator Benjamin Tillman of South Carolina and Governor John Peter Altgeld of Illinois, denounced gold and Cleveland. In response, David Hill of New York declared: "I am a Democrat, but I am not a revolutionist. My mission here to-day is to unite, not to divide—to build up, not to destroy." The silver platform, he insisted, would destroy the party in the East.

One of the last speakers was the young Nebraskan, Bryan. The crowd, knowing his reputation for eloquence, was expectant.

Starting with a modest disclaimer of any special insight, Bryan announced that "the humblest citizen in all the land, when clad in the armor of a righteous cause, is stronger than all the hosts of error." Bryan challenged the eastern view that free silver would disrupt the business of the nation. Gold, he said, had already disturbed the business of the West and South. He would not, he declared, "say . . . one word against those who live upon the Atlantic coast, but the hardy pioneers who have braved all the dangers of the wilderness . . . these people . . . are as deserving of the consideration of our party as any people in this country." After reviewing the other planks of the silver group's platform, Bryan moved on to the issue of silver. "The Battle," he proclaimed, was between "the struggling masses" and "the idle holders of idle capital." The Democratic idea is that if you "make the masses prosperous, their prosperity will find its way up through every class which rests upon them." The gold Democrats claimed that the great cities were in favor of the gold standard; the silverites replied that the cities rested on the foundation of the nation's "broad and fertile prairies." "Burn down your cities and leave our farms and your cities will spring up again as if by magic; but destroy our farms and the grass will grow in the streets of every city in the country." Then came Bryan's electrifying conclusion: "You shall not press down upon the brow of labor this crown of thorns, you shall not crucify mankind upon a cross of gold."

The Election of 1896   A half hour of bedlam followed the address, western and southern delegates cheering and parading up and down the aisles of the Chicago coliseum. When brought to a vote, the silver platform passed overwhelmingly. The next day the delegates began to ballot for their presidential candidate. On the fifth roll call, Bryan became the Democratic candidate.

The Bryan nomination posed a dilemma for the Populists, who met at St. Louis shortly after the Democrats adjourned. Was Bryan, as some argued, a Populist in all but name, and would supporting him give the People's Party its best chance of getting its program enacted? So-called Fusionists favored this course. On the other side were those Populists who opposed reducing their program to the single issue of silver. No doubt Bryan's rhetoric was populistic, but was he a real reformer? No, better to nominate a separate ticket, even at the risk of electing McKinley. The delegates at St. Louis "split the difference," it was said, nominating Bryan for President and choosing their own vice-presidential candidate.

After Chicago, many disgruntled eastern Democrats returned home determined to sit on their hands in the fall. A few, however, were too outraged at their defeat to remain simply inactive. In September these gold Democrats met in convention and nominated a National Democratic Party ticket.

The campaign that now ensued was one of the most exciting in the nation's history. The struggle was largely sectional. If Bryan had won, in all likelihood there would have been a shift of political emphasis toward the needs of the South and West. On the other hand, it is hard to believe that any major change in relations between labor and capital, or

BRYAN, BRYAN, BRYAN, BRYAN
by Vachel Lindsay

The Campaign of Eighteen Ninety-six, as Viewed at the Time by a Sixteen-Year-Old

I brag and chant of Bryan, Bryan, Bryan,
Candidate for president who sketched a silver Zion,
The one American Poet who could sing outdoors,
He brought in tides of wonder, of unprecedented splendor,
Wild roses from the plains, that made hearts tender,
All the funny circus silks
Of politics unfurled,
Bartlett pears of romance that were honey at the cores,
And torchlights down the street, to the end of the world. . . .

Prairie avenger, mountain lion,
Bryan, Bryan, Bryan, Bryan,
Gigantic troubadour, speaking like a siege gun,
Smashing Plymouth Rock with his boulders from the West. . . .

Election night at midnight:
Boy Bryan's defeat.
Defeat of western silver.
Defeat of the wheat.
Victory of letterfiles
And plutocrats in miles
With dollar signs upon their coats,
Diamond watchchains on their vests
And spats on their feet.
Victory of custodians,
Plymouth Rock,
And all that inbred landlord stock.
Victory of the neat.
Defeat of the aspen groves of Colorado valleys.
The blue bells of the Rockies,
And blue bonnets of old Texas,
By the Pittsburgh alleys.
Defeat of alfalfa and the Mariposa lily.
Defeat of the Pacific and the long Mississippi.
Defeat of the young by the old and silly.
Defeat of tornadoes by the poison vats supreme.
Defeat of my boyhood, defeat of my dream.

any major shifts in wealth and power, would have resulted from victory. It is not even certain that Bryan as President could have succeeded in getting the nation to abandon the gold standard.

Be that as it may, Bryan and his supporters saw the campaign as a crusade for the people, and wherever "the boy orator of the Platte" went, he urged his audiences to support the cause of the "toiling masses." In the West and South, Bryan gathered great crowds who cheered him as an evangelist. But in the East he made little headway. A sober speech before a large audience in New York's Madison Square Garden, designed to quiet eastern fears, was a disappointment and thereafter the Nebraskan entertained small hope of winning the East.

Meanwhile, McKinley conducted a dignified "front porch" campaign. Delegates would come to the McKinley home in Canton, Ohio, with prepared questions and remarks, and the Republican candidate would respond in a neighborly way. The Republicans were gorged with cash raised by Mark Hanna from among fearful industrialists and bankers. This enabled them to send out scores of speakers to follow Bryan to rebut his charges, and to mail out millions of pamphlets and broadsides warning the public that a Bryan victory meant revolution and the collapse of the dollar.

The popular McKinley's presidency was cut short when he was assassinated by an anarchist. The black leader W. E. B. Du Bois took the opportunity to connect the anarchism of the assassin, Leon Czolgosz, with the anarchy of lynching:

"In the midst of the season of deepest grief, when the heart of a nation is shedding tears of sorrow as perhaps it has never before done for an individual, is it not a fitting time to stop to take our bearings that we may know whither we are drifting? With united voice we condemn the individual who was the direct cause of removing the, perhaps, most tenderly and universally loved President the nation has ever had. But in all sincerity, I want to ask, is Czolgosz alone guilty? Has not the entire nation had a part in this greatest crime of the century? What is anarchy but a defiance of law and has not the nation reaped what it has been sowing? According to a careful record kept by The Chicago Tribune, 2,516 persons have been lynched in the United States during the past sixteen years. . . . We cannot sow disorder and reap order. We cannot sow death and reap life."

McKinley   The Republican campaign had its more positive side. McKinley was depicted as the herald of prosperity. The Republican tariff would restore good times and usher in the era of "the full dinner pail." Republican campaigners also spoke for unity and an end to ethnic and class conflict in the nation.

McKinley's victory in November was fairly decisive. Garnering 7.1 million votes to his opponent's 6.5 million, he carried much of the Midwest, Northeast, and West Coast, leaving Bryan chiefly the southern, plains, and mountain states. And even the South was not solid for the Democratic candidate; for the first time in a generation Delaware, Maryland, West Virginia, and Kentucky went Republican. Even more significant was Bryan's failure to capture the traditionally Democratic cities. Many wage earners, perhaps following the lead of Gompers's AFL, refused to support free silver. The tariff was attractive to workers wishing their industry protected against foreign competition. Bryan's evangelical style, his identification with the rural regions, his homespun character failed to captivate the urban masses. Nor did the Democratic candidate, any more than Populist candidate Weaver in 1892, inspire the more successful farmers of the older Midwest.

McKinley's victory brought to the White House the last veteran of the Union army to become President. Every Republican Chief Executive from Grant onward had served with the Union forces: McKinley differed from the others in not having been a general. The election was a turning point in the political history of the era. Thereafter the Republicans forged ahead of their opponents and became the majority party of the nation. Over the next thirty-five years the Democrats would win the presidency only twice, and the first time largely as the result of a severe Republican split. Voting percentages declined; more and more Americans lost interest in the act of voting.

By the time of McKinley's inauguration the country was experiencing a vigorous economic revival. Prices for farm commodities and other products began to rise by 1897, bringing prosperity to farmers and businessmen and providing a lively labor market for wage earners. During the next decade, except for a brief setback in 1907, the economy advanced rapidly, raising living standards and soothing discontent. In 1900 the silver issue was laid to rest for thirty years by passage of the Gold Standard Act, confirming and reinforcing the American commitment to gold as the backing for the American dollar, and providing some help to farmers in need of loans by authorizing national banks in rural communities.

And there was one other reason why the outsiders ceased to raise their voices in loud protest. Within a year of McKinley's inauguration, the country was at war with Spain over Cuba. Before long, patriotism and the appeal of imperial glory had captured the imaginations of Americans. When new protests appeared, they would come from different people and be couched in a different vocabulary.

A New Spirit

So ended, for practical purposes, the agrarian revolt of the era. It left as a legacy a chapter in the distinctive history of American radicalism, a story of movements that have aimed to empower small landholding and propertyless individuals and gather them into cooperative enterprises. It also left a contribution to American literature and folklore. L. Frank Baum's *The Wonderful Wizard of Oz*, not published until 1900, with its imagery of silver slippers, a wicked witch of the East where dwell financiers, the industrial worker made of tin who is mistakenly afraid that he has no heart, and a remaining complex of characters that tell of the struggle with the controllers of money. And in the years when farm radicalism, the silver controversy, and an increasingly articulate labor movement were in the public consciousness, a number of practical reformers along with leaders in religious and academic speculation were shaping new ways of thinking about social and moral problems. Many of them were on the fringes of political life; yet their work contributed to major strands in early twentieth-century social and political thought.

Dorothy Gale and the Wicked Witch of the West. In Frank Baum's book *The Wonderful Wizard of Oz*, written by a Nebraska populist in the 1890s, Dorothy wore silver slippers, symbolic of free silver. The wicked witch of the West is said to represent malign nature. *(Courtesy, MGM)*

The WCTU   One movement was by no means on the fringes. Abstinence from alcohol, voluntary or enforced by law on the state level, had been an objective of a highly visible wing of social reform for much of the century. Opponents of alcohol had also championed other reform objectives, among them abolition of slavery. The Women's Christian Temperance Union, founded in 1874 following a series of local women's crusades against drinking, achieved a special status among all women's organizations. By the 1920s it would attain a membership of over a half million, which made it one of the largest women's groups. In the late nineteenth century, the WCTU organized women from all over the country but especially the Midwest.

The WCTU had reformist implications far beyond the single issue of drinking. Alcohol abuse was perceived, rightly, as a threat specifically

Carry Nation became famous for her ax-wielding attacks on saloons. She meant to draw attention to the struggle, and so gladly went to jail—where she is headed in this photograph, taken in Enterprise, Kansas, in 1901. *(Courtesy, Kansas Historical Society)*

to the family and generally to social health. Attacking drunkenness therefore meant defending morality and public order as a whole. In time, for example, saloons came to be seen as evil not merely because they dispensed liquor but because they were centers of vice and social disintegration. They drew husbands away from their families, offered fancy women a place to seduce men, and provided a headquarters for political machines and their corrupt deals. Americans fearful of immigration associated liquor and saloons with alien cultures and favored prohibition as a means of control over immigrant populations. Frances Willard, leader of the organization, gained an interest in political rights for women so that they could force respect for their causes. The WCTU became an advocate of granting women the vote so that they might carry their special domestic virtues into the public sphere. Frances Willard along with the WCTU developed a subtle understanding of the demoralizing effects of poverty and their contribution to drunkenness. She became a member of the Knights of Labor and called for betterment of the lot of workers.

In all this, the WCTU is to be ranked among the groups committed to "social housekeeping," or subjecting public institutions and especially the unmanageable cities to the high standards of domestic purity and order. Cleaning up the city and its social and political ills was to be conceived as a project comparable to cleaning a house. Concern for the children who were victims of urban poverty and squalor was an expression of nurturing. For the betterment of the city, women labored for goals as humble as improvement of lighting and sewage systems, as lofty as art museums. Some objectives might require agitation for regulatory law; others could be the work of private organizations. The idea that cities could be remade by reforms addressing themselves at once to personal morality and to the social good was a conviction that would endure in American public life.

Settlement Houses   In 1889 Jane Addams and her friend Ellen Gates Starr, borrowing the idea of settlement houses from Great Britain, opened Hull House in Chicago's run-down Nineteenth Ward. Settlement houses, arising in many cities, made careers for women in social service, education, and political activism. The settlements provided nurseries and playgrounds for children, adult education for parents, and opportunities for study for visiting experts. Women and men residents entered reform politics and used their education in the settlements to develop plans for sanitary legislation, factory reform, labor legislation, and a host of municipal programs. One Christmas, the residents at Hull House were puzzled when neighborhood children refused gifts of candy, until they learned that the children were working six days a week in a candy factory. From the settlements, middle-class Americans could learn to appreciate the culture of the new immigrants and become aware of the armies of working women and children whose labors made life more comfortable for the favored classes.

Work in settlement houses provided middle-class women with a firsthand introduction to the problems of urban society. For all their sympathy for immigrants, these settlement workers normally sought to help the immigrants to adapt to American life, which meant in some measure to adopt American values. Settlement women tried to teach poor immigrant women how to keep house properly, how to feed their children, and how to provide them with health care. In their efforts, the settlement workers frequently came into conflict with the urban political bosses who sought to organize the immigrant communities according to different principles. Settlement workers like Jane Addams decided that women must have the vote in order to implement correct public standards. In this respect, settlement workers were of one mind with Frances Willard, who argued that women must do everything—including things that had previously been viewed as unfitting for women—to bring their own values to society.

Florence Kelley, who for many of her generation exemplified the best of the reform spirit, began her pathbreaking career when in 1891 she left New York for Hull House. There she helped lead to the creation in 1893 of the first state law regulating the hours and working conditions of women and children, and Governor John Peter Altgeld appointed her the first chief of factory inspection. Altgeld, according to her recollection, wanted the law enforced to the hilt, but the district attorney for Cook County, which includes Chicago, refused to prosecute any of the cases she and her staff brought. She thereupon acted in conformity with her approach to social reform, and to life in general. She enrolled in Northwestern University's Law School, completed her law degree by 1894, and successfully prosecuted the factory safety law violators herself.

When Governor Altgeld was defeated for reelection in 1897, Florence Kelley lost her job of chief factory inspector. She proceeded to help organize a new kind of public interest lobby, the Illinois Consumers' League in 1898. The League published a "white list" of companies that lived up to the law and urged its members, most of them middle- and upper-class women, to boycott manufacturers who did not have the League's seal of approval. There was scarcely a progressive cause in which Florence Kelley did not take a leading role. Newton D. Baker, a fellow reformer and later Woodrow Wilson's secretary of state during World War I, summed up her ability to inspire a whole generation of young women, and men: "Everybody was brave from the moment she came into the room."

Intellectuals

In the later years of the nineteenth century, a few intellectuals were rethinking fundamental questions in law, society, and psychology. Much of their work must have read at the time as mostly academic and speculative. But in years to come, when the Populist revolt had faded along with the issue of silver coinage, reformers seeking to base their ideas in a firm understanding of society and human nature would be turning to intellectuals and scholars for help.

Florence Kelley has left a remarkable account of her introduction to Hull House:

"On a snowy morning between Christmas 1891 and New Year's 1892, I arrived at Hull-House, Chicago, a little before breakfast time, and found there Henry Standing Bear, a Kickapoo Indian, waiting for the front door to be opened. It was Miss Addams who opened it, holding on her left arm a singularly unattractive, fat, pudgy baby belonging to the cook, who was behind hand with breakfast. Miss Addams was a little hindered in her movements by a super-energetic kindergarten child, left by its mother while she went to a sweatshop for a bundle of cloaks to be finished.

We were welcomed as though we had been invited. We stayed, Henry Standing Bear as helper to the engineer several months, when he returned to his tribe; and I as a resident seven happy, active years until May 1, 1899, when I returned to New York City to enter upon the work in which I have since been engaged as secretary of the National Consumers' League.

I cannot remember ever again seeing Miss Addams hold a baby, but that first picture of her gently keeping the little Italian girl back from charging out into the snow, closing the door against the blast of wintry wind off Lake Michigan, and tranquilly welcoming these newcomers, is as clear today as it was at that moment.

Henry Standing Bear had been camping under a wooden sidewalk which surrounded a vacant lot in the neighborhood, with two or three members of his tribe. They had been precariously employed by a vendor of a hair improver, who had now gone into bankruptcy leaving his employees a melancholy Christmas holiday. Though a graduate of a government Indian school, he had been trained to no way of earning his living and was a dreadful human commentary upon Uncle Sam's treatment of his wards in the Nineties."

William James   William James, elder brother of the great novelist Henry James, was at Harvard for thirty-five years. A serious knowledge of art, a degree in medicine, travel in Europe, and even early experience on a scientific expedition to the Amazon went into the profile of this scholar with a rare flexibility of mind. His charm, vivacity, and urbanity sparkled in his lectures and his popular prose. He was the most widely known American intellectual since Ralph Waldo Emerson.

James's seminal work, *Principles of Psychology* (1890), was an extraordinarily effective critique of the determinism and pessimism that characterized Social Darwinism, with its view that evolution and change were a process over which human beings had no control. In this and his later work, he presented a way of looking at existence that came increasingly to be known as pragmatism. Founded in the writings of several philosophers, among them Chauncey Wright and Charles Sanders Peirce, pragmatism holds that an idea is to be tested by its ability to give order and clarity within the flux of human experience.

James's version of pragmatism made use of the concept of the stream of consciousness, the stream of thoughts and sensations that flows through us. As James saw it, this gushing river is an unending source of uniqueness and creativity. Each of us is free to impose moments of order on the stream, seeking ideas that give form to some cluster of sensations and thoughts within it, relentlessly testing out and recycling ideas that do not provide a satisfactory order. For James balanced freedom with a rigorous method of examining the usefulness of ideas. True ideas, in effect, are true not in having some kind of inner coherence or truth but in helping their possessor to negotiate the endless detail presented in consciousness. In this sense, James was to be the exemplar of the reform spirit of the early twentieth century, in which both social theorists and politicians strove to order what seemed an unending and chaotic flow of social and economic events.

The New Scholarship   John Dewey's development of progressive education was a prime example of the new ways of thinking. Pragmatism invited a young generation of social critics to view a particular social problem not as formal textbooks would describe it, but by means of continual experimentation. They were urged to try out one theory or practical reform after another until the reformer finds a program that exactly answers to the detail of the problem. Dewey's way of teaching children sounds like training them to do precisely that kind of experimentation. Children learn, Dewey argued, by constant encounter with their environment, constant adjustment to its facts and demands. How could their education teach them to gather data about the world around them, to form and modify hypotheses, and to apply these to practical tasks?

Dewey began, of course, by experimenting. In 1896 at the University of Chicago, he and his wife, Alice Chipman Dewey, founded their Laboratory School. There students, by pursuing the activities required in agriculture, crafts, and industry under the supervision of subtle and effective teachers, discovered their need for the various kinds of knowledge that make up the subjects usually taught in schools. In the pro-

On joining the faculty of the University of Chicago in 1894, John Dewey, a child of rural Vermont, took up the challenge of adapting American education practices and ideals to the rapidly urbanizing society that he saw all about him. His subsequent move to Columbia University's Teachers College in 1904 reinforced his commitment to his version of "progressive education."
(Courtesy, Brown Brothers)

gressive school students discovered directly what they needed to know about their social environment, just as others had once discovered such things as part of their farm chores, their encounters with nature, their dealings with other people. Progressive education, which has influenced American educational practice ever since, did not meet all the goals Dewey had charted. Nonetheless, it enabled schools to introduce an increasingly diverse and foreign-born school population to enduring parts of the American ethos, and to motivate students by showing them that their curriculum could relate itself concretely to their future lives.

In the field of law, the pragmatic ferment was apparent in the writings of Oliver Wendell Holmes, Jr., later to serve thirty years on the United States Supreme Court. Holmes, from the 1880s onward, expounded what came to be called "legal realism." He interpreted the law as a practical instrument for dealing with public and private disputes rather than as a body of sacred, immutable principles passed down in awesome splendor from Roman and medieval times. The job of lawyers, according to Holmes, was to predict as best they could what judges would decide in particular cases and to advise their clients accordingly. A knowledge of legal reasoning and precedent was valuable in the service of that utilitarian purpose rather than as an end in itself. Similarly, a judge's decisions ought to reflect the practical situation. The law, like everything else in the world, changes with the changing times. The legal past is a guide to society's expectations and therefore important in making decisions, but so are the statistics, the data, the empirical information about the present that ought to be taken into consideration in deciding a case. Louis D. Brandeis, the great "people's lawyer" of the early years of the new century, took this doctrine seriously in the case of *Muller v. Oregon,* which he argued before the Supreme Court in 1908. Brandeis was defending state laws limiting hours of labor for women, and in this defense—its presentation is known as the Brandeis Brief—he emphasized the sociological and economic effects on women of long working hours. And he made little reference to legal precedent. The court was persuaded in this case, although for many years such "Brandeis briefs" were more popular in law schools than before judges.

Political scientists late in the nineteenth century and into the twentieth moved away from theoretical issues of natural rights or the character of sovereignty. They turned their attention to the actual workings of institutions like Congress—as in Woodrow Wilson's *Congressional Government*—or the activities of pressure groups, explored in Arthur F. Bentley's *The Process of Government*. At Columbia University, the political scientist John W. Burgess began to examine the economic motives behind political decision-making. Instead of deducing correct economic behavior from the laws of classical theories, economists like John R. Commons and Richard T. Ely at the University of Wisconsin began to collect economic statistics and to study in close detail corporations, railroads, and the banking system. Thorstein Veblen, the renowned economist, argued in such works as *The Theory of the Leisure Class* (1899) and *The Theory of Business Enterprise* (1904) that businessmen were motivated by greed, that the economic system did not regulate itself by natural laws, and that government experts should

Many twentieth-century American liberals trace their lineage to John Dewey, who once wrote:

"Politics is the shadow cast by big business over the country."

Oliver Wendell Holmes, whose belief that the law should be treated as a utilitarian tool rather than a body of immutable principles, captured the pragmatic spirit of the Progressive Era. *(Courtesy, Scribner's Archives)*

develop policies for giving direction to the economy. *An Economic Interpretation of the Constitution of the United States,* a 1913 study of that revered document by historian Charles Beard of Columbia University, interprets it as the product not of pure and virtuous political philosophy but, at least in part, of late eighteenth-century financial interests hoping to profit from a stronger central government.

Sociologists studied urban life, prostitution, labor organizations, and poverty. Lester Frank Ward, a Brown University sociologist, rejected the older theories of laissez-faire and Social Darwinism. The evolution of society, he argued in books like *Dynamic Sociology* (1883), was not controlled by fate or cosmic natural laws. Human beings, through rational planning, could change the course of social evolution and guarantee human progress. Other sociologists made similar claims. The *Hull House Maps and Papers* (1895), a study of Chicago's Nineteenth Ward by a group of economists, socialists, and social workers connected with the activities of Jane Addams's settlement work, exemplified the many studies of American life that provided the basis for reform. With its chapters on working conditions, schools, housing, charities, settlements, and other institutions, this volume was a guidebook for reform.

As the academic study of politics, economics, and social conditions began to center on the actual crowded facts of living social systems, practical legislators and administrators would learn to consult scholars for help in designing policies.

The spiritual soul of urban progressivism was the Social Gospel movement. In huge urban slums like Hell's Kitchen in New York City, Protestant clergymen built neighborhood churches in an attempt to proselytize the largely Catholic and Jewish immigrant masses. But traditional religion somehow seemed out of place in the tenements. Poverty, disease, unemployment, family strife, and crime assumed a greater urgency than the conversion of souls. Much of urban Christianity in the late nineteenth and early twentieth centuries became committed to improving the economic plight of poor people.

The Social Gospel

In the 1870s occurred one of the waves of religious revivalism that have repeated themselves in American history. Its best known leader was Dwight Moody. Like other American revivals, this one was not narrowly sectarian and took little interest in precise theology. Its aim was to awaken in the individual an experience of faith as the beginning of personal renovation. To that end it employed dramatic, eloquent, and quite sincerely committed preachers speaking to crowds, some drawn by curiosity, others by a serious predisposition to believe. The movement made for a great increase in church membership in the years to follow.

What, however, is to follow conversion? American evangelical Protestant churches have been accused of paying too little attention to the life of virtue, compassion, and charity that is supposed to flow from faith. The engagement of antebellum Protestants in antislavery activity is a partial refutation of that claim. No discernible movement parallel to that of abolitionism came out of the revival currents of the 1870s. But at the time of the revival and afterwards, a theology was appearing that found in concrete earthly existence both the presence of sin and a command to moral action. Washington Gladden's *Working People and Their Employers*, published in 1876, is an indictment of modern industrial capitalism, laissez-faire, and Social Darwinism. Gladden argued that poverty was neither a result of vice on the part of the poor nor the inevitable product of social evolution. People were often victimized by social and economic forces beyond their control. The government and the churches should join hands, Gladden urged, to provide assistance to the urban poor. Walter Rauschenbusch, a Baptist minister working in

Hell's Kitchen in New York City, widened the argument. The Kingdom described in the Gospels, he insisted, is to be an earthly as well as a heavenly kingdom, a reign of justice and virtue. In engaging in the fight against the selfishness and brutality of economic conditions, the individual enters immediately into the Kingdom and at the same time works for its full coming to the world.

The Social Gospel also found expression in the rise of Roman Catholic social reform. In 1893 Pope Leo XIII issued the encyclical *Rerum Novarum*. A document that did not depart from Catholic theological conservatism, it addressed the economic ills of its age and expressed the church's concern over them. *Rerum Novarum* had a wide influence within sectors of the Roman Catholic Church in this country. At least a few visible clerics felt themselves liberated to discuss issues that the church had seemed fearful of confronting. Prominent priests and Catholic laymen like Patrick Ford, John Ryan, and Raymond McGowan wrote widely and called for a variety of governmental and trade union solutions to the problem of poverty.

The new academic inquiries, the quickening social conscience within religion, the social reformism that had an expression in the settlement houses: all these were to reach their largest development a few years after the defeat of Populism. Together they made for an early twentieth-century period of political and social ferment that historians commonly call the Progressive Era.

Suggested Readings

Recent scholarship includes Nick Salvatore, *Eugene V. Debs* (1982), Lawrence W. Levine, *High Brow/Low Brow: The Emergence of Cultural Hierarchy in America* (1988), Judith Ann Trolander, *Professionalism and Social Change* (1981) on settlement houses, Roy Rosenzweig, *Eight Hours for What We Will* (1982), Steven Hahn, *The Roots of Southern Populism* (1983), Mari Jo Buhle, *Women and American Socialism,* (1982), John L. Thomas, *Alternative America: Henry George, Edward Bellamy, Henry Demarest Lloyd and the Adversary Tradition* (1983), Sean Denis Cashman, *America and the Gilded Age* (1984), Barton C. Shaw, *The Wool-Hat Boys: Georgia's Populist Party* (1984), Susan Levine, *Labor's True Women: Carpet Weavers, Industrialization, and Labor Reform* (1984), Carlos Schwantes, *Coxey's Army* (1985), Shinshan Henry Tsus, *The Chinese Experience in America* (1986), Daphne Pata, ed., *Looking Backward, 1988–1888: Essays on Edward Bellamy* (1988), and LeRoy Asby, *William Jennings Bryan* (1987).

Irwin Yellowitz in *Industrialization and the American Labor Movement, 1850–1900* (1977) tells of the efforts of labor unionists in the late nineteenth century to halt or modify the mechanization of production that threatened to disrupt older ways of work. Also useful is Herbert Gutman's collection of essays, *Work, Culture, and Society in Industrializing America* (1976). Alice Kessler-Harris has written a history of working women, *Out to Work* (1982).

For an overview of politics in this era, see Michael E. McGern, *The Decline of Popular Politics: The American Party, 1865–1928* (1986), and H. Wayne Morgan's *From Hayes to McKinley: National Party Politics, 1877–1900* (1971). Robert D. Marcus examines the structure of the Republican Party toward the end of the nineteenth century in *Grand Old Party* (1971). Lawrence Goodwyn, *Democratic Promise: The Populist Movement in America* (1976) presents an interpretation of Populism, emphasizing the place in it of its left wing, the Southern Alliance.

In *One Kind of Freedom: The Economic Consequences of Emancipation* (1977), Roger L. Ransom and Richard Sutch argue that the credit and landholding systems of the postwar South bore much responsibility for the lack of progress in the region. Having no ownership or secure possession of the land they worked, poor blacks and whites had no incentive to improve it. But blacks suffered more from simple white racism than from an unfair economic system.

See also David B. Tyack, *The One Best System: A History of American Urban Education* (1975), Lawrence A. Cremin, *American Education: The Metropolitan Experience, 1876–1950* (1988), Dorothy Blumberg, *Florence Kelley* (1971), Kathy Deiss, *Cheap Amusements: Working Women and Leisure in Turn-of-the-Century New York* (1986), Mary Jo Deegan, *Jane Addams and the Men of the Chicago School, 1892–1918* (1988), and Mina Carson, *Settlement Folk: Social Thought in the American Settlement Movement, 1885–1930* (1990).

Were the Populists Backward-Looking?

Lawrence Goodwyn

Populism in America was not an egalitarian achievement. Rather, it was an egalitarian attempt, a beginning. If it stimulated human generosity, it did not, before the movement itself was destroyed, create a settled culture of generosity. Though Populists attempted to break out of the received heritage of white supremacy, they necessarily, as white Americans, did so within the very ethos of white supremacy. At both a psychological and political level, some Populists were more successful than others in coping with the pervasive impact of the inherited caste system. Many were not successful at all. This reality extended to a number of pivotal social and political questions besides race—sectional and party loyalties, the intricacies of power relationships embedded in the monetary system, and the ways of achieving a politics supportive of popular democracy itself. In their struggle, Populists learned a great truth: cultures are hard to change. Their attempt to do so, however, provides a measure of the seriousness of their movement.

Populism thus cannot be seen as a moment of triumph, but as a moment of democratic promise. It was a spirit of egalitarian hope, expressed in the actions of two million beings—not in the prose of a platform, however creative, and not, ultimately, even in the third party, but in a self-generated culture of collective dignity and individual longing. As a movement of people, it was expansive, passionate, flawed, creative—above all, enhancing in its assertion of human striving. That was Populism in the nineteenth century.

But the agrarian revolt was more than a nineteenth-century experience. It was a demonstration of how people of a society containing a number of democratic forms could labor in pursuit of freedom, of how people could generate their own culture of democratic aspiration in order to challenge the received culture of democratic hierarchy. The agrarian revolt demonstrated how intimidated people could create for themselves the psychological space to dare to aspire grandly—and to dare to be autonomous in the presence of powerful new institutions of economic concentration and cultural regimentation. . . . That idea was a profoundly simple one: the Populists believed they could work together to be free individually. In their institutions of self-help, Populists developed and acted upon a crucial democratic insight: to be encouraged to surmount rigid cultural inheritances and to act with autonomy and self-confidence, individual people need the psychological support of other people. The people need to "see themselves" experimenting in new democratic forms.

In their struggle to build their cooperative commonwealth, in their "joint notes of the brotherhood," in their mass encampments, their rallies, their long wagon trains, their meals for thousands, the people of Populism saw themselves. In their earnest suballiance meetings—those "unsteepled places of worship"—they saw themselves. From these places of their own came "the spirit that permeates this great reform movement." In the world they created, they fulfilled the democratic promise—in the only way it can be fulfilled—by people acting in democratic ways in their daily lives. . . . [T]he substance of American Populism went beyond the political creed embedded in the People's Party, beyond the evocative images of Alliance lecturers and reform editors, beyond even the idea of freedom itself. The Populist essence was less abstract: it was an assertion of how people can *act* in the name of the idea of freedom. At root, American Populism was a demonstration of what authentic political life is in a functioning democracy. The "brotherhood of the Alliance" addressed the question of how to live. That is the Populist legacy to the twentieth century.

Reprinted from Lawrence Goodwyn, *Democratic Promise: The Populist Movement in America* (New York: Oxford University Press, 1976), pp. 541–43.

Populists were agrarian men with a limited understanding of the complexities of their era. They proposed solutions to current problems which often reflected their ignorance, their isolation from the best thought of the day, and their profound sense of frustration at the intractability of their social and economic environment. Clearly we today, in a still more complex world, cannot expect inspiration from such a parochial and limited social vision.

When confronted by a more abstruse and complex aspect of the economy, or when faced by the social change which accompanied industrialization, the farmer often embraced naive and simplistic answers.

Take the money and banking systems. The Populists were obsessed with finance. But wasn't this to be expected? Wasn't Populist concern with banks, greenbacks, and silver perfectly plausible given existing conditions? Weren't farmers primarily concerned with the practical matter of reversing the long-term trend of falling commodity prices? Only in part. There were such men: men who were chiefly concerned with high interest rates and the steady decline of staple prices, and who saw inflation as the "producer's" salvation. There was this pragmatic, bread-and-butter side of Populist financial attitudes. But there was another side which was peculiarly abstract and ideological. Many Populists viewed the money question as the key to all that was wrong with American life. Solve the money problem—by abolishing the national banks and by issuing government money—and you solved the problems of poverty and social injustice, as well as the question of who ran the government. To these men, exhortations to destroy the "banks," the "bondholder," and the "money power" were a substitute not only for serious thought about the nation's real financial inadequacies, but often for serious thought about the major social and political issues of the day.

Eliminate the money question from the Populist platform and you have virtually reduced it to its peripheral issues.

Consider next Populism and the contemporary "labor problem." The Populists did seek an alliance with labor, and they did express sympathy for labor's plight. But they could offer little to industrial labor because they were outside it, and could not understand it. Their solution to the labor problem, like their solution to so many others, consisted largely in destroying the money power and manipulating their finances. From the 1860's on, labor had been skeptical of monetary solutions of its problems, and in 1896 McKinley with the tariff, not Bryan with free silver, won the labor vote.

Consider, finally, the Populist response to the city. Perhaps Americans still have not come to terms with the city, but clearly the Populist attitude was peculiarly primitive and retrograde. That the supporters of the People's party did not like the cities is irrefutable. We have all seen the archetypal Populist cartoon of the transcontinental cow grazing on the prairies while being milked in New York. Who does not know those lines from the "Cross of Gold" speech about the grass growing in the streets of the cities if the farms are destroyed? And who is not aware of the disfranchisement, particularly in the South, of the urban areas by Populist dominated legislatures? Is this all circumstantial? Then hear the direct testimony of C. W. McCune's *National Economist:* "It has been shown again and again that the masses of the people in great cities are volatile and unstable, lacking in patriotism and unfit to support a wise and pure government. The city may be the best place to use them; but the finest types of muscle and brain are almost invariably furnished by the country. . . . If the country is drained to populate the cities, decay is sure to set in." Could the message be plainer?

There is no mystery about it. Populism had a dark side as well as a light one, and critics of the agrarian movement have merely detected and described it.

Adapted with permission of Irwin Unger.

President Theodore Roosevelt operating an American steam shovel at the Panama Canal, 1906.
(Courtesy, Library of Congress)

20

The Outward Thrust
1865–1909

THE PANAMA CANAL

Since 1513, when the explorers led by Balboa (the poet Shelley mistakenly took him for Cortés), "silent upon a peak in Darien," sighted the Pacific after having traversed the Isthmus of Panama, men and women had dreamed of a linkage between the great oceans. In time that dream envisioned a canal. But formidable jungle, tropical diseases, and differences in elevations between the two oceans had posed enormous engineering barriers. In the 1880s, the great French manager Ferdinand de Lesseps, who built the Suez Canal, tried and failed to conquer the Panamanian jungle. By 1889 his firm was bankrupt. The New Panama Canal Company was organized in 1894 to assume de Lesseps's assets and, perhaps, to complete the canal. But the financial climate in France during the depression of the 1890s and the reputation of Panama for tropical disease soon moved the company's ambitions to the more modest goal of selling its rights and its rusting machinery to the United States, where public opinion stoutly endorsed ownership of a canal. A dramatic incident in the Spanish-American War, when the U.S.S. *Oregon* was forced to steam around Cape Horn to join the Atlantic fleet off Cuba, convinced most doubters that a canal was imperative. The Clayton-Bulwer Treaty of 1850 between Great Britain and the United States had removed a cause of conflict between them by declaring that neither would have exclusive control over an isthmian canal or colonize the area surrounding it. In 1901 the two

HISTORICAL EVENTS

1850
Clayton-Bulwer Treaty

1867
Purchase of Alaska

1883
Congress approves rebuilding
naval fleet

1887
U.S. secures naval rights to
Pearl Harbor

1895
Cuban Civil War

1898
Battleship *Maine* sent to Cuba • the
Maine is sunk • Teller Amendment
• Spanish-American War
• Battle of Manila Bay • war over
• Hawaii annexed • Anti-Imperialist
League

1899
Peace treaty ratified • U.S. buys
Philippines from Spain • Philippine
insurrection

continued

countries adopted the Hay-Pauncefote Treaty, in which Britain gave up its restraint over American control of a canal and the Americans agreed to open such a canal to international traffic. That freed the United States to pursue its ambitions.

The new venture pinned its future on two talented adventurers: a swashbuckling French engineer named Philippe Bunau-Varilla and a shrewd New York lawyer, William Nelson Cromwell, who would earn every penny of the $800,000 fee he eventually collected from the company. Their first task was to dissuade Congress and public opinion from choosing a Nicaraguan site for the canal. Only Cromwell's intensive lobbying and a contribution of $60,000 to the Republican National Committee produced the substitution of "Isthmian Canal" for "Nicaragua Canal" in the Republican national party platform for 1900. In May 1902, with Congress about to vote, nature seemed to conspire with Cromwell and Bunau-Varilla. The Frenchman had lobbied mightily, arguing the hazard of Nicaragua's volcanoes; and within days of the final vote, Mt. Momotombo conveniently erupted. The next morning every United States senator found in his mail a copy of an old Nicaraguan stamp showing the mountain in a previous eruption: Bunau-Varilla had scoured the Washington stamp dealers. Panama narrowly won—with the proviso that diplomatic negotiations with Colombia, of which Panama was part, be successful.

President Theodore Roosevelt, by his own report, conducted the negotiations with Colombia "without the aid and advice of anyone." Through his secretary of state John Hay, Roosevelt concluded the Hay-Herran Treaty with Colombia, which offered an indemnity of $10 million and lease payment in perpetuity of $250,000 a year. In addition, there were provisions highly offensive to the sovereignty of Colombia, including the protection of the New Panama Canal Company against any claims by that country. Colombia rejected the treaty, out of pride, but also with a greedy eye to the French company's assets and to negotiating higher lease payments from the United States.

Roosevelt was furious. Negotiating with those "dagos," he claimed, was like trying to nail currant jelly to a wall. They were "those contemptible little creatures in Bogotá," those "jack rabbits," "foolish and homicidal corruptionists," "tricky oppressors" of Panama. Hay translated these racist sentiments into a diplomatic threat of retaliation—perhaps even war. Meanwhile, the President made widely known the pleasure he would take were the Panamanians to revolt against Colombia and form an independent nation agreeable to the treaty provisions that Colombia had rejected. While making plans to seize Panama if necessary, the President was willing to wait—although not so late as the

THE COUP d'ETAT.

Roosevelt and the Republican steamship arriving with guns and shovels to build the canal.

election of 1904—to see whether Cromwell and Bunau-Varilla could bring on a revolution.

They did. At $50 a head, members of the Colombia garrisons in Panama were bought off. Hay gave assurances that warships would be in the area to protect United States life and property if disruption occurred, that is, to prevent Colombian retaliation in the event of revolution. A young woman was delegated to create a national flag, groups of firemen and railroad workers were drilled, shots were fired in the air, and the republic was proclaimed. Someone backed a mule cart up to the subtreasury building, and the Colombia military were paid in gold: $30,000 to the general, who nearly drowned in the gallons of champagne poured over his head; $10,000 to most of the officers.

Washington received news of the revolution two days later and in precisely one hour and sixteen minutes recognized the new government. The Panamanians wasted no time in dispatching two ambassadors to sign the treaty with Washington, but Bunau-Varilla was taking no chances that the new owners of that narrow strip of real estate would become as greedy or as jealous of their sovereignty as had the Colombians; he named himself the Panamanian ambassador. Roosevelt agreed to receive his credentials, and Hay promptly signed the treaty for Panama. The Panamanian republic was all of thirteen days old. Roosevelt airily asserted that the entire process had been carried out "with the highest, finest, and nicest standards of public and governmental ethics." Payment of $25 million to the Colombian government in 1921 expressed a different judgment of the proceedings, agreeing more with another of Roosevelt's statements: "I took the canal zone and let Congress debate, and while the debate goes on the canal does also."

The Outward Thrust: Beginnings

American overseas expansion dates from before the Civil War, when American interest in the Pacific resulted in the famous visits of Commodore Matthew Perry's naval squadron to Japan in 1853–54 and the almost simultaneous effort of southerners to entice Spain to sell Cuba to the United States: the island would have been a rich addition to the slaveholding part of the country. Neither probe won the United States any territory, and during the Civil War foreign relations, like all other national concerns, were subordinated to the urgent goal of defeating the Confederacy and preserving the Union.

Reasserting the Monroe Doctrine

As secretary of state during the Civil War, William Seward had to pursue defensive policies against European opportunists seeking to take advantage of the Union's preoccupation with the rebellion. During these war years France sent troops to Mexico and established there the regime of a puppet emperor, the Archduke Maximilian of Austria. Meanwhile, Spain tried to regain control of the Dominican Republic and made demands on several South American countries. Seward deplored these violations of the Monroe Doctrine, the policy of excluding further European colonization in the Western Hemisphere, first announced by President James Monroe in 1823. He complained, expostulated, and protested, but he was forced to bide his time.

With the war's victorious conclusion, Seward quickly began to exert pressure on the French and Spanish. He warned the Spanish minister to Washington that if the country persisted in seeking an entrance into the Western Hemisphere, the United States would actively support the Latin American republics feuding with Spain. The Spanish quickly abandoned their ambitions in the hemisphere. France was a far more powerful nation, yet behind Seward were fifty thousand Union veterans under General Philip Sheridan's Texas command. If these linked up with the forces of Maximilian's Mexican opponent, Benito Juárez, the French puppet empire was done for. Seward demanded that the French set a time limit for ending their occupation of Mexico. By now the French emperor, Napoleon III, was convinced that the Mexican adventure was becoming too costly and he removed his troops. Juárez's forces quickly took over, captured Maximilian, and executed him. Having dealt with Europe's version of expansion, Seward was now free to turn to his own. He promised that his countrymen would have "control of the world." Wishing to make the nation's presence felt in the Pacific, Seward favored acquiring the Hawaiian Islands, then an independent kingdom. He also wanted to buy the Virgin Islands from Denmark and to establish a major United States naval base in the Dominican Republic.

The Purchase of Alaska   Alaska, that vast northwest corner of North America which provided Seward's one great expansionist success, was then a Russian colony, having been first explored and exploited by the Tsar's agents during the eighteenth century. A beautiful land, it had at most a few thousand inhabitants, almost all either Indian or Eskimo, and few known resources except furs. The fur trade had flourished at first under the Russian-American Company, but by 1865 most fur-bearing animals were gone and the company was in financial trouble. The Tsar made friendly overtures: our "two peoples," he remarked cordially in 1866, "have no injuries to remember." Not only was the region becoming a financial liability to the tsarist regime, but it was also too far from the Russian heartland to be militarily defensible. Better, then, to sell it to the Americans. Alaska as a United States colony would be a buffer between Russian Siberia and British Canada. Russia made an offer; Seward, with the annexation of all Canada also in mind, quickly accepted. Seward paid Russia $7.2 million for the cession, and in 1867 Russia formally transferred the territory to the United States.

All this had taken place at breakneck speed, before the American public could react. But Congress as a whole, not merely the favorably inclined Senate, had to appropriate the money to pay for the territory. And before the proposed appropriation came to a vote in the House of Representatives, the public had time to respond to the purchase. The response was at best mixed. A few expansionists, like Seward himself, saw the cession as another step toward the nation's eventual dominion over the entire continent. Some Americans favored the treaty because they felt kindly toward Russia, which had supported the Union during the Civil War. A still larger number of congressmen, apparently, found generous personal gifts from the Russian minister to be a convincing argument. Yet the opposition was strong and angry. One newspaper editor thought the treaty "a dark deed done in the night." Besides, what was this place for which Americans were paying millions? It was, said a critic, "a barren, worthless, God-forsaken region." It consisted of "walrus-covered icebergs"; it was the land "of short rations and long twilights."

In the end, Congress did appropriate the $7.2 million, but it was a near thing. Alaska had cost the United States about two cents an acre.

During Seward's time in the State Department, the United States also acquired the Midway Islands in the Pacific. He saw the new possession as a coaling station for American ships, a step toward the markets of Asia, which the transcontinental railroad in linking the eastern United States to the Pacific Coast made more accessible to American industry. But few Americans recognized Seward's vision, and until the great American naval victory of 1942, the American public would have little awareness of Midway.

Seward ceased to be secretary of state in 1869, when Grant suc-

In the late 1800s, the United States and Russia began to make expansionist moves in the Pacific. The cartoon, entitled "The Two Young Giants," is from the 1870s. (*Courtesy, Bettmann Archives*)

When the Tsar's minister told Seward that the Russians would sell Alaska, he eagerly pushed away the evening's card table:

"Why wait till tomorrow, Mr. Stoeckl? Let us make the treaty tonight!"

"But your Department is closed. You have no clerks, and my secretaries are scattered about the town."

"Never mind that," responded Seward. "If you can muster your legation together before midnight, you will find me awaiting you at the Department, which will be open and ready for business."

ceeded Johnson, and for the next decade or more the United States pursued a rather unaggressive foreign policy. Grant was interested in acquiring the republic of Santo Domingo, which shared a Caribbean island with Haiti, and the Dominican leadership was interested enough that the President got a treaty to that effect. Fear that the Dominican people would not assimilate with the rest of the American public was influential in the collapse of the project.

The United States settled disputes with Great Britain left over from the Civil War. The Treaty of Washington in 1871 provided for an international tribunal to assess the degree of British blame for allowing the escape of the Confederate raider *Alabama,* and this tribunal awarded the United States $15.5 million in damages. In 1878 the United States received rights to establish a naval base at Pago Pago in the Samoan Islands in the mid-Pacific. Yet on the whole, few Americans paid attention to international events. American foreign policy of the 1870s has been described as the "nadir of diplomacy." Expansion beyond continental limits seemed a preposterous idea. The *Chicago Tribune* noted soon after the Civil War: "we already have more territory than we can people in fifty years."

Overseas Expansion

Generations of Americans had wanted greatness for their nation, but a greatness that came of the perfection of its own institutions and the example it could set for the Old World. To stride forward beyond its own continental borders, to engage in the international politics that had been the province of aristocratic nations: that ambition a Jefferson or a Jackson or a Lincoln would have hardly dared imagine. By the 1890s, however, a number of influential Americans were restless to have the United States become a power among other world powers, a great presence on the world stage. Some believed that to this end it must acquire an overseas empire.

Arguments for Overseas Expansion   One philosophical basis for the change in outlook lay in the doctrines of Social Darwinism. One application of Darwinian ideas had reinforced the economic philosophy of laissez-faire. Another use likened individual countries to distinct organisms and proposed that in the inevitable competition those that were superior would triumph as superior forms flourish in biological evolution. The racism that attended this kind of thinking held that human characteristics were largely biologically determined. "Scientific" racists at the end of the nineteenth century were proclaiming a doctrine of Nordic supremacy that, they claimed, justified excluding the new immigrants from southern and eastern Europe. American Social Darwinists did not doubt that the United States, along with Britain and perhaps Germany, was admirably equipped to compete in the race for power, riches, and glory. Darwinian ideas of the process of evolution within nature do not, in

The "fitness" of the Anglo-Saxon "race," claimed the historian John Fiske, justified its expansion,

"until every land on the earth's surface that is not already the seat of an old civilization shall become English in its language, in its political habits and traditions, and to a predominant extent in the blood of its people."

fact, translate into a description of survival and progress among nations and ethnic groups, as responsible biologists could have told the ideologues who tried to apply the theory of evolution to political and military questions. But what should have been an obvious difference between the realm of evolutionary biology and the realm of national conflict was widely overlooked.

Imperialist Social Darwinism could be optimistic about the nation's future. But there were influential Americans, some of them responding to those same racist doctrines, whose writing breathed not optimism but gloom. Brooks Adams, grandson of one President and great-grandson of another, feared that his country was losing its virility and falling under the sway of plutocrats, rich men without vision or creativity—and hordes of non-Anglo-Saxon immigrants. Other Americans wondered whether a whole generation of peace was rotting the martial virtues. Americans, warned the naval theorist Alfred Thayer Mahan, were ceasing to be "fighting animals" and were "becoming fattened cattle fit only for slaughter."

The End of the Frontier

Pessimism had a source beyond Social Darwinist brooding. It fed also on the filling up of the West, the ending of the frontier experience that had been a component of American civilization since the earliest British settlements. The most famous argument that the end of the frontier was a turning point in American history came from the historian Frederick Jackson Turner, not long after the census of 1890, by a necessarily arbitrary definition, announced the frontier's virtual extinction.

The frontier, Turner declared, had encouraged democracy and initiative. With the thickening of population in the West, the United States had to begin a new phase. Turner did not say what this new phase would be like, but other Americans could imagine: in place of democracy, privilege and hierarchy; in place of initiative, sloth; in place of ethnic harmony among Americans of British and northern European stock, a babel of peoples and cultures.

A small group of the brightest men of the period decided that the only way to save the national character was to revive the martial spirit by an aggressive expansionism. Mahan, in his influential 1890 book *The Influence of Sea Power on History*, argued that a nation could achieve greatness only by sea power. Imperialism, Adams declared, would "grant a reprieve for individualism by continuing the frontier conditions that made it possible." Franklin Giddings, a sociology professor at Columbia, argued that unless it could turn to overseas expansion, the enormous energy of the American people might "discharge itself in anarchistic, socialistic, and other destructive modes that are likely to work incalculable mischief."

Adams, Mahan, and Giddings were all essentially intellectuals, but learning from them was a group of young politicians who in the next few years would have a great impact on the country. The most prominent of these was Theodore Roosevelt. Ever since his childhood Roosevelt had made a fetish of the "strenuous life." During the 1880s he was attracted by the cattle frontier, becoming a rancher in the Black

Alfred Thayer Mahan's *The Influence of Sea Power on History* contributed significantly to the rise of an imperialist ideology in the late nineteenth century.

The Civil War era had speeded the development of a number of new technologies that called for a revolution in naval strategy. These included the use of steam power on seagoing ships, the new production of cheap and highly durable steel, and chemical breakthroughs in the use of explosives. The old wooden, sail-driven fleet was clearly obsolete. But what was to take its place? The navy appointed hundreds of commissions to investigate these new developments and built a strange array of ships. Some were made of both wood and steel. Others had both steam and sails. All featured distinctive armaments. The navy had little idea of what to do with these ships. Those that combined steam and sail power were required by naval regulation to travel under sail a certain number of hours each day. The navy, in short, suffered from an embarrassment of technical riches which it had yet to figure out how to use.

Then Mahan wrote his book. *The Influence of Sea Power* provided a clear and convincing rationale for what the navy was for. Once, that is, it became clear what the navy needed to be ready to do, all of the technical problems became relatively easy to resolve and a modern navy became possible.

Hills. Roosevelt had no doubt that the long peace since 1865 had made Americans fat and complacent. At every chance for the country to get into a fight, he became enthusiastic. Then there was the young Indianian Albert Beveridge, who first came to the attention of the American public for his blatant advocacy of imperialism. In 1898, when he ran for the Senate, Beveridge brought his audiences cheering to their feet recounting how the "march of the flag" had taken the American people from the original boundaries of 1789 to the Pacific. It was now inevitable, he intoned, that the flag would wave over "an Isthmian canal . . . over Hawaii . . . over Cuba and the southern seas. . . ."

Francis Thurber, president of the United States Export Association, proclaimed that the expansion of American markets

"is absolutely necessary in view of our increasing productive capacity. . . . We must have a place to dump our surplus, which otherwise will constantly depress prices and compel the shutting down of our mills . . . changing our profits to losses."

Economic Reasons for Expansion

The fear of cultural and political stagnation had its counterpart, especially in the economically depressed 1890s, in the worry that the end of the frontier meant an end to expanding domestic markets for the enormous output of the American economy. During these years, businessmen and business spokesmen constantly urged the government to help industry find new markets abroad. "We must have more customers," explained a cotton manufacturer, to absorb "the excessive production of our mills."

Some scholars have concluded that these demands for overseas markets were in fact the primary motive behind the drive for empire at the century's end. Actually, very few of the business or farm groups advocated the grabbing of colonies. Yet these trade expansionists held much common ground with the outright imperialists. Both wanted the country to come out of its isolationism; both favored more use of American muscle in foreign relations. There were deeper resonances between the vision of commercial expansion and the other motives for the nation's coming out of its isolation. Commerce, and the industry behind it, represented for Americans much of what was most intelligent, virtuous, and benevolent in Western and more particularly American habits and institutions. Commercial outreach could substitute for more savage forms of national self-assertion, peacefully conveying to other peoples the material blessings and the enlightened moral behavior, as Americans perceived it, that had produced American industry and agriculture. Smug and provincial and yet innocent in its provinciality, an idea of this kind could contribute to the example of the United States as a redeemer nation.

The Redeemer Nation

Among the attitudes and ideas that prepared the way for the nation's outward thrust was a sincerely felt element of altruism, however misplaced. Every nation makes some claim to nobility; the American self-image has been that of a redeemer nation, meant to be an example of freedom and opportunity for all the world. At home, this implied a growth in freedom and prosperity; abroad, it involved championing the world's oppressed. All through the nineteenth century the United States government often depicted itself as a moral force in the world: in 1848, for example, when it protested the Austrian suppression of a liberal and national revolution in Hungary. The abolition of slavery removed that embarrassing contradiction to the country's view of itself as a champion of freedom, and the economic and technological forces pushing and drawing the United States outward toward the end of the century quickly allied themselves with the idea of the nation as a vehicle of civilization to the world.

In the era of expansionism, this notion of the redeemer nation cut both ways. It set a limit to American appetites: Americans could not easily condone outright conquest, nor could they readily swallow the role of a *Herrenvolk*, a super race that had the right to subdue others. Some Americans—those, for example, who believed in the mental and moral superiority of the northern European peoples—came close to accepting this idea, but they were never more than a small minority. And even the conviction of racial superiority often produced arguments against imperialism rather than for it. Peoples of alien race, tradition, and language could never be assimilated, so went the reasoning; therefore, let them alone. The redeemer nation self-image nonetheless did also serve to encourage a form of expansionism, especially when clothed in the vestments of religion. Even when they deplored physical conquest, Americans were often willing to condone cultural and religious conquest. The assumption was common that their combination of Protestant Christianity and material success was a boon to the world.

As far back as the 1820s, societies dedicated to bringing the Protestant word to the "heathens" of Asia and Africa had been sending missionaries east and west to foreign parts. The missionaries had achieved a particularly strong effect in the Pacific region. In Hawaii they transformed Polynesian culture utterly and for good or ill brought the islands headlong into the modern age. A far broader field for evangelization was the Celestial Kingdom of China, a vast society with an ancient, sophisticated, non-Christian civilization. American missionaries first arrived in China in the 1830s. By 1851, out of a total of about 150 Protestant missionaries in China, eighty-eight were American.

The primary purpose of the missionaries, of course, was religious: to gather souls for the Lord by converting the "heathen Chinese" to the true faith. But their work had effects far beyond this. For the missionaries brought not only the Bible but also Western ideas of democracy, the scientific method, material progress. The mission compounds took in Chinese orphans and taught them, along with the word of the Lord, Western concepts of sanitation and practical Western mechanical skills.

No mass conversions occurred, and by the late nineteenth century there were only a few thousand Christians out of China's vast millions. But the missionaries did succeed in creating a small elite imbued with Western ideas and skills. In response, there also appeared antibodies in the form of a deep hostility to the West.

At home the missionary societies had an important role in directing the attention of Americans overseas. Women played especially active parts in the societies for Foreign Missions, for which they raised funds. Some women became missionaries themselves, or traveled overseas with male relatives who were missionaries. On Sundays, in thousands of Protestant churches across the United States, worshippers listened to pleas for contributions for benighted China, or Samoa, or some other exotic land. One of the best-sellers of the 1880s was the Reverend Josiah Strong's *Our Country*, a volume that advocated a Christianized world under American auspices. Strong's message was not only religious. He also pleaded for Western "civilization" and Western material progress, and he promised that "commerce follows the missionary. . . ."

James G. Blaine

One manifestation of the new mood was the building of an oceangoing navy of steel vessels to replace the fleet left over from the Civil War. In 1883 Congress authorized a number of modern steel ships. The next year the Naval War College was established. The real turnabout came in the early nineties, with the building of two hundred additional warships that would give the nation the wide reach that befitted a major world power. Although at first Congress indignantly rejected this ambitious program, in the next few years it appropriated funds for constructing the first American battleships with large guns and wide cruising ranges. In 1880, the United States Navy ranked twelfth in the world; by 1900, the nation's fleet made it the third largest naval power. Also in the 1880s began a spirited diplomacy under the auspices of Secretary of State James G. Blaine.

Previously a powerful Republican senator from Maine, Blaine had been a major figure in American political life for two decades when he became President James Garfield's secretary of state in 1881. Garfield's death at the hands of an assassin within months after his inauguration ended Blaine's effort to organize a conference of Western Hemisphere nations to discuss economic cooperation. But when Benjamin Harrison, a Republican, succeeded the Democrat Grover Cleveland as President in 1889, Blaine once again became secretary of state, and the conference was on again.

The United States Navy, 1890–1905		
Year	Naval Expenditures	Percent of Federal Budget
1890	$22,006,206	6.9
1900	55,953,078	10.7
1901	60,506,978	11.5
1905	117,550,308	20.7

The White Squadron—battleships of steel painted white—built in response to Congress's call for a modernized navy in 1882. *(Courtesy, Navy Department, Washington, D.C.)*

Pan-Americanism

Blaine's Pan-Americanism was in some ways a refurbishing of the Monroe Doctrine. Blaine himself was a jingoist, meaning a strident nationalist, after a British tune "We do not want to fight / But, by jingo, if we do / We've got the ships, We've got the men / We've got the money, too." But he recognized that the United States could not be arrogant in its relationship with Latin America. This nation should, he believed, involve the Latin republics in their own defense in some sort of loose association with the United States. Blaine's more immediate goal was the improvement of trade relations. Although Latin America sent vast amounts of coffee, sugar, fruits, and other tropical and semitropical products to the United States, it bought most of its manufactured goods from Europe. When in 1889 Blaine once more found himself heading the state department, he worked hard to pull the Latin Americans away from Europe and toward the United States as their source of manufactures. As luck would have it, his Democratic predecessor had already called a second Pan-American conference, although he had not stayed long enough to preside over it; now Blaine was in charge.

Before the conference got fairly down to business, Blaine sent the Latin American delegates on a 6,000-mile railroad journey across the country, to impress them with the might and efficiency of the nation's industry. All this trip probably accomplished was to wear out the delegates. When the conference reconvened, Blaine proposed a customs union among all the American nations so that the goods of each could pass freely among all the rest without the payment of tariffs. He also suggested the establishment of arbitration machinery to settle disputes among the states of the hemisphere. Neither proposal was adopted, and the significance of the 1889 conference consists largely in the precedent it set for the later Pan-American movement and in its marking another beginning of the nation's emergence from isolationism.

American foreign policy toward Latin America during the Blaine years was not uniformly peaceful. Civil war erupted in Chile in 1891, and the United States took exception to the rise to power of the rebel Congressionalist Party. The State Department tried to halt the shipment of weapons and munitions to the new Chilean government, and the policy precipitated a series of demonstrations against the United States in Santiago and Valparaiso. In October 1891, the U.S.S. *Baltimore,* a naval cruiser, docked in Valparaiso on routine maneuvers and let several dozen sailors go on shore leave. They got drunk and precipitated a riot outside of a saloon. When the melee was over, two sailors were dead and seventeen wounded. The other sailors were arrested for disorderly conduct. President Benjamin Harrison denounced the Chilean government for allowing the event to happen and then demanded an apology. Chile refused until Harrison formally threatened to sever diplomatic relations and informally talked of going to war. In January 1892 the Chilean government apologized and paid an indemnity of $75,000. The incident was over.

But the crisis in Chile was the exception. Blaine's policy toward Latin America emphasized the economic issue of free trade among the American nations.

Critics of the United States have accused this country, not inaccu-

A poem published in the Detroit News *and adapted from an English music-hall song repeats the word that critics would apply to the promoters of expansion—jingoists:*

"We do not want to fight,
But, by jingo, if we do,
We'll scoop in all the fishing grounds
And the whole dominion too!"

rately, of pursuing in the twentieth century a "dollar diplomacy" that would subordinate the well-being of the other American republics to the needs of business in the United States. What Blaine earlier had in mind, apparently, was something milder, a peaceable flow of trade that should go to the benefit of the whole continent. And if an appetite for trade had been an occasion for imperialism and war, the ideal of peaceful trade offered itself as an alternative to strident nationalism. At its best it conceived of the world not as broken into competitive nations but as a single cooperative workplace. Some of the most brutal acts on the part of the United States toward Latin republics, in fact, have come not of trade hunger itself but of an ideological commitment to stamping out reformist or leftist movements. That commitment, to be sure, has been fueled in turn by the self-interest of the influential classes that profit from capitalism and commercial expansion.

Hawaii

The German Foreign Office complained of operations in the Samoan Islands:

"The United States was interpreting the Monroe Doctrine as though the Pacific Ocean was to be treated as an American lake."

At the time of Blaine's energetic management of the nation's foreign policy, American businessmen and American expansionists with no personal commercial interests at stake were beginning to look for new markets in Asia. But exploiting these markets required the acquisition of several strategically placed islands in the Pacific where ships could refuel.

The first opportunity to establish a base of operations came in the Samoan Islands, even though they were located south of what would become the major Pacific trade routes. Germany and Great Britain, however, were also interested in Samoa, and in March 1889 naval vessels from all three countries confronted one another in Apia Harbor. Only the arrival of a severe hurricane prevented a naval battle. A conference held in Berlin a few months later led to an agreement in which Samoa was declared independent but supervised by a cooperative protectorate of all three powers. During the next ten years, Germany, the United States, and Great Britain argued constantly over Samoan affairs, and in 1898, after a native rebellion against the local king, United States and British ships bombarded Apia Harbor. The instability finally ended in 1899 when the British agreed to surrender their claims to Samoa, and the United States and Germany divided up the islands between them.

As early as 1851 a San Francisco newspaper declared of Hawaii:

"The native population are fast fading away, the foreign fast increasing. The inevitable destiny of the islands is to pass into the possession of another power. That power is just as inevitably our own. . . . The pear is nearly ripe; we have scarcely to shake the tree in order to bring the luscious fruit readily into our lap."

The beautiful mid-Pacific chain of Hawaiian Islands, which Blaine also wished to annex, was located on a much more direct trade route to Japan and China. It had long attracted Americans—traders, whalers, and missionaries. The missionaries brought the Bible and a long shapeless gown designed to cover Hawaiian women. Sons of the missionaries stayed and became businessmen and sugar planters. In 1875 the kingdom of Hawaii negotiated a treaty with the United States by which, in exchange for the free admission of its sugar to the American market, it agreed not to allow territorial concessions to other foreign nations.

In the next decade, Hawaii prospered as a supplier of sugar to the United States. It was also pulled into the American political orbit, a process welcomed by the many Americans living in the islands. In 1887 Hawaii, in exchange for granting the United States the exclusive right to use Pearl Harbor as a naval station, secured an extension of the sugar agreement. By this time the American community in Hawaii had come to control about two-thirds of the islands' taxable real estate and to exert a strong influence on the policies of the Hawaiian government.

In 1890 the United States Congress removed the tariff on all imported sugar, ending Hawaii's advantage in the American market, and causing the Hawaiian economy to collapse. Meanwhile, the Hawaiian government was becoming, at least from the standpoint of the resident Americans, increasingly capricious, arbitrary, and tyrannical. When Queen Liliuokalani in 1891 succeeded her brother on the Hawaiian throne, matters became still worse. The physically formidable Queen despised the liberal constitution that the American residents had recently imposed on her brother, and early in January 1893 she issued a royal edict abolishing it in favor of one far more autocratic. The Americans and other whites in the islands feared that their expulsion, or at least the confiscation of their property, would soon follow. To forestall any such possibility they arranged a coup. Calling on the American minister, John L. Stevens, for support, they set up a provisional government and proclaimed it the legitimate authority in Hawaii. The presence of American servicemen called in by Stevens from a vessel in Honolulu Harbor kept the Queen from acting. Stevens then extended United States recognition to the revolutionary government. Soon afterward Liliuokalani abdicated, and Stevens declared Hawaii an American protectorate. He advised the State Department: "The Hawaiian pear is now fully ripe, and this is the golden hour for the United States to pluck it."

By this time a delegation of white Hawaiian residents had arrived in Washington to arrange for the islands to become part of the United States. Blaine was no longer secretary of state, but his successor John W. Foster was equally enamored of expansion and submitted a treaty of annexation to the Senate.

Then the headlong process of transferring Hawaii to the United States hit a snag. Many Americans were still not ready for the acquisition of an overseas empire. The case of Samoa was ambiguous, but Hawaiian annexation would be undisguised colonialism. Fortunately for the anti-annexationists, the Senate was at the moment a lame-duck body with little time to act. Before it could approve the treaty, the Harrison Administration gave way to that of Grover Cleveland, now about to begin his second term, the only President in the country's history to serve two nonconsecutive terms.

Cleveland was skeptical of expansion of any kind, and particularly suspicious of the course of events by which white Hawaiians were pushing the island into American hands. In 1893 he abruptly withdrew the treaty from the Senate and appointed a special commissioner, James Blount, to go to Hawaii on a fact-finding mission. Blount's report confirmed Cleveland's doubts. The Hawaiian revolution, the commissioner declared, had been fomented not by the native Hawaiians but by the whites, and would not have succeeded without improper American

Queen Liliuokalani of Hawaii, deposed in 1893 by what she regarded as a conspiracy of American interests. *(Courtesy, New York Public Library, New York City)*

One writer caught the public doubts about imperialism in Hawaii in racial overtones:

> " 'Shall we take Hawaii in, sirs?'
>   that's the question of the day.
> Would the speedy annexation of
>   that dusky country pay?
> Would the revenues from sugar and
>   from smuggled opium
> Counteract the heavy burdens that
>   with them are sure to come?"

intervention. These findings convinced Cleveland, and over the next few months he tried to return the Queen to her throne. But Lili-uokalani insisted that if and when she resumed power she would cut off the heads of the revolutionaries, a project Cleveland found entirely distasteful. Nor would the provisional government surrender power. In the face of this impasse, Cleveland chose to do nothing. For the moment Hawaii remained an independent republic, governed by its white residents. Annexation would come easily during 1898, a year of imperialist war and fevered national pride.

Venezuela

For years Venezuela and Great Britain had disputed the proper location of the boundary between Venezuela and British Guiana (now Guyana). To the British the disagreement seemed at first a minor matter; the Venezuelans, concerned with control of the mouth of the mighty Orinoco River and the possibility of finding gold in the disputed area, took it more seriously. In 1887 they suspended relations with Britain and turned to the United States for support, invoking the name of the "immortal Monroe." Early in the following decade they hired a publicist from the United States to write a pamphlet called "British Aggressions in Venezuela, or the Monroe Doctrine on Trial." This publication they circulated widely, paying particular care to get it into the hands of congressmen. During this period, the United States government suggested several times that the dispute be submitted to arbitration, but the British consistently refused.

There matters stood when Cleveland returned to office. The Democratic President was not a jingoist, but he and indeed many of his countrymen considered Great Britain arrogant and overbearing. Irish Americans, a constituency the Democrats had to court, in particular were hostile to England for its harsh rule of their ancestral homeland over many generations, and it had become a popular practice for politicians to "twist the lion's tail" with rhetorical denunciations of Britain. This bias alone would have been sufficient to make the administration favor Venezuela, but the Cleveland Administration was under pressure for other reasons to deal sternly with Britain. Republicans and other Americans believed that Cleveland's secretary of state, Walter Gresham, had responded weakly to Britain's seizure of the customs house at Corinto, Nicaragua, in 1894, on the pretext that the Nicaraguans had insulted the British consul. They were accusing the Democratic administration of cowardice.

In mid-1895 Gresham, preeminently a man of peace, died and was replaced by Richard Olney, a man of different temper. Soon after taking office he submitted to the British government a dispatch that caused an international furor. Asserting that the Monroe Doctrine was an integral part of American law, he demanded to know whether Britain intended to submit the Venezuela boundary dispute to arbitration. If it did not, the United States would consider it to be in violation of the Monroe Doctrine. This semi-ultimatum to Great Britain was aggressive enough in itself, but its effect was intensified by Olney's arrogant tone. "To-day the United States is practically sovereign on this continent," Olney

The young senator Henry Cabot Lodge of Massachusetts wrote in 1895:

"If Great Britain is to be permitted to . . . take the territory of Venezuela, there is nothing to prevent her taking the whole of Venezuela or any other South American state. If Great Britain can do this with impunity, France and Germany will do it also. . . . The supremacy of the Monroe Doctrine should be established and at once—peacefully if we can, forcibly if we must."

lectured Lord Salisbury, "and its fiat is law upon the subjects to which it confines its interposition."

The Olney note deeply offended the British, and Salisbury lectured the Americans back: the United States was mistaken in believing that the Venezuela boundary was a Monroe Doctrine issue; Olney had his history all wrong. As for arbitration, the answer was "No."

The British response made Cleveland "mad clear through," and late in 1895 he sent a warlike message to Congress, asking for funds to appoint an investigating commission to determine where the boundary should be drawn. The line so determined should then be forced on Britain, come what may. "I am fully alive to the responsibility incurred, and keenly realize all the consequences that may follow," the President ominously concluded. Congress unanimously appropriated $100,000 for the boundary commission. Meanwhile, the war spirit soared, with Civil War veterans volunteering their services and one Irish-American group pledging 100,000 men to fight the England that dominated their ancestral island.

Clearer heads finally prevailed. In England, too, leading politicians and molders of public opinion moved to calm things down. British policymakers had been startled by the fury of the American reaction. A war with the United States would expose Canada to dangerous attack, and Britain was already deeply embroiled in South Africa, in a dispute that would soon lead to the Boer War. At the same time, imperial Germany was beginning to challenge Britain internationally. To get into a war with the United States over a few thousand square miles of malarial jungle was pointless.

Before many weeks had passed, the worst of the crisis was over. When the boundary commission from the United States began its work, it found the British cooperative. Britain signed a treaty with Venezuela in early 1897 providing for an arbitration commission, as the United States had proposed. By the time the commission handed down its decision, few Americans cared very much. The confrontation had been resolved without war.

Cuba and War

In the Venezuelan boundary crisis, an American public opinion that since the nation's founding had been preoccupied with its own internal affairs was looking eagerly, belligerently outward for some assertion of power in world politics. Cuba was a still greater incitement.

The Cuban Civil War   For decades the "Pearl of the Antilles," one of Spain's few remaining possessions in the New World, had attracted the interest of people in the United States. Southerners had hoped to acquire Cuba as a slave state. Then after the Civil War a ten-year Cuban revolt against Spain drew the sympathy of people in the United States, who identified the Cuban struggle for independence with their own nation's revolution a century earlier. In 1878 the revolt was put down, and peace returned, temporarily, to the island. During the years of civil war, however, many sugar planters had suffered serious losses. Eager to get out, they sold their lands to citizens of the United States, who acquired valuable property in Cuba.

Civil war erupted once again in 1895. The rebels, anxious to involve the United States, attacked property owned by its citizens. Sometimes they spared property in exchange for ransoms that were then used for the revolution. Both sides resorted to brutal methods. The *insurrectos* dynamited passenger trains and took civilian hostages. The Spaniards, in turn, under General Valeriano Weyler, rounded up thousands of civilians and put them in "reconcentration" camps where they could not give aid and support to the rebels. Scarcity of food and medical supplies, combined with bad sanitation, soon killed hundreds.

Though rebels were a match for Spaniards in atrocities, people in the United States heard little of the *insurrectos'* misdeeds and much of Spain's. The daily press in the United States functioned as the revolutionaries' propaganda department. Particularly effective were the *New York World,* edited by Joseph Pulitzer, and the *New York Journal,* having as its editor William Randolph Hearst. In the later nineties these two papers engaged in a great circulation war. Every heavy-handed Spanish act produced headlines in one paper or the other, inciting its rival to find, or to invent, something even more brutal and sensational. In all this, the two were leading representatives of what has been called the "yellow press." The phrase, derived from Pulitzer's comic character "The Yellow Kid," depicted in that color, refers to the more sensationalistic journals of the time, thriving on tales of crime and other fascinating wickedness.

Americans were horrified at the mounting barbarism in Cuba. Some of the businessmen with investments on the island favored direct United States intervention, but their views were not typical within the business community. Since 1893, times had been bad, but by 1897 they were beginning to improve. United States involvement in a war with Spain over Cuba would threaten the recovery. In October 1897, the *Commercial and Financial Chronicle* noted that war would destroy "the trade prosperity we are all enjoying." But the business community's attitudes were not decisive. Sympathies were overwhelmingly in favor of *Cuba libre,* free Cuba. General Weyler's actions in Cuba seemed only the latest chapter in a centuries-long Spanish record of cruelty in the New World. "Butcher Weyler" recalled for one journalist Hernando Cortés and the other early *conquistadores,* whose brutality toward the Aztecs and Incas had decimated those native peoples.

It would be a mistake to see United States intervention in Cuba primarily as a propaganda victory for the yellow press. Without the deeply embedded hostility to the Spanish Empire, and without a growing concern over the end of the nation's open spaces combined with a growing sense of the nation's destiny and superiority, the press war between Hearst and Pulitzer would have meant little. The period from 1865 to 1898 was the longest stretch of peace in the nation's history. A new generation of young men had reached maturity without having experienced directly the horrors of death and mutilation that their forebears had known in 1861–65. By the late 1890s, many of these were

---

The New York Journal *wrote of*

"Weyler the brute, the devastator of haciendas, the destroyer of families, and the outrager of women. . . . Pitiless, cold, an exterminator of men. . . . There is nothing to prevent his carnal, animal brain from running riot with itself in inventing tortures and infamies of bloody debauchery."

Not to be outdone, a correspondent for Pulitzer's World *reported:*

"Blood on the roadsides, blood in the fields, blood on the doorsteps, blood, blood, blood! The old, the young, the weak, the crippled—all are butchered without mercy. . . . Is there no nation wise enough, brave enough, and strong enough to restore peace in this bloodsmitten land?"

almost eager for a good fight, especially in such a worthy cause as Cuban independence.

McKinley's Efforts to Avoid War Neither Cleveland nor his Republican successor, William McKinley, was an interventionist. At one point Cleveland told a group of belligerent congressmen that if Congress declared war against Spain he would "not mobilize the army." McKinley's reluctance to take action provoked Roosevelt to exclaim that the President had the backbone of a chocolate eclair. McKinley deplored Spanish policy and hoped to end Weyler's brutal repression. He did not see how if it continued the United States could fail to intervene directly. But he did not insist on Cuban independence, nor did he want to force Spain to move faster than it was politically possible for its leaders to do.

McKinley had his own political problems. The Republican Party, like the country at large, was torn between factions who favored caution and those who preferred war. McKinley knew that the best way to satisfy both was to conclude the conflict quickly. To this end, in June 1897 he sent Stewart Woodford, a level-headed New Yorker, to Madrid as American diplomatic representative. Woodford arrived in September and transmitted McKinley's wishes to the Spanish government. The United States must have assurances that repression would stop. This country would volunteer its good offices to settle the conflict between Spain and the Cubans, but if Spain refused, the United States would feel free to take action directly. The Spanish government promised to recall Weyler, whose harsh steps were popular with frustrated and politically powerful Barcelona shippers, and agreed that reforms in Spanish administration would be necessary, including some degree of Cuban autonomy. But Spain was slow to act. The American militants, hot for war, bombarded the President with demands that he brook no delay in ousting the Spaniards from Cuba.

By the beginning of 1898, McKinley, under intense pressure to intervene, ordered the battleship *Maine* to Havana, ostensibly as a friendly courtesy, but actually to protect the lives and property of United States citizens. The Spanish government was not pleased, but when the vessel arrived, Spanish officials received the *Maine* correctly and was hospitable to the officers and crew. It looked as if the visit might help the cause of peace.

While the *Maine* lay at anchor at Havana, relations between Spain and the United States took an abrupt bad turn. The Spanish representative to Washington, Enrique Dupuy de Lôme, was a proud and narrow aristocrat who despised the give-and-take of American politics. He was also indiscreet. In December 1897 he wrote a Spanish friend in Havana calling McKinley "weak and a bidder for the admiration of the crowd, besides being a would-be politician." The letter was intercepted by a Cuban rebel and sent to Hearst's *Journal,* where on February 9, 1898, a copy was printed below the headline "Worst Insult to the United States in Its History." Although the Spanish government quickly recalled de Lôme and apologized for his mistake, the harm had been done.

The Sinking of the *Maine*

Worse followed. On February 15 a massive explosion sank the *Maine* at its berth in Havana Harbor, with a loss of 260 sailors, almost its entire crew. During the next few frantic days, the President cautioned against too hasty a judgment. "I have been through one war," the former Union major remarked, "and I do not want to see another." The jingo press observed no such restraint. Certain that the explosion had come from outside the ship and had been set by Spanish agents, it demanded action. Hearst's *Journal* thundered "THE WARSHIP MAINE WAS SPLIT IN TWO BY AN ENEMY'S SECRET INFERNAL MACHINE. THE WHOLE COUNTRY THRILLS WITH WAR FEVER."

Mass meetings across the nation demanded that the country go to war, while around the country college students began to drill in preparation for a retaliatory attack. Congress, already bellicose, on March 9 appropriated an additional $50 million for the army and navy. Soon after, Senator Redfield Proctor of Vermont, just back from a tour of Cuba, further inflamed public opinion by confirming charges of Spanish brutality in the reconcentration camps. A United States commission reported that the explosion had been caused by a land mine, and could not have been internal.

To this day, no one knows who or what sank the *Maine*. It is hard to believe that the Spanish government, which feared intervention, was in any way responsible. Perhaps it was a lighted cigarette tossed into the ammunition hold. Current scholars have suggested that coal used on the ship gave off dust that was highly explosive; the coal bins were next to the ammunition hold. But the public had made up its mind.

A reluctant McKinley recognized that he had to act. A few days

William Randolph Hearst, owner of the New York Journal, *wrote in the paper's September 25, 1898, issue:*

"The force of the newspaper is the greatest force in civilization.

Under republican government, newspapers form and express public opinion.

They suggest and control legislation.

They declare wars.

They punish criminals, especially the powerful.

They reward with approving publicity the good deeds of citizens everywhere.

The newspapers control the nation because

THEY REPRESENT THE PEOPLE."

The wreck of the *Maine* in Havana Harbor, February 15, 1898, partially sunk in a still-unexplained explosion. Its destruction was used as a pretext to declare war on Spain. *(Courtesy, Scribner's Archives)*

after receiving the *Maine* commission report, he instructed Woodford in Madrid to demand an immediate armistice in Cuba and to insist on an end of the reconcentration camp policy. If peace terms were not achieved by October, Spain would have to accept McKinley's arbitration of the Cuban problem. As the President awaited the Spanish reply, congressmen and the public stormed for immediate action.

The Spanish reply was unsatisfactory. Madrid promised to investigate the *Maine* incident and to abolish the reconcentration camps in some areas, but it refused to suspend hostilities or allow arbitration by the United States. McKinley now knew that he had no choice and turned reluctantly to composing a war message. Still, he moved slowly, allowing the public to get angry and Spain to have second thoughts. On April 10, while Americans awaited war, the Spanish government agreed to suspend hostilities in Cuba. A few days earlier the President might have used this concession as an excuse to avoid a declaration. But now it was too late. On April 11, McKinley asked Congress to be allowed to use the army and navy to end the conflict in Cuba. Congress responded on April 19 with a four-part statement declaring that Cuba was free, that Spain must withdraw, that armed forces would be used to achieve these ends, and that the United States had no intention of annexing Cuba. That last section of this war document was the so-called Teller Amendment.

The Spanish-American War

The war that followed was one of the briefest in American history. Fighting began May 1, 1898, and on July 26 of the same year the Spanish government requested peace terms. Fewer than 400 of the 274,000 officers and men who served in the armed forces died as a result of enemy action. Of the more than 5,000 who lost their lives, most fell victim to illness or accident. The financial cost was small: about $250 million.

The Navy Takes the Philippines   A Spanish nation only a shadow of the great power that had once ruled half the world faced a young continental giant, by now the world's leading industrial power. The American navy had been thoroughly modernized, its morale was high, and it had vigorous leadership. The army was a weak and decrepit vestige of the mighty force that a little over three decades earlier had saved the Union.

The navy bore most of the burden of the war. Years of rebuilding since the early 1880s now showed their value. With four first-class battleships and many other vessels, the fleet outgunned the Spanish navy by a large margin. In Washington, Assistant Secretary of the Navy Theodore Roosevelt was a whirlwind of energy and intelligence who had been looking for this fight for many years. Though technically the subordinate of the secretary, Roosevelt was by far the more forceful man and, in the frequent absence of his Washington-hating chief, John D. Long, often served as acting secretary.

About two months before the outbreak of official hostilities,

In the Battle of Manila Bay, May, 1898, Admiral Dewey's Pacific squadron destroyed the Spanish fleet in the Philippines. *(Courtesy, New York Public Library Picture Collection)*

Roosevelt telegraphed Admiral George Dewey, in charge of the American Asiatic squadron, that he was to proceed to Hong Kong and keep his vessels fully coaled for an attack on the Philippine Islands, which Spain owned. On May 1, 1898, following the official declaration of war, Dewey steamed into Manila Bay, the harbor of the Philippine capital. Five times the American ships sailed past the inferior Spanish vessels stationed there, hurtling salvos with each pass. In a few hours the entire Spanish fleet consisted of smoking hulks. Then Dewey quickly smashed the land-based Spanish batteries. An English writer called the battle of Manila Bay "a military execution rather than a real contest."

Roosevelt along with Dewey wanted to prevent Spain from reinforcing its Atlantic fleet from the Pacific, but he had other purposes in mind as well. A disciple of Alfred Thayer Mahan, the naval historian and theoretician who believed that sea power was the basis of national greatness, Roosevelt wanted to strengthen his nation's ability to project its power in Asia. The Philippines, especially the harbor at Manila on the island of Luzon, would give the United States access to the eastern Pacific, the China Sea, and Indochina. So Dewey, in carrying out Roosevelt's orders, put the United States in the position to claim a Pacific empire.

The War in Cuba   In the main Caribbean theater of operations, matters moved more slowly. Volunteers flocked to the colors at McKinley's call; 223,000 men enlisted. The South's enthusiasm for the fight put an end, many contemporaries said, to the hostility that had prevailed between South and North ever since 1860. Volunteers came from every social stratum. Many black Americans by enlisting expressed their patriotism and temporarily escaped from southern poverty. William Jennings Bryan, McKinley's 1896 Democratic rival, enlisted as colonel of Nebraska's volunteers. Unable to stand by while others dashed about firing rifles, Roosevelt quit his post to lead the Rough Riders, a cavalry regiment of western cowboys and eastern swells that he had assembled himself.

Despite the enthusiasm, the army—small, lethargic, poorly led—

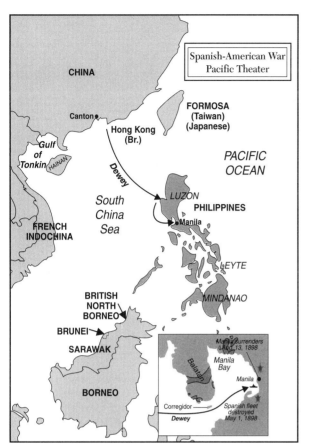

was not ready. Its civilian chief was Secretary of War Russell A. Alger, a Civil War veteran. Alger would serve as a convenient scapegoat for the nation's neglect of its army, and the inevitable military sloth of a great continental democracy.

Alger had promised the President that he could get 40,000 men to Cuba in ten days after the outbreak of war. It actually took seven weeks to get 17,000 men to the island. Thousands of volunteers poured into Tampa, Florida, without guns, uniforms, or other equipment, and were forced to wait in the hot spring weather to see action. Whole trainloads of equipment were backed up on sidings. The men soon got bored and restless; many contracted disease. Several weeks elapsed before the giant tangle could be unsnarled and troops put aboard transports for Cuba.

On June 22, the first United States troops finally landed at Daiquiri, near Santiago, amid near total confusion. At Las Guasimas there was a brief but bloody skirmish. The war's major battles took place on July 1–3. The terrain was hilly and wooded and the Spaniards, equipped with accurate Mauser rifles, were well entrenched. At Kettle Hill, close to the San Juan Hill with which he is usually associated since it was the larger objective of the United States forces, Roosevelt found himself at the head of his dismounted Rough Riders and a contingent of black troops. Always impetuous, he led them on a charge that swept the Spanish troops off the hill and opened the road to Santiago.

Meanwhile, the Atlantic fleet destroyed the Spanish fleet. The Spanish admiral, Pascual y Topete Cervera, had sailed from the Cape Verde Islands in late April headed for the Caribbean. For a while news of his departure created a panic along the east coast of the United States: was he planning to attack the mainland? He evaded capture and slipped into Santiago Harbor on May 19, short on coal and unable to go any farther. With the United States troops on the verge of capturing the town, he was faced with the choice of trying to escape or surrendering without a battle. Under pressure from the provincial governor, he reluctantly steamed out of Santiago into the waiting arms of the powerful flotilla. In a few hours the Spanish squadron was destroyed, with 300 of its sailors dead. The United States had not lost a ship and suffered only two casualties. The grossly uneven match attested to the effectiveness of the new navy. Two weeks later, Spanish officials surrendered Santiago. The fighting was over. One Spaniard reported to his commander that the Americans had "fired grapeshot and all kinds of projectiles on the Playa del Este and Cayo Toro until they set fire to the fort on Playa del Este, burning the house of the pilots . . . The American squadron in possession of the outer bay [of Santiago] has taken it as if for a harbor of rest, they being anchored as if in one of their own ports."

The Peace Treaty   When the Treaty of Paris between Spain and the United States, which included Spanish cession of the Philippines to the United States, came before the Senate for ratification, there was unexpected opposition. Despite the opinion shift of the previous months, some Americans were still strongly opposed to colonies. Hitherto United States expansion had been into empty territory, some critics held, where people of the European race and Anglo-Saxon institutions could form self-governing states like the original thirteen. Was it conceivable that these Filipinos, long governed by tyrannical Spain and unused to self-government, could ever become Americans? Implicit in this attitude was a fair amount of racial and cultural xenophobia, a conviction that the "little brown brothers," as McKinley called them, could not assimilate the institutions of northern Europeans. But there was a more generous aspect to anti-imperialism. The philosopher William James argued that Filipinos did not need any uplifting from the Americans. To suppose that they did was "sniveling, loathsome" cant. Acquiring the islands would be a "shameless betrayal of American principles." "What could be a plainer symptom of greed, ambition, corruption and imperialism?" James asked.

Outside Congress the anti-imperialists, many of them Mugwumps who had fought against political corruption during the 1870s and 1880s, organized the Anti-Imperialist League in November 1898. The league sent out thousands of broadsides and pamphlets to influential clergymen, politicians, businessmen, and farm leaders. These bore titles like "The Hell of War and Its Penalties" and "The Cost of a National Crime" and condemned the impending treaty. In Congress League officials fought such arch-imperialists as Henry Cabot Lodge and Albert Beveridge, who believed in the nation's Far Eastern destiny and its mission to uplift and relished the commercial and strategic advantages of possessing the Philippines. One argument for annexing the islands was the likelihood that if the United States did not take them, the Germans would.

A key figure in the Senate debate was William Jennings Bryan. Though skeptical of empire, the former Democratic standard-bearer believed that it was important to end the war officially. The impending presidential election, he claimed, could serve as a referendum on the annexation and if the vote went against the supporters of colonies, the decision to annex could be reversed. That made little sense: reversing an annexation would have been unlikely. Bryan's argument, however, probably changed the minds of a few Democratic senators and on February 6, 1899, the Senate ratified the peace treaty by a vote of 57 to 27, one vote more than the necessary two-thirds. For the Philippines, the United States paid Spain $20 million.

An American Empire

And so, as the old century ended, Americans found themselves with an empire; their country had now joined the great powers as a nation ruling over millions of non-Europeans. The new status brought satisfaction to many citizens who gloried in their country's added prestige. Europeans now clearly saw the United States in a new way, and the nation was dealing with them on new diplomatic terms. For much of its history the United States had exchanged with foreign countries no diplomatic representatives above the rank of minister, believing perhaps that the aristocratic rank of ambassador was not compatible with republican simplicity and virtue. But during the 1890s it had begun exchanging ambassadors. To that subtle change in self-image the United States could now add a very large one: it had stretched its reach across the great Pacific Ocean.

Revolt in the Philippines The final decision about whether to annex the Philippines rested with President William McKinley, who by his own admission had initially been unable even to locate the islands on a map of the world. As he recounted his thinking for a group of visiting clergymen, the President would recall that he had been unable to sleep, so tormented was he by the question. Kneeling next to his bed, he prayed for divine guidance and, after several nights, received the inspiration he sought. We could not give the islands back to Spain. That "would be cowardly and dishonorable." We could not give them to France or Germany: "that would be bad business and discreditable." Nor could we leave the Filipinos to themselves. They "were unfit for self-government" and "they would soon have anarchy and misrule over there worse than Spain's was." This left the United States with only one honorable course of action: "there was nothing left for us to do but to take them all, and to educate the

The war in the Philippines was the first of four the United States fought in Asia during the twentieth century. In Spoon River Anthology *(1915) Edgar Lee Masters writes a tombstone inscription for a fictional veteran of the war; the words exhibit the antiwar sentiment that has long vied in the United States with its martial opposite.*

HARRY WILMANS

I was just turned twenty-one,
And Henry Phipps, the Sunday-school superintendent,
Made a speech in Bindle's Opera House.
"The honor of the flag must be upheld," he said,
"Whether it be assailed by a barbarous tribe of Tagalogs
Or the greatest power in Europe."
And we cheered and cheered the speech and the flag he waved
As he spoke.
And I went to the war in spite of my father,
And followed the flag till I saw it raised
By our camp in a rice field near Manila,
And all of us cheered and cheered it.
But there were flies and poisonous things;
And there was the deadly water,
And the cruel heat,
And the sickening, putrid food;
And the smell of the trench just back of the tents
Where the soldiers went to empty themselves;
And there were the whores who followed us, full of syphilis;
And beastly acts between ourselves or alone,
With bullying, hatred, degradation among us,
And days of loathing and nights of fear
To the hour of the charge through the steaming swamp,
Following the flag,
Till I fell with a scream, shot through the guts.
Now there's a flag over me in Spoon River!
A flag! A flag!

Filipinos, and uplift and civilize and Christianize them, and by God's grace do the very best we could by them, as our fellow men for whom Christ also died." That most Filipinos were already Christians did not sidetrack McKinley's train of thought. And, when he reached his decision, he "went to bed, and went to sleep, and slept soundly."

McKinley had decided, in the words of Rudyard Kipling's 1899 poem urging just such a course, to "take up the White Man's Burden," to rule the Filipinos for their own good. The Filipinos, however, did not share his view that they "were unfit for self-government," and the guerrilla fighters there felt betrayed by the American decision to replace Spain as a colonial power.

Even as the Senate was considering the treaty with Spain, the Filipinos were rising in anger against the Yankees. Welcomed at first as liberators, they now seemed merely new conquerors no better than their predecessors. By the spring of 1899 a full-scale war, the Philippine insurrection, was raging over the archipelago. Under the leadership of Emilio Aguinaldo, the Filipino rebels attacked American troops, at first in conventional, pitched-battle fashion, and later, when these tactics proved disastrous against the better-armed Americans, in hit-and-run maneuvers. Some American troops responded by committing atrocities—acts that the Filipino insurgents were not above either.

Before long, reports were reaching the United States that American soldiers were butchering prisoners, while at least one American field commander had ordered his men "to kill and burn and make a howling wilderness of Samar," one of the rebel strongholds. Before the insurrection was put down and Aguinaldo wounded in mid-1902, some

A young soldier from Kingston, New York, wrote home:

"Last night one of our boys was found shot and his stomach cut open. Immediately orders were received from General Wheaton to burn the town and kill every native in sight; which was done to a finish. About 1,000 men, women and children were reported killed. I am probably growing hard-hearted, for I am in my glory when I can sight my gun on some dark skin and pull the trigger."

***On the Fighting Line Near Pasay, Philippine Islands, 1899.*
Photographer: James Ricalton for Underwood and Underwood.**
(Courtesy, California Museum of Photography, University of California, Riverside)

seventy thousand American troops, four times the number sent to Cuba, were engaged in fighting the Filipinos. The antiwar financier Andrew Carnegie, on reading that 8,000 Filipinos had been killed during the first year of the war, wrote an American official offering congratulations for "civilizing the Filipinos. . . . About 8,000 of them have been completely civilized and sent to heaven."

Congress in 1902 passed the Philippine Government Act, setting up a Philippine legislature elected by popular vote. The Jones Act of 1916 announced the intention of the United States to withdraw from the islands as soon as a stable government was established, and conferred on the Filipinos self-government in domestic matters. The act also provided for free trade with the United States, which brought a degree of prosperity but also subordinated the Filipino economy to American interests. Finally, in 1934, the Tydings-McDuffie Act made provisions for Philippine independence. Passed at the behest of anti-imperialists, beet-sugar producers who disliked the competition of Philippine sugar, and trade union leaders who wanted to end the influx of Filipino workers, the measure provided for eventual Filipino independence. In a "commonwealth" period the islands would be governed by their own legislature and elected governor. This was the islands' status when the Japanese invaded in early 1942. The Philippines received their independence in 1946 as provided by the act.

Guam, Puerto Rico, and Cuba   In 1900 the occupiers of Cuba helped set the island's finances in order, and doctors and public health authorities from the United States succeeded in wiping out the yellow fever that had afflicted the island for generations. Since Cuba was under only temporary occupation, no question of its technical governmental place within the empire of the United States was at issue. Guam and Puerto Rico, on the other hand, were possessions of the United States.

Guam was a small island with a small population and eventually became little more than an American naval base. Puerto Rico was large

Soldiers in the Philippines sang "Damn, damn, damn the Filipinos":

In that land of dopy dreams, happy peaceful Philippines,
Where the bolo-man is hiking night and day;
Where the Tagalogs steal and lie, where Americanos die,
There you hear the soldiers sing this evening lay;
Damn, damn, damn the Filipinos, cross-eyed kakiack ladrones,
Underneath our starry flag, civilize 'em with a Krag,
And return us to our own beloved homes.

and more densely populated. At first, Puerto Rican nationalism was quite weak, and most islanders seemed content to remain in the orbit of the United States. But what should be their status within that orbit?

In the *Insular Cases* (1901) the Supreme Court declared that while inhabitants of American possessions were entitled to enjoy some fundamental constitutional guarantees, they did not possess all the rights of citizenship. The Court noted, though, that Congress could choose to confer such rights if it wished, and in the next few years Congress did. The Foraker Act of 1900 had already provided for a partially elective legislature in Puerto Rico with an appointive governor. A treaty of 1903 between the United States and Cuba, however, included promises that the Cubans would not enter into any treaty with a foreign power that would impair Cuban independence, would not unilaterally contract any public debt beyond their ability to repay, would allow the United States to establish a naval base on Cuban soil, and ultimately would permit the United States to intervene to preserve Cuban independence. The Platt Amendment to the treaty established for the United States a virtual protectorate over the island: a right, in effect, to control Cuba's affairs, ostensibly to protect the island's safety and interests. The arrangement made a mockery of *Cuba libre,* the professed reason for the war with Spain. In 1917 Congress granted Puerto Ricans United States citizenship and gave them the right to elect both houses of the legislature. Puerto Rico was also to be part of the nation's free trade area; its products were to enter the mainland duty-free. A new treaty with Cuba in 1934 abrogated most of the offensive provisions of the older relationship between the two countries, but it did not remove our privilege of having a naval base in Cuba.

| **China's "Open Door"** | The United States had long exploited Chinese workers. European-born laborers were responsible |

for the massacre of twenty-eight Chinese coal miners in Wyoming in 1885. An obituary of Wan Lee expressed the meaning of a "chinaman's chance" on the West Coast: "Dead, my reverend friends, dead. Stoned to death in the streets of San Francisco, in the year of grace 1869 by a mob of half-grown boys and Christian school children."

American policy toward the Far East was based in substantial part on commercial self-interest. The Open Door policy, which held that no nation trading with China should try to exclude other nations from commerce, sensibly aimed at maintaining peace among the powers interested in trading there. It was even mildly benign toward China itself, seeking to ensure that China would enjoy what the Western powers believed to be the benefits of uninterrupted trade with them and that it would not be subject to military intervention on the part of any one country that wished to exclude others. Yet the Open Door policy also assumed that China would be for a long time a field for Western exploitation—peaceable and friendly exploitation, but not an equal relationship between a sovereign China and its sovereign trading partners. That policy in China had been as much English as American in origin, although it was Secretary of State John Hay who in 1899 sent notes to the major powers calling for it. After some Chinese staged the

Albert J. Beveridge, running for the Senate in Indiana in 1898, orated:

"American factories are making more than the American people can use; American soil is producing more than they can consume. Fate has written our policy for us; the trade of the world must and shall be ours."

Boxer Rebellion in 1900 to drive foreign "devils" into the sea, Hay sent another round of notes insisting on China's "territorial integrity," an act partly reflecting traditional friendship between that country and the United States.

In a formal sense the policy was anti-imperialist although the timing—the McKinley Administration issued the notes at the very time it was consolidating its grip on the Philippines—gives rise to questions about how seriously that aspect of the policy should be taken. As a practical matter too, the United States was in a poor position to carve out its own sphere of influence in China. Britain, Germany, Russia, and Japan had already staked out their claims and not much was left. So the United States had little to lose by calling for the Open Door. And it had much to gain.

Other Acquisitions   In 1903 the United States acquired, under discreditable circumstances, what was perhaps the most lucrative imperial prize of all, the Panama Canal. The last territorial acquisition was the Virgin Islands. Ever since the late eighteenth century those islands, which are located in the Caribbean, had been a Danish possession. By the early 1900s, her own imperial dreams long since shattered, Denmark decided to sell the islands, and Germany became the most interested buyer. But Germany had grown to be a world power, and the United States did not want the Germans establishing a foothold in the Western Hemisphere. When World War I broke out in Europe in 1914, Woodrow Wilson's administration decided to make an offer to Denmark. The two countries signed a treaty giving the United States sovereignty over the islands in return for a payment of $25 million. The Senate ratified the treaty in January 1917.

By that time the United States had lost interest in the rush to acquire more overseas territories. Colonies were disappointing. After the first flush there appeared little glory in empire; American destiny, it seemed, did not rest on colonial possessions after all. Nor was there any need, it seemed, for a social safety valve. Prosperity returned with the advent of the new century, and so did American confidence. Americans would invest millions of dollars abroad in the years before 1914. Some went to the Philippines, Cuba, and Puerto Rico, but even more flowed to Canada, Mexico, and other nations that were not colonies. Nor did the China market work out. It eventually proved an illusion, and direct government action was necessary to induce American businessmen to risk money in that nation, which was lacking a firm government and would fall into decades of revolution.

Theodore Roosevelt's World Vistas

Despite his reputation for bombast, President Theodore Roosevelt was a sophisticated diplomat with a sure grasp of the facts of politics, the uses and limits of power, and what the nation's worldwide interests were. He pursued these interests overseas with a combination of guile and deft skill that he encapsulated in his motto, "Speak softly and carry

This cartoon illustrates Theodore Roosevelt's "big stick" and global concerns. (*Courtesy, Scribner's Archives*)

a big stick." Only one nation, Great Britain, could impress American leaders with its power, and Roosevelt neither provoked the British nor took advantage of their growing preoccupation with Germany. Friendship with England freed Roosevelt for adventures in areas where strategic security and local weakness promised large gains with little risk. Gradually Roosevelt and the country, though little interested in colonization, took on a global role. American influence ranged from the Far East to the Balkans; the American fleet sailed all seven seas; American merchants roamed the planet.

The Russo-Japanese War   Japan, aiming at dominion over East Asia, was consolidating its grip on nearby Korea. Russian activities there, and growing Russian influence in nearby Manchuria, which the weakened Chinese were barely able to hold onto, triggered a war between these two emerging imperial powers. In 1904 Japanese sailors destroyed Russia's far eastern squadron with a surprise attack, a technique they would employ with equal success thirty-seven years afterwards at Pearl Harbor; six months afterwards a skilled Japanese attack pushed Russian troops out of Manchuria. Then Russia's Baltic Fleet, hastily sent into the war by a desperate government in St. Petersburg, was annihilated by Admiral Togo in the Tsushima Strait.

The United States in Latin America, 1895–1941

⬛○ U.S. possessions
⬜ U.S. interventions

UNITED STATES

Gulf of Mexico

MEXICO
Military intervention
1914,
1916–1919

Mexico City ✪
● Veracruz

CUBA
U.S. troops
1898–1902
1906–1909
1917–1922
Protectorate
1898–1934

BAHAMAS

ATLANTIC OCEAN

VIRGIN ISLANDS
Purchased from Denmark
1917

JAMAICA
(Br.)

Caribbean Sea

Santo
Domingo ●

**BRITISH
HONDURAS**

GUATEMALA

HONDURAS

EL SALVADOR

NICARAGUA
U.S. Troops 1909–1910
1912–1925
1926–1933
Financial supervision
1911–1924

HAITI
U.S. troops
1915–1934
Financial
supervision
1915–1941

**DOMINICAN
REPUBLIC**
U.S. troops
1916–1924
Financial
supervision
1905–1941

PUERTO RICO
Acquired from
Spain 1898

PACIFIC OCEAN

COSTA RICA

CANAL ZONE*
Control over canal
beginning 1904

VENEZUELA
Settlement of boundry
dispute
1895–1896

COLOMBIA

**BRITISH
GUIANA**

* Canal Zone not a possession
but controlled through a lease
from Panama.

PANAMA
Support of revolution
1903

The Japanese, everywhere victorious, kept secret the near-bankruptcy to which war had brought their fragile economy. In Washington, meanwhile, President Roosevelt worried that a jubilant Japan, unchecked by Russia, might close the Open Door in China and threaten the tenuous American colonial empire in the western Pacific. Eager to maintain a balance of power between the two antagonists once the fighting was over, he offered to mediate. Both belligerents accepted, hoping to gain more by talk than by renewed struggle.

Roosevelt cajoled the two enemies into a peace. According to the terms of the Treaty of Portsmouth, signed in that New Hampshire town on September 5, 1905, the Tsar granted Japan a "paramount interest" in southern Manchuria and Korea. Russia avoided the humiliation of an indemnity and ceded only half of Sakhalin Island, not all of it as leaders in Tokyo had wanted. Still, Japan's new protectorates did upset the balance of power in East Asia. Three times Roosevelt's intermediaries reached executive understandings with the Japanese. The Taft-Katsura Agreement of 1905 recognized Japan's power in Korea; in return, Japan foreswore "all aggressive designs whatever" on American colonies in the Pacific. Japan, meanwhile, had reason to be angry at the United States. In California, Japanese immigrants were subjected to a prejudice and hostility that went beyond the usual bigotry with which Americans have confronted newcomers. Roosevelt, for all his bluster, had a peculiar ability to get along with the proud Japanese nation. In the so-called Gentlemen's Agreement of 1907–8, Japan voluntarily limited the emigration of her laborers to the American West Coast. But California continued its hostile policies against the Japanese by limiting their right to own or lease farmland. In 1908 the Root-Takahira Agreement pledged both countries to respect the Open Door in China. Roosevelt realized that words could not always restrain the obstreperous Japanese, now a first-class world power, but he did keep on an even keel the relations between Japan and the United States.

The Algeciras Conference   A sense of the fragility of world peace prompted Roosevelt to intercede in Europe's affairs. Arguments over colonies had brought Europe's major powers to the edge of war, but never as dangerously as during the Moroccan crisis of 1904–5. French and British leaders had already worked out an entente that eventually ripened into alliance. They settled disputes over African territory by awarding protectorates to each other. The British gained a protectorate over Egypt. The French received a similar arrangement over Morocco. These colonial pretensions and the budding alliance angered Germany. That nation, like the other European powers, was hungry for a slice of the world that was now getting quickly divided, and the Germans resented any arrangement that seemed to be squeezing their country out of the competition. Kaiser Wilhelm flamboyantly called for an open door in Morocco, while his government demanded that France oust its foreign minister, Theophile Delcasse, the author of the alliance with Britain. Leaders in Paris bridled over such heavy-handed intervention in domestic affairs; the Germans hinted that any delay might bring war. Roosevelt skillfully maneuvered the angry parties into a conference at Algeciras, a resort

The Americans had experienced their own troubles with Morocco. In June 1904 Secretary of State John Hay cabled the American consul there: "We want Perdicaris alive or Raisuli dead." Perdicaris, an American citizen, had been kidnapped by Raisuli, a Moroccan bandit, and held for ransom. Perdicaris was released.

The French writer Andre Tardieu remarked in 1908:

"The United States is . . . a world power. . . . Its power creates for it . . . a duty—to pronounce upon all those questions that hitherto have been arranged by agreement only among European powers. These powers themselves, at critical times, turn toward the United States, anxious to know its opinion. . . . The United States intervenes thus in the affairs of the universe. . . . It is seated at the table where the great game is played, and it cannot leave it."

city in southern Spain. American delegates urged their British and French counterparts "to stand up to the Germans." Roosevelt meanwhile played to the Kaiser with long telegrams praising his "masterly politics." Once the conference formally opened, Wilhelm followed Roosevelt's lead. The President brought about an agreement that assured French control in Morocco, but managed still to convince the Germans that they had achieved "epochmaking success."

Most Americans probably did not realize the closeness of war or the extent of their President's involvement in the Algeciras meeting. Roosevelt had contributed in a major way to European peace, which, he privately wrote, "was essential to American security and prosperity." For his peacemaking efforts in Europe as well as Asia, the Nobel Committee awarded Roosevelt its Peace Prize for 1906.

Roosevelt's Corollary to the Monroe Doctrine   A delicate problem in international finance roused Roosevelt to further assertiveness. Some unscrupulous bond-brokers had persuaded many governments in Latin America to issue bonds whose proceeds too often financed lavish living for politicians rather than economic development for their countries. Gullible buyers in Europe snapped up the dubious issues because they promised a high rate of return. When the inevitable defaults occurred, European governments supported bond-holders who clamored for restitution. More than once, Roosevelt acted to restrain European nations from military enterprises in the Western Hemisphere. During the Venezuela affair of 1902–3, France, Britain, and Germany blockaded the country, demanding immediate, full payment for a defunct bond issue. Worried that the next step might be occupation, Roosevelt spoke strongly to Germany, whose leaders had talked of a "temporary possession" of territory. The President forced an arbitrated settlement. The tribunal appointed to hear the case ordered Venezuela to pay all its debtors, beginning with those from countries that had manned the blockade.

Soon afterward, Roosevelt defined a specific role for his nation. "The United States cannot see any European power occupy the territory of the Latin American republic," he told Congress, "not even if that is the only way to collect its debts." The United States would act in place of European nations on behalf of their legitimate interests, taking to itself an "international police power" to discipline "flagrant wrongdoing in the Western Hemisphere." The policy is known as the Roosevelt Corollary to the Monroe Doctrine. That famous Doctrine had warned Europe against expansion into the Western Hemisphere; Roosevelt was now indicating that the United States, by protecting the just claims of European countries, would keep them from having to exercise a military presence in the hemisphere.

Roosevelt's announcement was specifically in reference to a dangerous situation in the Dominican Republic. Some Americans and Englishmen had seized local customshouses there after the government negotiated a repayment scheme favoring French, Belgian, and Italian bondholders. Roosevelt ordered the marines into the capital of Santo Domingo, where they imposed a peace of sorts upon the feuding business community. The United States then negotiated a treaty with the local regime that handed control over customs to a retired United States colonel who divided up tariff receipts among the little nation's creditors. Anger among Dominican patriots prompted Roosevelt to use the United States navy "to keep the island in the status quo." Although financial solvency slowly returned under military occupation, nationalists in the Dominican Republic plotted against the intruders. One such attempt would bring another occupation of the island, from 1916 to 1924. The Roosevelt Corollary, designed to prevent European encroachment, had led the United States to meddle instead.

The Lodge Corollary to the Monroe Doctrine   Another twist on the Monroe Doctrine emerged in 1911 when the United States first learned that a Japanese banking syndicate was negotiating with the government of Mexico to purchase a piece of territory there. The Japanese planned to build a major port facility at the strategically significant Magdalena Bay. The State Department immediately lodged a protest, and the Senate passed a resolution sponsored by Henry Cabot Lodge expressing grave concern about any foreign corporation's constructing in the Western Hemisphere a facility that had a military potential. The protests brought the negotiations to an end. The Senate resolution, which became known as the Lodge Corollary, extended the Monroe Doctrine prohibitions to non-European powers as well as to foreign companies.

Suggested Readings

Two studies of Social Darwinism are Michael Ruse, *The Darwinian Revolution: Science Red in Tooth and Claw* (1979) and Cynthia Eagle Russett, *Darwin in America: The Intellectual Response, 1865–1912* (1976). On expansion into Asia see Stanley Karnow, *In Our Image: America's Empire in the Philippines* (1989). Milton Plesur's *America's Outward Thrust, 1865–1890* (1971), sampling newspapers, commercial journals, and other sources of public opinion, concludes that it was not merely economic interests but ideology that took the United States into the expansionism of the period. Other major books on foreign affairs in the late nineteenth century include Walter LaFeber, *The New Empire: An Interpretation of American Expansion, 1860–1898* (1963), David Healy, *United States Expansionism: The Imperialist Urge in the 1890s* (1970), and Charles S. Campbell, *The Transformation of American Foreign Relations, 1865–1900* (1976). Ernest May has written the original *American Imperialism: A Speculative Essay* (1968). Two works on the Spanish-American War are David F. Trask, *The War With Spain in 1988* (1981), and Frank Friedel, *The Splendid Little War* (1958). David McCollough is standard on *The Path Between the Seas: The Crea-*

tion of the Panama Canal 1870–1914 (1977). William Appleman Williams argues, in *The Roots of Modern American Empire* (1969), that behind the American imperialist push at the turn of the century was the American farmer, who wanted his country to open markets abroad. Williams shows how American ideals of self-determination blended with self-interest: keeping peoples free from domination by European powers would ensure the availability of their markets to American commerce; but the idea of the virtuousness of open markets made its own appeal. Roger Daniels has written *Asian Americans: Chinese and Japanese in the United States Since 1850* (1988).

See also Richard E. Welch, *The Response to Imperialism: The United States and the Philippine-American War, 1898–1908* (1979), Walter LaFeber, *The Panama Canal* (1979), Robert L. Biesner, *From the Old Diplomacy to the New, 1865–1900*, 2nd ed. (1986), Gerald F. Linderman, *The Mirror of War: American Society and the Spanish-American War* (1974), John Dobson, *America's Ascent: The United States Becomes a Great Power, 1880–1914* (1974), and Merze Tate, *The United States and the Hawaiian Kingdom: A Political History* (1965).

American Imperialism: Economic Self-Interest or Patriotic Mission?

Walter LaFeber

In less than a century and a quarter the United States had developed from thirteen states strung along a narrow Atlantic coastline into a great world power with possessions in the far Pacific.

Until the middle of the nineteenth century this had been, for the most part, a form of landed expansion which had moved over a large area of the North American continent. The Louisiana Purchase in 1803 had been followed by further important acquisitions in 1819, 1848, 1853, and 1867. But when William H. Seward entered the State Department in 1861, the nature of American expansion had begun to change. Under the impact of the industrial revolution Americans began to search for markets, not land. Sometimes the State Department seized the initiative in making the search, as in the Harrison administration. Frequently the business community pioneered in extending the interests of the United States into foreign areas, as in Mexico in the 1870's and in China in the 1890's. Regardless of which body led the expansionist movement, the result was the same: the growth of economic interests led to political entanglements and to increased military responsibilities.

Americans attempted to build a new empire, an empire which differed fundamentally from the colonial holdings of European powers. Until 1898 the United States believed that its political institutions were suitable only for the North American continent. . . .

In 1898, however, the United States annexed Hawaii and demanded the Philippines from Spain. These acquisitions were not unheralded. Seward had pushed his nation's claims far out into the Pacific with the purchase of Alaska and the Midway islands. . . .

One striking characteristic tied these acquisitions to the new territory brought under American control in 1898 and 1899, immediately after the war with Spain. The United States obtained these areas not to fulfill a colonial policy, but to use these holdings as a means to acquire markets for the glut of goods pouring out of highly mechanized factories and farms.

Hawaii had become an integral part of the American economy long before Harrison attempted to annex it in 1893. Missionaries had forged strong religious and secular links between the islands and the mainland, but of much more importance were the commercial ties. American capital, especially attracted by the islands' fertility during the depression years that plagued the mainland in the 1870's and 1880's, developed sugar plantations whose prosperity depended upon the American consumer. . . .

The Philippines marked the next step westward. In 1899 the Secretary of the American Asiatic Association analyzed the reason for the annexation of these islands in a single sentence: "Had we no interests in China, the possession of the Philippines would be meaningless." Mark Hanna, a somewhat more objective observer of the Far East than the gentleman just quoted, also desired "a strong foothold in the Philippine Islands," for then "we can and will take a large slice of the commerce of Asia. That is what we want. We are bound to share in the commerce of the Far East, and it is better to strike for it while the iron is hot."

Throughout the 1890's, debate had raged around the desirability of annexing yet another outlying possession. The growing desire for an American-controlled Isthmian canal partially explains the interest Hawaii held for some Americans. But it should be emphasized that in the 1890's, at least, Americans did not define their interests in a future canal as military; they termed these interests as economic. Policy makers viewed the control of strategic areas such as Hawaii or Guantánamo Bay in the same light as they viewed the Philippines, that is, as strategic means to obtaining and protecting objectives which they defined as economic.

Reprinted from Walter LaFeber, *The New Empire: An Interpretation of American Expansion, 1860–1898* (Ithaca, New York: Cornell University Press, 1963).

A few [critics] denigrated American imperialism as senseless aping of Europeans. But for the most part an overseas empire seemed to admit the United States to an elite club of powerful, advanced, and civilized nations. Preening Americans proclaimed themselves an imperial power and fondly traced the extent of their far-flung—if not massive—new empire. They also located their new-found genius for imperial exploits in their Anglo-Saxon ancestry.

As the British acquired the largest and richest shares of imperial bounty in Africa and Asia through wars of conquest and pacification that they called "our little wars," many white Americans—with the glaring exception of Irish-Americans—renounced their tradition [of] anglophobia (a legacy of the American Revolution and, especially, the War of 1812) to proclaim the kindredness of the English-speaking people and the natural superiority of Anglo-Saxons. The American nation became the expression of a single "race," the Anglo-Saxon, in a view that swept under the rug the Native American Indians, Irish, blacks, and Jews who had been Americans since colonial times and the Asians, Slavs, and Italians just now disembarking in increasing numbers.

Anglo-Saxon chauvinism was no novelty in the 1890s. Versions had flared up from time to time during the nineteenth century, and it was once again on the increase; the American Protective Association, a nativist, anti-Catholic organization, had been founded in Iowa in 1887. More recently Josiah Strong, a Congregational minister, had written an influential report on missions in 1885, *Our Country*, extolling the special gifts of Anglo-Saxons: they possessed a sense of fair play, the ability to gain wealth honestly, the enjoyment of broad civil liberties in democracies in which every man had an equal vote, the genius for self-government and for governing others fairly, and the evolution of the highest civilization the world had ever known and could ever know because the sun of empire moved from east to west, starting in China and ending, once and for all, in the United States. . . .

These American–Anglo-Saxon attributes, he said, were "peculiarly aggressive traits calculated to impress [their] institutions upon mankind." For Josiah Strong, Anglo-Saxon superiority obligated Congregationalists to convert the remainder of the world to American Protestantism. The seizure of territory was not one of his main concerns. But his rhetoric stressed aggression, thereby sounding other chords of Anglo-Saxonism that prevailed in the writing of Theodore Roosevelt. As early as 1895 Roosevelt had remarked that "this country needs a war," not to conquer territory but to restore manliness and military virtues. Pretending that the true Anglo-Saxon (or Nordic) spirit was that of the warrior, Roosevelt and novelists working in the enormously popular medieval genre, such as Charles Major (*When Knighthood Was in Flower* [2d ed., 1898]), and F. Marion Crawford (*Via Crucis: A Romance of the Second Crusade* [1898]), extolled the grandeur of combat. Crawford's knight characterizes Anglo-Saxons as "men who had the strength to take the world and to be its masters and make it obey whatsoever laws they saw fit to impose." Values like these proved exceedingly convenient during the era of seizing other people's lands.

In justifications of empire, Anglo-Saxonism combined variously with arguments for Anglo-American identity of interest, the white man's burden, manifest and ordinary destiny, and duty. In imperialist reasoning, opposition to expansion was utterly futile. For Alfred Thayer Mahan, expansion was "natural, necessary, irrepressible," and for Henry Cabot Lodge, there existed an "irresistible pressure of events." President McKinley spoke of the peculiarly American destiny that decreed Hawaiian annexation in 1898: "We need Hawaii just as much and a great deal more than we did California. It is manifest destiny." William Allen White recalled that "we were the chosen people . . . imperialism was in the stars." Americans must accept colonies and begin the regeneration of the world or see the world relapse into barbarism.

Nell Irvin Painter, *Standing at Armageddon: The United States, 1877–1919* (New York: W. W. Norton & Company, 1987). Reprinted by permission.

Women trapped in the Triangle Shirtwaist Factory fire on March 25, 1911, had to choose between being burned alive or jumping to near-certain death from windows eight stories high. The disaster took 146 lives. *(Courtesy, Brown Brothers)*

The Progressive Spirit 1900–1917

THE TRIANGLE SHIRTWAIST FACTORY FIRE

In 1900, when Joseph J. Asch began construction of his modern "fireproof" loft building at the corner of Greene Street and Washington Place in lower Manhattan, the shirtwaist had just become the vogue among American women. The ideal American woman now had to look like the Gibson Girl, as drawn by the artist Charles Dana Gibson: stately and aloof, with formal pompadour, heavy-lidded eyes, sensuous mouth, strong chin, full bosom, and wasp waist. She wore a sheer "shirtwaist," vaguely masculine in its high collar but billowing out to accentuate the bosom, then gathered in a mass of tucks, darts, and pleats to the narrow waist above a tailored skirt. The resulting look seemed peculiarly suited to an age in which women were going to work in increasing numbers: in a shirtwaist and skirt a woman looked tall, tailored, free. It became that generation's uniform, shared with the women of elite families by poor working girls, such as those who made shirtwaists in Mr. Asch's building.

The Asch Building was 135 feet high on a 100 by 100 foot plot. Construction was of steel frame and stone, but because the building was less than 150 feet tall its window frames, trim, and floors were all made—quite legally—of wood. It had no sprinkler system. The building had several elevators, but only two staircases, and a fire escape ending about 20 feet above a courtyard that, soon after the building's construction, became fully en-

continued

closed by other buildings. It had never been the scene of a fire drill. Except for some doubt over whether the fire escape legally constituted a third staircase, the structure passed fire inspection in October 1910.

At about 4:30 on Saturday afternoon, March 25, 1911, the workday was just ending for 500 employees—most of them young Italian or Jewish immigrant women—of the Triangle Shirtwaist Company, which occupied the top three floors of the building. Just as the cutters were hanging their patterns on the wires above the long worktables on the eighth floor, a flash fire broke out in a bin stuffed with rags beneath one of the tables. It quickly spread to the patterns and the freshly cut pieces of thin cotton and almost instantly passed out of control. Within minutes floors, tables, and partitions were aflame, windows were popping from the pressure, and smoke and fire spread relentlessly through the building. Attempts at an orderly exit turned to panic. Frightened workers discovered doors locked to keep control over employees, a stairwell with no exit to the roof, clawing crowds struggling to gain entrance to the elevators, masses of humanity pressed against metal doors that opened inward to the loft. Flames trapped scores of women and forced them to the windows. There they made a grim choice. A passerby below saw something that looked "like a bale of dark dress goods" falling from one window. "Someone's in there all right. He's trying to save the best cloth," remarked another observer. Then came the next bundle, and halfway down it seemed to open and reveal that it was no bolt of cloth, but a young girl. "Don't jump! Here they

WORKING FOR THE TRIANGLE SHIRTWAIST COMPANY

Pauline Newman, an organizer and educational director for the International Ladies' Garment Workers Union until her death in 1986, worked at the notorious Triangle Shirtwaist factory in New York. This is her account.

A cousin of mine worked for the Triangle Shirtwaist Company and she got me on there in October of 1901. It was probably the largest shirtwaist factory in the city of New York then. They had more than two hundred operators, cutters, examiners, finishers. Altogether more than four hundred people on two floors. The fire took place on one floor, the floor where we worked. . . .

We started work at seven-thirty in the morning, and during the busy season we worked until nine in the evening. They didn't pay you any overtime and they didn't give you anything for supper money. Sometimes

they'd give you a little apple pie if you had to work very late.

What I had to do was not really very difficult. It was just monotonous. When the shirtwaists were finished at the machine there were some threads that were left, and all the youngsters—we had a corner on the floor that resembled a kindergarten—we were given little scissors to cut the threads off. . . .

Well, of course, there were [child labor] laws on the books, but no one bothered to enforce them. The employers were always tipped off if there was going to be an inspection. "Quick," they'd say, "into the boxes!" And we children would climb into the big boxes the finished shirts were stored in. Then some shirts were piled on top of us, and when the inspector came—no children. The factory always got an okay from the inspector, and I

come!" men shouted on the sidewalks gesturing toward the arriving fire engines. Firemen spread life nets; the falling bodies tore them from their hands, smashing holes in the pavement. "Raise the ladders!" screamed the crowd assembling on the sidewalks. The ladders reached six floors. Then the firemen turned on the new high-pressure hose system. It reached eighty-five feet—only to the seventh floor. "Thud—dead! Thud—dead! Thud—dead!" so began the eyewitness story by United Press reporter William Gunn Shepherd. On Greene Street he saw people "jammed into the windows. They were burning to death in the windows. One by one the window jambs broke. Down came the bodies in a shower, burning, smoking, flaming bodies, with disheveled hair trailing upward." By a little before five o'clock the bodies had stopped falling. One hundred and forty-six people had died.

No one went to jail for the Triangle fire. The company's owners were tried for manslaughter, but the state could not prove that they knew the loft exits were kept locked. The fire and building departments blamed each other. The International Ladies' Garment Workers Union (ILGWU) and some of New York's wealthiest families combined to raise a relief fund for the stricken families. Almost the entire East Side gathered on April 5 for a memorial parade. Amid constant rainfall, about 120,000 people marched through the arch at Washington Square and up Fifth Avenue with neither bands nor banners save a single streamer reading "We Demand Fire Protection."

As a result of the disaster, New York City created the Bureau of

United Press reporter William Shepherd watched the fire:

"I looked upon the heap of dead bodies and I remembered these girls were the shirtwaist makers. I remembered their great strike of last year in which these same girls had demanded more sanitary conditions and more safety precautions in the shops. These dead bodies were the answer."

---

suppose someone at City Hall got a little something, too. . . .

I stopped working at the Triangle Factory during the strike in 1909 and I didn't go back. . . .

After the strike I worked with the union, organizing in Philadelphia and Cleveland and other places, so I wasn't at the Triangle Shirtwaist Factory when the fire broke out, but a lot of my friends were. . . . Of course, someone from here called me immediately and I came back. It's very difficult to describe the feeling because I knew the place and I knew so many of the girls. The thing that bothered me was the employers got a lawyer. How anyone could have *defended* them—because I'm quite sure that the fire was planned for insurance purposes. And no one is going to convince me otherwise. And when they testified that the door to the fire escape was open, it was a lie! It was never open. Locked all the time. One hundred and forty-six people were sacrificed,

and the judge fined Blank and Harris seventy-five dollars!

Conditions were dreadful in those days. But there was something that is lacking today. . . .

Now, I'm a little discouraged sometimes when I see the workers spending their free hours watching television—trash. We fought so hard for those hours and they waste them. We used to read Tolstoy, Dickens, Shelley, by candlelight, and they watch the "Hollywood Squares." Well, they're free to do what they want. That's what we fought for.

Source: Joan Morrison and Charlotte Fox Zabusky, eds., *American Mosaic: The Immigrant Experience in the Words of Those Who Lived It* (New York: E.P. Dutton, 1980), pp. 9–14. Copyright © 1980 by Joan Morrison and Charlotte Fox Zabusky. Reprinted with permission.

Fire Prevention, ending much of the divided responsibility that had made the inspection of factory buildings of such little effect. The state created a Factory Investigation Commission and placed it under the direction of two rising young urban politicians, Robert F. Wagner, Sr., and Alfred E. Smith. In four years of legislative work, the Commission made New York the most advanced state in the protection of factory workers. It is an old story, reform that follows a catastrophe instead of preventing it.

Society in the Progressive Era

The early twentieth century in the United States was a period of a reformist impulse that according to the usage of the time best takes the name "progressive." The word was then in wide employment, and some political figures were called progressives. In 1912 appeared a Progressive Party putting forth Theodore Roosevelt as its presidential candidate, and as late as 1924 a party championing the candidacy of Robert M. La Follette assumed the same title. Since political figures then and since labeled "progressive" differed fundamentally on specific reforms, the suggestion has been raised that the term and concept as applied to the era are meaningless. But it is possible to define for the first decade and a half of the century a number of distinctive reform ambitions, foremost among them an attempt on a national scale to give order to technical, economic, and social energies that seemed out of control. The assumption here will be that the Progressive Era usefully refers to a period stretching from the presidency of Theodore Roosevelt to the end of the First World War.

Political progressivism was rooted in a vital time of intellectual inquiry enriched by work that the philosophers William James and John Dewey and others had already been doing. The age was charged with the energies of an ever more sophisticated technology. Artistic experimentation added to the sense that the world could be made anew. The Social Gospel had awakened slumbering consciences among religious people. Hideous poverty remained, while an increasingly comfortable middle class was ready to listen to daring schemes of reformation at the national, state, and local levels. The politics of the period cannot be understood apart from these social currents.

Economic Growth

Accelerating Growth

The rising standard of living fed and was rooted in a growing economy rapidly eclipsing that of any other industrial nation. After the depression of the 1890s, economic growth accelerated at about six percent per year. Total physical production increased about seventy-five percent in the first decade of the twentieth century. Per capita income increased in real dollars from $496 to $608 in this same period. The burgeoning domestic economy was buttressed by the nation's increasingly favorable position in world markets. After 1892 the United States continuously enjoyed favorable trade balances, investment abroad quadrupling from about $635 million in 1897 to $2.7 billion in 1914.

By 1900 industry had assumed the leading role in the economy. Even more startling was the unprecedented prosperity enjoyed by farmers. Although agriculture's share of the national product was declining relative to that of industry, the long era of depression that had spurred the agrarian protest movements was now over. Later, the New Deal of the 1930s would officially establish the farmer's real purchasing power for the period 1909 to 1914 as the ideal standard. The government would attempt always to bring the farmer's buying power into "parity" or equality with it.

Public investment also contributed to increased economic growth. Between 1903 and 1913, the combined expenditures of federal, state, and local governments in such fields as education, roads, playgrounds, public health, and the civil service almost doubled, from $1.7 to $3.1 billion.

The New Cities
These tangible signs of prosperity and progress attracted to urban areas both rural Americans and European immigrants. In 1900 only thirty-eight cities had more than 100,000 people; in 1920 there were sixty-eight; in 1930 over a hundred. About seventy percent of the new urban population consisted of rural migrants and of immigrants largely from southern and eastern Europe. In the first decade of the twentieth century alone, 8.8 million immigrants entered the country. Declining death rates helped to increase the native population as well. Improvements in nutrition, sanitation, and public health facilities, along with a wave of immigration that included relatively few children, brought up the average age of the population from 22.9 in 1900 to 25.3 in 1920.

Yet for all the prosperity of these years Americans were experiencing a puzzling inflation. In the years between 1897 and 1917 the cost of living doubled while real wages lagged behind. Popular magazines like the *Ladies Home Journal* and the *Independent* ran articles by women talking about the social consequences of high prices for rent, food, and fuel. Few understood the phenomenon, but urban middle-class Americans indicted the trusts. As Woodrow Wilson put it: "The high cost of living is arranged by private understanding." Others believed that the wages won by organized labor were pushing up prices. Recent economic historians have argued that such inflation is normal and that the long nineteenth-century years of deflation had been an aberration. In those years large-scale investment in such industries as railroads, iron, and steel had brought an increase in production of goods and services and a consequent lowering in prices. During the progressive period new forms of long-term investment in both old and new industries deferred immediate production and pushed up prices. Whatever the cause, inflation convinced many Americans that there were important components of their lives over which they had no control.

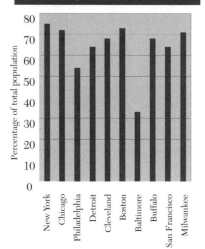

Percentage of Immigrants and Their Children in Population of Some Major Cities as of 1920

Corporations and Capital

Corporations   In 1898 there were just eighty-two relatively small trusts. By 1904, 318 large combinations with a total capital of $6 billion ran such industries as railroads, meatpacking, steel, copper, tobacco, and petroleum. In 1901 J. P. Morgan had formed United States Steel, the nation's first billion dollar corporation, absorbing 158 companies. By 1909 one percent of all the industrial firms in the country were producing forty-four percent of the nation's manufactured goods.

Many of the new combinations were themselves organized by investment banking firms like J. P. Morgan and Company and Kuhn, Loeb and Company, which emerged when heavy industry turned to Wall Street for credit. Finance capital meant that a few titans virtually controlled the credit resources of the country. In both 1893 and 1907, when the nation was at the brink of financial collapse, it was the Morgan firm that came to the rescue.

Responding to charges of a "money trust" circulating widely in the press, Congress decided to launch an investigation of the financial markets in the United States. A subcommittee of the House Committee on Banking and Currency, led by Representative Arsene Pujo of Louisiana, undertook the investigation during the spring of 1912. Dozens of leading financiers and bankers, including Morgan, were called to testify before the committee. When the hearings were concluded, the Pujo committee reported that the concentration of money and credit was increasing in the United States, and that such investment banking practices as interlocking directorates, stock purchases, the use of consortiums, and banking investment in railroads, insurance companies, and public utilities were likely to make the problem worse. Pujo also claimed that J. P. Morgan had enough power to cause a major financial panic and industrial depression.

The Pujo Committee hearings were taking place just when the National Monetary Commission was making its report. After the panic of 1907, Congress had passed the Aldrich-Vreeland Act to give the money supply a measure of flexibility. The legislation also established the National Monetary Commission, under the chairmanship of Senator Nelson Aldrich of Rhode Island, to study the currency system. In 1912 the commission recommended the creation of a national reserve association with branches around the country. The associations would have the authority to issue currency during times of economic contraction. Such a program, commission members believed, would prevent future financial panics or at least make them less severe. The National Monetary Commission report, along with the Pujo Committee investigations, helped create a political momentum that was to lead to the Federal Reserve Act of 1913 during Woodrow Wilson's administration.

As early as 1886, cartoonist Thomas Nast attacked trusts. Here the people's welfare is sinking as the Statue of Liberty is defaced. *(Courtesy, New York Public Library)*

The Newly Rich   Such enormous power frightened people. Though the new way of doing business gave order to several important industries, small local competitors increasingly lost out to large national—in some cases international— companies. Finance capitalists were accused of manipulating other people's money, and making great profits without producing any tangible goods or services. They lived somewhere, most of them in the East, far away and unconnected to the communities and sections their actions vitally affected. Their great wealth, displayed in monumental mansions surrounded by landscaped estates, overshadowed the moderately comfortable local gentry who composed most small-town elites. There was but limited comfort in learning of the bad taste with which the rich spent their money.

Making Things

American industry grew in these years in the sheer quantity of factories, shops, and human labor; but it grew more spectacularly in techniques and sources of energy. The improvement of engineering, the harnessing of electricity, the study of chemistry, the physical rearranging of factories, the rethinking of the very functions by which a hand and eye complete a job: these give some idea of the character of industry in its years of spectacular twentieth-century growth.

Frederick Winslow Taylor, an engineering and efficiency expert, was the apostle of what became known as the scientific management movement. He pioneered in time and motion studies of specific tasks with the aim of improving worker performance and increasing production. Breaking jobs down into their smallest components, Taylor looked for the best way of completing work with the perfect tool for the given task. He also labored incessantly at reducing unnecessary worker movements on the job. By redesigning floor plans, assembly line flow charts, and the shipping and handling process, Taylor eliminated excess movement. At the Midvale Steel Company in Pennsylvania during the 1880s, Taylor increased production by 300 percent and earnings for workers by more than twenty-five percent. Taylor soon established a very successful consulting business, and the Bethlehem Steel Company hired his firm to bring scientific management to the company. Through groundbreaking work on shoveling, Taylor made it possible for Bethlehem to cut its workforce of pig-iron shovelers from 600 to 140 and cut in half the cost of handling the material. Despite considerable opposition from fledgling labor unions suspicious of a system that clamped so tight a discipline on workers, scientific management spread rapidly in American factories and shops.

Taylor's Scientific Management   The full implications of Taylor's work awaited the early years of the twentieth century. By then a fascination with the sheer productive strength of industrialism was beginning to be supplemented with a recognition that its powers needed to be subdued to social order. At the same time the principles of order inherent in technology itself were coming to be more extensively explored. That exploration is in effect what Taylor's scientific management was about. A machine operates by the precise and economical arrangement of the forces within it. By much the same process, the worker on a factory floor was to apply body and mental forces in the most efficient way to the accomplishment of

Frederick Winslow Taylor conducted time and motion studies early in his life. As a boy, he had apparently invented the overhand pitch to deliver the ball with greater speed and precision. "Taylorism," like automation in a later era, alarmed some unions, who disliked the mechanical role he assigned to them. Inspectors would stand by a workstation with a clipboard in one hand and a stopwatch in another. But the effectiveness of Taylor's "scientific shop management" methods—which epitomized the Progressive Movement's drive for efficiency—contributed to material abundance.

the collective task. They were also to be trained in effective procedures and encouraged to make their own suggestions. From one point of view, scientific management further subjugated factory hands to machinery. From another, Taylorism was acknowledging, as capitalism had seldom before done, that trained and committed workers were essential to exact technological processes. Taylor urged, to the discomfort of employers, that workers be rewarded for their increases in productivity.

The Assembly Line   Assembly-line production—perhaps the central element in the later phases of the consumer society— awaited an expanded population, technological progress, prosperous times with available capital, and the imperative demands of wartime. Henry Ford preached "a standardized, low cost car for every adult person in America." Improving upon the production of interchangeable parts pioneered by Eli Whitney near the end of the eighteenth century, Ford developed the machinery for standardized quantity production of automobile components. The manufacture of cars was essentially a problem of assembly. Ford began with stationary assembly, and one hundred such assembly stations were set up. Within a few years, a conveyor belt speeded the process further, bringing the Ford chassis to the worker and moving it along at a constant rate. Each arrived at the appropriate moment and all were assembled in proper order into a complete car. Every worker accomplished a small and specialized task, infinitely repeated. This technique, Ford explained, "lifted the hard work off the backs of men and laid it on steel and motors." When the car reached the end of the line, it was driven off. Assembly time was cut from almost twelve and a half hours to slightly over one and a half, production skyrocketed, and prices dropped. The Model T was so popular that Ford produced it for almost twenty years, offering it in any color "so long as it's black." Increased car sales spurred the growth of the petroleum industry and improved the processing of rubber used for tires. Soon standardized interchangeable parts and the assembly line were making complicated machinery and machine tools for American industrial plants that were rapidly mechanizing.

The assembly line along with Taylor's scientific management were embodiments of what the architecture of Louis Sullivan, with its slender steel skeletons, had been announcing visually. Not raw power but power precisely and economically ordered was increasingly to be the character of modern technology.

Steel and Chemicals   Between 1899 and 1919 innovation in machinery and electrical engineering tripled the horsepower in factories and significantly increased the output per worker. The development in the 1890s of hydroelectric power and the invention of the steam turbine made possible the production of cheap and abundant electrical power. Electric motors, which had supplied only five percent of factory power in 1899, generated fifty-five percent in 1919.

Steel manufacture expanded greatly in the Progressive Era. By 1900 the open hearth furnace had replaced the older Bessemer process for more than half the production of steel and made a tougher, less

Henry Ford at the turn of the century. *(Courtesy, Library of Congress)*

Ford's assembly lines employed the best-paid factory workers in America in 1914. *(Courtesy, Scribner's)*

brittle metal. Steel production is basically a chemical process, and manufacturers produced a variety of alloys adaptable to numerous needs. The modernizing of railroads consumed steel for heavier rails and larger cars, and wooden bridges gradually gave way to steel. Western cattlemen increasingly used barbed wire fencing. Wire, nails, naval vessels, and the beams and girders of modern skyscrapers also used steel.

Innovations in the relatively new chemical industry raised the value of its products from $48 million in 1899 to $158 million in 1914. In 1911 Americans began production of "artificial silk," later called rayon. An electrolytic process for refining aluminum made this hard but light metal increasingly popular for kitchen utensils, automobile parts, and electrical equipment. Research into chemistry financed by commercial concerns ensured that manufacturing would continue to be innovative in the years to come.

Consumer Goods

A vast array of goods now presented itself to consumers of sufficient means. Refrigerator cars, innovations in canning, and the proliferation of home iceboxes enriched the previously dull American diet by putting a wide variety of foods on the table regardless of the season: a steady supply of fruit, vegetables, and meat. Modern pasteurizing plants gradually made milk safe to drink, even in cities. Chains like the Great Atlantic and Pacific Tea Company, with over a thousand stores by 1915, offered lower prices through large-scale purchasing, high volume, and the elimination of credit and the middleman—incidentally helping to standardize the quality of products available on the shelves. More and more Americans bought their household goods in the new 5&10¢ stores pioneered by F. W. Woolworth, or in the large department stores, aptly described as "palaces of consumption." Millions of others, especially rural Americans, met their clothing and household needs through the great catalogues distributed by Sears, Roebuck and Montgomery Ward, which helped to lessen the traditional isolation and monotony of farm life. Ready-to-wear clothing, an industry that thrived in this era, made fashionable styles and good fabrics available to all but the poorest Americans. Foreign observers complained that in the United States it was impossible to tell a person's class from his clothing.

Standards of cleanliness and comfort also rose as the inventions and appliances of the late nineteenth century, at first the luxuries of the well-to-do, became the necessities of the middle class. The introduction of the porcelain bathtub and flush toilet, along with the development of the septic tank, made the private indoor bathroom increasingly common in middle-class households. Home electrification, born in the 1880s with the development of the central power station, had spread rapidly by the turn of the century, and made possible a wide diversity of new appliances. The first electric household appliance, the flatiron, had its introduction at the Chicago World's Fair in 1893. Washing machines made laundering easier, although housewives now had higher standards of cleanliness, so that probably at least as much time continued to be

Winter 1896 catalog of Sears, Roebuck, famous as the "world's greatest silent salesman." *(Courtesy, Sears, Roebuck and Co., Chicago, Ill.)*

The first phonographs, available as early as the 1890s, played cylinders rather than flat records. This advertisement for a "graphophone" appeared in the 1901 Sears, Roebuck catalog.

GRAPHOPHONES OR TALKING MACHINES.

A Graphophone Exhibition.

You can hear in your own home all of the latest songs, instrumental music, speeches, etc., from the best artists in the metropolitan cities. The Graphophone or Talking Machine is a most wonderful invention, but until recently the prices were so high that their use has not become very general. All this is now changed and they are becoming so popular that thousands of private families are purchasing them for home entertainment. They also afford a most excellent means for money making by traveling from place to place and giving public exhibitions. By using the horn they can be distinctly heard in every part of a large hall. An outfit with records complete for an evenings entertainment can be purchased for a small amount of money. We list here but one style of machine, but the coin-in-the-slot machines as well as a large variety of records, etc., will be found listed in our special phonograph catalogue, which will be sent on application.

Graphophones, records, etc., will be sent C. O. D. when desired, on receipt of $2.00 with order as a guarantee of good faith. The balance can be paid at the express office after having examined the goods; but we advise sending the full amount of cash and save the 3 per cent. discount, also the return charges on the money.

spent in this traditional activity. Gas stoves facilitated cooking, and mechanical refrigerators began to supplant the widely used icebox by about 1912. Central heating, which spread rapidly after the large-scale production of the cast-iron radiator in the 1890s, brought the luxurious comfort of hotels both to individual houses and to new skyscraper apartments and office buildings in the cities.

Leisure Americans spent their leisure time in new ways. George Eastman developed the Kodak camera, first marketed in 1888 under the slogan "You press the button, we do the rest." Its almost immediate popularity turned photography from the skill of a few to an activity available to everyone for capturing everyday experience. The phonograph, with the new flat-disk record, first marketed for about $25, was by 1914 being produced at a rate of some 500,000 per year. With the development of the motion picture in the 1890s Americans also began attending the new nickelodeons (a name also applied to phonograph boxes fed with a nickel), where, for a nickel, the audience enjoyed short silent films. By 1908 there were 8,000 nickelodeons in the country. By 1920, the movies had become the most popular form of commercial amusement, and 17,000 theaters around the nation showed them to millions of viewers each week.

Getting Around

New forms of transportation and communication sped Americans to work, took them on their vacations, and lessened their isolation from one another. Alexander Graham Bell invented the telephone in 1876, soon bringing people within talking distance of one another. In cities and towns after 1890, electric street railways, or trolleys, replaced horsedrawn cars. These enabled the middle class to move to the newer suburbs of Boston, Chicago, and elsewhere beyond the traditional walking city. Thus began the segregation of work from living places so characteristic of American cities today. The period also encompassed the invention of the airplane and the first successful flight by the Wright brothers at Kitty Hawk, North Carolina, in 1903, although there was no significant development of commercial aviation until well after World War I.

Trains The Progressive Era was preeminently the age of the railroad. Business travel accounted for most passenger service, but the railroads were also successful in promoting pleasure excursions. Millions of Americans took to their vacation spots trains romantically named the *Adirondack Express* or the *Seashore*. Mythical personalities like Phoebe Snow, who extolled the cleanliness of the Lackawanna ("my dress stays white though I ride all night, when I take the road of anthracite"), advertised the ease and comfort of passenger travel. Innovation and new investment, particularly in the period from 1898 to 1906, allowed the railroads to overhaul their antiquated stock and track, improve the safety of rail travel, and build architecturally significant monuments like New York's Grand Central Station to handle the increased volume of traffic.

The glossy *National Geographic,* especially its frequent colorful articles on the West, helped lure American families into traveling long distances for pleasure. But perhaps the most important spur to increased long-distance passenger travel was the accelerated production of the ornate and luxurious Pullman sleeping, dining, and parlor cars. Pullman journeys rose from 5 million in 1900 to 25 million in 1914. In 1902 luxury rail travel arrived with the inauguration of nonstop all-Pullman trains, among them the *Twentieth Century Limited,* which traveled on a twenty-four-hour schedule between New York and Chicago.

Even comfortable accommodations might not have lured the millions of rail passengers without improvements in safety and efficiency. The introduction of the Westinghouse air brake made it possible to brake simultaneously, from inside the locomotive, all the cars of increasingly long and heavy trains. New types of more powerful steam locomotives and larger all-steel cars carried more passengers and freight at greater speed; new refrigerator and tank cars also added to the volume of freight. Accompanying the improvement in stock was the rebuilding of miles of dilapidated track and the addition of second, third, and even fourth mainline tracks and heavier rails. Hundreds of wooden trestles and bridges were replaced with ones that could support the newer, heavier locomotives. The automatic coupler, making it unnecessary to have workmen standing between cars, enabled railroads to exchange cars on a national basis and slightly reduced the incredibly high accident rate as well. Electrification of some lines in urban high-traffic areas and automatic block signals on some main lines also helped reduce the number of railroad accidents.

Automobiles   Adapting earlier German and English "horseless carriages," American bicycle-builders, mechanics, and repairmen like Henry Ford, R. E. Olds, Elwood Haynes, and Charles E. Duryea were constructing and selling by the mid-1890s workable motor-driven vehicles that would put the railroads into decline. By 1895 there were some 300 automobiles on the roads, perhaps one-third of them electric, then favored for their relatively quiet and clean ride and their maneuverability. By 1905—within a single decade—the number of registered vehicles had reached 77,988. Nonetheless, the automobile remained an object of popular suspicion, the toy of the mechanically inclined and a luxury of the rich. Autos, argued Woodrow Wilson in 1906, "are a picture of arrogance of wealth [that] spreads socialistic feeling." American capital continued to shun them, and manufacturers resorted to staging races to encourage their use. This somewhat inauspicious start did not deter a new magazine, *The Horseless Age,* from prophecies of a great future for automobiles.

Within a few years improvements in technology and production advances had put the automobile within financial reach of the average citizen. Even before World War I the mechanically simple and more powerful gasoline engine largely displaced steam and electric cars. Engines of four, six, or eight cylinders, along with cord tires, steering

***Rattling Ford Jokes.* A book of jokes featuring Ford's Model T: "What's the difference between a 1910 model Ford and a 1916?" "Six years."**

Ford and his Model T became an enduring part of American folklore. For several years beginning around 1914, the nation was overwhelmed with Ford jokes spreading like a respiratory infection from mouth to mouth, then hawked in paper-bound books: "two hundred good jokes for only fifteen cents." Many stressed the car's tinniness. A farmer who stripped the tin off his barn's roof and sent it to Ford received word that "While your car was an exceptionally bad wreck, we shall be able to complete repairs and return it by the first of the week." There were even Ford jokes about Ford jokes: a man in a theater refused to believe that a show was over, saying "That can't be—I haven't heard a Ford joke yet."

This delightful vignette, set chiefly in Cooperstown, New York, traces the enthusiasm of an extraordinarily indulgent father and his son impatiently awaiting delivery of their first automobile in 1909–1910.

Wednesday, Oct. 13, 1909.

My dearest Boy,

Alea Jacta Est, which meant when I was a boy, The Die is Cast. In other words, The Auto is OURS. Monday morning I went to the Cadillac Office, and paid $250. down, the remainder to be paid on delivery of auto, and thus secured the auto for next May 1st. I was afraid that they might have such a rush of orders that they could not fill them, and I might get left. I send you a copy of the contract. You will see there are quite a lot of extras. But they are necessary. . . .

Your loving father,
Charles F

[New York City]
Wednesday, Jan. 12, 1910.

My dearest Boy,

We received your telegram Sunday afternoon, telling that you had reached Millerton safely, and we felt much relieved. Your postal came yesterday, and the letter today. I shall send by express your comb and watch in a box with some fruit. To-day if possible.

Yesterday I went to the Auto show. The Cadillac looked fine, and I got some books with specifications describing it. I send you one, with some other pamphlets that are of interest. The Goodyear detachable-demountable tire was a wonder. You merely pushed the whole thing on the rim, gave it a kick, and it was all right. Some springs held it in position. Nothing could be simpler and easier. I send you a little comic book about autos and Goodyear tires, which I think you will enjoy. I bought still another gauge for tires, quite an original thing, so now I have three, enough to test all the tires in the country. . . .

wheels instead of tillers, and front radiators improved the appearance and performance of automobiles. With the introduction of the Model T in 1908, the Ford Motor Company offered at $950 an awkward-looking but sturdy vehicle with simple standardized mechanical parts that almost anyone could repair. Before many years assembly-line production was giving the Ford Motor Company a daily production capacity of 1,000 and an annual figure of almost 250,000. The base price eventually dropped to $290 and the popularity of the horseless carriage was assured.

The increasing popularity of the automobile encouraged a movement for improvement of roads. Until the turn of the century, state and local governments were the prime builders and custodians of the country's approximately two million miles of mainly unpaved rural roads. The bicycle craze of the 1890s and the general desire for rural improvement spurred farm, business, and citizens groups to agitate for better roads. Fuel taxes and automobile registration fees, state aid, and highway supervision would not develop fully until after World War I, but their beginnings occurred during the progressive period. The American romance with the automobile had begun.

1923 Model T. *(Courtesy, Ford Motor Co.)*

A New Middle Class: Ideas for Progress

The New Professions

A major part of the middle class was a creation of industrial society. It included the new bureaucratic, salaried employees: clerical workers and salespeople, professionals and technicians, government workers, and service

Sunday, January 16, 1910

Dearest Boy,

. . . . Thursday night Anita and I went to a Bridge Party, and on coming out found it snowing hard. It continued until Yesterday morning, making a pile over a foot high. The worst storm in years. But the sun yesterday and to-day shone with unusual brightness. I suppose you had some of this storm, probably more than we did. How deep was your snow? And now you must be enjoying coasting. We still enjoy seeing autos get stuck in the piles opposite our windows, and they have an awful time getting out. Just now horses have the best of it. . . .

May 24, 1910

My dearest Boy:

Last Friday I got very impatient, and finally wired to New York, asking how soon I might expect the AUTO. Soon after, I received the following answer:—"Received nothing but demis expect touring next week will wire." We all puzzled over the word demis and could make nothing out of it, until I pronounced the word differently from the way it looked, and then solved the mystery. Demis is the plural of Demi, which means "half," like a demi-tasse of coffee after dinner, meaning a small or half cup, and this demi meant a half tonneau or in other words a small car. According to this message I should expect a touring car this week. Well! perhaps! I have been disappointed so often that I am learning to expect nothing. . . .

Wednesday, June 1, 1910.

My dearest Boy.

Hurrah! Hurrah!—No! The auto has not yet arrived, but the Company has just written to me that they hope to ship it to me this week, and I feel much encouraged.

Saturday, June 11, 1910

My dearest Boy,

Just a last word. The Auto has come at last and is now in the Garage. I shall bring the car . . . Tuesday . . . and *you* can take it home. . . .

Your loving father

---

employees. These were the consumers ravaged by inflation to whom progressives—particularly in the cities—appealed. They also included the social workers, teachers, government scientists, and public officials whose professional activities often brought them in direct touch with the problems of poverty, sickness, exploitation, and corruption that the politics of the era struggled to address.

The older middle class of independent professionals and entrepreneurs had their own grounds for uneasiness. Many small businessmen, in particular, were enthusiastic progressives. They worried over the large corporations that seemed in control of their supplies and goods, fretted over railroad rates, feared unions, and distrusted the creaky national banking system heavily dominated by private bankers, many of them located on Wall Street. Independent professionals—lawyers, doctors, ministers—saw their independence erode and their world change. Ministers unable to match the styles of their rich parishioners or the expertise of secular authorities feared that they were being replaced as social arbiters. Salaried workers gradually took over such mechanical jobs as title-searching that had enabled many a lawyer to survive while waiting for more interesting work. The middle-class professions were prepared to defend the integrity of their specialized kinds of knowledge. The medical profession, for example, crusaded in the Progressive Era against quacks armed with bottled cures for diseases like diphtheria—as well as against midwives with folk knowledge that many male doctors lacked. A sharp upgrading of medical education, the rapid spread of immunization and antiseptic surgery, and great advances in public health made the Progressive Era formative years of American medicine.

Urban Progressivism

The Cities   Most of the initial efforts of the progressives were directed to cities. That was where were posed the greatest challenges to the progressive faith in scientifically managed social change. And it was the cities that seemed the most resistant to political reform.

British commentator Lord Bryce delivered a common view in 1889 when he wrote that its cities were the "one conspicuous failure" of American civilization. At the heart of this failure, or so Bryce and other critics believed, was the rise of machine politics.

Lincoln Steffens' *The Shame of the Cities* (1904) was the most famous progressive indictment of urban corruption. Steffens insisted that municipal corruption depended upon the active support of the most respectable and wealthiest citizens and upon the passive acquiescence of the middle class. One machine politician, Tammany Hall's George Washington Plunkitt, described good government campaigns as "morning glories" that faded in the noonday sun when the public wearied of the battle. Progressives knew this and went beyond goals of "good government" and devoted themselves to making urban government more efficient and serviceable. Unlike earlier reformers who concentrated primarily on reducing the cost of government by eliminating graft and bribery, the progressives had positive programs that might as easily expand government as streamline it.

Reformers began to modernize the nation's cities in the 1890s. One of the earliest of these urban leaders was Hazen Pingree, who became mayor of Detroit in 1889. He built schools and parks, forced reductions in gas rates and streetcar fares, reformed the local tax structure, and even introduced work relief during the depression of the 1890s. In Toledo, Samuel M. Jones, better known as "Golden Rule" Jones, built playgrounds and golf links, promoted municipal concerts, and established kindergartens in schools. He introduced the eight-hour day for some municipal employees and removed the police force from political influence. In Cleveland, Tom Johnson won his fight for the three cent fare on streetcars, passed effective public health ordinances, built recreational facilities, improved municipal garbage collection, reformed the police department, upgraded the city waterworks. These three men, whose example spread to cities across the country, were all successful businessmen who had turned to political reform. More than contenting themselves with simply being crusaders against the party machines, such reformers had a vision of government as a public business, to be run efficiently by skillful and educated people providing services and social justice for a wide range of citizens.

Many of the younger progressives, fresh out of college or the new graduate schools, entered public life hypnotized by these older reformers. Notable among Johnson's protégés was Frederic C. Howe. One of the first Americans to earn the Ph.D. degree, from Johns Hopkins, Howe was a young attorney in Cleveland when he joined Johnson's administration. He served on the city council and then in the Ohio state senate before returning to Cleveland and a position on the city's tax commission. Later he would become United States Commissioner of

WHAT HISTORIANS SAY

Richard Hofstadter, in *The Age of Reform,* argues that the significance of writers like Lincoln Steffens was largely symbolic. Crusading journalists would spell out the excruciating details of political corruption or economic exploitation for middle-class readers who believed, Hofstadter claimed, that the mere exposure of these wrongs somehow would cause them to disappear. Hence, he argued, muckraking led to few practical reforms.

An extension of this analysis could note the largely symbolic character of many progressive-era reforms. Sociologist Joseph Gusfield describes the prohibition movement as a Symbolic Crusade more interested in enshrining old-fashioned virtues like sobriety and striking out at immigrants than in controlling the use of alcohol.

There is a tendency to denigrate the importance of symbolic actions, to imply that they are not as meaningful as nuts-and-bolts changes. But, as Gusfield points out, people attach great significance to symbols. In that sense they are perfectly real and worth pondering.

Immigration. In 1905 Howe wrote a book that became the bible of urban progressivism, *The City: The Hope of Democracy*. The progressively governed city, Howe believed, would significantly broaden the services it offered to residents. It would collect garbage, supply water and electricity, extend the reach of the public schools through kindergartens, and open new parks and playgrounds. It was to regulate housing through model tenement laws and ensure the public health by inspecting milk. It would take over ownership of so-called natural monopolies, "the street railways, gas, water, electric-lighting, telephone, power, and heating companies." The rule, wrote Howe, should be "that whatever is of necessity a monopoly should be a public monopoly."

No city, not even Cleveland, fully measured up to Howe's ambitious reform agenda, but a great many made significant progress. New York took the lead in establishing minimum standards for housing, Detroit in operating public utilities. As reform mayor Hazen Pingree summarized his administration's achievements, the city was "no longer lighted by gas, but has its own electric lighting plant and is magnificently illuminated at less than half the old rates. The gas furnished to its citizens has been reduced at least one-third in price and much improved in quality." Streetcar fares had come down, telephone rates reduced, parks improved, schools built, and the city's wharves rebuilt. Many American cities were quite well governed during the Progressive Era, especially middle-sized and small cities that rarely had to deal with machine politics.

Middle-Class Urban Reform   Urban progressives came largely from the middle class that had long felt shut out of power in the cities, creating alliances with the churches, the settlement houses, the social workers, teachers, lawyers, doctors, and small businessmen. Most rejected the decentralized, ward-based government that had characterized the old regimes. In place of a council or board of aldermen, with each member controlling a little fiefdom in his neighborhood, they wanted a strong mayor supported by the middle class of the entire city. In many smaller cities progressivism went farther, obliterating the old political structure and centralizing executive and legislative functions in a commission form of government, or hiring a professional manager to run the city. Progressives sought to separate governing from politics; their reforms looked more to modernization and efficiency than toward the democracy of which they so glibly spoke. Indeed, in many cities fewer citizens voted after these progressive reforms than before. On the other hand, all classes in the cities received more services, and the quality of government improved. The Progressive Era initiated a long period in which city schools, hospitals, parks, police and fire departments, welfare agencies, and city-owned utilities made life better for generations of urbanites.

Woman Reformers   Throughout the age of muckrakers and early twentieth-century progressivism, the women's movement gained strength, although in a variety of ways and with disagreements over the goals for which women should work.

Frederic C. Howe believed that human beings could shape and improve their world. A close adviser to Mayor Tom L. Johnson of Cleveland, Howe remembered in his autobiography, Confessions of a Reformer:

"The political renaissance was now surely coming. It would not stop with economic reform; it would bring in a rebirth of literature, art, music, and spirit, not unlike that which came to Italy in the thirteenth century. The colleges were to lead it; it was to have the support of the more enlightened business men; it would call forth the impoverished talents of the immigrant and the poor. The spirit of this young America was generous, hospitable, brilliant; it was care-free and full of variety. The young people in whom it leaped to expression hated injustice. They had no questions about the soundness of American democracy. They had supreme confidence in the mind. They believed, not less than I had always believed, that the truth would make us free."

In 1916, Jeannette Rankin, a former suffrage organizer, became the first woman elected to Congress. Her vote against U.S. entry into World War I cost her the chance for election to the Senate in 1918. In 1940, she once again won election to Congress from Montana. True to her lifelong pacifism, she cast the only vote against American entry into World War II. (*Courtesy, UPI/Bettmann*)

The fight for political and civil rights gathered force following 1890, culminating in the 1920 passage of the Nineteenth Amendment. But during the final three decades of the nineteenth century, women's participation in general movements for social and cultural reform both for themselves and for society at large would be more extensive than their engagement in the fight for political rights.

In important ways, progressive reforms can be seen as efforts to make industrial society safe for women and their children. Much of the progressivism that required governmental intervention and foreshadowed the welfare state resulted from women's special concerns and campaigns.

Black women too were participating in the increased activism of their sex, as active on behalf of their communities as white women were in aid of theirs. Among them were Ida Wells Barnett, Fannie Barrier, and Josephine St. Pierre Ruffin. Black women joined clubs to administer to the needs of the poor, the sick, the old. Such groups also promoted the idea of the black woman as an important social and moral force in the black community. Lugenia Hope in Atlanta pioneered in clearing and supervising playgrounds for black children. The National Federation of Colored Women's Clubs undertook a great number of activities. The Women's Convention of the Black Baptist Church raised money for dormitories so that young black women could attend colleges far from their homes. The Young Women's Christian Association had black chapters that were especially active among young black college women, who were expected to use their educations for the "uplift" of their families, their communities, and their race.

Women's Groups

In this same period another large movement of middle-class women organized the General Federation of Women's Clubs. The movement originated in New York in 1868 when a group led by Jennie June Croly organized a club to provide themselves with the intellectual stimulation they had missed by being excluded from men's clubs. It rapidly expanded to include more than literary circles. Women throughout the country organized into groups to participate in a variety of interests and good causes. By 1910 these local clubs, linked through the national organization but pursuing separate activities, included more than 800,000 members. Ex-President Grover Cleveland, writing in *The Ladies' Home Journal,* echoed the sentiments of many men when he insisted that women should not join clubs other than those with "purposes of charity, religious enterprise, or intellectual improvement." But thousands of women who had joined clubs for just those purposes were slowly led to demand more and more rights for themselves and other women simply to guarantee the success of their charitable, intellectual, and religious purposes. The General Federation of Women's Clubs was drawn farther into the public sphere when it lobbied for progressive causes such as conservation, consumer legislation, child labor laws, and other legislation benefiting children. One club campaign produced over a million letters in support of the Pure Food and Drug Bill in 1906.

The National Consumer's League—modeled after an English organization—became a powerful lobby for legislation protecting women and children. Under the able leadership of Florence Kelley, the league boycotted manufacturers employing children, and pushed through the Ten Hour Law in Oregon that Louis Brandeis would defend successfully before the Supreme Court. The Women's Trade Union League paired wealthy women and reformers to aid working women in their efforts to organize unions.

Birth Control and Factory Legislation   In 1915 Margaret Sanger formed the National Birth Control League to work for the improvement and legalization of birth control. Middle-class, educated people had access to birth control information, but most poor people did not. Laws made it illegal on grounds of obscenity to distribute birth control literature. In 1923 Margaret Sanger set up the first birth control clinic in New York City, staffed by women volunteers and women doctors. Other clinics were soon opened in cities outside New York. Women were interested in birth control because they saw it as a way toward happier and healthier family life; they also believed it would reduce poverty and disease. Supporters of birth control understood that their message would appeal to those who wanted to keep down the immigrant population. Yet the combined work of the woman reformers and the clinics forged one of the few links between the poor working woman and the more affluent middle-class woman.

Birth control pioneer Margaret Higgins Sanger, one of eleven children, saw her exhausted mother die at age forty-nine. Her National Birth Control League was the forerunner of the Planned Parenthood Federation of America. *(Courtesy, Culver Pictures)*

Middle-class women's groups in general were instrumental in pushing for protective legislation for women workers. In their view, all women shared biological characteristics that made them gentler and more fragile than men, but also more moral. They insisted that women be recognized and treated as a special social group. Women needed protection, not equality with male workers. It is not entirely clear how completely working women, who needed to make as much money as possible, agreed with these women's groups. If protective legislation brought important benefits to women, it also imprisoned them in a segmented labor market. But it is impossible to exaggerate the contributions that middle-class women's organizations contributed to the passage of protective legislation for women workers. In this respect, as in so many others, organized middle-class American women were developing considerable skill in assuring the triumph of some of their own values in American society.

Suffrage   Gradually the women's groups and the constituents of their reform movements coalesced around the issue of votes for women, convinced not only that it was right but that it would improve political and social life. But there was much resistance. That liquor interests and large corporations financed the fight against suffrage reinforced the woman reformers' sense that their movement and progressivism were vital to each other. After 1914 the General Federation of Women's Clubs came out squarely for women's suffrage, giving the cause fresh respectability.

Alice Paul and Lucy Burns, who had journeyed to England and admired the militant struggle women were waging there, formed the Congressional Union to oppose President Woodrow Wilson on the

One suffragette would remember:

"A student at Vassar tried to get up a suffrage meeting, and the college President refused to let her hold the meeting. So she organized a little group, and they jumped over a wall at the edge of the college and held the first suffrage meeting at Vassar in a cemetery. Imagine such a thing happening at a women's college. . . . You can hardly believe such things occurred. But they did."

Suffragist Rose Winslow smuggled out descriptions of the treatment she and Alice Paul, militant founder of the National Woman's Party, endured in prison. The process of forcible feeding she mentions, which involved inserting a 20-inch-long tube through the nostril to the stomach while the patient was restrained, was painful as well as demeaning.

"We have been in solitary for five weeks. . . . I have felt quite feeble the last few days—faint, so that I could hardly get my hair brushed, my arms ached so. . . .

All news cheers one marvelously because it is hard to feel anything but a bit desolate and forgotten here in this place.

All the officers here know we are making this hunger strike that women fighting for liberty may be considered political prisoners; we have told them. God knows we don't want other women ever to have to do this over again."

suffrage issue. Starting in January 1917, Union members picketed in front of the White House for a year and a half in behalf of a constitutional amendment requiring all states to allow women the vote. Shortly after the picketing began, the United States entered World War I. The women were faced with a difficult decision. Would it be unpatriotic to continue their protest? When they chose not to stop working for the vote, police arrested many picketers and while some newspapers were sympathetic, most were not. By the end of the year 218 women had been charged and ninety-seven went to jail. Many of these women were prominent. Stories circulated about physical abuse and forced feeding; these drew more attention to the cause and gained some further sympathy. Not all of the women's organizations agreed with these militant tactics. Carrie Chapman Catt, president in 1915 of the National American Woman's Suffrage Association, counseled sticking with the slow process of educating and changing public opinion.

The movement finally managed to persuade President Wilson to support a constitutional amendment. Wilson's decision was not altogether selfless. In states that had already given women the vote, women's rights groups were urging them to cast their ballots against local Democratic candidates until the President decided to support a constitutional amendment ensuring the suffrage across the nation as a whole. The political pressure mounted on Wilson until he finally, but reluctantly, lent his support to the amendment.

In 1920 the Nineteenth Amendment became part of the Constitution: the right of citizens of the United States to vote could never again legally "be denied or abridged by the United States or by any State on account of sex." The struggle had taken over seventy years. The effects of the political victory went far beyond politics. With the vote, women had the means to enlarge their world outside the home and the church. Yet little immediate change occurred. Many women did not vote; many who did simply shared the opinions of their husbands and fathers, and voted accordingly.

The Muckrakers

A new journalism arose around the start of the twentieth century to make a vast public aware of society's problems. Technological innovations in publishing—cheap, high-quality paper, improvements in the printing of photographs—allowed inexpensive, mass-circulation magazines to flourish, beginning in the 1890s. New currents in literature also encouraged the realistic portrayal of American society. A creative and enterprising publisher, Samuel S. McClure, assembled a stable of ambitious, college-educated journalists and gave them the time and expense money for thorough research on articles about American life. In *McClure's* magazine they produced a series of startling exposés.

Lincoln Steffens wrote articles later collected in his book *The Shame of the Cities;* Ida M. Tarbell revealed the questionable practices that had created the Standard Oil trust; Ray Stannard Baker investigated railroads, labor unions, racial problems; Burton J. Hendricks exposed the inner workings of the insurance companies; Samuel Hopkins Adams attacked medical frauds. All listed names and carefully described illegal or immoral activities; the absence of successful libel suits against them attested to their journalistic accuracy. Theodore Roosevelt attacked these new journalists, recalling the passage in Bunyan's *Pilgrim's Progress* about the "Man with the Muckrake, the man who could look no way but downward with the muckrake in his hand"; but his attack gave them the name that they accepted as a badge of honor: "to muckrake" became a common verb for the art of exposing social wrongs.

In the decade after 1902 over 2,000 muckraking articles were written by journalists, professors, reformers, ministers, public officials, and the like. Muckraking dominated the magazines particularly from 1902 to 1906. *McClure's* continued to be the leading journal, but important articles appeared as well in *Collier's Weekly, American Magazine, Everybody's, Cosmopolitan, Arena, Pearson's*, and many other magazines selling for between five and fifteen cents a copy.

The typical article combined a careful accumulation of facts with heavy Protestant moralizing, rather than concrete suggestions for reform. The basic tactic was to induce shame. "The spirit of graft and of lawlessness," wrote Lincoln Steffens, perhaps the greatest of the muckrakers, "is the American spirit. The people are not innocent. . . . My purpose was. . . . to see if the shameful facts, spread out in all their shame, would not burn through our civic shamelessness and set fire to American pride." The tactic worked: Steffens's exposures of American cities left a trail of civic renewal in their wake as respectable citizens mobilized—for a while at least—to throw the rascals out.

Americans enjoyed their orgy of guilt and reveled in the discovery of how bad things were because they believed themselves capable of setting things right. This appetite for learning the worst was gradually sated and, partly in response to some prodding by advertisers, muckraking faded from American magazines after 1912. By then national politics had caught up with the issues the magazines exposed. The muckrakers had focused the diffuse uneasiness of the American public on concrete problems. The progressive crusades of the times had their goals defined and explained by the muckrakers.

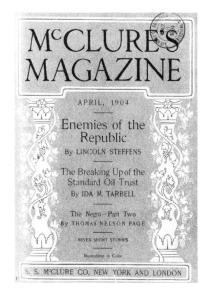

(Courtesy, Culver Pictures)

Workers

Along with the rise of organized capital came a similar, if less spectacular, growth of organized labor. The growing number of industrial workers, some thirty-five percent of the labor force in 1900, toiled—when there were jobs—an average of fifty-nine hours a week for wages of less than $2 a day. And many workers' real income actually declined in the period. Wives and children also entered the factories, contributing even lower wages to the precarious maintenance of their families. In 1910 some two million children and about one in four American women held jobs, many in agriculture but also in industry. Few of these children attended school. Life for working-class families was hard, hazardous, and insecure. The United States still had the highest rate of industrial accidents in the world. In 1917 over 11,000 workers were killed, and nearly 1.4 million injured. Increasing numbers of immigrants, composing the majority of workers in many major industries like steel, contributed more than their share to these statistics. Many of them were single men willing to take manual and unskilled jobs for minimal compensation. Even skilled workingmen, the elite in many industries, began to find themselves replaced by new machinery. Others found that Frederick Taylor's scientific management was redesigning their time-honored informal craft skills. Taylor personally alienated many labor leaders with his description of his prize pig-iron shoveler as a man "more or less of the type of an ox."

Labor Unions   Although the ranks of unionized workers had been decimated in the setbacks of the 1890s, the American Federation of Labor—founded in 1886 to represent the interests of skilled workers in national trade unions—survived and expanded rapidly during the prosperous times of the Progressive Era. In the seven-year period from 1897 to 1904, its membership grew from 250,000 to 1,670,000. Perennially led by Samuel Gompers, who preached and practiced a partnership with capital, the AFL regarded the strike and boycott as last resorts and tried to avoid partisan political action. Gompers worked to free organized labor from such legal restraints as injunctions issued by courts against strikes and boycotts. But he preferred to win tangible, practical benefits, such as higher wages, shorter hours, and safer jobs. The way to achieve these, he thought, was to force business to engage in collective bargaining with unions. Labor unions and employers entered into agreements for the improvement of working conditions. Such unionism was "craft, job conscious, business and wage conscious," not class conscious.

New unions appeared during the early 1900s and some of the older unions began to gain ground. The International Ladies' Garment Workers Union was formed in 1900 to organize female workers in the garment industry, and in 1914 the Amalgamated Clothing Workers Union appeared to organize male workers in the same industry. The railroad brotherhoods continued to add membership in the early 1900s, as did unions like the United Mine Workers and the Amalgamated Association of Iron, Steel, and Tin Workers.

Initially, the AFL did little to organize women. From about 1910 on, it made more serious efforts, but the AFL leadership remained committed to the convention that, under normal circumstances, men should earn wages and women should stay at home. The Women's Trade Union League, which had been founded in 1903 at an AFL meeting, attempted to organize women workers. For its first decade, the WTUL worked closely with the AFL, but eventually relations between the two organizations became strained. In 1915 the WTUL, apparently acquiescing in the AFL view of woman's place, abandoned direct organization and turned to pressuring for state and local government regulation of the conditions of women's work. The history of the WTUL captures the difficulty of organizing women workers as the

Unions were sometimes distinctly less than patient with foreigners disinclined to learn English. One AFL group took as its motto:

"If you are an American at heart, speak our language.
If you don't know it, learn it.
If you don't like it, MOVE."

nation industrialized. Much of its female leadership held middle-class ideas of reform that looked to rational "social housekeeping" and failed to perceive women as full wage-laborers. Much of the male leadership of the AFL remained fixed on the goal of winning gains for male workers, for whom the good life meant having a wife at home and not facing the competition of female labor hired at low wages.

Socialism Many socialist labor leaders argued instead that workers should develop class consciousness, organize a labor party with candidates supporting their own interests, and fight capitalism. Some even opposed working for improved conditions and shorter hours because these were palliatives that perpetuated the inherently evil capitalist system. Always a minority of organized workers, socialists were influenced by European radical ideologies or by evidence that the real miseries of industrial life were not yielding to the policies of "business unionism." This was the term they derisively gave to the conventional American union movement in its dependence on bargaining over wages and working conditions. Although Gompers fought socialists who wished to influence the AFL—"economically, you are unsound; socially, you are wrong; industrially, you are an impossibility"—by 1912 socialists led about one-third of AFL affiliates and controlled unions of miners and machinists. Socialist Party candidates won office in more than 300 cities across the nation, including Milwaukee, Schenectady, and San Francisco. Eugene V. Debs, former president of the American Railway Union, polled over 900,000 votes as the Socialist candidate in the 1912 presidential election.

The IWW Debs and most other moderate socialist leaders, like the New York lawyer Morris Hillquit and Milwaukee editor Victor Berger, never advocated revolution. Yet in 1905, after a series of bloody strikes in the West that the AFL failed to support, they helped create the militant Industrial Workers of the World, led by William D. "Big Bill" Haywood. The Wobblies organized migratory laborers and lumbermen, western miners, northeastern textile workers, and other laborers who did not conform to the craftworker model favored by the AFL. They sought to create a united labor organization of all trades, skill levels, and races and ethnic groups: One Big Union. Organization of the whole labor force was to build a new voluntary cooperative human society even as its strikes and sabotage destroyed the capitalist and governmental structures of the old.

The Wobblies lived the free, anarchic style that symbolized the society they hoped to bring about. One of their tactics was to go to town, begin reading the Declaration of Independence in public, and then protest when any attempt was made to stop them. When they took their fight for free speech to the streets of Spokane, Fresno, and San Diego, they were bitterly repressed, and established labor leaders representing the best-paid sector of the workforce opposed them for their disruptive tactics and their concern for the unskilled. The IWW gained few victories. One successful deviation from its practice of operating outside the system was the 1912 wage increase won for 30,000 textile

William "Big Bill" Haywood, one of the founders of the IWW, stated: "It is our purpose to overthrow the capitalist system by forcible means if necessary." Joe Hill, the legendary IWW songwriter, played an inspirational role as these stanzas indicate:

If the workers took a notion
　　They could stop all speeding trains;
Every ship upon the ocean
　　They can tie with mighty chains.

Every wheel in the creation
　　Every mine and every mill;
Fleets and armies of the nation,
　　Will at their command stand still.

workers in Lawrence, Massachusetts. Even at its peak the IWW probably never had more than 60,000 members, and after 1913 its membership declined. Vigilante action and federal prosecution for pacifism during World War I finished it as a visible force by 1920. Yet its interest in immigrants, blacks, and the marginal and unskilled workers spawned by modern mass industry made it a forerunner of the Congress of Industrial Organizations (CIO) of the 1930s.

Union Growth and Corporate Welfare By 1917 membership in 133 national unions reached a total of 3,104,000, representing about twenty percent of all industrial workers. Unionized women, particularly in the clothing industries, grew in numbers from 76,700 in 1910 to 386,900 in 1920. Most of the national unions were in the AFL, the vast majority of them amalgamated unions of workers in interrelated trades rather than pure craft unions. The four railroad brotherhoods of over 400,000 skilled workers remained independent of the AFL. Unions gained in mining, the building trades, and the clothing and transportation industries. Spectacular strikes—like that of the United Mine Workers under John Mitchell in 1902 and the International Ladies' Garment Workers' "Uprising of the Twenty Thousand" in 1909—consolidated union power in important industries.

Big business was inclined to see the virtues of Gompers' conservative unionism, and corporate leaders like George Perkins, of the House of Morgan, and Andrew Carnegie joined with him in 1900 in the National Civic Federation to promote industrial peace. But the National Association of Manufacturers, formed in 1895, though aiming to make industry civil and responsible toward workers was also opposed to all unionization. The American Anti-Boycott Association went to the courts to oppose labor's strikes and boycotts. In an effort to discourage unions and promote loyalty and efficiency among workers, some businessmen turned to welfare schemes. To corporations, welfare frequently meant amenities like restrooms, recreation areas, and classes in language, music, and the arts, but some businesses also introduced benefit associations for the sick and injured, pension funds for the disabled and aged, and group insurance. A few offered profit-sharing plans. Company unions instituted welfare capitalism by giving employees a voice, sometimes more apparent than real, in running the plant.

Many members of the middle class, too, feared the violence and "conspiracy" of strikes and boycotts and feared foreign agitators. They felt caught, and helpless, between big business and big labor.

The New Black Militancy

W. E. B. Du Bois The year of Booker T. Washington's death, 1915, marked a significant point in American black history. Events in Europe, discrimination and segregation at home, and the black exodus to northern cities prepared the way for W. E. B. Du Bois's challenge to the established progressive gospel of

Washington. Militant rhetoric, legal and political aggressiveness, and a commitment to a black elite distinguished Du Bois from Washington. Together the two define alternative strategies within the progressive reform spirit. Du Bois represented political insurgency and Washington a reliance on measured, negotiated means of advocacy. Du Bois's criticism of Washington fixed for future times his image of the earlier leader as a compromiser with white supremacy.

An exceptional student and a descendant of an old, established black family, Du Bois in 1889 began a socially isolated life at Harvard College and graduate school. He found satisfaction in scholarship and was influenced and stimulated by William James and George Santayana. He earned a doctorate in history, the first American black to be awarded such a degree from Harvard. Travel and study in Europe completed his education and confirmed Du Bois's view of himself as an American black with a special destiny.

At Atlanta University in 1897 Du Bois supervised sociology programs and directed conferences on blacks sponsored by the university. Through this program, he published a series of monographs aimed at social reform. He insisted on the cultivation and promotion of a "talented tenth." College-trained young black people would become community leaders, business organizers, and members of a cultural avant-garde. A sociological survey conducted for the University of Pennsylvania, Du Bois's *The Philadelphia Negro* is still noted today as a significant piece of research. It emphasizes the need for the black upper class to encourage the progress of the race. Du Bois's ideology, along with Booker T. Washington's doctrines, prompted middle-class black urban women to take up club work as a means to self-help. In their adoption of the formula of opportunity, ambition, frugality, and perseverance, these women seemed closer to Washington. Yet in their commitment to social organization, which recalls the ideology of *The Philadelphia Negro*, they were in the spirit of Du Bois.

In a collection of essays, *The Souls of Black Folk*, Du Bois in 1903 presented black Americans in all their variety to the white public. The black poet James Weldon Johnson described it as having "a greater effect upon and within the Negro race in America than any other single book published in this country since *Uncle Tom's Cabin*."

William Edward Burghardt Du Bois, 1869–1963. *(Courtesy, National Portrait Gallery)*

The Niagara Movement and the NAACP	In his biography of John Brown, in his response to the Atlanta race riot of 1906, and in his lectures, Du Bois spoke not in the measured tones of *The Souls of Black Folk* but with the fervor of a forceful propagandist impatient for the attainment of equality.

Under Du Bois's leadership, the Niagara Movement, which argued against the accommodationist tactics of Washington, was founded in 1905 at Niagara Falls, Ontario. The organization's "Declaration of Principles" demanded suffrage and civil rights, and called attention to southern peonage. The next year the delegates made a barefoot pilgrimage to the site of John Brown's execution. The movement's elitism thwarted its founder's hopes for wide support, and by 1911 it had petered out. Du Bois continued to agitate.

The Niagara Movement provided the groundwork for the estab-

W. E. B. Du Bois founded
the Niagara Movement. The
"talented tenth" of blacks would
extend their hands to all blacks.
(Courtesy, Library of Congress)

lishment in 1911 of the National Association for the Advancement of
Colored People, which contained an interracial membership. The social workers Lillian Wald and Jane Addams and *Nation* editor Oswald
Garrison Villard were among the prominent whites involved. The organization took what was then a radical position on matters of racial
equality and segregation, denouncing the political and economic subordination of blacks. In association with the NAACP, Du Bois edited *The
Crisis*. Both the organization and the magazine increased his prestige
and influence. Throughout the 1920s and 1930s Du Bois increasingly
articulated a socialist ideology that many NAACP board members
could not accept.

An Ethnic Mosaic

The newcomers to the United States during the progressive years and
after thickened the flow of the so-named new immigration from southern and eastern Europe that had startled Americans in the previous
years. Between 1900 and 1930, 19,000,000 newcomers came in the
largest migration in American history. In the peak year of 1907 alone,
over 1,285,000 people disembarked at American ports. Between 1896
and 1915 Italy sent over 500,000 annually, while 2,700,000 Russians,
two-thirds of them Jews, settled in the United States. By 1914 a million
Poles had come. Some immigrants migrated to American jobs in the
spring and returned home in the fall, but most stayed. Many Jews
brought their families with them, but the majority of Italian men came
alone, sending for their families when they could.

The new immigration continued to be drawn to the United States
by both hardship at home and American economic opportunity. Po-
groms—anti-Semitic violence—and economic restrictions pushed Jews
out of their east European villages or *shtetlach*. Italians, particularly in

the parched southland of their country, could scarcely eke out a living on the small, barren plots. Polish peasants also suffered overcrowding on their lands. Some immigrants were attracted by the sight of their countrymen returning from America "well dressed, with an overcoat, a cigar in the mouth," and others received word of successful friends and relatives. Agents of employers in search of cheap labor recruited many with the promise—the reality was often far different—of good jobs and comfortable lives. *Padrones* rounded up gangs of willing Italians to go to work on the railroads, mines, and farms. And steamship companies induced millions to undertake the arduous journey. By 1890 the Hamburg-Amerika line and others like it had established networks of thousands of European and American agencies to ensure regular supplies of passengers. By 1900 two-thirds of immigrants traveled on prepaid tickets, the money remitted from the United States.

Almost all immigrants started at the bottom as manual or unskilled workers. By the turn of the century they formed the bulk of the labor force in each of the nation's basic industries. Italians worked in construction and railroads; Jewish men, although few had been tailors in Europe, flocked into the garment factories or did sweat piecework at home, many with the help of their wives and children. Poles and Slavs concentrated in iron and steel. Exploiting enmities among nationalities, and even among different groups from the same countries—many northern Italians hated southern, assimilationist German Jews wanted nothing to do with Orthodox eastern European Jews—employers sometimes hired a variety of ethnic groups to discourage unionization. Almost all newcomers earned shockingly low wages: eight cents an hour, thirteen hours a day, six days a week, was not uncommon. At the slightest expression of discontent they might be replaced by even more recent immigrants. Their inability to understand warnings of danger shouted in an unfamiliar tongue contributed to the appalling rate of industrial accidents.

Immigrants arriving at Ellis Island, New York, ca. 1900.
(Courtesy, Scribner's Archives)

Immigrants in the Cities   Immigrants lived where they could get work and few traveled beyond the Altantic ports and major industrial cities. That had been the case from the early days of the new immigration in the 1880s. About two-thirds of the Jews settled in New York, Chicago, Philadelphia, and Boston. The lower East Side, "in the shadow of the Brooklyn Bridge," was the largest Jewish community in the world. Italians also concentrated in the industrial Northeast, while large numbers of Poles lived in Chicago. The writer Robert Hunter found in 1904 that thirty-five percent of the people in New York were foreign-born, and over eighty percent of foreign parentage. In thirty-three of the largest cities the immigrant population outnumbered the native-born. Most immigrants settled in dense ethnic communities, segregated in the inner cities and isolated from the mainstream of American life. The major cities were mosaics: New York's East Harlem had twenty-seven different groups, including blacks and Chinese, while Czechs, Germans, Italians, Irish, Jews, Syrians, and Poles all peopled Chicago's Nineteenth Ward.

Packed into tenements and slums abandoned by Americans of earlier immigrant stock who had moved up and out of the central city,

Boarders and relatives crowded into already inadequate tenement quarters. One magazine recounted:

"A family with two children rents an apartment of three rooms and then goes ahead and rents out the kitchen and the living room to two or three boarders. Sometimes there would be shifts, people would sleep in the daytime, and the same place would be used by somebody else at night."

the new arrivals suffered many miseries. Privacy, even for birth, sickness, and death, was virtually unknown. In the absence of sanitation and ventilation, such diseases as tuberculosis, diphtheria, and scarlet fever spread. Infant and maternal mortality were high. Hunger, language barriers, and the desire for an easier life lured young girls into prostitution. In many cities few children attended school full time, and many who did sat in overcrowded classrooms, read battered books, and afterward played in the streets. Working children labored in factories and sweatshops, work that stunted their growth and robbed some of them of vitality forever. Family ties were strained or broken, but many immigrant wives—notably among Italians and Jews—chose to work at home to maintain family life. Filthy streets and exorbitant street railway fares assaulted the new strangers outside their homes. In the industrial cities immigrants could live and die in squalor. Suffering had been the lot of earlier immigrants. But in the progressive period, the suffering came to the attention of reformers prepared to see immigrant life and its ills in their relationship to the country's destiny as a whole.

Yet immigrant experience also evoked an opulent variety of social and cultural institutions in response to the bewildering new environment. Some of these embodied the everyday details of life and celebration that are to be expected of any ethnic group. Others had to do with politics and ideology, or the practical effort to survive, or the new means of enjoyment and community provided by the new land. Papers for ethnic communities were found everywhere. The Jewish daily *Forverts* and the Italian *Il Proletario,* among others, spoke for labor. Others, probably most, simply expressed in a familiar language the attitudes and aspirations of their readers, informed them about community activities, and introduced them to American ways. Cafés and saloons gave a respite from toil and functioned as communications centers for the neighborhood. Mutual aid societies provided sickness and death benefits. Members of fraternal orders like the Odd Fellows, and of service organizations like the Sons of Italy and the Ancient Order of Hibernians, helped one another through hard times. Religious feast days were occasions of colorful celebration. Hebrew schools passed on Old World language, history, and customs to new generations. Although leisure time was limited, immigrant wards supported an energetic popular culture. East Harlem had Yiddish theaters and Italian marionette shows, not to mention movie and vaudeville houses. In some of the smaller industrial towns, nickelodeons and libraries provided relaxation for tired workers and their families. In many places, settlement houses were neighborhood centers with men's and women's clubs, day nurseries, gyms, art, music, and language classes, meeting halls, and discussion groups.

The Immigration Restriction League asked:

"Do you want this country to be peopled by British, German, or Scandinavian stock, historically free, energetic, progressive, or by Slav, Latin, and Asiatic races, historically down-trodden, atavistic, and stagnant?"

Nativism   Many Americans greeted their new countrymen with little enthusiasm and blamed the ills of the cities on them. In the later days of the nineteenth century, much of the hostility to immigrants had been anti-Catholic. Now the opposition was adding a vocabulary of social reform and social science. Some argued that cleaning up the slums and improving city services required getting rid of corrupt ward politicians, who bought the immigrant's vote for a turkey at Christmas or a little money when times were bad. Child-savers, prison reformers, and charity workers noted the high proportion of foreigners among juvenile delinquents, criminals, paupers, and the insane. Organized labor charged the new arrivals with being strike-breakers who lowered wage levels and reduced living standards to their own "pigsty mode of life." Complaining that immigrants were hard to organize, labor sought laws to restrict the employment of unnaturalized aliens in factories. Despite an increasingly rigorous checklist of physical, social, and mental characteristics that officials at the new Ellis Island depot used to detain undesirables after 1898, some Americans worried about social and biological degeneration. Restrictionists proposed literacy tests to keep out the "unassimilables." They buttressed their beliefs with scholarly arguments. Even respected sociologists and economists like Edward A. Ross and John R. Commons worried about "race suicide" and the "harmful" effects of the high immigrant birth rate.

The House-Senate Dillingham Report in 1911 declared the "new immigration" to be "unassimilable," and suggested the need for a quota system. Many old-stock Yankee Protestants shared these fears. Americans who wanted nothing to do with the "races of Europe" pressed for laws restricting immigration. Labor unions also clamored for a legislative cap on the influx. In 1896 President Grover Cleveland had vetoed a bill imposing a literacy test as a prerequisite to entering the United States, and President William Howard Taft did the same in 1913. Congress passed another literacy test measure in 1915, which President Woodrow Wilson vetoed. In January 1917 Congress revived the literacy test and Wilson once again vetoed it, but this time Congress overrode the veto, making the literacy test the law. It required new immigrants to demonstrate their ability to read in English or in their native language. Those who could not read were denied entry.

"Americani-zation" Progressives in the settlement houses sought, in the words of Mary Simkhovitch, to "get the slant of the [immigrant] neighbors" while easing newcomers into American life with language courses and civic instruction. Randolph Bourne, a young disciple of John Dewey, celebrated their diversity and predicted a "cosmopolitan federation, national colonies of foreign cultures" in a future "Trans-National America." Considerably less appreciative of European cultures were groups like the North American Civic League for Immigrants, which was originally formed to provide help in adjusting to the new environment, but eventually concentrated on steering newcomers away from threatening radical groups. The YMCA ran perhaps the most successful Americanization programs.

Many immigrants themselves responded ambivalently to efforts to Americanize them. Abraham Cahan's fictional David Levinsky gradually abandons all the outward signs and observances of Judaism. Many Americanized second-generation children, like the hero in *The Odyssey of a Wop*, experienced excruciating embarrassment at the trappings

The well-known poet Thomas Bailey Aldrich set the fears to meter:

Wide open and unguarded stand our gates,
And through them presses a wild, motley throng—
Men from the Volga and the Tartar steppes,
Featureless faces from the Huang-Ho,
Malayan, Scythian, Teuton, Kelt and Slav,
Flying the old World's poverty and scorn;
These, bringing with them unknown gods and rites,
Those, tiger passions, here to stretch their claws,
In street and alley what strange tongues are these,
Accents of menace alien to our air,
Voices that once the Town of Babel knew!
O Liberty, white Goddess! Is it well
To leave the gates unguarded?

An alternate view came from the British playwright Israel Zangwill, who urged Americans to regard the new immigrants as a challenge. In his 1908 play, *The Melting Pot*, Zangwill wrote: "America is God's Crucible, the great Melting Pot where all the races of Europe are melting and re-forming!"

Cartoon delineating the movement for immigration restriction. It culminated in a congressional law of 1921 limiting new immigrants to three percent of each group living in the U.S. in 1920, and a law of 1924 setting the year at 1890.

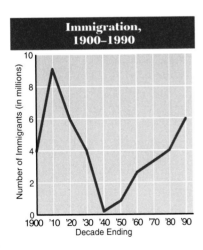

Immigration, 1900–1990

of the Old World in their homes: "I am nervous when I bring friends to my house: the place looks so Italian." For all their good will, in the end the Americanizers imposed a standard of immigrant performance that made those who did not conform look like the deviants of whom some nativists warned. In the wake of World War I, hostility to foreigners was to surface again in a particularly virulent form.

Mass Culture and Assimilation

Some authoritarian patriots hoped the Americanization crusade would simply make the new immigrants more like themselves. But subtle forces at work in the American cities were far more effective in encouraging assimilation.

Except for a few massive concentrations of immigrants—the Jews and Italians of New York, the Irish of Boston and New York, the Poles of Chicago, the Chinese of San Francisco—these neighborhoods were becoming more mixed. In the mill towns of New England, for example, the Irish, Italians, Portuguese, and French Canadians worked together in the factories and lived within a few blocks of one another. The same was true of the Slavs, Italians, and Irish in the Pennsylvania mines; of the Italians, Slovaks, and Romanians in the Cleveland steel mills; the

Learning a strange language was one of the greatest problems new immigrants faced. Many attended night-school classes after a full day's work at their jobs. *(Courtesy, Erving Galloway, New York)*

Jews, Syrians, and Italians in the needle trades of New York City; or the Poles, Irish, Lithuanians, Germans, Czechs, and Italians in the Chicago packinghouses. In the immigrant cities, churches, synagogues, businesses, public schools, parochial schools, and ethnic societies were concentrated spatially, and people were able to see clearly the difference between their own and other ethnic communities. But at the same time, the immigrants and their children had contact with people from other ethnic groups, and in those meetings in the mixed neighborhoods the forces of assimilation worked their magic. Soon their children learned to speak English and communicated freely with one another.

Immigrants and their children were on the move. The idea of a stable population, with the same people spending their whole lives trapped in urban ghettoes, does not explain urban life in the United States. Poor immigrants were highly mobile people, moving from city to city or neighborhood to neighborhood. In older pedestrian times the rich had lived downtown, close to the seats of political, religious, and economic power, while the poor were near the warehouses and railroad terminals where they worked. But as factories appeared downtown and streetcars, subways, and elevated trains crisscrossed the city and reached outside its limits, the rich relocated to the suburbs. The poor then filled the vacuum, often turning the large abandoned single-family homes of the rich into multifamily tenements. Even then the immigrants did not live out their lives in one neighborhood. As quickly as they could save enough money, they purchased homes in the outskirts of the city or in the suburbs and traveled downtown to work. Although the Irish, Italian, German, Slavic, and Jewish neighborhoods survived in the cities, they were rarely occupied by the same people for more than a few years. New immigrants would crowd into the same tenements while older immigrants and their children moved to newer neighborhoods. Those new neighborhoods were even more likely to be mixed ethnically, with even more contact among different groups in the markets, stores, workplaces, and public schools.

The new industrial economy, with its mass production of goods, was creating a consumer culture in which all Americans—native-born as well as immigrants—participated. Companies competed to sell their products, and advertisements in newspapers, magazines, and billboards bombarded consumers with one message: buy. As Americans of all ethnic backgrounds purchased the same clothes, shoes, and appliances, their styles became more similar. The new film industry, with its nickleodeons, storefront theaters, and movie palaces, created more standardized forms of entertainment. These trends, which would accelerate in the 1920s, especially after the invention of the radio, had their beginnings in the Progressive Era.

The Artistic Perception

Economics, social science, settlement-house work, and practical politics were learning during the Progressive Era to see social problems with something of the analytical closeness of the sciences. It was appropriate to the times to have available as well a literature and a diversity of visual arts that perceived the world through the medium of science and technology.

A George Luks portrait of a coal miner, 1924, an impressive example of the Ashcan School of American painting, which typically combined working-class subject matter and social conscience. *(Courtesy, Amherst College)*

Art and Photography   The most obvious case of an act of perception that by use of modern technology becomes art is photography. Early in the twentieth century, Alfred Stieglitz used the camera to catch images of wretched urban life. Craftsmen like Stieglitz brought recognition that the camera, through the capture of a gritty city scene, can see with such sharp exactness as to show viewers what their naked eyes had never seen before. It is not contradictory that the studio of Stieglitz, wielder of an instrument that appears to do no more with objects than report them with simple straightforwardness, was the gathering place of painters who were experimenting with radically complex ways of seeing objects. John Marin, for example, painted the Brooklyn Bridge not as the untrained eye takes it in but as splashes and streaks of color that represent the restless energy it embodies.

Another kind of painting, meanwhile, was doing something midway between the plain reporting done by the camera and the imaginative interpretations of reality offered by Marin and other abstract artists. A body of artists who have been termed the Ashcan School, taking as their spokesman Robert Henri, was painting the city in a way that reports its everyday life—in effect, its common, unadorned ashcans—but with a blur of colors and forms that make the objects seem composed of light. George Luks's *Hester Street*, presenting New York's lower East Side Jewish street life, shows a crowded thoroughfare busy with talk. But for all the vividness and concreteness of the scene, the faces are distant: the viewer is looking at a moment of life that will quickly pass into another moment.

The directness of photography, the abstractions of Marin's group, the haunting glimpses of city living offered by the Ashcan School: they

In *The Steerage*, the photographer Alfred Stieglitz—himself the son of immigrants—captured the poignancy and drama of a new wave of immigrants embarking on the journey to America. *(Courtesy, The Art Institute of Chicago)*

were alike in their attempt to make the eye an instrument of analysis. They were therefore consonant with a time in which science was analytically dissecting the given world and telling the educated public that it is far different from what it seems on the surface to be. In 1913 occurred New York City's famous Armory show, in which works of both the Ashcan and the abstract artists were exhibited along with canvases from some of the most important European painters. The best remembered of these is Marcel Duchamp's cubist *Nude Descending a Staircase*, depicting motion by means of slabs of color.

Architecture and Literature   As simple and direct in its way as photography, modern architecture provided its own interpretation of the technical advances of the age. The kinds of design begun by Louis Sullivan and others late in the nineteenth century made a remarkable discovery: that steel beams and girders have their own grace, and that the building can be beautiful in revealing to the eye, rather than hiding behind elaborate facades, the manner in which it is held up. Modern architecture expressed the spare, plain strength of steel, and it demonstrated that the sight of exact construction can bring as much pleasure to a viewer as complex ornamentation can. It caught the spirit of a time and people committed to investigation, work, and building things.

Literature too was in the spirit of its time of scientific exploration. Earlier there had emerged in the United States and abroad a school of fiction known as realism. Its objective was to picture life neither romantically nor brutally, and instead to portray the simple and ordinary so as to bring out its moral meanings. A leading practitioner in this country was William Dean Howells. Around the turn of the century there appeared—again both in Europe and in the United States—a variety of fiction that is usually termed naturalism. Its inspiration was the scientific discovery, in Darwinism and other fields, of the vital forces at work in nature, and it perceived human life as a manifestation of these. Naturalism is often thought of as nothing other than bleak and pessimistic, reducing human life to its animal component. This is not true.

Naturalism and Science   An instance of the complexity of naturalism is Stephen Crane's *The Red Badge of Courage* (1895). This story of the young, green Union soldier Henry Fleming is an examination of courage, an analysis as cool and detached as a laboratory test. Henry is moved by emotions that might be expected of any creature. For much of the novel he simply reacts to what is going on around him; and fear drives him to desert his comrades. But Henry is also propelled by shame and conscience, which carry him back to the front lines from which he had fled. And courage, enforced by a rush of energy and aggression such as combat veterans frequently describe, brings him to take up a battleflag from a fallen soldier and lead a successful assault on a rebel position. Crane pictures the biological urges that condition the humanity of Henry Fleming, but the author ends by affirming that humanity, revealed in the final act of valor that asserts itself in the face of mere biology.

How indebted a work of fiction could be to the science of the day, and how far fiction could lift its vision above a merely biological interpretation of life, have an example in a novel that Frank Norris published in 1901. Set in the vast wheatfields of California, *The Octopus* tells of the struggle of a group of farmers against a railroad. Norris presents the fight as an event within the great background of nature herself. The land produces the wheat, as though in its richness it cannot help but do so. The wheat must flow to the hungry; the railroad is the means of its flowing. Ultimately nature is discovered to be not cruelly mindless but beneficent and life-giving. If photography and skyscrapers represented the leaner, drier capabilities of the artistic mind of the early twentieth century, *The Octopus* illustrated its capacity to see existence in all its bounty.

Very much a part of the artistic developments of the progressive period was the flourishing of Greenwich Village, New York City's best-known bohemian district. It drew not only painters and novelists but political visionaries. It did so in the belief that a well-crafted political idea is itself a work of art as well as a guide to a society in which the human imagination will be fully liberated. Bill Haywood of the Industrial Workers of the World was a celebrity there—fittingly, for the style of the Wobblies, those western migrants with their easy disregard for authority, suggested the kind of freedom that Village artists sought.

Suggested Readings

Recent books on the social history of the Progressive Era include Moses Rischin, *Grandma Never Lived in America; The New Journalism of Abraham Cahan* (1988), Beverly Beeton, *Women Vote in the West* (1986), Ruth Rosen, *The Lost Sisterhood* (1982), Alice Kessler-Harris, *Out to Work* (1982), Alan Kraut, *The Huddled Masses: The Immigrant in American Society, 1860–1921* (1982), and Louis Harlan, *Booker T. Washington* (1983). Allen F. Davis wrote the perceptive *American Heroine: The Life and Legend of Jane Addams* (1973).

Robert Wiebe's interpretation of the Progressive Era is an essential work: *The Search for Order* (1968) makes progressivism a response to the breakdown of the "island communities" in American society, the emergence of an industrial economy of interdependent parts. The progressive social critics, as Wiebe explains them, believed that the new economy, with its technological sophistications and its capacity for change, needed to be subject to continual administration by experts, and the reform they advocated was toward giving government this role. For a case study, see Daniel Nelson's *Frederick W. Taylor and the Rise of Scientific Management* (1980). Richard Hofstadter's *The Age of Reform* (1955) represented at its time of publication a break with the tradition of scholarship that grouped together differing reform movements in American history as expressions of a common and virtuous democratic impulse. Hofstadter, who liked to conjecture that the opposite of received truth is the fact, is still full of insights for the receptive reader.

The work of the muckrakers is anthologized in Harvey Swados, ed., *Years of Conscience* (1962). David M. Chalmers, *The Social and Political Ideas of the Muckrakers* (1964) and Harold S. Wilson, *McClure's Magazine and the Muckrakers* (1970) are useful studies. Bradley Robert Rice examines the working of the commission system, a plan that a number of American cities adopted early in the twentieth century as a means of bringing efficiency to city government. In *Progressive Cities: The Commission Government Movement in America, 1901–1920* (1977), Rice claims that the commissions did not respond sufficiently to the need for social reform and the provision of welfare services. Henry F. May, in *The End of American Innocence* (1959), finds the beginnings of "modern" America in the years just before the First World War.

On feminism see Lois Banner, *Women in Modern America* (1974) and William O'Neill, *Everyone Was Brave: The Rise and Fall of Feminism in America* (1969). Aileen Kraditor studies the arguments both for and against woman suffrage in *The Ideas of the Woman Suffrage Movement* (1981). Thomas Reed West's *Flesh of Steel: Literature and the Machine in American Culture* (1967) defines in the culture of modern technology an element of discipline and one of energy and force. Thomas Haskell in *The Emergence of Professional Social Science* (1977) describes a division in the American Social Science Association between older members who saw a simple causation in social events and a younger generation convinced that causes are complex and hidden.

Other useful books include Samuel Haber, *Efficiency and Uplift: Scientific Management in the Progressive Era* (1964), James T. Kloppenberg, *Uncertain Victory: Social Democracy and Progressivism in European and American Thought, 1870–1920* (1986), Nancy S. Dye, *As Equals and Sisters: Feminism, the Labor Movement, and the Women's Trade Union League of New York* (1980), Susan A. Glenn, *Daughters of the Shtetl: Life and Labor in the Immigrant Generation* (1990), Rosalind Rosenberg, *Beyond Separate Spheres: The Intellectual Origins of Modern Feminism* (1982), and Martin Sklar, *The Corporate Reconstruction of American Capitalism, 1890–1916: The Market, the Law, and Politics* (1988).

Booker T. Washington: A Great Compromiser?

Louis R. Harlan

[Note: This debate on the merits of Booker T. Washington's approach to the race issue is in part inspired by W. E. B. Du Bois's criticisms of him. For accounts of Washington and Du Bois, see pp. 584–88, 710–12, and 732 of your textbook.]

It is ironic that Booker T. Washington, the most powerful black American of his time and perhaps of all time, should be the black leader whose claim to the title is most often dismissed by the lay public. Blacks often question his legitimacy because of the role that favor by whites played in Washington's assumption of power, and whites often remember him only as an educator or, confusing him with George Washington Carver, as "that great Negro scientist." This irony is something that Washington will have to live with in history, for he himself deliberately created the ambiguity about his role and purposes that has haunted his image. And yet, Washington was a genuine black leader, with a substantial black following and with virtually the same long-range goals for Afro-Americans as his rivals. . . .

Washington's bid for leadership went beyond education and institution-building, however. Symbolic of his fresh approach to black-white relations were a speech he gave in 1895 before a commercial exposition, known as the Atlanta Compromise Address, and his autobiography, *Up From Slavery (1901)*. As Washington saw it, blacks were toiling upward from slavery by their own efforts into the American middle class and needed chiefly social peace to continue in this steady social evolution. Thus, in the Atlanta Compromise he sought to disarm the white South by declaring agitation of the social equality question "the merest folly" and proclaiming that in "purely social" matters "we can be as separate as the fingers, yet one as the hand in all things essential to mutual progress." . . .

Washington's concessions to the white South, however, were only half of a bargain. In return for downgrading civil and political rights in the black list of priorities, Washington asked whites to place no barriers to black economic advancement and even to become partners of their black neighbors "in all things essential to mutual progress." Washington saw his own role as the axis between the races, the only leader who could negotiate and keep the peace by holding extremists on both sides in check.

Washington sought to influence whites, but he never forgot that it was the blacks that he undertook to lead. He offered blacks not the empty promises of the demagogue but a solid program of economic and educational progress through struggle. It was less important "just now," he said, for a black person to seek admission to an opera house than to have the money for the ticket. Mediating diplomacy with whites was only half of Washington's strategy; the other half was black solidarity, mutual aid, and institution-building. He thought outspoken complaint against injustice was necessary but insufficient, and he thought factional dissent among black leaders was self-defeating and should be suppressed.

Washington brought to his role as a black leader the talents and outlook of a machine boss. He made Tuskegee Institute the largest and best-supported black educational institution of his day, and it spawned a large network of other industrial schools. Tuskegee's educational function is an important and debatable subject, of course, but the central concern here is Washington's use of the school as the base of operations of what came to be known as the Tuskegee Machine. It was an all-black school with an all-black faculty at a time when most black colleges were still run by white missionaries. Tuskegee taught self-determination. It also taught trades designed for economic independence in a region dominated by sharecrop agriculture. . . .

Washington did try to change his world by other means. Some forms of racial injustice, such as lynching, disfranchisement, and unequal facilities in education and transportation, Washington dealt with publicly and directly.

Louis R. Harlan, "Booker T. Washington and the Politics of Accommodation," in *Black Leaders of the Twentieth Century*, John Hope Franklin and August Meier, eds. (Urbana University of Illinois Press, 1982), p. 2–4, 12.

Popular and powerful, [Booker T. Washington] symbolized the strengths and critical weaknesses within the Afro-American community at the turn of the century.

Washington's sudden emergence as a major figure came in September 1895, when he delivered a short address at the Cotton States and International Exposition in Atlanta. Little in the speech, which Du Bois later termed the "Atlanta Compromise," represented a radical departure from what other moderate black educators and elected officials had already argued. He observed that one-third of the South's population was black, and that any "enterprise seeking the material, civil, or moral welfare" of the region could not disregard the Negro. Blacks should remain in the South—"Cast down your bucket where you are"—and participate in the capitalist economic development of that area. During the Reconstruction era, blacks had erred in their priorities. "Ignorant and inexperienced," blacks had tried to start "at the top instead of at the bottom"; a Congressional seat "was more sought than real estate or industrial skill." To the white South, Washington pledged the fidelity of his race, "the most patient, law-abiding, and unresentful people that the world has seen." And on the sensitive issue of racial integration and the protection of blacks' political rights, Washington made a dramatic concession: "In all things that are purely social we can be as separate as the fingers, yet one as the hand in all things essential to mutual progress. . . . The wisest among my race understand that the agitation of questions of social equality is the extremest folly." Washington's "compromise" was this: blacks would disavow open agitation for desegregation and the political franchise; in return, they would be permitted to develop their own parallel economic, educational, and social institutions within the framework of expanding Southern capitalism.

White America responded to Washington's address with universal acclaim. President Grover Cleveland remarked that the speech was the foundation for "new hope" for black Americans. More accurate was the editorial of the Atlanta *Constitution:* "The speech stamps Booker T. Washington as a wise counselor and a safe leader." Black reactions were decidedly mixed. . . . [B]lack editor W. Calvin Chase described the speech as "death to the Afro-American and elevating to the white people." A.M.E. Bishop Henry M. Turner believed that Tuskegee's principal "will have to live a long time to undo the harm he has done our race." The Atlanta *Advocate* condemned Washington's "sycophantic attitude." . . .

Through Washington's patronage, his black and white supporters were able to secure posts in the federal government. Washington's influence with white philanthropists largely determined which Negro colleges would receive funds. The Tuskegee Machine never acquiesced in the complete political disfranchisement of blacks, however, and behind the scenes Washington used his resources to fight for civil rights. In 1900 he requested funds from white philanthropists to lobby against racist election provisions in the Louisiana state constitution. He privately fought Alabama's disfranchisement laws in federal courts, and in 1903–04 personally spent "at least four thousand dollars in cash" to promote the legal struggle against Jim Crow. Nevertheless, the general impression Washington projected to the white South was the Negro's subservience to Jim Crow, lynchings, and political terror. One of Washington's strongest critics in this regard was Alexander Crummell. The black scholar disliked Washington's emphasis on Afro-American industrial training at the expense of higher education. But more important, he viewed Washington's entire accommodationist political program as opportunistic, and believed that Tuskegee's principal was nothing but a "white man's nigger."

Upton Sinclair's graphic description of conditions in the Chicago stockyards upset the public more for what it revealed about the meat Americans consumed than for the plight of the workers. The meatpackers, it was said, used "everthing about the hog except the squeal." *(Courtesy, Scribner's Archives)*

Progressivism in Peace and War 1900–1918

THE JUNGLE

The Beef Trust was a ready target of public anger. The emergence of the packinghouses and the refrigerated railroad car had rapidly transformed the sale of meat from one of the most local of industries to a nationwide enterprise. The old-time butcher who slaughtered and dressed his own meat had been a familiar figure in American life. Most butchers were, according to American folklore, rotund and ruddy, walking testimonials to the quality of the meat they sold.

Upton Sinclair's novel *The Jungle* (1906) is remembered chiefly as an exposé of the packinghouses and for its role in the passage of the Meat Inspection Act of 1906. People talked knowingly of Butcher Watson's or Butcher Smith's chops, convinced that in watching the man carefully cutting up the animals, they had a guarantee of quality. At the turn of the new century a label reading "Armour" or "Swift" evoked no such confidence. But exposing the meatpacking industry was not Sinclair's main purpose for writing *The Jungle*. A recent convert to socialism, he had received a $500 advance to write the book from *The Appeal to Reason*, the nation's leading socialist newspaper. Choosing to write about packinghouse workers who had just lost a strike in the summer of 1904, he went to Chicago, infiltrated the stockyards, and composed a novel exposing their workers' miseries.

Sinclair's socialist connections gave him access to workers' homes, and by dressing poorly and toting a dinner-pail like them he could wander at will through the packinghouses. He soon had the material for a tract, though not the characters for a novel. Then, one Sunday afternoon, wandering through the "Back of the Yards" neighborhood, Sinclair chanced on a wedding party in the rear of a saloon and joined the group as an observer of the festivities: "There were my characters—the bride, the groom, the old mother and father, the boisterous cousin, the children, the three musicians, everybody."

The Jungle is the story of struggling immigrants destroyed by American industry. The hero, Jurgis Rudkus, goes through a series of industrial horrors that wrecks his entire life and finally brings him to socialism. But it was not Sinclair's plea for socialism that impressed the public. What made the book a best-seller, quickly translated into seventeen languages, was its graphic description of the packinghouses. President Theodore Roosevelt quickly responded to the public outcry aroused by *The Jungle*. Reading the book and inviting Sinclair to the White House, he worked out a plan to investigate Sinclair's charges against the packers. The investigation confirmed all that Sinclair had written.

The packers had made large contributions to Roosevelt's campaign fund in 1904 and could not believe that he would go through with strict legislation. But Roosevelt had the goods on them and released the tamer part of his investigators' discoveries. The Beef Trust senators began negotiating; and the President—who did not actually want to hurt the industry or overly damage its sales of meat products abroad—compromised rather more than Sinclair liked. Still, Roosevelt had achieved a significant piece of legislation. In his memoirs he takes full credit for the Meat Inspection Act of 1906 and makes no mention of Sinclair. As a socialist, Sinclair was at odds with Roosevelt's ideology, and he had a way of giving unwanted advice: Roosevelt wished that the writer would "go home and let me run the country for a while." Sinclair himself said that the passage of the act "was some satisfaction to me, but not my main interest. . . . I aimed at the public's heart and by accident hit it in the stomach."

State Progressivism

The progressive mind at the turn of the twentieth century favored a more humane and rational organization of the economic and technical forces of the times. It had some of its earlier expressions at the local and state level. As early as the 1890s urban progressives in the state legislatures were demanding new laws to carry out reform programs, including various forms of home rule.

The city reformers found friends in the state government among rural and small-town members seeking to control railroad rates, reduce tariffs, improve rural life, increase farm credit, and attack trusts and banks. Rural progressivism became a powerful force in the Midwest and Far West, as well as in parts of the South, and eventually even entered eastern states, among them Massachusetts and New Jersey.

Progressives, both urban and rural, recoiled against the emergence of new and, in their eyes, dangerous sources of power. These included urban political machines, which through voter fraud and other corrupt practices seemed to make a mockery of the idea of self-government, and giant corporations, which appeared to have the power to control both wages and prices. Progressives labeled these giant businesses and their political allies "the interests," while they called themselves the defenders of "the public" or "the public interest." Some, unlike their political cousins of a later age, were also hostile to labor unions, seeing them as another of the large concentrations of power that warred against simple democracy.

Political Reforms   While some progressives were pressing, especially at the city level, for clean and efficient mechanisms of government administration removed from the clash and vices of democracy, others worked to expand popular participation in the political process. Progressives stocked their arsenal for this campaign with a number of weapons. The Australian or secret ballot dated from the 1880s in the United States; by the time of the First World War every state had adopted it. Laws limiting the uses and amounts of money spent in campaigns also spread in the first decade of the new century. The direct primary gave all members of a political party the opportunity to participate in the choice of the party's candidates, and was popular among innovations designed to make politics a less boss-ridden process. The direct primary soon replaced the system of local conventions, which the bosses could manipulate. The initiative, referendum, and recall were experiments in direct democracy. The initiative is a process in which a number of citizens, by signing a petition, can offer a new law for consideration by the entire electorate. The referendum is a direct popular vote on whether to accept a proposed law. The recall refers to a popular vote that can remove officials from office before the expiration of their terms.

The ultimate effect of these structural reforms has been a subject of controversy. Some political scientists believe that in loosening party organization the direct primary actually weakened the democratic process and increased the importance of money in elections. The initiative and referendum, they point out, can require expensive organizing and lobbying campaigns that shut out the common citizen. The question of how best to further democracy, or for that matter whether beyond a certain point it should be furthered, is a recurrent issue in American politics.

State Governors   State-level progressivism began as a major force in 1900, when Robert M. La Follette became governor of Wisconsin. A central issue in Wisconsin was the way the state taxed railroads. They were the largest property owners in the state, and their taxes were based upon their annual earnings

Upton Sinclair. *(Courtesy, Culver Library)*

In Sinclair's depiction of meatpacking:

"There was never the least attention paid to what was cut up for sausage; there would come all the way back from Europe old sausage that had been rejected, and that was moldy and white—it would be doused with borax and glycerine, dumped into the hoppers, and made over again for home consumption. There would be meat that had tumbled out on the floor, in the dirt and sawdust, where the workers had tramped and spit uncounted billions of consumption germs. There would be meat stored in great piles in rooms; and the water from leaky roofs would drip over it, and thousands of rats would race about on it. It was too dark in these storage places to see well, but a man could run his hand over these piles of meat and sweep off handfuls of the dried dung of rats. These rats were nuisances, and the packers would put poisoned bread out for them; they would die, and then rats, bread, and meat would go into the hoppers together. . . . There were things that went into the sausage in comparison with which a poisoned rat was a tidbit. There was no place for the men to wash their hands before they ate their dinner, and so they made a practice of washing them in the water that was to be ladled into the sausage."

The most famous of the reform leaders in the states was Wisconsin's Robert M. "Fighting Bob" La Follette. (*Courtesy, State Historical Society of Wisconsin*)

rather than upon the assessed value of their property. This meant that during the depression following the panic of 1893 the railroads' tax burden dropped, from seventy-two percent of the state's tax revenues in 1892 to forty-seven percent in 1897. For all other property owners, however, taxes remained the same or went up. So La Follette was able to tap into deep pools of popular resentment when he made the railroads' privileged position a major issue. After legislative opponents defeated his initial moderate reform package, La Follette, stamping, demanding, and scolding, created a majority for reform and then ruled it tightly. Stubborn, humorless, and fiercely independent, La Follette became a reform boss, ruthless in the use of patronage, absolute in his demand for loyalty, implacable in dispatching his enemies in the good cause of honest government.

La Follette pushed through a wide range of political reforms: the direct primary, antilobbying laws, and civil service acts. Determined to make state government efficient and useful as well as honest, he called on outstanding academic experts to draft legislation, sit on commissions, and generally improve the quality of government. The University of Wisconsin became known as a center for research into social problems and solutions. And there was a lot to do in Wisconsin. La Follette's reform program included a strong railroad-rate commission, sharp increases in the taxes paid by corporations and railroads, conservation and water power measures, state banking regulation, and a host of other social and economic reforms. Under his prodding, Wisconsin became the first state to pass a graduated income tax. Theodore Roosevelt, always ready with an apt phrase, called Wisconsin "the laboratory of democracy."

Other states followed. Albert Baird Cummins in Iowa, Joseph Folk in Missouri, Jeff Davis in Arkansas, Hiram Johnson in California, Hoke Smith in Georgia, Charles Evans Hughes in New York, and Woodrow Wilson in New Jersey were among the governors of the era who adopted the Wisconsin Idea, as it was labeled. In various degrees these politicians succeeded in modernizing their state governments and passing political and economic reform legislation. During much of the nineteenth century, state government had addressed little energy to the development of large social and economic policy. Revitalization of state government was one of the major achievements of the Progressive Era.

In Denver, Colorado, Judge Ben Lindsey made it a practice to treat children not as criminals but as victims of their environment, and pressed for playgrounds, vocational education, and other means of improving their futures. Such efforts within states nourished progressivism on the national level.

Theodore Roosevelt Becomes President

As the nationwide economy became increasingly close-knit, there were still other reforms that only the federal government could undertake. Only it could effectively guarantee the safety of medicines; only it could regulate interstate commerce. Working against these progressive hopes was a series of Supreme Court decisions that had substantially weakened the Interstate Commerce Commission and virtually destroyed the Sherman Antitrust Law. Early in the new century, the leadership of a national progressive movement began to emerge. A number of progressive governors like "Fighting Bob" La Follette entered the United States Senate, and in 1901 Theodore Roosevelt became President.

The Last Nineteenth-Century President

President William McKinley's election victories in 1896 and 1900 established the Republicans as the majority party in national political life. Democrats and Republicans were no longer fighting with the narrow partisan intensity of equal competitors. That, along with the divisions within the Democratic Party that the Bryan campaign had brought, turned politics away from the old partisan issues that had grown out of the Civil War and Reconstruction. New publics—the concerned citizens of the cities and towns eager to assume more control of their surroundings, women active in social movements, the new professionals, the increasingly self-aware immigrant groups—could support a new national politics fixed on the issues of industrialism, urban life, and the growing interdependence of all communities across the nation. McKinley remained in some sense a politician of the old kind. Standing close behind him, however, cautiously nursing hopes for the presidential nomination in 1904, Vice President Theodore Roosevelt was eager to enter the twentieth century.

Then the President, on September 6, 1901, attended the Pan-American Exposition at Buffalo. There a cloudy-minded young man, Leon Czolgosz—whose knowledge of anarchism scarcely extended beyond the popular information that anarchists had a habit of assassinating rulers—pumped two bullets into McKinley. A black onlooker seized the assassin's gun, but he was too late. On September 14, the President died, the last chief executive to have survived in combat the bullets of the southern rebels, and the second Civil War veteran to be struck down while in the presidency. Roosevelt, informed while in Vermont, sped by special train to Buffalo. His ambition, and the great difference between the two men in age and ideology, impressed contemporaries. Rumors circulated of a cursing J. P. Morgan, his face a flaming red, staggering to his desk in fear that the government might wage war on his interests.

The First Full-Term Twentieth-Century President

Just under forty-three years old when he took office, Theodore Roosevelt was by far the youngest President in American history up to that time. He contrasted sharply with the staid chief executives of the previous quarter century. Articulate, excitable, and energetic, with a range of interests extending far beyond politics, he and his young family, particularly his beautiful daughter Alice, lent a glamour and excitement to national events. Already famous as a military hero, he immediately captured a vast public, becoming its beloved "Teddy." A young girl in the 1870s had written in her diary of the adolescent Theodore: "He is such fun . . . the most original boy I ever knew." Throughout his life, he remained fun

A song stressed Roosevelt's eagerness for the White House, his aristocratic background, and his reputation for horsemanship. (The new President actually learned of McKinley's death while in Vermont.)

He jumped on his horse and pulled down through Maine:
He said to his horse you've got to outrun this train [carrying McKinley's body];
Buffalo to Washington.
Now Roosevelt's in the White House drinking out of a silver cup.
McKinley's in the graveyard, he'll never wake up.
He's gone; he's gone.

Theodore Roosevelt. *(Courtesy, Brown Brothers)*

"For better it is," wrote Teddy Roosevelt in 1899, "to dare mighty things, to win glorious triumphs, even though checkered by failure, than to take rank with those poor spirits who neither enjoy much nor suffer much, because they live in the gray twilight that knows not victory nor defeat."

for millions of his adorers. Perhaps, too, he remained a most original boy as well: "You must always remember," wrote a friend, "that the President is about six." The ebullient man with the thick pince-nez glasses over his large nose, the face as square as his moralism, the gleaming teeth, the vigorous gesturing style was a cartoonist's delight. A college classmate long before had wondered "whether [Roosevelt] is the real thing, or only the bundle of eccentricities he appears." The public soon discovered that he was the real thing, a skillful leader and shrewd politician as well as a colorful character.

Theodore Roosevelt had been born in 1858, the first child of a public-spirited New York merchant and a southern lady. The Roosevelts' Manhattan brownstone was scarcely a log cabin, and the young Roosevelt was hardly an instinctive democrat. Even at Harvard he chose his company carefully. Graduating twenty-first in his class of 158—a creditable showing—he wrote his sister that "only one gentleman stands ahead of me." His precocious interest in nature and love of the outdoors almost led him to a career in science. Perhaps he was too much the dilettante for such a calling. Young Theodore needed a career to satisfy his enthusiasms for literature, sports, society, and nature, to meet his father's high ideals of public service, and to give him a limitless field in which to compete. For he was one of the most competitive of men, whether in boxing, hunting, politics, or literature.

With time out for exploring the Dakotas and for literary endeavors, Roosevelt pursued a career of public service. He received appointments to various offices for which his energy and connections made him suitable: the United States Civil Service Commission, the Board of Commissioners of the New York City Police, and assistant secretary of the navy (1897–98). Meanwhile, he was available when the Republican machine needed a reform candidate, as happens periodically to every political machine however wicked its usual behavior. In 1886 he was an unsuccessful Republican candidate for mayor of New York City. In

1898, after he had become famous in the war with Spain for leading the Rough Riders in their charge up Kettle (or, as tradition has it, San Juan) Hill, and with the state party facing a scandal, he was elected governor of New York.

Roosevelt acquitted himself well as governor, just as he had in his other offices. Well organized, hardworking, and with a flair for the dramatic, he was successful and popular. He showed that he could battle to improve the public service without wholly alienating the professional politicians. His New York State progressivism was a modest eastern version of the Wisconsin Idea.

Reformers put in office by machine politicians rarely serve more than one term. New York Republican boss Tom Platt, thoroughly tired of struggling with the moralistic governor whom fate and scandals had forced on him, easily maneuvered Roosevelt out of the statehouse and into the vice presidency, a usually trivial office and to Roosevelt's mind maddeningly dull for a "comparatively young man." McKinley's previous Vice President, Garret A. Hobart, had died in office.

Roosevelt, propelled into the White House by McKinley's death, was superbly suited for the presidency. He was ready to preach to a nation that wanted a new kind of secular preacher. He had advanced ideas about the needs of an industrial society, but he would couch them in words of a plain and traditional morality. His zest for competition led him to revive disused powers of the office. He was in touch with the new generation and its new ideas, yet he was a Republican regular in a time of clear Republican majorities. Most of all, he was a good speaker at the end of a period of great American oratory, a telling phrase-maker in an age of popular literacy, and good copy in one of the most vigorous eras of American journalism.

"I wish to say that it shall be my aim to continue, absolutely unbroken, the policy of President McKinley for the peace, prosperity, and the honor of our beloved country," Theodore Roosevelt promised his cabinet just before taking the presidential oath. Roosevelt had many good reasons to avoid any sudden upsets at the beginning of his accidental administration. The McKinley Administration's identification with prosperity, after the harsh depression of the 1890s, meant that any upset of business confidence would be blamed directly on the White House, which might then get a new occupant after the 1904 election. The focus of power in Washington was, meanwhile, not in the White House, but at the other end of Pennsylvania Avenue, especially in the United States Senate.

Theodore Roosevelt's daughter Alice added to the aura of glamour and excitement surrounding the President. *(Courtesy, Library of Congress)*

Roosevelt vs. the Senate   The Senate was the keystone that joined and held together the overarching powers of business and the Republican Party. Organized under tight party discipline to a far greater extent than it had been earlier or would be later, the upper House was ruled by a handful of powerful Republicans. Nelson W. Aldrich of Rhode Island, John C. Spooner of Wisconsin, Orville H. Platt of Connecticut, and William B. Allison of Iowa—called "The Four" by contemporaries—ran the formal machinery of the Senate. Mark Hanna of Ohio had been the administration's man in the Senate during the McKinley presidency and was the party's great fundraiser. All directly represented the major industries, frankly seeking subsidies and favors for their pet interests while standing firm against any reforms that might disturb "confidence," meaning the happiness of big business. Roosevelt worried them; they could see his assertive personality, knew his active governorship of New York, and were old enough to remember that the presidency could be transformed into an immensely powerful office, as during the Civil War.

Roosevelt had no intention of remaining within the mold the leadership had cast for his office. But he wisely refrained from hopeless confrontation with The Four. He saw that he would have to begin with activities remote from legislation in order to develop a public and to exercise the larger possibilities of the office. He would turn the presidency—as he wished to turn all life—into drama. Even his everyday routine was designed to invoke wonder and fasten attention on the White House. At his desk every morning by 8:30, he saw dozens of groups each day, not just senators and other party dignitaries, but writers, reformers, social workers, scientists, even labor leaders. The great Spanish cellist Pablo Casals performed in the White House, as he would do again sixty years later when John F. Kennedy was in office. And Roosevelt saw people during breakfast, lunch, and dinner, and during his daily horseback ride through Rock Creek Park. Scarcely a month after moving into the White House he defied white-supremacist custom, inviting the most celebrated black leader of the era, Booker T. Washington, to sit down at lunch with him. When white southerners protested the symbolic gesture bitterly, Roosevelt announced that he would have Dr. Washington "to dine just as often as I please"—though the politic President was never again pleased to do so.

The Roosevelt Leadership

Roosevelt and the Trusts Five months after taking office, the President took his first large action. It was on the "absolutely vital question," as he would later call it, of government regulation of the large corporations. J. P. Morgan provided Roosevelt's opportunity when, late in 1901, he formed the Northern Securities Company. The new holding company controlled the Northern Pacific Railroad and the Great Northern Railroad. This $400 million combination was essentially a peace treaty that Morgan imposed on all the groups competing for rail traffic in the Northwest. The first important holding company, it brought together the Hill, Harriman, Rockefeller, and Morgan interests. It extended across the country the Morgan rail monopoly of the eastern lines, bringing unified management and the threat of higher rates to a large part of the nation's shippers. Though unpopular with the public, it seemed safe from attack, since in *United States v. E. C. Knight Company* (1895) the Supreme Court had sharply restricted the scope of the Sherman Antitrust Act. Roosevelt, consulting only Attorney General Philander C. Knox, ordered him to file suit for the dissolution of the holding company. Morgan, at the White House, according to a common account, spoke to the President as one business executive to another, suggesting that Roosevelt's "man," the

"The President's Dream of a Successful Hunt." *(Courtesy, Library of Congress)*

attorney general, and "my man" settle the whole matter, apparently as two lawyers setting the boundaries of a turf dispute. Roosevelt had another idea of the dignity and power of the federal government. The Supreme Court, in effect reversing the Knight decision, upheld the President in *Northern Securities Company v. United States* (1904).

The image of trustbuster that Roosevelt gained in his confrontation with Northern Securities and other companies was more important than any particular antitrust actions he undertook. It offended him that J. P. Morgan could apparently not see the moral distance between a business and the government of the United States. Yet once he had asserted in principle the regulatory power of government, Roosevelt was eager to negotiate a "gentlemen's agreement" to approve in advance new acquisitions to the vast Morgan empire. Running with both the hounds and the hares, Roosevelt made his point without alienating either the Senate or the business community.

After the Northern Securities case, Roosevelt had considerable success with Congress. It agreed to establishing within the Department of Commerce and Labor, which was then being organized, a Bureau of Corporations that would collect statistics and investigate the activities of corporations. The Elkins Act, passed with railroad support in 1903, outlawed rebates to large shippers and increased the powers of the Interstate Commerce Commission. Together these acts created an enduring American legend, a President prepared to take on big business.

TR and Labor   Roosevelt sought to find moral grounds for distinguishing good corporations that increased services and efficiency or lowered prices from bad ones that limited competition and raised prices. He reached the same position on labor unions, which had also flourished in the years of trust building and inflation after 1897. In 1902, when old conflicts between the operators and the workers again erupted in the coal fields, Roosevelt had an opportunity to push the presidency into relations between labor and management in a way that would establish his conception of a "square deal" for all sides. The Square Deal was the first of a number of twentieth-century administrative slogans, a precedent for the New Deal, the Fair Deal, the New Frontier, and the Great Society.

In 1900 the anthracite coal workers had threatened a massive strike. Anthracite was the hard coal used to heat houses and workplaces, and despite the ready availability of a usable substitute, bituminous or soft coal, Americans feared for the misery that might come once the coal cars stopped rumbling over the Pennsylvania hills. To head off this election-year threat, Mark Hanna persuaded the operators to make concessions to the union. Two years later, however, when John Mitchell, the United Mine Workers' president, called for a new wage scale, the operators determined to crush the union. They rejected all overtures for negotiation, refusing not only a wage increase but any recognition, formal or informal, of the union.

Told that the miners had to contend with miserable conditions, the leader of the operators, George F. Baer, insisted that the miners "don't suffer; why, they can't even speak English." Despite the rising bitter-

There is little question that TR's aversion to trusts was sincere. Just before the election of 1904 he had written in a private letter:

"Corporation cunning has developed faster than the laws of nation and State. Corporations have found ways to steal long before we have found that they were susceptible of punishment for theft. Sooner or later, unless there is a readjustment, there will come a riotous, wicked, murderous day of atonement. There must come, in the proper growth of this nation, a readjustment. If it is not to come by sword and powder and blood, it must come by peaceful compromise. These fools in Wall Street think that they can go on forever! They can't!"

A song written during his second administration presents the popular Roosevelt image.

Not long ago the railroads owned the
    whole United States,
Their rates were high to farmers, but a
    trust could get rebates,
Who stopped this crime of freight rebates among the railroad men?
Who fixed it so the railroads carry people now and then?
It's Theodore, the peaceful Theodore;
Of all the rulers great or small
He is the greatest of them all.

A peaceful procession of striking coal miners makes an orderly demonstration at Shenandoah, Pennsylvania, during the 1902 coal strike. *(Courtesy, Library of Congress)*

John Mitchell, the leader of the Coal Strike of 1902, appealed to Teddy Roosevelt because he struck chords of responsibility. Here he denounces "sympathy" strikes whereby other unions strike to support their brothers and sisters.

"I have, during all my life in the labor movement, declared that contracts mutually made should during their life be kept inviolate; and while at times it may appear to the superficial observer or to those immediately concerned that advantage could be gained by setting agreements aside, such advantage, if gained, would, in the very nature of things, be temporary, and would ultimately result in disaster; because a disregard of the sacredness of contracts strikes at the very vitals of organized labor. The effect of such action would be to destroy confidence, to array in open hostility to our cause all forces of society, and to crystallize public sentiment in opposition to our movement."

ness of his men, whose gains of two years before had vanished with inflation, Mitchell remained moderate in his demands and restrained in his tactics. On May 12, 1902, the miners began the largest strike to date in American history. Mitchell kept his men in order, also seeing to it that the soft-coal workers stayed in the mines digging coal to compete with anthracite and contributed part of their paychecks to the strike fund.

Roosevelt hoped at first to bring an antitrust prosecution against the six railroad corporations that owned seventy percent of the mines and controlled the movement of the coal to market, but Attorney General Knox did not consider the case strong enough. As summer dragged into fall with the price of coal soaring and the public in fear of a cold snap, first Mark Hanna and then Roosevelt made efforts to end the strike. But the operators steadily rejected all overtures. The New York City schools closed down for lack of fuel. Finally Roosevelt, "at my wits' end how to proceed," and supported even by conservative Republican leaders, took the novel course of inviting to the White House the leaders of both the operators and the union.

It was a dramatic scene as these men who were not speaking to each other assembled, and Roosevelt, in a wheelchair from a recent accident, pleaded for a settlement. Mitchell offered to accept binding arbitration, but Baer, a few months before having announced that "God in his infinite wisdom" had appointed the coal owners to their post, vilified Mitchell and (in Roosevelt's careful prose) "in at least two cases assumed an attitude toward me which was one of insolence."

Threatening a military seizure of the mines unless the owners agreed to arbitration, Roosevelt got Morgan, the most influential American financier, to agree to back arbitration. The men went back to work and the threat of warfare in the coal country faded. The board of arbitration Roosevelt set up gave the workers a ten percent pay hike and corrected some minor abuses, but on the larger issue of recognition the union lost totally. The board passed on the cost of the settlement to the public by granting the operators a ten percent increase in prices.

Nonetheless, Roosevelt had broken decisively with the federal practice of intervening only in the interests of public order, and therefore on the side of management. Government as a third force in disputes between labor and management was now an accomplished fact. Roosevelt had at last provided a response to the middle-class fear of being squeezed to pieces between labor and capital. Whether or not he had made the system work much better, he made labor and the public feel better.

The Second Term

The Election of 1904

Roosevelt's nomination for a term on his own was a foregone conclusion. He had won the hearts of the people and the heads of the leaders. The Democratic opposition, having nowhere to go, went nowhere. Outflanked on the left by Roosevelt's initiatives, they turned away from William Jennings Bryan to nominate a colorless New York judge, Alton B. Parker. During his campaign, Roosevelt declared that in the anthracite coal strike he had gotten a square deal for both strikers and owners, and "Square Deal" was to become a catch term for his second administration. Flawless political management simply added to Roosevelt's huge personal acclaim. The Republican National Committee collected almost three-quarters of its gifts from large corporations, and Roosevelt swept to an overwhelming victory. His one blunder came on election night when, as part of his victory statement, he announced that "under no circumstances will I be a candidate for or accept another nomination." Roosevelt, who would be only fifty years old when he left office, was to have abundant cause to regret this noble pledge.

The second Roosevelt Administration was quite different from the first—in some ways far more successful, in other ways less so. Roosevelt's initiatives grew bolder, while opposition within his own party rose. As he widened the national agenda of reform, he began to strain the Republican alliance.

In the months after his election, Roosevelt announced a comprehensive set of goals. Noting that the Elkins Act of 1903 had failed to end the rebate evil, he called for the strict regulation of railroads; he wanted greatly to increase the power of the Interstate Commerce Commission and limit court review of its actions. He also proposed employers' liability laws, a minimum wage for railroad workers, and for the District of Columbia—which the federal government directly ruled—a variety of regulations, covering child labor, factory inspection, and slum clearance, designed to make it a model of progressive legislation for the states.

The Hepburn Act

The Republican Congress wanted none of this. "Congress will pass the appropriation bills and mark time," predicted Speaker Joseph G. Cannon, the plain-spoken autocrat who ruled the House of Representatives.

In spite of all the progress in the Progressive Era, patent medicines were still widely used. Often they contained a large percentage of alcohol; one label, for example, boasted that its contents would feel "like a ball of fire moving up and down your chest."

These ads are from the 1897 Sears, Roebuck catalog:

SPECIAL FAMILY REMEDIES.

The following few well known household remedies and other useful articles are carefully put up in our own laboratory, in a convenient form expressly for family use. We guarantee their strength, freshness and purity. Each and every one of them is a necessary article in every house, for when they are wanted they are wanted quick. When they are in reach they often save severe pain, avert sickness and sometimes save life, and the expense of having them is very small when purchased from us. Study the list well.

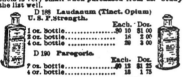

D 188 Laudanum (Tinct. Opium).
U. S. P. Strength.

	Each.	Doz.
1 oz. bottle	$0 10	$1 00
2 oz. bottle	18	2 00
4 oz. bottle	30	3 00

D 190 Paregoric.

	Each.	Doz.
7 oz. bottle	$0 12	$1 25
4 oz. bottle	18	1 75

D 248   Electric Ring for Rheumatism.

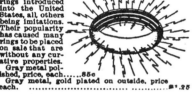

These are the first rings introduced into the United States, all others being imitations. Their popularity has caused many rings to be placed on sale that are without any curative properties. Gray metal polished, price, each.....35c. Gray metal, gold plated on outside, price each. $1.25

D 184 Worm Cakes. This is a very satisfactory remedy for destroying worms and removing them from the system. It is in convenient form for children to take, which they readily do, thinking it is a candy. Full instructions how to give them, and other useful information in each box. Price 20c; Doz.................$2.25

D 186 Root Beer. A healthy and delicious beverage. One bottle makes 5 gallons of not only a healthy temperance beverage but one of the most pleasant and invigorating that can be found for the warm weather, producing a gentle stimulation throughout the entire body without any deleterious effects. It is also a blood purifier, easily prepared and costs very little. Per bottle, 12c; Doz.................$1.25

D 172 Pink Pills for Pale People, the great blood builder. Cures pale and sallow complexions. Suppression of the Periods. Rheumatism and all diseases arising from mental worry, overwork, early decay, etc. Full directions on circular around the box. Price, 25c; Doz. boxes.................$2.00

D 154 Little Liver Pills. This is a very small pill, easily swallowed even by children. It acts specially on the Liver, regulating the flow of the bile and causing the bowels to act in a regular manner. It is especially a good pill for any one inclined to biliousness, and a sure cure for headaches and stomach troubles arising from too much bile in the stomach. Per bottle, 13c. Per doz. bottles... ....$1.00

D 156 Microbe Killer. This is Dr. Pasteur's Microbe Killer, which, if taken once or twice a day, will prevent La Grippe, Catarrh, Consumption, Malaria, Blood Poison, Rheumatism and all disorders of the blood. It acts as an antiseptic, killing the germs which are the cause of these diseases. This preparation of Dr. Pasteur's will eradicate any form of disease and purify the whole system. ¼ gallon bottles, each, 97c.; per doz.....................$11.50

Roosevelt quickly decided to concentrate on regulation of the railroads, one of the two questions then exciting the Middle West and the West. The other was the tariff, a sensitive economic issue all over the country that the Republican leadership, happy with the current high rates, refused to touch.

Roosevelt's strategy was to threaten the leadership with a tariff bill in order to force concessions on railroad regulation. Cannon eventually swallowed his distaste for railroad regulation and allowed the House to pass stringent bills by huge majorities. But the Senate was more conservative. As yet no constitutional amendment provided for direct election of senators, and senators chosen by state legislatures could afford to give their services freely to big business. Senator Aldrich used all his formidable parliamentary skills to block a strong bill. But the President, continuing to whip up the wrath of the small shippers and farmers and rallying middle-class opinion to the cause, kept a steady pressure on the Senate. He played off radicals and conservatives against each other, finally accepted a few painful compromises, and got a useful bill.

The Hepburn Act, as passed in 1906, allowed the Interstate Commerce Commission to set railroad rates on the complaint of a shipper, these to be subject to court review. It permitted the ICC to examine the railroads' books and prescribed bookkeeping standards. What it did not do was to permit the ICC to conduct valuations of the worth of a road's physical property, a power that Robert La Follette had argued was essential to the fixing of fair rates. The judicial review permitted under the act was broad: the courts could pass not only on the procedures of the commission but on whether the rates set were "reasonable." The act was nonetheless epoch-making. For the first time, a governmental body was empowered actually to set rates, and for the first time such an agency could open the books of the companies.

Consumer Legislation The whole question of consumer protection also had its origins in the Progressive Era. The quality of processed food and drugs had never before been much of an issue.

Most Americans traditionally lived on farms in rural areas; they raised, cooked, and ate their own food. All that changed in the cities. Urban dwellers purchased food in local stores, and they knew little about where it had come from, how it had been processed, or how long it had been on the shelf. That problem of food processing was especially acute in the marketing of meat. Rural Americans had always raised, processed, and preserved their own beef, pork, and poultry. They knew which animals had been sick, which ones had been healthy, and how much time had passed since the animals had been slaughtered. But buyers of meat in city stores or butcher shops had none of that information. New preserving processes and the introduction of artificial flavorings and colorings in food and meat had made it increasingly uncertain what exactly the public was purchasing. In the cities food poisoning, from salmonella to the deadly botulism, became increasingly common.

City people experienced a similar problem with drugs. Back on the farm, they had used herbs and folk medicines, family healing practices handed down from one generation to another. The real efficacy of the potions, of course, was debatable, but at least the cures were usually not worse than the diseases. Rural Americans might from time to time hear marvelous claims from snake-oil peddlers selling magic medicine from the backs of wagons. But in the cities people were more vulnerable to the mass marketing and mass advertising techniques of pharmaceutical companies. It was not uncommon for those companies to exaggerate the potency of certain drugs, market veterinary products for human use, or distribute new drugs that had not been adequately tested, or even tested at all.

For years the lone voice in the consumer wilderness had been that of Dr. Harvey W. Wiley, the chief chemist for the Department of Agriculture. He regularly tested food and drug products and was appalled at what he considered to be unsafe chemical tampering with the public health. Wiley demanded federal regulation of the food processing and drug manufacturing industries.

With the support of President Theodore Roosevelt and the public impact of Upton Sinclair's muckraking novel *The Jungle,* Congress addressed the problem and in June 1906 passed landmark legislation. The Pure Food and Drug Act prohibited the manufacture, sale, or transportation across state lines of foods and drugs that had been adulterated or carried fraudulent labeling. The Meat Inspection Act was targeted at cleaning up the packinghouses. It established sanitary regulations for meatpacking plants and provided for federal inspection of all companies selling meats in interstate markets.

Brownsville   In Roosevelt's second term occurred an incident that marred his record on racial relations. In August 1906, black soldiers rioted in Brownsville, Texas, in reaction to white-racist provocations. Without attempting to separate the rioters from the innocent, Roosevelt had all 167 members of three black companies dishonorably discharged. Not until more than six decades later were the men awarded honorable discharges, and by then few were alive to enjoy the righting of a wrong.

Roosevelt's reasons are unclear. Among Americans with military experience, he was notably well disposed toward black soldiers. In Cuba his Rough Riders had fought alongside black troops. After his country's declaration of war against Germany in 1917, he was to appeal, unsuccessfully, for authority to raise a force to fight in Europe, and he included in his plans a black unit. Perhaps the army veteran in him, joined to an impatient quickness with any disorder or insubordination, led him to an act of discipline unqualified by justice.

Origins of the Conservation Movement   Several important conservationists of the nineteenth and early twentieth century had been well in advance of the thinking of President Roosevelt, whose own ideas were in turn ahead of those of most Americans. Frederick Law Olmsted, a landscape architect most famous for planning New York's Central Park, had promoted the crea-

tion of city parks because they fostered health and offered a refuge from the pace of urban life. John Wesley Powell, an adventurer who floated down the Colorado River, mapped and classified the resources of much of the West and offered a plan to develop arid regions responsibly. George Perkins Marsh wrote in the pathbreaking *Man and Nature* (1864) about the "improvident waste" of natural resources. Once nature was dominated by man, Marsh believed, it could not revert to its primitive condition and so remained forever impoverished. John Muir, founder in 1862 of the Sierra Club and leader of the effort to establish Yosemite National Park, decried the dominance of man over nature and wished to restore the primacy of the natural environment. George Catlin, a painter and one of the earliest environmentalists, envisioned "a Nation's Park, containing man and beast, in all the wild and freshness of nature's beauty." Catlin wished no other memorial than credit for having elaborated the concept of a park for the nation. Yellowstone in the northwest corner of Wyoming Territory first realized his dreams in 1872 when President Grant gave the nation a great treasure of lakes, clear rivers, forests, geysers, and incredible beauty all around. Sequoia Park and Mount Rainier Park followed in the 1890s. By the turn of the century the conservation movement was ripe for national leadership.

Roosevelt and Conservation   From his founding of the "Roosevelt Museum of Natural History" in an upstairs bookcase sometime before he reached the age of ten, Theodore Roosevelt had maintained a continuous passion for nature. His interest was both scientific and romantic. In his public life it translated into a concern for the conservation of natural resources. The government should "make the streams and rivers of the arid region useful by engineering works for water storage," he wrote in supporting what became the Newlands Act of 1902 to reclaim arid lands in the West. The goal of conservation policy, Roosevelt said, was to ensure that the use of natural resources would be "in such manner as to keep them unimpaired for the benefit of the children now growing up to inherit the land." Always the emphasis was on use, on policies that would employ the country's natural wealth efficiently and without destruction of it. In this the conservation movement differed from the more recent preservationists who want the wilderness and its resources not to be put to careful use but rather to be kept untouched. After centuries of reckless exploitation of a seemingly inexhaustible treasury of land, water, plants, animals, and minerals, making conservation a national movement was TR's most decisive precedent for the new century. He established national parks, wildlife refuges, and monuments, set aside hundreds of millions of acres as national forests and nationally-controlled mineral lands, and put federal land and water policy on a solid and coherent basis.

"Is there any law that will prevent me from declaring Pelican Island a Federal Bird Reservation?" President Roosevelt inquired in 1903. Told that there was not, he announced, "Very well, then I so do declare it." In the next six years, he so declared fifty more times, establishing a substantial network of federal wildlife refuges. Congress, particularly westerners, reacted harshly to his setting aside 150 million

President Roosevelt encapsulated his conservation policy in a message to Congress on December 3, 1907:

"To waste, to destroy, our natural resources, to skin and exhaust the land instead of using it so as to increase its usefulness, will result in undermining in the days of our children the very prosperity which we ought by right to hand down to them amplified and developed."

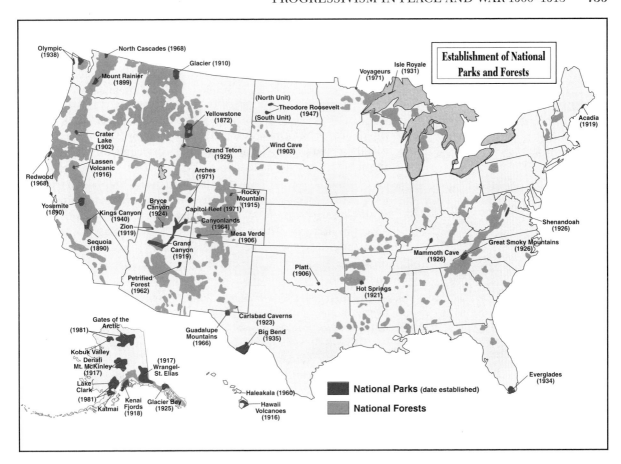

Establishment of National Parks and Forests

Olympic (1938)
North Cascades (1968)
Glacier (1910)
Voyageurs (1971)
Isle Royale (1931)
Mount Rainier (1899)
(North Unit)
Theodore Roosevelt (1947)
(South Unit)
Acadia (1919)
Yellowstone (1872)
Crater Lake (1902)
Grand Teton (1929)
Wind Cave (1903)
Lassen Volcanic (1916)
Arches (1971)
Redwood (1968)
Rocky Mountain (1915)
Yosemite (1890)
Bryce Canyon (1924)
Capitol Reef (1971)
Shenandoah (1926)
Kings Canyon (1940)
Zion (1919)
Canyonlands (1964)
Mesa Verde (1906)
Great Smoky Mountains (1926)
Sequoia (1890)
Grand Canyon (1919)
Mammoth Cave (1926)
Petrified Forest (1962)
Platt (1906)
Hot Springs (1921)
Gates of the Arctic (1981)
Carlsbad Caverns (1923)
Guadalupe Mountains (1966)
Big Bend (1935)
Kobuk Valley
Denali Mt. McKinley (1917)
(1917) Wrangel-St. Elias
Lake Clark (1981)
Kenai Fjords
Katmai
Glacier Bay (1925)
Haleakala (1960)
Hawaii Volcanoes (1916)
Everglades (1934)

National Parks (date established)
National Forests

acres of land as national forests, imposing limits on their exploitation while Gifford Pinchot, his chief forester, developed regulations on their cutting. In 1907 an amendment to the Agricultural Appropriations Act (which Roosevelt had to sign to keep the Forestry Service going) forbade the laying aside in six western states of any additional forest reserves. Roosevelt and Pinchot hurriedly established twenty-one new forest reserves totaling sixteen million acres while the bill sat on the President's desk. Only after officially proclaiming the new reserves did Roosevelt sign the appropriations bill, amid rising protest against "executive usurpation" and complaints from the Far West that the policy was retarding the region's economic development.

An issue that surfaced during Roosevelt's second term defines a distinction among conservationists who wish to preserve nature for human use and others who endow nature with an inherent value superior to the needs of agriculture or industrial development. San Francisco, seeking water for drinking and hydroelectric power, asked the permission of the federal government to dam Hetch Hetchy Valley in Yosemite Park and turn it into a reservoir. John Muir and others wanting to save the valley for its beauty opposed the plan. Pinchot considered the vital interests of San Franciscans to be superior to the pleasures of visitors to the stupendously beautiful Hetch Hetchy. The

John Muir, the ardent conservationist, wrote in his book The Yosemite:

"Dam Hetch Hetchy! As well dam for water-tanks the people's cathedrals and churches, for no holier temple has ever been consecrated by the heart of man."

question was not settled until Congress in 1913 gave its approval to San Francisco.

Roosevelt's Growing Radicalism

Toward the end of his second term Roosevelt—noting the continued rise of labor, the growing strength of socialism, the clear distrust of the wealthy in the public mind, the discomfort over rising prices, and the desire for reform—preached an increasingly radical message. He called for "industrial reform" to give the workingman a "larger share of the wealth." Yet the battle over forest reserves was one of the last successes of Roosevelt's second administration. Only Teddy's indomitable good spirits and self-righteousness saved him from discouragement, for his legislation proceeded no further. Nor were Roosevelt's actions always in harmony with his words. He gave informal approval to the Morgan interests when they proposed having United States Steel purchase the Tennessee Coal and Iron Company, a financially troubled competitor whose acquisition would give the House of Morgan control of over sixty percent of iron and steel production. Unlike Standard Oil or the Santa Fe Railroad, U.S. Steel was a good trust in Roosevelt's mind because it had cooperated with his Bureau of Corporations.

Roosevelt remained by far the most popular man in American life. He had succeeded in convincing millions both that he understood the new bustling world of giant industry, big labor, international rivalries, and mass immigration and that he retained and found applicable to this new world the moral values of a simpler time. His hand-chosen successor, the portly William Howard Taft, whom Roosevelt billed as "a stout defender of my policies," would have to be far more nimble than he looked to meet the demand for reform that Roosevelt had evoked.

Taft

President Taft enjoying a round of golf. *(Courtesy, Library of Congress)*

"Get on the Raft with Taft, Boys"

As secretary of war, Taft had become an informal "assistant President," carrying out presidential policies close to Roosevelt's heart, particularly in supervising the construction of the Panama Canal and in completing various initiatives in foreign policy. "If only there were three of you!" he had exclaimed to Taft upon appointing him. That would have been just under a half-ton of William Howard Tafts, for he weighed comfortably over 300 pounds. The one Taft available to Roosevelt performed many functions in addition to his duties at the War Department.

Yet for all his closeness to Roosevelt and his administrative experience, Taft was in some ways a curious choice. He had, as one historian puts it, risen "to the presidency through the appointive route." A loyal Republican lawyer from a distinguished Cincinnati family, Taft became the first governor general of the Philippines, a role in which he achieved outstanding success in quieting Filipino unrest and establishing limited self-government. In 1904 Roosevelt brought Taft into his cabinet, where he quickly became the first among equals. But his ability to lead the Republican Party and to provide the public with the image of presidential leadership that Roosevelt had created was far more questionable. "Politics, when I am in it, makes me sick," Taft admitted in 1906. Still, William Jennings Bryan's energy at the head of the Democratic ticket was no match for Taft's well-financed campaign of 1908, and the Ohioan rolled up a million-vote popular margin.

At state and local levels, the Republicans did not fare quite so well. Taft ran ahead of the local Republican tickets. In all but a few states in which progressive Republicans dominated the party, the Democrats, though defeated in the presidential race, demonstrated renewed strength. And the progressive Republicans would be demanding that the new President continue Roosevelt's pressure against the stand-patters in the House and Senate.

New Reforms   Taft received little credit from contemporaries for carrying out Roosevelt's reform policies. He deserved much recognition for doing just that.

Taft enforced the Sherman Act with far more vigor, if less drama, than had Roosevelt. Roosevelt in eight years had brought forty-four antitrust suits; Taft's Attorney General George W. Wickersham in four years brought sixty-five. Roosevelt had carefully avoided the issue of tariff revision, but Taft plowed into this thicket, securing an unsatisfactory—and politically disastrous—bill, the Payne-Aldrich tariff, which in fact did reduce some rates though in general it was a high-tariff law. The Hepburn Act of 1906 was the first measure to put some teeth into railroad regulation; the Mann-Elkins Act of 1910, which Taft supported and helped lobby into law, was a great white shark. "Bully! Bully!" Taft, for once in a Rooseveltean mood, exclaimed to reporters upon hearing that the bill had passed. Mann-Elkins enabled the Interstate Commerce Commission to initiate rate changes and to regulate telephone, telegraph, cable, and wireless companies, and placed squarely on a railroad seeking to raise a rate the burden of proof that the old rate was inequitable. The act's practical effect for some years was to prevent the railroads from raising rates. Liberal historians have praised Mann-Elkins for its securing effective control of rates. As a conservationist, Taft set aside even more forest lands than had his predecessor. Taft had a record on labor issues that he could vigorously defend:

> We passed a mining bureau bill to discover the nature of those dreadful explosions and loss of life in mines. We passed safety appliance bills to reduce the loss of life and limbs to railroad employees. We passed an employers' liability act to make easier recovery of damages by injured employees. We have just passed through the Senate a workman's compensation act . . . requiring the railroads to insure their employees against the accidents of a dangerous employment. We passed the children's bureau bill calculated to prevent children from being employed too early in factories. We passed the white phosphorus match

Taft was a lackluster campaigner. A popular song written for the campaign of 1908 sang more loudly of Roosevelt than of the candidate.

The greatest man that ever ran the
    greatest land on earth
Is Teddy R., whose shining star is only
    in its birth.
We'd like some more of Theodore, but
    Theodore has said,
That TAFT was meant for President to
    follow in his stead.

CHORUS:
Get on the raft with Taft, boys
Get in the winning boat,
The man worthwhile, with the big glad
    smile,
Will get the honest vote. . . .

bill to stamp out the making of white phosphorus matches which results in dreadful diseases to those engaged in their manufacture.

Taft might have added that he had appointed as chief of the new Children's Bureau a veteran labor reformer, Julia Lathrop, the first woman in American history to be appointed a bureau chief.

Perhaps most important of all was Taft's initiating of the process that resulted in the adoption of the Sixteenth Amendment, which in effect allowed the federal government to impose graduated personal income taxes that would rise proportionately with income. It is hard to see how without this levy any of the welfare state measures of later years could have been financed.

Nonetheless, Taft has gone down in history as both a conservative and a failure as President. (He would be more successful later as chief justice of the United States, from 1921 to 1930.) He carried out far too many progressive reforms to rank as a successful conservative, while his political ineptitude and his personal style made him a stranger to the progressives. Taft signed the Payne-Aldrich Tariff Bill of 1909 containing modest increases and infuriated the progressives. But his most dramatic clash with progressives, dramatic because it pitted him directly against one of Roosevelt's closest friends, was in the Ballinger-Pinchot affair.

The Ballinger-Pinchot Controversy   Richard A. Ballinger, Taft's new secretary of the interior, was a western lawyer respectful of the western view that favored making lands available for immediate development. Though committed to upholding federal law on conservation, he began soon after he took office to reverse what he considered to be illegal actions during Roosevelt's presidency in withdrawing public lands. Taft, referring tartly to the "transcendentalists" in Chief Forester Pinchot's office who had exceeded the law, allowed Ballinger to return over a million acres to private hands. The President and Ballinger would be better known for that than for their far more extensive preservations of federal lands. Pinchot, in retaliation, publicized the findings of an investigator in the General Land Office that Ballinger, before becoming secretary of the interior, had been involved in a shady land transaction that delivered an enormous windfall in Alaskan coal lands to a Morgan-Guggenheim syndicate.

Taft bought none of this; he exonerated Ballinger, although he went out of his way to state his continuing desire that Pinchot remain as chief forester. Pinchot, however, was not appeased, and he began a surreptitious press war against Ballinger and the President. Then he had a progressive senator read on the Senate floor a letter from Pinchot accusing Ballinger of being an enemy of conservation. Taft fired Pinchot, and he then had to defend his action before a joint congressional committee investigating the affair. As he had feared, his defense of the secretary of the interior came across to the public as opposition to conservation and therefore to Roosevelt's policies.

Roosevelt returned from a much publicized African hunting trip in June 1910 bearing the hides of dozens of large animals and the hopes of the thousands of progressives now in conflict with Taft. Conservationists smarting over the Ballinger-Pinchot affair, progressive editors disappointed in Taft and angered as well by his plans to raise sharply the second-class postal rates that magazines paid, westerners disappointed with the Payne-Aldrich tariff, all looked to Roosevelt for an alternative. The ex-President promised that he would "make no comment or criticism for at least two months." But a vow of silence was the hardest possible promise for Roosevelt to keep. Within a week the newspapers were full of his opinions, and in less than two weeks they would note that he had conferred with both Pinchot and Senator La Follette, Taft's worst enemies.

The New Nationalism   Late that summer Roosevelt, fearing an "ugly" party split, delivered two major speeches designed, he claimed, to provide "a common ground upon which Insurgents and Regulars can stand." But the speeches, particularly one at a gathering of Civil War veterans at Osawatomie, Kansas, had everything to horrify the regulars and cheer the progressives. Calling for a "New Nationalism" that would greatly extend the powers of the federal government, particularly over the corporations, and sharply criticizing the courts that stood in the way of such a program, the address made it obvious that Roosevelt had grown more radical. Taft complained that the speech "frightened every lawyer in the United States" and began identifying himself as a conservative.

With the Republicans in disarray, divided between western progressives and eastern conservatives, between Roosevelt men and Taft loyalists, the 1910 congressional elections warned of the dangers the party would face two years later. The House of Representatives went Democratic for the first time since 1892; state and local victories introduced to the public a fresh set of attractive, reform-minded Democrats such as Woodrow Wilson, a Virginian who had been president of Princeton University and was now governor of New Jersey. Among Republican candidates, it was western progressives who fared well, and Taft already considered progressives "assistant Democrats" rather than true members of his party.

The last act in this curious drama of personal and ideological division came in 1911, when Taft ordered an antitrust suit against the United States Steel Company. One prominent piece of evidence for the monopolistic character of U.S. Steel was the corporation's acquisition in 1907 of the Tennessee Coal and Iron Company, a deal that Roosevelt had tacitly approved and, so Teddy recalled, he had discussed with his secretary of war several times. Privately he excoriated Taft's "small, mean and foolish" act; publicly he attacked Taft's "archaic" attempt to break up the trusts when a better policy would be to regulate them effectively. It was an issue on which Taft was more the progressive opponent of monopolistic business than Roosevelt. But matters of style and political alliance have made Roosevelt remembered as the progressive, Taft as the reactionary.

Theodore Roosevelt was veering to the political left as early as 1910 when he wrote:

"The national government belongs to the whole American people, and when the whole American people are interested, that interest can be guarded effectively only by the national government. The betterment which we seek must be accomplished, I believe, mainly through the national government."

The Election of 1912

A Four-Party Race In 1912 progressive energies were surging. Of the four most visible candidates who took the field in 1912—Taft for the Republicans, Woodrow Wilson for the Democrats, Roosevelt for the newly established Progressive Party, and Eugene V. Debs for the Socialists—even the most apparently conservative among them, President Taft, could claim large credit for progressive ideas. By 1912, Roosevelt and Taft were publicly accusing each other of broken faith, dishonesty, and hypocrisy. As Roosevelt swept the presidential primaries (he even won Taft's home state of Ohio) and Taft used his patronage to pick up the delegates in the nonprimary states, the party split widened. The belligerent Roosevelt, confident that he had the support of the majority of Republicans, attended the national convention decked out in his Rough Rider outfit, topped by a giant sombrero. But the President's men, who controlled the party machinery, awarded themselves all the many disputed delegate seats and nominated their man with ease—while Roosevelt's supporters began to plan a new party.

The emergence of alternative parties—and in 1912 there would be two politically significant ones, the Socialists and the Roosevelt forces—can signify and make for political vigor, when ideas and programs are too insistent and various to be contained within the older organizations. So it was to be in 1912.

Furious at his loss to these "political thugs," and convinced that it was due to corruption in the selection of delegates, Roosevelt was ready to forsake the allegiance of a lifetime and bolt the Republican Party. When supporters guaranteed financial backing for a new party, the Progressive Party was born. Adopting the symbol of the bull moose—Roosevelt had once described himself as being as fit as a bull moose and the remark stuck—the party's national convention had the flavor of a religious revival. Roosevelt offered a "confession of faith"; delegates sang "Onward Christian Soldiers" and "The Battle Hymn of the Republic." The platform endorsed a wide range of progressive reforms, including unemployment insurance and old age pensions, woman suffrage, a tariff commission, tight regulation of the trusts, and national presidential primaries. The platform was stating the agenda for a generation of reform; by splitting the Republican Party, however, it was ensuring that the Democratic Party would be the agent of reform.

After forty-six ballots interspersed with furious negotiations, the Democratic Party finally managed to nominate its ideal candidate, Woodrow Wilson, a native southerner who was attractive to many different elements within the party. As an intellectual, he was a fit match for Roosevelt. He had been a Gold Democrat in 1896, which pleased some, and had become a progressive by 1912, which pleased others. Most of all, he had been a Democratic executive who carried out a progressive program in New Jersey, a state that was eastern and Republican as well as infamous for its corruption and conservatism.

While Taft defended his record and Debs made earnest pleas for socialism, Roosevelt and Wilson clashed over a question that had been

Theodore Roosevelt, "Strong as a Bull Moose," became the candidate of the Progressive Party in the 1912 election. (*Courtesy, Roosevelt Memorial Association, New York City*)

shaping itself during the progressive years: should the nation accept the increasing centralization of its economic and political life or should it break up concentrations of power?

The "New Nationalism" vs. the "New Freedom" Borrowing language from Herbert Croly's *The Promise of American Life* (1909)—which he had read during his African safari—Roosevelt argued that Americans should recognize that the increasing organization and interrelatedness of their society was both inevitable and good. The trusts were good insofar as they could impose order on the nation's economy, and should therefore not be broken up. Instead, the government ought to regulate them more tightly and therein bring still more order and purpose to national life. In that spirit the government should take on responsibility for social welfare and for relations between labor and management. This New Nationalism, as the campaign termed it, was in a Republican tradition that as early as the party's founding had envisioned a unified country, its economy nourished by the federal government, as opposed to a country that was no more than a collection of states and localities.

Wilson's response—the product of long hours of discussion with Louis D. Brandeis, a great legal mind of the age—was the New Freedom. Wilson demanded vigorous, effective antitrust activity that would open the avenues of commerce to new talent and energy. The rules of fair business dealing would be carefully established, and violators subjected to harsh penalties. Wilson was somewhat vague on how he would accomplish this restoration of competing small units, and as the campaign proceeded he lessened his stress on breaking up the trusts. But the idea appealed to people frightened by bigness both in industry and in government.

In the election Republican voters split, the progressives going for Roosevelt and the regulars for Taft. The Democrats won forty-two percent of the popular vote—not a majority, but a sizable plurality. Roosevelt gained a little over a quarter of the voters, and Taft a little less than a quarter. Even the Socialist candidate won nearly a million voters. Wilson had slid between two halves of a majority party to win the presidency. But even as a minority President he possessed a clear mandate for reform.

Woodrow Wilson

Like his great rival, Thomas Woodrow Wilson had decided while still a boy that he wanted to be a member of the governing class, but unlike TR he had no relish for the rough and tumble of politics. Instead he longed "to do immortal work." As a youth growing up in a South devastated by war and then embittered by Reconstruction, he found his models of greatness not in state or national leaders but in his father, a Presbyterian minister, and in the British prime minister, William Gladstone. Raised in relative comfort and able to move in the highest circles

Ex-President Taft escorting Woodrow Wilson to his inauguration. *(Courtesy, Underwood-Stratton, New York City)*

of southern society because of his father's calling, Wilson dreamed of becoming a great public figure, an American Gladstone. Wilson memorized speeches and practiced delivering them in his father's empty chapel. His Presbyterian background was to contribute to making him rigid in dealing with Congress, most notably in the dispute over the League of Nations.

Wilson's college career, first at Davidson and then at Princeton, followed this same pattern. As he polished his oratorical skills, he read British and American history with great interest. He lamented "the decline of American oratory." The cause, Wilson wrote in a senior essay, was that in Congress decisions were made in committees whose members negotiated the contents of bills. In the British Parliament, to the contrary, bills were approved or rejected in open debate. Wilson's preference for what he thought to be the British system was lifelong, and it meant that he would disapprove of much of the American political machinery even when he was actively seeking to lead his state or country.

After Princeton Wilson studied law at the University of Virginia. But he had no desire to try cases "in an atmosphere of broken promises, of wrecked estates, of neglected trusts, of unperformed duties." So he returned to school, this time to the new graduate school at Johns Hopkins University, where he earned a doctorate in 1885. His dissertation, published as *Congressional Government* that year, is a striking clue to the way Wilson's mind worked: he wrote this study in Baltimore, just a short train ride from Washington, but never attended a single congressional session or committee hearing. He praised the British system for uniting the legislative and executive powers in the person of the prime minister and extolled the superiority of parliamentary to congressional debate.

After a teaching career, in 1902 he became president of Princeton, a position from which he could address a national audience on the issues of the day. A believer in Anglo-Saxon superiority, he supported efforts to segregate public facilities in the South and criticized the "mongrel" races of southern and eastern Europe who formed the majority of the new immigration.

At Princeton Wilson recruited an outstanding faculty. In these respects Wilson succeeded brilliantly. But he soon found himself embroiled in a series of battles that would virtually drive him out of the university by 1910. One of the most important involved Princeton's exclusive eating clubs, which functioned snobbishly as fraternities. Wilson wanted to build a series of quadrangles where students from each class and some resident faculty members would live, eat, and study together. Many alumni voiced their disapproval, and, since their contributions were essential to the financial well-being of the university, their opposition persuaded the trustees to withdraw support for Wilson's plans.

At the same time a new opportunity beckoned. If New Jersey's Democrats could find the right candidate, a candidate with a national reputation who could appeal to progressives while still able to work with the machine, they could win the gubernatorial contest in 1910.

Woodrow Wilson at Princeton.
(Courtesy, Princeton University)

Wilson was able to appeal to progressives, but he broke his alliance with the conservative bosses, and as governor accomplished an impressive string of progressive legislative triumphs. Wilson's successes made him a plausible candidate for the Democratic presidential nomination in 1912.

Another Reform President

In the election of Woodrow Wilson, as in that of Theodore Roosevelt, progressivism triumphed nationally. Wilson's inaugural address called for reform of the tariff and the banking and currency system, for regulation of industry, and for conservation. Under conservation Wilson included the preservation of human resources. This notion that the government was to treat human beings as resources, promoting their health and development as assets to the national economy and society, was common among progressives.

Portrait of President Woodrow Wilson by Sir William Orpen. *(Courtesy, Library of Congress)*

Tariff, Taxation, Banking
Early in his administration Wilson, having called Congress into special session for reform of the tariff, did something that no President since George Washington had done: he appeared before Congress to present his program. The Underwood Tariff that he thereupon got through the national legislature cut rates; the same bill also imposed a federal graduated income tax—a progressive measure that the newly adopted Sixteenth Amendment to the Constitution made possible. Wilson kept Congress in session through the summer in order that it could achieve reform of banking and currency. The product was the Federal Reserve Act of 1913. A major contributor to the popular sentiment for this measure was an investigation by a congressional committee, with Representative Arsene Pujo as its chairman, of the "money trust," the forces that managed finance and credit.

The act was the most impressive domestic measure of Wilson's administration. Yet its scope indicates something of the limits of American reformist ambitions when they translated themselves into actual legislation. The Act did make large changes. It set up a Federal Reserve system of twelve banks that would issue currency to private banks in exchange for secured notes that those banks received from their borrowers. A Federal Reserve Board, its members appointed by the President, was to set the rates for the exchange. All this provided for a more flexible currency, somewhat less dependent on the price of gold than currency had been; and it established some public control over the banking system. But it was not a radical measure. It accepted and left almost completely intact the institution of private banking, and Wilson appointed to the Reserve Board bankers sympathetic to the banking business. In wishing to restructure the banking system so as to lessen the control of Wall Street over it without a large growth in federal power, Representative Carter Glass had been closer than Wilson to the original spirit of the New Freedom, which had projected a breaking up of big units and thereby the empowerment of smaller businesses.

Farm Legislation

Other policies of the Wilson years had, in their application, a similar character of both reforming and accepting the basic nature of American business institutions. During Wilson's first term Congress passed several pieces of legislation designed to assist farmers in increasing production, improving the marketing of their crops, and gaining access to new sources of credit. These programs, in effect, treated farmers not as manual workers on the land but as business people, minicapitalists.

The Smith-Lever Act of 1914, as an example, greatly strengthened the Department of Agriculture's extension services by creating a cooperative program with the state land-grant colleges. The federal government provided matching funds to state governments to build extension agencies in each county and help educate farmers in the latest techniques of scientific agriculture. But by working with the more prosperous farmers and by encouraging mass production on the farms, it unintentionally pointed agriculture in the direction that New Deal policies, again unwittingly, would later take it: toward consolidation into larger farming businesses and driving out small producers.

Two other major pieces of farm legislation were adopted during Wilson's administration. The Warehouse Act of 1916 permitted licensed, bonded warehouses to store various commodities for farmers. The federal government designated the warehouse receipts as negotiable financial instruments that could serve as collateral for loans. Giving farmers a reliable source of working capital made it possible for them to hold crops off the market until prices were favorable. The Federal Farm Loan Act, also passed in 1916, created a Federal Farm Loan Board and twelve regional Federal Land Banks, which were designed to provide long-term loans to farmers at interest rates well below those offered by commercial banks.

Antitrust Legislation

The Federal Trade Commission Act, which Congress passed in 1914, was one of two laws that, in the spirit of Wilson's New Freedom, strengthened the federal government's power to break up trusts that were thought to squeeze out small businesses. The legislation dissolved Theodore Roosevelt's Bureau of Corporations and replaced it with a new Federal Trade Commission. The FTC had the authority to investigate corporate operations and issue rulings outlawing unfair and monopolistic business practices.

Three weeks after creating the FTC in September 1914, Congress passed the Clayton Antitrust Act. It contained stronger provisions for breaking up business trusts than the Sherman Antitrust Act had embodied. One way that companies in effect combined was to put some of the same directors on the boards of the collaborating firms. The act outlawed these interlocking corporate directorates among companies issuing stocks and bonds that added up to more than $1 million. It forbade stock purchases and price discriminations in which the major objective was to lessen competition. It held corporate officials personally liable when companies violated federal antitrust laws. The Clayton Act also exempted labor unions from its provisions, outlawed most federal court injunctions in labor disputes, and legalized labor's right to strike and engage in picketing and boycotts. Although subsequent court decisions would weaken the Clayton Act, for the moment its provisions protecting organized labor appeared to promise fundamental change in the relations between workers and employers. Samuel Gompers termed it the "Magna Carta of Labor."

| **Social Legislation** | Wilson's first administration passed a series of laws designed to protect consumers and workers. The |

Harrison Narcotic Act of 1914 identified a number of pharmaceutical products that were not to be sold without a doctor's prescription. With the President's blessing, Senator Robert La Follette of Wisconsin pushed the Seaman's Act through Congress in 1915. At the time maritime workers were among the most exploited members of the country's labor force. The legislation established rules for fair treatment of the workers and for improving safety conditions. The Adamson Act of 1916 established the eight-hour day for railroad workers and guaranteed them time-and-a-half pay for overtime. The Workmen's Compensation Act of 1916 set up an insurance program for federal government employees. The insurance would compensate workers for injuries related to their jobs and provided death benefits to the families of workers killed on the job.

To provide more jobs, to eliminate the exploitation of children, and, according to some historians, to make northern industries more competitive with southern enterprises, among which child labor was common, Congress passed the Keating-Owen Act in 1916. It banned the transportation across state lines of products of child labor. In 1918 the Supreme Court in *Hammer v. Dagenhart* would find the law an unconstitutional extension of the authority of Congress to regulate interstate commerce. Congress tried again in 1919, this time imposing a punitive tax on goods manufactured by child labor. This too the Court threw out. In the productive year 1916, the Federal Roads Act provided a structure and precedent for funding a network of roads accommodating the new motorized traffic. The government would share costs with states establishing a road-planning system.

| **The Progressive Record** | What emerged from Roosevelt's and Wilson's progressivism, and from the actions of President Taft's administration, was a collection of federal programs |

that imposed on business a degree of social responsibility and made it an active partner of government. This was not an entirely new concept. The nineteenth-century grants of federal lands to railroads for the building of lines needed by the nation as a whole had constituted a somewhat similar partnership. Presidential progressivism did, however, much expand the practice of putting business to the service of the public, adding some fairly sharp restraints on private enterprise. The Wilson presidency did nothing for black Americans; and in fact this Democratic administration, tied to a party that had the white South as one of its major bases, extended segregation in government.

President Woodrow Wilson wrote in The New Freedom (1913):

"There was a time when corporations played a very minor part in our business affairs, but now they play the chief part, and most men are the servants of corporations. . . . In this new age we find that our laws with regard to the relations of employer and employee are in many respects wholly antiquated. . . . Workingmen . . . generally use dangerous and powerful machinery, over whose repair and renewal they have no control. . . . Rules must be devised for their protection, for their compensation when injured, for their support when disabled."

The Era of Dollar Diplomacy 1909–1917

The expulsion of Spain from Cuba and Puerto Rico in 1898, as well as the acquisition of the Panama Canal in 1903, gave the United States unprecedented power in the Caribbean, while the Open Door notes of 1899 and the Root-Takahira Agreement of 1908 seemed to guarantee the United States access to China. The administrations of William Howard Taft and then Woodrow Wilson used the power of the United States government to promote the nation's business interests abroad, particularly in the Far East and in Latin America. Officials in the departments of state and commerce were charged with the responsibility of expanding opportunities and increasing profits for private businesses. Historians have dubbed the policy "dollar diplomacy." It can be understood in either of two ways: as representing the subservience of the United States government to the ambitions of business, or as expressing the government's determination to use business as a projection of the nation's power and pride.

Despite the intense efforts of Philander C. Knox, Taft's secretary of state, dollar diplomacy did not get very far in China. In 1909 a consortium of European bankers began plans to finance construction of large railways in southern and central China. American bankers, excluded from the consortium, complained to the federal government, and President Taft worked personally to get them included in the project. Knox also tried to get the Chinese government to accept a huge loan from American bankers to inaugurate a program of currency reform. The proposals of President Taft and Secretary Knox aroused the suspicions of Russia and Japan, both concluding that the United States was trying to carve out its own sphere of influence in China. The Russian and Japanese protests between 1910 and 1913 frightened off American banking interests, who did not want to invest money in politically unstable areas.

But dollar diplomacy, stillborn in Asia, thrived in Central America and the Caribbean. Presidents Taft and Wilson presided over a foreign policy that treated the Caribbean virtually as their country's lake. The economic influence of the United States pervaded the region. The United Fruit Company, for example, was a corporation, based in the United States, that owned dozens of huge banana plantations in Central America, as well as railroads to transport the crop to Pacific and Atlantic ports. It wielded more power than most of the governments in Central America. The American Sugar Refining Company was equally powerful in Cuba. Those companies, and others like them, wanted governments in place throughout the region that would guarantee their assets, and they expected the United States to support and protect them. Eventually, United States marines marched through Nicaragua, Haiti, the Dominican Republic, and Mexico. Woodrow Wilson saw nothing wrong with such conduct: "I'll teach them to elect good men," he bragged. Humanitarians hoped to reform corrupt, poor countries, while strategists became convinced that stability in the region was vital to the security of the United States.

President William Howard Taft described "Dollar Diplomacy" on December 3, 1912:

"The diplomacy of the present administration has sought to respond to modern ideas of commercial intercourse. This policy has been characterized as substituting dollars for bullets. It is one that appeals alike to idealistic humanitarian sentiments, to the dictates of sound policy and strategy, and to legitimate commercial aims."

Nicaragua, Haiti, and Mexico
The dictator of Nicaragua threatened during 1909 to cancel a valuable mining lease held by a company based in the United States and to permit the Japanese to build a canal across his country. The threat was bluster. But the dictator's aims to create trouble in neighboring countries and the existence of an insurgency inside Nicaragua persuaded Taft to move to overthrow the regime. When two United States citizens caught dynamiting ships in the San Juan River during a street revolution were executed, Taft broke diplomatic relations and financed a makeshift government dominated by the United States. New York City bankers regulated the country's finances. A mining company employee asked Taft in 1912 to send a "legation guard" of 2,700 marines to "keep order." The troops stayed for more than two decades. A treaty signed in 1916 granted the United States an exclusive right both to build any canal and to lease naval bases on Nicaragua's Atlantic and Pacific coasts.

In Haiti Woodrow Wilson carried the game just short of annexation. Perennial misgovernment there had declined into near chaos by 1915. In less than four years, seven presidents—some of them eventually killed by explosives or poisoning—had looted the public treasury. Revolution became almost permanent. President Vilbrum Sam, who defaulted in early 1915 on some $24 million in debts owed to western Europeans and United States citizens, launched a vendetta against his opponents, killing 167 of them. Outraged townspeople in Port-au-Prince killed and dismembered Sam. Wilson ordered in the marines. Several thousand of them occupied the capital. New York City bankers, now familiar with the techniques of financial control, once again traveled to the Caribbean. A hastily elected local government signed a treaty that gave control of foreign policy to the United States. Some Haitians revolted; marines crushed them. Haiti remained a virtual protectorate for almost twenty years.

A dictator, Porfirio Díaz, had ruled Mexico since 1876. Roosevelt's secretary of state, Elihu Root, rhapsodized that Díaz was a "great man to be held up for the hero worship of mankind," but Mexicans rejected the advice. Nationalists objected to economic concessions that had given away oil and mining rights to companies based in Britain and the United States. A collection of middle-class reformers, socialists, Indians, adventurers, and radical Catholics called for land reform, national ownership of raw materials, and racial equality. Díaz retired and confusion followed. Power drifted into the hands of Francisco I. Madero, a gentle, indecisive, eccentric man unable to give direction to an emerging revolution. Demanding immediate redistribution of land, regional leaders like Emiliano Zapata and Pancho Villa assembled armies south and north of the capital. Worried by this growing threat to their economic interests, foreign companies appealed for help to the United States ambassador. So did the domestic Catholic hierarchy, who hinted of Madero's ineptness, and the country's ambitious military chief, Victoriano Huerta, understood. Huerta organized a palace revolt, took control of the regional armies, and installed himself as lifetime Presi-

Huerta's brutal rise occurred just before Woodrow Wilson took office on March 4, 1913.

"I will not," the new chief executive said, "recognize a government of butchers." Relying on sources prone to exaggeration, Wilson wrote: "Entire villages have been burned, their inhabitants—men, women, and children—slaughtered and mutilated indiscriminately; plantations have been ravaged and burned, trains have been blown up and derailed, and passengers slaughtered like cattle; women have been ravished and men mutilated with accompaniments of horror and barbarity which find no place in the chronicles of Christian warfare."

Pancho Villa with his troops, 1914. A bandit chieftain and political opponent of Mexican leader Venustiano Carranza, Villa tried to provoke U.S. intervention in Mexico as a way of discrediting Carranza. *(Courtesy, Brown Brothers)*

dent of Mexico. His agents murdered Madero and imposed a military dictatorship over most of the country.

The new President Wilson refused to talk with Huerta's diplomats, arguing that from now on the United States would deal only with "republican governments based upon law, not irregular force." This novel policy, which judged a nation's morality, departed from past recognition procedures, which required only that a regime be in control of its territory. Wilson hoped to isolate Huerta, and persuaded the British to follow his lead. Instead, a diplomatic standoff ensued. Words could scarcely hurt Huerta, who used Yankeephobia to prop up his faltering regime.

Barely a month after Wilson assumed office, Mexican authorities arrested a group of United States sailors in Tampico. The arrests were legitimate, for the men had drifted into a restricted area by mistake. But their commander, Admiral Henry T. Mayo, demanded an apology and a twenty-one gun salute to the Stars and Stripes. Nine days later, Wilson delivered an ultimatum: salute the flag or face the consequences. Huerta's government was now sustained on feeling against the Yankees and he refused. So the President ordered marines to occupy Mexico's chief Gulf port, Veracruz. Street fighting produced a large number of casualties, sixty of the invading troops and over 500 Mexican. Many people in the United States, unaware that relations with their neighbor had so deteriorated, were stunned. The marines remained in Veracruz for six months.

The Tampico incident and occupation of Veracruz humiliated Huerta, disgracing him in the eyes of most nationalists and preventing any foreign help for his regime. His power disintegrated. Venustiano Carranza, who had gathered an army outside Mexico City, easily occupied the capital. Like Madero, Carranza was a middle-class reformer buffeted by the winds of revolution; like Huerta, he was a vigilante, not a legitimate ruler. So the chaos in Mexico and the deadlock with President Wilson continued. Then Pancho Villa, a restless adventurer from the far north, raised a rebellion against Carranza. The *villistas* added an anticlerical seasoning to the revolutionary brew of economic reform and extended the violence. On January 11, 1916, Villa attacked a train at Santa Ysabel and slaughtered sixteen citizens of the United States; two months later he raided the New Mexico town of Columbus, burning it to the ground and killing seventeen people. He calculated that an armed intervention by the United States would destroy Carranza just as it had Huerta. Reacting as Villa had hoped, Wilson ordered General John J. Pershing across the border with 6,600 men in pursuit of the guerrilla bandit. The *villistas* eluded the army, so Wilson next called out 150,000 national guard troops to seal off the entire southwestern border. Time passed. Pershing rushed fruitlessly around Mexico's northern provinces; Carranza held on in Mexico City. Early in 1917, at the approach of war with Germany, Wilson quietly withdrew federal forces from Mexico, granted Carranza full recognition, and abandoned his efforts to instruct a nation in democracy. Preoccupied with their revolution, Mexicans withdrew into a bitter hostility toward the United States. So ended that interlude of imperialist good intentions. The cloak of empire fitted awkwardly upon the shoulders of the United States.

Neutrality 1914–1917

The War in Europe Military people and intellectuals, including Wilson, assumed that those "great watery moats" of the Atlantic and Pacific protected their country from major international troubles. But the war in Europe, which broke out in 1914, worried Americans when trench warfare stalemated in northern France. German predominance over continental Europe might harm American economic interests and be the basis for an attempt later at world dominion. An Anglo-French victory, on the other hand, might freeze Americans out of vast markets in the Allies' growing empires.

Both the Central Powers—Germany, Austria-Hungary, and later Turkey and Bulgaria—and the Entente or Allied nations—Britain, France, Italy, and Russia until the Bolsheviks commandeered its revolution—had planned for a quick, decisive war. After the murder of the Archduke Franz Ferdinand of Austria on June 28, 1914, the need to keep armies mobilized one step ahead of potential enemies accelerated into a general war by early August. A huge German army plunged through Belgium and into northern France, trying to outflank French troops and capture Paris from behind. Rather than hold fast on the Rhineland border, French generals moved their units westward. As each army tried to get beyond the other, a virtual race to the North Sea resulted. Thereafter, both sides settled into trench warfare, a tactic particularly favorable to the defense. The war stalemated: battles became a bloody attrition. On the huge plains of eastern Europe, armies found more room for maneuver, but here, too, the forces became locked together. Poorly trained Russian troops moved ponderously against smaller but better-equipped German and Austrian armies. Neither side was gaining a victory, though the Kaiser's troops slowly advanced.

The American public preferred neutrality. "Our people," Wilson was later to say, "did not see the full meaning of the war. It looked like a natural raking out of Europe's pent-up jealousies." Orders for war goods stimulated an American economic boom. Why, then, did the United States change from a determined neutral in 1914 to a belligerent in 1917? The answer lies in considerable part in the way that the Germans had to fight the war on the sea.

Submarine Warfare As land forces braced against each other in a long, sullen, man-crushing standstill, Germany and Britain struggled for control of the ocean commerce, the means by which the balance might be thrown to one of the contenders. Britain declared the entire North Sea a military region and mined its waters. The captains of neutral ships had to stop for sailing directions at Dover, where British officials often found pretexts to keep them there: the usual device was a greatly expanded notion of what

NOTICE!

TRAVELLERS intending to embark on the Atlantic voyage are reminded that a state of war exists between Germany and her allies and Great Britain and her allies; that the zone of war includes the waters adjacent to the British Isles; that, in accordance with formal notice given by the Imperial German Government, vessels flying the flag of Great Britain, or of any of her allies, are liable to destruction in those waters and that travellers sailing in the war zone on ships of Great Britain or her allies do so at their own risk.

IMPERIAL GERMAN EMBASSY
WASHINGTON, D. C., APRIL 22, 1915.

Before the *Lusitania* was torpedoed, this notice appeared in the classified sections of Washington newspapers.

The Nation *denounced the sinking of the* Lusitania:

"It is a deed for which a Hun would blush, a Turk be ashamed, and a Barbary pirate apologize. . . . The laws of nations and the law of God have been alike trampled upon. The torpedo which sank the *Lusitania* also sank Germany in the opinion of mankind."

constituted contraband. Germany retaliated by declaring its own war zone in the North Sea, where its submarines, or U-boats, would attack any vessel. The British armed their merchant marine and prepared it to fight. Thereby they trapped the Germans in a dilemma. The fragile submarines, so small they carried a crew of only a few men, could not obey the rule that a warship must give warning to the merchant vessel and must take on its passengers: steel merchant ships could easily ram the U-boats. Successful use of the submarine required breaking principles adopted before this stealthy but frail craft existed; otherwise the Germans would have to allow the Allies a commerce that could provide for a German defeat. It was this dilemma that would ultimately put Germany at irreconcilable opposites to the United States.

Early in 1915, when Germany prepared for unrestricted submarine warfare in the North Sea, Wilson responded with a warning, holding the Germans "strictly accountable" for the property and lives of any American citizens lost as a result. Then, on May 7, 1915, came news that a German U-boat had sunk the famous *Lusitania*, grandest ship of Britain's Cunard Lines, on its way from New York to Liverpool. Americans were not told that the *Lusitania* had been carrying munitions, and that it was not the torpedo but secondary explosions from the war materials that caused the ship to sink rapidly. Nearly 1,200 people died, 128 of them American citizens. The act outraged Americans. "The torpedo which sank the *Lusitania*," *Nation* magazine editorialized, "also sank Germany in the opinion of mankind." A wave of anti-German hysteria victimized innocent Germans living in the United States. Wilson protested the sinking so vigorously that Secretary of State William Jennings Bryan, an advocate of peace, resigned. Germany backed down, ordering U-boat captains not to attack passenger liners in the future. Still, damage to German prestige was immense. President Wilson himself told his cabinet: "Gentlemen, the Allies are standing with their backs to the wall fighting wild beasts."

The year 1916 tested American neutrality even more. Stalemated land war prompted leaders in Berlin to expand the ocean war. About fifty U-boats swarmed into the North Sea, attacking naval patrols and

armed merchant ships. On March 24, 1916, an overeager German commander torpedoed an unarmed French channel ferry, the *Sussex*. Wilson reacted with a virtual ultimatum: the United States would break diplomatic relations if Germany ever again attacked civilian ships. Though furious at Germany, Wilson was also angry with Britain. During the summer of 1916, the British Cabinet issued a blacklist of neutral firms that had traded with the Central Powers. The British announced that they would confiscate whatever goods of such firms their ships could seize. It was a blatant violation of rights. Peeved with both sides and anxious about the presidential election in the fall, Wilson took up peacemaking. His close adviser Colonel House traveled several times to Europe, where he hinted that if one side refused an armistice, the United States would join forces with its enemy. Both sides thereupon presented peace proposals, but they were so far apart that reconciliation was impossible.

Opposition to the War Among the groups opposing American involvement in the European conflict were isolationists, who on principle wanted the country to keep isolated from the politics and ambitions of Europe. The United States, they believed, had a particular task, to perfect social and political democracy, which other nations might then profit from. Isolationism had considerable sway among the progressives, in part because of the strength that the progressive movement possessed among midwestern German Americans. In later years, isolationism would become increasingly a creed among conservatives. But at the time of the First World War isolationists were concerned not with keeping American resources out of the hands of needy foreigners but with preserving free American institutions as an example to what isolationists, condescendingly but sincerely, saw as the less enlightened peoples of the Old World. Akin to isolationist thinking about the war was that of the socialists—again, many were of German background—who looked on the conflict as a reactionary capitalist and nationalist war that was merely setting workers to killing their brother workers on the battlefield, when all the world's working class should be sharing in the creation of a new just order.

Along with isolationists and socialists were such advocates of peace as Jane Addams. In the optimistic American and western European years preceding the war, humanitarian individuals and organizations had hoped that the spread of constitutional government and the softening of social manners in the nineteenth century would make possible the abolition of war. Even as the bombs and artillery of the European battlefields were smashing against such beliefs, social reformers were calling for the same ordered civility among nations that they had worked for in domestic life.

Peace, Preparedness, and War President Wilson's attempts to secure an armistice in Europe did not inspire confidence among his critics. They viewed Germany as a threat to American security, and they insisted that the country at least prepare militarily for war that might come in spite of the President's peacemaking. Theodore Roosevelt accused Wilson of weakness,

One of the most popular songs of 1915 was "I Didn't Raise My Boy to Be a Soldier."

I didn't raise my boy to be a soldier
I brought him up to be my pride and joy
Who dares place a musket on his shoulder
To shoot some other mother's darling boy?
Let nations arbitrate their future troubles,
It's time to lay the sword and gun away
There'd be no war today,
If mothers all would say,
"I didn't raise my boy to be a soldier."

President Woodrow Wilson's statements about the world war underwent an evolution:

"The United States must be neutral in fact as well as in name. . . . We must be impartial in thought as well as in action."

August 19, 1914

"There is such a thing as a man being too proud to fight."

May 10, 1915

"America cannot be an ostrich with its hand in the sand."

February 1, 1916

"Armed neutrality is ineffectual at best. . . . The world must be made safe for democracy."

April 2, 1917

and General Leonard Wood, head of the National Security League, began organizing volunteer militia units throughout the country and putting his soldiers through weekend training programs. Congress responded by passing preparedness measures. President Wilson initially opposed the preparedness campaign, but in time he began calling for an increase in the armed forces. Official preparedness gave progressives a chance to put the new graduated income tax to work. In 1916 Congress increased the size of the army to over two hundred thousand men and raised spending for warships.

Mediation efforts meanwhile sustained Wilson as the peace candidate. The Republicans passed over the bellicose Teddy Roosevelt and selected a moderate—former New York governor Charles Evans Hughes. The Democrats praised Wilson's progressive reforms and proclaimed that he had kept the country out of war. Hughes had a difficult time convincing the electorate that his views were much different from Wilson's. In a close vote, Wilson defeated Hughes.

The German Imperial Government announced that unrestricted submarine warfare would resume on February 1, 1917; two days later, Wilson severed diplomatic relations. A determined antiwar group in Congress blocked the President's call for arming merchant ships, but by late February a rush of events compelled most of them to accept the inevitable. German submarines sank a British Cunard liner, the *Laconia,* and torpedoed three American freighters, killing several Americans. Soon after, British intelligence officers made public a startling secret. Germany's foreign minister, Arthur Zimmermann, had promised the Mexicans a chance "to reconquer lost territory in New Mexico, Texas and Arizona" if they declared war on the United States. Stunned, angry Americans now eagerly followed where Wilson reluctantly led. On April 2, 1917, the President asked Congress for a declaration of war. The resolution passed four days later. "The Yanks are coming!" a newspaper headlined.

Within a few weeks, the first Yanks were in Europe, comrades to the British and French troops but, according to Wilson's fastidious phrasing, not technically their allies. The President wished to keep his country at a certain distance from European politics. We were, he insisted, merely "associated" with the Allies.

At War 1917–1918

The Arsenal of Democracy   While some progressives had embraced isolationism, the war enlisted the services, and beyond these the spirit, of progressivism. That movement, as a political and ideological force, embodied an appetite for central planning. The war offered that appetite a feast. Despite the years of fighting in Europe, the United States was not ready for war. No one in government had plans for mobilizing an American army or for converting industry to military production. Treasury officials and bankers paled at the complexities of war finance. If the nation was to become an arsenal of democracy, it must organize its economic power and invigorate its morale. That is exactly what progressives would do.

Wilson and most members of Congress wanted a national army, not a collection of volunteer corps gathered locally as during much of the Civil War. A conscription law—the "draft," Americans have become accustomed to calling it—garnered into a national pool of potential soldiers nearly 25 million men between eighteen and forty-five years old. Of these, nearly three million were inducted and another two million volunteered. Raising an army proved easier than equipping one. The army had stockpiled in April 1917 only 600,000 rifles and 900 heavy guns, field weapons essential to trench warfare. American industrialists quickly converted their plants to munition and small arms production, but the British and French had to supply almost eighty percent of the artillery used by American forces. Nor did Yankee ingenuity meet the challenge of the war's new weapons, the tanks and the airplane. By the armistice, just sixty-four tanks had rolled off American production lines, while poor design and even worse management plagued aircraft construction.

The Allies, though, needed money more than military knowledge, and here the Americans responded hugely. War finance at first set off a bitter dispute in Congress: conservatives wanted high taxes on consumer goods, while progressives in both parties fought for large inheritance, personal income, and excess profits taxes. Congress in the War Revenue Acts settled for taxing away nearly two-thirds of large personal and corporate income. The extraordinary taxes brought in about $10.5 billion, some one-third of the war's total cost. The government borrowed the rest. The Treasury sold to the public some $25 billion of liberty bonds. This niagara of dollars financed the American armies, but additional billions poured overseas in loans to pay for armaments for the Allies and to prop up British and French currencies.

| The Bureaucratic State | When the United States entered World War I in 1917, few people had any idea of the impact the war would have on the economy and public policy. The war brought the federal government into the economy in ways that had been unimaginable only a few years before. |

Together, the Lever Act of 1917 and the Overman Act of 1918 gave the President absolute authority over farm production, commodity prices, and the uses and prices of industrial raw materials. To guarantee the uninterrupted shipment of goods, President Wilson created the Railroad Administration and virtually assumed complete control over American railroads. The Food Administration, with Herbert Hoover as its chief, supervised rationing programs and helped augment American food production. The Fuel Administration stimulated coal production by bringing marginal mines into service.

Prohibition, favored by some progressives, gained from the war. The public was reminded of the Germanic character of beer. To conserve food needed for the war, Congress restricted the use of grain for liquor, though allowing beer of limited quantity and alcoholic content. In 1917 Congress passed the Eighteenth Amendment, prohibiting the

After the declaration of war on April 2, 1917, the Selective Service Act was passed in May.

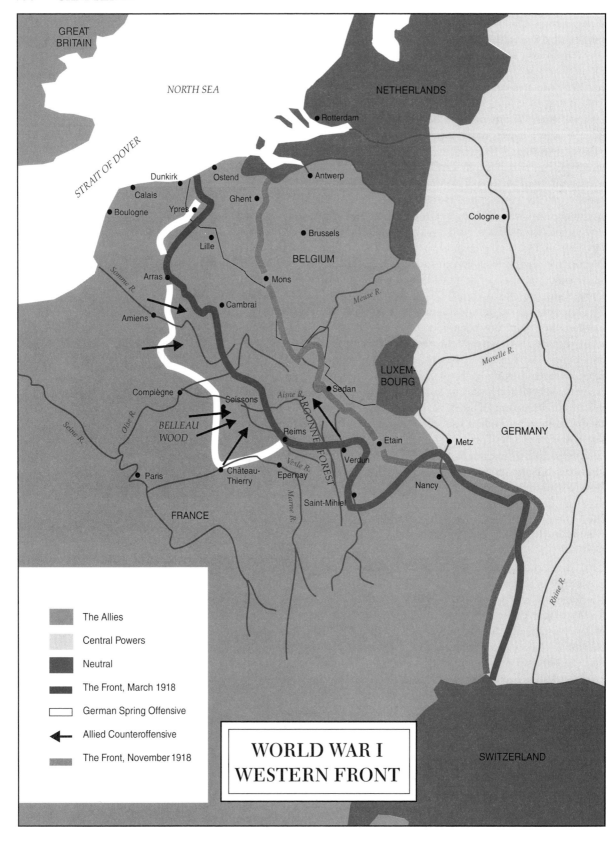

The Allies

Central Powers

Neutral

The Front, March 1918

German Spring Offensive

Allied Counteroffensive

The Front, November 1918

WORLD WAR I WESTERN FRONT

manufacture, sale, and transportation of liquor as a beverage, and soon afterward it was ratified.

To prevent debilitating labor strikes that would disrupt war production, Wilson created the National War Labor Board and gave it the power to arbitrate disputes between management and labor. His War Labor Policies Board guaranteed labor's right to bargain collectively and set minimum wages and maximum hours in defense industries. The War Industries Board was given broad authority over industrial prices, allocation of raw materials, and production priorities so that it could guarantee sufficient war goods and meet domestic economic needs. The War Finance Corporation was to make loans to war industries.

The war was enormously profitable to the United States. Able to sell huge amounts of war goods in Europe but protected by the Atlantic Ocean from the ravages of war, the economy blossomed. By the end of the war the United States had become the greatest economic power in the world.

The Eastern Front   For the Central Powers of Germany and Austria, the fighting went well. In late October 1917 an Italian army disintegrated under hellish artillery fire and hand-to-hand combat near Caporetto. Submarine warfare mauled British shipping all that fall. Only after months of hard lessons did the Allies have enough ships and enough knowledge to convoy merchant ships safely to port. On the Eastern Front, meanwhile, Russia's ability to stay in the war seemed less and less likely. Battles there had wiped out much of the country's fledgling industry; only large munitions shipments from Britain and the United States kept dispirited, poorly led Russian troops in the field.

In February 1917, socialists and middle-class liberals had taken over the government of Russia from Tsar Nicholas. When the Tsar called for troops to oust the usurpers, none responded; they were too disillusioned by military failures, and autocracy was no longer acceptable. Americans at first regarded the overthrow of the tsars in a positive light. But radical groups demanded from the new democratic government an immediate peace and sweeping economic reforms. Germans abetted the growing chaos by slipping Lenin, leader of the revolutionary Bolshevik Party, back into the capital city. Once there, he orchestrated the chant, "Peace, Land and Bread," into a program for revolution. The prospect of an anti-capitalist Russia abandoning the war panicked the Allies. Wilson and Prime Minister Lloyd George pressured Russian leaders such as Alexander Kerensky to keep on fighting, regardless of public sentiment. But more and more Russian troops simply deserted. The Eastern Front would soon disintegrate.

The German High Command, now under the leadership of Erich Ludendorff, massed its troops for a decisive assault. German troops overran the Baltic provinces and occupied much of Ukraine. Already discredited and disillusioned by the war, moderates fell to a palace revolution staged by the Bolsheviks in November 1917. Lenin then capitulated to the Germans. A peace treaty, signed at Brest Litovsk in March 1918, surrendered nearly half of European Russia to the Kaiser.

President Wilson portrayed the Germans as "wild beasts."
(Courtesy, Imperial War Museum, London)

World War I, especially on the Western Front, was a war of position and defense. Troops on both sides, like these French soldiers, lived in elaborate trenches that turned into a sea of mud when it rained. The men tried to protect themselves with barbed wire and gas masks against new and terrifying technology. But there was little defense against the machine gun that mowed down the troops as they charged from their trenches. *(Courtesy, Roger-Viollet, Paris)*

One American soldier wrote of finding

"a country of flat plowed field, pollard willows and deep muddy ditches. Then we come along, and in military parlance 'dig ourselves in.' That is, with the sweat of the brows of hundreds . . . working by night narrow trenches five feet deep at least and with the earth thrown up another two and a half feet as a bank on top. These trenches are one and a half to two feet wide, and curl and twist about in a maddening manner to make them safer from shell-fire. Little caves are scooped in the walls of the trenches, where the men live about four to a hole, and slightly bigger dugouts where two officers live. All the soil is clay, stickier and greasier than one could believe possible. It's like almost solid paint, and the least rain makes the sides of the trenches slimy, and the bottom a perfect sea of mud—pulls the heels off your boots almost."

The Western Front

Soon after the Russians withdrew, the Germans attacked violently all along the Western Front. Their dangerous offensive lasted five months. During March and April Ludendorff's most battle-ready troops stormed across Allied lines in northern France and Belgium. British counterattacks stopped their advance, but only after Germans had penetrated some thirty miles, more ground than either side had gained since the beginning of trench warfare in 1914. This near disaster prompted the Allies to set up a unified command under French general Ferdinand Foch and accelerated the movement of American troops into the war. Soon nearly 250,000 fresh, hastily-trained American soldiers were taking to the lines every month, over two million by the fall of 1918.

Meanwhile, the Germans attacked again, this time east of Paris. In just three days, the enemy reached the strategic village of Château-Thierry on the Marne River, only fifty miles from the capital. A French army, now well fleshed out by American divisions, blocked further advance; then the Americans by themselves pushed the Germans out of Belleau Wood, reestablishing the front. By midsummer 1918, the grand German offensive was broken. With Americans streaming up to the lines, the military advantage shifted permanently to the Allies. That fall, Foch launched a counterattack along a 200-mile front, aimed at destroying Germany's supply lines behind the Meuse River. General John Pershing, now commander of an exclusively American army, fought on the easternmost flank, for five weeks slugging through the Argonne Forest. The Yanks finally triumphed, wiping out German armies long entrenched in the difficult terrain. In late October Pershing's forces captured the railways that had supplied German forces. British and French troops had already destroyed German positions north of Paris, and German armies everywhere reeled back across France into Belgium. As the Western Front crumbled, the German High Command surrendered any hope of victory. "Open armistice negotiations as soon as possible," Ludendorff telephoned the Kaiser. The belligerents agreed to the armistice on November 11, 1918. Guns along the Western Front fell silent.

Thus ended a combat that is remembered for its special horrors of stationary trench warfare, of attacks across open ground in the face of machine guns and barbed wire, of lungs eaten with poison gas, and most memorably, of earth turned to bleak cold mud. That image of nature scorched would return with Hiroshima and Nagasaki and then with Vietnam. Among the Allies, the bullets and bombs and front-line illnesses had killed 900,000 British, over a million French, and upwards of two million Russian troops. Their associate, the United States, lost 48,000, about ten thousand fewer than in Indochina a half century later.

"The Yanks Are Coming"

The United States had contributed a boisterous morale to the war. The spirit of the Yankee doughboys rekindled hopes for victory that the long lethal grind of trench warfare had dulled. At home, too, Americans steeled themselves for the unfamiliarity of violence with an enforced light-heartedness and a harsh patriotism. George M. Cohan, the Broadway star, had earlier written a stirring musical, composing one song "You're a Grand

FROM THE FRONT

American Ex. [peditionary] Forces [AEF]

Dear Wife:

We pulled out about the 19th of Sept, moving towards the Argonne Forest. Finly we came to thair trenches and thair we got lots of prisiners, another fellow and myself got 13 out of one little dugout. We seen a machine gun setting in the mouth of the dugout so we stopped and decided what to do. So I asked him what he wanted to do, go get the machine gun or stay thair and keep his eye on the dugout until I could crawl up and get the gun, so he decided he would let me go.

Thair at that line of trenches one of the boys threw a hand grenade in on a Hun as he started to come out without his hands up and killed him. Well, it was along about eleven o'clock in the day now and as we hadnt had any breakfast we were getting quite tired and hungry.

In a short while we started to advance and by that time Jerry was sending shells over in a jiffy. Right thair was when I saw what war really was. The fellow on my right got hit. It was my luck that I was caught right in an open place so I dropped behind an old stump and thair I had to stay as it looked as if they were going to mow the old stump down. Well, I thought that I was a gone sucker sure. I laid thair until dark looking every minute for Fritzie to sneek up on me but he didn't come. Seven of us was sent back to gather up some ammunition and the Germans saw us and threw the shells into us. Three shells came all at once right on top of us. The man in front of me fell and the one in rear of me. The concussion from the explosion knocked me down and when I went to get up I was bured in dirt and rock and I thought I was killed as they almost knocked me senseless. Will leave out quite a bit that I witnessed now as it is too bad to write. We had 250 men when we started over the top on the 26th of Sept. and when we came out thair want but about 80 of us left. Gee, I did feel lucky, which all of us did that were still alive. Love to you.

Your Husband, Pvt. Jesse M. Maxey

Old Flag!" so spirited that Congress awarded him a Medal of Honor. Another ballad, "Over There," cheerfully promised, "The Yanks are coming, the drums rumtumming," and "We won't come back until it's over, over there!"

Along with the enthusiasms of war, bigotries were sprouting. Hatred of Germans and all things Germanic swept across the country, particularly in Pennsylvania and the upper Middle West where millions of German ancestry lived. Mobs stormed German language newspapers: some closed permanently. Schools and universities dropped courses related to the "enemy's" culture, even classes in German literature and music. Town elders changed street names; ball park vendors rechristened their frankfurters "hot dogs." For opposing the war, Frank Little of the IWW in Montana was lynched, and elsewhere war resisters were persecuted. The government did not endorse the more primitive spasms of popular war emotion. But its own actions contributed to the mood, which lingered even after the end of the war.

The Committee on Public Information   The mindless conformity that was settling upon much of the population has often been attributed in part to the Committee on Public Information, a governmental agency set up to enlist support for the war. At its head was George Creel, a progressive Denver journalist. The Committee disseminated government propaganda in newspapers and journals and distributed posters and other illustrations designed to incite patriotic emotions. It put the movie industry to making prowar films, and even sent out speakers to exhort

This song of World War I was a favorite.

A POOR AVIATOR LAY DYING.

A poor aviator lay dying.
At the end of a bright summer's day.
His comrades had gathered about him.
To carry his fragments away.

The airplane was piled on his wishbone,
His Hotchkiss was wrapped round his head;
He wore a spark-plug on each elbow,
'Twas plain he would shortly be dead.

He spit out a valve and a gasket,
And stirred in the sump where he lay,
And then to his wondering comrades,
These brave parting words he did say:

"Take the magneto out of my stomach,
And the butterfly valve off my neck,
Extract from my liver the crankshaft,
There are lots of good parts in this wreck."

"Take the manifold out of my larynx,
And the cylinders out of my brain,
Take the piston rods out of my kidneys,
And assemble the engine again."

their audiences to do their part. Scholars willingly lent their talent to the CPI. Creel's organization informally indicated to newspapers what they should print and what they should not. That a government would wage a massive campaign to tell the public what to think and whom to kill is repellant to civil liberties, and so the name of Creel came to be identified with war hysteria.

Creel's committee had good ground to work with. Before the entrance of the United States into the conflict, the American people had already been predisposed to see the Germans as the evil power. The British ran an exceptionally effective propaganda machine recruiting major writers and operating extensively in the United States. The British had the advantage of speaking the native language of most Americans. Meanwhile, German submarine warfare against merchant ships outraged the public. Especially potent in setting popular opinion against the Germans was sympathy for Belgium, invaded at the beginning of the war. Stories, since discredited, of German atrocities against Belgians added to the image of the brutal Hun. The teaching of the German language was frequently prohibited in public schools, and some German dishes like sauerkraut were given new names like "liberty cabbage." Like other modern wars, this one drew in much of the population. Women knitted for the troops. Men and women worked in the Red Cross, and some went overseas to bring medical services to the soldiers, while the evangelical Salvation Army and the YMCA provided the doughboys with such amenities as were available in combat zones. At home, Americans took pride in observing the little but important economies that aimed to conserve needed resources. Families cultivated "victory gardens" to feed themselves and thereby release food for the troops. Conservation required careful observances of meatless or wheatless days. Such activities constituted the most common ways Americans shared in the great enterprise.

Rechristened German–American Words	
Original	*Rechristened*
hamburger	salisbury steak liberty steak liberty sandwich
German shepherd	Alsatian shepherd
Hamburg Avenue Brooklyn	Wilson Avenue Brooklyn
Germantown, Nebraska	Garland, Nebraska
East Germantown, Indiana	Pershing, Indiana
Berlin, Iowa	Lincoln, Iowa

Governmental Repression   Much of what the government requested of the people, then, was within reason for a nation engaged in a major war. But the administration was also carrying on one of the largest campaigns of repression in American history. The Espionage Act of 1917 outlawed not only actions clearly aiding the enemy but any willful bringing about of insubordination in the military, and it empowered the postmaster general to ban from the mails whatever materials called for disobedience to the draft laws. The Sedition Act of 1918, an amendment to the earlier law, forbade abusive language attacking the American form of government, the Constitution, the flag, or the military forces. Both of these laws could mean just about anything the authorities wanted them to. The government along with state and local officers defined as enemies socialists, anarchists, pacifists, whoever saw the war as immoral or against the interests of the working classes. In 1917, for example, federal agents and New York City bomb-squad police raided *Mother Earth*, the paper issued by the Russian-born anarchist Emma Goldman. She and her companion Alexander Berkman were imprisoned for their work with the No-Conscription League. *The Masses*, a journal that had combined the artistic and the political radicalism of the prewar years, was among the publications banned from the mails. The Socialist Party leader Eugene Debs went to prison for opposing the draft, though he had neither practiced nor advocated violence.

The *Schenck* and *Abrams* Decisions (1919)   *Schenck v. United States* was an appeal from a socialist who had been convicted for a pamphlet that urged enlistees to resist the draft. The pamphlet angrily described conscription as benefiting only capitalism, but suggested no more than political opposition. Schenck's appeal claimed that his conviction violated the First Amendment's protection of freedom of speech and the press. The great legal scholar Oliver Wendell Holmes, Jr., speaking for the Court in upholding the government's prosecution of Schenck, argued that the meaning of the Constitution must be understood in the light of particular circumstances. Speaking the word "fire" is protected by the First Amendment; but the "most stringent protection of free speech would not protect a man in falsely shouting fire in a theatre and causing a panic." In normal times, Holmes conceded, the pamphlet would enjoy the protection of the Constitution. But it threatened to obstruct the draft, which was a legitimate governmental measure in the dangerous time of war.

The revolutionary excesses of the Bolsheviks, and their withdrawal from the war, earned them the animosity of the Allies along with the United States. Wilson sent troops to Russia to join Allied soldiers essentially to oppose the Bolshevik regime. In a series of pamphlets Abrams and four fellow immigrants from Russia attacked American intervention in that country and called for workers in the United States to defend the Bolshevik revolution. Bullets and bayonets that workers were making would be turned against the workers' revolution in Russia. Convicted under the amended Espionage Act, the defendants made essentially the same appeal to the Supreme Court as Schenck's: that the words for which they had been prosecuted had the protection of the First Amendment. The Court, citing among other precedents the *Schenck* case, upheld the conviction.

In his dissent from the Court majority, Holmes did not back away from his reasoning in *Schenck*. He continued to argue that whether speech is protected by the Constitution depends on intent and circumstances. But a call to resist interference in the Russian revolution, he insisted, did not represent a clear intent to damage the war mobilization against Germany and did not amount to a clear and present danger.

Resistance on the Left   Among those who resisted the general war spirit were American socialists, who stood by their belief that in modern times, only capitalists could profit from war, selling munitions to the armed forces and investing in the many industries that expand in wartime. Socialists, even those who maintained a benign love of their homeland, would have nothing to do with nationalism, and insisted that workers should unite with their brothers and sisters across national borders: "The International," proclaims the great socialist anthem, "shall be the human race." Members of the Socialist Party in the United States who opposed the war showed more ideological consistency than their European socialist and social-democratic comrades who had chosen after 1914 to follow the flag, German or French or British, rather than the logic of their convictions. Religious pacifists maintained their creed, and some of them went to jail for refusing to cooperate with the conscription system. The international pacifist Fellowship of Reconciliation defended war resisters who were victims of the sedition laws.

Women and the War

Among politically active women, opinion on the war divided. Prior to the American declaration of war the suffrage movement in general had been opposed to the conflict. Carrie Chapman Catt in 1915 was an organizer of the Woman's Peace Party. After the entrance of the United States into the fighting, she along with most other women and her National American Woman Suffrage Association switched to support of the war. Even then Jane Addams and the feminist Charlotte Perkins Gilman condemned the war. The more militant National Woman's Party, headed by the Quaker Alice Paul, was not ready at any rate to absorb the wartime mood of submission to authority. Members of the party picketed the White House, in one instance chaining themselves to the fence and inviting arrest. By 1920 Congress had passed and the necessary number of states had ratified the Nineteenth Amendment, guaranteeing the right of women to vote.

Women parading for suffrage.
(Courtesy, Library of Congress)

The war accelerated important changes in women's role in the labor force. The decline in the importance of the farm sector, together with the growth of the corporation, the expansion of such forms of white-collar employment as advertising, and the coming of electrical industries had altered the employment of women as well as men. The war itself brought only a modest increase, 6.3 percent, of women in the labor force, but it did deepen new patterns of female employment. Women clerks, secretaries, advertising employees, and telephone operators increased significantly in numbers. And the number of white women in service jobs, especially domestic service, declined significantly. Black women remained heavily concentrated in service and agricultural labor. But a small percentage of black women workers did break into manufacturing jobs that had previously been rigidly closed to them. Although business after the coming of peace would not force women altogether out of the labor force to make way for returning veterans, many were dismissed from some of the higher-paying jobs related to the war. The war years confirmed the steady, if still slow, growth in female participation in the labor force.

Libertarian Dissent

Regimentation in the military, in universities, and above all within a conformist public brought a reaction among Americans who, whatever they thought of the war, thought well of liberty. Roger Baldwin and Norman Thomas, later the leader of the Socialist Party, founded the National Civil Liberties Bureau, soon to become the American Civil Liberties Union. It did the best it could to defend victims of governmental repression. Randolph Bourne, a progressive journalist, protested the willingness of his fellow intellectuals to lend their talents to the war. The young social critic Harold Stearns soon after the war's end spoke for a mentality that he associated with liberalism: scientific, experimental, possessed of an "inner discipline" that is superior to the outward compulsions of law. Such virtues, he believed, are the proper counters to conformity and war psychology.

Recoiling from one of the world's maddest enterprises, a generation of writers returned from the battlefields to create an impressive literature. Representative of them were Erich Maria Remarque in Germany, Henri Barbusse in France, the British war hero and antiwar activist Siegfried Sassoon, and in the United States John Dos Passos, e e cummings, and Ernest Hemingway. In *The Enormous Room,* cummings caught one of the most powerful images of the war's victims, confined by governments and populations unable to tolerate dissent or difference of any kind. A volunteer in an American unit of the French army, he and a friend were confined on suspicion of disloyalty. Among their inmates were the broken, the simple, the flotsam of the war. Cummings wondered what act of beauty or innocence these had committed that would make the French government, the representation of the war's cruel stupidity, treat them so.

Suggested Readings

Recent works on progressivism include Nick Salvatore, *Eugene V. Debs* (1982), Arthur S. Link and Richard McCormick, *Progressivism* (1983), Dewey W. Grantham, *Southern Progressivism* (1983), and John Milton Cooper, Jr., *The Warrior and the Priest: Woodrow Wilson and Theodore Roosevelt* (1983). See also Cooper's survey text, *Pivotal Decade: The United States, 1900–1920* (1990). Brandeis's influence is traced in Melvin I. Urofsky, *Louis D. Brandeis and the Progressive Tradition* (1981).

Gabriel Kolko, in *The Triumph of Conservatism* (1963), argues that much of the support for regulation of business came from big business itself, which wished for a safe and orderly existence under government regulation in place of the discomforts of uncontrolled competition. In *The Corporate Ideal in the Liberal State, 1900–1918* (1968), James Weinstein stresses the role of corporations in drafting reform legislation. R. B. Nye, *Midwestern Progressive Politics* (1951), David Thelem, *The New Citizenship: Origins of Progressivism in Wisconsin, 1885–1900* (1972), and R. S. Maxwell, *La Follette and the Rise of Progressives in Wisconsin* (1956) analyze progressivism on a state level. Other state studies include Spencer O. Olin, *California's Prodigal Son: Hiram Johnson and the Progressive Movement* (1968), Robert F. Wesser, *Charles Evans Hughes: Politics and Reform in New York State, 1905–1910* (1967), and Richard Lowitt, *George Norris: The Making of a Progressive* (1963). James Green's *Grass Roots Socialism* (1978) is perceptive,

and see Aileen Kraditor, *The Radical Persuasion, 1890–1917* (1981).

Good studies of Roosevelt include John M. Blum, *The Republican Roosevelt* (second edition, 1977), and George E. Mowry, *The Era of Theodore Roosevelt, 1900–1912* (1958). See also James Pensik, *The Ballinger-Pinchot Affair* (1968) and David Sarasonn, *The Party of Reform: The Democrats in the Progressive Era* (1989). Standard on their subjects are Donald F. Anderson, *William Howard Taft: A Conservative's Conception of the Presidency* (1973) and Arthur S. Link, *Woodrow Wilson and the Progressive Era, 1900–1917* (1954).

Stephan Thernstrom pursues *The Other Bostonians: Poverty and Progress in the American Metropolis, 1860–1970* (1973); see also Tamara K. Hareven and Randolph Langenbach, *Amoskeag: Life and Work in an American Factory City* (1978).

Still standard on the First World War is Ernest R. May, *The World War and American Isolation* (1959). A briefer treatment can be found in Ross Gregory, *The Origins of American Intervention in the First World War* (1971). An excellent study is Frank E. Vandiver, *Black Jack: The Life and Times of John J. Pershing,* (1977). Black soldiers who fought in the war are depicted in A. E. Barbeau and F. Henri, *The Unknown Soldiers* (1974), while David Kennedy treats the home front in *Over Here* (1980).

In Search of Progressivism

Peter G. Filene

"What was the Progressive Movement?" This deceptively simple question, posed in different ways, holds prominent rank among the many controversies which have consumed historians' patient energies, spawned a flurry of monographs and articles, and confused several generations of students. [O]ne may suspect that it is a false problem because historians are asking a false question. This essay seeks to prove the latter suspicion—more precisely, seeks to prove that "the progressive movement" never existed. . . .

As soon as some . . . issues are examined in detail, the progressive profile begins to blur. The most familiar debate focused on federal policy toward trusts and has been immortalized in the slogans of "New Nationalism" versus "New Freedom." In 1911 Theodore Roosevelt bitterly rebuked those of his alleged fellow-progressives who wanted to split industrial giants into small competitive units. This kind of thinking, he claimed, represents "rural toryism," a nostalgic and impossible desire for an economic past. . . .

Another example of progressive disunity concerns the struggle to achieve women's suffrage, a cause that has generally been attributed to the progressive movement. Yet progressive Presidents Roosevelt and Wilson entered late and grudgingly into the feminists' ranks. More general evidence emerges from a study of two Congressional votes in 1914 and 1915, both of which temporarily defeated the future 19th Amendment. Using a recent historian's list of 400 "progressives," one finds progressive Congressmen almost evenly split for and against women's suffrage.

[T]he intellectual atmosphere before World War I consisted of a faith in moralism and progress—and almost everyone breathed this compound eagerly. In order to distinguish progressives from others, then, one must specify their values more strictly. Activism . . . at first seems to serve well. Unlike conservatives of their time, progressives believed that social progress could and should come at a faster rate via human intervention, particularly governmental intervention. Yet this ideological criterion works paradoxes rather than wonders. It excludes not simply conservatives, but Woodrow Wilson and all those who subscribed in 1913 to his "New Freedom" philosophy of laissez-faire and states rights. In order to salvage Wilson as a progressive, one must expand the definition of progressivism beyond optimism and activism to include a belief in popular democracy and opposition to economic privilege.

Historians have discovered numerous businessmen who qualify as progressive by their support for federal economic regulation and civic improvement. But these same individuals diverged sharply in ideology. They doubted man's virtuousness, believed that progress comes slowly, trusted in leaders rather than the masses as agents of progress, and generally preferred to purify rather than extend democracy. In short, their progressive activism blended with a nonprogressive skepticism and elitism. Do these reform-minded businessmen deserve membership in the progressive movement? [The historians James] Weinstein and Gabriel Kolko go further, arguing that these businessmen formed a salient, if not dominant, thrust of influence and ideas within progressivism; they were not merely supporting actors. . . .

The present state of historical understanding seems to deny the likelihood of a synthesis as convenient and neat as "the progressive movement." In their commitment to making sense of the past, however, historians will continue to search for conceptual order. Perhaps, after further studies of specific occupations, geographical areas and issues, a new synthesis will appear. But if that is to occur, the "progressive" frame of reference, carrying with it so many confusing and erroneous connotations, must be put aside. It is time to tear off the familiar label and, thus liberated from its prejudice, see the history between 1890 and 1920 for what it was—ambiguous, inconsistent, moved by agents and forces more complex than a progressive movement.

Reprinted by permission of *American Quarterly* XXII (Spring 1970), 20, 21, 22, 23, 25, 26, 34.

Daniel T. Rodgers

[P]rogressives did not share a common creed or a string of common values, however ingeniously or vaguely defined. Rather what they seem to have possessed was an ability to draw on three distinct clusters of ideas—three distinct social languages—to articulate their discontents and their social visions. To put rough but serviceable labels on those three languages of discontent, the first was the rhetoric of antimonopolism, the second was an emphasis on social bonds and the social nature of human beings, and the third was the language of social efficiency. . . .

Of these languages, antimonopolism was the oldest, the most peculiarly American, and, through the first decade of the century, the strongest of the three. When Tom Johnson took on the streetcar franchises, when Frederic Howe plumped for municipal ownership of natural monopolies, when the muckrakers flayed the trusts, there was nothing essentially new in the grievances they dramatized or the language they employed. The disproportionately large number of single taxers in the early progressive crusades was clue enough that this line of attack on "privilege" and "unnatural" concentration of wealth ran back through the Populists, through Henry George, and on at least to Andrew Jackson. But this understanding of economics and politics in terms of graft, monopoly, privilege, and invisible government had almost always before been the property of outsiders: workers, farmers, Democrats, Populists. What was new in the Progressive years was that the language of antimonopolism suddenly gained the acceptance of insiders: the readers of slick magazines and respectable journals, middle-class family men, and reasonably proper Republicans. . . .

[T]he most common explanations most Americans gave to political, economic, and social questions at the end of the century were couched in terms of largely autonomous individuals: poverty and success were said to hinge on character; the economy was essentially a straight sum of individual calculations; governance was a matter of good men and official honesty. Part of what occurred in the Progressive era was a concerted assault on all these assumptions, and, in some measure, an assault on the idea of individualism itself. That was what the era's "revolt against formalism" was all about: not a revolt against formal categories of thought, for progressive intellectuals were full of them, but against a particular set of formal fictions traceable to Smith, Locke, and Mill—the autonomous economic man, the autonomous possessor of property rights, the autonomous man of character. In its place, many of the progressives seized on a rhetoric of social cohesion.

The last of the three clusters of ideas to arrive—so very different in outward form from the other two—was the one we associate with efficiency, rationalization, and social engineering. The language of social efficiency offered a way of putting the progressives' common sense of social disorder into words and remedies free of the embarrassing pieties and philosophical conundrums that hovered around the competing language of social bonds. . . . [I]t was the merger of the prestige of science with the prestige of the well-organized business firm and factory that gave the metaphor of system its tremendous twentieth-century potency—and it was presumably for this reason that that metaphor flourished more exuberantly in the United States, along with industrial capitalism itself, than anywhere else. . . .

What made progressive social thought distinct and volatile, if this reading is correct, was not its intellectual coherence but the presence of all three of these languages at once. If we imagine the progressives, like most of the rest of us, largely as users rather than shapers of ideas, this was the constellation of live, accessible ways of looking at society within which they worked, from which they drew their energies and their sense of social ills, and within which they found their solutions. It did not give those who called themselves progressives an intellectual system, but it gave them a set of tools which worked well enough to have a powerful impact on their times. To think of progressive social thought in this way is to emphasize the active, dynamic aspect of ideas. It is also to admit, finally, that progressivism as an ideology is nowhere to be found.

Daniel T. Rodgers, "In Search of Progressivism," *Reviews in American History* 10 (December 1982), 123, 124, 126, 127.

Charles A. Lindbergh. *(Courtesy, Library of Congress)*

The New Era

LINDBERGH'S TRANSATLANTIC FLIGHT

At almost 8:00 a.m. on May 20, 1927, after a sleepless night, Charles A. Lindbergh, carrying five sandwiches, climbed into the cockpit of his small plane, which was loaded with as many extra containers of gasoline as it could carry. He left his parachute on the ground to conserve twenty pounds of fuel. The engine seemed sluggish as Lindbergh slowly maneuvered down the muddy runway of Roosevelt Field, New York, and his wheels left the ground dangerously late. He managed to clear a steamroller at the end of the field and then missed some telephone wires by less than twenty feet. As he crossed Long Island Sound and Connecticut, Lindbergh's speed reached only one hundred miles an hour. Chasing the horizon, the plane used more and more fuel, which eased the strain on the engine and the trembling wings. It was when he left Massachusetts and headed toward Nova Scotia that Lindbergh first sensed the danger of his unique solo flight—he had never before passed over a large body of water. Below him lay the awesome span of the Atlantic. His single propeller droned on.

Suddenly, over the rugged countryside of Cape Breton Island, the weather turned bad. Cross winds, driving rain, and turbulence buffeted the tiny craft; the primitive weather forecasts had suggested nothing of this. But just as unpredictably the sky cleared. Lindbergh dipped his wings over St. John's, Newfoundland, before heading out over two thousand miles of rough ocean. Night came on swiftly, and now he had to fly with a compass and an altimeter, but no lights, no flares, no means of reaching human beings. Fog descended along with wintry gusts,

continued

Lindbergh's autobiography observes of ice clouds:

"They enmesh intruders. They are barbaric. . . . They toss you in inner turbulence, lash you with hailstones, poison you with freezing mist. It would be a slow death, a death one would have long minutes to struggle against . . . climbing, stalling, diving, whipping, always downward toward the sea."

HISTORICAL EVENTS

1924
Johnson Act of 1924 • Jacksonville Agreement • Dawes Plan • U.S. troops leave Dominican Republic

1925
Brotherhood of Sleeping Car Porters formed

1927
Lindbergh makes first solo transatlantic flight • Radio Act of 1927

1928
Kellogg-Briand Pact

1929
Agricultural Marketing Act • Wall Street crashes

1930
Clark Memorandum • Hawley-Smoot tariff

1931
Reconstruction Finance Corporation • Germany defaults on all loans • Japanese attack Manchuria • Britain devalues the pound

1932
Federal Home Loan Bank Act • Japanese attack China

1933
• Twenty-first Amendment repeals Eighteenth • almost one-fourth of labor force unemployed • all international debtors except Finland default on loans from U.S.

and Lindbergh climbed to 10,000 feet. He became sharply aware of the cold. Using a flashlight, he saw ice forming on the wings and knew he was in an ice cloud. Lindbergh soon emerged into clear air under a dome lighted by stars.

Twenty-six hours after leaving Long Island, the young flyer sighted a land bird and knew he was approaching Ireland. He swooped down over a fishing boat and asked for directions, but received no response from the astonished crew. At last, there it was: a rocky shore and green fields. But the aviator flew on—over England, over the Channel, over France—until he saw the lights of the Eiffel Tower dead ahead. Lindbergh circled it to mark his victory and, thirty-three hours after takeoff, set down at Le Bourget Field, where a mob engulfed his plane even before the propeller stopped. After a night's sleep he called his mother 4,000 miles away to confirm his safe arrival.

Greeted at home by massive ticker-tape parades, he was the nation's last hero. "He has displaced everything that is petty, that is sordid, that is vulgar," orated Charles Evans Hughes at a dinner for Lindbergh in New York. Lucky Lindy had shown a decade of glitter, sensationalism, and quick profits that it was not rotten, that it could put ethics and achievement above wealth, that modesty and courage could still excite admiration.

Lindbergh entitled his story of flying solo across the Atlantic *We*—the aeronautical "we," the flying pronoun—for his achievement depended on a machine, his airplane the *Spirit of St. Louis*. Lindbergh symbolized an earlier time, but at the same time became an emblem of change, yoked to the new technology that was remaking the nation. That the machine, in all its metallic impersonality, could also be a partner in danger represented the complexity of the American encounter with modern technology. Americans were calling the Ford car the Tin Lizzie.

The Fourteen Points and the League of Nations

The Fourteen Points   Wilson's war message to Congress, designed to rally domestic public opinion, had pledged "to make the world safe for democracy." Such generalities had little to do with secret Allied agreements that granted to Britain a dominant role in the Middle East and to France its long-coveted frontier on the Rhine. Even before the United States entered the war, Wilson had called for "a peace without victory," a peace between equals that avoided mutual hatreds and the seeds of future war. Then partly to counter Bolshevik propaganda, partly to thwart his Allies' imperialist schemes, and in part to reinvigorate Western morale, Wilson presented an attractive set of war aims. In a speech to Congress on January 8, 1918, he outlined his Fourteen Points, which defined a new world order of justice, peace, and prosperity: freedom of the seas, removal of trade barriers, disarmament, national self-determination in central and eastern Europe, and a new era of collective security. This last idea, institutionalized in a League of Nations, was supposed to lessen the likelihood of any future wars. All countries would pledge to resist any single nation guilty of aggression, and the prospect of certain defeat would deter the potential wrongdoer. Critics pointed out that such provisions masked Anglo-American movement toward global domination. But Wilson's ringing rhetoric thrilled public opinion at the time on both sides of the Atlantic. A new dawn seemed close to breaking.

A Grand Vision Woodrow Wilson's League of Nations was to be a social contract among nations, leading the peoples of the world out of an old age of wars and fragile peace. The United States, in fulfillment of its historic mission, would be the agent of regeneration. Because it was the embodiment and champion of humane and libertarian values, its pursuit of its own safety and eminence was for the good of the world community it sought to renew. Or so the Wilsonians believed. Wilson's great importance for twentieth-century foreign affairs lies in his casting of the American national interest in an ideal of liberal internationalism.

Postwar policy was anti-Bolshevist. In Siberia, the United States in the winter of 1919 joined Britain, France, and Japan in an unsuccessful intervention and suffered considerable casualties. Against Lenin's vision of a world revolution, Wilson set a vision of a world system of parliamentary republics and unhindered international commerce—ordered by the League and led by the United States.

Wilson was probably wise to go to Paris to negotiate the Treaty of Versailles that ended the war and divided the former German and

President Wilson proposed in the League

"a general association of nations . . . for the purpose of affording mutual guarantees of political independence and territorial integrity to great and small states alike."

The "Big Four"—Prime Minister Lloyd George of England, Premier Orlando of Italy, French Premier Clemenceau, and President Wilson—who forged the Treaty of Versailles ending World War I. *(Courtesy, Library of Congress)*

Austrian empires in eastern Europe into a number of new nations. He displayed more breadth of purpose at the peace table than did any other major world leader, and he took with him a host of intellectual advisers to provide him with timely analyses of problems to be solved.

Yet he did not, perhaps could not, prepare the Senate and the American people for acceptance of his work, particularly for the many compromises between ideals and European national interest. Wilson lost in his attempt to scale down to reasonable size the reparations from Germany demanded by the Allies, but thought that a future American presence on the reparations commissions would ensure a fairer settlement. He was perhaps most effective in resisting excessive territorial encroachments on Germany by the Allies, and setting political boundaries that conformed in the main to lines of nationality. Wilson did not support Japan's demand for a racial equality clause in the Treaty and lost face among liberals by agreeing to let that country keep the Chinese province of Shantung. A paternalistic mandate system gave to modern countries a number of presumably backward and unwesternized territories they were to govern and prepare for eventual self-rule. Though the mandate system was partly a means of dividing among the victors the spoils of war, it subjected the governing powers to various restrictions and demanded of them responsible administration of the mandated territory. On balance Wilson achieved a tolerable treaty redeemed, in his estimate, because it contained the Covenant of the League of Nations.

| **The Fight Over the League** | At the end of the war the vast majority of Americans favored some form of a League of Nations. But this support splintered when they had to agree on a particular League. |

Republicans were the first to be estranged. Wilson's appeal on October 25, 1918, for a Democratic Congress invited a partisan response on postwar policies. By failing to take senior Republicans with him to Paris, and by leaving them ignorant of his progress there, he widened the gulf. The off-term elections produced a Republican Congress. Wilson assailed anti-League senators, calling them "bungalow minds" whose heads were "knots tied to keep their bodies from unraveling." Wilson apparently assumed at Versailles and thereafter that it was the Senate's duty to stamp its formal approval on such momentous presidential negotiation. That was added incitement to the Republicans—led by Senator Henry Cabot Lodge, majority leader and chairman of the Foreign Relations Committee—to insist on modifications of the League Covenant.

The immigrant vote, much of it traditionally Democratic, became as bitterly opposed to the treaty as the most intractable isolationists. Several nationalities resented its impact on their motherlands. The heavily Democratic Irish saw the League as an instrument for oppression at the hands of the British, who, through the membership of their dominions, such as Australia or South Africa, would control a sizable number of votes in the League Assembly. German-Americans sought revenge against Wilson for the war and the reparations settlement.

Opposition to President Wilson's League of Nations mounted, and the Senate finally defeated his plan that would have allowed the United States to join. *(Cartoon by Rollin Kirby, New York World, April 14, 1921)*

Americans of Italian descent resented the award of the city of Fiume to the new state of Yugoslavia. Jews disliked the eastern European territorial settlements, the failure at Versailles to create a Jewish homeland, and the administration's treatment of Jewish radicals.

Wilson's willingness to barter away advantage at Versailles in exchange for a secure League lost him the support even of many fellow idealists. Unwilling to accept his argument that a League could correct inequities in the treaty, they became convinced that the President had betrayed his famous Fourteen Points outlining the basis for a just peace.

By the fall of 1919 wartime idealism had fallen victim to the continuing and fruitless League debates in and out of the Senate. By the time Senator Lodge finished his Foreign Relations Committee hearings, much of the public thought of the League not as an instrument for peace but largely as a vehicle for unending war. The Republicans argued that Article X of the League Covenant—a statement guaranteeing national boundaries—would simply mean one police action after another, with the United States obliged to contribute. Wilson invited Republican senators to the White House and tried fruitlessly to reason with them.

Going to the People   Wilson even drew up four reservations to the Covenant, which he planned to offer if it was necessary. He had meanwhile a major strategy. Following the British tradition, he would go to the people. Although weakened by influenza, he began a speaking tour in September to generate support for his League. He delivered some thirty major speeches, pointing out the economic benefits the League would bring, arguing that Article X was a moral rather than a legal commitment, and generally portraying the League as man's best hope. On September 25 he suffered a physical breakdown in Pueblo, Colorado, and shortly after that he had a paralyzing cerebral hemorrhage. Had Wilson died in 1919 and become a martyr, his dream of American participation in a League might have become a reality. As it was, secluded in the White House, he became an object of gossip and slander.

The Versailles Treaty with the League Covenant attached first came before the Senate in November 1919. The critical vote was on whether to accept entrance with reservations, which protected Senate prerogatives and such traditions as the Monroe Doctrine. Loyal Wilsonian Democrats opposed to the reservations joined their votes to those of isolationists opposed to the treaty as a whole, and it was defeated. The Senate voted again: perhaps enough members in favor of a League would finally accept compromise. Three of the first four Democrats previously in opposition voted for the Treaty. The final vote was forty-nine in favor and thirty-five against—just seven short of the necessary two-thirds.

Wilson asked that the election of 1920 be a "solemn referendum" on the League. But the candidacy of a handsome Ohio senator, Warren Harding, overwhelmed the Democratic ticket of Ohio governor James Cox and vice-presidential candidate Franklin Delano Roosevelt. Sena-

"Sometimes people call me an idealist. Well, that is the way I know I am an American. America is the only idealistic nation in the world."
—President Woodrow Wilson, September 8, 1919

President Wilson has been accused of "infanticide," of slaying his own sickly brainchild, the League of Nations. As President in November 1919 he wrote to loyal Senate Democrats:

"In my opinion . . . [the Lodge resolution] does not provide for ratification but, rather, for the nullification of the treaty. I sincerely hope that the friends and supporters of the treaty will vote against the Lodge resolution of ratification."

So the League with the Lodge reservations attached—its only hope of passage—went down to defeat.

tor Harding rode an anti-Wilson tide and won the election by almost a two-to-one popular margin. The new Republican Vice President, Calvin Coolidge, observed that the election marked "the end of a period which had seemed to substitute words for things." The League was dead.

Demobilization and the Red Scare

Conversion to Peace The end of the First World War had left the government with the problem of how to return the country's economy and society to a peacetime basis. The President said that "people would go their own way." They would want a relaxation of wartime restraints and Wilson, who viewed the public as the final repository of support for his League of Nations, had no wish to alienate them.

Demobilization, when it came, was rapid. Almost immediately following the armistice the government discharged 600,000 veterans. Four million more returned to the peacetime economy during the next year; most of them reached their homes by the summer of 1919, some carrying gas masks or helmets as souvenirs. Commitments to government war spending inevitably continued into peace, and no early postwar deflation occurred. In 1920 Congress did pass legislation that helped demobilize the economy from its wartime footing and also constituted a final burst of Wilsonian progressivism. But like that of Wilson's earlier presidential years it was a progressivism of a character less of his New Freedom than of Theodore Roosevelt's New Nationalism, a concern not for dismantling large enterprises but for bringing them under close federal regulations.

The Transportation Act, also known as the Esch-Cummins Act, returned the nation's railroads to private control but at the same time expanded the powers of the Interstate Commerce Commission, allowing it to set minimum and maximum railroad rates. By establishing a Railway Labor Board, the law also came close to authorizing compulsory government arbitration of disputes between labor and management in the railroad industry. The Water Power Act brought the federal government into the hydroelectric power industry. Progressives had long been demanding government regulation of monopolies, and the Water Power Act represented a beginning. The legislation created the Federal Power Commission and gave it authority over all public land water as well as over navigable streams, lakes, and rivers. The Merchant Marine Act, also termed the Jones Act, to the contrary loosened regulation. It repealed the wartime legislation giving the federal government much authority over the shipping industry. The Shipping Board helped the industry make the transition to private control.

The economy was unsettled. As industries once bloated by war shrank, many people moved from one job to another. The high cost of living was a constant irritant; some consumer prices had almost doubled between 1914 and 1920 and rose fastest in the postwar period. It was a time not of high unemployment but of economic dislocation.

The Red Scare

The emotion of a modern war, the perfect fusion of lofty idealism with the baser feelings of chauvinism, had settled easily upon a nation technologically advanced enough for total mobilization and still naive enough to believe in splendid adventures with noble goals. The aftermath of the war was an assault on that innocence. Having finished a war it had thought it could handle on the simplest and purest moral terms, the nation discovered that those terms meant little to Europe. At home, the worst emotions of the war remained and sought out new enemies on which to spend themselves. Among them was Bolshevism.

The Socialist Party, once a thriving organization under the leadership of Eugene Debs, had fallen into disrepute for its opposition to the war. Debs himself, prosecuted under Wilson's harsh Sedition Act, remained silent in jail. Mobs and wartime legislation crushed the more radical Industrial Workers of the World. By 1919 many socialists had joined either the native Communist Party of America or the Communist Labor Party, composed mainly of foreign-born urban Americans. Both parties, which soon united, amounted to considerably less than one percent of the population. Their very existence, however, provided some business groups, anxious to keep labor from extending its wartime gains, with a convenient image to fix on to the labor movement and social protest as a whole. In his last years, Debs denounced the call from Moscow for world revolution and was at odds with the domestic Communist Party.

In the winter of 1919 the city of Seattle, Washington, experienced something almost totally unfamiliar in American history, a general strike. In sympathy with striking longshoremen, the unions that ran the city— streetcar employees, clerical workers, even firemen—walked off their jobs, leaving Seattle paralyzed. A Committee of Public Safety, which sounded vaguely foreign and revolutionary, maintained essential services. But the strikers could not agree on demands, public opinion turned against them, and Mayor Ole Hanson brought marines into the city to end the strike.

After the Seattle strike Mayor Hanson's office received a package wrapped in brown paper. Since the mayor was in Colorado selling war bonds that were still being issued after the end of the war, it was put aside and some liquid leaked out, burning a wooden table. The package was a homemade bomb. A similar missive went to the home of a southern senator favoring more stringent immigration restriction and blew the hands off his black maid. A New York City postal employee read about the packages and remembered putting some others aside for insufficient postage. Marked with a "Gimbel's Brothers" return address, they were found at the main post office in New York City or in transit. Newspapers compiled a "bomb honor list" that included Supreme Court Justice Oliver Wendell Holmes, financier J. P. Morgan, and Attorney General A. Mitchell Palmer. Whoever mailed the packages apparently intended that they should arrive around May Day, the labor holiday. In June a bomb-thrower blew himself up with his own missile on the steps of Palmer's house in Washington. After this incident Palmer, once known as a progressive, became notorious for rounding up aliens and endeavoring to deport them.

The Red Scare that followed the Great War caused panic and violence throughout the nation. *(Courtesy, Chicago Historical Society)*

The evangelist Billy Sunday said of Communists:

"If I had my way, I'd fill the jails so full of them that their feet would stick out the windows . . . [or] I would put them on ships of stone with masts of lead."

A victim of racial rioting in Chicago, July 1919. *(Courtesy, Scribner's Archives)*

In the summer of 1919 a bloody race riot occurred in Chicago, where many blacks had migrated from the South to fill unmet labor needs during the world war. A black youth unable to swim had clung to a railroad tie that drifted into an area of Lake Michigan reserved for whites. Whites swam menacingly toward him: he moved away for a few strokes, then sank and drowned. When police refused to arrest any whites and instead took a protesting black into custody, a riot ensued, killing twenty-three blacks and fifteen whites. Riots occurred in other cities, and in the course of 1919 some seventy blacks were murdered, including at least ten veterans of the recently ended world war.

In September the whole Boston police force went out on an unprecedented strike. The mayor fired the strikers, the President called the strike "a crime against civilization," and Calvin Coolidge, at that time the governor of Massachusetts, said that there was "no right to strike against the public safety by anybody, anywhere, anytime." In Washington state that November an IWW member provoked into shooting an American Legionnaire was taken from prison by a mob that beat and castrated him, hanged him from a bridge, and riddled his body with bullets. In early January 1920, the New York State Assembly refused to seat five legally elected Socialists. For once in a period when law and mobs were persecuting radicals, distinguished citizens did protest an act of repression. A number of them denounced the Assembly's action.

Labor Strife   Labor unrest before the war had taken particularly militant form in the Colorado coal fields in 1913. Banding together in tent communities, strikers and their families demanding, among other things, recognition of their union settled down for a long struggle. On April 20, 1914, the state national guard, siding with the owners, joined with company police in firing on the tent city at Ludlow, and fourteen inhabitants were killed, eleven of them children. For days after the Ludlow Massacre miners in southern Colorado were in open insurrection. At a time of widespread strikes two years later in San Francisco, which had the most active labor movement in the

This photograph of Ludlow, Colorado, April 21, 1914, shows the aftermath of the state militia attack that destroyed a tent colony of striking miners. The "Ludlow Massacre," which killed fourteen people (including eleven children), demonstrated the intensity of violence in western company towns. *(Courtesy, Western Historical Collection, Denver Public Library)*

country, someone threw a bomb during a parade backed by business interests in support of military preparedness, and several spectators died. The prominent union leader Tom Mooney of the iron molders, along with Warren Billings and other labor activists, were convicted of the crime on dubious evidence. Amidst national and international protest among liberals and radicals, President Wilson appealed to the governor of California, who commuted Mooney's death sentence. But it was not until 1939 that he and Billings were released from prison.

American engagement in the European war and the consequent protection that the federal government extended to unions cooled labor conflict for the moment. The coming of peace reheated it. Unions determined to maintain advantages they had enjoyed during the war and to push the closed shop, an arrangement whereby a business will hire only union members. Leaders of management, resolved to restore their earlier dominance, denounced the closed shop as an assault on liberty, and promoted the "American Plan," the open shop. Over 4,000 strikes ensued during the year 1919.

The men who ran the steel industries were among the least enlightened in all management. In 1910, thirty percent of the labor force in steel had worked a seven-day week; seventy-five percent had worked a twelve-hour day, some even laboring on two consecutive twelve-hour shifts every other Sunday when they changed from day to night work. The average work week for the whole industry was sixty-eight hours. During the war the industry, to avoid government intervention, agreed to pay time-and-a-half for work beyond an eight-hour day, and a severe labor shortage raised wages faster than inflation could erode the gains. Unions flourished; by the war's finish, more than 100,000 steelworkers belonged. The great steel strike began on September 23, 1919. Management, knowing that it was the stronger party, refused to meet with union leaders at all. The national organization was unready, lacking money and adequate preparation for a venture thrust upon it by militant locals. By January the strike was dead.

The Palmer Raids

The Red Scare culminated in the Palmer raids of January 2, 1920, when Justice Department agents, striking simultaneously in dozens of cities, rounded up thousands of aliens. Held incommunicado for days in violation of their civil rights, they would have been shipped to Europe had Palmer got his way.

The opposition of Acting Secretary of Labor Louis F. Post, a political progressive who now held technical power over deportations, saved many of Palmer's victims from being thrown out of the country. When nativist congressmen sought to impeach Post in the House, he reminded them of the Bill of Rights and refused to budge. At the same time that Post was declining to effect Palmer's will, the nation was turning to other issues. By the spring of 1920 the Red Scare was on the wane, soon to be replaced by concern over a serious depression that lasted until 1922 and then by the revolution in customs and values that occupied the nation in the 1920s. A bomb that killed dozens in Wall Street in 1920 was correctly regarded as the work of a crank, and there was no widespread attempt to associate it with a conspiracy of radicals.

Sonia Kaross would remember what happened to her during the Palmer Raids:

"We were living in Philadelphia and had been at a chorus rehearsal. We came home—it must have been eleven or twelve—and went to bed. One o'clock, there was banging on the doors. It woke up the whole building. There were police cars and all kinds of detectives all over the street. They came in and took all my books, all my letters, whatever they found.

Then they took my husband and me away. I was almost seven months pregnant. The police threw me in the wagon. And I was locked up with five or six prostitutes. I got sick from all the excitement and the way the police handled me. Those prostitutes, I want to tell you, were the nicest people. I didn't fully understand what was going on. I thought: Well, I'm just getting sick. But they realized that I might lose the baby. They raised an awful rumpus. They were screaming, hollering, knocking on the door. They were yelling, 'This woman is dying! Get her an ambulance!' But nobody responded. All night they banged the door while I lay there suffering. Well, my companions in jail saved my life, but they couldn't save the baby's. Before the ambulance came it was morning, and the baby was dead. . . .

We were charged with being undesirable. . . . I was elected a delegate . . . from the Young Socialist League, and they had found that out. . . . We had no rights. . . . There was such a wide gap between the native Americans and the foreign-born."

The Red Scare was in essence the equivalent in domestic matters of the nation's rejection of Versailles. As Americans shifted away from involvement in the rest of the world, they turned upon foreigners in their own land.

Lingering Effects   The Bolshevik revolution and the establishment of a one-party Communist regime in the Soviet Union added a burden that has pressed upon American socialists ever since. Now a system calling itself "socialist" was manifestly imposing centralization and repression on Russia. Not even the relentless war of words and bullets that Communists and democratic socialists would wage upon each other since then, in country after country, managed to reveal to the American public the irreconcilable opposition between socialism and the thing that in Russia took that name.

The conviction that radicalism and socialism are alien to the nation's culture, the absence of a long-standing and fairly sizable political left, is a peculiarity of American politics. The decline of the Socialist Party after the First World War and the ferocity with which Americans came to reject the very idea of a radical left meant that their politics would lack the diversity, the sharpness and intelligence of philosophical debate that have prevailed among other Western nations.

Traces of the Red Scare or of the mentality that had produced it affected the twenties. The newly-formed American Legion grew rapidly, preaching "one country, one language, one flag." While the Legion was a legitimate organization of veterans, some of its members collected themselves into such mobs as the one that lynched the IWW member in Washington State. A burgeoning Ku Klux Klan reached a membership of some two to four million by 1924. The trial of two Italian anarchist immigrants, Bartolomeo Vanzetti and Nicola Sacco, for the robbery and murder in 1920 of a paymaster in South Braintree, Massachusetts, was reminiscent of the Red Scare. While a modern ballistics study indicates that Sacco was probably guilty, the fish peddler Vanzetti may have been innocent. What is memorable about the trial is its xenophobic atmosphere. The judge privately referred to the defendants as "those anarchistic bastards," and his conduct of the trial was scarcely less prejudiced.

Before his execution in 1927 Vanzetti delivered a moving oration:

"We were tried during a time that has now passed into history. . . . I am suffering because I am a radical and indeed I am a radical. I have suffered because I was an Italian, and indeed I am an Italian; I have suffered more for my family and for my beloved than for myself; but I am so convinced to be right that if you could execute me two times, and if I could be reborn two other times, I would live again to do what I have done already."

City vs. Country

For many traditionalists in the farms and the small towns, the city stood for all that was alien to American life. Descended from generations of Americans, they worried about the communities of "foreign" stock and identified the city with vice, most notably alcohol.

Prohibition   For a short time, the alcohol question came close to being the single most intoxicating ingredient in American politics on the national level. In 1919 the nation adopted the Eighteenth Amendment to the Constitution, and it went into effect the next year. The measure prohibited the manufacture, sale, transportation, import, and export of liquor. By the mid-twenties, the defenders and opponents of prohibition were at angry odds over whether the Amendment should be repealed. Each side connected the issue with larger cultural matters. Many though not all prohibitionists associated alcohol with Roman Catholics, immigrants, corrupt worldliness, and pleasure-seeking: with a whole range of forces that were centered in the big cities and threatened the nation's plain old-fashioned morals. Numbers of immigrant-stock Catholics in turn associated prohibition with nativist prejudice and Protestant bigotry. New York City gave the country Alfred E. Smith, a Catholic of Irish descent who opposed prohibition and as governor of New York State signed bills legalizing Sunday baseball and the bloody sport of boxing.

Prohibition in Practice   Prohibition's history dates back to the mid-nineteenth century and before, when Americans consumed huge amounts of liquor. During the Progressive Era the dry organizations drew support from the eugenics movement, which argued the banning of alcohol for improving the race; from women who saw their husbands spend wages in saloons or wished to "uplift" the urban poor; and from nativists who viewed the movement as a symbolic battle against the new immigrants as well as the Irish. Then came the First World War. Along with wartime hostility to German-American brewers came more serious considerations: alcohol was a wasteful use of grain that could feed the army and war-torn Europe; the purchase of whiskey was a luxury diverting money from the war effort; and alcohol, so it was thought, interfered with the efficiency of the labor the war so desperately needed. And so the country went dry during the war and then, with the passage of the Eighteenth Amendment, elected for permanent abstinence. Or so it thought.

In many cities prohibition popularized drinking by forcing it to be secretive and therefore romantic. While the immigrant poor could make their own home brews, the young middle class—both male and female—had fun in dark speakeasies. Movies depicted drinking by the hero and his girlfriend. But the quality of available liquor declined as well as the quantity. Now there came mixtures called Old Stingo or Cherry Dynamite, concocted often with a dash of iodine, sulphuric acid, creosote, or embalming fluid. Poisoned liquor occasionally killed someone who could not afford the steady flow of Canadian Club that entered from the North, sometimes on sleds drawn by dog team, or spirits brought in by Caribbean and Atlantic rumrunners.

Organized crime had existed well before the twenties: by taking over the illegal distribution of liquor the gangs flourished. Prohibition's fairest flower was Al Capone, a Chicago mobster responsible for hundreds of deaths. The St. Valentine's Day Massacre, the result of a gang war in Chicago, Capone called "bad public relations." For some Americans of immigrant background a life of crime was a route to higher status.

One of the popular beliefs about the period is that prohibition did not work. Statistics reveal that prohibition did cut down the amount of drinking, and alcoholism also declined. The problem is that this came at a great price. Prohibition made for an increase in organized crime in the dank criminal underworld. It put a strain on the resources of the police. It deprived the government of the tax revenues that might have been collected on legal alcohol. It deepened the hostility between Catholics and Protestants, between immigrant-stock and old-stock Americans. It gave the prohibitionist and hate-mongering Ku Klux Klan one more issue to feed on.

By the later 1920s, then, the social and financial costs of prohibition were outrunning its benefits. Drys had promised that it would empty jails and mental institutions, and therefore lower taxes. Local taxes did not fall, and some wealthy Americans, calculating that a tax on legal alcohol would ward off increases in income taxes, began to spend money to get the Eighteenth Amendment repealed. As the Great Depression cast its shadow the public was turning against the great experiment. An increased need for tax revenue and a turning of public attention to grim realities brought in 1933 the Twenty-first Amendment, repealing the Eighteenth.

Fundamentalism   The politics of traditionalism also drew fundamentalists, those Protestants who hold to belief in the literal meaning of Scripture. The preachers and lecturers of fundamentalism would talk about the growing power of the Catholic Church, drawing its strength from the immigrants and their offspring in the urban centers. Or they would announce that the great cities were the place of skepticism and agnosticism, and warned of modernist Protestant theologians who refused to accept the Bible in its clear and simple sense. Hinterland moralists were convinced that the cities, infected with atheism and false religion, had gone also into more general decadence. New York City housed cultural enterprises like the opera and the ballet that many rural Americans thought snobbish and unmasculine. More particularly, traditionalists identified the city with Tammany Hall.

Fundamentalism had its own particular public event in the decade. In the small town of Dayton, Tennessee, John Scopes had taught his public high school biology students, in disobedience of state statute, that man had descended from an ape-like creature. William Jennings Bryan—hopelessly naive about religion—offered himself as a witness for the prosecution and was intellectually pounded by the great criminal lawyer, Clarence Darrow, an agnostic.

In one sense, the encounter of 1925 merely pitted authority against authority—"the Bible teaches" against "Science says"—for many street-corner evolutionists, like much of American society, took science to be a giver of revelations rather than a complex method of doubt, inquiry, and tentative hypothesis.

A witness for John Scopes remembered later:

"The important question [Darrow] asked was whether Scopes' teaching for evolution had affected my religion in any way. He asked if I still attended church and Sunday school and believed in the Bible. I said I was still religious."

Immigration Restriction and the New Klan   Hostility to immigrants was reinforced during the First World War, which brought violence against German Americans. And the activities of antiwar radicals evoked the old image of the immigrant revolutionary, a large specter during the Red Scare. Native labor, suffering hard times in the depression of 1920–1922, complained that competition with immigrants was pulling down wages.

Despite the appetite of the economy for cheap labor, among businessmen there was some distrust of immigrants as being open to labor radicalism. Social workers sometimes betrayed a subtle distaste for their clients.

The white-sheeted, anti-immigrant fraternal order of the Ku Klux Klan flourished during the decade. Founded in 1915 in Georgia as an imitation of the Reconstruction Klan, the new organization gathered its two to four million members chiefly during the early twenties. In the South it directed much of its fury against blacks; over the country as a whole it was militant against Catholicism and immigration. The Klan's popularity came from the lure of secrecy and from association with religious and patriotic institutions.

One of the Klan's efforts was to keep Governor Al Smith of New York from winning the Democratic presidential nomination in 1924. The Klan did its part to spread anti-Catholic rumors that the Pope, crowded in the Vatican, aspired to new headquarters in the Mississippi Valley and that his minions were tunneling their way under the Atlantic Ocean to give orders to Smith in New York. The Klan declined when financial and sexual scandals struck some of its leaders in the mid-twenties.

Another ground of nativism, quite urban and academic in character, was the pseudo-scientific racism that was having its vogue at this time. The social psychologist William McDougall of Harvard studied results of World War I intelligence tests, which showed lower I.Q. scores for southern Europeans. Having little knowledge of the distortions that differences in environment and cultures make in such tests, he concluded that they demonstrated the superiority of northern Europeans over other peoples.

The immigration law of 1921 imposed an annual nationality quota: three percent of the number of each group in America in 1920. The Johnson Act of 1924 reduced the quota from three to two percent, and set the date back to 1890 for computing it. The thrust was against the

One of the Klan's most popular songs, sung to the tune of "The Battle Hymn of the Republic," combined symbols of religion and patriotism:

We rally round Old Glory in our robes
    of spotless white,
While the Fiery Cross is burning in the
    silent, silv'ry night,
Come join our glorious army in the
    cause of God and Right,
The Klan is marching on.

So powerful was the Ku Klux Klan in the mid-1920s that its members felt emboldened to march openly and defiantly down the streets of major cities— even down Pennsylvania Avenue in Washington, in the shadow of the Capitol of the United States.
(Courtesy, Library of Congress)

Annual Immigrant Quotas under the Johnson Act, 1925–27	
Germany	51,227
Great Britain	34,007
Ireland	28,567
Sweden	9,561
Norway	6,453
Poland	5,982
France	3,954
Italy	3,845
Czechoslovakia	3,073
Denmark	2,789
Soviet Union	2,248
Switzerland	2,081
Holland	1,640
Africa	1,100
All others	8,132

cities and the recent immigrants. The Japanese were badly treated in the 1924 law; through a diplomatic bungle the Gentlemen's Agreement with Japan, by which unskilled workers were barred except for those with families already here, was abrogated and Japanese immigration totally banned. It was an insult to a proud people, and an incident in a continuing history of insults to Japan that prepared the ground for World War II.

The Jazz Age

The Idea of the "Twenties"   People have a way of thinking by decades, as though "the twenties," "the thirties," or "the sixties" each defines by some logic of numbers a distinct cultural situation. The 1920s was especially susceptible to this, for the decade is marked off nearly at its edges by the Great War and the Great Depression. It was a colorful time that became quickly and heavily stereotyped. Under a rhetoric of individualism, in fact, the United States was collectivizing its productive and financial institutions. An ideology of calling for economy in government coexisted with an expansion of bureaucracy. The country talked isolationism and extended its influence abroad.

Defined by some of its most striking qualities, the "twenties" did not even open with 1920 or 1921, but was launched well before then. There had been bohemians in Greenwich Village, Chicago, and San Francisco as early as 1910. American women had begun to assert themselves, leading in the field of social work, entering a few of the professions, and demanding the vote. As early as 1914, H. L. Mencken coined the term "flapper" for a new, less inhibited type of woman. Unsettling literary influences were coming in from abroad: D. H. Lawrence in England, the decadent symbolists in France, the mystic novelists and short story writers in Russia. Experiments in poetic form were particularly notable. Some young people began to think of them-

King Oliver's famous Creole Jazz Band of the 1920s poses for a striking picture. (*Courtesy, Hogan Jazz Archives, Tulane University*)

selves as "modern" and as a new generation, and to denounce their elders as Puritans. World War I sped these and other changes.

The Arts   The decade, a triumphant time in art and literature, introduced or continued the work of durable figures: Eugene O'Neill, Gertrude Stein, Ezra Pound, e e cummings, Sinclair Lewis, Sherwood Anderson, Ernest Hemingway, F. Scott Fitzgerald, John Dos Passos, Theodore Dreiser, Robert Frost, Hart Crane, Robinson Jeffers, Edna St. Vincent Millay, and many others. The American theater enjoyed a highly creative period, and there was active experimentation, both artistic and technical, in the young medium of the movies.

An inspiration to literary endeavor was the great and much misunderstood Viennese physician Sigmund Freud. Recently, Freud has come to be discovered as a student of civilization and its intricate psychological strategies for mastering the dark primal forces of the mind. More interesting to the few people of the twenties who had a superficial acquaintance with his ideas was his apparent belief in sexual liberation. But in directing attention to the shadows beneath the surface of the human psyche, Freudianism encouraged writers to seek introspectively for these in their fictional characters and in themselves.

Among the richest artistic flowerings of the era was the Harlem Renaissance. Representing in part an integration of white and black culture during the 1920s, it was an assertion of black pride, an expression of white fascination with Africa, and a part of the larger American cultural upheaval of the time. The Harlem Renaissance demonstrated a new awareness of blacks by whites and an opportunity for intellectuals of both races to mingle in salons (many of them organized by wealthy white women), studios, and theaters. Countee Cullen, James Weldon Johnson, Claude McKay, Zora Hurston, and Langston Hughes were prominent within the Harlem Renaissance, which also included black literary and political magazines—*Harlem*, *The Messenger*, *Fire*—theater and art groups, and political associations.

An important radical who wrote for *The Messenger* (1917–28) was A. Phillip Randolph, who urged blacks to join unions and to vote for socialist candidates. In 1925 Randolph founded the Brotherhood of Sleeping Car Porters and become its president. During the New Deal of the 1930s the Brotherhood was to win a good union contract with the Pullman Company. In 1941 Randolph threatened a mass march on Washington to protest the boycotting of blacks from defense jobs. President Roosevelt promised to prevent such discrimination and that march was never held. But Randolph lived to preside over the March on Washington of 1963, a high point of the civil rights movement.

The Great Migration   The Harlem Renaissance was notable not only for its artistic achievements but for marking the presence in the North of a black population previously associated almost wholly with the South. Harlem itself was the most striking new center of northern black urban life.

Between 1870 and 1890 some 80,000 black Americans had moved out of the South, and 200,000 more left between 1890 and 1910. That

SHARE-CROPPERS
by Langston Hughes

Just a herd of Negroes
Driven to the field,
Plowing, planting, hoeing,
To make the cotton yield.

When the cotton's picked
And the work is done
Boss man take the money
And we get none.

Leaves us hungry, ragged
As we were before.
Year by year goes by
And we are nothing more

Than a herd of Negroes
Driven to the field—
Plowing life away
To make the cotton yield.

Langston Hughes. (*Courtesy, New York Public Library*)

The South during the Progressive Era had been rigidly segregated. One black woman would recall:

"You could not go to a white restaurant; you sat in a special place at the movie house; and, Lord knows, you sat in the back of the bus. It didn't make any difference if you were rich or poor, if you were black you were nothing. You might have a hundred dollars in your pocket, but if you went to the store you would wait at the side until all the clerks got through with all the white folks, no matter if they didn't have change for a dollar. Then the clerk would finally look at you and say 'Oh, did you want something? I didn't see you there.'

They did want our money, that was true enough, but otherwise we were dirt in the street. If you'd go in to get some shoes, some stores would not let you try them on before you bought them. If you wanted to have a new hat, they might make you put a handkerchief on your head before you tried it out. They thought we were dirty; they thought we leave stains, maybe that was it; and they didn't want to drink out of the same water fountain. There were women who would go into stores to buy a fur coat but they couldn't use the rest room."

A black man in Philadelphia recounted his new life there:

"Well Dr. with the aid of God I am making very good I make $75 per month. I am carrying enough insurance to pay me $20 per week if I am not able to be on duty. I don't have to mister . . . every little white boy comes along I havent heard a white man call a colored a nigger you no now—since I been in the state of Pa. I can ride in the electric street and steam cars any where I get a seat. I dont care to mix with white what I mean I am not crazy about being with white folks, but if I have to pay the same fare I have learn to want the same acomidation. and if you are first in a place here shopping you dont have to wait until the white folks get thro trading yet amid all this I shall ever love the good old South and I am praying that God may give every well wisher a chance to be a man regardless of his color."

Black northern newspapers served as a source of information to southerners, as exemplified in this letter to the Chicago *Defender:*

Sherman, Ga., Nov. 28, 1916.
Dear sir:

This letter comes to ask for all infirmations concerning employment. . . . Now I am in a family of (11) eleven more or less boys and girls (men and women) mixed sizes who want to go north as soon as arrangements can be made and employment given places for shelter and so on (etc) now this are farming people they were raised on the farm and are good farm hands I of course have some experience and qualefication as a coman school teacher and hotel waiter and along few other lines.

I wish you would write me at your first chance and tell me if you can give us employment at what time and about what wages will you pay and what kind of arrangement can be made for our shelter. Tell me when can you best use us now or later.

Will you send us tickets if so on what terms and at what price what is the cost per head and by what route should we come. We are Negroes and try to show ourselves worthy of all we may get from any friendly source we endeavor to be true to all good causes, if you can we thank you to help us to come north as soon as you can.

year there were more than 850,000 black people living in the northern cities. Large communities appeared in the North complete with their own elite groups of lawyers, teachers, ministers, doctors, nurses, social workers, businessmen, and businesswomen. Successful black newspapers appeared, such as the *Chicago Defender*, the *Pittsburgh Courier*, and the *New York Amsterdam News*.

Migration to the North accelerated when the South was hit by an economic recession in 1914 and by the cotton-destroying boll weevil attacks in 1915. Thousands of jobs disappeared in the South just as northern and midwestern industries were booming during World War I. Black people headed north by the hundreds of thousands. Between 1910 and 1920 the black population of the North increased from 850,000 to 1.4 million people, and by 1930 it had grown to more than 2.3 million. Two million more were to leave the South during the Great Depression and World War II, and black ghettos would appear in cities throughout the Northeast and Midwest.

Because of the great migration, there were now two black pop-

A black family from the South
arrives in Chicago in 1910.
(*Courtesy, Historical Pictures Service,
Chicago*)

ulations in the United States, one rural and southern and the other
northern and urban. Booker T. Washington had represented southern
blacks; new leaders appeared whose primary constituency consisted
of the urban, northern communities. The two most prominent were
W. E. B. Du Bois and Marcus Garvey.

**Marcus
Garvey
and Pan-
Africanism**

Pan-Africanism, a special vision of Du Bois, was
particularly popular after World War I. Du Bois
dreamed of a great free central African state to
encompass a "unity of the colored races." An
NAACP session in 1919 endorsed Du Bois's grand
scheme, but it received no popular support. Du Bois's movement
eventually clashed with that of Marcus Garvey, whose showmanship,
flash, and ability to evoke emotion won him a following. Garvey has
been described as a "charlatan" and a "crook" and as "the greatest thing
that happened to a black man."

Born in Jamaica in 1887 of peasant parents, Garvey attended local
secondary schools. A youthful experience of rejection by the white
daughter of a Methodist minister taught Garvey that "there were different races, each having its own separate and distinct social life. . . ."
Garvey pursued a short-lived printing career, then became involved in
the Jamaican labor movement.

Before he came to the United States, Garvey's most significant
achievement was the founding in Jamaica of the Universal Negro Improvement Association. Its purpose was to unite "all the Negro peoples
of the world into one great body to establish a country and government
absolutely their own." Arriving in the United States, Garvey proceeded
to raise funds and interest other blacks in his plan for the formation of
a black economic community. By 1919, Garvey's UNIA claimed thirty
branches in American cities and the organization flourished until 1927.

**Black separatist Marcus Garvey
and his followers were one of
many factions of the black
movement during the 1920s and
1930s. Other groups, such as the
NAACP, worked to bring blacks
and whites together rather than
segregating them further.**
(*Courtesy, Archive Pictures*)

Garvey spread his ideology through the publication of a weekly newspaper, *The Negro World*. Printed in Spanish, French, and English, the paper celebrated black heroes of the past, recalled slave rebellions, and promoted the grandeur of Africa. Garvey's insistence on racial pride had a tremendous effect among black northerners.

Garvey in 1919 established a steamship company, the Black Star Line. Only blacks were entitled to buy shares in the company and thousands made the investment. Garvey announced that "the Black Star Line will sail to Africa if it sails in seas of blood." The three ships of the line eventually were lost at sea, and the company went bankrupt. But Garvey then established a Negro Factories Corporation, along with another steamship company, and plans for the settlement of American blacks in Liberia testify to Garvey's unflagging spirit.

New York City's Assistant District Attorney questioned Garvey about the sale of unincorporated stock in the Black Star Line. The Jamaican was also involved in libel suits instigated by comments printed in *The New World*. His legal problems culminated in a trial for using the mails with intent to defraud. Found guilty, Garvey lost an appeal in 1925 and the Supreme Court refused to review his case. He served three years of a five-year sentence and was deported to Jamaica, where he continued his efforts toward fulfillment of his grand scheme. In 1935 he moved to London, dying there in poverty five years later.

Towns in Literature Amidst the growth of cities, the expansion of the literary and other arts, and the transformation of northern urban life by black and immigrant cultures, writers looked back in time or inland in space to the country and small-town life that some disdained. In their number were Sinclair Lewis and Sherwood Anderson.

Set early in the twentieth century, Lewis's *Main Street* (1920) is about the efforts of the mildly feminist Carol Kennicott to bring a higher culture to Gopher Prairie, or at least to survive her own boredom there. *Main Street* depicts a town still untouched by the upheaval of values that followed World War I. Lewis was able to reproduce the monotonous tones and platitudinous content of everyday speech, along with the town's routinized life and drab appearance. The same authenticity in talk and manners, and in the small feelings that make up the surface of consciousness, gives strength to *Babbitt* (1922), a satirical novel about a businessman in a much larger midwestern city, the fictional Zenith.

The affection that grounded Lewis's depiction of the American inland is mostly hidden in these early works, and indeed Lewis may not have fully discovered it in himself until later. *Winesburg, Ohio* (1919), Sherwood Anderson's collection of tales about a small midwestern town, is openly lyrical. The characters are isolated from one another, and in their aloneness, deepened by the isolation of Winesburg itself, each develops some intensity of longing or ambition, or other private obsession that Anderson turns into prose poetry.

Another avenue to an understanding of the American town is advanced in a sociological work, *Middletown* (1929), a study of Muncie, Indiana, by Robert and Helen Lynd. Middletown was no longer a

Gopher Prairie, if it had ever been one; it was closer to the Zenith of *Babbitt,* and indeed hinted at what much of American society would soon become. The idea of the small town survived the reality. Suburbs, residential and industrial, metropolitan areas, and new demographic categories like neighborhood and region, created by the automobile and other forms of transportation, were replacing the older, simpler categories of town and city. The role of Middletown's women was changing. Of 446 girls in the three upper high school classes in 1924, eighty-nine percent were planning to work after graduation. The whole family structure and the dominance of the home were giving way under the influence in part of the automobile, as the ride in the country replaced the visit in the parlor.

Radio   The society that remained in the nation's rural Gopher Prairies was under a friendly invasion. The radio had long been in use by ship operators and amateurs, but the first station to do regular broadcasting was KDKA in Pittsburg, which in 1920 began covering election returns. Radio was an instant hit in the United States. More than 500 new radio stations began broadcasting in 1922. The Radio Act of 1927 brought the airwaves under federal control. By the late 1920s, radio networks like the Columbia Broadcasting System (CBS) and the National Broadcasting Company (NBC) had established local affiliated stations, linked them by telephone to network headquarters in New York City, and were broadcasting soap operas, situation comedies, sports, and news programs across the country. Americans everywhere began listening to the same programs, laughing at the same jokes, hearing the same advertisements, and recognizing the same personalities. Radio did more than any other medium except possibly motion pictures to create a mass culture in the United States.

Silent Movie Classics   Long before television's domination of the mass media, audiences of the twenties were living vicariously through the larger-than-life images that flickered enticingly across the screens of movie theaters throughout the United States. The burgeoning film industry became big business. True to the spirit of American industry, films became a commodity valued according to their box office success. By the end of the decade at least one ornate movie house could be found in town after American town. White-gloved doormen and uniformed ushers, baroque lobbies, balconied theaters—all testified to the public's total enthusiasm for the country's favorite form of entertainment.

The filmmakers picked subject matter that would attract all classes. Movies of the twenties reflected the transformation in social values that prevailed in the years following World War I. Scenes of sex and drinking were frank and tolerant. Yet the heroes and heroines of movies embodied the virtues: courage, generosity, kindness, honesty, and responsible conduct. Particular actors and directors in Hollywood films seized the imagination of American moviegoers. Charlie Chaplin advocated dramatic revisions of the social structure. Chaplin became a star in 1914 with *Tillie's Punctured Romance,* and he continued to dominate silent comedy throughout the 1920s. In *The Sheik* Rudolph

Charlie Chaplin, who dominated film comedies in the early days of the industry, in *The Gold Rush.*
(Courtesy, Scribner's Archives)

A Mrs. B.I.H. of Cheyenne, Wyoming, wrote a typical letter in 1926 to her local paper protesting the emphasis on sex in the movies:

"I just wonder why all actresses wear so little. Don't they have shame? They go so near naked there is nothing left to the imagination. I don't object to love scenes, but let the ladies keep their bodies covered."

Valentino embodied the romantic, sensual hero. Among other European stars whose passionate images stirred American fantasies, Greta Garbo was legendary, playing numerous roles of temptress. At the end of the decade, talkies—Al Jolson's *The Jazz Singer* (1927) was the first major one—transformed the experience of moviegoing, at once depriving it of the verbal imagination that the public had needed to bring to it and adding to the artistic resources of the film.

Republican Ascendancy

Warren Harding: Strengths and Weaknesses

In 1920 the Republican President Warren Harding, likeable and hardworking, had inherited from Woodrow Wilson a disintegrating presidency and a drifting foreign policy. He also faced a severe postwar depression, growing out of tight money policies and cutbacks in federal spending, that was worsening as he entered the White House. Harding appointed three important progressives to his cabinet: Charles Evans Hughes to State, Henry C. Wallace to Agriculture, and Herbert Hoover to Commerce. Astute programs from these three helped him slowly to recreate confidence among businessmen. A President's Commission on Unemployment, called by Hoover, marked the first time in United States history that the federal government acted in a considerable way to curb hard times. Another innovation was the Sheppard-Towner Act of 1921, which offered federal funds for state programs in prenatal and child health. By the end of 1922 there was a consensus that good times for business lay ahead. The Fordney-McCumber Act of that year restored high tariffs. In his first two presidential years, Harding by his bland, reassuring manner gave the nation a respite from factional strife and a sense that old values were still alive.

But Harding's personal cronies brought his downfall. Secretary of the Interior Albert Fall accepted sizable loans from oilman Edward L. Doheny, who sought advantages in the stock market from leasing government oil lands in Elk Hills, California, and Teapot Dome, Wyoming. Fall eventually went to jail, but nothing was proven against Attorney General Harry Daugherty, who was also implicated. Beginning in 1923 there were suicides and resignations among Harding appointees below the cabinet level. Charles R. Forbes, head of the newly-formed Veterans' Bureau, made off with $250,000 and was sentenced to Leavenworth prison for two years. If Harding had not died of heart disease in August 1923, a death hastened perhaps by his knowledge of the impending scandals, he would have had a hard time winning reelection. Calvin Coolidge, the Vice President who succeeded to the presidency on Harding's death, muted the effect of the scandals by appointing an independent investigating committee under the chairmanship of a Democratic senator, Thomas J. Walsh.

The Teapot Dome and Elk Hills oil scandal rocked the Republican administration in 1924, resulting in the prosecution or resignation of several of Harding's appointees. *(Cartoon by Clifford Berryman, Courtesy, Library of Congress)*

A born compromiser, Harding had tried to maintain some moderation in his ideological position; Coolidge almost always sided with big business. He encouraged Secretary of the Treasury Andrew Mellon to reduce taxes, especially on the wealthy. Mellon, a wealthy industrialist from Pittsburgh, also worked to reduce both the national debt and government expenditures.

Conservative Coolidge   Coolidge slept a lot, suffered indigestion, and enjoyed his reputation for being the spare, laconic Yankee who took as his motto "Don't hurry to legislate." His ideal day, H. L. Mencken remarked, was one on which nothing whatever happened. He would not permit economic and social problems to intrude much on his equanimity or his moral sense. He honestly thought they would go away. Some did. Pungently honest, Coolidge was a good symbol of rectitude in an era that was experimenting with pleasure: a "Puritan in Babylon," he has been called.

The Coolidge era venerated business. People credited it with providing the appliances, radios, cars, electricity, and indoor plumbing that finally became commonplace in the decade. Coolidge asserted: "The man who builds a factory builds a temple . . . the man who works there, worships there." Bruce Barton, an advertising executive, compared Jesus Christ to a great business executive whose parables are effective advertisements. Jesus also embodied the ideal of public service. Business was, in fact, no longer publicly looking like the expression of ruthless and competitive forces that during the nineteenth century had not bothered to disguise their character. It was now articulating ideas of welfare capitalism that had been maturing for at least two decades. Large corporations began pension plans, profit sharing, and early forms of unemployment insurance, also providing their employees with such amenities as cafeterias. And in place of the power barons of nineteenth-century industry, business was now increasingly in the hands of managers whose importance signified the increased complexity of industrial, commercial, and economic processes.

The predominance of big business almost assured that its tradi-

At a press conference Coolidge once said:

"We have got so many regulatory laws already that in general I feel that we would be just as well off if we didn't have any more."

In this visual equivalent of later sound bite journalism, Coolidge epitomizes the traditional rural identification of the presidency. *(Courtesy, National Archives)*

John L. Lewis of the United Mine Workers gained his greatest prominence during the 1930s, but he ably fought for miners during the prosperity of the 1920s that they did not share. *(Courtesy, Library of Congress)*

tional opponent, organized labor, would suffer in the twenties. It did. Membership in the AFL declined sharply to a scant three million. The Railway Brotherhoods felt the sting of an unfriendly government: the Railway Labor Board approved a twelve percent reduction in the wages of railway shopmen, and Attorney General Daugherty ended the resulting strike with an injunction. Hardest hit of all were soft-coal miners. Highly competitive market conditions brought union-busting and bloodshed, particularly in the Appalachian South. The Jacksonville Agreement, engineered in 1924 by John L. Lewis of the miners and Secretary of Commerce Hoover, broke down after bringing a brief interlude of peace. The Supreme Court added its weight against labor in *Bailey v. Drexel Furniture Company* (1922), which declared unconstitutional a federal tax on products manufactured by children. The next year in *Adkins v. Children's Hospital* the Court decided against a District of Columbia law setting minimum wages for women.

Public finance also reflected the conservatism of Coolidge's administration. Secretary of the Treasury Andrew Mellon was convinced that fiscal responsibility on the part of the federal government would inspire business confidence and strengthen the economy, so he implemented budget cuts that by 1928 had created a net surplus of $8 billion. Mellon used the money to reduce the national debt. He believed that tax cuts on the rich would also benefit the economy, since the well-to-do would tend to reinvest the money. Congress in the 1920s passed special revenue acts that reduced corporate and personal income tax rates, gift taxes, inheritance taxes, and luxury excise taxes.

Farmers   In 1920 the government's wartime price support for farmers ended at the same moment the European market was shrinking. Large operators bought out small ones, and three million people left the farms between 1921 and 1928. Prices varied immensely from one crop to another. Wheat suffered precipitous price cycles and grave problems of surplus; tobacco and dairying flourished. Cattle and hog prices fluctuated. Shifts in consumption away from breads and toward dairy products and in international demand away from wheat and cotton in particular threatened special groups of farmers, as did severe droughts and flooding.

In the twenties one half of the farmers produced over ninety percent of the agricultural product. The lower half owned small farms, sometimes of submarginal land, or were tenants or sharecroppers. Many were deficient in skills and unable to adjust to new tools or changed demands of the market, while others simply could not afford such farm implements as tractors. The real bottom of agriculture, and a huge one, included black and white southern sharecroppers along with farm laborers and migratory workers. These forgotten Americans had no political power, and remained practically invisible.

All politically successful ideas for agriculture reform in the twenties promised one thing: higher prices. A number of laws designed to help agriculture passed Congress in the early twenties. They provided higher tariffs; more government credit; regulation of the grain exchanges, packers, and stockyards; and the freeing of farm cooperatives from prosecution under antitrust laws. Sweeping plans dominated the debates in the middle and late twenties, each conceptually subtle and mechanically complicated.

The most important scheme was for controlling the marketing of farm goods abroad. Its authors were George N. Peek and Hugh S. Johnson, two farm machinery industrialists of Moline, Illinois. In the form of several slightly divergent bills all called McNary-Haugen after congressional sponsors, this proposal remained before Congress from the mid-twenties to 1929. Two such bills survived both houses of Congress, only to be vetoed by President Coolidge. The McNary-Haugen bills provided for a government marketing corporation to purchase all surplus agricultural production in major crops at a high price. In its original form, the plan defined the price as being at "parity" with prewar prices. In compensation for losses the government might incur in selling its surpluses abroad, the processors were to pay the government an equalization fee making up the difference between the home price and the world price. Tariffs would protect the farmer against foreign competition. The artificially created scarcity at home would impose higher prices on consumers. The plan could have worked only in an expanding world market; in the existing, contracting one it would have forced retaliatory tariff action by foreign governments and added to inflation at home.

Herbert Hoover offered an alternative proposal: cooperative marketing. He wished not only to leave many managerial decisions to the farmers, but also to let the free market set prices. Yet Hoover wanted farmers to rationalize their production, and to control their marketing in behalf of both higher and more stable prices. He advocated government aid for large marketing cooperatives—similar to trade associations in other industries—made up in each case of farmers producing a given commodity. He hoped that a given cooperative could successfully recommend annual production quotas to individual farmers, make marketing agreements with purchasers, rationalize marketing by calculated storage and by better processing, and possibly even expand markets by advertising. In 1929 during Hoover's presidency Congress passed the Agricultural Marketing Act, which authorized a Federal Farm Board to implement it. The Board made loans to cooperatives. After the collapse of farm prices in 1930, stabilization corporations purchased to the limits of their funds in a vain attempt to hold up wheat and cotton prices. By 1932 they were broke. But as minor price-support programs they set a precedent for supports in the New Deal, and it is hard to say how effectively they would have worked in more prosperous times.

Power and Peace: Diplomacy 1921–1929

East Asian Problems The most vexing foreign problem for the new Republican administrations of the 1920s came in East Asia, where Japanese ambitions challenged both China's integrity and American security. The disruptions brought by the Bolshevik revolution had destroyed Russia's traditional check upon Japanese expansion, while world war weakened the area's major colonial powers, Britain, France, and the Netherlands. Japan's alliance with England forestalled unilateral action by the United States. In this favorable diplomatic circumstance, ministers around Japan's emperor began to fashion a sea-based empire in the western Pacific and dreamed of still grander glories on the mainland: dominion over the industrial heartland of East Asia, Manchuria, and the huge populations of central China.

Disarmament   Disarmament readily attracted the public imagination. In the aftermath of war, many people thought that weaponry itself created a climate for violence.

At the Washington Naval Conference of 1921–22 Secretary of State Charles Evans Hughes made skillful use of the political hunger for disarmament and created a temporary strategic balance in the Pacific. The conference produced three major agreements, each named after the number of countries participating in it. The Five-Power Pact embodied Hughes's proposal that the five great naval powers limit future building so as to preserve their battle fleets at a constant ratio of total tonnage: Britain and the United States, 525,000 tons each; Japan, 315,000 tons; France and Italy, 175,000 tons each. In the Four-Power Pact, Britain, France, Japan, and the United States each promised to respect the island possessions of the other signatories in the Pacific and to consult, presumably for joint action, in the event any outsiders challenged this status quo. The Nine-Power Pact, signed by all the major colonial powers in East Asia, pledged each to respect the principles of the Open Door in China, including that country's right to self-determination.

The three agreements distributed losses and gains. The United States won naval equality with Britain and formal recognition of the Open Door principles, but both Western powers had to agree not to fortify most of their island possessions in the west Pacific, effectively ceding to Japan naval superiority there. Britain jettisoned its centuries-old naval dominance but gained guaranteed security for its extensive Pacific possessions and escaped from any trouble its alliance with Japan, now formally abrogated, could have brought. The Japanese lost territorial prerogatives in China but won secure control over an island empire in the Pacific. A newspaper remarked that the secretary of state had "frozen over the Pacific."

Hughes also dealt with many diplomatic questions left over from war. Not until the end of 1921 did Secretary Hughes begin to answer letters from the League of Nation's headquarters in Geneva, Switzerland. Two years later he sent an American delegation to an opium conference sponsored by the League. His successors broadened this policy of joining in nonpolitical functions, and by 1932 the United States had participated in fifty such gatherings. The Senate in 1926 approved a treaty for United States membership in the World Court, a body that ruled in controversies disputing nations agreed to bring before it. But the Senate adopted reservations so sweeping that other members of the court refused to accept them.

At the beginning of his full presidential term, Calvin Coolidge appointed Frank Kellogg to replace the retiring Hughes. Kellogg deftly handled a tricky negotiation with his French counterpart, Aristide

Briand. Peace factions in the United States, long discontented at their country's cautious foreign policy, called on a willing Briand to publish an open letter on the tenth anniversary of the entry of the United States into World War I. The letter called for a Franco-American treaty between the two countries renouncing war. Kellogg, quickly realizing that the proposal would in fact bring the two nations close to a military alliance that he did not want, cleverly countered with an offer to all nations to join in "outlawing war forever." Some sixty-four powers in 1928 ultimately signed what became known as the Kellogg-Briand Pact, which deepened the illusion of international stability.

Latin America   Kellogg dealt less convincingly with difficulties in Nicaragua. Bickering over the presidency there descended into a fierce struggle, and Coolidge sent several thousand marines into the small country in 1926. Nicaragua under Augusto Sandino unsuccessfully waged against the invaders an armed resistance that left Sandino a national hero and martyr from whom the later Sandinistas took their name. When the puppet ruler supported by Coolidge's administration seemed more intent upon looting the public treasury than in building democracy, troops from the United States policed a national election. Then the marines trained a local militia, a job they did so well that after they left in 1933 its chief, the ruthless Anastasio Somoza, seized power.

The Republicans navigated an even stormier course in Mexico, where social revolution continued. A new constitution in 1917 had claimed all subsoil wealth as the property of Mexico's people. The secretary of state finally denounced Mexico as "a center of Bolshevik activity," but Coolidge sent to Mexico City Dwight Morrow, a friendly, skillful negotiator who restored a measure of amity between the two nations. Morrow's compromises postponed a clash between foreign oil and Mexican nationalism until the late 1930s, when Mexico seized all United States concessions with only modest compensation.

Coolidge and Kellogg moved generally toward greater neighborliness with Latin America. In 1924 the occupying troops sent by Washington left the Dominican Republic, though United States administrators supervised government finances there until 1940. The United States paid Colombia an indemnity of $25 million for its loss of Panama. Late in his term Coolidge asked J. Reuben Clark, an official in the State Department, to outline the precise limits of the Monroe Doctrine. His brief, published in 1930 as the Clark Memorandum, argued that "the Doctrine states a case of the United States versus Europe, not of the United States versus Latin America." This was a repudiation of Roosevelt's Corollary to the Monroe Doctrine, which had justified unilateral intervention in Latin American countries.

War Debts   High American tariffs blocked sales of many Euro-
and   pean goods and kept debtors from earning dollars,
Reparations   so what could they use to repay wartime era loans?
                    The Allies also argued that the money represented the contributions of the United States to the war effort and an unequal one at that: Americans had lost dollars, but Europeans lost millions of

lives and suffered frightful physical destruction. In any event, most of the money had been spent in the United States, where it stimulated industry and kept employment high. American Presidents and public opinion bluntly rejected pleas for cancellation. In Coolidge's famous remark, "They hired the money, didn't they?"

Worried by rumors of default, Congress early in 1922 created the World War Foreign Debt Commission, headed by Secretary of the Treasury Mellon, to negotiate specific repayment schedules. This group adjusted interest rates and other technical details to each debtor's capacity to repay. Most European leaders, privately supposing they could simply collect reparations required from Germany for the war and pass them along to the United States, went along with this proposal. Overall, the Debt Commission reduced by about half the combination of original debts and accrued interest.

Meanwhile, foreign officials together with private American bankers stabilized the German economy and set up a schedule of German reparations to European countries that were supposed to go in step with European war debt payments to the United States. In 1924, following the trying French occupation of the Ruhr Valley after a German default on reparations payments, Germany and its former enemies ratified the Dawes Plan. Germany pledged to put into reparations its profits from railroads and mines. British and American bankers promised loans to speed recovery in the Rhineland, the center of German industry. In late 1928, Germany and its creditors reorganized reparations again under the guidance of the banker and industrialist Owen D. Young. The Young Plan limited payments to the next fifty-nine years on a sliding scale determined by Germany's economic health. Nothing in this cluster of agreements shored up their rickety economic base. Reparations and war debts could be paid only if countries allowed an influx of foreign goods.

The Election of 1928

The Democratic Party, badly split between its rural and its urban component, went nowhere in the 1920s. At the famous 1924 Convention in New York City, delegates voted for 103 ballots before turning to a colorless compromise candidate, John W. Davis. Only a third party of progressives led by Senator Robert La Follette and supported by Debs and the Socialist Party gave ideological variety to the 1924 campaign; he won almost twenty percent of the vote, nearly as much as Davis.

Some three years later, at about noon on a showery day in South Dakota, August 2, 1927, thirty or so reporters in attendance on President Calvin Coolidge filed into the mathematics classroom of the Rapid City High School. Coolidge was already there, and when the door was closed he told the newsmen "the line forms on the left." As they passed by, the slight man from Vermont who had recently lost his son to sudden death handed each a slip of paper that read: "I do not choose to run for President in nineteen twenty-eight." The country by and large accepted the statement at face value, and Secretary of Commerce

Herbert Hoover came correctly to mind as the likely Republican presidential nominee in 1928.

Al Smith   The more familiar story of the 1928 campaign concerns Governor Alfred E. Smith of New York, the unsuccessful Democratic nominee. Born on New York's lower East Side, Al Smith was a faithful Roman Catholic, a practicing opponent of prohibition, and a product of New York City's Tammany Hall. In the thinking of many Americans, a more threatening combination could not be imagined. Smith's presence on the ticket sparked the worst bigotry in any recent presidential campaign, especially but not exclusively in the South.

Smith, an amateur and a provincial in national politics, was not entirely without responsibility for the manner in which the issue of religion became inflamed. He displayed his Catholicism in ways that were irrelevant to the core of his faith but could offend Protestant sensibilities. He was public in his Catholicism: he kept an autographed picture of the Pope in his Albany office, publicly kissed the ring of a visiting papal prelate, and received words of political encouragement from the pope himself by way of his talkative wife, who visited Rome in 1925. Smith, moreover, drank and served liquor in the Albany executive mansion during prohibition. When the governor appointed as his presidential campaign manager John J. Raskob, an outspoken anti-prohibitionist closely identified with the Catholic church, many Americans assumed that he wished to flaunt what was most controversial about his candidacy. The next Catholic presidential candidate, John F. Kennedy in 1960 would be at once more open and more reassuring in addressing the religious issue.

Herbert Clark Hoover had none of Smith's disadvantages and a large career already behind him: a Quaker orphan who had made himself into a millionaire working on the frontiers of five continents, a supplier of relief to Belgium and later to much of Europe and the

Al Smith, Catholic and anti-prohibitionist, many perceived as the candidate of New York City and the corrupt political machine, Tammany Hall. *(Cartoon by Gale, August 31, 1928. Courtesy, the* Los Angeles Times*)*

One voter complained to Franklin D. Roosevelt, who had made a nominating speech for Al Smith at the Democratic Convention:

"Birds of a feather flock together, and if you uphold Smith and help him get in it is obvious you are in Tammany's pay. Of course he may be better than the ordinary man but Tammany has not become honest.... Everyone knows that Tammany uses Public School surplus to supply parochial schools so god knows what they will do when he gets to be President.... If you ever heard the Knights of Columbus oath I am sure you a Protestant would be through with [Roman Catholics]. They say it is all right to steal or cut out the bellies (the exact words used) of Protestants.... Why people are saying that he will make us have war with Mexico and he will so he can kill off some Protestants.... We can't trust them, don't you know that their church and the Pope come first, and they will be subject as it was to them first, and to America and her ideals second.... You ought to know the corruption there is in New York with Smith having a private telegraph wire to Tammany Hall, so of course he'll have a private wire to Tammany if he is made President.... An eyewitness saw him carried on the train dead drunk after his mother's funeral. He'd make a fine President, getting the Protestants drunk like he did when he was speaker or leader of the floor, in Albany, just so they would vote his way. And everyone knows his sons had to get married. And what kind of a woman would that be in the White House? Some difference from Mrs. Coolidge, who is educated and refined, and cultured. Mrs. Smith's father was a saloon keeper, and kept Prostitute Houses and yet you'd help those kind of people get in. Well, all I can say is God help you and all of us, if they do get in."

Hoover worried about "the exaggerated idea the people have conceived of me. . . . if some unprecedented calamity should come upon the nation, I would be sacrificed. . . ."

Soviet Union. During the twenties Hoover had converted his commerce department into an instrument for promoting a free-flowing international trade intended to replace the relationships of force and war. It was also a center of communication among manufacturers, and a purveyor of a concept of socially responsible business self-regulation in the public interest. Hoover was the Great Engineer and the Great Humanitarian. In an era of prosperity the nominee of the party in power would undoubtedly win by a wide margin—and he did. With his Middle American background and his success in technology, Hoover was an agreeable blend of tradition and progress. People expected much of him: "He sweeps the horizon of every subject. Nothing escapes his view," a delegate had observed.

Hoover and the Great Depression

For many years before Herbert Hoover became President, he had been warning against the "crazy and dangerous" stock market, while President Calvin Coolidge to the contrary told press conferences that stock prices were not high enough. As Hoover feared, much was wrong with the American economy. While it resisted inflationary temptations and increased the real income of all classes, a larger proportion of the new wealth went into the hands of the very rich. When the stock market ended its dazzling ascent and slumped downward, vast quantities of consumer goods now beyond the purchasing power of average householders quickly piled up in warehouses and factories.

Causes   Was the Great Depression a crisis in confidence as Hoover grimly assumed and as a modern school of economists argues? Was the chief cause the weak banking system, another culprit that Hoover singled out? Did a shrinking in the supply of money in circulation cause the Depression? Or as John Kenneth Galbraith suggests in his witty account *The Great Crash*—a book rarely to be found in airport terminals—was the market crash an intricate effect and cause of economic instability? These explanations need not be in conflict with one another. Confidence did collapse and banks did fail and the money supply did shrivel as the stock market crumbled. The probable effect of each of these conditions was to accelerate the others. And together they worsened the Depression. But the illness of the economy did not begin with the Wall Street crash of 1929.

A host of new consumer goods industries emerging or expanding during the decade had run into problems of overproduction well before the stock market crashed. Vacuum cleaners, linoleum, and washing machines eased the lives of homemakers; the automobile quickened the mobility of people and objects; and radios bolstered communications and recreation. Autos and movies had been around since early in the century, and telephones even longer; but now they were far more widely accessible. These products, in turn, stimulated such producer goods industries as steel, rubber, oil, glass and textiles, as well as government building of highways and airports. But this economic growth fed on paying in installments for the more expensive of the new

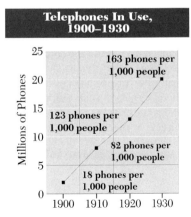

The telephone changed business and social life and even dating customs for the middle class.

household products. As people went more deeply into debt, they could not continue to purchase; and by the later 1920s, many who could afford durable consumer goods already had them. The postwar consumer spree began to level off. Yet many durable goods producers were basing their production projections on their previously escalating sales. As purchasing leveled in the period from 1925 to 1929, these industries soon found themselves overproducing. A recession began, with the resultant layoffs and further drops in consumption. Some 5,000 banks failed before 1929.

These events not only preceded the stock market crash but helped cause it. Speculation in stock prices had begun in the mid-1920s on the solid basis of profits and the stock dividends that companies paid to investors. But in time it turned to sheer gambling. People bought stocks at high prices on the assumption that everyone else would then want to buy them at higher prices on the guess that still others would thereupon be happy to buy them at still higher prices. To raise the money for purchase of stocks, people bought on margin: paying in cash as little as ten percent of the price of a stock and being indebted for the rest. Businessmen, finding few profits in expanding production, flooded their wealth onto the market, and this drew money away from investment in the fundamental production that constitutes the health of an economy.

Motor Vehicle Registration, 1900–1930	
Year	Motor Vehicle Registration
1900	8,000
1905	78,800
1910	468,500
1915	2,490,000
1920	9,239,100
1925	20,068,500
1930	26,749,860

The Course of Decline After serious collapses in late October 1929, the stock market staged a recovery, particularly early in 1930. Not until mid-1930 did stock prices fall steadily, week by week, until their low point in 1933. Employment began to drift downward in 1930 and reached very serious proportions in the winter of 1930–31; by 1933 almost one quarter of the labor force was without work.

In 1930, meanwhile, President Hoover had signed a staggeringly high tariff in order to repay a campaign promise to farmers. The Hawley-Smoot tariff raised to well over fifty percent tariff rates that the Fordney-McCumber schedules had already put at more than thirty-eight percent. This unilateral American protectionism stunned Europe. Already pressed by the drying up of American loans following the Wall Street crash, Europeans found themselves unable to sell in the American market. Their retaliatory tariffs damaged American exports, especially farm products. Europe and the United States were stifling international trade and further battering productive industries already badly pounded. The inability of Europeans to sell on the American market also deprived them of the funds to pay debts to both European and American banks, including loans that American institutions had made to the Allies during the world war. When Austria's largest bank, itself indebted to American banks, folded in the spring of 1931, Hoover got a one-year agreement on both sides of the Atlantic for a moratorium on all war debts and on reparations payments by Germany. The moratorium became permanent, and had the effect of nearly complete defaults. Five thousand American banks closed their doors between 1929 and 1932.

Hoover was more willing and quicker than most politicians, in-

Though Herbert Hoover made sincere efforts to end the Depression, his opposition to direct federal relief programs convinced the voters that he was insensitive to their suffering. In 1932, they sent him fishing.
(Courtesy, National Archives)

A popular song, "Brother, Can You Spare a Dime," carried the lament of a World War I veteran:

Once I built a railroad, made it to run,
Made it race against time.
Once I built a railroad, now it's done—
Brother, can you spare a dime?

Once in khaki suits,
Gee, we looked swell,
Full of that Yankee Doodle-de-dum.
Half a million boots were sloggin'
    through Hell,
And I was the kid with the drum.

Say, don't you remember, they called
    me Al—
It was Al all the time.
Say don't you remember I'm your pal—
Buddy, can you spare a dime?

cluding the Democratic Congress that met in 1931, to use the government to cushion the fall. Right after the crash he urged business to maintain wages. He increased spending for public works at all levels of government. Within the limits of economic solutions then entertained by leading economists Hoover moved swiftly; but he refused to step outside these boundaries. And as chief executive at the outset of the Great Depression, Hoover could hardly present himself as the solution to it. This shy President, who knew the importance of confidence, could not bring himself to manufacture it.

Hoover's opposition to direct federal relief programs furnishes our worst memory of him. He accused progressive senators of "playing politics at the expense of human misery" by recommending expensive relief programs, and he hinted darkly at the evils of the public dole as practiced in Great Britain. In fact, it was some of the best things in Hoover's past that stood in his way. His relief projects in the era of World War I had trained him to believe that people voluntarily contribute their money and time, that good will and expert knowledge could solve the most enormous problems of logistics and supply. He feared hordes of government subsidy seekers, who would indeed crawl out of the woodwork in years to come. He believed that more fortunate Americans would come to their neighbors' aid. Not selfishness or indifference but a misplaced faith in public generosity kept Hoover from engaging in the more extensive programs of relief that were in fact necessary.

Reconstruction Finance Corporation Hoover set up government agencies to encourage and coordinate private and local relief efforts. His main measures to combat the Depression were the Agricultural Marketing Act, the Reconstruction Finance Corporation, and the Federal Home Loan Bank Act.

The agricultural legislation, which was passed in the spring of 1929, was not intended for relief. Once the Depression began, however, the fund was used to stabilize the market, and it had the helpful effect of slowing the descent of farm prices. It was, in effect, largely a relief agency.

The Reconstruction Finance Corporation had a grander vision. Adopted late in 1931 after a similar private scheme had failed and patterned after the War Finance Corporation that had made loans to industries during World War I, the RFC could loan up to $2 billion to banks and other agencies. For once, Hoover had overcome his fear of the duplication, slowness, and wastefulness of bureaucracy. But he worried that business interests would wish to manipulate it. Under Hoover, in 1932, the RFC began to loan substantial sums to the states for relief, loans he knew would never be repaid.

To lessen what was fast becoming a catastrophic unemployment problem in the construction industry, Hoover had Congress pass in July 1932 the Federal Home Loan Bank Act. It created a system of federal home loan banks to discount home mortgages. The Federal Home Loan Banks received $125 million in capital to discount the home mortgages of building and loan associations, insurance companies, and savings banks. Hoover believed that the ability of private lending institutions to secure new sources of capital would encourage them to make more construction loans and revive the industry. But it had little effect.

Hoover was not the grumbling reactionary that New Dealers later portrayed. Depression forced him to abandon a host of reforms that he had planned to pass into law. One radical piece of legislation that he did achieve was a steeply graduated income tax. Many of Hoover's programs, such as the RFC, anticipated the New Deal, though Roosevelt was to go much farther. Hoover gave private enterprise a chance to cure the Depression, and its timidity and self-protectiveness in the face of the crisis revealed that the government was going to have to take the initiative. By 1932 the election of a Democrat was inevitable.

Depression Diplomacy: Hoover and the World 1929–1933

As international problems became more complex, the American people turned inward, preoccupied by greater worries of their own. President Hoover dreamed of further disarmament, economic collaboration, conciliation in Latin America, even modest collective security efforts. Yet obstinate Congresses and the Depression stymied Hoover's internationalism. The times and the man were uniquely mismatched.

An Economic House of Cards
During 1930 and the first half of 1931, the international economy collapsed. National banks in central Europe had borrowed funds from private banks in New York and London to relend to domestic businesses. As depression ruined sales both at home and abroad, the German and Austrian central banks discovered that on many of their loans they could collect neither interest nor principal. Scared by the prospect of financial collapse, foreign investors sold property and securities. Others frantically tried to exchange paper marks for gold or other currencies that popular mythology conceived as being solid. These pressures forced Germany to default on all its loans, public and private, and to abandon the gold standard—meaning that holders of German marks could no longer exchange them for gold—during the summer of 1931. Many British banks had invested heavily in high-risk, high-yield German ventures that now were worthless. Depositors rushed to withdraw their money from London banks, and soon Britain too had left the gold standard. Prime Minister J. Ramsay MacDonald decided to devalue the pound—to reduce its worth compared to that of other currencies. This made British goods cheaper in foreign currencies and stole markets from other countries still burdened by expensive gold currencies.

Hoover believed in a sound currency in which paper money was solidly backed by gold reserves. Britain's aggressive, unorthodox use of monetary devices frightened him into financial alliance with the only other major gold power, France. During talks with French Premier Pierre Laval in October 1931, Hoover secured a pledge from the Bank of France to support the dollar with its own gold. In return, the

President had hinted that he might cancel war debts entirely if the Allies canceled German reparations. This arrangement temporarily strengthened the dollar. And the Allies soon gathered at Lausanne, Switzerland, where they pared German reparations to a token $700 million. This chain of events embarrassed both Hoover and Roosevelt, now in the midst of a presidential campaign. Both men realized that canceling German reparations and Allied debts was economic good sense, but both appreciated equally the political folly of saying so. Even after the election they shied away from decisive action, so all the nation's debtors except Finland defaulted during 1933.

The Hoover Doctrine   Economic crisis also upset the delicate naval and political balance in East Asia. On September 18, 1931, Japanese armies in Manchuria, stationed there to guard the strategic South Manchurian Railway owned by Japan, attacked around Mukden and soon routed the Chinese. This early triumph emboldened local commanders to begin a systematic conquest of all Manchuria. Victory there, they hoped, would discredit moderate leaders at home and commit Japan to armed expansion in China proper. Early in 1932, aircraft bombed villages and raided China's largest city, Shanghai. All Manchuria fell to the invaders that spring, when a puppet ruler signed a protective alliance with Japan. Its generals next assaulted the provinces of north China. Chiang Kai-shek, the leader of the ruling Nationalist Party, could not stop the Japanese advance. A weak political base and a persistent Communist rebellion led by Mao Zedong inhibited Chiang's ability to resist. He turned to the United States and the League of Nations for help.

Peace machinery clanked slowly into motion. Faced with the first serious challenge to collective security, the League dispatched a fact-finding group to Manchuria under Lord Lytton. While its members tramped over rough terrain and interviewed village elders, Britain's foreign secretary, Sir John Simon, endeavored to put pressure on Japan. France and Italy nervously offered token help; Simon did not even ask Germany and the Soviet Union. The issue became starkly simple: would the United States and Great Britain in defense of the Nine-Power Pact and the principle of collective security risk war with Japan? Secretary of State Stimson hinted that the answer might be "yes," but Hoover overruled him. Hoover politely declined Simon's idea, taking up instead the device of refusing to recognize the Manchurian regime installed by Japan. Stimson notified the signatories of the Nine-Power Pact only that the United States "can not admit the legality of conquests in violation of treaty commitments." Most other countries rallied to this Hoover-Stimson Doctrine. Late in 1932, the Lytton Commission Report found Japan guilty of aggression; the League of Nations formally condemned Japan; Japanese delegates left Geneva. But wrist-slapping did not halt Japan's aggression against China. The situation illustrated what many years later the United Nations would demonstrate: whatever may be the status of international agreements, countries in the absence of self-interest will not often take decisive action against aggression. Maneuverings and plots continued intermittently until 1937, when a local skirmish near Peking grew into a full-scale war of conquest.

An American teacher in Shanghai wrote in a letter on January 29, 1932:

"Today the Japanese have been bombing Shanghai. We're getting our first sample of what war on populations can mean,—non-combatants blown up by bombs, shot down in the street, or burned alive in the great fires the battle has set. These may destroy the city before they can be checked. What part will be taken by Americans and British is uncertain. Eventually these events of the last week or so will lead to war,—if not this year, then in ten years, or twenty. When I was a college student writing orations, I thought we should soon come to permanent peace. Now I know we won't, in my lifetime."

Hoover's secretary of state, Henry L. Stimson, wrote an identical note to Japan and China pointedly referring to Japanese aggression in Manchuria.

"[The United States] does not intend to recognize any situation, treaty, or agreement which may be brought about by means contrary to the covenants and obligations of the Pact of Paris [the Kellogg-Briand Peace Pact of 1928]."

Good intentions led Hoover into ineffective efforts at disarmament. Early in his term, he invited British Prime Minister MacDonald to Washington for wide-ranging talks that soon began to look like an Anglo-American effort to settle the world's major problems. As they sat on a log near a stream at Hoover's private retreat in the hills of northern Virginia, the two rhapsodized about peace and disarmament. They agreed on details for another naval limitations conference to be held in London during 1930. That meeting granted ocean tonnage parity to the United States for all classes of ships, long an American objective, but isolationist senators worried that secret clauses might ally the country with England. They demanded all documents pertaining to the negotiations. Hoover refused, citing executive privilege.

The Senate eventually ratified the work of the London Naval Conference, but the new treaty was far less effective than its predecessors. France and Italy did not join, and an escalator clause allowed building past agreed limits under certain circumstances. Japan did sign, but in Tokyo the ratification fight was so bitter it was only a matter of time before that country pulled out of the agreement. The signatories altogether ignored enforcement measures.

Suggested Readings

Newer books on the era include Paul K. Conkin, *The Southern Agrarians* (1988), Nancy Cott, *The Grounding of Modern Feminism* (1987), Carole Marris, *Farewell—We're Good and Gone: The Great Black Migration* (1989), Michael C. C. Adams, *The Great Adventure: Male Desire and the Coming of World War I* (1990), Cary D. Wintz, *Black Culture and the Harlem Renaissance* (1988), and Lloyd Ambrosius, *Woodrow Wilson and the American Diplomatic Tradition: The Treaty Fight in Perspective* (1987).

On the Versailles Treaty, see Charles L. Mee, Jr., *The End of Order: Versailles 1919* (1980). Ralph A. Stone, in *The Irreconcilables: The Fight Against the League of Nations* (1970), investigates the reasons that motivated each of the sixteen senators who refused to ratify the treaty. Woodrow Wilson's vision is presented in Arthur S. Link, *Woodrow Wilson: Revolution, War, and Peace* (1979) and N. Gordon Levin, *Woodrow Wilson and World Politics* (1968). See also Link's multivolume biography, *Wilson* (1947–).

A good general survey of the twenties is William E. Leuchtenburg, *The Perils of Prosperity, 1914–1932* (1958). David Burner has written two books on the era's politics: *The Politics of Provincialism: The Democratic Party in Transition, 1918–1932* (1968) and *Herbert Hoover: A Public Life* (1979). Francis Russell's *The Shadow of Blooming Grove: Warren G. Harding in His Times* (1968) and Donald R. McCoy's *Calvin Coolidge: The Silent President* (1967) each to some extent rehabilitates the reputation of its subject.

On the importance of the automobile, see J. B. Rae, *The Road and the Car in American Life* (1971) and James J. Flink, *The Car Culture* (1975). For the literature of the era, see Alfred Kazin, *On Native Grounds* (1942) and F. J. Hoffman, *The Twenties* (1955). Nathan J. Huggins portrays *The Harlem Renaissance* (1972), as does David Levering Lewis, *When Harlem Was in Vogue* (1981). Mark Schorer's *Sinclair Lewis* (1961) is definitive. Other studies of twenties literary figures include Carlos H. Baker, *Ernest Hemingway: A Life Story* (1969) and Henry D. Piper, *F. Scott Fitzgerald: A Critical Portrait* (1972). Robert Sklar, *Movie-Made America* (1975) and Lary May, *Screening Out the Past* (1980) discuss the rise of motion pictures.

Other important books include James R. Grossman, *Land of Hope: Chicago, Black Southerners, and the Great Migration* (1989), Robert Strauss Feuerlicht, *Justice Confirmed* (1977), Ellis Hawley. *Tthe Great War and the Search for a Modern Order, 1917–1933* (1979), David Montgomery, *The Fall of the House of Labor* (1982), Emily Rosenberg, *Spreading the American Dream* (1982), Neil Gabler, *An Empire of Their Own: How the Jews Invented Hollywood* (1988), Philip Rosen, *The Modern Stentors: Radio Broadcasting and the Federal Government, 1920–1933* (1980), Beth L. Barley, *From Back Porch to Back Seat* (1988), and Lizabeth Cohen, *Making a New Deal: Industrial Workers in Chicago, 1919–1939* (1990).

Wilsonian Internationalism: Curse or Blessing?

Thomas J. Knock

Thus, on the evening of April 2, 1917, Wilson asked Congress to recognize that a state of war existed between their country and the German empire. . . .

After outlining the measures necessary for getting the country's war effort underway, he turned to more transcendent matters. His thoughts, he said, were still the same as when he had addressed the Senate on January 22: "Our object now, as then, is to vindicate the principles of peace and justice in the life of the world as against selfish and autocratic power and set up amongst the really free and self-governed peoples of the world such a concert of purpose and of action as will henceforth insure the observance of those principles." Yet he emphasized several times, in all of this, the United States had no quarrel with the German people themselves; it was not they, but their military masters, who had brought on the war. "A steadfast concert of peace can never be maintained except by a partnership of democratic nations. No autocratic government could be trusted to keep faith within it or observe its covenants."

He continued: "The world must be made safe for democracy. Its peace must be planted upon the tested foundations of political liberty. We have no selfish ends to serve. We desire no conquest, no dominion. We seek no indemnities for ourselves, no material compensation for the sacrifices we shall freely make. We are but one of the champions of the rights of mankind. We shall be satisfied when those rights have been made as secure as the faith and the freedom of nations can make them."

Then in words that one observer compared to Shakespeare's for their rhetorical grace and power, Wilson compressed into a final peroration his vision of the American historical mission, in all its arrogance and innocence—a summons to the New World to return to the Old to vindicate the creed for which it had broken away a hundred and forty years before:

"It is a distressing and oppressive duty, Gentlemen of the Congress, which I have performed in thus addressing you. There are, it may be, many months of fiery trial and sacrifice ahead of us. It is a fearful thing to lead this great peaceful people into war, into the most terrible and disastrous of all wars, civilization itself seeming to be in the balance. But the right is more precious than peace, and we shall fight for the things which we have always carried nearest our hearts—for democracy, for the right of those who submit to authority to have a voice in their own governments, for the rights and liberties of small nations, for a universal dominion of right by such a concert of free peoples as shall bring peace and safety to all nations and make the world itself at last free. To such a task we can dedicate our lives and our fortunes, everything that we are and everything that we have, with the pride of those who know that the day has come when America is privileged to spend her blood and her might for the principles that gave her birth and happiness and the peace which she has treasured. God helping her, she can do no other."

Of all the outpouring of public commentary, none better captured the thoughts and emotions of Wilson's admirers and critics at that moment than the *New Republic,* "Our debt and the world's debt to Woodrow Wilson is immeasurable," the editors wrote. "Only a statesman who will be called great could have made American intervention mean so much to the generous forces of the world, could have lifted the inevitable horror of war into a deed so full of meaning. . . . Through the force of circumstance and through his own genius he has made it a practical possibility that he is to be the first great statesman to begin the better organization of the world."

Reprinted from Thomas J. Knock, *To End All Wars: Woodrow Wilson and the Quest for a New World Order* (New York: Oxford University Press, 1992).

Only after much soul-searching did Woodrow Wilson call Congress into special session on April 2, 1917, to hear his message of war. What he was asking contradicted much that he stood for. In his May 1914 address to the same body he had recalled George Washington's advice to avoid entangling alliances. That summer of 1914 the European war broke out. For a time, Wilson tried to keep his country out of it. The ideals of the Founding Fathers afforded him—and more particularly the isolationists who warned more strongly than he against siding with the Allies—a solid ground on which to base their argument. Isolationists wanted the United States to remain aloof from the rest of the world, or at least from the corruption that they associated with reactionary and imperialist European regimes. But events pressed Wilson—or, so historians hostile to him would argue, he pressed events—to so angry a confrontation with Germany that by April 1917 he saw no way out of entering the war. His decision probably stemmed from his increasing recognition of the significance of European power relationships to American security. He was never convinced, even after the April 2 speech, that war was the answer. He had become certain, however, that it was inescapable. To salvage the situation, he set out to convert the savage bloodletting into a crusade to make the world safe for democracy. War, in Wilson's thinking, was to be justified now for its moral result.

Throughout the twentieth century, isolationism would continue to attract many Americans. In its later forms, isolationism has gotten a bad reputation, and that is in good part the fault of isolationists themselves. Hostility to impoverished immigrants, hostility to foreign aid aimed at relieving suffering abroad, surliness toward any possibility of intervention that might ease the lot of other peoples but at some expense to the United States: these have been more recent isolationist postures.

That mentality is not to be confused with that of the isolationists who tried to prevent our country's entrance into the First World War. Progressive isolationists who opposed Wilson did not have the antagonism to foreigners displayed by later advocates of staying within our own borders. Nor did they adopt for domestic issues the right-wing Republican economics favored by late twentieth-century isolationists, an economics designed to protect the wealth of the wealthy. To the contrary, progressive isolationists of the time of the First World War wished to put government actively to nourishing the well-being of the people and to strengthening the institutions of democracy. It was not, they believed, in siding with capitalist and imperialist Britain against capitalist and imperialist Germany that the United States could make its contribution to the world. Our best course instead was to serve as a peaceful example of social and political democracy.

The words of President Wilson's war address to Congress are indeed powerful and sincere. But their warning of "civilization . . . in the balance," its fate hanging on the outcome of the conflict, belongs to the inflated and self-delusionary mind that comes with all wars. In the hands of early twentieth-century Germany and Austria-Hungary, civilization would have continued to do quite nicely. In the United States, the Wilson administration in time of war was conducting perhaps the most extensive repression in the nation's history. Civilization was not the winner. Wilson's prose, his driven conscience, and his capacity for generous vision deserved a better cause than that to which he had committed his country.

The Bonus Marchers of 1932. *(Courtesy, Library of Congress)*

The New Deal

THE BONUS ARMY OF 1932

In the spring of 1932 few newspaper readers paid much attention to reports that some 300 unemployed First World War veterans were traveling in Union Pacific freight cars rocking and swaying over the Rockies from Portland, Oregon, to Pocatello, Idaho. Some of them accompanied by their families, they were headed for Washington, D.C., to persuade Congress to approve early payment of a soldier's bonus not scheduled for distribution until 1945.

Congress had ignored their pleas. Now the Bonus Army picked up fresh recruits at almost every city, and finally became national news when the B & O Railroad tried to stop it in the "Battle of East Saint Louis." Local railroad union leaders averted bloodshed by moving truckloads of men, women, and children across Illinois to the Indiana border. Then each state governor hurried the band as swiftly as possible across his territory, and so the travelers crossed Indiana, Ohio, Pennsylvania, and Maryland until they reached the District of Columbia. There they met other veterans from every state in the Union, a total of more than 20,000 people.

President Herbert Hoover allowed the veterans to settle in abandoned buildings, and on the largest site, Anacostia Flats. He quietly provided them with army food, clothing, beds, tents, and medical supplies—characteristically keeping secret his humanitarian acts.

Like Hoover, Governor Franklin D. Roosevelt of New York disapproved early payment of the bonus. He offered his state's veterans both transportation home and guaranteed employment.

HISTORICAL EVENTS

1930s
The Great Depression • radio shows, movies, and games help keep spirits up

1932
Bonus Army riot • Franklin Roosevelt elected President

1933
Banking system collapses • The Hundred Days (March 4 to mid-June) • Emergency Banking Relief Act • Glass-Steagall Act creates Federal Deposit Insurance Corporation (FDIC) • Home Owners Refinancing Act • Civilian Conservation Corps (CCC)• Federal Emergency Relief Administration (FERA) formed • Civil Works Administration (CWA) • Agricultural Adjustment Administration (AAA) • Farm Credit Act • Tennessee Valley Authority (TVA) • National Recovery Administration (NRA)

1934
National Housing Act establishes the Federal Housing Administration (FHA) • Bankhead Cotton Control Act of 1934 • Tobacco Control Act of 1934 • Securities and Exchange Commission (SEC) • Federal Communications Commission (FCC) • Upton Sinclair runs for governor of California

continued

While the bonus bill passed the House on June 5, 1932, two days later the Senate defeated it. Hoover thereupon initiated federal loans to provide transportation home to any veteran who applied. But 10,000 stayed on, waiting for something to happen.

On July 9 some 250 Californians arrived, led by a navy veteran, Roy W. Robertson, who camped out with his men on the Capitol lawn. While in the service Robertson had broken his neck falling out of a hammock. Wearing a brace supported by a tall steel column rising almost a foot above his shoulders, he gave the eerie impression of a man with his head perpetually in a noose. For three days and four nights his men took turns slowly walking single file in a "Death March" vigil around the Capitol building. His head held high in the rigid brace, Robertson was a study in determination. While fellow veterans occupied the building's steps, Congress adjourned and its members escaped by subterranean passageways.

Army Chief of Staff General Douglas MacArthur stood ready for trouble with a sizable regular army force. The moment came when the administration on July 28 forced the eviction of veterans from a small downtown area of government buildings scheduled for demolition. A riot ensued between a gathering of as many as 5,000 veterans and fewer than 800 police. One veteran was dead; another lay fatally wounded.

MacArthur ordered his troops to assemble at the Ellipse behind the White House. Hoover specifically directed MacArthur only to move the rioting veterans out of the business district and back to their camps. But MacArthur saw "revolution in the air." Ignoring the President's orders, he sent his troops across the bridge into the Anacostia Flats. The whole Anacostia camp became ablaze with light: setting fire to their own huts was the veterans' final symbolic act of defiance. A young military aide,

General Douglas MacArthur disobeyed President Hoover's orders and engineered a confrontation that ended in the burning of the Bonus Army shacks in the muddy Anacostia Flats. *(Courtesy, National Archives)*

Dwight D. Eisenhower, saw "a pitiful scene, those ragged, discouraged people burning their own little things." Soldiers fired the remaining empty huts. Fleeing the capital, the veterans became refugees from a government more immobile than heartless, more ignorant than cruel. Hoover, the great humanitarian who had fed the starving Belgians during World War I, received all the blame in the election—and Depression—year of 1932. The incident helped assure an overwhelming victory for the Democratic candidate, Franklin Roosevelt, in the presidential contest that year.

Down and Out in the Land of Opportunity

On the Road   Many people, in this time still remembered as that of the Great Depression, tried to escape an unpromising future. Americans moved about in numbers that recall the days of the frontier. In the course of the decade the rural populace declined by more than a fifth; by 1940 about sixty percent of the people lived in urban areas. Drought and a slump in commodity prices prodded many midwesterners toward California or into middle-sized towns. Whole families, unable to find work or to continue paying rent or the mortgage, piled into the old car and took to the highway, bewildered driftwood carried from town to town by a tide of unemployment. Migratory workers usually moved with the seasons, but some simply rushed into regions where rumor pointed to jobs. For nearly a sixth of the population, depression meant permanent emigration, always leaving someplace, never really going anywhere. Perhaps as many as five million people became vagrants, perpetually unemployed, perpetually hounded out of towns. These hoboes gathered together in camps remote from state troopers. "It's the big trouble," a young girl explained. "That's why I'm on the rails." Nearly two million youngsters like her understood the slang: depression had turned them into twentieth-century nomads riding steel trails. The Union Pacific Railroad reported in 1933 that freight cars had killed hundreds of boys and girls.

Pictures of poor farm workers Dorothea Lange or Walker Evans photographed impart something of what poverty did to people. Hard times lashed out first at the unskilled, those with the least resources to tide them over. Some areas suffered more than others: the southern Appalachians with its depleted mines; the Great Plains made barren by wind erosion and drought; the old southern cotton belt with too many people on too little good land. Grayness and worry settled over the poor and the lower middle class.

Family Tensions   Loss of employment, or the threat of it, altered the fundamental form of the nuclear family. The equation of home and family diminished when banks foreclosed mortgages. Parents became so discouraged that between 1935 and 1940 the number of new babies fell below the rate of zero

A pair of hoboes walking the rails.
(Courtesy, Scribner's Archives)

Joe Morrison, a coal miner, described riding the rails:

"In '30 and '31 you'd see freight trains, you'd see hundreds of kids, young kids, lots of 'em, just wandering all over the country. Looking for jobs, looking for excitement. . . . That one thing that was unique was to see women riding freight trains. That was unheard of, never had been thought of before. But it happened during the Depression. Women gettin' places by ridin' freight trains. Dressed in slacks or dressed like men, you could hardly tell 'em. Sometimes some man and his wife would get on, no money for fare.

You'd find political discussions going on in a boxcar. Ridin' a hundred miles or so, guys were all strangers, maybe two or three knew each other, pairs. There might be twenty men involved. They would discuss politics, what was happening. What should be done about this, that and so forth."

In the cities, unemployed workers selling apples on street corners became an all-too-common sight. *(Courtesy, AP/Wide World Photos)*

population growth. Young couples postponed children until times should improve, and the number of marriages decreased by nearly one fourth. Only because of a drop in the death rate to eleven per thousand—boosting life expectancy to sixty-three years—did the population increase as much as seven percent in the course of the decade. Evidence exists that the scarcity of food, which for most people did not become so acute as it is in the world's most impoverished regions, was a factor in the cut in the death rate within a population that even then had inclined to overweight. The number of divorces dropped sharply, perhaps because legal costs, child support, and alimony were beyond the reach of so many people. Still, there were instances of starvation, and public health standards declined.

The Depression burdened family life in less tangible ways. Across the country, indigent relatives moved in with more fortunate aunts or brothers or cousins. Generations crowded in on one another, grandmothers and mothers arguing over how to raise children or run the household. Youngsters were suddenly confronted with orders from many adults, not just two. Most available jobs for men went to unskilled laborers at low wages; railroads, for example, paid only $10 a week for work on road gangs. As a result, many fathers sat at home, losing their traditional authority over the family while their sons worked.

During the Depression, dominant American values strongly opposed married women's participation in the labor force at a period in which so many male heads of families were without jobs. But by the 1930s, middle-class American families also had developed a strong consumer ethos—a belief that the constant purchase of goods is a mark of worth—that in some instances made a married woman's extra income appear indispensable to the well-being and standard of living of the family. These attitudes did not present married women's work as good in itself, nor did they result in campaigns for equal pay for women. But they expanded the notion of woman's role to include bringing in enough extra money so that the family could afford a car, college for children, and small luxuries that were increasingly being redefined as needs. Under these conditions, many middle-class women remained in the labor force during the Depression, normally in jobs that had already been defined as female, but many of them in jobs that had previously belonged to lower-class or black or Hispanic women. There was a general tendency for white women to push other women out of the labor market. In addition, the labor of women of all classes, especially their unpaid labor in the home, more and more became crucial to the very survival of their families. Women made small budgets stretch further by making things that they had previously bought: food, clothing, home furnishings. And many women bore the main share of the burden of taking in relatives who were out of work, or young or elderly people who could not get work, or young couples who could not afford to set up independent households.

Inventive Americans discovered new ways to earn a living. During the twenties, people had avoided jury duty; now they shoved their way into court buildings eager for the allotted $4 a day. An army of new-fledged salesmen went from door to door, peddling everything imaginable, and in cities they spread out their wares along the street curbs. Arguments went on over whether permanent investment in a shoeshine kit would produce more income than hawking apples or newspapers. The International Apple Shippers Association, faced with a large surplus, sold its product on credit to the unemployed; 6,000 people sold apples on New York City streets in 1930. Sunday papers sold from door to door in apartment houses offered an income, and more and more newsboys walked the city streets. Enterprises given up earlier as an uneconomical use of labor—vegetable and fruit pushcarts, for example—reappeared.

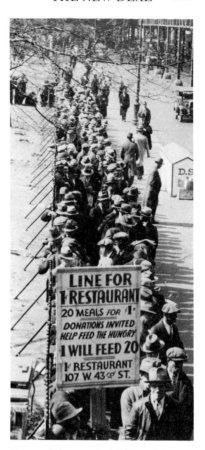

Some of the most vivid images from the Depression were the breadlines for free or cheap meals. *(Courtesy, F. D. R. Library, Hyde Park)*

Middle- and Upper-Class Americans in the Depression

Even in the worst Depression years, most American workers had jobs. Essential skilled laborers, both farm and factory, or those in the few powerful unions generally rode out the decade with few scars. Schoolteaching, especially in college, was usually a stable, much-prized job, even when some salaries dropped. Government work became the most desirable of all: Washington, D.C., possessed the healthiest economy of any city in the nation. If such workers bought few luxuries, they seldom worried about the necessities. For small businessmen lucky enough to survive, the Roosevelt era restored a measure of stability. Though banks hoarded money, making long-term expansion almost impossible, grocers, druggists, and oil dealers, for example, could rely upon a small but stable income and assets slowly rising in value. Many merchants, in fact, took advantage of abysmally low prices to invest in land or the stock market.

Clerks, typists, and many white-collar workers outside of government fared less well. Even professionals such as lawyers and doctors lost income as the earnings of their clients lagged.

"We're all going down to the Trans-Lux to hiss Roosevelt." The very wealthy would distrust the new President, Franklin Roosevelt, sometimes calling him an enemy of his class.—*The New Yorker*, July 8, 1936.

The Rich   Except for the worst months at the end of 1932 and the beginning of 1933, the Depression scarcely touched the very rich, that top five percent of the population who owned three-fourths of the nation's wealth. The stock market crash had fallen hardest on risk takers rather than holders of carefully diversified investments. Dividends and rents shrank during those long, weary years, but prices also declined. Ice cubes still tinkled against cut glass at parties, which with the repeal of the Eighteenth Amendment had now moved away from speakeasy brownstones and back into expensive apartments. Well-dressed women copied Parisian styles, wearing long scarves, low hemlines and close-fitting hats. The rich collected objects of art during the thirties. Porcelain, antique silver, paintings, French furniture, and jewelry flooded into the United States as the wealthy bought treasures from Europe's harder-pressed upper classes. Winter vacationing on the shores of the Caribbean became popular, Miami and Havana being the new watering holes for the very fashionable. More and more islands built resort hotels and legalized casino gambling. On the mainland, conspicuous consumption continued, though not the public lavishness of the twenties. General Motors reported large declines in its sales of Chevrolets, but none at all for Cadillacs.

Class Themes in Depression Movies   The Great Depression put fifteen million people out of work, brought businesses to a standstill, and sent banks to the brink of disaster. It is therefore surprising that, broke or not, tens of millions of Americans every week proved that for them film-going was not a luxury but a necessity.

The classic gangster movies, such as *Little Caesar* (1930), *Public Enemy* (1931), and *Scarface* (1932), were all propelled by a single dynamic. They emphasized the individual—the self-made man who seeks somehow to transcend his environment. The disorder of the heroes' lives reflected the turmoil and confusion of the early Depression years. *Little Caesar* (played by Edward G. Robinson), the first of a long succession of films in this genre, is the story of Rico, a man outside the law and at the same time a personification of the American dream. Rico's life follows the pattern of a nineteenth-century Horatio Alger success story. Starting his career as a nobody, he climbs to the pinnacle of achievement in his own milieu. Once at the top, however, he dies— the only acceptable ending for a man who lives outside the law. In the sordidness and frustrations of their lives, the characters depicted in these movies represented the many victims of widespread social chaos and deterioration.

Depression movies had a lighter side. The Marx brothers, W. C. Fields, and Mae West all represented versions of the anarchic character in comic guise. W. C. Fields in *The Fatal Glass of Beer* mocks the family. Mae West jokes irreverently about sex in *I'm No Angel*. In *Duck Soup* (1932) the Marx brothers do away with logic and sequence. In the

W. C. Fields.

Paul Muni's role in *I Am a Fugitive from a Chain Gang* suggests the despair encountered by many Americans during the Great Depression.

mid-1930s screwball comedies appeared, at once teasing about social conventions and romantic about love. Perhaps none did it better than the very first of this type, Frank Capra's *It Happened One Night* (1934). Two dozen or so of these comedies appeared during the later part of the decade, with such stars as Cary Grant, Carole Lombard, Katherine Hepburn, Irene Dunne, and Clark Gable. Musicals of the 1930s also presented romantic escapism and one or another version of the success story. Three of the most popular, *Forty-Second Street*, *Gold Diggers of 1933*, and *Footlight Parade*, were all constructed around Depression themes.

The escapist screwball comedies and musicals contrasted with films that depicted social and economic problems. Labor dissension, slum conditions, and, of course, unemployment were among the issues appearing on screen. John Ford's filming of John Steinbeck's novel *The Grapes of Wrath* (1939) was notable for its sympathetic portrayal of farm workers, "Okies" driven by dust storms from Oklahoma.

The Roosevelts

FDR   The new governor of New York, Franklin D. Roosevelt, beat out his predecessor Al Smith for the Democratic presidential nomination in 1932. To demonstrate that the polio that had crippled him in 1921 could not scar his vitality, Roosevelt delivered sixty speeches on a national tour by railroad. His talks, vague in substance and dynamic in delivery, were well received by Depression audiences. One telegram to Hoover at the end of the campaign captured the voters' sentiment: "Vote for Roosevelt and make it unani-

Franklin Roosevelt. *(Courtesy, F. D. R. Library)*

One quatrain caught a popular feeling toward the outgoing President:

O 'Erbert lived over the h'ocean
O 'Erbert lived over the sea;
O 'Oo will go down to the h'ocean,
An' drown 'Erbert 'Oover for me?

Franklin Roosevelt as a boy.
(Courtesy, F. D. R. Library)

mous." While the programs put forward in the campaign speeches of the two candidates differed in only a few respects, Roosevelt took all but six states—with a margin in the popular vote of seven million—against an incumbent President himself elected overwhelmingly four years earlier.

The Democrat who defeated Hoover in the 1932 election possessed a personality suited to the times. Franklin Delano Roosevelt would speak of the nation's troubles only to express confidence that they could be banished. He did not hold himself back from the people but seemed eager to meet each one personally. One woman, trying to express to her grandchildren in later years her feeling toward Roosevelt, has remarked that if the President had come into her kitchen for morning coffee she would have been perfectly comfortable and not the least bit surprised. A young soldier, standing outside the White House at night after hearing of the President's death, said, "I felt as if I knew him. I felt as if he knew me—and I felt as if he liked me." Someone remarked that Roosevelt could say "my old friend" in ten languages while Hoover could say it in none.

Born in 1882 to a wealthy and aristocratic family in Dutchess County, New York, Franklin had grown up as the sheltered only child of an aging, indulgent father and a domineering but intensely loving mother. His monopoly on parental affection, and the luxury and material comforts of the family estate at Hyde Park, made him secure and self-assured. At the Reverend Endicott Peabody's Groton School Roosevelt learned the values of the "better" classes: patriotism, public service, and a simple and unobtrusive Christianity. Both at Groton and later at Harvard, he lived a life of gentility, manners, and fellowship rather than of serious intellectual effort. But he was competitive. As friends of his youth have recalled, he took his cousin Theodore as a model and planned to follow TR's career to the presidency.

Franklin began well by winning election to the New York State legislature and then, before the First World War, achieving TR's old job of assistant secretary of the navy. He accepted the 1920 Democratic nomination for Vice President. The defeat of the ticket that year was only a temporary check to Roosevelt's ambition. But the following year he contracted an illness that could have broken him: a case of polio that left his legs badly and permanently crippled. This the buoyant aristocrat met gallantly. That would become something of an asset during the 1932 campaign, suggesting that in his optimism, his courage, and his knowledge of affliction he was equal to combating the Depression.

Four years before the presidential campaign Roosevelt had won election for governor of New York, following Al Smith into the office. There he backed important if not drastic reforms in agriculture, public utilities, welfare, and conservation, making New York one of the states most vigorous in its attempts to cope with the Depression. By 1932 he had experience in governing and a national reputation for being a reformer. While Roosevelt's gubernatorial program, like those he would later initiate or support in the presidency, were never organized into a logical, coherent philosophy, they gave an impression of energy and action. The pursuit of pet programs, frequent last-minute meetings with advisers, and quick responses to emergencies were to comprise whatever platform is detectable in his presidential years. The essence of the New Deal to come was perhaps best summed up by a revealing bit of FDR's campaign wisdom: "The country needs bold, persistent experimentation. It is common sense to take a method and try it. If it fails, admit it frankly and try another. But above all, try something." Whatever else it did, this approach promised movement in a country mired in despair.

After being nominated on the fourth ballot by the Democratic convention, Roosevelt surprised and thrilled the delegates by flying through stormy weather from New York State to Chicago in a Ford Trimotor to accept their nomination in person. Almost immediately after his election he won an important ally, the press, by opening his news conferences to offhand questions and joking with reporters, rather than simply delivering answers to written questions as his predecessor had done. Using radio as a new political tool, Roosevelt in the presidency delivered "fireside chats" to the nation, explaining his policies and plans in a conversational, easily understood manner, and projecting his personality into millions of homes.

| **Eleanor Roosevelt** | The First Lady also lent a special aura to the administration. Eleanor Roosevelt involved herself more deeply in public life than any previous President's |

wife had done, establishing a personality that competed for public attention with that of her remarkable husband.

Eleanor was also a Roosevelt, niece of Theodore and distant cousin of Franklin. Perceiving herself as unattractive and awkward, the young Eleanor had been extremely shy. Her beautiful mother called her "Granny" and made fun of her in front of visitors. The mother died when Eleanor was eight. Her father Elliott, though kind, soon drank himself to death. Her parents' early deaths, which left her to grow up with a grandmother and without many playmates, deepened her withdrawal. After marrying her confident and attractive cousin Franklin in 1905, Eleanor gave birth in rapid succession to six children who, in upper-class fashion, were brought up by servants. As the years passed, however, she gradually gained greater self-confidence; and she began to take a more and more active interest in her husband's career and in public affairs generally. Mrs. Roosevelt's public role became increasingly visible as Franklin proceeded from office to office.

After the Roosevelts settled into the White House in 1933, Eleanor shocked those who expected another in the tradition of virtually invisible first ladies. With her husband unable to walk or to travel easily, she often became the President's eyes and ears. Although their relationship was no longer intimate, and her dearest friends were female social activists, Eleanor had Franklin's respect and trust; he encouraged her to see people and problems firsthand and report to him. She showed up in so many places that her adventures became legendary. One cartoon of the period showed coal miners deep underground looking up to say, "Here comes Mrs. Roosevelt."

She produced after 1935 a newspaper column called *My Day*, which purposefully remained rather chatty and trivial although it occasionally floated a political balloon, and she published several books on

Eleanor Roosevelt. (*Courtesy, F. D. R. Library*)

One woman wrote to Eleanor Roosevelt from Troy, New York, in 1935:

"About a month ago I wrote you asking if you would buy some baby clothes for me with the understanding that I was to repay you as soon as my husband got enough work. Several weeks later I received a reply to apply to a Welfare Association so I might receive the aid I needed. Do you remember?

Please Mrs. Roosevelt, I do not want charity, only a chance from someone who will trust me until we can get enough money to repay the amount spent for the things I need. As a proof that I really am sincere, I am sending you two of my dearest possessions to keep as security, a ring my husband gave me before we were married, and a ring my mother used to wear. Perhaps the actual value of them is not high, but they are worth a lot to me. If you will consider buying the baby clothes, please keep them (rings) until I send you the money you spent."

The daughter of a railroad worker in Cleveland recalled her own family's experience during the Great Depression:

"I remember all of a sudden we had to move. My father lost his job and we moved into a double garage. The landlord didn't charge us rent. . . . We had a coal stove, and we had to each take turns, the three of us kids, to warm our legs. It was awfully cold when you opened those garage doors. We could sleep with rugs and blankets over the top of us [and] dress under the sheets. . . . In the morning we'd get out and get some snow and put it on the stove and melt it and wash around our faces. . . . [We] put on two pairs of socks on each hand and two pairs of socks on our feet, and long underwear and . . . Goodwill shoes. Off we'd walk, three, four miles to school."

Secretary of Labor Frances Perkins, the first woman cabinet member. *(Courtesy, National Portrait Gallery)*

broad political questions. Ordinary people responded to her evident sympathy for their plight.

From the first months of her husband's administration, Eleanor Roosevelt's activities provoked criticism. Americans hostile to her liberalism found improper her involvement in public affairs. Later Eleanor defied the segregation customs of her time and intervened personally when prejudice barred the black singer Marian Anderson from Constitution Hall, owned by the Daughters of the American Revolution. She supported the American Youth Congress, which a red-hunting House committee claimed to be dominated by Communists. When challenged, Eleanor was quick to assert her independence and to deny any responsibility to the electorate since "I have never been elected to any office." Yet had she been in an elective post, she would not have needed to fear being unseated. A January 1939 Gallup poll reported that sixty-eight percent of the population approved of Mrs. Roosevelt, a higher rating than her husband achieved. Repeatedly, ordinary people remarked on how neighborly she seemed. In 1939 she raised a stir by roasting hot dogs for the King and Queen of England.

The Hundred Days

By the time of Roosevelt's inauguration the Depression had gone on for more than two years. Millions were now unemployed. In his inaugural address the new President proclaimed that "the only thing we have to fear is fear itself" and promised "to wage a war against the emergency." The so-called Hundred Days from March 4 to mid-June 1933 marked the first major campaign in that war.

It was one of the most productive bursts of lawmaking in American history. Perhaps the only element that unified the legislation of the Hundred Days and beyond was the personality of the President. Roosevelt brought to Washington a "Brains Trust" of college professors including Raymond Moley, Adolf A. Berle, Jr., and Rexford G. Tugwell from Columbia University and Felix Frankfurter of Harvard Law School. But none of these intellectuals put his stamp on the New Deal as a whole; nor did they collectively give order and system to the administration's programs. Moley, for example, soon broke with the President. Roosevelt's cabinet reflected his penchant for variety. Secretary of the Treasury Henry Morgenthau was a model of caution. At Agriculture was Henry A. Wallace, the son of Harding's secretary of agriculture, and at Interior Harold L. Ickes, both Republican progressives. And running the Department of Labor was an urban liberal, Frances Perkins, the first woman cabinet officer in United States history. Roosevelt freely mixed diverging ideas and interests.

The Banking Crisis The nation's paramount and paralyzing immediate trouble was the condition of its banks. Between Roosevelt's election in November 1932 and his inauguration on March 4, 1933, the American economy had slid even lower. During this interregnum more than a quarter of the labor force was out of work. Neither the defeated President nor the waiting President-elect could initiate major policies. The banking system, under pressure since 1931, collapsed in the first months of 1933. Depositors stood in line at banks in every part of the country to demand their savings; such runs emptied the cash drawers of more and more weaker institutions, forcing them to shut down. On February 14 the governor of Michigan closed that state's banks for eight days. By Roosevelt's inauguration, state governments had closed or placed under restriction nearly all the nation's financial institutions.

The banking crisis eased Roosevelt's task. Everyone from the conservative businessman to the most liberal reformer admitted the need for drastic action; for a time all bowed to his lead almost without question.

On March 6 the President dramatized his new leadership by declaring a four-day national bank holiday. On March 9, the first day of the special session of Congress called by Roosevelt, the Emergency Banking Relief Act was introduced, passed, and signed within hours, with congressmen shouting their support before the final version was complete. The act confirmed the President's power to do as he had already done, provided guidelines for reopening sound banks, and strengthened federal authority over the currency. These measures, backed by Roosevelt's firm public insistence on the soundness of the banking system, enabled about seventy-five percent of member banks in the Federal Reserve System to reopen within three days, and boosted stock market prices fifteen percent in the next two weeks.

Despite threats in Roosevelt's inaugural address about driving the money changers from the temple, the new banking laws were drafted in collaboration with the big banks. As would happen again and again, Roosevelt's angry speeches produced fairly tame legislation. Other financial laws of the Hundred Days included the Economy Act—a futile effort to reduce federal expenditures and to balance the budget; the Federal Securities Act, requiring full disclosure to investors of information on new securities issues; and the second Glass-Steagall Act (Banking Act of 1933), creating the Federal Bank Deposit Insurance Corporation (FDIC) to guarantee a minimum amount of bank deposits up to $5,000 and expanding the membership and authority of the Federal Reserve System. The panic eased as the public began returning its money to the banks.

Relief   One of Roosevelt's favorite programs addressed the problem of unemployment among young men. The Civilian Conservation Corps (CCC) employed men aged eighteen to twenty-five in reforestation, highway, anti-erosion, and national park projects under the direction of army officers. At its peak the CCC payroll contained the names of 500,000 conservation soldiers, and by 1941 it had employed a total of over 2,000,000 young men.

Another relief measure was the Federal Emergency Relief Administration (FERA). Run by Harry Hopkins, soon to be one of the best known New Dealers, it provided money to states for relief projects. Near the end of 1933, months after the Hundred Days, Congress

American Banks and Bank Failures, 1920–1940		
Year	Total Number of Banks	Bank Failures
1920	30,909	168
1929	25,568	659
1931	22,242	2,294
1933	14,771	4,004
1934	15,913	61
1940	15,076	48

One enrollee in the Civilian Conservation Corps recalls:

"I was sent to Utah. I'll never forget the ride up the mountains in this battered old truck. We had an old grizzled army sergeant in charge. When we got to the area, it was just thick woods. 'Where's the camp?' I asked. The sarge waved his hands around the trees. 'This is it. Break out the axes and chop like hell if you don't want to sleep on the ground.' We chopped and built cabins and even a mess hall. For the next three years I grew up, physically and mentally and spiritually, in that beautiful country. It was one of the most rewarding experiences of my life. Before I left I was offered a job as a ranger. To this day I wonder whether I was a fool in turning it down and coming back east. A large number of the CCCs stayed on. Some own ranches today."

set up an even bolder agency. The Civil Works Administration (CWA) gave money to states and localities that put the unemployed to building roads, schools, and playgrounds. Again, Hopkins was the administrator.

Agriculture and Flood Control
The Agricultural Adjustment Act, creating the Agricultural Adjustment Administration (AAA), aimed at restoring the security and the purchasing power of farmers. After an unhappy experiment in plowing under crops and killing piglets to cut surpluses and raise prices, the administration attempted to accomplish reductions by paying subsidies to farmers for the voluntary reduction of acreage and production in certain basic commodities. The AAA would obtain funds for these subsidies from a tax on the processors of listed farm products. The act also provided funds for refinancing farm mortgages through Federal Land Banks. The Farm Credit Act, also of 1933, went much farther, offering loans for agricultural production and marketing and allowing farm mortgages to be refinanced on longer terms, at low interest. Together, these two laws did for farmers what another act of the Hundred Days—the Home Owners Refinancing Act, which created the Home Owners Loan Corporation (HOLC)—did for other debtors. Within less than two years, the government had refinanced about twenty percent of all home and farm mortgages, offering both immediate relief and some hope of future security. To stimulate the construction industry, Congress passed the National Housing Act in June 1934 establishing the Federal Housing Administration. The FHA had the authority to insure loans made by banks and savings and loan associations to middle-income families who wanted to repair their homes or build new ones.

The Tennessee Valley Authority (TVA)
Among the most striking New Deal programs passed during the Hundred Days was a sweeping experiment in regional planning for the valley of the Tennessee River. During the First World War the federal government had constructed a large hydroelectric power facility and two munitions plants at Muscle Shoals, Alabama. When after the war the government was unable to obtain a reasonable price for these facilities from private interests, Senator George W. Norris twice shepherded through Congress, in 1928 and 1931, legislation allowing the federal government to operate the plants to provide power and fertilizer for the region's inhabitants. Republicans Coolidge and Hoover vetoed these measures on the grounds that they would compete with private enterprise. But Roosevelt, who visited Muscle Shoals in January 1933, saw the possibilities for a broad development of the valley through the careful control and use of water resources. Congress in that year created the Tennessee Valley Authority (TVA), an independent public corporation with the authority to build dams and power plants, to produce and sell electric power and nitrogen fertilizers, and to sell explosives to the federal government. The TVA was to provide a yardstick for judging the rates charged by privately owned utilities. But its planners had larger

ambitions. Roosevelt and Norris hoped to further the entire social and economic well-being of the region through erosion and flood control, land reclamation, reforestation, recreational development, and the encouragement of mixed industry. By 1944 nine dams on the main river and many on tributaries had greatly improved the economy of six states. The TVA was for many years one of the most successful of all planning programs.

The National Industrial Recovery Act (NIRA)   At the heart of Roosevelt's plans for reviving industry was the National Industrial Recovery Act (NIRA). It attempted to stimulate business activity by halting the downward spiral of prices and wages.

It encouraged representatives of various industries to draw up "codes of fair competition" establishing fair wages, working conditions, and prices. Once created and approved by the President, these codes were to be exempt from antitrust actions and enforceable by law. The National Recovery Administration (NRA), for the first year headed by the brash General Hugh Johnson, had the difficult task of policing the codes and encouraging consumers to buy only from those businesses that participated.

President Roosevelt in an informal pose. (*Courtesy, Scribner's Archives*)

Sections of the NIRA aimed at more direct assistance to sufferers from the Depression. One provision set up a Public Works Administration (PWA) for direct public employment in the construction of roads and public buildings and a variety of other projects. The PWA, under Interior Secretary Harold Ickes, spent over $4 billion on 34,000 ventures. The NIRA gave labor unions a long-desired legal basis. Section 7-A guaranteed workingmen the right "to organize and bargain collectively through representatives of their own choosing." A National Labor Relations Board, with Senator Robert Wagner of New York at its head, was charged with assuring the right of collective bargaining. Organizers cleverly, if not quite accurately, used this legal prop to persuade workers that the President wanted them to join a union, and an era of intensive unionization and strife between labor and management got under way. Prominent within it was John L. Lewis of the United Mine Workers.

For years, the coal miners under Lewis's leadership had been among the most active unionists. In response to labor unrest in the West Virginia coal fields in 1921, President Harding ordered troops to put down the miners. During the early 1930s, miners in Harlan County, Kentucky, stood off management in some of the bitterest labor strife in American history. The character of coal mining had been a matter of dispute among labor activists, its union leaders claiming that it was a skilled craft; and coal had been admitted into the aristocracy of labor represented by the AFL. But by the 1920s, coal miners were beginning to think of themselves as an industrial union, a union embracing a whole industry, including its unskilled workers. In the Depression decade industrial unionism, the more radical form of organization, had Lewis as its most insistent champion. Despite resistance within the AFL toward this more daring strategy, that older federation did allow the establishment of the Committee on Industrial Organization; before the Depression was over it would split from the AFL and became the Congress of Industrial Organizations, retaining the familiar initials CIO.

After the Hundred Days

More Help from Washington

The First Hundred Days brought excitement to the national government and a sense of movement to the country as a whole.

The repeal of Prohibition contributed to the new mood. The First World War had provided for Prohibition the argument that the nation had better uses for grain than to make spirits; now the Depression furnished against it the argument that the sale of alcoholic beverages would bring desperately needed tax revenues. On December 5, 1933, the Twenty-first Amendment to the Constitution achieved ratification, repealing the Eighteenth Amendment. People stood in saloons with glasses raised awaiting the hour of a new era, crowds sang "Happy Days Are Here Again," and bootleggers went out of business.

Congress continued to churn out legislation all through 1933 and 1934. Many new laws simply expanded the legislation of the Hundred Days. The AAA had depended on voluntary crop reduction, but the Bankhead Cotton Control Act of 1934 and the Tobacco Control Act of 1934 required cutbacks for these specific crops, fixing a national production limit and then providing farmers with individual allocations. An effect was to cut back on the use of pesticides that had made for greater productivity. These laws therefore happened unintentionally to be environmentally sound. A number of federal agencies now long familiar to Americans were the products of congressional activity in 1934. The Securities and Exchange Commission (SEC) was established to regulate the trading of stocks and bonds and to discourage the manipulation of values or overspeculation. The Federal Communications Commission (FCC) had the task of overseeing all interstate and foreign uses of telegraph, cable, and radio. Each of these agencies has directly or indirectly affected millions of Americans.

The Depression Persists

Despite this rich harvest of legislation, the Depression refused to fade away under the brilliance of Roosevelt's smile. The economy did revive somewhat, but there was little long-term recovery. Manufacturers, for instance, increased their inventories, driving up industrial production, because they expected labor costs to rise under the NIRA; this gave an appearance of rapid success for the New Deal while actually providing no sustained improvement. By the spring of 1935, when Roosevelt had been in office two years, nearly 20 percent of the labor force remained unemployed and national income had risen only slightly from the depths of 1933.

Any administration and any plan of action would have faced great difficulty in ending the Depression, but Roosevelt's policies met special problems. Some portions of hastily drafted New Deal legislation failed

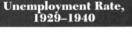

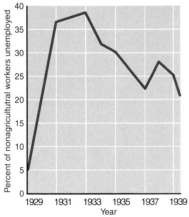

Although the unemployment rate declined during the New Deal years, the number still unemployed remained tragically high until World War II brought full employment.
(Source: *U.S. Bureau of the Census*)

to withstand legal challenge. Roosevelt's taste for a balanced budget got in the way of his desire to increase purchasing power and put people to work through spending on public works. Many programs simply did not work, and some conflicted with others.

For a time, the NRA was a popular institution signifying national cooperation in the face of the Depression. Its emblem, the Blue Eagle, proudly appeared in windows of stores and businesses that were adhering to the NRA codes. But the NRA faced particularly substantial problems. It produced codes for separate industries, written largely in isolation and usually under the influence of big corporations. Progressives worried about this revival of monopoly; small businessmen resented the power it gave to big business. General Hugh Johnson, for all his enthusiasm, proved to be an incompetent administrator, and was removed after a year. The NRA did much to end child labor and encouraged labor unions. But as a device to bring economic recovery it had clearly failed even before May 1935, when the Supreme Court in *Schechter v. United States* declared unconstitutional the legislation creating the NRA. That law, claimed the Court, had conferred on the executive branch powers to regulate the economy that under the Constitution could belong only to Congress.

The AAA encountered its own difficulties. Farmers did reduce acreage in order to receive federal subsidies, but they took out of production their poorest land and on their better acreage sometimes actually increased the size of their crops. Farm income rose, but marginal farmers and farm tenants were pushed off the land. The AAA, administered in the South by local appointees, did little for blacks. In 1936, the Supreme Court in *United States v. Butler* found it to be an unconstitutional congressional use of the taxing power.

FDR's dilemma was real. Many of the nation's economic institutions required serious reform, and public bitterness toward the corporations made the political demand for reform overwhelming. Yet if capitalism was to be the essential mechanism of recovery—and Roosevelt never intended to challenge capitalism—recovery required a renewal of business investment, and serious changes in regulations and policies would frighten the rich away from investment.

In the 1930s Dorothea Lange pioneered a new realism in photography—grim, unvarnished, and poignant. Nowhere did she better capture the shattering effects of the Great Depression than in these pictures of a heavily mortgaged Georgia cotton farmer. *(Courtesy, Library of Congress)*

The Second Hundred Days

The Works Progress Administration (WPA)

At the beginning of 1935, Roosevelt's annual message to Congress called for new initiatives in resources policy, provision of relief, slum clearance, and some form of social legislation to protect against sickness, unemployment, and penniless old age. Yet by the time Congress prepared to adjourn for the summer, it had passed only the Emergency Relief Appropriation Act. This bill established the Works Progress Administration (WPA), which became the very symbol of the New Deal. To some a giant boondoggle, to others it was a vast, imaginative use of federal dollars to provide work for the unemployed. In eight years, the WPA spent $11 billion—then a giant sum even for the federal government—employing over eight million people in nearly one million projects. It constructed and repaired roads, bridges, parks, airports, and public buildings, hired artists and writers to spread culture to even the tiniest villages, and performed a bewildering array of services, some priceless when the project was well designed, some doubtless a waste. However humanitarian, however useful in pump-priming the economy, the WPA remained essentially a relief measure.

Then Roosevelt seized the moment. A series of executive orders established several important agencies: the Resettlement Administration, to help poor farm families and to establish greenbelt towns for low-income city dwellers; the Rural Electrification Administration (REA), an extraordinary success that vastly speeded the use of modern appliances by farm families; the National Youth Administration (NYA), which offered jobs to young people, helping millions to survive and hundreds of thousands to complete college. The President also demanded that Congress remain in session during the sweltering summer of 1935. Congressmen prodded from the White House entered upon the Second Hundred Days, enacting laws that have had a permanent effect on American society.

The Social Security Act of 1935 ultimately established a vast system of pensions and unemployment insurance, providing a modest cushion against unemployment, dependency, and old age.

The Wagner and Social Security Acts   The National Labor Relations Act of 1935, long pressed by Senator Robert Wagner of New York but only now supported by FDR, radically shifted the balance of power in labor-management relations by guaranteeing labor's right to organize. The Wagner Act reestablished and even strengthened labor rights gained under the NRA and lost at the hands of the Supreme Court. The National Labor Relations Board established by the act could supervise elections among workers, certify duly elected unions as bargaining agents, and collect data on management's unfair labor practices, including refusal to bargain. Thereafter the rise of organized labor, while still tested in bloodshed during strikes as well as court battles, proceeded without serious interruptions. The newly powerful mass unions quickly became an essential element of the New Deal coalition.

The Social Security Act of 1935 had consequences equally far-reaching. It established a vast system providing a very modest cushion for most Americans against unemployment, dependency, and old age. Coverage was limited: domestics, agricultural workers, and people working in businesses of fewer than eight employees were excluded. Nonetheless, the act signaled a basic change in the country's direction and outlook—the United States was becoming a welfare state. It had at last joined other industrial nations in providing social insurance against the worst shocks of modern economic life.

Said FDR of the New Deal measure that has struck the deepest roots in American society:

"No damn politician can ever scrap my social security program."

Additional Legislation   The Banking Act, the Holding Company Act, and the Wealth Tax Act were all aimed squarely at Roosevelt's opponents, and they represented his response to the public hostility toward big business and banks reflected in the popularity of such demagogues as Senator Huey Long of Louisiana. The Banking Act opened the way for closer central control over the banking system. The Holding Company Act, aimed at breaking up

giant utilities combinations, and the Wealth Tax Act aroused some of the fiercest controversy in that summer of 1935. The newspaper baron William Randolph Hearst decreed that all his editors should henceforth refer to the New Deal as the Raw Deal because of the wealth tax, and the public utilities invested over a million dollars on bogus telegrams to Congress opposing the Holding Company Act.

Some historians have referred to the Second Hundred Days as a second New Deal fundamentally different from the first. They see the first New Deal as more conservative and sympathetic to business and the second New Deal as a coalition against business. But whatever elements of planning, or regulation, or basic safeguards for individuals Roosevelt championed and experimented with, his thinking and that of most of his public never went beyond seeking adjustments within the system of private enterprise, within the system that had produced both the nation's wealth and its Great Depression.

Outside the New Deal

The Democrats picked up a total of nine seats in the House and Senate in the 1934 elections, an uncommon gain for the party in power in a non-presidential year. But despite the popularity of the New Deal, the times were uncommonly diverse in visible political movements.

The Right   On the far right stood American fascists, lavishing hatred on Jews, blacks, Communists, and foreigners, and talking of saving democracy, Christianity, free enterprise, and America. William Dudley Pelly's Silver Shirts won a temporary and unsavory fame.

Unlike the fascists, who desired sweeping changes that would institutionalize their prejudices, political conservatives wanted little change of any kind. Conservatives made up a substantial portion of the business community, the professions, the press, and the Republican Party. By the autumn of 1933 conservatives, after having cooperated during the crisis of the Hundred Days, began to organize in opposition to Roosevelt. They charged the New Deal with extravagant spending, overtaxation, and meddling bureaucracy. They warned that the administration was trampling on the Constitution and marching to socialism. Many conservatives charged that recovery had been about to occur when Roosevelt took office, and that his foolish programs were unsettling the economy and prolonging hard times. The well-financed Liberty League issued anti-New Deal propaganda, attracting several prominent Democratic conservatives, including the former presidential nominee Al Smith.

The Left   The American Communist Party extended its membership and influence in the early thirties while using the militant rhetoric of hostility to capitalism that the Soviet Union was then demanding of its puppet parties throughout the world. By the later 1930s the new Soviet strategy of the Popular Front—cooperation with liberal democracies against Hitler—had turned the Communists to a more restrained rhetoric. Yet beneath their strategies of restraint they continued in their conviction that liberals, progressives, and the non-communist left were self-deluded servants or ineffectual critics of a dying capitalist order and would have to be crushed or remade when communist revolution came.

The First World War and the Red Scare had decimated the Socialist Party, but it continued to exist in the thirties under the leadership of Norman Thomas. Roosevelt, thought the Socialists, was a decent and well-meaning man though not a strong leader, and the New Deal presented merely a conglomeration of weak measures. Roosevelt was wasting a precious historical moment, when a major reshaping of the system was possible. As Norman Thomas put it, the New Deal was like an attempt "to cure tuberculosis with cough drops." The Socialists meanwhile fought the Communists, arguing for an egalitarian social and economic order founded in freedom as opposed to the one-party totalitarian rule practiced in Moscow.

In 1934 Upton Sinclair, author of *The Jungle* and other muckraking novels, left the Socialist Party and with the help of the unemployed obtained the Democratic nomination for governor of California. In a program known as "End Poverty in California" (EPIC), Sinclair called for turning silent factories and fallow farmlands into nonprofit cooperatives that, he hoped, while operating inside the capitalist system would provide large-scale relief and convert millions to socialism. Although Sinclair at first had the implicit approval of the White House as the party nominee, California interests and state Democratic leaders soon organized a modern advertising campaign to tar him as communistic, atheistic, and un-American. Sinclair was badly defeated at the polls. Other protest movements rose to champion agricultural interests. Milo Reno, a longtime agricultural radical, supported the traditional populist solution of currency inflation, and demanded government guarantees of the farmer's production costs and a further extension of farm mortgages. His Farm Holiday movement proposed agricultural strikes, and his followers attracted attention by blocking highways, dumping milk on the roads, and forcibly preventing eviction sales.

Huey Long   Huey P. Long, from the hardscrabble hills of northern Louisiana, had gone from traveling salesman to lawyer to railroad commissioner to governor at the age of thirty-five, and finally United States senator. Possessing an intelligence unburdened by scruples, he taxed oil profits as governor and used the taxes (after keeping a share for himself) to provide schoolbooks, health services, and other benefits to the people of Louisiana, including poor blacks. By 1934 he held virtually dictatorial power in Louisiana, establishing a base for national ambitions. He aimed at forming a coalition of the poor, black as well as white; his slogan was "Every Man a King."

Huey Long. (*Courtesy, Library of Congress*)

An early supporter of Roosevelt, Long quickly moved away to advance his own program, which he termed "Share Our Wealth," and denounced Roosevelt as a stooge of Wall Street. He suggested seizing all private assets above $5 million and taxing at one hundred percent the portion of annual incomes over $1 million. The money collected would be redistributed to provide every American family a homestead and a yearly income of between $2000 and $3000 as well as pensions and educational benefits. The uninhibited, brash but clever Kingfish gleefully gained as an associate Gerald L. K. Smith, a shouting evangelical preacher who helped build his following. By 1935 twenty thousand Share-Our-Wealth clubs claimed several million members, and Long was taking aim at the presidency—writing a book entitled *My First Days in the White House*. Some believe that Long hoped to achieve the presidency in 1936, but more likely he sought to lay the basis for a triumph in 1940. The question became moot when, on September 8, 1935, an assassin fatally wounded Long in the marble corridors of the Louisiana state capitol, destroying both Long and his movement.

Father Coughlin and Doctor Townsend   Rivaling Long in national influence during the early thirties was the "Radio Priest," Father Charles Coughlin. In his mellifluous voice he had been broadcasting a weekly religious message since 1926, but in the thirties his messages became increasingly political. At first an enthusiastic supporter of the New Deal, he came to dislike Roosevelt's financial policies and was soon searching for sensational topics to hold his audience among low-income people, particularly urban Catholics in the Midwest. Coughlin called Roosevelt a "great betrayer" and a "liar," and he eventually gave expression to an anti-Semitism suggestive of European fascism. Coughlin, his audience estimated at between thirty and forty-five million listeners, seemed a major political threat.

The New Deal had another challenger less menacing than Long or Coughlin: a white-haired, retired doctor living in California, Francis E. Townsend. Disturbed by the terrible effects of depression and unemployment on the elderly, Townsend proposed that the government give each person over sixty a pension on the conditions that the recipient refrain from a paying job and spend the entire amount within the month. The presumption was that such spending would create jobs for younger workers and stimulate economic recovery. Critics noted that Townsend's plan would require the expenditure of about $25 billion, or half the national income, to support ten percent of the population. Yet Townsend had tapped an important new interest group in politics, the elderly, who made up an increasingly large segment of the population.

In 1936 the Townsendites, Coughlin's National Union for Social Justice, and the remnants of Long's movement would come together in the Union Party to oppose Roosevelt. Although the Union Party won only a few hundred thousand votes in the election, it as well as Huey Long's popularity a year earlier reflected serious dissatisfactions with the New Deal's progress in ending the Depression. The despair of 1932 had turned to hope in 1933, and that hope had bred frustration. But Roosevelt was a political master. By early 1935 he was moving to expand the New Deal dramatically in ways that would confound all his opponents in 1936.

The Election of 1936

In 1936 the Democrats renominated Roosevelt at their convention in Philadelphia and promised more reform. If the Supreme Court blocked economic regulation by the government, the platform hinted darkly, Congress and the people must seek "a clarifying amendment" to the Constitution. Then on the evening of June 27 the President delivered to a radio audience of millions one of the great speeches of American political history. "In the place of the palace of privilege," he told his excited listeners, "we seek to build a temple out of faith and hope and charity." Castigating "economic royalists," he grandly called the country to its mission: "There is a mysterious cycle in human events. To some generations much is given. Of others much is expected. This generation of Americans has a rendezvous with destiny."

Not all Republicans were ready to concede a Roosevelt triumph. Despite the severe drubbing of the 1934 congressional campaign, those who survived thought that the welfare politics of 1935 and 1936 had alienated conservatives in the border South and Far West. Townsend, Coughlin, and Gerald L. K. Smith all pumped out anti-Roosevelt propaganda to their followers in critical states like California and Michigan, and Republicans could hope that the three would draw votes away from Roosevelt. The Depression continued with persistent double-digit unemployment that also gave the Republicans hope of winning. The GOP finally turned to Governor Alfred Landon of Kansas, a man with few enemies and one of the few Republicans still in office. Best known for fiscal caution—Landon had balanced the Kansas budget every year—the nominee along with his party platform nevertheless boldly approved unemployment relief, farm subsidies, collective bargaining, and antitrust action. But Republicans still denounced the style, if not the substance, of the New Deal as "socialistic" and as "unconstitutional dictatorship."

Robert Spencer wrote of a tour to the nation's capital in the thirties:

"In 1937 Marguerite and I were married and we began our honeymoon in Washington, D.C. Of course we wanted to see the White House.

There was no gate, fence, concrete barrier, not even guards, so we drove in right up to the portico, parked, and took a stroll around the grounds. No one interrupted our walk until a man in civilian clothes came out of the White House and politely requested us to move our car because the President was waiting to leave. When we asked if we could take a photograph first, the President's aide agreed, as long as we hurried. . . .

Not too long ago we traveled again through Washington and were saddened by the security that is now necessary to protect the President, Congress, and other government officials and buildings."

Almost everyone realized that the popularity of the New Deal and Roosevelt's personal magnetism guaranteed a Democratic sweep. But few could believe the election eve prediction of James Farley, the President's campaign manager: "Roosevelt will carry every state except Maine and Vermont." He was exactly correct. That coalition of farmers, workers, and middle-class wage earners who had voted against Hoover in 1932 now even more strongly validated New Deal reforms, and black Americans—those among them who were permitted access to the ballot—were shifting from their traditional support of the Republican Party. The Democratic administration, drawing much of its support from the white Democratic Solid South, was timid about challenging southern race customs; but blacks along with other poor and unemployed people benefited from New Deal measures. Roosevelt won over sixty percent of the popular vote, and all the electoral college votes but eight. Only eighty-eight Republicans remained in the House of Representatives. The election of 1936 transformed national politics for a generation. It institutionalized the New Deal, cementing a coalition of Democratic voters that ensured the party's dominance in the United States for many years thereafter. In only four years out of the next forty would the Republicans hold a majority in Congress.

Roosevelt and the Supreme Court

Even as Roosevelt's reelection was appearing more and more certain, the Supreme Court had been striking broadly at the government's legal power to regulate the economy. The "nine old men," as some angry Democrats called them, having thrown out the NRA and the AAA, overturned in June 1936 a New York law that legislated minimum wages for women. The state, they said in *Morehead v. New York ex rel. Tipaldo,* had encroached upon the exclusive federal jurisdiction over interstate commerce. Roosevelt's massive triumph that autumn gave him, it seemed, the political sinew to remove the obstacle that had blocked the will of President, Congress, and people.

The Court-Packing Scheme Early in 1937, Roosevelt suddenly released a White House plan to reform the entire federal judiciary. Thirty-five additional district judges could speed decisions in lower courts. The age of six Supreme Court justices—all over seventy—slowed its deliberations, the proposal argued. For every justice of that age who did not retire, Congress should allow the President to appoint another judge to assist him. The ill-disguised purpose of the maneuver was clear: Roosevelt wanted to add to the Court liberals certain to approve New Deal reforms.

The popular President now encountered a sudden barrage of opposition. Most Republicans and many conservative Democrats condemned Roosevelt, some publicly, as a dictator. They feared that the court-packing scheme might subordinate the judiciary to the executive. But Roosevelt's abrupt manner on this issue angered many liberals as well. Chief Justice Charles Evans Hughes testified during Senate hearings that the Court regularly completed some ninety percent of its

The American people rejected President Roosevelt's "court-packing" scheme aimed at obtaining Supreme Court rulings more sympathetic to the New Deal. *(Courtesy, F. D. R. Library)*

docket every year. Additional justices, he charged, would slow the Court's work, for "more must discuss, more must decide." The Court now moved to approve another minimum wage law, then made a series of unexpected decisions: it accepted social security benefits, then startled even labor leaders with a confirmation of the Wagner Act. A conservative justice, Willis Van Devanter, retired during the spring; Roosevelt's replacement, presumably, would tilt the Court toward a five to four liberal majority. The final blow to Roosevelt's plan came that summer with the death of Joseph T. Robinson, floor manager for the bill in the Senate. Thwarted by the politically astute chief justice, his own clumsy tactics, and congressional independence, Roosevelt quietly admitted defeat.

The President later claimed that he had "lost a battle but won the war." Between 1937 and his death, Roosevelt appointed seven new justices, all liberals. For the first time since the Civil War, the judges widened the scope of government activity, particularly its right to regulate the economy. The Court also soon vigorously expanded First Amendment freedoms and began the great judicial revolution in civil rights that was to result in the destruction of the system of Jim Crow in the ensuing decades. During the middle third of the twentieth century, in fact, the Court would become the most reformist branch of government.

The Waning of the New Deal

A substantial number of Americans, including some who voted for FDR, had never lost their inbred conservatism. The Court fight, a sharp economic downturn, and the approach of war in Europe largely halted liberal efforts at social engineering. In Congress an alliance of southern Democrats, determined to protect economic and social practices, and northern Republicans, equally determined to preserve business prerogatives, effectively blocked further challenges to the status quo. Debate raged between isolationists and interventionists over the nation's role in world affairs. Reform lost some of its public, and much of its urgency.

The Sit-down Strikes   While the government was less active, labor's drive in 1936 and 1937 toward national organization had a permanent success that both gave the New Deal an institutional base and solidified opposition to it. At the end of 1936, CIO workers at the General Motors Fisher Body plant in Flint, Michigan, seized the factory, sitting down instead of walking out. The new strategy of sit-down strikes spread across the nation, achieving more success for unionization in a year than labor had accomplished in decades. Businessmen were fearful of having their equipment damaged along with their hopes of industrial recovery. Both the federal and the state governments refrained from the use of force that had once been their response to labor militancy. So industry after industry yielded to the workers' new aggressiveness. Some workers threw pop bottles or nuts and bolts, and in a few incidents heads were cracked and blood flowed. Four people were killed in the Republic Steel strike of 1937. But much of American industry was organized in scarcely a year. In 1936 before the great strikes began, scarcely four million workers had belonged to unions. By the end of 1937, the figure was over seven million. The nation entered World War II with over eleven million workers organized. The workers had found a home; the New Deal had found its steady political support both in funds and in votes.

The Depression Worsens   During the winter of 1937–1938, the Depression suddenly intensified. Record crops glutted markets, and many farmers stopped buying manufactured goods. Federal spending and taxation policies also affected the economy. The Social Security Act, which had been passed in 1935, was not going to pay any benefits for a few years and even then would be dispensing only small amounts. In order to build up its

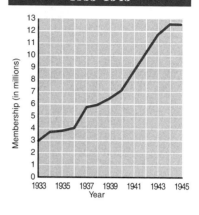

Labor Union Membership, 1933–1945

Membership (in millions) vs. Year

A strike in Michigan. Republic Steel president Tom M. Girdler was quoted as saying: "I won't have a contract, verbal or written, with an irresponsible, racketeering, violent, communistic body like the CIO, and until they pass a law making me do it, I am not going to do it." *(Courtesy, AP/Wide World Photos)*

In this very unusual picture of Franklin Roosevelt showing his leg braces, he is flanked by his wife and mother. *(Courtesy, F. D. R. Library)*

Migrant Mother, Nipomo, California, **by Dorothea Lange.** *(Courtesy, The Museum of Modern Art, New York)*

reserve fund, however, the Social Security Administration began collecting taxes late in 1936, which put a temporary drain on purchasing power. Also, Roosevelt's administration, anticipating a continuing strengthening of the economy, slashed federal relief programs. Both of these measures together pulled down to only $800 million in 1937 the net federal contribution to the national income; in 1936 the sum had been more than $4.1 billion. As federal spending declined and taxes went up, consumer purchasing power fell sharply and the economy slipped badly.

Between October 1937 and May 1938, industrial production fell more than a third, durable goods production more than half, and business profits more than three-quarters. National income was down by 13 percent, employment by 20 percent, payrolls by 35, and industrial stock averages by 50.

The economic decline precipitated an intense debate within the administration. Several of the President's economic advisers now urged a fresh round of relief spending. Influenced by the theories of the great British economist John Maynard Keynes, they argued that government spending could compensate for a fall in private purchasing and thereby encourage fresh private investment. Others pressed Roosevelt to reduce expenditures and thereby to calm businessmen holding to the orthodox conviction that government's role in the economy should be small. Roosevelt compromised by calling for a $3 billion public works program. Too small to be a major boost to the economy, it was just the right size for Congress, which passed it in only two months.

A new farm bill, the second AAA (1938), allotted acreage quotas to individual farmers; in return for confining their production to a part of their land, the Department of Agriculture bought up their crops at artificially high prices. These subsidies, called parity payments, aimed at boosting income to levels prevailing between 1909 and 1914, known as a time of agricultural prosperity. Most farmers willingly joined the voluntary program. To reduce its own surplus holdings and to alleviate the effect of higher food prices on the poor, the government distributed food stamps to the unemployed.

Then, after a long struggle, the administration finally pushed through Congress the Fair Labor Standards Act of 1938, which set the minimum wage at twenty-five cents per hour and limited the work week to forty-four hours. The law also barred from interstate commerce goods manufactured by child labor. That was an addition to one emphatically liberal measure of 1937. Complementing the earlier Federal Housing Administration Act, which guaranteed home mortgages for the middle class, the Wagner-Steagall National Housing Act sought to fill the huge demand for low income housing and to revive the long depressed construction industry. The law provided loans to local governments for construction programs.

Assessing the New Deal   What had the New Deal accomplished? In some respects, almost nothing. Partly out of fear of losing its southern white mainstay, the Democratic Party had failed to address the evil of racism. The administration, for example, allowed discriminatory hiring practices in programs it funded. Not only black Americans but the poorest of the poor in general got the least from governmental programs: migrants, as an instance, did not come under Social Security. The AAA programs for acreage and crop reduction actually harmed many of the poor: sharecroppers and hired workers, black and white, were expelled from land they had tended without owning. Nor did the New Deal end the Depression. That came with the mobilization of the economy for war. But these comments on the limits of the New Deal would be meaningless except against the measure of the remarkable changes the Roosevelt years effected. Relief programs took the raw edges off the Depression. Roosevelt's temporary jobs programs were better than mere welfare relief, giving to beneficiaries not only money but the dignity of a job. Close to the center of the New Deal, in fact, was the building of a democracy of workers: putting people to work, guaranteeing collective bargaining for unions, providing relief for the temporarily unemployed and pensions for Americans after a lifetime of effort.

Ignoring It All

Leisure at Home   Americans did not gloom their way through ten years of depression. Economic troubles were so common and widespread that a kind of camaraderie sprang up. People took up a variety of pastimes.

Parlor games changed to meet the need and the opportunity for inexpensive, readily available entertainment. Card-playing, especially the new game of contract bridge, became immensely popular. After Ely Culbertson and his wife beat Sidney Lens and Oswald Jacoby in a 150-game "Battle of the Century" on radio, over twenty million people learned the Culbertson system of point count and bidding. Other inexpensive crazes—jigsaw puzzles, Monopoly, Ping-Pong—helped many adults keep their minds off their problems.

Outside the home, bingo games, slot machines, pinball boards, and prize contests offered a chance to get something for (almost) nothing. A lucky bingo card, often selling for only a penny, might win a ham or a new shirt. Slot machines, then legal throughout most of the country except the East Coast, returned on the average seventy-five cents on each dollar. Thousands danced on weekends in local "hippodromes" to the sounds of swing music—happy tunes with a quick beat—made famous by Benny Goodman. Doing the Big Apple or the Lindy under twirling specks of light reflected overhead from hundreds of little mirrors calmed worries about the next paycheck.

Radio   For American stay-at-homes the most ubiquitous entertainment came over the air waves. The number of radio sets quadrupled during the decade to over forty million. Most households listened three or four hours each day to a wide range of programs. Dance music from New York City nightclubs or popular singers like Kate Smith filled many hours, but most popular of all was comedy; after all, what was more needed? George Burns and

The New Deal sponsored a number of reforms such as the Social Security system and unemployment compensation that together formed the building blocks of the welfare state in the United States. Controversy yet stirs over these and other welfare programs and their supposed incompatibility with the traditional American commitment to free enterprise.

In fact, however, every industrial nation in the world provides the same welfare programs. Every industrial society has had to come to terms with the industrial revolution. The Great Depression of the 1930s was simply the occasion for the United States to come to this same recognition. Even today the United States is the only industrial nation that does not provide comprehensive national health insurance. And the United States spends less of its total wealth on welfare programs than any other country except Japan, whose employers traditionally do not lay off workers during bad times.

The point of these comparisons is not to defend the American welfare state from all of its critics, but to point out that some of these criticisms have no basis in reality. It can be argued that the American welfare state is wasteful or ineffective but not so easily that it is too large. It is proportionately the smallest in the world.

When Rudy Vallee sang "Life is just a bowl of cherries," he was counseling his listeners not to take the Depression too seriously.

Life is just a bowl of cherries,
Don't make it serious,
Life's too mysterious.
You work, you save, you worry so,
But you can't take your dough when you go-go-go,
So keep repeating, it's the berries. . . .

During the 1930s New York City White Towers sold burgers for a nickel. *(Courtesy, Culver Pictures)*

Gracie Allen drew laughs with their routines about a dizzy but insightful housewife; Jack Benny and Mary Livingstone joked about his stinginess. Ethnic comedies like *The Goldbergs* introduced millions to the habits and cultures of one of the country's many minorities. One program above all fascinated Americans during the thirties: *Amos 'n' Andy*. While this series about two black men, played by whites, presented stereotyped racial attitudes, it had the general aim of poking fun at the dilemmas of individuals caught in situations beyond their control. As radio broadcast major-league baseball contests and Broadway show tunes, it did much to homogenize the nation, to create universal symbols.

Getting Away from It All As the Depression lengthened the free time that American technology had already begun providing more and more of, the country still spent about ten percent of its national income on vacationing and recreation. Even more than the new streamlined trains with air-cooled Pullman cars, the country's highways took people to inexpensive vacation spots such as national parks and seashores. Automobile ownership actually increased during the thirties, as the appearance of modest tourist camps and motels enticed millions onto the roads, their cars burning the cheap fuel of the times. Auto trailers also began to appear in large numbers.

The Works Progress Administration spent huge amounts on local parks, swimming pools, tennis courts, and beaches. States contributed as well to the nearly $1 billion lavished on new recreation areas. In New York, Public Works Commissioner Robert Moses opened for public use

THOMAS WOLFE

In his novel Of Time and the River *(1935) Thomas Wolfe evoked the folk nationalism that helped America through the Depression. Wolfe sang*

. . . the thunder of imperial names, the names of men and battles, the names of places and great rivers, the mighty names of the States. The name of The Wilderness; and the names of Antietam, Chancellorsville, Shiloh, Bull Run, Fredericksburg, Cold Harbor, the Wheat Fields, Ball's Bluff, and the Devil's Den; the names of Cowpens, Brandywine, and Saratoga; of Death Valley, Chickamauga, and the Cumberland Gap. The names of the Nantahalahs, the Bad Lands, the Painted Desert, the Yosemite, and the Little Big Horn; the names of Yancey and Cabarrus counties; and the terrible name of Hatteras.

Then, for the continental thunder of the States: the names of Montana, Texas, Arizona, Colorado, Michigan, Maryland, Virginia, and the two Dakotas; the names of Oregon and Indiana, of Kansas and the rich Ohio; the powerful name of Pennsylvania, the name of Old Kentucky; the undulance of Alabama; the names of Florida and North Carolina.

In the red-oak thickets, at the break of day, long hunters lay for bear—the rattle of arrows in laurel leaves, the war-cries round the painted buttes, and the majestical names of the Indian Nations: the Pawnees, the Algonquins, the Iroquois, the Comanches, the Blackfeet, the Seminoles, the Cherokees, the Sioux, the Hurons, the Mohawks, the Navajos, the Utes, the Omahas, the Onondagas, the Chippewas, the Crees, the Chickasaws, the Arapahoes, the Catawbas, the Dakotas, the Apaches, the Croatans, and the Tuscaroras; the names of Powhatan and Sitting Bull; and the name of the Great Chief, Rain-In-The-Face. . . .

The rails go westward in the dark. Brother, have you seen starlight on the rails? Have you heard the thunder of the fast express?

Of wandering forever, and the earth again—the names of the mighty rails that bind the nation, the

miles of bathing beaches on Long Island and built roads and bridges to reach them. Depression weakened the popularity of spectator football, of necessity a costly amusement, although some institutions took advantage of cheap labor to construct enormous stadiums such as the Yale Bowl, built to hold fifty-five thousand people. Among spectator as opposed to participant sports, big-league baseball remained important. But the athlete of the decade was the black boxer, Joe Louis. Son of an Alabama sharecropper, the Brown Bomber turned pro in 1934 and defeated the former heavyweight champion Max Baer the next year. Millions followed his career on the radio as he won bout after bout, losing only to Max Schmeling, the great German fighter. In 1937 only three years after his debut, Louis knocked out James Braddock to win the world heavyweight championship. The next year, Louis again met Schmeling. Patriotic Americans, and especially blacks, hoped ardently to see him defeat the white man who, Hitler bragged, had proved Nazi theories about the Aryan "master race." Their hopes were realized. Louis destroyed Schmeling in the first round.

Crime   Despite the solace of religion, sports, and parlor games, a sense of decline afflicted the daily life of most citizens. The ending of prohibition and the onset of hard times sliced in half the revenue from organized crime. But crimes against property increased during the thirties, as did arrests for vagrancy and drunkenness. Personal assaults declined, although an old American type reappeared, the bandit or outlaw who panicked whole regions with sprees of violent revenge against society. Some outlaws, like Clyde

---

wheeled thunder of the names that net the continent: the Pennsylvania, the Union Pacific, the Santa Fé, the Baltimore and Ohio, the Chicago and Northwestern, the Southern, the Louisiana and Northern, the Seaboard Air Line, the Chicago, Milwaukee and Saint Paul, the Lackawanna, the New York, New Haven and Hartford, the Florida East Coast, the Rock Island, and the Denver and Rio Grande. . . .

The names of the mighty rivers, the alluvial gluts, the drains of the continent, the throats that drink America (Sweet Thames, flow gently till I end my song). The names of men who pass, and the myriad names of the earth that abides forever: the names of the men who are doomed to wander, and the name of that immense and lonely land on which they wander, to which they return, in which they will be buried—America! The immortal earth which waits forever, the trains that thunder on the continent, the men who wander, and the women who cry out, "Return!"

Finally, the names of the great rivers that are flowing in the darkness. . . .

The names of great mouths, the mighty maws, the vast, wet, coiling, never-glutted and unending snakes that drink the continent. Where, sons of men, and in what other land will you find others like them and where can you match the mighty music of their names?—The Monongahela, the Colorado, the Rio Grande, the Columbia, the Tennessee, the Hudson (Sweet Thames!); the Kennebec, the Rappahannock, the Delaware, the Penobscot, the Wabash, the Chesapeake, the Swannanoa, the Indian River, the Niagara (Sweet Afton!); the Saint Lawrence, the Susquehanna, the Tombigbee, the Nantahala, the French Broad, the Chattahoochee, the Arizona, and the Potomac (Father Tiber!)—these are a few of their princely names, these are a few of their great, proud, glittering names, fit for the immense and lonely land that they inhabit.

Barrow and his moll Bonnie Parker, were pathetic people too buffeted by depression and ignorance to understand why they compulsively, happily robbed banks and killed. John Dillinger reveled in the notoriety of being J. Edgar Hoover's FBI Public Enemy Number One. Law officers staged elaborate ambushes of such figures: federal agents gunned down Dillinger outside a movie theater in Chicago and police assassinated the Barrow gang along a back road in Louisiana.

Persistent Optimism Americans still dreamed of a better future. Twenty million people visited the Century of Progress exposition in Chicago during 1933 and 1934 to stare at the technological gadgetry and wonder over the possibilities of science. Five years later, an even more ambitious undertaking, the Golden Gate International Exposition in San Francisco, looked to a future of swift transportation and near-simultaneous communication. These *papier maché* fantasies had their grandest expression at the gigantic New York World's Fair of 1939. Nearly fifty million people strolled around the "Trylon and Perisphere": a 728-foot needle pyramid and a 180-foot globe that symbolized "The World of Tomorrow." Huge exhibits, sponsored by businesses and governments from all over the world, portrayed the panorama of a future built around cooperation and the rational use of the earth's resources for the benefit of all mankind. These earnest hopes were shortly dashed by the beginning of yet another war among the great powers—a war that, in one of history's profound strokes of irony, would finally bring to an end the decade-long Great Depression. The Trylon and the Perisphere were soon melted down to make war weapons.

The Arts and the Spirit of the 30s

The best remembered literature of the Great Depression differs from the experimental achievements of the 1920s. At that earlier time much of fiction had centered in psychological explorations, portrayals of soldiers struggling to maintain integrity and sanity in face of the meaningless conflict, examinations of the culture of the country's backwaters. Now writing became lyrical in its depiction of an American land and folk together struggling to recover from the Great Depression. The poetry of Archibald MacLeish presents a tough people, mixed of many ethnic strains, building a nation on the wide and lonely continent; the wealthy have excluded themselves from that democratic project. At the end of the decade appeared its most familiar novel, John Steinbeck's *The Grapes of Wrath*, the tale of the Depression-driven Joad family as it migrates from its lost acres in Oklahoma to seek work in California, where its troubles worsen. Moving across the land, Steinbeck's Joads are the land's people, adrift on it when they should be its possessors.

Other arts capture like themes. In the hands of Margaret Bourke-White and Walker Evans, photography accomplished unadorned studies of the victims of the Depression. *Let Us Now Praise Famous Men* (1941) contains photos by Evans of impoverished farmers in the South; with them is James Agee's famous text. Commenting on the southern

The Empire State Building, finished in the early 1930s, had space for 25,000 tenants. But much of the rental area remained empty until the following decade.
(*Courtesy, Brown Brothers*)

poor, Evans also celebrates the craft of photography for its direct treatment of its subjects: the smallest detail of the interior of a farmer's shack, caught as only the camera could catch it, reveals the personality of its tenant. *The River* (1937), Pare Lorentz's film documentary on the Mississippi Valley and the efforts of the New Deal to save it from erosion, is accompanied by a prose poem that relates the story of destruction and reclamation while repeating the names of the rivers, names that themselves make poetry of the land. The spirit of the era appears above all in the murals that artists hired by the WPA painted on post office walls and elsewhere, representations of muscular workers giving shape to their country. Though the inspiration for many of the murals came doubtless from left of the New Deal, they are in character with that massive, energetic, and diverse effort to put the nation together.

Suggested Readings

Some new books on the 1930s include Richard Brestman and Alan M. Kraut, *American Refugee Policy and European Jewry, 1933–1945* (1987), Susan Ware, *Partner and I: Molly Dewson, Feminism, and New Deal Politics* (1987), Maurine Beasley, *Eleanor Roosevelt and the Media* (1987), Pening Migdal Glazer, *Unequal Colleagues: The Entrance of Women into the Professions, 1890–1940* (1987), George M. Jimsen, *Harry Hopkins* (1987), Robert Eden, ed., *The New Deal and Its Legacy* (1989), the very readable Frank Freidel, *Franklin D. Roosevelt: A Rendezvous with Destiny* (1990), and the anti-New Deal book by Gary Dean Best, *Pride, Prejudice, and Politics: Roosevelt Versus Recovery* (1990).

William Leuchtenburg's *Franklin D. Roosevelt and the New Deal, 1932–1940* (1963) is an excellent comprehensive survey; his *In the Shadow of FDR* (1983) is an interesting account of Roosevelt's influence on subsequent administrations. Paul Conkin's *The New Deal* (3rd rev. ed., 1992) is critically alive and surrounds the period with controversy. On the Depression itself a readable study centers on the stock market crash, John Kenneth Galbraith, *The Great Crash* (rev. 1979); Robert Sobel's *The Great Bull Market* (1968) is more analytical. Donald Lisio is thorough on the Bonus Army in *The President and Protest: Hoover, Conspiracy, and the Bonus Riot* (1974). Joseph P. Lash has written a sympathetic biography of the widely admired Eleanor Roosevelt, *Eleanor and Franklin* (1971). Alan Brinkley looks at opposition to the New Deal in *Voices of Protest: Huey Long, Father Coughlin, and the Great Depression* (1982). Thomas K. McCraw goes thoroughly into the fortunes of the Tennessee Valley Authority, one of the most important New Deal innovations: *TVA and the Power Fight, 1933–1939* (1971). Elliot A. Rosen questions the generosity of some recent historians to Herbert Hoover. In *Hoover, Roosevelt and the Brains Trust* (1977), Rosen claims that Hoover had a commitment to individualism that his ideas of cooperation did not at all modify. Rosen also argues that before Roosevelt took office he and the Brains Trust had thought out a general coherent public policy for coping with the economic crisis. Rosen's claim contradicts the familiar belief that the New Deal had no consistent ideas and made itself up from one moment to the next. Otis Graham analyzes the important topic of federal economic planning in *Toward a Planned Society: From Roosevelt to Nixon* (1976).

See also Robert S. McElvaine, ed., *Down and Out in the Great Depression* (1983), Arthur M. Schlesinger, Jr., *The Age of Roosevelt*, 3 vols. (1957–1960), Harvard Sitkoff, *A New Deal for Blacks* (1978), Lois Scharf, *To Work and to Wed* (1980), and Susan Ware, *Beyond Suffrage* (1981), Richard Pells, *Radical Visions and American Dreams* (1973), Warren Sussman, ed., *Culture and Commitment* (1973), and Richard Wright, *Native Son* (1940).

A New Deal But Not a New Deck?

William Leuchtenburg

In eight years, Roosevelt and the New Dealers had almost revolutionized the agenda of American politics. . . . In 1932, men of acumen were absorbed to an astonishing degree with such questions as prohibition, war debts, and law enforcement. By 1936, they were debating social security, the Wagner Act, valley authorities, and public housing. The thirties witnessed a rebirth of issues politics, and parties split more sharply on ideological lines than they had in many years past. . . .

Franklin Roosevelt re-created the modern Presidency. He took an office which had lost much of its prestige and power in the previous twelve years and gave it an importance which went well beyond what even Theodore Roosevelt and Woodrow Wilson had done. Clinton Rossiter has observed: "Only Washington, who made the office, and Jackson, who remade it, did more than [Roosevelt] to raise it to its present condition of strength, dignity, and independence." Under Roosevelt, the White House became the focus of all government—the fountainhead of ideas, the initiator of action, the representative of the national interest.

Then Roosevelt greatly expanded the President's legislative functions. In the nineteenth century, Congress had been jealous of its prerogatives as the lawmaking body, and resented any encroachment on its domain by the Chief Executive. Woodrow Wilson and Theodore Roosevelt had broken new ground in sending actual drafts of bills to Congress and in using devices like the caucus to win enactment of measures they favored. Franklin Roosevelt made such constant use of these tools that he came to assume a legislative role not unlike that of a prime minister. He sent special messages to Congress, accompanied them with drafts of legislation prepared by his assistants, wrote letters to committee chairmen or members of Congress to urge passage of the proposals, and authorized men like Corcoran to lobby as presidential spokesmen on the Hill. By the end of Roosevelt's tenure in the White House, Congress looked automatically to the Executive for guidance; it expected the administration to have a "program" to present for consideration. . . .

If the test of good administration is not an impeccable organizational chart but creativity, then Roosevelt must be set down not merely as a good administrator but as a resourceful innovator. The new agencies he set up gave a spirit of excitement to Washington that the routinized old-line departments could never have achieved. The President's refusal to proceed through channels, however vexing at times to his subordinates, resulted in a competition not only among men but among ideas, and encouraged men to feel that their own beliefs might win the day. . . . Most of all, Roosevelt was a successful administrator because he attracted to Washington thousands of devoted and highly skilled men. . . .

[T]he New Deal added up to . . . more than an experimental approach, more than the sum of its legislative achievements, more than an antiseptic utopia. It is true that there was a certain erosion of values in the thirties, as well as a narrowing of horizons, but the New Dealers inwardly recognized that what they were doing had a deeply moral significance however much they eschewed ethical pretensions. Heirs of the Enlightenment, they felt themselves part of a broadly humanistic movement to make man's life on earth more tolerable, a movement that might someday even achieve a co-operative commonwealth. Social insurance, Frances Perkins declared, was "a fundamental part of another great forward step in that liberation of humanity which began with the Renaissance."

William Leuchtenburg, *Franklin D. Roosevelt and the New Deal* (New York: Harper and Row, 1963). Reprinted by permission.

The welfare legislation [of the New Deal], large in hopes generated, often small in actual benefits, hardly represented a social revolution. Except for temporary relief, it added only a small burden to the national budget and none of the welfare programs significantly redistributed the wealth of the country. . . . Welfare, by stilling the voice of dissent and by stimulating consumption and higher profits, represented a type of government insurance for a capitalist economy. . . . But the meager benefits of the early Social Security system were insignificant in comparison to the building system of security for large, established commercial farms. . . .

The story of most New Deal frustration remains untold. The thirties was indeed a reform decade, a period when sensitivity to injustice, to vast structures of privilege, to the terribly empty life of most people, prevailed as never before. Much of the concern remained outside government, in critics of the New Deal, in radical political movements, in artists of varied mediums, in a few philosophers. But many reformers worked in or with New Deal agencies, particularly the relief and rehabilitation agencies. They were always in the minority and had to fight an unending battle within their own agencies. But the outside battle was the main one. As they struggled to carry out their programs, dealing directly with the exploited people who loved Roosevelt, they often found their task impossible. The economic and social institutions of a Democratic South, as an example, presented a continuing source of frustration, particularly in the treatment of blacks. . . .

The enemies of the New Deal were wrong. They should have been friends. Security was a prime concern of the insecure thirties. Concern for it cut across all classes. Businessmen, by their policies, desperately sought it in lowered corporate debts and tried to get the government to practice the same austerity. Even when ragged and ill-housed, workers opened savings accounts. The New Deal, by its policies, underwrote a vast apparatus of security. . . . But like stingy laborers, the frightened businessmen did not use and enjoy this security and thus increase it. New Dealers tried to frame institutions to protect the economy from major business cycles and began in an unclear sort of way to underwrite continuous economic growth and sustained profits. Although some tax bills at least hinted at restrictions on high profits, the New Deal certainly never attacked profits. During the thirties, taxes did not contribute to any leveling of income. Because of tax policies, even relief expenditures were disguised subsidies to producers, since future taxes on individual salaries or on consumer goods would pay for most of the relief. Thus, instead of relying on higher wages to create increased consumer demand, possibly at the short-term expense of profits, the government created the demand through relief expenditures, without taking the cost out of the hides of businessmen in the way they expected and feared.

The crusade almost always ended in some degree of futility. . . .

But nothing in [Roosevelt's] leadership was capable of transforming the desires of these loyal reformers into a new structure of political power. It may have been impossible, even had he tried. Master of politics, he was also captive to politics. Thus the story of many New Deal agencies was a sad story, the ever recurring story of what might have been. . . .

Paul Conkin, *The New Deal*, 3rd ed., 1992. Reprinted by permission of Harlan Davidson, Inc. pp. 58, 66, 73–76 passim.

Der Führer—Adolf Hitler. *(Courtesy, Library of Congress)*

25
Diplomacy and War
1933–1945

KRISTALLNACHT

On October 28, 1938, the German government rounded up about 18,000 Polish Jews living in Germany. Thousands of storm troopers snatched children from the streets, plucked the ill out of hospitals, herded the victims into trains and trucks. Allowed only to take the clothes on their backs and ten marks (about $4), they were dumped across the Polish border to find shelter in the no-man's land between these hostile nations' frontier outposts.

The deportees suffered terrible hardship, particularly those at Zbaszym, whose plight attracted worldwide attention. In a letter to his seventeen-year-old son Herschel, who had escaped from Germany to Paris, Zindel Grynszpan described his family's suffering. Wild with grief, the son bought a pistol and went to the German embassy in Paris. He was sent to the desk of a minor official, Ernst vom Rath—himself under investigation for suspected Jewish ancestry. Convinced he could not see the ambassador, Grynszpan shot vom Rath.

As the German official lay dying, it is said, the German S.S. teletyped orders to cities throughout Germany for a "spontaneous" pogrom. Vom Rath's death on the afternoon of November 9 was the signal; at 2:00 the next morning began *Kristallnacht,* the "night of broken glass." Some two hundred synagogues were burned, thousands of shops looted or destroyed, and twenty thousand Jews thrown into concentration camps. Thirty-six Jews were murdered, and many Jewish women were raped. While the

HISTORICAL EVENTS

1933
World Economic Conference • Roosevelt-Litvinov accord • Good Neighbor Policy

1934
Reciprocal Trade Agreements Act • Lázaro Cárdenas elected president of Mexico • Senate investigates munitions makers

1935
Neutrally Act • Italians invade Ethiopia

1936
Hitler marches into the Rhineland • Spanish Civil War

1937
Hitler allies with Mussolini's Italy • Japanese sink U.S. gunboat *Panay* in China

1938
"the night of broken glass" (November 9) • Wagner-Rogers refugee legislation fails in U.S. • Cárdenas confiscates major oil lands in Mexico • Hitler attacks Austria • Munich Pact (September 29) • Hitler occupies the Sudetenland

continued

destruction continued, the German government issued a set of decrees that essentially expropriated all property of German Jews and barred Jews from virtually all but the most menial employment.

American religious and civic groups and hundreds of newspapers demanded that something be done. German propaganda minister Joseph Goebbels replied coolly to worldwide protests: "If there is any country that believes it has not enough Jews, I shall gladly turn over to it all our Jews." The United States government retorted with a mild diplomatic gesture of calling back its ambassador to Germany "for consultation" (a gesture less serious than a formal recall). President Roosevelt expressed his shock at a news conference, but was evasive on the question of whether the United States would accept more refugees. Trade with the Third Reich continued.

In response to the night of broken glass the Netherlands, Belgium, and Great Britain admitted several thousand refugee children, inspiring a movement among clergymen to urge the same in the United States. Senator Robert F. Wagner of New York and Representative Edith Nourse Rogers of Massachusetts proposed the Wagner-Rogers Bill, which would have admitted up to 20,000 German refugees under the age of fourteen as an addition to the next two years' regular German quota. Advocates of the bill assured a joint House-Senate Committee that "none will come here save those who are, in the opinion of trained specialists, good material for American citizenship." They pointed out how few refugees the United States had recently absorbed and gave assurances that there was a surplus of good homes for these children. Mrs. Calvin Coolidge and Herbert Hoover were among the people offering to sponsor these children.

The bill, however, was in trouble from the start. The congressional hopper was crammed with sixty different anti-alien bills, including one—officially endorsed by the American Legion—to abolish all immigration to the United States for ten years. The Roosevelt Administration retained a tomblike official silence. The President was then struggling to pry from Congress funds to build naval bases and to expand the Army Air Corps in preparation for the country's possible involvement in another world war. Despite Roosevelt's genuine concern over the fate of all of central and eastern European Jewry, whose future he described at this very time as "exceedingly dark," he let the Refugee Bill die along with many refugees.

The United States never met Goebbels's challenge. The American public believed not only that it had enough Jews, but that it had more than enough aliens in general. Not until 1944 did Americans seriously notice the atrocities, and by then there were pathetically few refugees to save. In December 1944, after American troops had already reached some of the death camps, a public opinion poll showed that most Americans still believed that the Nazis had killed fewer than 100,000 Jews instead of some six million—or probably more—Jews, gypsies, and homosexuals. The United States admitted about 250,000 Jewish refugees in the entire period. The American government, which made military detours to preserve the art of the Japanese city of Kyoto and the architecture of Rothenburg in Germany, sent no bombers to destroy the ovens at Dachau and Auschwitz or train trackage to them, although the administration had evidence available that amply suggested what the ovens were being used for.

The World Economic Conference

Foreign affairs were but an afterthought on March 4, 1933, a windy, steel-gray day in Washington, D.C., as silent, anxious Americans gathered on Capitol Hill or listened on the radio to a new President. Recovery at home, the problem of unemployed workers, closed factories, bankrupt banks—it was these that preoccupied Franklin Delano Roosevelt, not distant drums in the Far East or continental Europe.

Yet the new leaders in Washington were not true isolationists. Roosevelt and the Democrats, long identified with Wilsonian internationalism, repeatedly glanced abroad for cures to the nation's economic ills. While Congress debated New Deal recovery measures, a debate that lasted until early summer, Roosevelt restlessly took up a proposal left over from the Hoover Administration for a world economic conference.

Ever since a financial panic forced Great Britain off the gold standard in 1931, world leaders, especially in France and the United States, had groped after an international solution to the spreading economic crisis. By the time the World Economic Conference convened in London on June 12, 1933, no coherent strategy had emerged. The delegates knew that Roosevelt's experimental plans were at odds with those of the so-called Gold Bloc, those nations like France whose economic interests required continuation of the gold standard. Discussions in London drifted on for a few weeks, but the gathering that could have ended the crisis of confidence only worsened it by spoiling the hopes it had raised. Even Secretary of State Cordell Hull, a devout Wilsonian committed to expanding world trade by lowering tariffs, decided that "The best contribution America can make to world prosperity is its own domestic recovery."

And so the country turned inward to seek its economic salvation— a luxury the United States thought it could afford in the impregnable security behind the world's great oceans. Still, the New Deal did make several modest attempts at easing the effects of the Great Depression by addressing international economic issues. To make American goods

Sophia Litwinska remembered Auschwitz, largest of the Nazi extermination camps, which had begun to operate in 1940 (estimates of the numbers who died at Auschwitz vary from one to two-and-one-half million):

"There was Block No. 4, the hospital block. . . . We had to leave our beds very quickly and stand quite naked to attention in front of the doctors. . . . All those who could not leave their beds had their numbers taken, and it was clear to us that they were condemned to death. Those whose bodies were not very nice looking or were too thin, or whom those gentlemen disliked for some reason or other, had their numbers taken, and it was clear what that meant. . . . About half-past five in the evening trucks arrived and we were loaded into them, quite naked like animals, and were driven to the crematorium.

The whole truck was tipped over in the way they do it sometimes with potatoes or coal loads, and we were led into a room which gave me the impression of a shower-bath. There were towels hanging round, and sprays, and even mirrors. I cannot say how many were in the room altogether, because I was so terrified, nor do I know if the doors were closed. People were in tears; people were shouting at each other; people were hitting each other. There were healthy people, strong people, weak people and sick people, and suddenly I saw fumes coming in through a very small window at the top. I had to cough very violently, tears were streaming from my eyes, and I had a sort of feeling in my throat as if I would be asphyxiated.

At that moment I heard my name called. I had not the strength to answer it, but raised my arm. Then I felt someone take me and throw me out from that room. . . . I was subsequently taken to the political department and apparently I had been taken out of the gas chamber because I had come from a prison in Lublin, which seemed to make a difference, and apart from that, my husband was a Polish officer."

more competitive in world markets, Roosevelt in his first year in office devalued the dollar by approximately forty percent. At the insistence of Secretary of State Hull, Congress passed the Reciprocal Trade Agreements Act of 1934, which provided for negotiated tariff reductions. During the 1920s, tariff increases around the world had stifled international trade and contributed to the global economic decline, and the effort to reduce tariff rates was designed to stimulate world production. For an added stimulant Roosevelt established the Export-Import Bank in 1933. But by and large, the immensity of the Depression simply forced international matters into the background.

Recognizing the Soviet Union

Ever since Woodrow Wilson refused to recognize the Communist regime, Americans had found many justifications for ignoring the Soviet Union. Wilson himself doubted that a new government which made such radical pronouncements would survive in a country so wedded to a feudal past. Then, too, the Russians had angered the West in many ways. Lenin signed a separate peace with Imperial Germany early in 1918, releasing large numbers of German troops for an onslaught against the Western Front. The Communists brooked no opposition to their plans for a proletarian paradise; police murdered thousands of potential subversives, including the Tsar and his family. And the Soviet leaders announced the start of a world revolution against capitalism.

The idea of world revolution collapsed soon after brief revolts in Hungary and Germany; by the thirties, Stalin was committed to "building socialism in one country," his own. Soviet financial sins seemed less offensive when France, and later almost all of the countries owing money to the United States, defaulted on their public debts. Roosevelt

Lenin and Stalin, ca. 1920. The United States formally recognized the Soviet Union in 1933, sixteen years after the Bolshevik revolution. *(Courtesy, Brown Brothers)*

himself thought it foolish to continue to withhold recognition from a regime that was stable; he also calculated that a rapprochement between the Soviet Union and the United States might restrain Japan in the Far East. As businessmen had once dreamed of the China market, so others now looked to the Russians. Stalin had been dumping Soviet grain on world markets at absurdly low prices in a desperate effort to pay for expensive technological equipment; a trade agreement might boost sales for Yankee industry and keep Russian grain at home, to the benefit of both countries.

Roosevelt's first overtures to the Russians brought Stalin's Commissar for Foreign Affairs, Maxim Litvinov, to Washington for talks. On November 16, 1933, the President and Litvinov reached an accord that formalized relations between the two countries. Wall Street bankers wanted payment of Russia's prewar bonds; the representatives from the Soviet Union sought compensation for damages caused by American troops during Wilson's intervention in their civil war. The Roosevelt-Litvinov accord also included a pledge by the Russians not to "spread Communist propaganda" in the United States, and guaranteed religious freedom and the right to a fair trial to Americans living in the Soviet Union. Roosevelt sent William Bullitt as his first ambassador to the Soviet Union. Meanwhile, Litvinov stayed on in Washington as the Soviet ambassador. But negotiations about claims collapsed, and Stalin ignored both the civil liberties of Americans (as he did those of Russians) and his promise to halt subversive activities in the United States. Bullitt unsuccessfully tried to interest the Russians in American culture; at one point he distributed baseball bats and gloves to the somewhat bewildered citizens of Moscow. Businessmen and farmers, too, were disappointed: trade between the United States and the Soviet Union actually declined after 1933, and the Russians continued to dump huge amounts of grain on world markets.

The Good Neighbor

"In the field of world policy," Roosevelt had pledged during his inaugural address, "I would dedicate this nation to the policy of the good neighbor—the neighbor who respects the rights of others." Hoover already had turned away from the interventions in Caribbean affairs characteristic of Theodore Roosevelt, William Howard Taft, and Woodrow Wilson. At the Seventh International Conference of American States, which met at Montevideo, Uruguay, during December 1933, Latin American leaders challenged the Roosevelt Administration to renounce unilateral intervention in the Western Hemisphere. Cordell Hull, chairman of the delegation from the United States, was expected to do what his predecessors had always done in such situations: veto the agenda. But instead the secretary of state proclaimed that "No state has the right to intervene in the internal or external affairs of another," and signed a formal convention condemning intervention, while retaining a loophole permitting the United States to move against "outlaw" regimes.

Alarmed by Hitler's rhetoric and by the rise of fascism in Japan and

Eleanor Roosevelt wrote of her husband:

"One of Franklin's major interests was in changing the hard feelings that existed between us and our Latin-American neighbors. He had always felt that our attitude was that of an objectionable big brother and that we could create better feeling by a wiser and more neighborly policy."

Europe, Roosevelt concocted the practice of "consultation": whenever an outside force threatened "the peace and independence" of the Western Hemisphere, the nations of the New World would attempt to react in concert. Most Latin American states, already frightened by events elsewhere, welcomed the implied protection almost as much as they rejoiced in the ending of a unilateral Monroe Doctrine. Consultation worked smoothly during the tense years of World War II; on three occasions before 1942 the countries of the New World met together, the last time to declare war against the Axis powers. (Argentina alone held to neutrality until early 1945, seeing in fascism a possible solution to its economic troubles.)

The Caribbean   Roosevelt's concern for national security made it hard for him to be a good neighbor to Cuba. This 700-mile-long island commands the defense of the nation's southern coasts; instability there had always prompted intervention. A treaty of 1904 formally obligated the United States to maintain internal order and when President Gerardo Machado's dictatorial ways threatened to bring civil war, Roosevelt sent diplomat Sumner Welles to calm the island. Machado was forced to resign, but this failed to restore calm, and Roosevelt then sent warships into the area.

Elsewhere in the Caribbean, where United States security concerns were less pressing, Washington's diplomats acted with more restraint. By late 1934 Roosevelt, following a plan laid down by Hoover, withdrew the last contingent of marines from Haiti. A "fiscal representative" stayed behind to ensure repayment of debts to creditors in the United States. In Puerto Rico, Roosevelt's governors-general—especially former brains-truster Rexford Tugwell—diversified the island's economy and struggled against widespread illiteracy. A mini-New Deal, emphasizing public works, relieved some of the Depression gloom in the largest city, San Juan. But not until the postwar years would tourism, together with large-scale emigration to the mainland, invigorate the Puerto Rican economy.

Mexico   Roosevelt's good-neighborliness survived its greatest interwar test, which came in Mexico. In 1934 Mexican voters elected as president Lázaro Cárdenas, who wanted to accelerate the mildly socialist revolution begun in 1912. He nationalized most foreign-owned land suitable for farming, turning it over to local communities, and organized industrial workers into a single giant union. Then early in 1938, Cárdenas confiscated most major oil lands in Mexico from their British and Yankee owners. In theory, he was acting to force the companies to accept a new labor contract. But Cárdenas almost at once offered to buy out the oilmen. Although the companies conducted private negotiations with the government, Roosevelt refused to pressure the Mexicans, and just two weeks before Pearl Harbor the two nations settled all outstanding differences.

The Good Neighbor policy, so richly praised, was more than rhetoric, yet less than revolution. Roosevelt withdrew the remaining symbols of his country's dominance, those troops stalking the streets of small countries to the south, and resisted temptation in Mexico. In return, much of Latin America followed Washington's careful steps toward war in the early 1940s. The Monroe Doctrine now became a multilateral device for deflecting threats from the Old World. The Americas could live as good neighbors, though only as long as Washington felt its interests to be secure.

Neutrality and the Descent into War

The World Economic Conference, the recognition of the Soviet Union, the Good Neighbor Policy—all these were merely adjustments to present realities rather than any sort of New Deal in foreign affairs. Roosevelt shrank from adventures abroad that might jeopardize economic recovery or his new political coalition. In those days before the Cold War with the Soviet Union, Presidents shared decision-making about foreign affairs with Congress, and legislators reflected the attitudes of their constituents. Probably a majority of Americans who thought about the question at all during the thirties were steadfast isolationists, believing involvement overseas to be futile and dangerous.

Reassessing the "Great War" Contributing to the spirit of isolationism was George Norris, a progressive Republican from Nebraska, who persuaded his colleagues in the Senate to investigate the role of "those merchants of death," the munitions makers, in the country's decision to enter World War I. Norris, like many progressives in both parties, believed that big businessmen started wars for their own profit. So Norris maneuvered the unknown, and therefore presumably neutral, Senator Gerald P. Nye of North Dakota into the chairmanship of a special committee named in 1934 to ferret out the truth.

In months of highly visible hearings, Nye and his colleagues proved the obvious: American businessmen had made millions selling arms during the war. It seemed far-fetched to suggest that a great nation would go to war solely to protect the investments of a few citizens, yet much of the American public accepted this interpretation. Revisionist historians like Charles A. Beard and Walter Millis added academic prestige and the authority of footnotes to a dubious hypothesis. The complex legalities of neutral rights, the novelty of submarine warfare, Wilson's own fierce moralism, the country's national interests, all were ignored by people now certain that businessmen had tricked the United States into a needless war.

The Neutrality Acts Congress reacted predictably, and speedily, to the isolationist mood. No doubt happy at last to take the initiative in national affairs, the legislators passed a series of neutrality acts.

The first, passed in 1935, provided that whenever the President proclaimed that a state of war existed anywhere in the world, United States arms shipments to belligerents on both sides had to cease. No American ships could transport war material, and Americans might be warned against traveling on neutral ships. Roosevelt himself thought the act would "drag us into war instead of keeping us out," but still he signed the bill rather than risk making the presidential election of 1936 a fight over isolation instead of a referendum on the New Deal. Congress quickly added a second neutrality act forbidding American bankers to lend to belligerents.

In 1937 a third act forbade Americans to travel on belligerent ships, even at their own risk. Nations at war might purchase nonmilitary goods in the United States, but only on a basis of what became known as "cash and carry": the purchasing nation could not buy on credit, but must pay cash only. That same year Roosevelt did officially ignore the outbreak of hostilities between China and Japan in order to ship munitions to the Chinese, the country's traditional friend in the Far East.

The Rise of Fascism   While Congress talked a rhetoric of neutrality, regimes in Germany, Italy, and Japan glorified the state as man's greatest institution and war as the state's greatest enterprise. Many people were attracted to such notions, which went by the name fascism, as the ideology of the Italian regime was called; the word derives from *fasces*, the ax surrounded by bound rods that had constituted the ancient Roman emblem of authority. Germany's prosperity mocked the persisting depression in England, France, and the United States. The future, many thought, lay with ordered regimes and not with outdated notions of personal liberty. Adolf Hitler in Germany, Benito Mussolini in Italy, and Francisco Franco in Spain would triumph amid the decline of democracy, establishing a new order.

Italy's Benito Mussolini (center) was the first fascist dictator, taking power in the 1920s. *(Courtesy, Strazza Photo)*

In Italy, Mussolini boasted, "We have buried the putrid corpse of liberty." The Italian invasion of Ethiopia in 1935 was an early instance of fascist foreign policy, and the failure of the League of Nations to respond with anything stronger than an unenforceable call for economic sanctions against Italy defined the League as an ineffective organization. In Germany, fascism was early coupled with an intense racism. Writing in *Mein Kampf*, a book that roughly sketched out his dreams and his hatreds, Hitler had blamed "subhuman" Jews for defeat in World War I. In the utopian future as the Nazis envisioned it, "mongrel" races would serve their natural superiors, a master race of Germans who were to rule a European empire for a thousand years. The nation must earn this magnificent destiny by obedience and sacrifice.

Fascist regimes gained their successes while their rivals were inactive. Though possessing the greatest standing army in Europe, France feared war. Germany's demographic advantage, its greater population and birth rate, meant that a fresh conflict could end in France's defeat. A vast empire spread over a quarter of the globe on six continents drained Britain's power away from Europe. The long-term success of the Bolshevik revolution in Russia had alarmed Europe's propertied classes. Fascists played on these anxieties, accusing the Communists of destroying religious values and robbing the middle class of its modest wealth. Stalin's cruelty and his ruthless collectivization of rural lands created its own horror. British prime ministers often argued that a strong central Europe would serve to prevent Soviet

Francisco Franco achieved another victory for fascism in the Spanish Civil War of the late 1930s. *(Courtesy, United Press International)*

expansion. Paris conservatives chanted at rallies, "Better Hitler than Blum"—Blum being a moderate socialist who became premier of France in 1936.

Adolf Hitler

The Rhineland and Spain

Adolf Hitler was possibly the most sophisticated or most gambling German diplomat since Bismarck. He steadily maneuvered his way toward imperial domination in Europe.

Gradually Hitler destroyed those parts of the Versailles Treaty that had forced Germany into a position of inferiority. He began to rearm on both land and sea; he meddled in Austrian affairs, bringing that country closer to Germany; then, in 1936, he marched his new though still small army into the Rhineland, the territory bordering France that the victors in World War I had forbidden Germany to rearm. Hitler further isolated France in 1937 when he signed an alliance with Mussolini's Italy. Then the two Axis powers intervened in the Spanish Civil War on behalf of Francisco Franco. In Spain, the dictators experimented with new techniques of war, especially air attacks designed to demoralize civilian populations. Airplanes had replaced ships at sea as the dominant strategic weapons, a development that would work to Britain's disadvantage. Britain and France refused to aid the Spanish republicans, and the American Congress applied its neutrality legislation to civil as well as international wars, thereby depriving the United States of any role at all. Aside from volunteers such as the Americans who formed the Abraham Lincoln Brigade, the republicans in Spain had no foreign resource to help them but the Soviet Union, which gave aid to Communists within the antifascist coalition of socialists, anarchists, and other defenders of the republic. And the Spanish Communists, when they had the chance, brutally asserted their dominance over the non-Communist forces within the coalition. By 1939 the Fascists had won the conflict in Spain.

Certain that the Western democracies would not block him, the Nazi chancellor was continuing his war of nerves elsewhere. Just across German frontiers, he wailed, millions of Germans languished under oppressive regimes. Until they could rejoin the fatherland, Europe could have no peace. Nazi agents sparked pro-German rallies in these areas, and many ethnic Germans responded enthusiastically. Austrians saw union with Germany both as economic salvation and as a return to former imperial glory; Germans living in the Sudetenland, a part of Czechoslovakia bordering Germany, longed to escape what they perceived to be second-class citizenship in a second-class country; Germans in Poland protested that country's treatment of its minorities. Hitler exploited these discontents.

Austria and Czechoslovakia

In early 1938 Nazi sympathizers so bedeviled the regular government in Austria that its leaders called for a plebiscite. The people, they thought, would reject union with Germany. Hitler reacted quickly, sending an army

The principal conferees in the historic Munich Conference, intended to address the dispute between Germany and Czechoslovakia: Prime Minister Neville Chamberlain (left), Adolf Hitler, and Benito Mussolini (third and fourth from left). *(Courtesy, United Press International)*

Chamberlain returns with the "peace" pact, September 30, 1938. *(Courtesy, Wide World)*

into Austria before the voting in March. Storm troopers marched through Vienna, reinforcing a martial image abroad as well as terrorizing the Austrian populace. The Western powers had not really recovered from this coup—which at one stroke made Germany the leading nation in Europe—when Hitler began to pressure the Czechs. He wanted the Sudeten Germans and the mountain areas where they lived. The minority Germans refused Czech offers of negotiation while Hitler's speeches became more and more hysterical and his armies gathered along the frontier. By early fall, war seemed inevitable: if Hitler attacked, the Czechs would fight back, and the French and Russians would have to come to their aid. British ministers sought to head off a war between Germany and the Western democracies. Prime Minister Chamberlain flew several times to meet Hitler in Germany, where he finally secured an agreement at Munich in late September. Hitler immediately occupied the Sudetenland, but promised to settle all future disputes without war. The "peace in our time" that Chamberlain announced soon collapsed. Four months later Hitler marched into the rest of Czechoslovakia and then, during the summer of 1939, he took up a refrain that had become commonplace within his regime. "So long as Germans in Poland suffer grievously, so long as they are imprisoned away from the Fatherland," he said, "Europe can have no peace."

The War Begins   Everyone realized now that Hitler was determined upon great conquests, not mere revisions of the status quo. But an odd twilight lingered over Europe; everyone, even the Germans, hesitated about going the final distance to war. Chamberlain's government issued a unilateral guarantee of Polish independence. This maneuver, probably designed to bring the Russians closer to Britain, failed. By late August 1939 Stalin had signed a nonaggression pact with Hitler, thereby spurning an Anglo-

French offer of a formal alliance. In the United States the Communist Party, which at Moscow's direction had faithfully proclaimed the Popular Front in resistance to fascism and nazism, now faithfully praised Stalin's agreement with Hitler and argued against American interference in European politics. But for some Communists, that was too much. Disillusionment with the Soviet Union had already been growing. The trials in Moscow of loyal Communists who had somehow offended the regime made clear its ruthlessness. Stories came back from Spain of the Communists' military repression there of their antifascist comrades-in-arms. And now the Soviet Union had become virtually allied with the fascist enemy. Disgruntled American Communists and well-wishers turned away from the party.

On September 1, shortly after the signing of the pact wtih Stalin, the Nazis attacked Poland with the new weapons of *Blitzkrieg,* "lightning war." Airplanes strafed Polish troops and urban centers, while German motorized divisions sped across eastern Europe's wide plains; badly organized and poorly equipped, the Poles fell back on all fronts. Then the Russians invaded from the east, and within six weeks Stalin and Hitler were dividing the country between them. Britain and France had declared war on Germany a few days after the German invasion, but they could scarcely save Poland or, for that matter, take up an offensive. French generals, remembering the lessons of World War I, worshiped at the altar of defensive warfare. A hastily gathered British army did land in western Europe, but it numbered only about 300,000 soldiers.

The Soviet Union meanwhile succeeded in further discrediting itself in American and western European circles otherwise prepared to think well of it. For a combination of historical and geopolitical reasons, it invaded without provocation its small neighbor Finland. For much of the winter of 1939–1940, the Finns held out with a stubbornness that captured the admiration of the West. But the overwhelming force of the USSR ensured a Soviet victory.

Germany was not quite ready for war with its western foes and stalled for time. Then the *Sitzkrieg,* or "sitting war," also termed the "phony war," ended abruptly in 1940. Hitler attacked Denmark, then Norway. A new British prime minister, Winston Churchill, pledged to destroy the Nazis, not negotiate with them. But the revered Maginot Line—a defensive system the French had set up along part of their border with Germany and thought to be unbreakable—crumbled against a new *Blitzkrieg,* and within six weeks Hitler had conquered France, trapping its armies in a great semicircular sweep through Belgium and driving the British off the continent in an improvised evacuation at Dunkirk. Hitler was master of Europe, and only England fought on against him. The west and north of France, including Paris, came under direct Nazi rule. The rest of the country was governed by a regime, its capital in the city of Vichy, that was neutral but friendly toward Germany. In resistance to the Germans was an underground in France, and outside the nation, the Free French, headed by Charles de Gaulle. Free French airmen based in Britain flew in bombing raids over their homeland.

Hitler told his commanders:

"When you start a war, what matters is not who is right, but who wins. Close your hearts to pity. Act with brutality. Eighty million Germans must get what is their due. Their existence must be made secure. The stronger man is in the right."

The Far East   The Far East had also descended into war. Leaders in Japan, a militarist state where philosophers glorified war and political and military leaders hungered for a self-sufficient Japanese Empire, dreamed of dominating all Asia. Raw materials from the European colonies there and control over all China could satisfy even the most ambitious imperialism. Soon after consolidating their control in Manchuria, the Japanese stepped up pressure against Chiang Kai-shek's Nationalist government in Nanking.

The Chinese rallied against this new threat of foreign invasion—Chiang and Communist leader Mao Zedong even agreed to suspend their civil war—and leaders in Tokyo backed down. Yet the presence of Chinese and Japanese troops in north China guaranteed that incidents which might lead to war could be triggered at any time. The future depended upon which of two factions came to dominate Japan's aristocratic government, the moderates who favored only economic expansion or the militarists who promoted war. For the moment, however, everyone in the West was transfixed by Hitler's adventure in Europe.

From Neutrality to Undeclared War, 1937–1941

From these climactic events the American people only wished to retreat. When the Japanese sank the United States gunboat *Panay* in December 1937, on the Yangtze River in China, the reaction of over seventy percent of Americans asked in an opinion poll was that the United States should withdraw from the Far East. Roosevelt was convinced that his country eventually must join Britain and China in the fight against fascism in Europe and Asia. But he had to cope with an isolationist public. In any case, the United States possessed only a tiny army, and its navy, though growing, was spread over two oceans. Still, the country drifted toward war, nudged by Roosevelt's convictions, a reinvigorated interventionist movement, and the reality of the fascist menace.

Isolationists vs. Interventionists   Roosevelt sounded a warning. On October 5, 1937, during a speech delivered in Chicago, he denounced Japan's war against China and likened the spread of violence to a disease that peace-loving nations must halt. His call to "quarantine the aggressors," such as Italy in the invasion of Ethiopia, led to questions about exactly what he meant. The President refused any clarification. This was perhaps just as well, for two-thirds of the legislators on Capitol Hill opposed sanctions, most agreeing that economic retaliation was only "a back door to war."

Yet Americans began to attend to military matters. Only three weeks after Hitler's invasion of Poland in September 1939, representatives of all the republics in the Western Hemisphere gathered at Panama. Pledging joint action against any threat to their security, they issued the Declaration of Panama, which marked out a war-free zone three hundred miles out to sea, surrounding the neutral Americas. Meanwhile, Roosevelt had succeeded in modifying some of the neu-

In his "Quarantine the Aggressors" speech delivered in Chicago in October 1937, President Roosevelt said:

"The epidemic of world lawlessness is spreading. When an epidemic of physical disease starts to spread, the community approves and joins in a quarantine of the patients in order to protect the health of the community against the spread of the disease. . . . War is a contagion."

trality acts. He believed that Britain and France could defeat the Nazis if the United States supplied them generously. In this way, outright American participation in any hostilities could be avoided. The Neutrality Act, passed in November 1939, repealed the embargo on arms shipments abroad—a considerable gain for the Allies—although no loans could be extended to fund the purchase of American goods and the purchasers most use their own ships to carry the weaponry: the "cash and carry" policy remained intact. Over the next six months, the British bought several billion dollars worth of munitions.

Then the Nazi *Blitzkrieg* of May 1940 shocked American politicians into action. Roosevelt asked for increases in the army and navy and huge expenditures for military equipment—capped by a pledge to build 50,000 planes a year. Congress passed the necessary appropriations. Widespread anti-militarist sentiment, the army's reputation for harsh treatment, and new openings in private industry discouraged volunteers. A Selective Service Act became law on August 25, 1940, but was limited in effect to only one year. In the summer of 1941 the House extended the draft by only one vote. Nonetheless, about 1,600,000 men were conscripted during the next year under the first peacetime draft in American history.

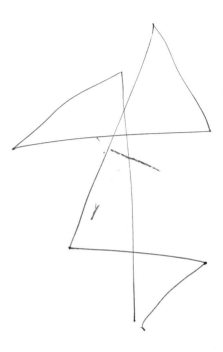

The Election of 1940   The debate over the war became part of the presidential campaign of 1940. Meeting in Philadelphia only days after the French surrender, the Republicans nominated Wendell L. Willkie of Indiana, a progressive midwestern businessman who turned his back on the strong isolationist bloc within the GOP. A former Democrat, Willkie himself supported most New Deal reforms and approved aid to Britain. Roosevelt, who wanted an unprecedented third term but was worried about being accused of excessive ambition, maneuvered the Democratic convention into drafting him.

Roosevelt, choosing as his vice-presidential candidate his secretary of agriculture Henry A. Wallace, shunned active campaigning for two months. He stayed in the White House, directing a large-scale buildup of American defenses. Then, shortly after Hitler launched a massive air attack against England, Churchill asked for United States destroyers. Roosevelt was anxious to help, but isolationists had amended a naval appropriations bill to forbid any transfer of equipment unless the service chiefs certified that it was not needed for national defense. So Roosevelt made a deal: fifty aged destroyers went to Britain in exchange for long-term American leases on military bases in Newfoundland, Bermuda, and the Caribbean. This trade vastly improved the country's defense posture, outflanking the isolationists, and at the same time ended neutrality. Now the United States was neither at war nor at peace with Nazi Germany: it was supplying Britain short of war.

At this point, Willkie shifted his campaign strategy against Roosevelt, charging that the President's policy "surely meant wooden crosses for sons and brothers and sweethearts." Suddenly Willkie's crowds grew more and more enthusiastic, and Democrats around the country worried about the rise in antiwar sentiment. Roosevelt, who had shrewdly appointed two prominent Republicans to his cabinet, then toured the Northeast, repeating in New York City the rationale for aid to Britain and finally pledging in Boston, "I have said this before, but I shall say it again and again and again: Your boys are not going to be sent into any foreign wars." These words blunted Willkie's charges. The President also said that a defense of the United States required the defense of Britain. Roosevelt won another term by another landslide, but Willkie did reduce the President's popular vote margin.

Lend-Lease   Just after his victory, Roosevelt faced a strategic situation of great complexity. Feisty British pilots and a new invention, radar, had denied Hitler that superiority in the air necessary for a cross-channel invasion. But despite their defeat in the Battle of Britain, as the air war over the island kingdom was called, the Germans were now the masters of central and western Europe. Hitler loosed "wolf packs," patrol after patrol of submarines, against Britain's merchant marine. Slow strangulation, he hoped, could achieve what the quick blow had not. Strangulation loomed from still another source: the cash-and-carry provisions of American neutrality acts. The British could buy only with cash, and British dollar resources had dwindled to about $2 billion.

Roosevelt reacted strongly and swiftly. Recalling the simple human duty to "lend a garden hose" to a neighbor whose house "had caught fire," the President declared that "We must be the great arsenal of democracy." The United States would supply the material, Britain the men, for the war against fascism. In January 1941 Roosevelt laid his

Prime Minister Winston Churchill inspects the ruins at Coventry Cathedral, bombed by the Luftwaffe in October 1941. President Roosevelt's Lend-Lease program helped the British survive while they fought alone against Germany. *(Courtesy, British Information Services)*

Lend-Lease proposal before Congress, along with an impassioned declaration of the need to preserve the Four Freedoms: freedom of speech, freedom of worship, freedom from want, and freedom from fear. By March 1941 Lend-Lease—under which the United States was to lend Britain some $7 billion in goods—had passed Congress.

So began a period of involvement that in time brought the United States into open war. Hitler marked off a huge area of the North Atlantic between Iceland and Britain as a war zone, where submarines aided by spotter aircraft attacked merchant shipping headed for Britain. Almost 500,000 tons of allied ships a month disappeared beneath the waves. When the Nazis sank an American freighter, the *Robin Moor*, on May 21, 1941, the President ordered the navy to convoy American ships across the "neutral" area almost to Iceland. Senator Robert Taft of Ohio protested: "Convoys mean shooting and shooting means war." In August 1941 Churchill met with Roosevelt in Newfoundland. After secret meetings aboard a United States cruiser and a British battleship, the two leaders issued a communique, soon called the Atlantic Charter. A blueprint of sorts for the postwar world, this document pledged self-determination for all people, freedom from want and fear, freedom of the seas, equal commercial opportunities, and disarmament. By September fifteen nations including the Soviet Union had endorsed the principles of the Atlantic Charter.

On September 4, 1941, in Icelandic waters, a German submarine attacked but did not sink an American destroyer, the *Greer*, which had been sending the British information about the position of the sub, and the President announced a policy of "active defense." The navy now would guard the sea lanes all the way to Iceland for all ships, opening fire on sight at any German vessels or aircraft. When an American warship was sunk in October with over a hundred lives lost, the folksinger and political radical Woody Guthrie wrote a ballad about it: "What were their names, tell me, what were their names? Did you have a friend on the good *Reuben James*?" Roosevelt then pushed through Congress a measure that armed American merchant ships and permitted them to carry cargo directly to British ports. Isolationists protested, but public sentiment now agreed with the President that the nation must aid Britain at all costs. That cost was indeed high: by the fall of 1941 the United States had abandoned its neutrality laws and joined in the Battle of the Atlantic. The "arsenal of democracy" already had entered a shooting war. "Never before since Jamestown and Plymouth Rock," said Roosevelt in a fireside radio chat, "has our American civilization been in such danger."

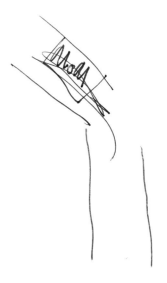

In his fireside chat on the radio after the Greer *incident President Franklin Roosevelt said:*

"In spite of what Hitler's propaganda bureau has invented, and in spite of what any American obstructionist organization may prefer to believe, I tell you the blunt fact that the German submarine fired first upon this destroyer without warning, and with deliberate design to sink her."

Japan

Tension with Japan   During 1938, and well into 1939, Japan and the United States had tried to ignore each other. Tokyo continued its military adventure in China, certain that the economic health of its empire required exclusive access to resources there; the United States still insisted upon the traditional

Open Door policy. Events in Europe diverted attention from this deadlock for many months.

The outbreak of war in Europe forced Britain to cut back its commitments to Chiang Kai-shek. Almost at once, Roosevelt moved to take on a stronger role in Asia. Convinced that Japan's leaders would never dare fight the United States, he adopted a policy of firmness, pressuring them constantly to withdraw from China. For two years, from late 1939 until late 1941, the United States gradually severed its commercial and financial relations with Japan in a slowly escalating economic war. Embargoes on scrap iron and steel, industrial chemicals, and oil, aid to China's war effort, and the freezing of Japanese assets in the United States all reflected Roosevelt's determination. Most of the leadership in Tokyo was not yet prepared to go to war against the Americans, especially since the Soviet Union remained a potential danger on Japan's western flank.

Germany and Japan were now allies, and Hitler's conquests in Europe made the Japanese less cautious. The fall of France and the Netherlands bewitched most of Prime Minister Fumimaro Konoye's cabinet: raw materials from French Indochina and the Dutch East Indies could replace those embargoed by the United States. Still, moderates in Japan and many naval leaders shrank from action that could provoke war. So when Roosevelt widened the embargo, Konoye temporarily turned to diplomacy.

Konoye suggested a face-to-face meeting with Roosevelt, but the President refused unless the issue of China was settled beforehand. This requirement, amounting in effect to a demand that Japan retreat from all its conquests since 1937, toppled Konoye and brought to the premiership a militant expansionist, General Hideki Tojo. Like many of his fellow army officers, he sought war.

Pearl Harbor, December 7, 1941

A huge fleet of Japanese aircraft carriers had left the Kuril Islands on November 25 for Pearl Harbor, Hawaii, and a massive army mobilized in southern Indochina for an attack on British Malaya, the strategic key to Southeast Asia. American intelligence, both in the Pacific and in Washington, had predicted an attack on Singapore, while fog and the absence of radar camouflaged Japanese ships moving toward Hawaii. At the same time the American naval commander there, Admiral Husband E. Kimmel, ordered all American aircraft carriers out to sea and grouped airplanes together on runways as a safeguard against sabotage. Then, a little before 8 a.m. local time on December 7—just as the Japanese ambassador was supposed to be cutting off negotiations in Washington—hundreds of Japanese planes attacked the greatest American naval installation, destroyed most of the planes bunched on the ground, and then turned toward the fleet. One dive bomber intentionally crashed into a ship. A second wave of bombers appeared an hour later to continue the assault almost unopposed, so completely were the Americans surprised. The United States's eight battleships were disabled, the *Oklahoma* and *Arizona* sunk outright. More than 2,300 Americans died.

Still, the survival of the American aircraft carriers meant that the

Rick Blaine, played by Humphrey Bogart, deserts isolationism and his romantic love Ilsa, played by Ingrid Bergman, to serve his country selflessly. *Casablanca* (1942).

attack on Pearl Harbor, a major Japanese tactical victory, was in effect a strategic defeat for Japan. The purpose of the assault had been to destroy the Pacific naval power of the United States, which the Japanese recognized as a potential threat to their imperial ambitions. But since the attack, while laying waste to the American battleship fleet, left the carriers untouched, the United States would be able to counterattack long before Japan could greatly strengthen its defensive positions. On a political level, the attack on Pearl Harbor was in another way also a strategic disaster for Japan. It inflamed American public opinion to a desire for revenge that bordered on blood lust. That rage would eventually lead to the detonation of atomic bombs over the Japanese cities of Hiroshima and Nagasaki.

On the day after the attack on Pearl Harbor, President Roosevelt, appearing before the jointly assembled House and Senate, called the attack "a day which will live in infamy," and Congress declared war against the Empire of Japan. FDR reacted in the same way he had during the banking crisis of 1933. He started at once to do the things he had to do—and with perfect assurance that the country would be able to meet any situation whatever. Hitler and Mussolini, joined to Japan in the Tripartite Pact, then declared war on the United States. Americans were now at war with the three largest Axis powers, as they were called. Almost all Americans, including the isolationists, at once closed ranks behind the President; "the only thing to do now is to lick hell out of them," isolationist Senator Burton Wheeler wrote, catching the national mood.

As in the First World War the countries opposed to Germany became known as the Allies. The three major Western Allies were the United States, Britain, and the Soviet Union. The Soviet Union had been Hitler's ally until June 1941, when Nazi Germany suddenly launched a massive invasion of Russia, and the Russians were now bearing the full weight of a German attack. On New Year's Day 1942,

One witness to Pearl Harbor was sixteen years old, employed as a pipe fitter apprentice at Pearl Harbor Navy Yard.

"On December 7, 1941, oh, around 8.00 a.m., my grandmother woke me. . . . I was four miles away. I got out on my motor-cycle and it took me five, ten minutes to get there. . . . I was asked by some other officer to go into the water and get sailors out that had been blown off the ships. Some were unconscious, some were dead. So I spent the rest of the day swimming inside the harbour, along with some other Hawaiians. I brought out I don't know how many bodies and how many were alive and how many dead. Another man would put them into ambulances and they'd be gone. . . .

The following morning, I went with my tools to the *West Virginia*. It had turned turtle, totally upside down. We found a number of men inside. The *Arizona* was a total washout. Also the *Utah*. There were men in there, too. We spent about a month cutting the superstructure of the *West Virginia*, tilting it back on its hull. About three hundred men we cut out of there were still alive by the eighteenth day."

the United States, Britain, and the Soviet Union, together with twenty-three other nations at war against the Axis powers, signed the Declaration of the United Nations, each committing itself to uphold the Atlantic Charter and promising not to make a separate peace.

The Home Front

The Nation Begins to Fight

War and the preparations of war revived to some extent a reform impulse in American society that had withered in the late 1930s. Global conflict not only honed the skills of government bureaucrats and academic intellectuals, making both more expert in social planning, but also changed radically the status of blacks and women. The population shifted northward to industrial centers in Chicago, Cleveland, Pittsburgh, New York, and New Jersey, and westward to defense plants in southern California. A new sense of noble purpose and community replaced the malaise of the Depression years. War saddened but also invigorated the nation.

In the first months of war, while American newspapers spoke with

Women working on an airplane fuselage. *(Courtesy, McDonnell Douglas)*

a chatty optimism, Hitler's troops were camped outside Moscow, almost in sight of the golden glint of the Kremlin's ancient churches. In North Africa the Nazi legions of General Rommel, the Desert Fox, had by midsummer swept nearly to the gates of Alexandria, Egypt, threatening to seize the Suez Canal that connected Britain with much of her empire. German submarines infested the Atlantic, their skilled commanders sinking ships far more rapidly—nearly 750,000 tons a month—than the Allies could replace them. In 1942 the Germans destroyed 1,664 ships. Elated by success, Admiral Doenitz wanted to send every U-boat he had to the eastern seaboard of the United States, where a mere dozen subs had sunk fifty-seven percent of American tankers in a few weeks. But Hitler preferred to rely on his attacks of intuition. "Norway," he said emphatically, would be his "zone of destiny." "Norway?" the admiral asked incredulously. The Führer rolled his eyes toward the map. Nonetheless, Germany had accomplished the amazing feat of waging war effectively on three fronts.

Meanwhile, the Japanese in 1942 descended upon the British, Dutch, and American possessions in Asia. An army moving overland down the Malay Peninsula captured the key British naval base of Singapore. Now the Japanese roamed almost at will across East Asia, conquering Burma, most of the East Indies, and the Philippines, where General Douglas MacArthur, commander of United States forces in the Pacific, directed a gallant but futile defense. When the Philippine stronghold of Bataan fell after a three-month siege, Japanese soldiers forced Filipinos and Americans to evacuate quickly and without adequate food or water. Thousands died on this infamous Bataan death march.

Last-ditch battles on Bataan Peninsula and Corregidor, together with a rearguard naval action in the Java Sea, could do no more than slow the Japanese advance. By summer, both Australia and India lay open to attack. A few Japanese fishing vessels even shelled Los Angeles in early 1942, but the Pacific's vast expanses protected the American West Coast from any serious assault. The United States had now to gear up its industrial might for a war of attrition.

| **Mobilizing the Economy** | Mobilization proved a cumbersome task. The experiences gained in depression were no guide. In the years of economic hardship the nation had worried |

about unemployment; now it worried about labor shortages as industries expanded to produce war goods and workers were drained into the military. Inflation, not falling prices, now bedeviled government economists. Congress again granted the President sweeping powers to organize the economy.

Roosevelt immediately set up a central agency, the War Production Board, to oversee all industry. WPB chief Donald Nelson faced a difficult problem. Most businessmen did not want to make heavy investments in military plants that would probably be useless at war's end, yet business would never accept any suggestion that the government itself manufacture war goods. Nelson finally swung private industry toward conversion with the carrot of guaranteed profits and the stick of banning all nonessential production. Even then, bottlenecks appeared,

Donald Knox lived through the Bataan death march:

"We moved down the ridge a ways when we saw this GI. He was sick. I figured he had come out of the hospital that was in the tents out under the trees. He was wobbling along, uneasy on his feet. There were Japanese infantry and tanks coming down the road alongside us. One of these Jap soldiers, I don't know whether he was on our side or if he deliberately came across the road, but he grabbed this sick guy by the arm and guided him out across the road. Then he just flipped him. The guy hit the cobblestone about five feet in front of a tank and the tank pulled on across him. Well, it killed him quick. There must have been ten tanks in that column, and every one of them came up there right across the body. When the last tank left there was no way you could tell there'd ever been a man there. But his uniform was embedded in the cobblestones. The man disappeared, but his uniform had been pressed until it had become part of the ground."

A government poster urging the conservation of gasoline.
(Courtesy, National Archives)

Most meat and gasoline required rationing "points," a certain number of which were distributed to families.

so he organized a committee to allocate scarce raw materials. A scrap-rubber campaign aroused popular enthusiasm—a set of rubber galoshes appeared in the White House mail—but produced little usable rubber; not until 1943 did a massive expansion of synthetic rubber plants, together with wartime rationing, make it possible to meet industrial demands.

On April 18, 1942, Roosevelt created the War Manpower Commission to see that priorities were established and enforced on the use of human resources during the war. The President also directed that until the war was over, the normal work week would be forty-eight hours. The government soon became concerned about the possibility of crippling labor strikes. Not wishing simply to outlaw strikes and leave workers subject to the whims of management, President Roosevelt created the War Labor Board in January 1942. The board established guidelines for wages, hours, working conditions, and collective bargaining rights, and under this federal protection union membership expanded rapidly to more than fifteen million people. The War Labor Board decided that wage increases would be scaled to the cost of living. The board first implemented that decision in 1943 when 180,000 workers of Bethlehem, Inland, and Republic steel companies—called Little Steel—received a fifteen percent raise, which the War Labor Board determined was the increase in the cost of living from January 1, 1941, to May 1, 1942. This became known as the Little Steel formula.

Women entered the war industries in full force. Between 1940 and 1944, five million women helped meet the demands of war production, replacing men who had gone overseas. During this period, women entered jobs that had previously been barred to them, especially in heavy industry. The government waged massive campaigns to encourage women, including married women, to join the ranks of labor. The image of Rosie the Riveter gained widespread appeal. But after the war, women would withdraw from many of the jobs they had held during it.

The massive federal spending and shortages of consumer goods led inevitably to serious inflation during the early years of the war. On January 30, 1942, the Emergency Price Control Act went into effect, establishing the Office of Price Administration to fix prices, except on farm products, and to control rents in areas where defense needs were creating housing shortages. Leon Henderson was appointed to head the agency. The rationing of tires had already started at the end of 1941, and during the rest of the war a number of other products—sugar, rubber, butter, coffee, gasoline, meat, cheese, processed foods, and shoes—were added to the rationing program to prevent inflation and black marketeering. Each citizen received a quota of special ration stamps; retail goods cost both dollars and stamps.

World War II had a great impact both on the size of the American economy and on the role of the federal government in regulating and stimulating it. Between 1941 and 1945, federal spending added up to more than $321 billion, twice as much as all federal spending from 1789 to 1941. The Gross National Product grew by more than seventy-five percent. In only a matter of a few years, the federal government became the premier sector of the economy. Strikes during the war lost the country only one tenth of one percent of total working time. The American economy produced an extraordinary volume of goods during the war—275,000 military aircraft, 75,000 tanks, 650,000 pieces of artillery, 55,239,000 tons of merchant shipping, and more than 1.5 million tons of synthetic rubber. General prices increased only thirty-one percent during the four years of the war, compared to sixty-two percent during the less than two years of World War I.

The Citizen Army   In all, nearly twenty million American men and women went into uniform. Huge training camps transformed farmland outside cities and towns into miniature battle fronts or vast barracks for citizen-soldiers. The Depression had made physical training doubly difficult. Poverty had condemned many to inadequate diets and so to weak bodies; and few doctors, nutritionists, or physical trainers had gone through college during the 1930s. The only people accustomed to handling large numbers of young men, it turned out, were the nation's high school coaches. Thousands of them left local playing fields for basic training camps in the South and California, so many that for several years the traditional Saturday football and basketball games disappeared in small towns. GIs—so called because everything they owned was government-issued—received four to six months of physical conditioning, good food, and patriotic propaganda.

Critics worried that this mass experience in military uniformity might weaken the nation's individuality and diversity. The citizen army, though, quickly dispelled such fears. Soldiers spoke of "SNAFU": "situation normal, all fouled (or whatever) up." Officers rounded up for service—"ninety-day wonders" hastily trained in special camps—did not glorify war. (Some commanders forgot this character of their armies. George Patton, a dynamic general whose bold tank maneuvers destroyed the enemy in Africa and southern Italy, once struck and humiliated a young soldier suffering from combat fatigue. Public anger temporarily forced him from his command, and he later publicly apologized.) Military service, Americans assumed, was a temporary thing, a necessary duty to be abandoned at the moment of victory. They were fighting a war to preserve American liberties, not weaken them.

Though millions of Americans left familiar jobs or the unemployment lines to work in weapons factories or for wartime bureaucracies and all citizens paid swollen tax bills, the fighting itself was far distant. No bombs fell on American cities, no armies threatened invasion. War was work: many adults held one full-time and one part-time job. War was also scarcity: guns, ships, aircraft, bombs, and ammunition spilled into distant battle fronts, leaving few goods behind to meet the standard of living that even during the Depression years many Americans had come to think of as their normal due. A healthier effect of wartime needs was the return of the victory gardens of the First World War. Shortages sometimes had unexpected consequences. Disappearing supplies of cloth, for example, prompted government officials to order a reduction of yardage in women's clothes, whereupon the skimpy two-piece bathing suit replaced the one-piece skirted model popular during the 1930s.

One woman found that wartime work was changing her life:

"My mother warned me when I took the job that I would never be the same. She said, 'You will never want to go back to being a housewife.' She was right, it definitely did. At Boeing I found a freedom and an independence I had never known. After the war I could never go back to playing bridge again, being a clubwoman and listening to a lot of inanities when I knew there were things you could use your mind for. The war changed my life completely."

Men and women worked side by side in defense plants. *(Courtesy, Scribner's Archives)*

Here was a typical experience for a young black in the army:

"I was drafted into the Army at the age of nineteen through the Selective Service. . . . They segregated us, and when we went into basic training we had to eat separately, we were put into separate barracks, and separate uniforms from the white soldiers, but we always had a white soldier as commander. We did have some Negro officers, but they always had a white commander over them.

Everything was segregated, and they kept it that way until 1943, when I was overseas . . . , then they began integrating the troops. General Eisenhower was the Supreme Allied Commander in Europe, and actually we were losing the war, all because of segregation. Those German soldiers would sneak upon American soldiers, kill them and take their equipment, then disguise themselves by using Americans uniforms to get into the camps—they killed many soldiers that way. The white soldiers were so prejudiced they trusted anything with a white face, yet they would not trust their own fellow Negro American soldiers."

Discrimination Against Blacks and Japanese Americans

Although struggling to defeat racist regimes in Germany and Japan, white American civilians extended into the war effort their own bigotry against blacks. Many defense contractors hired blacks only when whites were unavailable. New Deal bureaucrats pledged not to challenge "local social patterns."

The armed forces segregated blacks into separate barracks and units, and excluded most of them from the more respected military assignments. And the Air Corps and Marines—self-styled elite forces—accepted few blacks. In the segregated armed forces of the day all-black units loaded arms and ammunition on ships. In 1944, in the worst home-front disaster of the war, 202 black men at a navy depot north of San Francisco were blown up doing this dangerous assignment. Some white workers died, too, but the white officers responsible for the unsafe working conditions survived.

Urban blacks suffered unfamiliar harassments in small towns near training camps. Lloyd Brown has written of an incident in Salina, Kansas. He and several friends, all in uniform, entered a restaurant. "You boys know we don't serve colored here," the waiter told them. Brown remembers: "We just stood there, staring. For sitting at the counter having lunch were six German prisoners of war. The people of Salina would serve these enemy soldiers and turn away black American GIs."

Japanese Americans living in California, along with others of Asian origin there, had long endured discrimination. Tokyo's attack on Pearl Harbor set off hysteria against them as subversives. Local army commanders ruthlessly rounded up 100,000 Japanese and corralled them into "relocation centers" hundreds of miles inland. "A Jap's a Jap . . . whether he's an American citizen or not," General John DeWitt explained. Many lost all their property and their businesses, an injustice unremedied for decades until Congress in the 1980s compensated some of those still living.

"Relocation" was the polite term for the policy of rounding up all

YOSHIYE TOGASAKI

Ms. Yoshiye Togasaki, a Californian, recalled her wartime imprisonment in a concentration camp for Japanese Americans:

We could not go to public swimming pools in San Francisco, and they tried to segregate the schools, you know. It was not quite the same discrimination as the blacks in the South experienced, because we were not excluded from most public facilities, but we were definitely set apart. We might have white friends in school, but they did not socialize with us outside of school. We did not date whites, we did not go to parties or dances with them.

They thought of us as inferior, at least many of them did. We were called J-A-P-S. And of course there was the problem that nobody recognized you as a citizen. So we had to struggle that much harder to reach our goals. I certainly had to do my share of struggling to become a doctor. . . .

The rule was that everyone was evacuated who was at least one-sixteenth Japanese. . . .

I went to Manzanar. It was built from scratch by the military, and so it resembled a military place. Families had no privacy, and they were split apart. I was particularly upset with that aspect of it. A mother and children might be in one place, the father in another, and maybe teen-age daughters would be thrown in with four or five bachelors.

Although engaged in a war to defeat racist regimes in Japan and Germany, the United States succumbed to wartime hysteria, interned Japanese Americans living in California, and relocated them far inland. *(Courtesy, National Archives)*

of the Japanese and herding them into concentration camps. The ostensible justification for this policy was the need to protect American naval and other military installations from espionage. Most of the Japanese in this country had settled along the West Coast, and many were fishermen and so had small boats and short-wave radio sets. The real basis for "relocating" the Japanese, it is clear in retrospect, was continuing prejudice against Asians, which was especially strong in California. The Supreme Court refused to intervene even though the policy amounted to imprisoning tens of thousands of American citizens without trial or even formal accusation. All second-generation Japanese Americans were citizens; every person born in the United States is by that very fact a citizen. Thus the Bill of Rights was, in effect, suspended for the duration of the war, and even afterward the Japanese Americans faced sometimes insurmountable obstacles in reacquiring lost property.

It was also a very dirty place. Manzanar at one time had been a pear orchard, before Los Angeles took over all of the water rights of the area. When that happened, the orchard went dry, and the place became very dusty. The wind would blow from the south, and then it would turn around and blow from the north, and it was a very fine grit that covered everyone and everything. It was in the beds and in the food. We took showers, of course, but that was an unpleasant task. The showers were all open, and you can imagine how the women were embarrassed with that. . . .

Many of the older people had lived in the United States most of their lives, and the nisei (second-generation Japanese Americans) were full citizens. They were law-abiding people, they were hard-working, they loved the United States, and now they were treated like traitors. . . .

All of Manzanar was a stockade, actually—a prison. We were in jail. There was barbed wire all around, there were great big watch towers in the corners, and there were spotlights turned on during the night. You could not cross the boundaries, unless you were authorized on a work detail or something. The guards carried rifles. There was a teenager at Manzanar who walked out into the desert one day. He was not running away, he just walked in plain sight. Who in God's name would try to escape in broad daylight? He was mentally deranged. And he got shot. They shot him in the back. So we all knew exactly where we stood.

**John Atherton, *A Careless Word,
Another Cross.*** *(Courtesy, The
Museum of Modern Art, New York)*

**Wartime
Entertainment** Film and radio brought the war home. Americans watched and listened. MovieTone news clips preceded double features everywhere. Edward R. Murrow won overnight fame for his dramatic broadcasts that, as German bombs exploded eerily in the background, he would begin with the words, "This . . . is London." Hollywood filmmakers produced a record 982 movies in three years. No *All Quiet on the Western Front* caught the spirit of the war; instead, a wearying genre of patriotic films repeated a litany of American virtue, enemy perfidy, and the final triumph of a righteous people. Still, movies like the classic *Casablanca* with Humphrey Bogart and Ingrid Bergman made effective drama of war. And the oppressive atmosphere lent itself to such triumphs of film noir as *Double Indemnity* (1944) and *Mildred Pierce* (1945). In that day of radio, schoolchildren looked forward to an afternoon fare that included *Terry and the Pirates* (also a comic strip), *Hop Harrigan*, and *Jack Armstrong* (the All-American Boy), featuring small bands of heroes who in adventure after adventure took on the Axis foe.

Superman, going to war like the other comic-strip heroes, gave his audience satisfying images of invincible power. Joe Palooka, formerly a boxer, enlists in the army in 1941: "No, I ain't gonna be an officer," he tells his girlfriend, Rosie, "just a buck private. I don't deserve t' be an' don't know enuff t' be." The next year, as Joe stands with a pal on dangerous anti-sniper duty, their dialogue sums up a nation's recent conversion: "Yeah, Joe, I was an isolationist. I really believed I was right then." "A man's certainly entitled to 'is b'lifs, George." "But when the big test came I realized how wrong I was. . . ."

In *Terry and the Pirates,* an older pilot, Colonel Flip Corkin (loosely based on an authentic army air hero, Colonel Philip G. Cochran), lectures Terry in the strip of October 17, 1942: "You'll get angry as the devil at the army and its so-called red tape . . . but be patient. . . . Somehow, the old eagle has managed to end up in possession of the ball in every war since 1776—so just humor it along . . . remember, there are a lot of good guys missing from mess tables in the South Pacific, Africa, Britain, Asia and back home who are sorta counting on you to take it from here. Good night, kid!" (Terry salutes as Corkin waves.) And the leader of the "pirates" in the strip, the sinister sexpot known as the Dragon Lady, turns after years of crime to patriotism: "Follow me against the invader who threatens to engulf China!" Her band replies, "We fight for Dragon Lady! We march with Dragon Lady against foreign armies!"

The nation's young people indulged themselves with fads: yo-yos, mismatched shoes, slumber parties, and bubblegum. Frank Sinatra gave teenagers a singing idol. On the night before New Year's Eve 1942, Sinatra appeared at New York's Paramount Theater, where the audience of high school girls alternately shrieked and swooned as "the Voice" crooned favorites like "Fools Rush In" and "Night and Day." Wherever he appeared, girlish screeching created pandemonium; souvenir hunters tore his clothes and preserved his footprints in mud; a concert in 1944 required some 400 police to control a crowd of 30,000. Parents and psychiatrists professed bewilderment: this puny kid with greased hair and flamboyant antics so completely contradicted the all-American image of helmeted, soft-spoken GIs. Well-publicized love affairs and a garish life in southern California made Sinatra an American celebrity entertaining as much offstage as on.

Some attributed the wacky Sinatra craze to an anomaly of war: few young men remained at home. College women worried about their prospects for an "MRS. degree," then one of the major reasons parents sent daughters to colleges. One coed at the University of Nebraska complained, "They're all either too old or too young or too sick." (Men not drafted for physical reasons, even if quite legitimate, often suffered unjust scorn as "4-F'ers.") Most women, to the dissatisfaction of later feminists, did not use the opportunity of war for feminist reform. Women yearned for normal times. Hasty trips to the altar produced a growing number of divorces, then a severe social stigma. American women, then, continued to value most the traditional roles of wife and mother.

The Early War in Europe and the Pacific

The Pacific War   Vice-Admiral William F. "Bull" Halsey struck at the Marshall and Gilbert islands, held by the Japanese. Army Air Corps bomber squadrons, led by Jimmy Doolittle, raided Tokyo itself on April 18, 1942. Only a month later, aircraft from the *Lexington* and *Yorktown* thwarted an attack on Port Moresby, New Guinea, in the Battle of the Coral Sea. Navy leaders in Tokyo sent a huge armada into the Central Pacific to capture Midway Island, which they thought would cut American communications with Asia. Admiral Chester Nimitz, commander of the Pacific forces, ordered Rear Admirals Ghormley and Spruance to meet the Japanese there, and for three days in early June a giant battle raged in the air: the fleets themselves were some 400 miles apart. American pilots sank four carriers and two heavy cruisers, and put four destroyers out of commission. Admiral King, in charge of all American naval forces, called the battle "the first decisive defeat suffered by the Japanese Navy in 350 years." And by the end of January 1943, after some of the most difficult fighting in the war, Papua, New Guinea, was in Allied hands.

An even more difficult battle was occurring in the nearby southern Solomons, where Ghormley ordered an assault on Guadalcanal and Tulagi island by the First Marine Division. The marines landed on August 7, 1942, but within forty-eight hours the naval force that had landed them was attacked and smashed in the worst defeat in the history of the United States Navy, the Battle of Savo Island. In several other minor engagements in the ensuing two months the American navy could not relieve the marines. Cut off from supplies and untrained for the kind of fighting they faced, the marines hung on grimly against three attempts by the Japanese to drive them into the sea. Casualties were heavy, supplies dwindled, and defeat seemed certain.

Then, on November 12, a naval task force moved against the Japanese naval units enveloping the island of Guadalcanal. In a three-

In a fireside chat early in 1942 President Franklin Roosevelt said:

"The Malayan Peninsula and Singapore are in the hands of the enemy: the Netherland East Indies are almost entirely occupied. . . . Many other islands are in the possession of the Japanese. But there is good reason to believe that their southward advance has been checked. Australia, New Zealand, and much other territory will be bases for offensive action—and we are determined that the territory that has been lost will be regained."

Weblan Midain

day battle the Japanese lost two battleships, a cruiser, two destroyers, and ten transports. The Americans also lost heavily: two cruisers and seven destroyers; two admirals were killed. But the battle prevented the landing of Japanese reinforcements and so weakened the position of the Japanese that they had to begin evacuating Guadalcanal. The army's Americal Division moved in, and by mid-February, 1943, the Japanese had left the island.

Joseph Stalin. *(Courtesy, Library of Congress)*

War in Russia and North Africa

In June 1941 Hitler had launched a huge offensive against Russia. Leningrad was encircled and the Sixth Corps under General Paulus ramrodded south into Ukraine and beyond, toward the oil fields of central Asia. As the war dragged on, Stalin appealed urgently to his allies for some action to counter German strength in Russia, preferably an invasion of France across the English Channel. Lower-echelon military planners in the United States agreed, but their chiefs knew that the British and Americans could at best secure a beachhead in France, not open a major front there. Some indirect evidence suggests, also, that they hoped Hitler would exhaust Germany's armies against Stalin, and thereby considerably ease their own task. Worried that an early assault with American supplies might bog down into a stalemated front reminiscent of World War I, Churchill flatly rejected any scheme to invade France. His concern, instead, was to preserve the British Empire and its lifeline in the Mediterranean.

Rather than risk decisive action on the continent, the British Eighth Army in Egypt, under General Bernard Montgomery, and a hastily-trained American force commanded by Dwight Eisenhower attacked German positions in North Africa. The giant pincer movement of Operation TORCH began in early November 1942, Montgomery moving west, Eisenhower landing in Morocco. General Rommel slowly retreated, conserving his forces to defend Tunisia—since Roman times the strategic key to North Africa and the Mediterranean Sea. But British and American tanks relentlessly closed around him, and his troops surrendered on May 12, 1943.

Elsewhere, too, during the fall and winter of 1942 to 1943, the Allies halted the Axis advance and took the initiative. In the most important theater of war, the Russian front, Hitler's legions had driven rapidly forward, reaching the Caucasus in the South and the Volga River in the East. But immensely long supply lines, a foolishly harsh occupation policy that used many soldiers for garrison duty, and a devastatingly cold winter slowed, then stopped, German armies. The turning point came at Stalingrad. General Paulus laid furious siege to the city throughout the fall, but the Russians staved off the Germans in hand-to-hand, building-by-building fighting. At the peak of winter Stalin, buoyed by the arrival of American lend-lease from Iran, launched a surprise counterattack. The Russians encircled the Sixth Army, and the Germans lost 600,000 soldiers, some killed and the remainder captured. The great victory came on February 2, 1943, now a national holiday throughout Russia, and marked the beginning of a Soviet offensive that ended in Berlin. In lives lost Russia bore by far the largest cost of the war: some twenty million compared to half a million Americans.

Coalition Diplomacy, 1943–1945

In early 1943 the British and American leaders met at Casablanca, and decided that Germany must surrender unconditionally. This promise probably reassured the Soviet Union. Some commentators have argued that the prospect of total defeat encouraged the Germans to fight to the bitter end, so that the demand for unconditional surrender needlessly prolonged the war. Yet the alternative, a negotiated settlement with Hitler, was neither realistic nor morally thinkable.

In 1943 George Patton's Third Army and Montgomery's British troops swept across Sicily and part way up the Italian peninsula; both commanders received secret offers of surrender from King Victor Emmanuel. Ignoring Russian protests, Roosevelt and Churchill negotiated separately with these agents, finally accepting terms ensuring that democratic forces would dominate postwar Italy. Already suspicious of every Anglo-American move, Stalin was infuriated. The government now recognized by the Allies joined them against Germany. The Nazis propped up Mussolini in an alternative shadow regime.

Arguments broke out even between the Americans and the British. Churchill insisted that the Western Allies should first invade "the soft underbelly of Europe"—strike northward through the Balkans and Italy into Austria and Czechoslovakia. Churchill was thinking of slicing across the path of a Soviet advance into eastern Europe, on which he could guess the USSR had designs. American Army Chief of Staff George C. Marshall angrily replied that "No American is going to land in that god-damned" region. Instead, the Americans argued, an invasion across France into the Rhineland would more quickly end the war, and more surely keep the industrial heartland of western Europe out of Russian control. After several particularly strained meetings among Big Three planners and foreign ministers, Churchill, Roosevelt, and Stalin agreed to meet at Tehran in the late fall of 1943. On their way to the Iranian capital, Churchill and Roosevelt stopped at Cairo, where they conferred briefly with Chiang Kai-shek. The three leaders demanded unconditional surrender from the Japanese, vowing to deprive that country of all its empire. Manchuria and Formosa would be returned to China and the islands of the Pacific handed back to their former imperial masters or given to the United States.

At Tehran during the last days of November, the world's leaders discussed both military strategy and postwar relations. The Americans outlined their campaign against Japan in the Pacific, and the Soviet Union promised to join the war there after Germany's defeat. Stalin pressed the other leaders vigorously for an invasion of France, but he was unable to obtain firm commitments. Agreement came more easily on less immediate matters. The three men pledged to partition Germany, reducing it to a third-rank military power. To prevent future wars, a United Nations would oversee collective security. The Allies

U.S. soldiers looking for snipers in ruins of German building.
(Courtesy, Scribner's Archives)

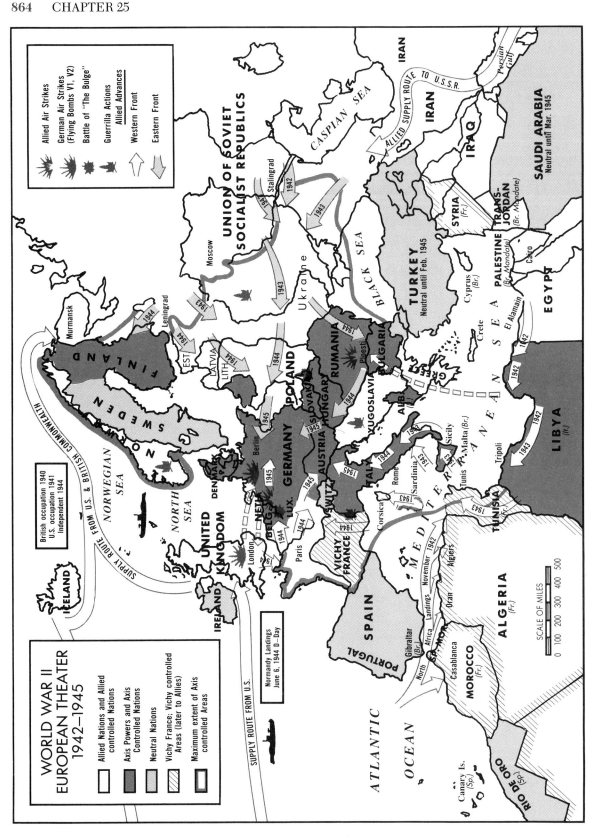

WORLD WAR II EUROPEAN THEATER 1942–1945

Allied Nations and Allied controlled Nations

Axis Powers and Axis Controlled Nations

Neutral Nations

Vichy France; Vichy controlled Areas (later to Allies)

Maximum extent of Axis controlled Areas

SCALE OF MILES

0   100 200 300 400 500

Normandy Landings June 6, 1944 D–Day

SUPPLY ROUTE FROM U.S.

British occupation 1940
U.S. occupation 1941
Independent 1944

SUPPLY ROUTE FROM U.S. & BRITISH COMMONWEALTH

Allied Air Strikes

German Air Strikes (Flying Bombs V1, V2)

Battle of "The Bulge"

Guerrilla Actions   Allied Advances

Western Front

Eastern Front

would jointly administer all liberated countries until representative institutions were set up.

1944: The Final Struggle

Bombs rained on German cities as the Anglo-Americans during 1944 opened an immense three-pronged campaign against Hitler's western stronghold. Their air war, which had carried destruction to Germany itself as early as 1942, entered a new phase. Radar bombsights tripled the destructive power of nighttime raids, and new long-range fighters permitted daytime sorties. Round-the-clock bombing, made possible by immense amounts of equipment and men from the United States, targeted German aircraft plants, communications systems, and chemical factories. Incessant bombing doubtless discouraged many Germans, already fatigued by years of warfare, but its strategic effectiveness remains questionable. Some attacks, like those against Düsseldorf and Dresden, nearly destroyed entire cities; a total of almost three million tons of bombs fell on Hitler's Reich from 1942 to 1945.

In those pre-atomic days, however, wars were still decided on the ground. The battle for western Europe began in earnest on January 22, 1944, when an Anglo-American army landed at Anzio behind the German front in Italy. But this effort soon bogged down. That spring a slow, hard advance began against the German divisions south of Rome. It linked up with the Anzio beachhead and then, on June 4, captured Rome itself. The Germans retreated to their so-called Gothic Line, some 150 miles north of the city, where the fighting stabilized.

OVERLORD   On June 6, D-Day, just two days after the fall of Rome, began the campaign code-named Operation OVERLORD, the biggest amphibious landing in history. Dwight

One American medic had more than his share of work:

"By the time I got to Normandy, several villages had already been captured. We'd just set up a tent hospital. It was unbelievable. . . . A sergeant came in and said, 'Captain, you better come out and take a look at this.' I went out, and as far as the eye could see, for miles up the highway, there were ambulances waiting to get in. We had a four-hundred-bed hospital and we were already filled. Then he said, 'I want you to look out there, too.' I looked around and there lying in the field are several hundred wounded. So I said, 'Sergeant, get me about twenty syringes and twenty shots of morphine and we're goin' out for a walk.' It was a bright, beautiful summer day. The two of us wandered from group to group. I had a vision in my mind of the Civil War, with all the wounded in the fields. In little groups. Those Mathew Brady photographs. Relived on this field."

The Normandy beachhead, June 1944. (*Courtesy, Acme Photo*)

This soldier's letters home to his wife tell a large story of World War II:

Camp Polk, La.
April 28, 1943

My Darling,

I never could have believed that my love for you could grow to any greater proportions but it has darling. . . . Your kindness is all so endearing so inexplicably adorable. I have never loved you like this before. . . .

Frank

[England]
March 30, 1944

Hi Hon,

Somehow when I write out the 'United States of America' it gives me a sort of a moral boost. Writing it, looking at it, and reflecting on the powerful meaning of that word 'united' is good for a person. The immediate reflection and knowledge that it is no trite symbol and that these 48 are really one with one common purpose is some gigantic thought to encompass. Compare the continent of North America with its 175 million odd and see what other continent is so singular in purpose. Australia, mebbe! but then it is a midget—Europe, Asia, Africa and even the presently peaceful continent South of us is disrupted with powers and claimants to power, with rulers and claimants thereof. It seems that the word 'united' should be the one reassuring, encouraging word, the word that must cause the defeatist and skeptic some worried moments. Class dismissed—

I love you,
Frank

April 26, 1944

Dearest Polly:

Well when I get to thinking of home I just get homesick as the dickens but one consoling thought is that the thing is bound to be half over and I guess I can do the balance of my time in this army on my head. The day we plan for will, please God, someday dawn and when I get off that train. . . . But it may be a boat in New York, or a plane in Pittsburgh—but who cares as long as I see you.

I love you,
Frank

Eisenhower, Supreme Commander of the Western forces, directed the attack on the French coast of Normandy. Air bombardments softened up beach defenses (Hitler's famous "Westwall") and disrupted German communications; the night before the major assault, three airborne divisions landed behind German lines, there to disrupt defense strategy; finally, at 7 a.m. on June 6, some 125,000 soldiers scrambled onto the beaches of Normandy. The Allies had put great effort into convincing Hitler, successfully, that their principal landing site would be farther north, around the city of Calais, with the result that the main German force, General Rommel's Seventh Army, stayed away for several critical days. Despite enormous casualties, which sometimes reached a hundred percent at places like Omaha Beach, the Allies established their beachhead. Within five days, sixteen more divisions landed. The invaders now occupied some eight miles of coastline.

Unlike the Italian campaign, that in France quickly took on the character of a *Blitzkrieg* in reverse. There General Patton's Third Army raced into Brittany and down the Loire Valley, while another Allied force under Montgomery drove eastward to Paris. Under orders not to retreat, the German Seventh Army counterattacked, was trapped at Falaise, and managed to extricate only a few of its troops as Polish, Canadian, British, and United States soldiers snapped shut the jaws of the trap. Now the road to Paris lay open, and on August 25 its citizens rebelled against the Nazis. British and Canadian soldiers streamed along the coast into Belgium and the Netherlands; troops of the United States headed for Luxembourg. The Allied rush halted in early September at the Siegfried Line, a string of powerfully defended forts protecting Germany against a Western invasion. But France, like Italy, was now on the side of the Allies.

Germany's Final Offensive On December 16, 1944, General Gerd von Rundstedt attacked along the thinly held front in the Ardennes Forest. Spearheaded by tanks, the offensive carried rapidly forward. Then a column of American troops blunted the advance and held the besieged city of Bastogne. This Battle of the Bulge was a very near thing for the Allies, although it proved to be Germany's last major effort on the Western Front. The Germans tenaciously defended their Rhineland cities that winter against the Allied troops across the Rhine River, but on March 7, 1945, the Allies captured the strategic bridge at Remagen. Their armies crossed over the Rhine into Germany. The end was near.

Meanwhile, the Soviet Union had destroyed Hitler's main force on the plains of eastern Europe, where the Nazis had concentrated nearly eighty percent of their military strength. Despite huge losses at Stalingrad, Hitler launched still another offensive against Russia in July 1943. But increasingly scarce supplies and poor morale robbed his legions of their elusive victory. The Eastern Front became a vast war of attrition. American equipment and Russian blood guaranteed Allied triumph. As his dreams faded, a monomaniacal Hitler threw every possible unit, every possible weapon, against the Soviet advance. Nothing availed. Russian soldiers pushed the Germans out of Ukraine in March 1944 and then that summer drove into Poland. The people of Warsaw, like those in Paris, rebelled at the approach of their liberators. But Stalin halted his advance supposedly to regroup his scattered forces, while the Nazis slaughtered the Polish patriots, having already wiped out the city's fiercely resisting Jewish ghetto. Stalin welcomed this outcome, for it killed many combat-hardened and loyal Poles who might otherwise have battled a seizure of the country by Communists obedient to the Soviet Union. That fall, the Red Army drove into the Balkans, routing Germans in Romania and Bulgaria. By the end of 1944 Soviet troops were inside East Prussia and at the gates of Budapest. All that remained was the final drive on Berlin.

A Two-Pronged Strategy in the Pacific

Guadalcanal and Papua had been more than the first successful offensive actions by American ground forces in the Pacific. They had proved that amphibious landings backed by naval concentrations and heavy air support could work, that Americans could learn jungle fighting and fight the Japanese on such ground. The battle intensified a major and long-continued debate in the American high command. Admiral Nimitz used the example of Guadalcanal to argue that taking the islands one by one would be too risky and costly, that such Japanese island fortresses as Rabaul in the Bismarcks and Truk in the Carolines were impregnable, and that the logistic problems of such a campaign were insurmountable. He favored an attack on Japan by the Central Pacific route—straight across the open reaches of the ocean, relying on carriers rather than ground-based aircraft for attacks on the less heavily fortified islands of the Central Pacific: the Gilberts, the Marshalls, and the Marianas. MacArthur, to the contrary, insisted that the effort should be concentrated in the southwest Pacific area, where ground-based aircraft could support a drive from Papua and the Solomons along New Guinea through the Netherlands East Indies to the Philippines, and from there to Japan. The Joint Chiefs were also divided, but eventually, largely because it was becoming apparent that the American economy was producing enough to support two offensives, President Roosevelt decided to accept both recommendations.

This "two roads to Tokyo" offensive began in 1943. The naval plan pushed westward and MacArthur's progressed toward the northwest. By the end of the winter of 1944, Kwajalein in the Marshalls had capitulated after a bitter struggle and Truk was neutralized from the air. By May, American forces had also reached the western end of New Guinea. In June 1944 the American Fifth Fleet, under Admiral Raymond A. Spruance, supported one army and two marine divisions at Saipan Island in the Marianas. Within one week of the initial assault, the counterattacking Japanese fleet was crushed in the Battle of the Philippine Sea and other related air actions. Carrier aircraft destroyed over five hundred Japanese planes. Having crushed the Japanese air force in the Central Pacific and turned back Japan's fleet, American forces completed the capture of Saipan and neighboring Tinian and Guam. From these islands, very long range American B-29 strategic bombers could reach Japan.

Meanwhile, in the China-India-Burma theater—designed at first

May 6, 1944

Dearest Darling,

All day I have been fighting the feeling which has been dominating me of late. I keep continually thinking of home and longing for home in the worst way. All your letters of how beautiful my daughter is becoming by the day. The realization that I am missing all these months and years of her formative growth is actually gnawing at my heart. . . .

I love you,
Frank

May 9, 1944

Dearest,

. . . The invasion [D Day], I read, is a topic of daily conjecture among the people at home and I guess you are a mite worried. Well, sweetheart, don't worry, please. It is possible I may be a member in the assault but no more possible than that I may someday die. . . .

Frank

Darling [Frank]

I miss you so very much, sweetheart, and right now I'm just plain worried. If only we'd get a letter from you. The days seem so long when there is no word from you. While you are away, darling, the mailman has to be my 'favorite guy'—

I love you,
Polly

Frank never came home. He died late in the day on D-Day, on Omaha Beach near the bluff, as he and the men in his unit, part of the initial assault wave, prepared the way for the entry of the 2d Infantry Division. It was these men who, with their supplies, were later to establish the beachhead that would permit the Allies to penetrate Europe.

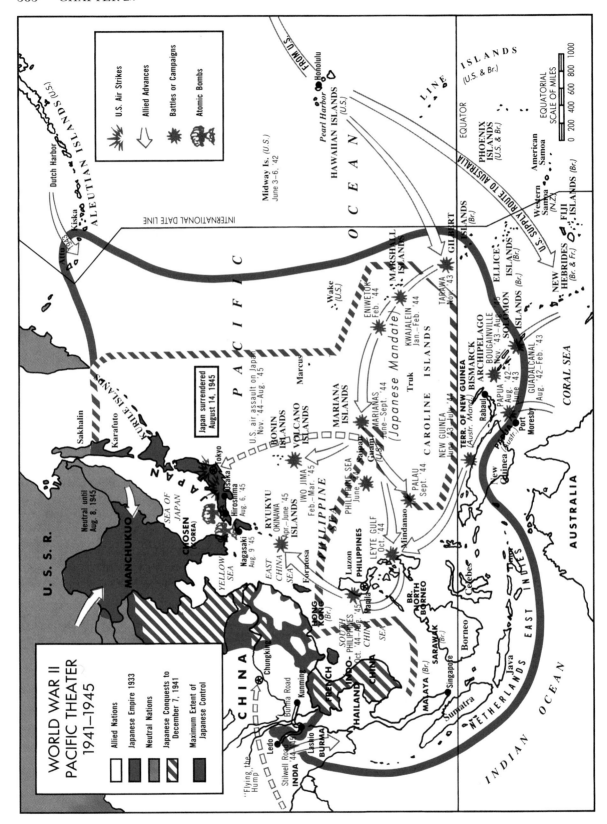

WORLD WAR II
PACIFIC THEATER
1941–1945

Allied Nations
Japanese Empire 1933
Neutral Nations
Japanese Conquests to
December 7, 1941
Maximum Extent of
Japanese Control

U.S. Air Strikes
Allied Advances
Battles or Campaigns
Atomic Bombs

only to keep China in the war, and later to provide bases for B-29 attacks against Japan—Allied troops were attempting to open the Burma road so that supplies could be taken into China by land. But geography, weather, and logistics worked against the Allies, and the Burma campaign bogged down. It would be 1945 before effective land communication replaced the flights of Americans over "the hump" from India as the principal means of access to China. Chinese troops under Chiang Kai-shek had not been pulled together into a single effective army. By the late summer of 1944 it was clear that not even effective bomber bases could be maintained and supplied in China, and late in the year the Japanese made it doubly clear by a massive attack that demolished the airfields that had been so laboriously constructed the preceding year.

On October 20, 1944, MacArthur's forces landed in the Philippines along a twenty-mile beachhead at Leyte. A Japanese naval force moved in to attack the Americans, and the largest naval battle in history ensued. The Americans sank four Japanese carriers, two battleships, and nine cruisers.

While MacArthur's forces were mopping up in the Philippines, Nimitz's forces were pressing north toward Japan. In early February the air forces began softening up another tiny stepping-stone to Japan, the island of Iwo Jima, lying only 750 miles southeast of Tokyo, close enough to allow the bombers the fighter support necessary for making heavy attacks on Japan. An intensive naval and air bombardment of Iwo Jima was conducted, and three days later the Americans landed. On February 23, 1945, the famous American flag-raising on Mount Suribachi took place. Iwo Jima was the bloodiest battle in United States Marine history: 4,189 marines were killed and 15,308 wounded. The American high command reckoned that the advantage had been worth the cost, for in March American B-29's began receiving fighter support from Iwo Jima airfields for their bombing missions over Japan.

American soldiers encountered jungle fighting in parts of the Pacific. *(Courtesy, Scribner's Archives)*

Yalta and the Postwar World

Diplomacy acquired an urgency until now reserved for the battlefield. Despite preliminary agreements about unconditional surrender, the partition of Germany, and a joint occupation of liberated areas, troubles among the Allies intensified as the western and the Soviet forces approached each other. The Western Allies worried about the principles of self-determination in eastern Europe, where the Red Army was prepared to install regimes controlled by the Kremlin. Since the British and Americans were sure to dominate the industrialized parts of Germany, the Soviet Union wanted reparations; yet reparations presumably must come principally from the Rhineland and Bavaria, precisely the areas that would be under Western control. United States military experts calculated that the war against Japan required Soviet help. Another meeting of the Big Three was necessary for sorting out these complicated and increasingly political postwar issues.

Planning for the Postwar World

In 1944 Roosevelt, though garnering a less impressive popular majority than in his previous three campaigns, had won election to his fourth presidential term. Political caution had made him choose as his vice-presidential candidate Harry S Truman of Missouri, who replaced the more radical and more controversial Henry A. Wallace. His Republican opponent, New York's governor Thomas E. Dewey, was known especially for having been as a New York City district attorney an energetic warrior against organized crime. The war had overshadowed the contest, which as an encounter between a liberal Democrat and a liberal Republican yielded little in the way of significant argument.

Roosevelt was quite ill with cardiovascular problems as early as 1944 when this picture was taken. *(Courtesy, F. D. R. Library)*

In February 1945 the newly inaugurated FDR came together with Churchill and Stalin at the Black Sea resort of Yalta for eight days of difficult talks. Each wanted something from the others. Worried by military estimates that the Pacific war might require two more years and a million American casualties—MacArthur predicted 50,000 casualties on the first day of the invasion of Japan—Roosevelt sought help from his Allies. Stalin was determined to erect subservient governments along Soviet borders, especially in eastern Europe, Iran, and China. Churchill looked forward to an enlarged British Empire, perhaps in the Middle East, and financial aid from the United States. Churchill and Stalin had already mapped out spheres of influence in the Balkans, a plan that Roosevelt was not fond of. Nevertheless, a spirit of amity signaled by the appearance of carafes of vodka at the breakfast table prevailed. On broad declarations of principle, there was ready accord. All agreed that Germany would never again cause war. All agreed that a conference would meet in San Francisco on April 25, 1945, to work out institutional arrangements for a United Nations. All claimed to agree that the liberated countries would have self-determination. But no friendship came out of Yalta.

Many Americans at times since 1945 have blamed Roosevelt for dooming eastern Europe to Communist slavery. But both the presence of the Red Army and Stalin's demands for security in that region made it unlikely that any regime could exist there that the Soviet dictator considered unfriendly. The President understood, as other westerners did not, that the area by and large did not contain the conditions for a middle-class, democratic alternative to Stalinist domination. The three leaders issued a Declaration on Liberated Europe, which guaranteed free elections and self-determination. This solved a public-relations problem in England and the United States, but just as clearly opened the way for Stalin, whose ambitions for eastern European countries had nothing to do with self-determination there.

The conference's ideas about Germany and the Pacific presented great problems for the postwar era. His country desperately weak, Stalin was greedy for Germany's industrial plants, those factories that lay almost exclusively in the western zones. He accepted an Anglo-American plan that divided the country into four sectors—north-central Germany for Britain, the south for the United States, the Rhineland for France, and the pastoral east for the Soviet Union—on condition that Moscow receive $10 billion in reparations "in kind," that

is, in goods rather than money. The Western Allies accepted this sum as a basis for discussion. All four powers would garrison the capital, Berlin, although it lay deep within the Soviet sector, and would jointly decide Germany's future. Stalin promised Roosevelt that the Soviet Union would enter the war against Japan as soon as possible, but his price was high: virtually the return of that Russian dominance in northern China exercised by the tsars before 1905. Without the cooperation that war had forced among the powers, the compromises of Yalta would soon collapse into the conflicts of the Cold War.

The End of the War   Within three months Roosevelt, a symbol of Allied unity, was gone. So was Nazi Germany, the common danger. During that early spring of 1945, Anglo-American and Soviet troops closed in on Hitler's last strongholds. General Eisenhower vetoed Montgomery's plan to drive straight for Berlin. The general, more interested in winning the war than in politicking about the future, considered this British plan likely to prolong the conflict if Nazi armies escaped to a southern redoubt in Bavaria. Instead, Eisenhower wanted to surround and destroy German armies in the Rhineland, then push south of the capital toward the Elbe River. Churchill argued furiously with Eisenhower that "We should shake hands with the Russians as far to the east as possible." Roosevelt did not resolve the issue, for the exhausted President was now in Warm Springs, Georgia, resting for the coming United Nations Conference. Around noon on April 12, he complained of a terrible headache; that afternoon he lay dead of a cerebral hemorrhage. Eisenhower now followed his own plan. Soviet and American troops met at the Elbe, some 200 miles south of Berlin, on April 27. That same day Hitler committed suicide, and Soviet soldiers raised the hammer-and-sickle flag over his command post. German armies in Italy, Austria, Holland,

The young GIs waiting for the invasion of Japan realized that their futures had suddenly changed:

"When the bombs dropped and news began to circulate that the invasion of Japan would not take place, that we would not be obliged to run up the beaches near Tokyo, assault-firing while being mortared and shelled, for all the fake manliness of our façades, we cried with relief and joy. We were going to live. We were going to grow up to adulthood after all."

When Japan's formal surrender was announced on August 15, V-J Day, Americans at home went wild with joy. A Mexican American girl in Corpus Christi, Texas, heard a sound that a year earlier would have meant a warning:

"When the war ended the sirens sounded again. Corpus Christi has a bluff. There's uptown and there's a downtown. The sailors that were there were in white because it was hot and they rolled. They would roll down this bluff on to the street and nobody was stopping them. The whole city went wild."

"Any girl . . . in downtown San Diego got kissed and thrown in Horton Plaza Fountain," Patricia Livermore would recall. "I got thrown in ten times."

This famous photograph catches a sailor and a young woman celebrating the end of the war in Times Square, New York City; neither has ever been identified. *(Courtesy, Wide World)*

and Denmark, some one million men, stopped fighting during the next week. On V-E Day, May 7, 1945, the German high command surrendered unconditionally.

On April 1 Nimitz's forces had moved to within 370 miles of Japan by invading Okinawa, a sixty-five-mile long island in the Ryukyus, near the Japanese homeland and close enough to open all Japan's skies to American fighters as well as bombers. The Japanese fought desperately at Okinawa, and the United States Navy, covering the land assault, took a heavy beating from 3,500 Japanese kamikaze pilots, who dived their explosive-laden planes directly into American vessels in a glorious sacrifice of life for the emperor. American casualties were 11,260 killed, 33,769 wounded.

Then, in August, 1945, came the dropping of atomic bombs, on the sixth on the city of Hiroshima and on the ninth, Nagasaki. On August 10, Japan offered to surrender.

A boy from Union, New Jersey, was in the midst of the celebrating:

"I can remember going into New York City and the whole harbor was one great big banner. In those days there were a lot of piers along Manhattan Island where the ships came in . . . and when they would come in the tug boats would run around and they'd be spraying water up. They'd shoot this water way up in the air and blow the whistles and all of the docks had great big banners on them—'welcome home' and 'victory.'

Everything was red, white and blue. The troop ships came in with thousands and thousands of guys jammed on them. These are the old luxury liners, the ships that before the war used to carry passengers back and forth to Europe. They tore out all of the luxury suites and crammed these guys in them and painted them gray. . . . We used to have a railroad track fairly close to our house and at night we'd hear the troop trains come through and they'd stop there and everybody would run out with bottles of wine and trade them for souvenirs."

Suggested Readings

Recent works on the era include Stephen E. Ambrose, *Eisenhower: Soldier, General of the Army, President-Elect, 1890–1952* (1983), Forrest C. Pogue, *George C. Marshall* (1987), Ruth Milkman, *Gender at Work: The Dynamics of Job Segregation by Sex During World War II* (1987), Waldo Heinrichs, *Threshold of War: FDR and American Entry into World War II* (1987), and William Klingman, *1941* (1988).

For American policy toward the persecution of the Jews, see Henry L. Feingold, *The Politics of Rescue: The Roosevelt Administration and the Holocaust, 1938–1945* (1970) and David S. Wyman, *Paper Walls: America and the Refugee Crisis, 1935–1941* (1968). Albert U. Romasco, *The Politics of Recovery* (1983), studies the politics of international economic reform. On Latin America see Irwin Gellmen, *Good Neighbor Diplomacy* (1979). Various strains of isolationism are studied in Manfred Jones, *Isolationism in America, 1935–1941* (1966).

Robert Dallek's *Franklin D. Roosevelt and American Foreign Policy, 1932–1945* (1979) is a balanced study. America's road to the Second World War is the subject of William L. Langer and S. Everett Gleason's monumental volumes, *The Challenge to Isolation, 1937–1940* (1952) and *The Undeclared War, 1940–1941* (1953). On wartime battles and strategy there is Richard Ernest and Trevor N. Dupuy, *Encyclopedia of Military History* (revised edition, 1977). A useful account of the confusion surrounding the day of infamy is Roberta Wohlstetter, *Pearl Harbor: Warning and Decision* (1962). John J. Stephen, *Hawaii Under the Rising Sun* (1984) studies Japanese planning for an invasion of Hawaii. A good survey of wartime diplomacy is Gaddis Smith, *American Diplomacy during the Second*

World War (1965). Richard Polenberg argues that the war made for great changes in American society, among them a further mechanization of agriculture, an increase in the membership of labor unions, a weakening of the ideology of racism, and a growth in government: *War and Society: The United States, 1941–1945* (1972). Roger Daniels gives a survey of the persecution of Japanese Americans during the war in *Concentration Camps, USA* (1971); see also Jacobus ten Broek et al., *Prejudice, War and the Constitution* (1954).

Fighting and winning the war are also covered in Clayton R. Koppes and Gregory D. Black, *Hollywood Goes to War: How Politics, Profits, and Propaganda Shaped World War II Movies* (1987), John Keegan's *The Second World War* (1996), Sherna B. Gluck, *Rosie the Riveter Revisited: Women, the War, and Social Change* (1987), Gerald D. Nash, *The American West Transformed: The Impact of the Second World War* (1985), Dominic Capeci, Jr., *Race Relations in Wartime Detroit* (1984), David S. Wyman, *The Abandonment of the Jews* (1984), John W. Dower, *War Without Mercy: Race and Power in the Pacific War* (1986), and John Martin Blum, *V Is for Victory* (1982).

See also Akira Iriye, *The Origins of the Second World War in Asia and the Pacific* (1987), Stephen E. Ambrose, *D-Day, June 6, 1944* (1994), Allan Berube, *Coming Out under Fire: The History of Gay Men and Women in World War Two* (1990), Charles A. Lindbergh, *The Wartime Journals* (1970), Albert E. Cowdrey, *Fighting for Life: American Military Medicine in World War II* (1994), Michael S. Sherry, *In the Shadow of War: The United States Since the 1930s* (1995), and Gerhard Weinberg, *World at Arms: A Global History of World War II* (1994).

Did the United States Provoke the Japanese into World War II?

Hosoya Chihiro

Hard-liners in the U.S. government such as Stanley Hornbeck, Cordell Hull, Henry Stimson, and Henry Morgenthau, who favored economic sanctions against Japan in the years immediately preceding the Japanese attack on Pearl Harbor, seriously miscalculated the impact of such a policy on Japan. Instead of deterring the Japanese from pursuing an expansionist policy, these economic sanctions exacerbated U.S.-Japanese relations, encouraged Japan's southward expansion, and provoked Japanese hard-liners to risk war with the United States. The advocates of the hard-line policy toward Japan misunderstood the psychology of the Japanese, particularly the middle levels of the military, the Japanese decision-making process, and Japanese economic realities. They also rode roughshod over the prudent proposals of the soft-liners in the U.S. State Department such as the director of the Far Eastern Division, Maxwell Hamilton, and Ambassador Joseph Grew in Japan.

The demand of the hard-liners for economic sanctions against Japan played into the hands of the ultranationalists in the Japanese government. The latter argued that the imposition of economic sanctions by the United States necessitated risk and expansion by Japan. In such a climate Japanese moderates found it impossible to counsel caution and accommodation. Their counterparts in the U.S. government similarly learned that they were no match for those who foolishly believed that Japan would not dare attack the United States and that economic reprisals would so cripple Japan that she would acquiesce to American pressures. . . .

The American hard-liners' policy of first proposing and then imposing economic sanctions to deter a Japanese southern advance and war failed badly. To understand how it produced the opposite effect it is necessary to consider two miscalculations about the Japanese made by the hard-line faction of the U.S. government. One was that Japan would seek to avoid war with the United States at all costs. The other assumption followed from the first, namely that Japan would inevitably submit to unbending American resolution. However, economic pressure did not restrain Japan from a southern advance. Instead it accelerated a Japanese southern policy even at the risk of possible war with the United States. . . .

The hard-line faction concluded that, in light of the disparity in strength between Japan and the United States, Japanese decision makers could not rationally decide on war. In this regard they made the mistake of applying to the Japanese in unaltered form the western model of decision making based upon rational behavior. Lack of knowledge about the psychology of the Japanese people and especially of the middle-echelon military officers in the period immediately preceding the war led the hard-line faction to miscalculate Japanese psychology. That psychology was marked by a predisposition to making crucial decisions in the face of extremely great, even illogical, risks—as was expressed in Tōjō Hideki's often quoted statement that "sometimes a man has to jump with his eyes closed, from the temple of Kiyomizu into the ravine below." This predisposition was also characterized by an absolute abhorrence of submission.

Hosoya Chihiro, "Miscalculations in Deterrent Policy: U.S.-Japanese Relations, 1938–1941," in *Pearl Harbor Reexamined: Prologue to the Pacific War,* eds. Hilary Conroy and Harry Wray (Honolulu: University of Hawaii Press, 1990), pp. 51, 60, 61, 62.

Michael Barnhart

Stanley Hornbeck, chief of the State Department's Far Eastern Division and, after 1938, political adviser for East Asian affairs, has often been the object of criticism, even derision, for his role in America's relations with Japan before Pearl Harbor. . . .

These arguments are wide of the mark. Nearly alone among the top American policymakers, Hornbeck had a clear sense of what America's interests were in East Asia, what power the United States could wield in that corner of the world, and what policies could best use that power to achieve those interests. Moreover, Hornbeck was consistently correct in his assessments of Japan's aims in the Far East.

Hornbeck believed that his country's interests were best expressed by the Open Door policy. For Hornbeck, the chief principle of that policy was respect for the territorial and administrative integrity of all nations. This was no high-sounding altruism. As long as no nation achieved hegemony over East Asia, the fundamental security of the United States would not be endangered.

Hornbeck realized that the United States was not likely to use military force to uphold this tenet. The nation's direct stake in Asia, unless hegemony actually threatened, was too small. Hornbeck maintained, however, that any effort to influence Japan or China had to be backed by a strong military. Hornbeck did not approve of bluffs. The United States, he argued throughout the decade before Pearl Harbor, ought to make clear its positions and be prepared to support them. Military force was the ultimate, but not the only, instrument of support. Hornbeck recognized that the enviable economic strength of America—and the economic vulnerability of Japan—gave another weapon of great potency to the government he served. . . .

Hornbeck's watchful concern grew to alarm. After literally scores of new laws, including the powerful National General Mobilization Law, were passed by the Japanese Diet, Hornbeck rightly concluded that the military and expansionist elements were using the patriotism generated by the war in China to revolutionize the Japanese economy and place it firmly under martial control. He feared that the result would be a militaristic Japan that would devote all its energies to aggression. This in turn would compel the United States to enlarge its own naval forces in self-defense. Hornbeck fully realized the expense that would be involved and was all the more appalled that the Japanese buildup was fueled largely by exports of American scrap iron, machine tools, and petroleum products to Japan. . . .

Until 1940 he labored largely in vain. After Japan used American-made equipment in the bombings of Chinese civilians, public pressure compelled the Roosevelt administration to call for a "moral embargo" on exports of aircraft, air munitions, and aeronautical equipment to Tokyo. The embargo did not, however, have the force of law. . . . Shipments of all types of scrap iron and an array of exotic alloy metals were stopped after Japan allied with Nazi Germany and Fascist Italy in September. Embargoes on machine tools and industrial equipment shortly followed. . . .

Informal negotiations, going on since April [1941], still offered some hope for avoiding armed conflict. These reached their end in the final offer, called Proposal B, from Japan in late November. The Japanese asked for a restoration of U.S.-Japanese trade relations before the asset freeze of July (meaning a resumption of American oil shipments), American help to enable Japan to procure materials, including oil, from the Dutch East Indies, and an American promise not to "hinder" peace efforts between Japan and China (meaning an end of American aid to the Chinese). In exchange, the Japanese offered to withdraw their troops from the southern half of Indochina.

Hornbeck opposed acceptance. Proposal B, if agreed to, promised the virtual defeat of China while the United States provided Japan with additional stockpiles of oil! The United States government rejected Proposal B.

The result was the unforeseen attack on Pearl Harbor and the equally unforeseen Japanese victories of the spring of 1942. Nevertheless, historians should not allow perfect hindsight to cloud their judgments of the past. . . .

Frequently the argument is raised that the United States ought to have pursued a less hard-line policy so to have encouraged the resurgence of Japanese "moderates." These moderates, it continues, then would have redirected Japanese policy back toward a closer alignment with the West or, at the least, have agreed to some sort of *modus vivendi* that would have averted war.

This reasoning does not stand scrutiny. . . . The sad fact is that there were no Japanese moderates with the will or ability to deflect their country from the course chosen for it by the military and the aggressive civilian leaders. . . . Hornbeck was right.

Michael Barnhart, "Hornbeck Was Right: The Realist Approach to American Policy toward Japan," *in Pearl Harbor Reexamined: Prologue to the Pacific War,* eds. Hilary Conroy and Harry Wray (Honolulu: University of Hawaii Press, 1990), pp. 65–71.

The atomic bomb explodes over Hiroshima, August 6, 1945. *(Courtesy, United States Air Force Photo)*

26
Postwar Politics and the Cold War

HIROSHIMA AND NAGASAKI

Hiroshima—the name means "broad island"—had never suffered conventional bombing during the war. On the morning of August 6, 1945, a lone American bomber, the *Enola Gay*, approached the city, lazy in the sky, from the southeast. As the B-29's bombardiers released the five-ton atomic bomb it carried, the sky above Hiroshima was blue and serene, the air flooded with glittering sunlight. An all-clear air raid signal had just sounded, and the inhabitants were going about their daily business. Suddenly there came a great flash of light, described as "brighter than a thousand suns," followed by the lacerating heat of a giant fireball, then the sound of a blast bringing the force of hurricane winds, and finally, the now-familiar multicolored mushroom cloud rising high above the city.

The bomb, with a destructive force equivalent to that of twenty thousand tons of TNT, exploded 1,800 feet above the center of the flat city built mostly of wood. Within a radius of two miles of ground zero, the destruction was total: metal and stone melted, and human beings were incinerated. Then fire spread everywhere. The nine-square-mile city almost disappeared. As many as 200,000 Japanese died, either immediately or some time after, from the bomb and the resultant fires. Human suffering from burns was terrible. The trimmed and nurtured landscape that the Japanese had loved was scorched to dead soil and rubble, and with its scorching, survivors felt as though nature herself had died.

HISTORICAL EVENTS

1938
House Un-American Activities Committee (HUAC)

1944
GI Bill of Rights • Dumbarton Oaks Conference

1945
First use of atomic bomb • United Nations meets in San Francisco • Big Three meet at Potsdam • First (and only) use of atomic bomb, on Hiroshima and Nagasaki

1946
Nationwide strikes • Council of Economic Advisers created • Baruch Plan fails • Republicans gain control of Congress

1947
To Secure These Rights published by civil rights committee • George Kennan proposes containment policy • Truman Doctrine • The Marshall Plan (European Recovery Program) proposed • National Security Act of 1947 • Department of Defense and Central Intelligence Agency created • Taft-Hartley Act of 1947

continued

HISTORICAL EVENTS

1948
Truman elected President
• Communists seize Czechoslovakia
• Berlin Airlift begins • Truman prohibits discrimination in hiring federal employees and orders end to racial discrimination in the military

1949
Truman proposes the Fair Deal
• North Atlantic Treaty Organization (NATO) formed • National Housing Act of 1949 • People's Republic of China formed under Mao Zedong
• Chiang Kai-shek sets up exile regime in Taiwan • Soviet Union tests atomic weapon

1950
National Security Council Paper No. 68 • Senator McCarthy begins his campaign against Communism
• American troops sent to Korea
• Eisenhower appointed military commander of NATO

1951
Korean front stabilizes along the 38th parallel • MacArthur relieved of his command

1952
Eisenhower elected President

1953
Korean armistice begins in June

1954
McCarthy loses support in Army–McCarthy hearings

Three days later, another atomic bomb was dropped, this time on Nagasaki, Hiroshima's neglected historical sister. The captain who piloted the plane wrote: "Does one feel any pity or compassion for the poor devils about to die? Not when one thinks of Pearl Harbor and of the Death March on Bataan." Mass open cremations followed; perhaps 100,000 more people died then or later.

Only gradually did the world come to realize that an even more wretched curse had been visited on the two cities in the form of a slow, painful, invisible contamination—radiation poisoning. The course of the disease consisted of vomiting, diarrhea, fever, loss of hair, skin ulcerations, and purple spots on the body from internal bleeding. Unknown numbers died later of cancer.

For President Harry Truman, the decision to use the bomb had been plain. The bomb from its inception had been intended as a weapon to be used against the nation's enemies. Besides, it might save many tens of thousands of American lives by shortening the war. And after all, the Japanese had struck us at Pearl Harbor without warning. Some advisers had suggested exploding a demonstration bomb in an uninhabited area in the Pacific to convince the Japanese of the new weapon's terrible power. But government scientists feared that the bomb might prove a dud, and there existed a very limited number of bombs to detonate.

On August 10, the day after Nagasaki was destroyed, the Japanese agreed to surrender.

The use of the atomic bomb deprived the United States of some of the moral superiority it had held through the war. No longer could we speak of totally evil Axis powers confronting

Hiroshima after the blast.
(Courtesy, United States Air Force Photo)

totally righteous Allies. The United States was the first and only country to commit such an act of monumental devastation with a single weapon against a primarily civilian population. "O, it is excellent," Shakespeare writes, "To have a giant's strength; but it is tyrannous / To use it like a giant." In recent times critics have argued that the use of the bomb was unnecessary, that Japan was beaten anyway and ready to surrender. Some have even suggested that the principal reason the United States employed the bomb was to demonstrate its military superiority to the Soviet Union, that it was thus the first act of the Cold War as much as the last of the war against Japan.

One point deserves some consideration: perhaps these actual demonstrations of even these miniature atomic bombs' awesome power served to instill a degree of caution in the world's leading powers. The proliferation of atomic weapons and the availability of nuclear raw materials, however, put that restraint at risk.

Harry S Truman

A Missouri Democrat   One of President Roosevelt's closest aides, Steve Early, said only: "Harry, please come over to the White House right away." Several hours before on that day, April 12, 1945, in Warm Springs, Georgia, President Franklin D. Roosevelt had died of a massive cerebral hemorrhage.

Almost a legend by 1945, Roosevelt, through his reassuring manner no less than his virtuoso leadership, had guided a nation through depression and global war. Now, when Vice President Harry Truman arrived at the White House, he was met by Eleanor Roosevelt, who said simply, "Harry, the President is dead." "I felt," Truman was to remark a little later, "like the moon, the stars and all the planets had fallen on me."

Harry S Truman. *(Courtesy, UPI)*

Harry S Truman of Missouri considered himself a plain man, taking pride in his honesty and self-reliance. His mother had inculcated a resoluteness in this middle-class child: do your best and don't worry about it afterwards. The family farm prospered during the Progressive Era; Truman served creditably as an artillery captain in World War I; the postwar recession ruined a haberdashery venture in Kansas City. Out of work, Truman gratefully accepted from Tom Pendergast, the head of a Kansas City political machine, an endorsement to run for county judge. A reputation for integrity and a folksy campaign style won the election, and Truman settled into the comfortable life of presiding over a quiet court.

A dispute among Democratic bosses in Missouri gave Truman a chance to run for United States senator in 1934. His political finesse and a workmanlike record carried him to Washington, where he vigorously supported Roosevelt and the New Deal. Senate leaders back in Washington put Truman in charge of a watchdog committee on the conduct of the war, a difficult job he performed with sober dispatch. But no aura of destiny surrounded him, at least not before 1944.

In that year, a bitter squabble broke out in the Democratic Party over the vice-presidential nomination. Liberal Democrats supported the incumbent, Henry A. Wallace. But powerful midwesterners, southerners, and big-city bosses considered Wallace too radical, and combined their considerable forces to replace him. Busy with the war, and not wishing to offend, an ailing Roosevelt allowed the 1944 Democratic Convention to pick Truman, a good New Dealer and a good campaigner from an important border state. The election that fall made Truman Vice President; Roosevelt's death made him President.

A Quicksilver Peace: From Allies to Adversaries

Truman and the World

As Vice President, Truman had been excluded from any role in policy and decision making. Now, inexperienced in foreign affairs, and surrounded by advisers far more knowledgeable than he, the new Chief Executive had to gather the reins of government into his own hands. Events tumbling over one another in the last months of the war and the first days of peace enabled Truman to establish his authority almost immediately.

The United Nations Charter reflected the new President's determination. At the Dumbarton Oaks Conference in 1944 and again at the Yalta Conference early the following year, Roosevelt and the Allied powers had pledged to replace the discredited League of Nations with a new, more effective instrument of collective security. But when they gathered in San Francisco during April 1945, just as Truman was taking over in Washington, negotiations turned unpredictable and difficult. Friction over Poland and disputes over procedure led Truman abruptly to inform Stalin that the United States would go ahead with the United Nations project with or without the Soviet Union. Stalin relented. The Charter allowed all member nations to discuss any question and vote in the General Assembly, but the Assembly's recommendations required approval from the Security Council. This supercabinet had five permanent members: the United States, Britain, France, the Soviet Union, and China, represented by the Nationalist, anti-Communist government of Chiang Kai-shek. Sitting with them were to be six temporary members (later increased to ten) elected periodically by the General Assembly. The Security Council would meet to deal with the world's crises. Each member had the power to veto decisions of the Council's majority. A Secretariat administered dozens of economic, social, financial, and relief agencies, all to have their headquarters with the rest of the UN in New York City.

The Potsdam Conference

New rivalries quickly crushed hopes for worldwide cooperation. At a meeting in July 1945 of the Big Three at Potsdam, near Berlin, Truman, Stalin, and Clement Attlee (who had defeated Churchill as British prime minister and replaced him halfway through the conference) pondered the future of eastern Europe, the occupation of Germany, and the war against Japan. They demanded an unconditional surrender from the Japanese,

The United Nations General Assembly Building, New York, completed in 1952. *(Courtesy, United Nations)*

and Stalin again promised to send Soviet troops against the Japanese in Manchuria and North China. In other areas, the problems proved intractable. Huge Soviet armies in the Balkans and eastern Europe added compelling force to Stalin's demand for "friendly regimes" there. Unable to compromise, the three men simply postponed decisions about Poland, Hungary, Romania, Austria, Yugoslavia, Bulgaria, and Greece. The future of Germany proved an even more divisive issue. Stalin, already angered by Washington's refusal of a postwar loan to rebuild his war-shattered country, demanded a joint occupation of all Germany and immense reparations from the defeated nation. The British and Americans succeeded in reaffirming a zonal occupation, coinciding roughly with the distribution of Allied troops at the time. Stalin satisfied himself with a promise from the other Allies to turn over twenty-five percent of western Germany's factories and movable equipment as reparations in kind.

Eleven years later Truman recorded his memories of Stalin at Potsdam:

"A large number of agreements were reached only to be broken as soon as the unconscionable Russian Dictator returned to Moscow! And I liked the little son of a bitch. . . ."

Domestic Whirlwinds: Demobilization and Reform

Conversion to Peacetime   Roosevelt's death and the end of the war threw American politics into prolonged uncertainty. Democrats argued among themselves over civil rights, labor policy, and demobilization. Yet the Republicans, divided over foreign policy and weakened by so many years of defeat, seemed unlikely to provide a strong, effective alternative. Some Americans wanted to dismantle what they called "the welfare state." Others looked forward to a postwar extension of the New Deal, particularly in health care, housing, and full employment. Mingled with hopes and promises of a new era of peace and affluence was anxiety. Some of the nation's economists predicted that a flood of twelve million returned veterans into the labor market and the shutting down of ten million jobs that the war had brought would return the prewar depression.

These disturbing predictions complicated the task of converting the nation's economy to peacetime. In part to move the veterans back into the labor force, Congress passed the GI Bill of Rights. It offered them a range of benefits, including college tuition, vocational training, low-interest home loans, small business loans, health care, and even weekly unemployment checks if necessary. Four out of five GIs went back to school, many to colleges that welcomed them gratefully after fifteen years of half-empty classrooms. For the first time in American history, many males now looked forward to a university education as a matter of course. The GI Bill was one of the greatest programs of the immediate postwar period. It would succeed in easing the absorption of the discharged veterans into the nation's economy and paid them back, at least in part, for their wartime sacrifices.

Initially the postwar period seemed to strengthen traditional gender relations. The media preached the virtues of domesticity and women at home. But despite the strength of domestic values, the percentage of married women and mothers who worked for a wage or a salary climbed steadily. Many women worked to contribute extra income to their families. Even during the conservative 1950s, the numbers of women in the labor force would increase steadily. What was not to change swiftly were popular attitudes that endorsed inequality of pay, approved segregation of the labor force by gender, and expected women to assume full responsibility for domestic work and child care. Not until the maturation of the new women's movement at the end of the 1960s and beginning of the 1970s would these questions even be frequently raised, and mostly by and for women who were not poor, not black, and not Hispanic.

Throughout United States history, at least until the years of the New Deal, the federal government had assumed a very small role in regulating the economy. Few Americans even believed it was the responsibility of government to guarantee full employment and stable prices. The Great Depression and World War II changed all that, especially after the results of wartime spending made it clear that the federal government, through large disbursements of funds, could affect the course of the economy. Events, then, had forced Washington to adopt and come to like the economic practice advocated by the British scholar John Maynard Keynes. At the end of World War II, Truman's administration wanted to make the transition to a peacetime economy as well as continue the social and economic programs inaugurated by the New Deal. Liberal Democrats also wanted the federal government to assume permanent responsibility for guaranteeing full employment in the United States.

The legislation designed to achieve those goals was the Employment Act passed by Congress in 1946. It created the Council of Economic Advisers to assist the President in developing economic policy, established a Joint Economic Committee of Congress to monitor those policies, and gave the federal government responsibility for maintaining full employment. It was tacitly understood that the government should use spending and taxation policies to stimulate employment and to control prices.

Labor Trouble, Inflation, and Political Bickering   Labor-management relations deteriorated rapidly. The wartime agreement not to strike, along with the decline that postwar inflation inflicted on purchasing power, had put the average wage earner well behind the rest of the country in real personal income. Union members demanded pay hikes. President Walter Reuther of the United Automobile Workers argued that if workers' real wages did not increase, they could not buy enough to absorb the production anticipated by American business. Large profits drawn from wartime government contracts, he insisted, could and should finance higher pay without any boost in retail prices. Management, to the contrary, feared being locked into long-term wage contracts with labor unions when the economic future of the nation seemed so uncertain. At the end of 1945 the disagreement turned to conflict. In November workers walked off their jobs in all General Motors plants. Electrical workers, meatpackers, and steelworkers followed during January 1946. That spring John L. Lewis ordered out the United Mine Workers, which threatened to close down a wide range of satellite industries dependent upon soft coal. These strikes were settled, but in late May a strike shut down the country's railroads. Faced with the prospect of economic chaos, Truman reacted quickly. The President promised that unless the strikers returned to work he would draft them and order the army to run the trains. The railway brotherhoods relented at once.

Chrysler workers on strike. Relations between management and labor deteriorated in the postwar period, as inflation and unemployment rose. (*Courtesy, United Auto Workers*)

The congressional elections of 1946 rebuked those who wanted to maintain Roosevelt's legacy. The Republicans turned popular dissatisfaction with the economy into a stunning victory that gave them control of both the Senate and the House of Representatives for the first time in sixteen years. After the Republicans triumphed in November, everyone expected a difficult two years in domestic politics—with a progressive President now confronting conservative legislators. Nonetheless, Senator Robert Taft, the Republican leader, did indicate that Congress might address at least one progressive concern. "You don't get decent housing from the free enterprise system," he observed. And in foreign affairs bipartisanship made for action and innovation.

Atomic Diplomacy

The American atomic monopoly reinforced an American sense of total security. It also must have made the Soviet leadership even more insecure. More than ever Stalin thought he needed compliant regimes in those nations that bordered the Soviet Union in eastern Europe, central Asia, and the Far East. His maneuvers in these areas strengthened American hostility. Truman and his new secretary of state, James Byrnes, labored on proposed peace treaties to resurrect a unified but neutral Germany as a buffer state against Stalin. Remembering two German invasions of Russia in less than thirty years, Stalin responded by disrupting, postponing, and ignoring these negotiations. By the middle of 1947, the two opposing sides had tacitly divided Europe: Italy and the heavily industrialized western portions of Germany in the Western sphere of influence; eastern Europe and most of the Balkans in the Soviet sphere.

The Baruch Plan   In June 1946, Bernard Baruch, on behalf of the Truman Administration, submitted a daring plan to the United Nations for the international control of atomic energy. An agency independent of any country would operate all uranium mines and production plants. It was also to oversee nuclear research, monitor all explosions, and administer the peaceful use of atomic energy. Composed of scientists from many lands, the new body would inspect unhampered all atomic installations everywhere and punish violators. No veto could block its decisions.

Stalin rejected this idea and instead called for the immediate destruction of all nuclear weapons and a multinational treaty outlawing nuclear war. He might have liked that to occur. But he was in fact convinced that the United States was determined to exploit its economic and political power and would never agree to the abolition of its nuclear arsenal. His own scientists would soon develop an atomic device, an equalizer as he saw it, necessary to the safety of the Soviet Union in response to the huge American lead in both atomic technology and industrial production. Hence the lack of any Soviet veto in the Baruch Plan made the plan doubly objectionable to him. The Allies were becoming relentless adversaries.

Containing Communism   An early indication of how matters were shaping up between the United States and the Soviet Union were the plans that Secretary of the Navy James V. Forrestal outlined for American naval bases scattered throughout the Mediterranean. More specific about the nature of the emerging conflict was Winston Churchill's charge in a speech at Fulton, Missouri, that an "iron curtain" had descended across the continent "from the Baltic to the Adriatic," sealing off the Communist world from the West. (Forty-six years later another Russian leader, Mikhail Gorbachev, would return to Fulton to speak of the raising of the iron curtain.)

In Moscow, George Frost Kennan, a mid-level counselor at the United States Embassy there, reported an ominous warning from Stalin: "The present capitalist world order makes peace impossible." Kennan drafted a long dispatch to the State Department, describing Russian paranoia about the outside world. The Soviet leaders, he concluded, "are committed fanatically to the belief that it is necessary to disrupt the internal harmony of our society and to break the international authority of our state, if Soviet power is to be secure." The proper response—which Kennan anonymously proposed in a famous article of

Communism, according to George Kennan, was like

"a toy automobile wound up and headed in a given direction, stopping only when it meets with some unanswerable force . . . a fluid stream which moves constantly, wherever it is permitted to move . . . [until] . . . it has filled every nook and cranny available to it in the basin of world power."

1947 by Mr. X in the prestigious journal *Foreign Affairs*—was for the United States to "contain" Communist power by rebuilding American military might as a "counterweight" to Soviet "expansive tendencies." Kennan's Mr. X essay is widely perceived as the defining statement of American containment policy in the opening years of confronting the Communists.

Since early 1945, the Soviet Union had given moral support to local Communist guerrillas in Greece, while England aided the embattled Greek monarchy with money and troops. But in 1947 the British ambassador told Truman that his country could no longer sustain the financial burden. At the same time, Stalin was leaning heavily on Turkey to gain control of the Bosporus Straits. The Soviet Union seemed likely to replace the British throughout the eastern Mediterranean. Thereupon, Truman boldly went to Congress for $400 million in military assistance for Greece and Turkey. "It must be the foreign policy of the United States," he explained, "to support free peoples who are resisting attempted subjugation by armed minorities or by outside pressures." A new secretary of state, former Army Chief of Staff George Marshall, heartily approved this so-called Truman Doctrine. Greece and Turkey survived and became firm allies of the Western powers. The Truman Doctrine fully placed the United States in a Cold War against the Soviet Union. No longer would our foreign policy be a matter of sallies beyond our borders, to which we would then return. We were committing ourselves to a complex and steady course of diplomatic, economic, and military engagement.

Containment in Action

The Marshall Plan   Economic catastrophe and a growing sense of frustration in western and central Europe seemed likely, many feared, to push the whole continent into Stalin's embrace. The war's destruction made recovery in western Europe appear remote, and the unusually harsh winter of 1946–47 edged the suffering populace toward despair. Already French and Italian Communists had demonstrated impressive voting strength.

The administration moved quickly to halt what it believed to be the spread into western Europe of Communism controlled by Moscow. In a commencement address at Harvard University, Marshall proposed the rescue of Europe's economic health. "There can [otherwise] be no political stability and no assured peace," he declared. "Our policy is directed against . . . hunger, poverty, desperation and chaos." Instantly applauded throughout a troubled Europe, Marshall's project for massive aid was a breathtaking act of policy and imagination.

Within three weeks, British, French, and Soviet leaders gathered in Paris to work out specifics for the European Recovery Program. But the Russians, angered by what they saw as a scheme to undermine their influence and position in Europe, quickly left the conference, denouncing the ERP as "an imperialist plan to subjugate independent nations."

Secretary of State George C. Marshall (left), seen here with U.S. Ambassador to Britain Lewis Douglas. The Marshall Plan rebuilt western Europe's economy. *(Courtesy, United Press International)*

Truman had many motives for this spectacular scheme to aid the economic recovery of western Europe. Humanitarianism blended almost imperceptibly with hopes for anti-Communist and American advantage. A prosperous Europe would provide markets for United States manufacturers; successfully democratic societies in the West would halt any drift toward Communism there and dampen the appeal of that ideology elsewhere in the world. Still, the Marshall Plan encountered significant opposition from the new Congress. Some internationalists considered unilateral action a dangerous affront to the Russians. At the other pole was isolationism, an attitude once associated with a number of political progressives but now tilted to the right, a strong force in a national legislature now dominated in both houses by the Republicans. Determined to lower taxes and reduce the role of government in American life, isolationist conservatives detested massive aid to Europe, and feared alliances and commitments that would compromise American independence. Nonetheless the Marshall Plan moved steadily through Congress. In this as in other policies of the postwar years, the American confrontation of international Communism was chiefly a liberals' rather than a conservatives' enterprise.

In early 1948 sixteen western European nations submitted a comprehensive report, outlining their specific needs and asking for $20 billion during the next four years. Hearings began several months later before a sympathetic Foreign Relations Committee chaired by Senator Arthur Vandenberg, a Michigan Republican from the liberal internationalist wing of his party. Suddenly, on February 25, 1948, Communists staged a successful coup d'état in Czechoslovakia. The seizure of this industrialized country convinced Congress and many officials of Stalin's aggressive designs. Within six weeks, the legislators had voted $17 billion in Marshall aid. American money and materials flooded western Europe for the next four years, creating a recovery so fast and so complete that Communist parties, strong at the war's end, rapidly declined in political power.

United States Foreign Aid, 1945–1955

$ Billions

| 1945–50 | 1951–55 |

■ Economic Aid
■ Military Aid

The Berlin Airlift   All during 1947 the Soviet Union had bickered with the British and Americans over Germany's future. Stalin—understandably after losing twenty million troops to the Nazis—aimed for a weak, neutral Germany, forever unable to wage modern war. To that end the USSR advocated joint control over Germany's industrial areas. The Western powers wanted an economically strong Germany that could be an active trading partner and again fuel the economies of western Europe. As the Marshall Plan moved toward adoption, Britain, the United States, and later France made plans to merge their three zones into a single political and economic unit. A furious Stalin then impeded Western ground access to Berlin, isolated some 110 miles inside the Soviet occupation zone. In response the western Allies speeded up plans for a single regime in western Germany. On June 25, 1948, the Red Army blocked all ground access to Berlin. Soviet propaganda clarified Stalin's aims: to force the West to give up its plan to unify western Germany or risk losing its advanced position in Berlin.

For nearly a year, the Soviet military cut off Western ground

contact with Berlin. Realizing that a mistake might precipitate a third world war, Truman responded with a sophisticated use of air power. Hundreds of British and American planes flew in essential supplies to some two million people trapped in Berlin behind the Soviet blockade. The technical skills of the pilots and flight crews, together with the great courage of the Berliners, matched the determination of Moscow. The commander of American troops in Europe, Lucius D. Clay, announced that the USSR "can't drive us out by any action short of war." Eleven months passed. Suddenly Stalin proposed a scheme that in effect masked his surrender, promising to respect Berlin's independence in return for the resumption of regular meetings of the largely ceremonial Council of Foreign Ministers.

NATO   The Berlin crisis of 1948 and 1949 had a tremendous impact upon Washington's foreign policy. The State Department quickly opened talks aimed at establishing a defensive alliance with Britain, France, Italy, the Netherlands, Denmark, Norway, Portugal, and Canada. Despite the continuous prod of the Berlin blockade, opposition to a comprehensive alliance developed in the Senate. Senator Taft opposed the idea because it "committed this country to the policy of a land war in Europe." Nonetheless, the North Atlantic Treaty Organization (NATO) passed in the legislatures of Britain and the United States. Article 5 provided that "an armed attack

Post–World War II partition of Germany.

against one or more of the signatories . . . shall be considered an attack against them all."

This formula made explicit the need for a standing American army. The National Security Act of 1947 brought all the armed forces under the administrative control of a new Department of Defense. James Forrestal became its first secretary and began the long task of molding the rival services into a cooperative military enterprise. A Joint Chiefs of Staff worked under the secretary, although at times its members leap-frogged over him by appealing to sympathetic congressmen or directly to the public. Intelligence functions and personnel were brought together in the Central Intelligence Agency (CIA). The secretaries of state, defense, and the treasury became members—with a large number of experts and special assistants—of the newly formed National Security Council, which coordinated decision making about pressing questions of military intervention.

Rearmament, the Marshall Plan, and the NATO alliance revolutionized United States foreign policy. A nation that had never had a standing army of any substance in peacetime, and had not entered a formal military treaty alliance since the compact with the French during the Revolution, now took on heavy overseas commitments, both economic and political. The United States boasted the muscle to defend those interests with force if necessary.

Politics as Usual: The Election of 1948 and Its Aftermath

Congress and the President, together fashioning precedent-shattering military and diplomatic policies, continued to quarrel on domestic issues. Truman confronted an alliance of conservatives on Capitol Hill, who not only blocked future reform but also aimed at undoing important parts of the New Deal. "We have got to break" argued its leader, Senator Robert Taft of Ohio, "with the corrupting idea that we can legislate prosperity, equality and opportunity." Southern Democrats, seriously alarmed by Truman's increasing commitment to civil rights, often joined with the Republicans.

The Taft-Hartley Act   A battle erupted early in 1947, almost as soon as the new Eightieth Congress convened, over the future of labor unions. Many Americans were blaming both high prices and scarcities on the greed of big unions. That militant leaders like John L. Lewis of the United Mine Workers called for strikes in defiance of court orders added to the unpopularity of unions. Many conservatives were philosophically opposed to unions, believing that they wielded unwarranted power over American labor and disrupted the free market. The anti-labor mood of the postwar 1940s, combined with conservative control of Congress, produced the Taft-Hartley Act of 1947.

This complicated statute outlawed major tools of the labor movement: the closed shop, a contract with management requiring workers to join a union before taking a particular job; the secondary boycott, in which a union picketed firms not directly involved in a labor dispute but doing business with a company that was; and the check-off, under which employers agreed to deduct union dues from paychecks. In addition, the act banned contributions from unions to political campaigns and required workers to notify management of a strike in advance and to postpone any walkout for eighty days if it "affected an entire industry" or "imperiled the national health or safety." Taft-Hartley thus blunted labor's most powerful weapon, the strike, and limited the control of union leaders over the rank and file. Truman vetoed the bill at once, arguing that it would "encourage distrust and suspicions and . . . threaten our democratic society." The next day, Congress overrode his veto. Republicans everywhere were elated: Taft-Hartley redeemed a major campaign promise, reversed the course of New Deal reform, and appeared to have humiliated Truman. But labor unions pledged a struggle to repeal what they called "the slave labor law."

Congress and the President battled as well over inflation and tax policy. The GOP wanted to lower income taxes, maintaining that the money left in the private economy would go into investment and consumer spending, which in turn would quicken the economy to everyone's benefit. Twice during 1947 Congress passed bills reducing taxes by some twenty percent; Truman vetoed both of them. The President argued that a tax cut would aggravate inflation. Although most economists agreed with him, political pressures during the elec-

"The New Deal is kaput," gloated the conservative *New York Daily News* in 1949, like "the Thirty Years' War or the Black Plague or other disasters. . . . [Its demise] is like coming out of the darkness into sunlight. Like feeling clean again after a long time in the muck."

tion year of 1948 enabled Congress to override Truman's veto of a third tax cut bill. The angry President noted that the reductions benefited the upper classes more than working people, and that Congress still had not acted on proposals for control of wages and prices. These immediate economic issues were rapidly becoming the stuff of an exciting presidential election.

Thomas E. Dewey, who some said looked like the man on a wedding cake, was heavily favored to defeat President Truman in the 1948 election. But Truman's whistle-stop campaign won the day. *(Courtesy, AP/Wide World Photos)*

The Election of 1948—the Republicans

Observers did not give the embattled President much of a chance in the 1948 election. The Republican primary battles gradually narrowed to two men: Senator Taft and Governor Thomas E. Dewey of New York, the nominee in 1944. Though at ease with Taft's more conservative philosophy, most Republicans worried that the stilted oratory and unyielding views of the "somber senator" might needlessly risk GOP defeat. Dewey had been a successful governor of a large state, and still carried a certain glamour from his earlier role of racket-busting district attorney who had prosecuted Murder, Incorporated, an organized gang of assassins for hire. Having a strong civil rights record and connections to organized labor in New York, he belonged to the more liberal wing of the Republican Party. Dewey campaigned effectively, stressing a moderation that essentially embraced the New Deal while suggesting that few further reforms should be initiated. Sophisticated politicking quickly isolated Taft, who withdrew on the third ballot, making Dewey's nomination unanimous.

The GOP platform reflected the sentiments of Dewey's camp. Influenced by the Berlin crisis which broke out during the convention, the party readily endorsed an essentially liberal internationalist foreign policy, lauding "collective security against aggression." The Republicans took credit for the Taft-Hartley Act as "a sensible reform of the labor law" and promised more tax reductions. But the party platform did not attack the New Deal, and even called for federally sponsored slum clearance and low-cost housing projects along with civil rights legislation.

The Election of 1948—the Democrats

As the lure of victory unified Republicans on a strategy of moderation, Democrats were battling over ideology. Henry Wallace pushed for conciliation with the Soviet Union; other liberal Democrats supported containment of the Communists. Their leaders, particularly the mayor of Minneapolis, Hubert H. Humphrey, also struggled to commit the party to civil rights. Southern Democrats protested this attack on local traditions and countered with a tough rejoinder: respect states' rights or risk a destructive southern desertion of the party. A battle over civil rights raged during the convention. The liberals won what would prove a historic victory: the platform pledged the party "to eradicate all racial, religious and economic discrimination." They also pushed through promises of federal aid to education, national health insurance, repeal of Taft-Hartley, and increases in the minimum wage and in social security coverage. The 1948 Democratic platform was an agenda for reform. The convention nominated Truman unanimously.

Other Political Parties   Angered by the Democrats' antisegregation platform, the Alabama and Mississippi delegations walked out of the convention and at a meeting in Birmingham several days later organized a States' Rights Party, popularly known as the Dixiecrats. This convention, attended primarily by reactionary elements long familiar to the South, nominated for President the governor of South Carolina, James Strom Thurmond. A blunt platform declared opposition to any force that threatened to interfere with local "social custom," which meant, of course, white supremacy. Dixiecrat leadership came mostly from state and local Democratic politicians in the deep South. Meanwhile, Henry Wallace, running as the candidate of the newly formed Progressive Party, denounced containment. The Communist Party in the United States officially endorsed Wallace during August.

The Democrats, already facing a resurgent Republican Party, were now threatened with serious defections. The Dixiecrats might deprive the Democratic Party of its normally secure southern base. Wallace's candidacy could draw votes away from the party's left wing in New York State. The Americans for Democratic Action, a new organization of liberal anti-Communist Democrats, worked to lessen the influence of Wallace.

The Whistle-Stop Campaign   Ever a fighter, Truman in this time of great political peril to him surprised the country by calling the Eightieth Congress back into session during late July, challenging the Republicans to enact their own convention platform, which was clearly more liberal than the Republican members of Congress. GOP congressmen at first vacillated and then blundered, when several senators proposed ending farm price supports as a means of reducing taxes. Throughout his grueling thirty-thousand mile whistle-stop campaign Truman laced into the "party of privilege" and "old mossbacks in a do-nothing Congress." He spoke plainly and directly, pounding the Republicans for weakening labor, hurting farmers, and cutting taxes for the wealthy: "The Republicans are committed to a program to benefit special interests—the powers of big business and monopoly. The only people who have prosperity under the Republicans are those who live on the fat profits made by [the exploitation of] workers, farmers and the common everyday citizen." From the platform of his train's rear car, Truman reminded his audience of his own country background. Organized labor supported Truman vigorously, if only because of his veto of Taft-Hartley, and farmers everywhere recalled the "Hoover" Depression. To Roman Catholic audiences Truman spoke of his tough anti-Communism. He courted Jews by quickly recognizing the new state of Israel.

President Truman had implemented a federal civil rights program that for its time was the most comprehensive in United States history. Late in 1946 he established the President's Committee on Civil Rights to study discrimination in the United States. The committee published its report *To Secure These Rights* in 1947, and Truman accepted many of its sweeping recommendations. He asked Congress in 1948 to establish a permanent federal civil rights commission, a permanent fair

"Give-em-hell" Harry drew increasing criticism from Republicans, but for the most part their efforts to counter Truman were ineffective.
(Courtesy, Library of Congress)

employment practices commission, a congressional committee on civil rights, and a civil rights division in the Justice Department. He also proposed a federal antilynching law and legislation prohibiting discrimination in interstate transportation and in voting rights.

The proposals were ahead of their time and made little progress through a Congress controlled by a coalition of conservative Republicans and southern Democrats. But Truman moved ahead with his own civil rights program, using executive orders. In July 1948 the President prohibited discrimination in the hiring of federal employees, and later that year he signed an executive order that began the process which would end racial discrimination in the military

Dewey's advisers badly underestimated the sophistication of Truman's strategy, and polls predicted a Republican landslide. Early returns on election night seemed to confirm Dewey's anticipated victory. The New Yorker won the Northeast, except the Democratic bastions of Massachusetts and Rhode Island. The Dixiecrat Thurmond would almost surely capture South Carolina, Alabama, Mississippi, and Louisiana. The headline of the conservative Chicago *Tribune's* early edition read, "DEWEY DEFEATS TRUMAN." At home in Independence, Missouri, Truman simply told his family not to worry and went to bed. As the President slept, ballot-counters recorded a startling trend. Not only did Truman win all the border South and Texas, but also, in the early morning, the rural vote in Ohio, Illinois, and Iowa put these states into the Truman column. Now the candidates were running even. Still, Dewey seemed a sure winner, for the Far West traditionally supported the GOP. Yet California and Washington went for Truman and gave him the election.

The Fair Deal, 1949–1952   Now President in his own right, Truman left no one in doubt about his liberalism. His State of the Union message in January 1949 announced a sweeping agenda of domestic change: aid to education, national health insurance, a new farm program, regional development projects, civil rights legislation, wider coverage for social security, public housing, a reorganization of the federal bureaucracy, and repeal of Taft-Hartley. Truman labeled this whopping list of social welfare proposals the Fair Deal. At the time prospects for its passage seemed good. A strong economy would finance the President's new programs. And the Democrats had captured control of both houses of Congress.

Even before the outbreak of war in Korea some eighteen months later, however, the Fair Deal faltered. The long-standing conservative coalition of Republicans and southern Democrats in Congress made the House and Senate less friendly to Truman's ideas than would be expected of legislative bodies with nominally Democratic majorities. Conservatives halted the President's initiatives in national health insurance, civil rights legislation, federal aid to education, increases in farm subsidies, and a repeal of Taft-Hartley. Yet on some issues Truman enjoyed a clear popular support that overwhelmed his congressional opponents. New social security laws covered nearly eleven million more people, and doubled benefits to offset postwar inflation. The administration pushed through an increase in the minimum wage from

40 cents to 75 cents per hour. Desperate shortages prompted Congress to pass the National Housing Act of 1949, which subsidized slum clearance projects and built almost one million houses for low-income families. Legislators also granted Truman authority to streamline the federal bureaucracy. Following the recommendations of a commission headed by former President Herbert Hoover, Truman reduced the number of agencies and improved staff work.

The United States and East Asia

Reconstructing Japan Truman's presidency, attempting to bring about a larger democratization of American society, had its parallel in the government that General Douglas MacArthur imposed upon postwar Japan. Catastrophic defeat in war had disgraced the military clique that had long ruled the country. Americans moved swiftly, methodically, to crush the old elite. Democratic ideals and capitalist profits must replace feudal values and Japan's monopoly industry. Although authority after the surrender was nominally in the hands of a four-power commission, it was General Douglas MacArthur, commander of the only Allied armed forces in the region, who made all decisions. Ruling almost without restraint for several years, MacArthur reformed the educational system, rewrote the Japanese constitution, broke up the great cartels, and encouraged trade unions and a two-party political system. The Japanese, realizing the totality of their defeat and ready to abandon the past, eagerly accepted these changes. Western styles swept the nation; businesses welcomed American methods and investment; and citizens enjoyed a civil liberty and social mobility that traditional Japan would never have provided.

The Fall of China, 1945–1949 American plans for a new order in the postwar Pacific included China as an ally. But events in China between the end of the war and 1949 changed that.

The Chinese revolution, begun in 1911 by intellectuals and urban leftists, entered its last stages after World War II. During the interwar period a regime of powerful entrenched interests led by Chiang Kai-shek had maintained control over most of China, warding off the challenge of the Communists, whose ideology was even more authoritarian. Largely suspending their civil conflict during the war against Japan, the adversaries after 1945 entered their final struggle. Chiang and his Nationalist regime relied upon military and financial aid from the United States, while the Communists took comfort in Marxist predictions of inevitable triumph.

Chiang's ramshackle, corrupt regime alienated both peasants and urban workers. Persistent inflation convulsed the economy. Mao Zedong's Communist guerrilla armies rooted themselves deep in the village structure of rural China, where Communist promises of peace and land won many converts. With sophisticated propaganda and a dedicated, well-trained fighting force, the Communists slowly advanced southward for the strongholds north and west of Beijing. Tru-

Mao Zedong and Chiang Kai-shek in happier times. (*Courtesy, United Press International*)

man and most Asian experts in the State Department believed that Mao and his Communists would probably win any prolonged conflict.

The United States, Truman decided, must mediate if Chiang and his Nationalists were to survive. In late 1945, he sent Army Chief of Staff George C. Marshall, recently retired, to secure a cease-fire. Promises of vast reconstruction aid, it was thought, could persuade the two sides to join in a coalition regime. Marshall arranged a truce that winter but in the spring, when military operations could resume, both sides broke the agreement. Discouraged, Marshall was recalled to the United States at the end of 1946. Truman was by that time preoccupied by events in Europe, but several months later he sent to China another general, Albert C. Wedemeyer. Only far-reaching administrative reforms, Wedemeyer reported, could end the corruption that so alienated the Chinese people. Yet the Nationalists rejected all of Wedemeyer's suggestions. Like Marshall before him, Wedemeyer told Truman that only direct military intervention, perhaps millions of American soldiers, could rescue the Nationalist cause. Largely because of propaganda by the "China Lobby"—a collection of anti-Communist conservatives in Congress and industry—Truman did continue to send money and equipment to Chiang. But after 1947 Washington concentrated upon containing Communism in Europe. No one was ready for a land war in Asia.

Less than two years later, newspapers across the United States announced the fall of China. Mao captured Beijing in 1948 and crossed the Yangtze River early in 1949. Chiang's armies disintegrated, many of the troops surrendering without a fight or simply melting away into the countryside. The mainland became the People's Republic of China—or "Red China," as Americans nicknamed it. Chiang set up an exile regime on the island of Taiwan off the shores of China, vowing to return someday to the mainland. The "fall" of China shocked Americans. The very word "fall" implied loss, defeat. Who was to blame? The China Lobby denounced the President and called for "a holy crusade against godless Communism in the Far East." Senator Taft, usually levelheaded, suggested that some experts in the State Department were "pro-Communist." Dean Acheson, who had succeeded the ailing Marshall as secretary of state in 1949, outraged such critics with his suggestion that the United States recognize the new regime. "We are all on the same planet," he declared, "and must do business with each other." Many Americans, inexperienced in the complexities of foreign affairs, looked for scapegoats—a search that quickly degenerated into a quest for "subversives" within the United States. Conservatives, having lagged behind most liberals in committing the country to military and economic confrontation of Communism, were rushing ahead in verbal anti-Communism.

National Security Council Paper Number 68   The final "loss" of China came just a month after another major Cold War setback, the Soviet explosion in September 1949 of an atomic device, which meant that the United States no longer had its monopoly on nuclear weapons. The Truman Administration in the spring of 1950 finally put together a new blueprint for Cold War strategy. National Security Council Paper No. 68 claimed that the Communists were aiming at world domination. They were seeking to achieve their goal, the paper argued, by a process of gradual, step-by-step conquest. It followed that American national security could be preserved only through maintenance of the global status quo, and so the United States was now obliged to patrol the world to contain the expansion of Communism. This new mission required a huge increase in military force. Rearmament must proceed regardless of cost, even if it consumed as much as a fifth of the nation's production. The Democrats also realized that NSC 68, whether its assumptions were sensible or not, was good politics: its hard line suited the anti-Communist mood of the country, and the heavy defense spending it required would stimulate the economy. That there might come to be not one Communism but many, that movements labeled "Communist" might differ in character and objectives from country to country, scarcely occurred to Americans. Communism, the public and most of its leaders believed, was a single force worldwide directed by Moscow. At one point after 1949 a plan was considered in the State Department to pull Mao away from the Soviet Union and into a friendship with the United States. But a militant anti-Communism along with a belief that Chinese Communism was a servant of the Soviet Union made such a plan untenable, and it was discounted almost immediately.

Yet even the implacable anti-Communism of Truman, Secretary of State Dean Acheson, and the liberals in general was not enough for emerging militant conservatives. The policy of containment, they complained in a reversal of the conservative isolationism of the early postwar period, was a cowardly acceptance of the existence of Communism in the regions it already controlled. American policy must commit itself to the destruction of Communism on every square foot of the globe. For this policy conservatives had few specific suggestions. And they did not seriously entertain the idea of crashing American troops through the Iron Curtain in a war of global liberation. What they really wanted was ideological spotlessness: a manner though not a program of uncompromised belligerence toward Communism everywhere; a rejection of

Stop Communism in the Philippines. A U.S. government poster. *(Courtesy, Library of Congress)*

A World War II veteran describes in 1949 what was coming to be a crusade for superpatriotism:

"During the war I was wounded. When I came back, I worked for the Veterans Administration in New Jersey. It was about a year and a half later when the attorney general, Tom Clark, issued a list of organizations that were supposed to be 'subversive.' These were organizations that, according to him, advocated the overthrow of the government by unconstitutional, violent means. . . .

I received a letter from the Veterans Administration saying that because of my membership in the Socialist Workers Party, my employment was to be terminated. The notice that I was to be fired stunned me more than anything I experienced during the war. . . . The thing that made it ridiculous was that I had no access to any kind of confidential information that could in any way benefit the enemies of this country."

Mickey Spillane caught the Cold War temper when he had his hardboiled detective hero, Mike Hammer, say in 1951 in One Lonely Night, *which sold three million copies:*

"I killed more people today than I have fingers on my hands. I shot them in cold blood and enjoyed every minute of it. . . . They were commies . . . red sons-of-bitches who should have died long ago. . . . They never thought that there were people like me in this country. They figured us all to be soft as horse manure and just as stupid."

friendship with even non-Communist regimes on the left, along with a renunciation of the welfare state, which some conservatives perceived as a pale cousin to Communism. In their hostility to radicalism in general, right-wingers were at poles from numbers of an early generation of officers at the Central Intelligence Agency who wanted to fund or otherwise support the socialist, anti-Communist left in foreign countries as a counter to Communist influence. Later the CIA was to gain a reputation for opposition to all varieties of the left, whether Communist or not.

A Second Red Scare

After 1945 Americans never recaptured the sense of normality that had followed World War I in the 1920s. Strategic security evaporated in a nuclear age. Oceans no longer isolated the New World from troubles in Asia and Europe. The Soviet possession of atomic power, along with Mao Zedong's victory over Chiang Kai-shek in 1949 in China, provoked dread. Many Americans simply could not understand how a nation endowed in 1945 with a mighty army, navy, and air force and a fully operating industrial plant amid a world in ruins could, in such a short space of time, find itself facing such threats and feeling so insecure. Surely something must be wrong; sinister and mysterious forces inside the country and the government must have subverted the easy security that was an American birthright.

The House Un-American Activities Committee This second Red Scare—the first had been just after World War I—began slowly. Early in 1947, Truman set up regional loyalty boards to unmask "potential subversives" within the sprawling federal bureaucracy. Over the next six years, however, only 384 alleged "security risk" employees were dismissed, most of them homosexuals. The House Un-American Activities Committee (HUAC), which had been set up in the 1930s, followed along Truman's lead by investigating and interrogating suspected Communists about their presumed efforts to infiltrate American society. Trade unions, colleges, and the Hollywood movie industry were all thought to be jammed with Communists and "fellow travelers," a popular term for anyone who seemed to be in any degree of collaboration with Communists. Truman's attorney general warned that American Reds "are everywhere—in factories, offices, butcher stores, on street corners."

Private citizens and organizations also engaged in the Red Scare. Entertainment moguls blacklisted performers accused of holding unpopular opinions; anti-labor politicians called for tighter regulation of unions. Red-hunters looked for political dissenters among college teachers. Truman lambasted "subversives" during his 1948 presidential campaign. *Marvel Comics* warned: "Beware, commies, spies, traitors, and foreign agents—Captain America is looking for you yellow scum." A gumball machine in Wheeling, West Virginia, was quickly impounded when it was found to dispense geography lessons under the hammer-and-sickle Soviet flag, reading: "U.S.S.R. population 211,000,000. Capital Moscow. Largest country in the world."

The Hiss Case   In the midst of the frenzy, a sensational testimony provided some limited evidence of a Soviet espionage network. Whittaker Chambers, a senior editor of *Time* magazine, told of his membership in the Communist Party for some years before the war. He named seven people who might be still active in the Soviet underground. One of the accused, Alger Hiss, then president of the prestigious Carnegie Institution for International Peace and a former official in the State Department, denied the charge. While under oath, he said, "I have never been a member of the Communist party. . . . I have never laid eyes on Chambers." Hiss then sued Chambers for libel. But the former Communist produced evidence that lent credence to his charge that Hiss had given him copies of secret government documents during the 1930s. Chambers claimed to have microfilm copies of these papers composed on Hiss's typewriter hidden in a pumpkin on his farm in Maryland, and he revealed them to a startled court. This disclosure prompted a federal grand jury to indict Hiss for perjured testimony before a congressional committee. Hiss was convicted, and he went to jail. The evidence against Hiss was overwhelming.

Before the eighteen-month furor about Hiss died down, British agents arrested Klaus Fuchs, a physicist who had evidently supplied the Soviet Union with information about Anglo-American atomic research during the war. Many blamed Fuchs's treachery for the Soviet Union's unexpectedly rapid development of nuclear power. During his trial, he implicated several Americans, including Julius and Ethel Rosenberg, two members of the New York City Communist Party. Ethel's brother, David Greenglass, who had been an army sergeant at Los Alamos, had supposedly turned over detailed diagrams of America's first atomic bomb to the Rosenbergs, who in turn, Greenglass charged, had given them to the Soviet consul in New York City. The Rosenbergs made moving declarations of their innocence, but after a sensational trial both were sentenced to die.

Whatever the actual degree of Soviet infiltration, the fear that many people harbored was way out of proportion with reality. "How much more are we going to take?" orated Homer Capehart, a conservative Republican senator. "Fuchs and Hiss and hydrogen bombs threatening outside and New Dealism eating away at the vitals of the nation. In the name of Heaven, is this the best America can do?"

Senator Joseph R. McCarthy   Into the furor strode the bizarre figure of Republican Senator Joseph McCarthy of Wisconsin. A crude bully, McCarthy had scored upset victories for local and national office with campaigns of innuendo against his opponents. As a senator, he had not distinguished himself. But on February 8, 1950, he addressed a meeting of the Republican Women's Club in Wheeling, West Virginia. Waving a piece of paper on which he implied he had the names of 205 subversives, McCarthy charged that Communists had "thoroughly infested" the

Whittaker Chambers testifying against Alger Hiss before the House Un-American Activities Committee, August, 1948. *(Courtesy, United Press International)*

In 1954 Senator Joseph McCarthy—here muffling the microphone as aide Roy Cohn whispers—took on the U.S. Army. The tempestuous hearings gave voters and colleagues dim views of "McCarthyism" and led to a 67 to 22 Senate vote condemning him. *(Courtesy, AP/Wide World Photos)*

State Department. "The reason we find ourselves in a position of impotency," he explained to his receptive audience, "is because of traitorous actions by those who have been treated so well by this nation." McCarthy expanded on this theme throughout the spring and summer of 1950, accusing both high officials and simple clerks of Communist sympathies. He never proved any of these "documented cases." Culling old, mostly outdated information about Soviet spy rings, some of it from discredited sources, McCarthy relied upon his gift of rhetorical embellishment.

During the next four years, the junior senator from Wisconsin verbally abused Presidents, the much-respected George C. Marshall, and many skilled experts in government service. Charge followed charge so fast and in a voice so tight with conviction, so mesmerized by its own message, that critics hardly knew how to begin to respond. Richard Rovere, a reporter for *The New Yorker,* dismissed McCarthy as "a pool room politician grandly seized with an urge to glory." Many others, including intellectuals like Daniel Boorstin and politicians like Senator Robert Taft, endorsed McCarthy. He condemned the Democrats for "twenty years of treason," and many Americans believed him. How else, they wondered, could Communism have triumphed in eastern Europe and China? GOP conservatives especially lauded McCarthy's cause, and various Republican newcomers won major elections by smearing opponents with the charge that they were soft on Communism. Richard Nixon destroyed the reputation of his opponent, Helen Gahagan Douglas, during the 1950 race for the Senate in California by permitting underlings to refer to "the pink lady." (Her lieutenants in turn labeled him a fascist and an anti-Semite.) McCarthy himself mercilessly attacked Senator Millard Tydings of Maryland, an early foe of Red-baiting, and was probably responsible for Tydings's defeat. More and more, McCarthy's critics silenced themselves.

Sensationalist newspapers played up the senator's cause; he was, after all, good copy, and publishers learned that publicity ensured protection from his vitriolic attacks. In reality McCarthy never commanded quite the mass following that he seemed to have. His main supporters were conservative Republicans. And in 1954, after he claimed that the army "coddled" Communists, he lost support and earned the censure of the Senate. His heavy drinking had made him reckless, and he died of liver disease in 1957.

Medics struggled with the cold in Korea:

"Everything was frozen. Plasma froze and the bottles broke. We couldn't use plasma because it wouldn't go into solution and the tubes would clog up with particles. We couldn't change dressings because we had to work with gloves on to keep our hands from freezing.

We couldn't cut a man's clothes off to get at a wound because he would freeze to death. Actually, a man was often better off if we left him alone."

The Korean War, 1950–1953

In early January 1950, Secretary of State Acheson spoke of the nation's "defense perimeter," those areas the United States considered vital to its own security. Attacks against Alaska, Japan, the Ryukyu Islands, or the Philippines, he explained, would mean instant retaliation. The secretary of state seemed to be excluding from this umbrella of protection two former Japanese holdings on the Asian mainland, Korea and French Indochina (Vietnam, Cambodia, and Laos). Both countries seemed headed in China's direction: local Communists backed by outside Communist powers were challenging regimes that the United States favored. French soldiers had already fought unavailingly for four years against a guerrilla rebellion in Indochina led by Ho Chi Minh. Korea, too, had disappointed leaders in Washington. By late 1948 the United States was supporting the reactionary government of President Syngman Rhee, while the USSR countered by establishing a Communist government in the North. Although the Americans and then the Soviet Union withdrew their troops, skirmishes broke out constantly along the 38th parallel, the dividing line between the two Korean states. Both North and South dreamed of a reunited country, and civil war seemed likely at any time.

North Korea Invades the South   Unclear signals from the United States seemed to indicate that Washington was not seriously considering the Korean peninsula inside the American sphere of defense in East Asia. Stalin apparently calculated that the United States would not fight to rescue Rhee, so he encouraged the North Koreans, shipping them small arms, advanced Soviet tanks, and advisers to train a sophisticated ground force of ten North Korean divisions, one motorized. On June 25, 1950, these troops attacked South Korea along a broad front. Truman quickly implemented NSC 68, telling the American people that "to conquer independent nations, Communism has now resorted to armed invasion and war." He responded along a wide front. The Seventh Fleet steamed toward Taiwan to protect it from possible Communist Chinese attack. American money and military equipment flooded into Indochina to help the French preserve their colonial authority there. And in Korea itself, an American army landed to repulse the North Korean invaders. Congress passed huge appropriations not only for the war in Korea but also for massive rearmament. This determined, wide-ranging response caught Stalin off guard: the Soviet Union was boycotting Security Council sessions when Truman pushed a resolution through the United Nations calling for joint action to punish "unprovoked aggression in Korea." In the three years of fighting that followed, a United Nations force, composed mostly of South Korean and American troops but supplemented by contingents from many other nations, would conduct this largest venture in international peacekeeping that the UN was ever to undertake.

Counterattack and Stalemate   The military situation in Korea at first looked bleak. The North Koreans rapidly pushed southward, overwhelming Rhee's ill-trained troops. Although GIs from Japan quickly joined in defense of the South, the North Koreans had conquered most of the peninsula by mid-August, trapping the United States Eighth Army in a 140-mile semicircle around Pusan. On September 15 General Douglas MacArthur launched a brilliant amphibious assault at Inchon, a port well behind enemy lines. Meanwhile, the newly supplied Eighth Army punched its way out of the Pusan perimeter. By early October, American forces had cleared all South Korea of Communist troops.

This rapid success elated Truman, who now, however, overreached

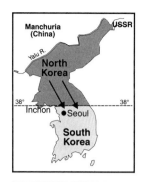
June 25, 1950

Sept. 14, 1950

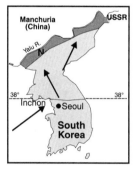
Nov. 25, 1950

July 27, 1953

Military advances and stalemate in the Korean War, June 1950 to July 1953.

An incident in Korea suggests many in the Vietnam War:

"There was the crack of carbines, a burst or two of automatic fire, somewhere away to the right, and a peasant woman crumpled into the ditch by the roadside with her two babes crawling upon her. . . . One babe sat on her belly, small hands reaching up to her face, stroking, pulling at her lips, growing frantic, inconsolable, its screams agonizing, as it knew, as it tried to suckle the warm still heavy breasts, to wake the dead. The other child sat in a kind of torpor of dejection at his dead mother's feet.

Someone tried to divert the young child with an apple. Nothing could stem this infant grief. It smote us all down, reminding us of the unforgettable meaning of war. A medical truck had been ordered up, and a corporal took the children in his arms to the beginning of their orphan lives, and the woman was alone in the ditch."

After being relieved of his command by President Truman, General Douglas MacArthur was hailed as a hero on his return to the United States in 1951. Here, he waves to an enthusiastic crowd in San Francisco. *(Courtesy, Library of Congress)*

himself. Once again turning to the United Nations, the President received approval for "steps to insure stability throughout Korea"—that is, to destroy the North Korean regime altogether, an objective beyond the original plan of clearing Communist troops out of the South. American armies rushed northward, crossing the 38th parallel and nearing the Yalu River that separated Korea from China. "All resistance," MacArthur told Truman at a meeting on Wake Island on October 14, "will [soon] end."

This time the general's calculation proved disastrous. North Korea bordered China's industrial heartland, Manchuria. For weeks Chinese Premier Chou En-lai had been warning the West that his people would not "supinely tolerate seeing their neighbors invaded by imperialists." Still the American troops drove forward. Then, on October 26, Chinese troops were discovered south of the Yalu River. In late November eighteen Chinese divisions attacked in terrifying force, tearing apart MacArthur's widely scattered armies. By early December the troops of the United Nations were in full retreat. In January 1951 the UN armies halted the Communists at a line that divided the two Koreas into much the same territories that the 38th parallel had done. Here the front stabilized and the war became a stalemate. Although hard fighting continued over the inhospitable terrain, neither side gained much advantage for the rest of the war.

MacArthur Oversteps His Authority Driven to destroy what he called "an alien, despised Communism," MacArthur wanted to bring all possible force to bear against Chinese troops in Korea: bombing the bridges across the Yalu River, opening a second front with Nationalist troops from Taiwan—even, if necessary, using atomic weapons. This course, which could have brought a major land war in Asia, went directly against Truman's policy of limited engagement, of keeping the conflict from expanding beyond the Korean peninsula. But MacArthur was insistent in pressing for it.

On April 11, 1951, Truman relieved MacArthur of his command for what appeared to be a determination to change the government's strategy. The immediate issue was clear: "If I allowed him to defy the civil authority," Truman said, "I myself would be violating my oath to uphold and defend the Constitution." Secretary of Defense George Marshall and the Joint Chiefs of Staff agreed that MacArthur had overstepped the line that for long had preserved American politics from interference by the military. But some Republicans, espousing a right-wing ideology that had now turned from isolationism to a diffusive militancy toward all Communist regimes, used MacArthur's popularity to attack the administration's policy of containment and limited warfare. Congressional hearings, televised across the nation, broadcast their anger at MacArthur's dismissal. MacArthur enjoyed a hero's welcome. His appearance before Congress was a personal triumph. Although the old soldier himself soon faded away, the larger issue raised by the controversy remained: should the United States merely contain its adversaries or go further to liberate those "captive nations," as Senator Taft melodramatically phrased it, "struggling under the yoke of Communist tyranny."

The Election of 1952

The Democrats' Liabilities

By 1952 the country seemed stagnant, mired in limited war in Korea and, many thought, betrayed by subversives at home. Political corruption meanwhile darkened the shadows of mistrust. A Senate subcommittee unearthed evidence that a presidential aide had influenced the awarding of government contracts, directing business to several friends. In gratitude, one of them had sent him a freezer, then a glamorous new appliance, worth $500. Some other bureaucrats, the Senate committee discovered, charged a flat five percent fee for favorable action. Truman, never personally involved in any of these scandals, vigorously prosecuted the wrongdoers, firing his attorney general. The issues of Korea, Communism, and corruption pushed down Truman's popularity rating to less than thirty percent.

Many midwestern Republicans again vigorously supported the candidacy of the conservative Robert Taft. But inside the Republican Party war raged between conservatives and liberals, a sharper conflict perhaps than that between Republicans and Democrats. Republicans from urban states along the East Coast worried that Taft's outspoken hostility to New Deal reforms and his reputation for hostility to labor might alienate millions of voters. Especially worried about Taft's isolationism, they persuaded General Dwight D. Eisenhower to resign his command of NATO forces in Europe and enter the race.

General Dwight D. Eisenhower

Born in Texas and reared in the modest surroundings of Abilene, Kansas, Dwight D. Eisenhower was a product of what would later be called Middle America. The young Eisenhower had secured entrance to West Point and, despite a mediocre academic record, distinguished himself in campus leadership. At Command and General Staff School in Fort Leavenworth, Kansas, he graduated first in his class after a year's study in 1925–26. As a soldier, Eisenhower did not affect the bluff arrogance and the disdain for civilian direction that can go with the military temperament. Eisenhower's military and strategic skill was demonstrated during the Second World War by his conduct during the 1942 North African invasion and later when he was supreme commander of Allied forces.

After the war, Eisenhower served as Army Chief of Staff and then as president of Columbia University. There he instituted the American Assembly, a forum for discussion of major national problems, and, as he would recollect with some pride, an academic "Chair of Peace." Late in 1950 President Truman appointed him military commander of NATO.

The general at first resisted those who urged him to enter the race for the presidency. He believed that a military man was unsuited for national politics. Ultimately, Eisenhower's decision in 1952 to resign his post of NATO commander and seek the presidency—so his memoirs assert—came from a fear that the foreign policy commitments of Senator Robert A. Taft of Ohio might otherwise prevail. Taft, still holding to the isolationism that many conservative Republicans had argued for a few years earlier, denied that the United States had a duty to extend its

President Dwight D. Eisenhower.
(Courtesy, Wide World Photos)

institutions abroad. The Republican Convention nominated the easy-going and politically promising "Ike." For Vice President the party chose Richard M. Nixon, who as a young congressman had won fame for his investigation of Alger Hiss.

Adlai Stevenson A serious contender in the Democratic primaries was Estes Kefauver of Tennessee, prominent as head of a Senate committee investigating organized crime in the cities and within labor unions. The committee exposed widespread prostitution, illegal gambling, and shake-down rackets. Television beamed the dramatic testimony of underworld figures like Frank Costello—who endlessly "took the Fifth" (Amendment) while nervously tapping his fingers—to a nation both fascinated and repelled by real-life gangsters. But the Democrats settled on a presidential candidate at least as cerebral as Taft: Governor Adlai E. Stevenson of Illinois. As governor he had increased funds for schools and roads, wiped out downstate gambling operations, and modernized the state bureaucracy. The 1952 campaign sparkled with Stevenson's cultivated, witty speeches that he wrote himself. But though the governor campaigned hard, he could not hope to overcome Eisenhower's popularity.

Stevenson actually had wanted Eisenhower to win the Republican nomination, fearing the effect of Taft's foreign policy ideas on the Western alliance. For Stevenson, like Eisenhower, represented an internationalist position that the Truman Administration had itself sustained. That internationalism was in part a benign acceptance of the nation's responsibility to enter the world community. But even in the language of the mild and hesitant Stevenson it could ring with belligerence. Speaking to a Kansas audience, for example, Stevenson explained that we were fighting in Korea "so we wouldn't have to fight in Wichita."

The Election of 1952 Eisenhower worked to heal wounds in the Republican Party between its right wing and its more liberal elements. He welcomed Taft to a breakfast at Morningside Heights, Columbia University, after which they agreed on the essentials of domestic policy. Easily projecting his folksy style across the land, the general spent more time campaigning in the South than had any previous Republican candidate. He deleted from an important speech a remark criticizing Senator Joe McCarthy, and he did little to support his old boss, General Marshall, against McCarthy's attacks. In September a storm broke when the *New York Post* charged vice-presidential candidate Nixon with accepting money from friendly businessmen for personal expenses. There were rumors that Eisenhower intended to drop Nixon from the ticket. Nixon rebutted the claim—Stevenson had a similar fund to supplement the salaries of public officials—and in a highly sentimental and effective speech broadcast on nationwide television he demonstrated a command of what was to be an important political medium. Since Eisenhower, unlike the more conservative members of his party, seemed content with the accomplishments of the New Deal and its Fair Deal extensions under Truman, the campaign lacked rancor on domestic questions. Neither candidate was anxious to press the issue of civil rights.

The results on election day, November 7, startled no one. After October 24, when Eisenhower promised that if he won he would "go to Korea," the polls had shown his margin to be widening. Eisenhower won fifty-five percent of the popular vote, and even carried the southern states of Virginia, Florida, and Texas. He received a majority vote from all income groups and drew unexpected support from normally Democratic Roman Catholics. What Eisenhower offered in the 1952 campaign, and would achieve in the first term of his presidency, was something the country needed: an easing of tensions after the hectic recriminations of the Truman years.

Soon after the new President took office, a time of political calm began. The Korean armistice in midsummer 1953 and the Senate censure of McCarthy for his increasingly outrageous charges in 1954 removed from politics the two most abrasive issues. So confidently stable did the national temper become, under the tranquil leadership of this most unbelligerent statesman, that the name of Eisenhower is remembered as defining an era. Eisenhower continued most of the policies of economic regulation, social welfare, and internationalism associated with his Democratic predecessors. He did more. By removing these policies from partisan debate, first in the campaign and then later in relations with congressional Democrats, who sometimes supported him more strongly than did his own party, Eisenhower the Republican made internationalism and the Democratic New Deal permanent parts of the national consensus.

Suggested Readings

Books published lately on this period include Michael J. Hogan, *The Marshall Plan* (1987), Burton Kaufman, *The Korean War* (1986), Robert James Maddox, *From War to Cold War: The Education of Harry S Truman* (1988), William E. Pemb, *Harry S. Truman* (1989), Kenneth T. Jackson, *Crabgrass Frontier: The Suburbanization of the United States* (1985), and M. J. Heale, *American Anti-Communism: Combatting the Enemy Within, 1830–1970* (1990).

Alonzo Hamby gives a rather favorable interpretation of Truman's domestic policies in *Beyond the New Deal: Harry S Truman and American Liberalism* (1973). Maeva Marcus examines the events of Truman's seizure of the steel mills during the Korean War, and goes into the constitutional issue that the Supreme Court confronted in its invalidation of Truman's act: *Truman and the Steel Seizure Case: The Limits of Presidential Power* (1977). See also Robert J. Divine, *Conflict and Crisis: The Presidency of Harry S Truman, 1945–1948* (1977). Allen Weinstein in *Perjury: The Hiss-Chambers Case* (1979) goes over the evidence bearing on the guilt or innocence of Alger Hiss, convicted of perjury for having falsely denied to a congressional committee the charge made by Whittaker Chambers that Hiss had engaged in espionage for the Communists. The author concludes that Hiss was probably guilty.

Martin Sherwin writes with insight of *A World Destroyed: The Atomic Bomb and the Grand Alliance* (1975). Barton J. Bernstein also studies this critical issue in *The Atomic Bomb* (1976) while Gregg Herken in *The Winning Weapon: The Atomic Bomb in the Cold War, 1945–1950* (1980) analyzes the importance of nuclear weapons in making policy. Thomas G. Paterson presents an illuminating study of the problems and policies that led to the Cold War and the continuing antagonism between the United States and the Soviet Union: *Soviet-American Confrontation: Postwar Reconstruction and the Origins of the Cold War* (1973). John Lewis Gaddis also explores these issues carefully in *The United States and the Origins of the Cold War, 1941–1947* (1972). Joyce and Gabriel Kolko, covering the same period, strongly condemn American policy: *The Limits of Power: The World and United States Foreign Policy, 1945–1954* (1972). John W. Spanier reviews *The Truman-MacArthur Controversy and the Korean War* (1959).

Other important books include Walter LaFeber, *America, Russia, and the Cold War, 1945–1960,* 6th ed. (1990), Akira Iriye, *The Cold War in Asia* (1974), Stephen Ambrose, *Rise to Globalism,* 5th ed. (1988), John Lewis Gaddis, *Strategies of Containment* (1982), and Ronald Steel, *Walter Lippmann and the American Century* (1980).

Why Did We Drop the Atomic Bomb?

Paul Fussell

Most of those with firsthand experience of [World War II] at its worst were relatively inarticulate and have remained silent. Few of those destined to be destroyed if the main islands had had to be invaded went on to become our most eloquent men of letters or our most impressive ethical theorists or professors of history of international jurists. The testimony of experience has come largely from rough diamonds like James Jones and William Manchester, who experienced the war in the infantry and the Marine Corps. Both would agree with the point, if not perhaps the tone, of a remark about Hiroshima made by a naval officer menaced by the kamikazes off Okinawa: "Those were the best burned women and children I ever saw." . . .

On the other hand, John Kenneth Galbraith is persuaded that the Japanese would have surrendered by November without an invasion. He thinks the atom bombs were not decisive in bringing about the surrender and he implies that their use was unjustified. What did he do in the war? He was in the Office of Price Administration in Washington, and then he was director of the United States Strategic Bombing Survey. He was 37 in 1945, and I don't demand that he experience having his ass shot off. I just note that he didn't. In saying this I'm aware of its offensive implications *ad hominem.* But here I think that approach justified. What's at stake in an infantry assault is so entirely unthinkable to those without experience of one, even if they possess very wide-ranging imaginations and sympathies, that experience is crucial in this case.

The dramatic postwar Japanese success at hustling and merchandising and tourism has (happily, in many ways) effaced for most people important elements of the assault context in which Hiroshima should be viewed. It is easy to forget what Japan was like before it was first destroyed and then humiliated, tamed, and constitutionalized by the West. "Implacable, treacherous, barbaric"—those were Admiral Halsey's characterizations of the enemy, and at the time few facing the Japanese would deny that they fit to a T. One remembers the captured American airmen locked for years in packing-crates, the prisoners decapitated, the gleeful use of bayonets on civilians. The degree to which Americans register shock and extraordinary shame about the Hiroshima bomb correlates closely with lack of information about the war.

And the savagery was not just on one side. There was much sadism and brutality—undeniably racist— on ours. No Marine was fully persuaded of his manly adequacy who didn't have a well-washed Japanese skull to caress and who didn't have a go at treating surrendering Japs as rifle targets. Herman Wouk remembers it correctly while analyzing Ensign Keith in *The Caine Mutiny:* "Like most of the naval executioners of Kwajalein, he seemed to regard the enemy as a species of animal pest." And the enemy felt the same way about us: "From the grim and desperate taciturnity with which the Japanese died, they seemed on their side to believe they were contending with an invasion of large armed ants." Hiroshima seems to follow in natural sequence: "This obliviousness on both sides to the fact that the opponents were human beings may perhaps be cited as the key to the many massacres of the Pacific war." Since the Japanese resisted so madly, let's pour gasoline into their emplacements and light it and shoot the people afire who try to get out. Why not? Why not blow them all up? Why not, indeed, drop a new kind of big bomb on them? Why allow one more American high school kid to see his intestines blown out of his body and spread before him in the dirt while he screams when we can end the whole thing just like that?

On Okinawa, only weeks before Hiroshima, 123,000 Japanese and Americans *killed* each other. "Just awful" was the comment not of some pacifist but of MacArthur. One million American casualties was his estimate of the cost of the forthcoming invasion. . . .

Experience whispers that the pity is not that we used the bomb to end the Japanese war but that it wasn't ready earlier to end the German one.

[L]et us move from combat experiences to historical research and inquire what *Truman was experiencing* and what he was thinking about as he sat behind his desk in the Oval Office in the spring and early summer of 1945.

Research in the President's Official File, and in the diaries, correspondence and records of his closest wartime advisers, reveals that while the war was an ever-present consideration, its conduct was not among Truman's primary tasks. The record of military successes, Roosevelt's deteriorating health, a growing concern with postwar problems and Truman's inexperience had shifted much of the daily management of the conflict away from the White House during 1945. The new President would officiate over victory, but he would not be credited with having led the nation to it. The problems of the postwar world loomed larger before Truman than they ever had before Roosevelt, and they occupied more of his time. *His* performance would be judged on what he accomplished *after* the war.

The Soviet Union was the primary postwar problem. Joseph Stalin was breaking the Yalta Agreement, the Secretary of State reported to the President at their first meeting on April 13, and soon after, Averell Harriman, Ambassador to Moscow, characterized Soviet behavior as nothing less than a "barbarian invasion of Europe. . . ."

As the bomb moved toward completion, a dangerous (though now familiar) illusion was nurtured in the White House: the idea that the bomb was a panacea for America's diplomatic as well as its military problems. As preparations for the Potsdam Conference got underway, assurances that the weapon would work became increasingly important to the President. . . . And then, Truman agreed, in an early linkage of arms control and diplomacy, that after the first bomb had been successfully used against Japan, a fitting exchange for an American offer to the Russians for the international control of atomic energy would be "the settlement of the Polish, Rumanian, Yugoslavian, and Manchurian problems." And even before this discussion, Secretary of State-designate James F. Byrnes had told Truman that the bomb "might well put us in a position to dictate our own terms at the end of the war."

Truman inherited the basic policy that governed the atomic bomb, just as he inherited every other policy related to the war, a point that commentators on both sides of the debate often ignore. It was therefore *possible* to use the bomb only because Roosevelt had made preparations to do so. Truman was *inclined* to use the bomb because of those preparations. But he *decided* to use it because there seemed no good reason not to. On the contrary, the bombs were available and the Japanese fought on; the bombs were available and precedents of burned cities were numerous; the bombs were available and $2 billion had been spent to create them; the bombs were available and revenge had its claim; the bomb was available and the Soviet Union was claiming too much. Its use held out not only the hope of shocking Tokyo into submission but also the possible dividend of jolting Moscow into cooperation.

But a critical question remains: Were the bombings of Hiroshima and Nagasaki the quickest way to end the war? A considerable body of evidence suggests that the decision to use the bomb, which involved a decision to reject another recommended initiative, *delayed* the end of the war.

American cryptographers had broken the Japanese diplomatic code before the war, and senior members of the Administration were aware of a struggle between peace and war factions within the Japanese government. Based on this privileged information, and on his knowledge of Japanese politics gained from long experience as Ambassador to Japan, Acting Secretary of State Joseph C. Grew urged Truman during the final days of May to modify the unconditional-surrender policy. It was an insurmountable barrier for the peace faction, he explained, for no Japanese government would surrender without assurances that the Emperor would not be deposed or the dynasty eliminated. But Truman decided to reject Grew's advice, and an important question is *why*?

One answer is that he would not accept the political consequences that were likely to result from a public retreat from a policy that had become a political shibboleth since Roosevelt introduced the idea in 1943.

Another answer is that he preferred to use the atomic bomb.

A black woman in a southern town during the 1950s watches Klansmen in full regalia.
(Courtesy, AP/Wide World Photos)

27
Consensus and Division: 1953–1965

THE GREENSBORO SIT-INS

None of them was over eighteen. Ezell Blair, Jr., David Richmond, Franklin McCain, and Joseph McNeil were younger than the youthful American revolutionaries of the 1770s. Their carefully planned revolutionary act was polite: they asked for Coca-Cola. Customers in range of the Woolworth's department store lunch counter noted their neat clothes and grooming. To all appearances they were normal American college students right out of the 1950s. Some were to employ Cold War rhetoric to justify their act, suggesting that racial justice at home would enhance their nation's struggle against Communism in the Third World, and later one of them, as a veteran of the Vietnam War, would heatedly defend his country's engagement in that conflict. But on Monday, February 1, 1960, the relatively progressive city of Greensboro, North Carolina, was still segregated, and at Woolworth's the four freshmen from the black North Carolina Agricultural and Technical College did not get their Cokes.

After leaving Woolworth's they formed a circle on the sidewalk and said the Lord's Prayer. Their return the next day with sixteen fellow students brought national wire service attention. On the third day, there were sixty-three. An elderly white woman seeking the white ladies' room encountered two black girls and exclaimed, eyes wide with alarm, "Nigras, Nigras everywhere!" On Thursday three white students from North Carolina Women's College joined the sit-ins. After that white youths mobbed the

continued

HISTORICAL EVENTS

1953
Earl Warren appointed Chief Justice • Stalin dies

1954
Brown v. Board of Education of Topeka

1955
Montgomery bus boycott • summit meeting at Geneva • peak of the baby boom

1956
Interstate and Defense Highway System Act • Eisenhower reelected • Hungarian rebellion • Jack Kerouac publishes *On the Road* • Allen Ginsberg reads "Howl!"

1957
Little Rock desegregates schools • Sputnik I • Khrushchev becomes premier of the USSR • Eisenhower Doctrine

1958
National Defense Education Act • Lebanon civil war

aisles and heckled the demonstrators, and in a mild departure from the original character of the event the A & T football team confronted gangs who waved Confederate flags. "Who do you think you are?" asked an angry white. "We the Union army," a player responded. On Friday, with more than 300 students participating, the movement started to spread to other stores, and within a few days it had traveled to other cities. In response to Greensboro a network of civil rights activists already in place began marching into the combat it had been planning and waiting for. Within two months the sit-ins had invaded fifty-four segregated establishments in nine southern states. The activists, most of them black but including numbers of white students, were taking up leadership of the civil rights movements from traditional older figures. John F. Kennedy, increasingly an inspiration to the young, endorsed the sit-ins during that year's presidential campaign.

The civility of the Greensboro demonstrations did not reassure respectable southerners. North Carolina's governor Luther Hodges, soon to be appointed secretary of commerce in the Kennedy Administration, told the press that the sit-ins threatened law and order. The Chancellor of the Women's College, having persuaded the female demonstrators to refrain from further participation, convened a meeting with the local black colleges that, after Woolworth's temporarily closed its doors, resulted in an unproductive truce. Moral privileges, a Greensboro business leader explained, could not "be obtained by force or intimidation, but must be secured through the medium of orderly negotiations, reason and mutual respect." It took a resumption of the demonstrations to desegregate the Woolworth's lunch counter.

The Greensboro sit-ins did not mark an increase in resolve on the part of the southern civil rights movement: a number of sit-ins had already occurred in the late fifties without benefit of the national attention that was to add confidence to the later action. But 1960 was precisely the time when the movement accelerated into the relentless, unbroken assault of the following years on southern racism, its confrontations and setbacks and victories reported in the press like dispatches from the battlefield.

The Nation at Midcentury

The nation over which Eisenhower presided, beginning in 1953, was offering to much of its people an unprecedented prosperity and security. Between 1940 and 1950 the gross national product had nearly doubled, to some $350 billion; real personal income increased by half; unemployment rarely reached five percent of the workforce.

The distinctively American pace of innovation speeded up after the war. New industries such as plastics emerged in the Northeast, southern California, and the Great Lakes region. Giant chemical corporations, spurred by government contracts during the war, prospered even more as synthetics created a rush of new consumer goods: plastics replaced wood and metal; detergents and insecticides eased housework; drugs cured illness. The appliance and electronics industries in particular galvanized the postwar economy. Always entranced by gadgets, Americans welcomed air-conditioners, advanced gasoline-powered and electric lawn mowers, and automatic washing machines. Television sets, three million by 1950, could unify the country instantly and at the same time persuade viewers to buy the fruits of technology. An infant computer industry promised a future of startling efficiency. Rapid advances in aviation shrank the country.

The Suburbs   Together, the mobility that has been traditional to American culture and the affluence that flourished in the postwar years created the suburb. As early as 1947, twenty miles outside New York City, a Long Island builder put up ten thousand homes, all identical except for their front doors. Each house in Levittown sold for $7,500, including appliances and landscaping, well within the financial resources of most of the working middle class. Another Levittown rose near Philadelphia the next year, and by 1950 suburbs had exploded around major cities. The population pressures of a baby boom that had begun at the war's end quickened their growth. During the 1930s economic conditions had limited families, but now three or even more children seemed normal. Federal tax benefits for home owners and liberal mortgage terms for veterans under the Federal Housing Administration and the Veterans Administration soon turned meadowlands into suburbs.

The long rows of matchbox houses were more than shelters; they became a new way of life. Clustered together, Americans soon organized themselves into a bewildering variety of groups. Scout troops multiplied, and Little League baseball engaged children; local politics preoccupied many adults; church membership increased substantially; PTAs brought parents into school activities; small businessmen joined chambers of commerce; hobbyists gathered monthly or weekly. Soon enough, strip zoning created massive corridors of storefronts, drive-ins, and used-car lots. Critics spoke of the intellectual sterility of the homogeneous suburbs, their conformity, their materialism. Yet millions of workers were rescued from city tenements, while educational standards improved and entertainment appeared in unparalleled varieties. Some Americans hoped that the spread of suburbia and its values might soon erase poverty altogether as new industries hired more and more workers to produce more and more consumer goods. In fact, many suburbanites in their all-white communities closed their eyes to that other nation of urban blight, racial bigotry, organized crime, and regional poverty. More aware of taxes and their own local interests, they largely shunned progressive reforms and big government. Yet they were not especially receptive to ultraconservative attacks on the welfare state. Suburbanites, who themselves benefited from government pro-

This photograph shows an idealized picture of family life in the 1950s. It suggests the theme of "togetherness," a word coined by *McCall's* magazine in 1954. (*Courtesy, Magnum*)

This young mother in New Rochelle, a suburb of New York City, was photographed in 1955. Some 24,000 American women responded to a 1960 *Redbook* magazine article entitled "Why Young Mothers Feel Trapped." (*Courtesy, Magnum*)

grams, did not begrudge a measure of federal and state assistance to others.

Hispanics

By mid-century, when middle-class whites were settling into what was supposed to be a life of singular progress and contentment and a civil rights movement was soon to gather blacks, it was increasingly apparent that Latin American people had become an integral part of the United States. Puerto Ricans and Cubans brought Hispanic culture to eastern cities. Great numbers of Mexican immigrants settled in California and the Southwest, regions once part of Mexico and since then containing many inhibitants of Mexican descent. By convention and convenience, citizens of this country who are of that background are termed "Mexican American." It is an instance of the troublesome practice of using "American" to refer exclusively to citizens of the United States. Mexican citizens, Guatemalans, and the rest of the peoples south of the Rio Grande, being inhabitants of the American continent, speak of their homelands as American. But the awkwardness of "United States" as an adjective has dictated that for certain purposes "American" will designate the northern republic alone.

Mexican Americans Between 1900 and 1930, the numbers of Mexican Americans in the United States had increased from 100,000 to between one and 1.25 million. Many were pushed from Mexico by revolution there; others came seeking jobs. Railroad construction in the Southwest, combined with the Chinese Exclusion Act of 1882, left openings for railroad crews. The railroad also expanded economic competition and opportunities. As the Colorado irrigation project poured water into the Southwest, fruit, vegetable, and cotton agriculture increased, and until 1930 about sixty percent of all Mexican Americans in the country were farm workers. Many moved north into the fruit valleys of Yakima and Wenatchee in Washington, while others went to the mills and packing plants of St. Louis and other cities.

As early as the 1920s, the largest number of immigrants were crossing the open border between the United States and Mexico illegally. They did so because they could not afford the head tax and visa or feared they would not pass the required literacy test in English for work in this country. Contracted haulers who avoided border patrols delivered many of them to crop growers, who preferred them because they worked for lower wages. Small growers especially became dependent on them. Life for the undocumented migrants—or "wetbacks" as they came to be called in slang—still is particularly tenuous. They not only suffer private discrimination against "Mexes" and wetbacks but live in constant fear of local and immigration authorities and even of the schools and social services agencies.

The demand for the labor of Mexican Americans increased during World War I: many of them enlisted in the armed forces. But Mexican Americans became much less welcome during the Great Depression.

Elliot West, author of Growing Up with the Country: Childhood on the Far Western Frontier, *finds*

"Indians and Hispanics may have been militarily subdued, but when we start to reconstruct the details we find that . . . those cultures have been remarkably resilient. If much has been lost, much has survived, and there has been a vigorous exchange between the conquered and the conquerors, a cross fertilization of customs, ideas, material culture, language, and world views."

Abelardo Delgado, born in Chihuahua, Mexico, emigrated to the United States in 1943. He was a leading figure in the Chicano political movement of the late 1960s and early 1970s. His poem "Stupid America" was published in 1969.

Stupid america, see that chicano
with a big knife
in his steady hand
he doesn't want to knife you
he wants to sit on a bench
and carve christfigures
but you won't let him.
stupid america, hear that chicano
shouting curses on the street
he is a poet
without paper and pencil
and since he cannot write
he will explode.
stupid america, remember that
   chicanito
flunking math and english
he is the picasso
of your western states
but he will die
with one thousand masterpieces
hanging only from his mind.

Other Americans, out of desperation, took the labor-intensive jobs in agriculture as well as the industrial jobs that the Mexican Americans had formerly held. New Deal jobs programs prohibited employment of noncitizens, which further threatened the income of the undocumenteds. The government deported half a million of them.

Those who remained in the United States continued to face the same kind of discrimination that blacks endured in such privately-owned businesses as restaurants and theaters and in public transportation and swimming pools. In the summer of 1943, riots broke out in Los Angeles: the "zoot suit" riots. The disturbances were provoked by American servicemen who prowled the streets looking for Mexican Americans dressed in the zoot-suit fad of the time: baggy pants, long coats, and wide-brimmed hats. The media characterized these young Mexican Americans as shiftless gangsters who were not giving their fair share to the war effort. The victims were arrested; their attackers were not.

During World War II, the demand for labor increased and again the United States encouraged Mexican labor. Between 1942 and 1947, the United States and Mexican governments arranged the *bracero* program, which recruited a quarter of a million field hands on annual contracts. The program lapsed for a year and then revived between 1948 and 1964, bringing 4.5 million Mexican citizens temporary employment here.

After 1945 undocumented immigrants came in greater numbers than before, probably outnumbering those entering legally as immigrants or under the *bracero* program. Deportation was stepped up in the early 1950s, as hostility to the foreign-born attended the Red-hunting of the era. Between 1950 and 1955 nearly four million left the country. Congress in the 1980s adopted stiff penalties for those who hired illegal aliens and gave amnesty to some who had been in the country for a specified period.

Puerto Ricans   Since 1917 Puerto Ricans, whose island was ceded to the American victors in the war with Spain, have been citizens of the United States. But since the culture of Puerto Rico is substantially different from that of the mainland, their migration more closely resembles that of earlier European immigrants. After World War II, the economic boom on the mainland attracted unskilled and semiskilled workers from the island, where unemployment was high and wages low. Between 1940 and 1950 the Puerto Rican population on the mainland of the United States quadrupled to 301,000. Throughout the 1950s, recruiters went to the island seeking workers for industries, often sweatshops. Puerto Rican communities began to grow in Pennsylvania, Illinois, New Jersey, Connecticut, and New York.

Several influences have pulled Puerto Ricans to the continental United States. Improved medical services at home brought down the death rate while the birthrate continued high. Population was increasing rapidly in an economy based on the seasonal production of sugar, tobacco, and coffee, all of which left the majority of workers unemployed for a great part of the year. Transportation has also been an important factor in migration to the mainland. Before World War II,

Miguel Torres wrote of his persistent attempts to enter the United States illegally from Mexico to make a better life for himself:

"I was born in a small town in the state of Michoacán in Mexico, but I wanted to come to the United States to work. . . . I went to Tijuana in Mexico. There's a person there that will get in contact with you. They call him the Coyote. . . . The Coyote rounded up me and five other guys, and then he got in contact with a guide to take us across the border. We had to go through the hills and the desert, and we had to swim through a river. I was a little scared. Then we came to a highway and a man was there with a van, pretending to fix his motor. Our guide said hello, and the man jumped into the car and we ran and jumped in too. He began to drive down the highway fast and we knew we were safe in the United States."

the journey was expensive and unpleasant. After the war, commercial air travel enabled individuals to fly between the island and the states for relatively modest sums.

Cubans   Few Cubans lived in the United States when the island nation, ninety miles off Florida's coast, ceased in 1898 to be a possession of Spain. While Cuba gained technical independence, the United States was to dominate it politically and economically. Yet this did not lead to a great movement of Cubans to the mainland. The island was able to employ most of its population in mining, tourism, or the large sugar industry.

After World War II the number of Cuban immigrants began to increase greatly. From 1951 to 1960 almost 79,000 Cubans came to the United States, mostly through Miami or New York City. An unsteady political situation impelled these Cubans to seek a new home. The corrupt Batista government was challenged during this decade and finally overthrown by a new dictator, Fidel Castro, and his followers in 1959. What began in that year as a trickle of Cuban refugees, many of them strong Batista supporters such as police and army officials, was by the middle of 1962 a flood. Between 1961 and 1970, some 208,000 Cubans left their homeland to seek refuge in the United States from a regime that brought some improvement in social and economic conditions for Cuba's poor but also imposed political repression.

During the era of Eisenhower's presidency, then, the country was settling into social blocs differing in important details from what had preceded. Suburbs, along with comfortable urban neighborhoods, were making for a population of prosperous whites more similated to one another than in the days of greatest immigration of European ethnicities. While Irish, Slavic, Jewish, and other enclaves continued to exist in the cities, maintaining distinctive folkways, the more noticeable ethnic communities now were Hispanic. Black Americans, gaining somewhat from the general prosperity and from the welfare state but much less so than whites, were on the verge of the most important social revolution since the abolition of slavery. But neither blacks nor Hispanics had the visibility of the white suburbanites who were appearing to social commentators as the typical Americans. They seemed, at any rate, to be the citizens most in the spirit of the comfortable presidency of Eisenhower.

At the fringes of American society, meanwhile, dwelt masses of the poor, Hispanic, black, and white.

The Civil Rights Movement

The Warren Court: Part I   One of the most important actions of Eisenhower's administration came early and with no recognition of its significance. In 1953 he appointed Earl Warren chief justice of the United States. Warren, a Republican former governor of California, was to preside over the Supreme Court until

1969, a time of increasingly militant confrontations over race relations and, in the later years, of unprecedented dissent from American foreign policy.

The National Association for the Advancement of Colored People (NAACP), through a team of lawyers headed by Thurgood Marshall, had been hammering away at school segregation for years before 1954. But the Supreme Court responded only by tightening the requirement for equality within a concept enunciated in *Plessy v. Ferguson* (1896), a case involving a Louisiana statute segregating public transportation. That doctrine held that public facilities could be "separate but equal": that states could impose segregation as long as both races enjoyed comparable facilities. Then the Warren Court, overturning *Plessy*, unanimously held in *Brown v. Board of Education of Topeka* that "separate educational facilities are inherently unequal." In its unanimous decision the Court mentioned psychological damage to black children forced into separate schools. The basic constitutional issue, Chief Justice Earl Warren wrote, was whether segregation in schools on the basis of race, even though all other factors were equal, deprives the minority group of equal educational opportunity. "We believe that it does," the nine judges asserted, arguing in effect that a policy which demonstrably does psychological damage to one group and not to another is unequal and discriminatory. Since the Fourteenth Amendment guaranteed the "equal protection of the laws," segregation was clearly unconstitutional. Aware that desegregation of schools was not a simple matter, the Court ordered the following year that steps be taken to implement the decision "with all deliberate speed." While *Brown* considered only the effect of segregation on the minds and emotions of schoolchildren, the clear implication was that all social segregation imposed by law is a damaging affront to the dignity of the minority race.

The Court majority headed by Warren repeatedly intervened in American social life. The *Brown* decision was the first of a number of judgments that brought critics to claim that the Court was usurping legislative power and willfully imposing its own blueprints of reform. Yet the Warren Court was not unique in its energy. The great chief justices beginning with John Marshall had gained renown not only for the elegance of their constitutional arguments but for their involvement in social or political transformation. Surely the Court's decision in *Plessy v. Ferguson* savored as much of political motivation as the Warren Court's rejection of that position in *Brown v. Board of Education*. Defenders and critics of the Warren Court divided ultimately not over the Court's methods but over the social wisdom of its decisions.

Little Rock and Montgomery

Eisenhower never put the moral prestige of his office clearly behind the Court's decision. He believed that the battle against intolerance had to be won in "the hearts of men," not in legislative chambers. Yet when violent resistance to school desegregation erupted in Little Rock, Arkansas, in 1957, Eisenhower did not hesitate to enforce federal supremacy. A state court had blocked an integration plan ap-

President Dwight Eisenhower later wrote:

"Civil rights supporters . . . seemed never to consider that troops could not force local officials to operate the schools; private schools could be set up, and Negroes, as well as many others, would get no education at all."

Angry jeers from whites rain down on Elizabeth Eckford, one of the first black students to arrive for registration at Little Rock's Central High School in 1957. Arkansas troops turned black students away from the school until President Eisenhower overruled the state and called in the military to enforce integration. *(Courtesy, Wide World Photos)*

Soldiers under federal command guarding black students as they enter Little Rock's Central High School.

proved by the Little Rock School Board, claiming that violence would break out if it went into operation. After a federal court ordered integration, Governor Orval Faubus mobilized the Arkansas National Guard to bar entrance to black students. In response Eisenhower placed the National Guard under federal authority and also ordered paratroopers from the United States Army into Little Rock. With bayonets fixed, the troops broke up a segregationist mob and stood guard while the integration plan went into effect.

Eisenhower was not acting out of a strong commitment to integration. He was temperamentally conservative, and he had a conservative's belief in the unbending authority of the Constitution. That document as the courts had interpreted it forbade public school segregation. The governor of Arkansas was disobeying the federal court, and so Eisenhower acted. But his action was more radical than he. It implied an overturning of what had been the relationship between federal and state government on the issue of race. Not since the end of Reconstruction had the federal government in any major way imposed its authority upon the southern states in their pursuit of white supremacy. Until Little Rock if a state wished to disobey the Constitution in matters of racial equality it had been at liberty to do so. President Eisenhower reversed that federal policy of inaction. Thenceforth, civil rights lawyers knew that they had a potential ally in the federal government.

Far more revolutionary in its effect on the future of civil rights was the Montgomery, Alabama, bus boycott of 1955. For some time the leadership of the black community in Montgomery had planned a protest against the insulting details of racial segregation on the city's buses, by which black people were required to sit in the rear section of a bus and the driver could order them about. Black women such as Jo Ann Robinson had taken much of the initiative in planning for resistance. Rosa Parks, whose arrest for refusing to move from her bus seat was the immediate cause of the boycott, had been a committed civil rights activist. The Reverend Martin Luther King's eloquence strengthened the subsequent struggle in his hometown of Montgomery, and his adherence to nonviolent resistance gave the boycott a character that would influence other protest movements. After about a year of black abstention from bus-riding, the boycott was followed by a court victory that forced the end of segregation on the city's buses.

Martin Luther King, Jr., wrote:

"I have a dream that my four little children will one day live in a nation where they will not be judged by the color of their skin but by the content of their character."

Economic and Social Policy in the 1950s

Unemployment   Unemployment was the central economic issue of the decade; up to 7.7 percent of workers were without jobs, and recessions of growing severity marred the times. The end of the Korean War and a sharp cut in military expenditures brought on the first recession in 1953–54. An easy money policy adopted by both the Treasury and the Federal Reserve Board, combined with a tax cut and an increase in old age and unemployment payments, eventually managed to offset the economic decline resulting from postwar layoffs. But the administration, worried over inflation, reacted slowly to another recession in 1957–58. When unemployment rates remained at seven percent during the congressional elections, Republicans suffered disastrous consequences. Even in 1960, though a presidential campaign hung in the balance, inflation troubled Eisenhower more than unemployment. What the economy needed, according to the Democrats, was growth. Growth would pull down prices by flooding the market with goods. It would decrease poverty without dislocating the rest of the economy. And it would provide new jobs even as technological improvements cut down the number of workers needed for a given operation. But that growth did not occur; the national economic growth rate remained below levels then prevailing in western Europe.

Eisenhower's administration no doubt wanted to curb rising prices, but it could not do it with voluntary restraints, especially since the steel industry resisted. Large firms aimed not for competition at home and abroad, but for secure growth based on rising prices in a carefully planned market, or for an "administered price." During the 1950s American investments in new plants and equipment shrank well below that in European economies. In the 1950s, Republicans friendly to the wishes of business appeared fearful of stimulating more rapid economic growth, while at the end of the decade, Democrats, less frightened by inflation, made growth their major objective.

As usual, the poor suffered most during the economic doldrums. Blacks, Indians, Hispanics, and growing numbers of the elderly were, in writer Michael Harrington's apt word, "invisible"—physically shut away and forgotten in slums, on reservations, in migrant workers' camps, in filthy nursing homes as medical indigents. Mass-produced clothing, which replaced the rags of earlier generations of the poor, hid their true economic condition. These same groups were also politically invisible, lacking a voice even in the Democratic Party, which had its institutional base in the unions.

Aid to public education was so popular, and the need for class-

The merger of the American Federation of Labor and the Congress of Industrial Organizations in 1955 created a sixteen-million member labor union. *(Courtesy, AP/Wide World Photos)*

rooms so great, that most people expected Eisenhower to implement his campaign pledge of direct federal aid to schools as "the American answer." Yet he failed to do so. Congress did pass one important education measure, the National Defense Education Act of 1958. But both the act's provisions and Congress's motivation seemed far removed from concern over the quality of local education. During the anxious period following the 1957 Russian launching of Sputnik I, the national government had quickly decided to improve college-level education, primarily in the applied sciences and engineering. Implementing this decision, NDEA provided loans, scholarships, and fellowships directly to students and a lesser amount in grants to the colleges themselves. The NDEA did mean that education had now become a concern of the federal government.

A most important domestic achievement of the Eisenhower Administration was the program to build a system of interstate highways. After World War II, when trucks became the preferred method of freight shipment in the United States and automobiles the most desired means of travel, traffic problems grew especially severe. Congestion in cities made it particularly difficult, and expensive, to ship goods across the country. Urban planners and transportation engineers began proposing the construction of limited-access, high-speed expressways. President Eisenhower endorsed the idea, and in June 1956 Congress passed the Interstate and Defense Highway System Act. The law provided for $32 billion over a thirteen-year period to construct a 41,000 mile interstate highway system and make improvements on other federal highways.

A Philosophy of Moderate Conservatism

Eisenhower's determination not otherwise to expand the federal budget expressed itself in the struggles over environmental bills. In 1960 the President vetoed a water pollution bill that would have established federal grants to build sewage treatment plants. He argued that pollution was "a uniquely local blight," and that responsibility rested with state and local governments. In 1962 Rachel Carson in *Silent Spring* would awaken environmental concerns about worldwide pollution of the oceans. Caution and philosophical objections guided Eisenhower's approach to social and ecological issues; the Republican President varied in his response to other kinds of federal spending. Public works projects that promoted the economic development of the country—what economists call the "capital infrastructure"—received quick, almost enthusiastic approval despite often costly drains on government funds. The Middle West welcomed plans for construction by Canada and the United States of the Saint Lawrence Seaway, a dream of Herbert Hoover's brought to fruition in 1959, thirty years after he recommended it to Congress.

The Eisenhower Administration, then, was neither in the reformist grain of the Democratic years that had preceded it nor in league with the lingering band of conservatives who hoped to repeal the New Deal. Quietly, in the very absence of any pronouncement on the subject, the Eisenhower presidency allowed the welfare state to become a permanent part of the American consensus.

Ike bluntly cautioned his conservative brother Edgar:

"Should any political party attempt to abolish social security and eliminate labor laws and farm programs, you would not hear of that party again in our political history. There is a tiny splinter group, of course, that believes that you can do those things, . . . a few Texas oil millionaires, and an occasional politician and businessman from other areas. Their number is negligible and they are stupid."

The Elections of 1956 and 1958

Stevenson Again   The 1956 campaign featured the same presidential candidates as in 1952. Stevenson presented a vision of possible disengagement from the Cold War; he recommended a unilateral halt to nuclear testing and an end to the draft. At the same time, however, he implied that Eisenhower had sacrificed our national security in exchange for a balanced budget and had failed to answer Soviet ideology with an articulate program and philosophy. Early in 1956 Stevenson told a Los Angeles audience that the use of federal troops to enforce school desegregation court orders would be "a fatal mistake." Like his hero Abraham Lincoln, Stevenson put national unity before racial justice. Many black newspapers backed Eisenhower, who later ran well in black precincts. Stevenson's shining reputation for articulateness has been preserved as in amber, but he was a man far removed from the issues that would prevail in the mid-sixties.

In the last days of the campaign the crisis in the Middle East, in which the country looked to presidential leadership, further strengthened Eisenhower. His margin of victory did not reach the fabled triumph of FDR twenty years before, but a tally of 457 to 73 electoral votes and a nine million popular vote margin gave the Republicans much reason for self-congratulation. It was a far more conclusive triumph than that of 1952. Even the Democratic Solid South crumbled; Stevenson lost Virginia, Florida, Louisiana, and Texas.

Had they read the congressional returns more carefully, however, the Republicans might have been somewhat less jubilant, for they had not built a lasting national majority. In 1956 Eisenhower ran 6.5 million votes ahead of the Republican congressional candidates. All through the fifties, in fact, the Democrats gradually regained congressional seats they had lost in 1952.

A Democratic Resurgence   The congressional elections of 1958 produced a landslide for the Democrats. The 1957 recession suggested that perhaps only under the Democrats could a stable prosperity be sustained. The Republicans unwisely chose 1958 to push "right to work" or open shop laws forbidding any kind of compulsory union membership. The Eisenhower agricultural program favored large farms that employed the latest technology and indirectly forced more and more small farmers to sell their holdings and to become tenants or move into the cities. The Soviet Union had launched two Sputniks in October 1957; the second one demonstrated that it had perfected the rocket fuel necessary for space exploration, and that the booster rocket could propel a nuclear weapon at high speed to a radius of 4,000 miles. These developments shocked whoever may have presumed that under a military man the United States would of course hold its own in competition against the Soviet Union. Questions about the administration had also appeared with the dismissal of Eisenhower's closest adviser, Sherman Adams, for accepting gifts.

The era, moreover, was stirring from its torpor with the publication of muckraking articles about automobile safety, air and water

The Democrat, Adlai Stevenson, though he won enormous loyalty from his followers, could not overcome Eisenhower's popularity and lost both the 1952 and 1956 presidential elections. *(Courtesy, Wide World Photos)*

pollution, the shortcomings of American schooling, and the injustice of the country's race relations.

Eisenhower's Foreign Policy

Eisenhower's efforts in foreign policy were more impressive than his work at home. A peace-loving man, he quickly ended the Korean War on terms that Truman had found unacceptable. The President settled for a truce that divided the country where the opposing armies had stopped, not far different from the old division of Korea into North and South. The threat to use atomic weapons that he had employed to bring the Communists into peace negotiations was pure Cold War stridency. But the truce itself meant that the country's most successful recent general had become the first President to halt a modern war short of victory. What he achieved was not a formal peace but a truce, sealed at Panmunjom in July 1953. The truce has held ever since.

At the same time, the Soviet Union moved toward improved relations with the West. Freed of Stalin's arbitrary cruelty by his death in March 1953, and perhaps sobered by Truman's determined containment politics and the unexpected strength of decadent capitalism, Georgy Malenkov, Stalin's nominal successor, sought a measure of calm between Moscow and the anti-Communist world. He received support from Foreign Minister Vyacheslav Molotov, Defense Minister Nikolay A. Bulganin, and Nikita Khrushchev, first secretary of the Communist Party. A three-year struggle for dominance ensued among Stalin's successors, a contest Khrushchev won largely because of timely support from Soviet marshal Georgy Zhukov, a war hero who controlled the Red Army. Khrushchev's triumph over his rivals seemed to increase the possibility of a more stable world order. Some of the sharpest confrontations between the USSR and the West would come in the years of Khrushchev's premiership of the Soviet Union and domination of the Communist apparatus there. Yet he articulated in a new way the possibility of a peace, however edgy, between the Communist and the Western bloc. He announced the doctrine of peaceful coexistence and economic competition, both direct repudiations of Bolshevik militancy.

In Washington, a new tenor and even a new substance entered the making of foreign policy. The President's immense following and his military reputation made it possible for him to pursue a policy of armed and tense but civilized truce with the Communist world. Eisenhower turned over the day-to-day control of foreign affairs to the somber John Foster Dulles. The secretary of state's vocabulary of unbending anti-Communism, his rhetorical willingness to go to the brink of nuclear war in order to contain Communism went counter to the details of his actual foreign policy, which did not bring the nation anywhere near to any brink.

Not long into his presidency, Eisenhower managed to complete a real peace between West Germany and France. Dulles negotiated the Paris Accords, which guaranteed French security and at the same time brought West Germany into the NATO alliance. This act provoked the Soviet Union into the Warsaw Pact, an alliance system in eastern

Eisenhower knew the horrors of war. He recalled the harrowing experience of entering the Falaise Gap zone in Normandy in 1944:

"It was literally possible to walk for hundreds of yards at a time, stepping on nothing but dead and decayed flesh. . . . I hate war as only a soldier who has lived it can, only as one who has seen its brutality, its futility, its *stupidity*."

Europe. This clear organization of the continent into two blocs actually appeared to make for an increase not in danger but in stability.

Both Eisenhower and Dulles relied heavily on the deterrent power of nuclear weapons as opposed to conventional forces. Admiral Arthur Radford, chairman of the Joint Chiefs of Staff, called it the "New Look" defense policy. This strategy produced "more bang for a buck" in the colorful words of economy-minded Charles Wilson, the secretary of defense. Yet the nuclear approach generally meant that in some future crisis requiring confrontation with the USSR, the United States was going to have to choose between doing nothing and threatening atomic catastrophe, obliterating both sides. However perilous the nuclear standoff might be in the years to come, it often made for stability, diplomacy, and mutual retreat.

Summit Meeting	In the most dramatic departure from the techniques of the Truman and Acheson years, Eisenhower sought direct meetings with Soviet leaders—

a diplomatic device unused since 1945. Meeting at Geneva in late July 1955, the United States, the Soviet Union, Britain, and France discussed disarmament, an increase in communication between East and West, and German unification. The USSR, fearful with reason of a strong and fully independent Germany, would not agree to allowing East Germany, then ruled by Soviet power, to slip from under that control and unite with anti-Communist West Germany. That was no surprise. The greater disappointment was the failure to achieve progress toward disarmament. At Geneva Eisenhower outlined his "open skies" proposal: mutual aerial surveillance and an exchange of military blueprints so that arms reductions, when negotiated, could be reliably verified. The USSR politely scuttled the idea. Yet the summit launched the hopeful "spirit of Geneva."

The Hungarian Rebellion	In 1956 the Soviet empire in eastern Europe nearly collapsed. On June 28 some 15,000 Polish factory workers revolted in Poznan. While the Kremlin

hesitated, the Poles demanded that Wladyslaw Gomulka take over the government. A patriot and Communist who opposed hasty collectivization, Gomulka refused to compromise with Soviet leaders clearly caught off guard. After a series of maneuvers, he forced Moscow to accept a government under his leadership. Gomulka's success triggered the devastating Hungarian rebellion, which sought political independence as well as economic reform. On October 23, a demonstration supporting Polish liberation quickly changed into a huge crowd of workers, soldiers, and students who demanded the return of Imre Nagy, a former minister. Nagy, a Communist who opposed Soviet economic methods and Moscow's political domination, formed a new government on the Polish model. But demonstrations turned into armed rebellion in favor of Nagy's attempt to eliminate the remnants of Soviet rule. Encouraged by signs of support from the West, the revolutionaries hoped for complete independence from the Soviet Union. When the Hungarians persisted in trying to escape its orbit, Moscow brought in a heavy military force to crush the rebellion.

Secretary of State Dulles explained his policy:

"The ability to get to the verge without getting into the war is the necessary art.. . . . If you try to run away from it, if you are scared to go to the brink, you are lost."

Worried about nuclear confrontation and tacitly recognizing Soviet dominance in eastern Europe, the West never considered intervention. In any case, the Western powers were preoccupied at the moment with the Suez Canal.

Suez and Sputnik   On November 5, 1956, England, France, and Israel launched a joint attack on Egypt, ostensibly to reopen the Suez Canal, which President Gamal Abdel Nasser had nationalized in July. Other issues lay behind the question of the canal. To the Israelis, the attack was a preventive war against Egypt, which along with other Arab nations had been in a standing conflict with the Jewish state. France hoped to recoup its prestige after frustrations in Vietnam and Algeria. Only Britain hesitated. Though anxious to topple Nasser, whose action against British interests in the Suez created a dangerous example to other Arab states, London understood the enormous military risks. British officials misread Eisenhower's mild warnings and concluded that he would not object. The United States, anxious to avoid identifying itself with European colonialism, abruptly condemned the operation. Eisenhower even threatened to bankrupt the British pound unless Prime Minister Anthony Eden withdrew British troops. Beset on all sides—the entire Arab world had broken off diplomatic relations—the British prime minister accepted a proposal by Canada and the United States for a United Nations peacekeeping force in the Sinai peninsula.

The next jolt occurred outside the field of politics. On October 4, 1957, the first space satellite, the Russian Sputnik, carrying a pioneering little dog—the first life in earth's outer reaches—beeped the beginning of the space age and seemed to tip the technological balance in favor of the Soviet Union. Economies in the Defense Department, together with an exaggerated reliance upon manned bombers, had limited the American missile development program. Despite the quiver that ran through the Western world, the new earth satellite had little strategic significance; the United States far surpassed the USSR in military technology and gross national product. Yet Soviet rocket engineers had given their government a strong propaganda weapon.

The Middle East   In 1957 Dulles enunciated the Eisenhower Doctrine for the Middle East, offering not only economic assistance but American soldiers to governments protecting their territorial integrity against Communism. The new policy resulted from the rapid erosion of the West's position throughout the strategically significant Near East. Egyptian leader Gamal Abdel Nasser's attempt to unify the region accelerated the trend toward militant nationalism.

In Lebanon during 1958, a confused, intricate civil war erupted setting Christians against Muslims, opponents of Egypt's President Nasser against his supporters, and urban Beirut with its Western flavor against the provincial culture of the hill areas. The pro-Western president of Lebanon asked the United States for military support to end the civil war. Eisenhower invoked his new doctrine and dispatched 3,500 marines, a force that eventually grew to 14,000. The intervention, so brief and well-executed, deserved commendation at least for its technical skill. While American troops helped keep peace, American diplomats aided in hammering out an accord that would restore harmony and balance to Lebanon for the next fifteen years. But a larger purpose of the landing failed; the attempt to set up an alternative to Nasser in the Middle East collapsed around Arab fears of renewed colonialism and the reluctance of Arab countries to combine with outside powers against one another.

Berlin and the U-2 Incident   Eisenhower deftly handled another crisis, potentially the most serious of the decade, when the Soviet Union in 1958 threatened the Western presence in Berlin. The President's resolve to stand firm without overreacting quickly diminished tension. As if to reiterate the common resolve to avoid war, Khrushchev paid a successful visit to the United States in 1959, and met a cordial Eisenhower at Camp David, Maryland. Observers spoke of the "spirit of Camp David," the dissipation of mistrust. But to the embarrassment of Eisenhower, Khrushchev in 1960 announced the shooting down over its territory of a U-2 spy plane. The downed plane had been among the aircraft that the United States, in violating Soviet air space, had been flying over the USSR to report on the state of military preparedness there. Khrushchev canceled a summit meeting in Paris with Eisenhower. It was a bad though fleeting moment in Western prestige and diplomacy.

President Eisenhower and Soviet Premier Nikita Khrushchev at Camp David, 1959. *(Courtesy, AP/Wide World Photos)*

The Social Spectrum

It is customary to present the Eisenhower years that preceded the Kennedy presidency as a time of blissful tranquility. The times had indeed been tranquil, if they are compared to what followed them. But they were in their own way as innovative as any comparable span of years in American history. A technology and economy that demanded literate skills swelled the college population and would swell it still further as the postwar baby boom came to university age. Technical advances were also preparing the way for new consumer goods that have shaped the behavior of Americans ever since. The beat literature of the 1950s, along with the communal style of life, defined a rebellion that is also remembered today in the shape it took among the communes of the late sixties. The energies of black rhythm and blues, white country music, and jazz were compounding into rock and roll, a prelude to the hard rock of the 1960s. And above all there was a peaceful black uprising at Montgomery, Alabama, and elsewhere, overturning patterns of subordination that whites had taken entirely for granted, and doing so with a method of nonviolent resistance almost unprecedented in the American experience.

The Service Economy   Most people associate work with making or growing something. But it is a peculiarity of advanced industrial societies that much of their most skilled and imaginative work goes not into production of visible goods but into services. In the affluent years that followed World War II, the American economy and technology spawned countless jobs of this kind: teaching, radio and television announcing, acting, retailing, the staffing of hotels and motels, restaurants, health spas, movie theaters. Accountants, technicians, clerical workers, and administrators, moreover, are all essential to the making of objects they will never see.

The Consumer Society   Away from working hours the participant in the modern economy has become a new creature: the consumer. Consumers in the 1950s and 1960s were barraged with every sales technique Madison Avenue could devise. Some observers decided that consumerism demonstrated the superiority of American life to that of those societies, especially the Soviet Union, where people still struggled to obtain necessities. Others concluded that consumerism embodied the shallowness of the nation's culture and compromised its ability to present itself as superior to the culture of Communist countries.

This consumer society was going to be well-stocked with customers. The birth rate for each 1,000 people reached a high 24.1 in 1950 and peaked at 25.0 in 1955 before declining steadily until the 1980s. The bumper crop of children necessitated building new public schools; overcrowded classrooms brought about school financing crises and a national furor over "why Johnny can't read," as the title to a well-known book puts it. These postwar children, in elementary school when the Soviet Union launched its Sputnik satellite in 1957, became the target of elaborate programs of curriculum reform, with particular emphasis on mathematics and the sciences. The baby boom would also furnish an immense audience for television and create an enormous market for rock and roll music, automobiles, surfboards, clothes, skin creams, magazines, movies, and innumerable other commodities. By the mid-1960s enrollment in public higher education had tripled since 1945. The postwar generation created the base for student movements and much of the cultural experimentation of the 1960s.

As these children reached their majority, they entered a world breathtaking in its gadgetry: copiers, credit card billing, cassette tape recorders, computers, direct distance dialing, TV dinners, drive-in banking. Inexpensive, high-fidelity recordings of all kinds of music became available, along with improved phonographic equipment. Paperback books, bringing to mass audiences not only a variety of cheap leisure reading but also ready access to serious and scholarly work, improved high school and college curricula.

Mass Culture   Critics reacted to a culture that seemed to express itself in television's trite situation comedies and popular music's banal lyrics. Newton Minow, chairman of the Federal Communications Commission under President Kennedy, called television a "vast wasteland." Some critics feared that mass culture might be the harbinger of a dangerous social and political stupor. The sociologist David Riesman in *The Lonely Crowd* described a mass society of "other-directed" Americans doing nothing much more serious than looking to their peers for the right tastes and interests in music, clothes, and other trivia of popular culture. Riesman contrasted these people with earlier generations of "inner-directed" individuals, self-motivated and independent. While Riesman actually looked with some sympathy on the amiable culture of other-direction and implied that character and creativity could express themselves even within its terms, his study suggested that modern conditions threaten independence and individuality. Riesman was among the subtlest of many commentators who examined the white middle classes in their suburbs, their work, and their leisure, concerned with whether middle-class comfort and social blandness were taking the strong, rough edges off the American spirit. If a single solution offered itself to social critics it was that a toughened educational system might supply the difficulties and challenges that appeared to be disappearing from the rest of American life. Yet within a few years, children of the suburbs would be the rebels of the 1960s. Something within the culture of suburbia, it seems, was more capable of producing political commitment and cultural dissent than observers during the Eisenhower era could have thought possible.

This song "Little Boxes," protesting conformity in the suburbs, was written by Malvina Reynolds.

Little boxes on the hillside,
Little boxes made of ticky tacky
Little boxes on the hillside,
And they all look just the same.

There's a green one and a pink one
And a blue one and a yellow one
And they're all made out of ticky tacky
And they all look just the same.

American Subcultures

The "Beats"   Beyond the confines of both traditional high culture and the spreading, popular "mass" culture, a distinctive body of writing originated during the 1950s. It was nurtured among the artists of San Francisco and Greenwich Village. The popular press used "beat," and then "beatnik"; a few beats explained it as short for beatific, indicating a state of ecstacy and understanding. Jack Kerouac spoke for the beats in *On the Road* (1956) and a series of other novels. His unbroken flow of prose chronicled beat culture semi-autobiographically, detailing the experiences of cross-country road trips, evading the police, appreciating black jazz, discovering marijuana and Buddhism, and generally avoiding the incomprehensible larger society. Allen Ginsberg and another poet, Gary Snyder, also popularized mystical Asian religion and philosophy among avant-garde groups. Ginsberg, possibly because of his radical background and avowed homosexuality, maintained a more distinctly political position than most beats; he became a fixture at antiwar demonstrations in the sixties, chanting rhythmic Indian mantras to calm the police.

Allen Ginsberg, coming from a radical middle-class family in Paterson, New Jersey, bummed his way around the world several times before reading to a San Francisco audience in 1956 a central statement of beat culture, a long poem entitled "Howl!" Its opening lines read:

I saw the best minds of my generation
    destroyed
by madness,
        starving hysterical naked,
dragging themselves through the negro
    streets at dawn looking for
        an angry fix

Rock and Roll   Along with the beats, rock and roll demonstratored the possibilities of cultural innovation in a society that critics feared had lost its sources of energy. Early rock and roll relied on two musical strains with long traditions and independent audiences. The primary appropriation, black rhythm and blues, gave the drive, the beat, and the solid, earthy feeling of the music. Rhythm and blues in turn had roots in black jazz, gospel, and blues music, all representing an autonomous market for recorded music until the advent of rock and roll. Some rhythm and blues performers, Little Richard and Fats Domino among them, successfully moved to the newer and larger white audience. But white performers and recording studios simply picked up and bleached much rhythm and blues without pay-

Elvis **by Andy Warhol (1964), a
pop tribute to the king of rock
and roll.** *(Courtesy, Leo Castelli)*

ment or acknowledgment. White country music, the other musical source of rock and roll, contributed some vocal patterns, the distinctive lead guitar sound, and many of the most important performers. The Everly brothers and Buddy Holly came directly from the country tradition, and Elvis Presley, the dominating figure of early rock, worked in the Grand Ole Opry in Nashville. Before his first major recording contract in 1956 and the release of "Heartbreak Hotel"—a hit with country, popular, and rhythm and blues audiences—Presley had been an acclaimed country performer. Rock and roll possessed a vitality with which a new generation readily identified.

**Popular
Diversions**

Some adolescent devotees of rock and the hot rod consciously separated themselves from the adult world. In the movie *Rebel Without a Cause* James Dean dramatized and romanticized the subculture, playing the rebellious, drag-racing high school adolescent who defies his middle-class parents and the police in resolving his identity crisis.

Neither knowing nor prepared to care about Allen Ginsberg, and having no wish to enter any culture of the alienated, countless Americans read *Reader's Digest,* with a monthly circulation of about ten million. The most popular books of the fifties were not Kerouac's novels but the *Reader's Digest Condensed Books,* abridgments of best-sellers. The biggest box-office attractions of the fifties were not James Dean films but romantic comedies starring Rock Hudson and Doris Day, and such spectacular movies as *The Ten Commandments.* Among adult Americans not Elvis but Lawrence Welk held sway, serving waltz-like, romantically light champagne music over prime-time national television. In a stadium or facing a television set, tens of millions of Americans sat and watched baseball, football, and basketball.

By far the largest commercial culture empire of the fifties was Walt Disney Productions, Inc. In earlier times Disney had achieved success by producing highly innovative animated cartoons and feature movies. By the fifties, he had left the drawing board to oversee a colossal business enterprise, producing cartoons, comic books, a weekly television series, and a host of other projects. In 1955 Disney fulfilled his lifelong dream by opening "Disneyland" in Anaheim, California, which created a fantasy world that could appeal to almost everyone. Disneyland seems to reflect that side of American society, safe, tranquil, vaguely unreal, that coexisted with the less visible beats, the black rhythm and blues artists, and the nonwhite communities of the poor.

Religion

Many in the 1950s took comfort in the steady rise in church membership, increasing more rapidly than the total population. Between 1950 and 1956, Roman Catholics added five million members, Protestants eight million. Billy Graham, a central figure in evangelical Protestantism, crusaded across the nation and throughout the world. Graham functioned as a popularizer of Christianity rather than as a theologian. Even in the 1950s that are now remembered as so placid, however, religion was astir. In Protestant theology, neoorthodoxy was applying to human nature some of the hard and skeptical analysis that is to be found in traditional Christianity. In the South, meanwhile, black churches were at the core of a growing resistance to white supremacy, bringing to the rebellion a Christian compound of militancy, patience, and cooperation.

JFK

The Kennedy Promise

Millions of Americans remember the hope and energy that attended the presidency of John Kennedy. He possessed intelligence, good looks, a Harvard education, a war hero's record, and a beautiful wife. For all its overuse, the word "image" is inescapable in any discussion of the Kennedy years. The President was widely admired by university people who perhaps credited him with more intellectual curiosity then he possessed. In his crispness of speech and manner, Kennedy seemed to embody the intelligence and creative energies of the technological forces that critics a few years earlier had feared were turning society passive and complacent.

The Massachusetts senator of the 1950s gave clues to the later man. Wishing not to antagonize his Irish Catholic supporters, and perhaps half agreeing with the methods of Joseph McCarthy, he kept silent on the Wisconsin red-baiter in the early 1950s. When Eleanor Roosevelt at the end of the decade asked him to go on record against the late senator—an act that would have brought him needed convention support—Kennedy had the honesty to recognize that to do so then, after his years of silence, would be hypocritical. He was refreshing and unpredictable.

When he first entered national politics in 1956 as a candidate for the vice presidency, Kennedy allowed his adviser Ted Sorensen to leak a memorandum arguing that a Catholic candidate would strengthen rather than harm a national ticket. Kennedy also let himself be cast as a northerner friendly to the South and willing to let that section move slowly on the race issue. Though he lost his vice-presidential bid at the 1956 Democratic Convention to Senator Estes Kefauver of Tennessee, in 1958 he won reelection to his senate seat in Massachusetts by 875,000 votes, the largest majority in the state's history.

The Election of 1960

Shrewd political methods and an able staff gave Kennedy by 1960 a commanding lead in the race for the Democratic presidential nomination. Party leaders worried about his religion and his youthfulness, but he proved himself in the primaries.

Many northern Democrats and labor leaders were chagrined at Kennedy's choice of Lyndon B. Johnson of Texas as his running mate, but they had nowhere to turn. The Republican party had nominated their old enemy, Vice President Richard Nixon.

Condemning Kennedy on religious grounds, Norman Vincent Peale, Nixon's own pastor, in effect gave credence to the view that the Catholic candidate was a victim of prejudice. Methodist leaders gave Kennedy a dramatic opportunity to prove to a skeptical audience of Houston ministers—and by way of television to the nation at large—

Jacquelyn and John F. Kennedy, the first Catholic and the youngest man to be elected to the White House. *(Courtesy, John F. Kennedy Library)*

Kennedy's inaugural address is the subject of much controversy. Its measured cadences suggest a belligerence at odds with his more prudent conduct of foreign policy. Here are some of his more famous words:

"Let the word go forth from this time and place, to friend and foe alike, that the torch has been passed to a new generation of Americans—born in this century, tempered by war, disciplined by a hard and bitter peace, proud of our ancient heritage—and unwilling to witness or permit the slow undoing of those human rights to which this nation has always been committed, and to which we are committed today at home and around the world.

Let every nation know, whether it wishes us well or ill, that we shall pay any price, bear any burden, meet any hardship, support any friend, oppose any foe to assure the survival and the success of liberty.

This much we pledge—and more."

The young folksinger Bob Dylan caught the demonstrative spirit of the times in one of his songs:

Come mothers and fathers
Throughout the land
And don't criticize
What you can't understand.
Your sons and daughters
Are beyond your command
There's a battle
Outside and it's ragin'
It'll soon shake your windows
And rattle your walls . . .
For the times they are a-changin'.

Reprinted by permission.

Nonviolence required enormous self-discipline of the civil rights workers.

Among the methods that gained a good deal of visibility during the civil rights struggle itself along with the later antiwar protests was that of nonviolence. Nonviolence does not refer to passivity in the face of power: it involves to the contrary some deliberate breaking of a law or custom—sitting in a segregated restaurant, blocking the entrance to a building, or the like. Perhaps the great majority of its practitioners used it exclusively as a tactic, to be employed as long as it was effective, to be replaced by the force of law and the courts if these could be enlisted on the side of civil rights. But since nonviolence requires that in the face of provocation the protester will resist both the impulse to become violent and the impulse to flee, the practice came to mean for some an exercise in self-control and self-reformation, as demanding in its own way as military training or the routines of a religious order.

that they had no religious reasons to fear him. Here Kennedy stood in sharp contrast to Al Smith. Smith had rejected as bigotry the very question of whether his faith might interfere with obligations to the country's laws and institutions; Kennedy welcomed queries and responded openly and at length.

In the course of the campaign Kennedy appeared the more activist candidate. When Kennedy endlessly said it was time "to get moving again," he referred principally to the national economy. But economic expansion also had its implications for foreign policy. Kennedy repeatedly charged that the Soviet Union held a lead over the United States in the development of missiles. He managed to link the issues of national prestige and economic growth, implying that Nixon, as a high official in the decent but placid Eisenhower Administration, could bring the country neither. Kennedy's charm and confident handling of the complexities of public problems cast him as a man who would handle the nation's problems with imagination and dash. Nixon agreed to a series of television debates in which Kennedy appeared fresher and more vibrant, thus confirming in the minds of voters the contrast between him and the exhausted Republican candidate. Kennedy won the election narrowly and became the youngest President to be elected in American history.

Kennedy and the Civil Rights Movement

On the issue of civil rights, the major domestic issue of the 1960s, John F. Kennedy brought to the presidency a record of compromise. From 1956 to 1960 he sought support from the most segregationist governors. During the presidential campaign of 1960, Kennedy castigated Eisenhower for tolerating segregation in federally financed housing, and his telephone message of sympathy to Mrs. Martin Luther King while her husband sat in an Atlanta jail in one of his innumerable protests against segregation was an important symbolic gesture. He appointed a black, Robert C. Weaver, to be federal housing administrator. But Kennedy, fearful of losing support for other programs, sent no new civil rights legislation to Congress in 1961 and 1962.

Bloody incidents in 1961 involving freedom riders at Birmingham and Montgomery, Alabama—whites and blacks desegregating interstate transportation—forced Washington into action. Attorney General Robert Kennedy, the President's brother, told the Birmingham office of the Greyhound Bus Company to get in touch with "Mr. Greyhound" and said: "I am—the Government is—going to be very much upset if this group does not get to continue their trip." The government sent 400 federal marshals to Montgomery to protect the contingent of freedom riders, some of whom had been beaten, and obtained an injunction against the Ku Klux Klan and other groups that were interfering with the rides. And after a while the attorney general decreed that the Interstate Commerce Commission ban segregation in bus terminals that served out-of-state passengers.

In the fall of 1961 and the summer of 1962 civil rights efforts

This Greyhound bus carrying the first Freedom Riders into Alabama was set afire by a mob outside the town of Anniston. (*Courtesy, AP/Wide World Photos*)

stalled in Albany, Georgia. Black demonstrators there learned some of the limits of nonviolence. When Martin Luther King came to that city, he told the largest gathering yet assembled at Shiloh Baptist Church: "Don't stop now. Keep moving. Don't get weary. We will wear them down with our capacity to suffer." And in harmony with Gandhi's precepts activists filled the jails. But the shrewd police chief Laurie Pritchett confined most of them in neighboring towns where they were nearly invisible, also instructing his force in the methods of nonviolence and making arrests across racial lines. Among his tactics was to get down on his knees and pray with the demonstrators, then lock them up. He thereby deprived the demonstrators of the scenes of white-supremacist violence, enacted before the national media, that elsewhere his more primitive southern compatriots happily supplied.

Coverage by the media made the nation aware of this time of confrontation, of violence from segregationists, of the posing of absolute moral issues. Forward momentum continued in the fall of 1962 with the enrollment at the University of Mississippi of its first black student, James Meredith. A white mob took over the campus, and when federal marshals were besieged in their attempt to enroll Meredith, Kennedy sent in federal troops. Vivian Malone entered the University of Alabama under milder conditions in the spring of 1963.

The only strategy that worked for blacks in Birmingham, Alabama, during May 1963 in their opposition to massive discrimination there, public and private, was the forcing of massive arrests. The city met the demonstrators with fire hoses, police dogs, and electric cattle prods. Kennedy, foreseeing the "fires of frustration and discord . . . burning in every city, North and South," responded with legislative proposals. The President requested a partial ban on discrimination in public places, asked that the Justice Department be given powers to sue for school desegregation upon request, and urged broader powers to withhold funds from federally assisted programs in which discrimination occurred. Late in 1963 a bomb went off in a black Birmingham church just before Sunday school, killing four schoolgirls. Congressional civil rights leaders pushed Kennedy farther, persuading him to give the attorney general power to intervene in all civil rights cases.

The civil rights movement was a model for other groups.

The civil rights movement was an object lesson in how to effect change. Or so it seemed to other groups in the 1960s. Many of the leaders of the students' and women's movements had gotten their start in the civil rights crusade. There they learned tactics like the sit-in and the protest march (both used with great effectiveness by the labor movement in the 1930s). And there they learned that American institutions could be altered by such forms of direct action. The student radicals adopted, in their struggle against the Vietnam War, the style of confrontation politics they had found in the civil rights crusade.

And just as blacks gained a new sense of themselves through participation in it, so too women, students, gays, ethnic groups, welfare recipients, senior citizens, Spanish-speaking Americans, and others all sought a new self-consciousness in the late 1960s. Ethnics rediscovered their cultural heritage, women engaged in "consciousness raising," and older Americans campaigned for a more favorable image of the elderly.

LETTER FROM BIRMINGHAM CITY JAIL

by the Reverend Martin Luther King, Jr.

King's attack on white moderates who counseled patience is a classic.

My dear fellow clergymen, while confined here in the Birmingham City Jail, I came across your recent statement calling our present activities "unwise and untimely." Seldom, if ever, do I pause to answer criticism of my work and ideas. If I sought to answer all of the criticisms that cross my desk, my secretaries would be engaged in little else in the course of the day and I would have no time for constructive work. But since I feel that you are men of genuine good will and your criticisms are sincerely set forth, I would like to answer your statement in what I hope will be patient and reasonable terms. . . .

You deplore the demonstrations that are presently taking place in Birmingham. But I am sorry that your statement did not express a similar concern for the conditions that brought the demonstrations into being. I am sure that each of you would want to go beyond the superficial social analyst who looks merely at effects, and does not grapple with underlying causes. I would not hesitate to say that it is unfortunate that so-called demonstrations are taking place in Birmingham at this time, but I would say in more emphatic terms that it is even more unfortunate that the white power structure of this city left the Negro community with no other alternative.

King, wrote one white woman, had captured the

"devotion of the masses of Negroes. . . . My wash lady tells me every week about how she hears the angel's wings when he speaks, and God speaks directly through him and . . . he speaks directly to God."

The March on Washington

Martin Luther King was the most widely recognized of the civil rights leaders, many of them ministers in black evangelical churches who in the late fifties had organized themselves into the Southern Christian Leadership Conference. But unknown or lesser-known individuals within and outside SCLC performed acts of equal heroism in lonelier isolation than King. Still, in his promotion of the idea of nonviolent resistance, and in his eloquence, King held a special place in the rights movement. When 250,000 people, about one-third of them white and the rest black, marched on Washington in August 1963 to be counted for civil rights legislation, King addressed them: "I have a dream that one day on the red hills of Georgia the sons of former slaves and the sons of former slaveholders will be able to sit down together at the table of brotherhood. I have a dream that one day even the state of Mississippi, a desert state sweltering with the heat of injustice and oppression, will be transformed into an oasis of freedom and justice."

The President's assassination that November brought an outpouring of grief in black communities. Construing civil rights legislation as a memorial to Kennedy aided its passage; Congress easily approved the first major law in 1964, and others followed in 1965 and 1968.

The New Frontier: Substance or Style?

In his handling of economic problems Kennedy had some success. In the 1960 campaign he had charged the Eisenhower Administration with failing to maintain as high a national growth rate as that of western Europe. Until the third quarter of 1962 Kennedy's policies held the cost of living steady, bringing neither substantial new unemployment

In any nonviolent campaign there are four basic steps: (1) collection of the facts to determine whether injustices are alive; (2) negotiation; (3) self-purification; and (4) direct action. We have gone through all of these steps in Birmingham. There can be no gainsaying of the fact that racial injustice engulfs this community. Birmingham is probably the most thoroughly segregated city in the United States. Its ugly record of police brutality is known in every section of this country. Its unjust treatment of Negroes in the courts is a notorious reality. There have been more unsolved bombings of Negro homes and churches in Birmingham than any city in this nation. These are the hard, brutal, and unbelievable facts. On the basis of these conditions Negro leaders sought to negotiate with the city fathers. But the political leaders consistently refused to engage in good faith negotiation.

Then came the opportunity last September to talk with some of the leaders of the economic community. In these negotiating sessions certain promises were made by the merchants—such as the promise to remove the humiliating racial signs from the stores. On the basis of these promises Reverend [Fred] Shuttlesworth and the leaders of the Alabama Christian Movement for Human Rights agreed to call a moratorium on any type of demonstrations. As the weeks and months unfolded we realized that we were victims of a broken promise. The signs remained. As in so many experiences of the past, we were confronted with blasted hopes, and the dark shadow of a deep disappointment settled upon us. So we had no alternative except that of preparing for direct action, whereby we would present our very bodies as means of laying our case before the conscience of the local and national community. . . .

nor inflation. A severe drop in the stock market began in May 1962. It threatened the somewhat shaky prosperity and persuaded Kennedy to embark upon a venturesome new policy. The patient counsel of Kennedy's chief economic adviser, Walter Heller, had convinced Secretary of the Treasury Douglas Dillon, a Republican in the Democratic administration, of the need for federal action. For the first time during a period of relative prosperity, an administration proposed a budget deficit through reduction in taxation, which was then much more acceptable to business than new spending. The Congress concurred. Under President Lyndon Johnson in 1964 the cut went into effect.

Businessmen had already profited from the Kennedy policies. The President signed tax credits and a generous depreciation allowance in 1962, and reduced corporate income taxes by twenty percent in 1963. But in April 1962 Kennedy so confronted the steel industry that, for many businessmen, his name would join that of the despised Franklin Roosevelt. Late in the afternoon of April 10, Roger Blough of United States Steel told Kennedy that even as they spoke press releases were announcing a steel price rise. The President was furious. He had persuaded the unions to be content with a modest wage hike on the understanding that prices would remain steady. Blough seemed both to deceive and to insult the President of the United States. Kennedy privately quoted his father's denunciation of businessmen as "sons of bitches" and launched an unprecedented government attack on the industry. The Defense Department threatened to switch its contracts over to the small companies that had not yet raised prices; the Justice Department and the Federal Trade Commission spoke of antitrust measures; the Treasury hinted at a tax investigation. It was a massive application of presidential power. Big steel canceled the increase in prices, at least for the moment.

A Darkening Plain:
Kennedy's Foreign Policy

Limited War Kennedy foresaw an end of direct superpower confrontation and the coming of an age of wars of national liberation in the course of which Communists would try to wrest control in the Third World. Kennedy joined his chairman of the Joint Chiefs of Staff, General Maxwell Taylor, in calling for a more mobile and technically skilled armed forces capable of fighting in limited wars. Kennedy's background made him especially receptive to the new brand of warfare: a naval hero, a reader of James Bond stories, the creator of the Green Berets, he combined a fascination for military technology with a feeling for military dash and style. Yet at the same time Kennedy seemed to believe that he could bring about an easing of international confrontation. That belief was not exactly contradictory to an interest in building a more sophisticated and mobile armed forces. The Kennedy people shared with earlier Cold War Democrats a conviction that conservative Republicans had brought primitive anti-Communist emotions to the conflict with the Soviet Union. They saw themselves as substituting for those emotions the cooler and more controlled temper appropriate to a technically advanced military and society.

That concept of what the twentieth century, the United States, and the new administration were all about gained its best expression in the Peace Corps. The idea was to send dedicated and knowledgeable Americans to impoverished regions of the world, there to apply to practical projects their skills in nursing, teaching, agriculture, or engineering. Volunteers were supposed to understand that their work would be difficult, under conditions of physical discomfort unfamiliar to middle-class Americans. The implicit assumption was that in the Third World cool technical expertise, as opposed to crude anti-Communist ideology and to crude military dominance, would be the appropriate American response both to Communism and to poverty.

Richard Reeves, the author of an excellent biography of JFK, quotes him on the Bay of Pigs:

"I just approved a plan that had been recommended by the CIA and by the Joints Chiefs of Staff. I just took their advice. Now in retrospect, I know damn well that they didn't have any intention of giving me the straight word on the thing. They just thought that if we got involved on the thing, that I would have to say go ahead, you can throw all our forces in there, and just move into Cuba: . . . Well, from now on it's John Kennedy that makes the decisions."

The Bay of Pigs In April 1961 President John F. Kennedy, relying on a plan developed by the Central Intelligence Agency under the Eisenhower Administration, gave orders for an assault on Cuba. The invasion force was made up of Cuban refugees. The CIA trained the men, some 1,400 of them, high on a coffee plantation in the Guatemalan mountains. It was a fool's dream. Cubans were overwhelmingly content under Fidel Castro. After overthrowing in 1959 the longtime dictator, Fulgencio Batista, Castro had alleviated suffering caused by decades of right-wing corruption. While Castro was himself a dictator, increasingly Communist in orientation, who imprisoned and executed political enemies, the Cuban people had no interest in joining an insurrection against him. Yet most people in the United States and Kennedy's administration mistakenly believed that any people who had lived under Communism yearned to overthrow the yoke of tyranny.

The CIA chose the landing spot, the *bahia de cochinos*. It was a swampy area separated by eighty miles of jungle from the Escanaba

Mountains, where the "freedom fighters" had been instructed to hide in the event of trouble. (Maps of the area contained the little grasslike symbols for swampland that any trained Boy Scout could have read.) Most of the ammunition and radio equipment was carried in a single ship, which was blown up before it landed. Freighters supplied by the United Fruit Company—famous symbol of Yankee imperialism—had their hulls ripped by coral reefs at the landing area. Castro's troops quickly defeated the landing attempt, and Kennedy displayed enough restraint not to involve the United States military more deeply in an effort to rescue the operation.

One of Kennedy's responses to problems in Latin America was to press for an Alliance for Progress, a $10 billion, decade-long program of economic aid to Latin America. He pushed harder for greater military spending, and in 1961 Congress responded with an increase. Kennedy discounted the argument that building up an arsenal of new weapons would provoke the Soviet Union into its own buildup. Nevertheless, the USSR did respond with a similar increase in its defense expenditures.

The Berlin Crisis of 1961   In June 1961 Kennedy and Khrushchev met in Vienna, where they accomplished little except an exchange of views. As Kennedy judged his rhetoric, Khrushchev seemed intransigently committed to disrupting world order, for he threatened to sign a peace treaty with East Germany without waiting for joint agreement on the part of the Western powers. Declaring the eastern part of Germany to be an independent nation, no longer governed by the Soviet Union as an agent of the postwar arrangement among the victors in World War II, could have been equivalent to saying that the Western Allies no longer had a voice in that region. In that case the German Communists, backed by the USSR, might seal off Western access to West Berlin, still under the protection of Britain, France, and the United States.

The encounter discouraged Kennedy. Upon returning home he increased draft quotas, called up the reserves, and demanded a civil defense program that led to a popular frenzy for bomb shelters. When Khrushchev in August acceded to the construction of the Berlin Wall, sealing off East Berlin from the Western sector and preventing inhabitants of East Germany from going to the West, Kennedy sent 1,500 troops from West Germany down the Autobahn to West Berlin, and Vice President Johnson came to pledge American lives to the defense of the city. But Kennedy was careful to restrict American reaction to gestures not calculated to bring war.

In September 1961 Russia began to detonate nuclear bombs of enormous power; the United States followed in the spring of 1962. The older policy of massive retaliation established chiefly by Dulles now existed perilously alongside a new Kennedy policy of "flexible response," which envisioned a willingness to use conventional weapons in wars against Communist forces. On every continent ambitious third powers threatened to upset the world balance and precipitate the ultimate conflict between the Soviet Union and the United States.

In distant Southeast Asia, the existing regimes in both Laos and

The Family Fallout Shelter.
(Courtesy, AP/Wide World Photos)

South Vietnam were endangered by native Communist forces. In Laos the President, remembering the Bay of Pigs, avoided direct intervention.

The Cuban Missile Crisis   In Cuba, Khrushchev was anxious to provide a semblance of defense for the island. Under pressure from the Soviet military, in the late spring of 1962 the USSR placed intermediate-range missiles in Cuba. United States air surveillance first revealed the sites as their construction neared completion. Kennedy quickly decided that he could not tolerate interference in an area so patently within his country's sphere of influence. Although quite congruent with international law, and no real military threat to the United States, the placing of missiles was a major challenge to the political and diplomatic status quo. Khrushchev's justification was that the missiles would protect a sovereign Cuba against a United States invasion—a possibility Kennedy's Bay of Pigs venture made believable even in the opinion of our allies. But his act brought the world in October 1962 close to nuclear war.

The President's military consultants recommended an immediate air strike, which would inevitably wipe out Soviet advisers along with the missiles. But the military and Attorney General Robert Kennedy, the President's brother, disagreed. He argued that it was not in the American grain to launch an air attack against a small island unable to retaliate. The United States would be faithless to its past if it attacked Cuba much as the Japanese had attacked Pearl Harbor.

The President decided on a less drastic course; he instituted a naval blockade against Russian ships bringing additional missile equipment to Cuba. The United States permitted a harmless tanker to penetrate the quarantine area, but then, as millions waited breathlessly, the first ship carrying technical equipment turned back. During the week Khrushchev and Washington engaged in a series of exchanges, each party careful neither to back fully down nor to push the other too far. By the end of the week Moscow had agreed to remove the missiles, while Washington promised not to invade Cuba. That crisis was over.

Some critics blamed Kennedy for bringing the world to the edge of nuclear war. Khrushchev, they said, had displayed the greater maturity by accepting humiliation. But Kennedy, too, had exercised restraint in the face of a reckless Soviet provocation. Before his countrymen Kennedy appeared a courageous and mature statesman.

Secretary of State Dean Rusk said the Americans were "eyeball to eyeball" and said smugly that the Russians "blinked."

An Easing of Tensions   After the fall of 1962, the antagonism between the Soviet Union and the United States shifted to the Third World. There confrontation would continue but with less immediate risk of incinerating the globe. Direct relations between the two superpowers underwent a kind of thaw. A "hot line" ensured instantaneous communication between the Kremlin and the White House for times of crisis. Kennedy, in a speech at American University in June 1963, looked to a new era of cooperation between the two countries. In that year, too, the Soviet Union rejected a Chinese call to global militance and proposed instead peaceful coexistence. By now it was clear that Communist China and the USSR were not allies but potential enemies. That too calmed Cold War militancy in the United States. For it meant that the West was not facing a dangerously unified Communist bloc, and it demonstrated that Communism was not a single indivisible ideology. Finally, the Test Ban Treaty of 1963 outlawed atmospheric testing of nuclear weapons. Ratification by the necessary two-thirds of the Senate came with the aid of Everett Dirksen, a Republican senator whose support broke the opposition by his party's conservative colleagues. The treaty repudiated the relentless confrontation that right-wingers had been hoping for all through the 1950s.

Dallas   Kennedy gave promise later in 1963 of responding to more domestic needs in the next years of his administration. He was planning a wide-ranging assault on poverty that embraced in part the retraining of the unemployed, the elimination of illiteracy, and the expansion of public works. Then he went to Dallas. Riding unprotected in an open car, Kennedy was an easy target for an assassin's bullet. Lee Harvey Oswald, confused and angry in his politics, was evidently the killer. The presidential plane promptly flew the body home to Washington. Chief Justice Earl Warren directed a comprehensive but hurried report on the killing, which uncovered no evidence of conspiracy. Subsequent efforts to link Oswald with one or more additional marksmen or conspirators remain merely speculative.

The achievement of the Kennedy Administration lay elsewhere than in a relatively meager legislative record. Kennedy's ultimate success with the economy and the fruitful negotiation of the Test Ban Treaty brightened the end of his thousand days. But like some other Presidents he gave something intangible to the country. He gave a style that could invite trivialization but also invited its admirers to fresh hope and purpose, when, for example, he proposed that Americans be the first human beings to land on the moon. By the end of Kennedy's administration many college students were uninterested in a life of mere security and accumulation of material goods; they desired something more idealistic and therefore more rewarding—the Peace Corps, for example. In the years to come, those desires would splinter, seizing here on some radical political vision, looking there to an alternative community, or slipping into drugs, or returning to hitherto forsaken material goals.

Lee Harvey Oswald fits a chilling model of assassins driven by their secret hopes of success: victims of disrupted childhoods; loners having no commitment to an idea or a cause except insofar as it can further aggrandize their own will and their own sense of importance. Conspiracy theories deny exactly that uncertainty and chanciness in life that the Oswald story amply illustrates, the uncertainty that he lacked the patience or discipline to accept.

LBJ

President Kennedy once told an off-the-record press conference that he did not have much hope for solving America's problems. Kennedy's pessimism about what was possible for mankind, a side of his intellectual sophistication not sufficiently appreciated, inevitably narrowed his perspective and his goals. Lyndon Johnson's strength—and his weakness—lay in a faith that America could accomplish anything. Johnson's pride, daring, and technical skill reached their greatest effectiveness in attacking stubborn domestic ills. During his years in office Congress passed more laws than in any earlier era for civil rights, health, educa-

Lyndon Baines Johnson receiving the oath of office following President Kennedy's assassination in Dallas, November 22, 1963. *(Courtesy, AP/Wide World Photos)*

tion, the arts and sciences, the eradication of poverty, and aid for the cities.

Lone Star Rising

Johnson's confidence originated in the New Deal of Franklin Roosevelt. Raised in the hill country of central Texas, Johnson himself had witnessed poverty at first hand. His calculating ambition was evident at Southwest Texas State Teachers College, where he dominated the student body. Afterward he taught briefly in a rural school and learned of the needs of poor Mexican Americans. He campaigned successfully for a congressional seat in 1937. With the coming of the Eisenhower era Johnson, now in the Senate, moved to the political center; in 1953, by virtue of his impressive legislative skill and bland ideology he won the post of Senate majority leader. Everything he did was the work of a masterful politician. In 1960 he became a presidential candidate. After Johnson's candidacy failed, Kennedy thought it desirable to have the popular southerner as a running mate.

The Great Society

While the Kennedy and Johnson administrations carried New Deal liberalism into the 1960s, the general prosperity of the times meant that their proposals could be far more ambitious than FDR's. Whereas Roosevelt had committed the government to do what it could to relieve poverty, Lyndon Johnson promised to abolish it.

People were unemployed. So the government, through proper economic policies, would stimulate the economy and create new jobs. Jobs called for skills the unemployed lacked. So the government would train them. Children from disadvantaged families did poorly in school. So the government, with programs like Upward Bound and Higher Horizons, would provide them with additional cultural opportunities. Hot lunch programs would guarantee that they received the proper nutrition.

The Great Society rested upon a simple idea. The United States, the richest nation in the world, could afford to abolish poverty, end discrimination, and guarantee everyone a decent life. The Great Depression, and the limits it had imposed on what the government could do, was over. So what was once only a dream could become reality. So argued LBJ and many of the American people agreed.

In the days following the assassination of Kennedy, Johnson behaved with skill and tact. He persuaded all of Kennedy's advisers to stay on, at least for the moment. Johnson's aggressive political mastery carried social programs much farther than Kennedy would most likely have taken them. He gathered into his policy much of what had lately existed for a decade, and he completed and presided over a powerful liberal coalition. Such coalitions as Johnson's are familiar in American history, accomplishing in a few years of intense activity what reformers had wanted for many years.

The Election of 1964   To Republican Party leaders the nomination of Barry Goldwater for President in 1964 was a calculated risk. A year so bleak for the Republicans could put to the test a proposition, long held by the political right wing, that there was a large potential electorate made up of frustrated voters who would awaken to a belligerently conservative candidate.

During the course of the campaign Goldwater revealed a knack for making a handicap of honesty. In Appalachia he insisted on attacking the poverty program; in Knoxville, Tennessee, he declared in favor of selling part of the Tennessee Valley Authority; in St. Petersburg, Florida, a city filled with retired people, he criticized social security; in North Dakota he told farmers that a decline in price supports would be good for them. Before an audience composed chiefly of first- and second-generation immigrants, vice-presidential candidate William Miller on Labor Day criticized liberal immigration policies.

All the pollsters agreed that November 4 would be a cold day for Goldwater. He carried only his home state of Arizona, in addition to Mississippi (where he won 87 percent of the vote), Louisiana, Alabama, South Carolina, and Georgia. The Democrats maintained their margin of two to one in the Senate and picked up thirty-eight seats in the House. Such were the immediate results of the Republican candidate's strategy of working to bring the still largely Democratic South solidly into the Republican Party. Yet the candidacy may have marshaled a set of ideas that would find a more effective political voice in later years. The race issue had not yet ripened to cause a backlash against the Democrats among whites in the North.

John F. Kennedy and Lyndon Baines Johnson. *(Courtesy, Wide World)*

Goldwater accepted the nomination in the spirit that would dominate his campaign:

"Anyone who joins us in all sincerity we welcome. Those who do not care for our cause, we don't expect to enter our ranks. . . . Extremism in the defense of liberty is no vice! . . . Moderation in the pursuit of justice is no virtue!"

The Great Society was never achieved, but the effort accomplished a great deal. Jobs were created; discrimination, if not ended, was combated; millions benefited from the new programs. Yet within a few years, it was commonplace to assert that the Great Society had been nearly a total failure. What had happened? The question is complex, but elements of the answer seem clear.

One is that the "war on poverty" raised expectations that could not be realized. Jobs were not being created quickly enough. Programs took a long time to implement and then often did not work. Job training programs, for example, admitted only a limited number, had difficulty keeping trainees in the program, and failed to place in permanent jobs a significant percentage of the graduates. Impatience sometimes turned to frustration and then to bitterness and hostility. Riots broke out in many cities. Meanwhile, many other groups in the society took the riots as evidence that it was a waste of time to try to help these people. What was needed, they insisted, was a program to strengthen the police. "Law and Order" became a powerful slogan for use by opponents of the Great Society.

Taxes

The first landmark of the Great Society was the tax reduction bill of 1964, which had been in the works for some time. Reducing income tax rates a total of $11 billion gave individuals and corporations an increase in spending power. The theory was that the resulting growth in investment and consumer demand would spur production, slacken unemployment, and ultimately swell federal revenues since the government would have a wealthier economy to tax. Unemployment fell in 1965 to the lowest level in eight years, and federal revenues actually rose, revenues that the Democratic administration put in part into measures for the relief of poverty. On the other hand, the tax cut, along with other incentives to activate business and the pressures of massive spending for the war in Indochina that the United States was waging, contributed to the inflationary economy of the late 1960s and the 1970s.

The Economic Opportunity Act

President Johnson had seen much of poverty during his youth; its alleviation became a major goal. Kennedy's poverty programs had included the retraining and rehabilitation of the unemployed, area redevelopment, youth employment, the eradication of illiteracy, and accelerated public works in poverty regions. Early in 1964, months before the election, Johnson brought together these programs and others, declaring a "war on poverty," an attractive theme for a presidential campaign. After hearing from the Council of Economic Advisers that twenty percent of all American families were poor by standard measures, Congress passed the Economic Opportunity Act of 1964, appropriating $800 million for the first year. Programs under the Office of Economic Opportunity (OEO) differed from past efforts in design as well as in size. Local community action agencies, the central innovation of the program, received $300 million. In each community, advisory boards, comprised of local business and political interests and representatives of the poor themselves, administered the funds. Another major emphasis of OEO programs was on the young. The Job Corps, an urban version of the New Deal's Civilian Conservation Corps, established for young slum-dwellers and rural poor alike facilities offering remedial education and vocational training. The Neighborhood Youth Corps provided summer jobs paying $50 a week for high school students, with an eye toward pacifying edgy ghetto youth. A work-study program assisted many college students. Volunteers in Service to America (VISTA), a domestic equivalent of Kennedy's Peace Corps, sent teams of idealistic people into communities across the country to assist in government programs.

Following the 1964 election came an ingenious manipulation of Congress by the President, who continued to capitalize on the memory of Kennedy as well as on his own legislative skills. Johnson showered Congress with Great Society proposals.

Education and Medicare

Aid to public education was next on Johnson's list. The President effectively steered the legislation through Congress, which passed $1 billion in aid for elementary and secondary schools, concentrating on districts with pu-

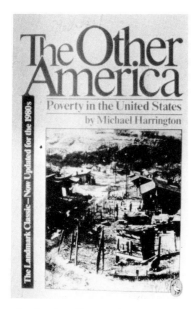

This book influenced Presidents Kennedy and Johnson.

pils from low-income families. Johnson flew to the small Texas school-house where he had once taught and there signed the bill.

Another of Johnson's major legislative goals was Medicare, health care for the elderly funded through social security. The basic plan provided funds for hospitalization and doctors' fees for people over sixty-five; a supplemental voluntary plan permitted individuals to enroll for coverage of additional doctors' bills and laboratory fees. Within two years, seventeen million Americans had taken advantage of this oppor-tunity. Legislation in 1965 and 1966 set up the Medicaid program, which extended federal medical care to other large categories of needy people—dependent children, the blind and disabled, and many low-income families. Although Medicare and Medicaid laws set upward limits of coverage and required patients to assume responsibility for a deductible amount, they constituted a major victory for the adminis-tration.

Environmental Legislation Not satisfied with the Water Quality Act of 1965, which provided demonstration grants for sewage control, Johnson demanded $6 billion for a six-year national program with the federal government ultimately imposing water purifying standards. The Clean Water Restoration Act of 1966 authorized $3.5 billion to be spent over five years. (Presidents Johnson and Nixon would use less than one-third of these funds.) Under Johnson legislation set standards for exhaust emission on combustion engines, but left the enforcement date to government discretion. The deadline for nearly fume-free combustion engines was later advanced to the twenty-first century. Johnson's environmental bills set important precedents that later administrations, after considerable resistance from various industries, were to extend somewhat in scope and in rigor of enforcement.

Civil Rights and Civil Liberties

The civil rights movement was by 1964 so large among black people, so fortified by white volunteers, and so consistent in its moral demands that even Democratic politicians fearful of driving southern whites from the party had to acknowledge the movement in a major way. In June 1964 the Senate voted 71 to 29 to end a southern filibuster; it was the first time Congress had invoked cloture during a civil rights debate. Then a new civil rights law passed by an even wider margin. Only five Republicans from outside the South, including Barry Goldwater, and even fewer non-southern Democrats, opposed the bill.

The Civil Rights Acts of 1964 and 1965 The new law covered a wide range of subjects, gen-erally promising more than it could deliver. The most controversial portion, Title II, outlawed dis-crimination in hotels, motels, restaurants, theaters, and all other public accommodations engaged in interstate commerce; a provision exempting "private clubs" without defining "private" made evasion of the law fairly simple. The law also created an Equal Employment Opportunity Commission with broad powers to investigate and review complaints but with little power to enforce compliance. Despite its weaknesses, the Civil Rights Act of 1964 represented a signal victory for the activists and friends of the civil rights movement. The provisions covering public accommodations were generally obeyed.

The Voting Rights Act of 1965 empowered the attorney general to appoint federal examiners to supervise voter registration in states and counties that had used such devices as literacy tests to exclude potential voters. By the end of 1965, examiners had been appointed in thirty-five counties, and within five months black registration in deep South states increased forty percent. The Voting Rights Act worked in tandem with the Twenty-fourth Amendment, ratified in 1964, which eliminated poll taxes in federal elections. Together they provided a base of voters in some areas for the election of the first black officials since Reconstruction.

Black Power and Ghetto Riots

Johnson made his most controversial civil rights request in January 1966. He wanted laws prohibiting discrimination in the sale or rental of all housing and punishing interference with the rights of Americans in education, employment, jury service, and travel. Congress responded with legislation, but resistance was hardening among white home owners and northern working-class whites. When Martin Luther King led a group of demonstrators into an ethnic suburb of Chicago, a mob met them filled with a rage King claimed never to have encountered before, even in Mississippi or Alabama.

At the same time a militant black power movement, expressing at moments a hostility to whites that sounded similar to white racism, was coming to replace in the public consciousness the civil rights movement of the early 1960s. Its hero was the martyred Malcolm X, killed by assassins in 1965. Malcolm had written against the ideas of King: "There is no such thing as a nonviolent revolution. The only kind of revolution that is nonviolent is the Negro revolution. The only revolution in which the goal is loving your enemy is the Negro revolution. It's the only revolution in which the goal is a desegregated lunch counter, a desegregated theatre, a desegregated park, and a desegregated public toilet; you can sit down next to white folks—on the toilet. That's no revolution." Ghetto rebellions, most notably those in Los Angeles in 1965 and in Detroit two years later, frightened even voters who lived far from black neighborhoods. Later in his life Malcolm X himself renounced racial hatred.

One of the most radical of the civil rights organizations of the 1960s had begun as the Student Nonviolent Coordinating Committee (SNCC). In the early and middle 1960s, black activists in SNCC, such as Robert Parris Moses, worked under dangerous conditions in Mississippi to encourage blacks to register to vote. Local authorities attempted to frighten blacks away from voting, and dozens lost their lives amidst the most murderous repression in the country. In the summer of 1964, Freedom Summer as it was called, almost a thousand northern

A legendary figure of the movement, Robert Parris Moses, returned to a SNCC office in Greenwood, Mississippi, to find it empty and ransacked by Klansmen. Exhausted from his day's work, Moses made up a bed in the corner and went to sleep. The volunteer who had escaped the white mob a few hours before by climbing to the roof of a nearby building has remarked of this reticent leader:

"I just didn't understand what kind of guy this Bob Moses is, that could walk into a place where a lynch mob had just left and make up a bed and prepare to go to sleep, as if the situation was normal. So I guess I was learning."

volunteers of college age, most of them white, went to the state at the invitation of SNCC to aid in voter registration. More specifically, that campaign was enrolling black Mississippians in the Mississippi Freedom Democratic Party (MFDP) as an alternative to the state's regular Democratic Party, which was under white control. In the most widely publicized killing of the summer a black activist, James Chaney, along with the northern white volunteers Michael Schwerner and Andrew Goodman was killed by a local white death squad.

Of the Freedom Summer project of 1964, which brought to Mississippi northern Kennedy-generation students to help register blacks, Fannie Lou Hamer wrote: "The big thing about the summer of '64 was that people learned white folks were human."

The Democratic Convention refused to seat the Mississippi Freedom Democratic Party delegation, selecting instead the regular white Mississippi delegates and offering the insurrectionist slate an unacceptable compromise. White and black civil rights volunteers shared a sense of betrayal that had a part in radicalizing both. More particularly, it contributed to the black power movement that became articulate in 1966, especially in the voice of Stokely Carmichael.

The Immigration and Nationality Act of 1965

The growing national concern with race, ethnicity, and civil rights, as well as changing immigration patterns and economic concerns in the United States, also led to extensive reforms in existing immigration laws. Ever since 1924, American immigration laws had established annual quotas by country for new immigrants. But the quotas were biased. Countries in northern and western Europe had relatively large quotas while countries in southern and eastern Europe and Africa had small quotas. Asian immigrants were excluded altogether. The McCarran Act of 1952 eliminated the Asian exclusion but still retained the other quotas. Then in 1965, the Immigration and Nationality Act reversed the forty-year-old policy of imposing ethnic quotas based on national origins.

Under this act the United States permitted a total of 170,000 people from the Eastern Hemisphere to immigrate each year, no more than twenty thousand people to come from any one country. Preferences went to refugees, people with family members already in the United States, and professional and skilled workers. The act, for the first time in United States history, limited immigration from the Western Hemisphere to 120,000 people per year, primarily to please the large labor unions that were concerned about immigration from Mexico. Western Hemisphere immigrants were allowed to enter without categorical preference or limits from any given country. A 1976 amendment to the act extended to immigrants from the Western Hemisphere the preference system and a limit of twenty thousand people per country. Perceiving Cubans as victims of massive political oppression, lawmakers exempted Cuban refugees from the limits. The measures showed no similar compassion for people living in anti-Communist Western Hemisphere regimes employing torture and death squads. Of course, large-scale immigration from Mexico continued, much of it by

Another prominent member of SNCC was Fannie Lou Hamer, who with Robert Parris Moses helped to mobilize a challenge to the all-white Mississippi delegation to the 1964 Democratic National Convention. Speaking for her largely black alternate slate of delegates, the MFDP, she told the television camera about her first attempt to register:

"[The policeman] said, 'You bitch, we gon' make you wish you was dead.' I heard the highway patrolman tell the black man [a prisoner], 'If you don't beat her, you *know* what we'll do to you.' The first Negro began to beat, and I was beat until he was exhausted. . . . All this is on account we want to register, to become first-class citizens, and if the Freedom Democratic Party is not seated now, I question America."

The American Birth Rate, 1960–1990

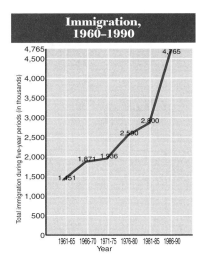

Immigration, 1960–1990

evasion of the Immigration and Naturalization Service. By the mid-1990s there was a strong movement, much of it bipartisan, once again to curtail immigration.

Supreme Court Chief Justice Earl Warren. *(Courtesy, Library of Congress)*

The Warren Court: Part II   The black revolution of the 1960s inevitably directed judicial attention toward the system of law enforcement, and some of the most controversial decisions of the Warren Court concerned criminal procedure and the rights of the accused. In *Gideon v. Wainwright* (1963) the Court guaranteed the right to legal counsel in all felony cases. At a trial in which insolvency forced him to carry on his own defense, Clarence Earl Gideon, a white southerner with a long criminal record, had been convicted of breaking and entering a Florida poolroom. His handwritten appeal to the Supreme Court combined a moving personal history with imperfect legal terminology. The guarantee in *Gideon* of courtroom counsel regardless of capacity to pay expanded to the police station three years later in *Miranda v. Arizona,* wherein the Court affirmed a prisoner's right to see an attorney before answering questions, besides requiring the police to inform the prisoner of a range of legal rights.

Other decisions protected rights of speech and privacy. With one notable exception the Court consistently refused to uphold obscenity convictions. More shocking to conventional sensibilities than permissiveness toward pornography was a series of decisions that in 1962 and 1963 outlawed compulsory Bible reading and similar religious activities in public schools. The Court rejected such practices not only for abridging the separation of church and state, but also for imposing, if only symbolically, a particular morality on the individual student.

One of the Warren Court's most notable dicta was the principle "one man, one vote." In a series of legislative apportionment cases beginning with *Baker v. Carr* (1962), the Court required that both

Clarence Earl Gideon used this handwritten letter (right) to bring his appeal to the attention of the Supreme Court. In the *Gideon* case the court ruled that even poor defendants have the right to legal counsel. *(Courtesy, National Association for the Advancement of Colored People)*

> I was sentenced to the State Penitentiary by The Circuit Court of Bay County, State of Florida. The present proceeding was commenced on a petition for a Writ of Habeus Corpus to The Supreme Court of The State of Florida to vacate the sentence, on the grounds that I was made to stand Trial without the aid of counsel, and, at all times of my incarceration. The said Court refused To appoint counsel and therefore deprived me of Due process of law, and violate my rights in The Bill of Rights and the constitution of the United States.
>
> Clarence Earl Gideon
> 5th day of Jan 1962 Petitioner
> Laurence C Duzza
> Notary Public

Gideon's Letter to the Supreme Court
John F. Davis, Clerk, Supreme Court of the United States

houses of the legislature in each state reflect the actual distribution of population in that state. This ruling ended some of the more extreme cases in which rural areas enjoyed a power disproportionate to their population.

The final two years of Johnson's administration were a time of political stalemate. Appropriations for the war on poverty remained fairly constant, but no new programs were initiated. Congress slashed the administration's foreign aid requests. To decrease the deficits caused by Vietnam war spending, the President in 1967 asked for a ten percent tax surcharge, claiming that the surcharge was necessary if the federal government was to provide both "guns and butter," foreign and domestic spending. Congress grudgingly passed the measure in 1968, but also forced budget reductions that began to cut into the butter. Symbolic of the new congressional mood was the defeat of an appropriation for a ghetto rat-control program; the debate centered not on the amount of money, a relatively small $100 million, but on the extent of the federal government's legitimate interest in social welfare. In 1968 Congress enacted the Omnibus Crime Bill, allocating funds to upgrade local police forces, broadening the wiretapping authority of law enforcement agencies, and attempting to restrict some of the Supreme Court's guarantees of the rights of the accused.

The most important political event in the mid-1960s took place not at home but in Vietnam. For Americans that war started in earnest in 1965. The movement to democratize American society that, beginning before Montgomery, had reached its fullest energy in the Great Society, now lost its momentum.

Suggested Readings

Recent books on the era include Maurice Isserman, *If I Had a Hammer. . . . The Death of the Old Left and the Birth of the New Left* (1987), Robert Divine, *The Johnson Years,* II (1987), Charles Eagles, ed., *The Civil Rights Movement in America* (1986), Richard Powers, *Secrecy and Power: The Life of J. Edgar Hoover* (1983), Paul K. Conkin, *Big Daddy of the Pedernales: Lyndon B. Johnson* (1986), Gerald T. Rice, *The Bold Experiment: JFK's Peace Corps* (1985), C. Eric Lincoln and Lawrence H. Mamiya, *The Black Church in the African American Experience* (1990), and, on civil rights, *Freedom Bound* (1990) by Robert Weisbrot, David Burner, *Making Peace with the 60s* (1996).

Recent studies of Eisenhower emphasize his caution in domestic programs, his restraint in the use of presidential powers, and the absence in his foreign policy of dangerously large involvements. See, for example, the two-volume biography by Stephen Ambrose. On John Kennedy see the two-volume biography by Herbert Parmet, *Jack: The Struggles of John Fitzgerald Kennedy* (1980) and *JFK: The Presidency of John Fitzgerald Kennedy* (1983) and David Burner and Thomas R. West, *The Torch Is Passed: The Kennedy Brothers and American Liberalism* (1984). Arthur Schlesinger, Jr., describes John and Robert Kennedy as expressing the best ideas and possibilities of their times: *A Thousand Days* (1965) and *Robert F. Kennedy and His*

Times (1978). Carl Brauer holds that Kennedy supported the civil rights activists strongly and effectively and within the limits imposed by politics and the legal system: *John F. Kennedy and the Second Reconstruction* (1977). Another controversial topic of the Kennedy presidency is covered by Robert A. Divine, ed., *The Cuban Missile Crisis* (1971), and a well-known effort to analyze the crisis is Graham Allison, *Essence of Decision* (1971). A sharply critical book on Kennedy is Garry Wills, *The Kennedy Imprisonment* (1981). On Lyndon Johnson see Doris Kearns, *Lyndon Johnson and the American Dream* (1976), Eric Goldman, *The Tragedy of Lyndon Johnson* (1969), and Merle Miller, *Lyndon: An Oral Biography* (1980). Robert Caro critically details Johnson's early life in his massive *The Path to Power* (1982) and *Means of Ascent* (1989). *Lone Star Rising* (1991), the first volume of Robert Dallek's life of Johnson which can be taken as a refutation of Caro, covers the Texan through 1960.

Richard Kluger's *Simple Justice* (1976) studies the great *Brown v. Board of Education* case and the struggle to implement the Supreme Court's order to desegregate public schools. Taylor Branch has written a magisterial biography of Martin Luther King entitled *Parting the Waters* (1988). William G. McLoughlin studies the moralism of the sixties in *Revivals, Awakenings, and Reform* (1978).

JFK—A Question of Character?

Thomas Reeves

Good character is an essential framework for the complex mixture of qualities that make an outstanding President and a model leader for a democratic people. Character is a question of values, inclinations, and judgment, all of which are brought to bear in the day-to-day work of leadership.

The real Kennedy—as opposed to the celebrated hero espoused by the Kennedy family, the media, and the Camelot School—lacked greatness in large part because he lacked the qualities inherent in good character. He failed to be a true moral leader of the American people because he lacked the conviction and commitment that create such exemplars of character for all to emulate. . . .

Jack was still incapable of monogamy at the time of his assassination. And it is just as likely that news of the dark side of the president's personal and official activities might have ruined Kennedy's second term and brought the nation another kind of grief and mourning than that which tragically did ensue.

America needs great presidents, which means that this country must find and elect people of high moral character, as well as intelligence and experience. Character and conduct are clearly linked, and the personal weaknesses of a chief executive can often turn out to be public liabilities. It is wise to encourage the careful scrutiny of presidential aspirants that has become the practice in recent years. It is neither priggish nor unrealistic to seek to determine, to the best of our ability, which presidential aspirants live by values that we hope they will uphold in public, values such as honesty, responsibility, fairness, loyalty, and respect for others. Indeed, the pursuit seems simply sensible.

At the same time, the American people must resist the temptation to be won over by a handsome face, expensive campaign efforts, and thrilling rhetoric. In the early 1960s, we became involved in a sort of mindless worship of celebrity; it was a love affair largely with images. . . .

Kennedy died a hero. This has less to do with the facts about Jack than with the image erected during and after his life by romantic, misguided, and sometimes cynical partisans. . . .

A major lesson that emerges from a careful look at Jack Kennedy's life concerns the moral responsibility of our presidents. From the nation's beginnings, in the exemplary George Washington, who thought about such things, there has been an implicit contract between the chief executive and the American people, an understanding that the nation's highest public official should exhibit such virtues as dignity, moderation, disinterestedness, self-mastery, resoluteness, strength of will, and personal integrity. Washington indeed was regarded as an "exemplification of moral values," a president widely perceived to be great because he was good. The public later attributed the same virtues to Abraham Lincoln. . . .

During the Thousand Days, Kennedy arrogantly and irresponsibly violated his covenant with the people. While saying and doing the appropriate things in the public light, he acted covertly in ways that seriously demeaned himself and his office. He got away with it at the time, and the cover-up that followed kept the truth hidden for decades. That this could happen again makes it imperative that we search for presidential candidates who can, by example, elevate and inspire the American people, restoring confidence in their institutions and in themselves. Kennedy's political skills are desirable, to be sure: the charisma, the inspiring oratory, the wit, the intelligence, the courage. But all of these qualities must be connected to an effort to live and lead by those values, known and declared for centuries, that link good character with effective leadership. The United States—and now the world—cannot settle for less.

Professor Thomas Reeves is right that Presidents set a public tone. The President is a symbol of the time, an exemplar of its virtues or a living statement of its vices. And in this capacity a presidency does not merely reflect on the faults or strengths of the era but molds the character of the citizenry. But that means that it is the public character of an administration and its Chief Executive, the image that the President projects out of public acts, that should be at issue.

The image that Kennedy shaped was one of the best that any recent President has had to offer. It recommended by example resoluteness tempered and strengthened by a refusal to act on emotion. It had, moreover, the essential, wholly legitimate value of being an image that the population could respond to. Consider the contrast between Kennedy's tenure and that of President Carter, a man of exemplary character who unlike other Presidents insisted that human rights are human rights, even when our allies violate them. If any President deserved to have the attention and understanding of the country, it was Carter. And this man of conscience got nowhere in the White House as an instructor of the American people.

Foreign policy gave the image of the Kennedy presidency much of its shape. Against the political right, with its frenzied vocabulary, its broodings about the metaphysical evil of Communism, its conviction that the Communist world was monolithic and indivisible, Kennedy was able to present a far more convincing image of strength as a compound of force and restraint. Restraint after the failure at the Bay of Pigs, restraint and measured reaction to the building of the Berlin Wall, restraint when during the blockade of Cuba a harmless Soviet freighter went through the American lines: all this defined Kennedy's foreign policy as much as did its more confrontational elements. The Peace Corps was wholly coherent with the more general temperament of Kennedy's foreign policy. It sent into impoverished regions of the world soldiers of peace armed with advanced academic or technical intelligence and a determination to carry out difficult assignments. The Test Ban Treaty was a fitting conclusion to an administration that calculated the means to a carefully monitored peace, while phobic conservatives fumed.

Meanwhile there was the civil rights movement, which the administration gave little indication of understanding. The rights movement had its own compound of forcefulness and, in the discipline of nonviolence, self-restraint. It practiced an impassioned liberation, while the administration was more at home with the cooler phenomena of the age: futuristic technology, advanced education, expert knowledge. The one spoke in the prophetic voice of Martin Luther King, Jr., the other in the flat factual radio messages of an astronaut in space. But together the Kennedy image and the rights revolution conquered the hearts and conscience of a young generation.

Whoever the private Kennedy may have been—cheating husband, father of a tight-knit family, or both, passive creature of events or their initiator—it was from the visible and composite figure in the White House that the nation as a whole could receive its moral lessons. That figure, defining itself in policies, exemplified the virtue of a purposeful self-control. For our own time, after a period of self-indulgence and facile patriotism urged on by Republican administrations and a decadence for which neither freemarket conservatives nor lifestyle liberals have any convincing solution, the virtues of the Kennedy era would be a valuable rediscovery.

Ohio National Guardsmen advance on demonstrating students, Kent State University, Kent, Ohio.
(Courtesy, AP/Wide World Photos)

28
American Society and the Vietnam War

THE KENT STATE MASSACRE

Kent State University in northeastern Ohio could have stood as a symbol of the growth of higher education in the 1960s. Although it was common for public universities to expand in this era, few had mushroomed like Kent State. During the 1960s, enrollment tripled to over twenty thousand students. Rapidly constructed new buildings could not keep pace with new enrollment. Students began to complain of alienation from this large campus. The annual mudfight on the first warm spring night was still a tradition; the football team was important. But even Kent State, a middle-American school that had been silent when Harvard and Columbia were erupting in the spring of 1968, had become politicized at the end of the decade.

Serious radical activity began at Kent State in November 1968 when the Black United Students and Students for a Democratic Society sat in to protest the presence on campus of recruiters from the Oakland, California, police. In April 1969, SDS members attacked the administration building demanding the abolition of the Reserve Officers Training Corps (ROTC). A week later, their suspension hearing turned into a fistfight between fraternity men and members of SDS that brought the Ohio Highway Patrol onto the campus to arrest fifty-eight students. Several SDS leaders went to jail for six months and the organization was banned from the campus.

On the evening of April 30, 1970, President Richard M. Nixon

HISTORICAL EVENTS

1945
Ho Chi Minh declares Vietnam's independence

1954
Dien Bien Phu falls to Vietnamese Communists • Geneva accords signed • SEATO formed

1962
The Port Huron Statement by Students for a Democratic Society (SDS)

1963
Buddhists begin protests against Saigon regime • Premier Diem assassinated

1964
Gulf of Tonkin Resolution • Free Speech Movement at Berkeley

1965
"Rolling Thunder" • first major anti-war demonstration (April)

1967
Over 500,000 U.S. troops in Vietnam • 200,000 rally against the war • Six-Day War in the Middle East

continued

went on national television to announce that as part of our withdrawal from the war in Vietnam we had invaded neighboring Cambodia. "All the kids were around TV sets in the dorm," the Kent State student government president at the time recalls. "They had horrified stares on their faces."

Fearing trouble, local police slapped a curfew on the town and called in the National Guard. Ohio Governor James Rhodes, who had expended more for National Guard service in the past two years than the total of the other forty-nine governors, readily complied. By the time the Guardsmen arrived, already exhausted from six days service at a truckers' strike, radical students had actually given them an occasion to be there: on the night of May 2, a group of students burned the rickety old wooden ROTC building.

The campus mood was surly. Communication between local officials, the Guard, and the university was awkward at best. The Guardsmen were ill-equipped for their duty, which was essentially crowd control. Their weapons were absurdly disproportionate to the job. Well-trained, well-directed Guard units in other states were supplied with non-lethal pellets and were forbidden to carry loaded weapons until directly ordered to do so by their commanders. In Ohio, the Guard troops kept their guns in "locked, loaded, and ready" position. Any tired, nervous young guard could—literally—trigger catastrophe. The weapon was the M-1, with bullets that pass through an eighteen-inch tree trunk at close range or travel for two miles. The odds on killing bystanders in an altercation were high.

On Monday, May 4, Kent State entered the history books. Students had conflicting information about what might happen: all assemblies on campus were forbidden, they heard. Yet classes were still scheduled and so was a noontime rally. Sometime after 11:00 a.m. someone began tolling a bell and about 1,500 students started gathering for the possible rally. Soon the Guard tried to disperse the crowd, which responded first with obscene chants and then, here and there, with flying stones. Wind and noise drowned out commands. A reporter standing with some Guardsmen heard an officer call: "Fix bayonets, gas masks, load [rifles]." With the students about one hundred yards away from this small contingent of troops, the gas canisters began to pop. No weapons were left except bayonets and the awesome M-1s. Some of the troops dropped to a kneeling position and pointed their rifles at the crowd. Some students ran up the hill behind them, coming closer than before to throw their rocks—perhaps now to somewhat more effect. At the top of the hill the Guardsmen stopped, turned, and in the next thirteen seconds fired sixty-one shots, killing four students and wounding nine.

A veteran of the war in Vietnam seeing the helicopter above

and the bloodshed imagined himself back in Vietnam. "I didn't realize the guys were shooting at the kids," one Guardsman has reported, "until I saw this kid's chest break into blood." By 5:00 p.m. the campus was empty. Dangling from a dormitory window near Blanket Hill were several bedsheets tied together to form the backdrop for a large sign with the word WHY? Why indeed? An observer can point to the inappropriateness of using the National Guard; to Nixon's speech on Cambodia (the following day he referred to student dissidents as "bums"); to the hysteria of local officials who called in the Guard; to the governor's overuse of them; to the sour mood of 1970 as the nation unhappily faced the prospect of final defeat in Indochina.

A few days later at Jackson State University in Mississippi, nervous local police riddled the facade of a dormitory with bullets that killed two students. As though in confirmation of what black commentators had been saying about the relative indifference of the white majority to even the grossest incidents involving blacks, an event very similar to that at Kent State but at a black school received only light press coverage.

Vietnam to 1960

The French in Vietnam
The war that in the mid-sixties replaced civil rights as the most volatile issue of the time was a result of an earlier imperial venture. Since the middle of the nineteenth century, Southeast Asia's fertile rice fields, mineral deposits, and strategic position have attracted rival empires and ideologies. In Indochina, which includes Vietnam, Laos, and Cambodia, France established itself. In the southern third of Vietnam, the French assumed direct control and began an intensive program of economic development in mines and plantations largely run by Vietnamese labor. Elsewhere, French authorities enlisted the Vietnamese elite. These two groups set up a Grand Council that taxed the Vietnamese, protected monopolies, and turned over to a handful of Frenchmen and Vietnamese land farmed by the peasants.

Almost from the beginning some Vietnamese opposed this economic exploitation and what they feared to be an attempt to replace old Vietnamese ways with French culture. When Paris vetoed moderate reforms during the early 1920s, nationalists adopted more militant tactics. In 1930 Ho Chi Minh, who had earlier studied Marxism in France, organized the Vietnamese Communist Party. Ho favored radical reforms and, ultimately, the expulsion of the French from Vietnam. But he was patient. After other nationalist groups led uprisings in the 1930s and were brutally and successfully suppressed by the French, Ho and his fledgling Communist movement moved into the vacuum of nationalist movements. During the Japanese occupation of Indochina from 1940 to 1945, Ho built upon these foundations to create the Vietminh, a united front of anticolonialists. And when Japan's power

Ho Chi Minh, Communist leader of Vietnam from 1945 through the Vietnam War, wrote that the Communists "swam like fishes in the peasant sea." *(Courtesy, AP/Wide World Photos)*

Vo Nguyen Giap (on the left), the military strategist of the Vietminh, standing with Ho Chi Minh, the leading Vietnamese political tactician. The photo was taken in September 1945 shortly after Ho read the Vietnamese Declaration of Independence and established the Democratic Republic of Vietnam. *(Courtesy, AP/Wide World Photos)*

disintegrated during early 1945, his Vietminh guerrilla forces seized northern border provinces and a popular revolution swept the colony. The Vietminh, the only tightly organized party uncorrupted by collaboration either with the French or with the Japanese, formed a government on September 2, 1945, when Ho Chi Minh declared Vietnam's independence.

President Franklin Roosevelt tended to favor an end to colonial rule. But the new French Republic under General Charles de Gaulle demanded a return of all French possessions. Late in 1945, British and French occupation troops forcibly installed in Saigon a nominally independent Vietnamese government effectively under French control. The Vietminh immediately launched a guerrilla counteroffensive against what rapidly became a French war of reconquest.

From 1947 to 1950 the French exerted great military pressure throughout Indochina, but still could not break Vietminh dominance in the countryside. President Harry Truman inherited Roosevelt's distaste for France's neocolonialist adventure. Initially, the Americans had no role in Indochinese affairs. But when late in 1949 the Communist Mao Zedong defeated Chiang Kai-shek and established the People's Republic of China, and in June 1950 Communist North Korea invaded South Korea, the United States became determined to block Communist victory in Indochina. If Indochina were lost to the Communists, so President Truman's National Security Council argued, neighboring Thailand would be next. This would upset the balance of power in Southeast Asia, and Communism might then reach out for either India or the rich islands of Indonesia. In 1950 Truman extended massive military aid to the French.

Communist control of the movement for Vietnamese independence left the United States in a curious dilemma. The best way to defeat the Vietminh would be to replace the French in Vietnam and the other Indochinese nations of Cambodia and Laos with non-Communist, nationalist regimes, but this contradicted another American motive in supporting France in Indochina. Washington's diplomatic needs in Europe required French support, and the French did not want to surrender to anyone, Communist or nationalist. So we supported the French.

Dien Bien Phu — Many non-Communist Vietnamese nationalists turned to the Communists as the strongest resistance force. Other Vietnamese fought on the side of France. The French had superior firepower and were well trained in the mode of conventional European combat, but Ho's native forces knew the land and fought an effective guerrilla war of attrition. General Vo Nguyen Giap moved the bulk of his Vietminh toward Laos in an attempt to win territory and to lure away from their coastal strongholds the French armies under General Henri Navarre. Navarre, to prevent future attacks against Laos and to restrict Vietminh movements toward the south, converted an obscure interior outpost at Dien Bien Phu into a major fortress, defended by French troops and Vietnamese who supported them. By March 1954 when the battle began that would bring the first Indochina war to a stalemate, France had concentrated there nearly 16,000 of its best troops, built an airstrip to supply the fort, and set up massive artillery. Navarre was confident that at last he could wipe out the Communists' main force. Yet Giap's forces outnumbered Navarre's nearly three to one, and, with the aid of thousands of Vietnamese who backpacked ammunition into the remote area, he had assembled superior firepower around the hills of Dien Bien Phu. Though the French retained control of the air, bombing strikes could not destroy the well-hidden Communist embankments, which soon knocked out the French airstrip. Then Giap encircled the post. The garrison fell to the Vietminh army, and its commander committed suicide. The French military effort to reassert colonial control had collapsed.

Americanizing the War   While most of the world's diplomats moved toward ending the war, Secretary of State John Foster Dulles took the first steps toward prolonging and Americanizing it. The Eisenhower Administration had already seriously considered active military intervention, not only to save Dien Bien Phu but also to bolster the entire French effort. Washington abandoned ideas of direct interference only after the French government itself refused to continue the war, believing the military situation in Vietnam to be hopeless. If the United States were to launch an anti-Communist crusade in Southeast Asia, it would have to find a vehicle other than French colonialism.

Only one day before the fall of Dien Bien Phu, nations involved in Indochina except for the United States convened in Geneva, Switzerland, to settle the conflict. After six weeks the representatives reached agreement. The Vietnamese Communists, flush with victory, wanted complete control of all Vietnam. They achieved much less, largely because the Soviet Union and China forced Ho Chi Minh to accept Western terms. Once again, broader international relations had critically affected the fate of Vietnam. In the aftermath of Stalin's death, the Soviet Union's new leadership wished to explore the possibilities of easing relations with the West. The Chinese, for their part, had no desire to see a swift repeat of the bloody stalemate with the United States that had been the recently concluded Korean War. The Geneva accords granted independence to the three Indochinese states of Laos, Cambodia, and Vietnam. Vietnam was temporarily divided at the 17th parallel. At the time, the territory north of the parallel was under Communist control, while the southern part of the country was in the hands of nationalist but anti-Communist Vietnamese. The agreement provided that elections throughout Vietnam within two years would determine the country's permanent political future. None of the new states was to permit foreign troops or bases on its soil or to join an outside alliance.

Rather than a compromise, Washington wanted an anti-Communist alternative state in Vietnam. Eisenhower's State Department announced that the United States, which had not signed the Geneva accords, intended to adhere to its terms, but would treat North and South Vietnam as separate entities. Then, in September 1954, Secretary Dulles negotiated the Southeast Asia Treaty Organization

One American observer commented of Dien Bien Phu:

"Here you were out in the middle of a jungle, and you have extremely heavy antiaircraft fire coming from positions that we didn't believe the Viet Minh could establish or maintain. We thought no one could put heavy weapons in there except the French, who had flown them in on C-119s and C-54s. But the Viet Minh, who had no air, had somehow put in 105s and 75 millimeters, and heavy mortars and all the rest of it, in what we thought was impenetrable jungle."

(SEATO), a milder version of the NATO alliance, pledging mutual assistance "in accord with constitutional process." The original signatories—France, Great Britain, the United States, Australia, New Zealand, the Philippines, Pakistan, and Thailand—later extended the pact's protection to include Cambodia, Laos, and South Vietnam. Convinced that his only other option was disengagement and the gradual fall of all Southeast Asia to Communism, Eisenhower pledged vast economic and military aid to the native but increasingly elitist South Vietnamese premier, Ngo Dinh Diem. In 1956 the United States supported Diem's open break with the Geneva settlement, his refusal to allow South Vietnam to reunite with the North. Washington had committed itself to the creation and then to the defense of a separate, anti-Communist South Vietnam.

The Diem Regime in South Vietnam

Supporting Diem would eventually backfire, for he took American money and built a corrupt personalist regime. At first, however, the new leadership seemed promising. Between 1954 and 1957 the country, generously supported by American financial aid, made substantial economic growth and even achieved some land reform in the interest of the poor peasantry as opposed to the wishes of the privileged classes. The government suppressed gangsters in Saigon and brought under control the religious sects, many of whose leaders had set up independent fiefdoms in the countryside. But Diem never gained broad popular support, and because the rural areas remained in the hands of opponents, he adopted increasingly repressive tactics.

The northern regime initially hoped that Diem might simply weaken badly. By 1959, though, the Communist movement in South Vietnam was so damaged and demoralized that North Vietnam authorized direct military action against Diem, which brought immediate and significant success. By the end of the decade Washington had dispatched some 685 American "advisory" personnel to Vietnam—the limit permitted by the Geneva accords; but the nonmilitary alternative, economic growth and thorough land reform, neared collapse in the absence of cooperation from Diem. While Eisenhower "could conceive of no greater tragedy than for the United States to become involved in an all-out land war in Asia," his secretary of state announced that "the free world would intervene in Indochina rather than let the situation deteriorate."

President Ngo Dinh Diem (second from the right), dressed in his customary white suit, seen with his finance minister, Tan Hun Phuong, after receiving an American aid check for $11,720,000. U.S. Ambassador G. Frederick Reinhardt stands at the right in this 1955 photo.
(Courtesy, AP/Wide World Photos)

Kennedy and Vietnam

In the early sixties the Diem government approached chaos. Social and economic reform halted, and even retrogressed, as Diem concentrated on maintaining his power and eliminating all opposition. In response, thousands of southern insurrectionists joined the newly organized Communist National Liberation Front (NLF), and many took the trek north for military training. Diem dubbed the forces Vietcong, for Vietnamese Communists. Support from the Kennedy Administration, which eventually sent to Vietnam nearly 16,000 American advisers, along with artillery and fighter-bombers, kept the Diem regime alive. Kennedy's secretary of state Dean Rusk confidently asserted: "This great country can do anything when it puts its shoulder to the wheel." Washington also expanded the elaborate clandestine war against North Vietnam that it had begun in 1955. Kennedy now ordered secret agents to sabotage lines of communication throughout the North, and American advisers directed military raids across Hanoi's frontiers and into Laos. At first these tactics appeared successful: during 1962 the NLF lost some of its territorial gains. Although several of Kennedy's partisans have insisted that he—unlike Lyndon Johnson—would have avoided full-scale conflict, his decisions enlarged American goals in Vietnam without assuring their achievement.

In South Vietnam, Diem increasingly reverted to trusting only a small, inner circle of family and friends. Most of these were Roman Catholic, the religion of choice for Vietnamese families who had wished to rise to high status during French rule. Diem's Roman Catholic sister-in-law, Madame Nhu, gained notoriety for her cynical dismissal of Buddhist "barbecues"—Vietnamese who set themselves on fire as a form of political protest. Beginning in May 1963, the Buddhists organized strong demonstrations against the Saigon regime; in an attempt to squash this threat, the government attacked Buddhist temples and pagodas throughout South Vietnam in August. When it became clear that the army raids had alienated the urban middle class, most religious sects, and intellectuals, the United States abandoned its support of the premier, while Ambassador Henry Cabot Lodge encouraged a cabal of generals to overthrow the Diem family. On November 2, 1963, the

A Buddhist priest immolates himself in protest against the Diem regime's religious persecution. Buddhist protests were a leading factor in toppling the Diem regime in 1963.
(Courtesy, United Press International Photos)

group assassinated Diem and set up a new government under Major General Nguyen Khanh. The Vietcong made rapid gains.

The United States might have used the Diem crisis as a convenient reason for withdrawing from the war. Robert Kennedy during a cabinet meeting urged a course of disengagement, and *Time*'s editors suggested the possibility of neutralizing all of the region as Laos had been neutralized. But Secretary of Defense Robert McNamara and the chairman of the Joint Chiefs of Staff, General Maxwell Taylor, visited Vietnam in September and reported that most American tasks there would be accomplished in fifteen months, with perhaps a thousand troops returning home by the end of 1963. Pursuing the war seemed a course that prudently weighed cost against advantage.

Johnson Escalates the War

By the time President Johnson took office in November 1963 he had inherited not only the war itself but also Kennedy's principal advisers on foreign affairs. The United States had many troops in South Vietnam and its new government was completely dependent on American economic and military aid. The new President approached Vietnam on the basis of his knowledge of World War II and Korea. It was, he thought, a simple matter of halting aggression.

The Gulf of Tonkin Resolution   A pretext to attack North Vietnam—the so-called Gulf of Tonkin crisis—occurred during early August 1964. The navy had helped South Vietnam to conduct extensive operations against shore installations in North Vietnam. A spy ship, the destroyer *Maddox*, loaded with electronic equipment, had supported these raids, often cruising inside the twelve-mile limit decreed by Hanoi. After one such incursion manned by South Vietnamese but supported by Americans, Hanoi sent several PT boats into the Gulf of Tonkin. The *Maddox*, now over twenty miles from the coast, may have been fired upon first by North Vietnamese ships, and the American ship then launched torpedoes. Johnson remarked privately: "For all I know, our navy was shooting at whales out there." Two days later, on August 4, as *Maddox* and another destroyer, *C. Turner Joy*, cruised in the same general area, they reported a second attack by North Vietnamese boats. It is not clear whether the attack actually took place or whether the Americans imagined it in the intense darkness, amid possible malfunctions of sonar or radar equipment.

But in Washington, Johnson publicly denounced "unprovoked aggression" and used the temporary feeling of crisis to extract congressional approval for a project the administration had contemplated for several months. To ensure his freedom of action and demonstrate American unity in an election year, Johnson secured a sweeping authorization "to take all necessary measures . . . to prevent further aggression." Both Houses adopted the de facto declaration of war, the House with no dissenting votes, the Senate by a vote of 88 to 2. Only a few isolated senators, Wayne Morse of Oregon in particular, questioned its ultimate purpose or the advisability of open-ended commitments.

Gulf of Tonkin Resolution, August 7, 1964

This resolution, which passed the Senate with only two dissenting votes and the House of Representatives with no opposing votes, gave President Johnson a degree of legal cover for his subsequent escalation of the American presence in Vietnam. The occasion for it was the military clash between the United States and North Vietnam that had just taken place in the Gulf.

To promote the maintenance of international peace and security in southeast Asia.

Whereas naval units of the Communist regime in Vietnam, in violation of the principles of the Charter of the United Nations and of international law, have deliberately and repeatedly attacked United States naval vessels lawfully present in international waters, and have thereby created a serious threat to international peace; and

Whereas these attacks are part of a deliberate and systematic campaign of aggression that the Communist regime in North Vietnam has been waging against its neighbors and the nations joined with them in the collective defense of their freedom; and

Whereas the United States is assisting the peoples of southeast Asia to protect their freedom and has no territorial, military or political ambitions in that area, but desires only that these peoples should be left in peace to work out their own destinies in their own way: Now, therefore, be it

Resolved by the Senate and House of Representatives of the United States of America in Congress assembled, That the Congress approves and supports the determination of the President, as Commander in Chief, to take all necessary measures to repel any armed attack against the forces of the United States and to prevent further aggression. . . .

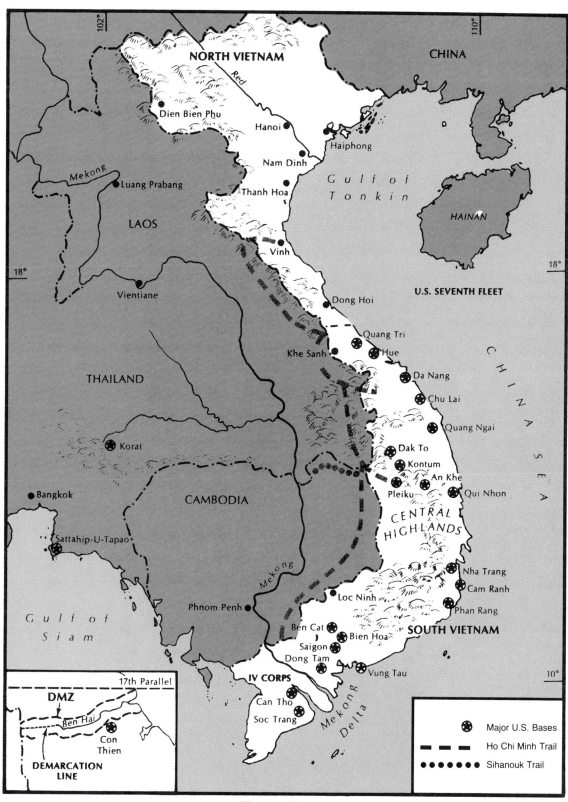

Vietnam War.

Pointing to a scar in the shape of Vietnam, LBJ in this cartoon seems to be indicating the wound from which he never recovered. (*Courtesy, David Levine and the* New York Review of Books)

One Vietcong soldier wrote in his diary:

"It is the duty of my generation to die for my country."

Escalation of the War

By early 1965, a major American air offensive named Rolling Thunder was under way. Immediately a basic difficulty arose. The South Vietnamese Army was incapable of adequately defending air bases used by American bombers in the South, as a series of aggressive Vietcong attacks made plain. The first actual American combat forces, no longer advisers to the South Vietnamese, came ashore in March 1965 to protect American aircraft. But who would protect the protectors? American field commanders, chafing under the restrictions of passive "base security" tasks, argued for a strategy of actively scouring the countryside for their Vietcong tormentors. The result eventually led to the "search and destroy" strategy and, inevitably, to the sharp increase of American combat forces in South Vietnam as Rolling Thunder proceeded against the North.

Johnson decided to fight the war tactically, somewhere between the extremes of what he thought of as a disgraceful withdrawal and the quick, massive attacks against North Vietnam and the Vietcong advocated by the joint chiefs of staff. He believed that a calculated, steady increase in force would convince his opponents that they could not win.

But Ho Chi Minh, the North Vietnamese, and the Vietcong were willing to make extraordinary sacrifices and sustain huge losses. When it became clear to the Johnson Administration that the Communists were not going to back down, the President switched to attrition—the United States would kill so many Vietcong and North Vietnamese soldiers that their military units would simply be unable to engage in battle. President Johnson and General William Westmoreland intended to kill the Communists faster than the Vietnamese population could replace them. Westmoreland kept talking about this "crossover point." It would take several years of fighting before the United States realized that the arithmetic of attrition did not add up. The American war machine would not be able to kill Vietnamese soldiers faster than the enemy could replace them. Washington military planners tripped over another misconception. For strategic and tactical reasons, in any guerrilla war the military defending the established government must be many times the size of the insurgents. Experts in guerrilla warfare estimated that United States and South Vietnamese forces would have to outnumber North Vietnamese and guerrilla troops about ten to one.

Problems in Pursuing the War

Stymied by the insufficiency of Rolling Thunder and by Hanoi's refusal to cave in at an American bargaining table, Johnson massively escalated the ground war in Vietnam during the spring of 1966. For nearly twenty-four months, the world witnessed this nation's military attempt to pursue a will-o'-the-wisp victory and to ensure a non-Communist South Vietnam. But obstacles multiplied.

In South Vietnam disagreements over military tactics and economic reforms plagued the junta that had replaced Diem. Even after two generals, Nguyen Van Thieu and Nguyen Cao Ky, emerged on top, Saigon could not heal the split between countryside and city that the insurgency widened. But at a meeting in Honolulu during February 1966 with Thieu and Ky, Johnson extracted promises that the junta would permit an elected government and begin large-scale land redistribution. It was a delicate diplomatic maneuver, for while Johnson to force compliance threatened to cut off American aid, the two Vietnamese leaders knew that they were the President's only option. American insistence upon the appearance, if not the reality, of democracy, together with the temporary eclipse of Communist progress during the massive United States buildup of 1966, finally brought about nationwide elections for a Constituent Assembly. But this "constitutional convention" was rigged: no Communist delegates attended and the regime blocked neutralist candidates such as the still-restive Buddhists.

The more the United States bombed North Vietnam, the more Ho scattered his factories, infiltrated the South, and whipped up war fever in the North. American bombers, moreover, quickly discovered that they lacked advantageous targets. North Vietnam itself was an especially poor subject for bombing. The economy was predominantly agrarian, lacking dependency on industries that in modern warfare are the most vulnerable to aerial attack. The country had an elaborate system of dikes to control flooding along the Red River, but the United States decided not to bomb them, since the flooding and starvation that would have resulted are considered international war crimes. Fears about reactions in the Soviet Union and China prevented an assault against the major port of Haiphong, for such an attack would probably have resulted in the deaths of Soviet and Chinese military and civilian personnel. Memories of the Chinese invasion of Korea remained strong.

Henry Kissinger, the American diplomat, observed:

"The conventional army loses if it does not win. The guerrilla wins if he does not lose."

The only really significant target available for attack was the so-called Ho Chi Minh Trail, which stretched into Laos and from Laos into the northern reaches of South Vietnam, the main thoroughfare for North Vietnam's shipment of troops and supplies to South Vietnam. In the early 1960s, the Trail had been little more than a path, but North Vietnam put a huge investment into developing it. By the early 1970s the Trail was actually an elaborate system of 12,000 miles of paved and unpaved roads and paths over which thousands of trucks, wagons, and people traveled every day. A five-inch pipeline from North Vietnam, through Laos, and into South Vietnam shipped petroleum products.

American aircraft regularly bombed the Ho Chi Minh Trail, but once again the arithmetic of attrition did not compute. On any given day, the United States could keep about 400 aircraft over the Trail for a period of one hour. The terrain of the Trail consisted of mountainous jungles that made accurate bombing very difficult. The Vietnamese Communists moved as much of their freight as possible at night. As North Vietnam's air defense systems became more sophisticated, American pilots who had one hour to spend over their target had to take much of that hour dodging surface-to-air missiles (SAMs) or attacking the missile launching sites instead of bombing the supplies moving down the Trail.

Meanwhile, the ground war in South Vietnam remained locked in a stalemate despite repeated United States reinforcements. By the end of 1967 over half a million American troops guarded major cities and many rural outposts, but the Communists dominated much of the countryside. When combat units embarked upon search and destroy

The Ho Chi Minh Trail was at first a series of footpaths which North Vietnamese troops took to the South. The trails, some of which traveled through the neighboring countries of Laos and Cambodia, were, as seen here, often quite narrow and primitive, but were modernized as the war went on. *(Courtesy, AP/Wide World Photos)*

An American military adviser on patrol with South Vietnamese troops. By 1968, over half a million U.S. troops were fighting the unconventional war against Vietcong guerrilla forces. *(Courtesy, U.S. Army)*

One American soldier related:

"You always had to watch your back, because there was no front line there, and you had women and kids as warriors, too, and you really didn't know who was trustworthy and who wasn't."

missions, North Vietnamese regulars shunned combat and Vietcong guerrillas hid among the population. Young Americans from city ghettos and green suburbs had to learn, and learned quickly, skills of jungle fighting that combined high technology with the primitive art of walking noiselessly over forest foliage.

Johnson's program to "win the hearts and minds of the Vietnamese people" was similarly indecisive. To "pacify" the countryside, Washington had launched a number of initiatives such as the Combined Action Platoon program. American troops would move into a village, secure it with a series of fortifications, and train the villagers as militia. Although the tactic sometimes protected the village from Vietcong attack, the ill-equipped militia were rarely a match for dedicated North Vietnamese regular units. And the intrusion into their villages along with the forced evacuation of some hamlets made for further antagonism to Americans. During the 1960s the United States forced more than two million South Vietnamese civilians to leave their homes. That is another reason why political victory was proving as elusive as military success.

Student Protests

Johnson's policy in Vietnam was soon facing an opponent as difficult to master as the Communists. He was confronting the most energetic student movement in American history.

By the time of John Kennedy's presidency, much had come about that could quicken the passions of middle-class young white Americans. They had the inspiration of the civil rights movement. Rock and roll was soon going to join or blend with coffeehouse folk songs to produce the varieties of music that would attend the student rebellions like a sound track. Beat literature offered images of cultural rebellion.

SDS and FSM   The early student movement emerged between the 1962 founding convention of the Students for a Democratic Society and the 1964 Free Speech Movement (FSM) at the University of California at Berkeley. The SDS convention in Port Huron, Michigan, issued what came to be recognized as the "Port Huron Statement." The document called for social reform, not social revolution. It coupled with explicit opposition to Communism its criticism of the nation's role in the Cold War. The Statement's demand for educational reform bespoke a belief in the university as a vehicle for social change. Its systematic critique of American society went with an insistence on nonviolence and a loyalty to traditional American ideals. The Free Speech Movement at Berkeley, though ostensibly for specific political rights such as bringing in speakers and distributing political literature on university property, presented a challenge to the concept Chancellor Clark Kerr called "The Multiversity." While servicing large numbers of students, Kerr's modern university remained closely tied to business and government, performing the research and analysis tasks that supported defense industries, domestic social policies, and corporate technology.

Student movements came at a receptive time. In the early 1960s students were enrolling in colleges and universities in far greater numbers than ever before. Some states advanced an unprecedented one-half of all high school students to some form of college study. California, New York, and Texas led the nation in the expansion of their universities, state colleges, and two-year junior colleges. Their numbers and a degree of common experience gave some college students a sense of collective identity and potential power.

SDS, increasingly radical, came to demand "participatory democracy," a dismantling of centralized bureaucracies and the forming of little democracies throughout American life. Communities should control schools, students should have power in universities, citizens should supervise the police, and workers should have a part in running their plants. SDS helped organize the first major antiwar demonstration. It took place in Washington in April 1965, and surprised everyone by drawing 25,000 people. Campus SDS chapters began campaigns

Mario Savio, standing on the steps of Sproul Hall, tells Berkeley students about the Free Speech Movement. *(Courtesy, UPI/Bettmann Newsphotos)*

The growing antiwar movement attacked the war's purpose and morality as well as the administration's "arrogance of power." *(Courtesy, AP/Wide World Photos)*

The sign perched on *Alma Mater*'s lap at Columbia University refers to calling in the police to clear buildings occupied by students. *(Courtesy, Claus Meyer, Black Star)*

against research sponsored by the Department of Defense, against ROTC, and against employment scouting on the campus by the Dow Chemical Company, which manufactured napalm—a burning jelly used in Vietnam that fastens onto the skin. Campus radicals attacked military recruitment officers as a visible link between the university and American foreign policy. On a few leading campuses, successful campaigns produced a denial of academic credit or university facilities to ROTC, which in effect eliminated these programs.

Confrontation with college administrators and with the world outside the campus sharpened. When small groups resorted to the occupation of buildings and were met with tear gas and police squadrons, broader revolts ensued in 1968 at Columbia and other universities. The size of antiwar demonstrations in major cities escalated immensely. These levels of protest created divisions within student movements. At a stormy convention in 1969, SDS split into several factions.

A tiny few became intrigued with real violence. The Weatherman, taking their name from Bob Dylan's "You don't need a weatherman to know which way the wind blows," tried in the "days of rage" in 1969 to disrupt the streets of Chicago. Soon Weatherman and others became interested in bombs. Several went off in buildings the bomb-wielders thought were symbolic of American capitalism or the war effort. The attempt was to bomb only empty buildings, but in 1970 in a New York City townhouse an accidental explosion killed three people who were operating a primitive bomb factory.

Another branch of the antiwar movement meanwhile was employing the tactics and spirit of nonviolent resistance developed in the civil rights actions. In October 1967, a group including the Roman Catholic priests Daniel and Philip Berrigan invaded the offices of the selective service board at Catonsville, Maryland, and poured animal blood on records. They then waited for the police to arrest them. Elsewhere, numbers of people registered for the draft publicly destroyed their selective service cards, expecting to be arrested. In the same month as the Berrigan raid, another form of nonviolent resistance occurred outside the registration center at Oakland, California. For several days, protesters ducked police and blocked traffic—a nonviolent act if compared with what some opponents wanted to do, and nonviolent if compared with the war.

Democratic Party Opposition   By 1967 Senator J. William Fulbright, who earlier had guided the Gulf of Tonkin resolution through the Senate, now attacked the administration's "arrogance of power." "Power," observed Fulbright, "tends to confuse itself with virtue." He believed that its history of victory, prosperity, and power gave the United States a sense of omnipotence and righteousness that could distort reality, as it was doing in Vietnam. The nation had been foolish, Fulbright argued, to assume that Western institutions and political methods could establish themselves in an alien culture. While Fulbright and other critics worried about misplaced motives, a mushrooming antiwar coalition directly questioned the war's morality. In October 1967, a rally of 200,000 students, leftists, and other Americans demonstrated in a march through the nation's capital. An important portion of the Democratic Party had rejected Johnson's leadership.

1968: Year of Turmoil

The Tet Offensive   Early in the year the Vietnamese customarily observed a month of truce: Tet, the month is called. At the end of January 1968, during Tet, the American embassy and all the major cities of South Vietnam came under attack. Parts of Saigon fell to the enemy and most of the northern city of Hue fell to Vietcong and North Vietnamese control for several days. Carnage spread in this time of truce: in Hue, from a campaign of murder waged by the Communists; in a number of cities, from the massive South Vietnamese and American counteroffensive that eventually restored the urban areas to Allied control. The Vietcong still dominated the rural areas. The Tet offensive ended in a victory for the South Vietnamese and American armies. But the scope and drama of the Communist offensive made for a kind of defeat in the United States. "What the hell is going on?" exclaimed the grandfatherly television anchorman Walter Cronkite upon hearing the news about Tet. "I thought we were winning the war." Keeping the news simple, Cronkite and other journalists portrayed Tet as an American defeat.

Brigadier General Nguyen Ngoc Loan of South Vietnam executing a Vietcong suspect during the Tet offensive. *(Courtesy, AP/Wide World Photos)*

General Westmoreland immediately flew to the United States and asked for 200,000 more reinforcements, a request that coincided with a major review of war policy in Washington. At this point, Johnson's decision was relatively straightforward. He could not send more men to South Vietnam without endangering the nation's commitments elsewhere and producing severe strains on the inflated American economy. Dismayed and disillusioned, he entrusted to a study group chaired by a personal friend, Clark Clifford, the search for an alternative. Since military victory was not in sight, the Clifford committee turned to diplomacy as a solution.

The simplest solution to the war—withdrawal from it—the administration resisted. Its own conscience caught it in a ruthless logic, the logic of war. The more deeply the South Vietnamese allies committed themselves to the conflict, trusting to the United States to support them, the more terrible it would be to desert them. And so the United States must go on encouraging them to fight. And the more Vietnamese and Americans died, the more terrible it would be to quit the war with nothing gained. And so the killing must go on.

In an anti-guerrilla war among people any one of whom might be a friend, an enemy, or simply a poor peasant who wanted to be left alone, widespread indiscriminate killing of civilians became inevitable. The best known American act of this kind was at My Lai in Song My. In that village suspected of harboring guerrillas, troops lost self-control and committed atrocities not revealed to the American public until 1970. According to the testimony of a rifleman who witnessed the spring 1968 My Lai slaughter of hundreds of civilians: "Lieutenant Calley and a rifleman pushed the prisoners into the ditch. . . . There was an order to shoot by Lieutenant Calley, I can't remember the exact words—it was something like 'Start firing.' Meadlo turned to me and said: 'Shoot, why don't you shoot?' He was crying. I said, 'I can't, I won't.' Then Lieutenant Calley and Meadlo pointed their rifles into the ditch and fired. People were diving on top of each other; mothers were trying to protect their children."

In a dramatic television appearance on March 31, 1968, Johnson officially announced the results of the Clifford policy review. The United States would halt bombing north of the 19th parallel in an effort to bring about serious peace negotiations. Westmoreland was to receive only token reinforcements. In addition, South Vietnam would gradually take over active prosecution of the war, an approach President Nixon was later to expand. It became known as "Vietnamization." On May 10, peace talks opened in Paris. But peace would elude the negotiators.

| The Democratic Primaries | Senator Eugene McCarthy of Minnesota, a handsome gray-haired man of fifty-three, seemed a study in political detachment and nonchalance. But when |

Attorney General Nicholas Katzenbach told the Senate Foreign Relations Committee in August 1967 that a President could no longer lose time by consulting the Congress on whether to involve the country in war, McCarthy lost his customary composure. Angrily he told Katzenbach that such extensive executive authority deprived the Senate of any decision-making role in foreign policy. Late in November McCarthy decided to oppose the President in the coming spring primaries.

The first contest came in New Hampshire on March 21, when snow still covered the ground. An energetic band of young students carried the antiwar message across the state. Gene McCarthy, in his dry and self-contained manner something of a New Englander himself, made sober and highly factual arguments against the war. In the vote, McCarthy's Roman Catholicism must have counted, for about two-thirds of the state's Democrats shared his faith. The senator won 42 percent of the two-party vote, almost as much as Johnson's write-in total of 49 percent. The vote registered not disapproval of the war so much as dissatisfaction with the failure of the United States to win it. It was unprecedented for an opponent to come so close to winning a primary in the party of an incumbent President during a war.

Three days later, in what appeared to some as shameless opportunism, Senator Robert Kennedy of New York announced that he, too, would oppose the President in primary contests. The timing of the entry reflected his political practicality: he doubted that the aloof McCarthy had the political manner and energy to unseat Johnson. Kennedy's campaign lost its initial momentum when Lyndon Johnson delivered his television speech just two days before the Wisconsin primary. The President declared that he would not only rapidly de-escalate the war and cut back bombing of the North, but also turn down army requests for more troops. In an almost casually presented coda that startled his listeners, he remarked that since he did not want political squabbling to hinder the search for peace, he would not seek reelection in November.

Deprived of their most effective campaign issue—the President

LBJ's surprise announcement: "I shall not seek and will not accept . . . another term as your President." *(Courtesy, AP/Wide World Photos)*

himself—Kennedy and McCarthy then had to campaign, to a great extent, against each other. In the process of their bickering the peace movement fragmented. McCarthy, never an admirer of the Kennedy clan, was offended at RFK's fascination with power. Kennedy thought McCarthy lazy, snobbish, and politically ineffectual. The two competed for the support of the young, who could be of assistance in the remaining primaries. McCarthy, after winning decisively against Johnson in Wisconsin, lost to Kennedy in Indiana and Nebraska. Then McCarthy made an unexpected comeback by winning easily in Oregon. One final primary would in large part determine the winner; Kennedy promised to drop out of the race should McCarthy defeat him in California on June 4. Kennedy won by a few percentage points, but on the very night of the primary election he was murdered by a Jordanian immigrant, Sirhan Bishara Sirhan.

Hubert Humphrey and the Democratic Convention   Vice President Hubert Humphrey just two decades before had forced a split in the Democratic Party when he led the forces demanding that the party make a commitment to civil rights. And he was known as a spokesman for labor and for the most aggressively liberal wing of the party, a fighter for welfare programs. But when asked as Vice President what had happened to the program he once had battled for, he answered simply and correctly: "We passed it." And antiwar liberals were perplexed at his attitude toward the conflict. The voluble Humphrey welcomed opportunities to explain the intervention in Vietnam. Before an AFL-CIO convention he associated the critics of the war with appeasers of Hitler. He dismissed the significance of corruption in South Vietnam's government, claiming it merely to be comparable to that in American cities.

Humphrey's position on the war, in fact, accorded with his brand of Democratic liberalism. For one thing, he was a good Democrat, convinced that the fortunes of liberalism depended on the strength of the Democratic Party; and he was loyal to the President. And his anti-Communism—he was right at least about the ruthlessness of Vietnamese Communism—came straight out of years of Cold War liberalism.

At the Chicago convention that city's mayor Richard Daley encouraged an effort to draft the surviving Kennedy brother, Edward, a Massachusetts senator, and McCarthy offered to withdraw in his favor. It was the last hope of the amorphous peace movement. Edward Kennedy might have denied the nomination to Vice President Humphrey, who was so closely identified with Johnson. Thousands of young people demonstrating outdoors reminded the delegates of their passionate dislike of the administration and of its policy in Vietnam. Several large states would have supported Kennedy, and in the psychology of a national convention enthusiasm for him as a potential winner might have put him across. But Kennedy refused to run.

At the convention a platform provision calling for a halt to all bombing in Vietnam failed by a 3 to 2 vote. Outside the convention hall in Grant Park, the Chicago police battled the young, engaging in what a later government report terms a "police riot." Inside, Senator Abra-

Antiwar protesters outside the Democratic Convention in Chicago, 1968. *(Courtesy, AP/Wide World Photos)*

ham Ribicoff of Connecticut told the delegates about the outside skirmishes and lashed out at the "Gestapo tactics of the police." After the riots, Humphrey's nomination by a 2 to 1 margin over McCarthy seemed anticlimactic.

Richard Nixon and George Wallace The strongest Republican contestant for the 1968 presidential nomination was former Vice President Richard Nixon. After losing to Kennedy in 1960, Nixon had moved to California and two years later failed in his bid for the governorship. During the 1964 presidential campaign he supported Barry Goldwater and thereby survived the year with political currency among party regulars. In mid-decade he practiced law in New York City, defending the right to privacy in *Time Inc. v. Hill* (1966). In 1968 he hewed to the political center and won victories in the spring primaries. Ronald Reagan of California tried to whittle away Nixon's southern support, and Nelson Rockefeller of New York hoped that preconvention polls would show him as the strongest candidate. But neither strategy succeeded. Nixon won on the first ballot.

Alabama's feisty Governor George Wallace, running as the candidate of the American Independent Party, got on the ballot in all fifty states. Wallace had become the candidate of the South on the strength of a single slogan: "Segregation now—Segregation tomorrow—Segregation forever." But now he reached out for a broader and more general campaign theme and insisted he was no racist. He blasted "bearded bureaucrats," "pointy-headed professors," and "poor-folks haters": his campaign resembled a class movement, speaking to divisions in taste, style, values, and education. The Wallace campaign employed the slogan "law and order." Above all, Wallace took as his target the Supreme Court under Chief Justice Earl Warren. Wallace denounced court decisions that outlawed school prayers, protected the rights of accused criminals, and strengthened the civil rights of minorities. As late as the second half of September the Gallup poll credited Wallace with about twenty percent of the vote.

Labor unions portrayed Alabama as a low-wage, open-shop state.

Supporters of George Wallace, Lansing, Michigan, 1968. *(Courtesy, John Barnard)*

Richard M. Nixon and Spiro Agnew, the Republican Party ticket chosen at the 1968 convention. *(Courtesy, United Press International Photos)*

Wallace's vice-presidential candidate, General Curtis LeMay, proved a liability. "We seem to have a phobia about nuclear weapons. . . ," he said. "I don't believe the world would end if we exploded a nuclear weapon." Wallace's presence in the campaign permitted Nixon to portray himself as a middle-of-the-road candidate.

Nixon almost lost the 1968 election. At the end of October peace talks began in earnest in Paris and the bombing of North Vietnam ceased; had these signs of the war's diminution come a bit sooner, Humphrey might have won. Wallace's votes, on the other hand, were cast by conservatives who might otherwise have favored Nixon.

Nixon: Years of Triumph

In 1969 Nixon came to the presidency after eight years of Democratic rule. In contrast to Lyndon Johnson, Nixon opposed a deeper involvement of the federal government in the solution of social problems, racial discrimination, or poverty. Instead he directed his appeals toward a "silent majority" of middle-class people who had tired of paying taxes to support welfare measures. Capitalizing on their discomfort over student and black protest and the rising crime rate, Nixon, though less stridently than Alabama Governor George Wallace, appealed for "law and order."

In his inaugural address Nixon asserted that the government could not solve all problems and called upon the young to lower their voices. The new President would turn out to be quite friendly to the basic institutions of the welfare state. But his appointments did not represent the diversity of groups and interests that a leader wanting to bring the country together could have been expected to recognize. The cabinet assembled to heal division and turmoil in the nation contained no blacks, Jews, women, or Democrats. The President stocked the White House with long-time followers whose essential qualification was loyalty to Richard Nixon. William P. Rogers, one of Nixon's closest friends, took office as secretary of state, and Professor Henry Kissinger of Harvard University succeeded Walt Rostow as head of the National Security Council. Later Kissinger became secretary of state.

The Nixon Doctrine and SALT I   The first elaboration of the President's foreign policy, the Nixon Doctrine of 1969, stated that the United States was reducing its military role in Asia but would continue to respect its world obligations. Concrete applications took the form of troop reductions in Korea and an agreement to return Okinawa to the Japanese.

The question that required immediate attention in 1969 was strategic arms limitation talks with the USSR. The United States had earlier planned for such discussions. But in the spring of 1968, when Johnson was still in office, the Communist government of Czechoslovakia in Prague under Alexander Dubcek broke with the practice of Communist regimes and opened up the country to freedom of expression. When the Soviet Union invaded Czechoslovakia and suppressed the Prague uprising, Washington postponed arms talks with Moscow.

Nixon preferred to engage in negotiations from a position of strength, and so proposed in March 1969 a plan for a shield against enemy missiles. Democratic senators objected to the cost and questioned the effectiveness of this antiballistic missile program, but the Senate passed it by a single vote. Some who voted in favor believed that Nixon would hold off deployment for fear of jeopardizing talks with the Soviet Union. And the veiled threat of an ABM system seemed to work: in October the Russians did begin SALT talks in Helsinki, Finland, "SALT" being the acronym for "Strategic Arms Limitation Treaty." The Soviet Union was chiefly interested in stopping deployment of the ABM. Aware of this, American negotiators pressed for the inclusion of limits on offensive nuclear weapons. They succeeded. The result was a 1972 treaty now called SALT I.

World Conditions   The major powers also reached important agreements on Berlin early in 1971. In part this resulted from the growing strength of the Social Democrats and Chancellor Willy Brandt of the Federal Republic of Germany, the official title of West Germany. Brandt, who as mayor of West Berlin had been a tough opponent of the Communist East that surrounded West Germany, was nonetheless well disposed to bargain with the Communist world. He began talks with the Soviet Union, the German Democratic Republic, as Communist East Germany called itself, and other eastern European nations. He also softened West Germany's trade stance toward Communist Poland. An agreement allowed unimpeded access to West Berlin, with provisions for two million West Berliners to visit relatives periodically and to transact business in East Germany.

Latin Americans increasingly demanded economic and political independence from the United States. In 1968, Peru had seized the International Petroleum Company, prompting Johnson's administration to enforce laws that cut off aid in the event of insufficient compensation. But Peru went on to nationalize other companies, while Ecuador seized fishing vessels of the United States, claiming they had violated Ecuadoran territorial rights, and Chile elected a Marxist president, Salvador Allende. These events strongly indicated a lessening of United States influence in Latin America. Burdened by commitments in Asia, the Nixon presidency could not provide significant economic assistance, especially when Congress consistently reduced the foreign aid budget. In Africa, Nixon maintained neutrality in the Nigerian civil war, but when it ended he tried to provide aid to both sides to ease the suffering and starvation, particularly severe among the Ibos of rebellious Biafra.

The Arab states of the Middle East demanded that the Israelis withdraw from Jordanian, Egyptian, and Syrian territories occupied in the Six-Day War of 1967. Many Israelis wanted to hold permanently such areas as the west bank of the Jordan, including East Jerusalem, the Arab section of Jerusalem controlled by Jordan before the Six-Day War. In January 1969 sporadic attacks by Israelis and Arabs occurred almost daily despite a cease-fire. President Nasser of Egypt offered a plan that called for Israeli withdrawal and a declaration of nonbelligerency, the territorial integrity of all countries in the Mideast including Israel, freedom of navigation on international waterways, and a just solution to the Israeli domination of Palestinian lands and people. Israel, however, rejected Nasser's proposal and resisted American pressures to ease its position on withdrawal. Both sides accepted a cease-fire. This only shifted the focus to Palestinian Arab guerrillas and almost continuous acts of terrorism, including several spectacular airplane hijackings. These led to studied, deadly effective Israeli retaliation. The hot and cold war between Israel and the Arabs was the most explosive situation in a world otherwise moving slowly toward peace.

Renewed Ties with China   In his most surprising reversal of foreign policy, Nixon opened the door to China. In his State of the World message on February 26, 1971, he cited the People's Republic of China by name and proposed an increase in trade and the beginning of a "serious dialogue." The People's Republic, seeking friends in its confrontation with the Soviet Union, invited an American table tennis team and three newsmen to visit Beijing. Shortly afterward, Chou En-lai, the Chinese prime minister, stated that more American newsmen would be admitted. At the same time President Nixon announced an easing of the trade embargo against China and the removal of American export restrictions on several nonstrategic items. In Nixon's view this was a significant way to "remove needless obstacles" to more contact between the American and the Chinese people.

The magnitude of the new thaw became obvious when Nixon reported in a short television address that Henry Kissinger had met with Chou En-lai in Beijing from July 9 to 11, 1971. Then Nixon announced a planned visit to Beijing. He stressed that the visit would not be at the expense of old friends, meaning the Nationalists, the anti-Communist government that had been driven from mainland China to the island of Taiwan but claimed still to be the country's legitimate regime. Yet the Nationalist leaders in Taiwan were dis-

President Nixon's historic trip to China in 1972 and his meeting with Mao Zedong ushered in a new age of détente between the two nations. *(Courtesy, AP/Wide World Photos)*

pleased. When Nixon suggested that both Chinas have representation in the UN, both the Nationalists and the Communist Chinese rejected it. Subsequently, despite half-hearted American opposition, the General Assembly voted to seat the People's Republic of China and to expel the Nationalist Chinese.

After months of preparation, the President landed in Beijing on February 20, 1972. Foreign minister Chou En-lai greeted him. At the end of the week Nixon and Chou En-lai issued a communique pledging peaceful coexistence and recognizing Taiwan as an "internal" Chinese problem. In effect, Nixon had granted the fact of a single China; he even promised eventual withdrawal of American forces from Taiwan.

The historic trip to China by a conservative President who was supposed to be a hard-line opponent of all Communist regimes jolted right-wing Americans. And the reconciliation with China did represent a softening of the conservative view of the Communist world. But the policy was also hard, balance-of-power politics of the kind that Kissinger favored: American friendship with China gave the Soviet Union more to worry about. Moscow was now thoroughly isolated. That may have spurred the USSR toward the détente with the United States that Nixon was also seeking in the SALT talks, an increase in cooperation in space, and other diplomatic arrangements. Nixon announced that he would visit Moscow in May 1972 in order to discuss all major issues that divided the two countries. The trip to Moscow took place as planned, and with considerable fanfare. Despite the grave domestic crisis created by the Watergate affair in 1973, Soviet Premier Brezhnev made a return visit to the United States.

By now, peaceful relations between the West and the two major Communist powers was a practical fact, belying the Cold War rhetoric that was to continue until the last days of the Soviet Union. Under conservative American administrations, hostility thereafter was directed not against China or the USSR but against Third-World leftist regimes and movements that conservatives in the United States disliked. An illustration came in the later days of Nixon's presidency, when the CIA managed to bring about a military coup against the Chilean government of Allende.

Henry Kissinger was President Richard Nixon's secretary of state. (*Courtesy, The White House*)

Nixon and Vietnam

Nixon did not want to lose the Vietnam War. Certain that American troop reductions were necessary, he was nevertheless determined to buy Saigon as much time as possible to build itself up before the last GI left. Part of this strategy led to a massive American and South Vietnamese invasion of Cambodia in late April 1970 designed to destroy enemy supplies and sanctuaries. Protests and strikes against the Cambodian venture spread throughout the nation, especially on college campuses. At Kent State University in northeastern Ohio, events took a terrible course. Three days after the killings of four students there and two subsequently at Jackson State in Mississippi, some eighty colleges had closed down, while in New York City construction workers badly beat up a group of antiwar demonstrators.

The Prisoner of War Issue One of the most sensitive issues in the peace negotiations was the fate of prisoners of war. Many American pilots shot down over North Vietnam had been POWs for four or five years. As their relatives began to insist on concessions to win their release, both supporters and opponents of the war embraced the POW issue for their own ends. On November 23, 1970, the administration authorized massive air strikes on North Vietnam and sent a rescue team to a suspected prisoner of war camp. When the news seeped out that no POWs had been rescued, the antiwar people sharpened their criticism, insisting on full withdrawal to win the POWs' rapid release. In Paris the shrewd Vietcong and North Vietnamese took advantage of this question by making offers to release prisoners in return for a definite date on complete American withdrawal from Indochina.

Nixon's administration would not set a date for a final pullout; indeed, in February 1971 the South Vietnamese with United States assistance launched an offensive in Laos. Although providing air support for South Vietnamese combat forces, the American command insisted that no United States combat soldiers aid in the operation. Nixon explained the invasion as a means of carrying out Vietnamization, the policy of turning the war over to the South Vietnamese. Even though the South Vietnamese soon abandoned the Laos invasion, the administration insisted that it had been a success. On April 7, 1971, President Nixon announced a further withdrawal of 100,000 troops by December 1971. By that time United States troop strength had fallen to 133,000, down from the half million of a few years earlier, but almost half of American soldiers lost in Vietnam and, of course, countless Vietnamese died during the protracted withdrawal under Nixon.

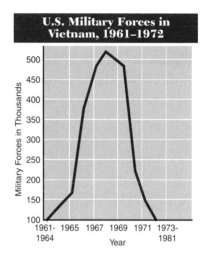

The Long Road Toward Peace

On April 1, 1972, after three days of intense bombardment, North Vietnamese regulars crossed the demilitarized zone to attack South Vietnam with great force. A few days of unsuccessful resistance demonstrated that the South Vietnamese needed help. The United States began the first night attacks on the Hanoi–Haiphong area since March 1968 and the first use of B-52s in this region. On May 8 President Nixon announced that the United States would mine North Vietnamese ports and systematically attack all supply lines.

"Peace Is at Hand" A flurry of pronouncements near the end of October revealed progress in the Paris peace talks. On the twenty-fourth, administration sources stated that bombing north of the 20th parallel had been temporarily halted. The next day North Vietnam announced an agreement that could be signed immediately. Forced by this statement to offer some explanation, Kissinger declared on October 26, 1972, "Peace is at hand," and suggested that one more negotiating session should wrap up the cease-fire. But at least one party to the war had not yet agreed to anything. President Thieu of South Vietnam demanded the withdrawal of all

North Vietnamese troops from the South before any cease-fire. It rapidly became clear, moreover, that on several points necessary to the peace, Hanoi's understanding differed from Washington's.

Renewed Fighting and a Peace Agreement at Last   To break the latest deadlock, beginning on December 17 the United States launched against North Vietnam the heaviest bombing campaign yet. For two weeks, with a thirty-six-hour break for Christmas, American planes bombed targets closer than ever before to urban populations and to the Chinese border. Huge B-52s carried on carpet bombing, the dropping of bombs by several planes simultaneously in an area over a mile long. This damaged many buildings in Hanoi not themselves targets, including foreign embassies and a major hospital. World opinion recoiled in shock. Yet Hanoi's reaction seemed restrained, as did that of Beijing and Moscow.

A peace agreement, signed on January 23, 1973, was an uneasy compromise. The United States tacitly consented to allow a substantial North Vietnamese troop presence in the South. Hanoi was forced to drop its demands for Thieu's resignation and agree to permit substantial American aid to Saigon to continue. Finally, on March 29, with the release of the last known prisoners of war and the departure of the last substantial American troop units from Vietnam, the United States apparently ended its direct military role in Vietnam.

Two years later the war, now chiefly among the Vietnamese themselves, ended with the fall of Saigon to the Communists, and the hasty evacuation of the city by westerners and those anti-Communist Vietnamese lucky enough to get out. Communists also won in Cambodia and Laos. The conflict had produced, in the words of one journalist, "no famous victories, no national heroes and no stirring patriotic songs"—or rather, it had brought the Americans none of those things.

Troubles at Home

Apart from the winding down of the war in Vietnam, Nixon's foreign policy proceeded smoothly. But at home he faced endless frustration. The President's largest problem was an economy threatened by inflation and by increasing deficits in the balance of payments. Congress, however, was not about to accept Nixon's plans for reduced spending. While most Democrats approved of cuts in defense appropriations, they objected to domestic cutbacks, and stalemate ensued.

The President soon asked for a striking program of welfare reform. His welfare proposal would guarantee $1,600 annually for a family of four regardless of state contributions. Families could earn an additional $720 a year with no loss in benefits, but beyond this, assistance would decrease fifty cents on each dollar earned at a job until wages reached $3,920. The more the recipient got paid at a regular job, the less he would get from the government. But the drop in government payments would not be so great as the rise in earned income, and therefore the individual would have reason to seek higher paying work.

The administration was attempting to correct what it saw to be one of the worst features of welfare, its discouraging recipients from seeking work. The program was not enacted. More successful was Nixon's plan for revenue sharing, which involved turning tax dollars back to state and local governments, many of them in serious financial difficulty. The mayors of large cities were particularly interested, for the flight of the middle class and businesses to the suburbs had eroded their tax base.

The Nixon Court   In recent years, the filling of vacant seats on the Supreme Court has become a politically charged business, for the Court in its ability to interpret laws or to throw them out as unconstitutional is a powerful instrument for directing or retarding social change. Nixon's first appointee to the Court, Chief Justice Warren E. Burger, faced little opposition as the successor to Earl Warren. Clement Haynsworth and Harrold G. Carswell were Nixon nominees who failed to win confirmation in the Senate. Democrats complained the President was putting up candidates merely on the strength of their being southerners and conservative. Denying this, Nixon then nominated Harry Blackmun of Minnesota, who won approval 94 to 0. In 1971 the Senate did approve a southerner, Lewis Powell of Virginia, along with William Rehnquist, an assistant attorney general in the Justice Department and a former Goldwater supporter.

The new Supreme Court refused to back down from the strong civil rights decisions issued since 1954. It ruled unanimously that school districts must end segregation "at once" and operate integrated school systems "now and hereafter." In other important decisions, the Court negated residency requirements for welfare recipients, and held that ethical as well as religious reasons were a sufficient basis for conscientious objection to war, and therefore for exemption from the draft. On April 20, 1971, the Court ruled 9 to 0 that school busing was a proper means of achieving school integration. Nixon wanted no more busing than the minimum required by law, and the issue was a major one in the 1972 primaries and campaign. Then the Court in 1973 held in *Roe v. Wade* that for the earlier stages of pregnancy a state could not prohibit a woman from getting an abortion; the vote was 7 to 2, with three of Nixon's four appointees in the majority. But a case in 1973, in which the Court gave localities more power to restrict pornography, indicated that it was more conservative than the Warren Court had been, and in future years that conservatism grew.

The Black Panthers and Attica   The 1960s had been an intensely public time when events on the streets and on campuses seemed almost daily to be making as much history as governments. Later in Nixon's administration the crowds would begin to withdraw from the streets. But for the first two or three years visual public events—"street theater," as radicals would perceive it—continued to compete for attention.

The Black Panthers were a black group professing revolutionary aims. There were theatrical courtroom outbursts in the cases of the "Chicago 8," indicted for conspiring to incite riot at the 1968 Democratic Convention in Chicago, and of the "Panther 21," a group charged with conspiracy to blow up buildings in New York City. The trial of the Panthers, postponed for over two months, resumed only when the defendants promised to restrain themselves. In the Chicago trial the conduct of Bobby Seale, the chairman of the Black Panther party, so infuriated Judge Julius Hoffman that he declared a mistrial and cited Seale for contempt of court. The other seven, although acquitted of the major charge of conspiracy, were convicted along with their lawyers on multiple counts of contempt of court, but secured a reversal of these through appeal.

The Black Panthers, suspected of conspiring to kill policemen, were a particular target of arrest and trial. In some large cities gun battles took place between Panthers and police. In December 1969 Chicago police, acting on information provided by the FBI, broke into an apartment and killed Fred Hampton, chairman of the Illinois Black Panthers. Although an interracial jury declared the killing justifiable, the government eventually dropped felony charges against the surviving Panthers, and in August 1972 a grand jury indicted the Illinois state attorney for blocking the prosecution of police officers responsible for the raid on Hampton's apartment. In almost every trial of Black Panthers from 1969 to January 1972 the juries failed to return convictions.

Among scattered outbreaks of prison violence and related demands for reform, none drew so much attention as that at Attica, New York. On September 9, 1971, one thousand inmates, most of them members of minorities, revolted and seized thirty-three guards as hostages. New York's Corrections Commissioner Russell Oswald negotiated with the prisoners for four days and acceded to twenty-eight demands for decent treatment but refused the request for amnesty. Then, with the consent of Governor Rockefeller, who had refused to meet with the prisoners, over one thousand state troopers and deputy sheriffs stormed the prison after helicopters dropped tear gas. Nine hostages and twenty-nine prisoners died. Gunshot wounds by the police had killed the hostages.

Edwin "Buzz" Aldrin, the second man to walk on the moon, as photographed by Neil Armstrong, the first, during the Apollo 11 mission, July 1969. *(Courtesy, NASA)*

Apollo 11   As early as December 1968 the space vehicle Apollo 8 had orbited the moon, and the flights of Apollo 9 and 10 followed soon after, testing the lunar module that was to make the landing. On July 16, 1969, Apollo 11 lifted off for the moon with astronauts Mike Collins, Neil Armstrong, and Edwin Aldrin aboard. Four days later as the Apollo 11 circled the moon, a smaller craft took Armstrong and Aldrin to the satellite's surface, and millions watched on television as Armstrong stepped onto the surface. As John Kennedy promised, Americans had landed on the moon before the end of the decade. Armstrong and Aldrin set up a seismometer to measure moonquakes, a solar wind screen, and an American flag; they brought home samples of rock showing the moon to be billions of years old. Subsequent flights provided more scientific information.

The moon flights were not greeted with the unquestioning enthusiasm that Lindbergh's solo flight across the Atlantic in 1927 had received. Perhaps television had made the nation more sophisticated, less susceptible to wonder. The matter-of-factness of the first steps on the moon, flashing on the same screens that showed advertisements and local weather reports, made the whole venture reveal itself as a magnificent technological achievement and an act of personal courage and discipline, but not a magical journey. And some Americans asked whether the resources that the country was hurling into space could have better gone to addressing the mundane problems of poverty, pollution, and worldwide overpopulation.

Regulation   Pressure mounted for programs against water and air pollution. Oil spills in the Santa Barbara channel in February 1969 offered an immediate opportunity to act against companies responsible for pollution. Environmentalists, at first upset with the appointment of Walter Hickel as interior secretary, were pleased by his call for stiffer laws governing offshore drilling. In his 1970 State of the Union message Nixon committed himself to improving the "quality of life." He proposed a $10 billion program to clean up the nation's waterways. The federal government would provide $4 billion and the states the other $6 billion. Nixon also responded to concern over air pollution. Conceding that his proposals were greater than any that had come before, most Democrats argued that they were nonetheless inadequate.

On August 15, 1971, Nixon took drastic action against inflation by instituting a freeze for ninety days of wages and prices. At the same time he proposed new tax cuts and called for programs that would add new jobs. The stock market leaped ahead. But labor leaders were not pleased. George Meany called the freeze discriminatory against his AFL-CIO workers, whose wages were frozen while industry received tax benefits. The freeze slowed but did not stop the pace of inflation.

The 1972   In the 1972 election Nixon, again more the liberal
Election   than he was perceived to be, announced lower draft
    calls, more federal aid to black colleges, greater purchases of farm surpluses, and new authority for the Civil Rights Commission to eliminate discrimination against women.

George McGovern received the Democratic presidential nomination from a convention that, in part as a result of his leadership, gave greater representation to women, minorities, and youth. By directing his appeal to the most cohesive and energetic factions within the Democratic Party—youth, peace activists, blacks—McGovern had won key primaries and the nomination, but at the same time the image he gained for being the representative of fringe and dissident groups almost ensured his defeat in November.

While Richard Nixon was maintaining a presidential calm, one of the most interesting political incidents in several decades occurred during the 1972 presidential campaign. During the summer of the election year an odd burglary took place that, though McGovern repeatedly brought it up, aroused little interest among the voters. On June 17 five men were captured inside Democratic National Headquarters in Washington while involved in a bugging and spying attempt.

Much as the pollsters predicted, Americans on November 7 gave

George McGovern, Democratic presidential nominee in 1972, appealed to party activists.
(Courtesy, United Press International Photo)

Richard Nixon 60.8 percent of the popular vote and 521 of 538 electoral votes; only Massachusetts and the District of Columbia went to George McGovern. President Nixon interpreted the overwhelming victory as a great personal mandate, as a prelude to a triumphant second term.

Watergate

Nixon and one of his advisers, John Erlichman, in a glum moment. *(Courtesy, Scribner's Archives)*

During the middle of Nixon's first term, some members of the White House staff had begun to use their power to pursue partisan vendettas. They pointed to the lawlessness of their opponents: antiwar demonstrators had pledged to stop the government; radicals had bombed the Capitol building; Daniel Ellsberg had stolen the Pentagon Papers, documents still secret though the government on its own had arranged them for public release. Nixon's assistants, most of them conservative young lawyers and former advertising men lacking political experience, ignored the traditional rules of Washington politics. By 1972 many of the President's men, claiming that the national interest required Nixon's reelection, justified crimes as necessary for national security.

The Committee to Re-Elect the President (CREEP) organized the burglary in June of Democratic Party offices at the Watergate Building in Washington. A White House official, G. Gordon Liddy, and a man working for him, E. Howard Hunt, recruited a group of anti-Castro Cubans; and CREEP's director of security, James McCord, led this small band of seven people on two raids. The burglars planted microphones and took pictures of files of the Democratic National Committee. During a second raid, a night watchman discovered their entry and called police. Moments later the burglars were under arrest. Evidence at the scene quickly connected them to Liddy and to CREEP.

CREEP Some newspaper reporters continued to investigate the Watergate incident. Amid media speculation, Nixon ordered a staff inquiry and told the public that "what really hurts is if you try to cover up" a crime. A federal grand jury indicted McCord and his accomplices, along with Liddy and Hunt. All pleaded guilty, and thus no trial or legal reckoning could be made. But Judge John Sirica, like many others, doubted that these brief judicial proceedings had solved the Watergate case. Then in mid-March 1973 McCord wrote to Sirica, charging that the White House had pressured the defendants into silence with offers of executive clemency and hush money. Government officials had approved the Watergate burglary, McCord claimed, and conspired also to cover up their own involvement. McCord's letter prompted the Watergate grand jury and the Senate's special Watergate committee, chaired by Sam Ervin of North Carolina, to probe further these mysterious White House activities.

Nixon loyalists could not contain the scandal. One of them, John Dean, thought that the President might blame the whole affair on him, and began to bargain with federal prosecutors from the grand jury. At about the same time, the former deputy chairman of CREEP, Jeb Stuart Magruder, admitted that he had lied in his appearances before the grand jury. He confessed that the bugging of Democratic headquarters was not "a wild scheme concocted by Hunt" but a much-discussed plan, which Attorney General John Mitchell had approved directly. Just at this point, another scandal broke. Two years before, a group of White House operatives authorized to plug security leaks (the "plumbers") had burglarized the office of a Los Angeles psychiatrist treating Daniel Ellsberg. At Ellsberg's trial for theft of government property, the prosecution admitted the illegal entry by the plumbers. The judge found this a violation of Ellsberg's civil rights and declared a mistrial.

Nixon tried to seal off the Oval Office from the spreading ooze of Watergate. Before a national television audience on April 30, 1973, he accepted the responsibility—but not the blame—for the actions of "overzealous subordinates." Absorbed in the business of running the country, he explained, he had failed to monitor their campaigning. He also announced the resignations of John Ehrlichman and H. R. Haldeman, "two of the finest public servants it has been my privilege to know." Dean also left the staff. Under pressure from Congress and even close friends, Nixon appointed a special prosecutor, Harvard law professor Archibald Cox, and promised him "complete independence" to investigate the Watergate affair. These acts provided only temporary surcease for the embattled President.

In the Senate Watergate hearings, Senator Sam Ervin with his shock of white hair and trembling jowls became a national symbol of honor and rectitude. The star witnesses, Magruder and Dean, told their stories. Magruder suggested presidential involvement in the cover-up, and Dean linked Nixon directly with illegal activities. Dean quoted the President as saying that it would be "no problem" to raise a $1 million hush fund and that payments should be made through E. Howard Hunt. Dean swore that Ehrlichman had instructed him to "deep-six" evidence in the Potomac River.

The White House Tapes Then the committee staff stumbled upon a stunning discovery. A former White House aide, Alexander Butterfield, testified that sophisticated recording equipment had taped most presidential conversations for the last two years. Presumably these reels could determine the extent of Nixon's role in the Watergate affair. The Senate committee, as well as Special Prosecutor Cox and the Watergate grand jury, requested segments of the tapes. The President argued that their disclosure would violate the confidentiality of the presidency and erode the separation of powers. A complicated legal battle ensued. Frustrated, Cox finally told a televised press conference that he would ask Judge Sirica to declare the President "in violation of a court ruling" for his delay in turning over a set of tapes. When Nixon fired Cox, the top two officials in the Justice Department quit in protest. This "Saturday Night Massacre" produced an outpouring of popular protest, appearing as it did that Nixon was trying to get Cox before Cox got Nixon.

Persistent scandal seemed to envelop Nixon. Just ten days before the Saturday Night Massacre, Spiro Agnew had resigned the vice presidency to escape a jail term for evading income taxes on bribes from Maryland building contractors. His blatant plea-bargaining—Agnew

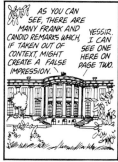

Although Nixon steadfastly denied his complicity in the Watergate affair, his tape recordings of White House conversations told a different story. In this "Doonesbury" cartoon of September 13, 1973, Garry Trudeau expressed one view.-*Reprinted by permission.*

A New Pattern of Abuse?

To the members of Nixon's administration—a group given to delusions of persecution even when things were going their way—the worst feature of the Watergate investigation was that they were being blamed for doing nothing worse than what earlier administrations had done. As a legal defense, this argument did not amount to much. As a historical claim, however, it deserves serious consideration.

The preceding forty years encompassed an enormous growth in the power of the executive branch. Initiative for legislation passed to the Executive; more and more typically, laws established goals such as a cleaner environment or lower unemployment but left to executive agencies the formulation of policies to realize the goals. The Cold War also strengthened the executive branch relative to the other two. Foreign policy came to be shrouded ever more deeply in secrecy. Secret agencies like the Central Intelligence. Agency further extended the executive policy of acting without congressional consent or knowledge.

Such great power invited abuse. And Nixon was not the first President to succumb to temptation. Virtually every abuse had precedents in other administrations. The FBI, for instance, had for thirty years been giving Presidents illegally obtained information about their political opponents. And the Internal Revenue Service had cooperated in harassing those same opponents.

What was new, if anything, in the Nixon presidency was that the pattern of abuse of power ceased to be that of occasional excess. Abuses of power became central to the whole approach to government, for Nixon apparently determined that the executive could become the entire government.

threatened a constitutional crisis unless promised leniency—clashed with his habit of protesting in grandstanding phrases against lawlessness. The smooth working of the Twenty-fifth Amendment soon installed Agnew's successor, House Minority Leader Gerald Ford, as Vice President. Popular with his fellow congressmen, Ford had a plainness and lack of public presence that made him seem always at the margin of events. He would serve briefly as Vice President and then as President, with an integrity plain to the point of colorlessness.

Continuing revelations now plagued Nixon. When the White House finally handed over a few tapes, prosecutors discovered the recordings contained sizable gaps, erasures that technical experts later judged intentional. During the winter of 1973, newspapers had told of Nixon's having become a millionaire while in the White House, paying only minuscule income taxes. Now Nixon accepted the judgment of a congressional committee and a ruling of the Internal Revenue Service that he owed nearly $450,000 in back taxes. Congressional investigators began probing federal expenditures for extensive remodeling of his estates at Key Biscayne, Florida, and San Clemente, California. The Watergate grand jury, now directed by a new special prosecutor, Texas attorney Leon Jaworski, indicted forty-one people for obstruction of justice and other crimes committed during the 1972 campaign. Convinced of Nixon's involvement, yet unwilling to confront constitutional issues, the jurors listed Nixon as an "unindicted coconspirator."

Pressed by public skepticism and a growing pile of subpoenas and court orders for more and more tapes, in late April 1974 Nixon released edited transcripts, not the actual recordings, of meetings concerning Watergate. Even Nixon's version—he had deleted a number of items that damaged his claims of innocence—showed a dubious morality. The new evidence implicated him in the cover-up and openly told of schemes for political revenge against "enemies."

The Final Days

Already at work on articles of impeachment was a judiciary committee of the House of Representatives, twenty-four Democrats and fourteen Republicans. Nixon made a last, double-edged counterattack. His lawyer fought to prevent release of further tapes. Nixon himself spoke to carefully selected audiences, often in the very conservative deep South, hoping for a show of public support. But his statement, "I am not a crook," shocked more than it soothed. And his lawyer-like argument that only criminal acts would justify impeachment sounded like a tacit admission of serious wrongdoing.

During late July and early August 1974, rapid events finally ended any doubts about the President's fate. The Judiciary Committee heard its Democratic and Republican counsels urge impeachment. On July 24 the Supreme Court ordered the White House to turn over sixty-four additional tapes. That same day the Judiciary Committee began its televised debate on impeachment.

It had been feared that Nixon's impeachment would rip the country apart. But to the contrary, people seemed calm, relieved that a constitutional process would soon end months of uncertainty. Though no irrefutable presidential involvement in Watergate had yet surfaced, most Democrats and a few Republicans argued that a pattern of presidential behavior and a mountain of indirect proof implicated Nixon in obstruction of justice. A Maine Republican compared the President's guilt to snow falling in the night: no one saw it happen, but the next morning it was there.

In compliance with the Supreme Court order, Nixon released additional tapes on Monday, August 5. Though they "might damage my case," he still maintained that he had done nothing to justify his removal from office. But almost no one in Washington believed him any more. Among other things, the new transcripts revealed that Nixon had been deceiving his own attorney. After seeing the new evidence, the President's chief of staff, Alexander Haig, began preparations for the accession of Gerald Ford to the presidency. The tape of a conversation on June 23, 1972—Nixon's first day back in Washington after the Watergate break-in—showed the President and Haldeman planning to cloak White House involvement in the crime. Here, after eighteen months of protestations of innocence, was the "smoking pistol." Nixon's defenders on the Judiciary Committee switched their votes, and leading Republican senators visited the White House, telling the President that his removal was a certainty. On August 8, 1974, Richard Nixon told the nation that he would resign, but he still confessed only "wrong judgment," not impeachable offenses.

President Nixon announcing the release of edited Watergate tapes in April, 1974; four months later he resigned his office.

Suggested Readings

Recent books on this period include Marilyn Young, *The Vietnam Wars, 1945–1990* (1991), Melanie Billings-Yun, *Decision Against War: Eisenhower and Dien Bien Phu, 1954* (1988), Larry Berman, *Lyndon Johnson's War* (1989), William Braeman, *William Fulbright and the Vietnam War* (1988), Andrew Rotter, *The Path to Vietnam* (1988), Stanley Karnow, *Vietnam: A History* (1983), Gabriel Kolko, *Anatomy of a War* (1986), Kathleen Turner, *Lyndon Johnson's Dual War* (1985), Bruce Palmer, Jr., *The 25-Year War* (1984), Mark Clodfelter, *The Limits of Air Power: The Bombing of North Vietnam* (1989), and the succinct James W. Gipson, *The Perfect War* (1986), which emphasizes war technology. Guenther Lewy argues in defense of the Vietnam War in *America in Vietnam* (1978). Neil Sheehan studies the war through the biography of John Paul Vann in *A Bright Shining Lie* (1988).

Two good books on events of the year 1968 are Irwin and Debi Unger, *America in the 1960s* (1988) and David Farber, *Chicago '68* (1988).

A good short survey of the Vietnam war is George Herring, *America's Longest War* (2nd ed., 1983). Another good introduction to the war is Frances Fitzgerald, *Fire in the Lake: The Vietnamese and the Americans in Vietnam* (1972). She tells of the disruption of traditional Vietnamese

society as a result of the war and the American presence. Michael Herr, a journalist in Vietnam, writes of the effect of the war on particular American soldiers: *Dispatches* (1977). David Halberstam, *The Best and the Brightest* (1972), contains a mountain of information based on extensive personal interviews. H. Y. Schandler, *The Unmaking of a President: Lyndon Johnson and Vietnam* (1977), explains why Johnson decided in March 1968 not to press the war harder. Schandler argues that the failure of the war came because of an effort to solve by military means a problem that was fundamentally political. Leslie Gelb and Richard Betts explore *The Irony of Vietnam* (1979).

Garry Wills has revised his perceptive *Nixon Agonistes: The Crisis of the Self-Made Man* (1979); see also Richard M. Nixon, *RN: The Memoirs of Richard Nixon* (1978). Carl Bernstein and Bob Woodward's *All the President's Men* (1974), Philip B. Kurland, *Watergate and the Constitution* (1978), John R. Labovitz, *Presidential Impeachment* (1978), and Stanley I. Kutler, *The Wars of Watergate* (1990) are important works. Henry Kissinger's own memoirs, *The White House Years* (1979), should be supplemented by David M. Barrett, *Uncertain Greatness: Henry Kissinger and American Foreign Policy* (1977).

Was the Generation of the Sixties Destructive?

Peter Collier and David Horowitz

From its earliest battle cry—"You can't trust anyone over thirty"—until the end of its brief strut on the stage of national attention, the Sixties generation saw itself as a scouting party for a new world. The "cultural revolution" it was staging would free inmates from the prison of linear thought. It was the social horticulturalist whose "greening of America" would allow the post-industrialist age finally to break through the crust of the Puritan past. It was the avenging angel that would destroy the evil empire of "Amerika" and free the captive peoples of the world.

It is hard to believe in epiphanies now, and it is hard not to wince at these homemade hankerings for Armageddon. Yet while the Sixties, that age of wonders, is over in fact, it is still with us in spirit. Nostalgia artists have made it into a holograph that creates beguiling images of the last good time—a prelapsarian age of good sex, good drugs, and good vibes. For unreconstructed leftists, the Sixties is not just an era of good fun but of good politics too—a time of monumental idealism populated by individuals who wanted nothing more than to give peace a chance; a time of commitment and action when dewy-eyed young people in the throes of a moral passion unknown in our own selfish age sought only to remake the world.

There is truth in the nostalgia. It is the *memory* of the era that is false. The vision we see when we look into the glass of Sixties narcissism is distorted. It may have been the best of times, but it was the worst of times as well. And by this we do not simply mean to add snapshots of the race riots at home and war in Vietnam to the sentimental collage of people being free. It was a time when innocence quickly became cynical, when American mischief fermented into American mayhem. It was a time when a gang of ghetto thugs like the Black Panthers might be anointed as political visionaries, when Merry Pranksters of all stripes could credibly set up shop as social evangelists spreading a chemical gospel.

The Sixties might have been a time of tantalizing glimpses of the New Jerusalem. But it was also a time when the "System"—that collection of values that provide guidelines for societies as well as individuals—was assaulted and mauled. As one center of authority after another was discredited under the New Left offensive, we radicals claimed that we murdered to create. But while we wanted a revolution, we didn't have a plan. The decade ended with a big bang that made society into a collection of splinter groups, special interest organizations and newly minted "minorities," whose only common belief was that America was guilty and untrustworthy. This is perhaps the enduring legacy of the Sixties.

The Sixties are still with us, therefore, as a nostalgic artifact that measures our more somber world and finds it wanting, and also as a goad to radical revival. It has become the decade that would not die, the decade whose long half-life continues to contaminate our own. . . .

Broadly speaking, if there was one event that triggered our reevaluations (and those of others who began to have second thoughts about the Leftism of the Sixties), it was the fate of Vietnam. There was no "new morning" as radicals had predicted, no peasant utopia. Instead, there was a bloodbath greater than the one we set out to oppose and a government worse than the one we had wanted to replace.

Some of the accomplishments were undeniably positive. There *was* an expansion of consciousness, of social space, of tolerance, of prospects for individual fulfillment. But there was a dark side too. In the inchoate attack against authority, we had weakened our culture's immune system, making it vulnerable to opportunistic diseases. The origins of metaphorical epidemics of crime and drugs could be traced to the Sixties, as could literal ones such as AIDS.

Peter Collier and David Horowitz, *Destructive Generation: Second Thoughts About the Sixties* (New York: Summit Books, 1989). Reprinted by permission.

During the '60s Mr. Collier and Mr. Horowitz were editors of the radical, high-flying *Ramparts* magazine. They are candid about the easy way they say *Ramparts* had with the truth, their willful ignorance of brutalities committed by Communist forces in Vietnam, their obstinate clinging to political orthodoxies. In the political milieu they inhabited, ideas, slogans and fantasies were recited as in the fevered dreams of half-sleep. They see themselves as having changed. Have they?

For Mr. Collier and Mr. Horowitz the matter is quite simple. Their radical politics of the '60s were wrong; their conservative politics of today are correct. This assumes that a correct position could have been found amid the realities of a repressive and brutal Vietnamese Communism, a weak and brutal anti-Communist Saigon and an American war that could only pile up bodies. What the authors might have found—what numbers of Americans on both sides of the Vietnam question had found or had possessed from the first— were skepticism, ironic perception, and judgment. But the only concept of discovery offered by the authors of "Destructive Generation" is that of switching sides.

They came to be Reagan supporters, backing the ex-President's Central American policy and attacking liberals and the left. But the large denunciations, the obsession with enemies, the delirium of half-sleep remain. The segment of the left that the authors fix upon is, in effect, their previous selves, which they denounce with the fervor of some party member undergoing public correction. They almost acknowledge that there were leftists who did not think in slogans, but that fact does not instruct them. The antiwar left and the community-action left, the icy liberal empiricists and impassioned Catholic pacifists, the whole brawling movement of the 1960s is shrunk to a strident reductionist polemic in the head of a Peter Collier or a David Horowitz.

Consequently, when the authors talk of the left today, they sound like their comrades of the '60s: sullen journalists discovering the enemy in his malicious and clever manipulation of events. Back then the enemy would have been capitalism or the White House or the Central Intelligence Agency controlling the nation's collective mind; more recently the two were finding agents of Castro or the Sandinistas everywhere and forever at work, starting this or that front, mounting support for the insurgents in El Salvador or against aid to the Nicaraguan Contras. . . .

Are the authors of *Destructive Generation* accurate in their appraisal of the present-day supporters of left revolutionary movements or opponents of this country's foreign policy? They are accurate about that portion of the left that they understand, the portion that is like they used to be. Where there are ideologies, there will be Horowitzes and Colliers, and their likenesses exist today in the ranks of the left and in the legions of the right.

The Reagan and Bush eras are attributable in part to the public identification of liberalism—the "L" word of the 1988 presidential campaign—and the responsible left with the travesty that Mr. Collier and Mr. Horowitz contributed to during their residency at *Ramparts*. Their earlier labors accomplished, they have joined in the exhuming and quartering of the corpse that two decades ago they helped mangle.

Reprinted by permission from *The New York Times Book Review*.

Rescue workers stand in front of the Alfred P. Murrah Federal Building following an explosion Wednesday, April 19, 1995, in downtown Oklahoma City. This catastrophe killed 168 people. *(Courtesy, AP Photo/David Longstrath)*

New Boundaries

THE OKLAHOMA CITY BOMBING

On the morning of April 19, 1995, a powerful explosion devastated the federal building in Oklahoma City. For days afterwards rescuers from across the country worked amidst the debris, some of it dangerously unstable, looking to find and dig out survivors. By a final count 168 people had died, including several children in a day-care center. Two suspects were quickly arrested, partly on the strength of sketches drawn from descriptions by employees of a shop where the two had rented the truck used in the bombing. The country was startled to discover that the biggest terrorist act in its history almost certainly was the work of American superpatriots. Timothy McVeigh was convicted and upon the jury's recommendation received the death sentence.

McVeigh was a skilled combat veteran of the Gulf War who after returning from the Mideast had suffered a bitter failure to become a Green Beret. He was discovered to have connections with a puzzling paramilitary phenomenon beginning to appear in rural areas. Groups of citizens angry with the government and the whole drift of the nation's policy were forming into armed camps. They aimed to oppose taxation, the Brady gun-control law, federal environmentalist regulation of what they conceived to be their property rights, even the very existence of the national government in its present condition. A common belief among their supporters was that sovereignty lies in the smallest units of the nation, notably local government or the individual. They looked to the traditional militia units: little neighborhood armies once charged with protecting their localities against Indian at-

HISTORICAL EVENTS

1953
Simone de Beauvoir publishes
The Second Sex

1963
Betty Friedan publishes
The Feminine Mystique

1964
Civil Rights Act prohibits discrimination in public places

1965
Civil Rights Act sends voting registrars to South

1966
National Organization for Women

1967
"Summer of love"

1968
American Indian Movement (AIM) founded

1969
Woodstock • Theodore Roszak publishes *The Making of a Counter-Culture* • Indians occupy Alcatraz • Stonewall Bar riot

1970
Recession ("stagflation") begins • Kate Millett publishes *Sexual Politics*

continued

continued

tacks or any other threats, and doing some of the fighting during the American Revolution.

Voluntary in membership, in their new form unconnected in any way with state authority, the militia had much that could appeal to inlanders hostile to the federal government. They brought the thrill of drilling with arms. Though not necessarily illegal, they had the character of spontaneous, rebellious resistance to government. Rooted in the immediate community, they represented a confrontation of the outsider, whether that be permissive liberal culture, federal interference, or a shadowy foreign world order reported to be flying unmarked black helicopters.

Among the incidents that fed the militia's rage was the siege in August 1992 by the FBI and other law enforcement bodies of Randy Weaver, a right-winger who, detesting public schools, lived with his family in a simple mountain cabin outside Ruby Ridge in Idaho. He had been charged with illegally selling two sawed-off shotguns, and in a firefight just before the siege an agent engaged in surveillance of the family was killed along with one of Weaver's sons. Another agent was wounded. In the course of the standoff, during which rightist supporters heckled the federal agents and the authorities built a road to convey tanks to the cabin, Weaver's wife was shot and killed as she held her baby in her arms and a friend of the family was wounded. In the end Weaver surrendered. But in the course of the operation the FBI, though trying to negotiate and avoid killings, had blundered. That and the defense's argument that Weaver's earlier arrest had been entrapment made the federal government look bad. He got a light sentence on minor charges and was soon free.

The FBI attack in 1993 upon the Branch Davidian compound in Waco, Texas, militia members perceived as a murderous assault upon the freedom and lives of plain Americans. The Oklahoma City bombing took place on the second anniversary of that event, which had killed ninety-three people, including twenty-five children. The FBI and the Bureau of Alcohol, Tobacco and Firearms were continuing objects of militia rage.

For months after the bombing, the militia movement was a hot topic in the news media and among politicians. Conservatives were looking into the behavior of federal agents at Ruby Ridge and Waco. Herein they were showing a libertarian concern that had escaped them when it was a question of the practices of the Central Intelligence Agency abroad. Liberal Democrats used the bombing to suggest that the antifederal rhetoric of the Republican Party had nourished the mentality of the militia.

The militia movement believes that the integrity of the self-sufficient community must be preserved against the outside. Today's militia members apparently want to be compared to the

Minute Men of the early days of the American Revolution. The two have at least one thing in common: a wish not better to reconnect their neighborhoods with the world beyond but to sever themselves from it. Proclaiming themselves to be individualists, militia members are prepared to surrender their individuality to their neighborhoods that contain not a diversity of minds but a single, unquestioned mind.

The Youth Culture

In the middle years of the 1960s, the student movement had supported the creation of a self-conscious and many-faceted youth culture. The demand for relevant and unprescribed education led to the establishment on some campuses of "free universities"—educational experiments, most of them noncredit, including open registration and courses ranging from traditional academic offerings or political study groups to transcendental meditation and macrobiotic cooking. "Underground" newspapers, made possible by inexpensive offset printing, appeared in every major city. The Berkeley *Barb,* the Los Angeles *Free Press,* the East Village *Other,* and the Atlanta *Great Speckled Bird* carried a mixed assortment: political analysis and polemics, music reviews, discussions of experimental ways of living, inventive graphic art work, and excursions into mysticism, Asian religion, and the effects of drugs believed to be mind-expanding.

Drugs, Sex, and Rock 'n' Roll   While one element of this new counterculture specifically merged with political radicalism, other members were quite aloof from politics. But the counterculture was in one sense political to its very core. Its members saw themselves as developing a way of life radically different from a stifling civilization of militarists, capitalists, and technocratic management. That civilization, so they argued, had produced the war in Vietnam. Even communes formed with no special political purposes required the democratic cooperation that the political left was seeking under the name of participatory democracy: an American future in which citizens would control the institutions bearing upon their daily life.

The beats and the earlier activists who had discovered American folk music provided some of the audience for the urban folk revival of the late fifties and early sixties that popularized authentic performers like Doc Watson, Mississippi John Hurt, and Jean Ritchie. The revival also produced a number of young, topical folksingers, among them Phil Ochs, Joan Baez, and Bob Dylan, who combined their musical talent with political commentary. Then the music hardened as it took in the metallic sounds of rock. Bob Dylan was booed off the stage during the 1965 Newport Rock Festival for using electric instruments in his back-up band, but before long hard rock had won wide acceptance among

HISTORICAL EVENTS

1983
U.S. sends troops to Grenada • 241 marines killed by car bomb in Lebanon and remaining troops are withdrawn • SDI plans announced

1986
U.S. launches air attack against Libya • Iran-Contra affair

1988
USSR withdraws troops from Afghanistan • George Bush elected President

1989
Berlin Wall torn down • Tiananmen Square demonstration in China

1990
East and West Germany united • Clean Air Act of 1990 • savings and loan crisis • Iraq invades Kuwait • Operation Desert Shield

1991
Operation Desert Storm • Rodney King beating • Boris Yeltsin elected president of the Russian Republic • Soviet Union formally dissolved

1992
Bill Clinton elected President • U.S. troops sent to Somalia

1993
NAFTA approved

1994
UN air attacks on Serb positions in Bosnia • Jean-Bertrand Aristide reinstated as president of Haiti • Republicans take both Houses

1995
Oklahoma City bombing • Bosnian peace talks held in Dayton, Ohio • U.S. troops are sent to assist UN forces in maintaining Bosnian peace

1996
Bill Clinton reelected President • Republicans take control of both houses of Congress

the young. By the time of the great music festival and gathering at Woodstock, New York, in 1969—still today a part of the folklore of the sixties—a variety of musical styles belonged to the counterculture.

Estimates of the number of college students who had at least tried marijuana reached by the late seventies as high as one-half. Stronger drugs found more limited use—LSD, hashish, mescaline, and amphetamines. The association of rock with drugs produced innumerable lyrics and a haunting style, softer than the hardest rock, known as acid or psychedelic rock—the special province of San Francisco groups such as the Grateful Dead, the Jefferson Airplane, and Big Brother and the Holding Company. San Francisco's Haight-Ashbury district became the center of 1967's summer of love as thousands of young people swarmed in from across the country. The Grateful Dead gave free concerts in the park; food was distributed by the Diggers, named after a seventeenth-century British sect advocating the abolition of private property. The summer of love also occasioned a minor business boom as hundreds of small entrepreneurs profited from the provision of drug-culture paraphernalia—black-light posters, water pipes, and chrome-plated roach clips. The head shops merchandising such items merely foreshadowed a systematic commercialization of youth movements, culminating in the advertising campaign to "hear the revolution on Columbia Records." Haight-Ashbury soon became a scene of drug addicts and crime.

Dotted across the country were communes, small groups of people living together. Probably the great majority were practical arrangements, among college students or others, for sharing expenses in an era of sexual freedom encouraged by The Pill, the oral birth control breakthrough of the 1960s. Groups of unmarried men and women could now begin to live openly under the same roof. But even in these communes there was the sense that something new was being tried, a free yet family-like association that could be a model for the rest of society.

Theodore Roszak, in *The Making of a Counter-Culture* (1969), wrote about his subject favorably but critically. Charles Reich's *The Greening of America* (1970) exulted that this youthful American generation was beginning to let nature sprout, green and spontaneous, in the sterile present. And today the ecology movement, having as one of its sources the counterculture, insists that the health of civilization depends on the preserving of nature and a careful integration with it.

Gay Rights   Cultural radicalism insisted on toleration and acceptance of varieties of personal behavior, and contributed to a significant modification of one form of bigotry. Gays have lived in jeopardy of their employment. Whether in private industry, government, or teaching, thousands of gay people used to be dismissed upon discovery of their sexual orientation. Worse still has been the social stereotype stamping homosexuals as emotionally ill. Hollywood films, for example, until recently almost invariably portrayed them as sick, vicious, or insipid. Adolescents in secondary school are still particularly savage toward gays, and as a result—so a suppressed Bush Administration report concludes—about one third of teenaged suicides are by gays. Using the civil rights movement as a model, gays have fought these stereotypes and have achieved some notable acceptance.

The Haight-Ashbury district of San Francisco was home to a large hippie community during the late 1960s. *(Courtesy, Wide World)*

In San Francisco, homosexual police and city council members now go about their daily routines like other American citizens. At the 1984 Democratic National Convention in that city, gays were welcomed into that political party and promised substantial funds to fight the sexually transmitted disease of AIDS, which fatally attacks the immune system.

So the current of cultural and political radicalism went in the sixties and after. The mildness of the Port Huron Statement passed to the later anger of SDS and the violence of the Weathermen. The simplicity of folk music translated into the steel clamor of hard rock. The experience of liberation in the days of the civil rights movement anticipated the more exploratory efforts in the counterculture to liberate consciousness. Yet the emphasis on the freeing and cultivation of personal experience could encourage a turning away from community into privacy. And by the 1970s many young Americans were adopting faddish philosophies that advocated one method or another of self-cultivation, to the near exclusion of politics or social concerns.

The Women's Movement

The Nineteenth Amendment to the Constitution, adopted in 1920, provided women with the right to vote. For a time thereafter, women actively participated in politics and social reform movements. After this relatively brief period the women's movement became either a local phenomenon or dormant, not to resurface until the 1960s. Yet during the decades in between the status of women underwent important changes. Some of the most significant occurred in the workforce.

Women in the Workplace During the Depression working women were blamed for taking jobs from men, but women were not flooding the labor market and they earned fifty to sixty-five percent less than men. World War II altered the image of the working woman. More than one out of every three worked for a wage, and almost half who did were married. Educated, white middle-class women were entering the wage-earning force in large numbers.

The end of the war provoked a shift in attitudes. Women were generally idealized as wives and mothers, told to use newly acquired managerial skills to organize the household, arrange the car pools, and run the PTA. Maintaining their family's mental and physical well-being became a full-time commitment for many women. Yet the number of female wage earners was higher than before the war, and continued to rise steadily. They were mainly working in occupations defined as female—clerical jobs, domestic service, elementary school teaching; many other occupations, especially the professions, were largely restricted to men. Women were acquiring a smaller proportion of college degrees than they had forty years before. Still, by 1960 the number of working women was nearly equal to that of men, and by the end of the decade almost nine out of every ten women, regardless of economic or

THE TRAPPED HOUSEWIFE

In Betty Friedan's The Feminine Mystique, *a woman testifies to the feelings of "desperation" that helped to inspire the feminist movement of the seventies and eighties. The mother of four children, she left college at the age of nineteen to get married.*

"I've tried everything women are supposed to do—hobbies, gardening, pickling, canning, being very social with my neighbors, joining committees, running PTA teas. I can do it all, and I like it, but it doesn't leave you anything to think about—any feeling of who you are. I never had any career ambitions. All I wanted was to get married and have four children. I love the kids and Bob and my home. There's no problem you can even put a name to. But I'm desperate. I begin to feel I have no personality. I'm a server of food and putter-on of pants and a bedmaker, somebody who can be called on when you want something. But who am I?"

social background, would be a part of the workforce at some time in their lives.

The women's movement in the late 1960s was closely related to the other reform movements of that period. The protest that the civil rights activists were raising against inequities in American life brought discrimination against women to public attention. And women, who found themselves relegated to secondary positions in the reform movements of the sixties, recognized that even liberalism and radicalism could reflect the injustices they were supposed to denounce.

The first major recognition of women's rights had come when President Kennedy set up the President's Commission on the Status of Women in 1961. Its purpose was to investigate institutional discrimination against women and to provide concrete recommendations for change. The report confirmed that there was widespread discrimination in both the public and the private sector, and it urged the passage of new legislative and administrative laws. Title VII of the 1964 Civil Rights Act prohibited job discrimination because of race, color, religion, sex, or national origin; it is still the most powerful legal tool women possess for fighting inequalities in work. A 1991 civil rights law added some additional protection against sexual harassment.

Literature was probing the status of women. In 1953 Simone de Beauvoir's *The Second Sex,* tracing the subordination of women throughout history, had been published in the United States. In 1963 Betty Friedan's *The Feminine Mystique* questioned the value and satisfaction middle-class women could derive from being housewives. This book, along with Kate Millett's *Sexual Politics* (1970) and Germaine Greer's *The Female Eunuch* (1971), had great impact on some women. Also influential was an anthology of shorter writings entitled *Sisterhood is Powerful,* which presented important articles on housework, marriage, minority-group women, the psychology of women, and a broad range of other topics.

Organizing Politically Women formed their own groups to press for an end to discrimination. In 1963 the Women's Equity Action League was formed to lobby for legislation concerning women's work and education. The National Organization for Women (NOW) was founded in 1966 with Betty Friedan as its first president; it quickly became the largest and most influential women's group. From the beginning the local chapters were autonomous. NOW concentrated on legal challenges, allowed men to join, and functioned as an umbrella covering many disparate tendencies. NOW committed much of its energies to passage of the Equal Rights Amendment, forbidding sexual discrimination on the part of federal or state governments, and to abolishing restrictions on abortion.

Women also carried their demands into state and federal courts, challenging statutes and practices that used sex as a legal classification. At least several states now provide for prosecution of a husband for raping his wife. Attention to these issues, along with others like the plight of battered wives and the need for child care services, have helped the movement reach women on all levels of society. Many activists avoided permanent organizations, forming groups and caucuses to battle within universities, social welfare agencies, neighbor-hoods, hospitals, and places of employment. In 1973 both houses of Congress approved the Equal Rights Amendment, but it failed to gain the necessary ratification in three-fourths of the states.

A Radical Feminism   A less structured movement composed largely of younger, unmarried women developed in parallel with the older, more established women's groups. These feminists held men to be the oppressors of women. They perceived male supremacy as continuous throughout history, perpetuated by stereotyped sex roles learned in childhood. The Red-stockings issued a manifesto in 1969 declaring male supremacy to be "the oldest, most basic form of domination; we need not to change ourselves, but to change men." From within these unstructured, deliberately leaderless groups came the technique of consciousness-raising—small, non-directed discussions in which women shared experiences and feelings concerning men, other women, children, jobs, and housework.

Many women worked to eliminate the traditional stereotype of feminine behavior, challenging sex role identity that begins with the pink blanket in the hospital bassinet. Contraception provided security against unwanted pregnancy and so allowed freer sexual expression. But the sexual permissiveness would also injure women. Some found their sex dehumanized, used to entertain men at topless bars, presented half-clad in multimillion dollar advertising campaigns to sell everything from automobiles to shaving cream. Popular music, and especially masculine rock lyrics—witness the Rolling Stones' "Stupid Girl" and "Under My Thumb"—celebrated primarily women's sexuality, not their intelligence, courage, or character. The lyrics of certain rap groups in the early 1990s were infinitely more demeaning to women.

Radical lesbians argued that existing heterosexual relationships exploited women and that only homosexuality could free women from this oppression. NOW was at first divided on homosexuality; many members felt the issue too controversial and destructive to the movement. But in 1973 NOW adopted a resolution on sexuality fully supporting "civil rights legislation designed to end discrimination based on sexual orientation."

Two young women at Mills College in California learn that their school will remain a woman's institution. *(Courtesy, Jane Cleland, East Setauket, NY)*

Minorities of Old American Heritage

It was predictable that the civil rights movement for black Americans, along with the general political ferment of the 1960s, would attract attention to other ethnic minorities who have suffered discrimination. Hispanic and Native Americans had already engaged in legal and political agitation, and both took further strength from the struggle for black rights. Both needed to come to terms with a dilemma shared among distinctive American ethnicities: how to reconcile their cultures with a common national language and institutions. Like the counterculture, Indian and Hispanic activists acted on the conviction that forms of personal and community expressiveness must be found outside the conformist terms of the larger society. But Indians and Chicanos along with other Hispanics faced problems of poverty and discrimination that required them to deal with the country's dominant institutions as threatening but potentially helpful forces.

The Chicano Movement   Mexican Americans, like other minorities, joined in the civil rights activism of the 1960s. Much of the movement originated among young Mexican Americans who styled themselves "Chicanos"—a shortened term for Mexicano. Many Chicanos sought greater control over their own educational, social, and law enforcement institutions.

In part, the Chicano movement asserted whatever was distinctive to Mexican American society. High school and college students in the Brown Berets called for Hispanic studies programs. Chicano culture gained recognition in theaters, among artists, and in the media. Alongside the celebration of cultural pluralism appeared separatist persuasions. The youthful urban-based Crusade for Justice, founded in Denver, Colorado, in 1965 by Rodolfo Gonzalez, proposed that Chicanos reacquire the Southwest as their own country. The group also sought jobs and social services for Mexican Americans. The more rural *Alianza*, founded by Reyes Lopez Tijerina in 1963, demanded the return of millions of acres in the Southwest to the descendants of those who had lost them despite guarantees in the Treaty of Guadalupe Hidalgo. The leader hoped to establish a string of city-states. To implement his demands, members of the *Alianza* occupied a courthouse in Tierra Amarillo, New Mexico, in 1967. After a massive manhunt, Lopez Tijerina was jailed in 1969, after which his movement declined.

More methodical politics also attracted activists. La Raza Unida, founded in Texas under the leadership of José Angel Gutierrez in 1972, aimed to create a separate political party to control local school boards and rural communities. While the movement gained momentum, it was unable to succeed in the cities. The most far-reaching and successful Chicano effort originated among migrant farm workers. Cesar Chavez,

Cesar Chavez, leader of the United Farm Workers, whose nationwide grape boycott in 1965 brought the plight of migrant farm workers to the attention of the nation. (*Courtesy, AP/Wide World Photos*)

its leader, had also helped establish the Community Service Organization. Migrant workers lived in camps, complete with drafty shanties and a few outdoor toilets and often a single water faucet for an entire camp. Committed like Martin Luther King to Gandhi's nonviolent tactics, and enlisting the support of the Roman Catholic hierarchy, Chavez worked to organize the migrants, a portion of the nation's labor force so poor and so transient that unionism had hardly touched it.

Perhaps drawing on a page from the AFL handbook, Chavez concentrated on the most skilled migrant workers, the grape pickers. In 1965 his United Farm Workers struck growers around Delano, California. The union picketed and Chavez sought a nationwide boycott of grapes. In 1966, one company came to terms, including a wage of $1.75 per hour. Within two years, eleven growers had signed, giving a $2.25 wage and some benefits. Civil rights workers, young people, and ministers aided Chavez's efforts. In 1968, Senator Robert Kennedy's active backing helped Chavez gain the national prominence the UFW needed, and by 1970, half of the hundred or more growers of table grapes came into line. Chavez then successfully unionized the lettuce growers.

Bilingualism   Like other ethnicities, Mexican Americans have struggled with the question of assimilation. Few immigrants came here to cease being who they were and to change their culture. As they accepted the new land and bought into its ways of acquiring and consuming, they little understood what adjustments they needed to make in their cultural heritage to attain those ways.

Nothing personifies the dilemma more than the question of whether state and federal institutions should provide separate Spanish-language facilities for speakers of that language. Not only Anglo-Americans but Hispanics have divided over the issue. Carter's administration

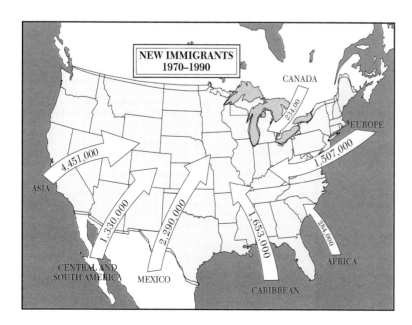

supported it; Reagan's and Bush's opposed it. Some argue that assimilation is inevitable and should take place sooner rather than later, so that the children of Hispanic parents will not be left indefinitely suspended between two languages and two cultures. By shunning the learning of proficient English, Hispanics are largely shutting themselves out of economic opportunities, including the law, medicine, corporate business, and most of the higher paid professions. Supporters of bilingual education claim that the maintenance of a Spanish-language alternative in public schools and other institutions, and thereby the sustenance of Mexican-American culture, will strengthen the pride of young Chicanos.

Native American Activism

The Dawes Severalty Act of 1887 that divided tribal lands among individual families failed to assimilate American Indians. By the 1920s, whites had purchased much of the affected land, while other 160-acre tracts had been divided many times among the heirs and would not support Indian families. Demoralization attended high disease and infant mortality rates, unemployment, illiteracy, malnutrition, and alcoholism.

During the 1920s, reformers in the Indian Defense Association convinced John Collier, a student of Indian life, that the policy embodied in the Dawes Act needed to be at least partially reversed. When he became commissioner of Indian affairs under the New Deal, Collier drew up the Wheeler-Howard Indian Reorganization Act (1934). This measure sought to have Indians regain lost reservation lands and tribally manage their own affairs, as well as formal relations with local and national government. The act also promoted loans for reservation development and funded the training of Indians for hire by the Bureau of Indian Affairs. In World War II the military used Indian languages and Indian translators, notably Navaho, for coded radio communications. During the war, Indian leaders founded the National Congress of American Indians, which at first represented over fifty tribes and eventually doubled in size. It was the first and largest nationwide Indian organization. While promoting education, employment, and health services for Indians and lobbying Congress for beneficial laws, the National Congress sought to develop reservation lands and resources and fought for Indian land claims against the government.

In the early 1950s, the relocation services program provided vocational and housing opportunities to Indians leaving their reservations. But most held unskilled city jobs and lived in wretched conditions. Many drifted back and forth between the city and the familiar and more communal reservation. A policy of terminating the reservations coincided with a lessening of federal support. Indians charged that President Eisenhower was balancing his budget by violating treaty responsibilities and leaving the Indians exposed once again to unfriendly and impoverished state governments. They maintained that termination opened Indian lands to exploitation by timber companies and land developers. The policy was soon abandoned and the government continued to thrash about in search of a coherent and consistent Indian policy.

An Indian encampment in front of the Washington state capitol in 1968 was part of the wider Indian movement calling for return of lands. *(Courtesy, AP/Wide World Photos)*

Native American Protests: the 60s and 70s

In 1961 over 400 Indians from nearly seventy tribes produced a Declaration of Indian Purpose: self-determination, return of reservation lands, improvement of living conditions, and staffing the Bureau of Indian Affairs with Indians. And under Presidents Kennedy, Johnson, and Nixon the national government again advocated cultural pluralism for Indians. Nixon appointed Louis Bruce the first Indian Commissioner of Indian Affairs, and ordered that the bureau operate directly under presidential supervision to become more responsive to the problems of Indians.

In 1968, Dennis Banks and Clyde Bellecourt founded the American Indian Movement (AIM). That the organization began in Minneapolis reflected how urban the Native American experience was becoming. Of the 800,000 American Indians, approximately one-third now live in cities. While AIM took up the cause of earlier reformers—reorganization of the Bureau, return of lands guaranteed by treaty, and Indian home rule—the tactics were much more militant. In 1969 Indians occupied the abandoned prison island of Alcatraz in San Francisco Bay. Led by a New York Mohawk, Richard Oakes, they demanded return of the island as partial payment for broken treaties. The publicity this event brought to the plight of urban Indians led to a series of Indian occupations of urban government property. In 1972, AIM members briefly took over the main offices of the Indian Bureau in Washington, D.C. The most significant protest occurred at Wounded Knee in South Dakota, where in 1890 troops had massacred over 200 Sioux. Radical members of the Oglala Sioux and leaders of AIM seized and held the town. Led by Dennis Banks and Russell Means, they demanded the restoration of treaty lands. After seventy-one days, two deaths, and several gunfights between the Indians and heavily-armed National Guardsmen and FBI agents, the protesters surrendered. Over 300 were arrested. Most, including Banks and Means, were acquitted on legal technicalities. By the end of the 1970s, Native Americans all over the country, often with much later success, began lawsuits to recover their treaty rights and lands.

In 1973 members of the American Indian Movement staged a 71-day protest at Wounded Knee, South Dakota, the site of the 1890 massacre of two hundred Sioux by U.S. soldiers. The use of guns in the takeover was reminiscent of the style of some black militants. *(Courtesy, Library of Congress)*

A Quiet Presidency: Gerald Ford, 1974–1977

On August 9, 1974, as Nixon went into many years of seclusion, his Vice President Gerald Ford took the presidential oath of office. The new Chief Executive found trust, even respect, from a country eager to put Watergate to rest. He and his staff intentionally shed the imperialist trappings of the Nixon years. "I'm a Ford, not a Lincoln," he quipped to White House reporters. Americans watched the President fix his own muffins for breakfast. Ford liked people: the folksy politician sometimes shook hands with surprised tourists waiting in long lines to visit the White House. He experimented with low-key talks on television to explain complicated economic issues and held as many press conferences and delivered as many speeches in eighteen months as

President Gerald R. Ford on his first morning in the White House, toasting the English muffins he and his wife Betty enjoyed for breakfast.

Nixon had in five years. The new President smiled a lot, mispronounced a few words, and soon charmed the nation. Within weeks after his inauguration, President Ford had pardoned Nixon for "any and all crimes."

South Vietnam Collapses

However much this open affability contrasted to Nixon's moody self-isolation, Ford could not escape his predecessor's legacies. Henry Kissinger, who during Nixon's presidency had moved from chief of the National Security Council to secretary of state, stayed on in that office. Yet even his wizardry did not slow the final collapse of South Vietnam. The cease-fire there so laboriously worked out had never really functioned. North Vietnam increased its troop levels in the South, contrary to the Paris agreements, and stepped up its propaganda campaign. Intermittent war returned again to most of South Vietnam. Nguyen Giap, Hanoi's legendary general, planned a giant assault by both Vietcong and North Vietnamese soldiers for the spring of 1975. Growing chaos in the South facilitated his scheme: Nguyen Thieu arrested opponents indiscriminately, banned political parties, closed down newspapers and television stations. The end came suddenly. Hard-pressed by enemy attacks, Thieu retreated from the three northernmost provinces of South Vietnam. Giap's troops turned retreat into

In April 1975, as the South Vietnamese army fled toward Saigon, hundreds of thousands of South Vietnamese citizens followed suit. Scenes like this one in Xuan Loc were reported as people attempted to board American helicopters that had brought supplies to the army. Few could be accommodated in this hopeless scramble. *(Courtesy, U.P.I.)*

rout. They overran the southern capital of Saigon on May 1, 1975, renaming it Ho Chi Minh City.

Just three weeks after the Communist victory in South Vietnam, the Khmer Rouge triumphed in neighboring Cambodia. During the confusion, overzealous Cambodian local commanders seized an American merchant vessel, the *Mayaguez,* and jailed its crew for smuggling contraband. Ford sent a naval task force and nearly 2,000 marines to rescue the thirty-one Americans involved. Either the show of force or a sincere Cambodian wish to make amends brought the release of the Americans. Kissinger traveled quietly in western Europe, reassuring NATO allies that the United States would never yield to neo-isolationists. The White House blocked all congressional efforts to cut military spending or reduce the number of American troops stationed overseas. Ford also committed an act notable for a politician: he followed his conscience in defiance of the popular will. Public opinion was hostile to the admission of refugees. The President let into the country thousands of Vietnamese, along with Cambodians and Laotians, in flight from victorious Communist forces.

Stagflation   As the American involvement in Vietnam faded and the resignation of President Richard Nixon ended, in the words of Gerald Ford, the "national nightmare," the United States might have expected a moment of calm. But that calm was marred by a curious new kind of economic discontent. The economy of the 1970s was unique in suffering from unemployment and inflation at the same time. Pundits named the problem "stagflation." During the decade the unemployment rate fluctuated between 5.8 and 11 percent, while inflation ranged from 6 to 13 percent.

Back in the late 1960s, when the Vietnam War was at its peak, the inflation spiral began modestly, and President Lyndon Johnson could have dealt with it by raising taxes. But because the Vietnam War was so unpopular at home, Johnson did not think it politically possible to raise taxes. So although steep increases in federal spending took place during the late 1960s and early 1970s, there were no offsetting tax increases. Consumer purchasing power helped drive up prices. But the biggest culprit in creating the economic trouble of the 1970s was the energy crisis.

The Energy Crisis and the Middle East   During the 1950s and 1960s, American oil consumption had boomed, but an increase in imports of cheaper foreign crude oil drove down American petroleum production. The United States became increasingly dependent on foreign suppliers, especially the Arab countries.

Ford took up Kissinger's formulas for stability in the Middle East. Leaders in the Arab world, particularly Egypt's Anwar Sadat, resented the relative inactivity of Moscow, once thought to be an ally, during the 1973 war with Israel that Egypt narrowly lost. Kissinger thought peace possible if the Arabs should come to realize that only Washington, not Moscow, could prod Israel into returning Arab lands Israel had occupied during the Six Days' War of 1967. He delicately negotiated into a

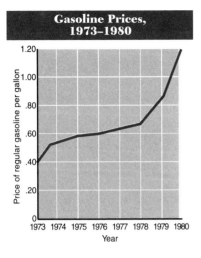

Gasoline Prices, 1973–1980

narrow band of agreement the wide space of hatreds separating Jew and Arab. By the fall of 1975, after more rounds of shuttle diplomacy, he secured a cease-fire. Sadat dropped old Egyptian dreams for uniting the Muslim world and rejected demands by Arab militants for Israel's destruction. In return for this long-sought right to exist, the Israeli Knesset promised to restore some of Egypt's lost territories in the Sinai peninsula. The United States underwrote the arrangement, pledging still more military aid to the Israelis and technological aid for the Egyptians. But Israel held most of its occupied lands.

Resenting Western friendship with Israel, the Arabs established oil embargoes. For the first time since World War II, consumers faced fuel shortages and long waiting lines to purchase gasoline. At the same time, the Organization of Petroleum Exporting Countries (OPEC) announced huge increases in oil prices. Before 1973, crude oil prices averaged only $3 a barrel, but by 1975 they would jump to more than $12 a barrel. Gasoline prices rose steadily in the years following the Arab oil embargo, as did the prices of coal and natural gas. Since energy is a principal ingredient in the manufacture and shipment of all products, producers had to increase their prices. The inflation rate in the United States leaped. At the same time, because consumers were spending so much more of their income on energy, they had less money to spend on other consumer goods, and the economy slowed. Companies began laying off workers in large numbers. The result was stagflation.

The Carter Years, 1977–1981

Carter vs. Ford
The presidential election of 1976 was the first in twelve years not haunted by the conflict in Vietnam. An unknown southern governor, Jimmy Carter, blitzed state primaries and captured the Democratic nomination. Ronald Reagan of California challenged his party's incumbent in the White House, Gerald Ford, and almost won.

In the campaign against Ford, Carter argued for full employment, the government if necessary acting as "an employer of last resort" for those unable to find work in the private sector. Carter offered to "avoid future Vietnams." Ford bumbled during a public debate with Carter, telling a stunned American audience that the Soviet Union "does not dominate eastern Europe." Carter won the election by reassembling Franklin Roosevelt's coalition of urban East and upper Midwest with southern Gulf and border states. Democrats swept congressional races, establishing a two-thirds majority in the House and a margin of 62 to 38 in the Senate.

Jimmy Carter
Carter promised an open presidency, a frugal and efficient White House staff, a chief executive in touch with the people. He began his presidency with symbols reminiscent of Andrew Jackson. Dispensing with traditional limousines, he and

his family walked down Pennsylvania Avenue after the inauguration. Carter tried to dismantle what has become known as the "imperial presidency." The phrase refers to the resolution on the part of recent administrations to invest the White House with majesty, an aura of secret doings of worldwide importance, and as much power as it can possibly wield, directed especially in foreign policy. But the former Georgia governor relied more and more upon his own staff, mostly young people from his home state with little national experience. Relations with Capitol Hill quickly deteriorated.

The President's attempts to deal with the nation's queasy economy speeded his decline. Carter did attempt to close loopholes in income taxes that favored the rich, deriding deductions like "the three martini business lunch." But lobbyists eventually killed most of his reform measures. A spurt in consumer spending boosted the inflation rate to thirteen percent by 1978 and 1979, scaring Carter away from expensive projects. The Federal Reserve Board tightened credit sharply. Interest rates rose to record levels in late 1979; even the most reliable borrowers paid over fifteen percent. Yet the expected slowdown did not soon materialize. The credit crunch did affect the automobile industry and housing starts, but retail sales and personal income pushed ahead while unemployment dropped under six percent. Carter unsuccessfully tried to talk down inflation with voluntary guidelines.

Energy Problems   Energy preoccupied President Carter. He proposed a two-track solution. Selective taxes could discourage gas-guzzling cars and promote home insulation. Lowered thermostats, more carpooling, government aid to mass transit, all could conserve scarce fuel. An extensive chain of nuclear power stations would further reduce dependence on fossil fuels and cut pollution at the same time. Most of these proposals succumbed to lobbying and—above all—public apathy. The accident at the Three Mile Island nuclear plant galvanized protests against atomic power, already much delayed by bureaucratic regulation. Environmentalists blocked planned conversion to coal, a far greater pollutant than oil. Solar power advocates denounced Carter for virtually ignoring the earth's only renewable source, sunlight. For four years interest groups debated, largely canceling one another out. Cosmetic conservation substituted poorly for what Carter once had called "the moral equivalent of war."

Human Rights   The Democratic President embraced détente with the Soviet Union, an American peace for the Middle East, and closer cooperation with old European allies. He completed the process of submitting to the Senate a treaty with Panama looking to the return of the Panama Canal Zone to that country. The action much aroused nationalist opposition in the United States, though the treaty did get barely by the Senate. But Carter added at least one element of his own. From the beginning, he spoke eloquently of "human rights." Breaking with the policy of both liberal and conservative predecessors, he put the United States into moral confrontation with right-wing regimes that employed repression and torture—

During the Carter years Middle Eastern countries joined to slow exports of oil, driving up fuel prices and causing long lines of cars to wait for gasoline. Some service stations ran out entirely.

regimes and tactics that the United States would once have accepted as necessary for the conquest of Communism.

Deregulation   For decades businessmen and Republican politicians had complained that excessive government regulation drove up the cost of doing business and contributed to inflation. During the Carter Administration Democrats adopted the idea of deregulation as a way of dealing with stagflation. They wanted to slow inflation without provoking worse unemployment, and it seemed that deregulation would cut business costs, restore price competition in some industries, and, as a result, slow the rise in prices.

Ever since the 1930s the Civil Aeronautics Board had regulated the airline industry. It determined the freight rates and ticket prices the airlines could charge and which routes the airlines could fly. Although regulation created a safe environment for capital investment in the industry, it also lessened any incentives among the carriers for competition and pushed up ticket prices. During the 1970s, primarily in California and Texas, new airlines appeared that were free of CAB controls because they flew only within one state. They were able to operate at profitable levels while offering extremely cheap fares to customers. In 1978 Congress passed the Airline Deregulation Act, providing for the phaseout of the CAB over a six-year period, free entry of airlines into new routes, and the basing of airfares on competition. The result, over the next several years, was a sharp decrease in ticket prices, an equally sharp increase in ridership, and the bankruptcy of several air carriers.

Congress passed the Motor Carrier Act of 1980 to deregulate the trucking industry. At the time the Interstate Commerce Commission controlled trucking, setting freight rates, determining routes, and limiting access to the business. These controls kept freight rates high. The new legislation withdrew from the government the power to control access, rates, and routes. The Rail Act of 1980 brought a measure of deregulation to the railroad industry by allowing railroad executives to negotiate mergers with barge and trucking lines without securing prior approval.

The Depository Institutions Deregulation and Monetary Control Act of 1980 deregulated the banking industry. The new legislation allowed banking institutions to compete with one another by paying whatever interest rates the market would bear and by allowing any of them to write home mortgages, extend commercial loans, and underwrite securities issues.

In time deregulation was to bring disaster to the banking industry, since it allowed banks and similar institutions to participate in the greedy irresponsibilities of the 1980s. Nor did it solve Jimmy Carter's political problem. Whatever might be the economic effects of deregulation in years to come, the President only had a few months before the election of 1980. Americans in the late 1970s were frustrated at their economic predicament. Carter often appeared on television for his version of Franklin Roosevelt's "fireside chat," but he usually spoke of belt tightening and the hard truth that Americans could not keep living in the future the way they had lived in the past. Carter's problem, of

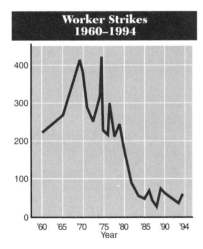

Deregulation probably contributed to the decline of organized labor's strength.

course, was that most Americans wanted to continue doing just that, and they wanted to hear the old, traditional messages of progress, prosperity, and power. With the election of 1980, Jimmy Carter would find himself in an impossible position because Republican candidate Ronald Reagan was telling the public just what it wanted to hear.

International Relations   Carter and his national security adviser, Zbigniew Brzezinski, were both anxious to control strategic nuclear weapons. The first SALT treaty under Richard Nixon had not cut into either superpower's stockpile; it only limited future production. The next logical step was balancing existing weaponry into a rough equilibrium. Three years of negotiating followed. Despite foot-dragging by the military services on both sides, a second SALT treaty was in place by early 1979. It provided caps on the total number of intercontinental ballistic missiles (ICBMs), missiles carrying multiple independent targetable re-entry vehicles (MIRVs) and other strategic nuclear weapons. Distrust of the Soviet Union slowed SALT II progress in the Senate; then the Soviet leader Leonid Brezhnev's invasion of Afghanistan stalled the ratification procedure altogether early in 1980. The collapse of further nuclear arms agreements illustrated the fragility of relations between the Soviet Union and the United States. Brezhnev resented Carter's call for human rights, which was directed against the Soviet Union and other Communist regimes as well as against right-wing anti-Communist governments.

Carter continued Kissinger's plans for an American presence in the Middle East. He pressured Israel for concessions to convince Arab moderates, like Egypt's Anwar Sadat, that the United States, not the Soviet Union, could best ensure return of their occupied lands. Runaway inflation in Israel and a nightmarishly backward economy in Egypt further encouraged the two enemies toward compromise. In 1978 at a ceremony at the White House after meetings at Carter's vacation home of Camp David, Sadat and his Israeli counterpart, Menachem Begin, finally signed a peace treaty. Egypt formally recognized Israel's right to exist; in turn, the Israelis restored the Sinai to the Egyptians. Other issues, like the future status of Jerusalem and the

The 1978 meeting of Israeli Prime Minister Menachem Begin (left), Egyptian President Anwar Sadat (right), and President Jimmy Carter at Camp David, Maryland, resulted in a historic treaty between Israel and Egypt, but did not bring peace to the volatile Middle East. *(Courtesy, AP/Wide World Photos)*

Palestinian refugees, remained unresolved. But hopes for stability in the Middle East, a region vital to American security and energy needs, quickly evaporated.

The Ayatollah Khomeini.

President Jimmy Carter wrote in his diary two days after the United States embassy was taken over in Tehran:

"It's almost impossible to deal with a crazy man [Khomeini] . . . and the world of Islam will be damaged by a fanatic like him should he commit murder in the name of religion. . . . We will not release the Shah, of course, as they demand."

The Ayatollah Khomeini
Washington long had supported the Shah of Iran in his efforts to modernize that country; huge amounts of Iranian crude oil were exchanged for sophisticated technological apparatus and military weapons. But religious fundamentalists among the country's Muslims, together with rebels angry at the Shah's dictatorial rule, combined to overthrow the monarchy early in 1979. Their leader, the Ayatollah Khomeini, turned his back on everything Western, cutting oil exports by one-third, reviving Islamic social customs, halting the drive toward modernization.

Then, in a dramatic campaign to consolidate his personal power, Khomeini unleashed a torrent of anti-American propaganda. "Students" stormed the American embassy in Tehran and held hostage Americans still working there. The militants demanded that the United States extradite the Shah, then at a hospital in New York City, to stand trial for crimes against the Iranian people. Until he returned, the Americans would remain hostage. Carter, publicly at least, refused to negotiate with the outlaws and slowly increased pressure against the Iranians, securing United Nations condemnation of the act and squeezing the country with economic sanctions.

In his dealings with the hostage crisis, sharpened by television pictures of mobs in Tehran mocking the United States, Carter usually exhibited patience. But in April 1980 he approved a reckless rescue operation that ended in failure with eight American lives lost. Otherwise he outwaited the Iranians and allowed the more sensible elements in that nation to negotiate the release of the hostages. On the inauguration day of Carter's successor, Ronald Reagan, they were released, and the United States had made no significant concession to the mobs.

Brezhnev meanwhile began a daring Soviet adventure in the Middle East. In December 1979 the Soviet Union attacked neighboring Afghanistan, invading the country with an army of up to 200,000 soldiers. A Marxist regime had come to power there some years earlier, but the same Islamic backlash that had seized Iran now operated against the pro-Russian rulers in Kabul. When tribal resistance almost toppled the new regime, its leaders appealed to Moscow for help. The Red Army overran the backward country but proved unable to deal with a guerrilla resistance movement reminiscent of that in Vietnam. The White House cut grain shipments to the Soviet Union, boycotted the 1980 Moscow Olympics, and finally decided to furnish the Pakistan dictatorship, a staunch American ally, with military weapons. Nothing budged the Soviet Union from the Afghan conquest.

More Stagflation
The rise to power of the Ayatollah Khomeini also had important effects on the American economy. During the last year of the Shah's regime, Iran had been one of the world's largest producers of petroleum. The revolution that brought the Ayatollah back to Tehran disrupted the Iranian economy and seriously reduced Iranian oil production. The shrinking world

oil supplies pressed oil prices skyward. Between 1979 and 1981, the price went from about $16 to as high as $36 a barrel. The effects in the United States were immediate. Gasoline rose from about 60 cents to $1.30 a gallon, and the prices of natural gas, kerosene, coal, and home heating fuel went up at similar rates. Again there appeared lines outside gasoline stations, violating the American expectation of being able to drive anywhere, at any time, with plenty of gas available along the way. The inflationary spiral got worse and as Americans pumped more money into their gas tanks and home heaters and therefore less into the rest of the economy, the country began slipping toward recession.

The Reagan "Revolution"

The New Right   Ronald Reagan, elected to the presidency in November 1980, represented the portion of Republican conservatism that had its roots in the new-money regions of the South and West, fertilized by funds from Texas and Oklahoma oil tycoons and southern California real estate developers. His Republicanism was of the freewheeling Sunbelt style. He was the standard-bearer of the New Right, a broad, loose coalition of conservative idealists, fundamentalist Christians, and neo-populist voters who deplored the liberal social, political, and economic forces of the sixties and hoped to see them reversed.

The New Right was ardent in support of free markets and a determined enemy of government intervention. Some of its adherents were disciples of Milton Friedman, the University of Chicago economist who spoke for a largely unhindered capitalism. In the 1970s many were pulled to the supply-side economic theories of Arthur Laffer, who argued for drastic tax cuts. The money left in private hands, Laffer assumed, would go into investment. The consequent increase in production could ease inflation while providing an increase in revenues for the federal government, which though taxing a smaller percentage of the country's wealth would have created a more productive and therefore wealthier country to tax.

President Ronald Reagan.
(Courtesy, Michael Evans, The White House)

The Religious Right   A major component of this New Right was religion. All through the seventies numbers of inhabitants of the nation's Protestant heartland, along with some members of the Jewish and Roman Catholic urban communities, had nursed their anger at social and moral permissiveness. Many pious communicants of the Protestant evangelical denominations that emphasized the literal truth of Scripture feared for Christian civilization. They recoiled from the irreverence of the young, the rising rate of divorce and illegitimacy, the growing assertiveness of feminists and gays, the spread of pornography, the gulping down of drugs, the increasing availability of abortion, and the breakdown of the family. Evangelical conservatives traced these evils to "secular humanism," a term they applied to the liberal temperament of a heterogeneous, pluralistic society. Under Jerry Falwell, a Baptist minister of Lynchburg, Virginia, the Moral Majority pledged to fight for federal laws to restrict abortion and check the spread of crime, pornography, and drugs, and to seek the reversal of federal court rulings against prayer in the public schools.

One final source of Reaganite inspiration was neoconservatism. The neoconservatives were former liberals repelled by what they perceived as the social and political excesses of the 1960s and early 1970s. They were also unhappy with Nixon's détente with the Soviet Union as continued under Ford and extended under Carter. They charged that the United States was allowing the Soviet Union to become a far more dangerous adversary than ever before. Hiding behind soft words about coexistence and arms limitations agreements like SALT I and SALT II, so argued the neoconservatives, the Soviet Union had surpassed the United States in arms. And it had been encouraged to engage in reckless adventures like the Afghanistan invasion and to support terrorism and revolutionary movements around the world.

The 1980 Election   The rising right-wing tide contributed powerfully to the 1980 presidential victory of Ronald Reagan. The Moral Majority worked for the Republican ticket, and conservative PACs (political action committees) targeted for defeat liberal senators and representatives. Reagan promised to work for stricter laws against pornography, drugs, and crime, oppose federal cooperation with abortion on demand, push a major increase in defense spending, and reverse American retreat around the world. During the Republican nomination race, Reagan's chief rival, George Bush, had called the supply-side theory—whereby lowered taxes would stimulate the economy— "voodoo economics," but a major tax cut remained part of the Republican agenda.

Energizing the political right, Reagan's candidacy dismayed many in the center and the left. Carter, the Democratic incumbent, was fighting an uphill battle for reelection. The Iran hostage crisis held him in thrall. At first the seizure of the American embassy personnel in Tehran back in November 1979 had encouraged national unity. But as the weeks and months passed without a resolution the administration came to look feeble and, after the disastrous attempt at a military rescue, reckless as well. And in the economy Carter had an even greater liability. Reagan received nearly 44 million popular votes to Carter's 34.7 million and won the electoral votes of all but four states. In the new Congress the Republicans would control the Senate for the first time since the 1950s and confront a reduced Democratic majority in the House. Conservatives claimed that the election was a conservative mandate. The Democratic defeat shook the confidence of liberals.

Reaganomics

Reagan's brief inaugural attacked both swollen government and swollen federal budgets and blamed them for the country's economic plight. "In this present crisis," he declared, "government is not the solution to our problem; government is the problem." He proposed cutting taxes and unleashing individual enterprise. He pronounced the United States "a beacon of hope throughout the world" and warned "the enemies of freedom" that they should not underestimate the nation's resolve to protect its "national security."

PATCO   The attitude on the part of Reagan conservatism toward unions, a long-standing component of the country's liberal coalition, had a demonstration when the members of the Professional Air Traffic Controllers' Organization (PATCO) went on strike for higher wages and for relief from the stress to which their job subjected them. The President fired them for violating the pledge against strikes that the controllers, like other federal employees, had been required to sign as a condition of working for the government. PATCO was one of the handful of unions that had endorsed Reagan in 1980. Soon unions found that the National Labor Relations Board, in the past a customary supporter of unions, and the Department of Labor as a whole were demonstrating a new sympathy for the self-interest of employers.

Tax Policy   The key to the administration's policy, and its first order of business, was a simultaneous tax cut and drastic reduction in the federal budget. David Stockman, director of the Office of Management and Budget, would eliminate "waste and fraud" and cut out expensive domestic programs inherited from the Great Society.

For his program the President needed opposition votes in the House, where the Democrats had a formal party majority. Reagan was widely admired in the South and West and by persuasion, charm, and the judicious use of patronage was able to win over a contingent of conservative Democrats, who became known as the Boll Weevils. Near disaster also came to the President's aid. On March 31, as he was leaving a Washington hotel, Reagan was shot and seriously wounded by an unbalanced young man. For a time the President's life was in serious danger, but he made an amazingly rapid recovery. During the crisis and his recuperation, press reports of his bravery, humor, and good spirits sent his popularity ratings soaring. When he appeared before a joint session of Congress in late April to support his economic policies, he received a standing ovation. Thereafter Reagan's tax and budget cut programs had relatively clear going.

The 1982 budget cuts slashed over $35 billion in domestic outlays from the proposed Carter budget while adding over $12.3 billion in defense. The new budget reduced education appropriations by almost fifty percent, canceled the Carter synthetic fuels program, and contracted proposed funding for housing, health, food stamps, school lunches, environmental protection, and the National Endowment for the Arts and its counterpart for the Humanities. The Economic Recovery Tax Act enacted a 25 percent cut in personal income taxes spread over three years, reduced the maximum income tax from 70 to 50 percent, sharply increased the individual exemption for inheritance taxes, and reduced the tax on capital gains.

The Professional Air Traffic Controllers' Organization (PATCO) was one of the few unions to support Reagan in the 1980 campaign. But when PATCO struck in August 1981, Reagan unhesitatingly fired the striking air traffic controllers, and he refused to hire them back when the strike collapsed. *(Courtesy, Bettmann Archives)*

The Reagan Economy

In 1982 the country suffered the most severe recession since the 1930s. The slump was not the administration's fault. In order to check the runaway inflation of the late 1970s, Paul Volcker, head of the Federal Reserve Board of Governors, had imposed heavy interest rates, in effect slamming down hard the nation's economic brakes. By late 1983 the recession had lifted and unemployment began to fall. By the following year, just in time for the presidential race, the country was enjoying a burst of prosperity combined with a slowing of price increases.

Reagan insisted that despite all the cuts in social programs, the administration would preserve a "safety net" to keep the truly poor and unfortunate from destitution. Economic growth, meanwhile, would benefit everyone.

That is not how it worked out. The economy did rebound and produced countless new jobs. They came just in time to absorb a flood of young adults. But a large proportion of the new employment slots were at low wages. Far more Americans proportionately would soon be working in fast food restaurants and supermarkets at a few dollars an hour than in steel mills and auto plants at $20 an hour as many had a decade before. Adult children could not expect on average to exceed their parents' income: a major component of the American Dream, which Reagan was supposed to have restored, was fading.

While those at the lower end of the income scale lost real income, the rich were gaining it disproportionately. By 1988, the top five percent of income receivers were paying a far smaller proportion of their income as taxes than before 1980. More important than tax breaks was the sheer size of the income explosion among top earners. Even if wealth is calculated without inflation, between the late 1970s and late 1980s the number of millionaires in the United States doubled.

If federal expenses were not to conform to the wishes of the administration, could it hope for a growth in tax revenue sufficient to control the deficit? Reaganite supply-siders had predicted that a cut in tax rates would so stimulate the economy that the government would in time actually be collecting more taxes. Federal budget receipts did rise—from $602 billion in 1981 to $909 billion in 1988—but this was not enough to offset a surge of spending, much of it going to the longest expansion in arms in peacetime history. To offset the perceived Soviet danger, the administration poured billions into the military. Between 1980 and 1985 defense outlays rose about forty percent. Annual federal deficits soared. In 1981 the deficit was $58 billion. By 1986 it was over $220 billion. In 1988, despite attempts under the Gramm-Rudman-Hollings Act that mandated automatic cuts in federal outlays, the total federal debt had risen to more than $2.3 trillion. Interest payments on the deficit absorbed billions of dollars of savings each year that might have been used for upgrading the nation's schools and highways and its private factories and machinery.

And Reaganomics did not restore American international competitiveness as promised. Instead, Americans seemed incapable of resisting foreign goods, such as Japanese cars and VCRs, and since foreigners wanted fewer American goods than formerly, United States trade deficits grew. For a century the country had run surpluses with its

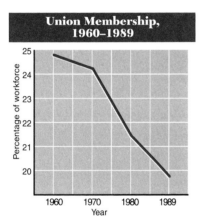

Union Membership, 1960–1989

foreign trading partners. This changed drastically during the 1970s and 1980s. By 1980 the yearly trade deficit was $40 billion; by 1988 it was $140 billion. These deficits had to be paid for by borrowing abroad. Before the end of the decade the United States was borrowing far more from foreign lenders to satisfy its insatiable appetite for foreign goods than it was lending. It was an international debtor, with billions of dollars going overseas to pay the interest on money owed.

Reagan Foreign Policy

At the core of early Reaganite foreign policy was the conviction that the Soviet Union was behind virtually all the world's disturbances and discords. The USSR, the President told a meeting of evangelical clergymen in 1983, was an "evil empire" with "aggressive impulses." The enormous arms buildup was the most tangible expression of this attitude. But much of foreign policy reflected the same feeling.

When early in Reagan's first term the Polish government, presumably in accordance with Moscow's wishes, suppressed the rebellion of Solidarity, an anti-Communist Polish trade union movement, Reagan imposed sanctions on the Soviet Union. After a Soviet fighter plane shot down a Korean civilian airliner that had strayed off course, Reagan denounced the USSR in terms that increased the ill feelings about an already wretched incident. In the Middle East, the administration tilted more toward Israel than any of its predecessors had done, perceiving that nation as a right-of-center ally against leftist movements.

Central America — Reagan blamed Soviet intrusion, much of it through its Cuban surrogate, for fomenting the spirit of revolt in Central America. The United States had traditionally considered Central America its backyard, where its will was unchecked. During Carter's administration, in both El Salvador and Nicaragua left-wing guerrilla movements had risen to challenge the existing conservative regimes. In Nicaragua, the Sandinistas, led by Daniel Ortega, overthrew the dictator Anastasio Somoza in 1979 and imposed an authoritarian regime. Reagan's administration saw the hand of Moscow and Cuba's Fidel Castro behind the Sandinistas and feared the spread of unfriendly regimes in the Western Hemisphere. Before long the United States was mining Nicaraguan harbors to keep Cuban and Soviet aid from reaching the Sandinistas, and was supplying guns, food, uniforms, and military advice to the Contras, a band of guerrillas seeking to overthrow the Ortega regime. Many people in the United States worried about involvement in a long, unwinnable war like that in Vietnam. Some suspected that Reagan was seeking merely to replace an authoritarian leftist government with an authoritarian rightist regime. Congress was also skeptical of the administration's Nicaragua policies and over the administration's protest worked to cut off all but humanitarian aid to the Contras.

Behind the particular quarrels between the administration and its critics over Central America lay a broader difference. The Carter presidency had abhorred the Communist systems for the whole range of repressions of freedom they carried out. But it had also abhorred the repressive acts of right-wing anti-Communist regimes, which had a particular taste for relentless and sophisticated torture. Reaganites, to the contrary, took their instructions from political theorists who made subtle distinctions between brutality imposed by the left, which they found to be Satanic, and brutality imposed by the right, which they decided to be not so very bad.

The Reagan White House was not totally insensitive to the evils of the right. It threw its influence behind the presidential candidacy of a moderate, Napoleon Duarte, in El Salvador, and urged a program there of redistribution of land. But in the end it was prepared to support any anti-leftist movement or government. It urged military assistance to Guatemalan regimes distinguished for their viciousness, while Congress balked. When Guatemala acquired later in the decade a barely civilian government thought to be somewhat more sympathetic to human rights, however, Reagan's administration did express its genuine approval.

In October 1983 the administration sent troops to the tiny West Indian island of Grenada, where a leftist coup had overthrown a government also on the left. After a few days of fighting with Grenadan and Cuban forces, the United States occupied the island.

World Affairs   The administration briefly entangled itself in Lebanon. That small nation north of Israel had become a battleground for many contending groups in the Middle East—Christian against Muslim; Shiite Muslim against Sunni; Jew against Arab; Syrian against Iranian. It was the headquarters of several terrorist bands, some of which had taken American journalists, academics, and businessmen as hostages to force Israel and the United States to meet their demands for release of Arab prisoners. What especially hurled that nation into turmoil was an Israeli invasion in 1982 with the aim of destroying bases of the Palestine Liberation Organization. Israel was unable to extricate itself from Lebanon, and its Lebanese Christian allies carried out a massacre of hundreds of Palestinian refugees for which world opinion held Israel accountable. Hoping to impose calm on that chaotic nation in 1982, the United States sent marines to Lebanon as part of an international peacekeeping force. In 1983, however, 241 marines were killed when a car bomb driven by an Islamic fundamentalist smashed into their barracks. Reagan soon after withdrew the American military forces, leaving Lebanon to descend even further into cataclysmic tribal and religious strife.

The Reagan Administration's main performance was in relations with the Soviet Union itself. The most pressing debate was over the placement of new intermediate range missiles in Europe to offset new, more powerful Soviet missiles aimed at NATO. Out of deference to world opinion, the administration continued the arms limitations talks with the Soviet Union, though choosing hard-line negotiators to replace the Carter liberals.

At the Geneva talks, the United States promised to revoke its proposed deployment if the USSR should withdraw its own. Instead, the Soviet representatives mounted a major offensive against the em-placement of the American missiles, claiming they were destabilizing weapons that would bring the world closer to nuclear war. Their most intense attacks were directed against Reagan's plan announced in 1983 to create a Strategic Defense Initiative, a defense system to be launched into space and intended to prevent intercontinental missile attack. Many Americans, including scientists, were skeptical of the effectiveness of Star Wars, a name for SDI taken from a popular science fiction movie. And even if technically feasible, many critics said, SDI would upset the policy of mutually assured destruction (MAD) that for a generation had made each superpower know that launching a first strike of nuclear weapons against the other would bring appalling retaliation. Reagan announced his intentions of sharing a completed SDI, which, if the defense could have worked as well as the administration projected, would have freed the Soviet peoples as well as the West from the danger of nuclear war. But opponents claimed that the very fact of building the system would introduce instability into relations between the superpowers.

After the West German parliament approved the deployment of American Pershing missiles, these weapons were finally rolled onto their launch pads. The Russians had been threatening for months to walk out of the arms talks if the American deployment was completed. Soon after, they did so. For the first time in a decade the superpowers would not be discussing arms limitations.

Society in the Reagan Era

The eighties were a time of quick money and rising criminality in business, a field of manipulation at the expense of solid productivity, innovation, and services.

Business had as its most visible money-makers the junk bond and the leveraged buyout. Both brought quick and enormous funds; neither had much to do with making or building or transporting anything good or useful. Junk bonds were corporate securities paying high interest and hitherto shunned by serious investors as too risky. Financiers convinced investors that these bonds were a safe place to put their money, and persuaded corporate executives that they were a superb tool for raising capital. Junk bonds soon caught on and became a favorite device for buying up large flourishing corporations. In leveraged buyouts, sharp-dealing financiers, armed with little cash but mountains of high-yield bonds, would buy out the existing stockholders. Once in possession of a firm they might sell off its profitable sectors at higher prices than the total cost of the business. The remaining parts of the firm were then left saddled with heavy debts and dim prospects.

The elimination of various government regulations of business gave rise to unscrupulous entrepreneurs. Carter initiated deregulation; Reagan pushed it much farther. In some industries its effects were good. But deregulation also allowed business racketeers to flourish. In the savings and loan industry, for example, greedy financiers gained control of vast savings insured by the government. Billions of dollars went into shaky real estate ventures and other dubious business deals. By the end of the decade the federal government found itself legally committed to compensating for the losses of savings and loan depositors that some estimates placed as high as half a trillion dollars.

The new breed of professionals and business executives who rode the wave of prosperity that swept the nation by the mid-1980s were termed "yuppies," an acronym for "young urban professionals." Armed with MBAs or degrees from law schools, they rushed to facilitate the corporate seizures and mergers, the savings and loan deals, the new opportunities in high-tech industry. Yuppies displayed all the characteristics of young men and women who made large amounts of money quickly: they had a reputation, earned or not, for being self-centered, self-indulgent, and convinced of their own brilliance.

Value of the Minimum Wage, 1965–95

The Underclasses   At the other end of society in the Reagan era was the "underclass," the decade's term for the poorest and most discouraged of the ghetto population. The civil rights movement and the subsequent surge of opportunity in business and the professions had helped a substantial group of educated black men and women. But the advances had left behind many black Americans who stagnated in the ghettos and fell prey to all the standard ills—poor health, crime, infant mortality, illegitimacy, family breakup, decrepit housing—and several new ones, most notably the crack plague. The advent of crack, a highly addictive form of smokable cocaine, destroyed lives and created a new class of criminals who preyed largely on their own people and brought a new level of violence to ghetto communities. There was now a two-tier black population: successful middle-class strivers seemed to represent a fulfillment of the nation's promise, while urban neighborhoods sagged in poverty and despair.

During the eighties streams of immigrants from Asia, the Caribbean, and Latin America poured into the United States. Many, like the immigrants of the past, were unskilled and found themselves relegated to the lowest levels of the urban poor. But some quickly moved up through higher education and business to achieve middle-class status. Inevitably, perhaps, the relative success of the newcomers encouraged resentment among the black poor.

Other outsiders also suffered setbacks during the eighties. The liberation mood of the 1960s had transformed American gays and lesbians. By the opening of the 1980s many had left the closet and publicly announced their sexual preferences. They also began to demand respect, along with equality of economic and legal treatment. Then early in the decade there struck a new, fearful disease, Acquired Immune Deficiency Syndrome (AIDS). Suddenly, more and more gay men began to come down with a mysterious ailment that destroyed their immune system and over many years afflicted them with terrifying infectious diseases that eventually led to death. The health authorities learned that the cause was a virus spread by sexual practices and by non-sexual exchange of blood products through drug injection. In the United States AIDS at least initially infected a far larger proportion of gay men than of the rest of society. For a time, especially among social conservatives who disliked homosexuality anyway, gays were treated as lepers who endangered straight society. By 1992 even larger numbers of drug addicts, particularly urban blacks, became victims of AIDS through the use of contaminated syringes.

Women's Issues   Women made advances in the professions and business during the 1970s and 1980s, yet for whatever reason the highest levels of both eluded them. There were many exceptions. Barbara Walters and Dianne Sawyer attained network anchor status on television. Women made considerable inroads into the academic profession. In July 1981 Reagan nominated Sandra Day O'Connor of Arizona as the first woman Supreme Court justice. And women made substantial gains in the military services. Still, some feminists charged, this was tokenism; the very top echelons of law, medicine, business were still dominated by what had come to be called an old boy network. And the 1973 Supreme Court decision *Roe v. Wade,* permitting abortion on demand during the first trimester of pregnancy, had aroused fierce opposition from conservatives, religious and secular, who regarded it as a license for murder. Sympathetic to the "pro-life" movement, the Reagan and succeeding Bush presidencies had promised to use their power to constrain federal funding and support for abortion. They did so by forbidding abortion at military hospitals and restricting the use of federal funds for welfare recipients' abortions.

Environment-alism   The record of Reagan and his successor George Bush on environmental issues often put them at odds with policies on consumer protection, conservation of wildlife and the wilderness, and controls on pollution. By 1980 there had formed an environmental lobby determined to exclude as many commercial operations as possible from the public domain and uphold higher standards of purity in the nation's environment. The Reaganites saw the environmentalists as driven by a combination of hysteria and bias against business and growth, and determined to restrain them.

The instruments of their policy were Interior Secretary James Watt and Ann Gorsuch Burford, head of the Environmental Protection Agency (EPA). Watt was a former lawyer for the Sage Brush Rebellion, a movement of western ranchers, timber barons, and mining operators hostile to federal control of western lands. Both administrators soon outraged the environmentalists. As interior secretary, Watt sought to open thousands of acres of wilderness to energy and mineral exploitation. He also sought transfer of federal lands to private interests. Ann Burford proceeded to lessen the environmental monitoring charged to her agency and effectively impeded the operation of the fund established by Congress for the cleaning up of toxic waste.

Neither official lasted long. Ann Burford left in March 1983 following revelations that a subordinate had connived with chemical firms to delay cleaning up toxic dumps. Replacing her as head of EPA was its first chief, appointed originally by Nixon, the respected William Ruckelshaus. In October 1983 the President removed Watt after the secretary made a crude remark that succeeded in insulting Jews, blacks, and the handicapped, all at the same time.

Reagan's Second Term

The growing gap between rich and poor, the savings and loan frauds, the corruption in Housing and Urban Development would not become common knowledge until Reagan's administration had ended. Meanwhile, the American public prepared to give the President a vote of confidence. By the summer of 1984 the country was prosperous. Inflation and unemployment were down and Americans, so they thought, were paying fewer taxes than they had paid in years. The Republican campaign slogan—"It's Morning in America"—caught the optimistic mood.

The End of Stagflation   The recession of 1982, although a severe setback for the American economy, did not hurt President Ronald Reagan politically, for he could still blame Jimmy Carter and the Democrats for the problem. As the election of 1984 approached, Reagan also found himself in the enviable position of riding the crest of an economic surge. By late 1983 and early 1984, the inflation rate slowed considerably, interest rates fell rapidly, and unemployment declined. Once again, American economic fortunes were closely tied to international oil prices. By 1984 the world was awash in a sea of oil.

In the years since the Arab oil boycott of 1973 and 1974, the industrialized countries had implemented a series of energy-saving measures that pushed down the demand for oil. The 1981 price, moreover, enticed new producers into the oil fields, raising global production. A war between Iran and Iraq, which erupted in 1981, increased world oil supplies, for both countries intensified their oil production to finance their battles. By 1984 oil prices were beginning a free fall. When Ronald Reagan entered the White House in 1981, international oil prices had stood at $36 a barrel. By 1984 they had fallen to $21, and within a year they would fall again, reaching $8 in late 1985. The prices of gasoline, heating fuel, natural gas, and coal dropped as well. The inflation rate in the United States fell with the decline of energy prices. As consumers were not putting so much of their disposable income into their gasoline and heating oil tanks, they enjoyed more purchasing power, and their demand for consumer products stimulated the economy and created millions of new jobs.

The Election of 1984   After winning the Democratic nomination at San Francisco over a field of candidates that included the first serious black contender, the Reverend Jesse Jackson, former Vice President Walter Mondale chose Congresswoman Geraldine Ferraro of New York as his running mate. That made her the first woman ever to be on a national presidential ticket. In his acceptance speech Mondale chided the Republicans on their debt-swelling fiscal policies and vowed to raise taxes to stem the deficit.

Neither tack worked. Some Americans admired Mondale's honest prescription for fiscal health; many women cheered the selection of Geraldine Ferraro. But the public as a whole was in no mood to be taxed further. Probably no Democratic candidacy or platform could have captured the public. The Republican ticket won by a landslide, carrying every state in the Union except Mondale's own Minnesota.

Tax Reform   After the election victory of 1984 and his inauguration to a second term early in 1985, President Ronald Reagan pushed for additional tax reform. Conservative economists had long argued that tax rates on the rich and well-to-do were so high as to discourage investment in the economy. No one, they argued, would be eager to risk money on an investment when the government stood to take most of the profits away in the form of capital gains taxes or personal and corporate income taxes. The administration also told the public that the existing Internal Revenue Tax Code was too complicated; most Americans agreed wholeheartedly.

The Tax Reform Act of 1986 emerged as a bipartisan effort to simplify the tax codes and to reduce the highest tax brackets in order to encourage saving and investment, as well as to eliminate the most notorious of the so-called tax shelters. Congress intended the legislation to be "revenue neutral"—raising no additional revenues for the government. The Tax Reform Act of 1986 did reduce tax rates. The law lowered the highest tax bracket from 50 to about 33 percent. The lowest rate paid was reduced from 19 to 15 percent. The average rate paid by middle-class families went from 37 to 27 percent. The legislation also eliminated deductions for consumer interest, investment tax credits to businesses, and real estate tax shelters.

The plan had assumed an almost automatic ratio between private wealth and private investment. The implicit assumption is that people will be frugal and energetic capitalists, putting their money into long-range productive investment. But the money freed up by the tax cut failed to show up in the economy in this way. Whether it was going into personal luxury spending, unwise investment, or flash ventures promising quick return, it was not nourishing fundamental production or research.

Iran-Contra   Reagan's administration became entangled in a complex scheme to achieve several foreign policy goals simultaneously. It wanted to free the hostages taken and held by Muslim terrorist groups in Lebanon. It wished to help pay the continuing costs of supporting the Nicaraguan Contras in the face of congressional refusal to vote funds. And it aimed to open channels with the Iranians with whom, ever since the embassy hostage crisis of 1979 and 1980, the nation had been on bad terms. None of this could be undertaken publicly. The United States was on record never to deal with terrorists and to punish those implicated in terrorism. In 1986 the United States launched an air attack against Libya, one of the Muslim states that, under Muammar Qaddafi, supported terrorist attacks against Americans in Europe and the Middle East. Washington was also bound by congressional action in its relations with the Contras,

History makers in the 1984 election: The Reverend Jesse Jackson, the first black to be a serious contender for the presidential nomination, and Geraldine Ferraro, the first woman to be nominated for the office of Vice President by a major party. *(Courtesy, AP/Wide World Photos)*

Lt.-Col. Oliver North testifying before the congressional committee investigating the Iran-Contra affair, July 1987. *(Courtesy, UPI/Bettmann News Photos)*

President Ronald Reagan explained Iran- Contra this way:

"I knew that there must be among our allies other countries that shared our concern about the threat to democracy in Latin America, and I believed we should communicate to them our strong convictions regarding the importance of tangible international support for the Contras. Several countries responded and extended help—a case of friendly nations believing we all had a stake in fighting for Democracy. I believed, then and now, that the President has the absolute constitutional right and obligation to share such thoughts and goals with leaders of other nations."

and Congress had balked at an open-ended military commitment in Central America. As for Iran, few Americans could see any grounds for serious dialogue. The Muslim fundamentalists under the Ayatollah Khomeini remained in power and still considered the United States "the Great Satan." So the scheme the administration devised had to be hidden from view.

The administration's foreign policy insiders, among them CIA director William Casey, national security adviser Admiral John Poindexter, and his aide, Colonel Oliver North, believed that secrecy was possible. The plan they concocted involved selling American weapons to Iran, at the time engaged in its desperate war with Iraq. In exchange, they thought, the Iranians would order their allies among the hostage-takers in Lebanon to release the American captives. Meanwhile, the profits from the arms sales could be used to finance covertly the money-starved Contras. A deal was struck, but it was botched. Iran bought American weapons, but only one or two American captives in Lebanon were released. Some of the money from the deal probably got to the Contras, but wily middlemen siphoned off a lot of it. News of the scheme got out late in 1986, and the administration now seemed engaged in hypocrisy, folly, and lawbreaking all at once.

Reagan denied knowledge of the plan. He had known about the arms sales, he said, but it was merely an attempt to open a dialogue with the Iranians; it was not ransom for hostages. Under growing pressure from critics, at the end of November he fired North and announced Poindexter's resignation. He agreed to appoint a special committee headed by former Senator John Tower to investigate the Iran-Contra affair, and chose a special prosecutor to seek out culprits and bring them to justice. Congress soon announced hearings to investigate the labyrinthine events.

The Iran-Contra affair damaged Reagan's reputation. The President, who had long basked in his Hollywood image of a tough frontier lawman, stood revealed as unable to form an open and convincing foreign policy. His testimony before the Tower commission reinforced this impression. Reagan remembered little of the arms deal discussions and admitted in effect that he delegated foreign policy making to others. Reagan's approval ratings soon declined.

And yet Reagan loyalists did not desert him. Many American conservatives approved the deal, especially the covert support of the Contras. When Oliver North appeared before the televised congressional hearings, many people cheered his flag-waving defense of the administration's hidden initiatives. (Later he would contradict Reagan's claim to know nothing of Iran-Contra.) Eventually, North, Poindexter, and others were indicted by the special prosecutor for violating various federal laws. But the cases dragged on past Reagan's second term and past the public's patience. And the results proved inconclusive: no defendant received a heavy sentence.

Wall Street   At the end of 1987 events on Wall Street further damaged the administration. On October 19, 1987, Wall Street crashed with a thunderous roar. That "Black Monday" stocks dropped 500 points in a few hours, the most disastrous one-day decline in the history of Wall Street. Black Monday pricked the over-blown confidence in Reagan era prosperity. Before many months the real estate swell began to flatten. Leveraged buyouts dwindled amid a cluster of Wall Street prosecutions for insider trading. Among the yuppie rich, some of them employed in law firms and brokerage houses that had done deals and sold junk bonds, prospects faded. The public was soon watching TV clips of the young brokers and traders at Drexel, Burnham, Lambert—Michael Milken's junk bond marketing busi-ness—moving out with their attaché cases and computers as the firm closed its doors.

Détente   Between 1982 and 1985 the Soviet Union under-went a remarkable progression of leadership from the rigid, old-line Communist, Leonid Brezhnev, to the undogmatic reformer Mikhail Gorbachev. A Marxist and a Soviet patriot, Gor-bachev sought within those limits to promote *glasnost,* or openness, an end to the intellectual and political repression in Soviet society. He also aimed to replace the faltering Soviet command economy with a more efficient and productive system drawing on individual incentives and private initiative. This was called *perestroika*.

From 1985 onward relations between the Soviet Union and the West improved remarkably. Reagan, his talk of an evil empire notwith-standing, proved a flexible and moderate negotiator. Right-wing admir-ers of Reagan have liked to claim that his toughness toward the Soviet Union had something to do with the crumbling of Communism there. But Western toughness in the past had merely largely confined the spread of the Soviet empire. It is not Reagan's posturing but his open-ness toward Gorbachev that is more likely to have aided in destroying the repressive Soviet system, for Reagan's civility to him gave Gor-bachev international credibility.

In the course of a series of summit meetings the two leaders resumed the arms control process terminated after the American Pershing missile deployment at the end of 1983. In December 1987 Gorbachev arrived in the United States prepared to sign an agreement eliminating all Soviet and American intermediate range missiles on the same terms that the United States had offered five years before at Geneva. His visit was a triumph of public relations. A friendly man with a winning smile, he stopped his limousine on the streets of Washington and got out to shake hands with passersby. The INF (intermediate nuclear forces) treaty, finally signed by the Senate in June 1988, elimi-nated entirely a whole class of nuclear weapons, an unprecedented achievement.

The process of improving relations continued. The United States and the Soviet Union were soon promising to reduce conventional arms in Europe and to take major strides toward scaling down their strategic nuclear arsenals. Moscow also agreed to leave Afghanistan and, by the spring of 1988, had withdrawn all its troops. The waning of the Cold War was even felt in Central America. Accepting the initiative of the President of Costa Rica, Sandinista leader Daniel Ortega agreed to

Mikhail Gorbachev. *(Courtesy, Library of Congress)*

hold free elections that would include his Contra opponents. The receding of the Iran-Contra fiasco and the remarkable advances in relations with the Soviet Union somewhat revived Reagan's reputation. By the time he was ready to leave office and retire to his home in Los Angeles, most Americans once more admired him.

The Bush Years

In 1988 Vice President George Bush had little serious opposition in winning his party's nomination for the presidency. As his running mate he chose Dan Quayle, a young senator from Indiana. The Republican platform defended Reagan's administration and confirmed its resistance to abortion rights.

President George Bush. (*Courtesy, The White House*)

The 1988 Election

The campaign was one of the dirtiest on record. The Willie Horton television clip appealed to the public's worst fears and hatreds. Horton was a criminal who, while on release from a Massachusetts prison, had raped a white woman. The TV spot suggested that the Democratic presidential candidate, Massachusetts governor Michael Dukakis, was directly responsible. Republicans also showed pictures suggestive of a polluted Boston Harbor, implying that Dukakis as governor of the state was to blame. The Democrats attacked Quayle as an intellectual lightweight with a poor academic record and a privileged rich boy whose parents had got him into the National Guard to evade the Vietnam War.

The candidates also spoke to more legitimate issues. Bush distanced himself a little from his predecessor by talk of "a kinder, gentler" nation that would succor the downtrodden. But this need not cost money. Instead, it would be accomplished by a multitude of private service and charity initiatives—"a thousand points of light." The Republican candidate supported policies to end abortion on demand. He also appealed to the tax aversion of the American people. His most telling phrase was "Read my lips; no new taxes." Dukakis did not respond quickly enough to devastating Republican attacks, and he refused until too late to emphasize the class issues that had traditionally aroused Democrats and focused instead on "competence." Bush won decisively.

The Bush Presidency

In his first months in office Bush impressed many Americans with his amiability, but he seemed unable to get much accomplished. He proposed measures to improve the quality of American education and raise environmental standards, but then refused to seek additional funding for his programs. His one environmental accomplishment, the Clean Air Act of 1990, had been largely thrust upon him by Congress. The federal budget deficits worsened, but he had promised not to raise taxes.

The unraveling savings and loan scandal troubled Bush's early months. It was only at the beginning of his administration that the media and public realized the full extent of the fraud, waste, and incompetence that had saddled the nation with hundreds of billions of dollars of obligations to repay cheated S&Ls depositors. Congress created an agency to take over the S&Ls, manage the sell-off of remaining assets, and rescue depositors. By 1990 it looked as if the whole savings and loan system was on the verge of bankruptcy with the middle class paying the price. The President alone could not be blamed for the debacle, but the slack regulation had occurred during the big-money Reagan years, when Bush was Vice President, and it seemed a part of that time of quick wealth. Bush got into further trouble when he reneged on his promise in 1990 to resist any new taxation. Faced with the worsening budget deficit and the restraints it imposed on all new governmental initiatives, he finally relented. In a budget conference of congressional leaders, he called for additional revenues. Students of government finance saw the action as realistic and statesmanlike, but to conservative Republicans it seemed a betrayal of the party's most sacred pledge.

Bush's Foreign Policy   In foreign policy the news for Bush was far better. Remarkable changes were coming with a rush in eastern Europe. In 1989 Soviet dominance in the East Bloc simply collapsed. By the end of the year popular uprisings had overthrown puppet Communist regimes and led to new, non-Communist governments in the former satellites. The most significant change of all took place in East Germany, the German Democratic Republic. In 1989 angry demonstrators overthrew the East German Communist regime, brought about the dismantling of the notorious Berlin Wall, the most vivid symbol of the Cold War, opened the long-closed border between the two Germanies to free movement, and began to demand the reunification of the German nation.

The Berlin Wall, erected by East German Communists in 1961, was torn down by anti-Communist demonstrators in 1989. *(Courtesy, AP/Wide World Photos)*

Some Europeans and Americans who remembered the role of Germany in the period between 1933 and 1945 were not entirely happy at the prospect of a reunited German *Reich*. The Soviet Union too considered it dangerous. Yet the reunion was unstoppable. After giving assurances on borders to the Poles and promising to provide major economic aid to the Soviet Union, West German Chancellor Helmut Kohl, in the summer of 1990, was able to merge the two Germanies economically. In October 1990 the political union was achieved. A new nation of some sixty million now existed, the richest and most populous in all of western Europe.

The larger truth is that the Cold War was finally over. With the uprisings in the East Bloc the Warsaw Pact was defunct. There still remained the Soviet superpower with its nuclear arsenal, but by the early 1990s the Soviet Union was beset with enormous distracting internal problems. The Union was disintegrating. The Soviet economy was producing fewer goods than ever, and the Soviet people were increasingly restless. Meanwhile, the Soviet military was being cut drastically in size to ease the burden on the economy. And with a few exceptions the Soviet leadership, even that portion of it that professed some commitment to Communism, had lost any interest in the ideo-

U.S. President George Bush and Soviet President Mikhail Gorbachev. *(Courtesy, AP/Wide World Photos)*

President George Bush addressing American combat troops in Saudi Arabia:

"We are not here on some exercise. And we are not walking away until the invader is out of Kuwait."

logical and military warfare against the non-Communist world. By the summer of 1990 Americans were gleefully contemplating the size of the "peace dividend" that could be squeezed out of the bloated defense budget and used for peaceful domestic purposes.

Early in 1990 a success in Central America had come both for the administration and for its liberal opponents. Liberals in Congress, after halting Reagan's policy of military assistance to the Nicaraguan Contras, had insisted, and conservatives denied, that in the absence of military pressure from the outside Nicaragua could be prompted to hold open elections. In time, regional opinion and enormous confidence on the part of the Sandinistas in their own popularity did bring them to put their government to the electoral test. Just before the Nicaraguan elections, Bush indicated his willingness to make his peace even with the Sandinistas if they should win, as they were expected to do. But they lost, thereupon accepting their defeat; and liberals joined the astonished White House in celebrating the success of a peaceful outcome.

Crisis in the Gulf   In August 1990 Iraq, led by its reckless strong man, Saddam Hussein, invaded and occupied the oil-rich kingdom of Kuwait on its southern border. In 1980 Saddam had launched a disastrous war against Iran that lasted eight years, cost countless lives, and squandered billions of dollars. The war ended in a victory for Iraq but left that nation depleted and deeply in debt. The Iraqi invasion of Kuwait may have been motivated primarily by Saddam Hussein's need to replenish his country's empty coffers from Kuwaiti treasure and oil. But many of his neighbors, the United States, and other industrial countries dependent on Mideast oil feared that his next act would be to invade Saudi Arabia, the richest in oil of all the Mideast countries. Success would give Iraq enormous arbitrary power over the economic fate of much of the world. For a man of such brutal and heedless temperament, a ruler who had murdered with poison gas thousands of his own dissident Iraqi Kurds, such power seemed intolerable.

Prompted by Saudi and Kuwaiti pleas, economic self-interest, and his sense that Saddam Hussein, whom he compared to Hitler, must be stopped, President Bush persuaded the United Nations to call for a blockade of Iraq. The UN also approved the sending of massive military forces to Saudi Arabia to repel any Iraqi invasion. These troops, so Bush hoped, would ultimately persuade Iraq to leave conquered Kuwait. For the first time the full UN Security Council, including the People's Republic of China and the USSR, had voted with the West to endorse condemnation of an aggressor. Dozens of nations, including several important Arab states, sent supplies, ships, and troops to reinforce the predominantly American forces soon landing in the thousands in Saudi Arabia as part of Operation Desert Shield.

Saddam Hussein soon took prisoner thousands of civilians in Kuwait and Iraq, including many Americans, but released them late in 1990. When Iraq refused to leave Kuwait by a deadline of January 15 endorsed by the United Nations and the United States Congress, the

President began Operation Desert Storm, attacking the enemy on all fronts in open war. The majority of Americans, and a slight majority in the predominantly Democratic Senate, supported the President.

Desert Storm   The UN led by the United States finally began on the night of January 16 a ferocious assault by planes and missiles. Prime targets were Iraqi command and control centers, air fields, power stations, chemical and nuclear warfare facilities, and Scud missile sites. The Scuds were especially feared as terror weapons that, if directed at Israel, might provoke that nation to intervene. An Israeli counterattack against Iraq, however justified, seemed certain to divide the Arab world and might weaken the fragile anti-Iraqi coalition that Bush and Secretary of State James Baker had so painfully constructed. Saddam launched the Scuds against both Saudi Arabia and major Israeli cities. Fortunately for the coalition, Bush was able to induce the Israelis to hold their fire and accept some civilian losses as UN forces eliminated Scuds in mid-flight while others fell harmlessly to the ground.

The effect of the initial air attack was astonishing. High-technology American weapons devastated Iraqi targets while risking few American lives. Some 3,000 civilians were killed, and the enormous destruction of bridges, power stations, and other facilities would produce civilian hardships and deaths long after the war ended. In a matter of days the Iraqi air force was immobilized. Still, the Iraqis refused to evacuate Kuwait, and many Americans thought that a ground attack, risking thousands of UN lives, would be unavoidable. Especially feared was the elite Iraqi Republican Guard, the special troops who had so effectively resisted the mass wave attacks by the Iranians in the recent war between Iraq and Iran. Day after day, high-flying B-52 bombers pounded the dug-in Republican Guards in the hope that remorseless air attack might destroy their morale and reduce their fighting effectiveness.

Saddam Hussein of Iraq.
(Courtesy, AP/Wide World Photos)

Secretary of Defense Richard Cheney consults with military figures in Saudi Arabia, December 1990. *(Courtesy, AP/Wide World Photos)*

At home, once the actual fighting broke out, public opinion shifted massively in support of the war. A great surge of patriotism marked by soaring flag and bunting sales and a wide display of yellow ribbons tied to trees, doorknobs, and street lamps signified overwhelming support for the fighting men and women in the Middle East. The public was pleased by the effectiveness of high-priced arms technology. It also came to admire the role of blacks and Hispanics who formed such a large part of the armed forces, and of women, tested for the first time as part of the combat military. Two heroes emerged from the war, General Norman Schwarzkopf, commander of all the UN forces in the Middle East, and General Colin Powell, chairman of the American Joint Chiefs of Staff, the first black soldier to occupy so high a military position. The underside of this tide of patriotism was that the war became something of a Roman circus. While Iraqi troops endured massive daily bombings and coalition troops readied themselves for possibly massive casualties, American television presented the whole business as nightly entertainment, complete with breaks for commercials.

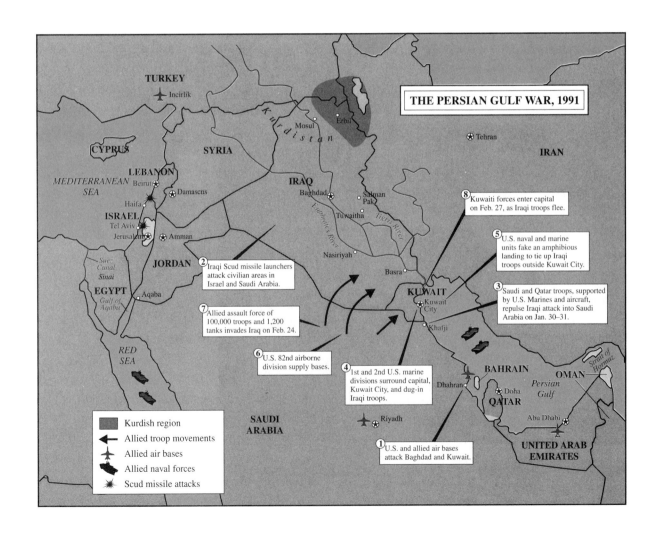

THE PERSIAN GULF WAR, 1991

8 Kuwaiti forces enter capital on Feb. 27, as Iraqi troops flee.

5 U.S. naval and marine units fake an amphibious landing to tie up Iraqi troops outside Kuwait City.

3 Saudi and Qatar troops, supported by U.S. Marines and aircraft, repulse Iraqi attack into Saudi Arabia on Jan. 30–31.

2 Iraqi Scud missile launchers attack civilian areas in Israel and Saudi Arabia.

7 Allied assault force of 100,000 troops and 1,200 tanks invades Iraq on Feb. 24.

6 U.S. 82nd airborne division supply bases.

4 1st and 2nd U.S. marine divisions surround capital, Kuwait City, and dug-in Iraqi troops.

1 U.S. and allied air bases attack Baghdad and Kuwait.

Kurdish region
Allied troop movements
Allied air bases
Allied naval forces
Scud missile attacks

On February 24 the coalition forces launched a ground attack against the Iraqis. While United States marines and coalition Arab troops attacked frontally across the border between Saudi Arabia and Kuwait, American, British, and French armored and infantry forces swung far to the west to outflank the main Iraqi army. Thousands of enemy troops surrendered without firing a shot. Many others fled northward toward Baghdad and were pounded mercilessly by coalition planes as they sought escape. In a hundred hours almost 4,000 Iraqi tanks were destroyed along with thousands of enemy vehicles and guns. A feared Iraqi chemical weapons attack never materialized. Coalition casualties were astonishingly low: only about one hundred Americans were killed in action.

A cease-fire ended the fighting on February 28. Iraq had been ejected from Kuwait after devastating that country. Enemy troops carried away almost everything portable, destroying much of Kuwait City and leaving behind hundreds of burning oil wells that continued to spew Stygian clouds of smoke into the atmosphere for almost nine months. The administration did not drive on to Baghdad to oust Saddam's regime. The dictator remained in power. Despite criticisms, Bush and his advisers refused to support rebels within Iraq, and before long thousands of Kurdish refugees had fled to the mountains and to Iraq's neighbors. A major international relief effort prevented mass starvation among them, but the Kurdish incident in particular raised at least some questions about how much had really been accomplished by the Gulf War.

The horror of modern high-tech warfare was highlighted by one American's bizarre account of plows, mounted on tanks and combat earthmovers, that buried thousands of dug-in Iraqi soldiers, some still alive and firing their weapons:

"What you saw was a bunch of buried trenches with peoples' arms and things sticking out of them."

Soviet Decline The Soviet economy, already in a shambles, was further deteriorating despite efforts by Mikhail Gorbachev to free it from some of the handicaps imposed by seventy years of centralized, totalitarian control. There was talk of famine when winter came, and the Bush Administration provided massive aid to keep the Soviet people from starvation. As its economy sank, the Soviet Union as a political entity also began to weaken. The Baltic republics—Lithuania, Latvia, and Estonia, all annexed forcibly by the USSR five decades earlier—declared their independence. Soon Ukrainians, Moldavians, Georgians, Kazakhs, and other peoples of the Union began to insist on self-rule. Meanwhile, Boris Yeltsin, a high Soviet official who had repudiated the Communist Party, was in June 1991 elected president of the Russian Republic in a landslide popular vote hailed in the West as the first free election ever held in Russia.

Then on August 19 a group of hard-liners, seeking to reverse the changes ushered in by Gorbachev and to prop up the rule of the Communist Party, staged a coup. Led by Yeltsin, the leaders of the Russian Republic rallied to Gorbachev and refused to yield control to the plotters. The democratic forces, backed by thousands of supporters in the streets of Moscow, faced down the tanks and soldiers of hard-liners, who soon surrendered and were placed under arrest. The coup's collapse restored Gorbachev as president of the Soviet Union. But he was now beholden to Yeltsin and no longer able to act alone.

The End of the Soviet Union

In the wake of the failed coup, the movement for drastic economic reform gained momentum, as did the forces tearing the Soviet Union apart. Communist rule had been the only effective force holding together the many nations of the Soviet Union; with its demise, the splintering of the empire became inevitable. Shortly before Christmas 1991, the Congress of People's Deputies formally announced the dissolution of the Soviet Union, creating in its stead the loose Commonwealth of Independent States. Wrangling among the member states soon raised serious questions about the Commonwealth's chances for survival.

The collapse of Soviet power changed the political equations in the Middle East and offered a chance to settle the conflict of decades between Israel and the Arabs. At the end of the Gulf War the most anti-Israel Arab states no longer had the support of their protector, the Soviet Union. In effect, the USSR had ceased competing with the United States in the region. And the Palestine Liberation Organization, chief agent of Palestinian national aspirations, had been profoundly weakened by its support of Iraq in the Gulf War. Secretary of State James Baker was able to bring together Israel, Syria, Jordan, the Palestinians, and Lebanon in a face-to-face conference held in Madrid in November 1991. The participants spent much of their time hurling insults and recriminations against each other. The Israelis, concerned with their national security, resisted any exchange of occupied land for peace and rejected major concessions to Palestinian national aspirations. The Palestinians, in turn, demanded the right to their own nationhood. Syria refused to consider any other arrangement than complete return of the strategic Golan Heights, lost to the Israelis during the Six Days' War of 1967. And yet as the initial meeting at Madrid adjourned, the world stood amazed that these antagonists for so many years had come as far as that.

The Peace Dividend

The United States had already achieved breakthrough agreements with the Soviet Union to reduce conventional arms and shrink the number of troops. The Bush Administration also took important unilateral steps to reduce the threat of nuclear war. With the USSR barely alive, was there any need for an enormous American military establishment? Could not billions be cut from the defense budget and used for vital purposes at home? Major weapons programs, including the Stealth Bomber, seemed likely to be canceled despite opposition by the administration. More than half of the 300,000 troops stationed in Europe were called home, and all the presidential contenders in the 1992 race promised greater reductions still in the nation's contribution to the North Atlantic Treaty Organization (NATO). It appeared that a "peace dividend," as it was called, a release of funds previously set aside for the Cold War, was now available for the relief of problems at home.

Among unmet domestic needs was education. A federal commission issued a "report card" showing that despite a succession of programs designed to check a long decline, American students had barely held their own during the 1980s in math and language skills. Bush endorsed programs that emphasized parental choice of schools and national testing rather than new spending. Bush also wished to be known as the environmental President. Yet his interior secretary authorized substantial clear-cutting of ancient forests on public lands in the West, and his administration did little to cooperate with international efforts to save the ozone layer in the outer atmosphere. Also demanding attention were the nation's roads, bridges, hospitals, and public buildings, which were becoming decrepit. Health care needed a major overhaul. The United States was spending a greater proportion of its gross national product on health care than any other industrial nation and the amount was rising rapidly each year. At the same time the system of private health insurance, even when joined with Medicaid for the indigent and Medicare for the retired, left millions of Americans without the means to pay the bills when they became ill.

Racial Issues   One racial issue that became politically hot was affirmative action, government policies to give preference to blacks and other minority members in college and professional school admissions, training programs, and jobs. These policies had enabled many blacks as well as women and some ethnic minorities to break into professional and occupational fields from which they had been generally excluded before. But for some whites it seemed reverse racism, a system that injured white males. During the Reagan years the conservative federal courts had whittled away at affirmative action programs. A central argument was that a governmental policy forcing preferential treatment violates the constitutional prohibition of racial discrimination by the federal and state government. Congressional liberals had introduced a new civil rights bill that passed the House in June 1991. President Bush charged that the bill imposed quotas and threatened to veto it. Abruptly, in early November, Bush accepted much of the Democratic bill.

Another administration strategy to change the course of the country's social policy was the nomination of Clarence Thomas to a seat on the Supreme Court. Thomas, a conservative black attorney from a poor rural southern background, had attended Yale Law School. Reagan appointed him head of the Equal Employment Opportunity Commission, the agency that administered affirmative action programs, and Bush then elevated him to a position of federal appeals judge. In July 1991 Bush nominated Thomas to replace the retiring liberal Thurgood Marshall as a justice of the Supreme Court. At the Senate hearings considering Thomas's appointment, charges abruptly surfaced that while at the Department of Education and at the Equal Employment Opportunity Commission, Thomas had sexually harassed a woman subordinate, Anita Hill, now a law professor at the University of Oklahoma and another black graduate of Yale Law School. The charges were aired publicly at a series of hearings before the Senate Judiciary Committee. As millions of thunderstruck viewers watched the fascinating proceedings, the dignified, well-spoken Anita Hill accused Thomas of using awesomely suggestive sexual language toward her and, at least by indirection, seeking sexual favors. Thomas angrily denied the charges and claimed that the hearing had become a "high-tech lynching."

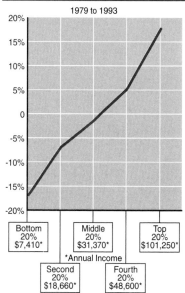

Growth in Real Family Income (in 1993 dollars, by income group)

1979 to 1993

| Bottom 20% $7,410* | Second 20% $18,660* | Middle 20% $31,370* | Fourth 20% $48,600* | Top 20% $101,250* |

*Annual Income

The Senate confirmed the nomination by a vote of 52 to 48. The closest confirmation vote for a Supreme Court nominee on record, it added another conservative vote to an already conservative Court. Observers expected that the impact would soon be felt as cases challenging liberal judicial interpretations.

A Sullen Politics

In the presidential campaigning that began early in 1992, the Democratic field quickly narrowed to two contenders. Jerry Brown, a former California governor, described American politics as perverted by short-sighted policy-making and political campaign financing that played to special interest groups. Arkansas Governor Bill Clinton offered a more conventional, less confrontational party politics designed to address a variety of popular and special interests. He easily defeated Brown in the primaries. At the July convention Clinton chose as his running mate Tennessee Senator Al Gore, a strong environmentalist whose record on that issue contrasted to that of both President Bush and Vice President Quayle. President Bush was briefly challenged by Patrick Buchanan, a conservative columnist who urged an isolationist foreign policy and attacked the President for succumbing to liberalism at home. But the Republican convention at Houston, Texas, selected the incumbents Bush and Quayle to run for office for the second time. The convention also tried what the party's right wing had expected to make a winning issue: speakers denounced Democrats and liberals as being alien to American family and moral values. It could have been a popular theme, but tests of public opinion after the convention indicated that the Republicans were perceived as having overdone it, sounding harsh and divisive.

Americans of each party, meanwhile, were showing a startling interest in the presidential candidacy of the Texas billionaire H. Ross Perot. He had no direct experience in government, and this was a

(From left to right) 1992 Democratic vice-presidential nominee Senator Al Gore of Tennessee, his wife Tipper, presidential nominee Bill Clinton, and his wife Hillary. *(Courtesy, AP/Wide World Photos)*

reason for his popularity. By the end of the campaign he would be stressing the need for debt reductions—the only one of the three candidates to say frankly that Americans were going to have to pay higher taxes.

Then, on April 29, occurred an event that might have shifted the focus of the campaign.

For a long time, the Los Angeles police had held a reputation for casually harassing black youths, stopping them at will and questioning them as potential suspects. Los Angeles was also a prey to violent and lethal gangs engaged in the drug trade. On March 3, 1991, after a high-speed car chase, a group of police repeatedly clubbed Rodney King while an onlooker unnoticed by the assailants videotaped the beating. Four policemen were put on trial, which the defense succeeded in getting removed to the comfortable white suburb of Simi Valley on the grounds that in the city a fair verdict would be difficult to obtain. Conviction seemed nevertheless certain: the crime was captured visually and in sound. On April 29, 1992, came the astonishing verdict: after some dissension among its members, the jury in effect acquitted the four.

Ghettos in Los Angeles exploded. Whites were beaten, including a truck driver whose near-fatal assault was recorded by video from a helicopter: in a heroic act, some black passersby rescued him. There was the usual looting and burning, which wrecked the neighborhood economy and the hopes of the innocent who live in the riot sections of the city. Fifty-eight deaths were reported. The several days of violence, which ended with the help of federal troops and the National Guard, had its dramatic moment: a simple, halting, and moving public appeal from Rodney King himself for an end to it.

H. Ross Perot, independent presidential candidate in 1992 who in November received nineteen percent of the popular vote.

The Election of 1992   Clinton as a campaigner offered a number of general ideas for economic revival, among them an injection of federal funds into efforts to renew and advance American technology. He also pledged to devise a scheme that would make basic health care available to the millions of Americans who could not afford to get sick.

The issue of family values having done them at most only a little good at their national convention, Republicans turned to attacking Clinton's character, particularly his opposition to the Vietnam War during the conflict. On election day, the Democrat won a sizable majority of the presidential electors and forty-three percent of the popular vote to Bush's thirty-eight and Perot's nineteen percent.

The Clinton Presidency

During the period of transition from the November elections to the inauguration of the new President, Clinton backed President Bush on a decision to order troops to Somalia, located on the east coast of Africa, where warring factions were seizing food for themselves and causing starvation among civilians. Bush was acting in cooperation with the United Nations. Soon the project of opening food lines had been completed. But the American and other troops had become embroiled in a project to bring orderly government to the country. After suffering American casualties in what appeared a pointless effort, the United States withdrew its contingent.

Clinton: Alarms, Diversions, and Retreats   The new Clinton Administration suffered for months an astonishing number of stresses and political difficulties. By the time his debt-reduction plan, combining taxation and cutting governmental programs, reached the House of Representatives, Clinton's ability to make a political difference was so weakened that he was barely able to muster a passing vote. Worse trouble threatened in the Senate. In addition to projecting a rise in income taxes for Americans most able to pay it, Clinton's plan had called for an energy tax. The tax encountered much hostility, especially from the oil industry, and in the Senate some members of Clinton's own party indicated that they could not support it. He compromised on a very low gasoline tax.

After a painful episode over a failed nomination for assistant attorney general for civil rights, Clinton selected for a seat on the Supreme Court a judge, Ruth Bader Ginsburg, who drew praise from Republicans as well as Democrats. A second appointment, that of the moderate Stephen G. Breyer, was confirmed in 1994.

Foreign Policy   Toward the end of 1993, President Clinton with the help of many Republicans achieved his first complete political triumph. He had inherited from President Bush the task of winning approval in the national legislature of the North American Free Trade Agreement, or NAFTA, dropping restrictions in trade among the nations of Mexico, Canada, and the United States. The strongest opposition came from the left wing of American politics: unions fearing competition from underpaid Mexican labor and human-rights advocates who believed that NAFTA would amount to an endorsement of the exploitation of Mexican workers. Support of NAFTA brought together Democrats of Clinton's persuasion and Republicans seeking world markets. In both the Senate and the House of Representatives, enough Republicans and Democrats voted for NAFTA to secure its passage.

In the spring of 1994 the President established a screening process that would permit entry to Haitian refugees who could show that their seeking to come to the United States was motivated not by economic considerations but by a reasoned fear of political persecution from that nation's repressive regimes. The United Nations with the strong backing of the Clinton Administration also tightened a trade embargo on Haiti to force change in its government. Later in the same year, the Haitian military rulership yielded to a new but short-lived government, under the returned dissident Jean-Bertrand Aristide.

The Communist government of China, while milder than Chinese Communism had previously been, continued to repress dissent. For a moment in 1989, a democracy movement had brought student demonstrators to Tiananmen Square in Beijing, demanding civil freedoms. The bloody suppression of the students by the government seemed to indicate that China would not in the near future go the way of the nations in eastern Europe emergent from Communist domination. Clinton for a time argued for restricting trade with China. But American business hungered for trade. In the end, Clinton renewed for China the trade status of most favored nation.

Still another question in foreign policy arose when a civil war in the African nation of Rwanda led since April 1994 to killings of civilians so widespread as to evoke the dread name of genocide. But chilled perhaps by the unsatisfactory outcome of the venture in Somalia, the international community hesitated to enter Rwanda to restore order and public safety.

Toward the three-sided warfare in eastern European Bosnia setting Muslims, ethnic Croats, and ethnic Serbs against one another, Clinton as a presidential candidate had advocated strong measures against rebel Serbs responsible for widespread atrocities. But then for a time in the White House he apparently backed away. Early in 1994 the North Atlantic Treaty Organization, acting in conjunction with the United Nations, began an only partly convincing show of force to dissuade the Bosnian Serbs from some of their more aggressive acts. There were air attacks on Serb positions. In Dayton, Ohio, peace talks were held in the fall of 1995 among the contending forces, and the Clinton Administration contributed ground troops to an international peacekeeping force.

Domestic Policy in the Mid-1990s   At home, President Clinton could take pleasure in the economy. Clinton could claim that his policies for reducing the federal deficit had sufficiently brought down interest rates as to send money churning through the economy.

Less cheering to the President were the ill fortunes of health care proposals designed by a task force headed by his wife, Hillary Rodham Clinton. They were shaped to make good medical treatment financially available to everyone who needed it. But after an effective campaign from conservatives, the plan died. Then, in November 1994, came a triumph for conservative Republicans in both state and congressional elections. Both houses of the national legislature became Republican. In the House of Representatives conservative members of the party set out to remake national policy, pushing for deep cuts in social spending, relaxation of environmental law, and a lowering of taxes.

A young Bill Clinton meets John F. Kennedy in Arkansas in 1960. *(Courtesy, Arnie Sachs, Sygma)*

The Election of 1996   Then, quite unexpectedly, the fortunes of the President and his party improved. Part of the reason was the new Republican House under its speaker Newt Gingrich. Assuming it had a mandate to reduce the size of the government, the House for a short time during the winter of 1995–96 refused to allot the funds to keep federal agencies going, determined to keep them closed until Clinton should approve the Republican schedule for a balanced budget. The country blamed the Republicans who were also willing more greatly than their Democratic adversaries to shrink the growth of Medicare and of federal aid to the children of the poor. The nation did appear satisfied with a welfare measure, which the President reluctantly signed. It put limits on the time an individual could receive federal welfare. But it did not provide a convincing plan for ensuring that jobs would be available for people whose checks had terminated. The concessions that Clinton made to conservativism, and at the same time a popular view of congressional Republicans as mean-spirited, revived his political strength. Even more favorable to the President's ratings was an increasingly vibrant economy.

In a skillful presidential campaign, Clinton and Vice President Al Gore stressed specific federal programs that could help Americans of all classes, particularly in sending their offspring to college. The Republican nominating process had one noteworthy feature at odds with the American past: a nativist who was also a Catholic. Patrick Buchanan attacked free trade and the flow of immigrants from Latin America. Robert Dole of Kansas, a legislative craftsman who resigned from the Senate to be the Republican presidential candidate, teamed with Jack Kemp, known for arguing that Republicans should design policies friendly toward the poor and marginalized. Dole promised a fifteen percent tax cut, which supporters claimed would stimulate the economy to increase federal revenues. Clinton, the big winner in the electoral college, took just under fifty percent of the popular vote, almost all the rest being split between Dole and Ross Perot, who this time won eight percent. Especially important to the Democratic victory were the votes of women. Republicans added two members to the Senate and, while exactly splitting with Democrats the combined popular vote for House candidates, held to a modest lead in the lower chamber. Most eligible voters stayed home. The election as a whole reflected a public wish neither for large new governmental programs nor for harsh measures against beneficiaries of existing ones.

National politics toward the end of the twentieth century might best be defined as stalled, seeking for issues. The Republicans, discovering that the ideology of the conservative revolution of 1994 did not have the approval of the country's majority, moved toward the center that administration Democrats had earlier occupied. President Clinton took few initiatives toward increasing social programs; his opponents took equally few toward shrinking them. In the absence of serious controversy, the public witnessed an undignified quarrel over the President's private life. Allegations of sexual misbehavior whetted the interest of Republicans along with Kenneth Starr, the special prosecutor investigating various matters of the President's conduct. Scarcely less gluttonous for sexual scandal were the media, which in their turn serve the appetites of the public. More significant were claims of questionable contributions to the Democratic and Republican parties.

Real issues did emerge. The ending of minority preferences in admissions to California's public universities quickened the debate over affirmative action. Supporters of affirmative action contended, accurately, that it opens opportunities to blacks and Hispanics who face such obstacles to advancement as the inadequacy of secondary schools in ghetto neighborhoods. Opponents observed, accurately, that affirmative action builds into the social system concepts of special entitlement contrary to the ideal of an egalitarian and integrated population. The question remained of how sensitive the nation's diplomacy should be to human rights abuses in foreign countries such as our profitable trading partner China. Conservatives and liberals had differing ideological preferences concerning which victims of repression to aid, while economic interests hesitated to attack the repressive policies of any regime that is friendly to American business. How best to further negotiations between Israelis and Palestinians, and how to stay the proliferation of nuclear weapons, also challenged the skills of American diplomats. Political parties seeking responsible discussion, then, have much to work with. Doing so will require subtle revisions of the political language with which Americans have been familiar.

Suggested Readings

Recent books include Jean Edward Smith, *George Bush's War* (1992) and Stephen R. Graubard, *Mr. Bush's War* (1992), Michael Paul Rogin, *Ronald Reagan* (1987), Samuel P. Hays, *Beauty, Health, and Permanence: Environmental Politics in the United States, 1955–1985* (1987), Erwin Hargrove, *Jimmy Carter as President* (1988), Fred Block et al., *The Mean Season: The Attack on the Welfare State* (1987), and Linda Killen, *The Soviet Union and the United States* (1989).

An important book on foreign affairs is William B. Quandt, *Decade of Decisions: American Policy Toward the Arab-Israeli Conflict, 1967–1976* (1977). On Jimmy Carter, see also the President's own *Keeping Faith* (1982) and James Wooten, *Dasher* (1978). Haynes Johnson, *In the Absence of Power* (1980), Lawrence Barrett, *Gambling with History* (1984), and Robert Dallek, *Ronald Reagan* (1984) attempt to fathom that President. Thomas R. West and David Burner study conservative journalists of the Reagan Era in *Column Right* (1988).

Christopher Lasch, *The Culture of Narcissism: American Life in an Age of Diminishing Expectations* (1978), employs Freudian terms to comment on the condition of American civilization, or that part of it which can be evoked as "narcissistic." Lasch distinguishes narcissism from simple selfishness: the narcissist, not having been provided with the interior restraints that would make it possible to direct the passions and desires, lacks an identity and searches self-indulgently for images of himself. Another important book is Robert Heilbroner, *An Inquiry into the Human Prospect* (1974).

An early study of energy questions is Anthony Sampson,

The Seven Sisters: The Great Oil Companies and the World They Made (1975). Tad Szulc studies *The Energy Crisis* (revised edition, 1978) while Daniel Ford is thorough on *Three Mile Island* (1982). Lester C. Thurow gives a broad view of the age of scarcity in the *Zero-Sum Society: Distribution and the Possibilities for Economic Change* (1981).

See also S. Kirkpatrick Sale, *SDS* (1973), Roger Kahn, *The Battle for Morningside Heights* (1970), Robert Wuthnow, *The Restructuring of American Religion* (1988), and David Marc, *Demographic Vistas: Television in American Culture* (1984). Alvin M. Josephy, Jr., *Now That the Buffalo's Gone* (1982), is a good introduction to Indian struggles and Rodoflo Acuna, *Occupied America: A History of Chicanos*, 3rd ed. (1988) is the best account of Chicanos in recent history.

Other books on the most recent years of American history include Peggy Noonan, *What I Saw at the Revolution* (1990), Haynes Johnson, *Sleepwalking Through History* (1991), David Stockman, *The Triumph of Politics* (1986), Jonathan Lash, *A Season of Spoils: The Story of the Reagan Administration's Attack on the Environment* (1984), Jane Hunter et al., *The Iran-Contra Connection* (1987), Steven Emerson, *Secret Warriors: Inside the Covert Military Operations of the CIA* (1987), Seweryn Braler and Michael Mandelbaum, eds., *Gorbachev's Russia and American Foreign Policy* (1988), Walter LaFeber, *Inevitable Revolutions* (1984), Kevin Phillips, *The Politics of Richard Poor* (1989), Hilda Scott, *Working Your Way to the Bottom: The Feminization of Poverty* (1985), and Randy Shilts, *And the Band Played On: Politics, People, and the AIDS Epidemic* (1987).

Why Did the Soviet Union Crumble?

Patricia Guerrin

Ronald Reagan's conservative Republican administration resolved to reverse a foreign policy that had attempted to accommodate the international Communist menace. The inauguration of Reagan's presidency in January 1981 was not a second too soon.

The foreign policy of previous years, and especially under Jimmy Carter, had suffered from a number of interrelated mistakes. One of them was an underestimation of the military capacity of the Soviet bloc, and therefore a neglect of needed weaponry. Another was a failure to see just how closely connected were the various Communist movements throughout the world: an ignorance, for example, of how closely the Sandinista regime in Nicaragua suited the geopolitical ambitions of Moscow. The indifference on the part of previous administrations to the threat that Cuba's Fidel Castro posed to Latin America measured their neglect of reality. Another failing was a refusal to see how different was Communism from any other form of government or political movement. This last had led in Carter's administration to a flawed human-rights policy based on a notion that the acts of repression under military or oligarchical regimes friendly to the United States were no different from the repression that people daily suffered under Communism.

Under Ronald Reagan the change of policy was swift and decisive. Crash expenditures on American armaments, most notably on the Strategic Defense Initiative, forced the Soviet economy into a competition that it could not endure. The invasion of Grenada in 1982, the aerial punishment of Libya in 1986 for its aid to terrorism, the support of the anti-Sandinista Contras, the denunciations of the Soviet Union: all this put the world on notice that the struggle with Communism was to be total, and threw Moscow on the psychological defensive. The degree of assistance that Reagan was able to give to the Contras lessened the hold of the Marxist Sandinistas on Nicaragua.

The results are history. Mikhail Gorbachev, the last Communist chief of the Soviet Union, inherited a broken economy, and his mild set of reforms grew beyond the control of the party, leading in time to the crumbling of Communism in eastern Europe and the USSR. On this continent, the Sandinistas in the time of George Bush fell in an election that had been forced upon them. In less than a decade, a world had been liberated.

By the end of the Communist era, the political right should have been in psychological shock. It came to the presidency in 1981 insisting, as it had for decades, that liberalism had never understood the true depth of the Communist evil, that only conservatives fully realized the spiritual crisis of the West in the face of an indivisible, unchangeable Communist peril. And within a few years, that unchangeable and indivisible peril had changed itself out of existence, disintegrated in the course of reforming itself. All the verbal profundity of American anti-Communist conservatism proved to have been strutting in the face of an enemy that had ceased long ago to be a serious danger to anyone outside its borders.

So closed the last chapter in a continuing quarrel between liberalism and the right over the nature of international politics. For decades, liberal administrations had stubbornly and patiently withstood Communism. They built alliances. When they could, they bargained with the enemy for enough peace to keep the world a little safer. When they thought it was necessary, they went to war. At all times, they demanded of the nation enough of its treasure to sustain the necessary military and foreign aid. They passed the Marshall Plan and created NATO; they sent forth the Peace Corps; they fought in Korea and Vietnam. It was an unbearable strain on the nerves of right-wingers. They hated the taxation; they hated the entanglements in diplomatic alliances; above all, they hated the grim, persistent patience of liberal foreign policy. Rightists wanted a more gratifying kind of anti-Communism, stronger in its posturings, its relentless denunciations of the Communist evil. What they did not want is difficulty.

Here Reagan's administration was quick to satisfy them. The Republicans had no intention of putting its affluent American constituency through the slightest effort and pain. Their actions were dramatic, but essentially safe. Reaganites would not tax the public for the Cold War: their strategy was to cut down on domestic programs, build up the military, and borrow the money. That way the prosperous classes could play for a moment at getting wealthier, and at no expense, while the administration played at being confrontational. And the human-rights policy of the Carter years, which required condemnation of repression in rightist and leftist regimes alike, was far too complicated and demanding for the Republican administration's taste.

Communism, meanwhile, was crumbling from inefficiency, expiring as it continued mechanically to speak the dead formulas of its ideology—until finally, in relief, its spokesmen gave up the formulas and the ideology. The sober resistance of the West for four decades, the struggles by dissidents within the Communist bloc, and finally the internal absurdity of Communism itself had defeated it.

Appendixes

The Declaration of Independence

When in the Course of human events, it becomes necessary for one people to dissolve the political bands which have connected them with another, and to assume among the Powers of the earth, the separate and equal station to which the Laws of Nature and of Nature's God entitle them, a decent respect to the opinions of mankind requires that they should declare the causes which impel them to the separation.

We hold these truths to be self-evident, that all men are created equal, that they are endowed by their Creator with certain unalienable Rights, that among these are Life, Liberty and the pursuit of Happiness. That to secure these rights, Governments are instituted among Men, deriving their just powers from the consent of the governed, That whenever any Form of Government becomes destructive of these ends, it is the Right of the People to alter or to abolish it, and to institute new Government, laying its foundation on such principles and organizing its powers in such form, as to them shall seem most likely to effect their Safety and Happiness. Prudence, indeed, will dictate that Governments long established should not be changed for light and transient causes; and accordingly all experience hath shown, that mankind are more disposed to suffer, while evils are sufferable, than to right themselves by abolishing the forms to which they are accustomed. When a long train of abuses and usurpations, pursuing invariably the same Object evinces a design to reduce them under absolute Despotism, it is their right, it is their duty, to throw off such Government, and to provide new Guards for their future security.—Such has been the patient sufferance of these Colonies; and such is now the necessity which constrains them to alter their former Systems of Government. The history of the present King of Great Britain is a history of repeated injuries and usurpations, all having in direct object the establishment of an absolute Tyranny over these States. To prove this, let Facts be submitted to a candid world.

He has refused his Assent to Laws, the most wholesome and necessary for the public good.

He has forbidden his Governors to pass Laws of immediate and pressing importance, unless suspended in their operation till his Assent should be obtained; and when so suspended, he has utterly neglected to attend to them.

He has refused to pass other Laws for the accommodation of large districts of people, unless those people would relinquish the right of Representation in the Legislature, a right inestimable to them and formidable to tyrants only.

He has dissolved Representative Houses repeatedly, for opposing with manly firmness his invasions on the rights of the people.

He has refused for a long time, after such dissolutions, to cause others to be elected; whereby the Legislative Powers, incapable of Annihilation, have returned to the People at large for their exercise; the State remaining in the mean time exposed to all the dangers of invasion from without, and convulsions within.

He has endeavoured to prevent the population of these States; for that purpose obstructing the Laws of Naturalization of Foreigners; refusing to pass others to encourage their migration hither, and raising the conditions of new Appropriations of Lands.

He has obstructed the Administration of Justice, by refusing his Assent to Laws for establishing Judiciary Powers.

He has made Judges dependent on his Will alone, for the tenure of their offices, and the amount and payment of their salaries.

He has erected a multitude of New Offices, and sent hither swarms of Officers to harass our People, and eat out their substance.

He has kept among us, in times of peace, Standing Armies without the Consent of our legislature.

He has affected to render the Military independent of and superior to the Civil Power.

He has combined with others to subject us to a jurisdiction foreign to our constitution, and unacknowledged by our laws; giving his Assent to their acts of pretended legislation:

For quartering large bodies of armed troops among us:

For protecting them, by a mock Trial, from Punishment for any Murders which they should commit on the Inhabitants of these States:

For cutting off our Trade with all parts of the world:

For imposing taxes on us without our Consent:

For depriving us in many cases, of the benefits of Trial by Jury:

For transporting us beyond Seas to be tried for pretended offences:

For abolishing the free System of English Laws in a neighbouring Province, establishing therein an Arbitrary government, and enlarging its Boundaries so as to render it at once an example and fit instrument for introducing the same absolute rule into these Colonies:

For taking away our Charters, abolishing our most valuable Laws, and altering fundamentally the Forms of our Governments:

For suspending our own Legislature, and declaring themselves invested with Power to legislate for us in all cases whatsoever.

He has abdicated Government here, by declaring us out of his Protection and waging War against us.

He has plundered our seas, ravaged our Coasts, burnt our towns, and destroyed the lives of our people.

He is at this time transporting large armies of foreign mercenaries to compleat the works of death, desolation and tyranny, already begun with circumstances of Cruelty & perfidy scarcely paralleled in the most barbarous ages, and totally unworthy the Head of a civilized nation.

He has constrained our fellow Citizens taken Captive on the high Seas to bear Arms against their Country, to become the executioners of their friends and Brethren, or to fall themselves by their Hands.

He has excited domestic insurrections amongst us, and has endeavoured to bring on the inhabitants of our frontiers, the merciless Indian Savages, whose known rule of warfare, is an undistinguished destruction of all ages, sexes and conditions.

In every stage of these Oppressions We have Petitioned for Redress in the most humble terms: Our repeated Petitions have been answered only by repeated injury. A Prince, whose character is thus marked by every act which may define a Tyrant, is unfit to be the ruler of a free People.

Nor have We been wanting in attention to our British brethren. We have warned them from time to time of attempts by their legislature to extend an unwarrantable jurisdiction over us. We have reminded them of the circumstances of our emigration and settlement here. We have appealed to their native justice and magnanimity, and we have conjured them by the ties of our common kindred to disavow these usurpations, which, would inevitably interrupt our connections and correspondence. They too have been deaf to the voice of justice and of consanguinity. We must, therefore, acquiesce in the necessity, which denounces our Separation, and hold them, as we hold the rest of mankind, Enemies in War, in Peace Friends.

We, therefore, the Representatives of the United States of America, in General Congress, Assembled, appealing to the Supreme Judge of the world for the rectitude of our intentions, do, in the Name, and by Authority of the good People of these Colonies, solemnly publish and declare, That these United Colonies are, and of Right ought to be Free and Independent States; that they are Absolved from all Allegiance to the British Crown, and that all political connection between them and the State of Great Britain, is and ought to be totally dissolved; and that as Free and Independent States, they have full Power to levy War, conclude Peace, contract Alliances, establish Commerce, and to do all other Acts and Things which Independent States may of right do. And for the support of this Declaration, with a firm reliance on the Protection of Divine Providence, we mutually pledge to each other our Lives, our Fortunes and our sacred Honor.

The Constitution of the United States

We the people of the United States, in Order to form a more perfect Union, establish Justice, insure domestic Tranquility, provide for the common defense, promote the general Welfare, and secure the Blessings of Liberty to ourselves and our Posterity, do ordain and establish this CONSTITUTION for the United States of America.

ARTICLE 1

Section 1.   All legislative Powers herein granted shall be vested in a Congress of the United States which shall consist of a Senate and House of Representatives.

Section 2.   The House of Representatives shall be composed of Members chosen every second Year by the People of the several States, and the Electors in each State shall have the Qualifications requisite for Electors of the most numerous Branch of the State Legislature.

No Person shall be a Representative who shall not have attained to the Age of twenty-five Years, and been seven Years a Citizen of the United States, and who shall not, when elected, be an inhabitant of that State in which he shall be chosen.

Representatives and direct Taxes shall be apportioned among the several States which may be included within this Union, according to their respective Numbers, which shall be determined by adding to the whole Number of free Persons, including those bound to Service for a Term of Years and excluding Indians not taxed, three fifths of all other Persons. The actual Enumeration shall be made within three Years after the first Meeting of the Congress of the United States, and within every subsequent Term of ten Years, in such Manner as they shall by Law direct. The Number of Representatives shall not exceed one for every thirty Thousand, but each State shall have at Least one Representative; and until such enumeration shall be made, the State of New Hampshire shall be entitled to chuse three, Massachusetts eight, Rhode-Island and Providence Plantations one, Connecticut five, New-York six, New Jersey four, Pennsylvania eight, Delaware one, Maryland six, Virginia ten, North Carolina five, South Carolina five, and Georgia three.

When vacancies happen in the Representation from any State, the Executive Authority thereof shall issue Writs of Election to fill such Vacancies.

The House of Representatives shall chuse their Speaker and other Officers; and shall have the sole Power of Impeachment.

Section 3.   The Senate of the United States shall be composed of two Senators from each State, chosen by the Legislature thereof, for six Years; and each Senator shall have one Vote.

Immediately after they shall be assembled in Consequence of the first Election, they shall be divided as equally as may be into three Classes. The Seats of the Senators of the first Class shall be vacated at the Expiration of the second Year, of the second Class at the Expiration of the fourth Year, and of the third Class at the Expiration of the sixth Year, so that one-third may be chosen every second Year; and if Vacancies happen by Resignation, or otherwise, during the Recess of the Legislature of any State, the Executive thereof may make temporary Appointments until the next Meeting of the Legislature, which shall then fill such Vacancies.

No Person shall be a Senator who shall not have attained to the Age of thirty Years, and been nine Years a Citizen of the United States, and who shall not, when elected, be an Inhabitant of that State in which he shall be chosen.

The Vice President of the United States shall be President of the Senate, but shall have no vote, unless they be equally divided.

The Senate shall chuse their other Officers, and also a President pro tempore, in the absence of the Vice President, or when he shall exercise the Office of the President of the United States.

The Senate shall have the sole Power to try all Impeachments. When sitting for that purpose, they shall be on Oath or Affirmation. When the President of the United States is tried, the Chief Justice shall preside: And no person shall be convicted without the Concurrence of two thirds of the Members present.

Judgment in Cases of Impeachment shall not ex-tend further than to removal from Office, and disqualification to hold and enjoy an Office of honor, Trust, or Profit under the United States: but the Party convicted shall nevertheless be liable and subject to Indictment, Trial, Judgment, and Punishment, according to Law.

Section 4.   The Times, Places and Manner of holding Elections for Senators and Representatives, shall be prescribed in each state by the Legislature thereof; but the Congress may at any time by Law make or alter such Regulations, except as to the Places of Chusing Senators.

The Congress shall assemble at least once in every Year, and such Meeting shall be on the first Monday in December, unless they shall by Law appoint a different Day.

Section 5.   Each House shall be the Judge of the Elections, Returns and Qualifications of its own Members, and a Majority of each shall constitute a Quorum to do Business from day to day, and may be authorized to compel the Attendance of absent Members, in such Manner, and under such Penalties, as each House may provide.

Each House may determine the Rules of its Proceedings, punish its Members for disorderly Behavior, and, with the Concurrence of two thirds, expel a Member.

Each House shall keep a Journal of its Proceedings, and from time to time publish the same, excepting such Parts as may in their Judgment require Secrecy; and the Yeas and Nays of the Members of either House on any question shall, at the Desire of one fifth of those Present, be entered on the Journal.

Neither House, during the Session of Congress, shall, without the Consent of the other, adjourn for more than three days, nor to any other Place than that in which the two Houses shall be sitting.

Section 6.   The Senators and Representatives shall receive a Compensation for their Services, to be ascertained by Law, and paid out of the Treasury of the United States. They shall in all Cases, except Treason, Felony, and Breach of the Peace, be privileged from Arrest during their Attendance at the Session of their respective Houses, and in going to and returning from the same; and for any Speech or Debate in either House, they shall not be questioned in any other Place.

No Senator or Representative shall, during the Time for which he was elected, be appointed to any civil Office under the Authority of the United States, which shall have been created, or the Emoluments whereof shall have been increased during such time; and no Person holding any Office under the United States shall be a Member of either House during his continuance in Office.

Section 7.   All Bills for raising Revenue shall originate in the House of Representatives; but the Senate may propose or concur with Amendments as on other bills.

Every Bill which shall have passed the House of Representatives and the Senate, shall, before it become a Law, be presented to the President of the United States. If he approve he shall sign it, but if not he shall return it, with his Objections, to that House in which it shall have originated, who shall enter the Objections at large on their Journal, and proceed to reconsider it. If after such Reconsideration two thirds of that House shall agree to pass the bill, it shall be sent, together with the objections, to the other House, by which it shall likewise be reconsidered, and if approved by two thirds of that House, it shall become a Law. But in all such Cases the Votes of both Houses shall be determined by Yeas and Nays, and the Names of the Persons voting for and against the Bill shall be entered on the Journal of each House respectively. If any Bill shall not be returned by the President within ten Days (Sundays excepted) after it shall have been presented to him, the Same shall be a Law, in like Manner as if he had signed it, unless the Congress by their Adjournment prevent its Return, in which Case it shall not be a Law.

Every Order, Resolution, or Vote to which the Concurrence of the Senate and House of Representatives may be necessary (except on a question of Adjournment) shall be presented to the President of the United States; and before the Same shall take Effect, shall be approved by him, or being disapproved by him, shall be repassed by two thirds of the Senate and House of Representatives, according to the Rules and Limitations prescribed in the Case of a Bill.

Section 8.   The Congress shall have Power To lay and collect Taxes, Duties, Imposts and Excises, to pay the Debts and provide for the common Defence and general Welfare of the United States; but all Duties, Imposts and Excises shall be uniform throughout the United States;

To borrow money on the credit of the United States;

To regulate Commerce with foreign Nations, and among the several States, and with the Indian Tribes;

To establish an uniform Rule of Naturalization, and uniform Laws on the subject of Bankruptcies throughout the United States;

To coin Money, regulate the Value thereof, and of foreign Coin, and fix the Standard of Weights and Measures;

To provide for the Punishment of counterfeiting the Securities and current Coin of the United States;

To establish Post Offices and Post Roads;

To promote the Progress of Science and useful Arts, by securing for limited Times to Authors and Inventors the exclusive Right to their respective Writings and Discoveries;

To constitute Tribunals inferior to the Supreme Court;

To define and punish Piracies and Felonies committed on the high Seas, and Offences against the Law of Nations;

To declare War, grant Letters of Marque and Reprisal, and make Rules concerning Captures on Land and Water;

To raise and support Armies, but no Appropriation of Money to that Use shall be for a longer Term than two Years;

To provide and maintain a Navy;

To make Rules for the Government and Regulation of the land and naval forces;

To provide for calling forth the Militia to execute the Laws of the Union, suppress Insurrections and repel Invasions;

To provide for organizing, arming, and disciplining the Militia, and for governing such Part of them as may be employed in the Service of the United States, reserving to the States respectively, the Appointment of the Officers, and the Authority of training the Militia according to the discipline prescribed by Congress;

To exercise exclusive Legislation in all Cases whatsoever, over such District (not exceeding ten Miles square) as may, by Cession of particular States, and the acceptance of Congress, become the Seat of Government of the United States, and to exercise like Authority over all Places purchased by the Consent of the Legislature of the States in which the Same shall be, for the Erection of Forts, Magazines, Arsenals, dock-Yards, and other needful Buildings—And

To make all Laws which shall be necessary and proper for carrying into Execution the foregoing Powers, and all other Powers vested by this Constitution in the Government of the United States, or in any Department or Officer thereof.

Section 9.   The Migration or Importation of such Persons as any of the States now existing shall think proper to admit, shall not be prohibited by the Congress prior to the Year one thousand eight hundred and eight, but a tax or duty may be imposed on such Importation, not exceeding ten dollars for each Person.

The privilege of the Writ of Habeas Corpus shall not be suspended, unless when in Cases of Rebellion or Invasion the public Safety may require it.

No Bill of Attainder or ex post facto Law shall be passed.

No Capitation, or other direct, Tax shall be laid unless in Proportion to the Census or Enumeration herein before directed to be taken.

No Tax or Duty shall be laid on Articles exported from any State.

No Preference shall be given by any Regulation of Revenue to the Ports of one State over those of another: nor shall Vessels bound to, or from, one State, be obliged to enter, clear, or pay Duties in another.

No Money shall be drawn from the Treasury, but in Consequence of Appropriations made by Law; and a regular Statement and Account of the Receipts and Expenditures of all public Money shall be published from time to time.

No Title of Nobility shall be granted by the United States: And no Person holding any Office of Profit or Trust under them, shall, without the Consent of the Congress, accept of any present, Emolument, Office, or Title, of any kind whatever, from any King, Prince, or foreign State.

Section 10.   No State shall enter any Treaty, Alliance, or Confederation; grant Letters of Marque and Reprisal; coin Money; emit Bills of Credit; make any Thing but gold and silver Coin a Tender in Payment of Debts; pass any Bill of Attainder, ex post facto Law, or Law impairing the Obligation of Contracts, or grant any Title of Nobility.

No State shall, without the Consent of the Congress, lay any Imposts or Duties on Imports or Exports, except what may be absolutely necessary for executing its inspection Laws: and the net Produce of all Duties and Imposts, laid by any State on Imports or Exports, shall be for the Use of the Treasury of the United States; and all such Laws shall be subject to the Revision and Control of the Congress.

No State shall, without the Consent of Congress, lay any duty of Tonnage, keep Troops, or Ships of War in time of Peace, enter into any Agreement or Compact with another State, or with a foreign Power, or engage in War, unless actually invaded, or in such imminent Danger as will not admit of delay.

ARTICLE II

Section 1.   The executive Power shall be vested in a President of the United States of America. He shall hold his Office during the Term of four years,

and, together with the Vice-President, chosen for the same Term, be elected, as follows:

Each State shall appoint, in such Manner as the Legislature thereof may direct, a Number of Electors, equal to the whole Number of Senators and Representatives to which the State may be entitled in the Congress; but no Senator or Representative, or Person holding an Office of Trust or Profit under the United States, shall be appointed an Elector.

The Electors shall meet in their respective States, and vote by Ballot for two persons, of whom one at least shall not be an Inhabitant of the same State with themselves. And they shall make a List of all the Persons voted for, and of the Number of Votes for each; which List they shall sign and certify, and transmit sealed to the Seat of the Government of the United States, directed to the President of the Senate. The President of the Senate shall, in the Presence of the Senate and House of Representatives, open all the Certificates, and the Votes shall then be counted. The Person having the greatest Number of Votes shall be the President, if such Number be a Majority of the whole Number of Electors appointed; and if there be more than one who have such Majority, and have an equal Number of Votes, then the House of Representatives shall immediately chuse by Ballot one of them for President; and if no Person have a Majority, then from the five highest on the List the said House shall in like Manner chuse the President. But in chusing the President, the Votes shall be taken by States, the Representation from each State having one Vote; a quorum for this Purpose shall consist of a Member or Members from two-thirds of the States, and a Majority of all the States shall be necessary to a Choice. In every Case, after the Choice of the President, the Person having the greatest Number of Votes of the Electors shall be the Vice President. But if there should remain two or more who have equal votes, the Senate shall chuse from them by Ballot the Vice-President.

The Congress may determine the Time of chusing the Electors, and the Day on which they shall give their Votes; which Day shall be the same throughout the United States.

No person except a natural-born Citizen, or a Citizen of the United States, at the time of the Adoption of this Constitution, shall be eligible to the Office of President; neither shall any Person be eligible to that Office who shall not have attained to the Age of thirty-five years, and been fourteen Years a Resident within the United States.

In Case of the Removal of the President from Office, or of his Death, Resignation, or Inability to discharge the Powers and Duties of the said Office, the same shall devolve on the Vice-President, and the Congress may by Law provide for the Case of Removal, Death, Resignation, or Inability, both of the President and Vice-President, declaring what Officer shall then act as President, and such Officer shall act accordingly, until the disability be removed, or a President shall be elected.

The President shall, at stated Times, receive for his Services a Compensation, which shall neither be increased nor diminished during the Period for which he shall have been elected, and he shall not receive within that Period any other Emolument from the United States, or any of them.

Before he enters on the execution of his Office, he shall take the following Oath or Affirmation:— "I do solemnly swear (or affirm) that I will faithfully execute the Office of President of the United States, and will, to the best of my Ability, preserve, protect, and defend the Constitution of the United States."

Section 2.   The President shall be Commander in Chief of the Army and Navy of the United States, and of the Militia of the several States, when called into the actual Service of the United States; he may require the Opinion, in writing, of the principal Officer in each of the executive Departments, upon any subject relating to the Duties of their respective Offices, and he shall have Power to Grant Reprieves and Pardons for Offences against the United States, except in Cases of Impeachment.

He shall have Power, by and with the Advice and Consent of the Senate, to make Treaties, provided two thirds of the Senators present concur; and he shall nominate, and by and with the Advice and Consent of the Senate, shall appoint Ambassadors, other public Ministers and Counsuls, Judges of the Supreme Court, and all other Officers of the United States, whose Appointments are herein otherwise provided for, and which shall be established by Law: but the Congress may by Law vest the Appointments of such inferior Officers, as they think proper, in the President alone, in the Courts of Law, or in the Heads of Departments.

The President shall have Power to fill up all Vacancies that may happen during the Recess of the Senate, by granting Commissions which shall expire at the End of their next Session.

Section 3.   He shall from time to time give to the Congress Information of the State of the Union, and recommend to their Consideration such Measures as he shall judge necessary and expedient; he may, on extraordinary occasions, convene both Houses, or either of them, and in Case of Disagreement between them, with respect to the Time of Adjournment, he may adjourn them to such Time as he shall think proper; he shall receive Ambassadors and other public Ministers; he shall take Care that the Laws be faithfully executed, and shall Commission all the Officers of the United States

Section 4.   The President, Vice President and all civil Officers of the United States, shall be removed from Office on Impeachment for, and Conviction of, Treason, Bribery, or other high Crimes and Misdemeanors.

ARTICLE III

Section 1.   The judicial Power of the United States, shall be vested in one supreme Court, and in such inferior Courts as the Congress may from time to time ordain and establish. The Judges, both of the supreme and inferior Courts, shall hold their Offices during good Behavior, and shall, at stated Times, receive for their Services, a compensation, which shall not be diminished during their Continuance in Office.

Section 2.   The judicial Power shall extend to all Cases, in Law and Equity, arising under this constitution, the Laws of the United States, and treaties made, or which shall be made, under their Authority;—to all Cases affecting ambassadors, other public ministers and consuls;—to all cases of admiralty and maritime Jurisdiction;—to Controversies to which the United States shall be a Party;—to Controversies between two or more States;—between a State and Citizens of another State;—between Citizens of different States,—between Citizens of the same State claiming Lands under Grants of different States, and between a State, or the Citizens thereof, and foreign States, Citizens or Subjects.

In all Cases affecting Ambassadors, other public Ministers and Consuls, and those in which a State shall be Party, the supreme Court shall have original Jurisdiction. In all the other Cases before mentioned, the supreme Court shall have appellate Jurisdiction, both as to Law and Fact, with such Exception, and under such Regulations as the Congress shall make.

The trial of all Crimes, except in Cases of Impeachment, shall be by Jury; and such Trial shall be held in the State where the said Crimes shall have been committed; but when not committed within any State, the Trial shall be at such Place or Places as the Congress may by Law have directed.

Section 3. Treason against the United States, shall consist only in levying War against them, or in adhering to their Enemies, giving them Aid and Comfort. No Person shall be convicted of Treason unless on the Testimony of two Witnesses to the same overt Act, or on Confession in open Court.

The Congress shall have power to declare the Punishment of Treason, but no Attainder of Treason shall work Corruption of Blood, or Forfeiture except during the Life of the Person attainted.

ARTICLE IV

Section 1. Full Faith and Credit shall be given in each State to the public Acts, Records, and judicial Proceedings of every other State. And the Congress may by general laws prescribe the Manner in which such Acts, Records and Proceedings shall be proved, and the Effect thereof.

Section 2. The Citizens of each State shall be entitled to all Privileges and Immunities of Citizens in the several States.

A Person charged in any State with Treason, Felony, or other Crime, who shall flee from Justice, and be found in another State, shall on demand of the executive Authority of the State from which he fled, be delivered up, to be removed to the State having Jurisdiction of the crime.

No Person held to Service or Labour in one State, under the Laws thereof, escaping into another, shall, in Consequence of any Law or Regulation therein, be discharged from such Service or Labour, but shall be delivered up on Claim of the Party to whom such Service or Labour may be due.

Section 3. New States may be admitted by the Congress into this Union; but no new State shall be formed or erected within the Jurisdiction of any other State; nor any State be formed by the Junction of two or more States, or parts of States, without the Consent of the Legislatures of the States concerned as well as of the Congress.

The Congress shall have Power to dispose of and make all needful Rules and Regulations respecting the Territory or other Property belonging to the United States; and nothing in this constitution shall be so construed as to Prejudice any Claims of the United States, or of any particular State.

Section 4. The United States shall guarantee to every State in this Union a Republican Form of Government, and shall protect each of them against Invasion; and on Application of the Legislature, or the Executive (when the Legislature cannot be convened) against domestic Violence.

ARTICLE V

The Congress, whenever two-thirds of both Houses shall deem it necessary, shall propose Amendments to this Constitution, or, on the Application of the Legislatures of two-thirds of the several States, shall call a Convention for proposing Amendments, which, in either Case, shall be valid to all Intents and Purposes, as part of this Constitution, when ratified by the Legislatures of three-fourths of the several States, or by Conventions in three-fourths thereof, as the one or the other Mode of Ratification may be proposed by the Congress; Provided that no Amendment which may be made prior to the Year One thousand eight hundred and eight shall in any Manner affect the first and fourth Clauses in the Ninth Section of the first Article; and that no State, without its Consent, shall be deprived of its equal Suffrage in the Senate.

ARTICLE VI

Debts contracted and Engagements entered into, before the Adoption of this Constitution, shall be as valid against the United States under this Constitution, as under the Confederation.

This Constitution, and the Laws of the United States which shall be made in Pursuance thereof; and the Treaties made, or which shall be made, under the Authority of the United States, shall be the supreme Law of the Land; and the Judges in every State shall be bound thereby, any Thing in the Constitution of Laws of any State to the Contrary notwithstanding.

The Senators and Representatives before mentioned, and the Members of the several State Legislatures, and all executive and judicial Officers, both of the United States and of the several States, shall be bound by Oath or Affirmation to support this Constitution; but no religious Test shall ever be required as a qualification to any Office or public Trust under the United States.

ARTICLE VII

The Ratification of the Conventions of nine States shall be sufficient for the Establishment of this Constitution between the States so ratifying the same.

Done in Convention by the Unanimous Consent of the States present the Seventeenth Day of September in the Year of our Lord one thousand seven hundred and Eighty seven, and of the Independence of the United States of America the Twelfth. In Witness whereof We have hereunto subscribed our names.

Signed by
George Washington
Presidt and Deputy from Virginia
(and thirty-eight others)

Articles in Addition to, and Amendment of, the Constitution of the United States of America. Proposed by Congress, and Ratified by the Legislatures of the Several States, Pursuant to the Fifth Article of the Original Constitution.

AMENDMENT I [1791]

Congress shall make no law respecting an establishment of religion, or prohibiting the free exercise thereof; or abridging the freedom of speech, or of the press; or the right of the people peaceably to assemble, and to petition the Government for a redress of grievances.

AMENDMENT II [1791]

A well regulated Militia, being necessary to the security of a free State, the right of the people to keep and bear Arms, shall not be infringed.

AMENDMENT III [1791]

No Soldier shall, in time of peace be quartered in any house, without the consent of the Owner, nor in time of war, but in a manner to be prescribed by law.

AMENDMENT IV [1791]

The right of the people to be secure in their persons, houses, papers, and effects, against unreasonable searches and seizures, shall not be violated, and no Warrants shall issue, but upon probable cause, supported by Oath or affirmation, and particularly describing the place to be searched, and the persons or things to be seized.

AMENDMENT V [1791]

No person shall be held to answer for a capital or otherwise infamous crime, unless on a presentment or indictment of a Grand Jury, except in cases arising in the land or naval forces, or in the Militia, when in actual service in time of war or public danger; nor shall any person be subject for the same offence to be twice put in jeopardy of life or limb; nor shall be compelled in any criminal case to be a witness against himself, nor be de-

prived of life, liberty, or property, without due process of law; nor shall private property be taken for public use, without just compensation.

AMENDMENT VI [1791]

In all criminal prosecutions, the accused shall enjoy the right to a speedy and public trial, by an impartial jury of the State and district wherein the crime shall have been committed, which district shall have been previously ascertained by law, and to be informed of the nature and cause of the accusation; to be confronted with the witnesses against him; to have compulsory process for obtaining witnesses in his favor, and to have the Assistance of Counsel for his defence.

AMENDMENT VII [1791]

In suits at common law, where the value in controversy shall exceed twenty dollars, the right of trial by jury shall be preserved, and no fact tried by a jury, shall be otherwise reexamined in any Court of the United States, than according to the rules of the common law.

AMENDMENT VIII [1791]

Excessive bail shall not be required, nor excessive fines imposed, nor cruel and unusual punishments inflicted.

AMENDMENT IX [1791]

The enumeration in the Constitution, of certain rights, shall not be construed to deny or disparage others retained by the people.

AMENDMENT X [1791]

The powers not delegated to the United States by the Constitution, nor prohibited by it to the States, are reserved to the States respectively, or to the people.

AMENDMENT XI [1798]

The Judicial power of the United States shall not be construed to extend to any suit in law or equity, commenced or prosecuted against one of the United States by Citizens of another State, or by Citizens or Subjects of any Foreign State.

AMENDMENT XII [1804]

The Electors shall meet in their respective States and vote by ballot for President and Vice-President, one of whom, at least, shall not be an inhabitant of the same State with themselves; they shall name in their ballots the person voted for as President, and in distinct ballots the person voted for as Vice-President, and they shall make distinct lists of all persons voted for as President, and of all persons voted for as Vice-President, and of the number of votes for each, which lists they shall sign and certify, and transmit sealed to the seat of the government of the United States, directed to the President of the Senate;—The President of the Senate shall, in the presence of the Senate and House of Representatives, open all the certificates and the votes shall then be counted;—The person having the greatest number of votes for President, shall be the President, if such number by a majority of the whole number of Electors appointed; and if no person have such majority, then from the persons having the highest numbers not exceeding three on the list of those voted for as President, the House of Representatives shall choose immediately, by ballot, the President. But in choosing the President, the votes shall be taken by states, the representation from each state having one vote; a quorum for this purpose shall consist of a member or members from two-thirds of the states, and a majority of all the states shall be necessary to a choice. And if the House of Representatives shall not choose a President whenever the right of choice shall devolve upon them, before the fourth day of March next following, then the Vice-President shall act as President, as in the case of the death or other constitutional disability of the President.—The person having the greatest number of votes as Vice-President, shall be the Vice-President, if such number be a majority of the whole number of Electors appointed, and if no person have a majority, then from the two highest numbers on the list, the Senate shall choose the Vice-President; a quorum for the purpose shall consist of two-thirds of the whole number of Senators, and a majority of the whole number shall be necessary to a choice. But no person constitutionally ineligible to the office of President shall be eligible to that of Vice-President of the United States.

AMENDMENT XIII [1865]

Section 1.   Neither slavery nor involuntary servitude, except as a punishment for crime whereof the party shall have been duly convicted, shall exist within the United States, or any place subject to their jurisdiction.

Section 2.   Congress shall have power to enforce this article by appropriate legislation.

AMENDMENT XIV [1868]

Section 1.   All persons born or naturalized in the United States, and subject to the jurisdiction thereof, are citizens of the United States and of the State wherein they reside. No State shall make or enforce any law which shall abridge the privileges or immunities of citizens of the United States; nor shall any State deprive any person of life, liberty, or property, without due process of law; nor deny to any person within its jurisdiction the equal protection of the laws.

Section 2.   Representatives shall be apportioned among the several States according to their respective numbers, counting the whole number of persons in each State, excluding Indians not taxed. But when the right to vote at any election for the choice of electors for President and Vice-President of the United States, Representatives in Congress, the Executive and Judicial officers of a State, or the members of the Legislature thereof, is denied to any of the male inhabitants of such State, being twenty-one years of age, and citizens of the United States, or in any way abridged, except for participation in rebellion, or other crime, the basis of representation therein shall be reduced in the proportion which the number of such male citizens shall bear to the whole number of male citizens twenty-one years of age in such State.

Section 3.   No person shall be a Senator or Representative in Congress, or elector of President and Vice-President, or hold any office, civil or military, under the United States, or under any State, who, having previously taken an oath, as a member of Congress, or as an officer of the United States, or as a member of any State legislature, or as an executive or judicial officer of any State, to support the Constitution of the United States, shall have engaged in insurrection or rebellion against the same, or given aid or comfort to the enemies thereof. But Congress may by a vote of two-thirds of each House, remove such disability.

Section 4.   The validity of the public debt of the United States, authorized by law, including debts incurred for payment of pensions and bounties for services in suppressing insurrection or rebellion, shall not be questioned. But neither the United States nor any State shall assume or pay any debt or obligation incurred in aid of insurrection or rebellion against the United States or any claim for the loss or emancipation of any slave; but all such debts, obligations, and claims shall be held illegal and void.

Section 5.   The Congress shall have the power to enforce, by appropriate legislation, the provisions of this article.

AMENDMENT XV [1870]

Section 1.   The right of citizens of the United States to vote shall not be denied or abridged by the United States or by any State on account of race, color, or previous condition of servitude—

Section 2.   The Congress shall have power to enforce this article by appropriate legislation.

AMENDMENT XVI [1913]

The Congress shall have power to lay and collect taxes on incomes, from whatever source derived, without apportionment among the several States, and without regard to any census or enumeration.

AMENDMENT XVII [1913]

The Senate of the United States shall be composed of two Senators from each State, elected by the people thereof, for six years; and each Senator shall have one vote. The electors in each State shall have the qualifications requisite for electors of the most numerous branch of the State legislature.

When vacancies happen in the representation of any State in the Senate, the executive authority of such State shall issue writs of election to fill such vacancies: *Provided,* That the legislature of any State may empower the executive thereof to make temporary appointments until the people fill the vacancies by election as the legislature may direct.

This amendment shall not be so construed as to affect the election or term of any Senator chosen before it becomes valid as part of the Constitution.

AMENDMENT XVIII [1919]

Section 1.   After one year from the ratification of this article the manufacture, sale, or transportation of intoxicating liquors within, the importation thereof into, or the exportation thereof from the United States and all territory subject to the jurisdiction thereof for beverage purposes is hereby prohibited.

Section 2.   The Congress and the several States shall have concurrent power to enforce this article by appropriate legislation.

Section 3.   This article shall be inoperative unless it shall have been ratified as an amendment to the Constitution by the legislatures of the several States, as provided in the Constitution, within seven years from the date of the submission hereof to the States by the Congress.

AMENDMENT XIX [1920]

The right of citizens of the United States to vote shall not be denied or abridged by the United States or by any State on account of sex.

Congress shall have power to enforce this article by appropriate legislation.

AMENDMENT XX [1933]

Section 1.   The terms of the President and Vice-President shall end at noon on the 20th day of January, and the terms of Senators and Representatives at noon on the 3d day of January, of the years in which such terms would have ended if this article had not been ratified; and the terms of their successors shall then begin.

Section 2.   The Congress shall assemble at least once in every year, and such meeting shall begin at noon on the 3d day of January, unless they shall by law appoint a different day.

Section 3.   If, at the time fixed for the beginning of the term of the President, the President elect shall have died, the Vice-President elect shall become President. If a President shall not have been chosen before the time fixed for the beginning of his term, or if the President elect shall have failed to qualify, then the Vice-President until a President shall have qualified; and the Congress may by law provide for the case wherein neither a President elect nor a Vice-President elect shall have qualified, declaring who shall then act as President, or the manner in which one who is to act shall be selected, and such person shall act accordingly until a President or Vice-President shall have qualified.

Section 4.   The Congress may by law provide for the case of the death of any of the persons from whom the House of Representatives may choose a President whenever the right of choice shall have devolved upon them, and for the case of the death of any of the persons from whom the Senate may choose a Vice-President whenever the right of choice shall have devolved upon them.

Section 5.   Sections 1 and 2 shall take effect on the 15th day of October following the ratification of this article.

Section 6.   This article shall be inoperative unless it shall have been ratified as an amendment to the Constitution by the legislatures of three-fourths of the several States within seven years from the date of its submission.

AMENDMENT XXI [1933]

Section 1.   The eighteenth article of amendment to the Constitution of the United States is hereby repealed.

Section 2.   The transportation or importation into any State, Territory, or possession of the United States for delivery or use therein of intoxicating liquors, in violation of the laws thereof, is hereby prohibited.

Section 3.   This article shall be inoperative unless it shall have been ratified as an amendment to the Constitution by conventions in the several States, as provided in the Constitution, within seven years from the date of the submission hereof to the States by the Congress.

AMENDMENT XXII [1951]

No person shall be elected to the office of the President more than twice, and no person who has held the office of President, or acted as President, for more than two years of a term to which some other person was elected President shall be elected to the office of the President more than once.

But this Article shall not apply to any person holding the office of President when this Article was proposed by the Congress, and shall not prevent any person who may be holding the office of President, or acting as President, during the term within which this Article becomes operative from holding the office of President or acting as President during the remainder of such term.

AMENDMENT XXIII [1961]

Section 1.   The District constituting the seat of Government of the United States shall appoint in

such manner as the Congress may direct:

A number of electors of President and Vice President equal to the whole number of Senators and Representatives in Congress to which the District would be entitled if it were a State, but in no event more than the least populous State; they shall be in addition to those appointed by the States, but they shall be considered, for the purposes of the election of President and Vice President, to be electors appointed by a State; and they shall meet in the District and perform such duties as provided by the twelfth article of amendment.

Section 2.   The Congress shall have power to enforce this article by appropriate legislation.

AMENDMENT XXIV [1964]

Section 1.   The right of citizens of the United States to vote in any primary or other election for President or Vice President, for electors for President or Vice President, or for Senator or Representative in Congress, shall not be denied or abridged by the United States or any State by reason of failure to pay any poll tax or other tax.

Section 2.   The Congress shall have the power to enforce this article by appropriate legislation.

AMENDMENT XXV [1967]

Section 1.   In case of the removal of the President from office or his death or resignation, the Vice President shall become President.

Section 2.   Whenever there is a vacancy in the office of the Vice President, the President shall nominate a Vice President who shall take the office upon confirmation by a majority vote of both houses of Congress.

Section 3.   Whenever the President transmits to the President pro tempore of the Senate and the Speaker of the House of Representatives his written declaration that he is unable to discharge the powers and duties of his office, and until he transmits to them a written declaration to the contrary, such powers and duties shall be discharged by the Vice President as Acting President.

Section 4.   Whenever the Vice President and a majority of either the principal officers of the executive departments, or of such other body as Congress may by law provide, transmit to the President pro tempore of the Senate and the Speaker of the House of Representatives their written declaration that the President is unable to discharge the powers and duties of his office, the Vice President shall immediately assume the powers and duties of the office as Acting President.

Thereafter, when the President transmits to the President pro tempore of the Senate and the Speaker of the House of Representatives his written declaration that no inability exists, he shall resume the powers and duties of his office unless the Vice President and a majority of either the principal officers of the executive departments, or of such other body as Congress may by law provide, transmit within four days to the President pro tempore of the Senate and the Speaker of the House of Representatives their written declaration that the President is unable to discharge the powers and duties of his office. Thereupon Congress shall decide the issue, assembling within 48 hours for that purpose if not in session. If the Congress, within 21 days after receipt of the latter written declaration, or, if Congress is not in session, within 21 days after

Congress is required to assemble, determines by two-thirds vote of both houses that the President is unable to discharge the powers and duties of his office, the Vice President shall continue to discharge the same as Acting President; otherwise, the President shall resume the powers and duties of his office.

AMENDMENT XXVI [1971]

Section 1. The right of citizens of the United States, who are eighteen years of age or older, to vote shall not be denied or abridged by the United States or by any State on account of age.

Section 2. The Congress shall have power to enforce this article by appropriate legislation.

AMENDMENT XXVII [1992]

No law, varying the compensation for the services of the Senators and Representatives, shall take effect, until an election of Representatives shall have intervened.

Admission of States to the Union

1	Delaware	Dec. 7, 1787	26	Michigan	Jan. 26, 1837
2	Pennsylvania	Dec. 12, 1787	27	Florida	Mar. 3, 1845
3	New Jersey	Dec. 18, 1787	28	Texas	Dec. 29, 1845
4	Georgia	Jan. 2, 1788	29	Iowa	Dec. 28, 1846
5	Connecticut	Jan. 9, 1788	30	Wisconsin	May 29, 1848
6	Massachusetts	Feb. 6, 1788	31	California	Sept. 9, 1850
7	Maryland	Apr. 28, 1788	32	Minnesota	May 11, 1858
8	South Carolina	May 23, 1788	33	Oregon	Feb. 14, 1859
9	New Hampshire	June 21, 1788	34	Kansas	Jan. 29, 1861
10	Virginia	June 25, 1788	35	West Virginia	June 19, 1863
11	New York	July 26, 1788	36	Nevada	Oct. 31, 1864
12	North Carolina	Nov. 21, 1789	37	Nebraska	Mar. 1, 1867
13	Rhode Island	May 29, 1790	38	Colorado	Aug. 1, 1876
14	Vermont	Mar. 4, 1791	39	North Dakota	Nov. 2, 1889
15	Kentucky	June 1, 1792	40	South Dakota	Nov. 2, 1889
16	Tennessee	June 1, 1796	41	Montana	Nov. 8, 1889
17	Ohio	Mar. 1, 1803	42	Washington	Nov. 11, 1889
18	Louisiana	Apr. 30, 1812	43	Idaho	July 3, 1890
19	Indiana	Dec. 11, 1816	44	Wyoming	July 10, 1890
20	Mississippi	Dec. 10, 1817	45	Utah	Jan. 4, 1896
21	Illinois	Dec. 3, 1818	46	Oklahoma	Nov. 16, 1907
22	Alabama	Dec. 14, 1819	47	New Mexico	Jan. 6, 1912
23	Maine	Mar. 15, 1820	48	Arizona	Feb. 14, 1912
24	Missouri	Aug. 10, 1821	49	Alaska	Jan. 3, 1959
25	Arkansas	June 15, 1836	50	Hawaii	Aug. 21, 1959

Population of the United States, 1790–1990

YEAR	NUMBER OF STATES	POPULATION	PERCENT INCREASE
1790	13	3,929,214	
1800	16	5,308,483	35.1
1810	17	7,239,881	36.4
1820	23	9,638,453	33.1
1830	24	12,866,020	33.5
1840	26	17,069,453	32.7
1850	31	23,191,876	35.9
1860	33	31,443,321	35.6
1870	37	39,818,449	26.6
1880	38	50,155,783	26.0
1890	44	62,947,714	25.5
1900	45	75,994,575	20.7
1910	46	91,972,266	21.0
1920	48	105,710,620	14.9
1930	48	122,775,046	16.1
1940	48	131,669,275	7.2
1950	48	150,697,361	14.5
1960	50	179,323,175	19.0
1970	50	203,235,298	13.3
1980	50	226,504,825	11.4
1990	50	249,632,692	10.2

The Vice Presidents and the Cabinet

SECRETARY OF STATE
(1789–   )

Thomas Jefferson	1789	Daniel Webster	1850	Elihu Root	1905
Edmund Randolph	1794	Edward Everett	1852	Robert Bacon	1909
Timothy Pickering	1795	William L. Marcy	1853	Philander C. Knox	1909
John Marshall	1800	Lewis Cass	1857	William J. Bryan	1913
James Madison	1801	Jeremiah S. Black	1860	Robert Lansing	1915
Robert Smith	1809	William H. Seward	1861	Bainbridge Colby	1920
James Monroe	1811	E. B. Washburne	1869	Charles E. Hughes	1921
John Q. Adams	1817	Hamilton Fish	1869	Frank B. Kellogg	1925
Henry Clay	1825	William M. Evarts	1877	Henry L. Stimson	1929
Martin Van Buren	1829	James G. Blaine	1881	Cordell Hull	1933
Edward Livingston	1831	F. T. Frelinghuysen	1881	E. R. Stettinius, Jr.	1944
Louis McLane	1833	Thomas F. Bayard	1885	James F. Byrnes	1945
John Forsyth	1834	James G. Blaine	1889	George C. Marshall	1947
Daniel Webster	1841	John W. Foster	1892	Dean Acheson	1949
Hugh S. Legaré	1843	Walter Q. Gresham	1893	John Foster Dulles	1953
Abel P. Upshur	1843	Richard Olney	1895	Christian A. Herter	1959
John C. Calhoun	1844	John Sherman	1897	Dean Rusk	1961
James Buchanan	1845	William R. Day	1897	William P. Rogers	1969
John M. Clayton	1849	John Hay	1898	Henry A. Kissinger	1973

Cyrus Vance	1977	Franklin MacVeagh	1909
Edmund Muskie	1979	William G. McAdoo	1913
Alexander M. Haig, Jr.	1981	Carter Glass	1918
George Shultz	1982	David F. Houston	1920
James A. Baker, III	1989	Andrew W. Mellon	1921
Warren Christopher	1993	Ogden L. Mills	1932
Madeleine K. Albright	1997	William H. Woodin	1933

George W. Crawford	1849
Charles M. Conrad	1850
Jefferson Davis	1853
John B. Floyd	1857
Joseph Holt	1861
Simon Cameron	1861
Edwin M. Stanton	1862

**SECRETARY OF THE
TREASURY (1789–   )**

Alexander Hamilton	1789	Henry Morgenthau, Jr.	1934	Ulysses S. Grant	1867
Oliver Wolcott	1795	Fred M. Vinson	1945	Lorenzo Thomas	1868
Samuel Dexter	1801	John W. Snyder	1946	John M. Schofield	1868
Albert Gallatin	1801	George M. Humphrey	1953	John A. Rawlins	1869
G. W. Campbell	1814	Robert B. Anderson	1957	William T. Sherman	1869
A. J. Dallas	1814	C. Douglas Dillon	1961	William W. Belknap	1869
William H. Crawford	1816	Henry H. Fowler	1965	Alphonso Taft	1876
Richard Rush	1825	David M. Kennedy	1969	James D. Cameron	1876
Samuel D. Ingham	1829	John B. Connally	1970	George W. McCrary	1877
Louis McLane	1831	George P. Shultz	1972	Alexander Ramsey	1879
William J. Duane	1833	William E. Simon	1974	Robert T. Lincoln	1881
Roger B. Taney	1833	W. Michael Blumenthal	1977	William C. Endicott	1885
Levi Woodbury	1834	G. William Miller	1979	Redfield Proctor	1889
Thomas Ewing	1841	Donald T. Regan	1981	Stephen B. Elkins	1891
Walter Forward	1841	James A. Baker, III	1985	Daniel S. Lamont	1893
John C. Spencer	1843	Nicholas Brady	1988	Russell A. Alger	1897
George M. Bibb	1844	Lloyd Bentsen	1993	Elihu Root	1899
Robert J. Walker	1845	Robert Rubin	1995	William H. Taft	1904
William M. Meredith	1849			Luke E. Wright	1908
Thomas Corwin	1850			J. M. Dickinson	1909
James Guthrie	1853			Henry L. Stimson	1911
Howell Cobb	1857	**SECRETARY OF WAR**		L. M. Garrison	1913
Philip F. Thomas	1860	**(1789–1947)**		Newton D. Baker	1916
John A. Dix	1861	Henry Knox	1789	John W. Weeks	1921
Salmon P. Chase	1861	Timothy Pickering	1795	Dwight F. Davis	1925
Wm. P. Fessenden	1864	James McHenry	1796	James W. Good	1929
Hugh McCulloch	1865	John Marshall	1800	Patrick J. Hurley	1929
George S. Boutwell	1869	Samuel Dexter	1800	George H. Dern	1933
William A. Richardson	1873	Roger Griswold	1801	H. A. Woodring	1936
Benjamin H. Bristow	1874	Henry Dearborn	1801	Henry L. Stimson	1940
Lot M. Morrill	1876	William Eustis	1809	Robert P. Patterson	1945
John Sherman	1877	John Armstrong	1813	Kenneth C. Royall	1947
William Windom	1881	James Monroe	1814		
Charles J. Folger	1881	William H. Crawford	1815		
Walter Q. Gresham	1884	Isaac Shelby	1817		
Hugh McCulloch	1884	George Graham	1817	**SECRETARY OF THE NAVY**	
Daniel Manning	1885	John C. Calhoun	1817	**(1798–1947)**	
Charles S. Fairchild	1887	James Barbour	1825	Benjamin Stoddert	1798
William Windom	1889	Peter B. Porter	1828	Robert Smith	1801
Charles Foster	1891	John H. Eaton	1829	Paul Hamilton	1809
John G. Carlisle	1893	Lewis Cass	1831	William Jones	1813
Lyman J. Gage	1897	Benjamin F. Butler	1837	B. W. Crowninshield	1814
Leslie M. Shaw	1902	Joel R. Poinsett	1837	Smith Thompson	1818
George B. Cortelyou	1907	John Bell	1841	S. L. Southard	1823
		John McLean	1841	John Branch	1829
		John C. Spencer	1841	Levi Woodbury	1831
		James M. Porter	1843	Mahlon Dickerson	1834
		William Wilkins	1844	James K. Paulding	1838
		William L. Marcy	1845	George E. Badger	1841

Abel P. Upshur	1841
David Henshaw	1843
Thomas W. Gilmer	1844
John Y. Mason	1844
George Bancroft	1845
John Y. Mason	1846
William B. Preston	1849
William A. Graham	1850
John P. Kennedy	1852
James C. Dobbin	1853
Isaac Toucey	1857
Gideon Welles	1861
Adolph E. Borie	1869
George M. Robeson	1869
R. W. Thompson	1877
Nathan Goff, Jr.	1881
William H. Hunt	1881
William E. Chandler	1881
William C. Whitney	1885
Benjamin F. Tracy	1889
Hilary A. Herbert	1893
John D. Long	1897
William H. Moody	1902
Paul Morton	1904
Charles J. Bonaparte	1905
Victor H. Metcalf	1907
T. H. Newberry	1908
George von L. Meyer	1909
Josephus Daniels	1913
Edwin Denby	1921
Curtis D. Wilbur	1924
Charles F. Adams	1929
Claude A. Swanson	1933
Charles Edison	1940
Frank Knox	1940
James V. Forrestal	1945

SECRETARY OF DEFENSE
(1947–   )

James V. Forrestal	1947
Louis A. Johnson	1949
George C. Marshall	1950
Robert A. Lovett	1951
Charles E. Wilson	1953
Neil H. McElroy	1957
Thomas S. Gates, Jr.	1959
Robert S. McNamara	1961
Clark M. Clifford	1968
Melvin R. Laird	1969
Elliot L. Richardson	1973
James R. Schlesinger	1973
Donald Rumsfeld	1974
Harold Brown	1977
Caspar Weinberger	1981

Frank Carlucci	1988
Richard Cheney	1989
Leslie Aspin, Jr.	1993
William Perry	1994
William Cohen	1997

POSTMASTER GENERAL
(1789–1970)

Samuel Osgood	1789
Timothy Pickering	1791
Joseph Habersham	1795
Gideon Granger	1801
Return J. Meigs, Jr.	1814
John McLean	1823
William T. Barry	1829
Amos Kendall	1835
John M. Niles	1840
Francis Granger	1841
Charles A. Wickliffe	1841
Cave Johnson	1845
Jacob Collamer	1849
Nathan K. Hall	1850
Samuel D. Hubbard	1852
James Campbell	1853
Aaron V. Brown	1857
Joseph Holt	1859
Horatio King	1861
Montgomery Blair	1861
William Dennison	1864
Alexander W. Randall	1866
John A. J. Creswell	1869
James W. Marshall	1874
Marshall Jewell	1874
James N. Tyner	1876
David M. Key	1877
Horace Maynard	1880
Thomas L. James	1881
Timothy O. Howe	1881
Walter Q. Gresham	1883
Frank Hatton	1884
William F. Vilas	1885
Don M. Dickinson	1888
John Wanamaker	1889
Wilson S. Bissell	1893
William L. Wilson	1895
James A. Gary	1897
Charles E. Smith	1898
Henry C. Payne	1902
Robert J. Wynne	1904
George B. Cortelyou	1905
George von L. Meyer	1907
F. H. Hitchcock	1909
Albert S. Burleson	1913
Will H. Hays	1921

Hubert Work	1922
Harry S. New	1923
Walter F. Brown	1929
James A. Farley	1933
Frank C. Walker	1940
Robert E. Hannegan	1945
J. M. Donaldson	1947
A. E. Summerfield	1953
J. Edward Day	1961
John A. Gronouski	1963
Lawrence F. O'Brien	1965
W. Marvin Watson	1968
Winton M. Blount	1969

ATTORNEY GENERAL
(1789–   )

Edmund Randolph	1789
William Bradford	1794
Charles Lee	1795
Theophilus Parsons	1801
Levi Lincoln	1801
Robert Smith	1805
John Breckinridge	1805
Caesar A. Rodney	1807
William Pinkney	1811
Richard Rush	1814
William Wirt	1817
John M. Berrien	1829
Roger B. Taney	1831
Benjamin F. Butler	1833
Felix Grundy	1838
Henry D. Gilpin	1840
John J. Crittenden	1841
Hugh S. Legaré	1841
John Nelson	1843
John Y. Mason	1845
Nathan Clifford	1846
Isaac Toucey	1848
Reverdy Johnson	1849
John J. Crittenden	1850
Caleb Cushing	1853
Jeremiah S. Black	1857
Edwin M. Stanton	1860
Edward Bates	1861
Titian J. Coffey	1863
James Speed	1864
Henry Stanbery	1866
William M. Evarts	1868
Ebenezer R. Hoar	1869
Amos T. Ackerman	1870
George H. Williams	1871
Edwards Pierrepont	1875
Alphonso Taft	1876
Charles Devens	1877

Wayne MacVeagh	1881
Benjamin H. Brewster	1881
A. H. Garland	1885
William H. H. Miller	1889
Richard Olney	1893
Judson Harmon	1895
Joseph McKenna	1897
John W. Griggs	1897
Philander C. Knox	1901
William H. Moody	1904
Charles J. Bonaparte	1907
G. W. Wickersham	1909
J. C. McReynolds	1913
Thomas W. Gregory	1914
A. Mitchell Palmer	1919
H. M. Daugherty	1921
Harlan F. Stone	1924
John G. Sargent	1925
William D. Mitchell	1929
H. S. Cummings	1933
Frank Murphy	1939
Robert H. Jackson	1940
Francis Biddle	1941
Tom C. Clark	1945
J. H. McGrath	1949
J. P. McGranery	1952
H. Brownell, Jr.	1953
William P. Rogers	1957
Robert F. Kennedy	1961
Nicholas Katzenbach	1964
Ramsey Clark	1967
John N. Mitchell	1969
Richard G. Kleindienst	1972
Elliot L. Richardson	1973
William Saxbe	1974
Edward H. Levi	1974
Griffin B. Bell	1977
Benjamin R. Civiletti	1979
William French Smith	1981
Edwin A. Meese, III	1985
Richard Thornburgh	1988
William P. Barr	1992
Janet Reno	1993

SECRETARY OF THE INTERIOR (1849–   )

Thomas Ewing	1849
T. M. T. McKennan	1850
Alexander H. H. Stuart	1850
Robert McClelland	1853
Jacob Thompson	1857
Caleb B. Smith	1861
John P. Usher	1863
James Harlan	1865
O. H. Browning	1866

Jacob D. Cox	1869
Columbus Delano	1870
Zachariah Chandler	1875
Carl Schurz	1877
Samuel J. Kirkwood	1881
Henry M. Teller	1881
L. Q. C. Lamar	1885
William F. Vilas	1888
John W. Noble	1889
Hoke Smith	1893
David R. Francis	1896
Cornelius N. Bliss	1897
E. A. Hitchcock	1899
James R. Garfield	1907
R. A. Ballinger	1909
Walter L. Fisher	1911
Franklin K. Lane	1913
John B. Payne	1920
Albert B. Fall	1921
Hubert Work	1923
Roy O. West	1928
Ray L. Wilbur	1929
Harold L. Ickes	1933
Julius A. Krug	1946
Oscar L. Chapman	1949
Douglas McKay	1953
Fred A. Seaton	1956
Steward L. Udall	1961
Walter J. Hickel	1969
Rogers C. B. Morton	1971
Thomas S. Kleppe	1975
Cecil D. Andrus	1977
James G. Watt	1981
William P. Clark, Jr.	1983
Donald P. Hodel	1985
Manuel Lujan	1989
Bruce Babbitt	1993

SECRETARY OF AGRICULTURE (1889–   )

Norman J. Colman	1889
Jeremiah M. Rusk	1889
J. Sterling Morton	1893
James Wilson	1897
David F. Houston	1913
Edwin T. Meredith	1920
Henry C. Wallace	1921
Howard M. Gore	1924
William M. Jardine	1925
Arthur M. Hyde	1929
Henry A. Wallace	1933
Claude R. Wickard	1940
Clinton P. Anderson	1945
Charles F. Brannan	1948
Ezra Taft Benson	1953

Orville L. Freeman	1961
Clifford M. Hardin	1969
Earl L. Butz	1971
John A. Knebel	1976
Bob Bergland	1977
John R. Block	1981
Richard E. Lyng	1986
Clayton Yeutter	1989
Edward Madigan	1991
Mike Espy	1993
Dan Glickman	1995

SECRETARY OF COMMERCE AND LABOR (1903–1913)

George B. Cortelyou	1903
Victor H. Metcalf	1904
Oscar S. Straus	1906
Charles Nagel	1909

SECRETARY OF COMMERCE (1913–   )

William C. Redfield	1913
Joshua W. Alexander	1919
Herbert Hoover	1921
William F. Whiting	1928
Robert P. Lamont	1929
Roy D. Chapin	1932
Daniel C. Roper	1933
Henry L. Hopkins	1939
Jesse Jones	1940
Henry A. Wallace	1945
W. A. Harriman	1946
Charles Sawyer	1948
Sinclair Weeks	1953
Lewis L. Strauss	1958
F. H. Mueller	1959
Luther Hodges	1961
John T. Connor	1965
A. B. Trowbridge	1967
C. R. Smith	1968
Maurice H. Stans	1969
Peter G. Peterson	1972
Frederick B. Dent	1973
Elliot L. Richardson	1974
Juanita M. Kreps	1977
Philip M. Klutznick	1979
Malcolm Baldrige	1981
C. William Verity, Jr.	1987
Robert Mosbacher	1989
Ronald H. Brown	1993
Mickey Kantor	1996
William Daley	1997

SECRETARY OF LABOR
(1913–   )

William B. Wilson	1913
James J. Davis	1921
William N. Doak	1930
Frances Perkins	1933
L. B. Schwellenbach	1945
Maurice J. Tobin	1948
Martin P. Durkin	1953
James P. Mitchell	1953
Arthur J. Goldberg	1961
W. Willard Wirtz	1962
George P. Schultz	1969
James D. Hodgson	1970
Peter J. Brennan	1974
John T. Dunlop	1975
W. J. Usery, Jr.	1976
Ray Marshall	1977
Raymond J. Donovan	1981
Elizabeth Dole	1990
Lynn Martin	1991
Robert B. Reich	1993
Alexis Herman	1997

SECRETARY OF HEALTH, EDUCATION, AND WELFARE
(1953–1979)

Oveta Culp Hobby	1953
Marion B. Folsom	1955
Arthur S. Flemming	1958
Abraham A. Ribicoff	1961
Anthony J. Celebrezze	1962
John W. Gardner	1965
Wilbur J. Cohen	1968
Robert H. Finch	1969
Elliot L. Richardson	1970
Caspar W. Weinberger	1973
Forrest D. Matthews	1974
Joseph A. Califano, Jr.	1977

SECRETARY OF HEALTH AND HUMAN SERVICES
(1979–   )

Patricia R. Harris	1979
Richard S. Schweiker	1981
Margaret Heckler	1983
Otis R. Bowen	1985
Louis W. Sullivan	1989
Donna E. Shalala	1993

SECRETARY OF HOUSING AND URBAN DEVELOPMENT
(1966–   )

Robert C. Weaver	1966
George W. Romney	1969
James T. Lynn	1973
Carla Anderson Hills	1974
Patricia Harris	1977
Moon Landrieu	1979
Samuel R. Pierce, Jr.	1981
Jack Kemp	1989
Henry G. Cisneros	1993
Andrew Cuomo	1997

SECRETARY OF ENERGY
(1977–   )

James R. Schlesinger	1977
Charles W. Duncan, Jr.	1979
James B. Edwards	1981
Donald Hodel	1982
John S. Herrington	1985
James Watkins	1989
Hazel R. O'Leary	1993
Frederico Peña	1997

SECRETARY OF TRANSPORTATION
(1967–   )

Alan S. Boyd	1967
John A. Volpe	1969
Claude S. Brinegar	1973
William T. Coleman	1975
Brock Adams	1977
Neil E. Goldschmidt	1979
Andrew L. Lewis, Jr.	1981
Elizabeth Dole	1983
James L. Burnley, IV	1987
Samuel Skinner	1989
Frederico Peña	1993
Rodney Slater	1997

SECRETARY OF EDUCATION (1979–   )

Shirley M. Hufstedler	1979
Terrel Bell	1981
William J. Bennett	1985
Lauro F. Cavozos	1988
Lamar Alexander	1991
Richard W. Riley	1993

SECRETARY OF VETERANS AFFAIRS
(1989–   )

Edward Derwinski	1989
Jesse Brown	1993

VICE PRESIDENT

John Adams	1789–97
Thomas Jefferson	1797–1801
Aaron Burr	1801–05
George Clinton	1805–13
Elbridge Gerry	1813–17
Daniel D. Tompkins	1817–25
John C. Calhoun	1825–33
Martin Van Buren	1833–37
Richard M. Johnson	1837–41
John Tyler	1841
George M. Dallas	1845–49
Millard Fillmore	1849–50
William R. King	1853–57
John C. Breckinridge	1857–61
Hannibal Hamlin	1861–65
Andrew Johnson	1865
Schuyler Colfax	1869–73
Henry Wilson	1873–77
William A. Wheeler	1877–81
Chester A. Arthur	1881
Thomas A. Hendricks	1885–89
Levi P. Morton	1889–93
Adlai E. Stevenson	1893–97
Garret A. Hobart	1897–1901
Theodore Roosevelt	1901
Charles W. Fairbanks	1905–09
James S. Sherman	1909–13
Thomas R. Marshall	1913–21
Calvin Coolidge	1921–23
Charles G. Dawes	1925–29
Charles Curtis	1929–33
John Nance Garner	1933–41
Henry A. Wallace	1941–45
Harry S Truman	1945
Alben W. Barkley	1949–53
Richard M. Nixon	1953–61
Lyndon B. Johnson	1961–63
Hubert H. Humphrey	1965–69
Spiro T. Agnew	1969–73
Gerald R. Ford	1973–74
Nelson A. Rockefeller	1974–77
Walter F. Mondale	1977–81
George Bush	1981–89
J. Danforth Quayle	1989–93
Al Gore	1993–

Presidential Elections, 1789–1996

Year	Candidates	Party	Popular Vote		Electoral Vote
1789	**George Washington**				69
	John Adams				34
	Others				35
1792	**George Washington**				132
	John Adams				77
	George Clinton				50
	Others				5
1796	**John Adams**	Federalist			71
	Thomas Jefferson	Democratic-Republican			68
	Thomas Pinckney	Federalist			59
	Aaron Burr	Democratic-Republican			30
	Others				48
1800	**Thomas Jefferson**	Democratic-Republican			73
	Aaron Burr	Democratic-Republican			73
	John Adams	Federalist			65
	Charles C. Pinckney	Federalist			64
1804	**Thomas Jefferson**	Democratic-Republican			162
	Charles C. Pinckney	Federalist			14
1808	**James Madison**	Democratic-Republican			122
	Charles C. Pinckney	Federalist			47
	George Clinton	Independent-Republican			6
1812	**James Madison**	Democratic-Republican			128
	DeWitt Clinton	Federalist			89
1816	**James Monroe**	Democratic-Republican			183
	Rufus King	Federalist			34
1820	**James Monroe**	Democratic-Republican			231
	John Quincy Adams	Independent-Republican			1
1824	**John Quincy Adams**	Democratic-Republican	113,122	(30.9%)	84
	Andrew Jackson	Democratic-Republican	151,271	(41.3%)	99
	Henry Clay	Democratic-Republican	47,531	(12.9%)	37
	William H. Crawford	Democratic-Republican	40,856	(11.1%)	41
1828	**Andrew Jackson**	Democratic	642,553	(55.9%)	178
	John Quincy Adams	National Republican	500,897	(43.6%)	83
1832	**Andrew Jackson**	Democratic	701,780	(54.2%)	219
	Henry Clay	National Republican	484,205	(37.4%)	49
	William Wirt	Anti-Masonic	100,715	(7.7%)	7
1836	**Martin Van Buren**	Democratic	763,176	(50.8%)	170
	William H. Harrison	Whig	550,816	(36.6%)	73
	Hugh L. White	Whig	146,107	(9.7%)	26
	Daniel Webster	Whig	41,201	(2.7%)	14
1840	**William H. Harrison** **(John Tyler,** 1841)	Whig	1,275,390	(52.8%)	234
	Martin Van Buren	Democratic	1,128,854	(46.8%)	60

Year	Candidates	Party	Popular Vote		Electoral Vote
1844	**James K. Polk**	Democratic	1,339,494	(49.5%)	170
	Henry Clay	Whig	1,300,004	(48.0%)	105
	James G. Birney	Liberty	62,103	(2.3%)	
1848	**Zachary Taylor**	Whig	1,361,393	(47.2%)	163
	(Millard Fillmore, 1850)				
	Lewis Cass	Democratic	1,223,460	(42.4%)	127
	Martin Van Buren	Free Soil	291,501	(10.1%)	
1852	**Franklin Pierce**	Democratic	1,607,510	(50.8%)	254
	Winfield Scott	Whig	1,386,942	(43.8%)	42
1856	**James Buchanan**	Democratic	1,836,072	(45.2%)	174
	John C. Frémont	Republican	1,342,345	(33.1%)	114
	Millard Fillmore	American	873,053	(21.5%)	8
1860	**Abraham Lincoln**	Republican	1,865,908	(39.8%)	180
	Stephen A. Douglas	Democratic	1,382,202	(29.4%)	12
	John C. Breckinridge	Democratic	848,019	(18.0%)	72
	John Bell	Constitutional Union	591,901	(12.6%)	39
1864	**Abraham Lincoln**	Republican	2,218,388	(55.0%)	212
	(Andrew Johnson, 1865)				
	George B. McClellan	Democratic	1,812,807	(44.9%)	21
1868	**Ulysses S. Grant**	Republican	3,013,650	(52.6%)	214
	Horatio Seymour	Democratic	2,708,744	(47.3%)	80
1872	**Ulysses S. Grant**	Republican	3,598,235	(55.6%)	286
	Horace Greeley	Democratic	2,834,761	(43.8%)	66
1876	**Rutherford B. Hayes**	Republican	4,034,311	(47.9%)	185
	Samuel J. Tilden	Democratic	4,288,546	(50.0%)	184
1880	**James A. Garfield**	Republican	4,446,158	(48.2%)	214
	(Chester A. Arthur, 1881)				
	Winfield S. Hancock	Democratic	4,444,260	(48.2%)	155
	James B. Weaver	Greenback-Labor	305,997	(3.3%)	
1884	**Grover Cleveland**	Democratic	4,874,621	(48.5%)	219
	James G. Blaine	Republican	4,848,936	(48.2%)	182
	Benjamin F. Butler	Greenback-Labor	175,096	(1.7%)	
1888	**Benjamin Harrison**	Republican	5,443,892	(47.8%)	233
	Grover Cleveland	Democratic	5,534,488	(48.6%)	168
1892	**Grover Cleveland**	Democratic	5,551,883	(46.0%)	277
	Benjamin Harrison	Republican	5,179,244	(42.9%)	145
	James B. Weaver	People's	1,024,280	(8.5%)	22
1896	**William McKinley**	Republican	7,108,480	(51.0%)	271
	William J. Bryan	Democratic; Populist	6,511,495	(46.7%)	176
1900	**William McKinley**	Republican	7,218,039	(51.6%)	292
	(Theodore Roosevelt, 1901)				
	William J. Bryan	Democratic; Populist	6,358,345	(45.5%)	155

Year	Candidates	Party	Popular Vote		Electoral Vote
1904	**Theodore Roosevelt**	Republican	7,626,593	(56.4%)	336
	Alton B. Parker	Democratic	5,082,898	(37.6%)	140
	Eugene V. Debs	Socialist	402,489	(2.9%)	
1908	**William H. Taft**	Republican	7,676,258	(51.5%)	321
	William J. Bryan	Democratic	6,406,801	(43.0%)	162
	Eugene V. Debs	Socialist	420,380	(2.8%)	
1912	**Woodrow Wilson**	Democratic	6,293,152	(41.8%)	435
	Theodore Roosevelt	Progressive	4,119,207	(27.3%)	88
	William H. Taft	Republican	3,486,383	(23.1%)	8
	Eugene V. Debs	Socialist	900,369	(5.9%)	
1916	**Woodrow Wilson**	Democratic	9,126,300	(49.2%)	277
	Charles E. Hughes	Republican	8,546,789	(46.1%)	254
1920	**Warren G. Harding** **(Calvin Coolidge,** 1923)	Republican	16,133,314	(60.3%)	404
	James M. Cox	Democratic	9,140,884	(34.1%)	127
	Eugene V. Debs	Socialist	913,664	(3.4%)	
1924	**Calvin Coolidge**	Republican	15,717,553	(54.0%)	382
	John W. Davis	Democratic	8,386,169	(28.8%)	136
	Robert M. La Follette	Progressive	4,814,050	(16.5%)	13
1928	**Herbert C. Hoover**	Republican	21,411,991	(58.2%)	444
	Alfred E. Smith	Democratic	15,000,185	(40.7%)	87
1932	**Franklin D. Roosevelt**	Democratic	22,825,016	(57.4%)	472
	Herbert C. Hoover	Republican	15,758,397	(39.6%)	59
	Norman Thomas	Socialist	883,990	(2.2%)	
1936	**Franklin D. Roosevelt**	Democratic	27,747,636	(60.7%)	523
	Alfred M. Landon	Republican	16,679,543	(36.5%)	8
	William Lemke	Union	892,492	(1.9%)	
1940	**Franklin D. Roosevelt**	Democratic	27,263,448	(54.7%)	449
	Wendell L. Willkie	Republican	22,336,260	(44.8%)	82
1944	**Franklin D. Roosevelt** **(Harry S Truman,** 1945)	Democratic	25,611,936	(53.3%)	432
	Thomas E. Dewey	Republican	22,013,372	(45.8%)	99
1948	**Harry S Truman**	Democratic	24,105,587	(49.5%)	303
	Thomas E. Dewey	Republican	21,970,017	(45.1%)	189
	J. Strom Thurmond	States' Rights	1,169,134	(2.4%)	39
	Henry A. Wallace	Progressive	1,157,057	(2.3%)	
1952	**Dwight D. Eisenhower**	Republican	33,936,137	(55.1%)	442
	Adlai E. Stevenson	Democratic	27,314,649	(44.3%)	89
1956	**Dwight D. Eisenhower**	Republican	35,585,245	(57.3%)	457
	Adlai F. Stevenson	Democratic	26,030,172	(41.9%)	73
1960	**John F. Kennedy** **(Lyndon B. Johnson,** 1963)	Democratic	34,221,344	(49.7%)	303
	Richard M. Nixon	Republican	34,106,671	(49.5%)	219

Year	Candidates	Party	Popular Vote		Electoral Vote
1964	**Lyndon B. Johnson**	Democratic	43,126,584	(61.0%)	486
	Barry M. Goldwater	Republican	27,177,838	(38.4%)	52
1968	**Richard M. Nixon**	Republican	31,783,148	(43.4%)	301
	Hubert H. Humphrey	Democratic	31,274,503	(42.7%)	191
	George C. Wallace	Amer. Independent	9,901,151	(13.5%)	46
1972	**Richard M. Nixon**	Republican	47,170,179	(60.6%)	520
	George S. McGovern	Democratic	29,171,791	(37.5%)	17
1974	**Gerald R. Ford**	Republican	Appointed on August 9, 1974, as President after the resignation of Richard M. Nixon.		
1976	**Jimmy Carter**	Democratic	40,828,587	(50.1%)	297
	Gerald R. Ford	Republican	39,147,613	(48.0%)	240
1980	**Ronald Reagan**	Republican	43,899,248	(50.7%)	489
	Jimmy Carter	Democratic	35,481,435	(41.0%)	49
	John Anderson	Independent	5,719,437	(6.6%)	
	Ed Clark	Libertarian	920,859	(1.0%)	
1984	**Ronald Reagan**	Republican	54,451,521	(58.8%)	525
	Walter F. Mondale	Democratic	37,565,334	(40.5%)	13
1988	**George H. Bush**	Republican	47,946,422	(54.0%)	426
	Michael S. Dukakis	Democratic	41,016,429	(46.0%)	112
1992	**Bill Clinton**	Democratic	43,682,624	(43.2%)	378
	George H. Bush	Republican	38,117,331	(37.7%)	168
	H. Ross Perot	Independent	19,217,212	(19.0%)	0
1996	**Bill Clinton**	Democratic	45,628,667	(49.9%)	379
	Robert Dole	Republican	37,869,435	(41.5%)	159
	H. Ross Perot	Independent	7,874,283	(8.6%)	0

Glossary

abolitionism: The campaign, strengthened by religious passion, for the immediate end of slavery. Among the most famous abolitionists were William Lloyd Garrison and Theodore Dwight Weld. Themselves always in the minority, abolitionists combined with more compromising opponents of slavery to form a wide antislavery movement in the North by the eve of the Civil War.

agrarian: Relating to agriculture

amnesty: General pardon granted usually for political offenses.

Anglo: A term in the Southwest for English-speaking whites.

antebellum South: The South in the decades before the Civil War.

antinomianism: The belief among Christians that salvation depends on the indwelling presence of the Holy Spirit, not obedience to earthly laws and codes.

apocalypse: A revelation or discovery. Christianity teaches that the final victory will be realized through the redemptive powers of Christ's Second Coming. Revelations, the Bible's final chapter, provides an apocalyptic vision of that fateful, final day.

appeasement: Giving concessions to enemies to maintain peace.

apprentice: A person bound to work for a time in exchange for instruction in a trade.

aqueduct: A device to transport water from a remote source.

arbitration: Parties to a dispute submit their case to the judgment of an impartial person or group.

armistice: A truce agreement between military opponents. The armistice that ended World War I, for example, was signed on November 11, 1918.

Articles of Confederation: The form of national government in the early days of the United States. The Articles, adopted in 1777, gave each state so much independence that the central government had difficulties in collecting revenue and establishing a national policy.

artisan: A skilled craftsman such as a blacksmith or carpenter.

assembly line production: A method of assembling standardized, interchangeable parts into an automobile or other item of mass consumption. Workers are assigned small, specialized tasks along the route of assembly, which increases efficiency, reduces production costs, and consequently lowers prices for the consumer. Of the nation's industrialists, Henry Ford was most closely identified with this form of production, using a conveyor belt system and making automobiles affordable to the middle class buyer.

assimilate: To absorb a culturally distinct group into the prevailing culture.

astrolabe: An instrument that navigators used to calculate their ship's location by measuring proportional distance to stars.

baby boom: Sudden increase in the birthrate after World War II from about 1947 through the 1950s.

balance of payments: The margin between the value of a nation's exports and the value of its imports.

balance of power: A system of international relations in which opposing alliances of countries seek to balance each other's military and diplomatic power. The confrontation between NATO (the North Atlantic Treaty Organization) and the Soviet-dominated Warsaw Pact is an example. See also **collective security**.

Bank of the United States: A centralized financial institution designed to regulate the nation's economy through selective distribution of capital (loans and related transactions). As envisioned by Alexander Hamilton, the first Bank of the United States was to stimulate general economic growth through commercial investment, which in turn would make individual states more dependent on a strengthened national government. Andrew Jackson, in his assault upon the Second Bank of the United States, argued that such centralized control threatened the authority of the states and favored wealthy interests to the detriment of others.

banknotes: Paper money issued by private banks and backed by the assets of those banks but not by any governmental agency.

barrio: A Spanish-speaking community, often economically impoverished.

bear market: A period of declining prices in the stock market or in any market. Speculators who agree to sell at some point in the future at lower than current prices are called bears since they can make a profit only if prices fall. See also **bull market**.

beat culture: A movement of the 1950s that rejected the nation's dominant values and mass culture. Beats, or beatniks, found little of worth in the decade's aggressive and confident capitalism and the generally rapid pace of American life. Instead they espoused individualism and nonconformity, which included Eastern religions, improvisational jazz, marijuana, and life on the road.

belligerent: A nation formally at war.

benign neglect: The British policy of non-enforcement of regulations on the American colonies in return for loyalty and mutual economic benefit.

black nationalism: The belief that African Americans should seek an independent national or cultural existence. Marcus Garvey was the major proponent of this viewpoint in the 1920s. Black Muslims continue to promote this view. See also **pan-Africanism**.

Bleeding Kansas: A phrase to describe the violent struggle between proslavery and antislavery forces in the Kansas territory after passage of the Kansas-Nebraska Act. Outside activists from both camps urged migration to Kansas to gain majority control of the territorial government and its decisions concerning slavery. Two separate governments were established, vigilante violence spread, and Congress, which had attempted to avoid the slavery issue, was forced to deal with the much intensified struggle. See also **popular sovereignty**.

blockade: The use of naval force to shut off passage to and from a hostile port or country. Used by England in its wars against Europe and the United States, by the North against the South during the Civil War, and by the United States in the twentieth century against such nations as Cuba and Iraq, blockades are designed to cripple a nation's economy and war machine by cutting off needed supplies.

bloody shirt (waving the): Taken from the waving in political campaigning of a shirt, actually or apparently bloody, said to belong to a supporter of the federal government killed by white southerners. The term "waving the bloody shirt" came to refer to the practice on the part of some Republican politicians late in the nineteenth century of arousing feelings among northern voters against the South, widely associated with the Democratic Party.

blue laws: Local laws, typically promoted by Protestant reformers, designed to keep Sundays reserved exclusively for worship and religious contemplation. Various immigrant and Catholic communities viewed the laws as discriminatory because they closed places used by these groups for social gatherings and cultural activities.

bond: A certificate of debt guaranteeing payment of an investment plus interest by a specified future date.

border states: Those states located between the North and the deep South, such as Delaware, Maryland, Kentucky, and Missouri, where slavery was legal but the plantation system was not widespread. A major task of Lincoln during the Civil War was to keep the border states in the Union.

brains trust: A popular nickname for the advisers Franklin D. Roosevelt gathered during his New Deal administration in the 1930s. Trust was another term for monopoly.

broadside: An advertisement or public notice printed on one side of a sheet of paper.

bull market: A stock market in which values are rising, to the benefit of investors who have bet on an increase in prices.

bullion: Gold used as backing for currency. See also **specie**.

cajun: People of southwestern Louisiana descended from those expelled by the British in the eighteenth century from Nova Scotia (Acadia, of which cajun is a variant).

capitalism: An economic system in which the means of production and exchange are privately owned (although one or more governmental agencies may regulate both) and market exchanges establish prices. Also referred to as the "free enterprise system." See also **socialism**.

carpetbagger: Negative southern term for the northerners who came South after the Civil War to take part in Reconstruction.

cartel: Business organizations that cooperate to control the production, pricing, and marketing of goods.

cash crops: Agricultural produce grown for sale rather than for the farmer's own use. In the nineteenth century, cotton was the nation's most valuable cash crop.

Chautauqua: Educational, religious, and recreational activities for adults that began in Chautauqua, New York.

checks and balances: The principle embedded in the Constitution that each branch of government be able to prevent any other from unilaterally deciding policy or imposing its will. The President, for example, can veto legislation and Congress can, with a two-thirds majority, override that veto.

civil liberties: Those rights of the individual citizen, as enumerated in the Bill of Rights in the Constitution, that limit the powers of the government. The First Amendment to the Constitution, for example, prohibits Congress from making any law that would restrict the free exercise of religious liberty.

civil rights: Rights to legal and social equality that everyone is supposed to possess regardless of race, creed, color, country of origin, age, gender, sexual orientation, or disability.

closed shop: The practice, made illegal by the Taft-Hartley Law, of requiring employers to hire only trade union members. See also **open shop** and **union shop**.

collective bargaining: Negotiations between organized workers and employers to determine wages and working conditions.

collective security: A system of diplomatic arrangements in which countries agree to act in unison to defend any one party to the agreement that is under armed attack or the threat of it. The United Nations seeks to embody this system on a global scale. See also **balance of power**.

commodity market: Financial market where brokers buy and sell agricultural products determining the prices paid to farmers.

conscription: Also known as the draft; a system in which young men (but, so far, not young women) are chosen and required to serve in the military for a specified period of time.

contraband: Goods legally prohibited from being imported or exported.

cooperative: A business enterprise in which workers or consumers share in ownership.

cost analysis: Study of the cost of operations intending to make them more efficient.

covenant: An agreement, like the Mayflower Compact, uniting a group of people for an expressed purpose. These agreements formed the basis for town settlement and government organization in regions where Puritan or Separatist groups took root. When establishing a new town, settlers signed a document (covenant) stating the spiritual purpose of their community and agreed to abide by Christian beliefs in their daily lives.

craft or trade union: Labor union that organizes skilled workers engaged in a specific craft or trade.

crop lien: A claim against a growing crop, usually held by a store in exchange for extending credit.

cult of domesticity: The belief that women's proper role lay in domestic pursuits.

currency: Money, whether specie (that is, gold or silver) or paper. The total amount of money in circulation at any one time is the total of all currency not held in bank reserves, plus all outstanding credit orders.

dark horse (candidate): An office seeker regarded as a long shot in a race. A person who achieves unexpected support as a political candidate.

de facto: Existing in practice, not established by law.

deflation: A period of declining prices and, therefore, of increasing purchasing power. During the last quarter of the nineteenth century, the longest sustained deflationary period in the nation's history, prices fell by a quarter, or a third. See also **inflation**.

deism: The belief that God created the universe so that no divine intervention was necessary for its operation.

de jure: According to law.

depression: A severe economic slump in which the total amount of goods and services produced declines sharply. The decline in production decreases employment, the result is that the public has less money with which to purchase goods, and that further discourages production. A less severe decline is called a **recession**.

deterrence: Measures taken by one country to discourage another from attacking it.

direct primary: A primary where party voters choose their candidates directly.

disarmament: A policy of reducing the size of a nation's military. Countries may undertake such a policy as part of an agreement with one or more other states. In that case the policy is called multilateral disarmament. Or it may disarm alone. That is called unilateral disarmament. Disarmament may involve particular weapons or types of weapons, such as intermediate range nuclear missiles, or may entail a general reduction in a country's military.

Dixiecrats: The name given to southern Democrats who bolted the 1948 nominating convention in protest over a civil rights plank in the party's platform. Forming the States Rights Party and nominating James Strom Thurmond as a third party presidential candidate, the Dixiecrats put forward a conservative program that pledged to preserve "social custom."

Dollar Diplomacy: A policy adopted by the United States during the administration of William Howard Taft (1909–1913) that relied upon economic incentives to persuade Latin American countries to cooperate with the policy initiatives of the United States.

domino theory: If one nation comes under Communist control, then neighboring nations will also become Communist.

dry farming: Farming that uses available moisture efficiently.

dry goods: Textiles, clothing, and materials.

effigy: A likeness, usually three-dimensional.

the elect: According to Calvinism, the people preordained by God for salvation.

Electoral College: Under the Constitution voters cannot directly elect the President or Vice President. Instead the Constitution provides that states are to elect the members of the Electoral College, who in turn elect the President and Vice President. Electors are not obligated to vote for the candidate with the highest popular vote in their state although, with rare exceptions, they have done so.

emancipation: Release from slavery.

embargo: A government decree banning trade with other nations.

Enlightenment: Also known as the Age of Reason, this term refers to the scientific and philosophical achievements from the late seventeenth century to the outbreak of the French Revolution at the end of the eighteenth. "Enlightened" thinkers emphasized the power of human reason to discover scientific "laws" of human behavior.

entail: Legal limitation preventing property from being divided or alienated.

established church: The official church of a government or state.

fascism: A political doctrine, adopted in Italy in the 1920s and then in Germany under the Nazis in the 1930s, that exalted the state and military power.

federalists: Supporters of ratification of the Constitution; believers in a strong central government.

fellow-traveler: Person who sympathizes with the Communist party, but not a member.

feminism: The belief that women should have equal rights to those of men.

flapper: In the 1920s, a young woman with short hair and short skirt.

foreclosure: Confiscation of property by a bank when mortgage payments are delinquent.

franchise: Government grant allowing a private company or person to provide a public service.

franchise (or suffrage): The right to vote.

free soil: The political doctrine, embodied in the Wilmot Proviso of 1846 and the Free Soil Party in the presidential election of 1848, that western territories should be closed to slavery.

free trade: The policy of permitting other countries to sell their goods in a nation's domestic markets without paying fees or taxes, called tariffs. In the nineteenth century Great Britain adopted this policy with the expectation that the resulting free competition would reward its advanced manufacturing capabilities. See also **protectionism**.

freedmen: Generic term used in reference to all black men, women, and children freed from slavery during the Civil War. The Freedmen's Bureau, passed by Congress over Andrew Johnson's veto, was established to minister to the needs of these former slaves.

frontier: Technically, the line marking the extent of settlement in the western territories; more broadly the term refers to the early period of settlement before such instruments of civilization as schools and churches had been established.

frontier thesis: Frederick Jackson Turner's argument that the American frontier shaped the American character, more especially implanting habits of democracy, individualism, and enterprise.

fundamentalism: The belief in the literal truth of the Bible. For centuries it had been habitual for Christians to take the Bible as being literally accurate, but among some conservative Christians in the United States that way of reading Scripture became particularly insistent early in the twentieth century in reaction to scientific theory and to historical interpretation of the Bible. It is to this recent reaction that the term "fundamentalism" is applied.

gauge: Distance between the iron rails in a railroad track.

general store: A small store, common in rural areas, that sells a lot of different goods.

general strike: A strike by all union members in a particular area.

gold standard: A monetary policy in which the amount of currency in circulation is based upon the amount of a country's gold reserves. The gold standard is often associated with the term "hard money."

Gospel of Wealth: The view, most strongly associated with Andrew Carnegie, that the wealthy were "stewards" of their riches and were to use them to benefit society. Carnegie's own philanthropy emphasized education and world peace.

grandfather clause: Some southern states restricted suffrage to those whose ancestors could vote in 1867, depriving blacks of the vote.

Great Plains: The arid, treeless area of the United States between the Dakotas in the north to parts of Texas in the south.

Great Society: The label given to Lyndon B. Johnson's domestic program. Johnson, having grown up politically during Franklin D. Roosevelt's years in office, sought during his own presidency a program to fulfill the promise of the New Deal and complete the work left undone by John F. Kennedy's New Frontier.

greenbacks: Paper money first issued by the Lincoln Administration and not redeemable in gold.

habeas corpus: The right of anyone to be brought before a court to determine whether the person is being held legally.

hard money: Currency backed by specie or redeemable in it. See also **soft money**.

harrow: A farm machine of heavy frame and sharp teeth, used to smooth plowed ground.

holding company: A corporation that holds stock in other corporations and is therefore able to establish a monopoly.

impeachment: The first part of a process whereby a President, Vice President, or federal judge can be removed from office. The word refers to a finding by the House of Representatives, by a two-thirds majority, that there is reasonable evidence that the officeholder in question committed "high crimes or misdemeanors." After impeachment by the House, the official goes on trial before the Senate. If a majority of two thirds of that body present finds the charges to be true, the defendant is removed from office.

imperialism: The policy of one nation's conquering other portions of the world and exercising political dominion over them. The term can also be applied to economic or cultural domination of one society by another.

implied power: Power not specifically granted by the Constitution but allegedly needed to carry out the governing duties listed in the Constitution.

impressment: Seizing men and forcing them into military service; the British thereby obtained crews for its ships in the War of 1812.

indentured servant: An individual bound by a contract, called an indenture, to work for a specified period of time. During the length of the contract the servant is not free to leave his master's employ. Indentured service was common during the colonial era. Many entered into such contracts to finance their migration to North America. See also **redemptioners**.

industrial union: Labor union that organizes all workers in an industry, skilled or unskilled.

industrialization: The process of substituting machine for human power in the manufacture of goods. In the United States this first happened on a large scale in the cotton textile industry, water power providing the primary source of energy.

inflation: A period of rising prices and therefore of decreasing purchasing power. Debtors favor inflation since it permits them to repay loans in dollars that are worth less than the ones they borrowed. Creditors have a corresponding preference for **deflation**.

infrastructure: Basic units that a society needs to function, such as transportation systems, water and power lines, and public institutions.

initiative: A proposed law is voted on by the electorate after a required number of signatures are obtained.

injunction: A court order sometimes to force strikers to return to work.

integration: The policy of ending the legal or customary segregation (separation) of the races. It may also entail the adoption of active measures such as school busing to achieve racial balance.

internal improvements: The policy, first associated with the Federalists under Hamilton and later with the Whigs under Henry Clay, of getting the federal government to finance the construction of roads, railroad lines, canals, bridges, and other public works.

interposition: A states rights theory whereby the state interposes itself or comes between the people and the federal government to protect the rights of the people.

isolationism: The conviction that the United States could, and should, stay clear of "foreign entanglements." It was especially popular following the First World War. In its extreme form it called for the United States to abandon all unnecessary contact with the rest of the world; a more moderate version called upon the United States to act alone in protecting its interests.

Jim Crow: A colloquial name for the system of legal segregation of African Americans formally adopted in the South in the late 1890s and 1900s. See also **integration**.

junta: Military officers who rule a country after seizing power.

kitchen cabinet: Unofficial but important advisers of President Andrew Jackson.

laissez-faire: The economic doctrine, especially popular during the nineteenth century, that holds that the government should not interfere with the free working of economic markets.

lame duck: An officeholder who has not been reelected but has the remainder of a term to serve, or a President serving a second and therefore by law a final term.

land grant college: A college instituted and funded by

resources made available under the Morrill Land-Grant College Act of 1862. Each state was allotted federally owned land in proportion to the size of its congressional delegation, to be sold by the state for the establishment of an agricultural college.

lobby: To attempt to influence public officials for or against a specific cause.

loyalists: Those colonists who retained their allegiance to Great Britain during the American Revolution. They were also called Tories.

manifest destiny: The belief, especially popular in the 1840s, that the United States was destined to rule all or most of the Western Hemisphere. Supporters of the War with Mexico used it to justify the invasion of that country and the seizure of a third of its territory.

manumit: To free from slavery or bondage; emancipate.

Medicare: A program of health care for the elderly championed by Lyndon B. Johnson and passed into law in 1965. During the next two years legislation was passed extending benefits to the needy under the Medicaid program.

melting pot: America as a place where immigrants lose their distinctive cultural identities and are absorbed into a uniform culture.

mercantilism: An economic policy under which a nation seeks to maximize exports and minimize imports on the theory that there is a finite amount of wealth and that one nation's gain is therefore another's loss. As applied by Great Britain during the eighteenth century, the policy held that colonial trade should be regulated in the interests of the empire as a whole as London perceived that whole.

merchant marine: A country's commercial ships.

mestizo: One of mixed Spanish and Indian ancestry.

middle passage: In the triangular trade among New England, Africa, and the West Indies, the voyage between Africa and the West Indies, when ships carried slaves held in nightmarish conditions.

migrant workers: Laborers who travel from one area to another to obtain work.

militiamen: Ordinary citizens ready to serve in military in event of emergency.

millennialism: The religious doctrine that the Second Coming of Jesus Christ will begin a thousand-year-long reign of the just, or alternatively, that the Coming will follow the reign of the just. Millenarians have often tried to predict the exact date of the Second Coming.

Model T: Automobile produced by Henry Ford from 1908 to 1927 and sold at the lowest possible price.

monopoly: Effective control over the supply of a product or service such that the holder can dictate its price. Some economists distinguish between "natural" monopolies, such as over a city's water supply, which should be permitted and regulated, and "artificial" ones, such as John D. Rockefeller's Standard Oil Company.

Monroe Doctrine: The policy adopted by the United States in 1823, proclaiming that in the future no European nation may establish a colony in the Western Hemisphere. See also **Roosevelt Corollary**.

moratorium: Suspension of an activity.

muckrakers: Progressive era writers who wrote articles exposing corruption in industry and government.

muckraking: A derogatory term coined by Theodore Roosevelt for the investigative journalism of the Progressive Era.

Mugwumps: Republican reformers in the 1880s and 1890s, who might cross party lines.

mulatto: One of mixed black and white ancestry.

nationalize: To convert an industry from private to governmental ownership.

nativism: Hostility to immigrants that has typically fed upon anti-Catholic or anti-Semitic notions or upon the belief that foreigners are the source of political radicalism. It is sometimes linked to racism when the immigrant group in question is non-white.

naturalized: Granted full citizenship after having been born in a foreign country.

naval stores: Timber, tar, resin, pitch, and turpentine used in building wooden ships.

navigation acts: A series of measures enacted by the British Parliament to regulate colonial commerce. See **mercantilism**.

Nazism: The German variant of Fascism. Nazis under Hitler sought German supremacy in Europe, the extermination of "lesser" races such as Jews and Gypsies, as well as homosexuals, and a totalitarian social order.

neutrality: A position of non-alignment adopted by a nation with respect to a real or potential international conflict. At the start of World War I, for example, President Woodrow Wilson pledged the United States to be neutral.

nullification: The constitutional theory, most notably associated with John C. Calhoun, that individual states could nullify and declare void within their own borders those acts of Congress the state believed to violate the Constitution. Used early by James Madison and Thomas Jefferson in their arguments against the Alien and Sedition Acts, and culminating in the nullification of the United States Constitution itself during southern secession, this theory was put aside as legitimate constitutional interpretation with the defeat of the Confederacy and its radical assertion of states' rights. See also **secession**.

nullify: To declare invalid.

old-stock: Families in the United States for a lengthy period.

Open Door (policy): The policy, adopted by Theodore Roosevelt's administration, that called for all states to have equal access to markets in China. By the end of the nineteenth century, several European powers had established spheres of influence in China that included monopolies of portions of that country's international trade.

open shop: The practicing of hiring nonunion as well as union employees. See also **closed shop** and **union shop**.

pacifist: A person opposed to war or violence to resolve disputes.

pan-Africanism: The vision of the uniting of all "colored races" in a single, free African state. Promoted in one form by Marcus Garvey, the idea gained additional popular support among urban African Americans after World War I. It quickly lost momentum when Garvey fell prey to legal and financial troubles, culminating in his deportation to Jamaica in the late 1920s.

panic: A sharp economic downturn, believed to be caused by a sudden loss of confidence in one or more markets. Panics normally follow bursts of speculative investing in which values rise very rapidly and many speculators overextend their holdings by buying on credit.

peculiar institution: A southern euphemism for slavery.

piecework: Work, usually textiles, paid for according to the number of items turned out.

piedmont: Land at the foot of a mountain range.

platform: A formal statement of principles on which a political party bases its appeal to the public.

political machine: A single-party political organization that dominates government and controls policy and practice. Most closely associated with the Democratic party in large northern cities during the late nineteenth and early twentieth centuries, the machine used patronage and corruption to consolidate a political power base that in turn provided opportunity for profit. George Washington Plunkitt, a boss in New York City's Tammany Hall machine, justified these practices, claiming they were merely the product of "honest graft."

poll tax: A fee some southern states required as a prerequisite to voting to discourage black participation.

popular sovereignty: A concept of self-rule built into the Kansas-Nebraska Act and other pre–Civil War legislation. People in the newer organized territories were empowered to decide whether to establish or prohibit slavery. Stephen Douglas and other architects of the policy hoped in vain to avoid contentious congressional and national debate over the extension of slavery, but in practice tensions between North and South intensified as evidenced by episodes such as "Bleeding Kansas."

populism: A radical political movement centered in the agricultural regions of the South and West of the late 1880s and the 1890s. Populists called for the federal regulation of railroads, the direct popular election of senators, federally guaranteed credit for farmers, the free coinage of silver, and numerous other reforms.

portage: Carrying boats or supplies overland between waterways.

pragmatism: An American philosophy most closely associated with William James, Charles Peirce, and John Dewey arguing that the truth value of an idea is its utility in enabling the thinker to accomplish some purpose. This use of utility to assess truth is referred to as the "pragmatic test."

primogeniture: Legal right of the eldest son to inherit the entire estate of his father.

privateer: A ship of war owned and equipped by a private individual, yet sanctioned by a government to seize and plunder enemy vessels during war. Englishmen John Hawkins and Sir Francis Drake, for example, profited greatly in ventures against the Spanish during the sixteenth century, as did many Americans against the English during the War for Independence.

progressivism: A moderate political reform movement of the early twentieth century. Progressives sought to eliminate governmental corruption at all levels, to make cities safer and more liveable, and to use the federal government to correct abuses in business.

prohibition: The policy of enforcing temperance by outlawing the sale and nonmedicinal use of alcohol. The Eighteenth Amendment to the Constitution, adopted in 1919, established prohibition throughout the nation. The Amendment was repealed in 1933.

protectionism: The economic policy of placing special fees or taxes (tariffs) on foreign or imported goods. The idea, in addition to raising revenue, is to aid domestic manufacturers whose goods would enjoy a protected position in their home markets.

protective tariff: Tax on imported goods to make them more expensive than similar domestic goods.

protectorate: A country partially controlled by a stronger power that protects it from foreign threats.

public domain: Federally-owned land.

racism: The belief that humanity is divided into distinct racial stocks and that one race is superior to others.

recall: Voters' petition to remove an elected official from office.

recession: See **depression**.

redeemers: Southern Democrats who hoped to bring the Democratic Party back into power during Reconstruction.

redemptioners: Laborers who contracted their services to pay for passage to the New World. Unlike indentured servants, who contracted through agents while still in Europe, redemptioners agreed to terms only after the Atlantic crossing. Most of them upon arrival were given two weeks to secure alternative means of payment through friends or family. If this failed, the newcomer's services would then be auctioned off. While indentured servants came singly, redemptioners generally came as whole families or even as small communities.

referendum: The submitting to the public for approval of proposed law.

reparations: Payments exacted from Germany, principally by Great Britain and France, after World War I in payment for damage that, so the victors claimed, Germany had done during the war. The Treaty of Versailles of 1919 authorized the payments under a "war guilt" clause that assigned blame to Germany for causing the war.

revenue sharing: The policy of sharing federal tax dollars with state and local governments.

revivalism: A season of spiritual renewal among evangelical Christians. Revivalists, beginning with Jonathan Edwards in the eighteenth century, have called upon sinners to acknowledge their own sinful natures and throw themselves upon Jesus' infinite love and forgiveness. The revived believer is said to be converted and seeks to reorganize his life.

right-of-way: The right to build facilities that cut across land belonging to others.

romanticism: Movement characterized by interest in nature, emphasis on emotion and imagination, and rebellion against social conventions.

Roosevelt Corollary (to the Monroe Doctrine): In 1904 Theodore Roosevelt added to the Monroe Doctrine that the United States pledged to police the hemisphere to make sure, for example, that Latin American countries did not default upon debts to other nations.

scalawag: Negative southern term for white southerners who aligned with the Republican Party.

secession: As a specific term in American history, the act of the eleven states of the Confederacy in removing themselves from the Union; also the doctrine justifying that decision. The theory of secession held that the Union was made up of sovereign states each of which retained the right to go its separate way.

sectionalism: A term used to describe the growing division between the North, South, and West in the decades prior to the Civil War. Each section increasingly identified more with its own regional interests than with national concerns.

secular: Related to or oriented toward worldly, nonreligious issues.

sedition: Conduct or language against the authority of a government.

segregation: The policy of maintaining a racially separate society. In 1896 the Supreme Court, rendering its decision in *Plessy v. Ferguson,* ruled that segregated "separate but equal" public facilities did not violate the Fourteenth Amendment. In 1954 the Court reversed itself through its decision in *Brown v. Board of Education,* holding that separate facilities were "inherently unequal."

separatists: Dissenting Christians who believed that virtual separation from the Anglican Church and the establishment of independent congregations were necessary for the practice of a purified spiritual life.

settlement house: Community center run by social workers in slums to aid the poor.

shaman: Acting between the visible and invisible spirit world, a shaman healed the sick, conducted religious ceremonies, and foretold the future.

sit-down strike: Strike where workers refuse to leave their factories until demands are met.

slave codes: Laws regulating slaves in the Old South. Codes typically required slaves to possess a pass from their master in order to travel, prohibited slaves from learning to read, and banned slaves from testifying in court against whites. During Reconstruction these codes were revised, becoming known as black codes, as a means of controlling the freed slave population and subsequently enforced by newly formed vigilante groups, including the Ku Klux Klan.

Social Darwinism: The nineteenth-century social philosophy teaching that human progress mimics animal evolution, in which the strong and most "fit" win out, and that therefore government programs or private charities that seek to help the less "fit" such as the poor actually retard progress.

Social Gospel: Reform movement of the twentieth century led by Protestant clergymen, who advanced social justice for the poor.

socialism: An economic system in which the workers collectively own the means of production. In the former Soviet Union, collective ownership had translated into ownership by the state. Socialist thought in the West has envisioned control by smaller collective units with participation on the part of the individual worker.

soft money: Paper money not backed by specie (coin or hard money).

sharecropping: An agricultural system of tenancy in which landlord and tenant share the crop. The landlord provides the land and often credit for supplies; the tenant provides the labor. After the Civil War, this became a dominant system in the South.

specie: Gold or silver used as currency.

sphere of influence: Area where a foreign nation has considerable authority.

spoils system: The winning party in an election distributes government jobs to its supporters.

states' rights: Maximum self-government by the individual states.

subculture: A group of people united by ethnicity, social class, behavioral tendencies, or other defining characteristics that are identifiably distinct from the dominant culture. In the United States since the middle of the twentieth century, the term has often been used in reference to countercultural groups such as the beat generation of the 1950s or the cultural radicals of the 1960s.

subsidy: Financial aid from a government in support of an enterprise in the public interest.

suburbanization: The movement of urban dwellers to surrounding areas or "bedroom communities." Advances in transportation, especially the automobile, made it possible for individuals to live at considerable distances from the workplace. After World War II, suburban developments such as Levittown, Long Island, provided thousands of nearly identical, inexpensive homes for first-time buyers. Here, the "baby boom" flourished, and the power also of television, along with that of mass market consumerism, made American life appear increasingly standardized.

suffrage: The right to vote. During Reconstruction the Fifteenth Amendment was ratified, granting the vote to African-American males. Women remained without a federal guarantee of the vote until 1920 when, after a century of organized political pressure, the Nineteenth Amendment was ratified.

summit meeting: Conference of highest-rank officials of two or more governments.

sweatshop: A shop where employees work long hours at low wages under bad conditions.

tariff: A tax imposed upon goods or services imported into a country. When such taxes are used simply to help finance governmental operations, they are called revenue tariffs. When they are used to give domestic manufacturers a favored position by raising the prices of their foreign competitors, they are called protective tariffs.

tarring and feathering: Covering a person with hot tar and rolling the victim in feathers.

temperance: The campaign against the nonmedical use of alcohol. It was one of the largest reform movements of the nineteenth and early twentieth centuries.

Texians: Non-Hispanic settlers in Texas in the nineteenth century.

Third World: A term used to designate non-Western countries that have yet to industrialize. The United States and its industrialized trading partners, and the former Soviet Union and its former satellites, make up the first two worlds respectively.

tidewater: Low coastal land drained by tidal streams.

tribute: A payment of valuables made as a price of security.

trust: A combination of companies or other economic units that have joined to act in restraint of trade by setting prices or eliminating competition.

union shop: The practice of requiring new employees to join a trade union, usually within thirty to ninety days. Unlike the closed shop system, the union shop allows the employment of workers who are not members of a union at the time of their hiring; unlike the open shop, the union shop system forces them thereupon to join a union. See also **closed shop** and **open shop**.

vigilantes: Individuals who band together extralegally to enforce particular codes of behavior. In the South after the Civil War, white gangs lynched African Americans and whites who challenged the system of white supremacy; on the western frontier, vigilantes sometimes hanged cattle rustlers.

welfare state: The set of governmental programs that provides minimal care for the poor, the elderly, the disabled, and the unemployed. All industrialized societies have adopted welfare measures. In the United States the origins of the welfare state lie in Franklin Roosevelt's New Deal.

writs of assistance: General search warrants giving customs officers authority to search ships and storage houses for smuggled goods.

yellow journalism: Newspapers that exaggerate events or give prominence to scandals to attract readers.

SUCCEEDING IN HISTORY COURSES

By John McClymer

STUDYING HISTORY AND STUDYING FOR EXAMS

The instructor who designed this course hopes you will take advantage of the opportunity to learn about the American past. Your own objectives in taking the course may be somewhat different. You may be taking it because it fulfills some requirement for graduation or because it fits into your schedule or because it seems less objectionable than the alternative you could be taking.

In a better world, these differences between your objectives and those of the course would not matter. The studying you do to perform well on exams and papers would involve your learning a fair amount of history. And so your grade would certify that you had indeed left the course with a more informed and thoughtful understanding of the American past than you had when you entered it. In the world we must actually live in, the connection between studying history and studying for exams in history is not necessarily so clear or straightforward.

Many students manage to prepare themselves for mid-terms and finals without permanently adding to their understanding. There they sit, yellow hi-liting pens in hand, plodding through the assigned chapters. Grim-faced, they underline every declarative sentence. Then they trace and retrace their tracks trying to commit every yellowed fact to memory. As the time of the test draws near, they choke back that first faint feeling of panic by trying to guess the likeliest question. The instructor is never, they say to themselves, going to ask us to identify George Washington. But what about Silas Deane? And Pinckney? No, wait. There were TWO Pinckneys! That means there is almost certainly going to be a question about ONE of them. So it is that some students devote more energy to Thomas and Charles Cotesworth Pinckney than they do to George Washington. By such tactics they may get ready for the exam, but sabotage their chance of gaining any insight into American history.

Life does afford worse tragedies. This one, however, is remediable. And this introduction can help. It is designed to help you do well in the course, and to help you learn some history. It is, in fact, dedicated to the proposition that the easiest and most satisfying way to succeed in a history course is to learn some history. It makes very little sense, after all is said and done, to spend your time trying to keep the Pinckneys straight or running down a fact or two about Silas Deane. What will it profit you? You may pick up a few points on the short answer section of the exam, but those few points are a small reward for hours of studying. And, in the meantime, your essay on Washington as a political leader was distinctly mediocre. Clearly something is wrong.

Studying for exams is a poor way of learning history. Studying history, to the contrary, is an excellent way of preparing for exams. If you had, for example, thought about American relations with France during John Adams' presidency, you would very probably remember who Charles C. Pinckney was. And you would scarcely have had to memorize anything.

Conserve your yellow pens. All that hi-liting simply lowers the resale value of the book. If you underline everything you read, you will wind up with a book of underlinings. There may be some psychological comfort in that. All of that yellow does provide visible evidence that you read the material. But it will not leave you with a useful guide to what to review. You have hi-lited too much.

You have created a democracy of facts. All names, dates, and events are equally yellow. The Pinckneys and Silas Deane, in other words, have just become as noteworthy as George Washington or John Adams. You need, more than anything else, some way of determining what is important.

The next step may prove harder. You will have to give up trying to learn history by rote. A certain amount of memorizing may be unavoidable in a course, but ultimately it is the enemy of understanding. That is because many people use it as an alternative to thinking. Have you ever wished there were a better way? Well, there is. If you understand what Lincoln had hoped to accomplish with the Emancipation Proclamation, for example, you will not need to memorize its provisions. You will know why it did not promise freedom to any of the slaves in states (like Maryland or Missouri) that remained loyal to the Union. You will know why the Proclamation did not go into effect until one hundred days after it was issued. You will not, in short, stumble over a question like: "Whom did the Emancipation Proclamation emancipate?"

Facts are by no means unimportant. It is essential to have something to think about. But it is generally more fun to pay attention to ideas. Lincoln, to pursue this example, was interested above all else in restoring the Union. He was perfectly willing, he said, to keep slavery if that would accomplish his purpose; he was equally willing to abolish slavery if that would do the trick. So there is no mystery that in the Emancipation Proclamation he gave the states of the Confederacy one hundred days to return to the Union on pain of

losing their slaves if they did not. The same reason explains why the Proclamation did not apply to slave states still in the Union.

If you take care of the ideas, the facts will assemble themselves. That has to do with the way in which textbooks are written and courses taught. It also relates to how people learn.

No historian, including the authors of the text and your instructor, pretends that history is the story of everything that ever happened. Many things happened for which there are no surviving records. More importantly, scholars use the records that have survived in a highly selective way. Even though they are always interested in finding new information, and in finding new ways of using information already known, each individual work of history—be it an article, a doctoral dissertation, a monograph, a textbook, a course of lectures—represents hundreds and thousands of choices about what to include and what to omit. Much more is known, for example, about the signers of the Declaration of Independence than you will read in any textbook. The information you actually encounter in this course, as a result, is there because the text authors or your teacher decided for some reason to include it. Usually the reason is that this particular bit of information helps explain or illustrate some pattern of behavior or thought. Focus on these patterns. They are what you should be thinking about.

In doing so you will have the approval of learning theorists. They have found that while it is difficult for people to recall disconnected bits of data (for example, which Pinckney was an emissary to France during the XYZ affair), it is comparatively easy to remember details of coherent stories. This is not a very startling finding. Details make sense once you see how they fit together. Let us return to the example of the Emancipation Proclamation. Lincoln's actions followed from his political priorities in which the integrity of the Union outranked achieving peace or ending slavery; his analysis of the course of the war, and his perception of the choices open to him. Had Lincoln valued peace or ending slavery more highly than preserving the Union, had easy victory or actual defeat seemed near at hand, had other inducements to the states of the Confederacy to return to the Union seemed more promising, he would have acted differently. Once Lincoln's perception of the situation becomes clear to you, you will have little, if any, difficulty remembering what he did.

Neither compulsive underlining nor prodigious memorization will help you to understand these patterns. What will? Rephrase the question: What does it mean to read and listen intelligently? For most students, reading and listening are passive forms of behavior. They sit and wait to be told. Someone else, they expect, will provide the answers. Even worse is that they expect someone else will provide the questions. And, of course, they do. At best, this situation leaves them with a more or less adequate record of what someone else thinks they should know.

Most of what passes for studying involves not a conscientious effort to wrestle with the subject, but a determined effort to be prepared to answer likely questions. That is why we pay more heed to Silas Deane than to George Washington. It is why studying for exams is such a poor way to learn history.

Letting your teacher or the authors of the text do your thinking for you leads to tedium. Passivity is boring. Yet people rarely blame themselves for being bored. It cannot be your own fault. You are only "taking" the course. Someone else is "giving" it, and so you look to the instructor to liven things up a touch. Maybe some audio-visuals or a bit of humor, you think, would make the course less dreary. These hopes are misplaced, for while humor is a blessed thing and audio-visuals have their place, it is the substance of the course that should interest you.

Boredom is almost always a self-inflicted wound. Students are bored because they expect the instructor always to be interesting when it is they who must themselves take an interest.

Taking an interest involves learning to read and listen actively. Intellectual activity begins with questions—your own questions directed, in the first instance, to yourself and then to your teacher. Why is it, you might wonder, that the United States is the only industrialized country without a comprehensive national system of health care? Why were New England authors drawn to the innocence or the mysterious evil of the wilderness in nature and the soul? Why did slavery last so long in the American South? And why did a party system develop even though the founders were bitterly opposed to political parties?

You will not always find satisfactory answers. But you will have started to think about the American past. And when you do, something quite desirable happens to all of those facts. They will take on life and become evidence, clues to the answers you are seeking. The questions will give you a rational basis for deciding which facts are important. And George Washington will finally receive his well-deserved place over the Pinckneys.

All of this leads directly to the question of how you should study for a course. It is too easy to assume that the sole reason why students are sometimes ill-prepared is that they did not spend enough time getting ready. This is a half-truth, and a dangerous one. It ignores the inefficiency of much reviewing itself.

How do you get ready for an exam? Do you get out your textbook and notes and pour over them again and again until the time runs out or the sheer boredom of it all crushes your good intentions? If so, then you have lots of company—a consolation of sorts. Available, on the other hand, is a better way.

Find a quiet and comfortable spot. Bring along a blank pad and something to write with. Then jot down, just as they occur to you, whatever items you can remember about the course. Do not rush yourself. And do not try, at this stage, to put things in order. Just sit there and scribble down whatever pops into your mind. After a while you will have quite a large and varied mix of facts. Then see how much of this you can put together. You do not need to write out whole sentences or paragraphs. An arrow or a word or two will frequently be enough. You are not, after all, going to hand in these scribbles. You are just collecting your thoughts. Do not be concerned if this process seems to be taking up some of the limited time you have to study. It will prove to be time well spent.

Now look over what you have written. Where are the gaps? You will find that you know a fair bit about the material just from your previous reading of the text and from listening in class. But some topics will still be obscure. Now you know what you should be studying. Why study what you already know? And here is the nub of the matter, for an intelligent review focuses on what you need to refresh your mind about.

You will doubtless have noticed that this

strategy presupposes that you have read the text-book and taken good notes in class. Just what, you might wonder, are good notes? Many students think that the closer they come to transcribing the instructor's every word the better their notes are. They are mistaken, and for several reasons.

One is that unless you are an expert at short-hand, you will not succeed. Instead you will be frantically scrambling to catch up. At the end of class you will have a sore hand, a great deal of barely legible notes, and little if any idea of what the class was about.

Another reason not to attempt to transcribe lectures—taping them usually wastes time—is that you will spend much of your hour taking down information you either already know or can easily find in the textbook. How often do you need to see that Jefferson Davis was the president of the Confederacy?

The most important reason not to take down everything is that it prevents you from doing what you ought to be doing during class, listening intelligently. Your instructor is not simply transmitting information but also seeking to explain the principles of the discipline. It is these explanations you should be listening for, and your notes should concentrate on them. It is much easier to do this if you have read the relevant textbook chapters first. That way you will already know much of the information. And you will have some questions already in your mind, something to listen for. You can take notes sensibly. You can fill in explanations of points that had puzzled you, jot down unfamiliar facts, and devote most of your time to listening instead of writing. Your hand will not be sore; you will know what the class was about; and your notes will complement rather than duplicate what you already knew.

So far we have dealt mainly with the mechanics of studying—taking notes, reviewing for exams, and the like. Valuable as knowing the mechanics can be, the real secret to studying is learning how to think within the ultimate intentions and boundaries of the field. History is a way of thinking about the human condition. Scholars of literature quarrel about the essence of their topic, but together they study the imagination of writers and the means by which words sharpen and express that imagination. And so, as you learn the details of the subject and the ways those details relate to one another, think even more broadly what the field of study is all about. Consider both the specific causes of the Civil War and the universal motives of pride and greed and loyalty that found expression in those times.

HOW TO TAKE EXAMS

In the best of worlds examinations would hold no terrors. You would be so well prepared that no question, no matter how tricky or obscure, could shake your serene confidence. In the real world, it seems, preparation is always less than complete. "Of course," you say to yourself, "I should have studied more. But I did not. Now what?" This section will not tell you how to get A's without study, but it will suggest some practical steps that will help you earn the highest grade compatible with what you do know.

Before you begin answering any of the essay portion of the exam, look over the entire essay section. It is impossible to budget your time sensibly until you know what the whole exam looks like. And if you fail to allow enough time for each question, two things—both bad—are likely to happen. You may have to leave some questions out, including perhaps some you might have answered very effectively. How often have you muttered: "I really knew that one"? The other unhappy consequence is that you may have to rush through the last part of the exam, including questions you could have answered very well if you had left more time.

How do you budget your time effectively? The idea, after all, is to make sure that you have enough time to answer fully all the questions you do know. So the best plan is also the simplest. Answer those questions first.

Answering question #7 before #4 may seem odd at first, but you will soon enough get used to it. And you will find that, if you still run out of time, you at least have the satisfaction of knowing you are rushing through questions you could not have answered very well anyway. You will have guaranteed that you will receive the maximum credit for what you do know. Answering questions in the order of your knowledge has an immediate psychological advantage too. Most students are at least a little tense before an exam. If you answer the first several questions well, that tension will likely go away. As you relax, you will find it easier to remember names, dates, and other bits of information. If you get off to a shaky start, a simple case of pre-exam jitters can become full-scale panic. Should that happen, you may have trouble remembering your own phone number.

Let us suppose you have gotten through everything you think you know on the exam and still have some time left. What should you do? You can now try to pick up a few extra points with some judicious guessing. Trying to guess with essay questions is of little use. In all probability you will write something so vague that you will not get any credit for it anyway. You should try instead to score on the short-answer section.

Some types of questions were made for shrewd guesswork. Matching columns are ideal. A process of elimination will often tell you what the answer has to be. Multiple choice questions are almost as good. Here too you can eliminate some of the possibilities. Most teachers feel obliged to give you a choice of four or five possible answers, but find it hard to come up with more than three that are plausible. So you can normally count on being able to recognize the one or two that are there just as padding. Once you have narrowed the choices to two or three, you are ready to make your educated guess. Always play your hunches, however vague. Your hunch is based on something you heard or read even if you cannot remember what it is. So go with it. Do not take your time. If you cannot think of the answer, just pick one and have done with it. Try to avoid changing answers. A number of studies show that you are more likely to change a right answer than to correct a wrong one.

Identifications are the type of short-answer question most resistant to guesswork. Don't spend much time on questions for which you have little idea of an answer, but try to come up with something better than a slapdash hunch. (This does not contradict the advice about playing hunches on multiple-choice questions. Such questions offer alternatives, one of which may tickle your memory.) You want the exam as a whole to convey what you do know. Supplying a mass of misinformation usually creates a presumption that you do not know what you are talking about even on those sections of the exam for which you really do. So be careful about wild guesses. Be prepared to present your instructor with a solid assemblage of good factual answers that will indicate that while you have achieved a critical understanding of the themes of the course, you have also respected the facts to which those themes speak.

These suggestions are not substitutes for studying. They may, however, help you get the most out of what you know. They may, that is, make the difference between a mediocre and a good grade.

HOW TO WRITE BOOK REVIEWS

One goal of book reviews is to set forth clearly and succinctly who would benefit from reading the work in question. It follows that a good review indicates the scope of the book, identifies its point of view, summarizes its main conclusions, evaluates its use of evidence, and—where possible—compares the book with others on the subject.

You have probably written book reviews in high school or in other college courses. You may then be in danger of approaching this kind of assignment with a false sense of security. It sounds easy, after all, to write an essay of five hundred words or so. And you have written lots of other reviews. But did those other reviews concentrate clearly on the questions a good review must address? If they did not, your previous experience is not going to prove especially helpful. You may even have developed some bad habits.

Easily the worst habit is that of summarizing not the book's argument but its contents. Let us suppose you are reviewing a biography of George Washington. The temptation is to write about Washington rather than about the book. This is a path to disaster. Washington had an eventful but widely known career. You are not, in all probability, going to find much that is fresh or interesting to say about him. Meanwhile, you have ignored your primary responsibility, which is to tell the reader what this study has to say that is fresh or interesting.

So you need to remind yourself as forcefully as possible that your job is to review the book and not the subject of the book. Does the book fix narrowly on Washington or does it also go into the circle to which he belonged? Is the author sympathetic to him? Does the writer attempt to psychoanalyze him or stick to questions of his political leadership? Is the book in firm command of the available evidence (this requires you to read the footnotes)? Does the author have something new to say about Washington and his times? If so, how well documented is this new interpretation?

You should generally not comment on

whether you enjoyed the book. That is undoubtedly an important consideration for you, but it is of little interest to anyone else. There are occasions when you need to suffer in silence. This is one of them.

HOW TO SELECT A TERM PAPER TOPIC

Doing research, as you may already have had occasion to learn, is hard work. It is sometimes boring. Typically it involves long periods of going through material that is not what you were looking for and is not particularly interesting. It also involves taking detailed and careful notes, many of which you will never use. These are the dues you must pay if you are ever to earn the excitement that comes when you finally find the missing piece of evidence and make sense of things.

Not everything about doing research is boring. Aside from the indescribable sensation of actually finding out what you wanted to know are occasional happy accidents when you stumble across something that while not relevant to your research nonetheless pricks your imagination. Many a scholar studying an old political campaign has read up on the pennant races or fashions or radio listings for that year. These are, as one scholar puts it, oases in the desert of evidence. But, as he quickly adds, no one crosses the desert just to get to the oasis. The truth is that you have to have a good reason for getting to the other side. This dictates a topic you are genuinely interested in.

The point cannot be overemphasized. If you have a question you really want to answer, you will find it much easier to endure the tedium of turning all those pages. You will have a motive for taking good notes and for keeping your facts straight. If you are not interested in your topic, you are going to be constantly tempted to take shortcuts. And even if you resist temptation, you will find it hard to think seriously about what you do find.

So the topic has to interest you. That, you may be thinking, is easy to say. But what if your interest in the subject is less than compelling? Are you then going to be stuck with some topic you could care little about? The answer is No. No, that is, unless it turns out that you have no curiosity about anything at all; and if that is the case, you are probably dead already. Anything that can be examined chronologically is fair game for the historian.

Histories exist of sports and of sciences, of sexual practices and jokes about them, of work and of recreation. Surely your imagination can find a topic on which you and your instructor will agree. This being true, if you wind up writing on some question you are not passionately concerned with answering, you alone are at fault.

Once you have such a topic you need to find ways of defining it so that you can write an intelligent essay. "The Automobile in American Life" could serve as the subject for a very long book. It is not going to work as a subject for a term paper. You could not possibly search out so vast a topic in the time you have to work with. And your paper, however long, is not going to be of book length, so you would be stuck with trying to compress an immense amount of information into a brief essay. You need to fix on some element of the general topic that you can intelligently treat in the space and time you have to work with.

Students usually look at this problem backwards. They complain about how long their papers have to be. They should complain about how short they have to be. Space is a luxury you normally cannot afford. If you have done a fair amount of research on an interesting topic, your problem is going to be one of finding a way of getting into your paper all you have to say. Writing consists of choices about what you want to say. And if you have done your work properly, the hard choices involve deciding what to leave out.

"Fair enough," you may be thinking, "but I do not want to get stuck investigating some minute bit of trivia, the 'gear shift level from 1940 to 1953,' for example. I want to study the automobile in American life." Here we come to the core of the matter. Your topic must be narrowly defined so that you can do it justice, but it must also speak to the broad question that interested you in the first place. The trick is to decide just what it is about your topic—cars in this instance—that really interests you. Cars are means of transportation, of course, but they are also status symbols, examples of technology, and much else. Because of the automobile, cities and suburbs are designed in ways very different from how they were when people traveled by trolley or train. The automobile has dictated even teenage dating patterns. Having a driver's license, and regular access to a car, has become for some teenagers an obsession.

The point is that you have to think about your

topic and then decide what within it to examine. If you end up doing a treatise on differing methods of changing tires, you are your own enemy. You could have been studying sex and sexism in automobile advertising.

HOW TO LOCATE MATERIAL

Once you have worked up an interesting and practical topic for your term paper, you are ready to begin your research. For many students this means ambling over to the library and poking around in the computer catalog. This may not be the best way to begin. The librarians who catalog the library's holdings, while skilled professionals, cannot possibly anticipate the needs of every individual student. So they catalog books by their main subject headings and then include obvious cross-references. But much of what you need may not be obvious. So, for example, if you are interested in the causes of the Civil War, you will have no trouble finding under "U.S. History, Civil War" a title such as Kenneth Stampp's *And the War Came*. But will you find Roy Nichol's *Disruption of the American Democracy*? Your subject, however, may have a general guide, such as the *Harvard Guide to American History*. In that case, draw titles from it.

Now you have the beginnings of a decent bibliography. Your next act should be to introduce yourself to the research librarian. This person's specialty is helping people look for information. Yet many students never consult with a librarian. Do not pass up an opportunity to make your work easier. Often a librarian can point you to more specialized bibliographical guides, show you where to learn of the most recent books and articles, and help you refine your topic by indicating what questions are easiest to get information on.

You now have a reasonably extensive set of cards. And you can now safely consult the computer catalog to see which of these titles your library has. Prepare yourself for some disappointments. Even good undergraduate libraries will not have everything you need. They will have some (unless your library is very weak or your topic esoteric). Almost all college libraries participate in the interlibrary loan system. This system, which the library staff will gladly explain to you, permits you to get virtually any title you could wish for. The only catch is that you must give the library enough lead time. For books and articles that are not especially rare this normally means from a day or two to two weeks.

HOW TO TAKE NOTES

Sifting through the material you have found, you will need to take careful notes. As you do, you should write down on a notecard each piece of information you believe might prove relevant. For each piece of information you also will have to specify the full source.

Following these two bits of advice will save you much time and trouble. Finding information in your sources is trouble enough. You do not want to have to find it all over again when you sit down to write your paper. But this is often just what students have to do because they failed to write down some bit of data (which, perhaps, seemed only marginally important at the time) or took all of their notes on loose leaf paper and now must search through every page to find this one fact. It is far easier, over the long run, to have a separate card for each piece or group of closely related pieces of information. Tell yourself that you are the last of the big time spenders and can afford to use up index cards as though they were blank pieces of paper, which is what they are.

The general rule is that in compiling your research notes you should take extra care so that the actual writing will be as trouble-free as possible. It follows that you should take lots of notes. Do not try to determine in advance whether you are going to use a particular bit of data. Always give yourself the margin of safety. Similarly, do not try to decide in advance whether you will quote the source exactly or simply paraphrase it. If you take down the exact words, you can always decide to make the idea your own by qualifying it in various ways and putting it in your own words.

WRITING TERM PAPERS AND OTHER ESSAYS

You have no doubt already learned that next to mastery of the subject matter nothing is more important for earning good grades than effective writing. You surely know people who despite weak study habits get high grades. The reason may be their ability to write well.

Students who are not among that relatively small group who write well sometimes think it unfair that writing skills should count so heavily. The course, some complain, is American history and not expository writing, and so their prose should not influence their grade. But teachers continue to believe that the ability clearly and forcefully to express what you know is an indispensable measure of how well you have learned the subject. Writing well is an invaluable skill, and not only in college. Many of the most desirable jobs involve writing correspondence, reports, memoranda. The writing will never stop.

No matter how poorly you write, if you can speak English effectively you can learn to write it effectively. It is simply a matter of expressing your ideas clearly. This you can learn to do. It requires not genius but merely patience and practice.

Charity, St. Paul said, is the chief of all the virtues. In expository prose, however, the chief virtue is clarity. And like charity, it covers a multitude of sins. If your sentences, however homely, are clear, they will receive a sympathetic reading.

It has perhaps crossed your mind that on some occasions you are not very eager to get to the point. Sometimes you may not be sure just what the point is. Sometimes you do know, but are not convinced that your point is a very good one. At such times, a little obfuscation may seem a better idea than clarity. It is not. Nothing is more troubling than reading a paper in which the author tried to hedge bets or fudge ideas. The very worst thing you can do is leave it up to your reader to decide what you are trying to say. So no matter how weak your ideas seem to you, set them forth clearly. Something is always better than nothing. Most teachers are interested in helping students. It is much easier to help you if your instructor can figure out what you were trying to say.

And teachers delight in watching students improve. The reason is obvious: They see it as proof that they are doing a good job. They take special pleasure in the progress of students who start off poorly but steadily get better over the course of the semester. You can do a lot worse than be one of those students.

If you have the energy, learn to write gracefully. But in any event, write clearly.

WHEN AND HOW TO USE FOOTNOTES

Many students apparently believe that the only thing worse than having to read footnotes is having to write them. It is easy to understand why they feel that way, but they are making much ado about very little. Footnotes inform the reader where the information in the body of the paper can be found. That is the substance of the matter.

So when should you use a footnote? One occasion is when you are referring to someone's exact words whether by direct quotation or by paraphrase. (If your paper does not require footnotes, you need only mention the author's name at the time you quote.) The other is when you are referring to some bit of information that is not already well known or is someone's interpretation of the facts. How, you might wonder, can you tell whether or not something is already well known? A simple rule is that nothing you can find in a standard textbook needs to be footnoted. Hence, for example, you do not have to footnote that George Washington was the first President of the United States. You may need to footnote an exact quotation from his "Farewell Address." You do not need to footnote that Abraham Lincoln wrote the Gettysburg Address. If you are in doubt about a particular case, you still have two steps open to you. One is to ask your instructor, the reader you are seeking to inform in the first place. The other, if you find it impracticable to reach your teacher, is to use the footnote. Having an unnecessary footnote is a minor flaw. Not having a necessary one is a serious omission. So you can simply err on the safe side.

Now that you know when to use footnotes, you can consider the matter of how to use them. Several formats are in common use. Simply ask your instructor which one is preferred. If your teacher has no preference, invest in the inexpensive Modern Language Association (MLA) style sheet. It is brief, clearly written, reliable, and cheap. It is very unlikely you will encounter a question it will not answer. If you think your writing needs improvement, try Brandywine Press's *Thinking and Writing*. It costs less than ten dollars.

WHAT TO INCLUDE IN YOUR BIBLIOGRAPHY

Early in your research you compiled a list of possible sources. The temptation is to type out a bibliography from those cards. This is fine provided that you actually used all of those sources. Your bibliography should include all the sources you consulted and only those sources. So even though you have all sorts of cards, and even though your bibliography would look far more authoritative if you included sources you looked up but did not use, do not do so. It is most unlikely that padding your bibliography will impress.

A WORD
ABOUT PLAGIARISM AND
ORIGINALITY

Plagiarism is the act of claiming another's work as your own. It is about as serious an academic offense as you can commit. Many colleges require teachers to report all instances of plagiarism, and while the punishment can vary, it is always stiff. And of all the various ways of cheating, teachers find plagiarism the easiest to detect.

Some students plagiarize without realizing that this is what they are doing. They quote from a book or article without so indicating by quotation marks or citing the author and the work, or they paraphrase a passage without proper acknowledgment. They have unintentionally passed off someone else's work as their own. Sometimes this results in nothing worse than a private lecture from the instructor on the necessity of correctly attributing all information. Even so it is embarrassing, and it creates the impression that you do not know what you are doing. So be sure you indicate the sources not only of your information but also of the interpretations or ideas you include in your papers.

Teachers will often tell their students that their papers should be original. Scholars use this word in a somewhat different sense from what you might expect. In ordinary speech something is original if it is the first of its kind or the only one of its kind. Scholars mean something less dramatic. We refer to research as "original" if the researcher did the work. We do not mean that the conclusions have never been reached before or that no one else has ever used the same source materials. The way you put together familiar information and ideas may be original.

Do not hesitate to make use of ideas from other scholars. No one with any sense expects beginning students to make startling discoveries or to develop radically new perspectives. It is, accordingly, perfectly legitimate for you to use other people's insights. The only hitch is that you must always acknowledge where they came from.

Index

E

J

NOTES

NOTES